Victoria

Jon Murray
Mark Armstrong
Michelle Bennett
Joyce Connolly
Richard Nebeský

LONELY PLANET PUBLICATIONS
Melbourne • Oakland • London • Paris

VICTORIA

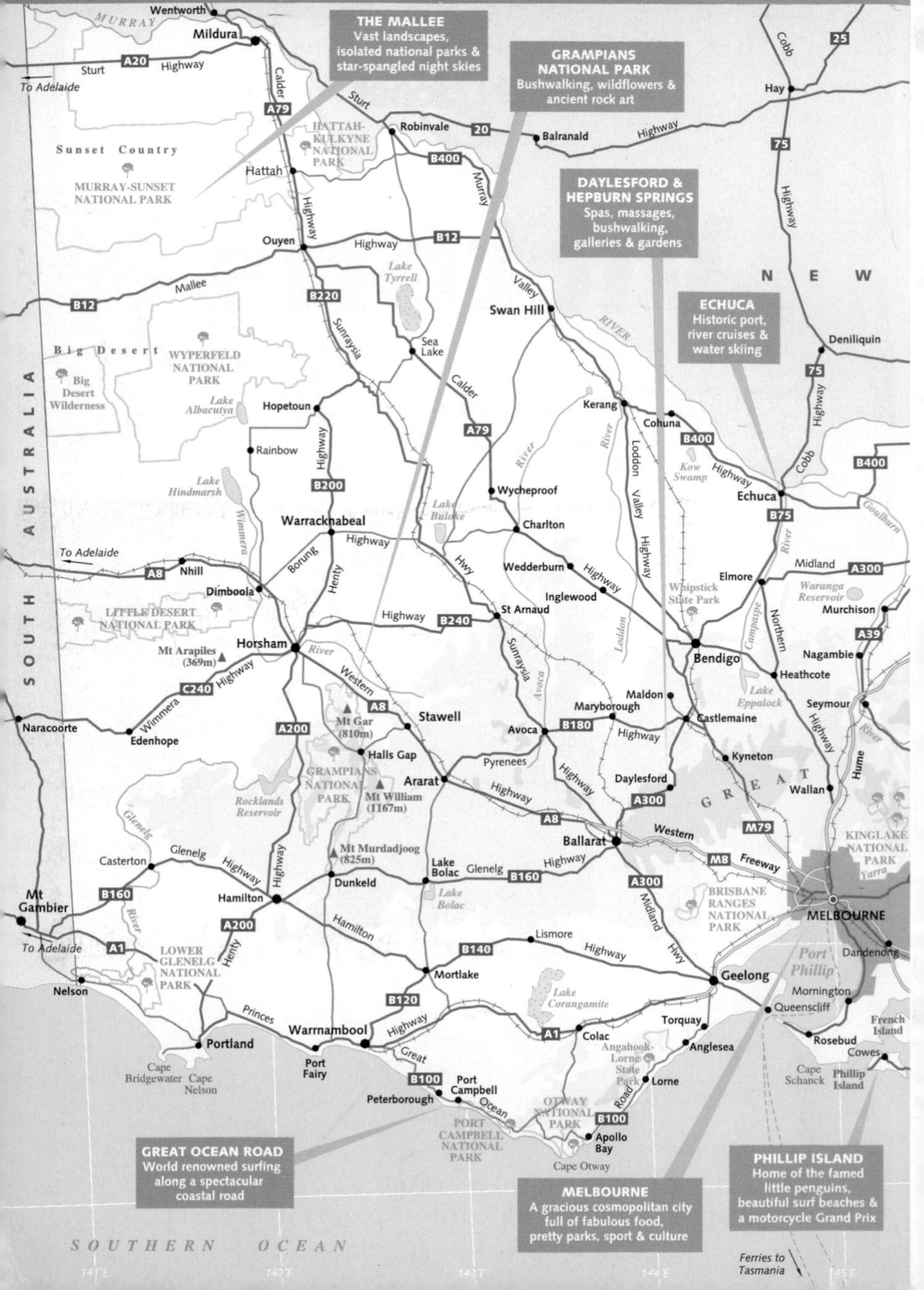
THE MALLEE
Vast landscapes, isolated national parks & star-spangled night skies
GRAMPIANS NATIONAL PARK
Bushwalking, wildflowers & ancient rock art
DAYLESFORD & HEPBURN SPRINGS
Spas, massages, bushwalking, galleries & gardens
ECHUCA
Historic port, river cruises & water skiing
GREAT OCEAN ROAD
World renowned surfing along a spectacular coastal road
MELBOURNE
A gracious cosmopolitan city full of fabulous food, pretty parks, sport & culture
PHILLIP ISLAND
Home of the famed little penguins, beautiful surf beaches & a motorcycle Grand Prix
SOUTH AUSTRALIA
NEW
SOUTHERN OCEAN
MURRAY
Wentworth
Mildura
Sturt
A20
Highway
To Adelaide
Calder
A79
Hattah
HATTAH-KULKYNE NATIONAL PARK
Robinvale
20
Balranald
Hay
Cobb
25
75
B400
Murray
Sunset Country
MURRAY-SUNSET NATIONAL PARK
Ouyen
B12
Mallee
Lake Tyrrell
B220
Sunraysia
Sea Lake
Swan Hill
Valley
RIVER
Deniliquin
Big Desert
Big Desert Wilderness
WYPERFELD NATIONAL PARK
Lake Albacutya
Hopetoun
Rainbow
Lake Hindmarsh
Wimmera
B200
Kerang
Cohuna
Kow Swamp
Loddon
Valley
Echuca
B75
Wycheproof
Lake Buloke
Charlton
Warracknabeal
Borung
Henty
To Adelaide
A8
Nhill
Dimboola
LITTLE DESERT NATIONAL PARK
Wedderburn
Inglewood
Whipstick State Park
Elmore
Midland
A300
Waranga Reservoir
Murchison
B240
St Arnaud
Horsham
Mt Arapiles (369m)
C240
Wimmera
Western
Bendigo
Campaspe
Northern
A39
Nagambie
Heathcote
Naracoorte
Edenhope
A200
Mt Gar (810m)
Stawell
Avoca
Maldon
Maryborough
B180
Castlemaine
Lake Eppalock
Seymour
Halls Gap
GRAMPIANS NATIONAL PARK
Mt William (1167m)
Ararat
Pyrenees
Kyneton
Daylesford
Wallan
Hume
Rocklands Reservoir
Glenelg
GREAT
Mt Murdadjoog (825m)
Ballarat
M79
Western
M8
Freeway
KINGLAKE NATIONAL PARK
Yarra
Casterton
Dunkeld
Lake Bolac
B160
BRISBANE RANGES NATIONAL PARK
MELBOURNE
Mt Gambier
Hamilton
Midland
Hwy
To Adelaide
A1
LOWER GLENELG NATIONAL PARK
Lismore
B140
Dandenong
Port Phillip
Nelson
Mortlake
Geelong
Mornington
Queenscliff
Lake Corangamite
B120
Princes
Portland
Warrnambool
Colac
Torquay
Anglesea
Rosebud
French Island
Cowes
Cape Bridgewater
Cape Nelson
Port Fairy
Peterborough
Port Campbell
B100
Great Ocean Road
Angahook-Lorne State Park
Lorne
Cape Schanck
Phillip Island
PORT CAMPBELL NATIONAL PARK
OTWAY NATIONAL PARK
Apollo Bay
Cape Otway
Ferries to Tasmania
141°E
142°E
143°E
144°E
145°E

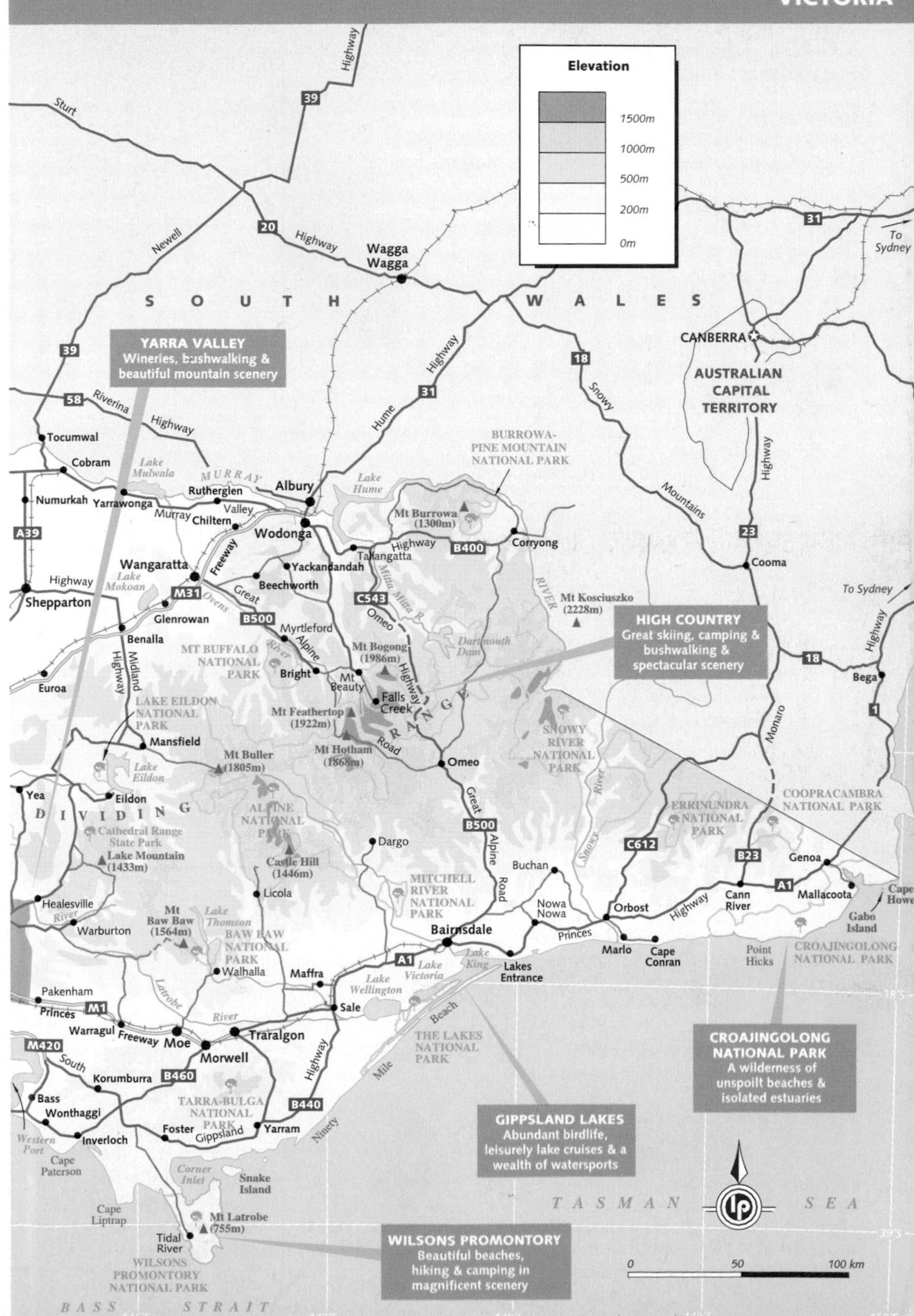

Elevation
1500m
1000m
500m
200m
0m
SOUTH WALES
CANBERRA
AUSTRALIAN CAPITAL TERRITORY
YARRA VALLEY
Wineries, bushwalking & beautiful mountain scenery
HIGH COUNTRY
Great skiing, camping & bushwalking & spectacular scenery
CROAJINGOLONG NATIONAL PARK
A wilderness of unspoilt beaches & isolated estuaries
GIPPSLAND LAKES
Abundant birdlife, leisurely lake cruises & a wealth of watersports
WILSONS PROMONTORY
Beautiful beaches, hiking & camping in magnificent scenery
Wagga Wagga
Albury
Wodonga
Wangaratta
Shepparton
Tocumwal
Cobram
Numurkah
Yarrawonga
Rutherglen
Chiltern
Beechworth
Yackandandah
Tallangatta
Corryong
Cooma
Bega
Glenrowan
Benalla
Euroa
Myrtleford
Bright
Mt Beauty
Falls Creek
Mansfield
Omeo
Eildon
Yea
Healesville
Warburton
Dargo
Licola
Buchan
Orbost
Cann River
Genoa
Mallacoota
Bairnsdale
Nowa Nowa
Lakes Entrance
Marlo
Cape Conran
Maffra
Sale
Walhalla
Pakenham
Warragul
Moe
Morwell
Traralgon
Korumburra
Bass
Wonthaggi
Inverloch
Foster
Yarram
Tidal River
Mt Burrowa (1300m)
Mt Kosciuszko (2228m)
Mt Bogong (1986m)
Mt Feathertop (1922m)
Mt Hotham (1868m)
Mt Buller (1805m)
Lake Mountain (1433m)
Castle Hill (1446m)
Mt Baw Baw (1564m)
Mt Latrobe (755m)
BURROWA-PINE MOUNTAIN NATIONAL PARK
MT BUFFALO NATIONAL PARK
LAKE EILDON NATIONAL PARK
ALPINE NATIONAL PARK
SNOWY RIVER NATIONAL PARK
ERRINUNDRA NATIONAL PARK
COOPRACAMBRA NATIONAL PARK
MITCHELL RIVER NATIONAL PARK
BAW BAW NATIONAL PARK
TARRA-BULGA NATIONAL PARK
THE LAKES NATIONAL PARK
CROAJINGOLONG NATIONAL PARK
WILSONS PROMONTORY NATIONAL PARK
Cathedral Range State Park
DIVIDING RANGE
TASMAN SEA
BASS STRAIT
To Sydney
0 50 100 km

Victoria
3rd edition – September 1999
First published – August 1993

Published by
Lonely Planet Publications Pty Ltd A.C.N. 005 607 983
192 Burwood Rd, Hawthorn, Victoria 3122, Australia

Lonely Planet Offices
Australia PO Box 617, Hawthorn, Victoria 3122
USA 150 Linden St, Oakland, CA 94607
UK 10a Spring Place, London NW5 3BH
France 1 rue du Dahomey, 75011 Paris

Photographs
Many of the images in this guide are available for licensing from Lonely Planet Images.
email: lpi@lonelyplanet.com.au

Front cover photograph
Lifeguards on Geelong Pier (Christopher Groenhout)

ISBN 0 86442 734 4

Printed by SNP Printing Pte Ltd, Singapore

Contents – Text

THE WESTERN DISTRICT 299

THE WIMMERA 314

THE MALLEE 335

THE MURRAY RIVER 342

GOLDFIELDS 374

THE HIGH COUNTRY 418

Contents – Maps

INTRODUCTION

FACTS ABOUT VICTORIA

FACTS FOR THE VISITOR

MELBOURNE

AROUND MELBOURNE

GREAT OCEAN ROAD & SOUTH-WEST COAST

THE WESTERN DISTRICT

THE MALLEE

MURRAY RIVER

GOLDFIELDS

THE HIGH COUNTRY

HUME FREEWAY & GOULBURN VALLEY

GIPPSLAND

THE LAKES DISTRICT

THE WILDERNESS COAST

MAP LEGEND

see back page

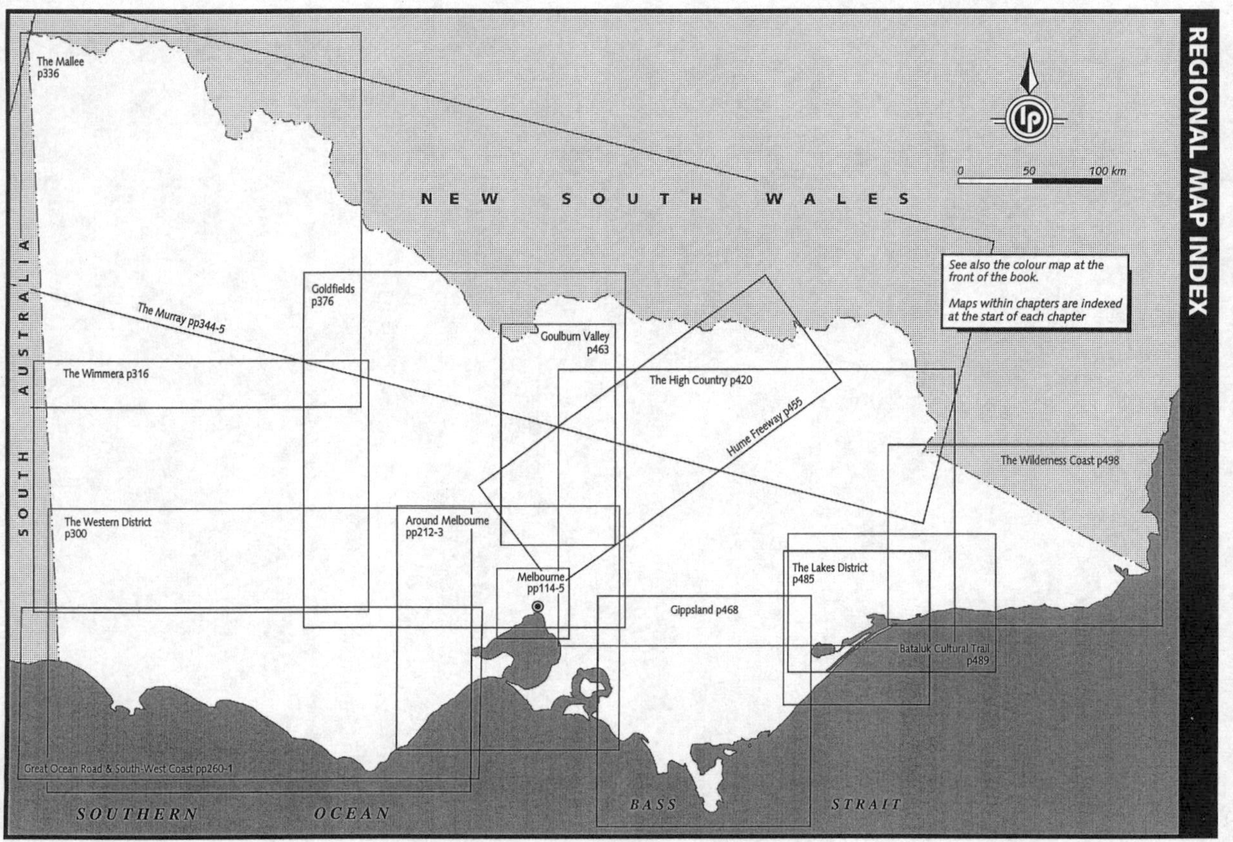
REGIONAL MAP INDEX
0
50
100 km
See also the colour map at the front of the book.
Maps within chapters are indexed at the start of each chapter
NEW SOUTH WALES
SOUTH AUSTRALIA
SOUTHERN OCEAN
BASS STRAIT
The Mallee p336
Goldfields p376
The Murray pp344-5
The Wimmera p316
Goulburn Valley p463
The High Country p420
Hume Freeway p455
The Wilderness Coast p498
The Western District p300
Around Melbourne pp212-3
Melbourne pp114-5
Gippsland p468
The Lakes District p485
Bataluk Cultural Trail p489
Great Ocean Road & South-West Coast pp260-1

The Authors

Jon Murray

Jon Murray spent time alternately travelling, and working with various publishing houses in Melbourne, Australia, before joining Lonely Planet as an editor then author. He co-authored Lonely Planet's *South Africa, Lesotho & Swaziland* and has written and updated books on destinations including West Africa, Papua New Guinea, Bangladesh and Hungary. He lives in country Victoria, on a bush block he shares with quite a few marsupials and a diminishing number of rabbits.

Mark Armstrong

In one of his former lives, Mark wrote and/or updated numerous LP guides including *Victoria*, *Melbourne*, *Queensland*, *Australia*, *Islands of Australia's Great Barrier Reef* and *Spain*. In his current state of enlightenment he lives with his wife Andrea in Melbourne, works as an account manager for an Internet company, goes surfing on weekends, and eagerly awaits the arrival of his first-born...

Michelle Bennett

Raised on the edge of an open-cut mine in Driffield, Victoria, Michelle learnt the fine art of cow milking at an early age on her parents' farm. At 17, she left the green pastures and headed for the big smoke of Melbourne to live it up (and study social geography). After graduating, she took off to travel throughout Asia and Europe, working in many fine pubs along the way. A job at a friend's graphic design studio lured her back to Australia and from there she went on to run a jazz club. After gaining a Masters degree in tourism development, Michelle joined Lonely Planet. She jumped at the chance to update part of this book, especially as it allowed her to indulge her obsession with guesthouses and B&Bs.

Joyce Connolly

Born in Edinburgh, Scotland, Joyce has been on the move from an early age; including time in the Netherlands where she developed an appreciation of Grolsch. Fuelled by the travel bug (and beer) she went to Luton to learn to be a professional tourist but instead fell into publishing in Oxford. In 1995, the urge to move on kicked in again and she set off to Australia in pursuit of Jason Donovan. She bumped into Jason in Bondi, but decided to share her Kombi with Reg, another true blue Aussie. After a year or so on the road together they returned to Melbourne, where they lived in a tent in St Kilda before becoming respectable employees of Lonely Planet. *Victoria* is Joyce's first writing assignment and she's looking forward to doing a lot more.

Richard Nebeský

Born one snowy evening in the grungy Prague suburb of Zizkov, Richard got his taste for travelling early in life when his parents dragged him away from the 'pretentious socialist paradise' of Czechoslovakia after it was invaded by the 'brotherly' Soviet troops. A stint on a campus was followed by a working wander trek around the ski resorts of the northern hemisphere and an overland odyssey across south Asia. He joined Lonely Planet in 1987, and since then has been the co-author of LP's *Central Europe* and *Eastern Europe* phrasebooks and the *Czech & Slovak Republics* guidebook. Titles he's helped to update include *Central Europe, Eastern Europe, Australia, France, Indonesia, Russia, Ukraine & Belarus, South-East Asia* and *Thailand*.

FROM THE AUTHORS

Jon Murray Jon thanks Naomi Richards for her diligent research and speedy writing of the Wimmera chapter.

Michelle Bennett Michelle would like to thank many at LP for their encouragement and support, especially Mary Neighbour, Jane Hart, Kath Dolan and the marvellous Mercury department, Gabrielle Green, Martin Hughes, Carly Hammond, Michael Weldon and Glenn Beanland. Thanks also to all the helpful folk at the tourist offices along the way, Sam Fadda at V/Line, Liza at Parks Victoria, Edwina Fowler, and the Bennett clan.

Joyce Connolly Biggest thanks go to Reg who made it so much fun, checked shower cubicles and blew our cover in Mallacoota. Thanks also to Caroline Carvahlo (for the Gemini), the Robin Hood Inn, Drouin (the folk who helped us when we locked our keys in the car), Janet Creaney, Michael McAuley, Chris and Louise for their company and photographic advice and finally my mum. Cheers also to Mary for the job, Tony for his patience and Helen for choosing Reg's photo.

Richard Nebeský Richard would like to thank the following people for extra help while researching this book: Colleen for much hospitality; Merrill and Russell for help and information; Ken Bell, Fae Valcanis, and staff at tourist information and NRE/Parks Victoria offices. Also a special thanks to the editor Tony and cartographer Helen.

This Book

The first two editions of this book were researched and written by Mark Armstrong. This edition was updated by a team of writers led by Jon Murray who coordinated the project and covered the introductory chapters, as well as Melbourne, Around Melbourne, Wimmera, Mallee, Murray River and Goulburn Valley & Hume Freeway. Jon was assisted by: Michelle Bennett, who covered the Great Ocean Road & South-West Coast, Western District and Goldfields chapters; Joyce Connolly, who updated Gippsland, the Lakes District and the Wilderness Coast chapters; and Richard Nebeský, who updated the High Country chapter.

From the Publisher

This 3rd edition of *Victoria* was edited and proofed by Tony Davidson with a great deal of assistance from Hilary Ericksen, who stepped into the breach when Tony was called away to welcome his son into the world. Martine Lleonart, Lyn McGaurr, Anne Mulvaney, Janet Austin and Sally O'Brien also contributed to the editing and proofing. Errol Hunt and Hilary Ericksen assisted with indexing, Lindsay Brown provided advice about flora and fauna entries, Adrienne Costanzo provided advice and information about places to eat and Paul Clifton advised about gay and lesbian life in Melbourne.

The mapping and design of the book was coordinated by Helen Rowley with mapping assistance from Barbara Benson. Thanks to Tim Fitzgerald for the climate charts, Guillaume Roux and Maria Vallianos for the stunning cover and to surfie Andrew Tudor for revealing his favourite surf beaches. Lonely Planet Images provided more gorgeous photographs than could possibly be used, and Matt King commissioned the intricate illustrations, which were done by Kate Nolan. Thanks also to Mark Griffiths, Paul Clifton and Chris Lee Ack for advice and to Tim Uden for his customary invaluable assistance during book layout.

Thanks to Mary Neighbour, Jane Hart and Glenn Beanland for their guidance and advice. Special thanks to Joyce Connolly and Richard Nebeský for their invaluable additional research and to Rob van Driesum for his contributions about the Macedon region and motorcycling in Victoria.

Acknowledgments

THANKS

Many thanks to the travellers who used the last edition and wrote to us with helpful hints, useful advice and interesting anecdotes:

Lachlan Anderson, Felicity Ballard, Marga & Theo van der Berg, Ren Berkerley, Hayden Berryman, Lesley Bonney, Janvander Breggen, Edmund Carew, Kate Cholweka, Deborah Collins, Margaret-Mary Corroll & Co, Waurick Dawson, Irene Esquivel, Pierluigi Fracasso, Gill Gaeuett, Job Heimerikx, Sjoerd Herder, Jan Hyde, Lesley Ireland, Evan Jones, Dan Landis, Charlotte Lobsack, Matt Lyall, Bo Maslen, Quimby Masters, Chris McClure, Neil Melville, John Morrow, Mary Munro, Megan Parish, Eva Pettersson, Karen & Ken Plunkett, Natascha Quadt, Alexandra Saidy, Phil & Teresa Savage, Dr Brian Skelton, Liz & David Smith, Zoe Smith, Joanne Tate, Kate Thompson, D A Toga, David Tognarini, Dr Klaus Truoel, Ray Wilkins, Gail Winberg, Helen Wraithmell, Carmen Zambri.

Foreword

ABOUT LONELY PLANET GUIDEBOOKS

The story begins with a classic travel adventure: Tony and Maureen Wheeler's 1972 journey across Europe and Asia to Australia. Useful information about the overland trail did not exist at that time, so Tony and Maureen published the first Lonely Planet guidebook to meet a growing need.

From a kitchen table, then from a tiny office in Melbourne (Australia), Lonely Planet has become the largest independent travel publisher in the world, an international company with offices in Melbourne, Oakland (USA), London (UK) and Paris (France).

Today Lonely Planet guidebooks cover the globe. There is an ever-growing list of books and there's information in a variety of forms and media. Some things haven't changed. The main aim is still to help make it possible for adventurous travellers to get out there – to explore and better understand the world.

At Lonely Planet we believe travellers can make a positive contribution to the countries they visit – if they respect their host communities and spend their money wisely. Since 1986 a percentage of the income from each book has been donated to aid projects and human rights campaigns.

Updates Lonely Planet thoroughly updates each guidebook as often as possible. This usually means there are around two years between editions, although for more unusual or more stable destinations the gap can be longer. Check the imprint page (following the colour map at the beginning of the book) for publication dates.

Between editions up-to-date information is available in two free newsletters – the paper *Planet Talk* and email *Comet* (to subscribe, contact any Lonely Planet office) – and on our Web site at www.lonelyplanet.com. The *Upgrades* section of the Web site covers a number of important and volatile destinations and is regularly updated by Lonely Planet authors. *Scoop* covers news and current affairs relevant to travellers. And, lastly, the *Thorn Tree* bulletin board and *Postcards* section of the site carry unverified, but fascinating, reports from travellers.

Correspondence The process of creating new editions begins with the letters, postcards and emails received from travellers. This correspondence often includes suggestions, criticisms and comments about the current editions. Interesting excerpts are immediately passed on via newsletters and the Web site, and everything goes to our authors to be verified when they're researching on the road. We're keen to get more feedback from organisations or individuals who represent communities visited by travellers.

Lonely Planet gathers information for everyone who's curious about the planet – and especially for those who explore it first-hand. Through guidebooks, phrasebooks, activity guides, maps, literature, newsletters, image library, TV series and Web site we act as an information exchange for a worldwide community of travellers.

Research Authors aim to gather sufficient practical information to enable travellers to make informed choices and to make the mechanics of a journey run smoothly. They also research historical and cultural background to help enrich the travel experience and allow travellers to understand and respond appropriately to cultural and environmental issues.

Authors don't stay in every hotel because that would mean spending a couple of months in each medium-sized city and, no, they don't eat at every restaurant because that would mean stretching belts beyond capacity. They do visit hotels and restaurants to check standards and prices, but feedback based on readers' direct experiences can be very helpful.

Many of our authors work undercover, others aren't so secretive. None of them accept freebies in exchange for positive write-ups. And none of our guidebooks contain any advertising.

Production Authors submit their raw manuscripts and maps to offices in Australia, USA, UK or France. Editors and cartographers – all experienced travellers themselves – then begin the process of assembling the pieces. When the book finally hits the shops, some things are already out of date, we start getting feedback from readers and the process begins again ...

WARNING & REQUEST

Things change – prices go up, schedules change, good places go bad and bad places go bankrupt – nothing stays the same. So, if you find things better or worse, recently opened or long since closed, please tell us and help make the next edition even more accurate and useful. We genuinely value all the feedback we receive. Julie Young coordinates a well travelled team that reads and acknowledges every letter, postcard and email and ensures that every morsel of information finds its way to the appropriate authors, editors and cartographers for verification.

Everyone who writes to us will find their name in the next edition of the appropriate guidebook. They will also receive the latest issue of *Planet Talk*, our quarterly printed newsletter, or *Comet*, our monthly email newsletter. Subscriptions to both newsletters are free. The very best contributions will be rewarded with a free guidebook.

Excerpts from your correspondence may appear in new editions of Lonely Planet guidebooks, the Lonely Planet Web site, *Planet Talk* or *Comet*, so please let us know if you *don't* want your letter published or your name acknowledged.

Send all correspondence to the Lonely Planet office closest to you:

Australia: PO Box 617, Hawthorn, Victoria 3122
USA: 150 Linden St, Oakland, CA 94607
UK: 10A Spring Place, London NW5 3BH
France: 1 rue du Dahomey, 75011 Paris

Or email us at: talk2us@lonelyplanet.com.au

For news, views and updates see our Web site: www.lonelyplanet.com

HOW TO USE A LONELY PLANET GUIDEBOOK

The best way to use a Lonely Planet guidebook is any way you choose. At Lonely Planet we believe the most memorable travel experiences are often those that are unexpected, and the finest discoveries are those you make yourself. Guidebooks are not intended to be used as if they provide a detailed set of infallible instructions!

Contents All Lonely Planet guidebooks follow roughly the same format. The Facts about the Destination chapters or sections give background information ranging from history to weather. Facts for the Visitor gives practical information on issues like visas and health. Getting There & Away gives a brief starting point for researching travel to and from the destination. Getting Around gives an overview of the transport options when you arrive.

The peculiar demands of each destination determine how subsequent chapters are broken up, but some things remain constant. We always start with background, then proceed to sights, places to stay, places to eat, entertainment, getting there and away, and getting around information – in that order.

Heading Hierarchy Lonely Planet headings are used in a strict hierarchical structure that can be visualised as a set of Russian dolls. Each heading (and its following text) is encompassed by any preceding heading that is higher on the hierarchical ladder.

Entry Points We do not assume guidebooks will be read from beginning to end, but that people will dip into them. The traditional entry points are the list of contents and the index. In addition, however, some books have a complete list of maps and an index map illustrating map coverage.

There may also be a colour map that shows highlights. These highlights are dealt with in greater detail in the Facts for the Visitor chapter, along with planning questions and suggested itineraries. Each chapter covering a geographical region usually begins with a locator map and another list of highlights. Once you find something of interest in a list of highlights, turn to the index.

Maps Maps play a crucial role in Lonely Planet guidebooks and include a huge amount of information. A legend is printed on the back page. We seek to have complete consistency between maps and text, and to have every important place in the text captured on a map. Map key numbers usually start in the top left corner.

Although inclusion in a guidebook usually implies a recommendation we cannot list every good place. Exclusion does not necessarily imply criticism. In fact there are a number of reasons why we might exclude a place – sometimes it is simply inappropriate to encourage an influx of travellers.

Introduction

Victoria is Australia's smallest mainland state. It's also a place of great contrasts – of ocean beaches and mountain ranges, deserts and forests, volcanic plains and endless sheep farms.

Its people are the most diverse in Australia, with immigrants from all over the world pouring in during the 19th century gold rushes, and again after WWII when Melbourne's Station Pier was the Australian equivalent of New York's Ellis Island.

There are more than 30 national parks – more than 12% of the state is classified as national park – and dozens of state parks, coastal parks and historical parks. The diversity is truly amazing, ranging from the lush cool-temperate rainforest areas of the Errinundra Plateau to the coastal wilderness areas of the nearby Croajingolong; from the mountainous majesty of the Alpine National Park to the flat desert wilderness areas in the north-west Mallee region.

One of the great things about these national and state parks and reserves is that there are so many ways of exploring and enjoying them. These areas are managed and protected, but they are there to be experienced and there are plenty of low-impact ways of doing that – camping, bushwalking, climbing, horse trekking, nature-watching, or for the more adventurous, ballooning, hang-gliding, canoeing and white-water rafting.

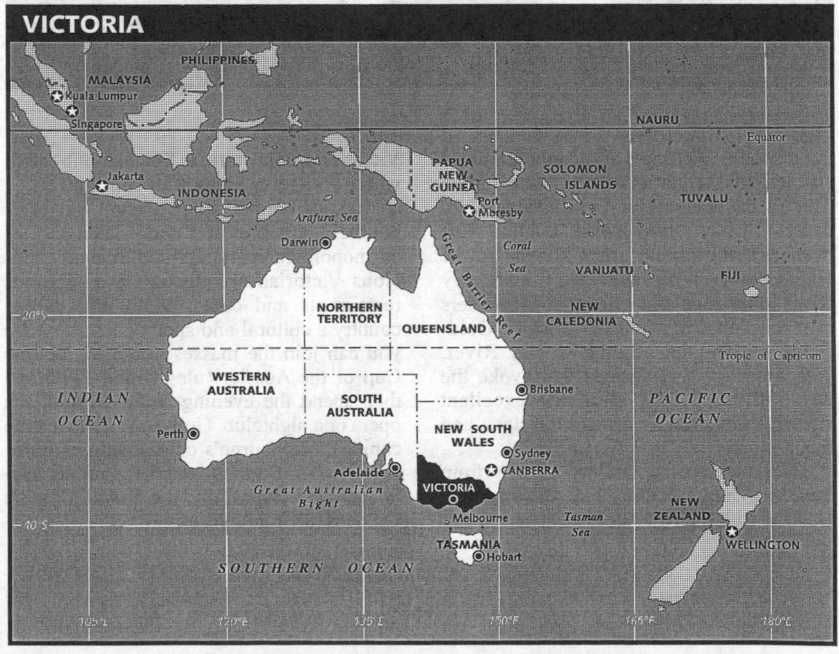

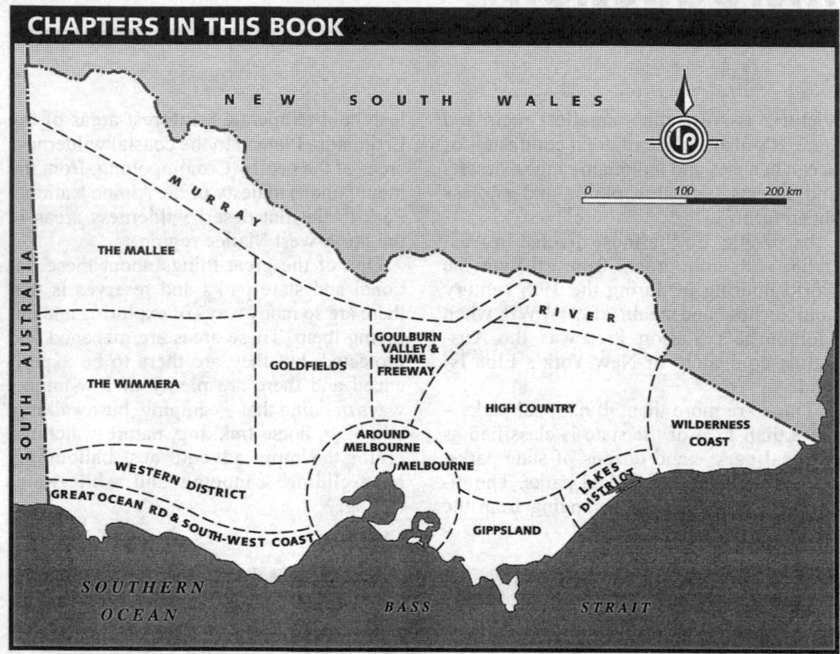

Of course, Victoria's attractions aren't restricted to the national and state parks. There's the spectacular Great Ocean Road coastal drive (past world famous surf beaches); the alpine areas known as the High Country, where the 'man from Snowy River' once rode and where snow-boarders blitz the slopes in winter; the historic Goldfields region; the mighty Murray River, with a string of townships that evoke the days of the paddle steamers; excellent wineries scattered all around the state; and much more.

Then there are the country towns – from large provincial centres like Bendigo and Ballarat with their rich gold-rush heritage of Victorian architecture, to tiny one-pub towns where you never know who you'll meet.

And, of course, there's good old Melbourne – a subtle and understated city of cosmopolitan charm, cultural diversity, gracious Victorian architecture and fabulous restaurants and cafes. Melbourne is the country's cultural and sports capital, where you can join the masses at the Melbourne Cup or the Aussie Rules Grand Final and then spend the evening at the theatre, the opera or a nightclub. Unlike most other state capitals, Melbourne's climate allows European trees to flourish, and the gracious public gardens, especially the Royal Botanic Gardens, are a highlight.

Facts about Victoria

HISTORY

The Dreamtime

Like most other peoples, Australian Aborigines have creation stories; the creation period is often called the Dreamtime. It was the time when spiritual beings travelled the land forming natural features and instituting laws and rituals.

But the Dreamtime is not simply the past – it is also the present and future. After creating life and everything associated with it, the spirits entered the land to dwell or formed themselves into natural features. This explains the strong spiritual link Aborigines have to particular tracts of land. Taking care of sacred sites is an essential part of maintaining life, health and social order.

Early Aboriginal History

Aborigines probably journeyed from South-East Asia to the Australian mainland at least 50,000 years ago, possibly much earlier.

The short-faced giant kangaroo (left) – rather larger than the eastern grey kangaroo (right) – became extinct around 35,000 years ago.

Although much of Australia is arid, the first immigrants found a much wetter continent, with forests and inland lakes teeming with fish. The native animals included 'megafauna' – gigantic marsupials such as 3m-tall kangaroos, giant koalas and wombats, and huge, flightless birds. The environment was relatively non-threatening, with few carnivorous predators.

Archaeological evidence suggests that Aborigines colonised the whole of the continent within a few thousand years. They were the first people in the world to manufacture polished edge-ground stone tools, cremate their dead and engrave and paint representations of themselves and the animals they hunted.

As the last ice age ended, around 15,000 to 10,000 years ago, sea levels rose and the Aborigines were isolated on the continent. Many of the inland lakes dried up and vast deserts formed, causing the majority of the inhabitants to live in coastal areas or along the relatively rare inland rivers.

When Europeans arrived, it's estimated that there were at least 300,000 people (possibly as many as a million) already living in Australia. Victoria was thought to have been home to around 15,000 people, but recent evidence suggests that the figure could be as high as 100,000. Diseases from Europe, which decimated Aboriginal peoples around Sydney Town, probably wiped out many Victorian Aborigines well before Europeans ventured south of the Murray River.

The Victorian people lived in some 38 different dialect groups who spoke 10 separate languages, with each of the dialect groups being further divided into clans and sub-clans. Each clan owned a distinct area of land, and its complex culture was largely based on a close spiritual bond with that land.

There was no need for agriculture. The land provided for them in abundance, and their survival and prosperity were a result of their deep understanding of a very rich environment.

The coastal tribes ate an amazing variety of plants and vegetables, supplementing their diet with seafood. Shellfish were collected and eaten on the beaches; evidence of these feasts in the form of huge shell middens has been found all along the Victorian coast. Inland tribes were expert hunters, using nets to catch kangaroos and possums, spears to kill emus, and boomerangs to bring down birds.

The tribes who lived along the coast and beside rivers also developed methods of trapping fish and eels. On the Murray River near Swan Hill, the people dug channels and built wooden grills to trap fish during floods, and at Lake Condah in the Western District complex stone channels were built to harvest migrating eels. Latticed weirs and funnelled baskets were also commonly used to catch fish.

Vast networks of trading routes existed across the huge continent. Sometimes the 'trade' was in goods, such as ceremonial clay, but often people met for cultural reasons.

Europeans Arrive

Captain James Cook is popularly regarded as the first European to 'discover' Australia but Portuguese sailors probably sighted the continent in the early 16th century. The earliest European coastal exploration, made by Dutch sailors who reached the west coast of Cape York and several places on the west coast, occurred about the same time.

The extreme south-eastern tip of the continent was sighted by Cook on 19 April 1770, and named Point Hicks. The *Endeavour* (Cook's ship) turned north and charted the coast. Nine days later the expedition found sheltered anchorage in a harbour they named Botany Bay. Cook continued north and again put ashore at Possession Island at the tip of Cape York to raise the Union Jack, rename the continent New South Wales (NSW) and claim it for the British in the name of King George III.

During their forays ashore the scientists recorded descriptions of plants, animals and birds, the likes of which had never been seen before, and attempted to communicate with the inhabitants, who all but ignored them. Cook later wrote of the Aborigines:

> They may appear to some to be the most wretched people upon the earth: but in reality they are far more happier than we Europeans...They live in a tranquillity which is not disturbed by the inequality of condition...they seem to set no value upon anything we gave them, nor would they ever part with anything of their own...

Despite the presence of the Aborigines, when the Europeans arrived in Australia they considered the 'new' continent to be *terra nullius* – a land belonging to no-one. Conveniently, they saw no recognisable system of government, no commerce or permanent settlements and no evidence of land ownership.

Convicts & European Settlement

Following the American Revolution, Britain was no longer able to transport convicts to North America. In 1786 Lord Sydney announced that the King had decided on Botany Bay as the destination for convicts under sentence of transportation.

In January 1788, the First Fleet sailed into Botany Bay under the command of Captain Arthur Phillip, the colony's first governor. Disappointed with the location of Botany Bay, Phillip immediately sailed to Sydney Cove on Port Jackson (Sydney Harbour). The Colony of NSW initially comprised the whole eastern half of the continent, but the area that comprises today's state of NSW was explored and settled first.

Although NSW was a convict colony it became obvious that Australia had the potential to be a wealthy colony with a more usual social structure than that at Sydney Cove in 1788. Of course, the social structure envisaged was a very British one, with a privileged class, preferably British-born and educated, controlling Australian-born colonials, with ex-convicts and a near-slave class of convicts at the bottom. Until the discovery of gold upset these plans, the wealth of the colony was to come from wool.

Europeans Cross the Murray

In 1803, a small party of convicts, soldiers and settlers under the command of Captain David Collins arrived at Sorrento (on Port Phillip) but abandoned the settlement in less than a year. A group of convicts escaped during this time and one, William Buckley, lived with a group of Kooris for over 30 years (see the boxed text). The arrival at Portland of Edward Henty, his family and flock of sheep from Van Diemen's Land in 1834 marked the first permanent European settlement in Victoria, but the astonishingly rapid influx of Europeans arrived overland from the north.

Two government sponsored journeys of exploration into the lands south of the Murray river revealed vast lands suitable for grazing cattle and, most importantly, sheep.

In 1824 Hume and Hovell made the first overland journey southwards from Sydney to the shores of Port Phillip. Their route was roughly that of today's Hume Highway. In 1836, the colony's surveyor-general, Major Thomas Mitchell, crossed the Murray (then called the Hume) near Swan Hill and travelled south-west to find the rich volcanic plains of the Western District. He wrote glowing reports of the fertile country and dubbed the region Australia Felix, or 'Australia Fair'. Mitchell's enthusiasm encouraged pastoralists to rush into Victoria, and within 10 years Europeans outnumbered Aborigines.

Aboriginal Resistance

With no need to build, no need to produce a surplus of food to survive winter, no concept of land as property that could be traded or conquered, and a cerebral religion with 50,000 years of development, the Aborigines' culture was highly sophisticated. But it was also practically invisible to the first Europeans.

Europeans took land as they wanted it and killed Aborigines who resisted. Usually, the cause of violence wasn't so much the taking of the land (Aboriginal culture had no notion that land *could* be taken) but reprisals for Aborigines killing sheep on the land.

At a local level, individual Aborigines resisted the invasion. Warriors including Pemulwy, Yagan, Dundalli, Pigeon and Nemarluk were feared by the colonists in their areas. But, although some settlements had to be abandoned, the weaponry and coherence of the European forces invariably won in the end.

Aborigines were generally regarded as a hindrance to the 'civilisation' and settlement of Victoria. Soon after the arrival of Europeans, their culture was disrupted, they were dispossessed of their lands, and they were killed in their thousands – initially by introduced diseases, such as smallpox, dysentery and measles, and later by guns and poison.

Estimates suggest that by 1860 there were only around 2000 Aborigines left alive in Victoria. It's a sad fact that the only Europeans to gain a detailed understanding of Aboriginal life were the few escaped convicts who lived with the tribes.

Founding of Melbourne

Two Tasmanians, John Batman and John Pascoe Fawkner, are widely acknowledged as the founders of Melbourne.

In 1835 a group of Launceston businessmen formed the Port Phillip Association with the intention of establishing a new settlement on Port Phillip. In May of that year, their representative, John Batman, purchased about 240,000 hectares of land from the Aborigines of the Dutigalla clan.

The concept of buying or selling land was completely foreign to the Aborigines, but in return for their land they received an assorted collection of blankets, tomahawks, knives, looking-glasses, scissors, handkerchiefs, various items of clothing and 50 pounds of flour. Once the treaty was signed, the other members of the association joined

Batman, and the settlement of Melbourne was established on the northern side of the Yarra River.

In October John Pascoe Fawkner and a group of Tasmanian settlers joined them. The son of a convict, Fawkner grew up in the harsh environment of a convict settlement. When he was 22, he received 500 lashes for helping seven convicts escape, and all his life he carried with him the scars of the lash and a hatred of the transportation system.

Fawkner was a driving force behind the new settlement. He was a self-taught bush lawyer, started several newspapers, and spent 15 years on the Legislative Council of Victoria, where he campaigned vigorously for the rights of small settlers and convicts and for the ending of transportation. By the time of his death in 1869, Melbourne was flourishing and he was known as the 'Grand Old Man of Victoria'. More than 15,000 people lined the streets to bid him farewell at his funeral.

History doesn't remember John Batman as kindly. Within four years of his shonky deal with the Aborigines, Batman was dead, a victim of his own excesses. Manning Clark describes him in *A History of Australia* as '...a man who abandoned himself wantonly to the Dionysian frenzy and allowed no restraint to come between himself and the satisfaction of his desires'.

While the initial treaty with the Aborigines had no legal basis, by 1836 so many settlers had moved to Port Phillip that the administrators of NSW had to declare the area open to settlement. The *Advertiser* newspaper wrote on 8 April 1838:

> The town of Melbourne is rapidly increasing in population and in building. There are at this present time not less than 10 brick houses in hand, some of them roofed in, and others, the walls partly built...

In 1839 the military surveyor Robert Hoddle drew up the plans for the new city, laying out a geometric grid of broad streets in a rectangular pattern on the northern side of the Yarra River.

By 1840 there were over 10,000 Europeans in the area around Melbourne. The

The Burke & Wills Expedition

In 1860, the Royal Society of Victoria and the Victorian Government organised an expedition to attempt the first crossing of the Australian continent from south to north. The expedition's leader, Robert O'Hara Burke, a police superintendent, was 39, had no exploration experience and was regarded as impulsive, eccentric, charming, short-tempered, reckless and brave; a contrary and fatal mix. While the expedition was hastily thrown together and poorly planned, it was also the most expensive in the history of Australian exploration, costing over £60,000, as well as seven lives.

Lavishly equipped, the party set off from Melbourne on 20 August 1860 and eventually set up a base camp at Coopers Creek. Burke, Wills, King and Gray then set out on a 2400km dash north across the centre to the Gulf of Carpentaria. They took provisions for three months, but the march took four and Gray died of exhaustion on the way back. The other three arrived back in Coopers Creek to find the base camp had been abandoned that very morning. Exhausted and near starvation, Burke decided they should try to reach a police station at Mt Hopeless, 240km away, instead of following their original track. They never made it. Burke and Wills died within a few days of each other, but King was kept alive by Aborigines until he was rescued by a search party.

As a local historian wrote, 'Burke was a death or glory man and he achieved both'.

Mark Armstrong

earliest provincial towns were established along the south coast at places like Portland, Port Fairy and Port Albert. The earliest inland settlements were sheep stations – small self-sufficient communities. As the new communities grew in size and confidence, they began to agitate for separation from NSW.

Separation & Gold Rushes

In 1851 Victoria won separation from NSW. The colony of Victoria was proclaimed with Melbourne as its capital. In the same year, gold was discovered at Bathurst in NSW. Fearing the young city's workers would desert for the northern goldfields, a committee of Melbourne businessmen offered a reward to anyone who found gold within Victoria – but even in their wildest dreams they couldn't have foreseen what would follow. The first gold strike was at Warrandyte in May 1851, and during the next few months massive finds followed at Buninyong and Clunes near Ballarat, Mt Alexander near Castlemaine and Ravenswood near Bendigo.

The subsequent gold rush brought a huge influx of immigrants from around the world. The Irish and English, and later other Europeans, Americans and Chinese, began arriving in droves and within 12 months there were about 1800 hopeful diggers disembarking at Melbourne every week.

The town became a chaotic mess. As soon as ships arrived in the harbour, their crews would desert and follow the passengers to the goldfields. Business in Melbourne ground to a standstill as most of the labour force left to join the search. Shanty towns of bark huts and canvas tents sprang up to house the population, which doubled within a decade. In 1852 the *Sydney Morning Herald* asserted:

> ...that a worse regulated, worse governed, worse drained, worse lighted, worse watered town of note is not on the face of the globe; and that a population more thoroughly disposed in every grade to cheating and robbery, open and covert, does not exist; that in no other place does immorality stalk abroad so unblushingly and so unchecked...that, in a word, nowhere in the southern hemisphere does chaos reign so triumphant as in Melbourne.

But a generation later, bolstered by the wealth of the goldfields, this ragged city had matured and refined itself into 'Marvellous Melbourne', one of the world's great Victorian-era cities. HM Hyndman, in his *Record of an Adventurous Life*, said of Melbourne in 1870:

> I have been a great deal about the world and I have moved freely in many societies, but I have never lived in any city where the people at large, as well as the educated class, took so keen an interest in all the activities of human life, as in Melbourne at the time I visited it. Art, the drama, music, literature, journalism, wit, oratory all found ready appreciation. The life and vivacity of the place were astonishing.

The gold rush produced enough wealth for Victoria to transform itself from a fledgling colony into a prosperous and independent state, but it also brought with it tensions that were to lead to significant social and political changes. In the early days of the rush, authorities introduced a compulsory licence fee, but in 1854 a group of miners at the Ballarat diggings rioted and burnt their licences in protest at the inequality of the fees. Twenty-five miners were killed during what was known as the Eureka Rebellion, but the aftermath was to forever change the political landscape in Victoria. (See the boxed text in the Goldfields chapter for more details.)

The gold rush years were a period of great prosperity and flamboyance, leading to a flowering of the arts and culture. Melburnians took some pride in the fact that theirs was not a convict settlement, and they used their new-found wealth to build a city of extravagant proportions. Among the new migrants came tradespeople from Europe who were trained in the great traditions of Renaissance building, and the city's architects readily put them to work. Large areas were set aside and planted as public parks and gardens. By the 1880s Melbourne was

The Chinese in Victoria

During the gold rush, diggers came to Victoria from all over the world. In particular, Chinese immigrants flooded into the state and headed for the goldfields. Their presence was greatly resented by the other diggers, and in response to demonstrations the government introduced a number of anti-Chinese policies, including a £10 per head entry tax and a quota on the number of Chinese each ship could bring into the state. In 1857 anti-Chinese sentiments spilled over in Ararat and at the Buckland River, and during race riots Chinese diggers were forcibly driven from the goldfields. But neither racist attitudes nor government policies could stem the influx, and between 1852 and 1859 the number of Chinese in Victoria rose from 2000 to 42,000, representing almost one-third of the goldfields' population.

By the end of the decade, however, much of the surface gold on the Victorian fields had been removed and many Chinese diggers returned home or moved on to new goldfields in New South Wales.

Today there are numerous reminders of the Chinese in Victoria. Many of the goldfields' cemeteries (notably those in Beechworth and Bendigo) have separate Chinese sections. Bendigo also has a historic Chinese Joss House and the impressive Golden Dragon Museum, and in Melbourne's Chinatown there's the Museum of Chinese Australian History.

Mark Armstrong

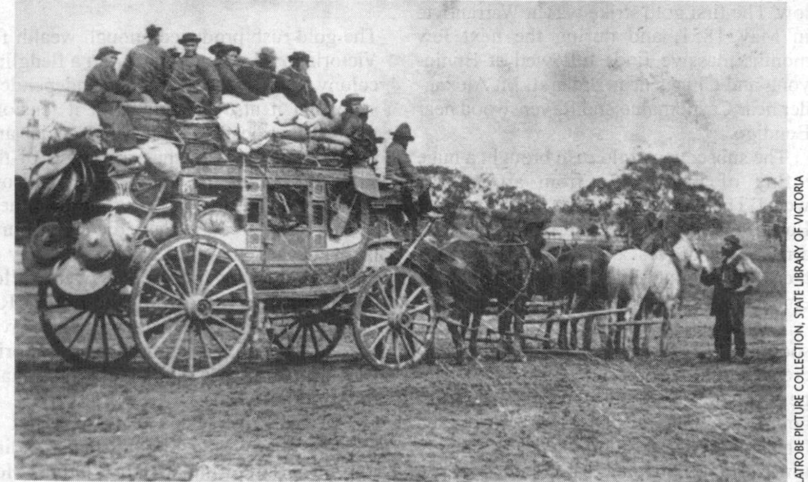

LATROBE PICTURE COLLECTION, STATE LIBRARY OF VICTORIA

Chinese people aboard a heavily laden stagecoach, en route to the goldfields.

being referred to as the 'Paris of the Antipodes'.

Similarly, from 1851 onwards provincial Victoria was quickly settled. The gold-rush wealth built major towns to house the sudden massive increase in the population, and the pastoralists and squatters spread their interests across the state.

This period of great prosperity lasted for 40 years. The 1880s were boom times for

Melbourne, but there was an air of recklessness. Money from the goldfields and from overseas was invested in real estate and building works, and speculation led to spiralling land prices that couldn't last. In 1888 Melbourne hosted the Great Exhibition in the opulent Exhibition Buildings. No expense was spared in the construction of the buildings or the exhibition itself, but this flamboyant showing-off to the world was the swan-song of Marvellous Melbourne.

In 1889 the property market collapsed under the increasing weight of speculation. In 1890 a financial crash in Argentina led to the collapse of several financial institutions in London and, overnight, investment in Australia dried up. The 1890s was a period of severe economic depression. In Melbourne, many buildings that were incomplete at the time of the collapse were never completed, and it was many years before the city recovered.

Aborigines Protection Act

Between 1861 and 1863, the Board for the Protection of Aborigines gathered many of the surviving Aborigines and placed them in reserves run by Christian missionaries – at Ebenezer in the north-west, Framlingham and Lake Condah in the Western District, Lake Tyers and Ramahyuck in Gippsland, and Coranderrk near Healesville. These reserves developed into self-sufficient farming communities and gave their residents a measure of independence, but they hastened the destruction of indigenous cultures.

The Aborigines Protection Act of 1886 stipulated that only full-blooded Aborigines or 'half-castes' older than 34 years of age could remain in the reserves – others had to leave and 'assimilate into the community'. The effect of the act was to separate families and eventually destroy the reserves themselves. By 1923 the only reserves in operation were Lake Tyers, with just over 200 residents, and Framlingham, with only a handful of people.

By the early 1900s, legislation designed to segregate and 'protect' Aborigines was passed. It restricted their right to own property and seek employment, and the Aboriginals' Ordinance of 1918 allowed the removal of children from Aboriginal mothers if it was suspected that the father was non-Aboriginal.

Children were still forcibly removed from their families as recently as the mid-1970s and today they are referred to as 'the Stolen Generation'. It's impossible to overestimate the pain caused by these abductions. It's equally difficult to understand current Prime Minister John Howard's refusal to apologise for them, despite the example of many church and state leaders, and many ordinary non-indigenous citizens.

Federation & After

With Federation, on 1 January 1901, Victoria became a state of the new Australian nation. Melbourne was the capital and the seat of federal government until it moved to Canberra in 1927. The Federal Parliament sat at the State Parliament Houses, and the State Parliament moved to the Exhibition Buildings. But Australia's loyalties and many of its legal ties to Britain remained. When WWI broke out, Australian troops went to fight in the trenches of France, Gallipoli and the Middle East.

There was more expansion and construction in Victoria in the 1920s, but all this came to a halt with the Great Depression, which hit Australia hard. In 1931 almost a third of breadwinners were unemployed and poverty was widespread. During the Depression the government implemented a number of major public works programmes and workers were put on sustenance pay ('susso'). Melbourne's Yarra Boulevard, the Shrine of Remembrance, St Kilda Rd and the Great Ocean Rd were all built by sustenance workers. By 1932, however, Australia's economy was starting to recover as a result of rises in wool prices and a rapid revival of manufacturing.

Post WWII

After WWII the Australian government initiated an immigration programme in the hope that the increase in population would strengthen Australia's economy and contribute to its ability to defend itself. 'Populate or Perish' became the catch phrase. Between 1947 and 1968 more than 800,000 non-British European immigrants came to Australia. The majority arrived by ships which landed in Melbourne first, and a large percentage of the new arrivals settled there. Since the 1970s immigrants have also been arriving from South-East Asia. (See the Population & People section later in this chapter for further information on immigration.)

On the political front, Victoria's post-WWII years were dominated by the conservative Liberal Party, which governed from 1955 to 1982, when the Labor Party came to power.

During the 1980s Victoria experienced boom times, just as it had 100 years earlier. Land prices rose throughout the decade, and thanks to monetary deregulation, banks were queuing up to lend money to speculators and developers. The city centre and surrounds were transformed as one skyscraper sprang up after another, leading some over-excited architects to refer to Melbourne as the 'Chicago of the southern hemisphere'. Even the worldwide stock market crash in 1987 didn't slow things down, but in 1990 the property market collapsed, just as it had 100 years earlier.

By 1991 Australia found itself in recession again, partly as a result of domestic economic policy, but also because Australia is particularly hard hit when international demand (and prices) for primary produce and minerals falls. Unemployment was the highest it had been since the early 1930s and Victoria, the industrial heartland, was the state hardest hit.

In 1992, a Liberal/National party coalition led by Jeff Kennett was elected in a landslide victory. The Kennett government has ruled the state with an iron fist. Its policies are succeeding in turning around the economy and Victoria should enter the new millennium in a reasonable economic condition. However, this has been achieved through a Thatcherite agenda and there are gaping holes in the health and education systems. The effects of privatising practically everything are beginning to be felt, and they are by no means uniformly positive.

The Mabo Decision & Native Title

In 1982, five Torres Strait Islanders led by Eddie Mabo began an action for a declaration of native title over the Queensland Murray Islands. They argued that the legal principle of *terra nullius* had wrongfully usurped their title to land, as for thousands of years Murray Islanders had enjoyed a relationship with the land that included a notion of ownership. In June 1992 the High Court of Australia rejected *terra nullius* and the myth that Australia had been unoccupied. In doing this, it recognised that a principle of native title existed before the arrival of the British.

The High Court's judgment became known as the Mabo decision, one of the most controversial decisions ever handed down by an Australian court. It was ambiguous, as it didn't outline the extent to which native title existed in mainland Australia. It received a hostile reaction from the mining and other industries and resulted in some fairly hysterical responses. But the Mabo decision was hailed by Aborigines and the then Prime Minister Paul Keating as an opportunity to create a basis for reconciliation between Aboriginal and non-Aboriginal Australians.

To define the principle of native title, the federal parliament passed the Native Title Act in 1993. Contrary to the cries of protest from the mining industry, the act gave Aborigines very few new rights. It limited the application of native title to land that no-one else owns or leases, and to land with which Aborigines have had continuous physical association since European settlement. Since 1998, when the Federal Liberal/National government outlined its infamous '10 Point Plan' to 'improve' the Native Title Act, the scales have been weighed even more heavily against Aborigines.

Victoria has little land that qualifies for Native Title claims compared with the larger states and their huge swathes of Crown land. Also, Koories in Victoria were decimated by the European invasion and the survivors were moved to concentration camps (aka reserves), so it is very difficult to prove continuous cultural connection with the land.

GEOGRAPHY

Australia is the world's sixth largest country. Its area is 7,682,300 sq km, about the same size as mainland USA and approximately 5% of the world's land surface.

Victoria is the smallest mainland state, and its area of 227,600 sq km makes up 3% of the continent's land mass. It is roughly equivalent in size to Great Britain. It is wedge-shaped, and stretches about 780km from east to west, with a coastline 1680km long.

Victoria is bordered to the south by the waters of Bass Strait (which joins the Southern Ocean and the Tasman Sea), to the west by South Australia and to the north by the Murray River, which forms the border with NSW.

There is a startling variety of landscape, ranging from the near-desert regions in the north-west to the cool-temperate rainforests in the south-east. There are five main geographic regions.

Western District Plains

The flat lands of the Western District, in the south-west of the state, comprise some of the best grazing land in the country partly because of its rich soil, the result of relatively recent volcanic activity. In fact it's the world's third-largest volcanic plain, with lava flows, volcanic peaks and crater lakes scattered throughout.

Murray/Darling Basin

North of the Western District are the Wimmera and Mallee regions, which together make up the Victorian section of the vast Murray/Darling Basin. The basin was formed from the beds of ancient and long-dry seas and lakes.

This is the driest, flattest and hottest part of Victoria, characterised by endless wheat fields and sheep farms, Mallee-type vegetation, salt lakes, and the wilderness national parks of the north-western corner.

Great Dividing Range

The mountains of the Great Dividing Range run parallel with Australia's east coast, from north Queensland down through NSW and into north-eastern Victoria, where they turn west to follow the Victorian coastline. West of Kilmore (north of Melbourne) the mountains begin to peter out, finally coming to an end near the Grampians.

The spectacular alpine areas in Victoria's north-east are collectively known as the High Country, and include numerous high plateaus and the state's highest peaks – Mt Bogong (1986m) and Mt Feathertop (1922m).

RELATIVE SIZE OF VICTORIA

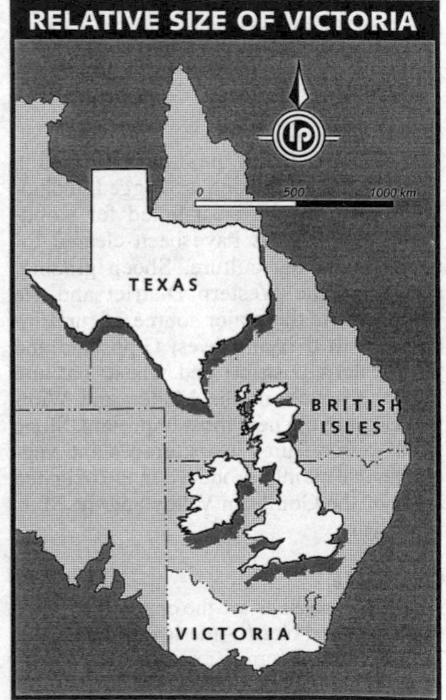

Gippsland

Gippsland, which stretches along the south-east of the state, includes the industrial Latrobe Valley with its extensive deposits of brown coal, the rolling hills and fertile dairy farms of south Gippsland, Australia's largest inland waterway system (the Lakes District), and remote national parks in the vast forests of East Gippsland.

Coastal Region

The coastline is diverse and ever-changing, with long sandy beaches contrasting with rugged headlands. The west coast includes the remote beaches of Discovery Bay and Portland Bay, the rock formations of the Port Campbell National Park, and resort-town beaches (with world-famous surf) along the Great Ocean Road. In the centre of the coastline are the three major inlets – Port Phillip , Western Port and Corner Inlet (which is north of Wilsons Promontory). East of Wilsons Promontory is the long sand bar known as the Ninety Mile Beach, and the remote far-eastern coastline is protected as part of the Croajingolong National Park.

Land Use

While about 35% of the state is covered in forests (many of which are logged, including some that are clear-felled for woodchips), large areas have been cleared for grazing and agriculture. Sheep grazing, mostly in the Western District and the Wimmera, is the major source of rural income, with dairying (west Gippsland and the Western District) and wheat, oat and barley production (the Mallee and Wimmera) being the next most important. Stone fruits, citrus fruits, pears, grapes and vegetables are mainly produced in the irrigated areas of the Goulburn Valley and the Murray River.

CLIMATE

Australia's seasons are the opposite of those in Europe and North America, so January is in the height of summer and July the depths of winter.

Victoria has a temperate four-seasons climate, although the distinctions between the seasons are often blurred by the unpredictability of the weather. There are three climatic regions: the southern and coastal areas, the alpine areas, and the areas north and west of the Great Dividing Range.

The climate charts give an indication of the average seasonal temperatures and rainfall for Melbourne, Mt Hotham and Mildura. Generally, the southern and coastal areas will be similar to Melbourne, the alpine areas (Mt Hotham) colder and wetter, and the northern and western areas (Mildura) warmer and drier. Rainfall is spread fairly evenly throughout the year, with the wettest areas being the Otway Ranges and the High Country, and the driest area being the north-western corner of the state. Because of exposure to frequent cold fronts and southerly winds, the coastal areas are subject to the most changeable weather patterns.

The alpine areas have the most extreme climatic conditions. In winter, most of the higher mountains are snow-capped and frosts are frequent, while in summer you can experience a warm or hot day and then at night the temperature may drop below freezing.

The weather is generally more stable north of the Great Dividing Range. The Wimmera and Mallee regions have the lowest rainfall and the highest temperatures.

In summer the average highest daily temperatures are around 25°C along the coast, around 20°C in the alpine areas, and up to 35°C in the north-west. In winter the average maximums are around 13°C along the coast, around 17°C in the north-west, and between 3°C and 10°C in the alpine areas.

ECOLOGY & ENVIRONMENT

If you come from Europe you might be amazed at how light the human impact has been. If you come from somewhere else in Australia, much of Victoria might seem thoroughly tamed. It isn't hard to find an empty beach, but you won't find an empty beach where you can camp for weeks undisturbed (it isn't even legal to try); it isn't hard to find a forest full of native animals,

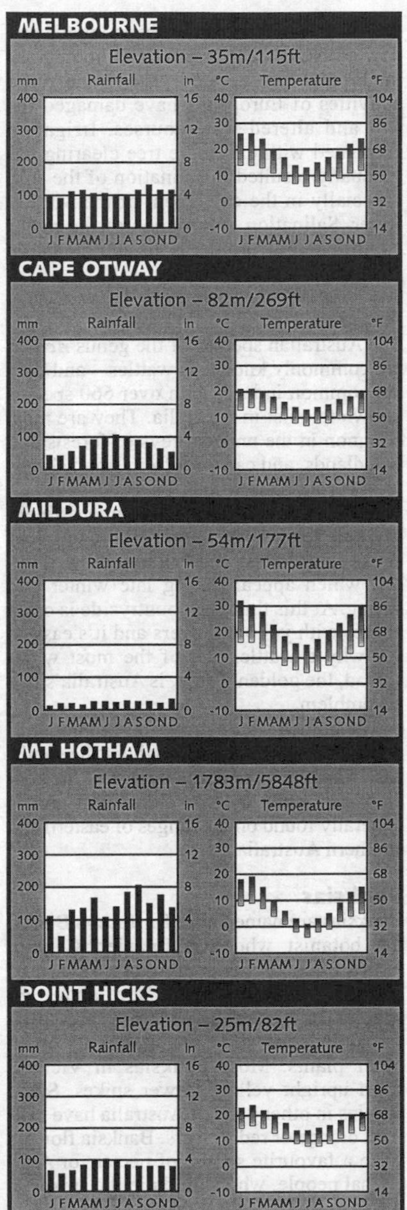

but few forests have not been logged and many animals have become extinct.

As in most countries, the land protected in parks and reserves is mostly land that was unsuitable for agriculture. Thus, it tends to be mountain forests and arid plains that are preserved. Victoria's parks are extensive and most are spectacularly beautiful, but some ecosystems have almost disappeared.

The grasslands of Australia Felix (see the History section earlier in this chapter) vanished soon after sheep were introduced. Sheep were the first hoofed animals to tread the light, fine topsoil, and they soon transformed it into a hard-packed mass that could not support native flora. This in turn resulted in the extinction of many animal species. Aborigines, killed or driven from the grazing land, could no longer selectively burn the plains. This practice, over tens of thousands of years, had shaped the environment.

More intensive agriculture, involving pesticides, fertilisers and irrigation, has also taken a toll.

Australian Conservation Foundation

The Australian Conservation Foundation (ACF) is the largest non-government organisation involved in conservation. The ACF covers a wide range of issues, including the greenhouse effect and depletion of the ozone layer, the negative effects of logging and land degradation, preservation of rainforests, and protection of the Antarctic.

The ACF's Melbourne office (☎ 9416 1166) is at 340 Gore St, Fitzroy.

Wilderness Society

The Wilderness Society is involved in issues concerning protection of the Australian wilderness, such as forest management and logging. In Melbourne, the Wilderness Society has a shop and office (☎ 9670 2867) at 355 Little Bourke St.

Australian Trust for Conservation Volunteers (ACTV)

This nonpolitical, nonprofit group organises practical conservation projects (such as tree planting, track construction and flora and fauna surveys) for volunteers to take part in. Most travellers who take part in ATCV join a Conservation Experience package, which lasts six weeks. The cost is $840, and further weeks can be added for $140; this includes food and accommodation. You can contact the head office in Ballarat on ☎ 5333 2290, or write to ATCV, PO Box 423, Ballarat, Vic 3350.

Energy

Most electricity is produced by coal-fired power stations in Gippsland's Latrobe Valley (it's said that the Latrobe Valley has Melbourne's pollution), although there is some hydroelectricity from the Snowy Mountains Scheme. There are no nuclear power stations.

Only a tiny fraction of households are powered by solar or wind generators. This chapter was written on a computer powered by solar panels.

Major gas and oil fields off Sale in Bass Strait mean that Victoria is self-sufficient in gas (except when the sole plant explodes, as it did in 1998) and petrol.

FLORA

Unlike the vast central regions of Australia, Victoria's landscapes are diverse. There's a rich range of native flora, from the mosses, lichens and tree ferns of the rainforests to the hardy mallee scrub of the semi-arid desert areas. Over 35% of the state is covered in forests – some native, and some commercial pine plantations. On the other hand, large areas have been cleared for agriculture.

The two most common native plant groups are the eucalypts and wattles (*acacias*). There are also 2000 species of native wildflower which vary from region to region, and provide colourful exhibitions, particularly during spring and summer.

Most of the state's landscapes now combine native Australian flora, which evolved over thousands of years in isolation from the rest of the world, and exotic species that have been introduced in the 200 years since the arrival of Europeans. During this time also, rainforests have been logged and new crops, pasture grasses and hoofed animals have proliferated. These and other activities of Europeans have damaged the soil and altered watercourses. Irrigation combined with excessive tree clearing has gradually resulted in salination of the soil, especially in the catchment of the Murray River. Salination is now one of the major environmental problems in south-eastern Australia.

Acacias

The Australian species of the genus *Acacia* are commonly known as wattles – and they are common indeed, with over 660 species known to exist in Australia. They are most common in the understoreys of forests and woodlands, and can vary from small shrubs to towering blackwoods.

Acacias have either deep green, finely divided leaves, or larger flattened leaf stalks (phyllodes) and bright yellow flowers, which appear during late winter and spring. At this time the countryside is often ablaze with yellow flowers and it's easy to see why a wattle, one of the most widespread, the golden wattle, is Australia's floral emblem.

The golden wattle grows best in hot, arid areas, but is common throughout the south-east. The blackwood, the largest of the acacias, can grow to over 30m high and is generally found on the ranges of eastern and southern Australia.

Banksias

Banksias are named after Sir Joseph Banks, the botanist who accompanied Captain James Cook on his exploratory voyage of eastern Australia. There are about 60 species in Australia, and they are often found in poor soils unsuitable for most other plants. Most Banksias in Victoria sport upright yellow flower spikes. Some species in other parts of Australia have brilliant orange or red flowers. Banksia flowers were a favourite source of nectar for Aboriginal people, who would dip the spikes in water to make a sweet drink.

Casuarinas

Also known as sheoaks, these hardy trees are almost as much a part of the Australian landscape as eucalypts. They grow in a variety of habitats, and are characterised by feathery needle-like foliage, consisting of branchlets; the true leaves are small scales at the joints of the branchlets.

Eucalypts

The eucalypts, or gum trees, are ubiquitous, except in the deepest rainforests and the most arid deserts. They vary in form and height from the tall, straight hardwoods such as jarrah, karri and mountain ash to the stunted, twisted snow gum with its colourful trunk striations. Mountain ash are the most majestic of this species, growing up to 90m in height; Victoria once claimed the world's tallest tree, but it was cut down before its height could be verified.

Eucalypts are evergreen, with tough fibrous leaves and thick protective bark. Of the 700 species of eucalyptus, 95% are native to Australia, the rest to New Guinea, the Philippines and Indonesia.

Grass Trees

Grass trees (*Xanthorrhea*) are easily recognised by their blackened twisted trunks, which testify the plants resiliance to fire, topped by a bushy crown of long grass-like leaves. Long woody flower spikes erupt with creamy yellow flowers that attract birds and insects alike.

Waratah

The scientific name of the spectacular waratah, *Telopea*, means 'seen from afar', and gives some idea of the impact it makes in the bush. It is more common in NSW, where it is the State's floral emblem, but a less spectacular waratah is also found in eastern Victoria.

FAUNA

Australia's most distinctive fauna are the marsupials and monotremes. Marsupials such as kangaroos and koalas give birth to partially developed young which they suckle in a pouch. Monotremes – platypuses and echidnas – lay eggs but also suckle their young.

Since the arrival of Europeans in Australia, many species of mammal have become extinct and more are endangered. Introduced non-native animals have been allowed to run wild and have caused a great deal of damage to native species and vegetation. Destructive feral animals in Victoria include foxes, cats, pigs, starlings, blackbirds, Indian mynahs and, best known of all, the notorious rabbit.

Birds

The Royal Australasian Ornithologists Union (RAOU) runs bird observatories in Victoria which provide accommodation and guides.

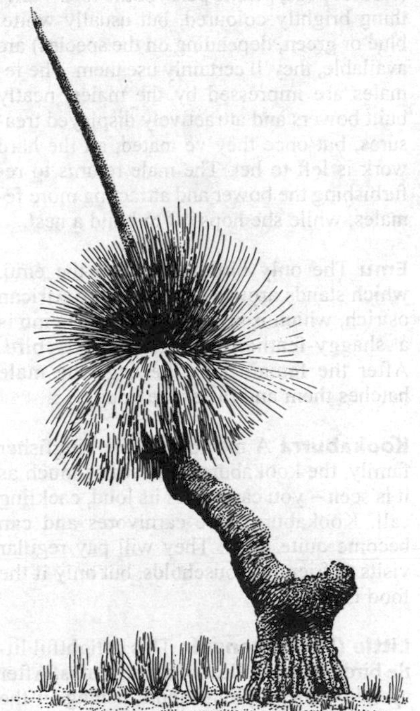

The grass tree, spectacular in flower, is common in many national parks.

Contact the RAOU (☎ 9882 2622), 415 Riversdale Rd, Hawthorn East, Victoria 3123.

Birds of Prey A variety of raptors – eagles, hawks, kites and falcons – are seen in rural Victoria. There's even a pair of peregrine falcons that nest among Melbourne's skyscrapers. The largest bird of prey is the wedge-tailed eagle, a majestic bird with a 2m wing span that is most often seen soaring at great heights or devouring road-kill such as wombat or kangaroo.

Bower Bird The bower bird has a unique mating practice. The male builds a bower that he decorates with various coloured objects to attract females. In the wild, flowers or stones are used, but if artificial objects (clothes pegs, plastic pens, bottle tops – anything brightly coloured, but usually white, blue or green, depending on the species) are available, they'll certainly use them. The females are impressed by the males' neatly built bowers and attractively displayed treasures, but once they've mated, all the hard work is left to her. The male returns to refurbishing the bower and attracting more females, while she hops off to build a nest.

Emu The only bird larger than the emu, which stands around 2m tall, is the African ostrich, which is also flightless. The emu is a shaggy-feathered, often curious bird. After the female lays the eggs the male hatches them and raises the young.

Kookaburra A member of the kingfisher family, the kookaburra is heard as much as it is seen – you can't miss its loud, cackling call. Kookaburras are carnivores and can become quite tame. They will pay regular visits to friendly households, but only if the food is excellent.

Little (Fairy) Penguin This delightful little bird is the smallest of all penguins. After spending the daylight hours fishing in the open ocean, these birds return to nesting burrows among the coastal scrub and rocks. One of Victoria's most popular tourist attractions is the Phillip Island Penguin Parade, where thousands of spectators watch penguins waddle up the beach to their burrows every night.

Lyrebird The superb lyrebird, found in Victoria's moist forest areas, particularly the Dandenongs, is famous for both its vocal abilities and its visual beauty. Lyrebirds are highly skilled mimics that copy segments of other birds' songs, or any other sound they hear, to create unique hybrid compositions. They have been known to mimic the sound of chain saws and trail bikes. During the courting season, with his spectacular tail feathers fanned out, the male puts on a sensational song-and-dance routine to attract a partner.

Mallee Fowl This fascinating bird is found in the Big Desert wilderness area in Victoria's north-west corner. See the boxed text in the Mallee chapter for details.

Magpie The black and white magpie, one of the most common birds in Australia, has a distinctive and beautiful warbling call. Magpies can be aggressively territorial when nesting (in spring) and aren't afraid of swooping and even striking at humans.

Parrots & Cockatoos There is an amazing variety of these birds throughout Australia. The noisy pink and grey galahs are among the most common, although sulphur crested cockatoos have to be the noisiest. Rosellas have one of the most brilliant colour schemes and in some parks in Victoria they're not at all afraid to take a free feed from visitors. The mainly red, yellow and blue eastern rosella is the most widespread in rural south-eastern Australia.

Dingo

Australia's native dog is the dingo, domesticated by the Aborigines and thought to have arrived with them 40,000 years ago. Dingoes now prey on rabbits and sometimes livestock, and are considered vermin by many farmers.

Kangaroos & Wallabies

There are several species of kangaroo, which are readily identified. Wallabies are smaller kangaroos. The extraordinary breeding cycle of the kangaroo is well adapted to Australia's harsh, often unpredictable environment.

The young kangaroo, or joey, just millimetres long at birth, claws its way unaided to the mother's pouch, where it attaches itself to a nipple that expands inside its mouth. A day or two later the mother mates again, but the new embryo does not begin to develop until the first joey has left the pouch permanently.

At this point the mother produces two types of milk – one formula to feed the joey at heel, the other for the baby in her pouch. If food or water is scarce, the breeding cycle can be interrupted until conditions improve.

Although kangaroos are generally not aggressive, males of the larger species can be dangerous when cornered. In the wild, boomers, as they are called, will grasp other males with their forearms, rear up on their muscular tails and pound their opponents with their hind feet, sometimes slashing them with their claws.

About three million kangaroos are legally culled each year in Australia, but probably as many more are killed for sport or by those farmers who believe the cull is insufficient to protect their paddocks.

Kangaroos can be a road hazard, especially at night – hitting one at 110 km/h is no joke.

Koala

Koalas are found along the eastern seaboard. Their cuddly appearance belies an irritable nature, and they will scratch and bite if sufficiently provoked.

Koalas initially carry their young in pouches but later the larger young cling to their mother's back. They feed only on the leaves of certain types of eucalypt and are particularly sensitive to changes in their habitat.

Today many koalas suffer from chlamydia, a sexually transmitted disease causing blindness and infertility. They suffer more, though, from loss of habitat, and there's a possibility of extinction.

Platypus & Echidna

The platypus and the echidna are the only living representatives of the most primitive group of mammals, the monotremes. Both lay eggs, as reptiles do, but suckle their young on milk secreted directly through the skin from mammary glands.

The amphibious platypus has a duck-like bill, webbed feet and a beaver-like body. Males have a poisonous spur on their hind feet. Recent research has shown that the platypus is able to sense electric currents in the water and uses this ability to track its prey.

Echidnas are spiny anteaters that hide from predators by digging vertically into the ground and covering themselves with dirt, or by rolling themselves into a ball and raising their sharp quills.

An echidna, rolled into a tight defensive ball, is a prickly problem for predators.

Possums

There is an enormous range of possums in Australia. The common brushtail is often found in towns and cities, where you'll find them in parks, sometimes tame enough to eat from your hand. Look for them at dusk.

Brush-tailed possums are common in Melbourne's parks and gardens.

Some possums are able to jump from tree to tree by extending flaps of skin between their legs. The feathertail glider is the world's smallest gliding mammal and is found in the tall eucalypt forest of eastern Victoria.

Wombat

Wombats are slow, solid, powerfully built marsupials with broad heads and short, stumpy legs. These fairly placid and easily tamed creatures are sometimes legally killed by farmers, who object to the damage done to paddocks by their large burrows and tunnelling under fences. The wombat can be seen in its natural setting in national parks such as Lower Glenelg on the South-West Coast and Wilsons Promontory in Gippsland.

Southern Right Whale

These majestic creatures gained their name as a result of being the 'right' whale to hunt. They migrate annually from Antarctica to Victoria to give birth in shallow waters and are no longer hunted. They can be seen at the Logan's Beach nursery off the coast of Warrnambool.

Snakes

Victorian snakes are generally shy and avoid confrontations with humans. A few, however, are deadly. The most dangerous are tigers, although common alpine copperheads, eastern brown snakes and red-bellied black snakes should also be avoided. Tiger snakes will actually attack humans. The best advice is to stay right away from all snakes. See the Health section in the Facts for the Visitor chapter for advice about dealing with snake bites.

Spiders

Most Australian spiders bite. The redback, which is fairly common in Victoria, is extremely poisonous and can be lethal. It's a small black spider with a red stripe on its back. You should also beware of the white-tailed spider, commonly found in fields and gardens, and sometimes inside buildings. It is about 2.5cm long, with a distinct white spot on its grey-black back. Some people have extreme reactions to its bite and gangrene can result. The funnel-web, a large aggressive ground dwelling spider, is more common in NSW, but has been reported in the far north-east of Victoria; its bite can also be lethal.

NATIONAL & STATE PARKS

Victoria has 34 national parks and 40 state parks – protected areas of environmental or natural importance. There is also a wide range of other protected areas including coastal and marine reserves and historic areas.

These parks are managed by Parks Victoria, which has a very useful 24-hour toll free information line (☎ 13 1963). You even get to speak to a human being, not a machine. Unfortunately, those human beings often rely on brochures to give you information, and the brochures are sometimes out of date. If you want detailed, current information phone the park's ranger station (most larger parks have one).

Offices of the Natural Resources & Environment department (NRE), which can be found in larger towns around the state, usually have some information on parks in their area, although the parks are no longer run by their department. Call Parks Victoria for the appropriate addresses. We haven't listed many NRE offices in this guide as the department is undergoing changes and there's a good chance that offices will move or close in the near future. The NRE Information Centre (☎ 9637 8080), 8 Nicholson St, East Melbourne, carries a good range of books and other information on parks and outdoor activities.

Perhaps the major feature of Victoria's park system is its tremendous diversity, including semi-arid desert regions, rugged coastal parks, fern-filled rainforests, river wetlands and flood plains, lakes and waterways, forests and mountain ranges, salt plains and sand dunes.

Public access to these areas is encouraged if safety and conservation regulations are observed. In all parks you're asked to do nothing that will damage or alter the natural environment. Approach roads, campgrounds (often with toilets and showers), walking tracks and information centres are often provided.

Some parks are so isolated or rugged that only experienced bushwalkers or climbers should venture in. Others, however, are among the state's most popular attractions, such as Wilsons Promontory, the Grampians and Port Campbell National Park.

Unfortunately, national parks haven't escaped the attention of the economic rationalists in government. There are moves to make those lazy parks pay their way. One of the most controversial is a plan for a major new complex at Wilsons Promontory.

State Forests

State forests are seen as a resource and are systematically logged. A long campaign to stop logging in East Gippsland's old-growth forests has prompted the state government to declare 'prohibited areas' which you need a permit to enter. These areas aren't usually signposted, but if you aren't a protester you're unlikely to be arrested if you're found there. Justice isn't entirely blind in this state.

GOVERNMENT & POLITICS

Australian Government

Australia is a federation of six states and two territories, and has a parliamentary system of government based on the Westminster model. There are three tiers of government: federal, state and local.

Australia's two main political groupings are the Australian Labor Party (ALP) and the coalition between the Liberal Party and the National Party. In theory, the Australian Labor Party is socialist, having grown out of the workers' disputes and shearers' strikes of the 1890s; the Liberal Party is traditionally conservative, representing the interests of free enterprise, law and order and family values; and the National Party (formerly the National Country Party) is traditionally the party of rural interests.

Victorian Government

State governments are theoretically Westminster-style governments in miniature, without powers to affect defence, foreign relations, income tax and a few other matters. In practice, power is becoming centralised in Canberra. State premiers are the equivalent of Westminster system prime ministers, although Victoria's current premier sees himself as the CEO of a large company, with the citizens as customers.

An Australian Republic?

In late 1999 Australians will vote on the question of becoming a republic. After bubbling along for a long time, the realisation that the British Queen is technically head of state, and is thus the person who should preside at the 2000 Olympic Games in Sydney, pushed the issue to the forefront.

A constitutional convention in 1998 debated the form of republic to be put to the people in a referendum. The proposed new head of state (replacing the British monarch, whose authority is represented by the Governor General of Australia) would be elected by a two-thirds majority of federal parliament and would probably be known as the President of Australia. (Some would prefer a more Australian title, such as The Big Bloke/Sheila.) The president would have powers similar to those of a governor general or a president of Ireland: ie much less than those of a president of the USA. The prime minister would remain the most powerful person in the country.

Unfortunately, the pro-republican side of the debate is split between those who support the model proposed at the convention and those who want the president to be directly elected by the people. (The 'Prez-Lotto' faction, which wanted a national lottery to decide the presidency, has sadly faded from the scene.) Australians are notoriously averse to voting 'yes' in referendums, especially if there is any sign of disunity between the proponents.

Mark Armstrong

Victoria's state government is based in Melbourne and is made up of the Legislative Council (the upper house, equivalent to a Senate or the British House of Lords) with 44 elected representatives and the Legislative Assembly (the lower house) with 88 elected representatives. Elections for the lower house are held every four years: voting is by secret ballot and is compulsory for everyone 18 years of age and over.

A Liberal/National party coalition, under the premiership of Jeff Kennett, currently governs.

ECONOMY

Victoria may be Australia's smallest mainland state, but it's also the most densely populated and the most intensively farmed, producing more than 20% of the country's agricultural products.

There are extensive natural resources. The Latrobe Valley has one of the world's largest deposits of brown coal and provides more than 80% of the state's energy requirements, while offshore fields in Bass Strait supply about half of Australia's crude oil and natural gas needs. More than 35% of Victoria is forested, and the timber industry is another major source of income. Most of the timber logged now comes from commercial softwood and hardwood plantations, although controversially some old-growth forests are still being logged.

Victoria's manufacturing industries once contributed around 25% of Australia's Gross National Product; the figure is now well under 5%. The major industries are clothing and footwear, textiles, automotive and transport equipment, paper, metal, coal and petroleum products.

Over 70% of the state's workforce is employed in the tertiary sector, particularly wholesale and retail trade and community services such as education and health. As in the rest of Australia, the tourism industry in Victoria is of growing economic importance.

POPULATION & PEOPLE

Victoria has a population of around 4.5 million people, making up about 26% of the total Australian population. Around 70% of people live in the Melbourne metropolitan area, 18% live in other urban centres and 12% live in rural areas.

Of the main regional population centres, Geelong, Ballarat, Bendigo, Shepparton, Warrnambool, Mildura, Wodonga, Morwell and Traralgon all have populations of more than 20,000. The north-west and the High Country are the most sparsely populated areas.

Victoria's population is the most culturally diverse in Australia. More than 60 different nationalities are represented, and almost one-quarter of the state's residents were born overseas.

There are around 20,000 Koories (Aborigines from south-eastern Australia) and Torres Strait Islanders, more than half of them living in Melbourne. Mildura, Robinvale, Swan Hill, Echuca, Shepparton, Bairnsdale, Orbost and Warrnambool all have significant Koori populations. There are also several independent Koori communities around the state, including those at Lake Condah (between Hamilton and Portland), Lake Tyers (east of Lakes Entrance), and Framlingham (north-east of Warrnambool).

The first wave of European settlers came predominantly from England, Scotland and Ireland.

After WWII thousands of immigrants arrived from war-torn Europe, bringing their own cultures, cuisines, ways of life and a passion that was lacking in what was previously a very conservative and Anglo-Celtic culture. Many were Jewish, survivors of the Holocaust, who wanted to start again as far from the horror as possible. Melbourne's large populations of Greek, Italian and Jewish people date from these times. Many others came from places like Turkey, Lebanon, Malta, Poland and Yugoslavia.

Since the mid-1970s, most immigrants have come from South-East Asia and the Pacific, many being refugees from Vietnam and Cambodia. On the whole these 'new Australians' have been remarkably well accepted and multiculturalism is a popular concept. One of Melbourne's greatest strengths is the richness of its cultural mix.

EDUCATION

Victoria's literacy rate is approaching 100%. Primary and secondary education is compulsory up to the age of 14. The state school system is secular and free, although economic rationalists in government have cut state school funding to the point where 'free' is only technically correct – state schools don't charge tuition fees but they charge for many other things. Many smaller schools have been closed or merged.

The Catholic education system has long been an important adjunct to the state system, and as standards have fallen in state schools, Catholic and other private schools are experiencing a boom.

Tertiary education, in universities and TAFE (Technical & Further Education) colleges is widely available, with campuses across the state.

One of the many reforms introduced by Gough Whitlam's (federal) Labor government in the 1970s was free tertiary education. This has steadily been chipped away by successive conservative governments, to the extent that students are now liable for hefty fees (payable by instalment after graduation) and many institutions offer places to students who can pay full fees in advance and who might not otherwise have qualified.

ARTS

Melbourne is regarded by many as the cultural capital of Australia. A town that unleashed people as diverse as Barry Humphries, Kylie Minogue, Sir Sidney Nolan, Olivia Newton-John, Nick Cave, Rupert Murdoch, Dame Nellie Melba, Peter Carey and Germaine Greer on the world can't be all beer and horse races.

Aboriginal Art

Aboriginal art is a traditional and symbolic art form. In ancient times, the main forms were body painting, cave painting and rock engraving, and it's only recently that Aboriginal artists have begun painting in more portable formats and using western art materials like canvas and acrylic paints.

The Museum of Victoria in Melbourne has an excellent collection of Aboriginal artefacts, and the National Gallery of Victoria has a collection of contemporary Aboriginal art. See the Shopping section of the

Melbourne chapter for information about buying Aboriginal art.

Dance

The Australian Ballet's school is in Melbourne, so there's considerable interest in ballet in the state. There's an awful lot of other dance going on, from classical (western and other cultures) to the most experimental. Chunky Moves is one of the state's permanent companies. Several internationally respected choreographers, including Lucy Guerin and Shelley Lasica, are based in Melbourne.

Music

Victoria's rich musical heritage covers the spectrum from rock to classics. Melbourne's lively rock music scene has been the launching pad for bands like Crowded House and Nick Cave & the Bad Seeds, while two Melburnians who achieved fame on the classical world stage were the singer Dame Nellie Melba and the composer Sir Percy Grainger.

Victoria hosts a wide range of music festivals throughout the year, featuring everything from jazz and blues to chamber music and alternative rock. Melbourne's music festivals include the Montsalvat Jazz Festival and the Melbourne Music Festival, and there are also plenty of excellent rural music festivals including the Port Fairy Folk Festival, the Queenscliff Music Festival and the Wangaratta Jazz Festival. New Years Eve at Erskine Falls (near Lorne) attracts big crowds and great bills with slightly eccentric headliners, such as Iggy Pop or Debbie Harry.

Victoria also has some great indigenous musicians including Archie Roach, Ruby Hunter and Tiddas.

Melbourne's dynamic music scene has consistently produced many of Australia's outstanding bands and musicians. See Entertainment in the Melbourne chapter for venues.

Classical Music The Melbourne Symphony Orchestra (MSO) and other orchestras and artists, local and international, perform at the Melbourne Concert Hall and other venues.

Opera The Victorian State Opera was recently merged with the Australian Opera, but there's still a major opera season in winter. Some performances sell out well in advance, but you can usually get a seat, at a price way below that of a European opera house.

A company to keep an eye on is the Chamber Made Opera, which produces quirky and often original pieces.

Musicals Melbourne has a long history of popular shows, from the days when Lola Montez sang on the goldfields (and was reputedly showered with nuggets). Big touring shows such as *Phantom of the Opera* and *Miss Saigon*, and local revivals of evergreens such as *South Pacific* are almost always on stage. Soon after his election premier Jeff Kennett became involved in lobbying to bring successful shows to Victoria. There was even talk of a *Sunset Boulevard* led economic recovery when the premier's Major Events committee was involved in securing that musical for Melbourne.

Literature

While Sydney writers Henry Lawson and AB ('Banjo') Paterson created the Australian national character as a self-reliant bush worker, Victorians were getting on with the business of making money on the goldfields and in the city.

CJ Dennis was a Victorian writer of the time, and his verse story, *The Songs of a Sentimental Bloke*, an urban idyll published in 1915, established him as a national writer with broad appeal. Dennis lived in the small town of Toolangi, north of Melbourne, from 1915 to 1935. Painter and writer Norman Lindsay grew up in the small town of Creswick (near Ballarat) and his books *Red Heap* and *Saturdee* offer very funny insights into a turn-of-the-century bush boyhood (there's hardly a girl in sight).

Other classic works of Victorian literature are *For the Term of His Natural Life* by Marcus Clarke, *The Getting of Wisdom* by Henry Handel (Florence Ethel) Richardson, *Picnic at Hanging Rock* by Joan Lindsay and *My Brother Jack* by George Johnston. Also, look for the work of Charmian Clift, Hal Porter, Alan Marshall and Frank Hardy. Hardy's *Power Without Glory* caused a sensation when it was first published in 1950. It was loosely based on the affairs and dealings of notorious Melbourne businessman John Wren and resulted in Hardy being prosecuted for criminal libel.

Among Victoria's contemporary writers, the best-known is probably Peter Carey (now living in New York), who won the Booker Prize for his novel *Oscar & Lucinda*. Helen Garner's works are mostly set in Melbourne, and include *The Children's Bach*, *Postcards From Surfers*, *Cosmo Cosmolino* and *Monkey Grip*. Some other contemporary Melbourne writers to look out for are Kerry Greenwood, Morris Lurie, Carmel Bird, Gerald Murnane and Rod Jones. Barry Dickens' novels are quirky, often hilarious and distinctively Melburnian.

AB (Banjo) Paterson created many literary icons, including *The Man from Snowy River*.

Architecture

Victoria's earliest buildings were built in the Old Colonial style (1788-1840), a simplified version of Georgian architecture. The earliest settled towns such as Portland, Port Fairy and Port Albert are the best examples of this period. In Melbourne few examples remain – St James' Cathedral (1840) in King St is the oldest public building.

Appropriately, the most prominent architectural style is Victorian (1840-90), which was an expression of the era's confidence, progress and prosperity. It drew on various sources including classical, romantic and Gothic, and as the era progressed designs became more elaborate, flamboyant and ornamental. Melbourne is acknowledged as one of the world's great Victorian-era cities. There are many outstanding examples of Victorian architecture in the city centre and inner suburbs, such as Carlton, East Melbourne, Parkville, St Kilda and South Melbourne. The provincial gold-rush centres such as Bendigo, Ballarat, Castlemaine and Beechworth are also renowned for their splendid Victorian architecture.

With the collapse of Melbourne's land boom in the early 1890s and the subsequent severe economic depression, a new style of architecture that came to be known as 'Federation' evolved. The Federation style was in many ways a watered-down version of Victorian architecture, featuring simplicity of design and less ornamentation. Its evolution was mainly driven by economic necessity, but it was also influenced by the pending federation of Australia (in 1901) and the associated desire to create a more distinctive and suitably 'Australian' style of design.

From around 1910, the most prominent style of residential architecture was a hybrid between the Federation and California Bungalow styles. The Art Deco style was also prominent from the 1920s, but after the Great Depression architecture became increasingly functionalist and devoid of decoration. Ubiquitous 'cream brick-veneers' housed the parents of the post-war baby boomers in mushrooming suburbs. One day these might gain National Trust recognition for their distinct style, and real estate agents might coo over their classic lines, but right now it seems a long shot.

In recent years, appreciation of these older styles of architecture has increased to the extent that local councils have actively encouraged residents to restore houses and buildings in sympathy with the period in which they were built.

In Melbourne the old Australian dream of a modest house on a quarter-acre (0.1 hectare) block is changing, partly because of economics and partly because of government policy.

In an effort to revitalise the city centre, apartment construction, and in the suburbs 'medium density' housing (ie building two houses where previously only one would have been allowed) has been encouraged often in spite of the objections of residents and even local government. Building a second residence (many of them in an ugly and inappropriate mock Georgian style) on a standard house block is now commonplace.

Painting

Melbourne's National Gallery of Victoria houses one of the most comprehensive art collections in the southern hemisphere. The Australian collection contains a significant number of works by Australian impressionists. Based at a bush camp in Heidelberg in the 1880s, Tom Roberts, Arthur Streeton, Frederick McCubbin and Charles Condor were the first local artists to paint in a distinctively Australian style rather than in imitation of the Europeans.

In the 1940s, another revolution in Australian art took place at Heide, the home of John and Sunday Reed in suburban Bulleen. Under their patronage, a new generation of bohemian young artists (including Sir Sidney Nolan, Albert Tucker, Arthur Boyd, Joy Hester and John Perceval) redefined the direction of Australian art. Today, you can visit the Museum of Modern Art at Heide – see the Melbourne chapter for details of other galleries in the city.

There are also some excellent provincial art galleries worth visiting as you travel around the state, particularly those of Ballarat, Benalla, Bendigo, Castlemaine, Geelong, Horsham, Mildura, Shepparton, Wangaratta, and Warrnambool.

Cinema

Melbourne is the birthplace of the Australian film industry and cinema historians regard an Australian film, *Soldiers of the Cross*, as the world's first 'real' movie. It was originally screened at the Melbourne Town Hall in 1901, cost £600 to make and was shown throughout the USA in 1902.

The next significant Australian film, *The Story of the Kelly Gang*, was screened in 1907, and the industry was flourishing by 1911. Low-budget films were being made in such quantities that they could be hired out or sold cheaply. Over 250 silent feature films were made before the 1930s when the talkies and Hollywood took over.

In the 1950s, the film *On the Beach* was shot in Melbourne. One of its stars, Ava Gardner, was less than enchanted by her surroundings and made the comment that Melbourne was the perfect place to make a film about the end of the world – at the time she may have been right.

With government subsidies during 1969 and 1970, the Australian film industry entered a renaissance, producing films that appealed to local and international audiences, such as *Breaker Morant*, *Sunday Too Far Away* and *The Devil's Playground*. Some Victorian productions from this period were *The Adventures of Barry McKenzie*, the *Alvin Purple* series, the *Mad Max* series, *Monkey Grip*, *Picnic at Hanging Rock* and *The Getting of Wisdom*.

Since the 1970s, Australian actors and directors like Mel Gibson, Judy Davis, Nicole

Kidman, Paul Hogan, Geoffrey Rush, Bruce Beresford, Peter Weir, Gillian Armstrong and Fred Schepisi have gained international recognition.

Kelli Simpson, whose film *Two Girls and a Baby* was well received at the 1999 Sundance Film Festival, is a new director to keep on eye on.

Theatre

Melbourne's main professional company is the Melbourne Theatre Company (MTC), which offers fairly middle-of-the-road works. There's also a huge variety of other companies that come and go, producing light and heavyweight classics and experimental works, and everything in between.

See the Melbourne chapter for information on where and when to sample local theatre.

TV Soap Operas

No discussion of culture would be complete without mentioning Victoria's TV soap operas such as *Neighbours* (see the boxed text below) and the now-defunct *Flying Doctors*, which launched the international careers of the likes of Kylie Minogue and Jason Donovan. *Prisoner* (known as *Prisoner Cell Block H* in the UK) was made in Melbourne. However, there's no remaining trace of the wobbly sets.

Ramsay St

A few years ago, an enterprising but unauthorised tour guide was taking fans of Melbourne's famous soap opera *Neighbours* to visit the set at 'Ramsay St'. Apparently the cast and crew didn't appreciate the interference, and one prominent cast member made his point to the tour-bus driver so passionately that assault charges were subsequently laid. Needless to say, 'Ramsay St' is no longer on tour itineraries.

Ramsay St is a real street with real residents who are a little tired of being gawked at. So much so that the producers of *Neighbours* employ security guards to watch the street.

Mark Armstrong

ABORIGINAL CULTURE

Because of early policies of 'dispersion' and later ones of assimilation, many Aboriginal languages and cultures have been lost forever and no Victorian people live a purely traditional lifestyle.

However, some groups are attempting to revive their cultures and there are Aboriginal cultural centres dotted around the state that are worth visiting, including the Brambuk Living Cultural Centre in the Grampians National Park, the Dharnya Centre in the Barmah State Forest northeast of Echuca, and the Nullwak Gundji Centre at Cann River.

There is an Aboriginal Resources Walk in the Royal Botanic Gardens in Melbourne; and the City of Melbourne publishes the excellent *Another View Walking Trail* brochure detailing a four to five-hour walking tour through the city that traces the links between Aborigines and the European settlers (available from information booths in the city).

RELIGION

A shrinking majority of people in Victoria are at least nominally Christian. Most Protestant churches have merged to become the Uniting Church, although the Church of England has remained separate. The Catholic Church is popular (about 30% of Christians are Catholics), with the original Irish adherents boosted by the large numbers of Mediterranean immigrants.

Non-Christian minorities abound, the main ones being Buddhist, Jewish and Muslim.

LANGUAGE

Australia contains many surprises for those who think all Aussies speak some weird variant of English. For a start many Australians don't even speak English – they speak Italian, Lebanese, Vietnamese, Turkish or Greek.

Traditional Aboriginal Culture

Society & Lifestyle Traditionally, the Aborigines were tribal people living in extended family groups or clans, with clan members descending from a common ancestral spirit. Tradition, rituals and laws linked the people of each clan to the land they occupied and each clan had various sites of spiritual significance, places to which their spirits would return when they died. Clan members came together to perform rituals to honour their ancestral spirits and the creators of the Dreaming. These traditional beliefs were the basis of Aboriginal ties to the land.

It was the responsibility of the clan, or particular members of it, to correctly maintain and protect the sites so that the ancestral beings were not offended and would continue to protect the clan. Traditional punishments for those who neglected these responsibilities were often severe.

Many Aboriginal communities were almost nomadic, others sedentary, one of the deciding factors being the availability of food. Where food and water were readily available, the people tended to remain in a limited area. The traditional role of the men was that of hunter, tool-maker and custodian of male law; the women reared the children, gathered and prepared food and were custodians of female law and ritual.

Environmental Awareness Wisdom and skills obtained over millennia enabled Aborigines to use their environment to the maximum. An intimate knowledge of the behaviour of animals and the correct time to harvest the many plants they utilised ensured that food shortages were rare.

Similar technology – for example the boomerang and spear – was used throughout the continent, but techniques were adapted to the environment and the species being hunted. At Lake Condah in Victoria, permanent stone weirs many kilometres long were used to trap migrating eels, while in the tablelands of Queensland finely woven nets were used to snare herds of wallabies and kangaroos.

The Aborigines were also traders. Trade routes crisscrossed the country, and along the way goods and a variety of produced items were dispersed. Many of the items traded, such as certain types of stone or shell, were rare and had great ritual significance.

Cultural Life The simplicity of Aboriginal technology contrasts with the sophistication of their culture. Complex traditional ceremonies depict the activities of their ancestral beings, and prescribe codes of behaviour and responsibilities for looking after the land and all living things. The link between the Aborigines and the ancestral beings are totems, each person having their own totem, or Dreaming. These totems take many forms, such as caterpillars, snakes, fish and magpies.

Those who do speak the native tongue are liable to lose you in a strange collection of Australian words. Some have completely different meanings in Australia than they do in English-speaking countries north of the equator; some commonly used words have been shortened almost beyond recognition. Others are derived from Aboriginal languages, or from the slang used by early convict settlers. (See the Transporting the Language boxed text).

There is a slight regional variation in the Australian accent, while the difference between city and country speech is mainly a matter of speed. Lonely Planet publishes *Australia – a language survival kit*, an introduction to both Australian English and Aboriginal languages. The Glossary at the back of this book contains some of the more commonly used words in the Aussie lingo.

Aboriginal Language

At the time the First Fleet arrived to establish the first European settlement in Australia, there were around 250 separate Australian languages spoken by 600 to 700 Aboriginal 'tribes', and these languages were as distinct from each other as English and French. Often three or four adjacent tribes would speak what amounted to dialects of the same language, but another adjacent tribe might speak a completely different language.

It is believed that all the languages evolved from a single language family as the Aborigines gradually moved out over the entire continent and split into new groups. There are a number of words that occur right across the continent, such as *jina* (foot) and *mala* (hand), and similarities also exist in the often complex grammatical structures.

Following the European invasion the number of Aboriginal languages was drastically reduced. At least eight separate languages were spoken in Tasmania alone, but none of these was recorded before the native speakers either died or were killed. Of the original 250 or so languages, many of which were mutually unintelligible, only around 30 are today spoken on a regular basis and are taught to children.

There are a number of terms that Aborigines use to describe themselves, and these vary according to the region. The most common term is Koori, used for the people of south-east Australia. Murri is used to refer to the people of Queensland, Nunga for those from coastal South Australia, and Nyoongah is used in the country's south-west.

Transporting the Language

Many English words have gained new meaning in Australia, some becoming virtually incomprehensible to non-Australians. Here's a sample, together with rough translations into more conventional English.

ankle-biter (also *tacker*; rug rat) – small child,
arvo – afternoon
avagoyermug – traditional rallying call, especially at cricket matches

back o' Bourke – back of beyond; middle of nowhere
backblocks – bush or other area far from the city
banana bender – resident of Queensland
black stump – where the *back o' Bourke* begins
blue (ie 'have a blue') – an argument or fight
bluey – swag; nickname for a red-haired person
bonzer – great; *ripper*
boomer – very big; a particularly large male kangaroo
bunfight – a quarrel over a frivolous issue, or one that gets blown out of proportion
bunyip – mythical bush spirit said to inhabit swamps and billabongs
burl (ie 'give it a burl') – have a try
bushbash – to force your way through pathless bush

Transporting the Language

chunder (also technicolour yawn, pavement pizza, curb-side quiche, liquid laugh, drive the porcelain bus, call Bluey) – vomit
cocky – small-scale farmer; cockatoo
cow cocky – small-scale cattle farmer
crook – ill; badly made; substandard
crow eater – resident of South Australia
cut snake – see *mad as a...*

dag (or *daggy*) – dirty lump of wool at back end of a sheep; an affectionate or mildly abusive term for a socially inept person
daks – trousers
don't come the raw prawn – don't try to fool me
duffing – stealing cattle (literally: altering the brand on the 'duff', or rump)
dunny – outdoor lavatory

earbash – talk nonstop

fair crack of the whip! (or *fair go!*) – give us a break!
flog – steal; sell; whip
fluke – undeserved good luck
from arsehole to breakfast – all over the place

galah – noisy parrot, thus noisy idiot

hoon – idiot; hooligan; *yahoo*; also 'to hoon' or 'hooning around', often in a vehicle – to show off in a noisy fashion with little regard for others

jumped-up (ie 'jumped-up petty Hitler') – arrogant; full of self-importance

kiwi – New Zealander

mad as a cut snake – insane; crazy; insane with anger
mate – general term of familiarity, whether you know the person or not (but don't use it too often with total strangers)

never-never – a place even more remote than *back o'Bourke*
no worries – she'll be right; that's OK

ocker – an uncultivated or boorish Australian
ocky strap – octopus strap: elastic strap with hooks for tying down gear and generally keeping things in place
off-sider – assistant or partner
on the piss (ie 'they're on the piss tonight') – drinking alcohol

perve – to gaze with lust
pineapple, rough end of the (also *stick, sharp end of the*) – the worst deal

Transporting the Language

razoo – a coin of very little value, a subdivision of a rupee ('he spent every last razoo'). Counterfeit razoos made of brass circulated in the goldfields during two-up sessions, hence 'it's not worth a brass razoo'
ridgy-didge – original; genuine; dinky-di
ripper (also 'little ripper') – good; great
root – sexual intercourse
rooted – tired
ropable – very bad-tempered or angry

septic tanks (also 'septics') – rhyming slang for Yanks; Americans
she'll be right – *no worries*; it'll be OK
sheila – woman, sometimes derogatory
shellacking – comprehensive defeat
shitbox – a neglected, worn-out, useless vehicle
shonky – unreliable
shoot through – leave in a hurry
slab – package containing four six-packs of *tinnies* or *stubbies*, usually encased in plastic on a cardboard base; also called a 'carton' when packaged in a box
squiz (ie 'take a squiz') – a look
stick, sharp end of the (also *pineapple, rough end of the*) – the worse deal
strides – daks, trousers

tacker – small child; *ankle-biter*; rug rat
thingo – thing; whatchamacallit; hooza meebob; dooverlacky; thingamajig
two-pot screamer – person unable to hold their drink
two-up – traditional heads/tails gambling game

up-north – New South Wales or Queensland when viewed from Victoria

wallaby track, on the – to wander from place to place seeking work (archaic)
walloper – policeperson (from 'wallop', to hit someone with a stick)
willy-willy – whirlwind, dust storm
wobbly – disturbing, unpredictable behaviour; (ie 'to throw a wobbly') a tantrum
wowser – spoilsport; puritan

yahoo – noisy and unruly person; *hoon*
yakka – work (from an Aboriginal language)
yobbo – uncouth, aggressive person
yonks – ages; a long time
yowie – Australia's yeti or big foot

Facts for the Visitor

HIGHLIGHTS

Perhaps Victoria's greatest feature is the diversity of its natural attractions. It's a compact state, and you can easily experience a stunning range of landscapes, areas and activities without having to travel too far.

Melbourne
This vibrant and cosmopolitan city is a great launching pad for explorations into the rest of the state.

Mornington and Bellarine peninsulas
Take the ferry across the bay, between the popular seaside resorts of Queenscliff, on the Bellarine Peninsula, and Portsea and Sorrento on the Mornington Peninsula.

Great Ocean Road
Drive one of the world's most spectacular coastal routes and visit towns such as Aireys Inlet, Lorne and Apollo Bay; then head inland to the lovely Otway Ranges; and on to the dramatic coastal rock formations of Port Campbell National Park.

Grampians
These mystical mountains in the heart of the Wimmera are famous for their natural beauty, great bushwalks, seasonal wildflowers and Aboriginal cultural centre.

The Mallee
North of the Wimmera, this is the most arid and sparsely populated region in Victoria, with extensive wilderness areas such as the Wyperfeld, Big Desert and Murray-Sunset national parks.

The Murray River
Experience the bygone days of the paddle-steamer era in Mildura, Swan Hill and Echuca.

Sovereign Hill
Visit this re-creation of an 1860s gold-mining township in Ballarat.

Daylesford/Hepburn Springs
Spend a very pleasant weekend enjoying the mineral spas, restaurants and cafes.

The High Country
This spectacular alpine region provides plenty of adventure: winter skiing, bushwalking, horse trekking, mountain biking, fishing, rock climbing, paragliding, hang gliding, ballooning and white-water rafting.

Gippsland
Explore the coastal beauty of South Gippsland, especially the natural delights of Wilsons Promontory – one of the best hiking and camping areas in the state.

For more information about these and other attractions, see the individual highlights section at the beginning of each chapter.

SUGGESTED ITINERARIES

Possible itineraries depend a lot on what you're interested in and when you will be in Victoria. Itineraries need not be complicated. Many people would be quite happy spending January on the beach at Lorne, or July skiing Falls Creek. Others might prefer a month in Melbourne during the spring frenzy of festivals and sport.

The suggested itineraries given here offer a reasonably comprehensive look at the state, travelling at a fairly relaxed pace. They're also a bit of a wish list by a researcher who has just been through the state far too quickly!

One Week

Two days in Melbourne, then drive the Great Ocean Road to Lorne or Apollo Bay. Inland to Halls Gap and the Grampians National Park, returning to Melbourne via Ballarat.

Two Weeks

A few days in Melbourne, then two days at Wilsons Promontory National Park. Head east to Bairnsdale and the Gippsland Lakes, maybe hiring a cruiser or a yacht, then inland to Omeo and across the High Country (though this road is closed in winter) via Mt Hotham or Falls Creek. Explore the historic towns surrounding Beechworth and the wineries around Rutherglen. Back to Melbourne quickly on the Hume Freeway or via Bendigo and the gold country.

Three Weeks

A few days in Melbourne, then west along the Great Ocean Road. Inland to the Grampians National Park, then north-east to Echuca via Bendigo. Down the Murray to Rutherglen then the historic Beechworth area. Across the High Country on the Omeo

Hwy (conditions permitting) and east to Croajingolong National Park. Return to Melbourne on the Princes Hwy, diverting onto the South Gippsland Hwy at Sale for a quick visit to Wilsons Promontory National Park or Phillip Island if there's time.

One Month or More

You'll be able to get a good idea of all the state's distinct regions. Read this book and decide where you want to spend the most time.

PLANNING

When to Go

The summer months from December to February are the busiest times for tourism in Victoria. Once the school holidays start in mid-December, families take to the roads en masse. Accommodation in the popular resorts, especially on the coast, is heavily booked (and more expensive), and the popular venues and restaurants are more crowded. As compensation, you can expect good weather – well, at least some of the time.

An amazing variety of events takes place in Melbourne during summer, including Test cricket matches at the Melbourne Cricket Ground (MCG), outdoor theatrical and musical productions in the Royal Botanic Gardens and the Myer Music Bowl, the Australian Open at the National Tennis Centre, international golf championships at Royal Melbourne and Huntingdale, the Australia Day celebrations, Midsumma Festival and the St Kilda Festival.

The autumn months, particularly March and April, are often the best time of year climatically. The days are warm and long and still, perfect for strolling through the botanic gardens or lying on your back on the grass, watching the leaves change colour. Melbourne's famous International Comedy Festival is held at this time of year. The Easter holiday period, which also falls during autumn, is one of the busiest times for tourism.

In winter, the skies tend to alternate between a soggy grey and a crisp clear blue. Winter temperatures average a maximum of 13°C and a minimum of 6°C – a good time to rug up and head off to a game of Australian Rules Football (the 'footy'). Alternatively, buy a pass to the Melbourne International Film Festival, or find an open fire somewhere and pull the cork on a bottle of Victorian Shiraz.

If you're into skiing, there are good snowfields within three hours drive of the city. The season usually runs from mid-June until mid-September.

Spring in Victoria, from September until November, means the weather is even more unpredictable than usual, the parks and gardens come to life, the world class Melbourne International Festival of the Arts begins – and, of course, there's the footy finals. Melburnians are fanatical about their football, and the build-up to the Australian Rules Grand Final, played on the last Saturday in September, is huge. There's also the Spring Racing Carnival, dominated by a horse race the whole country stops for – the Melbourne Cup, run at Flemington on the first Tuesday in November.

Along with the climate, it's also worth bearing the school holiday periods in mind. The school year is divided into four terms, and holidays are generally as follows: the longest break is the summer holiday from mid-December until the end of January; and there are also three two-week holiday periods which vary from year to year, but fall approximately from late March to mid-April, late June to mid-July and mid-September to early October.

Maps

The Royal Automobile Club of Victoria (RACV) publishes an excellent series of fold-up maps to the regions and towns of Victoria – these are available free to members. The *VicRoads Country Directory* ($29.95), published by the State Government road authority, has comprehensive road maps as well as maps of over 250 towns.

One of the best places for general maps is Map Land (☎ 9670 4383), 372 Little Bourke St, Melbourne.

For bushwalking, ski-touring and other activities which require more detailed maps, the topographic sheets published by the Australian Surveying & Land Information Group (AUSLIG) or VicMap are the ones to get. Many of the more popular sheets are available at shops that sell specialist bushwalking gear and outdoor equipment. Information Victoria (☎ 1300 366 356), 356 Collins St, stocks all Victorian topographic maps and fills mail orders.

What to Bring

With its notoriously unpredictable climate, packing for a visit to Victoria can be something of a challenge. Perhaps the best principle is to expect the unexpected – in summer, bring swimwear, shorts and light clothing, but also throw in some warmer clothing just in case. Melbourne's winters can be extremely cold, and at least one warm jumper (pullover, sweater) and a jacket would be a good idea.

Rainfall is spread fairly evenly throughout the year, so some wet weather gear could be handy irrespective of when you're coming.

Generally, Australians are casual dressers, although in some of Melbourne's more expensive and traditional restaurants men are still expected to wear a jacket and tie.

You need to be aware of the dangers of UV radiation. Australians have the highest incidence of skin cancer in the world, due in part to a hole in the ozone layer. In summer, a broad-brimmed sunhat, good sunglasses and effective sunscreen are all essential, especially for fair-skinned folk from cooler climates. Like safe sex, safe sun is an important health consideration – in both cases, use protection.

If you're planning to do any serious bushwalking, a pair of strong and comfortable walking shoes or boots is essential.

TOURIST OFFICES

Local Tourist Offices

Tourism Victoria is the government-run body responsible for promoting Victoria interstate and overseas; it has an office in the Melbourne Town Hall. See the Information section in the Melbourne chapter for details of other information services in the city.

In country areas, most of the larger towns have their own tourist information centres. The RACV's country offices also have information sections which include accommodation booking services.

For budget travellers, the best source of information is often the staff at backpackers' hostels. They can tell you about the best tours to take, what's on, where to go, what to see and how to get there.

Tourist Office Interstate

Tourism Victoria has an office in Sydney at 403 George St. For the cost of a local call you can get information and order brochures from anywhere in Australia: phone ☎ 1300 655 452.

Tourist Offices Abroad

The Australian Tourist Commission (ATC) is responsible for promoting Australia overseas and it has some useful tourist literature. Phone an 'Aussie Helpline' to order literature:

New Zealand
☎ 09-527 1629
UK (for all Europe)
☎ 171- 9405 200
USA (for North America)
☎ 661-775 2000

Otherwise you can order literature from the ATC website: www.aussie.net.au or contact your nearest Australian embassy or high commission.

VISAS & DOCUMENTS

Passport & Visas

All visitors to Australia need a passport and a visa. New Zealanders are issued with visas on arrival; all other visitors must obtain one in advance.

There are several different types of visa, depending on the reason for your visit, but most holiday visitors will need a standard tourist visa. Unless you have access to the Electronic Travel Authority system (see the following entry), you'll need an application form, which is available from Australian diplomatic missions overseas and many travel agents. You can apply either by mail or in person, and there is a US$33 fee for a three-month stay. You'll need to provide your passport and a passport photo with your application.

Visa regulations change from time to time. Your travel agent or Australian diplomatic mission will tell you of any changes, or check the Australian government's site at www.immi.gov.au on the Web.

Electronic Travel Authority (ETA) Visitors from certain countries who require a tourist visa for three months or less can apply through an IATA-registered travel agent. There are no forms or fees, as your ETA lives on a computer; you don't get a stamp in your passport.

ETA is available to citizens of the UK, the USA, Canada, most European and Scandinavian countries, Korea, Malaysia and Singapore. Other nationalities will probably be added to the list in the future.

Working Holiday Visas Young visitors from Britain, Ireland, Canada, Holland, Malta, South Korea and Japan may be eligible for a 'working holiday' visa. 'Young' means 18 to 26. You can work either full time or part time and for as much of the 12 months as you want to (or are able to), but you can't work for the same employer for more than three months. Visitors aged between 26 and 30 years can also apply for a working visa, but the conditions are much stricter – you have to be able to prove that having you work here will be 'mutually beneficial' to both Australia and your own country.

With a few exceptions, you have to apply for the visa in your home country. Some nationals can apply outside their own countries but no-one can apply in Australia.

See the section on Work later in this chapter for details of the availability of work.

Visa Extensions The maximum stay is 12 months, including extensions.

Visa extensions are made through Department of Immigration & Multicultural Affairs offices in Australia and, as the process can take some time, it's best to apply about a month before your visa expires. There is a non-refundable application fee of $145 – even if they turn down your application they can keep your money!

To qualify for an extension you must take out medical insurance and have a ticket out of the country. Some offices might want to see proof that you have enough money to stay in Australia, or statements from friends or relatives that you'll be staying with them.

The central Melbourne office of the Department of Immigration & Multicultural Affairs is at 2 Lonsdale St. Phone ☎ 13 1881 for information or ☎ 9235 3030 for a 24-hour recorded information service.

If you're trying to stay longer in Australia, the books *Temporary to Permanent Residence in Australia* and *Practical Guide to Obtaining Permanent Residence in Australia*, both published by Longman Cheshire, might be useful.

Travel Insurance

Ambulance services in Australia are self-funding (ie they're not free) and can be frightfully expensive, so you'd be wise to take out travel insurance. Make sure the policy specifically includes ambulance, helicopter rescue and a flight home for you and anyone you're travelling with, should your condition warrant it. Also check the fine print: some policies exclude 'dangerous activities' such as scuba diving, motorcycling and even trekking. If such activities are on your agenda, you don't want that policy.

Driving Licence & Permits

Foreign driving licences are valid as long as they are in English or are accompanied by a translation. An International Driving Permit (IDP), obtainable from your local automobile association, must be supported by your own licence anyway, so there's little point in getting one.

Bring proof of membership of your automobile association, which will give you reciprocal rights to the services of the RACV, including breakdown services.

Hostel Cards

A youth hostel membership card (HI/YHA) entitles you to various discounts and your card is valid for membership of the Australian YHA.

Student & Youth Cards

Carrying a student card will entitle you to a wide variety of discounts. The most common of these is the International Student Identity Card (ISIC) issued by student unions, hostelling organisations and 'alternative-style' travel agencies.

Other Documents

See the Health section later in this chapter for information on obtaining a Medicare card. If you're entitled to one you'll need to bring your health care card or other proof that you're enrolled in your country's health care system.

Hopefully, you won't lose your passport, but if you do it helps to have plenty of ID to convince your embassy to issue you with a new one.

EMBASSIES & CONSULATES

Australian Embassies & Consulates

Australian consular offices overseas include:

Canada
  High Commission:
  (☎ 613-236 0841) Suite 710, 50 O'Connor St, Ottawa K1P 6L2; also consulate in Vancouver

France
  Embassy:
  (☎ 01 40 59 33 00) 4 Rue Jean Rey, 75015 Cedex 15, Paris

Germany
  Embassy:
  (☎ 0228-810 3173) Godesberger Allee 107, 53175 Bonn 1; also embassy office in Berlin and consulate in Frankfurt

Indonesia
  Embassy:
  (☎ 21-522 7111) Jl HR Rasuna Said, Kav C15-16, Kuningan, Jakarta Selatan 12940; also consulate in Denpasar (Bali)

Ireland
  Embassy:
  (☎ 01-676 1517) 6 Fitzwilton House, Wilton Terrace, Dublin 2

Italy
  Embassy:
  (☎ 06-85 2721) Via Alessandria 215, Rome 00198; also consulate in Milan

Japan
  Embassy:
  (☎ 03-5232 4111) 2-1-14 Mita, Minato-Ku, Tokyo 108; also in Osaka

Malaysia
  High Commission:
  (☎ 03-242 3122) 6 Jalan Yap Kwan Seng, Kuala Lumpur 50450

Netherlands
  Embassy:
  (☎ 070-310 8200) Camegielaan 4, 2517 KH The Hague

New Zealand
  High Commission:
  (☎ 04-473 6411) 72-78 Hobson St, Thorndon, Wellington; also consulate in Auckland

Philippines
  Embassy:
  (☎ 02-750 2850) 1st-5th floors, Dona Salustiana, Ty Tower, 104 Paseo de Roxas Ave, Makati, Metro Manila

Singapore
  High Commission:
  (☎ 737 9311) 25 Napier Rd, Singapore 258507

South Africa
  High Commission:
  (☎ 012-342 3740) 292 Orient St, Arcadia, Pretoria 0083

Sweden
  Embassy:
  (☎ 08-613 2900) Sergels Torg 12, S-111 57, Stockholm C

Thailand
  Embassy:
  (☎ 02-287 2680) 37 South Sathorn Rd, Bangkok 10120

UK
  High Commission:
  (☎ 020-7379 4334) Australia House, The Strand, London WC2B 4LA; also consulate in Manchester

USA
  Embassy:
  (☎ 202-797 3000) 1601 Massachusetts Ave NW, Washington DC, 20036; also consulates in Los Angeles and New York

Embassies & Consulates in Victoria

Most foreign embassies are in Canberra, although many countries also have consulates in Melbourne. Many offer full consular services, including issuing visas. If the consulate you want isn't listed here, check the phone book under 'Consuls' or the *Yellow Pages* under 'Consulates & Legations'.

France
(☎ 9820 0921) 492 St Kilda Rd, Melbourne
Germany
(☎ 9828 6888) 480 Punt Rd, South Yarra
Greece
(☎ 9866 4524) 34 Queens Rd, Melbourne
Indonesia
(☎ 9525 2755) 72 Queens Rd, Melbourne
Italy
(☎ 9867 5744) 509 St Kilda Rd, Melbourne
Japan
(☎ 9639 3244) 360 Elizabeth St, Melbourne
Malaysia
(☎ 9867 5339) 492 St Kilda Rd, Melbourne
Netherlands
(☎ 9867 7933) 499 St Kilda Rd, Melbourne
Sweden
(☎ 9301 1888) 61 Riggall St, Broadmeadows
Thailand
(☎ 9650 1714) 277 Flinders Lane, Melbourne
UK
(☎ 9650 4155) Level 17, 90 Collins St, Melbourne
USA
(☎ 9526 5900) 553 St Kilda Rd, Melbourne

CUSTOMS

When entering Australia you can bring most articles in free of duty, provided that customs is satisfied they are for personal use and that you'll be taking them with you when you leave. There's also the usual duty-free per-person quota of one litre of alcohol, 250 cigarettes and dutiable goods up to the value of $400.

With regard to prohibited goods, there are two areas you need to pay particular attention to. Number one, of course, is drugs – Australian Customs have a positive mania about the stuff and can be extremely efficient when it comes to finding it. Unless you want to make first-hand investigations of conditions in Australian jails (they aren't very good), don't bring any with you.

Problem two is animal and plant quarantine. You will be asked to declare all goods of animal or vegetable origin – wooden spoons, straw hats, flowers. The authorities are naturally keen to prevent weeds, pests or diseases getting into the country – Australia has managed to escape many agricultural pests and diseases prevalent in other parts of the world. Fresh food is also unpopular, particularly meat, fruit and vegetables.

Weapons and firearms are either prohibited or require a permit and safety testing. Other restricted goods include products (such as ivory) made from protected wildlife species, non-approved telecommunications devices and live animals.

And when you leave, don't take any protected flora or fauna with you. Australia's unique birds and animals fetch big bucks from overseas collectors, and customs comes down hard on animal smugglers. Penalties include jail sentences and huge fines.

There are duty-free shops at Australian international airports and their associated cities. Treat them with healthy suspicion. 'Duty-free' is one of the world's most overworked catch phrases, and is often just an excuse to sell things at prices you can easily beat by a little shopping around.

MONEY

Currency

Australia's uses the decimal system of dollars and cents (100 cents to the dollar). There are $100, $50, $20, $10 and $5 notes, gold-coloured $2 and $1 coins, and silver-coloured 50c, 20c, 10c and 5c coins. The bronze 2c and 1c coins have been taken out of circulation, although prices can still be set in odd cents. Shops round prices up or down to the nearest 5c on your *total* bill, not on individual items.

There are no notable restrictions on importing or exporting currency or travellers cheques, except that you may not take out more than $5000 in cash (in any currency) without prior approval.

Exchange Rates

Over the years the Australian dollar has fluctuated quite markedly against the US dollar, from above US75c to below US60c. At the moment it's resurfacing after a big dive and seems to be settling at around US63c – great value!

Approximate exchange rates at the time of writing were:

Country	Unit		A$
Canada	C$1	=	A$0.98
euro	€1	=	A$1.54
France	FF1	=	A$0.23
Germany	DM1	=	A$0.79
Japan	¥100	=	A$1.19
New Zealand	NZ$1	=	A$0.80
Singapore	S$1	=	A$0.84
UK	UK£1	=	A$2.33
USA	US$1	=	A$1.43

Exchanging Money

Changing foreign currency or travellers cheques is no problem at almost any bank. Normal banking hours are Monday to Thursday from 9.30 am to 4 pm, and Friday from 9.30 am to 5 pm.

There are also foreign-exchange booths at Melbourne's international airport (Tullamarine), which open to meet arriving flights. Most large hotels will change currency or travellers cheques for their guests but the rates might not be so good.

You'll also find foreign-exchange booths in the city centre. These places are OK for emergencies – they have more convenient opening hours than the banks – but their rates generally aren't as good. The downside of changing money at banks is the fees they charge – around $5 to $7 per transaction.

Thomas Cook has four foreign-exchange offices in Melbourne's city centre, including one at 261 Bourke St (open daily). American Express (Amex) has two city offices; the one at 233 Collins St is open weekdays from 8.30 am to 5.30 pm and Saturday from 9 am to noon.

Travellers Cheques Amex, Thomas Cook and other well known international brands of travellers cheques are all widely used. A passport is usually adequate for identification.

Commissions and fees for changing foreign currency travellers cheques vary from bank to bank and month to month. It's worth making a few phone calls to see which bank currently has the lowest charges. Different banks charge different fees for different types of cheques. Most banks don't charge fees on Visa brand travellers cheques.

Credit Cards The most commonly accepted credit cards are Visa and MasterCard. Amex, and to a lesser extent Diners Club, are fairly widely accepted.

Credit cards are a convenient alternative to carrying cash or large numbers of travellers cheques. There are automatic teller machines (ATMs) throughout the country, and a credit card, preferably linked to your savings account back home, is the ideal way to organise your money for travelling. Visa and MasterCard are commonly accepted in ATMs – most machines display the symbols of the credit cards accepted. Cash advances are also available over the counter from all banks.

If you're planning to rent a car, a credit card is almost mandatory – many companies don't accept cash at all, unless you're prepared to leave an enormous amount of money as a deposit.

Local Bank Accounts If you're planning to stay longer than just a month or so, it's worth considering other ways of handling money that give you more flexibility and are more economical.

Most travellers opt for an account that includes a cash card, which you can use to access your cash from ATMs all over Australia. You put your card in the machine, key in your personal identification number (PIN), and then withdraw funds from your account. Westpac, ANZ, National and Commonwealth Bank branches are found nationwide, and it's possible to use the machines of other banks. Most reasonably sized towns have at least one place where you can withdraw money from a 'hole in the wall'. There is a limit on how much you can withdraw from your account each day. This varies from bank to bank but is around $1000 per day.

If you're planning to travel to more remote parts of the country, it may be worth opening a Commonwealth Bank account; it has fewer branches than the other national banks, but all post offices and postal agencies throughout Australia are agencies for the bank. You can either use a passbook with a blacklight signature or a card, although some of the more remote postal agencies only accept passbook accounts.

Many businesses, such as petrol stations, supermarkets and convenience stores, are linked to the EFTPOS system (Electronic Funds Transfer at Point Of Sale), and at places with this facility you can use your bank cash card to pay for services or purchases direct, and often withdraw cash.

Opening an account at an Australian bank is simple for foreign visitors if you do it within six weeks of arrival, when you just need to show your passport. After six weeks you're treated as an Australian and have to show a lot of extra ID as well as your passport.

Once you've opened your account, it takes about a week to get your card. Some banks will only forward the card to an address; you can't go back to the branch to pick it up.

If you don't have an Australian tax file number, interest earned from your funds is taxed at the rate of 48%.

Foreign Banks Quite a few foreign banks have branches in Melbourne. These include the Banque Nationale de Paris (☎ 9670 9500), 90 William St; the Bank of New Zealand (☎ 9641 4300), level 6, 395 Collins St; and Hong Kong Bank (☎ 9618 3888), 99 William St.

Costs

Compared to the USA, Canada and European countries, Australia is cheaper in some ways and more expensive in others. Manufactured goods tend to be more expensive but food is both high in quality and low in cost.

Accommodation is also reasonably priced. In virtually every town where backpackers are likely to stay there'll be a backpackers' hostel with dorm beds for around $14 to $16 and double rooms for around $40, or a caravan park with on-site vans from around $35 for two people. Most pubs in country towns have accommodation for around $20 per person, and an average motel room costs between $45 and $70 a night.

The biggest cost on any trip to Australia is going to be transport, simply because it's such a vast country. If there's a group of you, buying a second-hand car is probably the most economical way to go. Victoria isn't so big, but public transport is relatively poor so a car is handy here too.

Tipping

In Australia tipping isn't 'compulsory' the way it is in the USA or Europe. A tip is a recognition of good service rather than an obligation, and the amount you tip is usually weighted according to how good the service has been. It's only customary to tip in restaurants, and only then if you want to. If you do decide to leave a tip, 10% of the bill is considered reasonable. Taxi drivers don't expect tips, although if you tell them to keep the change they're unlikely to argue with you.

Taxes & Refunds

The Australian government is determined to introduce a goods and services tax (GST; the equivalent of a VAT) which will add about 10% to the cost of everything. The tax is being resisted in the Senate, so there's a chance that it will be defeated.

If the GST is introduced, it's likely that foreign visitors will be able to claim back the GST they've paid on goods they take out of the country. When you arrive in Australia, ask about the GST. If it is in operation there will be pamphlets at the airport information desk telling you how to make a claim (you might need special receipts etc).

POST & COMMUNICATIONS

Post

Australia Post is relatively efficient.

It costs 45c to send a standard letter or postcard within Australia. Air-mail letters/postcards cost 75/70c to New Zealand;

85/80c to Singapore and Malaysia; 95/90c to Hong Kong and India; $1.05/95c to the USA and Canada; and $1.20/$1 to Europe and the UK. Aerogrammes (prepaid air-mail letter forms) cost 75c to anywhere in the world.

Generally, post offices are open Monday to Friday from 9 am to 5 pm. The GPO in Melbourne, on the corner of Bourke and Elizabeth Sts, is open Monday to Friday from 8.15 am to 5.30 pm, and Saturday (for stamp sales only) from 9 am to noon. You can also buy stamps from most newsagents.

All post offices will hold mail, keeping it for one month before returning it to the sender, although for a small fee you can arrange to have mail forwarded to you. If you have an Amex card or buy Amex travellers cheques, you can have mail sent to you C/- American Express Travel, 233 Collins St, Melbourne 3000.

Telephone

Victoria's area code is 03. Dial this number first if calling from outside Victoria, but not for calls within Victoria (or Tasmania); omit the 0 if dialling from overseas.

Australia's phone system was formerly run by the government-owned Telstra, but these days the market for long-distance and international calls has been deregulated. The local call market will be deregulated in the future. Telstra's biggest competitor is Optus but a number of smaller players are emerging.

Local calls from public phones cost 40c for an unlimited amount of time. You can make local calls from Telstra payphone booths and also from the gold or blue phones which are often found in shops, hotels, bars etc.

Long-distance (Subscriber Trunk Dialling – STD) calls can be made from virtually any public phone. Many public phones accept Telstra Phonecards. The cards come in $5, $10, $20 and $50 denominations, and are available from retail outlets such as newsagents and pharmacies which display the Phonecard logo. Otherwise, have plenty of coins (any except 5c).

Some public phones take only bank cash cards or credit cards. The minimum charge for a call on one of these phones is $1.20.

Long-distance calls are charged according to distance, and rates vary depending on when you call. Currently, Telstra's lowest rates are on weekends and after 8 pm during the week.

International Calls – Public Phones

Practically every public phone allows you to direct dial international numbers. All you do is dial ☎ 0011 for overseas, the country code (eg, 44 for Britain), the city code (eg, 212 for New York) and the telephone number. Have a Phonecard, credit card or plenty of coins on hand. Public phones have less generous pricing structures for international calls than private phones. If you want to find out what your call will cost or the cheapest time to make a call, phone ☎ 12 552.

International Calls – Private Phones

The cost of an international call from a private phone varies enormously, depending on the country you're calling, the time of day and week, which carrier you use, whether the phone you're using subscribes to a pricing plan and whether the carrier has any special deals. To find out the current deals with Telstra, phone ☎ 1222; with Optus, phone ☎ 1300 300 937. A standard Telstra call from a private phone to the USA or the UK costs $0.91 a minute during the week and $0.49 on weekends, to New Zealand $0.72/0.45 and Japan $1.26/0.68.

Calling Cards There's a wide range of local and international phonecards. Several companies sell pre-paid cards which offer discounts on long-distance and overseas calls. Newsagents and other outlets stock them. These are different from Telstra Phonecards, as you don't insert them into the phone but dial a number given on the card and quote the card's ID number.

Lonely Planet's eKno Communication Card (see the insert at the back of this book) is aimed specifically at travellers and provides cheap international calls, a range of messaging services and free email – for local calls, you're usually better off with a local card. You can join online at www.eKno.lonelyplanet.com or by phone, from Victoria, dial ☎ 1800 674 100. Once you have joined, to use eKno from Australia, dial ☎ 1800 114 478.

Country Direct Country Direct is a service which gives travellers in Australia direct access to operators in more than 50 countries, in order to make collect or credit card calls. For a full list of these check any telephone book. They include:

Canada	☎ 1800 881 150
France	☎ 1800 881 330
Germany	☎ 1800 881 490
Japan (KD)	☎ 1800 881 810
Japan (IT)	☎ 1800 881 143
New Zealand	☎ 1800 881 640
Sweden	☎ 1800 881 460
UK (BAT)	☎ 1800 881 440
UK (Mercury)	☎ 1800 881 417
USA (ATTEST)	☎ 1800 881 011
USA (CM)	☎ 1800 881 100
USA (Sprint)	☎ 1800 881 877
USA (WorldCom)	☎ 1800 881 212

Operator Assistance Some useful numbers include:

Emergency (free call)	☎ 000
Domestic directory assistance (free call)	☎ 1223
International directory assistance (free call)	☎ 1225
Reverse charges	☎ 12550

Telephone Interpreter Service A free interpreter service is available in 23 languages. Call ☎ 13 1450, 24 hours a day.

Fax

You can send faxes from any post office, either to another fax or to a postal address. Faxes to another fax machine anywhere in Australia cost $4 for the first page and $1 for each subsequent page. Faxes to postal addresses within Australia cost the same, and will be delivered by the postal service, usually the next day. Overseas faxes cost $10 for the first page and $4 for each subsequent page.

You can also send faxes from many business services, photocopying shops and newsagents – these places are usually much cheaper than post offices.

Email & Internet Access

Melbourne has many Internet cafes and the like where you can access the Net, and some places to stay, especially hostels, also offer email. All public libraries are connected to the Net.

INTERNET RESOURCES

There are many Web sites devoted to things Australian, some are of interest to visitors to Australia and Victoria. Here's a selection:

Australian Tourist Commission
 www.aussie.net.au
 This site has plenty of information and some good links.

Tourism Victoria
 www.tourism.vic.gov.au
 Informative, but the businesses listed, eg in the tours section, have paid to be there and it is not at all comprehensive.

Information Victoria
 www.infovic.vic.gov.au
 This government site is intended to help Victorians, so it's more practical than the tourism body's site. There's a lot of information here.

Parks Victoria
 www.parks.vic.gov.au
 Details of all the state's parks.

YHA
 www.yha.org.au
 Contains information on all Australian YHA (HI) hostels.

Yorta Yorta People
 http://users.mcmedia.com.au/~yorta/yorta.htm
 The homepage of one of Victoria's largest Aboriginal clan groups.

Lonely Planet
 www.lonelyplanet.com.au
 Our own site is not specific to Victoria but it is still definitely worth a look. Well, we would say that, wouldn't we?

BOOKS

Almost every bookshop in the country has a section devoted to Australia, with everything from coffee-table books and the latest humorous scribbling of a sporting hero to history and literature.

Lonely Planet

Lonely Planet's *Melbourne City Guide* fits in more information than we have room for in this book. If you want to travel farther around Australia, Lonely Planet has state guides to New South Wales (NSW), the Northern Territory, Queensland, South Australia, Tasmania and Western Australia, as well as *Australia*, which covers the lot. There are also diving, bushwalking and outback driving guides.

Sean & David's Long Drive, a hilarious offbeat road book by Sean Condon, is one of the titles in Lonely Planet's Journeys travel literature series.

Guidebooks

The National Trust publishes *Walking Melbourne*. *Weekend Getaways* by Warwick Randall and *Robinson's Guide to B&Bs and Rural Retreats* are good accommodation guides.

There are a couple of good books on the Great Ocean Road: *The Great Ocean Road – A Traveller's Guide*, written, photographed and published by Rodney Hyett; and *Explore the Great Ocean Road* by See Australia Guides. See Australia Guides also publish *Discover Victoria's Goldfield Heritage*, a detailed guidebook to central Victoria.

Wildlife Watching in Victoria ($9.95), published by the department of Natural Resources and the Environment (NRE), is a region-by-region guidebook to the animals, birds and reptiles of the state, with more than 90 suggested viewing sites and descriptions of native fauna. *Parks*, by Jane Calder, is an excellent book covering Victoria's best parks.

Koories (Aborigines)

Koorie Plants, Koorie People by Nelly Zola and Beth Gott is an excellent little hardback, published by the Koorie Heritage Trust (☎ 9669 9058), 328 Swanston St, Melbourne. It details the traditional food, fibre and healing plants used in Victoria.

The award-winning *Triumph of the Nomads*, by Geoffrey Blainey, chronicles the life of Australia's original inhabitants, and convincingly demolishes the myth that the Aborigines were 'primitive' people trapped on a hostile continent.

The Other Side of the Frontier, by Henry Reynolds, uses historical records to give a vivid account from an Aboriginal viewpoint of the arrival and takeover of Australia by Europeans. His *With the White People* identifies the essential Aboriginal contributions to the survival of the early European settlers. *My Place*, Sally Morgan's prize-winning autobiography, traces her discovery of her Aboriginal heritage. In a similar vein is *Over My Tracks* by Evelyn Crawford (as told to Chris Walsh), a remarkable story of life in an Aboriginal family in the 1930s. *The Fringe Dwellers*, by Nene Gare, describes just what it's like to be an Aborigine growing up in a European-dominated society.

Ruby Langford's *Don't Take Your Love to Town* and Kath Walker's *My People* are also recommended reading for people interested in the experience of Aborigines.

History

For a good introduction to Australian history, read *A Short History of Australia*, a most accessible and informative general history by the late Manning Clark, the much-loved historian. His life work is the six volume *A History of Australia*.

Another good overview of Australian history is *A Shorter History of Australia* by the prolific historian and writer Geoffrey Blainey. Blainey's *The Tyranny of Distance* is a captivating narrative of European settlement, and Robert Hughes' bestselling *The Fatal Shore* is a colourful and detailed account of the history of the transportation of convicts. *Finding Australia*, by Russel Ward, traces the story of the early days, from the first Aboriginal arrivals up to 1821. It's strong on Aborigines, women and the full story of foreign exploration, not just Captain Cook's role.

Cooper's Creek, by Alan Moorehead, is a classic account of the ill-fated Burke and Wills expedition which dramatises the horrors and hardships faced by the early explorers. For an altogether easier expedition, see if you can find a second-hand copy of the reprint of Major Thomas Mitchell's journal *Three Expeditions into the Interior of Eastern Australia*. It will be expensive.

Mitchell's second-in-command, Granville Stapylton, also kept a journal but his wasn't intended for publication. It's a wonderful insight into the frustrations, fears and sheer boredom of playing second fiddle to a famous man. The journal was republished by Blubber Head Press as *Stapylton – With Major Mitchell's Australia Felix Expedition 1836*, edited by Alan Andrews, and might be found in antiquarian bookshops with a large price tag.

History of Melbourne Several books dealing specifically with Melbourne are available. *Old Melbourne Town* by Michael Cannon is an extensive and detailed history of the city's early years from the time of founding up until the gold rush. Cannon's earlier book, *The Land Boomers*, is a study of Melbourne during the 1880s.

Bearbrass – Imagining Early Melbourne, by Robyn Annear, is an unconventional and intriguing history – the author 'reinvents' the Melbourne of 1835 to 1851 and integrates the history with her own experiences of contemporary Melbourne.

The Rise and Fall of Marvellous Melbourne by Graeme Davison takes a look at the city from the time of founding in 1835 until the financial crash of the 1890s.

General

You don't need to worry about bringing a few good novels from home; there's plenty of excellent contemporary Australian literature – see Literature in the Arts section of the Facts about Victoria chapter.

NEWSPAPERS & MAGAZINES

Melbourne has two major daily newspapers. The *Age* is a quality newspaper which gives reasonable coverage of international news. The Saturday and Sunday editions have several review sections with plenty of weekend reading, and there are other interesting pull-out sections during the week. The *Herald-Sun* is a tabloid-style paper published in several editions throughout the day. The *Australian*, a national daily, is also widely available.

Most regions and towns have their own local newspapers, but they're often skimpy and not always daily.

For an introduction to the gay scene in Melbourne, pick up a copy of the fortnightly *Brother Sister* magazine, or the weekly *Melbourne Star Observer* newspaper. Both are free and available from gay cafes, bars and clubs. Also worth looking out for are *Lesbiana*, a monthly magazine for lesbians, and the handy *Gay & Lesbian Melbourne Map*.

International publications are available at the larger city newsagents such as McGills, 187 Elizabeth St, opposite the GPO. Papers from the UK, USA and South-East Asia are widely available and typically about three days behind. A large number of foreign-language papers are also published in Melbourne. The *Melbourne Trading Post*, published Thursday, is a good place to look if you want to buy or sell anything – it's available at all milk bars and newsagents.

Weekly magazines include an Australian edition of *Time* and the *Bulletin*, a conservative and long-running Australian news magazine which incorporates a condensed version of the US *Newsweek*.

TNT and *For Backpackers, By Backpackers*, are free magazines aimed at independent travellers, with lots of useful information. They are available where backpackers congregate – hostels, information centres etc.

RADIO & TV

Radio

Melbourne has more than 20 radio stations.

FM Most of the commercial stations on the FM band flog the standard 'hits and memories' format.

Two excellent non-commercial stations featuring alternative and independent music, current affairs and talk programmes are 3RRR (102.7) and 3PBS (106.7). Triple J

(107.5) is the Australian Broadcasting Corporation's (ABC) national 'youth network'. It specialises in alternative music and young people's issues and has some interesting talk shows. ABC Classic-FM (105.9) plays classical music, as does the non-commercial 3MBS (103.5), while 3ZZZ (92.3) and 3SBS (93.1) are multicultural stations broadcasting in a variety of foreign languages.

AM The ABC station Radio National (621) covers a diversity of topics with often fascinating features and has a 10-minute world-news service every hour on the hour, while the Melbourne-based ABC station 3LO (774) has regular talkback programmes, news on the hour and a world-news feature at 12.10 pm every weekday. The ABC's News Radio (1026) broadcasts non-stop news when it isn't broadcasting the proceedings of federal parliament.

3CR (855) is a non-commercial community radio station, and 3SBS (1224) is multicultural foreign-language station. Radio for the Print Handicapped (1179) broadcasts readings of daily newspapers and other useful programmes, and between 11.05 pm and 6 am broadcasts the BBC World Service.

3AW (1278) is the top-rating commercial talk station. It's pretty tame fare compared with the rantings of the 'shock jocks' in other states.

In country areas, most of the larger towns have their own commercial stations. ABC-3LO, Radio National, ABC-FM and Triple J can also be picked up throughout the state on various frequencies – pick up a copy of the free *Travellers Guide to ABC Radio*, available at ABC shops and radio stations.

TV

Melbourne has six TV stations. The three commercial networks, channels Seven, Nine and Ten, are just like commercial channels anywhere, with an unadventurous diet of sport, soap operas, lightweight news and sensationalised current affairs, plus plenty of sit-coms (mainly American).

Channel Two is the government-funded and commercial-free ABC. It produces some excellent current affairs and documentaries as well as showing a lot of sport, slightly heavier news and sit-coms (mainly British). The ABC also has a knack for making good comedy and drama programmes which receive critical acclaim and low ratings.

The best international news service is at 6.30 pm daily on the publicly funded Special Broadcasting Service (SBS, channel 28, UHF). SBS is a multicultural channel which has some of the best and most diverse programmes on TV, including serious current affairs, interesting documentaries and great films (with English subtitles when necessary).

For something completely different tune to Channel 31, which pays the bills by broadcasting horse racing but also produces some quirky and gloriously amateur local programming.

Most country areas receive an ABC channel and at least one of the commercial networks.

VIDEO SYSTEMS

Australia uses the PAL system (unlike Japan and the USA), so pre-recorded videos purchased here might not be compatible with your system at home. Check before you buy.

PHOTOGRAPHY & VIDEO

Film & Equipment

There are plenty of camera shops in Melbourne and a fair range in the larger provincial cities. Mini-labs offering one-hour processing of print film are common. While print film is available from just about anywhere, slide film can be harder to find. Camera shops in the larger towns are usually the best bet for Kodachrome or Fujichrome. Including processing, 36-exposure Kodachrome 64 or Fujichrome 100 slide film costs around $25, but with a little shopping around you can find it for around $20.

Remember that film can be damaged by heat, so allow for temperature extremes and do your best to keep film as cool as possible, particularly after exposure. Other film and camera hazards are dust and humidity.

In summer, allow for the intense light which washes out colours in photos taken between mid-morning and late afternoon. Conversely, in winter you'll want to use a fairly fast film – it can get quite gloomy.

As in any country, politeness goes a long way when taking photos or videos; ask permission before photographing people.

TIME

Victoria (along with Tasmania, NSW and Queensland) keeps Eastern Standard Time, which is 10 hours ahead of Greenwich Mean Time (UTC).

When it's noon in Melbourne, it's 6 pm the previous day in Los Angeles, 2 am the same day in London, 4 am in Cape Town, 10 am in Perth (Western Australia), 11 am in Tokyo, 11.30 am in Adelaide and Darwin, and noon in Brisbane, Sydney and Hobart.

In Victoria, NSW and South Australia clocks are put forward an hour for daylight saving time between the last Sunday in October and the last Sunday in March. Tasmania starts daylight saving time earlier and ends later; Western Australia, the Northern Territory and Queensland don't have daylight saving.

ELECTRICITY

Voltage is 240V and the plugs have three pins, but they're not the same as British three-pin plugs. Users of electric shavers or hair dryers should note that, apart from in fancy hotels, it's difficult to find converters to take either US flat two-pin plugs or the European round two-pin plugs. Adaptors for British plugs can be found in good hardware shops, chemists and travel agents.

WEIGHTS & MEASURES

Australia went metric in the early 1970s. Petrol and milk are sold by the litre, apples and potatoes by the kilogram, distance is measured by the metre or kilometre and speed limits are in kilometres per hour. There's a metric conversion table at the back of this book.

HEALTH

Australia is a remarkably healthy country. Basically, you don't have to worry about anything other than the normal health precautions you take at home. Visitors from cooler climates need to be aware of the potential dangers of hot weather, and everyone should be aware of occasional isolated outbreaks of mosquito-born viruses. The best defence against both heat and mosquitoes is to cover up.

As long as you haven't visited an infected country in the past 14 days (aircraft refuelling stops don't count), vaccinations are not required for entry.

Water

Melbourne has one of the highest standards of tap water in the world. Tap water is safe almost everywhere in the state.

Be wary of natural water, as it may have been infected by cattle or wildlife. The surest way to disinfect water is to boil it for 10 minutes. Simple filtering won't remove all dangerous organisms, so if you cannot boil water, treat it chemically. Chlorine tablets (Puritabs, Steritabs or other brand names) will kill many but not all pathogens. Iodine is very effective and is available in tablet form, such as Potable Aqua.

Medical Care

Medical care is first class and only moderately expensive. A typical visit to the doctor costs around $35. If you have an immediate health problem, contact the casualty section at the nearest public hospital or a medical clinic. However, if you're admitted to hospital and you are neither entitled to Medicare benefits nor covered by travel insurance, you'll be in for some very large bills indeed.

Medicare Visitors from Christmas Island, the Cocos Islands, Finland, Italy, Malta, the Netherlands, New Zealand, Norfolk Island, Sweden and the UK have reciprocal health rights in Australia. This means that you can obtain a Medicare card which entitles you to free treatment in public hospitals and potentially free treatment with any doctor.

The only catch is that you are entitled to treatment for an immediate problem, usually some sort of emergency, not for long-term or specialist services.

To get a Medicare card go to any Medicare office and show your passport and visa, plus your health care card from your home country. It takes about three weeks for your Medicare card to be issued, but you're entitled to health care from the date of your arrival.

Many doctors require you to pay the bill and get a refund from Medicare (available over the counter in a Medicare office), and many charge slightly more than Medicare refunds. If you don't want to do this, look for a doctor who advertises 'bulk billing', which means that the doctor bills Medicare directly.

Health Preparations

If you wear glasses or contact lenses, take a spare pair and your prescription. Don't forget to bring any medication you're already taking, and include prescriptions with the generic rather than the brand name (which may not be available locally).

A Medic Alert tag is worth having if you have a medical condition that is not easily recognisable (heart trouble, diabetes, asthma, allergic reactions to antibiotics etc).

The contraceptive pill is available on prescription only, so a visit to a doctor is necessary. Doctors are listed in the *Yellow Pages* phone book or you can visit the outpatients section of a public hospital. Condoms are available from chemists, many convenience stores and often from vending machines in the toilets of pubs.

If you're heading off the beaten track, at least one person in your party should have some knowledge of first aid, and you'll need a handbook and basic medical kit. St John Ambulance Australia has a selection of first-aid kits for car drivers, motorcyclists and bushwalkers, starting at around $50. They're available at St John offices and at the RACV.

Environmental Hazards

Victoria has its fair share of days hotter than 35°C in summer, especially inland. It is sensible on a hot day to avoid the sun between mid-morning and mid-afternoon. Infants and elderly people are most at risk from heat exhaustion and heat stroke.

People who first arrive in a hot climate may not feel thirsty when they should; the body and 'thirst mechanism' often need a few days to adjust. The rule of thumb is that an active adult should drink at least four litres of water per day in warm weather – more when walking or cycling.

Sunburn You can get sunburnt surprisingly quickly, even through cloud. Use a sunscreen, a hat, and a barrier cream for your nose and lips. Calamine lotion or Stingose are good for mild sunburn. Protect your eyes with good quality sunglasses, particularly near water, sand or snow. Sunburn during childhood is related to skin cancer in later life.

Heat Exhaustion Dehydration or salt deficiency can cause heat exhaustion. Take time to acclimatise to high temperatures and make sure you get sufficient (nonalcoholic) liquids. Think of your salt level too. Drinking an 'exercise' drink is better for you than taking salt tablets.

Heat Stroke This serious, sometimes fatal, condition can occur if the body's heat-regulating mechanism breaks down and the body temperature rises to dangerous levels. Long, continuous periods of exposure to high temperatures can leave you vulnerable to heatstroke. You should avoid excessive alcohol or strenuous activity when you first arrive in a hot climate.

The symptoms are feeling unwell, not sweating very much or at all and a high body temperature (39°C to 41°C). When sweating has ceased, the skin becomes flushed and red. Severe, throbbing headaches and lack of coordination will also occur, and the sufferer may become confused or aggressive. Eventually the victim will become delirious or convulse. Hospitalisation is essential, but meanwhile get patients out of the sun, remove their clothing, cover them with a wet sheet or towel and fan them continually.

Hypothermia Cold weather can be as dangerous as hot, and it isn't just in the snowy mountains that you're at risk. A wet day's bushwalking in winter can lower your body temperature to dangerous levels. Get out of the wind, put on dry clothes and have a warm drink. Despite the cliches about brandy, you should *never* give alcohol to someone suffering from hypothermia.

Infectious Diseases

Diarrhoea Simple things such as a change of water, food or climate can all cause a mild bout of diarrhoea, but a few rushed toilet trips with no other symptoms is not indicative of a major problem.

Dehydration is the main danger with any diarrhoea, particularly in children or the elderly as it can occur quite quickly. Under all circumstances *fluid replacement* (at least equal to the volume being lost) is the most important thing to remember. Weak black tea with a little sugar, soda water, or soft drinks allowed to go flat and diluted 50% with clean water are all good.

Sexually Transmitted Diseases Gonorrhoea, herpes and syphilis are among these diseases; sores, blisters or rashes around the genitals and discharges or pain when urinating are common symptoms. In some STDs, such as wart virus or chlamydia, symptoms may be less marked or not observed at all, especially in women. Syphilis symptoms eventually disappear completely but the disease continues and can cause severe problems in later years. While abstinence from sexual contact is the only 100% effective prevention, using condoms is also effective.

There are numerous other sexually transmitted diseases, for most of which effective treatment is available. There is no cure for herpes or AIDS. If you suspect anything is wrong, go to the nearest public hospital or visit the Melbourne Sexual Health Centre (☎ 9347 0244 or 1800 032 017 toll-free) at 580 Swanston St in Carlton – visits are free and confidential, and don't require a referral.

Medical Kit Check List

Following is a list of items you should consider including in your medical kit – consult your phamacist for brands available in your country.

- ☐ **Aspirin** or **paracetamol** (acetaminophen in the US) – for relief of pain or fever.
- ☐ **Antihistamine** – for allergies, eg hay fever; to ease the itch from insect bites or stings; and to prevent motion sickness.
- ☐ **Antibiotics** – consider including these if you're travelling well off the beaten track; see your doctor, as they must be prescribed, and carry the prescription with you.
- ☐ **Loperamide** or **diphenoxylate** – 'blockers' for diarrhoea; **prochlorperazine** or **metaclopramide** for nausea and vomiting.
- ☐ **Rehydration mixture** – to prevent dehydration, eg due to severe diarrhoea; particularly important when travelling with children.
- ☐ **Insect repellent, sunscreen, lip balm** and **eye drops.**
- ☐ **Calamine lotion, sting relief spray** or **aloe vera** – for easing the irritation caused by sunburn and insect bites or stings.
- ☐ **Antifungal cream** or **powder** – for fungal skin infections and thrush.
- ☐ **Antiseptic** (such as povidone-iodine) – for cuts and grazes.
- ☐ **Bandages, Band-Aids (plasters)** and other wound dressings.
- ☐ **Water purification tablets** or **iodine.**
- ☐ **Scissors, tweezers** and a **thermometer** (note that mercury thermometers are prohibited by airlines).
- ☐ **Cold** and **flu tablets, throat lozenges** and **nasal decongestant.**
- ☐ **Multivitamins** – consider for long trips, when dietary vitamin intake may be inadequate.

HIV & AIDS Infection with the human immunodeficiency virus (HIV) may lead to acquired immune deficiency syndrome (AIDS), which is a fatal, incurable disease. Any exposure to blood, blood products or body fluids may put the individual at risk. The disease is often transmitted through sexual contact or dirty needles – vaccinations, acupuncture, tattooing and body piercing are potentially as dangerous as intravenous drug use.

Fear of HIV infection should not preclude treatment for serious medical conditions.

The AIDS Line (☎ 9347 6099 or 1800 133 392 toll-free) provides information on AIDS and AIDS-related illnesses.

Cuts, Bites & Stings

See the Dangers & Annoyances section later in this chapter for information on snake and spider bites.

Cuts & Scratches Skin punctures can easily become infected and may be difficult to heal. Treat any cut with an antiseptic solution and Mercurochrome. Where possible, avoid bandages and Band-aids, which can keep wounds wet.

Bites & Stings Bee and wasp stings are usually painful rather than dangerous. However, in people who are allergic to them severe breathing difficulties may occur and require urgent medical care. Calamine lotion or Stingose spray will give relief and ice packs will reduce the pain and swelling.

Leeches Leeches may be present in damp rainforest conditions; they attach themselves to your skin to suck your blood. Trekkers often get them on their legs or in their boots. Salt or a lighted cigarette end will make them fall off. Do not pull them off, as the bite is then more likely to become infected. Clean and apply pressure if the point of attachment is bleeding. An insect repellent might keep them away.

Ticks You should always check all over your body if you have been walking through a potentially tick-infested area. Ticks can cause skin infections and more serious diseases. If a tick is found attached, press down around the tick's head with tweezers, grab the head and gently pull upwards. Avoid pulling the rear of the body as this may squeeze the tick's gut contents through the attached mouth parts into the skin, increasing the risk of infection and disease. Smearing chemicals on the tick will not make it let go and is not recommended.

Women's Health

Poor diet and even contraceptive pills can lead to vaginal infections when travelling in hot climates. Maintaining good personal hygiene, and wearing skirts or loose-fitting trousers and cotton underwear will help to prevent infections.

Yeast infections (thrush), characterised by a rash, itch and discharge, can be treated with a vinegar or even lemon-juice douche or with yoghurt. Nystatin suppositories are the usual medical prescription. Trichomonas is a more serious infection; symptoms are a discharge and a burning sensation when urinating. If a vinegar-water douche is not effective, medical attention should be sought. Flagyl is the prescribed drug. In both cases, male sexual partners must also be treated.

Some women experience irregular periods when travelling because of the upset in routine. Don't forget to take time zones into account if you're on the pill. If you run into intestinal problems, the pill may not be absorbed. Ask your physician about these matters before you go.

WOMEN TRAVELLERS

Victoria is generally a safe place for women travellers, although you should avoid walking alone in Melbourne late at night. Sexual harassment is rare, although the Aussie male culture does have its sexist elements. Don't tolerate any harassment or discrimination.

Female hitchhikers should exercise care at all times. See the section on hitching in the Getting Around chapter.

Women's Organisations The following organisations offer a range of advice and services exclusively for women:

Women's Health Information Centre (☎ 9344 2007), 132 Grattan St, Carlton
Women's Health Information Service (☎ 9662 3755; information line ☎9662 3742 from 9 am to 1 pm weekdays), Level 2, 210 Lonsdale St, Melbourne
Women's Information & Referral Exchange (☎ 9654 6844), Level 2, 247 Flinders Lane, Melbourne
Women's Refuge Referral (☎1800 015 188 toll-free, 24 hours)

GAY & LESBIAN TRAVELLERS

Homosexuality is legal and the age of consent, equal to that for heterosexuals, is 16.

The straight community's attitude towards gays and lesbians is, on the whole, open-minded and accepting. This is particularly the case in Melbourne, which has a high-profile gay community. In regional Victoria there's still a strong streak of homophobia, and violence against homosexual people, in particular gay men, is not unknown.

Melbourne has an increasingly lively gay and lesbian scene, with numerous bars, cafes, nightclubs and accommodation places in the inner suburbs of Fitzroy, Collingwood, Prahran, South Yarra and St Kilda. Around the state, places such as Daylesford and Hepburn Springs, Phillip Island, Bright, the Mornington Peninsula, Echuca and Lorne have accommodation catering for gays and lesbians.

The highlight of the local calender is the Midsumma Festival held each January/February, which showcases a wide range of theatrical, musical and artistic productions and events such as the Midsumma Carnival, the Pride march that ends at Luna Park, Red Raw, a big dance party held on the docks on the Saturday of the Australia Day weekend, and the Melbourne Queer Film & Video Festival. The Midsumma web site (www.midsumma.org.au) has more information.

For information on accommodation, places to eat, venues and health and support services for gays and lesbians see the relevant sections in the Melbourne chapter.

Gay & Lesbian Information Services The following organisations offer a range of advice and services for gays and lesbians. Bookshops are also useful sources of information and contacts (see the following Bookshop section).

Gay & Lesbian Switchboard (☎ 9510 5488), nightly between 6 and 10 pm (Wednesday from 2 to 10 pm), is a telephone information service with trained counsellors who offer advice and counselling, or you can just ring for a chat.
Gay & Lesbian Switchboard Information Service (☎ 0055 12504), a 24-hour recorded service that covers the entertainment scene as well as social and support groups.

DISABLED TRAVELLERS

Victoria provides an exciting range of accessible attractions. Highlights include the Penguin Parade (☎ 5956 8691) at Phillip Island, *Puffing Billy* (☎ 9754 6800) in the Dandenong Ranges, Healesville Sanctuary (☎ 5957 2800) and the Twelve Apostles along the Great Ocean Road.

Easy Access Australia – A Travel Guide to Australia, available from PO Box 218, Kew 3101 ($24.85), has a chapter on Victoria.

The following organisations offer a range of services for disabled people:

National Industries for Disability Services, operating through the Australian Council for the Rehabilitation of the Disabled (ACROD; ☎ 9687 7066), 81 Cowper St, Footscray, produces information sheets for disabled travellers, including lists of state-level organisations, specialist travel agents, wheelchair and equipment hire and access guides.
Paraplegic & Quadriplegic Association of Victoria (Para Quad; ☎ 9415 1200) can provide advice on access, equipment hire and attendant care.
Victorian Deaf Society (☎ 9657 8111)
Association for the Blind (☎ 9599 5000)
Independent Living Centre (☎ 9362 6111) might be able to help with equipment rental, and will certainly help with information.
Traveller's Aid Disability Access Service (☎ 9564 7690)

For information on equipment hire, accommodation and transport for disabled travellers see the Information, Places to Stay and Getting Around sections in the Melbourne chapter.

SENIOR TRAVELLERS

Many organisations offer discounts to seniors but usually only those with a government pension card which is only available to residents; however, it is always worth asking.

Discounts of 10% are available to pensioners for most express bus fares and bus passes. Travellers over 60 years of age can get up to 70% off the regular air fares. These discounts apply to both Australians and visitors; to qualify, present current ID showing your age.

TRAVEL WITH CHILDREN

Victoria is reasonably child friendly.

In cars, you are obliged to use appropriate restraints for infants and young children. If you're hiring a car make sure that these will be included when you book.

Large department stores and shopping malls usually have baby-changing facilities and most motels will provide a cot (often free).

If your kids can't swim (and even if they can), keep a very close eye on them at all times when they're near water. Not just at the beach or by rivers, but near dams and motel pools. Drowning is a tragedy that befalls far too many young children.

Lonely Planet's *Travel with Children* offers many handy hints on making travel enjoyable for both ankle biters and their parents.

USEFUL ORGANISATIONS

YHA (HI)

The YHA (☎ 9670 7991) has its helpful Melbourne office at 205 King St, on the corner of Little Bourke St.

Parks Victoria

This organisation is responsible for the management of Victoria's national parks and various other reserves. Parks Victoria was split from the NRE, which means that the offices of that department (which can be found in larger towns all over the state) no longer necessarily provide comprehensive information on parks. The good news is that Parks Victoria has a toll-free information number (☎ 13 1963).

Unfortunately, Parks Victoria doesn't have a physical location where you can collect brochures. You have to have them mailed to you. The NRE's Information Centre (☎ 9637 8080), 8 Nicholson St, East Melbourne, carries a good range of books and other information on parks and outdoor activities.

WWOOF

The idea behind Willing Workers on Organic Farms (WWOOF) is that you do a few hours work each day on a farm in return for bed and board. Becoming a WWOOFer is a great way to meet interesting people and travel cheaply. There are about 900 WWOOF associates in Australia, mostly in Victoria, NSW and Queensland.

To join WWOOF (☎ 5155 0218) send $30 for one person or $35 for two people travelling together and a photocopy of your passport data page to WWOOF Australia, DEP TM, Buchan 3885, and they'll send you a membership number and a booklet which lists WWOOF places all over Australia.

National Trust

The National Trust is dedicated to preserving historic buildings in all parts of Australia.

The Trust also produces some excellent literature, including a fine series of walking-tour guides to Melbourne and some of Victoria's historic towns. These guides are often available from local tourist offices or from National Trust offices and are usually free, whether you're a member of the National Trust or not. Membership is well worth considering, because it entitles you to free entry to any National Trust property for your year of membership. The Melbourne office (☎ 9654 4711) is in historic Tasma Terrace, Parliament Place, East Melbourne – just behind the Houses of Parliament on Spring St in the city.

DANGERS & ANNOYANCES

Theft

Victoria is a relatively safe place to visit, but you should still take reasonable precautions. Don't leave hotel rooms or cars unlocked, and don't leave money, wallets, purses or cameras unattended or in full view through car windows, for instance. Most accommodation places have a safe where you can store your valuables.

If you are unlucky enough to have something stolen, immediately report all details to the nearest police station. If your credit cards, cash card or travellers cheques have been taken, notify your bank or the relevant company immediately (most have 24-hour 'lost or stolen' numbers listed under 'Banks' or 'Credit Card Organisations' in the *Yellow Pages*).

Trams

In Melbourne, be *extremely* cautious when stepping on and off trams – a lot of people have been hit by passing cars, so don't step off without looking both ways. Pedestrians in Bourke St Mall and Swanston Walk should watch for passing trams too.

Car drivers should treat Melbourne trams with caution (see Getting Around in the Melbourne chapter). Cyclists should be careful not to get their wheels caught in a tram track, and motorcyclists should take special care when tram tracks are wet.

Swimming & Boating

Port Phillip Bay is generally safe for swimming – the closest you're likely to come to a shark is in the local fish & chip shop. The small blue-ringed octopus is sometimes found hiding under rocks in rockpools on the foreshore. Its sting can be fatal, so don't touch it under any circumstances! Many of the bay and coastal beaches are patrolled by life-savers in summer – patrolled beaches have a pair of red and yellow flags which you should always swim between. Boating on Port Phillip Bay can be hazardous, as conditions can change dramatically and without warning.

If you happen to get caught in a rip when swimming and are being taken out to sea, try not to panic. Raise one arm until you have been spotted, and then swim parallel to the shore – *don't* try to swim back against the rip, you'll only tire yourself.

Snakes & Spiders

Snakes are common in country Victoria. If you see one, leave it alone. To minimise your chances of being bitten, always wear boots, socks and long trousers when walking through undergrowth where snakes may be present. Don't put your hands into holes and crevices, and be careful when collecting firewood.

Snake bites do not cause instantaneous death and antivenenes are usually available. Keep the victim calm and still, wrap the bitten limb tightly, as you would for a sprained ankle, and then attach a splint to immobilise it. Then seek medical help, if possible with the dead snake for identification. Don't attempt to catch the snake if there is even a remote possibility of being bitten. The victim must not blunder about chasing the snake – it's essential that s/he keep as still and calm as possible.

Tourniquets and sucking out the poison are now comprehensively discredited.

Victoria's most dangerous spider is the redback. It has a very painful, sometimes lethal, bite – apply ice, treat as for snakebite and seek medical attention. The white-tailed spider should also be avoided. Some people have an extreme reaction to this spider's bite and gangrene can occur.

See the Flora & Fauna section of the Facts about Victoria chapter for descriptions of snakes and spiders.

Insects

Flies & Mosquitoes In summer, you'll have to cope with flies and mosquitoes. An insect repellent will help, but at times you might have to resort to the 'great Australian wave' to keep them at bay. A good spray for relieving the sting of mosquitoes or sunburn is Stingose.

Ticks & Leeches The common bush-tick (found in the forests and scrub country along the eastern coast of Australia) can be dangerous if left lodged in the skin. Remember to check yourself, children and dogs for ticks after a walk in the bush.

Leeches are common, and while they will suck your blood they are not dangerous. See the Health section earlier in this chapter for advice on how to deal with these suckers.

On the Road

Cows, kangaroos and even wombats can be a real hazard to the driver, especially at dusk and at night. Unfortunately, other drivers are even more dangerous, particularly those who drink. See the Getting Around chapter for more on driving in Victoria.

Bushfires

Bushfires happen every year in Victoria. Don't be the mug who starts one. In hot, dry, windy weather, be extremely careful with any naked flame – no cigarette butts out of car windows! On a Total Fire Ban Day (listen to the radio or watch the billboards on country roads) it is forbidden even to use a camping stove in the open. The locals will not be amused if they catch you breaking this particular law; they'll happily dob you in, and the penalties are severe. There's a good chance you'll go to jail for a long time.

If you're unfortunate enough to find yourself driving through a bushfire, stay inside your car and try to park in an open space, away from trees, until the danger passes. Lie on the floor under the dashboard, covering yourself with a wool blanket if possible. The front of the fire should pass quickly, and you will be much safer than if you were out in the open. It is very important to cover up with a wool blanket or wear protective clothing, as it is heat radiation which is the big killer in bushfire situations.

If you're out in the bush and you see smoke, even at a great distance, take it seriously. Go to the nearest open space, downhill if possible. A forested ridge is the most dangerous place to be. Bushfires move very quickly and change direction with the wind.

See the boxed text 'How to Survive a Bushfire'.

EMERGENCY

In a life-threatening emergency, telephone ☎ 000. This call is free from any phone in the country, and the operator will connect you to the police, ambulance or fire brigade. Other emergency numbers include:

Lifeline	☎ 13 1114
Maritime Search & Rescue	☎ 1800 641 792
Legal Advice	☎ 13 1384

LEGAL MATTERS

Australia's legal system developed from and is still broadly the same as that in the UK. Solicitors are the people you deal with initially on any matter and usually represent you in magistrates' courts. Barristers represent you in higher courts and are usually hired through your solicitor. There's one statewide police force, which deals with both traffic and crime.

Unless you're very unlucky or very silly, chances are your only contact with the law will be related to driving offences. Police have the power to stop your car and insist that you take a breath test for alcohol. You're required to carry your licence while driving; they'll ask to see it, and they might check your car for roadworthiness while they're about it.

First offenders caught with small amounts of illegal drugs are likely to receive a fine rather than jail. However, a conviction is recorded and this may affect your visa status.

Legal Aid is available only in serious cases and only to the truly needy. However, many solicitors do not charge for an initial consultation. The Law Institute has a referral service (☎ 9602 5000) which can recommend solicitors who specialise in the area of law that concerns you. To connect to the nearest solicitor (or one who is part of a fairly small networking scheme, anyway), phone ☎ 13 1384.

BUSINESS HOURS

Standard shop trading hours are Monday to Thursday from 9 am to 5.30 pm, Friday 9 am to 9 pm, and Saturday 9 am to 12.30 pm. Many shops in Melbourne's city centre and other major shopping centres also stay open until 9 pm on Thursday and until 5 pm on

Saturday – especially the larger retailers. Most retail shops close on Sunday, although many shops in tourist precincts such as Acland St (St Kilda), Chapel St (Prahran), Lygon St (Carlton) and Brunswick St (Fitzroy) are open every day. Places such as delicatessens, milk bars and bookshops often stay open late and on weekends. Many supermarkets are open until late at night, and some stay open 24 hours a day.

Most offices and businesses open Monday to Friday from 9 am to 5.30 pm, although some government departments close at 4.30 or 5 pm. Normal banking hours are Monday to Thursday from 9.30 am to 4 pm, and Friday from 9.30 am to 5 pm. Pub bottleshops generally stay open until 11 pm from Monday to Saturday, but close by 8 pm on Sunday.

PUBLIC HOLIDAYS

See the When to Go section earlier in this chapter for details on school holiday periods in Victoria. On public holidays, government departments, banks, offices, large stores and post offices are closed. On Good Friday and Christmas Day, newspapers are not published and about the only stores you will find open are the 24-hour convenience stores. Also note that some consulates close

How to Survive a Bushfire

Each year about 600 bushfires occur in forests and parks throughout Victoria. There are certain precautions that can be taken if you are caught in a bushfire; these are well summarised in *Don't Get Caught in a Bushfire*, a pamphlet published by the Department of Natural Resources and Environment (NRE).

It is better to avoid situations where you might be caught in fire, so before leaving on a trip to the bush in the summer, check the weather report and, if you plan to visit a park or forest, contact either a Parks Victoria or NRE office.

If you are caught in a bushfire while walking don't run unless there is a clear escape route. Don't try to outrun the fire uphill as a fire travels faster uphill than downhill.

You should seek shelter from the fire in a creek, wet gully, building, roadside drainage line, concrete bridge, deep wheel rut, rocky outcrop, open area with little or no vegetation, or an area that has been recently burnt, but not in a pool or any still water as there is a danger of being boiled alive. Next, clear the area around your shelter of any leaves, twigs or other easily flammable material. Cover any exposed skin with clothing (preferably woollen), soft earth or anything that will give protection from the heat. It's also important to keep low and breathe air close to the ground where it's cooler and there is less smoke. Don't leave the shelter until the fire has passed.

There is little chance of surviving an intense fire that is advancing if there is no shelter around you. In this case, at least try to move away from the hottest part of the fire. Only as a last resort, try to choose a place where the heat and flames are less intense and walk briskly through the fire to a burnt area.

Don't drive along a road that is obscured by fire and smoke, but don't leave your vehicle either. Park as far away as possible from any leaves or matter that can burn. All windows and vents should be closed and the headlights turned on. Lie on the floor and cover yourself with a blanket or any cloth that will shield you from the heat. It's vital to stay in the car until the fire has passed. If you have no choice but to continue in such conditions, proceed slowly with the headlights on and watch out for fallen trees, firefighting vehicles and fire personnel.

Richard Nebeský

for 10 days over the Christmas-New Year period.

Victoria has the following public holidays:

New Year's Day	1 January
Australia Day	26 January
Labour Day	first or second Monday in March
Easter	Good Friday and Easter Saturday, Monday and Tuesday: usually falls in late March or early April
Anzac Day	25 April
Queen's Birthday	second Monday in June
Melbourne Cup Day*	first Tuesday in November
Christmas Day	25 December
Boxing Day	26 December

* Melbourne Cup Day is a holiday only in the Melbourne metropolitan area. Some other urban centres (such as Ballarat, Geelong and Bendigo) have their own cup days which are local holidays.

When the proclaimed date falls on a weekend, the following Monday is declared a holiday (with the exception of Anzac Day and Australia Day). See the 'Festivals & Cultural Events' boxed text at the end of this chapter for a more comprehensive list of special events in Victoria.

WORK

If you come to Australia on a 12-month 'working holiday' visa you can officially work for the entire 12 months, but can only stay with the one employer for a maximum of three months. On the other hand, working on a regular tourist visa is strictly *verboten*. Some travellers do find casual work, but with an unemployment rate around 8% and youth unemployment rates much higher, it's becoming more difficult to get a job – legal or otherwise.

To receive wages you must have a tax file number, issued by the Australian Taxation Office. Application forms are available at all post offices, and you must show your passport and visa.

Try the classified section of the daily papers under 'Situations Vacant', especially the *Age* on Saturday and Wednesday. The staff and notice boards at some backpacker hostels can also be good sources of information.

Bar or restaurant work is the most commonly available, but quite a few agencies place travellers in office, teaching and medical jobs. Many advertise in travellers' magazines such as *TNT*, which is available at hostels and tourist information centres.

The federal government's agencies assisting the unemployed have been partially privatised, and the private agencies don't get paid for helping people who aren't eligible for unemployment benefits (such as overseas visitors). You can search the computer listings at a Centrelink office.

Fruit Picking

Fruit picking isn't highly paid and it can be tough. Picking grapes in 42°C heat isn't fun – some pickers call it 'paid torture'. As growers have trouble attracting locals to bring in the harvest, there are often jobs available. The table lists the main harvest times of the crops where casual employment is a possibility.

Crop	Time	Region
Peaches	Jan-Mar	Shepparton
Grapes	Jan-Apr	Mildura
Tomatoes	Feb-Apr	Shepparton, Echuca
Strawberries	Oct-Apr	Echuca, Dandenongs
Cherries	Nov-Feb	Dandenongs

ACCOMMODATION

There's a wide range of accommodation alternatives. Melbourne has everything from hostels to five-star hotels and most larger country towns have something to suit most budgets.

A typical small town has a basic motel, an old hotel or two and a caravan park with campsites and on-site vans or cabins.

The RACV's *Accommodation Guide* ($12, or $6 for members) is a comprehensive directory listing hotels, motels, holiday flats, guesthouses, B&Bs and even some backpackers' hostels in almost every town in the country. The RACV also publishes a *Tourist Park Accommodation* guide ($10, or $5 for members), which lists all the camping and caravan parks in the state. You can buy both for $18, $9 for members. The guides are updated every year, so the prices are fairly current. The RACV's branch offices around the state also offer accommodation booking services, as do some tourist information centres.

Camping & Caravanning

Pitching a tent is the cheapest form of accommodation. In some state and national parks camping is free, although the more popular parks charge a fee, usually around $9 for up to six people.

The good news is that there are plenty of caravan parks and they are quite cheap, with tent sites costing around $10 to $15 for two people. The bad news is that many cater predominantly for caravanners, and often have no cooking facilities or communal dining or recreation areas for tenters – you just get a tent site and toilet, shower and laundry facilities. There are plenty of exceptions, however, and many of the better caravan parks now have swimming pools, shops and campers' kitchens.

In general, caravan parks are well kept and excellent value, but they are usually located on the outskirts of towns, which means they can be a long way from the centre of the bigger towns.

Many parks have on-site vans which you can rent for the night (from $35). These give you the comfort of a caravan without the inconvenience of actually towing one. On-site cabins are also widely available (from $40 and way up), and these are more like a small self-contained unit. They usually have one bedroom, or at least an area which can be screened off from the rest of the unit.

Note that caravan park prices are strongly affected by seasonal demand. In any area with a hint of a tourist attraction (usually some sort of water – dam, river, sea), you'll pay much more in January, at Easter and in school holidays. Around Christmas and at Easter there might be a minimum stay of at least a few days.

Mobile Homes

The advantages of travelling in a Kombi, campervan or station wagon are that it's cheap – you don't have to pay for a bed – and you can sleep wherever you happen to be, without having to worry about booking a room. The main disadvantage is trying to find a shower in the morning. One option is to head for a caravan park, roadhouse or public toilet block (toilet blocks along the coast often have coin-operated hot showers).

Some towns, especially in popular coastal areas, have by-laws forbidding sleeping in vans by the roadside.

Hostels

Hostelling International Australia's overseeing body is currently still called the Youth Hostel Association (YHA), unlike many other countries where the hostelling organisations are now known under the new international standard name of Hostelling International (HI).

YHA hostels provide basic accommodation, usually in dormitories although more of them are providing twin and double rooms. The nightly charges are rock bottom – usually between $13 and $16 a night in a dorm, from around $35 for a twin or double. All hostels accept non-YHA members, at a slightly higher nightly charge.

For Australians, annual membership costs $27 plus a $17 joining fee (there are usually deals, such as discounted accommodation, to offset the joining fee). You can join at any hostel. Overseas visitors can buy an HI card (valid for one year) here for $27. If you're already a member of HI in your own country, your membership entitles you to use Australian hostels. Members are entitled to an impressive list of discounts at local and national businesses.

Most hostels have cooking facilities and a place where you can sit and talk. There are usually laundry facilities and often excellent notice boards. Many hostels have a maximum stay period – because some hostels are permanently full, it would hardly be fair for people to stay too long when others are being turned away. No YHA hostels have curfews or chores.

Accommodation can usually be booked directly with the manager, or through a Membership & Travel Centre. The YHA's Victorian head office (☎ 9670 7991) is at 205 King St, Melbourne 3000.

Backpackers' Hostels Melbourne has many, many backpackers' hostels, and they are becoming common in the more popular parts of rural Victoria. They vary enormously in style and standard, ranging from pub rooms to purpose-built hostels.

Many places employ backpackers for their day-to-day operation, and often it's not too long before standards start to slip. The best places are often the smaller hostels where the owner is also the manager.

Backpacker hostels also vary enormously in terms of their atmosphere – some of the bigger places in Melbourne are heavily party-oriented, with organised trips to pubs and clubs etc, but there are plenty of smaller, quieter places.

Prices are generally in line with YHA hostels although seasonal competition can push them up or down.

One practice that many people find objectionable – in independent hostels only, since it never happens in YHAs – is the 'vetting' of Australians and sometimes New Zealanders to determine whether they are genuine travellers. Some places demand to see a passport. This happens mostly where a hostel has had problems with locals treating the place as a dosshouse.

University Accommodation

Several university colleges in Melbourne, and some of the regional university towns, offer inexpensive accommodation during vacation periods. See the Melbourne chapter for details.

Guesthouses & B&Bs

These places represent the fastest growing segment of Victoria's accommodation market. Choices include everything from restored miners' cottages, converted barns and stables, rambling old guesthouses, upmarket country homes and romantic escapes to a simple bedroom in a family home. Tariffs (and standards) cover a wide spectrum, ranging from around $50 to $150 a double. Some extremely luxurious places charge over $300, usually with gourmet meals included.

Tourism Victoria publishes a good booklet called *Victoria's Bed & Breakfast Getaways*, available from most tourist offices. There are also several guidebooks dedicated to these places – see the section on Books earlier in this chapter. These publications mainly include the more expensive places, such as those you'd choose for a weekend getaway. For smaller, local places, more like the average B&B you'd find in the UK, see local tourist offices.

Pubs

The typical Aussie pub has a public bar (the traditional domain of the working man) at the front, a lounge bar and/or dining room at the rear and a number of small bedrooms upstairs, with shared bathrooms and toilets.

In Melbourne, there are very few pubs that still provide accommodation, but most country towns have at least one old pub with rooms for budget travellers. In some of these places, the old-fashioned rooms are drab, dirty or, at best, spartan. If you're paying around $20 a night, don't expect much more than a sagging single bed in a shoe box-sized room. On a brighter note, some of the better-kept country pubs have excellent rooms at reasonable prices, and most pubs include a cooked breakfast in the tariff – ask if this is the case when comparing prices.

Pubs don't usually have reception desks – you just ask at the bar whether they have a room.

In many older towns you'll find historic pubs which have been restored or renovated and offer charming and old-fashioned accommodation. Especially in the old goldmining centres, there are some magnificent examples of extravagant Victorian architecture. Staying in these places is a great way to experience country Victoria, and you'll meet many more interesting locals in the bar than you would if you stayed in a motel.

Motels

Motels are the most common type of accommodation. Almost every country town has at least one motel, and the larger towns have dozens to choose from.

A standard motel room has a double (or queen-sized) bed, a colour TV, bar fridge, tea and coffee-making facilities, private bathroom with a shower, and all bed linen and towels supplied. Most have some sort of air-conditioning.

Prices vary from place to place, but typically a budget motel charges from $45 to $55 a double, while newer and better motels cost around $70 to $100 a double.

Host Farms

Australia is a land of farms (known as 'stations' in the outback) and one of the best ways to come to grips with Australian life is to spend a few days on a farm. Many offer accommodation where you can just sit back and watch how it's done, while others like to get you more actively involved in the day-to-day activities.

The Host Farms Association (☎ 9650 2922), 6th floor, 230 Collins St, Melbourne, produces the excellent *Host Farm & Country Retreat Holidays* brochure, which is available from the association, the RACV and tourist information centres. The brochure gives details of over 150 host farms throughout Victoria and includes maps, tariffs, ratings and descriptions.

Other Possibilities

If you're looking for a self-contained flat or unit, the best contact points are the RACV, tourist information centres and local real estate offices.

You don't have to camp in camping sites. There are plenty of parks where you can bush camp for free. Victoria has lots of bush where nobody is going to complain about you putting up a tent – or even notice you.

There are also more unusual forms of accommodation, such as houseboat cruising on the Murray River (see the Mildura and Echuca sections in the Murray River chapter) or Lake Eildon (see the High Country chapter); hiring a yacht or motor-launch and sailing the Gippsland Lakes (see the Metung section in the Lakes District chapter); or a horse-drawn Gypsy caravan exploring the backroads of country Victoria at a leisurely pace (see the Bridgewater-on-Loddon section in the Goldfields chapter and the Strzelecki Ranges section in the Gippsland chapter).

If you want to stay longer, the first place to look for a share flat or a room is the classified ad section of the daily newspapers. Wednesday and Saturday are the best days for these advertisements. Notice boards in universities, hostel offices, certain popular bookshops and cafes in Carlton, Fitzroy and St Kilda are good places to look for flats/houses to share or rooms to rent.

FOOD

The Greeks, Yugoslavs, Italians, Lebanese and many others who flooded into Australia in the 1950s and 1960s brought their food with them. More recent arrivals include the Vietnamese, whose communities (and restaurants) are thriving.

You can have excellent Greek moussaka or souvlaki (and a bottle of retsina to wash it down), delicious Italian *saltimbocca*, *focaccia* and pasta, or good, heavy German dumplings; you can perfume the air with garlic after stumbling out of a French bistro, or try all sorts of Middle Eastern and Arab treats. The Chinese and their cuisine have been here since the gold-rush days, while more recently Indian, Thai and Malaysian restaurants have become part of the Aussie diet. And for cheap eats, you can't beat some of the Vietnamese places.

Fast Food

Food on the run? In Melbourne and the larger towns, you'll find all the major fast-food shops – McDonald's, KFC, Pizza Hut etc – all in prominent positions and blatantly signposted.

On a more local level, there are the ubiquitous milk bars on (almost) every corner, and most sell things such as meat pies, pasties, sausage rolls, sandwiches and milk shakes. Then there are the speciality sandwich bars, delicatessens and health-food shops – all worth looking out for if you're after something fresh and tasty. Other good alternatives are to search out bakeries for fresh bread, pies, pastries and cakes, or the local fruit shop.

Most towns and shopping centres also have a fish & chip shop (which usually also does good hamburgers, souvlakis etc). Compared with the UK equivalents, these places are gourmet delights, selling meat and fish that is recognisably meat and fish. A 'steak sandwich with the lot' will keep you going all day. Pizza places are also ubiquitous. And keep an eye out for the more exotic Indian, Lebanese, Turkish, Malaysian etc take-aways which are usually good and give value for money.

Pubs

Most country towns have more pubs than they need. For example, if a town has four pubs, typically one or two of them will be well run, with good meals and/or accommodation. The others will often be run down, dingy and derelict, so choose wisely.

Most pubs serve two types of meals. Bistro meals are usually in the $10 to $15 range, and are served in the dining room where you'll often find a self-serve salad bar with bread, condiments etc. Bar meals are served in the public bar and sometimes eaten at the bar. They are usually simplified versions of the bistro meals and cost around $5 to $10.

While pub food is usually fairly basic and unimaginative, it's often very good value, especially for steak dishes. The normal eating times are from noon to 2 pm and from 6 to 8 pm. Many country pubs don't serve meals on Sunday, especially Sunday night.

Cafes & Restaurants

Melbourne is one of the world's great cities for eating out. The city's high food standards have spread to many areas of country Victoria, and most larger towns have an excellent range of eateries for every style and budget. In some smaller places, however, you might only have a choice between a cafe (sometimes dubious), a Chinese restaurant (usually pretty bland) and the local pub (often excellent – and cheap – if you like steak).

Throughout Victoria, you'll find lots of restaurants advertising the fact that they're BYO. The initials stand for 'Bring Your Own' and it means that they're not licensed to sell alcohol but you are permitted to bring your own with you. This is a real boon for budget-minded travellers, because you can buy a bottle of wine from the local bottleshop or from a winery and not pay any mark-up. Some places have a small 'corkage' charge.

There are also many licensed restaurants that are also BYO, meaning that while they stock and sell a range of alcohol, you still have the option of bringing your own. Just to confuse the issue, some licensed restaurants are 'BYO wine only', which means you can bring your own bottles of wine, but if you want to drink beer, soft drinks, spirits etc, you have to buy theirs.

Self-Catering

Throughout Melbourne and Victoria you'll find a superb range of fresh and affordable produce – vegetables, fruit, meat, seafood, bread and much more. Melbourne's wonderful markets are the best showcases for the local produce, but in every suburb and country town you'll find good local stores which can supply your every culinary need.

Most supermarkets have seafood and meat departments as well as a fruit-and-vegetable section, and you can also buy some fresh produce in many milk bars and convenience stores.

Then there's a myriad of smaller speciality shops such as organic grocers, health-food shops and exotic delicatessens. Especially in Melbourne, you can find just about any type of food imaginable. There are Asian grocery stores where, once inside, you'll think you're in Saigon or Hanoi; Italian and Greek delicatessens crammed with hams, cheeses, olives – in fact everything from peppered anchovies to pickled zucchini; Latin American speciality stores with chorizo, tortilla, egg custard tarts and sardines; tiny cheese shops with every kind of cheese; and exclusive department stores specialising in imported food.

DRINKS

Nonalcoholic Drinks

The good news is that Melbourne's water (reputed to be the best in the world) is on tap everywhere – and it's delicious, clean and free! Most country areas also have good drinking water on tap.

Bottled water is also widely available, as are plain and flavoured mineral waters. Most shops stock a wide range of soft drinks, fruit juices and flavoured milk, while a milk shake from a local milk bar is an Aussie institution.

Almost every little cafe and restaurant in Melbourne serves 'real' coffee in any form to satisfy any caffeine addict. It's harder to come by in the provinces, although most larger towns have at least one good Italian cafe.

Alcoholic Drinks

Beer There's a bewildering array of beer available in bottleshops, pubs, bars and restaurants. There are local beers such as Victoria Bitter (VB), Melbourne Bitter, Carlton Draught, Foster's and Crown Lager; interstate beers such as Cascade Pale Ale, the Cooper's range, XXXX (pronounced 'four-ex') and Toohey's; and international beers such as Steinlager and Budweiser, among many others. Quite a few pubs have Guinness on tap.

It's worth keeping an eye out for the Australian 'boutique' beers. Most are just variations on lager, but they can be good. Some of the more interesting ones include: Redback, a Victorian wheat beer; Boags, a crisp, lightly flavoured beer in the style of Heineken or Steinlager; Cooper's Sparkling Ale, a cloudy, stronger-flavoured beer similar to some of the Belgian beers such as Duvel; or Newcastle Brown ale, which is similar to its English namesake.

Local beers have an alcohol content of around 4.9% (considerably higher than the average UK or USA lager), and light beers range from 2.7 to 2.9%.

Beer comes in bottles (750ml), stubbies (375ml) and cans (375ml). When ordering at the bar you ask for a 'glass' (200ml) or a 'pot' (285ml). With the increasing popularity of light beers, you might be asked by the barperson if you want a 'light' or a 'heavy'.

Wine There are more than 150 wineries scattered around the state. Victoria has a great climate for viticulture and excellent wines have been produced here since the days of the gold rush. The local industry flourished from the 1850s until the turn of the century, and in the last 20 years things have taken off again to the extent that many producers are successfully exporting their wine to the competitive US and European markets.

The main local styles are cabernet sauvignon, shiraz, riesling, chardonnay and sparkling *méthode champenoise* wines. Fortified ports and muscats are also prominent, especially in the north-east. The major wine areas include the Yarra Valley, the Mornington Peninsula, the Geelong region, Great Western and the Pyrenees, central Victoria, the Macedon Ranges and the north-east around Rutherglen and Milawa.

Most wineries welcome visitors and offer free tastings, although some have a tasting fee which is refundable if you buy.

Visiting wineries and drinking the local wines is a great way to experience the different regions of the state – and if you buy a few bottles, you can put Victoria's many BYO restaurants to good use and drink your purchases over a good meal. Strangely, you can often get the same wines at better prices from discount wine merchants in Melbourne than at the cellar door.

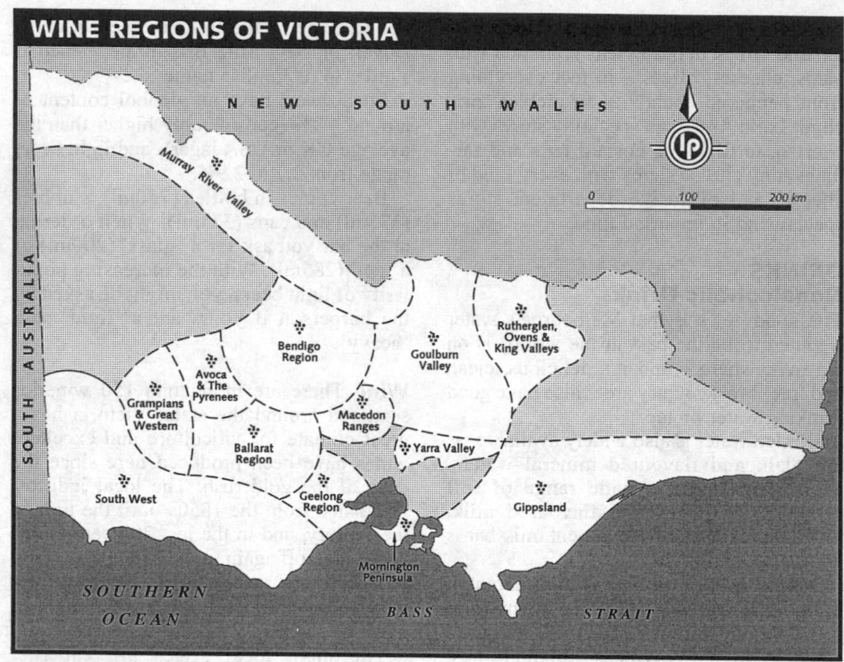

ENTERTAINMENT

There is a wide variety of entertainment available in a number of Victorian towns. Depending on the size of the place you're visiting, you should be able to enjoy film, theatre, dance, comedy, music, exhibitions, etc. As the state's capital, Melbourne is the undoubtedly the hub of the action, but you'll find that there's much going on in other places. For a preview of what's on offer and for venue details, check out the Entertainment section for Victoria's major towns.

Cinema

In Melbourne you will find big cinema chains, such as Village, Hoyts and Greater Union, each with its own multiplex. Most country towns have just the one cinema – some of these are glossy, modern cinema complexes, and others are almost museums.

In Melbourne you'll find a growing selection of art-house and independent cinemas, and these places generally screen 'art', classic and cult movies. Such venues also exist in a few country towns, most notably Castlemaine.

Drive-in cinemas used to be found all over Australia. They're a dying breed now, although there are still a few towns in Victoria where you can watch a movie from the comfort of your own car. There's one drive-in cinema in Melbourne – see the Cinema section of that chapter.

SPECTATOR SPORTS

If you're an armchair – or wooden bench – sports fan, Victoria has plenty to offer.

Football

The main type of football played is Aussie Rules and the season runs from about March to the fabled 'last Saturday in September'.

Melbourne is the national (and world) centre for Australian Rules, and the Australian Football League (AFL) administers the national competition. Ten of its 16 teams are from Victoria; the other sides are based in Perth (two teams), Sydney, Adelaide (two teams) and Brisbane. In Melbourne, crowds regularly exceed 50,000 at top regular games and 90,000 at finals.

Australian Rules is a great game to get to know. Fast, tactical, skilful, rough and athletic, it can produce gripping finishes when even after 100 minutes of play the outcome hangs on the very last kick. It also inspires fierce spectator loyalties and has made otherwise obscure Melbourne suburbs (Carlton, Essendon, Collingwood etc) national names. For information about seeing a game see the Spectator Sports section of the Melbourne chapter.

Soccer is a bit of a poor cousin: it's widely played on an amateur basis but the national league attracts only a small following. It's gradually gaining popularity thanks to the success of the youth and senior national teams.

Cricket

Outside the football season (October to March) there's cricket. The Melbourne Cricket Ground (MCG) is one of the world's great sports stadiums, and international Test and one-day matches are played there virtually every summer, as well as in the other state capitals. There is also an interstate competition (the Sheffield Shield) and numerous local grades. You won't need to book a seat for a Sheffield Shield game; for an international game call Ticketmaster (☎ 13 6100).

Other Sports

Basketball has grown phenomenally as a spectator sport since the formation of a national league. Baseball is another American sport that is slowly becoming more popular. Along the coast during summer there are surf life-saving carnivals, and world class surfing competitions such as that held each year at Bells Beach.

There's also yacht racing, some good tennis, including the Australian Open in January, and major golf championships, including the Australian Masters at Huntingdale in February. For information on events and tickets, call Ticketmaster (☎ 13 6100).

Gambling

Like other Australians, Victorians love to gamble, and hardly any town of even minor import is without a horse-racing track. You can bet on local and interstate horse and dog races at government-run Totalisator Agency Board (TAB) betting shops, which are found in most shopping areas – some are even in pubs.

Victoria's once conservative gambling laws have been radically changed, allowing the introduction of coin-fed gambling machines (called poker machines or 'pokies') in football clubs, pubs and other places. Melbourne's Crown Casino attracts punters in their thousands, as well as criticism from church and social welfare groups.

There are various numbers-for-prizes games, all administered by the Tattersall's company. There are Tatts branches everywhere, including most newsagents.

SHOPPING

Melbourne is a great shopping city. The Melbourne chapter has more details on where to buy many of the items listed below.

Large towns in country areas will be able to meet most of your needs but in smaller towns don't expect everything to be always available. Some shops can order things for you if you can wait a few days.

Aboriginal Art & Craft

Top of the list for any real Australian purchase would have to be Aboriginal art.

Prices of the best paintings are way out of reach for the average traveller, but among the cheaper art and craft works on sale are prints, baskets, small carvings, decorated boomerangs, didgeridoos, music sticks and some very beautiful screen-printed T-shirts produced by Aboriginal craft cooperatives – and a larger number of commercial rip-offs. It's worth shopping around and paying a few dollars more for the real thing.

Several of the Aboriginal cultural centres around the state, such as the Brambuk Living Cultural Centre in the Grampians, have a range of arts and crafts on sale.

Australiana

'Australiana', a euphemism for souvenirs, ranges from stuffed toys, especially koalas and kangaroos, to Australia-shaped egg flippers. The seeds of many of Australia's native plants are on sale all over the place. Try growing kangaroo paws back home, if your own country will allow them in. Australian wines are well known overseas, but why not try honey (leatherwood honey is one of a number of powerful local varieties), macadamia nuts (native to Queensland) or Bundaberg rum with its unusual sweet flavour. You can also get exotic tinned witchetty grubs, honey ants and other bush tucker.

Festivals & Cultural Events

Some of Victoria's major annual festivals, and some more interesting smaller events, are:

January

Melbourne

Australian Open, Melbourne Park (Grand Slam tennis championship)
Epsom Moonlight Cinema in the Royal Botanic Gardens
Melbourne Midsumma Festival (a gay and lesbian celebration, St Kilda)
Melbourne International Jazz Festival

Country Victoria

Cajun Blues Weekend, Falls Creek
Cobram-Barooga Apex Club Peaches & Cream Festival
Falls Creek Midsummer Singles' Week
Food, Wine & Wildflower Weekend, Falls Creek
Hanging Rock Gold Cup
Hydrangea Festival, Dandenong Ranges
Lavender Harvest Festival, Yackandandah
Lavender Harvest, Lavandula Lavender Farm, near Hepburn Springs
Leongatha Food & Wine Festival
Lorne Pier to Pub Swim
Red Hill Music Festival and Truck Show
SES Celebrity Duck Race, Swan Hill
Tranquillity Festival, Ocean Grove

February

Melbourne

Antipodes (Greek-Australian) Festival, Melbourne
Chinese New Year Festival, Chinatown, Melbourne
Maroondah Festival in the Foothills, Croydon
Melbourne International Motor Show, Southbank
Melbourne International Tattoo, Toorak (based on the Edinburgh Military Tattoo)
Nunawading Highland Gathering
Opera in the Park, Victoria Gardens, Prahran
Port Melbourne Festival
Richmond Lunar New Year Festival
Sidney Myer Free Concerts, Sidney Myer Music Bowl, Melbourne
St Kilda Festival
Sydney Road Street Party, Brunswick
Woolmark Melbourne Fashion Festival

Country Victoria

Australian International Airshow, Avalon
Ballarat Begonia Festival
Bruthen Blues Bash
Buninyong Gold King Festival
Bunyip Country Music Festival
Grampians Jazz Festival
Great Bendigo Bank Tram Race, Bendigo
Gunbower Aquatic Festival
Harvest Picnic at Hanging Rock
Kyneton Country Music Festival
Mildura Arts Festival
Mortlake Buskers' Festival
Pako Festival, Geelong West
Paynesville Jazz Festival
Rutherglen Festival for Old Bicycles
Seymour Alternative Farming Expo
Victorian Boomerang Throwing Championships, Wensleydale
Wunta Fiesta, Warrnambool (celebration of the fishing industry)

Aussie Clothing

While you're here, fit yourself out in some local clothes. Consider Blundstone or Rossi boots, anything from the RM Williams line (boots, moleskin trousers, shirts), some Yakka or King Gee work wear, a shearer's top or bush shirt, a greasy-wool jumper, a Bluey (a coarse woollen worker's coat), a Driza-bone (an oilskin riding coat) and an Akubra hat.

Australia also produces some of the world's best surfing equipment and surf/street wear, including brands such as Mambo, Hot Tuna, Mooks and Funk Essentials. Melbourne is also considered the capital for designer fashion.

Opals

The opal is Australia's national gemstone, and opals and opal jewellery are popular

Festivals & Cultural Events

March

Melbourne

- Australian Football League season starts
- Brunswick Music Festival
- Formula 1 Grand Prix, Albert Park
- Frankston Guitar Festival
- Melbourne Food & Wine Festival
- Melbourne International Dragon Boat Festival
- Melbourne Queer Film & Video Festival
- Moomba Festival
- Ringwood Highland Games
- Warrandyte Festival

Country Victoria

- Apollo Bay Music Festival
- Ararat Jail House Rock Festival
- Bairnsdale Riviera Festival
- Bendigo Madison/10,000 Carnival (athletics and cycling carnival)
- Birralee Goulburn Valley Children's Festival, Shepparton
- Blue Pyrenees Petanque Tournament, Avoca
- Geelong Highland Gathering
- Harcourt Applefest
- Inverloch Jazz Festival
- Jazz & Writers Festival, Berwick
- Landfest – Landcare Festival, Creswick
- Mansfield Harvest Festival
- Moe Jazz Festival
- Port Fairy Folk Festival
- Seymour Rafting Festival
- Sorrento Street Festival
- Thorpdale Potato Festival
- Tobacco, Hops & Timber Festival, Myrtleford
- Toolamba Giant Pumpkin Festival
- Toora King of the Mountain Family Festival, South Gippsland
- Yackandandah Folk Festival
- Yarra Valley Grape Grazing Festival
- Yinnar South Country Fair & Bush Dance

April

Melbourne

- Anzac Day dawn service, Shrine of Remembrance
- Boroondara Literary Festival
- Heritage Week (National Trust promotion of Melbourne's architectural heritage)
- Hot Air Ballooning Festival, Albert Park
- Melbourne International Comedy Festival
- Melbourne International Festival of Organ & Harpsichord
- Melbourne International Flower & Garden Show
- The Victorian Woodwork Festival, Templestowe

Country Victoria

- Anderson's Mill Food, Wine & Jazz Festival, Smeaton
- Australian Street Rod Nationals, Geelong
- Bell's Surfing Classic, Bell's Beach
- Bendigo Easter Fair
- Bright Autumn Festival
- Dargo Walnut Festival
- Eureka Jazz Festival, Ballarat
- Giant Easter Egg Hunt, Falls Creek
- Koroit Irish Festival
- Man From Snowy River Bush Festival, Corryong
- Magical Autumn in the Mystic Mountains, Marysville
- Maldon Easter Fair

Festivals & Cultural Events

Mallacoota Festival
(Easter; sometimes falls in March)
Mia Mia Kite Flying Championship
(13km from Heathcote)
Otway Harvest Festival, Forrest
Pyrenees Vignerons' Gourmet Wine & Food Anzac Day Race Meeting, Avoca
Stawell Athletic Club Easter Carnival
(including the 'Stawell Gift')

May
Melbourne
Great Australian Science Show, Southbank
Melbourne International Biennial
(visual art exhibition)
Puffing Billy Railway Great Train Race
(Belgrave to Emerald Lake)
St Kilda Film Festival

Country Victoria
Beechworth Harvest Celebration
Buninyong Film Festival
Festival of the Lakes
(Gippsland Lakes, Paynesville, Metung, Lakes Entrance & Bairnsdale)
Grampians Gourmet Weekend
May Racing Carnival, Warrnambool
(features Australia's longest horse race, the Grand Annual Steeplechase)
Yarra Valley Gladysdale Apple Festival, Gladysdale

June
Melbourne
Dance Masters of Australia Ballroom Dancing Championships, Springvale
Envirofest, Templestowe
Festival for Mind, Body, Spirit, Southbank

Country Victoria
Dandenong Ranges Winter Festival
National Celtic Folk Festival, Geelong
Official Opening of Ski Season
Queens Birthday Wine Weekend, Mornington Peninsula
Rhapsody in June, Port Fairy
Stawell Hot-Air Balloon Festival
Steam, Horse and Vintage Rally, Echuca
Winery Walkabout, Rutherglen

July
Melbourne
Melbourne International Film Festival
Melbourne Sheep and Wool Show, Ascot Vale

Country Victoria
Ballarat Winter Festival
Jazz on the Bay, Geelong
Red Cliffs Folk Festival
Sunraysia Orchid Club Winter Show, Mildura
Winterfest in Warburton
(which includes the Warbie Film Festival)

August
Melbourne
The *Age* Melbourne Writers' Festival
Exhibition of Victorian Winemakers
Melbourne International Orchid Spectacular, Keysborough

Country Victoria
Dirty Weekend in Beechworth
(mountain bike racing)
50 Day Daffodil Display, Olinda
Hamilton Sheep-vention
Sip 'n' Sup Wine Festival, Sunbury

September
Melbourne
Asian Food Festival
Australian Football League Grand Final
Melbourne Fringe Festival
(experimental art across all art forms)
Moon Lantern Festival, Richmond
Royal Melbourne Show, Ascot Vale

Country Victoria
Arthur's Seat Historic Hill Climb
(a vintage car event)
Horsham Grand Annual Show
Leongatha Daffodil & Floral Festival
Mildura Country Music Festival
Tesselaar's Tulip Festival, Silvan

October
Melbourne
Australasian and Pacific Motoring Show, Flemington
Festival of Health & Harmony, Southbank

Festivals & Cultural Events

Lygon Street (Italian) Festa, Carlton
Melbourne International Festival
(17-day arts festival incorporating the Writers' Festival)
Melbourne Marathon Festival, Albert Park
Melbourne Oktoberfest, Ascot Vale
National Zoo Month, Parkville
Spring Racing Carnival,
(October and November; featuring the Caulfield and Melbourne Cups)

Country Victoria

Australasian Goldpanning Championships, Maryborough (the World Goldpanning Championships will be held in Maryborough in 2001)
Australian Motorcycle Grand Prix, Phillip Island
Bendigo Orchid Club Spring Show
Festival of Gardens, Castlemaine
Great Australian Vanilla Slice Triumph, Ouyen
Halls Gap Festival of Flowers & Art
Herald Sun Tour
(Victoria's major cycling tour)
Main Street Mornington
Food & Wine Festival
Maldon Folk Festival
Mansfield Mountain Country Festival
Melbourne to Warrnambool Road Race
(the 'Holy Grail' cycling race)
Port Fairy Spring Music Festival
Sunraysia Jazz & Wine Festival, Mildura and district
Tea Tree Festival, Mornington
Wangaratta Festival of Jazz & Blues
World Animal Day, Beechworth

November

Melbourne

Foster's Melbourne Cup, Flemington
Frankston Celtic Festival
Garden & Multicultural Festival, St Kilda
Hispanic Community Festival, Johnson St, Fitzroy
Maribyrnong Festival
Oakleigh International Fiesta

Country Victoria

Bass Coast Beach Festival, Phillip Island
Beechworth Celtic Festival
Brown Brothers Wine & Food Weekend, Milawa
Festival of St Arnaud
Go Colac! Go Country! Festival, Colac
(incorporates the famous Ferret Cup)
Going Solar's Renewable Energy and Sustainable Living Fair, Musk
(near Daylesford)
Grampians Film Festival
Great Victorian Bike Ride
Meredith Country Festival
Pyrenees Vigneron's Petanque Weekend, Avoca
RACV Energy Breakthrough, Maryborough
(a 24-hour low energy Grand Prix)
Rosebud Family Festival
Victorian Strawberry Festival, Seville

December

Melbourne

Boxing Day Test (cricket) Match, Melbourne Cricket Ground
(begins on Boxing Day, continues for up to five days)
Royal Victorian Institute for the Blind Carols by Candlelight, Sidney Myer Music Bowl, Melbourne
Outdoor evening performances of Shakespeare,
Royal Botanic Gardens, Melbourne

Country Victoria

Bright New Year's Eve Family Gala
Daylesford Highland Gathering
Daylesford New Year's Eve Gala
Healing Arts Festival, Aireys Inlet
Moyneyana Festival, Port Fairy
Mozart on the Mountain Festival, Mount Buller
Red Cross Murray Marathon, Yarrawonga to Swan Hill (canoeing/kayaking marathon on the Murray River)
Yarrawonga Bachelor and Spinster Ball

For details of these and other festivals throughout the state see individual town listings, contact relevant visitor information centres or refer to the comprehensive *Victoria's Fantastic Festivals & Fun Events* by Barrie & Jill Richardson.

souvenirs. They are a beautiful stone, but buy wisely and shop around – quality and prices can vary widely from place to place.

Antiques

Look for early Australian colonial furniture made from cedar or Huon pine; Australian silver jewellery; ceramics – either early factory pieces or studio pieces (especially anything by the Boyd family); glassware such as Carnival glass; and Australiana collectables and bric-a-brac such as old signs, tins, bottles etc. *Carter's Price Guide to Antiques in Australia* is an excellent price reference which is updated annually.

Crafts

Victoria has many shops, galleries and markets displaying crafts by local artists, as well as goods from almost every region of the world. The local craft scene is especially strong in ceramics, jewellery, stained glass and leather craft. Pick up a copy of Craft Victoria's *Craft Shops & Galleries in Victoria*, available from their office (☎ 9417 3111) at 114 Gertrude St, Fitzroy, Melbourne.

Activities

There are plenty of activities for you to take part in. Victoria has a flourishing ski industry – a fact that some find surprising. Bushwalking is cheap, and there are many fantastic walks in national and state parks. If you're interested in surfing you'll find great beaches and surf. There's also scuba diving along the coast. You can go horseriding in the High Country and follow the route of the Snowy Mountains cattle people, whose lives were the subject of the film *The Man from Snowy River*, which in turn was based on the poem by Banjo Paterson. You can cycle all round Victoria; for the athletic there are long, challenging routes and for the not so masochistic there are plenty of possibilities for great day trips and longer rides through flat country.

Windsurfing, paragliding, rafting and hang gliding are among the many other sports available to travellers.

BUSHWALKING

Victoria has some great bushwalking. You'll find everything from short boardwalks through rainforest gullies to extended walking trails that take you across the state. The infrastructure is usually excellent, with marked trails, campgrounds with fireplaces, toilets and fresh water, and many park information centres.

The High Country, the alpine region in the north-east of the state, is the most spectacular and one of the most popular areas for bushwalking, particularly for experienced walkers. Other extremely popular areas include the Wilsons Promontory National Park (affectionately known as 'The Prom') in Gippsland, with many marked trails from Tidal River and Telegraph Bay that can take from a few hours to a couple of days; the Grampians, 250km west of Melbourne, where Victoria's only remaining red kangaroos hang out; and the Croajingolong National Park near Mallacoota in East Gippsland, which is rugged inland but has some easier coastal walks.

There are more than 30 active bushwalking clubs around the state. Many conduct regular walks and outings and most welcome newcomers. For a full list of clubs, contact the Federation of Victorian Walking Clubs (☎ 9455 1876), 332 Banyule Rd, Viewbank 3084. See their Web site at www.avoca.vicnet.net.au/~vicwalk or look in the relevant *Yellow Pages* under 'Clubs – Bushwalking'. The Internet newsgroup aus.bushwalking can also be useful.

Melbourne's outdoor and adventure shops in and around Hardware and Little Bourke Sts carry an excellent range of both imported and Australian-made gear and are also good sources of information. You can have backpacks and camping equipment repaired by Remote Repairs at 377 Little Bourke St, Melbourne, above the Mountain Designs shop.

The Department of Natural Resources & Environment (NRE) Information Centre in Melbourne stocks a range of walking guides, including *120 Walks in Victoria* by Tyrone T Thomas ($19.95) and *Melbourne's Mountains – Exploring the Great Divide* by John Siseman ($19.95).

Code of Ethics & Safety Precautions

With more and more people heading for the state's wilderness areas it is becoming increasingly important for bushwalkers to adopt and follow a 'minimum impact' code of ethics. There are also regulations enforced by Parks Victoria. Most of the following guidelines are basic common sense, but it's amazing how often you'll see people doing things that will cause damage to a sensitive environment.

- Stay on established trails, avoid cutting corners and taking short cuts, and stay on hard ground where possible.

- Before tackling a long or remote walk, tell someone responsible about your plans and arrange to contact them when you return.
- Keep bushwalking parties to small numbers (but never less than three people).
- When possible, visit popular areas at off-peak times.
- When camping, always use designated campgrounds where provided. When bush camping, look for a natural clearing and avoid camping under river red gums, which have a tendency to drop their branches without warning.
- Vehicles must stay on existing tracks or roads.
- All native plants and animals are protected by law.
- Don't feed native animals.
- Carry all your rubbish out with you – don't burn or bury it.
- Avoid polluting lakes and streams – don't wash yourself or your dishes in them, and keep soap and detergent at least 50m away from waterways.
- Use toilets where provided – otherwise, bury human waste at least 100m away from waterways (carrying a hand trowel is a good idea).
- Boil all water for 10 minutes before drinking it.
- Don't bring dogs or other pets into national parks.
- Carry a fuel stove and fuel for cooking.
- Don't light fires unless necessary – if you do, keep the fire small, use only dead fallen wood and use an existing fireplace. Make sure the fire is completely extinguished before moving on.
- On days of total fire ban, no fires whatsoever may be lit – this includes fuel stoves.

Long-Distance Walks

These longer walks range in length from 250km to over 750km, but you could also walk just a section to suit your itinerary or level of experience.

A wide range of information, including books, maps and brochures, is available on all of these walks, with details given in the following sections. If you need more specific details, the park rangers are often the best primary sources.

The Great South-West Walk This is the longest coastal walking trail in the state, covering a 250km loop from Portland to the South Australian border and back. Starting from the Tourist Information Centre in Portland, the walk follows the coastline all the way to the small township of Nelson, then heads inland beside the Glenelg River to the South Australian border before looping back to Portland.

To walk the full distance you'd need at least 10 days, although the walk is designed to allow people to walk shorter sections – anywhere from a few hours to a couple of days.

The first section (Portland to Nelson) heads south from Portland to Nelson Bay and Bridgewater Bay. At the Bridgewater Lakes you have the option of taking a detour via Mt Richmond National Park, rejoining the coast at Swan Lake Camp. The coastal trail traverses Discovery Bay, with its remote and beautiful beaches, sand dunes and inland lakes, all the way to Nelson. See the Discovery Bay Coastal Park section of the Great Ocean Road & South-West Coast chapter for details.

From Nelson, the walk follows the Glenelg River inland for about 45km through the Lower Glenelg National Park, and then crosses into the Cobboboonee State Forest before traversing open forest and farmland on the way back to Portland.

The walk is clearly marked and there are 15 bush campsites at varying intervals, all of which have fireplaces, toilets and fresh water. A gas or fuel stove is a good idea as firewood can be scarce.

For more information see Lonely Planet's *Bushwalking in Australia* or contact the Portland Tourist Information Centre or Parks Victoria.

Australian Alps Walking Track This spectacular track runs all the way from Walhalla, east of Melbourne, to Mt Pilot on the outskirts of Canberra – more than 760km. The Victorian section, formerly known as the Alpine Walking Track, has been linked up with trails through the Kosciusko National Park in New South Wales (NSW) to create this new walk.

The track passes through some of Victoria's most spectacular country, including the Baw Baw Plateau and the Bogong High Plains, and includes some of the state's finest walks. As with the other long-distance trails, only a handful of people cover the full distance, but you can easily choose sections of the track that suit your particular needs.

Most parts of the track traverse alpine areas, and as weather conditions can be extreme walks should only be undertaken by the experienced and adequately prepared. The best times of the year are late spring, summer and early autumn (ie November to March), but alpine conditions are extremely variable and you should be prepared for bad weather at any time of the year.

Publications covering the track include John Siseman's book *The Alpine Walking Track*. There is also a wealth of information on individual walks in the High Country, including various Parks Victoria brochures, Lonely Planet's *Bushwalking in Australia* and Tyrone T Thomas' *120 Walks in Victoria*.

The Bicentennial National Trail Running the full length of Australia's east coast, all the way from Cooktown in far north Queensland to Healesville on the outskirts of Melbourne, this trail is designed for long-distance walking and horse-riding. It incorporates roads, fire-trails and walking tracks through national parks.

The Victorian section traverses the spectacular High Country of the Great Dividing Range, from where it's possible to link up with the Australian Alps Walking Track to form a long-distance loop through the north-east of the state.

The Bicentennial National Trail Authority (Box 2235, Toowoomba, Qld 4350) publishes a brochure on the trail as well as 12 detailed books covering the entire route. Books covering the Victorian section are the *Bicentennial National Trail Guidebook No 11 (Kosciusko to Omeo)* and the *Bicentennial National Trail Guidebook No 12 (Omeo to Healesville)*, both of which cost $9.95. The NRE's Information Centre in Melbourne usually has copies in stock.

Other Walks

The following places are some of Victoria's outstanding walking areas – for more information, consult the text in the relevant regional chapters.

In & Around Melbourne
- Yarra River parklands
- Melbourne's parks and gardens
- Dandenong Ranges
- Yarra Valley, particularly around Warburton and Powelltown
- Brisbane Ranges National Park
- Anakie Gorge
- Toolangi area & Kinglake National Park
- Mornington Peninsula, particularly Point Nepean National Park and Cape Schanck Coastal Park
- Phillip Island, particularly around Cape Woolamai

Great Ocean Road & the South-West Coast
- Surf Coast Walk
- Angahook-Lorne State Park
- Otway National Park
- Port Campbell National Park
- Warrnambool area
- Port Fairy area
- The Great South-West Walk & Mt Richmond National Park
- Cape Nelson State Park

Wimmera & Mallee
- Grampians National Park
- Little Desert National Park
- Wyperfeld National Park

Goldfields
- Melville Caves and Mt Kooyoora State Park
- Daylesford/Hepburn Springs area
- Lerderderg Gorge
- Maldon area and Mt Tarrangower

High Country
- Kiewa Valley and Bogong High Plains
- Baw Baw Plateau
- Mt Buffalo National Park
- Mt Feathertop
- Beechworth area
- Bright area
- Marysville area
- Cathedral Range State Park

Gippsland
- Wilsons Promontory National Park
- Tarra-Bulga National Park
- Mitchell River National Park

Wilderness Coast
- Mallacoota area
- Croajingolong National Park
- Errinundra National Park

CYCLING

Bicycle helmets are compulsory in Victoria, as are front and rear lights for night riding.

It's possible to plan rides of any duration and through almost any type of terrain.

Wine regions such as Rutherglen and the Pyrenees Ranges are popular areas for cycling tours, and the High Country areas are much favoured by mountain bikers. There are also many organised tours available of varying lengths, and if you get tired of talking to sheep as you ride along, it might be a good idea to include one or more tours in your itinerary. Most provide a support vehicle and take care of accommodation and cooking, so they can be a nice break from solo chores.

Contact the helpful people at Bicycle Victoria (☎ 9328 3000, bicyclevic@ bv.com.au), 19 O'Connell St, North Melbourne, for more information; ask about their regular tours and events such as the Great Victorian Bike Ride (November) and the Easter Bike (April). The staff will be able to put you on to local clubs and tours. Members get free accident insurance, which might be useful if you're planning to do a lot of riding. Membership costs $46 a year. Check out their Web site at www.bv.com.au for details.

The book *Bicycling Around Victoria* (by Ray Peace, $19.95) is an excellent reference for cyclists, suggesting interesting rides in places like Williamstown and the Yarra Blvd as well as including suburban bike paths and some great rural rides. It's available in most bookshops and some bike shops.

Cycling has always been popular in Victoria and it's rare to find a reasonably sized town that doesn't have a shop stocking at least basic bike parts.

If you're coming specifically to cycle, it makes sense to bring your own bike. Check your airline for costs and the degree of dismantling/packing required. Within Australia you can load your bike onto a bus or train to skip the boring bits. Note that bus companies require you to partially dismantle your bike, and some don't guarantee that it will travel on the same bus as you. Trains are easier, but supervise the loading and if possible tie your bike upright – otherwise, you may find that the guard has stacked crates of Holden spares on your fragile alloy wheels. Not all services carry bikes. Check carefully with V/Line (☎ 13 2232) before travelling.

You can buy a reasonable touring bike here from about $600 (plus panniers). Many Melbourne bike shopes hire out bikes. A hybrid bike with panniers from touring specialists Christie Cycles (tel 9818 4011, 80 Burwood Rd, Hawthorn) costs $20/day or $75/week; tandems cost $30/day or $115/week (which includes both weekends). Mountain bikes with racks from St Kilda Cycles (tel 9534 3074, 11 Carlisle St, St Kilda) cost $20/day or $50/for a weekend, with panniers. Contact Bicycle Victoria for a current list of bike hire outlets.

You can get by with standard road maps almost everywhere in Victoria, but these don't show topography so you might want to use 1:250,000 topographic maps. If you're mountain biking off the beaten track you'll want 1:100,000 or 1:50,000 maps. Cycle tourists can drop in to one of the Melbourne Bicycle Touring Club meetings (every Thursday at 8 pm at 19 O'Connell St, North Melbourne) to get route tips for around the state. Visit the club's Web site at www.vicnet.net.au/~mbtc to see their current ride programme.

It can get very hot in summer, and you should take things slowly until you're used to the heat. Cycling in 35°C-plus temperatures isn't too bad if you wear a hat and plenty of sunscreen and drink *lots* of water. Be aware of the blistering 'hot northerlies', the prevailing winds that make a northbound cyclist's life uncomfortable in summer. In April, when the south-east's clear autumn weather begins, the Southerly Trades prevail.

Always check with locals if you're heading into remote areas, and notify the police if you're about to do something particularly adventurous. That said, you can't rely too much on local knowledge of road conditions – most people have no idea of what a heavily loaded touring bike needs. What they think of as a great road may be pedal deep in sand or bull dust, and I've happily ridden along roads that were officially flooded out.

See the 'Cycling Around Melbourne' boxed text in the Melbourne chapter for more information.

GOLF

Sadly, Melbourne's world famous sand-belt courses like Royal Melbourne, Victoria and Huntingdale are private members' clubs, so unless you have a letter of introduction from an overseas club with reciprocal rights or are on drinking terms with one of their members, you won't be able to test them out.

On the other hand, there are some excellent public courses in Melbourne (see the Activities section in the Melbourne chapter), and every country town worth its salt has at least one golf course. Some of the country courses are outstanding – Anglesea (with its famous grazing kangaroos), Barwon Heads, Sorrento, Kyneton and Gisborne. There are also some great courses (mostly financed by poker-machine gamblers) along the NSW side of the Murray River.

As in Melbourne, there are both public and private courses in country regions, but unlike Melbourne's private clubs most welcome visitors. At a public course, you'll pay around $12 to $20 for 18 holes, and club hire costs another $10 to $15. Private courses are generally a bit more expensive but they are usually of a higher standard.

TOURING WINERIES

Visiting wineries and sampling the product is very popular. Most winery regions produce pamphlets detailing opening hours, and some wineries (especially in the Rutherglen area) have fine restaurants and also accommodation, so you can sample as much as you like without risking your drivers licence.

SKIING

Skiing in Victoria goes back to the 1860s when Norwegian goldminers introduced the sport in Harrietville. It has grown into a multimillion dollar industry with three major ski resorts and six minor ski areas. None of these resorts is connected to another by a lift system, but it is possible for the experienced and well equipped cross-country skier to ski from Mt Hotham to Falls Creek across the Bogong High Plains. There is an annual race that covers this route.

The snowfields are north-east and east of Melbourne, scattered around the High Country of the Great Dividing Range. The two largest ski resorts are Mt Buller and Falls Creek. Mt Hotham is smaller, but has equally good skiing, while Mt Baw Baw and Mt Buffalo are smaller resorts which are popular with families and novice to intermediate skiers. Lake Mountain, Mt Stirling and Mt St Gwinear are cross-country skiing areas with no overnight accommodation. Mt Donna Buang, the closest snowfield to Melbourne, is mainly for sightseeing.

The roads to all ski resorts except Mt Baw Baw, Mt Stirling and Dinner Plain are fully sealed. In winter, it's compulsory to carry snow chains to all resorts irrespective of weather conditions (you may be turned back or fined if you haven't got them) and driving conditions can be hazardous.

The skiing season officially commences from the first weekend of June. Skiable snow usually arrives later in the month, and there's often enough snow until the end of September. Spring skiing can be good, as the weather may be sunnier and warmer and the crowds smaller.

The main ski organisations in Victoria are the Alpine Resorts Commission (ARC) (☎ 9895 6900), a government body responsible for managing the main ski resorts, the on-mountain information centres and ski patrols. Parks Victoria manages Mt St Gwinear and Lake Mountain.

Check the High Country chapter or ring the relevant information centres for more details.

Costs & Day Trips

If you're thinking about a day trip to the snow fields, Mt Buller and Mt Baw Baw are the closest options for downhill skiers, while cross-country skiers can choose from Lake Mountain, Mt Stirling or Mt St Gwinear.

Resort entry fees are usually $15 per car per day in winter, and for cross-country skiers there's at least a $5.25 trail-use fee at all resorts. As a rough guide, here's an estimate of some of the other costs you'll encounter during a day trip by car from Melbourne to the snow:

Petrol	$30-$50
Chain hire	$15
Equipment hire	$25
Clothing hire	$25
Lift tickets	$60
Meals, drinks & snacks	$15-$40

Note that these prices are approximates only, and that the hire rates given are for one day hire – rates are cheaper if you hire for longer periods.

Organised Tours

A potentially cheaper alternative for a day trip is to consider joining a package bus tour. During the season a company called Mt Buller Snowcaper Day Tours (☎ 1800 033 023 toll-free) offers day trips from Melbourne to Mt Buller on weekends ($99) and weekdays ($89) – the cost includes return transport from Melbourne, lift tickets and a beginner's lesson. Ski equipment can be hired for another $20, and clothing is available at an additional cost.

Accommodation

If you're planning to stay at the snow overnight or longer, you have a large and potentially confusing range of decisions to make – which resort to head for, whether to stay on or off-mountain, what type of accommodation to look for, and whether to buy a package deal (which can include meals and/or lessons, lift tickets, ski hire and transport).

For a package deal (or otherwise), you can book directly with a lodge, through a travel agent or through an accommodation booking service.

On-mountain accommodation tends to be expensive, but you have the advantage of stepping out of your door onto the slopes. Prices vary with the time of season and most places have three rate levels: weekend (Friday and Saturday nights), midweek (Sunday to Thursday nights) or a full week. If you just want somewhere to stay overnight, probably the easiest option is to go through one of the booking services. In July and August it is advisable to book your accommodation, especially for weekends. In June or September it's usually possible to find something if you just turn up.

A cheaper option can be to stay in one of the towns below the snow line and drive or catch a bus up, but don't forget to factor in the (high) cost of car entry or bus transport onto the mountain each day. For budget travellers, there are hostels on Mt Buller and Mt Buffalo and at Bright and Mansfield.

RICHARD NEBESKY

The Sun Valley quad chairlift at Mt Hotham

Food in the resorts tends to be expensive. If you're staying somewhere with kitchen facilities it might be worth stocking up with groceries before you get there.

SURFING

With its exposure to the relentless Southern Ocean swell, Victoria's rugged and spectacular coastline provides plenty of quality surf.

The surfing industry has undergone enormous growth in recent years, the attention centring on the Surfworld Plaza and Surfworld Museum at Torquay. Nearby, Bell's Beach plays host to the Pro Tour every Easter, bringing with it an international entourage of pro surfers, sponsors and spectators.

On the west coast you can take lessons with Go Ride a Wave (☎ 5263 2111), which holds lessons in Torquay, Anglesea and Lorne, or Westcoast Surf School (☎ 5261 2241) in Torquay. On Phillip Island try Island Surf School (☎ 5952 3443).

Telephone surf reports (☎ 19009 31996 or 19009 83268 for the Mornington Peninsula) are updated daily. A useful guide is *Surfinder Vic*, published by the Australian Surfriders' Association ($20) and available from surf and sports shops.

Equipment & Weather Conditions

Shorter boards will do the job for the beach breaks, but Victorian waves can get big and a good quiver, although a luxury for most, can come in handy. A longer board is definitely a necessity if you're going to surf the bigger, more powerful waves of the Shipwreck Coast.

Summer or winter, the water does not really lend itself to surfing in board shorts, so you will need a wetsuit. A full-length 3mm to 4mm thick wetsuit is the standard for winter, and booties, helmets and even wetsuit gloves might make that extra long session a bit easier.

The seasons provide varying wind and swell conditions. The slow moving high-pressure systems in summer generally produce a smaller swell with light winds, providing good opportunities for clean beach breaks. In the winter months the low-pressure fronts that push across the Southern Ocean generate larger swells, and if the wind is right the point breaks will be going off.

Where to Surf

The three most popular surfing areas are Phillip Island, the Mornington Peninsula and the west coast – all are less than a two hour drive from Melbourne. Farther east there is Inverloch, Wilsons Promontory, the Gippsland area, Lakes Entrance and Mallacoota.

Phillip Island Waves on the south or ocean side of the island work on north-east to north-west winds and south to south-west swells. On the Westernport Bay side of the island, waves work on east to south-east winds and larger swells.

A shallow section of sand and reef (a long bombora) runs from the Nobbies down into Westernport Bay. Affectionately known as the Bomby, it can provide a good indication of swell size and good breaks.

Woolamai Beach, Forrest Caves and Surfies Point all offer waves. Express Point, also known as EP's or Black's, is a tubing right-hand point break that should only be surfed at mid to high tides. Express Point should only be surfed by the experienced.

Berry's Beach, Kitty Miller Bay and the Penguin Parade have good surf. The Centre Crack at the Penguin Parade is sheltered in south-west winds but generally works on a larger swell. On bigger swells Cat Bay works on a south to south-east wind, while Right Point and Flynn's Reef work on easterly winds.

Mornington Peninsula There are several breaks inside Westernport Bay, one inside Port Phillip Bay and many good spots that face the open ocean. Within Westernport Bay, south to south-east swells will be best with north-west to west winds. Around Flinders, swells from the south and winds from the north will provide the best conditions. The coast from Cape Schanck to Portsea faces south-west and picks up the most swell on the Peninsula. It works best with south-west swells and north to north-east winds.

On the Westernport Bay side, check out Balnarring Point, Point Leo and Shoreham.

At Flinders, there are good reef breaks at the Gunnery, Meanos, Big Lefts and Cyrils. Big Lefts is quite a long paddle but can hold big swells up to 3m. Cape Schanck is well known for its big left-hand reef breaks on the western side of the lighthouse.

Between Cape Schanck and Point Nepean you will find beach breaks at Gunnamatta, St Andrews, Rye and Portsea.

The West Coast This stretch of coastline has plenty of breaks, from long reefs to peaky sandbars. Waves generally work on larger swells of about 2m, and north-west to west winds with southern swells will provide the best opportunities.

You can find beach breaks at Point Lonsdale, Ocean Grove, Barwon Heads, Torquay and Jan Juc. About 6km south of Torquay is the Bell's Beach Surfing Recreational Reserve. In this area check out Boobs, Winki Pop and Bell's Beach. Farther south of Bell's there are good breaks at Anglesea, Aireys Inlet, Mogg's Creek and Spout Creek. Lorne Point sometimes turns on a good right-hand reef break if there is enough swell. Along the Great Ocean Road south of Lorne you can see potential point breaks on almost every corner. More well known places include St Georges River, Cumberland River, Wye River, Kennett River and Skenes Creek.

The Shipwreck Coast, west of Cape Otway as far as Peterborough, offers possibly the most powerful waves in Victoria. It faces south-west and is open to the sweeping swells of the Southern Ocean. The swell is consistently up to a metre higher than elsewhere, making it the place to go if you're after big waves. However, extreme care must be taken as some breaks are isolated, subject to strong rips and undertows, and are generally only for the experienced surfer. It's probably best to surf with someone who knows the area.

Places to check are Johanna, Castle Cove and Gibson Steps. Still on the Shipwreck Coast, Port Campbell's Easter Reef is a well known big-wave spot, while farther west at Peterborough the Well and Massacres also hold big surf. The scarred coastline is also the home of the Twelve Apostles and you can continue on to Warrnambool, Port Fairy and Portland.

SCUBA DIVING

When it comes to scuba diving, Australia and images of the Great Barrier Reef mesh together so perfectly that it's hard to imagine it's worth dropping below sea level anywhere else in the country. In fact there is superb scuba diving all around the Australian coast, and some of Victoria's best diving is definitely word class. Of course, it can get a little chilly in Victorian waters and 7mm wetsuits or even drysuits are the order of the day. Nevertheless, dives operate year round and anyone who has been diving along the California coast will think Victorian waters are positively tropical.

Beneath its murky surface Port Phillip Bay has many excellent dive sites and an abundance of marine life. From Portsea and Sorrento on the Mornington Peninsula you can visit such notable dive sites as the Pope's Eye and Portsea Hole.

The Bellarine Peninsula is also popular with divers and Queenscliff is a good base from which to go diving. Other popular diving areas include Torquay, Anglesea, Lorne, Apollo Bay, Port Campbell and Portland (all along the Great Ocean Road); Flinders, Sorrento and Portsea (on the Mornington Peninsula); and Kilcunda, Wilsons Promontory and Mallacoota (along the east coast). There are dozens of shipwrecks along the Victorian coastline, many of which are popular dive sites, but note that the wrecks are protected from damage or disturbance by the Historic Shipwrecks Act.

Companies offering open-water courses and trips for certified divers include Diver Instruction Services (☎ 9840 7744) and Melbourne Diving School (☎ 9459 4111), both in Melbourne; and the Queenscliff Dive Centre (☎ 5258 1188) in Queenscliff. Check the *Yellow Pages* under 'Scuba Diving Schools' for others. Beginners' courses for open-water certification are run over either two weekends

Victorian Scuba Diving

Some of Victoria's best diving is found around the Heads, the narrow entrance to Melbourne's Port Phillip Bay. Portsea, on the eastern side of the Heads, and Queenscliff, on the western side, just 1½ hours from central Melbourne, are the two major centres for dives both inside and outside the bay. The massive flows of water into and out of the bay are both a blessing and a curse. The constant change of water makes for rich marine life and often excellent visibility but means that many dives can only be made at slack tide, the window of opportunity between incoming and outgoing tidal flows. Of course drift dives, where you're simply swept along with the tidal flow, take advantage of those swift flowing currents.

Popular dives around the Heads visit the complex series of reefs, rocks and bommies (bomboras; submerged reefs) which harbour colourful marine life. The long sweep of Lonsdale Wall, on the Queenscliff side of the Heads, is one of the bay's finest dives. Inside the bay are two artificial islands, built over 100 years ago to counter a feared invasion from Russia. South Channel Fort was actually completed but Pope's Eye never got farther than the foundations. Today the horseshoe-shaped artificial reef formed by these foundations is part of a marine reserve and home to a huge concentration of often fearless fish, swimming around the brightly decorated rocks and between long strands of kelp.

After diving at Pope's Eye many dive boats make a detour to a nearby wooden navigation structure, also dating from the Victorian era but now taken over by a friendly colony of seals. These Australian fur seals are keen to join divers if it looks like they're ready to play. Snorkelling trips to swim with the seals are made during the summer months. Port Phillip Bay also has a resident pod of dolphins which are often encountered by divers.

The bay's tricky currents, fast tidal flows and complex arrays of rocks and reefs have brought many ships to grief. The gold rush years were particularly dangerous, when a huge rush of ships converged on Melbourne's sketchily charted waters. As a result there are some great wrecks waiting for divers, topped by the *Eliza Ramsden* which went down in 1875 and lies in 20m of water. Remarkably, some of the best wrecks were deliberately sunk. In the 1920s scrap metal values were so low that there was no market for outdated ships and over 40 vessels were towed outside the Heads and scuttled in the 'Ships' Graveyard'. Pride of place in this sunken fleet goes to the four J-class submarines donated by the Royal Navy after WWI and dumped in the 1920s when they proved too expensive to maintain. The 26m 'shallow submarine', J4, is the most popular of the subs but the 'intact submarine', J5, at 36m, is a wonderful sight, decked out in bright yellow anemones.

Port Phillip Bay, with over 50 popular dive sites, is the state's busiest dive centre but there are plenty of other diving opportunities along the coast. To the east of Melbourne in Western Port, Flinders Pier is a popular shore dive where you stand an excellent chance of encountering the rare sea dragon, a colourfully elongated relative of the seahorse. Phillip Island and Wilsons Promontory, farther to the east, also have excellent diving.

To the west of Melbourne there's good diving at a number of centres including Portland, Port Fairy, Warrnambool and, especially, Port Campbell, where, if the weather conditions are cooperative, you can dive on a number of historic shipwrecks along the Shipwreck Coast, including Victoria's most famous wreck, the *Loch Ard.*

Tony Wheeler

(plus some evenings for theory) or five days: costs are around $450. Most companies require you to pass a medical before you can do a course.

SAILING

There are many sailing clubs around Port Phillip Bay – see Sailing in the Activities section of the Melbourne chapter. Other popular boating areas around the state include the large Gippsland Lakes system, Lake Eildon and Mallacoota Inlet in East Gippsland. At most of these places you can hire yachts and launches, which work out to be quite economical among a few people. There are also a few schools were you can learn to sail. In Melbourne, try the Jolly Roger School, or, to gain your Competent Crew certificate on yachts, you could try Geoff Steadman's Melbourne Sailing School (☎ 9589 1433).

CANOEING & KAYAKING

Canoeing and kayaking offer travellers the chance to see parts of Victoria they might otherwise not see – river gorges, lake edges and remote sections of wilderness such as along the Snowy River.

Trips can be as short as a couple of hours, or extended adventures. The Glenelg River in the south-west is well set up for a long trip as it has special riverside campsites for canoeists. Rivers are graded according to their degree of difficulty. Grade one (such as parts of the Yarra River) are easy-flowing rivers; grade five (such as the Indi River and parts of the Murray) are long, unbroken stretches of rapids, only suitable for very experienced canoeists.

Sea kayaking has become popular around the coasts and bays. Victorian canoeists have paddled across Bass Strait to Tasmania, while Port Phillip Bay is ideal for training trips. There are many opportunities to see wildlife such as sea lions, gannets, penguins and dolphins.

The Yarra River, which runs through much of Melbourne, has contributed in large measure to the popularity of canoeing in Victoria. The lower reaches are gentle and suitable for family outings. In the Upper Yarra there are a number of exciting possibilities, as the rapids – usually spaced well apart – reach grade three. All warnings should be heeded as the river is extremely dangerous when it's in flood. For information on this section of the river get hold of the pamphlet *Canoeing the Upper Yarra*, published by the Department of Sport & Recreation (☎ 9666 4200), 123 Lonsdale St, Melbourne.

For more information about canoeing courses, clubs etc contact the Victorian Board of Canoe Education (☎ 9459 4251), 332 Banyule Rd, Viewbank 3084.

Operators hiring out canoeing gear include Canoes Plus (☎ 9816 9411), 140 Cotham Rd Kew, Melbourne; Echuca Boat & Canoe Hire (☎ 5480 6208) in Echuca; and South West Canoe Service (☎ 08-8738 4141) and Nelson Boat Hire (☎ 08-8738 4048), both in Nelson near the estuary of the Glenelg River.

WHITE-WATER RAFTING

Guided white-water rafting trips are operated on various rivers in the Victorian Alps such as the Snowy, Thompson, Mitchell and Mitta Mitta. The trips run all year round, although the best times are during the snow melts from around August to December, when otherwise gentle streams can be transformed into raging white-water rapids.

Costs range from around $130 per person per day, with everything from day trips to five-day expeditions. Operators include Peregrine Adventures (☎ 9662 2800) and Snowy River Expeditions (☎ 5155 0220).

Paddle Sports (☎ 9478 3310), based in Preston in Melbourne, is another company offering guided rafting trips. If you'd rather do your own thing, Paddle Sports also hires out rafts that take from two to seven people, plus equipment.

HOUSEBOAT HOLIDAYS & PLEASURE BOATING

If you're interested in a floating holiday, various operators hire out houseboats for cruising the Murray River, Lake Eildon or

Mallacoota Inlet. Similarly, you can hire a yacht or a motor launch to sail or cruise the Gippsland Lakes or Lake Eildon. See the relevant chapters for details.

FISHING

Fishing is incredibly popular, and there are hundreds of places around the state where you can dangle a line – whether you want to fly fish for rainbow trout in a mountain stream, lure a yabby out of a dam, catch a deep-river redfin or hook a yellowtail kingfish from a surf beach.

To fish in most inland waterways, people older than 16 years need to purchase an Amateur Fishing License (AFL) – these cost $10 for 28 days or $20 for a year and are available from NRE offices and most tackle shops. Inland waterways where you can fish *without* an AFL include the Gippsland Lakes, the Bottom Lake at Mallacoota Inlet, Wingan Inlet, the Barwon River (inland from Barwon Heads) and Curdies Inlet at Peterborough.

You also don't generally need an AFL to fish in marine waters, except for Port Phillip Bay, where a licensing scheme is mooted.

Fishing-tackle shops and NRE offices are good places for info about fishing in Victoria. Size limits and seasons are specified in the free booklet *Recreational Fishing Regulations Guide*.

HORSE-RIDING & TREKKING

There are dozens of horse-riding ranches and farms throughout the state which offer rides from one hour (usually $20 or less) to a full day (around $80).

They include Lancefield Bush Rides & Tucker (☎ 5429 1627) at Lancefield, Blazing Saddles Horse Trail Rides (☎ 5289 7322) at Aireys Inlet, Grampians Coach House (☎ 5383 9255) at Brimpaen in the Grampians and the Herb & Horse (☎ 6072 9553) on the Upper Murray (east of Wodonga). Some places close to the city are listed in the Melbourne chapter. For details of other horse-riding ranches in country areas see the individual town listings or contact the local tourist office.

There are also quite a few commercial operators offering adventure horse treks, generally in the mountains of the High Country – anything from overnight rides to week-long packhorse expeditions.

The cost is generally between $100 and $130 per person per day, which includes meals and accommodation, camping gear or swags. Some of the better known operators are Bogong Horseback Adventures (☎ 5754 4849) at Mt Beauty, Bright-Freeburgh Trail Rides (☎ 5755 1370) at Bright, Giltrap's Mt Bogong Packhorse Adventures (☎ 02-6072 3535) at Mitta Mitta and Mountain Saddle Safaris (☎ 5165 3365) at Erica. Stoney's Bluff & Beyond Trail Rides (☎ 5775 2212) near Mansfield offers a three or four day ride in the mountains (around $450) and also an 18 day marathon down to the coast.

Beeton's Guide to Adventure Horse Riding is a good reference if you're interested in finding out more.

HANG GLIDING & PARAGLIDING

There are several hang gliding and paragliding schools in the state that cater for both novices and experienced fliers. They include the Eagle School of Hang Gliding (☎ 5750 1174), based at Porepunkah near Bright and, in Apollo Bay, Wingsports Hang Gliding & Paragliding (☎ 0419-378 616).

If you want a quick introduction to paragliding, you can do a two day course that will have you in the air on the second day and cost around $310 per person. A seven to nine day HGFA (Hang Gliding Federation of Australia) hang gliding licence course will cost around $150 per day. A 20 hour powered hang gliding course costs about $120 per hour.

Most operators also offer tandem flights in powered hang gliders (from $70 for a 15 minute flight), as well as tandem paragliding or hang gliding (from around $100). Add $10 for insurance.

HOT AIR BALLOONING

Ballooning, or the 'sport of the gods' as Marie Antoinette called it, is a popular if somewhat expensive way to start the day.

There are operators offering balloon rides all around the state, particularly in the High Country (Bright and Mansfield), the Yarra Valley, the Grampians and over Melbourne.

Most balloon flights take off just after dawn, which is the prettiest and most exhilarating time to fly, as well as the safest.

You're up for around $200 per person for about a one hour balloon ride, usually with a celebratory champagne breakfast afterwards. Operators include Balloon Sunrise (☎ 9427 7596) for flights over Melbourne, Balloon Aloft (☎ 1800 62 7661 toll-free) for flights over Mansfield or the Yarra Valley, and Grampians Balloon Flights (☎ 5358 5222) for flights over the Grampians or Melbourne.

ROCK CLIMBING

Victoria is world renowned for its climbing cliffs and crags. Mt Arapiles, in the Western District near Horsham, is famous among rock climbers from around the world as it has a huge variety of climbs for all levels of skill. Not far from here, in the Grampians National Park, rock climbing is increasingly popular as new areas like Mt Stapylton and Black Ian's Rock are developed. At Mt Buffalo, in the Victorian Alps, there is a great variety of good granite climbs, including those on the Buffalo Gorge wall.

Closer to Melbourne there are many developed areas. Sugarloaf and Jawbones are 112km out in Cathedral Range State Park, a popular weekend spot. Other popular climbing spots are the Camel's Hump (Mt Macedon), Werribee Gorge, Cape Woolamai (Phillip Island) and Ben (Mc)Cairn. These places offer a variety of climbs of varying grades of difficulty with names such as Cynical Pinnacle, Screaming Brainrot Ave, WD40, Desperate Living and Jug Abuse.

The outdoor and adventure shops in Hardware St in Melbourne's city centre are good sources of information. The Victorian Climbing Club, which meets at 8 pm on the last Thursday of most months at 188 Gatehouse St, Parkville, Melbourne, publishes a series of *Rockclimbers Handbooks* with detailed notes on the state's major climbs. For information write to The Secretary, GPO Box 1725P, Melbourne 3001.

In recent years, indoor rock climbing centres have sprung up in Melbourne and some regional centres. These offer a good introduction to climbing and are popular places to sharpen up skills before hitting the real thing. Check with tourist information centres or look under 'Indoor Sports' in the *Yellow Pages* for locations of climbing gyms.

Several operators in the Grampians and Natimuk (near Mt Arapiles) offer lessons and tours. See the Wimmera chapter for details.

CAVING

Victoria has some good areas for caving, including the limestone caves around Buchan in East Gippsland and the lava tubes and caves in the Western District. Note that caving is a potentially hazardous activity that should only be undertaken by experienced and properly equipped people.

The Victorian Speleological Association (☎ 9337 7680) has a fairly small membership but organises caving trips at least once a month, and interested newcomers are welcome. Contact the association by phone or write to GPO Box 5425CC, Melbourne 3001.

The spectacular limestone Princess Margaret Rose Caves (north of Nelson near the South Australian border) and the Buchan Caves (north of Lakes Entrance) are both open to the general public, with rangers conducting tours.

GOLD PROSPECTING

There's still a fair bit of gold in them thar hills, and looking for it is a popular pastime. People hoping to find big nuggets buy a metal detector and fossick around abandoned diggings. Panning for gold dust and small nuggets in creeks is less likely to make you rich (not that many fossickers become rich), but it's a very pleasant excuse to get into the bush.

You can hire gold pans in some towns in the old gold areas or buy one from a disposals shop. You also need a Miners Right – a licence to look for minerals and precious metals. They cost $18 at NRE offices.

Getting There & Away

For most international travellers, getting to Australia means flying, although it is sometimes possible to hitch a ride on a yacht or pay for a berth on a cargo ship.

AIR

The main problem with getting to Australia is that it's a long way from anywhere. Coming from Asia, Europe or North America there are lots of competing airlines and a wide variety of air fares, but there's no way you can avoid those great distances. Australia's international popularity adds another problem – flights are often heavily booked. If you want to fly to Australia at a particularly popular time of year (the middle of summer, ie around Christmas, is notoriously difficult) or on a particularly popular route (like Singapore-Melbourne), you need to plan well ahead.

First-time travellers to Australia may be alarmed to find themselves being sprayed with insecticide by the airline stewards. It happens to everyone. Some airlines don't spray from cans, but put the insecticide in the air-con.

Airport & Airlines

Melbourne airport services both domestic and international flights. The airport is in Tullamarine, 22km north-west of the city centre.

While plenty of airlines have direct flights into Melbourne, many flights stop off in Sydney. Sydney's airport is stretched way beyond its capacity and flights are frequently delayed on arrival and departure. Customs and immigration facilities are too small for the current visitor flow and are often overcrowded. Try to organise your flights to avoid Sydney.

Buying Tickets

If you're looking for a cheap ticket, go to a travel agent, not directly to the airline. The airline can usually only quote you the regular fare, but an agent can offer all sorts of special deals, particularly on competitive routes.

It's worth checking the Internet for flights, prices and availability. Some sites allow you to book online, which is up to $50 cheaper than buying through a travel agent. The *Age* has a good booking service on its Web site at www.theage.co.au/travel/intlairfare/html.

What's available and what it costs depends on what time of year it is, what route you're flying and who you're flying with. The high season for flights to/from Australia is generally between December and February. If you're flying on a popular airline or one where the choice of flights is very limited, the fare is likely to be higher or there may be no discounted fares available.

Similarly, the dirt-cheap fares are likely to be less conveniently scheduled, on less convenient routes or with less popular airlines. Spending 12 hours in a third-world transit lounge might save you some money but consider the wear and tear on your sanity.

Things to consider when choosing a ticket are its validity (you may not want a cheap return ticket if it's only valid for two weeks) and the number of stopovers you want. As a rule of thumb, the cheaper the ticket the fewer stopovers you'll be allowed.

In Melbourne, two travel agents to try for discounted airline tickets are STA (☎ 1300 360 960) and Flight Centre (☎ 13 1600 or 1800 069 063 toll-free for student travel). Both have offices around Melbourne (and around the world). The YHA travel office (☎ 9670 7991), 205 King St, is another good place to try.

Cheap international flights are also advertised in the travel section of the *Age* each Saturday. International airlines are listed in the *Yellow Pages*.

Round-the-World Tickets

Round-the-World (RTW) tickets have become very popular and many will take you

Air Travel Glossary

Baggage Allowance This will be written on your ticket and usually includes one 20kg item to go in the hold, plus one item of hand luggage.

Bucket Shops These are unbonded travel agencies specialising in discounted airline tickets.

Bumped Just because you have a confirmed seat doesn't mean you're going to get on the plane (see Overbooking).

Cancellation Penalties If you have to cancel or change a discounted ticket, there are often heavy penalties involved; insurance can sometimes be taken out against these penalties. Some airlines impose penalties on regular tickets as well, particularly against 'no-show' passengers.

Check-In Airlines ask you to check in a certain time ahead of the flight departure (usually one to two hours on international flights). If you fail to check in on time and the flight is overbooked, the airline can cancel your booking and give your seat to somebody else.

Confirmation Having a ticket written out with the flight and date you want doesn't mean you have a seat until the agent has checked with the airline that your status is 'OK' or confirmed. Meanwhile you could just be 'on request'.

Courier Fares Businesses often need to send urgent documents or freight securely and quickly. Courier companies hire people to accompany the package through customs and, in return, offer a discount ticket which is sometimes a phenomenal bargain. In effect, what the companies do is ship their freight as your luggage on regular commercial flights. This is a legitimate operation, but there are two shortcomings – the short turnaround time of the ticket (usually not longer than a month) and the limitation on your luggage allowance. You may have to surrender all your allowance and take only carry-on luggage.

Full Fares Airlines traditionally offer 1st class (coded F), business class (coded J) and economy class (coded Y) tickets. These days there are so many promotional and discounted fares available that few passengers pay full economy fare.

ITX An ITX, or 'independent inclusive tour excursion', is often available on tickets to popular holiday destinations. Officially it's a package deal combined with hotel accommodation, but many agents will sell you one of these for the flight only and give you phoney hotel vouchers in the unlikely event that you're challenged at the airport.

Lost Tickets If you lose your airline ticket an airline will usually treat it like a travellers cheque and, after inquiries, issue you with another one. Legally, however, an airline is entitled to treat it like cash and if you lose it then it's gone forever. Take good care of your tickets.

MCO An MCO, or 'miscellaneous charge order', is a voucher that looks like an airline ticket but carries no destination or date. It can be exchanged through any International Association of Travel Agents (IATA) airline for a ticket on a specific flight. It's a useful alternative to an onward ticket in those countries that demand one, and is more flexible than an ordinary ticket if you're unsure of your route.

No-Shows No-shows are passengers who fail to show up for their flight. Full-fare passengers who fail to turn up are sometimes entitled to travel on a later flight. The rest are penalised (see Cancellation Penalties).

On Request This is an unconfirmed booking for a flight.

Air Travel Glossary

Onward Tickets An entry requirement for many countries is that you have a ticket out of the country. If you're unsure of your next move, the easiest solution is to buy the cheapest onward ticket to a neighbouring country or a ticket from a reliable airline which can later be refunded if you do not use it.

Open Jaw Tickets These are return tickets where you fly out to one place but return from another. If available, this can save you backtracking to your arrival point.

Overbooking Airlines hate to fly empty seats and since every flight has some passengers who fail to show up, airlines often book more passengers than they have seats. Usually excess passengers make up for the no-shows, but occasionally somebody gets bumped. Guess who it is most likely to be? The passengers who check in late.

Point-to-Point Tickets These are discount tickets that can be bought on some routes in return for passengers waiving their rights to a stopover.

Promotional Fares These are officially discounted fares, available from travel agencies or direct from the airline.

Reconfirmation At least 72 hours prior to departure time of an onward or return flight, you must contact the airline and 'reconfirm' that you intend to be on the flight. If you don't do this the airline can delete your name from the passenger list and you could lose your seat.

Restrictions Discounted tickets often have various restrictions on them – such as needing to be paid for in advance and incurring a penalty to be altered. Others are restrictions on the minimum and maximum period you must be away, such as a minimum of 14 days or a maximum of one year.

Round-the-World Tickets RTW tickets give you a limited period (usually a year) in which to circumnavigate the globe. You can go anywhere the carrying airlines go, as long as you don't backtrack. The number of stopovers or total number of separate flights is decided before you set off and they usually cost a bit more than a basic return flight.

Stand-by This is a discounted ticket where you only fly if there is a seat free at the last moment. Stand-by fares are usually available only on domestic routes.

Transferred Tickets Airline tickets cannot be transferred from one person to another. Travellers sometimes try to sell the return half of their ticket, but officials can ask you to prove that you are the person named on the ticket. This is less likely to happen on domestic flights, but on an international flight tickets are compared with passports.

Travel Agencies Travel agencies vary widely and you should choose one that suits your needs. Some simply handle tours, while full-services agencies handle everything from tours and tickets to car rental and hotel bookings. If all you want is a ticket at the lowest possible price, then go to an agency specialising in discounted tickets.

Travel Periods Ticket prices vary with the time of year. There is a low (off-peak) season and a high (peak) season, and often a low-shoulder season and a high-shoulder season as well. Usually the fare depends on your outward flight – if you depart in the high season and return in the low season, you pay the high-season fare.

through Australia. Airline RTW tickets are often real bargains and, since Australia is pretty much on the other side of the world from Europe or North America, it can work out no more expensive, or even cheaper, to keep going in the same direction right around the world rather than U-turn when you return.

Official airline RTW tickets are usually put together by a combination of two airlines and permit you to fly anywhere you want on their route systems so long as you do not backtrack. Other restrictions are that you (usually) must book the first sector in advance, and cancellation penalties then apply. There may be restrictions on how many stops you are permitted, and usually the tickets are valid from 90 days up to a year. A typical price for a South Pacific RTW ticket is around US$2000.

An alternative type of RTW ticket is one put together by a travel agent using a combination of discounted tickets from a number of airlines. A UK agent like Trailfinders can put together interesting London-to-London RTW combinations including Australia for £800 to £1200.

Circle Pacific Tickets

Circle Pacific fares are a similar idea to RTW tickets, using a combination of airlines to circle the Pacific – combining Australia, New Zealand, North America and Asia. As with RTW tickets, there are advance purchase restrictions and limits to how many stopovers you can take. Typically, fares range between US$1900 and US$2200. A possible Circle Pacific route is Los Angeles-Hawaii-Auckland-Melbourne-Sydney-Singapore-Bangkok-Hong Kong-Tokyo-Los Angeles. You might find a cheaper ticket with fewer stops, eg Los Angeles-Tokyo-Kuala Lumpur-Melbourne-Los Angeles is sometimes advertised at around US$1400.

Departure Tax

A departure tax of $27 is payable by everyone leaving Australia. It's included in the cost of your ticket.

Within Australia

Australia's major domestic carriers are Ansett, which also flies a few international routes, and Qantas, which is also the international flag-carrier. Both have flights between Melbourne and all the Australian capital cities.

You don't have to reconfirm domestic flights on Ansett and Qantas, but you should phone on the day of your flight to check the details. For Ansett, call ☎ 13 1515; for Qantas, call ☎ 13 1223.

From time to time a new airline pops up to take on the major players. To date the newcomers have always failed, but they always prompt price wars, which are good news for travellers. There are rumours that yet another newcomer will appear in the near future.

Fares Ticket prices are determined by the airlines, so unlike the situation with international fares, travel agents will quote you exactly the same fare as the airlines themselves. Given this, the quickest and easiest approach is to book directly through the airlines, then pay for and collect your ticket from your nearest travel agent. Alternatively, if you have a credit card and you book more than three days in advance, the airline can forward your ticket to you by express post. For Ansett, call ☎ 13 1300; for Qantas, call ☎ 13 1313.

Discounted Fares Although full economy fares are quoted in this book, in practice very few people pay full fare for domestic travel. Discounted fares depend on various factors, including your age, whether you're studying, where you're going and how far in advance you book.

Full-time university or other higher education students get 25% off the regular economy fare on production of student ID or an ISIC card, but you can usually find fares discounted by more than that. Children (between the ages of three and 14) and secondary students get a 50% discount, and 'seniors' (travellers over the age of 60) get up to 70% off the regular fares.

Note that there are no longer stand-by fares, but there are discount fares that allow same-day travel on certain flights, usually those that are uncomfortably early or late.

The airlines also offer substantial random discounts on selected routes (mainly the heavy-volume routes, but not always) and at quiet times of the year.

International travellers (Australians and foreigners) can get a 25% to 40% discount on Qantas or Ansett domestic flights simply by presenting their international ticket (any airline, one way or return) when booking. It seems there is no limit to the number of domestic flights you can take, but there might be time limits, say 60 days after you arrive in Australia. Note that the discount applies only to the full economy fare, and so in many cases it will be cheaper to take advantage of other discounts offered.

Another thing to keep your eyes open for is special deals at certain times of the year. When the Melbourne Cup horse race is on in early November and the Aussie Rules Grand Final happens (also in Melbourne) at the end of September, lots of extra flights are put on. Special fares are offered to people wanting to leave Melbourne when everybody else wants to go there.

Advance Purchase Fares In many cases, the cheapest fares available are advance purchase deals. The basic rule with advance purchase fares is that the further ahead you book, the cheaper the flight. There are restrictions on changing flights and you usually have to stay away at least one Saturday night. The other major disadvantage is that advance purchase tickets are nonrefundable, so you lose all your money if you cancel, although you can buy health-related cancellation insurance.

As an example of how advance purchase fares work, the full economy return fare between Melbourne and Sydney costs $594. If you book the same ticket five days in advance the fare drops to $536; seven days in advance, $329; 14 days in advance, $269; and 21 days in advance, $239. The only discount on one-way fares is on bookings made five days in advance. This reduces the Melbourne-Sydney full economy one-way fare from $297 to $258 – which is more than a return fare booked three weeks ahead.

Air Passes With so much discounting, air passes do not represent the value they once did, although pre-buying a pass does save you the hassle of hunting around for special deals. However, there are a few worth checking out.

Qantas has the Boomerang Pass, available overseas only and theoretically not to Australian citizens. This involves purchasing coupons for either short-haul flights (eg Melbourne to Hobart) for US$175, or for long-haul sectors (eg almost anywhere to Uluru) for US$220. You have to buy a minimum of two coupons and after you arrive in Australia you can buy up to 10 more.

The Qantas Backpacker Pass can only be bought in Australia and is restricted to travellers with membership of the YHA or some other hostel groups, or some Greyhound Pioneer bus passes. You have to buy a minimum of three sectors and you can buy another two to six afterwards. There are some complex rules about minimum numbers of days at each stop, but these shouldn't inconvenience holiday visitors. Flying Melbourne-Perth one way, for example, would cost $258, much cheaper than the full economy fare. Melbourne-Perth return is a little cheaper than the equivalent 21 day advance purchase ticket.

Ansett has two similar passes.

North America

There is a variety of connections across the Pacific from Los Angeles, San Francisco and Vancouver to Australia, including direct flights, flights via New Zealand, island-hopping routes or more circuitous Pacific rim routes via Asia. Qantas, Air New Zealand and United fly USA-Australia, while Qantas, Air New Zealand and Canadian Airlines International fly Canada-Australia. An interesting option from the east coast is Northwest's flight via Japan.

To find good fares to Australia, check the travel ads in the Sunday travel sections of papers like the *Los Angeles Times*, *San Francisco Chronicle-Examiner*, *New York Times* and *Toronto Globe & Mail*. You can usually get a return ticket from the west coast from about US$1500 in low season, US$1600 in high season (Australian summer). Add a couple of hundred dollars for flights from the east coast.

In the USA, Council Travel and STA are good places to look for cheap tickets.

If Pacific island hopping is your aim, check out the airlines of Pacific island nations, some of which have good deals on indirect routes. Qantas can give you Fiji or Tahiti along the way, while Air New Zealand can offer these as well as the Cook Islands.

Sample one-way low-season fares from Melbourne to North America include: San Francisco A$1100, New York A$1300 and Vancouver A$1100.

New Zealand

Air New Zealand, Ansett and Qantas operate a network of trans-Tasman flights linking Auckland, Wellington and Christchurch to Melbourne. Typical fares range from NZ$500/550 one way/return in low season. One-way fares are not much cheaper than return fares but there is a lot of competition on this route so there is bound to be some good discounting going on. Ask your travel agent for current United Airlines fares.

The UK

The cheapest tickets in London are from the numerous 'bucket shops' (discount ticket agencies), which advertise in publications like *Time Out*, *Australasian Traveller* and *TNT*. The magazine *Business Traveller* also has a great deal of good advice on air fare bargains, and the *Evening Standard*'s travel section is also worth perusing. Most bucket shops are trustworthy and reliable, but the occasional sharp operator appears – *Time Out* and *Business Traveller* give some useful advice on precautions to take.

Trailfinders (☎ 020-7938 3366) at 46 Earls Court Rd, London W8, and STA Travel (☎ 020-7937 9962) at 74 Old Brompton Rd, London SW7, and offices around the UK, are good, reliable agents for cheap tickets.

The cheapest London to Melbourne flights are Britannia Airways charter flights that operate from November through March for an amazingly cheap fare of around £400. The cheapest bucket-shop tickets are around £350/600 one way/return. Such prices are usually only available if you depart the UK in low season (March to June); high-season fares, in September and mid-December, are around £600/750.

From Australia you can expect to pay at least A$900/1200 to London and other European capitals (with stops in Asia on the way) in low season and A$1500/2000 in high season.

Africa

The flight possibilities from these continents are not so varied and you're much more likely to have to pay the full fare. There are flights to Perth from Harare (Zimbabwe) and Johannesburg (South Africa), with connections to Melbourne. Return fares between Melbourne and Johannesburg start from around A$1900. A cheaper alternative from East Africa may be to fly from Nairobi to India or Pakistan and on to South-East Asia, and then to connect from there to Australia.

Asia

Ticket discounting is widespread in Asia, particularly in Singapore, Hong Kong, Bangkok and Penang. There are a lot of fly-by-nights in the Asian ticketing scene, so a little care is required. Also, the Asian routes fill up fast. Flights between Hong Kong and Australia are notoriously heavily booked, while flights to or from Bangkok and Singapore are often part of the longer Europe to Australia route, so they are also sometimes very full. Plan ahead.

Typical one-way fares from Singapore to Melbourne are around S$900.

From Melbourne, return fares start from A$1100 to Hong Kong, and anywhere between A$700 and A$1200 to Singapore, Kuala Lumpur and Bangkok.

South America

There are two routes between South America and Australia. From Chile, take Lan-Chile's Santiago-Easter Island-Tahiti flight then connect with Qantas or another airline to Australia. This costs about A$2000 to Melbourne. Aerolineas Argentinas flies from Buenos Aires to Sydney via the Antarctic Circle.

LAND

Bus

Travelling by bus is the cheapest way to get around Australia, and you get to see more of the wide red-brown land than if you fly. But don't forget that it's a big country – bus travel can be slow and tedious.

There is only one truly national bus network – Greyhound Pioneer (☎ 13 2030). McCafferty's (☎ 13 1499) is the next biggest operator, with services along the east coast as well as the loop through the centre to Alice Springs and Darwin. There are also a few smaller companies, such as Firefly (☎ 1800 631 164 toll-free), which operates discounted services between Melbourne, Sydney and Adelaide.

You can book directly with the bus companies, although it's often worth checking with travel agents, especially those catering to backpackers. See the Information section in the Melbourne chapter for a few places to try.

There are basically two types of fares – express fares and bus passes. Students, backpackers belonging to some sort of hostel group (eg YHA, VIP, Nomad) and pensioners get discounts of at least 10% off most express fares and bus passes.

Express Fares Express fares are for straight point-to-point travel. On these tickets stopover conditions vary from company to company – some give you one free stopover or allow you to stopover wherever they have a terminal, and others charge a fee for each stopover. If you want to make multiple stopovers, you'll end up paying full fares on each separate segment – in these cases a bus pass may work out to be better value.

There's hot competition between the various companies, which means that prices are constantly changing. As a guide, some approximate fares and travelling times to/from Melbourne include: Sydney $50 (12 hours), Adelaide $45 (10 hours), Perth $240 (46 hours), Brisbane $130 (23 hours), Cairns $270 (47 hours), Canberra $45 (8½ hours) and Alice Springs $325 (30 hours).

Bus Passes Greyhound Pioneer and McCafferty's have a wide variety of passes, so it's a matter of deciding which best suits your needs. Their networks are fairly similar throughout eastern and central Australia. At this stage only Greyhound Pioneer has services throughout Western Australia, although McCafferty's includes the Indian-Pacific train trip from Adelaide to Perth on some of its passes.

Warning

The information in this chapter is particularly vulnerable to change: prices for international travel are volatile, routes are introduced and cancelled, schedules change, special deals come and go, and rules and visa requirements are amended. Airlines and governments seem to take a perverse pleasure in making price structures and regulations as complicated as possible. You should check directly with the airline or a travel agent to make sure you understand how a fare (and ticket you may buy) works. In addition, the travel industry is highly competitive and there are many lurks and perks.

The upshot of this is that you should get opinions, quotes and advice from as many airlines and travel agents as possible before you part with your hard-earned cash. The details given in this chapter should be regarded as pointers and are not a substitute for your own careful, up-to-date research.

Broadly, there are three different types of passes: set-kilometre, set-route and set-days. Greyhound Pioneer's set-kilometre passes offer anything between 2000 and 20,000km. As an example, 10,000km (which would cover a great deal of the country) costs $735 and is valid for 12 months. An example of a set-route pass, on which you travel point-to-point but can make stopovers along the way, is Cairns-Melbourne, which costs $300 and is valid for 90 days. A set-days pass allows you to travel where you want on a certain number of days during a specified period. For example, travelling on 10 days out of 30 costs $640.

Alternative Bus Tours & Networks If you're travelling between Melbourne and either Sydney or Adelaide, you'll miss some great countryside if you fast-track down the main highways. There are some fun and scenic alternatives.

Wild-Life Tours (☎ 9747 1882) is a Melbourne-based company offering tours of the Great Ocean Rd and the Grampians (from $49 to $120) and also a one-way trip between Melbourne and Adelaide (either direction) via the Grampians (from $75) or via the Great Ocean Rd and the Grampians (from $119). You can stop over anywhere along the way.

The Wayward Bus (☎ 1800 882 823 toll-free, www.waywardbus.com.au) runs a variety of routes through south-eastern Australia, most of them connecting Melbourne with Adelaide or Sydney. This is a great way to travel and see some interesting places. You can stop over in as many places as you like or stay on the bus (and get off for sights and activities along the way) as it makes its way to Adelaide in three days via the Great Ocean Rd ($170), to Sydney via the High Country (and Canberra) in five days ($190) or to Sydney via the Lakes District and East Gippsland in five days ($170). There's also a route between Sydney and Adelaide running through Mildura. Fares don't include accommodation, but the bus always stops where there's a hostel or other cheap accommodation.

Another interesting alternative is Oz Experience (☎ 1300 300 028), which is basically a backpackers' bus line. It has frequent bus services up and down the east coast and through central Australia to all the major destinations, with off-the-beaten-track detours to outback cattle stations, national parks, wineries etc. Its passes (of which there are numerous types) are valid for either six or 12 months, in which time you can travel freelance all over its network.

Train

Australia's railway system is less comprehensive than the bus networks, and train services are less frequent and more expensive. However, interstate trains are now as fast or faster than buses and the railways have cut their prices in an attempt to be more competitive with both bus fares and reduced air fares.

Victoria's V/Line operates most interstate services in conjunction with government-owned railways in other states. However, there's now also a private company, Great Southern Railway, which runs the *Overland* (Melbourne to Adelaide), the *Ghan* (Adelaide to Alice Springs, but soon to continue on to Melbourne) and the Indian Pacific (Sydney to Perth). Book on ☎ 132 147 or through a travel agent.

As the interstate railway booking system is computerised, any station (other than those on metropolitan lines) can make a booking for journeys throughout the country. Currently that includes the Great Southern Railway trains, but things might change. For reservations telephone ☎ 13 2232 from anywhere in Australia; this will connect you to the nearest booking agent. Hours for this service vary slightly from state to state. In Victoria, the hours are 7 am to 9 pm daily.

Fares & Conditions Some interstate trains no longer have separate 1st and 2nd classes, although most have sleepers. Ticket prices are set by the railways, so you can't get better deals by shopping around.

Depending on availability, a limited number of discounted fares are offered on most trains. These cut 10 to 40% off the standard fares, and if you book early or travel at off-peak times, you'll usually qualify for one of these cheaper fares. There are concession fares for children under the age of 16 and Australian (only) students.

On interstate journeys you can make free stopovers – you have two months to complete your trip on a one-way ticket and six months on a return ticket.

There are no discounts for return travel – a return ticket is just double the price of a one-way ticket.

Rail Passes There are a couple of Australia-wide passes that you can use to get here, and around, once you are here. Both passes are available only to overseas visitors and must be purchased outside Australia. They are valid for economy class only.

With the Austrail Pass you can travel anywhere on the Australian rail network for a set number of days. The cost is $545 for 14 days, $705 for 21 days and $850 for 30 days. You can buy extra weeks at $280 each.

The Austrail Flexipass allows a set number of travelling days within a six-month period. The cost is $450 for eight days of travel, $650 for 15 days, $915 for 22 days and $1175 for 29 days. (An eight day Flexipass cannôt be used for travel west of Adelaide.)

Surcharges are payable on sleeping berths, and on certain trains, such as the *Ghan* and the *Indian-Pacific* (Sydney to Perth), there are compulsory meal charges as well.

Sydney Countrylink runs daily XTP trains between Melbourne and Sydney, with the Melbourne-Sydney service operating during the day and the Sydney-Melbourne service overnight. The trip takes 10¾ hours, and standard fares are $96 in economy, $154 in 1st class and $229 for a 1st-class sleeper.

Canberra To get to Canberra from Melbourne by rail you take the daily *Canberra Link*, which involves a train to Wodonga on the Victoria-New South Wales border and then a bus from there. This takes about eight hours and costs $49 ($64.50 with 1st class on the train).

Adelaide The *Overland* runs overnight and costs $182 in sleepers, $58 in seats. You can take your car on the *Overland* for $100. V/Line has a combined bus/train 'Link' service that costs $51 ($59.40 for 1st class on the train section between Melbourne and Bendigo).

Perth To get to Perth by rail from Melbourne you take the *Overland* to Adelaide and then the popular *Indian-Pacific* (which comes through Adelaide from Sydney). The Melbourne to Perth trip takes two days and three nights, and fares are $306 for an economy seat (it's a long time to sit in a seat!), $520 for a 'holiday sleeper' (seat to Adelaide, sleeper with shared facilities to Perth) or $805 for a 1st-class sleeper and all meals.

Car & Motorcycle

See the Getting Around chapter for details of road rules, driving conditions and information on buying and renting vehicles.

The main road routes into Victoria are: between Sydney and Melbourne you have a choice of either the Hume Hwy (870km, and freeway most of the way) or the coastal Princes Hwy (1039km, much longer and slower but also a hell of a lot more scenic). There's a similar choice if you're travelling between Adelaide and Melbourne, with either the fairly direct Western Hwy (730km) or the slower Princes Hwy coastal route (894km), the first section of which is known as the Great Ocean Rd.

If you're travelling between Brisbane and Melbourne, the quickest route is via the Newell Hwy (1890km).

SEA

Ferry

Operating regular services across Bass Strait to Tasmania is the big *Spirit of Tasmania* (☎ 13 2010) car and passenger ferry.

There are dozens of different fares, all of which include breakfast and a very good buffet dinner. Fares depend on the type of sleeping quarters and the time of year. Cheapest are the 'hostel fares' at $103/132 one way per person in the low/high season. The next level up costs $151/176 for a two or four berth cabin ($113/134 with student discount), with the most expensive option being $225/308 for a luxury suite. Return fares are double one-way fares. High-season prices apply during the Christmas school holidays and at Easter. Taking your car costs $30/40 in the low/high season.

The *Spirit of Tasmania* takes a leisurely 14½ hours to cross Bass Strait, and leaves Station pier in Port Melbourne at 6 pm every Monday, Wednesday and Friday and returns from Devonport at 6 pm every Tuesday, Thursday and Saturday. The ship arrives into both ports at 8.30 am.

In summer and part of autumn the *Devil Cat*, a huge, Star-Wars style catamaran, zooms across Bass Strait between Melbourne and George Town in just six hours. It's fast but not nearly as romantic as the *Spirit* and services are delayed or cancelled in very bad weather. The service is subsidised by the Tasmanian government, which is becoming edgy about continuing to do so. Peak and off-peak one-way fares are $170 ($40 car) and $160 ($35 car). The student fare is $134 in peak season and $120 in off peak.

For more information on other ways of getting to the Apple Isle, fly/drive packages etc, telephone or visit the Tasmanian Travel Centre (☎ 9206 7922) at 256 Collins St, Melbourne.

Yacht

It is quite possible to make your way round the Australian coast, or to/from other countries like New Zealand, Papua New Guinea or Indonesia, by hitching rides or crewing on yachts. Ask around at harbours, marinas or yacht clubs. It's often worth contacting the secretaries of sailing clubs and asking whether they have a notice board where people advertise for crew. Some of the major Australian clubs even run waiting lists for people wanting to crew on yachts. Look under 'Clubs – Yacht' in the *Yellow Pages* telephone directory. It obviously helps if you're an experienced sailor, but some people ship out as cooks (not very pleasant on a rolling yacht).

Cargo Ship

Many container lines do take a limited number of passengers, and while the voyage will be considerably more expensive than flying, the per-day cost is reasonable. Accommodation can be anything from the owners' suite to a bunk in a self-contained cabin.

The best source of information about routes and the lines plying them is the *OAG Cruise & Ferry Guide*, published quarterly by the Reed Travel Group in the UK. Your travel agent might have a copy.

A few companies take bookings for freighter travel. Given the complex nature of freight routes (delays and diversions are common) it might be best to deal with one of them. They include:

Freighter World Cruises
(☎ 818-449 3106) 180 South Lake Ave, Suite 335, Pasadena CA, 91101, USA

Strand Cruise & Travel Centre
(☎ 020-7836 6363) Charing Cross Shopping Centre Concourse, London WC2N 4HZ, UK

Sydney International Travel Centre
(☎ 02-9299 8000) Level 8, 75 King St, Sydney 2000, Australia

Getting Around

DOMESTIC AIR SERVICES

Because of the state's compact size, scheduled internal flights are somewhat limited. Regional airports impose taxes on ticket prices, from around $4 (Mildura) to $10 (Albury).

Kendall Airlines (book through Ansett on ☎ 13 1300) operates daily services between Melbourne and Mildura ($183 one way), Portland ($137) and Albury ($133). Southern Australia Airlines (book through Qantas on ☎ 13 1313) also flies between Melbourne and Mildura ($183). Unlike the advance purchase deals with Ansett and Qantas, Kendall and Southern Australia offer good advance purchase discounts on one-way fares as well as return fares.

There are also several small private airlines that fly to selected destinations – see the Getting There & Away sections in the various chapters for details.

TRAIN & BUS

V/Line

Extensive train and bus services within country Victoria are operated by V/Line. In Melbourne, long-distance trains operate out of the Spencer St station and long-distance buses operate out of the Spencer St coach terminal, on the north side of the train station.

Train/Bus Pass V/Line sells a pass that entitles you to travel on all its trains and buses for 14 days for $130. Overseas visitors can also buy a seven day pass for $75. You'd have to do a fair bit of travel to save money with the pass but it does save the hassle of buying tickets. You can't travel at peak times (basically weekday commuter times in and out of Melbourne, plus all day Monday and Friday) and you can't use the non-V/Line *Overland* and XPT trains.

Tickets & Reservations Book tickets by phone (☎ 13 2232) between 7 am and 9 pm daily. In Melbourne you can buy tickets in person at Spencer St and Flinders St train stations and some major suburban stations, and at most travel agents.

Most services do not require a reservation, although you will need one if you're travelling on an interstate train (eg the *Overland*) to a destination within Victoria.

Costs One-way economy fares are quoted throughout this book; 1st-class fares (available on trains only) are around 30% more than

Economy V/Line Fares from Melbourne

Note that standard return fares are double one-way fares.

Destination	Duration	One Way	Off-Peak Return
Ararat	3 hours	$26.90	$37.60
Bairnsdale	4 hours	$34.20	$47.80
Ballarat	2 hours	$13.80	$19.40
Bendigo	2 hours	$20.80	$29.20
Echuca	3½ hours	$26.90	$37.60
Geelong	1 hours	$8.60	$12.00
Mildura	9½ hours	$53.60	$75.00
Phillip Island	3 hours	$13.80	$19.40
Swan Hill	4½ hours	$43.40	$60.80
Warrnambool	3 hours	$34.20	$47.80

economy fares, and return fares are double the one-way fare. For the extra 30% you'll travel with a little more space and comfort than you will in economy.

There are various special deals on return fares, most of which give a discount of about 30%. Inter Urban fares are available for travel on weekdays between Melbourne and South Geelong, Bacchus Marsh, Ballarat, Kyneton, Seymour or Traralgon. You can't depart Melbourne between 4 and 6 pm, and you have to arrive in Melbourne after 9.30 am. Inter City fares apply to travel departing or arriving outside the Inter Urban area on Tuesday, Wednesday or Thursday. Weekend Saver Day Return fares apply to all services on weekends, but you must return the same day.

Children accompanied by an adult pay $5 for travel in the Inter Urban area and no more than $6 for travel anywhere else.

Major Routes Out of Melbourne, the principal V/Line routes are as follows, with economy fares from Melbourne:

South-west to Geelong ($8.60) then inland to Warrnambool ($34.20); a daily bus service runs along the Great Ocean Rd from Geelong through Lorne ($21.90) and Apollo Bay ($26.90), continuing through to Warrnambool on Friday (also on Monday during summer).

North-west to Ballarat ($13.80), Stawell ($31.60), Horsham ($41.30) and on to Adelaide in South Australia; buses run from Stawell to Halls Gap in the Grampians.

North through Bendigo ($20.80) to Swan Hill ($43.40); buses continue from Bendigo to Echuca ($26.90).

North to Shepparton ($23.30) and Cobram ($31.60).

North along the Hume Hwy to Albury-Wodonga ($38.90), continuing to Sydney; buses run from Wangaratta ($29.30) to Beechworth ($34.20) and Bright ($38.90).

East through Moe ($15.20) to Sale ($26.90); buses connect from Sale to Bairnsdale ($34.20), Lakes Entrance ($41.30), Orbost ($46.90), Cann River ($49) and Merimbula ($50).

Other Bus Services

The major bus companies, Greyhound Pioneer (☎ 13 2030) and McCafferty's (☎ 13 1499), operate bus services from Melbourne to Adelaide (via Ballarat and Horsham) and from Melbourne to Sydney (via the Hume Hwy). Greyhound Pioneer also operates buses along the coastal Princes Hwy between Melbourne and Sydney. If you're travelling from Melbourne through to Adelaide or Sydney you can make stopovers along these routes (at an extra cost).

For discounts and deals on bus travel check hostel noticeboards or contact a backpacker-oriented travel agency. A couple are listed in the Information section of the Melbourne chapter.

For an interesting alternative to travelling with V/Line or the major companies see the Organised Tours section later in this chapter.

TAXI

Most taxis in Melbourne are yellow and all have a large dome light on the roof. Taxi ranks are located at strategic places throughout Melbourne and the larger country centres – such as outside train stations. Taxis can also be hailed on the street or booked by telephone.

Flagfall is $2.60, and the standard tariff is 89c per kilometre and the detention rate, when the taxi is travelling at less than 21km/h, is 33c per minute. There is a $1 charge for telephone bookings ($2 between midnight and 6 am, $2.50 outside of Melbourne), and most cabs only take cash, American Express or Diners Card. Tipping is not expected, but always appreciated.

CAR

You can get around Melbourne and between the main country centres on public transport, but many of Victoria's finest features – the national parks, the remote beaches, the mountain regions, the backroad country towns – are not readily accessible by train or bus. So if you're planning to explore Victoria in detail or get off the beaten track, you'll need your own wheels.

Road Rules

Australians drive on the left-hand side of the road. Road rules are broadly the same as in other countries, but note that if you're turning left or right at an intersection you must give way to pedestrians (which isn't the case in the UK, for example) and that parallel parking on the wrong side of the street will get you a parking ticket (ditto).

Overseas licences (preferably with photo-ID) are acceptable if they are in English. If not you'll need to provide a translation.

There is a special hazard if you're driving in Melbourne – trams. See Getting Around in the Melbourne chapter.

Speed Limits The speed limit in built-up (residential) areas is 60km/h, sometimes rising to 75 or 80km/h on main roads and on the outskirts of towns, and dropping to 40km/h in specially designated areas such as school zones. Out on the open highway the speed limit is generally 100km/h (roughly 60 miles per hour), although on some freeways it rises to 110km/h.

Speed limits are more or less obeyed and police radar guns enforce them strictly.

Seat Belts Victoria's government was the first in the world to make the wearing of seat belts compulsory. Small children must be belted into an approved safety seat.

Alcohol *Don't* drink and drive – the blood-alcohol limit of 0.05% is strictly enforced by the police. Random breath tests occur throughout the state and penalties are severe, including losing your licence and having to pay a heavy fine. Probationary and learner drivers must display 'P' and 'L' plates and maintain a blood-alcohol reading of zero.

On the Road

Although it's more closely settled than most of the rest of Australia, Victoria is not criss-crossed by multi-lane highways. Apart from a few major routes, highways are just two-lane roads.

You don't have to get very far off the beaten track to find yourself on the narrower backroads, and anybody who sets out to see the state in reasonable detail will have to do at least some dirt-road travelling. If you aren't an experienced dirt-road driver, treat it like ice.

Signposting along the major routes is usually adequate, but again, if you're planning to explore in any detail you'll need a decent road map or two. The Royal Automobile Club of Victoria's (RACV) *Victoria State Map* is a pretty good general reference; if you need more detail, the RACV also publishes a comprehensive and accurate series of district maps.

Kangaroos and wombats are common hazards on country roads, and a collision is likely to kill the animal and seriously damage your vehicle. Swerving to miss an animal is potentially even more dangerous. Kangaroos are most active around dawn and dusk, and they travel in groups.

Route Numbering Most country routes are known by name – anything from 'the Goulburn Valley Hwy' to 'the back Glenlyon road' to 'that old right-of-way down past Ken's dam – the big one, not the small one, OK?'. However, that's changing with the gradual introduction of systematic route numbering.

'M' roads have divided carriageways (eg the Hume Freeway is the M38), 'A' roads are highways without divided carriageways (eg the Midland Hwy is the A300) and 'B' roads are almost as good (eg the Great Ocean Rd is the B100). 'C' and 'D' roads are lesser grades of roads, mostly sealed and usually two lanes wide.

It will be several years before the whole state is signposted, and much longer than that before locals will see the logic of calling, say, the road from Geelong to Portarlington anything but 'the Geelong-Portarlington road', as opposed to its new title of C123.

Fuel Service stations generally stock diesel, super (leaded) and unleaded fuel. Liquid petroleum gas (LPG, Autogas) is usually available in the major centres, but is much harder to find once you get off the major highways.

Expect to pay anywhere between 68c and 80c a litre for unleaded fuel (super and diesel cost a couple of cents more, LPG significantly less).

4WD or 2WD? There aren't many places in Victoria you can't get to in a conventional car. However, a 4WD will give you full access to the more remote national parks and state forests.

Buying a Car

Buying a used car involves much the same rules as anywhere in the western world but with a few local variations.

Firstly, used car dealers in Victoria are just like used car dealers from Los Angeles to London – they'd sell their mother into slavery if it turned a dollar. For any given car, you'll probably get it cheaper by buying privately through newspaper ads – try the *Age* classifieds on Wednesday or Saturday, or the weekly *Trading Post* – rather than through a car dealer. One advantage of buying through a dealer is that, if you spend more than $3000, you get a warranty of at least 3000km or two months.

Third-party personal-injury insurance (ie you're insured against injuries you cause other people) is included in the vehicle registration fee. This means that every vehicle (as long as it's currently registered) carries at least minimum insurance. You're wise to extend that minimum to at least third-party property insurance as well – minor collisions with Rolls Royces can be surprisingly expensive regardless of who is at fault.

In Victoria, a car has to have a safety check (Road Worthiness Certificate – RWC) before it can be registered in the new owner's name – usually the seller will indicate if the car already has a RWC. Don't let yourself be talked into buying a vehicle without a RWC – unless you're a mechanic, it almost *always* turns out to be much more hassle than it's worth.

It's much easier to sell a car in state in which it's registered, otherwise it has to be re-registered in the new state. It may be possible to sell a car without re-registering it, but you're likely to get a lower price.

For a fee ($90, or $120 for nonmembers), the RACV will check over a used car and report on its condition before you agree to purchase it. Arranging a mechanical test might seem like a hassle at the time, but it's a sensible investment that could save you a bundle of money and much heartache.

Be aware that an RACV test is likely to find a million things wrong with a cheap car. It's still a good idea to have the test, but talk over the results with the tester or another mechanic to see if the faults predict the car's imminent demise or are just minor annoyances that you can live with for a few months.

There are often cheap cars on offer at hostels and other places travellers hang out. Many of these have been around Australia a few times and haven't exactly been well looked after.

Buy-Back Deals One way of getting around the hassles of buying and selling a vehicle privately is to enter into a buy-back arrangement with a dealer. However, dealers will often find ways of knocking down the price when you return the vehicle, even if a price has been agreed in writing – often by pointing out expensive repairs that allegedly will be required to gain the dreaded RWC needed to transfer the registration. The main advantage of these schemes is that you don't have to worry about being able to sell the vehicle quickly at the end of your trip, and can usually arrange insurance, which short-term visitors may find hard to get.

One company that specialises in buy-back arrangements on cars and motorcycles, with fixed rates and no hidden extras, is Car Connection Australia (☎ 5473 4469, fax 5473 4520), based in Castlemaine in Victoria. Its program is basically a glorified long-term rental arrangement where you put down a deposit to the value of the vehicle and in the end you get your money back, minus the fixed 'usage' fee.

The bottom line is that a second-hand Ford station wagon or Yamaha XT600 trail bike will set you back a fixed sum of $1950 for any period up to six months; a good Toyota Landcruiser, suitable for serious outback exploration, is $4500, also for up to six months. Insurance is available at an additional cost. Prices include pick-up at Melbourne airport and a night's accommodation in Castlemaine to help you acclimatise, and you'll be sent on your way with touring maps and advice. You can also rent camping equipment (but not sleeping bags). Information and bookings are handled by its European agent: Travel Action GmbH (☎ 02764-78 24, fax 79 38), Einsiedeleiweg 16, 57399 Kirchhundem, Germany.

Renting a Car

The three major rental companies are Avis (☎ 1800 225 533 toll-free), Budget (☎ 13 2727) and Hertz (☎ 13 3039), with offices or agents in almost every large town. If you want to pick up a car or leave a car at the airport or organise a one-way rental, then the big firms are the best to deal with. The second-string companies, which are also represented almost everywhere, are Thrifty and National. Then there is a vast number of local firms or firms with outlets in a limited number of locations – check the *Yellow Pages* under 'Car &/or Minibus Rental'.

Rates with the major companies are typically around $53 a day for a tiny car (eg Ford Festiva) about $55 a day for a small car (Ford Laser, Toyota Corolla, Nissan Pulsar), about $70 a day for a medium car (Holden Camira, Toyota Camry, Nissan Pintara) or about $80 a day for a big car (Holden Commodore, Ford Falcon), all including insurance and unlimited kilometres. These rates are for one day's hire – the longer the hire period, the cheaper the daily rate. Also, keep an eye out for weekend specials and other offers.

Overseas travellers might be able to get a better deal if they pre-book and prepay through Avis, Budget or Hertz in their home country. They might not, though – do your homework!

Be aware that the insurance usually has an excess – if you have a prang, the excess is the amount you have to pay before the insurance company takes over. With some of the smaller companies the excess figure can be very high. Most companies prefer to rent to people over 21, and some require you to be over 25, although there are a few who will rent to 18-year-olds (often with high insurance premiums or a greater excess).

And then there are the 'rent-a-wreck' companies. They specialise in renting older cars, typically for around $35 a day. If you just want to travel around the city they can be worth considering.

4WD Renting a 4WD vehicle is within the budget range if a few people get together. The daily rate for a Toyota Landcruiser or similar is around $145, dropping to around $110 per day for rentals of a week or more. You'll only get about 250 free kilometres a day, with additional distance charged at around 20c a kilometre.

Companies that have 4WDs for hire out of Melbourne include Hertz (☎ 13 3039), Budget (☎ 13 2727), Thrifty (☎ 1300 367 227), Delta (☎ 13 1390) and Off Road Rentals (☎ 9543 7111).

Royal Automobile Club of Victoria (RACV)

The RACV (☎ 13 1955) provides an emergency breakdown service, literature, excellent maps and detailed guides to accommodation. They can advise you on regulations you should be aware of and give general guidelines about buying a car.

There are RACV offices around the state and almost every town has a garage affiliated with the RACV. If you're a member of an organisation such as AAA in the USA or the RAC or AA in the UK, you can use the RACV's facilities. But bring proof of membership with you.

MOTORCYCLE

Motorcycles are a very popular way of getting around. The climate is just about ideal for biking most of the year, though it might not always be dry (bring your rain gear) and winters can get chilly. Favoured motorcycle touring areas include the Great Ocean Rd, the Grampians, the upper reaches of the Murray River (east of Albury-Wodonga – the biker friendly hotel at Tintaldra makes a good base), the Grand Ridge Rd and the south-eastern coast. The wild mountain country north-east of Melbourne offers hidden townships and stunning scenery to those who don't mind gravel roads. For long, empty roads and big skies, put your feet up on the highway pegs and head for the north-west.

If you want to bring your own motorcycle into Australia you'll need a *carnet de passage*, and when you try to sell it here you'll get less than the market price because of bureaucratic problems in registering vehicles without Australian approval markings. Shipping from just about anywhere costs a fair bit, but might be worth looking into if you're serious.

One option is hiring, though there aren't many places where you can do this and it often costs less to hire a car.

Garner's Hire-Bikes (☎ 9326 8676) at 179 Peel St (on the corner of Queensberry St), North Melbourne, Vic 3051, has Victoria's biggest range of trail bikes and large road bikes for rent, with prices from $90/180/450 per day/weekend/week for a Suzuki TS185 trail bike all the way up to $240/440/1120 for a Harley-Davidson Softail Custom. There's a special deal on a Honda CB250, with weekly rentals at $273. Prices include helmet, gloves and jacket, plus insurance and unlimited kilometres. Victorian Motorcycle Hire & Sales (☎ 9817 3206) at 606 High St, East Kew, also has a wide range of bikes for rent.

If you want wheels for more than a few weeks, you might want to look at buying. Newspapers and the lively local motorcycle press have extensive classified advertisement sections where $2500 gets you something that will easily take you around Australia if you know a bit about bikes. But you'll have to sell it again afterwards.

An easier option might be a buy-back arrangement with a large motorcycle dealer (Elizabeth St near Franklin St in Melbourne is a good hunting ground). They're keen to do business, and basic negotiating skills allied with a wad of cash (say, $4000) should secure a good second-hand bike with a written guarantee that they'll buy it back in good condition minus 25% to 50% after your three month tour. Shop around. Popular models for this sort of thing are large-capacity, shaft-driven Japanese bikes, BMWs (cheap ones) and even Harley-Davidsons (very popular in Australia). Few dealers are interested in buy-backs on trail bikes.

You'll need a rider's licence and a helmet. During summer, beware of dehydration in the dry, hot air – force yourself to drink plenty of water, even if you don't feel thirsty.

The roo bars (outsize bumpers) on interstate trucks and many country cars should be a warning never to ride at night, or in the early morning and evening. Marsupials are nocturnal, sleeping in the shade during the day and feeding at night, and road ditches provide luscious grass for them to eat. Cows and sheep can also stray onto the roads at night.

It's worth carrying some spares and tools even if you don't know how to use them, because someone else often does. Ask the bike shop if you're not sure.

Be sure to carry water when heading off the beaten track. And finally, if something does go hopelessly wrong in a remote area, park your bike where it's clearly visible and observe the cardinal rule: don't leave your vehicle. Someone always comes along eventually.

If you're a reasonably competent off-road rider, you could consider one of the packages offered by Australian Trail Bike Tours (☎ 9842 4831), 134 Tunstall Rd, Donvale, Vic 3111. Tours include accommodation, food and backup, take two to five days ($160 to $495), and traverse some of the most spectacular tracks and fire trails of the High Country or Sunset Country depending on the season. Bikes (Yamaha TT250/350) are available for $130 a day.

BICYCLE

Victoria is a great place for cycling. There are bike tracks in Melbourne, and in the country you'll find thousands of kilometres of good roads that carry so little traffic that the biggest hassle is waving back to the drivers. Especially appealing is that in some areas you'll ride a very long way without encountering a hill. If you're silly enough to *like* hills, the High Country in summer will be paradise. See the section on Cycling in the Activities chapter for further information and for details on renting cycles.

HITCHING

Hitching is never entirely safe in any country, and we don't recommend it. Travellers who decide to hitch should understand that they are taking a small but potentially serious risk. Before deciding to hitch, talk to local people about the dangers, and it is a good idea to let someone know where you are planning to hitch to before you set off.

Successful hitching depends on several factors. Factor one is numbers. More than two people hitching together will make things very difficult, and solo hitching is unwise for men as well as women. Two women hitching together may be vulnerable, and two men hitching together can expect long waits. The best option is for a woman and a man to hitch together.

Factor two is position: look for a place where vehicles will be going slowly and where they can stop easily. The ideal location is on the outskirts of a town – hitching from way out in the country is as hopeless as from the centre of a city. Take a bus to the edge of town.

Factor three is appearance. The ideal appearance for hitching is a sort of genteel poverty – threadbare but clean. Looking too good can be as much of a bummer as looking too bad! Don't carry too much gear – if it looks like it's going to take half an hour to pack your bags aboard you'll be left on the roadside.

Factor four is knowing when to say no. Saying no to a car-load of drunks is pretty obvious, but you should also be prepared to abandon a ride if you begin to feel uneasy for any reason. Don't sit there hoping for the best: make an excuse and get out at the first opportunity.

It can be time-saving to say no to a short ride that might take you from a good hitching point to a lousy one. Wait for the right, long ride to come along. On a long haul it's pointless to start walking, as it's not likely to increase the likelihood of you getting a lift and it's often an awfully long way to the next town.

Trucks are often the best lifts but they will only stop if they are going slowly and can get started easily again. Thus the ideal place is at the top of a hill where they have a downhill run.

If you're visiting from abroad, a prominent flag on your pack will help, and a sign announcing your destination can also be useful. University and hostel notice boards are good places to look for hitching partners. The main law against hitching is 'thou shalt not stand in the road' – so when you see the law coming, step back.

Just as hitchers should be wary when accepting lifts, drivers who pick up fellow travellers to share the costs should also be aware of the possible risks involved.

BOAT

A couple of companies run ferry trips across the bay from Melbourne to the seaside suburbs of Williamstown and St Kilda. See Getting Around in the Melbourne chapter. A useful car and passenger ferry travels across the mouth of the bay between Sorrento and Queenscliff. See the appropriate sections in the Around Melbourne chapter.

ORGANISED TOURS

There are all sorts of tours around Victoria, though few cover the whole state in any sort of detail. Most are connected with a particular activity (eg bushwalking or horse riding tours) or area (eg the Great Ocean Rd or Phillip Island). If you're on the lookout for tours, the YHA or hostel notice boards are good sources of information.

Various companies offer conventional bus tours to the most popular tourist destinations outside of Melbourne – Sovereign Hill, Healesville Sanctuary, the Great Ocean Rd, Phillip Island etc. V/Line has some packages that might be useful if you don't have transport. They range from Day Tripper day tours from Melbourne to destinations such as Ballarat and Bendigo, to two-night Victorian Breakaways with accommodation packages.

Book these on ☎ 1800 811 452 (toll-free). The fairly hectic but interesting Around the Bay in a Day trip is worth considering – see the boxed text in the Around Melbourne chapter.

Steamrail Victoria (☎ 9397 1953, srv@railpage.org.au) started out as a bunch of railway enthusiasts indulging their hobby, and has grown to be a fairly large organisation with a range of old engines and carriages. They have regular day trips from Melbourne and longer outings as far afield as Mildura, with accommodation packages.

Several operators offer bus tours for backpackers and hostellers. Well-known outfits include Mac's Backpacker Bus (☎ 5241 3180) and Autopia Tours (☎ 9326 5536).

If you're travelling between Melbourne and either Sydney or Adelaide and want to see (and maybe stop over in) some of the best parts of Victoria along the way, there are some interesting alternatives to travelling with V/Line or the major bus companies. See the Bus section in the Getting There & Away chapter for details.

There is a wide range of activity-based tours, and some interesting smaller operators. Echidna Walkabout (☎ 9646 8249) runs day trips with bushwalking, wildlife watching and an introduction to Aboriginal culture ($95 or less), as well as trips to the Grampians, the Great Ocean Rd and the national parks of East Gippsland. Wild-Life Tours (☎ 5439 5086) is another small company doing the Great Ocean Rd and the Grampians, with the emphasis on wildlife. They also run between Melbourne and Adelaide. Another outfit that gets good feedback is Eco Adventure Tours (☎ 5962 5115), which began offering wildlife tours of the Healesville area but now travels farther afield.

Sunset 4WD Tours (☎ 5023 1047) runs 4WD tours of the Murray-Sunset, Wyperfeld, Big Desert and Hattah-Kulkyne national parks, with day trips (around $70 per person, $200 minimum) and longer adventures by arrangement. Great Ocean Rd Adventure Tours (☎ 5289 6841), based at Aireys Inlet, offers a wide range of tours (walking, mountain biking, canoeing) around the Great Ocean Rd and through the Otway Ranges, with prices starting around $30.

Bogong Jack Adventures (☎ 08-8383 7198) has a wide range of cycling, bushwalking and skiing tours through the Victorian Alps and wine regions, involving either camping or other accommodation and various levels of skill and fitness.

During summer, Walkabout Gourmet Adventures (☎ 5159 6556), based at Dinner Plain in the High Country, has a five day Alpine Gourmet Walkabout tour – the cost of $865 includes accommodation, all meals, walks and use of mountain bikes.

If you look in the *Yellow Pages* under 'Adventure Tours & Holidays' you'll find a variety of companies and travel agents catering to all sorts of tastes. They include Outdoor Travel (☎ 9670 7252), which organises things like adventure weekends in the High Country, skiing, hang-gliding, ballooning, rock climbing and bushwalking trips.

There are many other tours on offer. See the Activities chapter and the various chapters throughout this book for some more suggestions.

Melbourne

HISTORY

Melbourne, Australia's second-largest city, was founded and experienced its greatest period of development during the reign of Queen Victoria (1837 to 1901), and the city is in many ways a product of its formative era, both architecturally and socially. It's a traditionally conservative city of elaborate Victorian-era buildings, gracious parks and gardens, and tree-lined boulevards.

The first European settlers only arrived in 1835, but within just 50 years Melbourne had been transformed from a small village into a major city, and it remains the youngest city of its size in the world. In 1885, English journalist George Sala described Melbourne as:

> ...marvellous not merely for its civilisation and its wealth and vigour, but above all for its precocious growth.

The first European settlement was established on Port Phillip Bay at Sorrento in 1803, although within a year it was abandoned and the settlers moved down to Tasmania. In 1835 a group of Tasmanian entrepreneurs returned and established a permanent settlement near the site of today's city centre.

In 1851 the colony of Victoria became independent from New South Wales, and almost immediately the small town of Melbourne became the centre for Australia's biggest and most prolonged gold rush. The immense wealth from the goldfields was used to build a solid and substantial city that came to be known as 'Marvellous Melbourne'. This period of great prosperity lasted until the end of the 1880s, when the collapse of the property market led to a severe depression. See the Facts About Victoria chapter for more details about the history of Melbourne.

In the years since WWII, Melbourne's social fabric has been greatly enriched by an influx of people and cultures from around the world. Several building booms, most notably

HIGHLIGHTS

- A picnic on the lakeside lawns at the Royal Botanic Gardens
- Parks and boulevards full of elm trees, most free of Dutch elm disease
- Melbourne's trams
- The St Kilda to Williamstown ferry
- Boxing Day at the Test cricket match at the MCG
- Cycling, strolling, running or in-line skating along the foreshore between St Kilda and Albert Park
- Devonshire tea at the Studley Park or the Fairfield Boathouse, followed by a paddle along the Yarra River
- Cult movies at the old Astor cinema in St Kilda
- Sunday yum cha in Chinatown
- The delis at the Prahran Market
- Footy at the 'G' (the MCG)
- Riding along the Yarra's bike paths
- A beer, a band and a bite at the Espy (St Kilda's Esplanade Hotel)
- Affordable opera at the Concert Hall
- Exploring central Melbourne's lanes and arcades

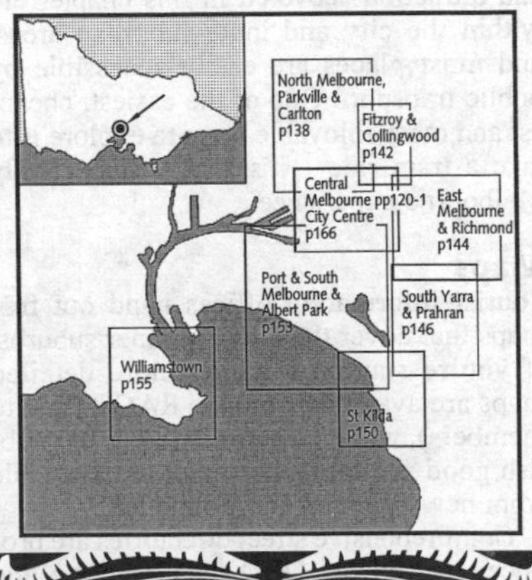

that of the 1980s, have altered the city physically so that it is now a striking blend of past and present, with ornate 19th century buildings sitting alongside towering skyscrapers.

Today Melbourne is perhaps best-known for its trams, its cafes and restaurants, the diversity of its inner-suburban 'villages', and events such as the Melbourne Cup and the International Festival of the Arts. It's a vibrant, multicultural city which is characterised by its people rather than any geographical feature. It combines a passion for the arts with an equally healthy passion for sports, food and wine, and 'the good life'.

Melbourne may lack the physical impact of its more flamboyant northern sister and take a little more time to get to know, but it has much to offer. After all, why else would Lonely Planet, with an entire world to choose from, be based here?

ORIENTATION

Melbourne's suburbs sprawl around the shores of Port Phillip, with the city centre on the north bank of the Yarra River, about 5km inland from the bay. The inner suburbs that surround the city centre (known as the CBD – central business district) are often likened to a ring of 'villages', each with its own particular character. If you want to get a true feel for Melbourne you'll need to venture beyond the city centre. Most of the places and attractions covered in this chapter are within the city and inner-suburban areas, and most places are easily accessible by public transport. One of the easiest, cheapest and most enjoyable ways to explore is to take a tram ride – it's also a distinctively Melbourne experience.

Maps

Tourist information offices hand out free maps that cover the city and inner suburbs. If you're staying a while, more detailed maps are available from the RACV (free to members), while companies like UBD publish good pocket maps which are available from newsagencies for around $5.

Comprehensive street directories are produced by Melway, UBD and Gregory's, and are available at bookshops and newsagents. The best option for travellers is probably the *Compact Gregory's* (around $15). The Melway street directory (around $38) is such a Melbourne institution that places are often located by simply stating the relevant Melway page and grid reference.

Map Land (see the Bookshops entry later) has a comprehensive range of maps.

City Centre

Since its founding the CBD has been bordered by the Yarra River to the south, the Fitzroy Gardens to the east, Victoria St to the north and Spencer St to the west. However, the huge Docklands project is considerably extending the western border, Federation Square is changing the eastern border and Southgate has finally helped the city across the river. See the New Melbourne section following.

Back in 1837, the city was laid out in a geometric grid one mile (1.61km) long and half a mile (805m) wide. It was known as the Golden Mile. The main streets running east-west are Collins and Bourke Sts, crossed by Swanston and Elizabeth Sts.

If you're arriving in Melbourne by long-distance bus or on the airport bus, you'll arrive in the city at either the Spencer St coach terminal on the west side of town (V/Line, Skybus, Firefly and McCafferty's buses) or the Melbourne Transit Centre at 58 Franklin St (Greyhound Pioneer Australia and Skybus buses) on the northern edge of the city centre.

The heart of the CBD is the Bourke St Mall, between Swanston and Elizabeth Sts. On the mall you'll find a tourist information booth, the Myer and David Jones department stores, and, on the corner of Bourke and Elizabeth Sts, the General Post Office (GPO).

Swanston St, running north-south through the city, was a pedestrian mall for a few years, but the city council has decided to reopen it to traffic. After crossing the Yarra River, Swanston St becomes St Kilda Rd, a tree-lined boulevard running all the way south to St Kilda and beyond.

Beside the river, on the corner of Swanston and Flinders Sts, is Flinders St train station, the main station for suburban trains. 'Under the clocks' at the station is a popular meeting place. The other major station, for country to interstate services, is Spencer St station, at the western end of Bourke St.

The New Melbourne Two huge projects are radically changing the shape of central Melbourne. At the eastern end, **Federation Square** and associated projects are reducing the Jolimont railyards which used to separate this end of the CBD from the river. Exhibition St is being extended and an eight hectare riverside park is being built.

At the western end of the city the gigantic **Docklands** project is grafting a big new inner suburb onto the CBD. The city's whole focus is changing, with the river suddenly becoming more important, after 150 years of neglect. The Docklands precinct is larger in area than the current city centre and will have 7km of river frontage. As well as office, residential, entertainment and commercial areas, it will include some 'gee whizz' features, such as a theme amusement park and a state-of-the-art stadium. The Colonial Stadium was nearly finished at the time of writing but the rest of the development will be longer in coming.

As with all major projects there is controversy. Docklands won't be a gated suburb, but it will be something of an upper-income ghetto. The stadium won't be large enough to hold the crowds that attend many football games, and to the relief of some, a proposal to build the world's tallest building, was scrapped when the developers failed to reach agreement with authorities. And as a tourist attraction, how many people make travel plans specifically to visit the current tallest building in the world? Quick – where *is* the current tallest building, and what is it called? (The answer is in the Rialto Towers Observation Deck section later in this chapter.)

Docklands will be served by train and tram, and there are proposals for ferry links to the city and some bayside suburbs.

A third, and equally controversial, giant project – CityLink – is changing the way Melbournians move around their city. See the Getting Around section later in this chapter for details of a tollway with no toll booths but big fines for not paying the toll.

Inner Suburbs

Each of the inner suburbs that encircle the city centre has its own personality, although all grew up during Melbourne's 19th century boom and are full of Victorian architecture. They were also the first home of many of the successive waves of immigrants.

To the north are North Melbourne and Carlton, the latter the first home of Melbourne's Italian community and Melbourne University. East of Carlton (and north-east of the city) is the bohemian suburb of Fitzroy, once the poorest area in the country but now Melbourne's arty alternative-lifestyle centre. East from Fitzroy is Collingwood, becoming trendy but still a recognisably working-class area where a large immigrant population rubs shoulders with old-time Aussies (and old-time immigrants).

East of the city, Richmond was once solidly Greek but is now dominated by the local Vietnamese community, while to the south-east (and across the river) is stylish South Yarra with its up-market fashion boutiques and restaurants.

South of the city is South Melbourne, Albert Park and other small bayside suburbs leading down to St Kilda, which has long been Melbourne's most diverse and permissive area. Soaring real estate prices and middle-class mores are driving out the more colourful residents, but there's still a hint of sin. Williamstown, south-west of the city at the mouth of the Yarra River, is a charming seaside suburb with a historic maritime flavour.

Greater Melbourne

The Yarra River wends its way through Melbourne from the Upper Yarra Reservoir (about 90km east of the city centre) to the head of the bay. The river divides the city in

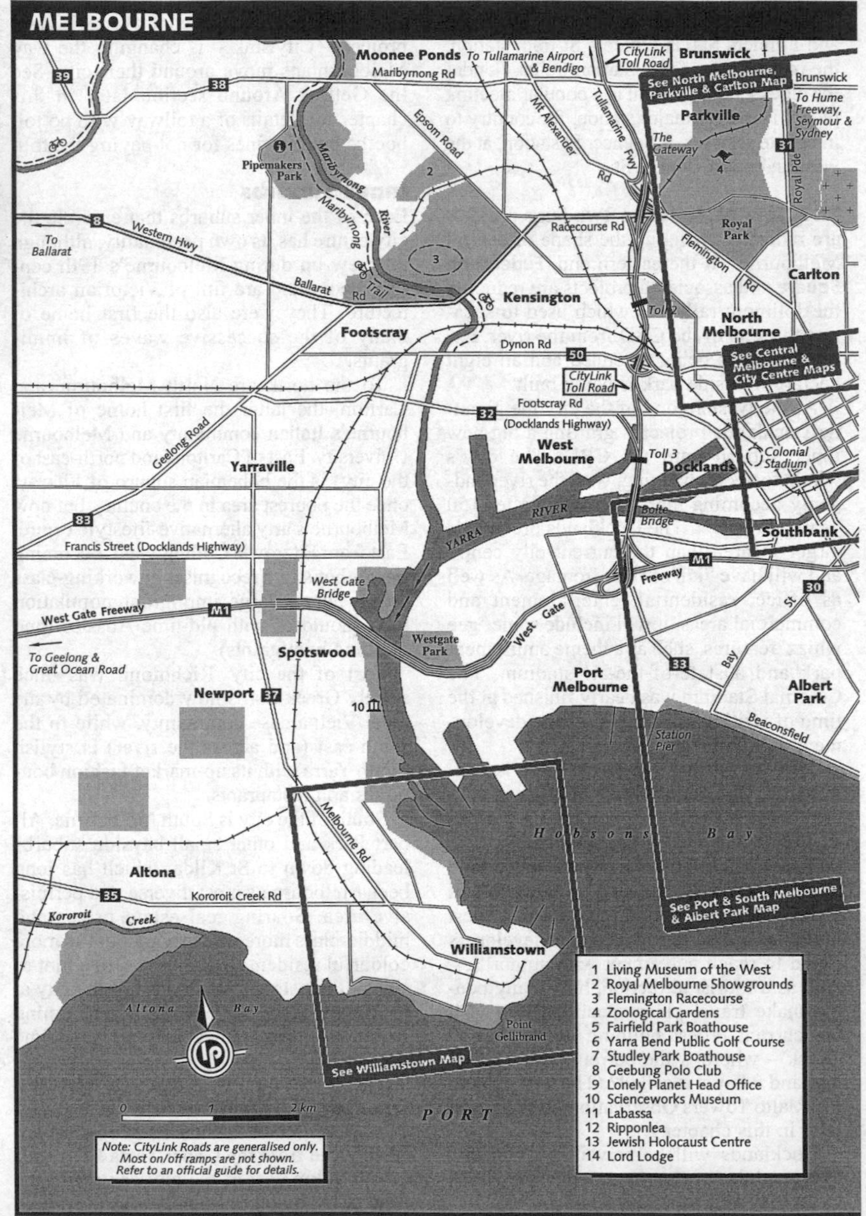
MELBOURNE
Moonee Ponds
To Tullamarine Airport & Bendigo
CityLink Toll Road
Brunswick
See North Melbourne, Parkville & Carlton Map
Brunswick
To Hume Freeway, Seymour & Sydney
Maribyrnong Rd
Epsom Road
Mt Alexander Rd
Tullamarine Fwy
Parkville
The Gateway
Royal Pde
Pipemakers Park
Maribyrnong River
Maribyrnong Trail
To Ballarat
Western Hwy
Racecourse Rd
Royal Park
Flemington Rd
Carlton
Ballarat Rd
Kensington
Toll 2
North Melbourne
Footscray
Dynon Rd
See Central Melbourne & City Centre Maps
CityLink Toll Road
Footscray Rd
(Docklands Highway)
Geelong Road
West Melbourne
Yarraville
Toll 3
Docklands
Colonial Stadium
Yarra River
Bolte Bridge
Southbank
Francis Street (Docklands Highway)
Freeway
West Gate Bridge
West Gate Freeway
West Gate
Bay St
To Geelong & Great Ocean Road
Westgate Park
Spotswood
Port Melbourne
Albert Park
Newport
Beaconsfield
Station Pier
Melbourne Rd
Hobsons Bay
Altona
Kororoit Creek Rd
Kororoit Creek
See Port & South Melbourne & Albert Park Map
Williamstown
Altona Bay
Point Gellibrand
See Williamstown Map
0 1 2 km
PORT
Note: CityLink Roads are generalised only. Most on/off ramps are not shown. Refer to an official guide for details.
1 Living Museum of the West
2 Royal Melbourne Showgrounds
3 Flemington Racecourse
4 Zoological Gardens
5 Fairfield Park Boathouse
6 Yarra Bend Public Golf Course
7 Studley Park Boathouse
8 Geebung Polo Club
9 Lonely Planet Head Office
10 Scienceworks Museum
11 Labassa
12 Ripponlea
13 Jewish Holocaust Centre
14 Lord Lodge

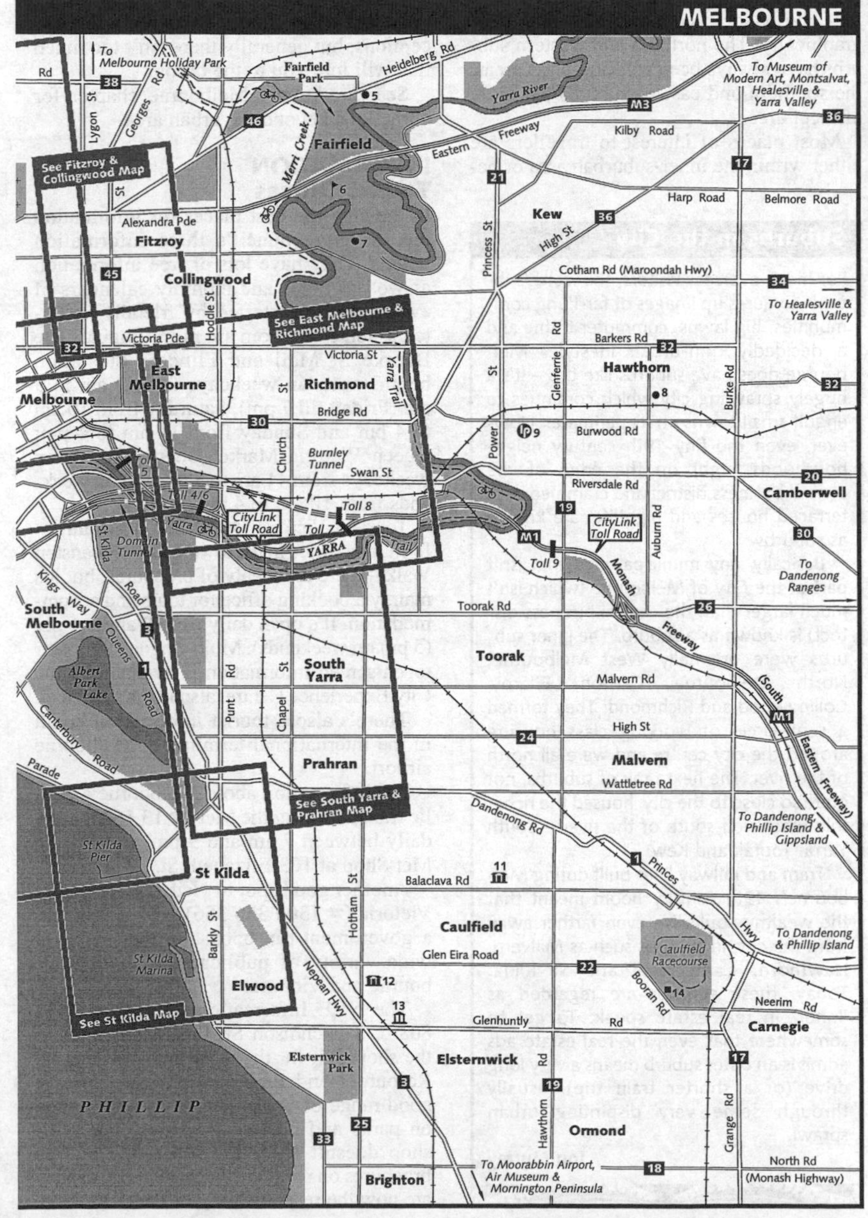
MELBOURNE
To Melbourne Holiday Park
Fairfield Park
Heidelberg Rd
Yarra River
To Museum of Modern Art, Montsalvat, Healesville & Yarra Valley
Merri Creek
Fairfield
Eastern Freeway
Kilby Road
See Fitzroy & Collingwood Map
Lygon St
Georges Rd
Alexandra Pde
Fitzroy
Collingwood
Harp Road
Belmore Road
Kew
High St
Princess St
Cotham Rd (Maroondah Hwy)
To Healesville & Yarra Valley
See East Melbourne & Richmond Map
Victoria Pde
Hoddle St
Victoria St
Yarra Trail
East Melbourne
Richmond
Melbourne
Barkers Rd
Hawthorn
Glenferrie Rd
Burke Rd
Bridge Rd
Burwood Rd
Power St
Church St
Burnley Tunnel
Swan St
Riversdale Rd
Camberwell
Toll 4/6
Toll 5
Toll 8
Toll 7
Toll 9
CityLink Toll Road
YARRA
Domain Tunnel
St Kilda Road
Auburn Rd
To Dandenong Ranges
Kings Way
South Melbourne
Queens Road
Toorak Rd
Monash Freeway
Toorak
Albert Park Lake
South Yarra
Malvern Rd
Punt Rd
Chapel St
(South Eastern Freeway)
High St
Canterbury Road
Parade
Prahran
Malvern
Wattletree Rd
See South Yarra & Prahran Map
Dandenong Rd
To Dandenong, Phillip Island & Gippsland
St Kilda Pier
St Kilda
Princes Hwy
Balaclava Rd
Hotham St
Caulfield
To Dandenong & Phillip Island
Barkly St
Glen Eira Road
Caulfield Racecourse
St Kilda Marina
Nepean Hwy
Elwood
Booran Rd
Neerim Rd
See St Kilda Map
Glenhuntly Rd
Carnegie
Elsternwick Park
Elsternwick
Hawthorn Rd
Grange Rd
PHILLIP
Ormond
North Rd (Monash Highway)
To Moorabbin Airport, Air Museum & Mornington Peninsula
Brighton

half, both socio-economically and geographically. The northern and western suburbs have always been working-class areas, the southern and eastern suburbs the more affluent areas.

Most places of interest to travellers are either within the inner-suburban area or beyond the urban fringe. There are a few exceptions, but generally there isn't too much that will lure you to the burbs.

See the Around Melbourne chapter for attractions beyond the urban area.

Suburbs in the City

For many overseas visitors, the word 'suburbs' conjures up images of far-flung communities, big lawns, commuter traffic and a decidedly non-urban lifestyle. Melbourne does have suburbs like this – it's a hugely sprawling city which continues to engulf small towns on its perimeter. However, even the tiny 19th century neighbourhoods, right on the edge of the central business district and crammed with terraced houses and nightlife, are known as suburbs.

Basically, any municipal area that isn't part of the City of Melbourne (which isn't much larger than the central business district) is known as a suburb. The inner suburbs were originally West Melbourne, North Melbourne, Carlton, Fitzroy, Collingwood and Richmond. They formed a semi-circle of working class housing around the city centre and were all north of the river. The next rank of suburbs, not quite so close to the city, housed the richer folk who lived south of the river – South Yarra, Toorak and Kew.

Tram and railway lines built during Melbourne's 19th century boom meant that the wealthy could live even farther away from the city, in suburbs such as Malvern, Hawthorn, Camberwell and St Kilda. Today, these suburbs are regarded as 'inner' in real estate speak. To get to somewhere that even the real estate ads admit is an outer suburb means a very long drive (or a shorter train trip), usually through some very dispiriting urban sprawl.

Jon Murray

INFORMATION

Tourist Offices

In the city, the best places for information are the city council's three information booths. They have lots of free information as well as maps and monthly calendars of events, and are staffed by friendly volunteers, some of whom are multi-lingual. The Bourke St Mall and Flinders St station booths open on weekdays from 9 am to 5 pm (Friday till 7 pm), Saturday from 10 am to 4 pm and Sunday from 11 am to 4 pm; Queen Victoria Market Booth is open on weekdays from 11 am to 5 pm and on weekends from 10 am to 4 pm.

Tourism Victoria (☎ 13 2842) has an information office in the town hall on Swanston Walk – there are plenty of brochures, but it's mainly a booking office for tours and accommodation. It's open daily from 9 am to 6 pm (5 pm on weekends). Multi-lingual computer touch-screen information is available at the City Experience Centre, also in the town hall.

There's also a tourist information booth in the international terminal at Melbourne airport.

For information about Melbourne's public transport, ring the Met (☎ 13 1638, open daily between 7 am and 9 pm) or visit the Met Shop at 103 Elizabeth St.

Another good spot to visit is Information Victoria (☎ 1300 366 356), 356 Collins St, a government-run bookshop that stocks a wide variety of publications about Melbourne and Victoria.

The NRE Information Centre (☎ 9637 8080), 8 Nicholson St, East Melbourne, is the shopfront for the department of Natural Resources and Environment and carries a good range of books and other information on parks and outdoor activities. The NRE shop doesn't carry the full range of free brochures on national and state parks, as they are now the responsibility of Parks Victoria.

Parks Victoria doesn't have a shopfront but it does have an informative web site (www.parks.vic.gov.au) and a telephone information service (☎ 13 1963) which will mail brochures to you.

Free Publications There are a number of free information guides, most of which are available from the tourist offices and the Royal Automobile Club of Victoria (RACV). They include booklets such as *This Week in Melbourne* and *Melbourne Events*, which have handy 'what's on' listings.

The best give-aways are those produced by Tourism Victoria. Their *Melbourne & Surrounds Official Visitors' Guide* has all sorts of helpful information, including a calendar of events, transport maps, attraction and accommodation listings, and a useful information section at the back. They also produce excellent glossy regional guides to Victoria.

It's worth picking up a copy of the Victorian edition of *For Backpackers by Backpackers* or *TNT*, small magazines that list cheap accommodation and eateries, attractions and events. They are available free from hostels and info centres.

See the Entertainment section for details of free entertainment magazines.

Money

See the section on Exchanging Money in the Facts for the Visitor chapter for details about banks and exchanges in Melbourne.

Post

The GPO, on the corner of Bourke and Elizabeth Sts, is open from 8 am to 6 pm on weekdays, and on Saturday (for stamp sales only) from 10 am to 1 pm. There's an efficient poste restante section. The National Philatelic Centre and post office, on the corner of Latrobe and Exhibition Sts in the city, is also open on Saturday from 10 am to 5 pm, as well as Sunday from noon to 5 pm.

Telephone

There are telephone booths all over the city, including those at the GPO and just behind the GPO on Little Bourke St. There's also a Telstra Centre with phones and phonecard machines for international calls at 94 Elizabeth St; it's open daily from 6 am to midnight.

The STD telephone area code for Melbourne, most of Victoria and Tasmania is 03. Omit the 0 if dialling from overseas.

There are a few call centres offering discount long-distance and international calls, including Global Gossip (☎ 9663 0511), 440 Elizabeth St, open daily between 8 am and midnight, and 24-hours around Christmas.

Email & Internet Access

Internet cafes come and go rapidly. Current places include: Cosmos Internet Services, Level 1, 247 Flinders Lane; Melbourne Central Internet Cafe, Level 2, Melbourne Central; the Binary Bar, 243 Brunswick St, Fitzroy (5 pm to 1 am daily); Cafe Wired, 363 Clarendon St, South Melbourne; and Internet Cafe St Kilda, 9 Grey St, St Kilda. Global Gossip (see Post and Communications earlier) also has Internet access.

Travel Agencies

There are some backpacker-oriented travel agencies that offer information on tours and activities, plus many brochures. They include Backpackers Travel Centre (☎ 9654 8477), Shop 19 Centre Place, 258 Flinders Lane; Backpackers World (☎ 9329 1990), 167 Franklin St; Travellers Contact Point (☎ 9642 2911), 29 Somerset Place (off Little Bourke St); and YHA Travel (☎ 6970 7991), 205 King St.

Bookshops

The largest bookshop chains include Angus & Robertson Bookworld, at 107 Elizabeth St; Collins Booksellers, at 115 Elizabeth St; and Dymocks, in Melbourne Central. They all have several other city shops and suburban branches, and carry a broad range of books. The major department stores also have comprehensive book sections.

Melbourne is blessed with excellent independent booksellers. Map Land, 372 Little Bourke St has the city's most extensive range of travel books and maps, as well as travel accessories. McGills, 187 Elizabeth St (opposite the GPO), is good for interstate and overseas newspapers and magazines, as well as general and technical books.

Other good city bookshops include: Hill of Content, 86 Bourke St; the Paperback, 60 Bourke St; the ABC Shop, in the Galleria on the corner of Elizabeth and Bourke Sts; the Technical Book Shop, 295 Swanston St (good for technical and specialist books); Mary Martin, in Australia on Collins, 260 Collins St, and across the river at Southgate and; Webers, 1st Floor, 423 Little Collins St.

Collected Works, 1st Floor, Flinders Way Arcade, sells mainly poetry. The Foreign Language Bookshop, downstairs at 259 Collins St, has a wide selection of dictionaries, grammar books and cassette tapes. The Little Bookroom, 185 Elizabeth St, is a long-established children's bookshop.

Hares & Hyenas is an excellent gay and lesbian bookshop with branches at 135 Commercial Rd, Prahran and 100 Smith St, Collingwood.

The NRE Information Centre, 8 Nicholson St, East Melbourne, has an excellent range of maps, books and posters on Victoria's national parks and wilderness areas.

The National Gallery Bookshop has an excellent range of art and Australiana books.

Outside the city centre, other recommended bookshops include:

Albert Park
- The Avenue Bookstore, 127 Dundas Place

Carlton
- Readings, 338 Lygon St

Fitzroy
- Brunswick St Bookstore, 305 Brunswick St
- Shrew Women's Bookshop, 37 Gertrude St

Prahran
- Greville St Bookstore, 145 Greville St
- Kill City, 126 Greville St (crime fiction specialist)

St Kilda
- Chronicles Bookshop, 91 Fitzroy St
- Cosmos Books & Music, 112 Acland St

South Melbourne
- Emerald Hill Bookshop, 336 Clarendon St

South Yarra
- Black Mask, 78 Toorak Rd
- Readings, 153 Toorak Rd

There are also some excellent second-hand bookshops. At Alice's Bookshop, 629 Rathdowne St in Carlton, you'll find a collection of early editions of *Alice in Wonderland* among others. The Grub St Bookshop at 317 Brunswick St in Fitzroy is also well worth a browse, as is Pig's Wings at 53 Barry St in South Yarra. Kay Craddock's, 156 Collins St, is a good antiquarian bookshop.

Laundry

Most accommodation places provide laundry facilities for their guests. There are no self-service laundries in the city centre, but there are quite a few in the inner suburbs. They include the City Edge Laundry at 39 Errol St in North Melbourne (opposite the Town Hall) and the St Kilda Beach Laundrette at 7 Carlisle St in St Kilda. Others are listed in the *Yellow Pages* phone book under 'Laundries – Self-Service'.

Left Luggage

There are luggage lockers on the ground and 1st floors of the international terminal at Melbourne airport, which cost $4 a day.

In the basement at Spencer St train station, left-luggage lockers cost $2 per day and the cloakroom costs $3.60 per item per day. There are also left-luggage facilities at the Elizabeth St entrance of Flinders St train station.

Medical Services

The Traveller's Medical and Vaccination Centre (TMVC; ☎ 9602 5788), Level 2, 393 Little Bourke St in the city, is open weekdays from 9 am to 5 pm (Monday, Tuesday and Thursday till 8.30 pm) and Saturday from 9 am to 1 pm. It has excellent information on the latest vaccinations needed for most countries. Appointments are necessary. There's another TMVC clinic in the private wing of the Royal Melbourne Hospital (enter from Royal Pde), open from 9 am to 5 pm on weekdays (to 8 pm on Wednesday).

The Melbourne Sexual Health Centre (☎ 9347 0244), 580 Swanston St, Carlton, provides free checkups and other medical services. Appointments are preferred.

The Victorian AIDS Council & Gay Men's Health Centre (☎ 9865 6700), 6 Claremont St, South Yarra, provides education, information and support for AIDS sufferers and operates a health centre.

Major public hospitals close to the city centre are:

The Alfred
(☎ 9276 2000) Commercial Rd, Prahran
Royal Children's
(☎ 9345 5522) Flemington Rd, Parkville
Royal Melbourne
(☎ 9342 7000) Grattan St, Parkville
Royal Women's
(☎ 9344 2000) 132 Grattan St, Carlton
St Vincent's
(☎ 9288 2211) 41 Victoria Pde, Fitzroy

Emergency

Phone ☎ 000 for emergency help from the police, ambulance or fire brigade. In the city centre, there's a 24-hour police station at 637 Flinders St (near Spencer St).

On the 2nd floor at 169 Swanston St in the city, the Travellers' Aid Support Centre (☎ 9654 2600) offers assistance for stranded travellers, information, advice, showers, toilets and, if you're in need, a cup of coffee and a sandwich. There's a youth worker on staff, and also support services for disabled, handicapped and aged people. The service is free, and is open on weekdays from 8 am to 5 pm and Saturday from 10 am to 4 pm.

Some other useful addresses and numbers include:

Chemist
Tambassis Pharmacy (☎ 9387 8830), corner of Sydney and Brunswick Rds, Brunswick (24 hours)
Leonard Long Pharmacy (☎ 9510 3977), corner of Williams Rd and High St, Prahran (8 am to midnight)
Dentist
Dental Emergency Service (☎ 9341 0222)
Interpreter Service
Translating and Interpreting Service, 24 hours (☎ 13 1450)
Personal Crisis
Crisis Line (24 hour telephone counselling) (☎ 9329 0300)
Lifeline Counselling (24 hours, six languages) (☎ 13 1114)
Automotive Breakdown
Accident Towing Service (☎ 13 1176)
RACV Emergency Roadside Service (☎ 13 1111)
Poisons
Poisons Information Centre (☎ 13 1126)

WALKING TOUR

The following walking tour is a good introduction to the city centre and some of its attractions (although to really get to know Melbourne you'll need to jump on a tram or two and explore beyond the city).

This tour starts at the intersection of Flinders and Swanston Sts, home to three of Melbourne's best-known landmarks. The grand old **Flinders St train station** is the main station for suburban trains. Built in 1899 on the site of Melbourne's first fish market, the station is quite impressive with its domes, towers and rows of clocks, and is splendidly lit at night. Across the road is one of Melbourne's best-known pubs, **Young & Jackson's**, which is famed mainly for the painting of *Chloe* hanging in the upstairs bar. Judged indecent at the Melbourne Exhibition of 1880, she has gone on to win affection among generations of Melbourne drinkers. The third landmark on this corner, **St Paul's Cathedral**, is a masterpiece of Gothic Revivalist architecture, and the interior is particularly noteworthy for its detailed tiled floors, stained-glass windows, restored organ and stonework.

Also on this corner the big new **Federation Square**, with more attractions, was still under construction at the time of writing.

Stroll up Swanston St, which has been closed to cars to create **Swanston Walk**, a tree-lined boulevard which pedestrians share with trams and commercial vehicles. When the trees grow it will be a good addition to Melbourne's swag of boulevards. In the block between Flinders Lane and Collins St is the **City Square**, yet again being redeveloped. Across Collins St is the **Melbourne Town Hall**, built between 1870 and 1880.

Continue up to Bourke St and take a left into the **Bourke St Mall**. Like Swanston Walk, it's difficult for a pedestrian mall to

CENTRAL MELBOURNE

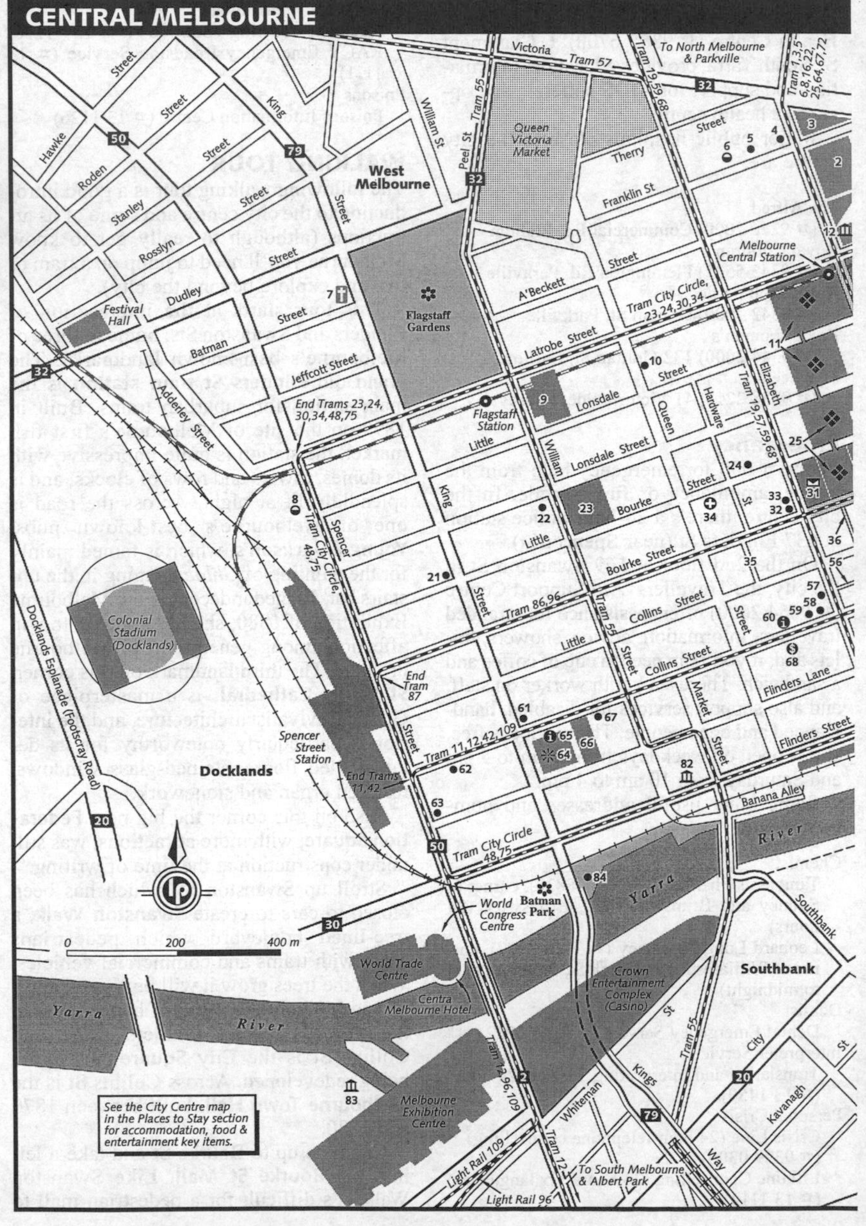

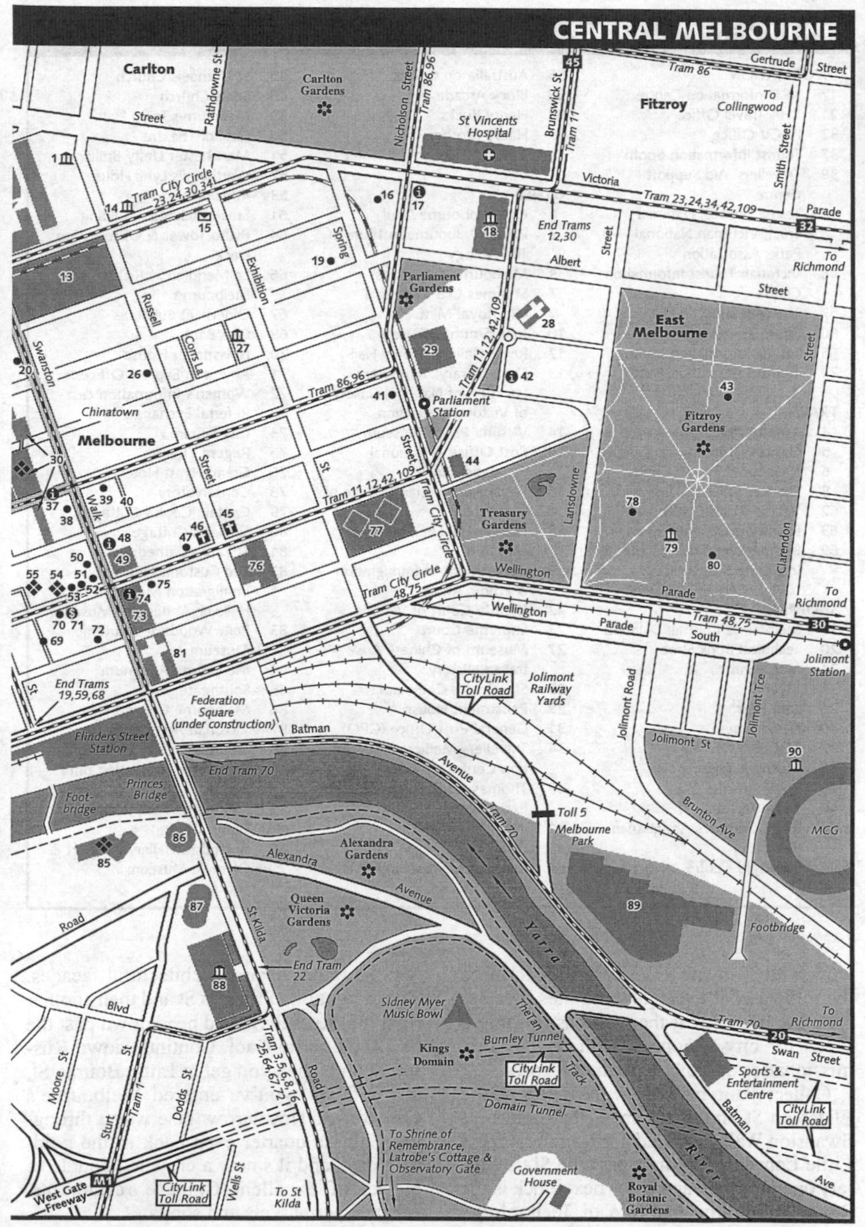
CENTRAL MELBOURNE
Carlton
Rathdowne St
Carlton Gardens
Nicholson Street
Tram 86,96
St Vincents Hospital
Brunswick St
Tram 11
Gertrude
Street
Tram 86
Fitzroy
To Collingwood
Smith Street
Street
Victoria
Tram 23,24,34,42,109
Parade
Tram City Circle 23,24,30,34
Exhibition
Spring
End Trams 12,30
Albert
Street
To Richmond
Street
Parliament Gardens
Russell
Tram 11,12,42,109
East Melbourne
Street
Corrs La
Swanston
Tram 86,96
Parliament Station
Chinatown
Melbourne
Street
St
Street
Tram City Circle
Lansdowne
Fitzroy Gardens
Walk
Tram 11,12,42,109
Treasury Gardens
Clarendon
Wellington
Parade
To Richmond
Tram City Circle 48,75
Wellington
Parade
South
Tram 48,75
Jolimont Station
St
End Trams 19,59,68
CityLink Toll Road
Jolimont Railway Yards
Federation Square (under construction)
Batman
Jolimont Road
Jolimont Tce
Jolimont St
Flinders Street Station
End Tram 70
Avenue
Princes Bridge
Foot-bridge
Tram 70
Toll 5
Melbourne Park
Brunton Ave
MCG
Alexandra
Alexandra Gardens
Avenue
Queen Victoria Gardens
Road
St Kilda
Yarra
Footbridge
End Tram 22
Blvd
Sidney Myer Music Bowl
Tram 3,5,6,8,16 25,64,67,72
Tram 70
To Richmond
Swan Street
Burnley Tunnel
Kings Domain
Road
Moore St
St
Tram 1
Dodds St
CityLink Toll Road
Track
Sports & Entertainment Centre
Domain Tunnel
Batman
CityLink Toll Road
Sturt
To Shrine of Remembrance, Latrobe's Cottage & Observatory Gate
Wells St
River
Ave
West Gate Freeway
CityLink Toll Road
To St Kilda
Government House
Royal Botanic Gardens
1
13
14
15
16
17
18
19
20
26
27
28
29
30
37
38
39
40
41
42
43
44
45
46
47
48
49
50
51
52
53
54
55
69
70
71
72
73
74
75
76
77
78
79
80
81
85
86
87
88
89
90
45
32
30
20
M1

CENTRAL MELBOURNE

INFORMATION
17 NRE Information Centre
21 YHA Travel Office
32 RACV Office
37 Tourist Information Booth
38 Travellers' Aid Support Centre
42 Tasma Terrace; National Trust; Victorian National Parks Association
48 Victorian Tourist Information Centre
57 The Met Shop
60 Information Victoria
65 Tourist Information Booth
74 Tourist Information Booth

TRAVEL
4 Ansett Office
5 Qantas Office
6 Melbourne Transit Centre
8 Spencer St Coach Terminal
62 V/Line Travel Centre
63 Bus Booking Centre
69 Backpackers' Travel Centre & Interstate Bus Services

SHOPPING
11 Melbourne Central; Daimaru
20 Technical Book Shop
24 Map Land
25 Myer
26 Sam Bear
30 David Jones
33 McGills
35 McKillop Street
36 Royal Arcade
40 Tivoli Arcade
47 Kay Craddock's Antiquarian Bookseller
54 Sportsgirl Centre
55 Australia on Collins
56 Block Arcade
58 Henry Bucks
59 Hardy Brothers
77 Collins Place; Sofitel Hotel

OTHER
1 Old Melbourne Gaol
2 Royal Melbourne Institute of Technology
3 Melbourne City Baths
7 St James Old Cathedral
9 Old Royal Mint
10 John Smith's House
12 RMIT Gallery; Storey Hall
13 State Library; Temporary Location of National Gallery of Victoria Colllection
14 Victoria Police Museum
15 Post Office & National Philatelic Centre
16 Royal Australasian College of Surgeons
18 Eastern Hill Fire Station & Museum
19 Department of Immigration & Ethnic Affairs
22 County Court of Victoria
23 Supreme Court
27 Museum of Chinese Australian History
28 St Patrick's Cathedral
29 Parliament House
31 General Post Office (GPO)
34 Travellers Medical & Vaccination Centre
39 Thomas Cook Foreign Exchange
41 Windsor Hotel
43 Dolphin Fountain
44 Old Treasury Building
45 St Michaels Church
46 Scots Church
49 Melbourne Town Hall
50 Capitol Theatre
51 Manchester Unity Building
52 Wertheim's Lyric House
53 Kodak House
61 Stock Exchange Building
64 Rialto Tower & Observation Deck
66 Le Meridien at Rialto Melbourne
67 Olderfleet Buildings
68 CBA Bank
70 Newspaper House
71 American Express Office
72 Women's Information & Referral Exchange
73 City Square
75 Regent Theatre
76 Grand Hyatt Hotel
78 Conservatory
79 Captain Cook's Cottage
80 Sinclair's Cottage
81 St Paul's Cathedral
82 Old Customs House; Immigration Museum; Hellenic Antiquities Museum
83 Polly Woodside Maritime Museum
84 Melbourne Aquarium
85 Southgate
86 Melbourne Concert Hall
87 Victorian Arts Centre
88 National Gallery of Victoria (closed for renovation until 2001)
89 Melbourne Park (National Tennis Centre)
90 Australian Gallery of Sport & Olympic Museum

work with 30-tonne trams barrelling through the middle of it every few minutes, but despite the tram threat the mall has become a focus for city shoppers, with its buskers, missionaries and big department stores.

Collect your mail from the GPO at the Elizabeth St end of the mall, then return to Swanston Walk and head north again. Across Little Lonsdale St you'll pass the **State Library** on your right, and in the next block is the **Royal Melbourne Institute of Technology**, with its rather bizarre architectural facades. Take a right into Franklin St and then another right into Russell St, and head down past the **Old Melbourne Gaol**. Continue down Russell St and when you get to Little Bourke St, turn left and you've entered Melbourne's **Chinatown**. This narrow lane was a thronging Chinese quarter even back in the goldrush days and it's now a crowded couple of blocks of excellent Chinese restaurants, Asian supermarkets and shops.

At the top end of Little Bourke St, turn right into Spring St, which has some of Melbourne's most impressive old buildings, including the lovely **Princess Theatre**, the gracious **Windsor Hotel** and the state **Parliament House**. Built with gold-rush wealth, this building served as the national parliament while Canberra was under construction. There are free tours. Farther down Spring St opposite Collins St, the **Old Treasury Building** is one of the finest 19th century buildings in the city. See the later Spring St section for details of both these.

Cross Spring St into Collins St, and on your left you'll see the soaring towers of Collins Place, which house the five-star **Sofitel Hotel**. The hotel's toilets on the 35th floor are well worth a visit – they boast spectacular views over the MCG, parklands and shimmering suburbs of Melbourne, and are one of the city's prime (unofficial) attractions. While you're up there, you could have a drink in the hotel's ritzy Atrium Bar.

Back on ground level, head around to Flinders Lane (south of Collins Place). The **'top end' of Flinders Lane**, between Spring and Swanston Sts, is said to be the closest thing Melbourne has to New York's Soho, and was once the centre of Melbourne's rag trade. It's an interesting area to explore, with numerous art galleries, fashion warehouses and offices, restaurants and cafes.

Continue down Flinders Lane as far as Swanston Walk and take a left. Continue past Flinders St train station, then turn right down the steps just before the river and stroll along the riverside. An arched footbridge takes you across the river to the **Southgate** complex, with its excellent restaurants, bars and cafes. South of Southgate is Melbourne's **Arts Precinct**, and across St Kilda Rd are the parklands of the **Kings Domain** – a marvellous area to wander through and explore, if you still have the energy.

A shorter walk concentrating on the redevelopment along the Yarra begins at the Arts Precinct and follows the river down past the **Casino** to Spencer St. You can cross Spencer St to visit the **Polly Woodside** then backtrack to cross the river and walk back up Flinders St by the river to the corner of Flinders and Swanston Sts.

TRAM TOURS

When you tire of walking, consider buying yourself a Zone 1 daily Met ticket (see the Getting Around section later in this chapter for information about Met tickets) and continuing your exploration of Melbourne by tram. For $4.40, you can spend the entire day travelling around the city and inner suburbs by tram – a bargain, and a great way to get a feel for Melbourne. The same ticket lets you use trains and buses too.

Try a ride on tram No 8. It starts along Swanston St in the city, rolls down St Kilda Rd beside the Kings Domain and continues up Toorak Rd through South Yarra and Toorak. Another popular tram ride is on No 16, which cruises all the way down St Kilda Rd to St Kilda.

Colonial Tramcar Restaurant

Two of Melbourne's most popular attractions are its trams and its restaurants, but when some oddball came up with the idea of combining the two, most people thought it was a weird gimmick that would never last. Well, several years down the track (sorry) the ***Colonial Tramcar Restaurant*** (☎ 9696 4000) is still a huge success with both visitors and locals – a great novelty idea backed up with good food and service. You can dine in comfort while taking a scenic evening tram cruise around Melbourne's streets.

A four-course lunch (1 to 3 pm) costs $65, a three-course early dinner (5.45 to 7.15 pm) costs $55 and a five-course dinner (8.35 to 11 pm) costs $80 or $90 on Friday and Saturday. Drinks are included in the prices.

The tram leaves from stop No 125 on Normanby Rd, near the corner of Clarendon St, South Melbourne.

CITY CENTRE

Swanston St

Swanston St runs through the heart of the city. Formerly a major traffic artery, it was closed to cars to create Swanston Walk, a boulevard lined with trees and street cafes and shared by pedestrians, trams and commercial vehicles. There's still a bit of tackiness about this stretch of Swanston St, and there is talk of reopening it to cars.

On the corner of Swanston and Collins Sts, the **Manchester Unity Building** is easily missed, but if you raise your eyes above street level you'll see a marvellous example of a Gothic 1930s building. One of Melbourne's earliest skyscrapers, it had the city's first escalators, and the original ventilation system was cooled in summer by tons of ice!

Melbourne Town Hall, opposite the Manchester Unity Building, is another fine building. Free tours are held at 10.30 am and 2.30 pm on Tuesday, Wednesday and Thursday but you must book (☎ 9658 9464). Until the Concert Hall, across the river in the Arts Precinct, was built, this was Melbourne's main concert venue.

Opposite Melbourne Town Hall at No 113 is the **Capitol Theatre**, built in 1925-27. Local architect and writer Robin Boyd called the theatre 'possibly the finest picture theatre ever built anywhere'. Unfortunately, the facade was demolished for an arcade 20 years ago, but if you ignore the trashy exterior and wander inside, you'll see what he meant. The ceiling, designed by the team of Marion Mahony Griffin and her husband Walter Burley Griffin (the architects of Canberra), is a kaleidoscopic creation that glitters like illuminated crystals.

On the corner of Swanston and Victoria Sts, the **Melbourne City Baths** were built in 1903, and to quote local architect Dimity Reed, 'the design is a flamboyant but disciplined extravaganza of towers and domes and red-and-white striped brickwork'.

State Library The State Library, with its classical revival facade facing Swanston St, between Little Lonsdale and Latrobe Sts, was built in various stages from 1854. When it was completed in 1913, the reinforced concrete dome over the octagonal **Reading Room** was the largest of its kind in the world. If you want somewhere peaceful to write letters or just contemplate life, the Reading Room is one of the most serene rooms in Melbourne. In 1871, Marcus Clarke wrote much of *For the Term of His Natural Life* in this room. The book is an Australian masterpiece about transportation and the penal system.

The library's collection is notable for its coverage of the humanities and social sciences, as well as art, music, performing arts, Australiana and rare books dating back to a 4000-year-old Mesopotamian tablet. The collection also includes the records from the Burke and Wills expedition, and various interesting items are on display.

The library is open daily from 10 am to 6 pm (9 pm on Monday and Wednesday), with reduced hours in summer. There are free tours at 2 pm on weekdays and on the first and third Saturday of the month.

Museum Victoria Once housed in the State Library building, Museum Victoria has finally outgrown its premises with a massive collection of over 12 million items, gathered since it was founded as the Museum of Natural History in 1854. A new museum is being built, controversially, in the Carlton Gardens by the Exhibition Buildings and will open early in the 21st century.

While cataloguing some of the old crates in the cellar prior to the move, staff were startled to find some birds collected in the Galapagos Islands by Charles Darwin during the momentous voyage of the *Beagle*.

Queen Victoria Women's Centre Housed in the surviving (and renovated) tower of the demolished Queen Victoria Women's Hospital, the centre (☎ 9663 8799) houses exhibition spaces, a cafe, lounge and women's health library. It's on Lonsdale St east of Swanston St and is open on weekdays from 8.30 am to 5.30 pm.

Collins St

Collins St is Melbourne's most elegant streetscape, although much of its original grandeur and history was lost during short-sighted periods of 'development'. Collins St has both a fashionable end and a financial end. The west end (from Elizabeth St to Spencer St) is home to bankers and stockbrokers, while the east or top end is mostly five-star hotels and exclusive boutiques. The top end was once known as the 'Paris End' because it was lined with plane trees, grand buildings and street cafes. The trees remain (and are beautifully lit at night by fairy lights), but many of the finer buildings are gone.

Facing each other on the north-west and north-east corners of Russell and Collins Sts are two of Melbourne's most historic churches, **Scots Church** (1873), No 140, the exterior of which has recently been cleaned, and **St Michael's Church** (1866). **Kay Craddock's Antiquarian Bookshop** at No 156 is a marvellous place for book lovers. The **Athenaeum Theatre**, at No 188, dates back to 1886 and was recently refurbished. There's a general library on the 1st floor which is open to the public. Across the road is the magnificent **Regent Theatre**, reopened with a major restoration after being saved from demolition.

Just across Swanston St, the **Sportsgirl Centre** is one of the city's best shopping centres, with a spacious, well-planned layout and an excellent food court on the 3rd floor.

The section of Collins St between Swanston and Elizabeth Sts contains some interesting examples for students of 1930s architecture, a period in which the emphasis lay more on facades and external ornamentation than on integrated design. Some of the better buildings are the former **Wertheim's Lyric House**, at No 248, **Kodak House**, at No 252, and **Newspaper House**, at No 247 – an 1880s warehouse which received a new facade in 1932.

The **Block Arcade**, which runs between Collins and Elizabeth Sts, was built in 1890 and is a beautifully intact 19th century shopping arcade. Its design was inspired by the Galleria Vittorio in Milan and features intricate mosaic tiled floors, marble columns, Victorian window surrounds and the magnificently detailed plasterwork of the upper walls. The arcade has been fully restored, and houses some exclusive specialist shops selling things like lingerie, crystal and glass, and designer clothing. Taking tea in the old-fashioned **Hopetoun Tearooms** is an elegant step back in time.

The financial sector begins across Elizabeth St, but this area isn't all banks and brokers. **Henry Buck's**, at No 320, is a gentlemen's outfitter of distinction and a great place if you're in the market for classic menswear, and at No 338, **Hardy Brothers** is one of Australia's most famous jewellers.

The financial sector also has some of Melbourne's best-preserved old buildings. The original facade of the **CBA Bank** building at No 333 was one of the most extreme examples of classicism of its time, but unfortunately the bank decided to 'update' its image in 1939, and the new facade represents the austerity of between-the-wars architecture. The interior is another matter, and you should wander inside to enjoy the restored magnificence of the domed foyer.

The three buildings on the corner of Collins and Queen Sts are fine examples of the extravagance of late Victorian architecture during Melbourne's land boom period, and you should wander into all three chambers and feast your eyes. The **Gothic Bank** is at No 376, the former **National Mutual Life** building at No 395 and the former **Bank of Australasia** at No 396.

The block between William and King Sts provides a striking contrast between the old and the new. The Gothic facade of the three **Olderfleet** buildings, at No 471-477, has been well preserved, and **Le Meridien at Rialto**, at No 495, is an imaginative five-star hotel behind the facades of two marvellous old Venetian Gothic buildings, with the original cobbled lane between them covered as an internal atrium. These older buildings are dwarfed by the soaring **Rialto Towers**, Melbourne's tallest building, nearby. The semi-reflective glass exterior looks stunningly different under varying light. See the following section on the Rialto's Observation Deck.

At the **Stock Exchange** building, at No 530, you can wander through the impressive central foyer and check out the glass-fronted lifts running up the outside of the atrium. Since the computerisation of the exchange there's not much to see in the public gallery apart from a big screen and some public terminals.

Rialto Towers Observation Deck This extremely popular lookout (☎ 9629 8222) is on the 55th floor of Melbourne's tallest building, the Rialto Towers on Collins St. It offers spectacular 360° views of Melbourne's surrounds, and there's a cafe if you want to linger. It's open daily from 10 am to 10 pm (until 11 pm on Friday and Saturday); entry costs $7.50 ($5 children) and includes a short film on Melbourne's history.

The Rialto is 253m tall, 200-odd metres shorter than the world's current tallest building, the Petronas Towers in Kuala Lumpur (Malaysia), and a whopping 400-odd metres shorter than the Grollo Tower, which was proposed for the neighbouring Docklands precinct, but had been cancelled at the time of writing. (In 2001 the Petronas Towers will be overtaken by the 460m World Financial Centre in Shanghai.)

Bourke St

The area in and around the centre of Bourke St is the shopping heart of the city, and the mall section between Swanston Walk and Elizabeth St is closed to traffic – like Swanston Walk, pedestrians share the Bourke St Mall with trams (share and beware).

The north side of the mall is dominated by the frontages of the Myer and David Jones department stores, and the tower-topped **GPO** on the corner of Elizabeth St. This elaborate and elegant building was built in stages, and if you look closely at the designs on the columns, you'll see that the three levels feature the classical Doric, Ionic and Corinthian forms respectively. On the other side of the mall, the **Royal Arcade** is lined with souvenir, travel, food and jewellery shops, but if you look up you'll see the fine detail of the original 19th century arcade. At the Little Collins St end, the tall figures of **Gog** and **Magog** stand guard. These mythological giants were modelled on the original figures in London's Guildhall, and have been striking the hour on the clock here since 1892.

The east end of the street beyond the mall has some great cafes and restaurants, interesting book and record shops, mainstream cinemas and more fashion boutiques.

Spring St

Standing at the eastern end of Collins St beside the Treasury Gardens, the **Old Treasury Building** is appropriately solid and imposing. It was built in 1858 with huge basement vaults to store much of the £200 million worth of gold that came from the Victorian goldfields, and was designed by the 19-year-old government draftsman JJ Clark, who went on to become one of the city's finest architects. It now houses an interesting exhibition on Melbourne's past and future, which opens from 9 am to 5 pm on weekdays and 10 am to 4 pm on weekends.

At 103 Spring St, between Bourke and Little Collins Sts, the **Windsor Hotel** is a marvellous reminder of the 19th century. Built in 1883, it is the city's grandest historic hotel.

Opposite, the **Parliament House of Victoria** building was started in 1856, when the two main chambers, the Lower House (Legislative Assembly/House of Representatives) and the Upper House (Legislative Council/Senate), were built. The library was built in 1860, Queen's Hall in 1879, and the original plans also included a dome over the entrance. The dome is still on the drawing board, and the side facades were never completed to plan. Despite being incomplete, this structure is still the city's most impressive public building. Australia's first federal Parliament sat here from 1901, before moving to Canberra in 1927.

GLENN BEANLAND

The tiled portico of Parliament House of Victoria

The interiors are superb and well worth seeing. The building is open on weekdays, with free tours when parliament isn't sitting. Ask about the story behind the second ceremonial mace that went missing from the Lower House in 1891 – rumour has it that it ended up in a brothel! The tour guide points out some fascinating design aspects and explains the symbolism underlying much of the ornamentation. Another way to see the houses is to visit when Parliament is sitting. The public galleries of both houses are open to the public – phone ☎ 9651 8568 to find out when Parliament is in session.

The small and pretty **gardens** behind Parliament House are open to the public, as are the **Parliament Gardens** to the north. The steps of Parliament House give great views of Bourke St, the Windsor Hotel and the elaborate facade of the restored **Princess Theatre**.

At the top of Spring St, the building of the **Royal Australasian College of Surgeons** stands alone, a marvellous and restrained example of 1930s architecture, which is unfortunately not open to the public.

Chinatown

Little Bourke St has been the centre for Chinese people in Melbourne since the days of the gold rush. It's a fascinating walk along the section from Spring St to Swanston St.

This is the only area of continuous Chinese settlement in the country, as well as one of Melbourne's most intact 19th century streetscapes. In the 1850s, the Chinese set up their shops alongside brothels, opium dens, boarding houses and herbalists, but nowadays it's mainly restaurants and discount traders.

The **Po Hong Trading Company**, on the corner of Cohen Place, is famous for its huge assortment of Chinese nick-nacks. It is housed in the former Chinese Mission Hall, built in 1894 by a Chinese evangelist.

The **Chinese Museum**, 22 Cohen Place, documents the long history of Chinese people in Australia. The entrance is guarded by Dai Loong, the huge Chinese dragon who comes out to party on Chinese New Year. It's open daily from 10 am to 4.30 pm (Saturday from noon); admission is $5 (children $3). The museum also conducts walking tours around Chinatown every morning, and these cost $15 (two hours), or $28 (three hours, including lunch at a Chinatown restaurant). Phone ☎ 9662 2888 for bookings.

There are many well-preserved old buildings and warehouses in Little Bourke St and the narrow cobbled lanes that run off it, and it can be fun just to wander around, especially if you're hungry. Sunday-morning yum cha is very popular with Australians of Chinese descent, and this is the busiest and most lively time to visit.

Queen Victoria Market

This market, on the corner of Victoria and Peel Sts, is equally popular with Melbournians and visitors. The market has been on the site for more than 100 years, and many of the sheds and buildings are registered by the Historic Buildings Council. It's a link with the past, but also a great place to buy just about anything, or just wander around soaking up the atmosphere (see Markets in the Shopping section for opening hours).

Food is something of an obsession for many Melburnians, and if you're interested in exploring behind the scenes, Queen Victoria Market Walking Tours (☎ 9320 5822) runs great two-hour tours around the market from Tuesday to Saturday. You get to visit all sorts of different stalls, meet a fascinating bunch of characters, and taste a variety of interesting goodies – great fun! The 'Foodies Dream' tour costs $18 – it's great if you're specifically interested in food, and you get to try weird and wonderful things like emu sausages and wallaby pies. Bookings are necessary. There's also a Heritage Tour ($12).

Old Melbourne Gaol

This gruesome old gaol, now a penal museum (☎ 9663 7228), is at the northern end of Russell St. It was built of bluestone in 1841 and was used until 1929. In all, over 100 prisoners were hanged here. It's a dark, dank, spooky place. The museum displays include death masks and histories of noted bushrangers and convicts, Ned Kelly's armour, the very scaffold from which Ned took his fatal plunge and some fascinating records of early 'transported' convicts, indicating just what flimsy excuses could be used to pack people off to Australia's unwelcoming shores. (See The Kelly Gang boxed text in the Goulburn Valley & Hume Freeway chapter for more about Ned.) It is open from 9.30 am to 4.30 pm daily, and admission is $8 (children $5, family $23, students $6). There are also tours of the gaol on Wednesday and Sunday nights at 7.45 pm (8.45 pm during daylight saving), costing $17 for adults, $9 for children – book through Ticketmaster (☎ 13 6100).

Immigration Museum & Hellenic Antiquities Museum

In the old Customs House (1858-70) on Flinders St between William and Market Sts, the Immigration Museum (☎ 9927 2732) tells (literally – there is lots of audio) the story of Melbourne's migrants. Station Pier, down in Port Melbourne, was where most immigrants to Australia left the boat, and Melbourne was the first Australian home to many. This excellent little museum is well worth a look, as is the restored Customs House building itself, which dates back to the days when ships sailed up the Yarra as far as the former Queen's Wharf at the end of Queen St. On the 2nd floor is the Hellenic Antiquities Museum, housing changing displays from Greece.

Both museums are open daily from 10 am to 5 pm. Admission to either is $7; to both it's $12. There's a cafe and disabled access from Market St.

Other Historic Buildings

Melbourne is an intriguing blend of the soaring new and the stately old, and a few places manage to combine the two sympathetically. The **Melbourne Central** shopping and office complex, on Latrobe St between Elizabeth and Swanston Sts, manages just that. The centrepiece is an old **shot tower**, which was built on the site in 1889. The complex was built around the tower, which is now enclosed in a 20-storey-high cone-shaped glass tower that is worth a visit. When you walk in you'll see lots of people looking up – when you look up, you'll see why.

The city's other historic buildings are too numerous to mention here. However, some of the more notable ones are the simple Georgian **John Smith's House** (1848) at 300 Queen St; the massive structure of the **Law Courts** buildings (1874-84) in William St between Little Bourke and Lonsdale Sts; the **Old Royal Mint** (1872) in William St, adjacent to the Flagstaff Gardens; and **St James Cathedral** (1842), which was moved to its present site at 419 King St in 1913, and is Melbourne's oldest surviving building.

Victoriana enthusiasts may also find some very small Melbourne buildings of interest – scattered around the city are a number of very fine cast-iron men's urinals (like French *pissoirs*). They mainly date from

RICHARD NEBESKY

A ride on a free City Circle tram is a great way to acquaint yourself with some of Melbourne's attractions

CHRIS MELLOR

Block Arcade, an exquisite city time-warp

GLENN BEANLAND

Olderfleet buildings, dwarfed by Rialto towers

RICHARD I'ANSON

'Under the clocks' at Melbourne's Flinders Street Station is a popular meeting place

RICHARD I'ANSON

The historic Shot Tower in Melbourne Central

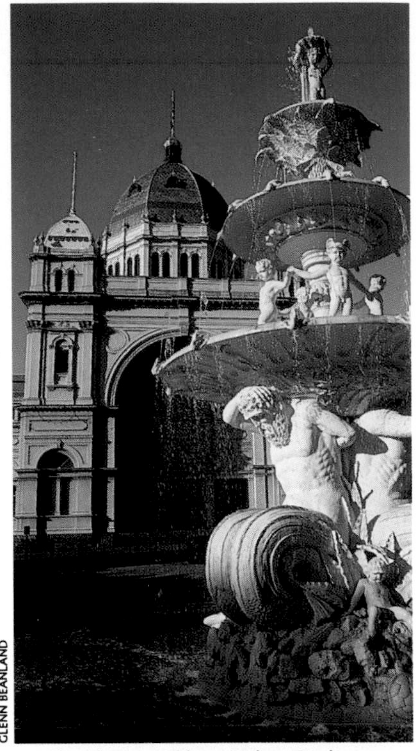

GLENN BEANLAND

Royal Exhibition Building, Carlton Gardens

CHRIS MELLOR

Melbourne's city skyline from St Kilda pier

1903 to 1914, and the one on the corner of Exhibition and Lonsdale Sts is classified by the National Trust.

SOUTHBANK

South across the river from the city centre, the area known as Southbank is a former industrial wasteland that was brilliantly transformed in the early 1990s by the **Southgate** development. An arched footbridge crosses the Yarra River from behind Flinders St train station, linking the city centre to the Victorian Arts Centre, the National Gallery and Southgate itself. Parisian-style riverside walks flank the river on both sides, and where you once would have seen saw-toothed roofs and smoke billowing from chimney stacks you'll now see dozens of people happily promenading along the riverside.

The Southgate complex houses three levels of restaurants, cafes and bars, all of which enjoy a marvellous outlook over the city skyline and the river. There's also an international food hall, an upmarket shopping galleria with some interesting speciality boutiques, and a collection of specially commissioned sculptures and other artworks that are well worth seeing.

Arts Precinct

This small area, on St Kilda Rd across the Yarra River from Flinders St train station, is the high-culture heart of Melbourne. It contains the National Gallery of Victoria, the Concert Hall and theatres of the Victorian Arts Centre, the Victorian College of the Arts, and the Malthouse Theatres.

National Gallery of Victoria The National Gallery of Victoria was the first part of the arts complex to be completed, back in 1968. While the 1960s isn't too many people's favourite period of architecture, the gallery is one of its better examples. The building was designed by Sir Roy Grounds and is constructed from bluestone and concrete. The stark, imposing, fortress-like facade with its moats and fountains has been enlivened by the addition of Deborah Halpern's quirky two-headed and three-legged sculpture *Angel*, which stands in one of the moats looking a bit like a mutated antipodean Loch Ness Monster.

The internationally renowned European section has an impressive collection of works by European masters including Rembrandt, Picasso, Turner, Monet, Titian, Pissarro and van Dyck. The sculpture courtyard and gallery has some fine works including sculptures by Auguste Rodin and Henry Moore. The gallery also has a good collection of contemporary Aboriginal art, large collections of Chinese art, an excellent photography collection, a display of period costumes, jewellery, prints, ceramics and much more. The gallery's full collection is too large for permanent display, so many temporary exhibits are featured.

The fine collection of Australian painters includes the work of the modernists Sir Sidney Nolan, Arthur Boyd, Fred Williams, Albert Tucker and John Perceval, and Australian impressionists including the Heidelberg School's Tom Roberts, Frederick McCubbin, Charles Condor and Arthur Streeton. Female Australian artists represented at the gallery include the impressionists Jane Sutherland and Clara Southern, as well as Margaret Preston and, in contemporary art, Rosalie Gascoigne, Bea Maddock and Janet Davison. Most of this collection will move to the new **Museum of Australian Art** in Federation Square. Surprisingly, this will be the first major gallery specifically devoted to Australian art.

The **Great Hall** is a highlight, and the best way to see its best feature is to lie on your back on the floor. Melbourne artist Leonard French spent five years creating the amazing stained-glass ceiling. The Gallery Shop is a good place to buy souvenirs, posters, books and postcards, and there's also a good restaurant here (see Places to Eat).

The gallery is open daily from 10 am to 5 pm and admission is free (down from $6.50 a few years ago). Free guided tours are given hourly between 11 am and 3 pm on weekdays, on Saturday at 2 pm and on Sunday at 11 am and 3 pm. The gallery also features special exhibitions, for which a fee is charged.

The National Gallery is closed for a complete refurbishment from the end of June 1999 and will reopen in late 2001, although most of its Australian collection will move to the new Museum of Australian Art in Federation Square, which will open in early 2001. However, some of the gallery's collection will be on display from late 1999 in the State Library, in the impressive old rooms recently vacated by the museum. Enter from Russell St.

Victorian Arts Centre The Victorian Arts Centre is made up of two separate buildings – the Melbourne Concert Hall and the Theatres Building – which are linked to each other and the gallery by a series of landscaped walkways.

The **Melbourne Concert Hall**, the circular building closest to the Yarra, is the main performance venue for major artists and companies, and the base for the Melbourne Symphony Orchestra. Most of it is below ground, resting in Yarra mud so corrosive that a system of electrified cables is needed to prevent it deteriorating. The **Theatres Building** is topped by the distinctive spire, underneath which are housed the State Theatre, the Playhouse and the George Fairfax Studio. The stylish interiors of both buildings are quite stunning, and are well worth visiting in their own right, although you should try to see a performance at the centre.

Both buildings feature the works of prominent Australian artists, and in the Theatres Building the **Westpac Gallery** and the **Vic Walk Gallery** are free gallery spaces with changing exhibitions of contemporary works.

There are one-hour tours of the complex ($8) at noon and 2.30 pm each weekday and at 10.30 am and noon each Saturday. On Sunday you can visit the backstage areas at 12.15 pm ($12). Phone ☎ 9281 8198 for details, as backstage tours aren't always available. Children under 12 aren't allowed backstage.

The **Performing Arts Museum** in the Theatres Building has changing exhibitions on all aspects of the performing arts – it might be a display of rock musicians' outfits or an exhibit on horror in the theatre. Admission is free and the museum is open whenever the building is.

Crown Casino

The operators, rather euphemistically, refer to this megalith as Crown Entertainment Complex. It was fleetingly the world's largest casino (it's still the biggest in the southern hemisphere) and it has had an enormous effect on Melbourne. A lot of money is spent in its many bars and restaurants which was once spent in suburban pubs and eateries, not to mention the money squandered on gambling.

The casino was opened with a flourish that suggested Melburnians were living in a new golden age, although shareholders quickly found that this was not so. It's incredibly garish, noisy and crass, but then, what else would you expect from a casino? As well as gambling facilities there are bars, cafes and restaurants, some of them cheap, a cinema and the Planet Hollywood nightclub.

The complex is open 24 hours a day and it's well worth a look if you're a fan of kitsch.

Melbourne Exhibition Centre

Jeff's Shed, as the Melbourne Exhibition Centre is popularly known, is on the south bank of the Yarra on Clarendon St. It hosts trade exhibitions, 'bridal fayres' and the like. It's architecturally interesting, not least for its angled, thrusting 'blade', which is a feature of several current projects around the city. This seems to be Melbourne's symbol for the new millennium. And why is it called Jeff's Shed? Because it was built under the auspices of Premier Jeff Kennett, and, well, it does somewhat resemble a shed.

Polly Woodside Maritime Museum

The *Polly Woodside* is an old iron-hulled three-masted sailing ship. She was built in Belfast in 1885, and spent the first part of her working life carrying coal and nitrate between Europe and South America. She made the rounding of Cape Horn 16 times and ended her career as a coal hulk, but was bought by the National Trust in the 1970s and restored by volunteers. It is now home to the Polly Woodside Maritime Museum (☎ 9699 9760) on the riverfront, close to the Spencer St bridge and across the river from the World Trade Centre.

Polly Woodside is now the centrepiece of a maritime museum park, and floats proudly in a dry dock in the centre of the park – a 'memorial to a breed of ships and men the world will not see again'.

The ship and museum are open daily from 10 am to 5 pm, and admission is $8 for adults and $4 for children.

Victoria Police Museum

Across the river in Building C of the World Trade Centre on Flinders St, the Victoria Police Museum is open on weekdays from 10 am to 4 pm. Entry is free and the museum has a small but interesting collection of police history and various displays including one of the four original sets of the Kelly gang's armour. (Kelly memorabilia moves around quite a lot. You might find that the armour is now in the Old Melbourne Gaol or the new museum.)

Melbourne Aquarium

Still under construction at the time of writing, this will be an exciting place to visit, with a huge tank extending into the Yarra River and glassed tunnels to walk through. The aquarium will be sited east of Kings Way, on the north side of the river.

OTHER GALLERIES

Apart from the marvellous collection at the National Gallery, Melbourne has a number of other good galleries.

At 7 Templestowe Rd in the outer suburb of Bulleen, the **Museum of Modern Art at Heide** (☎ 9850 1500) is on the site of the former home of John and Sunday Reed, under whose patronage the likes of Sir Sidney Nolan, John Perceval, Albert Tucker and Arthur Boyd created a new movement in the Australian art world.

The gallery has an impressive collection of 20th century Australian art. It is set in a sprawling park with an informal combination of deciduous and native trees, a carefully tended kitchen garden and scattered sculpture gardens running right down to the banks of the Yarra. Known as 'Heide', the gallery is open from Tuesday to Friday between 10 am and 5 pm and on weekends from noon. Admission costs $6/3 for adults/children. Heide is signposted off the Eastern Freeway. Otherwise, bus No 203 goes to Bulleen, and the Yarra bike path goes close by.

Montsalvat (☎ 9439 7712) is in Hillcrest Ave in Eltham (26km north-east of the city), the mud-brick and alternative lifestylers' suburb. This artists' colony was established by Justus Jorgensen in the 1930s when the suburb was all hills and bush.

Montsalvat features and sells the works of a variety of artists and craftspeople, and there's an eclectic collection of impressive stone and mud-brick buildings to explore. As well as hosting the Montsalvat Jazz Festival each January and the National Poetry Festival each December, Montsalvat is open daily to visitors from 9 am to 5 pm. Admission costs $5 for adults, $2.50 for children, and it's about a 2km walk from Eltham train station.

The **Australian Centre for Contemporary Art** (☎ 9654 6422), on Dallas Brooks Drive across the road from the main entrance to the Royal Botanic Gardens (see the Port & South Melbourne & Albert Park map), is well worth a visit, with regular exhibitions of cutting-edge contemporary art. It also hosts lectures, screenings and other events, and welcomes visitors. The centre opens Tuesday to Friday from 11 am to 5 pm and weekends from 2 to 5 pm. Entry is free.

Other public galleries include the **Linden Art Centre & Gallery** at 26 Acland St in St Kilda, the **Westpac Gallery** at the Victorian Arts Centre, the **RMIT Gallery** in the city, and the **Ian Potter Museum of Art** and **Griffin Gallery**, both at Melbourne University. **CCP** (the Centre for Contemporary Photography) has a gallery at 205 Johnston St in Fitzroy (near the corner of George St) with an interesting programme of exhibitions, including multi-media. Entry to each of these galleries is free.

See also Commercial Art Galleries in the Shopping section later.

OTHER MUSEUMS

The science and technology section of the Museum of Victoria, **Scienceworks Museum**, is at 2 Booker St in Spotswood, under the shadow of the West Gate Bridge (see the Greater Melbourne map). It was built on the site of the Spotswood pumping station, Melbourne's first sewage works, and incorporates the historic old buildings. This place has a fascinating array of tactile displays. You can spend hours wandering around inspecting old machines, poking buttons and pulling levers and learning all sorts of weird facts and figures. Scienceworks is open daily from 10 am to 4.30 pm – it's very popular with school groups and can get pretty crowded. Admission costs are $8 adults, $4 kids. The museum is a 15-minute walk from Spotswood train station down Hudsons Rd. It's signposted.

The **Jewish Holocaust Centre** (☎ 9528 1985), 13 Selwyn St in Elsternwick (close to Elsternwick train station and Rippon Lea), is a small but detailed museum with pictorial displays, documents and various items from the Nazi death camps of WWII. It tells a grim story, but one that must be told – the museum guides are survivors from the camps. School groups visit the museum daily, and it's open to the public Monday to Thursday from 10 am to 2 pm and Sunday from 11 am to 3 pm. There is no entry fee but donations are accepted.

At 174-180 Smith St in Collingwood, the **Australian Toy Museum** opens daily from 10 am to 5 pm. Out at Moorabbin airport in Cheltenham, the **Moorabbin Air Museum** has a collection of old aircraft, including a number from WWII. It's open daily from 10 am to 5 pm.

The **Victoria Racing Museum** at Caulfield Racecourse has an interesting collection of horse-racing memorabilia, and opens Tuesday and Thursday from 10 am to 4 pm and race days from 11 am to 4.30 pm.

The **Living Museum of the West**, set in the wetlands and parklands of **Pipemakers Park** in Maribyrnong, is a unique 'eco-museum' with display boards and photos documenting the heritage of the western suburbs. You can cruise up the Maribyrnong River to the museum – see the River Cruises section in Organised Tours later.

PARKS & GARDENS

Victoria has appropriately dubbed itself the 'Garden State' and Melbourne is surrounded by an array of public parks and gardens, thanks to the foresight of the city's founders.

Royal Botanic Gardens

Certainly the finest botanic gardens in Australia and arguably among the finest in the world, these form one of the best spots in Melbourne. There's nothing more genteel than having scones, jam and cream by the lake on a Sunday afternoon. The beautifully laid out gardens are right beside the Yarra River; indeed, the river once actually ran right through the gardens, and the lakes are the remains of its curves, cut off when the river was straightened to lessen the annual flood damage.

There's a surprising amount of wildlife in the gardens, including water fowl, ducks, swans, cockatoos, rabbits and possums. Peer over one of the small bridges and you'll probably see some eels, which have lived here since the lake was a bend of the Yarra. A large colony of fruit bats has taken up residence for the last 10 summers or more – look for them high in the trees of the fern gully. The bats are huge, noisy and smelly, but they are almost cute. You'll see why they are also known as flying foxes.

Pick up guide-yourself leaflets at the park entrances; these are changed with the seasons and tell you what to look out for at the different times of year. There are various entrance gates around the gardens, but the visitor centre is in the National Herbarium inside Gate F on Birdwood Ave (see the Port & South Melbourne & Albert Park map). Free guided tours depart from the visitor centre most days at 10 and 11 am. The gardens are open daily from sunrise to sunset and admission is free. The tearooms and kiosk beside the lake are open daily from 9 am to 5 pm (4.30 pm in winter).

Kings Domain

The Royal Botanic Gardens form a corner of the Kings Domain, a park that also contains the Shrine of Remembrance, Governor La Trobe's Cottage and the Sidney Myer Music Bowl. The domain is bordered by St Kilda Rd, Domain Rd, Anderson St and the Yarra River.

The whole park is encircled by a former horse-exercising track known as the **Tan**, now a 4km running track that is probably Melbourne's favourite venue for joggers. The track has an amusing variety of exercise points – a 'mixture of the stations of the Cross and miniature golf', someone once said.

A huge colony of grey-headed flying foxes lives in the Royal Botanic Gardens.

Beside St Kilda Rd stands the massive **Shrine of Remembrance**, built as a memorial to Victorians killed in WWI. Its design is partly based on the Temple of Halicarnassus, one of the seven ancient wonders of the world, and it wasn't completed until 1934. The inner crypt is inscribed with the words:

> This holy place commemorates Victoria's glorious dead. They gave their all, even life itself, that others may live in freedom and peace. Forget them not.

These words are heeded every Anzac Day, 25 April, when a dawn service at the shrine is attended by thousands, and also on Remembrance Day at the 11th hour of the 11th day of the 11th month – the time at which the Armistice of 1918 was declared. At this moment, a shaft of light shines through an opening in the ceiling to illuminate the Stone of Remembrance. The forecourt, with its cenotaph and eternal flame, was built as a memorial to those who died in WWII. Several other war memorials surround the shrine.

It's worth climbing to the top as there are fine views from the balcony to the city along St Kilda Rd and towards the bay. The shrine is open daily from 10 am to 5 pm.

The shrine faces up Swanston St, and until recently the building it faced at the top end of Swanston St was the Carlton & United brewery (now mostly demolished), which old diggers thought was pretty appropriate.

On Birdwood Ave near the shrine is **Governor La Trobe's Cottage**, the original Victorian government house sent out from the mother country in prefabricated form in 1840. Open daily except Tuesday and Thursday; admission is $2 for adults.

The cottage provides a dramatic contrast with the more imposing **Government House** where Victoria's Governor resides. It's a copy of Queen Victoria's palace on England's Isle of Wight, and was built in 1872. There are guided tours on Monday,

Wednesday and Saturday for $8 – you need to book on ☎ 9654 5528 (no tours from mid-December to the end of January).

On the other side of Birdwood Ave from La Trobe's humble cottage are the **Old Melbourne Observatory** (recently renovated) and the **National Herbarium** at the main entrance to the Royal Botanic Gardens. The Herbarium was established by Baron von Mueller in 1853 as a centre for identifying plant specimens.

Across the road from the herbarium, on Dallas Brooks Drive, is the **Australian Centre for Contemporary Art** (see Other Galleries earlier in this chapter). Up at the city end of the park is the **Sidney Myer Music Bowl**, a functional outdoor performance area in a natural amphitheatre. It's used for all manner of concerts in the summer months, although of late not rock concerts, due to too much trouble afterwards.

The small section of park across St Kilda Rd from the Victorian Arts Centre is the **Queen Victoria Gardens**, containing a memorial statue of the good Queen herself, a statue of Edward VII astride his horse, and a huge floral clock, as well as several more contemporary works of sculpture.

Fitzroy & Treasury Gardens

The leafy Fitzroy Gardens divide the city centre from East Melbourne. With their stately avenues lined with English elms, these gardens are a popular spot for wedding photographers – on Saturday afternoons there's a procession of wedding cars pulling up for the participants to be snapped.

Governor La Trobe's nephew designed the original layout in 1857 which featured paths in the form of the Union Jack. James Sinclair, the first curator, was landscape gardener to the Russian Tsar Nicholas I until the Crimean War cut short his sojourn. Sinclair amended and softened the original design, and the gardens are now a rambling blend of elm and cedar avenues, fern gullies, flower beds and lawns.

In the centre of the gardens are ferneries, fountains and a kiosk. By the kiosk is a miniature **Tudor village** and the **Fairy Tree**, carved in 1932 by the writer Ola Cohn. The painted carvings around the base of the tree depict fairies, pixies, kangaroos, possums and emus.

In the north-west corner of the gardens is the **People's Pathway** – it's a circular path paved with individually engraved bricks and is quite the nicest bit of whimsy in any park in Melbourne.

Captain Cook's Cottage is actually the former Yorkshire home of the distinguished English navigator's parents. It was dismantled, shipped to Melbourne and reconstructed stone by stone in 1934. The cottage is furnished and decorated as it would have been around 1750, complete with hand-made furniture and period fittings. There is an interesting exhibit on Cook's life and achievements during his great exploratory voyages of the southern hemisphere. The cottage is open daily from 9 am to 5 pm and admission is $3 (children $1.50).

Nearby, the **Conservatory**, built in 1928, is looking a little dated from the outside, but the glorious floral displays and tropical-rainforest atmosphere inside are well worth the $1 admission.

There's another cottage to visit in the Fitzroy Gardens, **Sinclair's Cottage**, once the home of the gardens' caretaker. It contains arts and crafts for sale.

The smaller **Treasury Gardens**, a popular lunchtime and barbecue spot, contain a memorial to John F Kennedy. In the early evening you'll probably meet **possums** here, on the lookout for some scrounged tucker. If you must feed them (and they are cute), give them fruit, not bread or crisps, which can cause them serious health problems.

Other Parks & Gardens

The **Flagstaff Gardens**, near the Queen Victoria Market, were first known as Burial Hill – it's where most of the early settlers ended up. As the hill provided one of the best views of the bay, a signalling station was set up here – when a ship was sighted arriving from Britain, a flag was raised on the flagstaff to notify the settlers. Later, a cannon was added and fired when the more important ships arrived, but once newspapers started publishing regular information about shipping, the signalling service became redundant. Free lunchtime concerts are now a frequent feature in the gardens, particularly in warmer weather.

The **Carlton Gardens** surround the historic **Royal Exhibition Building**, a wonder of the southern hemisphere when it was built for the Great Exhibition of 1880. Later it was used by the Victorian Parliament for 27 years, while the Victorian parliament

Free Melbourne

Experiencing some of the things that Melbourne has to offer needn't cost you anything. Most of Melbourne's parks and gardens are free to visit, including the Royal Botanic Gardens, St Kilda Botanical Gardens and the System Garden at Melbourne University. You can visit the MCC Pavilion Library & Museum, take a tour of the Parliament House of Victoria, or if you're interested in seeing how the legal system operates you can sit in on a court case; the Law Courts are in William St between Lonsdale and Little Bourke Sts.

Feeding swans in the Royal Botanic Gardens
Engraving from the *Illustrated Australian News*, 1882

LA TROBE PICTURE COLLECTION, STATE LIBRARY OF VICTORIA

There are lots of free art galleries. They include the National Gallery of Victoria (though not the special exhibitions) and Australian Centre for Contemporary Art (see the section on Art Galleries earlier for details of others). In the State Library, the municipal libraries or the universities you can go book-browsing and reading; a walk along High St or Malvern Rd in Prahran will give you the chance to do some antique-browsing; or you could try taking a tour of Melbourne's major cathedrals such as St Patrick's or St Paul's. The Shrine of Remembrance is free and offers good views of the city; a wander through the Melbourne General Cemetery in Carlton provides some interesting genealogical insights; and any of Melbourne's markets are worth a visit, to see what's on offer or just to people-watch.

If you want to do something energetic, you can crew a racing yacht on the weekend (see the Sailing section); or if you want to sample Australian Rules football, the gates are opened at three-quarter time (around 4 pm) and you can see the last quarter for free.

building was used by the National Legislature until Canberra's parliament building was finally completed. It is still used as a major exhibition centre, and the building has been recently restored. At night it is brilliantly lit in the same ceremonial manner as at the end of the 19th century.

The new **Museum of Victoria** is being constructed on the north side of the Exhibition Buildings. Although the museum site hasn't taken any parkland (some ugly additions and a carpark were demolished to make way for it), it will certainly change the streetscape significantly. It's a controversial location (it was supposed to be on the Yarra where the casino is) and design (it features yet another 'blade' – that hard-edged slope which is a feature of several new projects in Melbourne).

ALONG THE YARRA RIVER

Melbourne's prime natural feature, the 'muddy' Yarra River, is the butt of countless jokes but is actually a surprisingly pleasant river. It is slowly but surely becoming more of an attraction as new parks, walks and buildings appear along its banks. Despite being known as 'the river that flows upside down', it's just muddy, not particularly dirty.

This hasn't always been the case. During the gold-rush period, the Yarra River was everything from a water supply to an open drain. Raw sewage was emptied into the river until 1900, and industrial wastes from tanneries, soap works and later chemical companies were dumped into it as well. In recent years efforts have been made to clean up the river and beautify its surrounds, and the result is now looked upon with some pride by Melburnians.

When rowing boats are gliding down it on a sunny day, or you're driving towards the city on a clear night, the Yarra can really look quite magical. There are some beautiful old bridges across the river, and the riverside boulevards provide delightful views of Melbourne by day or night.

As it winds its way into the city, the Yarra River is flanked by tree-lined avenues – Batman Ave along the north bank and Alexandra Ave on the south. Farther east, the Yarra Blvd follows the river in several sections from Richmond to Kew – like the Great Ocean Road, the Yarra Blvd was a relief-work project of the Great Depression.

Boat cruises along the river depart from Princes Walk (below Princes Bridge) and from Southgate. A series of bike paths (see Cycling later) start from the city and follow the Yarra River, and bikes can be hired from various places. Studley Park Boathouse and Fairfield Park Boathouse are both popular spots where you can hire a canoe and paddle around, enjoy a leisurely Devonshire tea or have a walk beside the river.

Yarra Bend Park

North-east of the city centre, the Yarra River is bordered by the Yarra Bend parklands, much loved by runners, rowers, cyclists, picnickers and strollers. To get there, follow Johnston St through Collingwood and turn into the scenic drive of Yarra Blvd or, better still, hire a bike and ride around the riverside bike paths – a leisurely 40-minute roll. By public transport, take tram No 42 from Collins St east along Victoria St to stop No 28, then walk up Walmer St and over the footbridge; or take bus No 201 or 203 from Flinders St train station, both of which go up Studley Park Rd.

The park has large areas of natural bushlands (not to mention two golf courses, numerous sports grounds and a hospital) and there are some great walks. In parts of Studley Park, with the song of bellbirds ringing through the trees and cockatoos screeching on the banks, it's hard to believe the city's all around you. At the end of Boathouse Rd is the **Studley Park Boathouse** (☎ 9853 1972), open daily from 9.30 am to sunset. These timber buildings on the river bank date back to the 1860s, and now house a restaurant and cafe – there are also boats and canoes available for hire. Kanes suspension bridge takes you across to the other side of the river, and it's about a 20-minute walk from here to Dights Falls at the confluence of the Yarra River and Merri Creek, with some great views along the way. You can also walk to the falls along the southern river bank. On the way is the **Pioneer Memorial Cairn**, which commemorates Charles Grimes (the first European to see the Yarra River, in 1803) and the first settlers to bring cattle from Sydney to Melbourne (in 1836).

Farther up river, Fairfield Park is the site of the **Fairfield Amphitheatre**, a great open-air venue used for concerts and films among other things.

The **Fairfield Park Boathouse & Tea Gardens** (☎ 9486 1501) on Fairfield Park Drive, Fairfield, is a restored 19th-century boathouse with broad verandahs and a garden restaurant. It's open from 9.30 am to 5.30 pm on weekdays and from 9.30 am to sunset on weekends. (From May to September it only opens on weekends.)

YARRA PARK

Yarra Park is the large expanse of parkland to the south-east of the city centre. It contains the Melbourne Cricket Ground, the Melbourne Park National Tennis Centre, Olympic Park and several other sports ovals and open fields.

Melbourne Cricket Ground

The Melbourne Cricket Ground (MCG or just 'the G') is the temple in which sports-mad Melburnians worship their heroes and (to a markedly lesser extent) heroines. The MCG is one of the world's great sporting venues, imbued with an indefinable combination of tradition and atmosphere. The first game of Australian Rules Football was played where the MCG and its car parks now stand in 1858, and in 1877 the first Test cricket match between Australia and England was played here. The MCG was also the central stadium for the 1956 Melbourne Olympics, and it will figure prominently in the 2006 Commonwealth Games which Melbourne will host.

RICHARD I'ANSON

Cricket under lights at the MCG, with the city skyline in the background

The stadium will host some soccer matches during the 2000 Olympics and an artificial surface will be laid – heresy!

The Melbourne Cricket Club **Members' Pavilion** is the oldest stand and, if you're interested in sports, you can lose hours wandering through the pavilion's creaking corridors of sporting history. Its walls are lined with a collection of fascinating old sporting photos. The pavilion also houses the famous Long Room (members only) and the MCC Cricket Library and Museum, which has thousands of items of sporting memorabilia, books, records and ancient equipment. The pavilion, library and museum are open on weekdays from 10 am to 4 pm (except on match days) and admission is free – one of the best deals in town.

Australian Gallery of Sport & Olympic Museum

In front of the members' entrance to the MCG (near the corner of Jolimont St and Jolimont Terrace) this museum is dedicated to Australia's sporting passions. It's open from 9.30 am to 4.30 pm every day, and the admission – $9.50 adults, $6 children, $25 families – includes a one hour tour of both the MCG and the museum. Tours run hourly between 10 am and 3 pm, although they might be curtailed on match days.

Melbourne Park National Tennis Centre

A footbridge links the Melbourne Park National Tennis Centre (formerly Flinders Park) with the MCG, crossing the Jolimont Railway Yards from the members' car park. Opened in 1988, the centre hosts the Australian Open Grand Slam championship each January, and is also used as a concert

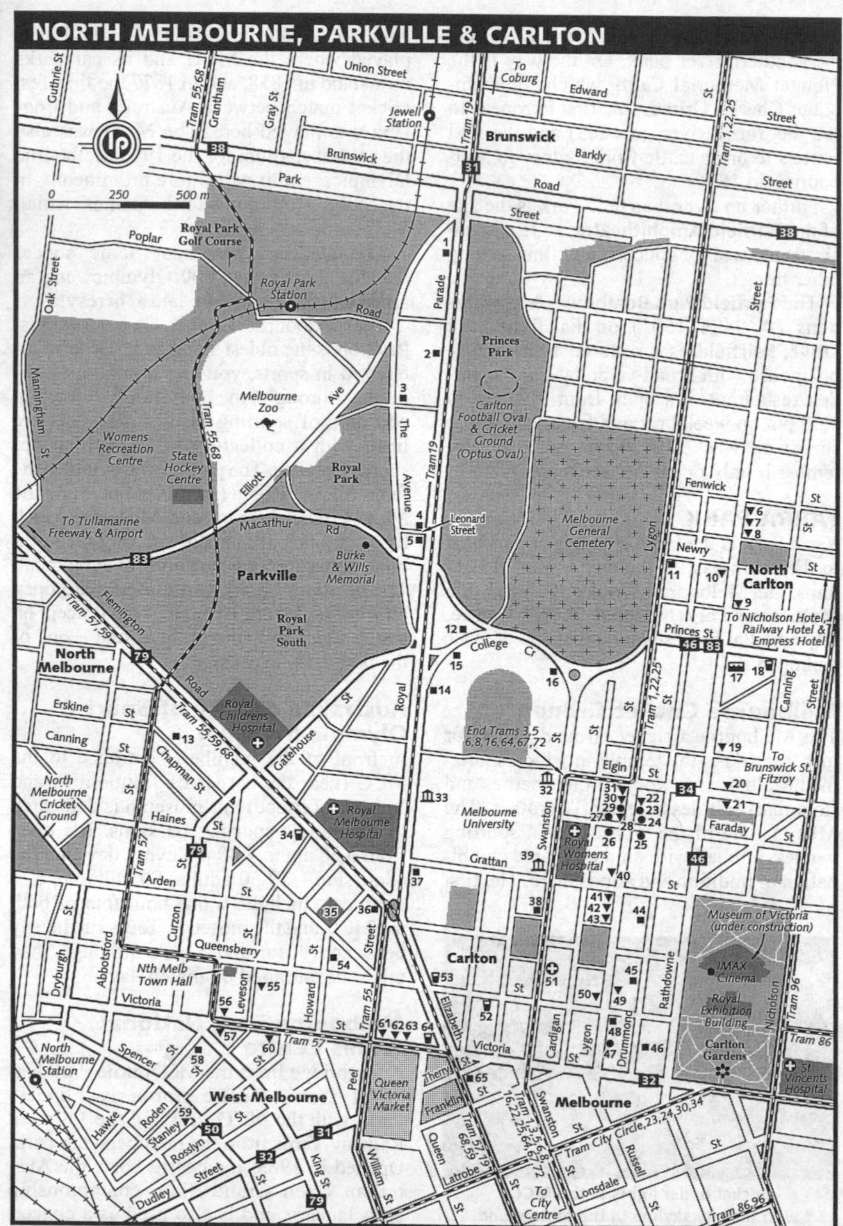
NORTH MELBOURNE, PARKVILLE & CARLTON
Union Street
To Coburg
Edward
Street
Jewell Station
Brunswick
Barkly
Park
Road
Street
Royal Park Golf Course
Poplar
Royal Park Station
Princes Park
Carlton Football Oval & Cricket Ground (Optus Oval)
Melbourne Zoo
Womens Recreation Centre
State Hockey Centre
Royal Park
Melbourne General Cemetery
To Tullamarine Freeway & Airport
Macarthur Rd
Leonard Street
Burke & Wills Memorial
Parkville
North Carlton
To Nicholson Hotel, Railway Hotel & Empress Hotel
Royal Park South
North Melbourne
College Cr
Princes St
Royal Childrens Hospital
End Trams 3,5 6,8,16,64,67,72
To Brunswick St Fitzroy
North Melbourne Cricket Ground
Royal Melbourne Hospital
Melbourne University
Royal Womens Hospital
Museum of Victoria (under construction)
IMAX Cinema
Royal Exhibition Building
Carlton Gardens
St Vincents Hospital
Nth Melb Town Hall
Carlton
North Melbourne Station
West Melbourne
Queen Victoria Market
Melbourne
Tram City Circle,23,24,30,34
To City Centre
0 250 500 m

venue. The centre court area is covered with a retractable roof. The centre has five indoor and 23 outdoor tennis courts available to the public (see Tennis in the Activities section later).

CARLTON & PARKVILLE

Up this end of town you'll find a cosmopolitan area that blends the intellectual with the gastronomic, the sporting with the cultural – and you'll also see some of the city's finest Victorian residential architecture.

These two suburbs are divided by the tree-lined Royal Pde. In Parkville there's Melbourne University and the Melbourne Zoo; in Carlton there's the Melbourne General Cemetery and some great restaurants in the Italian quarter around Lygon, Drummond and Rathdowne Sts.

Royal Park

Royal Park, a large expanse of open parklands, contains a number of sports ovals and open spaces, large netball and hockey stadiums, a public golf course and the Melbourne Zoo. In the corner closest to Melbourne University is a garden of Australian native plants, and a little farther north, just before MacArthur Rd, a memorial cairn marks the spot from which the Burke and Wills Expedition set off in 1860 on its fateful crossing of the interior. (See the Burke & Wills Expedition boxed text in the Facts About Victoria chapter.)

Melbourne Zoo

Melbourne's zoo is one of the city's most popular attractions, and deservedly so. Established in 1861, this is the oldest zoo in Australia and the third oldest in the world. In the 1850s, when Australia was considered to be a foreign place full of strange trees and animals, the Acclimatisation Society was formed for 'the introduction, acclimatisation and domestication of all innoxious animals, birds, fishes, insects and vegetables'. The society merged with the Zoological Society in 1861, and together they established the zoo on its present site.

NORTH MELBOURNE, PARKVILLE & CARLTON

PLACES TO STAY

1 Ramada Inn
2 Park Avenue Motor Inn
3 Ridley College
4 Whitley College
5 International House
11 Lygon Crest Lodgings
12 University College
13 Chapman Gardens YHA Hostel
14 Trinity College
15 Ormond College
16 Queen's College
36 Old Melbourne Hotel
37 Elizabeth Tower Motel
38 Rydge's Carlton
44 163 Drummond Street
45 Carlton College
46 Medley Hall
48 Downtowner on Lygon
54 Queensberry Hill YHA Hostel
58 Miami Motel
65 Stork Hotel

PLACES TO EAT

6 La Trattoria
7 La Porchetta
8 Kent Hotel
9 La Luna
10 Paragon Cafe
19 La Contadina
20 Jakarta
21 Abla's
22 Trotters
28 Tiamo
30 Brown's Bakery
31 Jimmy Watson's
40 Papa Gino's
41 Borsari Ristorante
42 Nyonya
43 Notturno
49 Casa Malaya
50 Toto's Pizza House
55 Eldorado Hotel
56 Peppermint Lounge Cafe
57 Amiconi
59 La Chaumiére
60 Warung Agus
61 La Porchetta
62 Viet Nam House
63 Dalat's

OTHER

17 Carlton Baths
18 Dan O'Connell Hotel
23 Lygon Court, Cinema Nova & Comedy Club
24 Johnny's Green Room
25 La Mama Theatre
26 Carlton Movie House
27 STA Travel
29 Readings Bookshop
32 Ian Potter Museum of Art
33 Sir Percy Grainger Museum
34 Redback Brewery-Pub
35 Metro! Craft Centre
39 Griffin Gallery
47 Trades Hall
51 Melbourne Sexual Health Clinic
52 Dream Nightclub
53 Arthouse
64 Public Bar

Set in spacious and attractively landscaped gardens, with broad strolling paths leading from place to place, the zoo's enclosures are simulations of the animals' natural habitats. The walkways pass through the enclosures – you walk through the bird aviary, cross a bridge over the lions' park, enter a tropical hothouse full of colourful butterflies and walk around the gorillas' very own rainforest. There's also a large collection of native animals in a native bush setting, a platypus aquarium, fur seals, lions and tigers, plenty of reptiles and lots more to see. You should allow at least half a day. There's also a good selection of not-too-tacky souvenirs, as well as quite a few snack bars and two bistros.

The zoo is open daily from 9 am to 5 pm; admission is $14 adults, $7 children and $38 for families. In January and February the zoo hosts twilight concerts (see the Entertainment section later in this chapter for details). To get there from the city, take tram No 55 or 56 from William St, or an Upfield-line train to Royal Park train station (no trains on Sunday!).

Melbourne University

Melbourne University is well worth a visit. The university was established in 1853, and a wander around the campus, in Parkville on the edge of the central city, will reveal an intriguing blend of original Gothic-style stone buildings and some incredibly unattractive brick blocks from more recent, less noteworthy 'functionalist' periods of architecture. The college buildings, to the north of the campus, are particularly noteworthy for their architecture.

The grounds are sprinkled with open lawns and garden areas, and during term, there's always something going on. There are often bands playing in North Court (behind Union House), or you could sit in on a lecture, go book browsing in the Baillieu Library, inspect the rare plants in the System Garden (between the Botany and Agriculture and Forestry buildings) or visit one of several free galleries and museums.

The **Ian Potter Musum of Art**, in the Physics building on the corner of Swanston St and Tin Alley, features contemporary exhibitions and opens Wednesday to Saturday from 12 noon to 5 pm (closed in January). The **University Gallery** in the former Physics building has a small but interesting collection of Australian art, and is open at the same times. On the Royal Pde side (next to the Conservatory of Music), the **Percy Grainger Museum** is dedicated to the life and times of Percy Grainger (1882-1961), an eccentric composer who lived an extraordinary life and travelled the world collecting and recording folk music on an old Edison recording machine. Grainger set up the museum before his death, and it contains his collections, instruments, photos, costumes and other interesting personal effects. The museum is open weekdays from 10 am to 4 pm and admission is free.

Lygon St

Carlton is Melbourne's Italian quarter, and Lygon St its backbone. Many of the thousands of Italian immigrants who came to Melbourne after WWII settled in Carlton, and Lygon St became the focal point of their community. Over the ensuing years, the street has gradually evolved into what is now referred to as Melbourne's Via Veneto.

Lygon St is the most highly 'developed' example of the multicultural evolution of Melbourne's inner-suburban streets. A fondness lingers for the older, less glamorous version, but as they say, you can't stop progress. The developers moved in and, with their out-with-the-old and in-with-the-new philosophy, gave Lygon St a facelift that didn't necessarily improve its looks. Lygon St lost its offbeat appeal and the bohemian element moved on to Brunswick St, Fitzroy and beyond.

But not all of the old Lygon St was lost. In among the tourist restaurants and exclusive fashion boutiques, you'll still find a few of the oldies: Readings Bookstore is still there, albeit in a new shop; places like Toto's, Tiamo, Papa Gino's and Jimmy Watson's have resisted the winds of change; you can still see art-house films at the Carlton Movie House (the 'bug house') or play pool at Johnny's Green Room; and La Mama, the tiny experimental theatre started by Betty Burstall in 1967, is still going strong in Faraday St.

Lygon St is one of Melbourne's liveliest streets. Day and night it is always filled with people promenading, dining, sipping cappuccinos, shopping and generally soaking up the atmosphere. Every November, Lygon St hosts the lively Lygon St Festa, a four-day food-and-fun street party.

Other Attractions

Two attractive and broad tree-lined avenues, **Drummond St** and **Royal Pde**, contain outstanding examples of 19th century residential architecture. Drummond St in particular, from Victoria St to Palmerston St, is one of the most impressive and intact Victorian streetscapes in the city. **Rathdowne St**, north of Victoria St, has a great little shopping area and some good cafes and restaurants. North Carlton and Brunswick (Sydney Rd and the northern ends of Lygon and Nicholson Sts) present the less commercial face of this cosmopolitan area.

Princes Park, to the north of Melbourne University, has a number of sports grounds including the Carlton Football and Cricket clubs' main ground (now known as Optus Oval), as well as a 3.2km fun-and-fitness exercise circuit. A visit to the **Melbourne General Cemetery**, next to Princes Park, is a sombre reminder that no matter how many laps of the fun-and-fitness circuit you do, you can't avoid the inevitable. The earliest gravestones date back to the 1850s, and the cemetery is a graphic and historic portrait of the wide diversity of countries from which people have come to settle in Australia.

FITZROY & COLLINGWOOD

Fitzroy is where Melbourne's bohemian subculture moved to when the lights got too bright in Carlton. It's a great mixture of artistic, seedy, alternative and trendy elements, and one of Melbourne's most interesting suburbs to live in or to visit.

In Melbourne's early years Fitzroy was a prime residential area, and the suburb contains some fine terraced houses from the mid-Victorian era, the most notable of which is **Royal Terrace** (1854) on Nicholson St, opposite the Exhibition Building. Later on, the suburb became a densely populated working-class stronghold with a large migrant population. The inner-city location and cosmopolitan atmosphere has attracted students, artists and urban lifestylers, creating the lively blend that now exists.

Brunswick St is Fitzroy's and probably Melbourne's most vibrant and lively street (St Kilda residents would disagree), and you shouldn't visit the city without coming here. This is where you'll find some of the best food, the weirdest shops, the most interesting people, the wildest clothes and the wackiest waiters. In particular, the blocks on either side of the Johnston St intersection have a fascinating collection of young designer and retro clothes shops, bookshops, galleries, nurseries, antique dealers and, of course, more cafes and restaurants than you can poke a fork at. (See the Places to Eat section later.) Tea aficionados shouldn't miss Tea Too at No 340.

Johnston St is the centre of Melbourne's small but lively Spanish-speaking community, with its tapas bars, the Spanish Club, and several Spanish delicatessens. It also hosts the annual Hispanic Festival every November.

Smith St forms the border between Fitzroy and Collingwood, and this is where the bohemians who think that Brunswick St is going the way of Lygon St have moved. Smith St in turn is becoming an exciting strip of food shops, bookshops, good pubs and restaurants. Where will the avant garde go when Smith St becomes too popular? There just aren't many old-style shopping strips left in the inner city.

Along Brunswick St north of Alexandra Ave in **North Fitzroy**, there are quite a few interesting and quirky shops to explore, more historic buildings, the Edinburgh Gardens and one or two good pubs in which to enjoy an ale. The **Fitzroy Baths** swimming pool, on Alexandra Pde between Brunswick and Smith Sts, is open from November until the end of April.

FITZROY & COLLINGWOOD

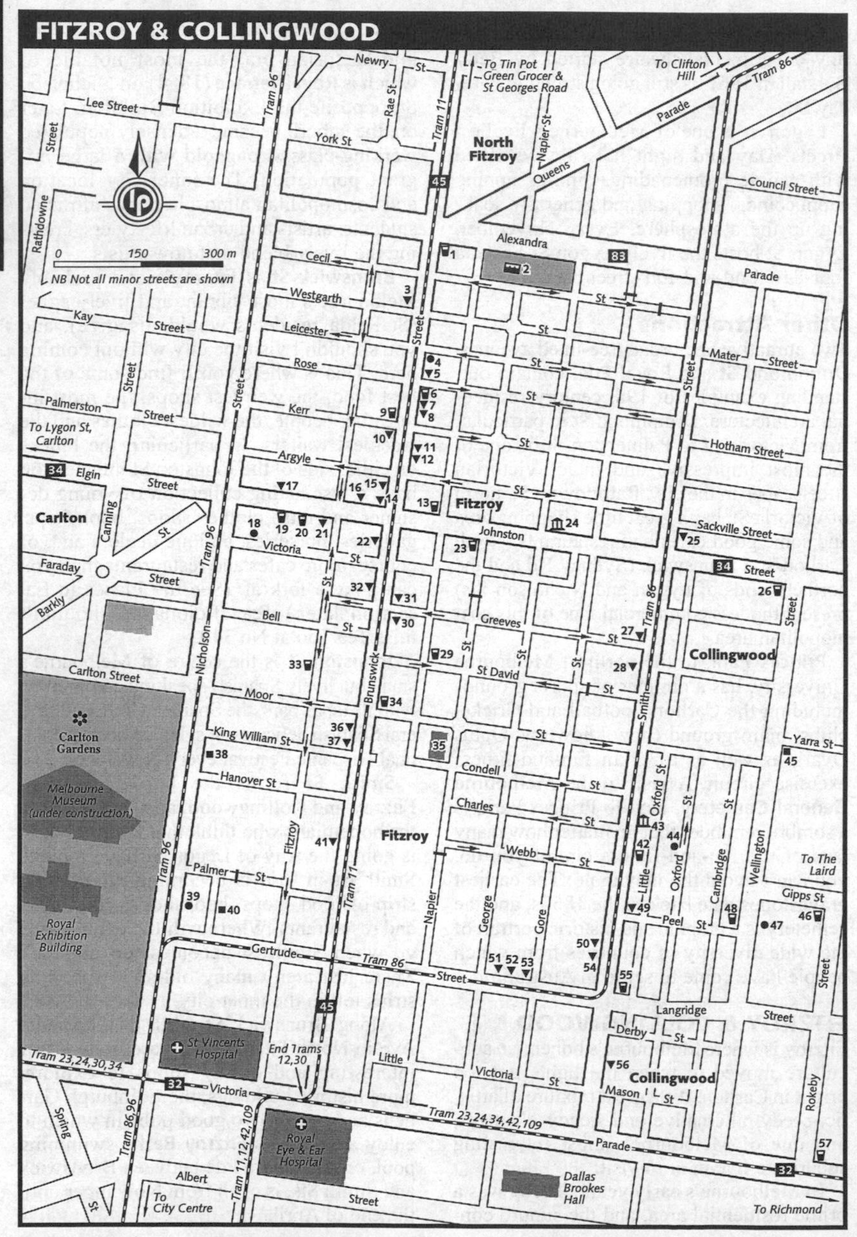

FITZROY & COLLINGWOOD

PLACES TO STAY
38 The Nunnery
40 Royal Gardens Apartments
45 Star Hotel

PLACES TO EAT
3 Cafe Retro
5 Vegie Bar; Bakers Cafe
7 Charmaine's
8 Joe's Garage; Babka Bakery-Cafe
10 The Fitz
11 Rhumbarella's
12 Gypsy Bar
14 The Provincial
15 Mario's
16 Bull Ring
17 Spanish Club (Hogar Español)
21 Carmen Bar
22 Thai Thani
25 Cafe Bohemio
27 Sinbad's Corner
28 Soul Food Vegetarian Cafe
30 Black Cat Cafe
31 Sala Thai
32 Guernica
36 Cafe Rumours
37 De Los Santos; Akari 177
41 Nyala
49 Grace Darling Hotel
50 Cafe Birko
51 Arcadia
52 Macedonia
53 Builders Arms Hotel
54 Vegetarian Orgasm
56 Smith St Bar & Bistro

ENTERTAINMENT/PLACES TO DRINK
1 Royal Derby
6 Punters Club
9 The Evelyn Hotel
13 Night Cat
19 Bar Salona
20 The Laundry
23 McCoppin's Hotel
26 The Tote
29 Rainbow Hotel
33 The Standard Hotel
34 Perseverence Hotel
42 The Club
46 Glasshouse Hotel
48 The Peel Dance Bar
55 The Barracuda
57 Prince Patrick Hotel

OTHER
2 Fitzroy Baths
4 Fitzroy Nursery & Artists Garden
18 Universal Theatre; Radio 3RRR
24 CCP Gallery
35 Fitzroy Town Hall
39 Royal Terrace
43 Australian Toy Museum
44 The Mill
47 Collingwood Indoor Tennis Centre

The baths were saved from closure by a huge community campaign; a similar campaign a generation earlier couldn't prevent the freeway eating up once-pretty Alexander Pde and cutting North Fitzroy from Fitzroy proper. A generation before that, few people were particularly concerned that whole blocks of inner Melbourne 'slums' were razed to make way for the ugly public housing towers that dominate the skyline. It's said that the planners just drove around Carlton, Collingwood, Fitzroy and Richmond, deciding on demolition sites without getting out of their cars.

Carlton & United Breweries, maker of beers such as Fosters and Victoria Bitter, has a visitor centre at the **Carlton Brewhouse** with some interesting displays. The brewhouse is actually in Abbotsford, a small suburb between Collingwood and Richmond, on the corner of Nelson and Thompson Sts (see the East Melbourne & Richmond map). It's open from Monday to Saturday and admission is $5 (including a tasting). On weekdays there are tours of the brewery at 10 and 11.30 am and 2 pm ($7.50). Book on ☎ 9420 6800.

EAST MELBOURNE

East Melbourne is a small residential pocket of elegant Victorian townhouses, mansions and tree-lined avenues. Clarendon, Hotham and Powlett Sts are all worth a wander if you're interested in seeing some of Melbourne's most impressive early residential architecture.

Tasma Terrace, in Parliament Place behind Parliament House, is a magnificent row of six attached Victorian terraces. The three-storey terraces were built in 1879 for a grain merchant, a Mr Nipper, and are decorated with enough cast-iron lace to sink a small ship. They also house the office of the **National Trust**, an organisation dedicated to preserving Australia's heritage. It's worth visiting the office – it has a range of information on National Trust properties, and the interior of the reception office is a great example of over-the-top Victoriana. The terrace next door has also been restored, and if you ask nicely they will show you the parlour and sitting room with its original Victorian furniture and artworks. The last terrace houses the **Victorian National Parks**

Association (☎ 9650 8296), a lobby group for conservation and the promotion of national parks. It also hosts regular bushwalks and nature walks in and around Melbourne – ring for details.

St Patrick's Cathedral, placed behind Parliament House in Cathedral Place, is said to be one of the world's finest examples of Gothic Revival architecture. It was designed by William Wardell, begun in 1863 and built in stages until the spires and west portal were added in 1939. The imposing bluestone exterior is floodlit to great effect by night, and is spectacular from Brunswick St to the north.

Diagonally across Gisborne St from the cathedral is the Eastern Hill Fire Station. The Old Fire Station building on the corner of Gisborne St and Victoria Pde was built in 1891. Its ground floor now houses the **Fire Services Museum of Victoria** (☎ 9662 2907), which has a historic collection of fire-fighting equipment – fire engines, helmets, uniforms, medals and photos – and is

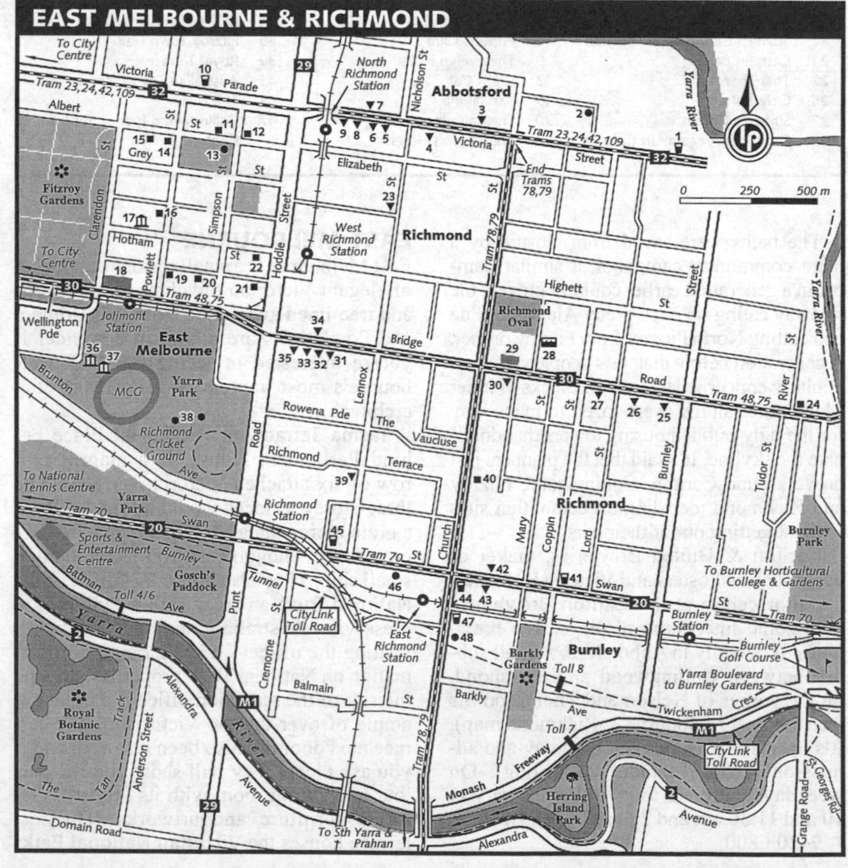

open on Friday from 9 am to 3 pm and on Sunday from 10 am to 4 pm; admission is $5 (children $2). Facing Albert St, the unattractive facade of the newer building has been brightened up with a mural designed by Harold Freedman, the same bloke responsible for the murals at Spencer St train station and the Australian Gallery of Sport. The mosaic mural depicts the history and legends of fire.

The **WR Johnston Collection** (☎ 9416 2515) is a private museum of the decorative arts of 18th century England, displayed in the collector's former home Fairhall at 152 Hotham St. Tours are held on weekdays and cost $12 ($6 concession), and you have to ring in advance to book.

RICHMOND

As Carlton is to Italy so Richmond is to Vietnam, although there are still many Greek Australians living here, hangers-on from the previous wave of immigrants to adopt the suburb. You might even find an Irish Australian from an earlier wave.

The suburb is another centre for Victorian architecture, much of it restored or in the process of restoration. With Richmond's working-class roots, many of the houses are small worker's cottages and terraces, although the Richmond Hill area (between Lennox, Church and Swan Sts and Bridge Rd) has some impressive old mansions.

The **Bridge Rd** and **Swan St** areas form something of a fashion centre, with shops where many Australian fashion designers sell their seconds and rejects alongside the outlets of some of Melbourne's best young designers. **Dimmey's** department store at 140 Swan St is an old-fashioned and chaotic wonderland of junk and bargains, and one of the cheapest and most bizarre places to buy just about anything.

Around the corner in Church St there's a completely different shopping experience at **Duttons**. Nothing costs much under $100,000 here – it's part car showroom and part car museum. It even sells racing cars from time to time. Strangely, the cafe here, ***Cafe Veloce***, is inexpensive.

In the adjacent suburb of Burnley, alongside the Yarra River, you'll find the **Burnley Golf Course**, the Burnley Horticultural College and the **Burnley Gardens** off Yarra Blvd, with their lovely lawns, lily ponds and exotic trees.

For a very quirky and very amateur look at Richmond, watch *Richmond 3121-oh!* on the very quirky and very amateur community television station, Channel 31.

EAST MELBOURNE & RICHMOND

PLACES TO STAY

11 Eastern Townhouse
12 Birches Boutique Apartments
14 Treasury Motor Lodge
15 Albert Heights Executive
16 Magnolia Court Boutique Hotel
18 Hilton on the Park
19 George Powlett Lodge
20 George St Apartments
21 Georgian Court Guesthouse
22 East Melbourne Apartment Hotel
24 Rydge's Riverwalk Hotel
40 Richmond Hill Hotel

PLACES TO EAT

3 Min Tan III
4 Thy Thy 1
5 Vao Doi
6 Thy Thy 2
7 Victoria
8 Tran Tran
9 Tho Tho
23 All Nations Hotel
25 Bill's Barrow
26 Thai Oriental
27 The Curry Club Cafe
30 Silvio's
31 Tofu Shop
32 Richmond Hill Cafe & Larder
33 Chilli Padi
34 Vlado's
35 Downtown Bar & Bistro
39 London Tavern
42 Elatos Greek Tavern
43 Kaliva; Salona

OTHER

1 Terminus Hotel
2 Carlton Brewhouse
10 Prince Patrick Hotel
13 East Melbourne Tennis Centre
17 WR Johnston Collection
28 Richmond City Baths
29 Richmond Town Hall
36 Australian Gallery of Sport
37 MCC Pavilion Library & Museum
38 Aboriginal Canoe Trees
41 Central Club Hotel
44 Swan Hotel
45 Corner Hotel
46 Dimmey's Department Store
47 Great Britain Hotel
48 Duttons; Cafe Veloce

SOUTH YARRA & PRAHRAN

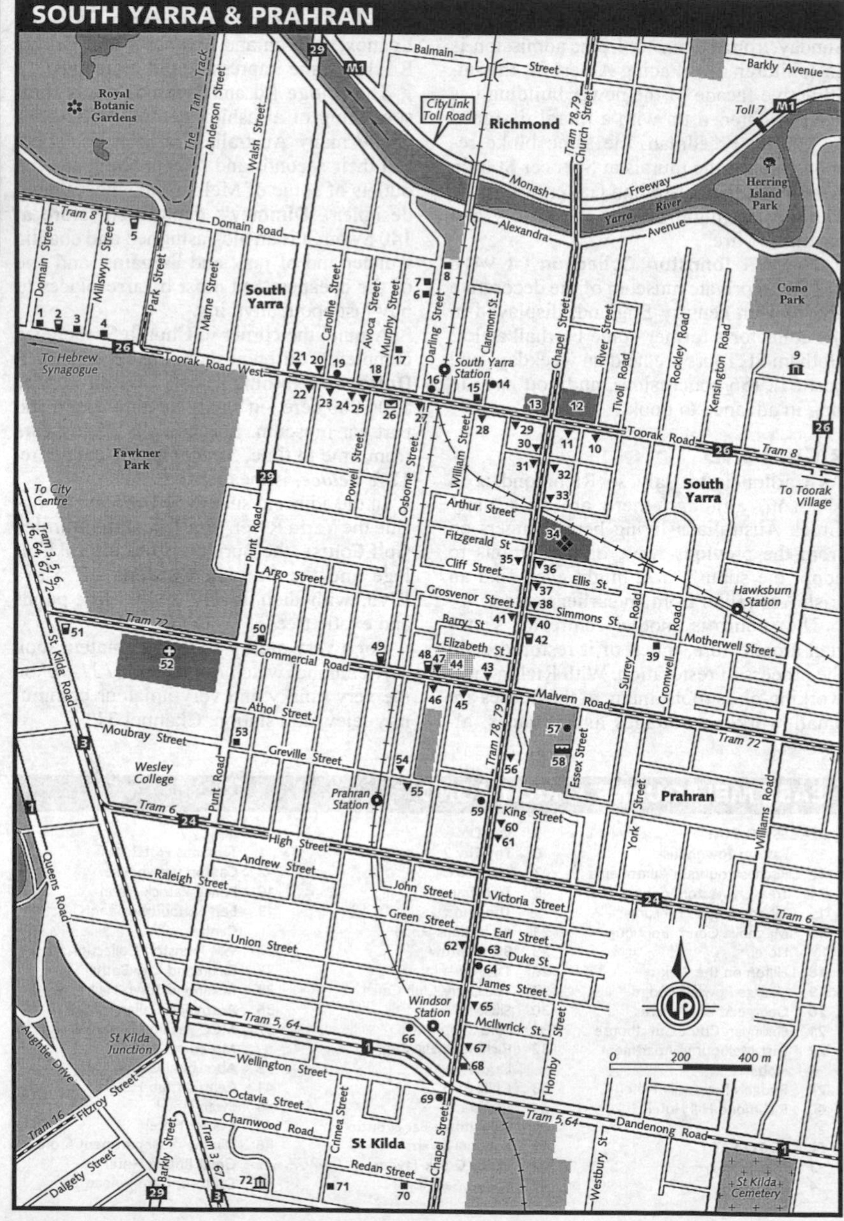

SOUTH YARRA & TOORAK

South Yarra and Toorak are on what's referred to as the 'right' side of the river – the high-society side of town. South Yarra is a bustling, trendy and style-conscious suburb – the kind of place where avid readers of *Vogue Living* will feel very at home. Farther east, Toorak is the poshest suburb in Melbourne and home to Melbourne's wealthiest (or at least the most ostentatious) home-owners. Although it can be interesting to drive around the tree-lined streets looking at the palatial homes, Toorak doesn't hold much interest for travellers.

While in South Yarra, visit **Como House** at 16 Como Avenue, one of Australia's finest colonial mansions. (See the Historic Houses boxed text) open daily from 10 am to 5 pm.

Toorak Rd

Toorak Rd forms the main artery through both suburbs, and is one of Australia's classiest shopping streets, frequented by those well-known Toorak matrons in their Porsches, Mercedes Benzes and Range Rovers (known as 'Toorak Tractors').

The main shopping area in South Yarra is along Toorak Rd between Punt Rd and Chapel St. Along here you'll find dozens of exclusive boutiques and specialist shops, cafes and restaurants, some great bookshops, such as Black Mask, Readings and Martin's, and the Longford Cinema.

The **Fun Factory**, on the corner of Toorak Rd and Chapel St, is a good place to take the kids, with things like roller skating, Dodgem cars, mini-golf and plenty of video games to keep them entertained. The **Como**

SOUTH YARRA & PRAHRAN

PLACES TO STAY

- 1 Tilba
- 3 Albany Motel
- 4 West End Private Hotel
- 6 Darling Towers
- 7 St James Motel
- 8 Domain Motel
- 15 Claremont Accommodation
- 17 South Yarra Hill Suites
- 39 Idlemere B&B
- 50 Hotel Saville
- 53 Lord's Lodge Backpackers
- 68 Nomad's Chapel St Backpackers
- 70 Redan Quest Lodgings
- 71 The Melbourne Guesthouse

PLACES TO EAT

- 10 Zampeli's
- 11 Vietnam Village; Corridor
- 18 La Porchetta
- 20 Soba
- 21 France Soir
- 22 Cotton Lounge; L'Ami
- 23 Winchell's Deli; Cafe Modi
- 24 Barolo's; Cosi
- 25 Frenchy's
- 27 Tamani Bistro; Pinocchio's; Cornercopia
- 28 Pieroni; Chinois
- 29 Tanah Ria
- 30 Caffe e Cucina
- 31 Kanpai; Chapelli's; That Little Noodle Place
- 32 Cafe Greco
- 33 Gratzi Coffee House
- 35 Kazbar
- 36 La Lucciola; STA Travel
- 37 La Camera
- 38 Frostbites
- 40 Caffe Siena
- 41 Kush
- 43 Sweet Basil
- 45 Blue Elephant; The Outlook
- 46 Chinta Ria; Soul Sisters
- 47 Cafe 151; Alternative; Sandgropers
- 54 Feedwell Cafe
- 55 Continental Cafe & Cabaret Club
- 56 Ankara
- 60 Globe Cafe
- 61 Saigon Rose
- 62 Patee Thai
- 65 Marmara
- 67 Cafe Marie

ENTERTAINMENT/ PLACES TO DRINK

- 2 Fawkner Club Hotel
- 5 Botanical Hotel
- 42 Chasers Nightclub
- 48 Three Faces Nightclub
- 49 Exchange Hotel
- 51 Chevron Nightclub

OTHER

- 9 Como House
- 12 Como Centre; Hotel Como; Como Cinemas
- 13 The Fun Factory; Soda Rock
- 14 Victorian AIDS Council & Gay Men's Health Centre
- 16 Readings Bookshop
- 19 Longford Cinema
- 26 South Yarra Post Office
- 34 Jam Factory; Borders Bookshop; Studio Cafe
- 44 Prahran Market; Let's Eat; Spargo's
- 52 Alfred Hospital
- 57 Prahran Skatebowl
- 58 Prahran Swimming Pool
- 59 Prahran Town Hall
- 63 Orange
- 64 Ibiza
- 66 Empire
- 69 Astor Cinema
- 72 Jewish Museum of Australia

Centre, on the opposite corner, is a sleek and stylish commercial development which houses upmarket boutiques and shops, offices, cafes, the Como Cinemas and the five-star Como Hotel.

At the St Kilda Rd end of Toorak Rd stands the copper-domed **Hebrew Synagogue**, built in 1930. On the south side of Toorak Rd between Punt Rd and St Kilda Rd is **Fawkner Park**, an attractive and spacious park with large expanses of grass, tree-lined paths, tennis courts and various sports ovals. It's a great spot for a stroll or a picnic or perhaps to kick a football around.

At the Toorak end of Toorak Rd is the smaller and more exclusive group of shops and arcades known as **Toorak Village**, between Wallace Ave and Grange Rd. This is the local convenience shopping area for some of Melbourne's wealthiest citizens – don't expect any bargains, but this is a great spot for window-shopping and people-watching. If you want to see how and where Melbourne's moneyed classes live, go for a drive through streets like St Georges Rd and Grange Rd – you'll see some of the biggest mansions in the country.

Chapel St

Chapel St is one of Melbourne's major and most diverse retail centres. The South Yarra end, between Toorak Rd and Commercial Rd, is probably Melbourne's trendiest and most stylish centre for retail fashion, and is virtually wall-to-wall clothing boutiques (with a sprinkling of hip bars and cafes). If you want to see fashion, this is where you'll see it – in the shop windows, sitting outside the cafes and walking the street.

The **Jam Factory** at No 500 is a large shopping and entertainment complex that has recently been redeveloped in a glitzy, somewhat controversial 'Hollywood-meets-Disneyland' style. It contains a wide range of specialty shops, a cinema complex, and plenty of bars and restaurants.

PRAHRAN

Prahran, surrounded by its more affluent neighbouring suburbs of South Yarra, Toorak and Armadale, is a blend of small Victorian workers' cottages, narrow, leafy streets and high-rise, government-subsidised flats for low-income earners. This area is populated by people from a broad range of ethnic backgrounds and is enlivened by a variety of cultural influences.

It has some lively streets, the most notable being **Chapel St**. Prahran's sector of Chapel St stretches from Malvern Rd down to Dandenong Rd, and is more diverse and less fashionable than the South Yarra sector. The delightful **Prahran Market** is just around the corner from Chapel St on Commercial Rd (see Markets in the Shopping section).

Commercial Rd is something of a focal centre for Melbourne's gay and lesbian community, and has a diverse collection of nightclubs, bars, pubs, bookshops and cafes.

East of Chapel St, Commercial Rd becomes **Malvern Rd**, and is the border between Prahran and South Yarra, another interesting shopping precinct, with a large number of antique shops and quite a few second-hand and bric-a-brac shops, clothes boutiques, nurseries and other hidden gems along its length. In Essex St (off Malvern Rd) is the Prahran Pool, and beside the pool is the popular Skatebowl, a council-run skateboarding centre with a large concrete bowl and metal ramp.

Running west off Chapel St beside the Prahran Town Hall, **Greville St** has a quirky collection of offbeat retro/grunge clothing shops, galleries, bookshops, junk shops and some good bars and cafes – well worth checking out.

ST KILDA

St Kilda is one of Melbourne's liveliest and most cosmopolitan areas, a fact jointly attributable to its seaside location and its chequered history.

In Melbourne's early days, St Kilda was a seaside resort, the fashionable spot for those wanting to escape the increasingly grimy and crowded city. Horse trams, and later cable trams, ran along St Kilda Rd carrying day-trippers, and by 1857 the railway line to St Kilda was completed. During the gold-rush period, many of the wealthier citizens built mansions in St Kilda, and Fitzroy St became one of the city's most gracious boulevards. Hotels were built, dance halls opened, sea baths and fun parks catered for the crowds, and St Kilda was *the* place to go in search of fun and entertainment.

As things became more hectic, the wealthy folk moved on to the more exclusive areas like Toorak and Brighton. With the economic collapse of the 1890s, St Kilda's status began to decline. Flats were built and the mansions were demolished or divided up, and by the 1960s and 1970s, St Kilda had a reputation as a seedy centre for drugs and prostitution. Its decadent image of faded glories (and cheap rents) attracted a diverse mixture of immigrants and refugees, bohemians and down-and-outers.

In recent years, St Kilda has undergone an image upgrade. It has returned to the forefront of Melbourne's fashionable suburbs, the place it occupied more than a century ago, but with a few characteristic differences. Its appeal is now a mix of the old and the rejuvenated, the ethnic and the artistic, the stylish and the casual. St Kilda is a place of extremes – backpacker hostels and fine-dine restaurants, classy cafes and cheap take-aways, seaside strolls and Sunday traffic jams. Despite its improved image, however, some elements of its seedy past remain, and it can still be somewhat perilous to wander the streets late at night, particularly for women.

Of interest is a historic **Corroboree Tree**, a 350-year-old Aboriginal ceremonial tree located between the Junction Oval and the intersection of Queens Rd and St Kilda Rd. The **St Kilda Botanical Gardens** were first planted in 1859 and have recently been upgraded and improved, and feature a new garden conservatory and the Alister Clarke Memorial Garden (a bed of roses). The gardens are tucked away off Blessington St, not far from the bottom end of Acland St, and are well worth searching out.

The *St Kilda Heritage Walk* brochure, with 22 historic points of interest, is available from the town hall on the corner of St Kilda Rd and Carlisle St. The walk concentrates on the foreshore and Esplanade area, although another interesting walk is to explore the St Kilda Hill area where some of the oldest and grandest buildings remain.

The **National Theatre** (☎ 9534 0221), a great old theatre on the corner of Barkly and Carlisle Sts, houses a ballet and drama school and stages a wide variety of productions – ring to find out what's on.

If you follow **Carlisle St** across St Kilda Rd and into St Kilda East, you'll find some great Jewish food shops, bakeries, European delicatessens and fruit shops – Carlisle St is much less trendy than the bayside areas, and the shops generally less expensive.

The **Jewish Museum of Australia** (☎ 9534 0083), 26 Alma Rd, houses displays relating to Jewish history and culture, as well as hosting regular exhibitions. It's open Tuesday to Thursday from 10 am to 4 pm, and Sunday from 11 am to 5 pm; entry costs $5/3.

The **St Kilda Festival**, held on the second weekend in February, is a great showcase for local artists, musicians and writers, and features street parties, parades, concerts, readings and *lots* more. Acland St is closed to traffic and filled with food stalls and entertainment, and in Fitzroy St all the restaurants bring their tables out onto the footpath. The finale of the festival and the weekend is a concert and fireworks display over the beach.

Fitzroy St

Originally a proud and stylish boulevard, Fitzroy St followed St Kilda's decline at the end of the 19th century and became a seedy strip of ill repute. Today, Fitzroy St is at the leading edge of St Kilda's revival and has been given new life by the opening of a growing number of stylish new bars, restaurants and cafes. It's one of Melbourne's most interesting eating and drinking precincts, and day and night the street is crowded with a fascinating blend of people.

Acland St

Farther south, the section of Acland St between Carlisle and Barkly Sts was famed for its continental cake shops, delicatessens,

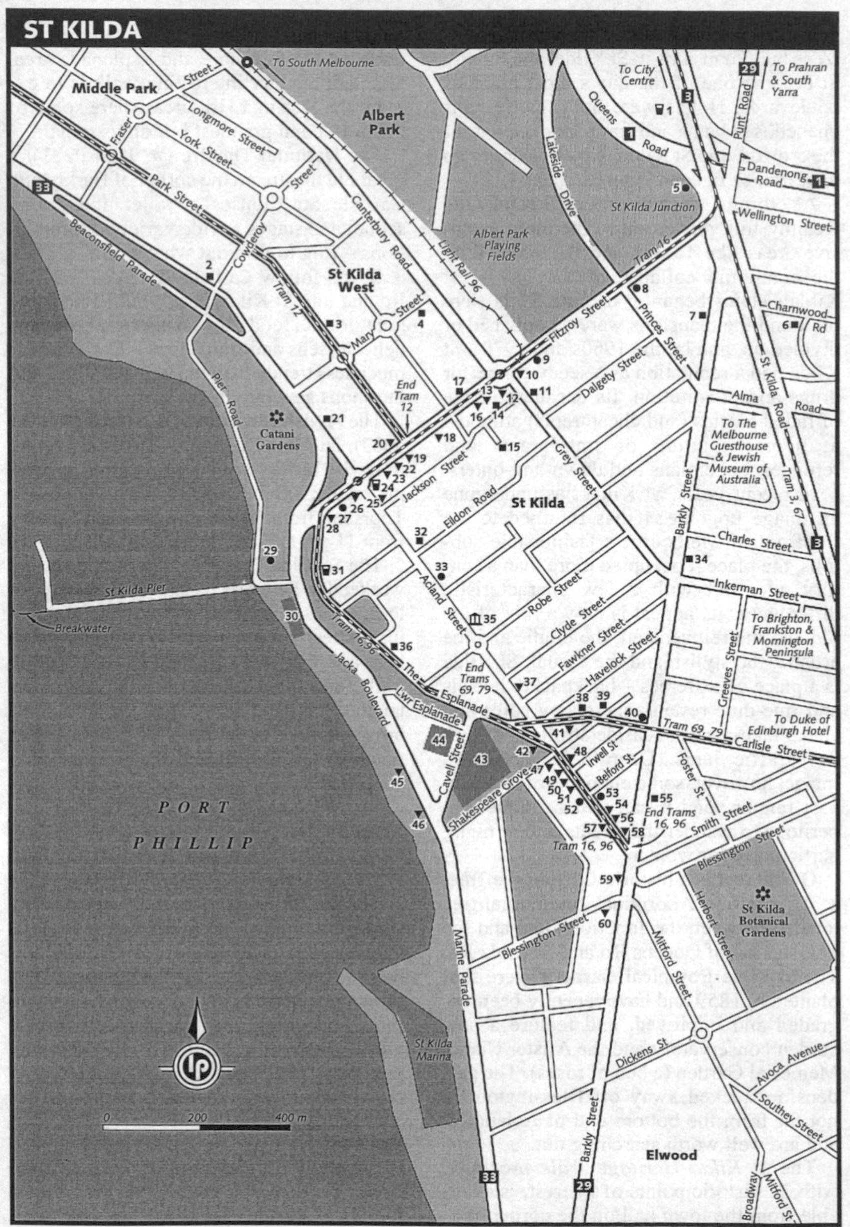

ST KILDA
To South Melbourne
Middle Park
Albert Park
To City Centre
To Prahran & South Yarra
St Kilda West
St Kilda
St Kilda Junction
Albert Park Playing Fields
Catani Gardens
St Kilda Pier
Breakwater
PORT PHILLIP
To The Melbourne Guesthouse & Jewish Museum of Australia
To Brighton, Frankston & Mornington Peninsula
To Duke of Edinburgh Hotel
St Kilda Botanical Gardens
St Kilda Marina
Elwood
End Tram 12
End Trams 69, 79
End Trams 16, 96
Tram 12
Tram 16
Tram 16, 96
Tram 69, 79
Tram 3, 67
Light Rail 96
Street
Longmore Street
York Street
Park Street
Fraser
Cowderoy
Beaconsfield Parade
Pier Road
Canterbury Road
Mary Street
Fitzroy Street
Queens Road
Lakeside Drive
Punt Road
Dandenong Road
Wellington Street
Princes Street
Charnwood Rd
Dalgety Street
Alma Road
St Kilda Road
Grey Street
Jackson Street
Eildon Road
Barkly Street
Charles Street
Inkerman Street
Acland Street
Robe Street
Clyde Street
Fawkner Street
Havelock Street
Greeves Street
The Esplanade
Lwr Esplanade
Jacka Boulevard
Cavell Street
Shakespeare Grove
Irwell St
Belford St
Carlisle Street
Foster St
Smith Street
Blessington Street
Herbert Street
Mitford Street
Marine Parade
Dickens St
Avoca Avenue
Southey Street
Broadway
Mitford St
0
200
400 m

Checkout Receipt

Porterville Public Library (Porterville)
05/28/11 11:01AM
Access to the Web catalog at
http://www.sjvls.org
Use Telecirc to renew books!
866-290-8681
****

RUSH, TIFFANY L

Loving Natalee : a mother's testimony of
1077611042 06/18/11

Bad cat /
1072361965 06/18/11

The Christmas spirit : memories of famil
59372085829821 06/18/11

Frommer's Vancouver & Victoria 2010, wit
50772082881460 06/18/11

Victoria.
1045327200 06/18/11

An eagle named Freedom my true story of
59372082028138 06/18/11

Porterville 559-784-0177

TOTAL: 6

Thank you for supporting
your public library.

ST KILDA

PLACES TO STAY
2 Robinson's by the Sea
3 Cabana Court Motel
4 Victoria House B&B
6 Charnwood Motor Inn
7 Crest international Hotel/Motel
11 St Kilda Coffee Palace
14 Kookaburra Backpackers
15 Enfield House
17 Hotel Tolarno; Bar & Bistro
21 Warwick Beachside
32 St Kilda Quest Inn
34 Olembia Guesthouse
36 Novotel Bayside Hotel
38 Carlisle Motor Lodge
39 Cosmopolitan Motor Inn
55 Barkly Quest Lodgings

PLACES TO EAT
10 The George Hotel, Public Bar and Gallery
12 Chichio's
13 Bar Ninety Seven; Chronicles Bookshop
16 Topolino's
18 Thai Panic Cafe
19 Leo's Spaghetti Bar
20 Cafe Menis/Bortoletto's
22 Hard Wok Cafe
23 Café Di Stasio
25 Chiata Ria – Blues
26 Street Cafe
28 Madame Joe Joe
37 Spuntino; Harley Court; Dog's Bar
41 The Galleon
42 Vineyard Restaurant
45 Stokehouse
46 Pavilion
47 Bala's
48 Chinta Ria – Soul; Cafe Goa
49 Cafe Manna
50 Red Rock Noodle Bar
51 Blue Danube; Scheherezade
54 Cicciolina
56 Noodle Box
57 Orienta on Acland
58 Big Mouth
59 Wild Rice; Claypots Seafood Bar
60 Rasa's Vegie Bar

OTHER
1 Mansion
5 Corroboree Tree
8 The Ritz
9 The George Cinemas
24 Prince of Wales Hotel
27 Rock 'n' Roll 'n' Skate Hire
29 Royal Melbourne Yacht Squadron
30 St Kilda Baths
31 Esplanade Hotel; Espy Kitchen
33 Theatreworks
35 Linden Art Centre & Gallery
40 National Theatre
43 Luna Park
44 Palais Theatre
52 Internet Kennel Cafe
53 Cosmos Books & Music

and central European cafes and restaurants such as Scheherezade and the Blue Danube. This part of Acland St became the focal centre for the wave of Jewish and other European refugees who settled in this area during Hitler's rise to power and after WWII, and their influence and presence remain strong. However, the older places are being swamped by stylish bars and eateries, making Acland St another of Melbourne's favourite food strips. The street also has good book and record shops, fish shops, clothing boutiques and gift shops, and on weekends in particular, Acland St is bustling with people who come from everywhere to enjoy the atmosphere.

North of Carlisle St, Acland St is mostly residential all the way to Fitzroy St – with a few exceptions. The grand old two-storey mansion at 26 Acland St has been converted into the **Linden Art Centre & Gallery**. Registered by the National Trust, the building houses a contemporary art gallery, artists' studios, workshops and performance spaces. Linden is open daily and admission is free.

At 14 Acland St is the home of the excellent **Theatreworks**, a local fringe theatre group (see Theatre in the Entertainment section).

Seaside St Kilda

St Kilda's foreshore has undergone the same rejuvenation as the rest of the suburb. The beaches have been cleaned up, the foreshore parks landscaped and bike paths built. The boats and yachts moored in the lee of the breakwater, the Canary Island palm trees planted along the foreshore and people promenading along the pier all add to the ambience. Two of St Kilda's most popular restaurants are superbly located in converted foreshore buildings: the stylish seafood restaurant the Pavilion was once a bathing pavilion, and the Stokehouse was originally an Edwardian teahouse.

St Kilda Pier and breakwater is a favourite spot for strollers, who often reward themselves with a coffee or a snack at Kirby's Kiosk, a restored 19th-century tearoom at the junction of the pier. On weekends and public holidays ferries run from the pier across the bay to Williamstown (see Getting Around later in this chapter). Bicycles can be hired at the base of the pier in summer. You can also take a boat cruise with **Penguin Waters Cruises** (☎ 0412 187 202) to see a local fairy penguin colony. Sunset cruises, including a BBQ and drinks, cost $30 from St Kilda Pier, $40 from Southbank.

On the foreshore south of the pier, the former **St Kilda Baths** site has been stalled in mid-renovation for years, thanks to a messy squabble between the developers and local residents.

The entrance of **Luna Park**, with its famous laughing face and twin-towers, on the Lower Esplanade, has been a symbol of St Kilda since 1912, and it has just been restored to an artistic approximation of its first incarnation. Luna Park, with its motto 'Just for Fun', is a somewhat dated and old-fashioned amusement park but that's a big part of the seaside charm. It has some great rides, including the roller coaster, disco swings, Dodgems, a Ferris wheel and ghost train. Admission is free if you want to wander in and look around. Each ride costs $3 for adults, $2 for kids; multiple-ticket booklets are available at slightly discounted prices. Opening times vary; ring the recorded information number (☎ 1902 240 112, 30c per minute) for details.

The **Palais Theatre** across the road was built in 1927. At the time it was one of the largest and best picture palaces in Australia, seating over 3000, and it's still a great venue for a wide variety of live performances.

Built in 1880, the marvellous **Esplanade Hotel** on the Upper Esplanade is the musical and artistic heart and soul of St Kilda, and perhaps the best-known pub in Melbourne. The actress Sarah Bernhardt stayed here back in 1891. Today the 'Espy' is much loved by St Kilda's locals, with its live bands (often free), comedy nights, great food and a uniquely grungy atmosphere. Due to its prime location and run-down state its future is constantly being threatened by developers who want to build huge towers on the site. See the Places to Eat and Entertainment sections for more details on the Espy.

The **Esplanade Art and Craft Market**, every Sunday along the Upper Esplanade, features a huge range of open-air stalls selling a great variety of arts, crafts, gifts and souvenirs.

SOUTH MELBOURNE

South Melbourne had humble beginnings as a shanty town of canvas and bark huts on the swampy lands south of the Yarra. The area was originally called Emerald Hill, after the grassy knoll of high ground that stood above the muddy flatlands. Nowadays, South Melbourne is an interesting inner-city suburb with a rich architectural and cultural heritage and quite a few sights worth seeing.

Clarendon St is the main street. It runs through the heart of South Melbourne from Spencer St in the city to Albert Park Lake. In the central shopping section, many of the original Victorian shopfronts have been restored and refitted with their verandahs, and you'll find all sorts of shops and quite a few pubs (the survivors from the days when the area boasted a pub on every corner).

Emerald Hill, between Clarendon, Park, Cecil and Dorcas Sts, was the first area built on and is now a heritage conservation area, with some fine old mansions and terrace houses, and the impressive **South Melbourne Town Hall** on Bank St, which has been restored. The **South Melbourne Market**, which dates back to 1867, is on the corner of Cecil and Coventry Sts (see Markets in the Shopping section).

The **Victorian Tapestry Workshop**, 260 Park St, produces large-scale tapestries which are the collaborative work of weavers and contemporary artists. At the workshop you'll be able to see the creation of 'one of Western civilisation's oldest and richest art forms'. Some pieces are available for sale.

The **Chinese Joss House** (1856), 76 Raglan St, is said to be one of the finest Chinese temples outside China. It was built by the Sze Yup Society as a place of worship for the Chinese who came during the

PORT & SOUTH MELBOURNE & ALBERT PARK

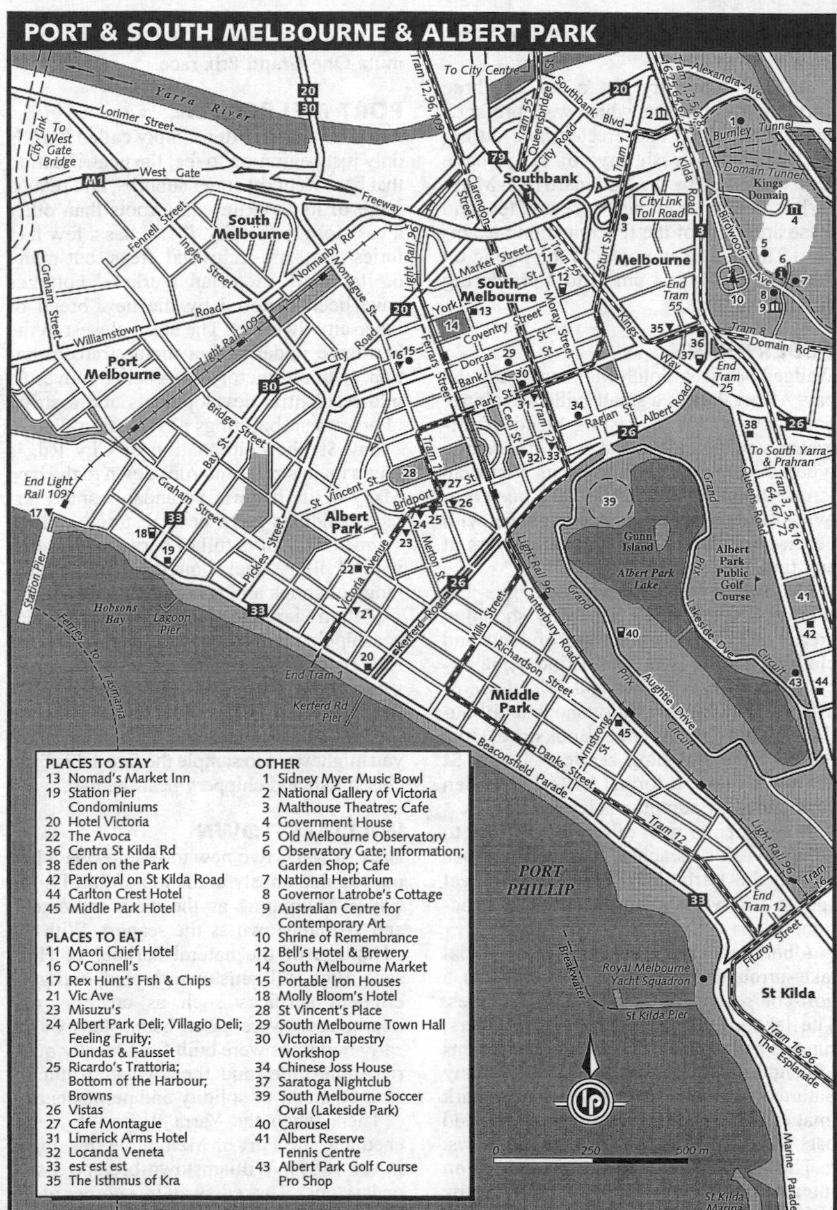

PLACES TO STAY
13 Nomad's Market Inn
19 Station Pier Condominiums
20 Hotel Victoria
22 The Avoca
36 Centra St Kilda Rd
38 Eden on the Park
42 Parkroyal on St Kilda Road
44 Carlton Crest Hotel
45 Middle Park Hotel

PLACES TO EAT
11 Maori Chief Hotel
16 O'Connell's
17 Rex Hunt's Fish & Chips
21 Vic Ave
23 Misuzu's
24 Albert Park Deli; Villagio Deli; Feeling Fruity; Dundas & Fausset
25 Ricardo's Trattoria; Bottom of the Harbour; Browns
26 Vistas
27 Cafe Montague
31 Limerick Arms Hotel
32 Locanda Veneta
33 est est est
35 The Isthmus of Kra

OTHER
1 Sidney Myer Music Bowl
2 National Gallery of Victoria
3 Malthouse Theatres; Cafe
4 Government House
5 Old Melbourne Observatory
6 Observatory Gate; Information; Garden Shop; Cafe
7 National Herbarium
8 Governor Latrobe's Cottage
9 Australian Centre for Contemporary Art
10 Shrine of Remembrance
12 Bell's Hotel & Brewery
14 South Melbourne Market
15 Portable Iron Houses
18 Molly Bloom's Hotel
28 St Vincent's Place
29 South Melbourne Town Hall
30 Victorian Tapestry Workshop
34 Chinese Joss House
37 Saratoga Nightclub
39 South Melbourne Soccer Oval (Lakeside Park)
40 Carousel
41 Albert Reserve Tennis Centre
43 Albert Park Golf Course Pro Shop

gold rush, and is open daily except Friday from 9 am to 4 pm.

At 399 Coventry St, a set of three **portable iron houses**, which were prefabricated in England and erected here during the heady gold-rush days of 1853, have been preserved by the National Trust. Many early colonial dwellings were prefabs, and these are some of the few remaining examples. The houses are open to the public on Sunday from 1 to 4 pm (2 to 4 pm during daylight savings).

ALBERT PARK

Wedged between South Melbourne and the bay, Albert Park is a small 'village' suburb, populated by an interesting blend of migrants, young families and upwardly mobile types. A large percentage of its Victorian terrace houses and cottages have been renovated and the suburb is a popular spot with beach-goers in summer and cafe-lovers at any time of the year.

On **Bridport St** between Montague and Merton Sts is a small but lively shopping area, with a high proportion of food and clothing shops. Here you'll find some excellent and stylish cafes and delicatessens, a few exclusive speciality shops and boutiques, and the Avenue Bookstore. Just north of the shopping centre is lovely **St Vincent's Place**, a formal Victorian garden surrounded by sumptuous terrace houses.

In summer, crowds of sun-lovers flock to Albert Park's beaches, especially those around the **Kerferd Rd Pier** – it's a great spot to observe Aussie beach 'kulcha' in action.

Albert Park Lake is a 2.5km-long artificial lake surrounded by parklands, sports ovals, a golf-course and other recreation facilities. The lake circuit is popular with strollers, runners and cyclists, and the sight of dozens of dinghies sailing across the lake on a sunny Saturday is one of Melbourne's trademark images. There are several restaurants and bars where you can sit and enjoy the views.

The road around the lake was used as an international motor-racing circuit in the 1950s, and since 1996 the revamped track has been the venue for the **Australian Formula One Grand Prix** race.

PORT MELBOURNE

Port Melbourne, often simply called Port, is only just beginning to feel the gentrification that has swept the inner suburbs, and retains more of its working-class roots than other areas close to the city. It still has a few factories and semi-industrial areas, but many of its small Victorian workers' cottages have been restored by the new breed of inner-city dwellers. The areas closest to the bay have undergone a major transformation, with old factory sites being converted into residential developments and a string of apartment buildings near Station Pier.

Bay St, the continuation of City Rd, is Port's main street, and runs down to the bay. Many of its historic verandah-fronted terrace buildings have been restored and revamped. Bay St is full of heritage character with a 'village' feel about it – there's a good range of shops and some great pubs.

Station Pier is Melbourne's major passenger shipping terminal and the departure point for ferries to Tasmania. It also has good views of the city and an old-fashioned kiosk. If you're a fan of Rex Hunt (an over the top football commentator and TV fishing guru) you might want to sample the fare at his franchised fish and chippery near the pier.

WILLIAMSTOWN

Back in 1837, two new townships were laid out simultaneously at the top of Port Phillip Bay – Melbourne as the main settlement, and Williamstown as the seaport. With the advantage of the natural harbour of Hobson's Bay, Williamstown thrived, and government services such as customs and immigration were based here. Many of the early buildings were built from locally quarried bluestone, and the township quickly took on an air of solidity and permanence.

Then, when the Yarra River was deepened and the Port of Melbourne developed in the 1880s, Williamstown became a secondary port. Tucked away in a corner of the bay, it was bypassed and forgotten for years.

In the last decade or so Williamstown, or Willy as it's often called, has been rediscovered and is experiencing a renaissance.

Nelson Place, which follows the foreshore and winds around the docklands and shipyards, was patriotically named after the British Navy's Admiral Horatio Nelson, famous for his victory in 1805 over the combined French and Spanish fleets in the Battle of Trafalgar. Nelson Place is lined with historic buildings, many of them registered by the National Trust, while the yacht clubs, marinas, boat builders and chandleries along the waterfront all add to the maritime flavour. Williamstown's other attractions include restaurants and cafes, some good pubs and bars, art and craft galleries and interesting speciality shops.

The **Visitor Information Booth** (☎ 9397 3791) on Nelson Place opens from 11 am to 3.30 pm on weekdays and 5 pm on weekends. Between Nelson Place and the waterfront is **Commonwealth Reserve**, a small park where a **craft market** is held on the first

and third Sunday of each month. It's also the main site for the Williamstown Summer Festival, held over the Australia Day weekend in January.

Moored at Gem Pier is the **HMAS Castlemaine**, a WWII minesweeper that was built at Williamstown in 1941 and has been converted into a maritime museum. It is staffed by volunteers from the Maritime Trust of Australia and contains interesting nautical exhibits and memorabilia, and is open on weekends from noon to 5 pm. Admission is $5. **Cruises** around the harbour on the *Little Gem* leave from the pier on weekends and cost $5.

The **Historical Society Museum**, housed in the old Mechanics Institute building (1860) at 5 Electra St, has displays of maritime history, model ships, antique furniture and some strange relics including a spring-loaded fly-disturber. The museum opens on Sunday from 2 to 5 pm and admission is $3.

Williamstown Railway Museum (☎ 9397 7412), operated by the Australian Railway Historical Society, is open on weekends and public holidays from noon to 5 pm, and on Wednesday during school holidays from noon to 4 pm. It's a good spot for kids and rail enthusiasts, with a fine collection of old steam locomotives, wagons, carriages and old photos, and mini-steam-train rides for kids. It's part of the Newport Railway Workshops on Champion Rd in North Williamstown, and is close to North Williamstown train station. Admission is $5 for adults, $2 for children.

On the corner of Nelson Place and Syme St, the **Customs Wharf Market & Gallery** houses an interesting collection of arts and crafts and speciality shops: it's open daily from 11 am to 6 pm and entry costs $1. On the corner of Osborne and Giffard Sts, the small but lovely **Williamstown Botanic Gardens** are also worth a visit.

North along the Strand at **Parson's Marina**, Williamstown Boat Hire (☎ 9397 7312) hires out boats for fishing and cruising, for around $25 an hour (with a two-hour minimum). It also hires tackle and sells bait.

The excellent **Scienceworks Museum** is just north of Williamstown in Spotswood (see Other Museums earlier in this chapter).

Williamstown Beach, on the south side of the peninsula, is a really pleasant place for a swim. From Nelson Place walk down Cole St.

Getting There & Away

From the city, Williamstown is about a 10-minute drive across the West Gate Bridge, or a short train ride – change at Newport; Williamstown station is close to the centre of town. The double-decker City Wanderer tour bus (see Organised Tours later in this chapter) will also get you there, but the nicest way to go is by ferry – see Getting Around later in this chapter.

A good bicycle path follows the foreshore reserve from the Timeball Tower and runs all the way to the West Gate Bridge, passing the Scienceworks Museum. An interesting option for cyclists wanting to get from the city side across to Scienceworks and Williamstown is the Punt (☎ 015 304 470), which ferries cyclists and pedestrians across the Yarra River from under the West Gate Bridge. The Punt operates from Friday to Monday and during school holidays between 10 am and 5 pm and costs $3/5 one way/return. Wave to attract the punter's attention.

OTHER BAYSIDE SUBURBS

Melbourne has some fairly good beaches close to the city, though there's no surf in the bay. The bay is reasonably clean and fine for swimming, although the water tends to look a little murky, especially after high winds and rain.

Starting from the city end, Albert Park, Middle Park and St Kilda are the most popular city beaches. Farther around the bay there's **Elwood**, **Brighton** and **Sandringham**, which are quite pleasant. Next comes **Half Moon Bay** which, for a city beach, is very good indeed, as is **Black Rock** nearby. Beyond here you have to get right around to the Mornington Peninsula before you find some really excellent bay beaches, especially around **Mt Eliza** and **Mt Martha**. The north end of Sunnyside Beach at Mt Eliza is a designated nudist area.

If you want to go surfing or see spectacular and remote ocean beaches head for the **Mornington Peninsula**, to the south-east, or the **Bellarine Peninsula**, to the south-west of the city, both a little over an hour's drive away.

ACTIVITIES

This section covers a range of activities in and around Melbourne – for more details and info on activities around the state, see the earlier Activities chapter.

Billiards/Pool/Snooker

There are lots of dim, smoky venues around town, many with full-sized billiards/snooker tables, which is a nice change from all those kiddie-sized tables in pubs. Popular places include King's Pool, 256 King St; the Cue, 277 Brunswick St, Fitzroy; the fabled Johnny's Green Room, 194 Faraday St, Carlton; and Masters, 150 Barkly St, St Kilda. The Victorian Billiards and Snooker Club (☎ 9388 1947) is at 203 Sydney Rd in Brunswick.

Bushwalking

Pick up a copy of the useful book *Walking Around Melbourne – Bushwalking by Public Transport* ($12.95, available at the NRE information centre) for details of day walks you can reach by jumping on a train or bus.

Canoeing

The Yarra River offers canoeists a variety of water from tranquil, flat stretches to rapids of about grade three (classified difficult and requiring some paddling technique). The best sections of river are in the upper reaches from Warburton to the lower reaches at Fitzsimmons Lane, Templestowe. The lower reaches are still scenic, offering respite from the city, but consist mostly of flat water.

Popular sections for those in kayaks and Canadians (open canoes) are Lower Homestead Rd to Wittons Reserve in Wonga Park, Pound Bend in Warrandyte, including the tunnel (at medium-water level and for experienced paddlers only), and Fitzsimmons Lane to Finns Reserve in Templestowe. In the lower reaches there's a canoe recreation area around Dights Falls in Abbotsford.

The pamphlet *Canoeing the Upper Yarra*, provided free by the Upper Yarra Valley and Dandenong Ranges Authority (☎ 5967 5222), gives all the do's and don'ts, locations and information on essential safety equipment. You should observe warning signs and water-level gauges. The YHA also organises canoeing trips.

For more sedate canoeing in the city, see the section earlier on Yarra Bend Park.

Cycling

See the Bicycle section in the Getting Around at the end of this chapter for details on cycling in Melbourne.

Fishing & Boating

You *can* fish in the Yarra and Maribyrnong rivers, but you're better off heading down to the bay and hooking a few snapper. Try the Port Melbourne, Albert Park and St Kilda piers. Tackle shops like the Compleat Angler, at 19 McKillop St in the city, are good places for advice.

Boats can be hired for fishing on the bay, but the conditions can be deceptively treacherous – don't go out unless you're sure of the weather. Try Williamstown Boat Hire (☎ 9397 7312) at Parson's Marina in Williamstown – the same people operate Southgate Boat Hire, at Berth 1 Southgate, with motor boats for cruising along the Yarra River. Another good boatshed is the long-established Keefers Boat Hire (☎ 9589 3917) in Beaumaris, about 30 minutes drive south-east from the city.

Canoes and boats can be hired along the Yarra River – see the Yarra Bend Park section earlier for details.

Golf

Melbourne's sandbelt courses such as Royal Melbourne, Victoria, Huntingdale and Kingston Heath are world famous. It is tough to get a round at these members courses, but there are also plenty of public courses where anyone can play. You will need to book on weekends. Green fees are around $12 to $20 for 18 holes, and most courses have clubs and buggies for hire (around $10 to $15). Some good public courses close to town are Royal Park (☎ 9387 3585) in Parkville near the zoo, Yarra Bend (☎ 9481 3729) in Fairfield and Albert Park (☎ 9510 5588) next to Albert Park Lake. Yarra Bend is the best of these.

In-Line Skating

In-line skating (also known as Rollerblading, although Rollerblade is a brand name) is booming and the best tracks are those around Port Phillip from Port Melbourne to Brighton. You can hire from places like Rock 'n' Roll 'n' Skate Hire (☎ 9525 3434), 11 Fitzroy St in St Kilda. Rock 'n' Roll charges $8 for the first hour (less for subsequent hours) and $25 for 24 hours.

Indoor Climbing

The are a number of places where you can hone your rock-climbing skills on indoor walls. The Mill (☎ 9419 4709), 78 Oxford St, Collingwood, is a very nice space and costs $25, including equipment.

Running

Melbourne has some great routes for runners. One of the favourites is the Tan track around the Royal Botanic Gardens. The bicycle tracks beside the Yarra and around the bay are also good runs, but watch out for bike riders and skaters. Albert Park Lake is another favourite, especially on Saturday when the sailboats are racing.

Melbourne's premier annual running event, the Melbourne Marathon, is held each October. Other major runs include the 5km and 10km women-only Sussan Classic each March/April, and the 8km Run to the MCG in April/May. For details of fun runs, check the calendar in the *Australian Runner* magazine or ring them on ☎ 9819 9225.

Sailing

With about 20 yacht clubs around the shores of Port Phillip Bay, yachting is one of Melbourne's most popular passions. Races and regattas are held most weekends, and the bay is a memorable sight when it's sprinkled with hundreds of colourful sails. Conditions can change radically and without warning, making sailing on the bay a challenging and sometimes dangerous pursuit.

Many yacht clubs welcome visitors to volunteer to crew on racing boats. Phone the race secretary at one of the major clubs if you're keen. (You might learn some new words, as I did after dropping a small but vital shackle-pin into the briny deep.)

The big four clubs are: Royal Melbourne Yacht Squadron (☎ 9534 0227) in St Kilda; Royal Brighton Yacht Club (☎ 9592 3089); Sandringham Yacht Club (☎ 9598 7444); and Hobson's Bay Yacht Club (☎ 9397 6393) in Williamstown. For more leisurely sailing, dinghies can be hired from the Jolly Roger School of Sailing (☎ 9690 5862) at Albert Park Lake.

You can learn to sail in Melbourne, in dinghies at the Jolly Roger School (☎ 9690 5862), or, to gain your Competent Crew certificate on yachts, with a school such as Geoff Steadman's Melbourne Sailing School (☎ 9589 1433).

If you'd rather be a spectator, head down to the Royal Melbourne (at the end of Fitzroy St in St Kilda) on the weekends, where you can watch the boats preparing for races and see them start and finish from out on the breakwater. Williamstown is also a good spot for spectators.

Melbourne's two main ocean races are the Melbourne to Devonport and Melbourne to Hobart, held annually between Christmas and New Year. The Melbourne to Hobart goes around Tasmania's wild west coast, unlike the more famous Sydney to Hobart which runs down the east coast.

Scuba Diving

See the Activities chapter for details of diving around Melbourne.

Surfing

The closest surf beaches to Melbourne are on the Mornington Peninsula and the Bellarine Peninsula. Bells Beach on the Great

Ocean Road near Torquay is recognised as a world-class surfing beach. Again, see the Activities chapter for more details.

Swimming

The Melbourne City Baths, on the corner of Swanston and Victoria Sts, has a 25m indoor pool plus a gym, spas, saunas and squash courts. The facilities open from 6 am to 10 pm on weekdays and 8 am to 6 pm on weekends. A swim, spa and sauna costs $6.50.

In the Albert Park lake's parklands is the new Melbourne Sports and Aquatic Centre. It's a great place for a swim, with a 75m-long lap pool and several other pools, including a wave pool, plus an indoor water-slide. It's open from 6 am to 10 pm on weekdays and 7 am to 8 pm on weekends. Entry costs $4 ($3 children).

Other pools close to the city include the outdoor Carlton Baths in Rathdowne St, Fitzroy Baths in Alexandra Pde, and Prahran Pool in Essex St; and the indoor Richmond Baths in Gleadell St and St Kilda Swimming Centre in Alma Rd. The outdoor pools are generally open from late October until April.

One exception is the Harold Holt Swimming Centre in High St, Glen Iris (which must be the only pool in the world named after a prime minister who drowned). It's a great facility and open year round, with indoor and outdoor pools, spas, saunas and aerobics.

Lastly, don't forget the bay – you can choose from many beaches and the water temperature is tolerable from mid-November to late March.

Tennis & Squash

Tennis-court hire is generally between $10 and $20 an hour. On weekends rates are often higher, and for floodlit or indoor courts you can pay between $17 and $24 an hour.

Except in January during the Australian Open, you can hire one of the 23 outdoor and five indoor courts of the Melbourne Park National Tennis Centre (☎ 9286 1244) on Batman Ave. For other public courts see the *Yellow Pages* phone book.

There are squash courts in the city at the Melbourne City Baths ($9 for half an hour in peak times, $6 in off-peak): for courts in other areas, check the *Yellow Pages*.

Windsurfing/Sailboarding

Close to the city, both Elwood and Middle Park beaches are designated sailboarding areas. A company called Repeat Performance Sailboards (☎ 9525 6475) at 87 Ormond Rd in Elwood hires beginners' boards for $15 an hour or $35 for half a day, and specialised equipment for between $45 and $75 a half day. It offers packages for longer hires.

ORGANISED TOURS

There's a huge array of tours on offer in and around Melbourne. Ask at the tourist information centres in the city if you're looking for something in particular. See the Organised Tours section in the Getting Around chapter and the Alternative Bus Tours section in the Getting There & Away chapter for more details on tours around the state, and beyond.

City Bus Tours

Companies like AAT Kings (☎ 9663 3377), Australian Pacific (☎ 9663 1611) and Gray Line (☎ 9663 4455) run conventional city bus tours, as well as day trips to the most popular tourist destinations like Sovereign Hill, Healesville Sanctuary, Phillip Island and the Great Ocean Road.

There are also a couple of popular double-decker buses offering tours around Melbourne. The City Explorer (☎ 9650 7000) does a continuous circuit around the city and inner suburbs, with 16 stops including the Melbourne Zoo, Metro! Craft Centre, Queen Victoria Market, Shrine of Remembrance and the Victorian Arts Centre. Passes are sold on board and one/two day passes cost $22/35 for adults, $10/15 for children or $50/80 for a family of five. There's an information kiosk outside the town hall, which is the first stop. The first circuit begins here at 10 am daily and the last at 4 pm.

The City Wanderer (☎ 9563 9788) does a similar circuit around the inner-city area, as well as heading over the West Gate Bridge to the Scienceworks Museum and Williamstown. One-day passes cost $20 for adults, $10 for children or $45 for a family of five. The first bus leaves the Town Hall at 10.30 am. Tickets for both buses get you discounts on entry to various attractions, and you can get on and off all day.

Special Interest Tours

A wide variety of special interest tours are run, including those of specific sites or areas such as the Queen Victoria Market or Chinatown. You'll find information about many under the entries in this chapter, but there are a few others that deserve special mention.

White Hat Tours (☎ 9662 9010) show you around historic Melbourne General Cemetery at 2 pm on Wednesday and Sunday for $10. On Saturday between 2.30 and 4.30 pm there's a Chocolate and Other Desserts Walk (☎ 9815 1228); between 12.30 and 2.30 pm the same day there's the more popular Chocolate Indulgence Walk (☎ 9815 1228). City Cycle Tours (☎ 9585 5343) offers guided tours of the city by bike (bicycles supplied or bring your own).

Tram Tours

In the city centre, free City Circle trams (☎ 13 1638 for information) travel along Flinders, Spring and Nicholson Sts to Victoria Pde and then back along Latrobe and Spencer Sts (there are also trams running in the opposite direction). Designed primarily for tourists, and passing many city sights along the way, the trams run daily between 10 am and 6 pm, every 10 minutes or so. There are eight refurbished W-class trams operating on this route. Built in Melbourne between 1936 and 1956, they have all been painted a distinctive deep burgundy and gold.

You can even dine on board a tram while taking a scenic night cruise around Melbourne's streets – see the Colonial Tramcar Restaurant boxed text.

There's also a restored 1920s tourist tram that runs from the city to the Melbourne Zoo on Sunday. This service leaves from the Flinders St end of Elizabeth St at 9, 10 and 11 am and noon each Sunday – phone the Met to confirm times.

River Cruises

Melbourne River Cruises (☎ 9614 1215) offers regular cruises along the Yarra River, departing every half-hour from Princes Walk (on the north bank of the river, east of Princes Bridge) and from Southgate. You can take a one hour cruise either upstream or downstream ($13 for adults, $6.50 for children) or combine the two for a 2½ hour cruise ($25/13). Southgate River Tours (☎ 9682 5711) offers an hour-long cruise upstream to Herring Island in the old steam-powered *Elizabeth Anne*, departing from Berth 4 at Southgate.

Maribyrnong River Cruises (☎ 9689 6431) has 2½-hour cruises up the Maribyrnong River to Avondale Heights, with a stopover at the interesting Living Museum of the West, costing $14 for adults and $4 for children. There are also one-hour cruises down to the West Gate Bridge and docklands ($7/4). Departures are from the end of Wingfield St in Footscray.

You can also take a cruise to the penguin colony at St Kilda pier – see the St Kilda section above for details.

Organised Walking Tours

Melbourne Heritage Walks (☎ 9827 1085) conducts informative and interesting walking tours of Melbourne. Focusing on fine arts, history and architecture, the two-hour walks operate on Wednesday from 10 am to noon and Sunday from 2 to 4 pm. The cost is $20.

Art and About (☎ 9696 0591) has an Arts City Melbourne tour ($25) at 10 am on the last Tuesday of the month that takes you through the ballet school and backstage at venues in the nearby Arts Precinct. It also has good walking tours around Aboriginal art galleries and tours concentrating on city architecture but they're for groups only.

The City of Melbourne publishes a series of seven *Heritage Walk* brochures, which

RICHARD I'ANSON

Meditation (1933), Fitzroy Gardens Conservatory, honours the sorrow of mothers who lost their sons in WWI

RICHARD NEBESKY

Exhibition Fountain (1880), at the original entrance to the Royal Exhibition Building, Carlton Gardens

RICHARD NEBESKY

Tiled seat, Brunswick Street, Fitzroy

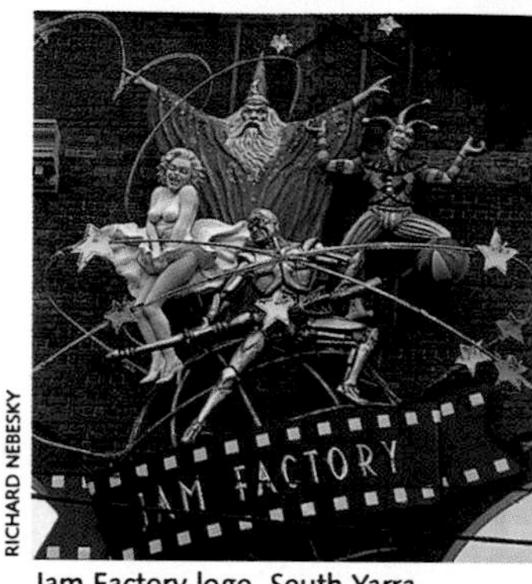

RICHARD NEBESKY

Jam Factory logo, South Yarra

RICHARD NEBESKY

Colourful bathing boxes line the beach at Brighton

RICHARD NEBESKY

Ian Potter Museum of Art, Melbourne University

GLENN BEANLAND

Art for sale at the Esplanade market, St Kilda

are available from the council's information booths.

The National Trust publishes the *Walking Melbourne* booklet, which is particularly useful if you're interested in Melbourne's architectural heritage.

SPECIAL EVENTS

Melbourne has festivals all year round, with themes such as film, comedy, arts, theatre, sporting events, food and wine, multiculturalism or just simple celebrations of life.

Historic Houses

If you're interested in Victoria's heritage, the National Trust (☎ 9654 4711) publishes a brochure that gives details of historic properties that are open to the public. In Melbourne they include the following:

RICHARD I'ANSON

Como House, South Yarra

Como House, overlooking the Yarra River from Como Park in South Yarra, was built between 1840 and 1859. The home, with its extensive grounds, has been authentically restored and furnished and is operated by the National Trust. Aboriginal rites and feasts were still held on the banks of the Yarra when the house was first built, and an early occupant wrote of seeing a cannibal rite from her bedroom window (she was probably mistaken).

Como House is open from 10 am to 5 pm every day and admission is $9 (students $6, children $5, family $20) and you can get there on tram No 8 from the city – get off at stop 33 on Toorak Rd and walk down Como Ave.

Rippon Lea is at 192 Hotham St in Elsternwick, close to St Kilda. It is also a fine old mansion with huge, elegant gardens inhabited by peacocks. Rippon Lea is open from 10 am to 5 pm daily, except Monday, and admission costs are $9 adults, $6 students, $5 children and $20 for families. The tearooms are open between 11 am and 5 pm on weekends only. The easiest way to get there is to take a Sandringham-line train to Ripponlea train station, from where you'll have a five-minute walk to the property.

Labassa (☎ 9527 3891), at 2 Manor Grove in Caulfield, is an elaborate French Renaissance-style, two-storey mansion noted for its richly detailed interior. It's well worth seeing, but is only open on the last Sunday of each month from 10.30 am to 4.30 pm – ring for details. Admission costs $7 for adults, $5 for children and $18 for families.

'What's on' lists are available from tourist information offices. Tickets to most major events can be booked through Ticketmaster (☎ 96645 7970 for inquiries, ☎ 13 6122 for sport, ☎ 13 6166 for theatre and the arts, ☎ 13 6100 for general events). Some of the festivals and events are listed below.

Summer

December The outdoor evening performances of plays such as *A Midsummer Night's Dream* and *Romeo and Juliet* in the Royal Botanic Gardens are a special summer highlight. Since 1937 Christmas in Melbourne has been celebrated with Carols by Candlelight, under the stars at the Sidney Myer Music Bowl. Book for both of these through Ticketmaster, and don't forget a rug, a candle and insect repellent. Another Christmas institution is the decorated windows at Myer's department store in Bourke St Mall.

If you're into cricket, head for the MCG on Boxing Day, when thousands turn up for the first day of the international Test Match.

January A public New Year's Eve party is often held at Southgate.

Each January, the Australian Open, a Grand Slam tennis championship, is held at the Melbourne Park Tennis Centre. The Summer Music Festival is based at the Victorian Arts Centre and features everything from the classics to rock music.

Australia Day is celebrated in all sorts of ways, including street parades, food fairs and fireworks at Albert Park Lake. For jazz lovers, the eclectic Montsalvat Jazz Festival is held over three days at a picturesque artists' colony in Eltham and various other venues around town. If you want to get out of town for Australia Day, pack a picnic basket and head to the rustic Hanging Rock Horse Races, held yearly since the 1870s.

February During February, the St Kilda Festival is a week-long celebration of local arts, culture and food. Also in February, the Australian Matchplay and the Australian Masters golf tournaments are held on the great sandbelt courses, while Vietnamese culture is celebrated with the Victoria St Festival. At the marvellous Harvest Picnic out at Hanging Rock, you can enjoy the pick of the crop of Victorian produce. Chinatown comes to life with the celebration of Chinese New Year and the Asian Food Festival. The Melbourne Music Festival is also held in February, and showcases local musicians at various venues.

The gay and lesbian Midsumma Festival is held in early February.

Autumn

March The 10 day Moomba festival, in early March, is one of Melbourne's favourite family events, with carnivals and fireworks, water-skiing, a Dragon Boat Festival and the zany Birdman Rally, all on the Yarra River. The Aboriginal meaning of Moomba is 'getting together and having fun' (which might or might not have sexual connotations).

The Formula 1 Grand Prix is held at the Albert Park circuit also in early March.

The Melbourne Food and Wine Festival is held over two weeks in late March.

Oh, and the football season kicks off in March too!

April It seems like almost everyone's a comedian in Melbourne, but in April when the brilliant International Comedy Festival takes over the town, the locals are joined by a swag of fabulous international acts.

The National Trust runs Heritage Week during April, devoted to increasing the appreciation of Melbourne's rich architectural heritage. Anzac Day, commemorating those who fell in war, is held on 25 April, the date that the Australian and New Zealand combined forces landed at Gallipoli during WWI, sustaining enormous losses. The day begins with a dawn service at the Shrine of Remembrance, followed by a march along St Kilda Rd into the city.

Easter is pretty quiet in Melbourne – half the population heads to the countryside in pursuit of various activities, such as tennis carnivals in country towns, the Easter Fair in Bendigo or to watch the world's best surfers in the Bells Beach Surfing Classic held just south of Torquay.

Winter

June June brings the Queen's Birthday weekend, when all ski resorts go into party mode to herald the official opening of the ski season (weather permitting!). At the same time, the International Film Festival opens and runs for two weeks, featuring the newest and the best in local and international film – luckily, Melbourne is one of the *café latte* centres of the world, so you can always top up on caffeine to get through the next session or two.

August August sees yet more food and wine shows in Melbourne – the Exhibition of Victorian Winemakers and the Sip 'n' Sup Wine and Food Festival in Sunbury, on the north-western edge of the metropolitan area.

Spring

September September/October epitomises Melbourne's eternal conflict – the world of art and culture versus the world of sport. The Australian Football League (AFL) Finals series builds up to an extravagant, colourful and noisy climax when the Grand Final is played on the last Saturday in September.

Also in September is the Royal Melbourne Show, when the country comes to town. Held at the Royal Melbourne Showgrounds in Flemington, it's a large-scale agricultural fair with a carnival atmosphere – livestock judging, equestrian events, wood-chopping competitions, rides and showbags (bags containing novelties, samples and confectionery) – and attracts 800,000 visitors yearly.

October Believe it or not, not everyone appreciates 'the footy', and Melbourne has an Anti-Football League that takes solace in the commencement of the Melbourne International Festival in October. Run over 16 days, the festival combines the best of the performing arts, visual arts and music, and incorporates the Melbourne Writers Festival and the Melbourne Fringe Arts Festival – don't miss the weird and wild street party in Brunswick St.

The Spring Racing Carnival runs through October and November, and the two feature horse races are the Caulfield Cup and the Melbourne Cup. October also features two professional cycling races, the Herald-Sun Tour 10 day event and the Melbourne to Warrnambool Classic.

On Phillip Island, the Australian Motorcycle Grand Prix is held.

November The Melbourne Cup horse race is always run on the first Tuesday in November. During Cup Week, Melbourne gets caught up in something called 'Spring Fever', which manifests itself as a frenzy of partying, gambling, social intercourse and high fashion.

For the Italian Lygon St Festa in November, the street is blocked to traffic and filled with food stalls, bands and dancers; the entertainment also includes the manic waiters' race.

Also in November is the Hispanic Community Festival, when Melbourne's small Spanish and South American communities take over Johnston St for a lively celebration of Latin culture.

PLACES TO STAY

You have a choice between caravan parks and backpacker hostels, pubs and motels, B&Bs and guesthouses, serviced apartments and a range of hotels. Once you've decided what you're looking for, the tricky part is deciding which area to stay in. The city centre is convenient and close to things like theatres, museums and the train and bus terminals, although it can be a little lifeless at night. The alternative is to stay in one of the inner suburbs that ring the city.

Accommodation can be booked directly, or you can make reservations through Tourism Victoria (☎ 13 2842), in the Melbourne Town Hall on the corner of Swanston Walk and Little Collins St. The more expensive hotels can be booked through travel agents, and that might get you a better rate than booking directly.

Note that during major festivals and events accommodation in Melbourne is often very scarce, and you need to make reservations well in advance. This will especially be the case during the Grand Prix, at which time you can also expect prices to rise substantially, even for the backpacker hostels.

If you decide to stay longer, look in the *Age* classifieds on Wednesday and Saturday under 'Share Accommodation'. You could also try the notice boards in the hostels, or places like the universities, Readings bookshop in Carlton, Cosmos Books and Music and the Galleon restaurant in St Kilda, or the Black Cat Cafe in Fitzroy.

PLACES TO STAY – BUDGET

Camping & Caravan Parks

There are a few caravan/camping parks in the metropolitan area but none are close to the centre and most are in unattractive areas. An exception is the ***Hobsons Bay Caravan Park*** *(☎ 9397 2395, 158 Kororoit Creek Rd, Williamstown)*. It's still a long way from the city centre (about 15km) but Williamstown is a pleasant little bayside suburb with a distinct personality. There's a reasonable train connection with the city or you can take a ferry to Southbank. Sites cost $15 and cabins are $40/45 a single/double. The caravan park is about 2km west of Williamstown's shopping centre and 2.5km west of the bayfront.

The closest place to the city centre is ***Melbourne Holiday Park*** *(☎ 9354 3533, 265 Elizabeth St, Coburg East)*, 10km north of the city. For two people camping costs from $18 and cabins from $47 (from $61 with ensuite bathroom).

There are caravan parks along the Mornington Peninsula (see the Around Melbourne chapter) that have the advantage of being near the bay, and are close to reasonable train links to the city. Of course, the really sensible answer is to forget about camping while you're in Melbourne and stay at a hostel.

Hostels

There are backpacker hostels in the city centre and most of the inner suburbs. St Kilda and the city vie for the biggest collection of hostel accommodation. Competition between hostels is fierce in winter but it can be hard to find a bed in the better places over summer. Several of the larger hostels have courtesy buses that do pickups from the bus and train terminals.

The following is a selection of hostels in the popular areas. They're all safe bets for your first night or two, after which you might want to look around for something that more closely matches your own style – there are lots to choose from. The prices listed are indicative only. Except at the YHA hostels, which have the same prices all year, you can expect to pay a little less in winter and a little more in summer. Most hostels offer cheaper weekly rates.

City Centre The city has some good hostels, which have the advantage of being central and close to the train station and bus depots. ***Toad Hall*** *(☎ 9600 9010, 441 Elizabeth St)* is within easy walking distance of the bus terminals. It's a quiet and well-equipped place with a pleasant courtyard and off-street parking ($5). A bed in a four or six-bed dorm costs from $16; single/double/triple rooms cost about $30/48/52. We've had a few complaints about unfriendly staff here, but given the high staff turnover at hostels it's likely that things have changed – and just as likely that the odd disgruntled employee will be found at any hostel.

Hotel Backpack *(☎ 3929 7525, 167 Franklin St)* gets good reports. ***Exford Hotel Backpackers*** *(☎ 9663 2697, 199 Russell St)* is a cheerful and well set-up hostel in the upper section of an old pub. Rates are marginally less than those at Toad Hall. The same people run the big, well-equipped ***Flinders Station Hostel*** *(☎ 9620 5100, corner Elizabeth St and Flinders Lane)*.

The ***City Centre Private Hotel*** *(☎ 9654 5401, 22 Little Collins St)* is clean and quiet, if somewhat prim. All rooms have shared bathrooms and there's a TV lounge and kitchen on each floor. Backpackers pay $18 in a three or four-bed room and doubles are $37; serviced singles/doubles are $37/50.

North Melbourne Melbourne's YHA hostels are both in North Melbourne, northwest of the city centre. Both offer discounts for a four-day or longer stay. From the airport you can ask the Skybus to drop you at the North Melbourne hostels.

The YHA showpiece is the ***Queensberry Hill Hostel*** *(☎ 9329 8599, 78 Howard St)*. This huge 348-bed place can feel a little soulless but it has excellent facilities, including modern bathrooms, a state-of-the-art kitchen, a rooftop patio with barbecues and 360° views of the city, and a security car park. Dorms cost $18; singles/doubles are $45/55, or $55/65 with private bathroom and there's a self-contained apartment for $95. Office hours are 7 am to 11 pm, although there is 24-hour access once you have checked in. Catch tram No 55 from William St and get off at stop No 11 (Queensberry St), or any tram north up Elizabeth St to stop No 8 (Queensberry St). Walk west on Queensbury St and turn right into Howard St.

Chapman Gardens YHA Hostel *(☎ 9328 3595, 76 Chapman St)* is smaller and older but can be a bit more intimate than Queensberry Hill. Dorms here cost $15, singles $33, twin rooms $36 and doubles $44. From Elizabeth St in the city, take tram No 50 or 57 along Flemington Rd and get off at stop No 19, then walk down Abbotsford St. Chapman St is the first on the left.

Some very good tours operate out of the hostels.

Carlton ***Carlton College*** *(☎ 1800 066 551 toll-free, 101 Drummond St, Carlton)* is a student residence in a very fine triple-storey terrace row – it becomes a hostel over summer. Dorm beds are $15 and singles/doubles are just $25/40. This place has more of a hostel atmosphere than the colleges listed in the later Colleges section.

Fitzroy Well located on the fringe of the city and opposite the Exhibition Gardens is the ***Nunnery*** *(☎ 1800 032 635 toll-free, 116 Nicholson St)*, one of the best budget accommodation options. It's a converted Victorian building with comfortable lounges, good facilities and a friendly atmosphere. The rooms are small but clean and centrally heated. Rates range from $18 in a twelve-bed dorm to $21 in a three-bed dorm; singles are around $40 and twins/doubles are around $55. Take tram No 96 heading east along Bourke St from the city centre, and get off at stop No 13.

Richmond ***Richmond Hill Hotel*** *(☎ 9428 6501, 353 Church St)* is a big Victorian-era building with spacious living areas and clean rooms. Dorm beds cost about $18, singles/twins are $40/50, and it has a B&B section with good single/double rooms from around $60/80.

South Yarra ***Lord's Lodge Backpackers*** *(☎ 9510 5658, 204 Punt Rd)* is on a fairly hectic main road. This is a large, rambling old two-storey mansion with a range of accommodation and prices a little lower than places in the city.

Windsor Nomad's new ***Chapel St Backpackers*** *(☎ 9533 6855, 22 Chapel St, Windsor)* is within walking distance of both South Yarra and St Kilda. It has dorms for $18, doubles for $50 and a double with an ensuite bathroom for $60. Breakfast is free.

St Kilda St Kilda is one of Melbourne's most interesting and cosmopolitan suburbs, and has a good range of budget accommodation as well as plenty of restaurants and entertainment possibilities. From Swanston St in the city, tram No 16 will take you down St Kilda Rd to Fitzroy St, or there's the faster light-rail service (No 96 from Spencer St and Bourke St) to the old St Kilda train station and along Fitzroy and Acland Sts.

Enfield House *(☎ 9534 8159, 2 Enfield St)* is the original and probably the most popular of St Kilda's hostels. It's a huge and rambling Victorian-era building with over 100 beds that somehow manages to have a good atmosphere. There's a variety of dorms, singles and twins. The hostel's courtesy bus

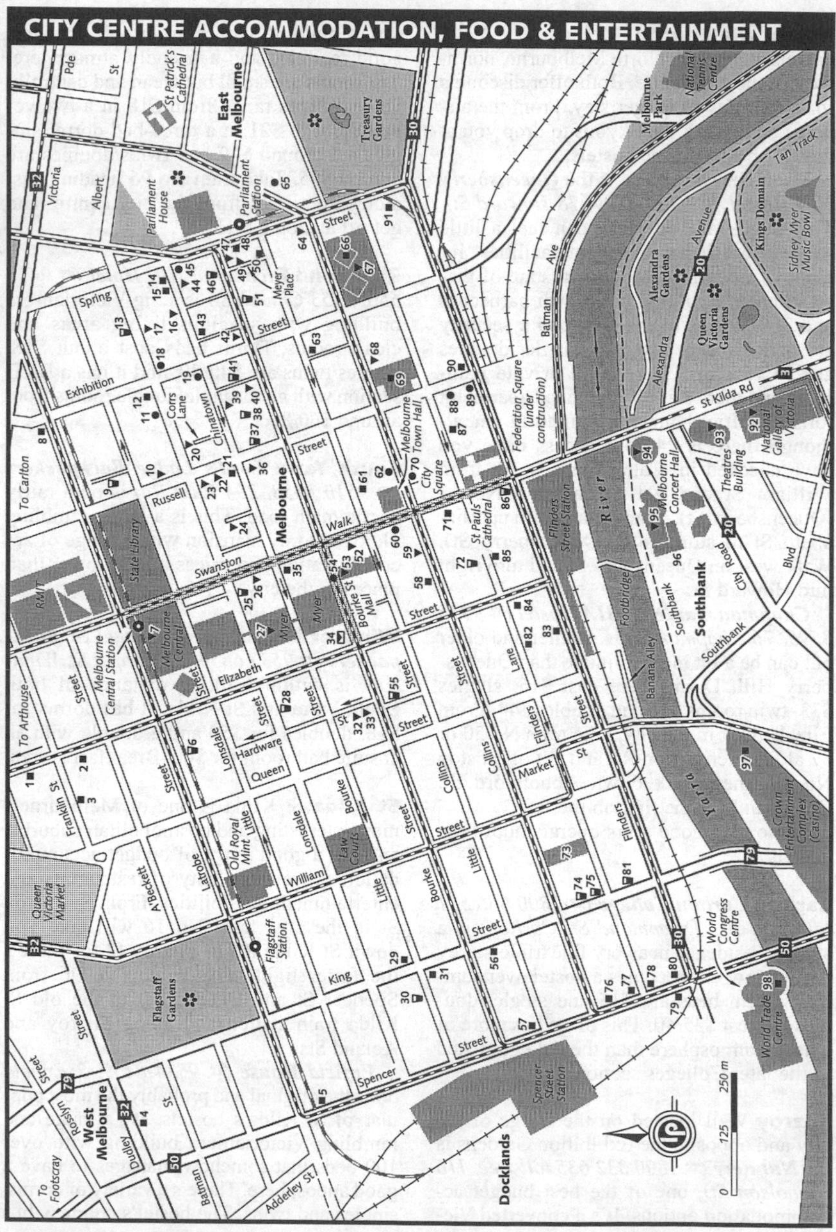
CITY CENTRE ACCOMMODATION, FOOD & ENTERTAINMENT
St Patrick's Cathedral
East Melbourne
Treasury Gardens
Parliament House
Parliament Station
National Tennis Centre
Melbourne Park
Tan Track
Kings Domain
Sidney Myer Music Bowl
Alexandra Gardens
Queen Victoria Gardens
Batman Ave
Federation Square (under construction)
Melbourne Town Hall
City Square
St Paul's Cathedral
Flinders Street Station
Yarra River
Melbourne Concert Hall
Theatres Building
National Gallery of Victoria
St Kilda Rd
Southbank
Footbridge
Banana Alley
Crown Entertainment Complex (Casino)
World Congress Centre
World Trade Centre
Spencer Street Station
Docklands
West Melbourne
Flagstaff Gardens
Flagstaff Station
Queen Victoria Market
Old Royal Mint
Law Courts
Melbourne Central
Melbourne Central Station
State Library
RMIT
Myer
Bourke St Mall
Chinatown
Corrs Lane
Meyer Place
To Carlton
To Arthouse
To Footscray
250 m

CITY CENTRE ACCOMMODATION, FOOD & ENTERTAINMENT

PLACES TO STAY

1 Hotel Y
2 Toad Hall
3 Hotel Backpack
4 Flagstaff City Motor Inn
5 Astoria City Travel Inn
8 Holiday Inn Park Suites
12 Rockman's Regency Hotel
14 City Limits Motel
15 Oakford Gordon Place
21 Exford Hotel Backpackers
29 All Seasons Paragon Hotel
31 The Friendly Backpacker
35 All Seasons Welcome Hotel
43 All Seasons Crossley Hotel
48 Windsor Hotel
50 City Centre Private Hotel
56 Kingsgate Budget Hotel
57 Savoy Park Plaza
58 Novotel Melbourne on Collins
61 Victoria Vista Hotel
63 Stamford Plaza Melbourne Hotel
66 Hotel Sofitel
69 Grand Hyatt Melbourne; Max's; Hyatt Food Court
71 City Square Motel
73 Le Meridien at Rialto Melbourne
76 Batman's Hill Hotel
77 Hotel Enterprize
78 Holiday Inn
79 All Seasons Premier Grand Hotel
80 Terrace Pacific Inn
82 Sebel of Melbourne
83 Euro-Asia Heritage Hotel
84 Flinders Station Hostel
85 Punt Hill Flinders Lane
87 Adelphi Hotel
90 Duke of Wellington Hotel
91 Sheraton Hotel
96 Sheraton Towers Southgate
97 Crown Towers
98 Centra Melbourne on the Yarra

PLACES TO EAT

7 Daimaru
10 Cafee Baloo's
16 Shark Finn Inn
17 Marchetti's Latin
20 Yamato
22 King of Kings
23 Stalactites
24 Supper Inn
26 Lounge
27 Myer
32 Campari Bistro
33 Schwobs
36 Dahu Peking Duck
39 Mask of China
40 Flower Drum
42 Pellegrini's; Florentino; Nudel Bar
44 Cafe K
47 Hard Rock Cafe
49 Waiter's Restaurant; Meyer Place
52 Gopals
53 David Jones
59 Sportsgirl Food Centre
64 Cafe Alcaston
67 Kenzan; Kino
68 Il Solito Posto
92 Garden Restaurant & Café
93 Cafe Vic
94 Treble Clef; Aromas Restaurant
95 Blue Train Cafe; Walter's Wine Bar; Simply French; Blakes; Bistro Vite; Wharf Food Market

OTHER

6 Hardware
9 Bennett's Lane
11 Lumiere Cinema
13 44
18 Comedy Theatre
19 Her Majesty's Theatre
25 Rue Bebelons
28 Club 383
30 Tunnel
34 General Post Office (GPO)
37 Billboard
38 Bernie's
41 International Lounge
45 Princess Theatre
46 Metro
51 Spleen
54 Half-Tix
55 Bass Station
60 Capitol Theatre
62 Atheneum Theatre
65 State Film Centre
70 Regent Theatre
72 Hell's Kitchen
74 Inflation
75 Grainstore Tavern
81 Sports Bar
86 Young & Jackson's Hotel
88 Russell St Theatre
89 The Forum

picks up travellers from the bus terminals, and from Station Pier where the Tasmanian ferries dock.

More like a boutique hotel than a hostel, the facilities at the excellent ***Olembia Guesthouse*** *(☎ 9537 1412, 96 Barkly St)* are very good and include a cosy guest lounge, dining room, courtyard and off-street parking. The rooms are quite small but clean and comfortable, and all have hand-basins and central heating. Dorm beds cost $18, singles are $40, and twins and doubles are $56. Book ahead.

St Kilda Coffee Palace *(☎ 1800 654 098 toll-free, 24 Grey St)* is a big, spacious place with its own cafe and a modern kitchen. Dorms range from $16 to $18 ($20 in a four bed dorm with its own bathroom) and doubles are $50. Around the corner, ***Kookaburra Backpackers*** *(☎ 9534 5457, 56 Jackson St)* is different from most St Kilda places in that it's very small. Dorms are $16 and double rooms $45.

Middle Park Well located between Albert Park Lake and Port Phillip Bay, the ***Middle***

Park Hotel *(☎ 9690 1958, corner Canterbury Rd and Armstrong St)* is a popular pub in a trendy little shopping centre. The upstairs rooms have been renovated and cost $15 in dorms, $25 for singles ($35 in larger rooms) and $50 for doubles, all with shared bathrooms.

South Melbourne Right beside the South Melbourne Market, within walking distance of Southgate and close to both light rail and tram lines, ***Nomad's Market Inn*** *(☎ 1800 241 445 toll-free, 115 Cecil St)* is not really in the centre of things but it's still very well located. And it's a pleasant hostel in a converted pub, which charges about $15 to $18 in dorms and $45 in doubles. Breakfast is included in the price.

Colleges

The University of Melbourne is a short distance to the north of the city centre, in Parkville. Other universities offer college accommodation but they are too far from the centre to be of any interest to most travellers. The following colleges at (or near) the University of Melbourne have accommodation during the vacation period from late November to mid-February and some also offer rooms during the semester breaks (July and the second half of September). You'll pay around $40 for B&B and about $10 extra if you want all meals. Ormond, Queen's and Trinity Colleges are impressive 19th century buildings – ask for a room in their old buildings.

The colleges are: ***International House*** *(☎ 9347 6655, 241 Royal Pde, Parkville)*; ***Ormond College*** *(☎ 9348 1688, College Crescent)* in the University grounds; ***Medley Hall*** *(☎ 9663 5847, 48 Drummond St, Carlton)*; ***Queen's College*** *(☎ 9349 0500, College Crescent)* in the University grounds; ***Ridley College*** *(☎ 9387 7555, 160 The Avenue, Parkville)*; ***Trinity College*** *(☎ 9347 1044, Royal Pde, in University grounds)*; ***University College*** *(☎ 9347 3533, College Crescent)* opposite the University; ***Whitley College*** *(☎ 9347 8388, 271 Royal Pde, Parkville)*.

Pubs

There are still some old pubs offering a varying range of accommodation in inner Melbourne.

A good budget option in the city is the ***Duke of Wellington Hotel*** *(☎ 9650 4984, corner Flinders and Russell Sts)*. Built back in 1850, it's one of Melbourne's oldest pubs but has been recently renovated and has comfortable upstairs rooms with shared bathrooms at $50/90 for singles/doubles, including breakfast. The ***Stork Hotel*** *(☎ 9663 6237, corner Elizabeth and Therry Sts)* is close to the Franklin St bus terminal and Queen Victoria Market, and has simple upstairs rooms from $39/49, and a small guest kitchen.

Hotels & Guesthouses

Moving up a level from the backpacker hostels, there are some good budget options in and around the city centre.

City Centre The hotels along Spencer St are convenient for the bus and train terminals. This was once a rundown area, but is changing fast. ***Hotel Enterprize*** *(☎ 9629 6991, 44 Spencer St)* is a refurbished hotel with budget singles/doubles from $50/60, or from $95/100 with ensuites.

Kingsgate Budget Hotel *(☎ 9629 4171, 131 King St)* is a big old place, with budget rooms with shared bathrooms from $29/45 and ensuite rooms from $60/80. Check the room before you commit yourself.

Hotel Y *(☎ 9329 5188, 489 Elizabeth St)*, run by the YWCA, is an award-winning budget hotel close to the Franklin St bus terminal. It has simple four-bed bunkrooms at $25, singles/doubles/triples at $79/87/99 and deluxe rooms from $99/110/120. The 'Y' has good facilities including a budget cafe, communal kitchen and laundry.

The big ***Victoria Vista Hotel*** *(☎ 9653 0441, 215 Little Collins St)* is a notch up from the cheapest city hotels, and a bit of a Melbourne institution. Budget rooms with shared facilities cost $45/60, standard rooms with ensuite and TV are $85/124, and executive rooms are $124 for singles or doubles.

City Square Motel *(☎ 9654 7011, 67 Swanston St)* is fairly simple, but it's well located and costs from $70/90/100 a single/double/triple. ***Miami Motel*** *(☎ 9329 8499, 13 Hawke St)*, north-west of the city in the semi-industrial area of West Melbourne (see the North Melbourne, Parkville & Carlton map), is a cross between a motel and a backpacker hostel. It's clean and simple, with rooms with shared bathrooms at $40/60 and rooms with ensuites at $68/84.

South Yarra Tram No 8 from Swanston St in the city takes you along Toorak Rd into the heart of the chic suburb of South Yarra.

The ***West End Private Hotel*** *(☎ 9866 5375, 76 Toorak Rd West)* has B&B with singles/doubles at $40/55 – it's pretty old-fashioned, but has a certain shabby charm.

Farther east, the vast ***Claremont Accommodation*** *(☎ 9826 8000, 189 Toorak Rd)* has bright rooms with polished-timber floors, heating and modern communal facilities. Singles/doubles with shared bathrooms start at $46/58.

St Kilda St Kilda used to have quite a few old boarding houses and private hotels that mainly housed longer-term residents. However, most of these have gone upmarket and there's now a shortage of budget places other than backpacker hostels.

Opposite St Kilda beach, ***Warwick Beachside*** *(☎ 9525 4800, 363 Beaconsfield Pde)* is a large complex of 1950s-style holiday flats. They're not glamorous, but they're quite well equipped, and there's a laundry and off-street parking. Costs range from $55 to $85 for a studio and from $90 to $110 for two bedrooms. Weekly rates are cheaper.

Charnwood Motor Inn *(☎ 9525 4199, 3 Charnwood Rd)* is on the inland side of St Kilda Rd and is a good motel in a quiet suburban street with singles/doubles at just $55/65.

PLACES TO STAY – MID-RANGE

Hotels & Motels

Most of the hotels in this section are rated at three stars, and they're pretty comfortable but often a little cramped. In the city centre there isn't much distinction between a hotel and a motel – you certainly won't find single-storey ranch-style motels with a parking space in front of each unit. Unless otherwise stated, rates quoted are for doubles, which often cost the same as singles.

City Centre ***All Seasons Welcome Hotel*** *(☎ 9639 0555, 265 Little Bourke St)* is good value at $95 a room. ***All Seasons Paragon*** *(☎ 1300 360 262, 600 Little Bourke St)* charges from $130. ***All Seasons Crossley***

Places to Stay – Gay & Lesbian

The Laird *(☎ 9417 2832, 149 Gipps St, Collingwood)*, one block east of Hoddle St, is an old pub that has been converted into a gay men's bar and nightclub. Upstairs there are rooms from $65. The ***Star Hotel*** *(☎ 9417 2696, 176 Hoddle St, Collingwood)* is a gay and lesbian pub with singles/doubles for $45/55.

More upmarket is ***163 Drummond St*** *(☎ 9663 3081, 163 Drummond St, Carlton)*, a stylishly restored B&B with small single rooms from $45, doubles with shared bathrooms from $70 and ensuite doubles for around $90. ***Palm Court B&B*** *(☎ 9427 7365, 283 Punt Rd, Richmond)* is another restored two storey Victorian terrace house with four double rooms, two bathrooms, a guest lounge and a pleasant barbecue courtyard. Singles/doubles start at $40/60.

Other places that advertise themselves as being gay-friendly include ***The Friendly Backpacker*** *(☎ 9670 1111, 197 King St)*, a hostel charging $20 a night in dorms, ***Hotel Tolarno*** in St Kilda and the ***Adelphi Hotel*** in the city centre – see the relevant Places to Stay sections for details. If you're intending to stay longer, you'll find accommodation notices in *Melbourne Star Observer* and *Brother Sister*, as well as on notice boards in many cafes and bookshops.

Hotel *(☎ 9639 1639, 51 Little Bourke St)* is a small four-star hotel in the heart of Chinatown with rooms from $140.

Batman's Hill Hotel *(☎ 9614 6344, 66-70 Spencer St)* has rooms starting at $140, and ***Terrace Pacific Inn*** *(☎ 9621 3333, 16 Spencer St)*, nearby, is reasonable and charges from $109.

The ***Euro-Asia Heritage Hotel*** *(☎ 9250 1888, 328 Flinders St)* is in a recycled old building and charges from about $150.

The ***Sheraton Hotel*** *(☎ 9205 9999, 13 Spring St)* dates back to the 1960s but has been refurbished to a reasonable standard. Rooms start at $110/120 a single/double. Note that this hotel is not part of the Sheraton chain – the hotel took the name before the 'real' Sheraton thought of registering the name in Melbourne.

City Limits Motel *(☎ 9662 2544, 20-22 Little Bourke St)* has rooms with kitchenettes costing from $99. ***Astoria City Travel Inn*** *(☎ 9670 6801, 288 Spencer St)* is close to the train station and has its own restaurant and renovated rooms from $84. Nearby, ***Flagstaff City Motor Inn*** *(☎ 9329 5788, 45 Dudley St)* costs from $90.

Parkville ***Elizabeth Tower Motel*** *(☎ 9347 9211, corner Royal Pde and Grattan St)* is opposite the university. This high-rise motel has its own restaurant and bar, and rooms start at $125. Farther north is the 2½ star ***Park Avenue Motor Inn*** *(☎ 9380 9222, 441 Royal Pde)*, which has a swimming pool, restaurant and convention centre, with units and apartments from $76/87 a single/double. One tram stop farther north again is the budget ***Ramada Inn*** *(☎ 9380 8131)*, 539 Royal Pde, with singles/doubles from $84/89.

Carlton ***Rydges Carlton*** *(☎ 9347 7811, 701 Swanston St)* is a five storey hotel built in 1970. It's comfortable and well run, and the facilities include a restaurant, bar and rooftop spa and sauna. Rates start at $130.

Downtowner on Lygon *(☎ 9663 5555, corner Lygon and Queensberry Sts)* has motel-style units from $120.

East Melbourne There are two convenient but uninspiring choices here. ***George Powlett Lodge*** *(☎ 9419 9488, corner George and Powlett Sts)* has older motel-style rooms with kitchenettes from $85/90. ***Treasury Motor Lodge*** *(☎ 9417 5281, 179 Powlett St)* charges from $100/105.

South Yarra ***Hotel Saville*** *(☎ 9867 2755, 5 Commercial Rd)* is a seven storey octagonal building with refurbished motel-style rooms from $84/88, plus its own bar and restaurant – and lots of traffic noise. ***St James Motel*** *(☎ 9866 4455, 35 Darling St)* is an older motel with singles/doubles costing from $75. The ***Albany Motel*** *(☎ 9866 4485, corner Toorak Rd and Millswyn St)* is a busy tourist motel opposite Fawkner Park and close to the Royal Botanic Gardens, with rooms from $75/80.

St Kilda The modern high-rise ***Novotel Bayside Hotel*** *(☎ 9525 5522, 14-16 The Esplanade)* overlooks the bay. It's no architectural masterpiece, but the position is excellent and the front rooms have great views of the bay. Rooms start at $160. Stylish ***Hotel Tolarno*** *(☎ 9537 0200, 42 Fitzroy St)* is in the renovated flats above the Tolarno Restaurant. It charges from $100 a double, plus $15 for a balcony.

St Kilda has plenty of motels, but some of them are fairly dodgy. More respectable places include ***Cabana Court Motel*** *(☎ 9534 0771, 46 Park St)*, with units from $99 to $120, and ***Cosmopolitan Motor Inn*** *(☎ 9534 0781, 6 Carlisle St)*, with rooms from $95. Another reasonably good option is ***Crest International Hotel/Motel*** *(☎ 9537 1788, 47 Barkly St)*, a larger motel that incorporates a conference centre, restaurant and bar, with rooms starting at $99.

Albert Park ***Hotel Victoria*** *(☎ 9690 3666, 123 Beaconsfield Pde)* has a great position overlooking the bay. It's an impressively restored and elegant hotel that dates back to 1888. Downstairs, it has a front bar, bistro and a rather grand formal dining room. Upstairs are 20 comfortable rooms with shared bathrooms for $60 a double, and 10 double ensuite rooms from $90, or $150 with a view of the bay.

St Kilda Rd & Queens Rd The hotels along this stretch mostly cater for corporate travellers. While it's largely a commercial area it can still be a good part of town to stay in.

Centra St Kilda Rd *(☎ 9209 9888, corner Park St and St Kilda Rd)* is an older hotel that has been fully refurbished. The front rooms have great views of the Shrine of Remembrance and parklands opposite, and tariffs start around $100.

The modern and stylish ***Eden on the Park*** *(☎ 9820 2222, 6 Queens Rd)* has 132 well-appointed and comfortable rooms. Standard rooms start at just $145 and suites at $190. Around the corner is ***Parkroyal on St Kilda Road*** *(☎ 9529 8888, 562 St Kilda Rd)*, a flashy four star hotel with rooms from $290.

The 4½ star ***Carlton Crest Hotel*** *(☎ 9529 4300, 65 Queens Rd)* is a large tourist hotel with rooms from $150.

Williamstown Right on the waterfront, by the Gem pier, ***Quest Inn*** *(☎ 1800 334 033 toll-free)* has studio apartments from $125, one-bedroom apartments from $145 and two-bedroom apartments from $165. It would be nice to stay here and catch the ferry into the city.

B&Bs & Boutique Hotels

There are some excellent B&Bs, many of which are at least as comfortable as a four star hotel but charge much less. Boutique hotels are often more like large B&Bs or upmarket guesthouses, sometimes occupying lovely old buildings.

East Melbourne On the fringe of the city, East Melbourne has a pleasant residential feel with its tree-lined streets and grand old Victorian terrace houses. ***Georgian Court Guesthouse*** *(☎ 9419 6353, 21 George St)* is an elegant and cosy B&B with singles/doubles at $59/69, or $89/99 with an ensuite; prices include a buffet breakfast.

Magnolia Court Boutique Hotel *(☎ 9419 4222, 101 Powlett St)* is a bright and friendly small hotel in two halves. The older wing, formerly a ladies finishing college, dates back to 1862. The rooms in the new wing are of a good standard, but don't quite have the same charm. Standard singles/doubles are $113/117, superior rooms are $145 for both singles and doubles, and two-room suites with cooking facilities are $165. The best option is the cute and tiny two room Victorian cottage ($165). The hotel has a breakfast room, heated outdoor spa and garden courtyard.

South Yarra Close to both Chapel St and Toorak Rd, ***Ildemere B&B*** *(☎ 9826 2921, 10 Motherwell St)* is a charming period home with one single ($85) and one double with its own private bathroom and sitting room ($135).

Tilba *(☎ 9867 8844, corner Toorak Rd West and Domain St)* is a small and elegant hotel that has been lovingly restored in gracious Victorian style. Stepping inside is like taking a trip back in time, and the 15 suites all feature old iron bedheads, leadlights, decorative plasterwork and period-style bathrooms. Tariffs range from $140 to $200 a double, depending on the size of the room – highly recommended.

Toorak ***Toorak Manor*** *(☎ 9827 2689, 220 Williams Rd)* is an excellent boutique hotel. Set in lovely gardens, it's a historic mansion that has been impressively converted. It has comfortable period-style rooms with ensuites, cosy lounges and sitting rooms. Tariffs start around $150 a double. Toorak Manor is a short walk from Hawkesburn train station.

Caulfield If you're a racing aficionado (or just like grand Victorian architecture), you might be interested in ***Lord Lodge at Caulfield*** *(☎ 9572 3969, 30 Booran Rd, Caulfield)*. It's adjacent to the Caulfield Racecourse (about 15km south-east of the city centre) and is by Colin Little's famous racing stables. An impressive historic home, it has three guestrooms, each named after famous racehorses that have come out of the stables. Prices here for doubles start at $120.

St Kilda Opposite the beach, ***Robinsons by the Sea*** *(☎ 9534 2683, 335 Beaconsfield Pde)* is an elegant and impressive Victorian-era terrace house with three double rooms with en-suite priced from around $130.

Victoria House B&B *(☎ 9525 4512, 57 Mary St)* is a very comfortable and well setup Victorian home with three double rooms, one of which has its own kitchen. It's a friendly place with pleasant gardens and an attractive courtyard, and good value with singles/doubles from $90/100. In a refurbished 1880s apartment block behind Fitzroy St, ***Brooklawn Mansions*** *(☎ 9537 2633, 5/95 Fitzroy St)* has three rooms for around $150 each.

Albert Park ***The Avoca*** *(☎ 9696 9090, 98 Victoria Ave)* is a large terrace house with good facilities, charging from $100/125 a single/double.

Williamstown Williamstown is mainly thought of as a day-trip destination, but if you want to stay overnight in this very pleasant bayside suburb then the ***Grange B&B*** *(☎ 9397 6288, 219 Osborne St)*, a beautifully restored Victorian-era home, is a good option. It's has one double bedroom with its own en suite and sitting room; rates start at around $140 a double.

PLACES TO STAY – TOP END

Apartment Hotels & Serviced Apartments

Melbourne has plenty of apartment-style hotels and serviced apartments. These are usually more spacious than regular hotels and, having their own kitchen and laundry facilities, they can be better value than an equivalently priced hotel, especially for groups.

City Centre The modern apartment-hotel ***Holiday Inn Park Suites*** *(☎ 9663 3333, 333 Exhibition St)* is a good alternative to hotels. All rooms have balconies, separate lounges, kitchens and laundries. There's a heated pool and sauna on the roof. One-bedroom suites start at $197 a night, two-bedroom suites at $222, and the penthouse is $875 a night.

Another good self-contained option in the city is ***Oakford Gordon Place*** *(☎ 1800 818 236 toll-free, 24 Little Bourke St)*. In a historic setting and built around a garden courtyard, the stylish self-contained apartments are very popular. There's a big range of rooms – examples are: single/double studios cost $130/160, one and two-bedroom apartments are $210/250; split-level suites are $350.

Punt Hill Flinders Lane *(☎ 9650 1299, 267 Flinders Lane)* has apartments from $160. ***Stamford Plaza Melbourne*** *(☎ 9659 1000, 111 Little Collins St)* has mostly one-bedroom luxury suites with a separate lounge room and kitchenette, starting at $240 a night.

Carlton ***Lygon Crest Lodgings*** *(☎ 9345 3888, 700 Lygon St)* is opposite the Mel-

Disabled Travellers Accommodation

Accessible accommodation in Melbourne is at best limited, and expensive, being provided primarily by four and five-star hotels. Canberra-based National Information Communication Awareness Network (NICAN; ☎ 1800 806 769 toll-free) has a database of accessible accommodation, or you can try ***Queensberry Hill YHA*** *(☎ 9329 8599)*, which has an accessible bathroom on each of its four floors. Two accessible motel units are available from the ***Victorian Disabled Motorists Association*** *(☎ 9386 0413)* in Station St, Coburg, north of the city centre. The ***Novotel Bayside*** *(☎ 9525 5522)* in St Kilda is a good but not cheap option with five accessible rooms.

bourne General Cemetery. These former flats have been refurbished to a good standard, and the one and two-bedroom apartments range from $110 to $165.

Fitzroy Fitzroy is fairly light on for accommodation, but ***Royal Gardens Apartments*** *(☎ 9419 9888, Royal Lane)* are well located in a quiet street, a block back from the Exhibition Building and close to Brunswick St. These 76 spacious and stylish apartments are built around a landscaped courtyard with a swimming pool, and there are one, two or three-bedroom configurations, costing $175, $210 and $269 respectively.

East Melbourne There are quite a few serviced apartments in this area. ***East Melbourne Apartment Hotel*** *(☎ 9412 2555, 25 Hotham St)* is a fairly stylish block of 1940s flats converted into studio apartments with good facilities and kitchenettes, ranging from $110 to $150 a night.

Eastern Town House *(☎ 9418 6666, 90 Albert St)* is a refurbished complex with good studio units costing from $99/107 for singles/doubles. Nearby the units at ***Albert Heights Executive*** *(☎ 9419 0955, 83 Albert St)* are a bit bigger and more motel-style, and cost from $100. ***Birches Boutique Apartments*** *(☎ 9417 2344, 1800 651 623 toll-free, 160 Simpson St)* has reasonable one-bedroom apartments from $103.

South Yarra South Yarra is the serviced-apartment capital of Melbourne. Most of them are blocks of flats that were built in the 1950s and 1960s and have been refurbished, some better than others. Several companies manage many blocks of apartments, and you're likely to be offered a better deal if you speak to HQ rather than the individual apartment managers. Try Oakford (☎ 1800 818 244 toll-free), Apartments of Melbourne (☎ 1800 681 900 toll-free) or Punt Hill (☎ 1800 331 529 toll-free).

One of the best options is ***South Yarra Hill Suites*** *(☎ 9868 8222, 14 Murphy St)*, an elegant apartment-style hotel in a quiet leafy street close to Toorak Rd. The hotel has 24-hour reception, a heated pool, spa and sauna, with one-bedroom apartments from $240 and two-bedrooms from $320.

A more affordable option is ***Darling Towers*** *(☎ 9867 5200, 32 Darling St)*, with good one-bedroom flats from about $75 a night.

St Kilda St Kilda also has some good serviced apartments. ***Barkly Quest Lodgings*** *(☎ 9525 5000, 180 Barkly St)* has 26 one-bedroom apartments costing around $105 per night for two people or $140 for four people (two of them on a fold-up couch). They're on a busy street, but the apartments are well renovated and fully equipped. The same company has ***Redan Quest Lodgings*** *(☎ 9529 7595, 25 Redan St)* in a quieter and more suburban part of St Kilda (see the South Yarra & Prahran map), with studio apartments with kitchenettes from $80. There's also ***St Kilda Quest Inn*** *(☎ 9593 9500, 1 Eildon Rd)* with one and two-bedroom apartments from $90 to $160.

Port Melbourne Near the top of the bay, ***Station Pier Condominiums*** *(☎ 9647 9666, 15 Beach St)* has modern, spacious apartments separated by landscaped gardens and boardwalks, with a pool and sauna, tennis court, conference facilities, and a stylish bar and restaurant with live jazz on Sunday afternoons. The one-bedroom apartments start from $230 a night, two bedrooms from $250; most rooms have bay views.

Hotels

Most four and five-star hotels are in the city centre. Because much of their custom is business travellers, they tend to have empty rooms on weekends, which they try to fill by good weekend deals. These vary from time to time – shop around.

City Centre – Four Star ***Adelphi Hotel*** *(☎ 9650 2709, 187 Flinders Lane)* is a stylish small four star hotel with a good range of facilities including a pool, a basement restaurant and a great rooftop bar with views of the city. Standard rooms are $240, deluxe rooms $260 and executive suites $440. ***Savoy Park Plaza*** *(☎ 9622 8888, 630 Little Collins St)* was built in the 1920s, but later became a police academy. It has recently been refurbished in period style, and has a modern Art Deco feel, complete with 1920s-style furnishings. Rooms start at $230 and suites at $370.

Centra Melbourne on the Yarra *(☎ 9629 5111)*, in the World Trade Centre complex on Spencer St, between Flinders St and the Yarra River, is a modern four star hotel with rooms from $180. ***Novotel Melbourne on Collins*** *(☎ 9650 5800, 270 Collins St)* is a four star tourist hotel with rooms from $220.

The ***All Seasons Premier Grand Hotel*** *(☎ 9611 4567, corner Flinders and Spencer Sts)* is part of the massive old Victorian Railways administration buildings, which have been converted into grand apartments and this hotel. Rooms start at $175. Across the road is the ***Holiday Inn*** *(☎ 9629 4111, corner Spencer St and Flinders Lane)*, with rooms from $175 and suites from $220.

City Centre – Five Star They call the ***Windsor Hotel*** *(☎ 9633 6000, 103 Spring St)* Melbourne's 'Grand Lady', and she is indisputably the matriarch of Melbourne's hotels. Other hotels are more opulent, more luxurious and have better facilities, but there are some things you can't manufacture, and a grand sense of history is one of them. Built in 1883 and restored during the 1980s, the Windsor is the epitome of old-world elegance. Beyond the top-hatted doorman, the foyer is all marble and mahogany, shaded lamps and potted palms. Rooms start at $500 and the suites, which have housed everyone from the Duke of Windsor to Rudolph Nureyev, range from $750 to $1600.

Grand Hyatt Melbourne *(☎ 9657 1234, corner Collins and Russell Sts)* is the most lavish of the big modern hotels, with 580 luxuriously appointed rooms. It features a cavernous foyer chiselled out of Italian marble, as well as a pool, spa, sauna, gymnasium and rooftop tennis court. Rooms start at $390 and suites range from $630 up to the Presidential Suite – a steal at $3300.

Hotel Sofitel *(☎ 9653 0000, 25 Collins St)* is another excellent hotel at the top end of Collins St. The hotel occupies the 30th to 49th floors of one of the twin towers of Collins Place, and the uninterrupted views are great. Rooms start at $530 and suites at $695.

Fronted by the historic and elaborate Gothic Revival facades of two buildings that date back to 1891 is ***Le Meridien at Rialto Melbourne*** *(☎ 9620 9111, 495 Collins St)*. Inside, the individually styled rooms overlook an enclosed central atrium that covers the original cobbled laneway between the two buildings. This laneway now houses bars, cafes and open-air restaurants. Rooms cost from $375 and suites from $525.

Rockman's Regency Hotel *(☎ 9662 3900, corner Exhibition and Lonsdale Sts)* prides itself on providing the level of personal service that only a small hotel can, and is particularly popular with visiting celebrities. The rooms are spacious and tastefully decorated, and the hotel is close to the main theatres and Chinatown. Rooms start at $230, suites at $450. ***Sebel of Melbourne*** *(☎ 9629 4088, 321 Flinders Lane)* is an intimate hotel that has an impressive style and personality. The staff are friendly, the rooms are spacious and the windows even open! Rooms range from $375 to $600.

Crown Towers *(☎ 9292 6868)*, part of the massive Crown Casino development on the southern bank of the Yarra, has rooms from $540 and suites from $900. Nearby, ***Sheraton Towers Southgate*** *(☎ 9696 3100, 1 Southgate Ave)* has rooms from $405 and suites from $515.

Hilton on the Park *(☎ 9419 2000, 192 Wellington Pde)* is a very pleasant 10-minute stroll from the city through the Treasury and Fitzroy gardens. Close to the MCG, the Hilton has rooms from $240 and suites from $400.

North Melbourne The ***Old Melbourne Hotel*** *(☎ 9329 9344, 5 Flemington Rd)* is a motel but it's rated at 4½ stars. It's a large (and not old) place and is a good option, with rooms from $157.

Richmond An impressive four star hotel is ***Rydges Riverwalk Hotel*** *(☎ 9246 1200, corner Bridge Rd and River St)*, beside the Yarra River. This place is better value and more spacious than city hotels in the equivalent price bracket, with tastefully decorated rooms starting at $170, and apartments at $200.

South Yarra *Hotel Como (☎ 9825 2222, corner Chapel St and Toorak Rd)* is an all-suite hotel that prides itself on providing 'exclusivity, security, impeccable service...' The brochure may be over the top, but so is the hotel. The design is subtle and distinctive, and the 107 suites are very stylish. Then there's the pool, spa, sauna and gym, and room-service meals from the adjacent Maxim's, a renowned local restaurant. It's also well located, near the trendy cafes, restaurants and boutiques of South Yarra. Suites range in price from $520 to $2000.

PLACES TO EAT

Melbourne is a marvellous place to have an appetite – and a terrible place to start a diet. Everywhere you go, there are restaurants, cafes, delicatessens, markets, bistros, brasseries and take-aways.

Melbourne's multiculturalism is reflected in the inexhaustible variety of its cuisines and restaurants. Food is something of a local obsession, and Melbourne is considered to be the country's eating capital. Sydney food and travel writer David Dale wrote, 'Melbourne has sensational food...I like to think of my trips to Melbourne as the equivalent of a Londoner saving up to spend one precious weekend a year in Paris, living on crusts and gruel for months afterwards'.

You don't have to go to that extreme – there are plenty of great places to eat that don't cost a fortune. Compared to many other parts of the world, you'll find that food and wine in Melbourne are great value for money and of the highest standard.

Most restaurants are either licensed to sell alcohol or BYO, meaning you can 'Bring Your Own' booze (and usually pay a small 'corkage' fee). Until recently, BYO licences were more prevalent than licences to sell liquor, but the relaxation of alcohol licensing laws in recent years has meant that many more cafes and restaurants are allowed to sell alcohol and this has seen a decline in the number of purely BYO places.

Gay-friendly cafes and restaurants abound in Melbourne, and these places are also good meeting and contact points. Some of the more popular eateries include ***Cafe Rumours*** in Brunswick St, Fitzroy, the ***Blue Elephant*** in Commercial Rd, Prahran, and the ***Globe Cafe*** in Chapel St, Prahran. See the following sections for more details.

For a reliable and inexpensive Italian restaurant, find the nearest member of the burgeoning La Porchetta chain, specialising in pizza and home-made pasta, with non-seafood main courses under $10. There are La Porchettas in many areas, including: Brunswick 317 Victoria St; North Carlton 392 Rathdowne St; North Melbourne 302 Victoria St; St Kilda 80 Acland St; South Yarra 93 Toorak Rd; Williamstown 193 Nelson Place.

For more good value places to try, see the 'Value-for-Money Eating' boxed text and if price isn't a consideration see the 'Dining in Style' boxed text, both in this chapter.

City Centre

Chinatown Area The area in and around Chinatown, which follows Little Bourke St from Spring St to Swanston St, is the city's best and most diverse food precinct. Here you will find acclaimed Chinese restaurants rubbing shoulders with cheap Chinese cafes, as well as Italian, French, Malaysian, Thai and many other types of restaurants. Part of the fun is wandering around exploring the narrow cobbled lanes that run off Little Bourke St, seeking out the city's hidden gems.

The Southgate and casino developments have hit this area particularly hard, and many places offer good special deals.

The ***Shark Finn Inn*** at No 50 Little Bourke St is very popular. ***Cafe K*** *(☎ 9639 0414)*, No 35, is a European-style bistro with very good dishes in the $15 to $20 range – you may need to book.

Value-for-Money Eating

Looking for the best bite for your buck? Lonely Planet's *Out to Eat – Melbourne* is the best guide to Melbourne's value eateries for any budget; if you're staying a while it will quickly repay your investment. The book takes its food seriously, but offers a fresh approach, with independent, wickedly unstuffy opinion on heaps of hand-picked restaurants, bars and cafes in Melbourne. Here's a selection from the guide's restaurant reviewers.

Try ***Kri Kri*** *(39 Lt Bourke St, ☎ 9369 3444)* for the best mezze this side of Athens. ***Sheni's Curries*** *(shop 16, cnr Russell St & Flinders Lane, ☎ 9654 3535)* has everyone queuing for fix a of subcontinental spiciness, with beef, lamb, chicken or fish curry and rice meals at $6.50 ($5 for vegetarian). The Hare-Krishna run ***Gopal's*** *(139 Swanston St, ☎ 9650 1578)* has three-course vegetarian meals for $5.50. ***Pellegrini's*** *(66 Bourke St, ☎ 9662 1885)* is a real Melbourne institution with pasta the way mama used to make it for $8 to $12.

At Southbank's ***Automatic Cafe at Crown*** *(ground level, Crown Towers, 8 Whiteman St, ☎ 9690 8500)*, you're guaranteed a good return on your money (not as risky as the tables). Modern Australian mains range from $4.90 to $9.95.

Eschewing the pavement touting tactics of Lygon Street's many Italian eateries, the more modest ***Carwan Afghan*** *(12 Lygon St Carlton, ☎ 9639 3429)* serves great kebabs, kormas and pulau for $11-15.

It is the dessert bar that distinguishes the ***Bangla Sweets & Curry Cafe*** *(199 Brunswick St, ☎ 9417 1877)* from other North Indian eateries. The cardamom flavoured rasmalai ($3) is a delicacy that will be like nothing you've tasted before!

For vegetarian cuisine, St Kilda's ***Wild Rice*** will rate highly for any Melburnian. Organic and biodynamic produce are concocted into delectable savoury bakes and casseroles for around $8.50. ***The Galleon*** *(9 Carlisle St, ☎ 9534 8934)* is as comfy as nanna's kitchen and great value too, and the ***Espy Kitchen***, deep in the bowels of the legendary Esplanade Hotel, serves terrific food to tuck into while waiting for your turn at the pool table.

Just off Little Bourke St is the highly acclaimed ***Flower Drum*** *(☎ 9662 3655, 17 Market Lane)*, one of Melbourne's finest (and most expensive) restaurants, serving up the best Cantonese food this side of Hong Kong. For southern Chinese chiu chow food, try ***The Mask of China*** *(☎ 9662 2116, 115 Little Bourke St)*, another outstanding and expensive restaurant. ***Dahu Peking Duck*** *(☎ 9639 1381, corner Little Bourke and Russell Sts, upstairs)* isn't in the same league as these heavyweights, but it's still well worth trying. A bonus is that it's spacious, calm and relaxed.

The low-key ***Yamato*** *(28 Corrs Lane)* turns out excellent, inexpensive Japanese dishes. ***King of Kings*** *(209 Russell St)* is a cheap (most dishes $5 to $10) and very popular Chinese place that stays open until 2.30 am. Another late closer is ***Supper Inn***, hidden away at 15-17 Celestial Ave. It is definitely worth searching out for its excellent, authentic and reasonably priced Chinese food.

Bourke St Area Off the top end of Bourke St, hidden away up a flight of stairs, the ***Waiters' Restaurant*** *(20 Meyer Place)* serves good, cheap Italian food in unglamorous but cosy surrounds. Back on Bourke St, at No 66, is another Melbourne institution – ***Pellegrini's***. This long-running bohemian Italian cafe/bar is a popular haunt and meeting place for struggling actors, writers, musicians and other subculture types. This narrow (and usually crowded) cafe serves up excellent coffee and simple Italian dishes the same way it did back in the 1950s. The food is not outstanding but the atmosphere keeps people coming back.

Grossi Florentino (☎ *9662 1811, 80 Bourke St)*, or Florries, as it's known to the ladies who lunch, has been an institution for 50 years. The upstairs restaurant is elegant and expensive, but ***Florentino Grill*** on street level is reasonable, if unadventurous, and ***Florentino Cellar Bar,*** downstairs, is a bargain; pastas under $10, and various snacks.

Nearby at No 76, busy ***Nudel Bar*** is dedicated to noodles from all sorts of European and Asian cuisines. The food is good and the prices reasonable – from $8.

Collins St Area Collins St has some of its own institutions, one of which is ***Cafe Alcaston*** *(2 Collins St)*, housed in one of the street's few remaining historical buildings. This place caters for breakfasts and lunches in rather noble surrounds, and attracts a suitably upmarket clientele.

Kenzan *(☎ 9654 8933)*, on the lower ground floor of Collins Place (behind the glass lift), is a stylish, popular, licensed Japanese restaurant highly regarded for its sushi and sashimi. Main courses cost around $18 and there are lunch specials.

Farther down at 113 Collins St (actually tucked down a laneway called George Pde), ***Il Solito Posto*** is a marvellous Italian bar and restaurant with a stylish but cosy ambience. It's a great place for a meal, or just to meet someone for a drink. You can eat cheap at the bar or dine in the restaurant. Nearby, the ***Grand Hyatt Melbourne*** complex houses several restaurants including the highly impressive ***Max's*** and the ***Hyatt Food Court***, with a good range of reasonably priced food stalls in spacious and stylish surrounds.

Other City Centre Areas Just north of Lonsdale St, ***Cafee Baloo's*** *(260 Russell St)* is perhaps the best budget eatery in the city centre. It's a funky little place with Indian/Italian food (strange combination but it works well). You pay around $6 for main courses and there are plenty of choices for vegetarians. It's open daily from noon to 10 pm.

Lounge *(243 Swanston St, upstairs)* is a groovy cafe/club with pool tables, a balcony overlooking Swanston Walk, and snags, stir-fries, satays and salads from $8 to $10.

Gopal's *(139 Swanston St)* is a vegetarian cafe run by the Hare Krishna sect. It's open for lunch and dinner and has extremely inexpensive food.

At the other end of the price spectrum, ***Marchetti's Latin*** *(☎ 9662 1985, 55 Lonsdale St)* tops many people's list of Melbourne's best restaurants. The Italian food is superb, the service always just right and the ambience uniquely chic, sophisticated and at the same time welcoming. Marchetti's is expensive, and very popular – you'll need to book well ahead.

The block of Lonsdale St, between Russell and Swanston Sts, is Melbourne's small Greek enclave. ***Stalactites***, on the corner of Lonsdale and Russell Sts, is a Greek restaurant best known for its bizarre stalactite decor and the fact that it's open 24 hours. Farther west you'll find another restaurant or two and some good cake shops.

As well as being the home of Melbourne's outdoor adventure shops, Hardware St is lined with cafes with open-air tables. At No 25 ***Campari Bistro*** is a busy Italian bistro with pastas for around $12 and other mains under $20. It's an old favourite for lots of Melburnians, and the staff inspire confidence – there's a smiling Italian *mama* or two. Nearby, ***Schwob's*** is a great place for a sandwich or roll, eat in or take-away.

The city's three major department stores – Myer, David Jones and Daimaru – each have marvellous food emporiums with a selection of goodies that should satisfy even the most obscure craving. Particularly worth searching out is the ***Daimaru Sushi Bar***, at level one in the Melbourne Central complex – the omelettes, sushi boxes and udon soups are sensational value.

Southgate & Arts Precinct

Since opening in the early 1990s, the Southgate development at Southbank, on the south side of the Yarra River, has quickly become one of Melbourne's most popular eating places. It enjoys a great setting overlooking the river and the city skyline, is close to the galleries and theatres of the Arts Precinct and the gardens of the Kings Domain, and has a broad range of bars, cafes and restaurants, most of which have outdoor terraces and balconies where you can dine alfresco in the warmer weather.

On the mid-level, the casual, trendy and noisy ***Blue Train Cafe*** serves breakfasts, pastas and risottos, wood-fired pizzas and salads, all at reasonable prices. Main courses are under $20 and there are lots of cheaper snacks. There are outdoor tables with good views. It's open daily from breakfast until late.

On the upper level is ***Walter's Wine Bar*** *(☎ 9690 9211)*, a classy establishment with fine views across the river. The wine list is extensive, and there's a large selection of wines by the glass. The food is simple modern Australian cuisine with main meals starting around $20. There's also a selection of less expensive snacks, or you can just drop in for a glass of wine. Right next door is ***Simply French***, a smart bar and brasserie charging a little more.

On the ground level, ***Blakes*** *(☎ 9699 4100)* serves modern and innovative food with mains in the $18 to $25 range, and the menu adds an interesting touch by recommending a wine to complement each meal – all wines are also sold by the glass (around $6). ***Bistro Vite*** is a casual and simple French bistro, where mains cost under $20. Next door, ***E Gusto*** is a stylish and traditional Italian bistro, with most mains in the $17 to $20 range.

The centre of the ground floor is taken up by the ***Wharf Food Market***, with scattered clusters of tables and chairs interspersed with a selection of excellent international food stalls. These places are all reasonably priced, the service is fast and if you're in a group there's no need for compromise – everyone can have something different.

In the Victorian Arts Centre, ***Treble Clef*** is in the Concert Hall overlooking the river and city skyline, and opens from 11 am until around midnight, serving snacks, light meals or more substantial main courses. The casual ***Cafe Vic*** in the Theatres Building has pre-performance meals or post-performance coffee and cake. ***Aromas Restaurant*** in the concert hall is more formal.

In the National Gallery there's the terrific ***Garden Restaurant & Cafe***, which opens daily from 11 am to 4 pm and serves lunches and morning and afternoon teas. The ***Malthouse Cafe***, in the Malthouse Theatre at 113 Sturt St, is a great little cafe with all sorts of tasty snacks and meals. It's a popular spot for a quick bite before or after a show, but it's also open during the daytime and attracts an interesting blend of actors, writers, directors and other arty types.

North Melbourne

North Melbourne, home to the YHA hostels, doesn't have the glamour or the range of some other inner suburbs, but there are some great places to eat if you're prepared to hunt.

Victoria St has a good range of places. ***Amiconi*** *(☎ 9328 3710, 359 Victoria St)* is one of the most popular eateries. This traditional little Italian bistro has been a local favourite for decades, and you'll probably have to book. Across the road at No 488, the ***Peppermint Lounge Cafe*** is a top spot for breakfast or lunch, with specials around $7.

Warung Agus, farther along at No 305, is a cosy and simple two-room restaurant that serves great Balinese food, with mains from $10 to $16.

For Vietnamese food, head down towards the Queen Victoria Market – across the road, ***Viet Nam House*** *(284 Victoria St)* and ***Dalat's*** at No 270 both have good cheap Vietnamese food, especially at lunch.

Don Camillo at No 215 is another little Italian place that's been here for yonks, and it serves the basics in large, very tasty portions. You'll pay about $15 for main courses. Nearby, the busy ***La Porchetta*** *(corner Victoria and Peel Sts)* is a budget bistro with pizzas and pastas from $5 and other mains under $12.

The ***Eldorado Hotel*** *(46 Leveson St)* is an old pub that has been revitalised into a fun, bustling 'cafe saloon'. The menu covers lots of territory – burgers, grills, chillies, pastas – and there's a pleasant covered courtyard. The open fires in winter make it a cosy place for a beer.

If you're looking for French food, try ***La Chaumière*** *(☎ 9328 1650, 523 Spencer St, West Melbourne)*. It recently moved from its long-standing premises into the dining room of the Royal Mail Hotel, but still offers good food at sensible prices (many mains under $20) with unpretentious service.

Carlton

Lygon St Lygon St was once affectionately thought of as the multicultural centre of Melbourne. That was back in the days when Melbourne was a dull city devoid of alternative culture, and Lygon St, with its fascinating blend of cosmopolitan immigrants and bohemian university students, was thought of as a glimpse of Europe. But, progress being progress, eventually the old Italian tailors and small shopkeepers moved out and the developers and entrepreneurs moved in. Many of them were descendants of the original Italian immigrants, returning to liven up the old suburb.

Nowadays Lygon St is all bright lights, big restaurants and flashy boutiques. No longer a trend-setter in Melbourne's restaurant scene, it now caters mainly to tourists and out-of-towners, although some of the long-running places are still worth searching out.

Tram Nos 1 and 21, which both run along Swanston St, will get you there from the city centre, or if you feel like walking, it's a very pleasant stroll up Russell St.

Toto's Pizza House at No 101 claims to be the first pizzeria in Australia. It's licensed, the pizzas are cheap and good and it stays open till after midnight. After your pizza, you could head up to ***Notturno*** at No 179 for coffee and cake. There are tables on the pavement, and it's open late.

Casa Malaya, across the road at No 118, is an excellent Malaysian restaurant with superb and reasonably priced food. Also good is ***Nyonya,*** up at No 191. Nyonya food, a blend of Malay spices and ingredients and Chinese cooking styles, originated in Singapore, and they do it well here. The setting is bright and cheerful and the prices are very good, with most mains in the $8.50 to $18.50 range.

Borsari Ristorante *(corner Grattan and Lygon Sts)* is worth a visit. It's a busy bistro with tables out on the footpath and traditional Italian cuisine. ***Papa Gino's***, at No 221, is a straightforward and long-running pizza-and-pasta joint with a good reputation.

A block farther north at No 303, ***Tiamo*** is another old Lygon St campaigner. It's an old-fashioned Italian bistro that's popular with Melbourne Uni students, and has tasty pastas for around $8.50 and great breakfasts just like mama used to cook. Around the corner in new premises, ***Shakahari*** *(☎ 9347 3848, 201 Faraday Street)* is one of Melbourne's oldest, and still one of the most innovative, vegetarian restaurants. Open the door and you'll be drawn in by those marvellous wafting aromas. The ingredients are fresh and seasonal, the main dishes are around $10 to $12, and you should save room for the remarkable desserts at $7.50.

At No 333, ***Jimmy Watson's*** *(☎ 9347 3985)* is one of Melbourne's most famed institutions. Wine and talk are the order of the day at this long-running wine bar/restaurant – the annual Jimmy Watson trophy is Australia's best-known red-wine award, so you can count on the wines being drinkable. This has always been a great spot for long, leisurely lunches, and nowadays it's also open at night. With one of Melbourne's top chefs at the helm, the small upstairs dining rooms are now used for fine dining.

Across the road, ***Trotters*** at No 400 is another popular little bistro, serving good breakfasts and hearty Italian fare in the $9 to $14 range. Lygon St also has plenty of dark little coffee houses, tempting, calorie-stuffed cake shops and great gelato bars.

Elgin St ***Jakarta*** *(118 Elgin St)* serves Indonesian-style seafood, with decor including statuary and a stone fish-pond. Main courses range from $16 to $20. Right across the road at No 109, ***Abla's*** *(☎ 9347 0006)* is Melbourne's best Lebanese restaurant by a mile. The food is great and it's almost always crowded. The banquet menus are good value at $25 a head for lunch and $30 for dinner.

Rathdowne St Rathdowne St, which runs parallel with Lygon St, has some good alternatives to its more crowded commercial cousin.

La Contadina Ristorante *(168 Rathdowne St)* serves traditional Italian food in a cosy atmosphere. Farther north, and on the other side of the road, is the ***Paragon Cafe*** at No 651. The food here is excellent, with pastas from $10 to $15, main meals like calamari fritti around $16.50, and a great range of cakes and desserts. Another block north at No 370 is the ***Kent Hotel***, a trendy bar/cafe with reasonable food for around $14. It tends to be noisy inside, but the outdoor tables are a great spot to be on a warm night. Up the road at No 392 is ***La Porchetta***, which has inexpensive pastas and pizzas. This, plus the fact that the food's pretty good, accounts for its enormous popularity with students from the university. If you can't get in there, try up the road at ***La Trattoria***, which attracts an older crowd and is slightly more expensive but still good value.

Fitzroy

Brunswick St You haven't really eaten out in Melbourne until you've been to Brunswick St. It's the most fascinating street in town, and for a couple of blocks north and south of Johnston St it's lined with dozens of great cafes, bars and restaurants offering a surprisingly wide range of cuisines. The prevailing mood is bohemian, studenty and arty but there are some high quality restaurants among all that expensive designer grunge decor.

With so many places to choose from, perhaps the thing to do is to promenade along the street and consider your options. Have a beer here, a glass of wine there, and study the menus and the crowds. Like trucks outside a good roadhouse, you can usually tell which restaurants are good by how crowded they are. There are far too many eateries along here to list in this book – following are just a few that worth checking out.

Most of the action is up around Johnston St, but there are quite a few interesting places down the city end near Gertrude St. ***Nyala*** *(113 Brunswick St)* serves exotic Ethiopian and Sudanese food in a casual bluestone and cane setting, with most main courses under $15. The combination plate has a good variety of dishes, which you scoop up with spongy bread known as *injera*. At No 177, ***Akari 177*** is a stylish but low-key licensed Japanese restaurant which is very popular. It has set lunches and early-dinner deals (order before 7 pm) which are both great value. ***De Los Santos*** nearby at No 175 is a good Spanish restaurant open for dinner nightly.

A little farther north is the ***Black Cat Cafe*** at No 252. This was among the first of the cool eateries in Brunswick St, and was into retro before the term was invented. The decor is very 1950s – lots of vinyl and laminex. The 'Cat' has a good snack menu with most dishes under $8 and a great range of drink, including spiders. ***Guernica***, No 257, offers both style and substance, with excellent modern dishes priced around $20.

This part of the street is well endowed with the flavours of the Orient. ***Sala Thai***, at No 266, has good Thai at reasonable prices (choose between a traditional table or cushions on the floor) and particularly good vegetarian dishes. ***Thai Thani***, at No 293, is another good option for spicy Thai food.

The Provincial *(☎ 9417 2228, corner Brunswick and Johnston Sts)* is unrecognisable as the old pub it once was. It's now sparse, spacious and stylish, with a front bar, a great Italian bistro, where you can watch the chefs at work, and a burger/Asian bar next door. ***Mario's***, at 303 Brunswick St, is another stayer in this street of rapid change, with an arty, devout clientele and stupendous Italian-based food for any time of day or night.

The ***Fitz*** at No 347 has been bypassed by the hippest of the hip, but it's still a good place for breakfast and other meals and snacks. ***Rhumbarella's***, across at No 342, is an arty, barn-sized cafe/restaurant with an art gallery upstairs. ***Babka Bakery-Cafe*** at No 358 is famous for its breads and pastries – it's also a great place for breakfast, with interesting dishes like corn fritters, bacon and tomato. For lunch try the delicious pies and sandwiches.

At No 366, ***Joe's Garage*** has a central bar, with benches and stools on one side and a dining area on the other. It's a friendly place with a great atmosphere and you'll find plenty of snacks for less than $10. Next door, ***Charmaine's*** has simply sensational ice creams, cakes and other indulgent delights.

On the corner of Rose St, the ***Vegie Bar*** exudes delicious aromas and has a great range of vegetarian meals for under $10 and snacks for around $2 – it's so popular that it has recently taken over the shop next door. Another Brunnie St favourite is ***Baker's Cafe*** at No 384 – it has plenty to choose from and reasonable prices.

A couple of blocks north on the Westgarth St corner, the very laid-back ***Cafe Retro*** is a spacious 1950s-style cafe.

If you venture across Alexandra Pde to North Fitzroy where Brunswick St joins St Georges Rd, you'll find another little pocket of interesting cafes and restaurants. ***Tin Pot*** *(284 St Georges Rd)* is a friendly place with good food at reasonable prices. Diagonally opposite, ***The Toucan Club***, in a wonderfully angular old post office, serves good, inexpensive food and has cabaret in the evening. Also nearby are the ***Moroccan Soup Bar*** *(☎ 9482 4240, 183 St Georges Road)* with great spicy vegetarian food, and the groovy ***Green Grocer*** *(217 St Georges Rd)*, which has a good cafe and sells organic fruit and vegetables.

Johnston St The stretch of Johnston St between Brunswick and Nicholson Sts once looked as though it would become Melbourne's Spanish quarter. However, the tapas bar fad died and several places closed, but there are still a couple along here. The ***Hogar Español Spanish Club*** *(59 Johnston St)* is still there. Its simple bar and restaurant are open to the public.

Carmen Bar *(☎ 9417 4794, 74 Johnston St)* is a hectic and down-to-earth restaurant with authentic Spanish food and live flamenco and Spanish guitar from Wednesday to Saturday night. The outdoor barbecue is popular in summer – buy your meat or fish at the counter and cook it yourself. Near Brunswick St at No 95 is the huge ***Bull Ring***, which is part Spanish restaurant, part tapas bar and part nightclub.

Gertrude St Gertrude St between Smith St and Nicholson St has an interesting collection of galleries, art suppliers, costume designers and antique shops, as well as a few good eateries. At No 193, ***Arcadia*** is a friendly little cafe, while at No 199 the very straightforward ***Macedonia*** does grills, goulash and other Balkan specialties at low prices. The arty and cosy ***Builders Arms Hotel*** *(corner Gertrude and Gore Sts)* is a top spot for an ale and a bite.

Smith St Smith St, which forms the border between Fitzroy and Collingwood, also has some good eateries. It's an interesting multicultural streetscape, a lot less fashionable than Brunswick St but still well worth exploring.

The ***Smith St Bar & Bistro*** *(14 Smith St)* is a very pleasant and stylish bar/restaurant, with a front bar with snacks, a spacious lounge area with couches and an open fire, and an elegant dining room with French/Italian mains in the $13.50 to $18 range.

Farther north at No 117, ***Vegetarian Orgasm*** is a bright and friendly vegie cafe with an interesting range of inexpensive dishes. ***Cafe Birko*** at No 123 is a rustic bar/restaurant with salads, stir-fries, risottos and pastas, while on the corner of Peel St, the ***Grace Darling Hotel*** is a great pub with cheap bar snacks and meals, and an excellent restaurant but it's closed on Sunday.

At No 275, the ***Soul Food Vegetarian Cafe*** is a popular vegan cafe with salads

Dining in Style

Melbourne has hundreds of great eateries to suit all budgets, but for a special occasion or a big splurge consider trying one of the following places, considered by Lonely Planet's *Out to Eat – Melbourne* team to be some of the city's best venues for fine dining. (Prices given are the approximate cost of a three-course meal for one person, excluding drinks.)

Many of Melbourne's top eateries are in the inner city area. On the 35th floor of the Hotel Sofitel, ***Le Restaurant** (☎ 9650 4242, 25 Collins St)* offers great views and innovative cuisine, utilising fine Australian produce ($80). On the lower ground floor at Collins Place, ***Kenzan** (☎ 9654 8933, 45 Collins St)* serves elegant Japanese food in a very Zen atmosphere; the fresh seafood is mouth-watering ($45). ***Il Bácaro** (☎ 9654 6778, 170 Little Collins St)* serves unforgettable Italian food in a charming, theatrical atmosphere ($47).

***Grossi Florentino** (☎ 9662 1811, 80 Bourke St)* is a Melbourne institution owned and operated by renowned restaurateurs, the Grossi family. Here you can indulge in some seriously romantic ambience and unbelievably good Italian cuisine ($50). ***Republique Brasserie** (☎ 9654 6699, 23 Bourke St)* is a comfortable, traditional white-tablecloth place, serving fairly conventional but delicious French cuisine ($45). ***Langton's Wine Bar & Restaurant** (☎ 9663 0222, 61 Flinders Lane)* is tucked away in a moody city lane, with modern decor and cuisine and a fine wine list ($47).

Close to Her Majesty's and the Princess theatres, ***Stella** (☎ 9639 1555, 159 Spring St)* is laidback and atmospheric with a touch of Moroccan style and a mix of contemporary dishes ($48). Nearby, the grand old ***Windsor Hotel** (☎ 9633 6004, 111 Spring St)* offers olde-worlde fine dining with impeccable service and beautifully presented food ($48). Not far from the National Gallery, in an elegant old Victorian building complete with chandeliers and murals, ***Scalaci at the Willows** (☎ 9867 5252, 462 St Kilda Rd)* is a fine restaurant serving delicious food by one of Melbourne's top chefs, Tansy Good ($42).

The Southgate development offers great river and city views, proximity to city theatres and the Concert Hall, and a number of fine restaurants. ***Blakes** (☎ 9699 4100, Shop GR2, river level)* combines Asian and Mediterranean influences in an eclectic menu that changes monthly ($52). ***Walter's Wine Bar** (☎ 9690 9211, Shop UR1, St Kilda Rd level)* serves superb modern Australian cuisine and has a great wine list to match ($47).

Further west along the river, the Crown Casino complex (8 Whiteman St, Southbank) is another hotspot for upmarket dining. ***The Duck** (☎ 9696 5432)* is a swanky modern restaurant and wine bar where the monochrome decor and contemporary food are equally well

and hot food for well under $10, and an organic grocer next door.

Closer to Johnston St, ***Sinbad's Corner*** is a little shop selling home-made felafel – the owner is from Alexandria – and $7 will get you one with the lot. Farther north again, across Johnston St at No 354, ***Cafe Bohemio*** is a quirky and laid-back Latin-American cafe with mains from $9 to $14.

Richmond

Victoria St Walk down Victoria St and you'll soon realise why this area has become known as 'Little Saigon'. Melbourne's growing Vietnamese community has transformed what was once a dull and colourless traffic route into a fascinating, bustling commercial centre. The stretch of Victoria St between Hoddle and Church Sts is lined with Asian supermarkets and groceries, the foot-

Dining in Style

designed ($53). ***Silks*** *(☎ 9292 6888)* is an opulent place serving high-end Cantonese cuisine ($55). ***Koko*** *(☎ 9292 6886)* is Melbourne's priciest Japanese restaurant, with panoramic views, rustic village charm and an indoor pond ($55).

South Melbourne is an ex-working class (now gentrified) area that's home to one of Melbourne's best and most exciting contemporary restaurants, ***est est est*** *(☎ 9682 5688, 440 Clarendon St)*, where the food is out-of-this-world and the wine list is extraordinary ($66). ***La Madrague*** *(☎ 9699 9627, 171 Buckhurst St)* is a rather conservative but charming French restaurant serving predictable but good food ($45).

In upmarket South Yarra, ***France-Soir*** *(☎ 9866 8569, 11 Toorak Rd)* serves classic French dishes, including superb steaks and desserts ($42). Nearby, ***Pomme*** *(☎ 9820 9606, 37 Toorak Rd)* is a charming establishment that dishes up 'modern British' food with imaginative flavour combinations ($63).

In fashionable St Kilda, ***The George Melbourne Wine Room*** *(☎ 9525 5599, 125 Fitzroy St)* is a delightful retreat with great service, a fantastic wine list and superbly prepared food ($47). Towards the bay, in the magically restored Prince of Wales Hotel, ***Circa*** *(☎ 9534 5033, 2 Acland St)* represents the best of modern architecture combined with the height of Australian cuisine and service ($52). Set in a restored teahouse right on the beach, ***The Stokehouse*** *(upstairs dining room ☎ 9525 5555, 30 Jacka Boulevard)* is immensely popular for its panoramic bay views and superb seafood ($45). ***Donovan's*** *(☎ 9534 8221, 40 Jacka Boulevard)*, a short stroll south-east along the boulevard, has cosy beach-house ambience but a very long waiting list for tables ($38).

In a beautiful Victorian mansion in Windsor, ***Jacques Reymond*** *(☎ 9525 2178, 78 Williams Rd)* is one of the *country's* most highly esteemed restaurants, run by the celebrated Jacques Reymond himself. Indulge here in truly sublime dishes that combine the very best of Australian produce with some Asian flavours and classical French cooking techniques ($70-$90).

There are gourmet highlights scattered throughout the inner suburbs. In Richmond, ***Vlado's*** *(☎ 9428 5833, 61 Bridge Rd)* is a meat-eater's paradise, famous for its superb steaks ($48). Fitzroy's Brunswick St is best known for lively cheap cafes, but ***Matteo's Ristorante*** *(☎ 9481 1177, 533 Brunswick St)* is a genteel establishment and one of the city's finest Italian eateries ($44). Across the bay in Williamstown, ***Aquis*** *(☎ 9397 2377, 231 Nelson Place)* offers sea views and a modern European-influenced menu in its elegant upstairs dining room ($45).

For more tips on dining out on any budget, check out Lonely Planet's *Out to Eat – Melbourne* restaurant guide.

paths are piled with boxes of exotic fruits and vegetables, and there are discount shops, butchers, fishmongers and dozens of bargain-priced Vietnamese restaurants.

If you're coming by car, be warned that parking spaces are at a premium. Otherwise, tram No 42 or 109 from Collins St in the city will get you there.

Don't expect vogue decor in the restaurants, but the food will be fresh, cheap and authentic, and the service lightning fast and friendly. You can have a huge, steaming bowl of soup that will be a meal in itself for around $4, and main courses generally cost between $5 and $9, so you can afford to be adventurous.

One of the original, and still one of the most popular places, is ***Thy Thy 1*** *(142 Victoria St)* hidden away up a narrow, uninviting set of stairs. This no-frills place is dirt-cheap, but the food is fresh and excellent and the clientele is very varied. The same people have a slightly more upmarket place called ***Thy Thy 2*** down the road at No 116. Try the pork, chicken, prawn or vegetable spring rolls, complete with mint and lettuce leaves for do-it-yourself construction.

Vao Doi at No 120 is another good place to try, as is ***Victoria*** across the road at No 311. The menu here also offers Thai and Chinese food, and no, you can't eat those big fish in the tank up the back – they bring the owners good luck. ***Tran Tran*** at No 76 is also popular.

Farther along at No 397, ***Minh Tan III*** looks a bit more upmarket than most other places and specialises in seafood, but you'll still get lunch for $6.

Back down at the city end of Victoria St at No 66, the modern ***Tho Tho*** is a surprisingly stylish bar/restaurant that would be more at home in South Yarra, but despite the slick decor the food here is still cheap with mains mostly $7 to $10.

Swan St Richmond's Swan St, in the block east of Church St, is something of an enclave for Greek cuisine. You'll find half a dozen or so Greek restaurants in this area, all reasonably priced and offering fairly similar menus: an assortment of dips such as tzatziki and taramasalata with pita bread, souvlaki and sausages, sardines and calamari, stuffed peppers and moussaka – all the old favourites! If you really want to pretend you're in the Greek Islands for the night, the pub on the corner of Swan and Church Sts sells retsina.

To get here from the city, take tram No 70 from Batman Ave, by the river, to the corner of Swan and Church Sts.

Elatos Greek Tavern *(☎ 9428 5683, 213 Swan St)* is one of the best places – lively, licensed and good value, and the seafood here is particularly good. Main courses cost about $12 and seafood about $16. Across the road the tiny ***Salona*** is also good, and is a little cheaper.

At No 256, ***Kaliva*** is fairly plain, although you can dine to live bouzouki music Thursday to Sunday nights.

Bridge Rd Bridge Rd, which runs parallel with and between Swan and Victoria Sts, also has some great food possibilities. Take tram No 48 or 75 from Flinders St in the city to these restaurants.

Starting at the city end, there's the ***Downtown Bar & Bistro*** *(14-16 Bridge Rd)*, a reasonably priced place serving pizzas, pastas, focaccias and other Italian tucker. Next door is ***Chilli Padi*** *(☎ 9428 6432)*, which serves authentic and excellent Malaysian food in an elegant setting. It has noodle and vegetable dishes from $7.50, and other mains from $13 to $18. There are good lunch specials.

Richmond Hill Cafe & Larder *(48 Bridge Rd)* is owned by Stephanie Alexander, whose late lamented Stephanie's Restaurant was one of Australia's finest. This establishment is nothing like the restaurant – it's a lively, casual place with nary a port-sipping judge in sight. The food is outstanding, with many dishes under $15. It's open from breakfast to past dinner daily except Sunday, when it closes at 5 pm.

At No 78 the ***Tofu Shop*** is definitely popular with the vegetarian and health-kick crowds. It can be a squeeze finding a stool at the counter at lunchtime, but the salads, vegetables, filled filo pastries and 'soyalaki' (a great invention) are tasty and filling.

Across the road at No 61 is the famed ***Vlado's*** *(☎ 9428 5833)*. This place has a reputation for serving the best steaks in the country, and if you're into prime red meat you'll be more than happy to pay round $70 a head. If you want something lighter, stay away – there's nothing else on the menu.

Across Church St you'll find ***Silvio's*** *(270 Bridge Rd)* serving up some of the best pizzas in town. Up at No 396, ***The Curry Club Cafe*** has inexpensive but unusually good Indian food. ***Thai Oriental***, farther down at No 430, has cheap and tasty Thai, Malay and Indian food. ***Bill's Barrow*** at No 462 is a good fruit and vegetable shop that stays open 24 hours a day, 365 days a year.

Lennox St Midway between Swan St and Bridge Rd, the ***London Tavern*** *(238 Lennox*

St) used to be Lonely Planet's local pub, until we moved office. It rose to local pub-food fame under a chef who liked India and curries, and despite his departure the menu still has some interesting dishes, plus there's a bright and sunny courtyard where you can eat outside.

Farther north is the great ***All Nations Hotel*** at No 64. It's hard to get to because of a series of one-way streets, but if you make the effort you'll be rewarded with some of the best pub food in town. It's an original, honest and friendly pub, the sort of place everyone wishes they had as a local. Meals range from $6 to $16.

South Yarra

Most of South Yarra's eateries are along Toorak Rd and Chapel St. The No 8 tram from the city will get you there.

If you love to shop and eat, you'll be right at home here. There are dozens of stylish cafes and restaurants, from the extravagant to the simple, but this is one of Melbourne's more affluent areas, so there aren't too many cheapies. The range of cuisines includes Italian, Asian and lots of places serving a bit of everything, from pasta and focaccia to noodles and curries. If you're not so hungry, just grab a pavement table and sip on a wine or coffee while enjoying the passing parade.

Toorak Rd Starting from the Punt Rd end at No 11, the bustling and stylish ***France-Soir*** *(☎ 9866 8569)* is one of the best French brasseries in town, with excellent food and mains in the $18 to $23 range. It's open for lunch and dinner, but you'll probably need to book.

Across at No 32, the ***Cotton Lounge*** is a big licensed cafe and bar with pasta and other mains around $9 to $12, and live entertainment on Friday and Saturday nights. Next door, ***L'Ami*** is a stylish little cafe and bar with mains such as pasta and risotto from $13. Breakfast is served, but it's closed on Sundays. Across at No 39, ***Soba*** is a cute little place with noodles, sushi and stir-fries at very reasonable prices.

Further along at No 58, ***Winchell's Deli*** offers breakfast specials from $5.50 and focaccia from $5. At No 62, ***Cafe Modi*** serves Italian mains from $12.50 and is licensed.

Cosi at No 70 is a swanky bar and restaurant with a rear courtyard; mains start at $21.50, but there are cheaper lunch options. Nearby at No 74, ***Barolo's*** is a narrow bistro, also with a courtyard, offering good pastas and interesting Italian-style mains. If you're feeling indulgent, pop into ***Frenchy's*** at No 76 for a coffee and sublime French pastry.

La Porchetta at No 93 is one of the best-value pizza/pasta joints in town, with pizzas and pastas from $4 to $8 and other mains from $10.

Pinocchio's at No 152 is a popular pizzeria. ***Tamani Bistro***, nearby at No 156, is an Italian place where time has stood still since the 1970s. It's good for a hearty, inexpensive meal and serves excellent coffee. Next door, ***Cornercopia*** is a grocery shop and licensed cafe with a great lolly bar.

Over the hill and across the railway line at No 172 is ***Pieroni***, a big upmarket bar/restaurant. You can get breakfast here from $5, or a pasta from $12, and it does kids' serves. Next door, ***Chinois*** *(☎ 9826 3388)* is one of Melbourne's most acclaimed restaurants, specialising in innovative east-meets-west cuisine. Its 'business lunch' menu is good value at $22.50 for two courses and a glass of wine, while the dinner menu is more expensive with mains ranging from $22 to $36.

Up towards Chapel St at No 210, ***Tanah Ria*** is a pleasant modern place serving noodles for around $8 and curries and stir-fries around $12. At the Fun Factory on the Chapel St corner, ***Soda Rock*** is a corny American 1950s-style joint with burgers around $6.

Across Chapel St (still on Toorak Rd), the ritzy Como building has plenty of upmarket and pricey eateries. For a more affordable feed, try ***Vietnam Village*** across the road at No 272, a modern bar and restaurant with lunch specials for $7. At No 278, the very funky ***Corridor*** serves pasta and risotto from

$13, plus other dishes. At No 300, ***Zampeli's*** is a big place that's open late and is good for a snack or coffee and cake.

Chapel St Don your designer sunnies and head down Chapel St – you'll find plenty of interesting cafes, bars and restaurants in among all the fashion boutiques between Toorak Rd and Commercial Rd.

Caffe e Cucina *(9827 4139)*, No 581, is one of the smallest, coolest and best cafe/restaurants in town, with great Italian meals in the $14 to $22 range. It's one of *the* places in Melbourne to see and be seen, so book ahead. Down at No 571 is the friendly ***Chapellis***, a bar/restaurant with good food – and it's open round the clock. Right next door at No 569 is ***Kanpai***, a popular little Japanese restaurant with modestly priced dishes. At No 565, ***That Little Noodle Place*** is an extremely hip, licensed cafe with noodle and rice dishes from around $10, and other interesting offerings. Across the road at ***Cafe Greco***, slide into a red leather-look booth for coffee and cake, or a main from around $10. At No 534, ***Gratzi Coffee House*** is a smart, contemporary little place with pavement seating and focaccias and salads around $8. A little farther down, the Jam Factory complex is home to a few eateries, including the popular ***Studio Cafe*** and a small cafe in the huge ***Borders*** bookshop. Opposite, at No 481, ***Kazbar*** is a stylish licensed cafe that has survived a few years on this fickle strip, serving excellent coffee, focaccia around $7.50 and innovative dishes at reasonable prices.

At No 478, ***La Lucciola*** is a small Italian bistro that's popular with locals and reasonably priced. ***La Camera***, at No 446, is another good Italian bistro with interesting artwork and snacks and meals in the $7 to $13 range.

Kush, No 427, is a hip cafe with light meals around $10. Across at No 426 is ***Frost Bites***, a cool converted pub with meals around $7 to $15 plus a huge range of frozen fruit cocktails on tap – wash your lunch down with a 'Viagra' (bourbon and lemonade). On the opposite corner, ***Caffe Siena*** is an eternally busy people-watching spot with meals around $10 to $20.

Prahran

Commercial Rd & Chapel St Commercial Rd is the border between South Yarra and Prahran. The Prahran Market (actually in South Yarra) is a terrific place to shop – go here for some of the best fresh vegetables, fruit and fish in Melbourne. Within the market complex, ***let's eat*** is an impressive and very cool 'food and wine emporium' where you can shop for gourmet produce, indulge in a snack, coffee, wine or cake, order takeaway or stay for a meal (pizza/pasta from $4.95, vegie curry $8.50, Atlantic salmon $16.50). Across the courtyard is ***Spargo's*** cafe, also good for a quick meal with a glass of wine or a coffee.

Before the market, at No 209, ***Sweet Basil*** *(☎ 9827 3390)* is a charming, modern Thai place where you can get noodle or curry dishes for around $13. It's open Tuesday to Sunday and is licensed.

Opposite the market, ***Blue Elephant*** *(194 Commercial Rd)* is a funky and eternally-popular little cafe with great-value meals such as salads, noodles and curries from around $10, and breakfasts from around $5. Next door, ***The Outlook*** at No 196 *(☎ 9521 4227, theoutlook@hotmail.com)* is a brilliant little place that combines cafe, gift and card shop, Internet access and a hair salon! Light meals are around $7, Internet access $7 an hour and haircuts from $15.

Nearby at No 176, ***Chinta Ria*** has good Malaysian meals ranging from $8 to $16, and good jazz and soul music in the background. Next door, ***Soul Sisters*** offers similar cuisine and atmosphere.

This stretch of Commercial Rd is a centre for Melbourne's gay and lesbian community, and down past the market there's a string of popular cafes and restaurants. At Nos 151 and 149 respectively, there are two small and stylish licensed cafes, ***Cafe 151*** and ***Alternative***. At No 133 is ***Sandgropers***, a friendly beach-style cafe with a wide choice of dishes at reasonable prices (try the Mars Bar cake for $5).

Heading south back on Chapel St, ***Ankara*** at No 310 is a narrow and inexpensive Turkish restaurant which features a belly dancer on Friday and Saturday nights. The ***Globe Cafe***, at No 218, has excellent food – Thai, Cajun, Indian, Italian and lots of other influences – and a sensational cake counter. It's open for breakfast (around $7), and lunch and dinner mains range from $12 to $15.

Saigon Rose, at No 206, serves inexpensive Vietnamese food in a pleasant setting. At No 135 ***Patee Thai*** is the best Thai restaurant in the area, with an exotic, intimate feel and meals around $10 to $15.

The Windsor end of Chapel St is undergoing something of a renaissance, with hip second-hand clothing boutiques springing up, and funky little cafes like the cheap and homey ***Orange*** *(126 Chapel St)* and the more sophisticated ***Ibiza*** *(116 Chapel St)*. At No 68, ***Marmara*** is another cheap Turkish place with great kebabs and delicious Turkish bread. For good food and good value, try the tiny and charming ***Cafe Marie*** at No 34.

Greville St Greville St, which runs off Chapel St beside the Prahran Town Hall, has an eclectic collection of grungy and groovy clothes boutiques, book and music shops, and a few good eateries. Beside the railway tracks at No 95 is the ever-popular ***Feedwell Cafe***, an earthy vegetarian cafe serving interesting and wholesome food in the $5 to $10 range. The ***Continental Cafe*** at No 132 has fabulous food at affordable prices and a sophisticated atmosphere – it's open from 7 am until midnight.

St Kilda

St Kilda has been transformed almost beyond recognition in the past decade or so, and in many ways its eateries are a reflection of both the past and the future. The past is a noisy hamburger joint, a fast-felafel bar or a well-worn Italian bistro. The future is an ultra-hip cafe with a clientele to match. This is the suburb with something for everybody.

Be warned that on summer weekends St Kilda is packed to overflowing with visitors from other suburbs.

St Kilda's two main eating precincts are along Acland and Fitzroy Sts, but there are also some good places down by the sea.

Acland St Up at the north-west end of Acland St, where it merges into a residential area, there's a cluster of places to eat and drink, including the ***Dog's Bar*** at No 54. This is the place where the truly hip (and somewhat monied) people hang out, and they usually come in droves. If you can get in, this popular and hectic bar also serves good food at reasonable prices.

Heading south-east down Acland St, turn left up Calisle St to reach the ***Galleon*** at No 9. It's a local favourite, and a hold-out against the super-slickness of modern St Kilda. It has quirky concrete-and-laminex decor, good music and everything from toasted sandwiches and apple crumble to chicken and leek pie – all at very reasonable prices. There's also a shared accommodation notice board.

The unassuming ***Vineyard Restaurant*** *(71 Acland St)* is a long-standing favourite among carnivores – the grills are huge and range from $13 to over $30. Salad is extra, but that's not really what you come here for. Around the corner on Shakespeare Grove (there can't be many less grove-like streets in Melbourne), ***Bala's*** is a small cafe-style place with an inexpensive Indian-influenced menu to eat in or take-away. Back on Acland St is the even smaller ***Cafe Manna***, a simple, friendly Indian place where most main courses are around $7. A thali costs $7.50 or $8.50 with meat.

Opposite, ***Chinta Ria – Soul*** *(☎ 9525 4664, 94 Acland St)* combines terrific Malaysian food with soul music images and sounds. Main meals are $8 to $15, and you'll need to book. There's another Chinta Ria, ***Chinta Ria – Blues*** *(☎ 9534 9233, 6 Acland St)*, at the other end of Acland St and others in Carlton and Prahran. Next door to Chinta Ria – ***Soul***, the quirky and opinionated ***Cafe Goa*** serves spicy Portuguese,

Indian and vegetarian dishes, most of which cost $9.50.

Back across the road at No 89, ***Red Rock Noodle Bar*** is a large, semi-hip place specialising in noodles and other east Asian dishes. The quality is a bit hit and miss: the squid salad ($6) was different and delicious, but the Red Rock noodles (about $11) were just average. For noodles without decor, head to the other end of Acland St for the ***Noodle Box*** at No 164.

The ***Blue Danube*** *(107 Acland St)* and ***Scheherezade*** *(99 Acland St)* serve central-European food in generous proportions. Blue Danube is more Hungarian and Scheherezade is more Jewish. These low-key cafes are good places to come when you're really hungry, with hearty dishes like borscht, goulash, cabbage rolls and gefilte fish to choose from. They're a reminder that St Kilda was (and still is, to some extent) a suburb of central European immigrants.

Farther down at No 153, ***Orienta on Acland*** doesn't offer great food but it is cheap, with Asian-style dishes at $5 for as much as you can put on your plate. Diagonally opposite, ***Cicciolina*** *(130 Acland St)* is a very popular modern bistro serving classic Italian food at mid-range prices. (And did you know that Cicciolina, the Italian artist/porn star-cum-politician, is in fact from Budapest?)

Big Mouth *(corner Acland and Barkly Sts)* has good service in its popular downstairs cafe (most main courses under $10) and upstairs restaurant (most main courses well under $20). Both are good places for people watching.

Across the street and round the corner, ***Wild Rice*** *(211 Barkly St)* is a very good organic/vegan cafe with inexpensive stir-fries, casseroles, burgers, salads and more, as well as a pleasant courtyard out the back. Next door, ***Claypots Seafood Bar*** sells an intriguing breakfast of fresh sardines, eggs and potatoes for $6, as well as other dishes for lunch and dinner. Around the next corner is the popular ***Rasa's Vegie Bar*** *(5 Blessington St)*, a tiny vegetarian bar with tofu or lentil burgers at $6.50 and vegetarian stir-fries, curries and pastas from $8. It's closed Monday and Tuesday.

Acland St is renowned for its fine delis and cake shops – the window displays emanate so many calories you're in danger of putting on weight just walking past.

Fitzroy St The beach end of Fitzroy St is crowded with eateries, most of which are open-fronted with tables spilling out onto the footpath. Up this end, the very chic ***Madame Joe Joe*** *☎ 9534 0000)* is one of the best of the new breed of St Kilda restaurants. It serves up fabulous Mediterranean-style food and is fairly pricey with mains at around $18 to $25, but great for a splurge. Farther along at No 23, the Street Cafe is a big and bustling cafe, bar and restaurant with something for everyone – sit out the front and play the see-and-be-seen game.

In the next block, at No 31, the slick and sophisticated ***Cafe Di Stasio*** *(☎ 9525 3999)* has a reputation for outstanding Italian food, although if you don't have *the* look (ie very hip or just plain rich) you might feel a little out of place here. If so, head for the tiny and cheerful ***Hard Wok Cafe*** at No 49, with Asian stir-fries, laksas and curries from $6 to $12. ***Leo's Spaghetti Bar*** (*55 Fitzroy St)* is something of a St Kilda institution, with a coffee bar, bistro and restaurant, while farther along at No 73 ***Thai Panic Cafe*** is a tiny Thai-food cafe with reasonable curries from $7 to $9.

On the corner of Fitzroy and Park Sts, ***Cafe Menis/Bortolotto's*** is dominated by a large and colourful St Kilda beach mural. The excellent food is Italian provincial, with main meals from $10 to $18.

Farther up, the wonderful ***Tolarno Bar & Bistro*** *(☎ 9525 5477)*, at No 42, features the quirky wall murals of local artist Mirka Mora. The restaurant specialises in Mediterranean-style cuisine, with mains from $12.50 to $20. Next door, the small bar/eatery offers snacks and meals for $7 to $18, including the best burgers in Melbourne ($9 with fries).

Back on the busy side of the street, the bustling ***Topolino's*** at No 87 is the place to go for a pizza or big bowl of pasta (try the spaghetti marinara for $12.50 – you won't go home hungry!), especially late at night when it's usually packed. It stays open until around sunrise. ***Bar Ninety Seven***, at 97 Fitzroy St, is a very fashionable bar/eatery with good food – wear sunnies by day, something black if you're coming at night. ***Chichio's***, at No 109, is a popular budget eatery that offers tasty main meals for $7.50 to $12.50.

On the corner of Fitzroy and Grey Sts is ***The George Hotel***. A hundred years ago, the George was one of St Kilda's grandest hotels, but as the years passed the old pub slid into disrepair and punkish ill repute. But, since being taken under the wing of local restaurant guru Donlevy Fitzpatrick, the George has returned to the forefront of St Kilda style. The corner bar/cafe is known as ***The George Melbourne Wine Room***, and features fine food and Victorian wines. The complex also includes a wine shop, the underground George Public Bar, also known as the Snakepit, and a foyer cafe, gallery, an adventure travel agency and hairdresser.

Seaside ***The Stokehouse*** *(☎ 9525 5555, 30 Jacka Blvd)*, down on the foreshore, has one of the best settings in town and is just about a 'must-see' for visitors to Melbourne. The restaurant section upstairs is fairly pricey but has fabulous views and outstanding food in the 'modern Mediterranean/Asian' style, while downstairs is a big, bustling bar/bistro with an outdoor terrace and tasty tucker like antipasto, burgers, fish and chips, and gourmet pizzas, all from $8 to $15. But nobody comes here just to eat – they come to see (sunsets over the bay, the passing parade of strollers, in-line skaters, joggers and cyclists, and all the beautiful people) and be seen.

Nearby, ***Donovan's*** *(☎ 9534 8221, 40 Jacka Blvd)* has an equally good position. It's a classy and popular licensed restaurant boasting a great outlook, and some of the best seafood in Melbourne. For those of us without gold Amex cards there's also a take-away section with great fish and chips and outdoor tables.

Last but by no means least is the remarkable ***Espy Kitchen*** way up the back of the Esplanade Hotel. It's always busy, the food is great (mains from $10) and after you've eaten you can play pool or check out one of the (often free) live bands.

Albert Park

If you're in Albert Park and hungry, just follow the tram line (No 1) that runs down to the beach. Most of the area's eateries are along this route.

Vic Ave *(135 Victoria Ave)* is a bustling Italian bistro with a courtyard out back – pastas are around $13, other mains $16 to $21. Farther up, ***Misuzu's*** *(7 Victoria Ave)* is a small and extremely popular 'village-style' Japanese cafe. It's probably the only eatery in this area that's worth a special trip to find. The food is outstanding and quite different from the standard fare in formal Japanese restaurants; the prices are very reasonable. It's open daily, except Monday, for breakfast, lunch and dinner.

Albert Park has a thriving and very trendy cafe scene, and there are some good daytime eateries around Bridport St and Victoria Ave (this shopping strip is called Dundas Place). Popular places include the ***Albert Park Deli***, the ***Villagio Deli*** and ***Dundas & Faussett***, all on Bridport St. All these places serve great coffee, cooked breakfasts, focaccias, filled croissants, salads, pastas and home-made cakes. You can eat in, take-away or sit out on the footpath and watch the trams roll by. ***Feeling Fruity*** sells great ice cream and pricey fruit salads; ***Browns*** is popular for coffee and pastry; and ***Bottom of the Harbour*** is the place for fish and chips.

Ricardo's Trattoria *(☎ 99 Dundas Place)* is a smart and popular open-fronted Italian bistro, and nearby on the corner of Bridport and Montague Sts, ***Vistas*** is rather more chic. Just off Dundas Place in Montague St, ***Cafe Montague*** is a fairly upmarket bistro that is never crowded.

South Melbourne

South Melbourne is home to advertising agencies and video production houses, so there are quite a few places to hit the expense account on a business meal. But it's also an old (and newly expensive) residential area, so there are some good local eateries. The main bunch of cafes is on Clarendon St between Park and York Sts, but there are some very good places off this strip.

est est est *(☎ 9682 5688, 440 Clarendon St)* offers superb food and well-trained staff, with prices to match. You could easily spend well over $60 on a meal. Less well-heeled, but still stylish, workers head to the ***Limerick Arms Hotel*** *(corner Clarendon and Park Sts)*. It's a revamped pub with a pleasant courtyard restaurant, and bar meals cost under $10.

If you transplanted a 1920s Aussie pub to provincial Italy, you'd end up with something like the ***Locanda Veneta*** *(273 Cecil St)* – a traditional bistro serving good food in a cosy atmosphere. Pastas start around $10 and main meals around $15. It makes you wish that more pubs had gone this road rather than resorting to postmodern glitz. An old-style Aussie pub that hasn't made any great leaps in style is the ***Maori Chief*** *(117 Moray St)*. It's very relaxed, caters to locals and serves good-value pub standards from around $11.

O'Connell's *(corner of Montague and Coventry Sts)* is known for its excellent food and inspiring menu. The restaurant is expensive but the bar isn't, and there are plenty of choices for vegetarians. The ***Isthmus of Kra*** *(☎ 9690 3688, 50 Park St)* is one of Melbourne's best Asian restaurants. It's a classy and elegant place with fine service, specialising in southern Thai cuisine with Malaysian influences. Main courses are mostly $14 to $20. You'll need to book.

Williamstown

Willy has a fine assortment of cafes and restaurants along Nelson Place, catering to the hordes of day-trippers. ***Hobson's Choice Foods*** *(213 Nelson Place)* is an extremely popular cafe with great food, all made on the premises – pies, brioches, breakfasts, sandwiches, vegetarian meals and lots more. Nearby at No 203 is the ***Scuttlebutt Cafe***, with interesting snacks and meals at reasonable prices. ***Kohinoor***, farther up at No 223, looks pretty basic but serves good-value Indian food with main meals from $7 to $12.

The next stretch of Nelson Place, beyond the Cole St roundabout, also contains its fair share of good pubs and eateries. The ***Atomic Bar*** has fairly inexpensive food plus a billiards club upstairs. On the Syme St corner is the Customs House Market & Gallery and next door is ***Sam's Boatshed***, a bar/eatery built around an old clinker boat. The open-air courtyard is a very pleasant spot to tuck into a wood-fired oven pizza.

The elegant ***Aquis Cafe & Restaurant*** *(☎ 9397 2377, 231 Nelson Place, upstairs)*, also on Nelson Place, has a cafe downstairs and a restaurant upstairs with views over the marina to St Kilda. It has modern, European influenced mains in the $14 to $24 range. The more casual cafe is cheaper.

The ***Strand*** *(☎ 9397 7474, corner the Strand and Ferguson St)* is stylish, simple and ultra-modern, with a small bar, an open-air courtyard and good views over the bay. The menu is predominantly seafood, with main courses in the $15 to $28 range, and there's an upmarket take-away fish and chip joint next door.

Another good option is the ***Anchorage*** *(☎ 9397 6270)*, 500m north along the Strand at No 34. This former boat shed sits over the water and has a cosy maritime feel, with timber decking, fishing nets hanging from the roof and a marvellous outlook across the bay to the city skyline. Main courses are around $22.

If you feel like an after dinner stroll and a drink, wander up to the end of Nelson Place. There, at No 1, ***Titanic Entertainments*** has a fairly large-scale model of the famous ship on its roof. It's a function and party venue but there's also a bar.

ENTERTAINMENT

The best source of 'what's on' information is the *Entertainment Guide* (*EG*), which comes out every Friday with the *Age* newspaper. *Beat*, *Inpress* and *Storm* are free music and entertainment magazines that have reviews, interviews and dates of gigs. They're available from pubs, cafes and venues.

Ticketmaster is the main booking agency for theatre, concerts, sports and other events. For inquiries ring ☎ 9645 7970, or ☎ 1800 338 998 (toll-free) from outside Melbourne. To make credit card bookings for sporting events ring ☎ 13 6122; for theatre and the arts events, ☎ 13 6166; and for other events, ☎ 13 6100. The telephone services operate Monday to Saturday from 9 am to 9 pm and Sunday to 5 pm. Besides taking bookings by phone, Ticketmaster has outlets in places such as Myer stores, major theatres and shopping centres.

If you want cheap tickets, visit the Half-Tix (☎ 9650 9420) booth in the Bourke St Mall, which sells half-price tickets to shows and concerts on the day of the performance. There are usually some great bargains going, but make sure you find out where you'll be sitting – they don't sell the best seats in the house at half price. Half-Tix opens Monday and Saturday from 10 am to 2 pm, and Tuesday to Thursday from 11 am to 6 pm and to 6.30 pm on Friday. It doesn't accept credit cards – cash only.

Bars

Melbourne has a great collection of ultra-fashionable bars. They are all individual, but generally have a few things in common such as stylised design, booze, good food and music, and very groovy clientele. If you're looking for style without frenetic activity, try the five-star hotels; if you're looking for activity without style, try an old-fashioned pub, if you can still find one – try the ***Standard Hotel*** *(293 Fitzroy St, Fitzroy)*.

Fashionable bars in the city include ***Meyer Place***, in tiny Meyer Place, off the top end of Bourke St, ***Lounge*** *(243 Swanston St)*, ***Bernie's*** *(1 Coverlid Place)*, off Little Bourke St near Russell St, ***International Lounge*** *(18-24 Market Lane)*, ***Rue Bebelons*** *(267 Little Lonsdale St)* and ***Spleen*** *(41 Bourke St)*. ***Hell's Kitchen*** *(20 Centre Place)* is another worth trying.

There are plenty of bars over the river in the casino, including ***Planet Hollywood***.

Brunswick St in Fitzroy, north of Johnston St, is a long string of 'entry level' fashionable bars – go for a stroll. Chapel St in South Yarra, south of Toorak Rd, is where the wealthier hang out.

The ***Terminus Hotel***, 605 Victoria St, Abbotsford, is a good place for a drink before or after a meal at one of the street's many, many Vietnamese restaurants. It feels a bit like being in the lounge room of a shared house circa 1970.

In St Kilda, the ***Dog's Bar*** at 54 Acland St is the original and still one of the most popular hangouts for social barflies. It has several good neighbours. The front bar at ***The George Hotel***, on the corner of Fitzroy and Grey Sts, is another popular local, and the ***Snakepit*** is a narrow and super-groovy underground bar in the same complex. Farther along Fitzroy St, ***The Mink Bar*** at the Prince of Wales Hotel is a very cool, expensive cocktail bar, which you might not get into. The main bar here has for decades been a hangout for gays, transvestites, showgirls, drunks and other St Kilda types. (I was once rescued from a psychopathic bouncer by a huge male Pacific Islander in a dress.) You'll be welcome at the friendly ***Tolarno Bar*** *(42 Fitzroy St)*.

Pubs & Live Music Venues

For the bigger local and international acts, Melbourne's main music venues are the National Tennis Centre, the Concert Hall at the Victorian Arts Centre, the Sports and Entertainment Centre with its quirky acoustics and the MCG for the occasional massive concert, such the Three Tenors or the Rolling Stones. Some (mainly classical) concerts are held at the outdoor Sidney Myer Music Bowl in the Kings Domain.

Melbourne has always enjoyed a thriving pub-rock scene and is widely acknowledged as the country's rock capital. The sweaty grind around Melbourne's pubs has been the proving ground for many of Australia's best outfits. Internationally successful bands like AC/DC, INXS, Crowded House and Nick Cave and the Bad Seeds all had their roots deep in Melbourne's pub-rock scene. Clubbing and DJs have shifted the focus from the live band scene in recent years, but it's still extremely healthy.

To find out who's playing where, look in the *EG*, *Beat* or *Inpress*, or listen to the gig guides on FM radio stations like 3RRR (102.7) and 3PBS (106.7). (These are both excellent independent radio stations.) Cover charges at the pubs vary widely – some gigs are free, but generally you'll pay $5 to $10.

Just about every pub in inner Melbourne has hosted bands at one time or another, and new venues crop up all the time; old ones close just as regularly. The following are mainly pubs and other venues that have had live music for a while, and are likely to stay in business.

In the city, ***Lounge*** *(243 Swanston Walk, upstairs)* is a hip, semi-alternative club that features everything from Latin rhythms to techno and hip-hop. Down on Flinders St, at the corner of Russell St, ***The Forum*** is a fabulous old cinema that's been renovated into a music venue. The ***Public Bar***, opposite the Queen Vic market at 238 Victoria St, has a nightly line-up of bands playing through until the early hours for about $4. Nearby on the corner of Queensberry and Elizabeth Sts, ***Arthouse*** is the place to head for if you're into death metal.

In Fitzroy, the ***Rainbow Hotel***, an old back-street pub at 27 St James St, has (free) live bands nightly, ranging from jazz, Cajun and blues to funk and soul. On the corner of Brunswick and Kerr Sts, the ***Evelyn Hotel***, with its funked-up interior, is still one of Fitzroy's major band venues, while across the road the very grungy ***Punters Club*** *(376 Brunswick St)* has bands most nights for $5 or less. (If the Punters can resist redecoration for a few more years it will probably find itself a cultural icon.) The ***Royal Derby*** *(corner Brunswick St and Alexandra Ave)* is another venue. The ***Builders Arms*** *(211 Gertrude St)* is another good Fitzroy watering hole.

In Collingwood, the ***Club*** *(132 Smith St)* attracts good bands and stays open until dawn-ish, while the ***Prince Patrick Hotel*** *(135 Victoria Pde)* alternates between being a band venue and a comedy venue. ***The Tote*** *(71 Johnston)* is another fine pub with bands.

Richmond has always been something of an enclave for grungy rock pubs; they include the famous ***Corner Hotel*** *(57 Swan St)* and the ***Central Club Hotel*** *(293 Swan St)*.

The ***Continental*** *(☎ 9510 2788)*, above the cafe of the same name at 134 Greville St, Prahran, is a sophisticated and popular venue where you have a choice of dinner-and-show deals ($35 to $65) or standing-room ($15 to $30). It's a small space where you can see a wide range of local and international acts close up. Not far away in

Rock 'n' Roll High School

In 1990 Stephanie Bourke decided to start a summer school for aspiring young female rock stars. From humble beginnings, the school has grown to become an icon in Melbourne's music scene and something of a mecca for female musos. Over the years numerous touring international bands have visited the school and some donate instruments.

The school is in an old red-brick house in the inner-city suburb of Collingwood. There are more than 250 students 'enrolled' here – mostly female, and mostly studying their various instruments on a casual or part-time basis. The school has been the birthplace of numerous bands, with names like Gritty Kitty, Hecate, Cherry Bombs and Tuff Muff.

The Rock 'n' Roll High School (☎ 9416 1663) is at 186 Easey St in Collingwood a couple of houses along from where Easey St intersects with Hoddle St. The school offers individual lessons in electric guitar, classical guitar, bass, drums, piano, flute, cello and voice. Phone the school for more info.

Mark Armstrong

Windsor, ***Empire*** *(174 Peel St)* is much larger but plays a similar range of acts, with clubbing nights as well.

In St Kilda is the famed ***Esplanade Hotel***, on the Esplanade of course, which has, often free, live bands every night and Sunday afternoons. It's also a great place just to sit with a beer and watch the sun set over the pier, or have a meal in the Espy Kitchen out the back. You can't leave Melbourne without visiting the Espy. Around the corner and up Fitzroy St you'll find the venerable ***Prince of Wales*** hotel at No 29. Good local bands play in a great, grungy venue, and there are sometimes insane Wrestlemania nights, with pro wrestling and bands (about $12). Call ☎ 9536 1166 to find out what's on. Young bands on the way up (or the way out) play up the street at ***Underbelly***, No 61.

The ***Limerick Arms***, on the corner of Park and Clarendon Sts in South Melbourne, is a friendly little pub with jazz bands on Thursday and DJs on Friday and Saturday.

For country music (usually in the country swing or rockabilly vein rather than modern Nashville) try the ***Railway Hotel*** *(800 Nicholson St, North Fitzroy)*.

Folk & Acoustic Music If you're into mellower music, the *EG* has an 'Acoustic and Folk' listing. One of the main venues is the ***Dan O'Connell Hotel***, *(225 Canning St, Carlton)*. As a measure of its Irishness, it claims to sell more Irish whisky than Scotch whisky. Another popular Irish pub is ***Molly Bloom's Hotel*** *(corner Bay and Rouse Sts, Port Melbourne)*, which has traditional Irish folk music seven nights a week. The ***Great Britain Hotel*** *(447 Church St, Richmond)* sometimes has folk (and even when it doesn't, it's a nice place for a drink).

Jazz & Blues There are some great jazz joints in Melbourne's city centre. Hidden down a narrow lane off Little Lonsdale St (between Exhibition and Russell Sts), ***Bennett's Lane*** is a quintessentially dim, smoke-filled, groovy jazz venue – well worth searching out. It's open every night (except Tuesday) until around 1 am, and until 3 or 4 am on weekends.

Quite a few pubs also have good jazz and blues sessions on certain nights – check the gig guide in the *EG*. They include the ***Spleen Bar*** *(41 Bourke St)*, ***Limerick Arms*** in South Melbourne; ***The George Hotel*** *(corner Fitzroy and Grey Sts, St Kilda)*, the cosy ***Commercial Hotel*** *(238 Whitehall St, Yarraville)*, the ***Rainbow Hotel*** *(27 St David St, Fitzroy)*, the ***Grace Darling Hotel*** *(corner Smith and Peel Sts, Collingwood)*, the ***Emerald Hotel*** *(414 Clarendon St, South Melbourne)* and ***McCoppin's Hotel*** *(166 Johnston St, Fitzroy)*. Some of the five-star hotels in the city, such as ***Rydges Melbourne***, ***Rydges Riverwalk*** and ***Sofitel***, have jazz in one of their bars.

During January (four evenings each week) and February (three evenings), the Melbourne Zoo in Parkville has an extremely popular 'Zoo Twilights' season of open-air sessions with jazz or big bands. Call the recorded information line (☎ 9285 9333, 24 hours) for details.

Brewery Pubs Pubs that brew their own beer ('boutique beers') were all the rage a few years back. A few places have survived, and while the beer is certainly not cheap, it makes a nice change from the standard mass-produced stuff. For homesick Europeans, these are the places to look for some *real* bitters. Popular brewery pubs include the ***Redback Brewery*** *(75 Flemington Rd, North Melbourne)*, the ***Geebung Polo Club*** *(85 Auburn Rd, Auburn)* and ***Bell's Hotel & Brewery*** *(157 Moray St, South Melbourne)*.

Clubs

Melbourne has a huge collection of dance clubs. The club scene is diverse and ever-changing, and what's hot today isn't necessarily hot tomorrow. Clubs range from the exclusive 'members-only' variety (where if you haven't got the right look or know the right people you don't get in) to barn-sized discos (where anyone who wants to spend money is welcomed with open arms). Cover charges range from $5 to $15, although some places don't charge at all.

Most places have dress standards, but it is generally at the discretion of the people on the door – if they don't like the look of you, they might not let you in.

Mainstream Clubs The city centre is home to most of Melbourne's mainstream clubs, and ***Metro*** *(20 Bourke St)* is a good place to start any exploration of club land. It's the biggest nightclub in the southern hemisphere, and with eight bars on three levels it's very impressive, especially on the busier nights. It sometimes hosts quite big international acts, such as Grace Jones or UB40.

King St in the city is a busy but somewhat seedy nightclub strip, with a cluster of places that include ***Inflation*** at No 60, the ***Grainstore Tavern*** next door and the ***Sports Bar*** at No 14. Another popular city club is the ***Tunnel*** *(590 Little Bourke St)*.

Outside the city centre, the ***Chevron*** *(519 St Kilda Rd)* in South Melbourne has been around for ever. It's a huge place with a mixture of DJs and live bands, a cocktail bar and cheap drink deals. Down in St Kilda there's the ***Ritz*** at 169 Fitzroy St, which is part band venue, part nightclub, or you could try ***Joey's*** *(upstairs 61 Fitzroy St)* – it's a seedy dive but it stays open until sunrise. ***Carousel***, an upmarket bar and restaurant overlooking Albert Park Lake from Aughtie Drive, also hosts club nights.

Billboard *(170 Russell St)*, ***Mercury Lounge*** at the casino, ***Silvers*** *(445 Toorak Rd, Toorak)* and ***Chasers*** *(386 Chapel St, South Yarra)* are more large, mainstream places with a variety of music on different nights. There are also a few clubs at the casino.

Alternative Clubs Melbourne has a vibrant alternative and indie club scene. Most venues host different club nights on different nights and names change as quickly as Melbourne's weather, so the only way to keep up is to check the alternative club pages in the entertainment papers.

Dream *(229 Queensberry St, Carlton)* is one of the best alternative venues – it goes Gothic on Friday, indie/alternative on Saturday and has gay/S&M nights on Sunday. Other good venues, all in the city, include ***Lounge*** *(243 Swanston St)*, ***Bass Station*** *(12 McKillop St)*, ***44*** *(44 Lonsdale St)* and ***Club 383*** *(383 Lonsdale St)* and, just south of the city, is ***Mansion*** *(83 Queens Rd, South Melbourne)*, which hosts the B&D ***Hellfire Club*** on Sunday.

In Fitzroy, the extremely hip ***Night Cat*** *(141 Johnston St)* is well worth a visit, with a great 1950s-esque decor and jazz, soul and other bands from Thursday to Sunday. Farther down Johnston St at No 48, ***Bar Salona*** is a small and funky Latin-style dance club that opens every night – until 3 am on Friday and Saturday. In South Melbourne, ***Saratoga*** *(46 Albert Rd)* is another small, dim nightclub – if you can get in, you might find yourself drinking and dancing with some of Melbourne's semi-famous musos, actors and comedians.

Gay & Lesbian Venues

The Saloon Bar at the ***Prince of Wales Hotel*** *(29 Fitzroy St, St Kilda)* is Melbourne's oldest gay bar, full of the quirky, grungy and glamorous and hosts the infamous 'Dollar Pots' every Monday night. Melbourne's gay precinct of Commercial Rd Prahran (locals call it the 'Gay Metre') houses ***Three Faces Nightclub*** *(143 Commercial Rd, Prahran)*, open Thursday to Sunday and attracting a young crowd, ***Diva Bar*** *(153 Commercial Rd)* open Tuesday to Saturday and others

Hardware *(285 Latrobe St)* is a bar, bistro and cabaret venue for gays, lesbians and friends; open nightly.

Collingwood has some good men's venues. ***The Peel Dance Bar*** *(corner Peel and Wellington Sts)* has Go Go dancers on podiums and DJs spinning trance, house and garage music. ***The Laird*** *(149 Gipps St)* is a men only pub catering to an older crowd with pool tables, a beer garden and theme nights. ***Jock's*** *(9 Peel St)* is a bar with entertainment (singers such as Eva Destruction). There's also the ***Star Hotel*** *(176 Hoddle St)*.

Also in Collingwood, the ***Glasshouse Hotel*** *(corner of Gipps and Rokeby Sts)* is a women's pub with entertainment (anything from bingo to bands) nightly except Monday.

Several other pubs and clubs have gay nights, such as ***Freakazoid,*** Saturdays from midnight, at the rear of the Chevron *(519 St Kilda Rd, Prahran)* and ***Toolbox*** for women on alternative Fridays at The Laundry *(50 Johnston St, Fitzroy).*

Cinema

Melbourne has plenty of mainstream cinemas playing latest releases, although if you've come from Europe or the USA they might be last season's latest. The main chains are Village, Hoyts and Greater Union, and the main group of city cinemas can be found around the intersection of Bourke and Russell Sts. Tickets cost around $9 during the day, up to $12 at night.

There's a huge collection of arthouse cinemas – there's even a chain (Palace Cinemas). Actually, these days 'arthouse' seems to mean current non-blockbuster films. It can be hard to find classics and truly weird films. Lovers of, say, Bergman or the Marx brothers, not to mention *The Blues Brothers* and *Eraserhead*, may find the pickings slim. However, ***Cinemateque*** has screenings at thé State Film Theatre *(☎ 9650 2562, 1 Macarthur St, East Melbourne)* each Wednesday night.

Independent cinemas include the not-to-be-missed Art Deco nostalgia of the big ***Astor*** *(☎ 9510 1414, corner Chapel St and Dandenong Rd, St Kilda)*, with double features for $10 every night (and great ice creams!). Other good alternative cinemas include the modern ***Kino*** *(☎ 9650 2100, Collins Place 45 Collins St)* and the ***Lumiere*** *(☎ 9639 1055, 108 Lonsdale St)* in the city centre; the intimate old ***Carlton Moviehouse*** *(☎ 9347 8909, 235 Faraday St,)* and ***Cinema Nova*** *(☎ 9347 5331, 380 Lygon St)*, both in Carlton; the ***Longford*** *(☎ 9867 2700, 59 Toorak Rd, South Yarra)*; the ***George Cinema*** *(☎ 9534 6922, 133 Fitzroy St, St Kilda)*; and the ***Trak*** *(☎ 9827 9333, 445 Toorak Rd, Toorak).*

Moonlight Cinema

From mid-December to early March, the Moonlight Cinema screens good movies outdoors in the Royal Botanic Gardens. These can be old favourites, from *Breakfast at Tiffany's* to *Taxi Driver* or recent box office or arthouse hits. Take along a rug to sit on and a picnic supper, or buy your food and drinks there. Screenings begin around 8.45 pm (depending on when it gets dark) and the gate (Gate D on Birdwood Ave) opens at 7.30 pm. Tickets cost $11.50 ($8.50 concession) at the gate or through Ticketmaster (☎ 136 100). For screening details phone ☎ 1900 933 899.

Outdoor cinema has caught on, and there are several others around the city, including screenings at the Myer Music Bowl and the Northcote Amphitheatre.

Mark Armstrong

The ***State Film Centre*** *(☎ 9651 1515, 1 Macarthur St, East Melbourne)* is a venue for film festivals, experimental and cultural works, and film-society screenings.

The cinemas at the universities also have interesting and inexpensive non-mainstream screenings. The closest are the ***Union Theatre*** *(☎ 9344 6976)* at Melbourne University and the ***Union*** *(☎ 9660 3713)* at RMIT.

Melbourne's IMAX Theatre *(☎ 9663 5454)* is by the new museum, near the Exhibition Buildings (enter from Rathdowne St). As usual with IMAX, the films aren't exactly masterpieces but the huge screen makes them spectacular. Finally, if you want to experience one of the world's last drive-ins, head out to the ***Village Drive-in*** at Newlands Rd, Coburg.

Check the *EG* in Friday's *Age* or newspapers for screenings and times.

Theatre

The ***Victorian Arts Centre*** *(☎ 9281 8000)*, in St Kilda Rd, is Melbourne's major venue for the performing arts. Flanked by the

Yarra River on one side and the National Gallery on the other, the complex houses the ***Melbourne Concert Hall*** and three theatres – the ***State Theatre***, the ***Playhouse*** and the ***George Fairfax Studio***.

If you're in Melbourne during the summer months watch out for the excellent open-air theatre productions staged in the Royal Botanic Gardens. See the *EG* listings or ring Bass for details.

Theatre Companies The Melbourne Theatre Company (MTC) is Melbourne's major theatrical company and performs at the Victorian Arts Centre. The MTC stages around 15 productions each year, ranging from contemporary and modern (including a large percentage of new Australian works) to Shakespearian and other classics.

Melbourne's other major theatre companies include the following:

Handspan Theatre (☎ 9427 8611)
Performing at various theatres, this group is Australia's foremost puppet-theatre company. Its work has a strong visual element, using effects like shadow screens and animation. Its adult shows are just as exciting as its children's shows.

La Mama (☎ 9347 6142)
La Mama Theatre, 205 Faraday St, Carlton – a tiny and intimate forum for new Australian works and experimental theatre, with a long-established reputation for developing emerging young writers.

Playbox (☎ 9685 5111)
Malthouse Theatre Complex, 113 Sturt St, South Melbourne – this outstanding company stages predominantly Australian works by established and new playwrights.

Theatreworks (☎ 9534 4879)
Theatreworks Theatre, 14 Acland St, St Kilda – combines community theatre and story telling with innovative productions.

In addition to those listed above, Melbourne's major theatres include:

Athenaeum Theatre (☎ 9650 1500)
188 Collins St, Melbourne

Comedy Theatre (☎ 9209 9000)
240 Exhibition St, Melbourne

Her Majesty's Theatre (☎ 9663 2266)
219 Exhibition St, Melbourne

National Theatre (☎ 9534 0221)
Corner of Barkly and Carlisle Sts, St Kilda

Princess Theatre (☎ 9299 9800)
163 Spring St, Melbourne – restored for the Australian production of *Phantom of the Opera*, Melbourne's most historic theatre was built in 1854 when Melbourne was awash with money from the gold-rush.

Regent Theatre (☎ 9299 9500)
191 Collins St, Melbourne – saved from demolition and restored to its former glory.

Trades Hall (☎ 9662 3511)
54 Lygon St, Carlton South – this bastion of left-wing politics is an occasional venue for good theatre and comedy – comedian Rod Quantock's wonderful Kennett Lectures might become an annual event.

Universal Theatre (☎ 9419 3777)
13 Victoria St, Fitzroy – offers a range of productions from comedy to narrative.

Melbourne also has a huge fringe and amateur theatre circuit, so much so that the magazine *Stage Whispers* is devoted solely to fringe and amateur news – see that magazine or the *EG* for listings of current productions.

Buskers, especially in Bourke St Mall and at Southgate, range from the mundane to the extraordinary. Sadly, some of the most popular acts get moved on from the mall because the crowds they attract block the trams.

Theatre Restaurants There are quite a few 'dinner-and-show' type places, where you'll meet the office party crowd; find them in the *Yellow Pages*.

Comedy

Melbourne prides itself on being the home of Australian comedy. Even the comedians who have used Melbourne as a launching pad to international stardom have fond memories of their home town and its influences. Looking forward to a return visit, Barry Humphries once said:

> Visiting Melbourne today is like entering the hushed bedchamber of a dying relative and telling him he looks great.

Among other things, Humphries' characters such as Sir Les Patterson, Sandy Stone and Dame Edna Everage taught Melburnians to laugh at themselves – and maybe that's why nobody takes themselves too seriously in this town.

During the International Comedy Festival, in April each year, the whole city is turned into a festival venue, and local comedians join international acts (including many from the Edinburgh Festival) to perform in pubs, clubs, theatres and city streets.

Melbourne has a few regular comedy venues and nightspots where stand-up comics show their wares. Look in the *EG* for weekly gigs.

Now that the venerable Last Laugh has closed, the ***Comedy Club*** *(9348 1622, 380 Lygon St, Carlton)* is the main venue in Melbourne for comedy. The ***Prince Patrick Hotel*** *(135 Victoria Pde, Collingwood)* is an old stager in the comedy scene. Other stand-up venues include the ***Waiting Room***, held each Sunday at 4 pm in the Esplanade Hotel's ***Gershwin Room*** *(11 the Upper Esplanade, St Kilda)*, ***Geebung Polo Club*** *(85 Auburn Rd, Auburn)* and the ***Nicholson Hotel*** *(551 Nicholson St, North Carlton)*.

Performing Arts

As Australia's cultural capital, Melbourne offers a huge range of performance in music, dance and theatre.

The Arts Precinct should be your first stop for major artists in the classical fields, with opera, ballet and orchestral concerts held all year (except January). The hard-working Melbourne Symphony Orchestra (MSO) performs almost every week between February and December, with most performances being held at the Melbourne Concert Hall. The season always includes internationally known guest artists.

The Victorian State Opera was recently merged with the Australian Opera (to the chagrin of Melburnians) but a full opera season is still held here. If the Chamber Made Opera company is presenting a new work while you're here, you're in luck – don't miss it.

Dozens of theatrical productions are staged each week, ranging from amateur productions to the latest experimental works. The major mainstream drama companies are the Playbox and the Melbourne Theatre Company – see Theatre in the Entertainment section for details. Handspan Theatre, an innovative puppet theatre, produces exciting shows for adults, as well as its excellent kids' shows.

Musicals, from Gilbert and Sullivan (very popular here) to the latest international extravaganza, are almost always playing. The Princess, Her Majesty's and Regent are the venues for big touring shows.

There's a rich dance scene but no company has a permanent venues. You'll catch ballet in the Arts Precinct but for modern works you'll have to keep an eye on the newspapers and the notice boards in cafes in St Kilda and Fitzroy.

Listed under the 'Readings' and 'Hear This' sections in the *EG* in the Friday edition of the *Age* newspaper, you'll also find things like book launches, religious discussions, educational lectures and public debates. Pub poetry is intermittently popular – check the papers.

Despite the city's multicultural population, there are only sporadic 'high art' performances from non-western cultures. However, there are plenty of opportunities to see folk performances.

Mark Armstrong

For information on comedy around town, listen to 'The Cheese Shop' show on radio 3RRR-FM (102.7) on Monday afternoons.

Poetry Readings

Some of Australia's best younger poets (and some of the older ones) read their poetry at ***La Mama*** in Carlton at 8 pm on the first Monday of most months.

Several pubs and other venues have performance poetry sessions on a regular basis, and newcomers are usually welcomed along to listen or even perform their own work. Venues include the ***Dan O'Connell Hotel*** *(225 Canning St, Carlton)*, the ***Empress Hotel*** *(714 Nicholson St, North Fitzroy)*, the ***Evelyn Hotel*** on the corner of Brunswick and Kerr Sts in Fitzroy, and ***Lounge*** *(Swanston St)* in the city. Check the 'Readings' listing in the *EG* for more details.

Children's Entertainment

The *EG* has a section called 'Children's Activities' that details what's on for children over each weekend – things like pantomimes, animal nurseries, sanctuaries and museum programmes. Other good options include bowling alleys, ice-skating rinks, video arcades and go-kart racing – there are a number of go-kart centres within half an hour's drive of the city, listed under Go-Karts in the *Yellow Pages* phone book.

Some of the favourite places to take kids include the ***Melbourne Zoo***, ***Luna Park*** on the Lower Esplanade in St Kilda, the ***Fun Factory*** in South Yarra and ***Puffing Billy***, a vintage steam-train that runs through the Dandenong Ranges (see the Around Melbourne chapter).

The Melbourne City Council runs an excellent child-minding centre at 104 A'Beckett St in the city (☎ 9329 9561) for children up to five years old. It charges $3.50 an hour or $35 a day.

Gambling

Gambling swept through Melbourne like a plague during the 1990s, leaving in its wake a trail of financial devastation and cultural destruction. That might sound like a puritanical and hysterical over-reaction, but the architects of Melbourne's so-called 'casino-led recovery' have a lot to answer for.

First came the introduction of poker machines. Overnight, hundreds of pubs and clubs were converted into 'gaming rooms' – live music venues, restaurants and bars had to make way for the pokies, and instead of bands, bistros and conversations, pubs were suddenly filled with people sitting moronically feeding money into coin slots, watching lemons spin round and round.

Then Melbourne got its own casino. Flooded on a daily basis with thousands of people wanting to get rid of their excess cash, the casino has quickly become an extremely effective tool for the redistribution of wealth – the rich get richer, while the poor pour money they don't have into the casino's coffers. And as the casino thrives, hundreds of other local businesses – restaurants, retailers, theatres etc – claim to be suffering as a direct result. Meanwhile the churches and welfare groups are left to try to clean up the social destruction.

Sex

Licensed brothels, most catering to heterosexual men, are legal in Victoria. The *Yellow Pages* and any taxi driver will help you find one. So-called 'escort agencies' serve most genders and orientations.

Illegal street prostitution, gay and straight, is fairly common in some inner city areas.

SPECTATOR SPORTS

When it comes to watching sports, Melburnians are about as fanatical as they come. The biggest events on the calendar are a horse race and a game of Australian Rules football.

Melbourne Cup & Spring Racing Carnival

Horse racing takes place throughout the year at one or other of Melbourne's courses – Flemington, Caulfield, Moonee Valley or Sandown – but spring is when it's most colourful and frenetic.

The Melbourne Cup, one of the world's greatest horse races, is the feature event of Melbourne's Spring Racing Carnival, which runs through October and finishes with the Melbourne Cup Carnival early in November. The carnival's major races are the Cox Plate Handicap, the Caulfield Cup, the Dalgety, the Mackinnon Stakes and the holy grail itself, the Melbourne Cup. Apart from these races, Derby Day and Oaks Day feature heavily on the spring racing calendar.

The two-mile (3.2km) Melbourne Cup, which is always run on the first Tuesday of November at Flemington Racecourse, was first run in 1861. Mark Twain, after seeing the race in 1895, wrote:

> And so the grandstands make a brilliant and wonderful spectacle, a delirium of colour, a vision of beauty. The champagne flows, everybody is vivacious, excited, happy; everybody bets...

If he were to visit now he'd probably write much the same.

The cup brings the whole of Australia to a standstill for the three or so minutes during which the race is run. Cup day is a public holiday in the Melbourne metropolitan area, but people all over the country are affected by Melbourne's spring racing fever.

Serious punters and fashion-conscious racegoers pack the grandstand and lawns of the Victoria Racing Club's beautiful Flemington Racecourse, once-a-year punters make their choice or organise cup syndicates with friends, and the race is followed on TVs and radios in pubs, clubs, TAB betting shops and houses across the land.

The race has in recent years attracted horses and owners from Europe, the USA and the Middle East, but New Zealand horses and trainers have had a stranglehold on the coveted gold cup for many years.

Many people say that to be in Melbourne in November and not go to the cup is like going to Paris and skipping the Louvre, or turning your back on the bulls in Pamplona! Tickets for reserved seats in the Lawn Stand can be booked through Ticketmaster (☎ 13 6122) and cost around $75, or you can just front up on the day and buy a general admission ticket for around $25.

The Footy

Without a doubt, Australian Rules football – otherwise known as 'the Footy' – is the major drawcard, with games at the MCG regularly pulling crowds of 50,000 to 80,000; the grand final fills the ground with 100,000 fans. If you're here between April and September you should try to see a match, as much for the crowds as the game. The sheer energy of the barracking at a big game is exhilarating. Despite the fervour, crowd violence is almost unknown.

The Australian Football League (AFL) runs the nation-wide competition, and while there are sides based in Perth, Adelaide, Sydney and Brisbane, Melbourne is still considered the game's stronghold. It's also the place where Aussie Rules Football was created – on 7 August 1858, the first game was played between Melbourne Grammar and Scotch College on the very spot where the MCG and its car parks now stand. The playing field was a rough 1.5km-long paddock, and each team had 40 players. There was no result after the first day, so the teams met on the following two Saturdays, at the end of which the game was declared a draw. Since then the footy rules have been (slightly) refined (see the Aussie Football – The Rules boxed text in this chapter).

Being the shrine of Aussie Rules, the MCG is the best place to see a match. The ground is steeped in tradition, and with the completion of the new Great Southern Stand it has the best spectator facilities. AFL Park is the other main stadium, but it lacks the atmosphere and tradition of the MCG and is way out in Mulgrave, in the south-eastern suburbs. It can be quite an experience to see a game at one of the suburban grounds such as Victoria Park in Collingwood or the Western Oval in Footscray. Here's where you get to literally rub shoulders with the fanatical one-eyed supporters who live and breathe football. For them, it's not just a sport, it's a religion.

Tickets can be bought at the ground for most games, and entry costs $13.50 for adults, $7.50 concession and $2 for kids under 14 (and you'll need another few dollars for the obligatory pie and a beer). Reserved seats, but general admission tickets, can be booked (this might be necessary at big games) through an agency such as Ticketmaster for $23.50.

Note that the Olympic Games in Sydney will disrupt the football year in Melbourne, as some preliminary soccer matches will be played at the MCG, so the Aussie rules final will be held earlier than usual in 2000.

Motor Sports

Fans of blokes (and the odd sheila) driving in circles very fast will be pleased to know that Melbourne hosts both the Australian Formula One Grand Prix and the Australian round of the World 500cc Motorcycle Grand Prix. The cars race around Albert Park Lake in March, and the bikes race at Phillip Island in in October. For people driving very fast in a straight line, head for the drag races at Calder Thunderdome, just outside the city on the Calder Freeway.

Cricket

The MCG is one of the world's great sports stadiums. For any cricket fan or general sports fan, a visit to the MCG is not only compulsory, it's something of a pilgrimage. During the summer, international Test matches, One-day Internationals, Sheffield Shield (the national cricket competition) and local district matches are all played here. General admission to international one-day matches is around $25, while reserved seats start around $32. You'll pay more for finals.

Tennis

For two weeks every January the National Tennis Centre (officially called Melbourne Park) on Batman Ave hosts the Australian Open tennis championships. Top players from around the world come to compete in the year's first Grand Slam tournament. Tickets for the early rounds cost about $15 for general admission (which allows you to wander around the various outside courts) or $25 for centre court. A ticket to the final rounds costs $80 to $90. To book phone Ticketek (☎ 13 2849).

Aussie Football – The Rules

Unique to Australia, Aussie Rules football is a fast-flowing, highly skilled and visually exciting game played by teams of 18 on an oval field with an oval ball that can be kicked, caught ('marked'), carried (if regularly bounced) or hand-balled (ie punched with one hand off the palm of the other – not thrown). To take a 'mark' a player must catch the ball on the volley from a kick – in which case the player gets a free kick. You can get six points for kicking the ball between two central posts (a goal) and one point if it goes between the side posts (a behind).

A game lasts for four quarters of at least 25 minutes each (there's lots of 'time on' added because of the frequent scoring and stretcher cases). A typical final score for one team is between 70 and 110.

Players cannot be sent off in the course of a game; disciplinary tribunals are held the following week. Consequently, there are some spectacular brawls on field – while the crowds, in contrast, are noisy but remarkably peaceful (a pleasant surprise for visiting soccer fans).

There are seven umpires for each game – crowds love to hate the 'men in white'. Three central umpires control the play, award free kicks and apply penalties, and two boundary umpires throw the ball back into play when it goes out of bounds. That leaves the goal umpires, the ones in the long white coats and funny hats. Watch for their theatrical hand signals when a goal or a behind is scored, after which they wave flags at each other for no apparent reason.

Mark Armstrong

Basketball

Basketball enjoyed phenomenal growth in the 90s (thanks, you'd have to suspect, to US-made soft-drink and sports footwear TV advertisements) and is still popular. National Basketball League games are of a high standard and draw large crowds, the main venue being Melbourne Park (the National Tennis Centre). The season runs from October to March and ticket prices start at $12.50 – book through Ticketek (☎ 13 2849).

SHOPPING

Melbourne claims to be the shopping capital of Australia. Hype or no hype, it's true that people do come from other parts of Australia just to shop in Melbourne.

For late-night staples, head to Coles Express, 6-22 Elizabeth St, open 24 hours. Coles supermarkets around the suburbs are open 24 hours at least some days of the week.

The major department stores are in the city centre. Myer has 12 floors of different departments in two buildings – the main entrance is in the Bourke St Mall at No 314. David Jones, with shops on both sides of the Mall, is slightly more upmarket and a good place to look for top quality goods. The Melbourne Central shopping complex houses dozens of speciality shops plus the Daimaru department store. In the centre of the complex, a massive cone-shaped dome encloses a National Trust-classified brick shot tower.

Victoria St, Richmond, affectionately known as Little Saigon, is the place to go for excellent Asian groceries, supermarkets, discount shops, restaurants and the flavours and feel of Vietnam and South-East Asia.

Most of Melbourne's more interesting shopping areas are in the inner suburbs and their attractions are outlined in the respective sections earlier in this chapter. But US visitors might be pleased (or not, depending on your politics) to find that Australia trades with Cuba, so Havana cigars are available. And having sampled some of the lack-lustre offerings from the rest of the Carribbean, sometimes masquerading under Cuban brand names, I can tell you that there's nothing like the real thing. Cigar shops mushroomed in Melbourne a few years ago when cigars became trendy, but for an established cigar merchant visit Alexanders (☎ 9827 1477 or 1800 635 505 toll-free), in the Tok H shopping centre, 459 Toorak Rd, Toorak.

Aboriginal Art

Although Melbourne's a long way from the outback, there are commercial galleries selling authentic Aboriginal art. In the city centre, try the Aboriginal Gallery of Dreamings (73-77 Bourke St), the Aboriginal Art Galleries of Australia (31 Flinders Lane), Aboriginal Handcrafts, 9th floor (125 Swanston St), Alcaston House Gallery (2 Collins St) and Emerald Hill Gallery (Level 8, 37 Swanston St).

Expensive paintings are likely to have well-established provenances. Unfortunately, cheaper items (maybe painted clapping sticks or T-shirts) might be made by non-Aboriginal people and the designs might have been stolen from Aboriginal artists. This isn't just a breach of copyright but could be a desecration of sacred designs. Try to buy items made by Aboriginal craft co-ops.

Antiques

If you're on the lookout for antiques, head for places like High St in Armadale, Malvern Rd in Malvern, Gertrude St in Fitzroy, and Canterbury Rd in Surrey Hills. Kozminsky Galleries, at 421 Bourke St in the city, was established back in 1851 and specialises in antique jewellery and collectables.

Aussie Clothing

Sam Bear, 225 Russell St, is a great place to go for tough, durable hats, clothing and footwear – just like the real shearers and jackaroos wear. It's also a good place for things like camping and walking gear, cheap beanies (woollen hats) and warm socks. (Check the changing rooms to see if they still have ancient Levi posters advertising flares.)

Some other good shops for Aussie gear are RM Williams, with a large shop in the shot tower at Melbourne Central (300 Lonsdale

St); the Thomas Cook Boot & Clothing Co at 60 Hoddle St in Abbotsford; and Hall & Co at 1019 High St in Armadale.

A couple of places in the city to try for surfing equipment and clothing are the Melbourne Surf Shop in the Tivoli Arcade at 249 Bourke St and Surf Dive 'N' Ski at 213 Bourke St and in Melbourne Central – both have been around nearly as long as Nat Young (an Aussie surfing legend).

Akubra hats are incredibly popular with travellers and are sold just about everywhere. Good city hat shops include City Hatters, beside the main entrance to Flinders St train station at 211 Flinders St, and Melbourne's Top Hatters at shop 19, 259 Collins St.

Australiana

Australian souvenirs are available from dozens of places around town, particularly in areas where tourists tend to hang out.

In the city, places worth checking out include the Australiana General Store, shop 32 in Collins Place, 45 Collins St; the Bodymap shop at 300 Lonsdale St and Monds Gifts and Souvenirs at 133 Swanston St.

Places to look for souvenirs or gifts with a lower tackiness quotient include the Metro! Craft Centre on the corner of Courtney and Blackwood Sts in North Melbourne, the Queen Victoria Market in the city and the gallery shop at the National Gallery. The Australian Geographic shop, in the Shot Tower at Melbourne Central, has some interesting items.

Commercial Art Galleries

Melbourne has dozens of private, commercial art galleries – the magazine *Art Almanac*, a monthly guide to all city and regional galleries, is available from the shop at the National Gallery and other galleries.

The top end of Flinders Lane in the city is something of an enclave for art lovers, and there are plenty of interesting galleries here, including Gallery Gabrielle Pizzi at No 141, William Mora at No 31, the Tribal Art Gallery at No 103, the Flinders Lane Gallery at No 137 and Anna Schwartz at No 185.

Fitzroy also has some good galleries, including Roar Studios at 115 Brunswick St, the Tolarno Gallery at 121 Victoria St and 200 Gertrude St (at 200 Gertrude St).

Also worth checking out in Prahran, are the Karen Lovegrove Gallery at 321 Chapel St and the Lula Bilu Gallery at 142 Greville St; and in Richmond, Christine Abrahams' Gallery at 27 Gipps St, and Niagara Galleries at 245 Punt Rd.

Duty-Free

Duty-free shops abound in the city centre. Remember that a duty-free item might not have had much duty on it in the first place and could be available cheaper in an ordinary shop.

Fashion & Clothing

In the city centre, the major department stores all have good ranges of both local and imported fashion. The Sportsgirl Centre, in Collins St between Swanston and Elizabeth Sts, has a great range of shops for female fashions, and the Australia on Collins complex nearby is also good. You'll find plenty of fashion houses along Bourke St, particularly in and around the mall, while Collins St is the home of the more exclusive and expensive designer boutiques. Shopping adventurers will have fun exploring the network of alleys, laneways and arcades that run through the heart of the city.

Bridge Rd and Swan St in Richmond are full of fashion warehouses, factory outlets and seconds shops – great places to head for fashion bargains.

Brunswick St in Fitzroy has lots of groovy, grungy and offbeat clothing shops in among all the cafes and restaurants. Greville St in Prahran is probably *the* most fashionable address for retro shops.

Chapel St in South Yarra is the most fashionable of Melbourne's fashion zones. The section between Toorak Rd and Commercial Rd is lined with ultra-trendy and generally expensive boutiques, and it's a fascinating area to visit, whether you come to shop or just to check out all the beautiful people.

Toorak Rd in South Yarra is the ultimate in style. This street is home to the most exclusive designers, specialist shops and galleries – even if you can't afford to buy anything, it's a fascinating street to wander along. You never know who or what you might see.

Lygon St in Carlton has the latest in upmarket and imported Italian clothes and shoes. High St in Armadale is another fashion shopping mecca, with quite a few designers sprinkled between the antique dealers and Persian-rug shops.

Film & Photography

In the city centre, there's a cluster of camera shops along Elizabeth St between Bourke and Lonsdale Sts. Little Bourke St (west of Elizabeth St) is another good area to look for camera gear. Some sell second-hand gear that they've taken as trade-ins, usually with a guarantee.

If you need your camera repaired, the Camera Clinic (☎ 9419 5247) at 19 Peel St in Collingwood has an excellent reputation. The Melbourne Camera Club (☎ 9696 5445), in South Melbourne on the corner of Ferrars and Dorcas Sts, meets every Thursday night at 8 pm and welcomes visitors.

Handicrafts

Melbourne's best craft gallery is the Metro! Craft Centre, in the old Meat Market on the corner of Courtney and Blackwood Sts in North Melbourne, not far from the Queen Victoria Market. It houses the state craft collection and other exhibitions, craft workshops, a bookshop and coffee shop. It's open Tuesday to Sunday from 10 am to 5 pm.

There are a number of good craft shops around town selling local and imported crafts, including the long-running Ishka Handcrafts with shops in South Yarra, Carlton, South Melbourne and Kew.

In many suburbs there are weekend craft markets like the Sunday market on the Upper Esplanade in St Kilda, and farther out there are craft places in Warrandyte and small towns in the Dandenongs.

Markets

The Queen Victoria Market, on the corner of Victoria and Elizabeth Sts in the city, is one of the best places to shop, not just for the huge range of goods and souvenirs, but also for the bustling atmosphere and exotic cast of characters. It has over 1000 stalls that sell just about everything under the sun, including fruit and vegetables, meat and fish, jeans, furniture, budgies and sheepskin products. It opens Tuesday and Thursday from 6 am to 2 pm, Friday from 6 am to 6 pm, Saturday from 6 am to 3 pm and Sunday from 9 am to 4 pm. On Sunday the fruit, vegetable, meat and fish stalls are closed and there are dozens more stalls selling jewellery, clothes, souvenirs, antiques and bric-a-brac.

Over summer, part of the Queen Vic is open on Wednesday nights until 10.30 pm for the Gaslight Night Market. There's plenty of food and entertainment.

Melbourne's other major markets are the South Melbourne Market in Cecil St, which opens on Wednesday, Friday, Saturday and Sunday; the wonderful Prahran Market in Commercial Rd, which opens on Tuesday, Thursday, Friday and Saturday; and the Footscray Market on the corner of Hopkins and Leeds Sts, which opens Thursday, Friday and Saturday.

There are also lots of good weekend markets selling crafts, clothes, second-hand goods etc. In St Kilda, the Esplanade Art and Craft Market operates every Sunday on the Upper Esplanade and has a good range of stuff on offer. One of the most popular 'trash and treasure' markets is the Camberwell Sunday Market (from dawn to mid-afternoon) in Station St, Camberwell, which has over 300 stalls piled with everything including the kitchen sink – you might even find that hot pink T-shirt you lost back in 1979. Other popular markets include the Sunday Market at the Victorian Arts Centre (Sunday from 10 am), with arts and crafts from around the state, and the small and slightly grungy Greville St Sunday Market (noon to 5 pm) in Prahran.

Music

Large city recorded music shops include the enormous Blockbuster Music shop at 152 Bourke St (also in the Jam Factory at 500 Chapel St in South Yarra). Interesting independent shops around town include Gaslight at 85 Bourke St (great alternative music, open nightly till late, and its annual calendar compels customers to do strange things like shop in the nude), Missing Link at 262 Flinders Lane and Au Go Go at 349 Little Bourke St. Discurio at 285 Little Collins St has the best range of classical, jazz, blues and folk music and literature.

In the inner suburbs, Greville Records at 152 Greville St, Prahran, Polyester Records at 387 Brunswick St, Fitzroy, and Readings at 366 Lygon St, Carlton, and 153 Toorak Rd, South Yarra, are other good shops to try if you're looking for something other than top 40.

JB Hi-Fi sells discounted tapes and CDs, and its shops include one in the city at 289 Elizabeth St.

Opals

Some gem and opal shops in town are Andrew Cody, 1st floor, 119 Swanston St; Altman & Cherny, 120 Exhibition St; John H Mules, 110 Exhibition St; and Rochi's Opals, 210 Little Collins St.

Outdoor Gear

The best area for outdoor shops is around the intersection of Hardware St and Little Bourke St in the city. In Hardware St you'll find places like Auski at No 9, the Melbourne Ski Centre at No 17 and Wetsports at No 83. In Little Bourke St, Mountain Designs is at No 377, Kathmandu is at No 373, Bogong Equipment is at No 374 and Paddy Palin is at No 360. Snowgum (formerly the Scout Outdoor Centre) is around the corner at 366 Lonsdale St, and the previously mentioned Sam Bear, at 225 Russell St, is also worth checking out.

These places generally stock top-quality outdoor gear – cheaper gear is available from the many army disposal shops (listed in the *Yellow Pages* phone directory).

GETTING THERE & AWAY

All international and interstate flights operate out of Melbourne airport at Tullamarine, while long-distance trains run from the Spencer St train station. There are two long-distance bus terminals in the city centre – the Spencer St coach terminal on Spencer St (V/Line, McCafferty's and Firefly buses) and the Melbourne Transit Centre at 58 Franklin St (Greyhound Pioneer Australia buses). The Skybus airport buses operate from both terminals.

For details of travel to/from Melbourne and places interstate and overseas, see the introductory Getting There & Away chapter: for details of travel between Melbourne and places within Victoria, see the introductory Getting Around chapter.

GETTING AROUND

To/From the Airport

Melbourne airport is at Tullamarine, 22km north-west of the city centre. It's a modern airport with a single terminal: Qantas at one end, Ansett at the other, international in the middle. There are two information desks at the airport: one on the ground floor in the international departure area and another upstairs next to the duty-free shops.

If you're driving, the Tullamarine Freeway runs from the airport almost into the city centre, finishing in North Melbourne. A taxi between the airport and city centre costs about $30.

The Skybus (☎ 9662 9275) operates frequent shuttle-bus services between the airport and the city centre, costing $10 for adults and $4.50 for children. Skybuses depart from Bay 30 at the Spencer St coach terminal and from the Melbourne Transit Centre at 58 Franklin St, with buses operating about every half-hour between 6.45 am and 10.45 pm – ring to confirm departure times. Buy your ticket from the driver; bookings are not usually necessary. If there's room you can take your bicycle, but the front wheel must be removed.

There is also a fairly frequent bus operated by Gull Airport Services (☎ 5222 4966) between the airport and Geelong. It costs $20 one way. The Geelong terminus is at 45 McKillop St.

Public transport between the city and the airport is limited. The Skybus is by far the best bet, but you could take tram No 59 from Elizabeth St to the Moonee Ponds Junction – from there, Tullamarine Bus Lines (☎ 9338 3817) runs bus Nos 478 and 479 to the airport several times a day; bus No 500 runs to the airport from Broadmeadows train station. You can do either trip on a zone 1 and 2 Met ticket. If you make the connections you could do it on a two-hour ticket ($3.90). If not you'll need an all-day ticket, which doesn't cost much less than the Skybus fare.

Public Transport

Melbourne's public transport system, the Met, incorporates buses, trains and the famous trams. It's in the process of being privatised (like just about everything else in the state) but the following information should still be pertinent.

There are about 750 trams and they operate as far as 20km out from the centre. Buses take routes where the trams do not go, and replace them at quiet weekend periods. Trains radiate out from the city centre to the outer suburbs.

For information on public transport, phone the Met Information Centre (☎ 13 1638), which operates daily from 7 am to 9 pm. The Met Shop at 103 Elizabeth St in the city (open weekdays from 8.30 am to 5 pm and Saturday from 9 am to 3 pm) also has transport information and sells souvenirs and tickets. If you're in the city, it's probably a better bet for information than the telephone service, which is usually busy. Train stations also have some information.

After the trams, buses and trains stop running (around midnight for most services) night buses depart from the City Square for many suburban destinations. The fare is a flat $5.

Tickets & Zones There's quite an array of tickets, and Melburnians are struggling to come to grips with the new automatic ticketing system, known as Metcard. On trams, 'connies' (conductors) have been replaced by machines. Once you've bought the ticket you have to validate it in another machine. However, it's practically impossible to fight your way to the validation machine if you're on a peak hour tram in the city centre. Roving 'customer service officers' will fine you $100 if you haven't managed to buy and validate a ticket.

The metropolitan area is divided into three zones, and the price of tickets depends on which zone(s) you will be travelling in and across. Zone 1 covers the city and inner-suburban area (including St Kilda), and most travellers won't venture beyond that unless they're going right out of town – on a trip to the Healesville Sanctuary, for example, or down the Mornington Peninsula.

Zone 1 tickets cost $2.30 for two hours, $4.40 for all day and $19.10 for a week (longer periods are available). You are allowed to break your journey and change between trams, buses and trains with these tickets.

Short Trip tickets ($1.50) allow you to travel two sections on buses or trams in Zone 1, or you can buy a Short Trip 10 Card ($12.50) which gives you 10 short trips. You can't break your journey on a short trip ticket.

Buying a Ticket Now for the tricky bit. How do you buy a ticket? Many small businesses, such as newspaper kiosks and milk bars, sell most tickets but not short trip tickets. Machines on trams sell *only* short trip and two hour tickets but only take coins. Machines at train stations sell many types of tickets but not short trip tickets. Large machines at train stations take coins, some notes and some bank cash cards; small machines at stations take coins only. (Many machines at stations are chronically out of order due to malfunction and vandalism.) Some stations have booking offices that sell most tickets. On buses you can buy short trip, 2 hour and all day tickets from the driver with coins and notes.

The Metcard system took many years and many millions of dollars to develop, and is regarded as a fiasco by just about everyone. If you add up the cost of the machines, the cost of security guards to guard the machines and the rampant fare evasion, it would probably have been cheaper to keep the conductors. Most connies were friendly types who were very helpful to visitors and locals alike.

Disabled Travellers The *Mobility Map* is available from tourist information booths in the Bourke St Mall and Rialto Towers, and from the Melbourne City Council's information desk (☎ 9658 9763) on the corner of Swanston Walk and Little Collins St (ring and they will post one to you).

Victoria's Public Transport Corporation (PTC) publishes *Disability Services for Customers with Specific Needs* and provides accessible rail services on V/Line Sprinter trains to the major rural centres of Geelong, Ballarat, Bendigo, Seymour and Traralgon. Hoist-equipped buses then link other centres and also Adelaide (via Ballarat). Contact V/Line's Disability Services section on (☎ 13 2232). Metropolitan trains carry a portable ramp in the driver's compartment. Just wait at the end of the platform where the front of the train will be.

See the following Taxi and Car Rental sections for further information.

Tram Melbourne's trundling trams are one of the city's most distinctive features. Tram routes cover the city and inner suburbs quite extensively. The majority of routes operate as back-and-forwards shuttle services, with the city centre acting as the hub of the wheel and the tram routes as the spokes. This makes it a good system if you want to get to somewhere from the city centre, but not so good if you want to travel across from one suburb to another. Tram stops are numbered out from the city centre.

There are also 'light rail' services to some suburbs. These are basically express trams running along disused rail lines.

In theory, trams run along most routes about every six to eight minutes during peak hour and every 12 minutes at other times. Unfortunately, trams have to share the roads with cars and trucks, so they are often delayed. It's not uncommon to wait 20 minutes for a tram – then see two or three arrive at once. Services are less frequent on weekends and late at night.

Be extremely careful when getting on and off a tram: by law, cars are supposed to stop when a tram stops to pick up and drop off passengers, but that doesn't always happen.

Free City Circle trams travel along Flinders, Spring and Nicholson Sts to Victoria Pde, and then back along Latrobe and Spencer Sts. Designed primarily for tourists, and passing many city sights along the way, the trams run daily between 10 am and 6 pm, every 10 minutes or so. Built in Melbourne between 1936 and 1956, the trams have all been refurbished and painted a distinctive burgundy and gold.

Train An extensive train network covers the city centre and suburban areas. Trains are generally faster than trams or buses, but they don't go to many inner suburbs.

Flinders St train station is the main suburban terminal, and each suburban line has a separate platform there. The famous row of clocks above the entrance on the corner of Swanston St and Flinders St indicate when the next train will be departing from each line. There's an information booth just inside the entrance.

During the week, trains on most lines start at 5 am and finish at midnight and should run every three to eight minutes during peak hour, every 15 to 20 minutes at other times, and every 40 minutes after 7 pm. On Saturday they run every half-hour from 5 am to midnight, while on Sunday it's every 40 minutes from 7 am to 11.30 pm. Of course, these are just rule-of-thumb times. In a perfect world (or if Mussolini were transport minister) all of the above would be accurate. In reality, expect deviations.

The city service includes an underground City Loop which is a quick way to get from one side of town to the other. The stations on the loop are Parliament, Museum, Flagstaff, Spencer St and Flinders St.

Bicycles can be carried free on trains during off-peak times and weekends.

Bus Generally, buses continue from where the trains finish, or go to places, such as hospitals, universities, suburban shopping centres and the outer suburbs, not reached by other services. If you find you can't get somewhere by train or tram, ring the Met – chances are they will have a bus going that way.

Car

Cars & Trams Car drivers should treat trams with caution – trams are about half the weight of an ocean liner and seldom come off second best in accidents. You can only overtake a tram on the left and must *always* stop behind a tram when it halts to drop or collect passengers (except where there are central 'islands' for passengers).

Melbourne has a notoriously confusing road rule, known as the 'hook turn', for getting trams through the city centre without being blocked by turning cars. To turn right at many major intersections in the city, you have to pull to the left, wait until the light of the street you're turning into changes from red to green, then complete the turn. These intersections are identified by a black-and-white hook sign that hangs down from the overhead cables.

Parking If you're lucky enough to find an on-street parking space in the city centre you'll pay about $2 an hour. Check parking signs for restrictions and times, and watch out for clearway zones which operate during peak hours. Parking in a clearway means big fines and maybe having your car towed away. Inner residential areas often have 'resident only' parking zones, or parking restrictions that run until midnight, rather than 5 or 6 pm as elsewhere. This makes parking near nightlife areas in Fitzroy or St Kilda nearly impossible – take a tram or a taxi.

Note that a sign telling you that you're allowed to park for, say, two hours, reads 2P.

There are over 70 car parks in the city, and the council produces a map-and-brochure guide to city parking – it's available from Melbourne Town Hall. Rates vary depending on the car-park's location, but you'll pay around $4 to $6 an hour or $14 to $25 a day during the week – less on weekends. There are often flat rates of $3 to $5 for parking after about 6 pm.

Car Rental Avis (☎ 1800 225 533 toll-free), Budget (☎ 13 2727), Hertz (☎ 13 3039) and Thrifty (☎ 1300 367 227) have desks at the airport, and you can find plenty of others in the city. The offices tend to be at the northern end of the city or in Carlton or North Melbourne.

For disabled travellers Avis rents hand controlled vehicles while Norden Transport Equipment (☎ 9793 1066) has self-drive vans, equipped with lifts, available for long or short-term rentals.

The *Yellow Pages* lists lots of other firms, including some reputable local operators who rent newer cars but don't have the nationwide network (and overheads) of the big operators. Some places worth trying are Delta (☎ 13 1390) and National (☎ 13 1045).

A number of rent-a-wreck-style operators rent older vehicles at lower rates. Their costs and conditions vary widely, so it's worth making a few inquiries. You can take the 'from $21 a day' line with a pinch of salt because the rates soon start to rise with insurance, kilometre charges and so on. Beware of distance restrictions; some companies only allow you to travel within a certain distance of the city, typically 100km. Try Rent-a-Bomb (☎ 9428 0088) in Richmond and Ugly Duckling (☎ 9525 4010) in St Kilda.

CityLink A huge new road network called CityLink should be operating by the time you read this. It's a private-enterprise freeway system with two main links: the western link runs from the Calder Hwy intersection of the Tullamarine Fwy down the west side of the city to join with the

Westgate Fwy; the southern link runs from Kings Way, on the southern edge of the CBD, to the Malvern section of the Monash Fwy (the renamed South-Eastern Fwy).

CityLink operates with a toll system. This wouldn't be such a bad idea except that there's no alternative freeway route between the airport and the city. While there are alternative routes that allow you to avoid the tolls, most are on narrow roads already choked with traffic.

For visitors, the annoying thing about CityLink isn't the cost but the inconvenience. Tolls are 'collected' electronically by overhead readers from a transponder card displayed in the car (an e-Tag). You don't have the option of paying cash and you can't buy a card once you're on the system. You have to go to a post office (anywhere in Australia) or another Melbourne outlet and buy either a day pass (unlimited access for $7.30) or open a CityLink account, which gets you an e-Tag. If you use CityLink without having bought an e-Tag or a day pass, you have until noon the next day to contact CityLink (☎ 13 2629) and pay $8.50 with a credit card. The penalty for travelling without paying is about $100.

There are many pricing sections along CityLink, but if you have an e-Tag the most you'll pay for one trip in one direction is $3.77 in a car and $1.89 on a motorbike. These rates will be lower during the introductory period.

Taxi

There are plenty of taxi ranks in and around the city. The main ones in town are outside the major hotels, outside Flinders and Spencer St train stations, on the corner of William and Bourke Sts, on the corner of Elizabeth and Bourke Sts, in Lonsdale St outside Myer and outside Ansett in Franklin St. Finding an empty taxi in the city on Friday or Saturday night can be difficult.

There are several taxi companies but all taxis are painted yellow. If you want to book a taxi, the major companies include Arrow (☎ 13 2211), Black Cabs (☎ 13 2227), Embassy (☎ 13 1755) and Silver Top (☎ 13 1008). All charge the same fares and all are bound by the same regulations. If you have a complaint about a taxi driver, call ☎ 9345 4321.

Accessible taxis for disabled travellers are plentiful. Try Black Cabs or Silver Top.

Ferry

Two companies operate ferries between the city and Gem Pier in Williamstown, with hourly departures from Southgate between 10 am and 5 pm. The one-way/return fare is $10/18. You can ask to be dropped at Scienceworks and the *Polly Woodside*. On weekends and public holidays there's a ferry between St Kilda Pier and Williamstown, departing St Kilda hourly between 11.30 am and 4.30 pm, and departing Williamstown's Gem Pier hourly from 11 am to 4 pm. The one-way/return fare is $6/10 (children half price).

Between October and June the restored 1933 steam tug *Wattle (☎ 9328 2739)* runs a ferry service on Sunday between Station Pier in Port Melbourne and Gem Pier in Williamstown. It leaves from Station Pier at 10.30 am, noon and 1.30 and 3 pm; the return fare costs $10 for adults and $7 for children.

Bicycle

Melbourne's a great city for cycling. It's reasonably flat so you're not pushing and panting up hills too often, and there are some great cycling routes throughout the metropolitan area. Two of the best are the bike path that runs around the shores of Port Phillip Bay from Port Melbourne to Brighton, and the bike path that follows the Yarra River out of the city for more than 20km, passing through lovely parklands along the way. There are numerous other bicycle tracks, including those along the Maribyrnong River and the Merri Creek.

Discovering Melbourne's Bike Paths ($14.95) has excellent maps and descriptions of the city's bicycle paths. The *Melway* street directory is also useful for cyclists. Note that bicycles can be taken on suburban trains for free during off-peak times. One note of caution: tram tracks are a major hazard for cyclists in Melbourne.

Cycling Around Melbourne

You're cycling beside the river through a grove of trees, bellbirds are chiming, colourful rosellas are swooping low over the path, and the tangy aroma of hops from the brewery is mingling with the chocolate smell from the biscuit factory. You're somewhere in the country, miles from Melbourne, right? Wrong – you're on the Main Yarra Trail, one of Melbourne's many inner-city bike paths constructed along the riverside green belts.

Used by commuters and tourists alike, this 38km cycling and walking trail winds along the Yarra River, past historic homes, natural bushland and sportsfields, often far from roads. The 19km Merri Creek path branches off the main trail, passing Studley Park Boat House, Australia's oldest operating boathouse, and Fairfield Boathouse, where you can reward yourself with a Devonshire tea in early 20th century surroundings. To the west of the city is the 22km Maribyrnong River Trail and to the south, along the waterfront, is the Bays Trail.

At least 20 other long urban cycle paths exist, all marked in the Melway *Greater Melbourne Street Directory*; your hostel or hotel will have a 'Melways', or try any library. The pocket guide *Discovering Victoria's Bike Paths* is a useful introduction to more than 2000km of paths around the state, but the maps can be hard to follow. Pick up a copy of the excellent *Cycling the Surf Coast Shire* map from any backpackers or call the shire council (☎ 03-5261 0600) for a guide to 32 rides around some of the seaside towns south-west of Melbourne.

Melbourne also has a growing network of on-road bike lanes; those in the inner city are marked on the free *City of Melbourne Bike Map*, available from the council (☎ 9658 9658).

On the outskirts of the city is the Lilydale to Warburton Rail Trail, one of the many new recreational paths built along disused railway lines; they have a steady gradient, good riding surface and invariably travel through bushland between quaint historical towns. Met trains run to Lilydale, the last stop on its line; bikes are carried free on weekends and off-peak times, or for a half fare at other times.

Many Melbourne bike shopes hire out bikes. A hybrid bike with panniers from touring specialists Christie Cycles (☎ 9818 4011, 80 Burwood Rd, Hawthorn) costs $20/day or $75/week; tandems cost $30/day or $75/week (which includes both weekends). Mountain bikes with racks from St Kilda Cycles (☎ 9534 3074, 11 Carlisle St, St Kilda) cost $20/day or $50/for a weekend, with panniers. Contact Bicycle Victoria for a current list of bike hire outlets. See Cycling in the Activities chapter for information on hiring bikes in Melbourne and cycling in the rest of the state.

Sally Dillon

Every cyclist has their own 'wheel-in-a-track' horror story.

Quite a few bike shops and companies have bikes for hire, and a good mountain bike, helmet and lock will cost about $20 a day. The following places are all worth trying: St Kilda Cycles (☎ 9534 3074), 11 Carlisle St, St Kilda; Cycle Science (☎ 9826 8877), 320 Toorak Rd, South Yarra; City Cycle Tours (☎ 9585 5343) Treasury Gardens; and Fitzroy Cycles (☎ 9639 3511) 224 Swanston Street, the city.

Around Melbourne

There are some good excursions within about an hour of the city. Melbourne sits below a backdrop of scenic hills and mountain ranges: to the east are the Dandenong Ranges, north-east there's the Kinglake National Park, and to the north-west, the Macedon Ranges and the mysterious Hanging Rock.

Then there's the Yarra Valley, well known for its wineries and the wonderful Healesville Sanctuary; the rugged ocean beaches of the Mornington and Bellarine Peninsulas (which are linked by car and passenger ferries); and of course Phillip Island with its famous penguin parade.

HIGHLIGHTS

- Queenscliff has old-fashioned guest-houses, historic hotels and restaurants. For a great splurge, stay and eat at Mietta's Queenscliff Hotel
- Hanging Rock for picnics, walks and the picnic race meeting
- Tours of the Macedon region wineries
- Healesville Wildlife Sanctuary
- The wineries, bushwalks and scenic beauty of the Yarra Valley
- The Dandenongs have beautiful gardens, tearooms, the *Puffing Billy* train ride and William Ricketts Sanctuary
- Dolphin cruises at Sorrento and swims in Port Phillip
- Lunch at Arthur's restaurant on top of Arthur's Seat on a sunny day
- Phillip Island's penguin parade

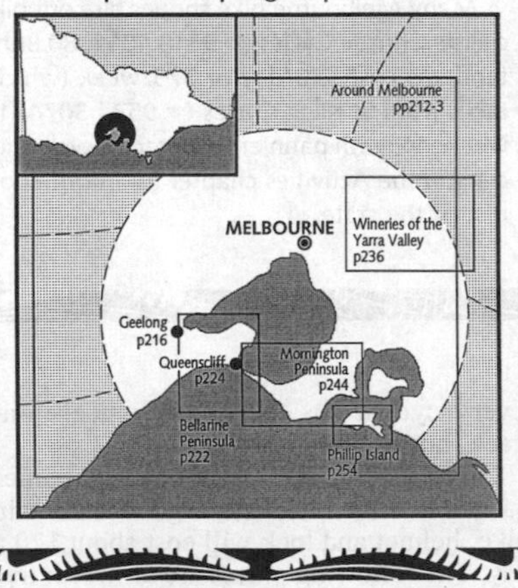

Melbourne to Geelong

It's a one hour drive down the Princes Freeway (M1) to Geelong. You can leave Melbourne over the soaring West Gate Bridge and enjoy the fine views of the city, and there are a few interesting stopovers and detours along the way.

RAAF NATIONAL AVIATION MUSEUM

Near Werribee is the National Aviation Museum at the RAAF base at Point Cook, with a variety of displays, including one on the WWI German ace, Baron von Richtofen. Its collection of 20 aircraft ranges from a 1916 Morris Farman Shorthorn to a 1970 F4 Phantom. Seven of the vintage planes still fly, and the resident aces use them for air shows. It's open Tuesday to Friday from 10 am to 3 pm and until 5 pm on weekends; admission is by donation.

WERRIBEE PARK MANSION & ZOO

Signposted off the freeway, about 30 minutes from Melbourne, is Werribee Park, with its free-range zoological park and the huge Italianate **Werribee Park Mansion** (☎ 9741 2444), built between 1874 and 1877. This flamboyant building is surrounded by formal gardens, including picnic and barbecue areas and the State Rose Garden, with 3000 plants in the shape of a giant Tudor rose. Entry to the gardens is free, but admission to the mansion costs $10 for adults and $5 for children. The mansion is open from 10 am to 4.45 pm. The mansion often hosts events, when a different fee structure applies.

The adjacent **Werribee Zoo** (☎ 9731 9600) is a free-range park with African herbivores – zebras, giraffes, hippos, rhinoceroses etc – in an Australian bush setting. Bus tours of the zoo cost $14 for adults and $7 for kids. On weekdays the buses depart half-hourly between 10.30 am and 3.30 pm. On weekends the buses run every 20 minutes and on summer weekends the parks stays open until 7.30 pm.

Met trains run to Werribee train station (Zone 1 & 2 ticket), and an infrequent bus service (six buses on weekdays, three on Saturday and none on Sunday) runs the 5km between the station and the park – ring the Met for details (☎ 13 1638).

YOU YANGS FOREST RESERVE

Another worthwhile detour off the Princes Fwy is to the You Yangs, a picturesque little range of volcanic hills just off the freeway. Ecologically, the park is quite degraded, but climbing up **Flinders Peak** gives fine views down to Geelong and the coast. Matthew Flinders scrambled to the top in 1802.

BRISBANE RANGES NATIONAL PARK

You can make an interesting loop to/from Melbourne west to the Brisbane Ranges National Park, and north to Bacchus Marsh, then return via the Western Highway. There are four good walking tracks (two to three kilometres) in the park, and the scenic **Anakie Gorge** is a popular spot for barbecues. You may see koalas in the trees near the car park and picnic area. **Fairy Park**, perched on a huge rock at the southern edge of Mt Anakie, has 100 clay fairy-tale figures.

Buy some apples if you head back through Bacchus Marsh, where the writer Peter Carey grew up (and read his surreal short story *American Dreams* before you go).

GEELONG

- **pop 125,400**

Geelong, Victoria's largest provincial city, sits on the shores of Corio Bay. For most Victorians, the word 'Geelong' conjures up AFL football and Ford: the city is the home of the Cats and a major car factory. For many Melbournians, 'Geelong' means being stuck in traffic on some very dispiriting roads, en route to the surf coast. The number of pawn and second-hand shops in the city centre tells you something about the state of the local economy.

If these seem good reasons to give the city a miss, think again. Central Geelong is a historic and attractive bayside city, with fine parks and gardens, some impressive museums and galleries, good restaurants, and modern shopping and recreational facilities. And a very lively nightlife.

History

In 1824 the explorers Hume and Hovell made the overland journey from Sydney to Melbourne, their expedition finishing at Point Wilson on the northern shores of Corio Bay. They returned to Sydney and reported with great enthusiasm on the area's fine qualities for grazing and agriculture, although it was another 11 years before their enthusiasm was acted on.

In 1835 John Batman formed the Port Phillip Association with the intent of establishing a new settlement around Port Phillip. On behalf of the association, Batman 'purchased' 40,000 hectares of land from the local Aborigines, including a large area around Corio Bay which the Aborigines called 'Jillong'. A small settlement was established on the shores of the bay, and the surrounding district was taken over by sheep graziers. Encouraged by the availability of fertile lands, more settlers came from both Sydney and Van Diemen's Land (Tasmania), and the town of Geelong grew

AROUND MELBOURNE

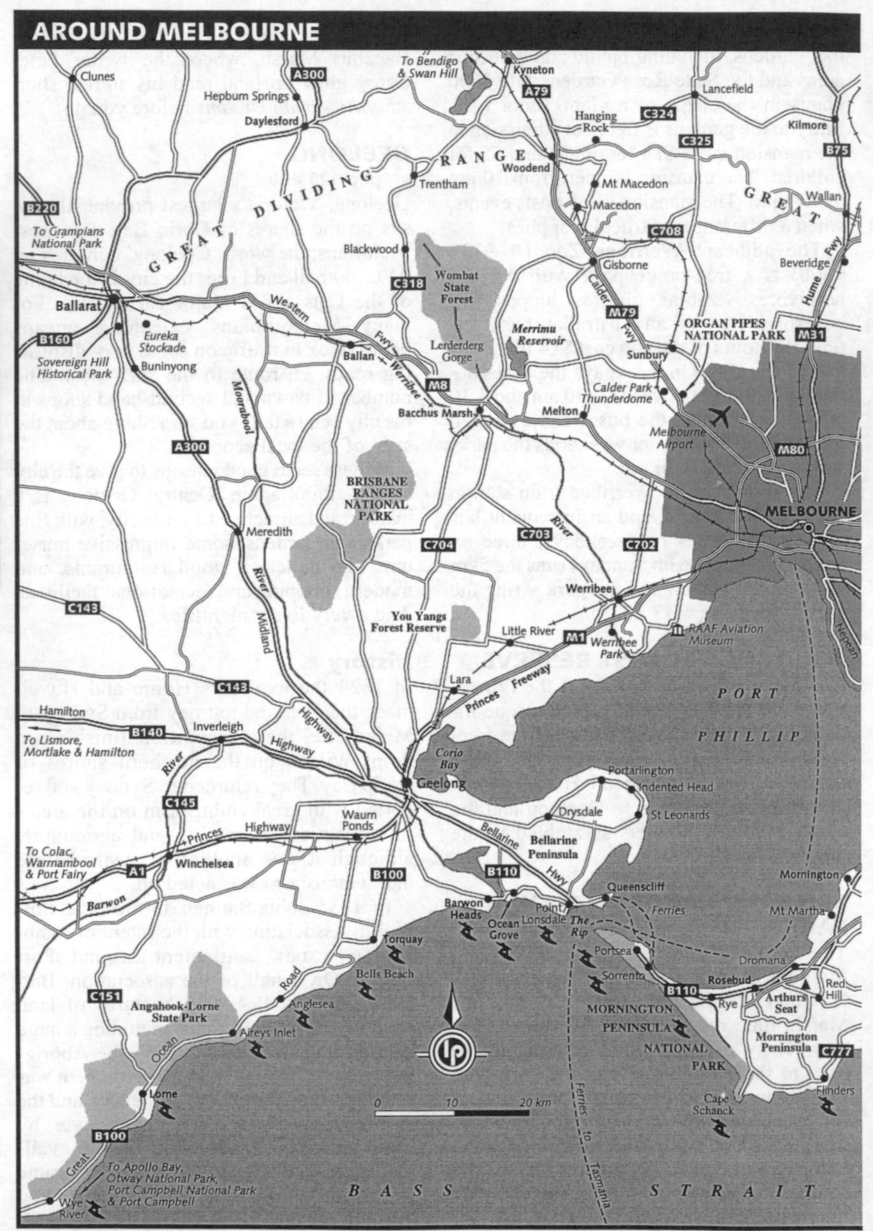

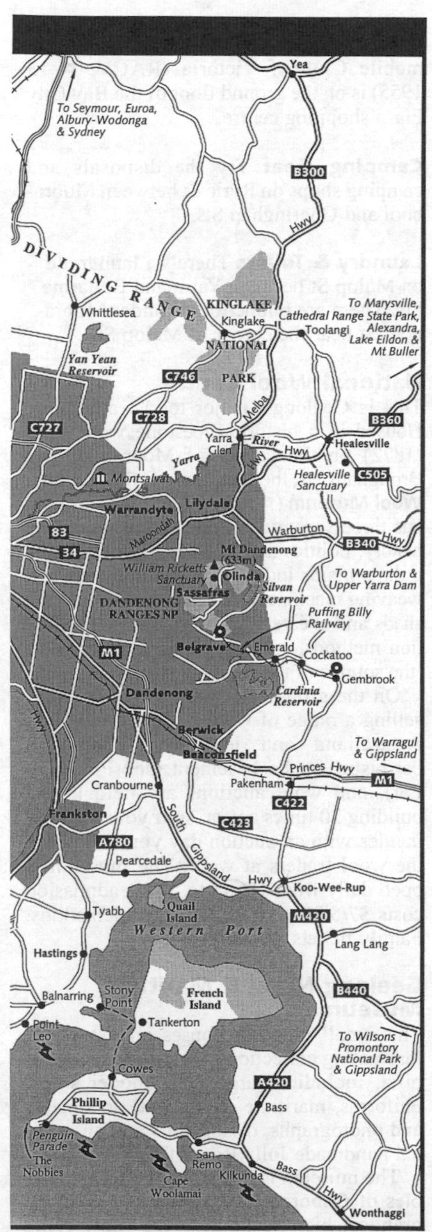

steadily until 1850, when the population was around 8000.

Like Melbourne, Geelong experienced boom times during the gold rush years. The city was one of the major gateways to the goldfields and the population trebled in the next decade as thousands of gold seekers arrived in ships and bought supplies before setting off inland to find their fortunes.

But gold or no gold, Geelong's future was assured by the richness of the Western District. Victoria's south-west quickly became one of the finest wool grazing and most fertile grain producing areas in Australia, and Geelong became the major port for the dispatch of wool and wheat from the district, much of which was sent back to England. However, because of a sandbar across the entrance to Corio Bay, large ships couldn't enter the port, which limited Geelong's progress for many years. This was rectified in 1893, when a channel was cut through to allow larger ships to enter the natural harbour, enabling the city to develop into a major industrial and shipping centre.

Today, a large proportion of Victoria's industrial and manufacturing sectors are based in Geelong. The main industries include car manufacturing, petrochemical refineries, agricultural products and machinery, aluminium refineries, and, of course, wool.

Orientation

Geelong is on the western shores of Corio Bay. The Barwon River winds through the city from the north-west to the south-east, passing about 2km south of the city centre.

The Princes Hwy (A1) enters from the north and passes close to the centre of town (where it's named Latrobe Terrace) before heading south-west towards Colac and Warrnambool. From the city centre, Aberdeen St heads west and becomes the Hamilton Hwy (B140), while 2km north of the centre the Midland Hwy (A300) heads north-west to Ballarat.

If you're driving in from the north, take the scenic foreshore route instead of the highway – even if you're just passing through. Turn left into Bell Parade (about 2km after the Ford factory) and follow the Esplanade along the foreshore. Geelong looks much more appealing from this perspective – yachts and boats bobbing in the bay, grand historic houses, and a series of foreshore reserves on the waterfront between Rippleside Park and Eastern Park.

The city centre is set back from Corio Bay. The main streets are Malop, Moorabool and Ryrie. The Bay City Plaza shopping centre, in the block bordered by Brougham, Yarra, Malop and Moorabool Sts, includes major department stores like Myer, Coles and Target, as well as a wide variety of smaller specialised shops.

Little Malop St is a shopping mall between Yarra and Moorabool Sts, and in the same street you'll find the Geelong City Hall, the art gallery and library, and the Performing Arts Centre.

Geelong train station is at the north end of Fenwick St in Railway Terrace – V/Line trains and buses arrive here, and other long-distance buses arrive at the Trans Otway Terminal on the corner of Ryrie and Fenwick Sts.

Information

Tourist Information The Geelong Otway Tourism Centre (☎ 5275 5797 or 1800 620 888 toll-free) is on the corner of the Princes Hwy and St Georges Rd, about 7km north of the centre. You'll see it on the left as you come in from Melbourne.

There are also tourist offices in the National Wool Centre on Moorabool St and in the Market Square shopping complex. There's also a Web site (www.greatoceanrd .org.au) that has information about the west coast.

Post The impressive old post office (1889) is on the corner of Ryrie and Gheringhap Sts.

Bookshops Good bookshops include the impressive old Griffith's on Ryrie St near Gheringhap St, and Barwon's, a second-hand and antiquarian bookshop on James St between Ryrie and Little Malop Sts.

Useful Organisations The Royal Automobile Club of Victoria (RACV; ☎ 13 1955) is on the ground floor of the Bay City Plaza shopping centre.

Camping Gear Try the disposals and camping shops on Ryrie St between Moorabool and Gheringhap Sts.

Laundry & Toilets There's a laundrette on Malop St between Yarra and Bellarine Sts. There are public toilets under Moorabool St near the corner of Malop St.

National Wool Centre

This is Geelong's major tourist attraction. Housed in a historic bluestone wool store (1872) on the corner of Moorabool and Brougham Sts, the focal point is the **National Wool Museum** (☎ 5227 0701). The museum has three separate galleries focusing on the history, politics and heritage of one of Australia's major industries, with spinning and weaving machinery, re-creations of shearing sheds and shearers' quarters, textile production methods, and a backing soundtrack of 'the sounds of the shearing shed'.

On the ground floor are souvenir shops selling a range of wool products, clothing, Australiana and jewellery. There's a bar/bistro in the basement (see Places to Eat), and wool auctions are held in the building 30 times a year, so if your visit coincides with an auction day you can watch the wool traders at work. The museum is open daily from 10 am to 5 pm; admission costs $7/5.80/3.50 for adults/students/kids. Family tickets are available.

Geelong Naval & Maritime Museum

This small museum houses an extensive, fascinating collection of maritime memorabilia, including large-scale model ships, uniforms, maritime equipment, documents and photographs, diving suits and an original handmade Jolly Roger flag.

The museum is housed in the former stables of **Osborne House**, one of Geelong's grandest historic homesteads (now lying empty) in Swinburne St in North Geelong. It's signposted from the highway. The museum is open daily, except Tuesday and Thursday, from 10 am to 4 pm, and admission is $2.

Geelong Art Gallery

In Little Malop St, this gallery has an extensive collection of mainly Australian art. Purchased in 1900, Frederick McCubbin's *A Bush Burial* is still the gallery's most famous painting. The 19th century collection also includes the work of Louis Buvelot, Eugene von Guerard, Tom Roberts and Arthur Streeton. The contemporary section includes works by Fred Williams, John Brack and Charles Blackman. Other collections include classical and contemporary sculptures, decorative arts and Asian artefacts. The gallery is open on weekdays from 10 am to 5 pm and weekends and public holidays from 1 to 5 pm; entry is $3 (free on Monday).

Historic Houses

Geelong has more than 100 buildings classified by the National Trust, several of which are open to the public.

The **Heights** (1855), 140 Aphrasia St in Newtown, was prefabricated in Germany and shipped out to Australia. The quaint white weatherboard house still contains some of the original furnishings. Other interesting features include a stone water tower, stables, a grooms' cottage and several hectares of beautifully landscaped gardens. The house is open Wednesday to Sunday between 1 and 5 pm; admission costs $5 for adults, $3 for kids and a family ticket costs $14. The National Trust shop here sells gifts, books, souvenirs and plants.

Barwon Grange (1856), in Fernleigh St, Newtown, is an impressive neo-Gothic brick homestead that overlooks the Barwon River. It was bought by the National Trust in the 1970s and has been fully restored, refitted and furnished in accordance with a list of contents dated 1856. The house is fronted by a broad verandah and surrounded by pretty 19th century gardens. It's open on Wednesday and weekends from 2 to 5 pm and admission costs $4 for adults, $2.50 for children and $10 for a family.

Corio Villa has an interesting story. The house was prefabricated in cast iron sections in a Glasgow (Scotland) foundry and shipped to Geelong, but by the time it arrived the original owner had died. The new buyer couldn't find any assembly plans, so his builders made a bit of a guesstimate and started welding the sections together. If you want to see how it turned out, the home is on the corner of Eastern Beach (the Esplanade) and Fitzroy St, overlooking Eastern Beach, but this place is privately owned and not open to the public.

Other historic properties include **Osborne House**, next to the Maritime Museum, and **Armytage House** (1859), 263 Pakington St in Newtown, a grand sandstone mansion.

Eastern Beach

This is the main city beach, and it's been one of the most popular swimming spots since the city was established. In the 19th century, private bathing boxes were built along the foreshore, and during the depression years a swimming complex was built by 'susso' (sustenance) workers. They laid thousands of stones along the foreshore and built a half-moon shaped enclosure to protect the beach from sharks. The bathing pavilions and promenade have been recently restored, and the complex now includes a restaurant, cafe and kiosk, sandy beaches, swimming pontoons and diving platforms, a children's swimming pool and playground, landscaped lawns and gardens with barbecues, and picnic facilities. On weekends and during the holiday seasons, fishing boats, aqua bikes, yachts and fun boats can be hired.

It's worth walking east along the shoreline to **Cunningham pier**, near the end of Moorabool St. Along the way are some very amusingly **painted bollards**. The pier has a new look, although a long walk to the end reveals only car-parking, a smorgasbord restaurant and a cafe.

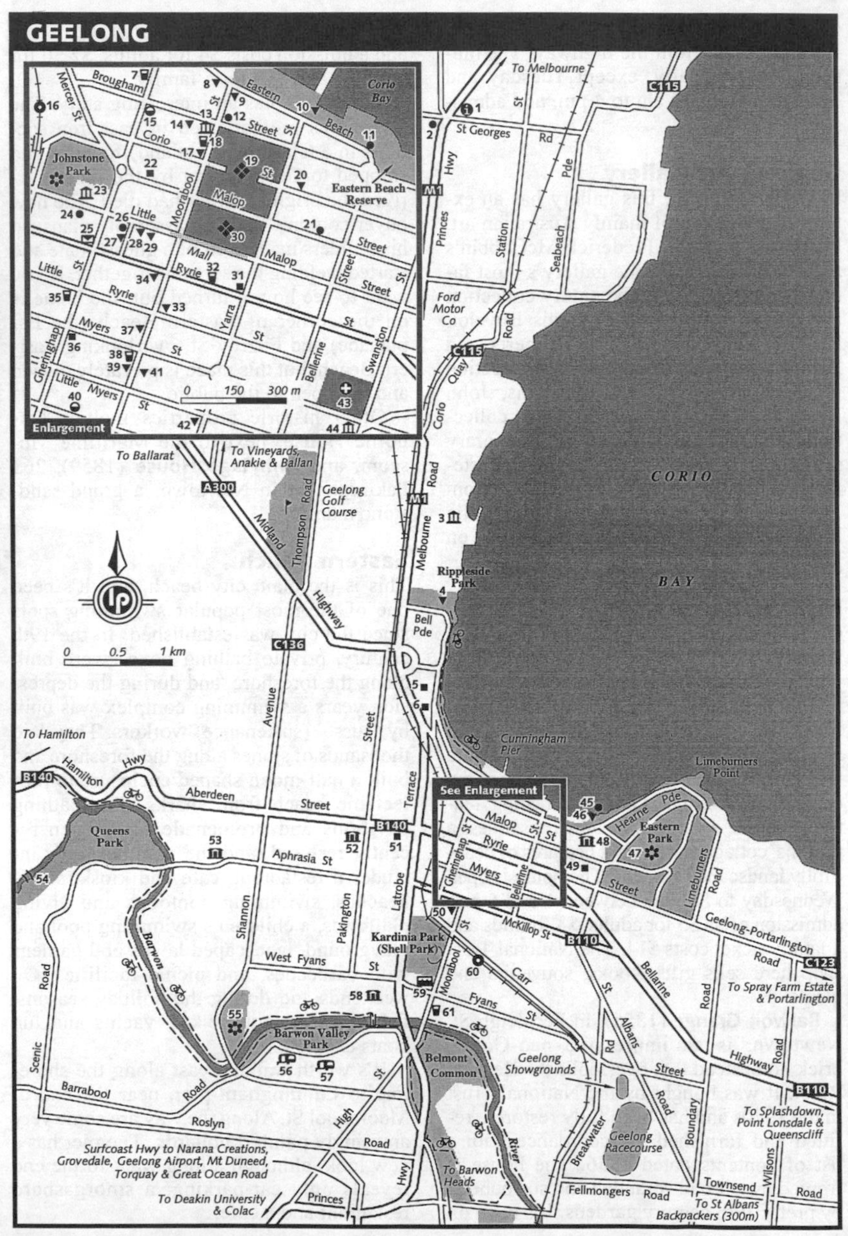
GEELONG
Enlargement
See Enlargement
Brougham
Mercer St
Eastern Beach
Corio Bay
Street
Corio
Johnstone Park
Moorabool
Malop
Little
Mall
Ryrie
Little
Myers
Gheringhap
Yarra
Bellerine
Swanston
Little Myers
St
Street
Eastern Beach Reserve
0 150 300 m
To Ballarat
To Vineyards, Anakie & Ballan
To Melbourne
St Georges
Rd
Princes Hwy
Station
Seabeach Pde
Ford Motor Co
Corio Quay Road
Melbourne Road
Geelong Golf Course
Thompson Road
Midland Highway
Rippleside Park
Bell Pde
CORIO
BAY
0 0.5 1 km
Cunningham Pier
Limeburners Point
Hearne Pde
Eastern Park
Limeburners Road
To Hamilton
Hamilton Hwy
Aberdeen Street
Queens Park
Aphrasia St
Shannon Avenue
Pakington Street
Latrobe Terrace
Kardinia Park (Shell Park)
Mckillop St
Geelong-Portarlington Road
To Spray Farm Estate & Portarlington
West Fyans St
Fyans St
Carr St
Bellarine Highway
Albans Rd
Boundary Road
Barwon River
Barwon Valley Park
Belmont Common
Geelong Showgrounds
Street
Road
Scenic Road
Barrabool Road
Roslyn Road
High St
Breakwater
Geelong Racecourse
To Splashdown, Point Lonsdale & Queenscliff
Surfcoast Hwy to Narana Creations, Grovedale, Geelong Airport, Mt Duneed, Torquay & Great Ocean Road
To Deakin University & Colac
Princes Hwy
To Barwon Heads
Fellmongers Road
Townsend Road
Wilsons Road
To St Albans Backpackers (300m)
M1
C115
A300
C136
B140
B110
C123

GEELONG

PLACES TO STAY
- 5 Hamilton Hume Motor Inn
- 6 Kangaroo Motel
- 22 Carlton Central Motel Hotel
- 31 Jokers on Ryrie
- 36 All Seasons Ambassador Geelong
- 49 Pevensey House
- 51 Lucas Innkeeper's Motor Inn
- 56 Billabong Caravan Park
- 57 Southside Caravan Park

PLACES TO EAT
- 4 Koaki
- 8 Gilligan's Fish & Chips
- 9 Sailors Restaurant
- 10 Fish Pier Restaurant
- 14 Lamby's Bar & Bistro
- 17 Pancake Kitchen
- 20 Scottish Chief's Tavern & Brewery
- 27 Wholefoods Cafe
- 28 Bamboleo
- 29 Cats
- 33 National Hotel
- 34 Fugisan
- 37 Spaghetti Deli
- 39 Hill Grill
- 41 Joe's Cafe
- 42 Wintergarden Cafe
- 46 The Beach House Cafe & Restaurant
- 50 Tousson

OTHER
- 1 Geelong Otway Tourism Centre
- 2 Norlane Waterworld
- 3 Geelong Naval & Maritime Museum; Osborne House
- 7 The Max
- 11 Geelong Sailing School
- 12 Customs House
- 13 National Wool Museum
- 15 Bus Port
- 16 Geelong Train Station
- 18 Wool Exchange Hotel
- 19 Bay City Shopping Centre
- 21 Laundrette
- 23 Geelong City Hall, Library & Art Gallery
- 24 Performing Arts Centre
- 25 Post Office
- 26 Barwon's Bookshop
- 30 Market Square Shopping Centre
- 32 Rebar Lounge
- 35 Lyric Nightclub
- 38 Geelong Hotel
- 40 Gull Airport Services Terminal
- 43 Geelong Hospital
- 44 Old Geelong Gaol
- 45 Eastern Beach Swimming Enclosure
- 47 Botanic Gardens; Old Customs House; Historic Lime Kilns
- 48 Corio Villa
- 52 Armytage House
- 53 The Heights
- 54 Buckley's Falls
- 55 Balyang Sanctuary
- 58 Barwon Grange
- 59 Geelong Memorial Swimming Centre
- 60 Geelong South Train Station
- 61 Barwon Club Hotel

Botanic Gardens

These beautifully kept gardens are a great place for a stroll or a picnic. Located in the centre of Eastern Park, they're surrounded by heavily treed parklands and overlook Corio Bay. Planting began here in 1858 when Daniel Bunce was appointed the first curator of the gardens. A canopy of established trees shades the paths, garden beds and fern glades, and just inside the entrance is a fan-shaped rose garden and a large plant conservatory.

Also within the gardens is the **Old Customs House**. This tiny cottage is said to be the oldest timber building in Victoria. It was built in Sydney in 1838 and transported here in sections – the interior contains historic displays from the days when it was used as a telegraph station.

Between November and March, Friends of the Botanic Gardens (☎ 5227 0387) conduct free guided walks of the gardens on Wednesday at 10.30 am and Sunday at 2.30 pm, departing from the front gate.

Other Parks & Gardens

Geelong has a large number of parks, gardens and reserves, particularly along the foreshore of Corio Bay and the banks of the Barwon River.

Eastern Park is the largest foreshore reserve, with many trees planted as early as 1859, including some quite rare species. The park is popular with joggers and walkers, and within the park are the botanical gardens, sports ovals, tennis courts and the Geelong East nine-hole golf course. On the eastern side of the park, at the end of Limeburners Rd, are the remains of three historic brick and stone **lime kilns** that were built here in 1852 and used to break down chunks of limestone.

Rippleside Park, on the foreshore off Bell Parade, has a children's playground, barbecues and picnic tables, a rock pool, a kiosk and a boat jetty. There are also barbecue facilities at various places along the foreshore reserve that runs around the shores of Corio Bay between here and Eastern Park. These reserves feature landscaped lawns sloping down to the water, shady bushes and large palm trees.

Johnstone Park, with its lawns and palm trees, bandstand, walking paths and memorial statues, is close to the centre of town on Little Malop St between Fenwick and Gheringhap Sts.

Belmont Common is the largest area of parkland along the Barwon River. It's on the south-western bank between Moorabool St and Barwon Heads Rd. Within the common are the Barwon Valley Public Golf Course, a riding club, a rifle club and various sports ovals There is also a **wetland reserve** off Barwon Heads Rd, which is maintained by the Geelong Field Naturalists Club and has over 100 different species of birdlife.

Farther west along the river is the **Balyang Sanctuary** on Shannon Ave in Newtown. This is an eight hectare bird reserve with a central lake – bring some bread and feed the ducks, swans and pelicans. Another popular riverside spot is **Buckley's Falls** off Scenic Rd in Highton. A picnic area overlooks a canoe slalom course, a walking track leads down to the small falls, and from a lookout you can see the water-driven Buckley's Falls Paper Mill across the river.

Narana Creations

Narana Creations (☎ 5241 5700) is an interesting Aboriginal arts and crafts gallery and cultural centre, selling hand-carved emu eggs and boab nuts, didgeridoos, posters, hand-painted T-shirts and more. It's also an information centre for people interested in local Aboriginal culture and history, with a resource library, videos and a big indigenous plant garden. The centre is near the airport at 410 Torquay Rd (the Surfcoast Hwy (B100) in Grovedale, on Geelong's southern outskirts. It's open on Wednesday from 9 am to 5 pm.

Other Attractions

If you're interested in Geelong's architectural heritage, pick up a copy of the brochure *City of Geelong Heritage Trail* from the Tourism Centre – it guides you around some of the more interesting old buildings, such as the 1856 **Customs House** in Brougham St, a classical building featuring the clean and simple architectural lines of the Georgian period. It still operates as the customs office for the Geelong port. The **Old Geelong Gaol** (corner of Myers and Swanston Sts), a grim Victorian-era building, is open on weekends from 1 to 4 pm.

The **Performing Arts Centre**, in Little Malop St opposite the art gallery, houses two theatres and is the major venue for theatre and music productions, and touring shows.

On hot summer days, there are a few places where you can cool off. **Waterworld**, on the corner of the Princes Hwy and Cox Rd in Norlane, is a massive swimming complex with two huge water slides, five pools, a gym, spa and sauna. **Splashdown**, in Coppards Rd, Whittington, just off the Bellarine Hwy (B110), has similar facilities. There's also the **Geelong Memorial Swimming Centre** just off Moorabool St, south of Kardinia Park.

Geelong Sailing School (☎ 5223 2733) offers a variety of courses, but all run over several weeks so they probably aren't useful to most visitors. However, the school also offers 'offshore passages', yacht trips to places along the Victorian coast. These are available by arrangement and cost from around $200 per person per day. It would be great to arrive at, say, Wilsons Promontory by yacht!

Special Events

Major festivals and events include the Pako Festival, a multicultural street festival held in February; the Australian Sprint Kart Championships, run at Beckley Park each Easter; Heritage and Wool Weeks, held in April; the Head-of-the-River college rowing regatta, held on the Barwon River each April; the Spring Festival, an arts and community festival, held during the first week of spring; and the Geelong Show, an agricultural and fun fair, held each October.

Places to Stay

Camping & Caravan Parks There are about ten caravan parks in and around Geelong. Closest to the centre are the four parks along Barrabool Rd on the south side of the Barwon River, which include the ***Billabong Caravan Park*** *(☎ 5243 6225)* and ***City Southside Caravan Park*** *(☎ 5243 3788)*. Campsites range from $12 to $14 and cabins cost $45 a double.

Hostels & Colleges ***St Albans Backpackers*** *(☎ 5248 1229)* is on a historic horse-stud property. The old coach house behind the main homestead has been converted into a hostel, with four-bunk rooms at $17 and one double at $34. The property is on Homestead Drive in Whittington, surrounded by a modern housing estate. Ring for a free pick-up from Geelong.

On the outskirts of Geelong towards Colac, Deakin University's ***colleges*** (☎ 5227 1100) also have cheap accommodation in the summer holidays.

Pubs & Motels ***Carlton Central Hotel*** *(☎ 5229 1954, 21 Malop St)* is an old-fashioned pub with reasonable singles/doubles/triples at $30/40/60, including a light breakfast. The ***Jokers on Ryrie*** *(☎ 5229 1104, corner Ryrie and Yarra Sts)* also has a few rooms at $25/45.

One of the cheapest and most central motels is the ***Kangaroo Motel*** *(☎ 5221 4022, 16 The Esplanade South)* with good budget units from $45/55. Nearby at No 13, the more upmarket ***Hamilton Hume Motor Inn*** *(☎ 5222 3499)* is opposite the waterfront and has a pool, a restaurant and modern units ranging from $85 to $150 a double.

Another central budget motel is ***Lucas Innkeepers Motor Inn*** *(☎ 5221 2177, 9 Aberdeen St)*, just west of the centre, with doubles from $59 to $90. Geelong's biggest hotel/motel is the four-star ***All Seasons Ambassador Geelong*** *(☎ 5221 6844, corner Gheringhap and Myers Sts)*. It's a five-storey hotel and conference centre with plenty of facilities and good views if you're facing the sea. The rooms are large if a little tired and cost from $110 a single or double. Suites cost $195.

B&Bs Geelong has some good B&Bs, as you might expect in a city with some fine 19th century homes. One of the nicest is ***Pevensey House*** *(☎ 5224 2810, 17 Pevensey Crescent)*, well located between Eastern Beach, the Botanical Gardens and the city centre. It's furnished with antiques and has a pool, and the four guestrooms costs $120/140. The Tourism Centre has information on other places.

Places to Eat

Geelong has a wide range of restaurants, cafes and pubs, most of which are spread around the city centre. There are plenty of choices along Moorabool St and in Little Malop St west of the mall, and pubs all over the city have very cheap counter lunches – some for $3.50. For a more upmarket pub meal, head for the ***Scottish Chief's Tavern & Brewery*** *(99 Corio St)*. The refurbished ***National Hotel*** *(195 Moorabool St)* also has cheap bar meals and a popular bistro section.

A couple of places with good lunch deals are ***Pancake Kitchen*** *(48 Moorabool St)* and ***Spaghetti Deli*** *(188 Moorabool St)*. ***Fujisan***, on Ryrie St near the corner of Moorabool, is a small place selling take-away sushi.

There's also a cluster of budget eateries and late-nighters on the Moorabool St hill. ***Hill Grill***, at No 228, is a rustic place with bare brick walls, tiled floors and a take-away counter. Nachos, pastas, grills and seafood dishes are mostly under $12. Opposite is ***Joe's Cafe***, a lively souvlaki-and-burger jukebox joint that stays open until 4 am.

The wonderful ***Wholefoods Cafe*** *(10 James St)* specialises in healthy natural tucker. They do great sandwiches, cakes and coffee, as well as vegetarian dishes (with some fish and chicken sneaking in as well). It's open all day from Monday to Friday, and on Friday nights for dinner.

Around the corner is ***Bamboleo*** *(86 Little Malop St)*. The owner is from Cadiz, and with its whitewashed walls, arches and traditional Andalusian cooking, it's like a slice of Spain transplanted to central Geelong. Tapas are $4 to $8, mains are around $12. At 90 Little Malop St, ***Cat's*** is a stylish licensed cafe with an interesting range of curries, pastas and vegetarian dishes in the $12 to $17 range.

There are some good places to eat while watching the bay. ***Sailors*** restaurant is on Eastern Beach Rd across from Cunningham pier. Farther west (and closer to the water) is the ***Fish Pier Restaurant*** which has fish dishes for around $20 as well as cheaper options. At the Eastern Beach swimming enclosure, ***The Beach House*** which is in the restored bathing pavilion has a restaurant, cafe and kiosk, as well as a great location. If you want cheaper bayside eats, try ***Gilligan's Fish & Chips***, across the road from Sailors.

Lamby's Bar & Cafe is a stylish place in a bluestone cellar beneath the National Wool Museum. During the day they have gourmet sandwiches, salads and light lunches, with specials from $5.

Head to ***Koaki*** *(☎ 5272 1925)* in Rippleside Park off Bell Parade, for Japanese food. The restaurant is simple and unpretentious, but it has a wonderful setting overlooking the bay and the food is very good.

Tousson *(☎ 5221 1375, 310 Moorabool St)* is set in a beautifully restored old bluestone building, and has a groovy cocktail bar and several very elegant dining areas. The food is excellent, with starters from $8 to $11.50 and mains from $12.50 to $19.50, and an extensive wine list, which includes many local wines.

Up on McKillop St at No 51, Geelong Wintergarden is a restored church housing craft, souvenir and antique shops, and the good ***Wintergarden Cafe***.

Entertainment

The large student population translates into a lively and reasonably varied nightlife, with most of the action in the city centre. The *Geelong Advertiser* publishes a gig guide – look in Friday and Saturday's entertainment sections; *Forte* is a free weekly paper detailing bands and other acts in Geelong, Ballarat and Bendigo. *That's Entertainment* is a free monthly magazine listing events in the theatre and the arts. You can find this at the tourist centre, and *Forte* at music shops around town.

A surprising number of small city pubs have live bands, especially on weekends, and many of them are in walking distance of each other. This is a good place for a pub band crawl. Check the gig guides or just use your ears.

Lamby's at the National Wool Museum, in Moorabool St, sometimes hosts quite big acts in a nice space, and the ***Wool Exchange Hotel*** across Moorabool St is another venue. The barn-sized ***Geelong Hotel*** *(214 Moorabool St)* usually has something happening, although that might be something like guest appearances by members of the Geelong football team. In South Geelong, the big ***Barwon Club Hotel*** *(509 Moorabool St)* has bands from Thursday to Sunday.

If you want to kick on until the early hours, try ***The Max***, a big but pleasant venue on Gheringhap St near the corner of Brougham. There are three floors with several bars and places to eat, and live music four nights a week. The ***Lyric Nightclub*** *(corner Gheringhap and Little Ryrie Sts)* is probably the top nightspot. It's in an attractive old bluestone church building and is part nightclub, part live band venue. The ***Rebar Lounge*** *(177 Ryrie St)* attracts a lot of students.

On winter Saturdays check to see if the mighty Cats are playing a home game (of AFL football, stupid) at Kardinia Park (recently renamed Shell Park), just south of the city centre on Moorabool St. You'll meet some very parochial local supporters. It's very much a family occasion (but no less fervent for that) and you'll understand why the whole city's mental health improves when the team is doing well. The *Geelong Advertiser* will tell you much more than you want to know about the team and its coming games.

Getting There & Away

Train V/Line runs frequent 'sprinter trains' between Melbourne and Geelong, departing every 20 to 30 minutes during peak hours and roughly hourly at most other times. The trip takes about an hour and the one-way fare is $8.60.

From Geelong, two to three trains each day continue on to Warrnambool ($24.50). There are also trains from North Shore train station (two stations north of Geelong) to Ballarat ($24.50) twice daily on weekdays and once on Saturday.

Bus V/Line buses operate from Geelong along the Great Ocean Rd as far as Apollo Bay ($18) via Torquay ($4.50) and Lorne ($11.20), with services three times daily on weekdays and twice daily on weekends. On Friday (and Monday during summer), a V/Line bus continues around the coast from Apollo Bay to Port Campbell and Warrnambool.

V/Line buses also depart for Ballarat ($9.80) five times a day during the week, thrice on Saturday and twice on Sunday. This service continues on to Bendigo via Castlemaine.

McHarry's Bus Lines (☎ 5223 2111) operates the Bellarine Transit service with frequent buses to the Bellarine Peninsula – see the relevant section later in this chapter for details.

Gull Airport Service (☎ 5222 4966), 45 McKillop St, runs 13 buses a day between Geelong and the Melbourne airport. The fare is $20.

All other long-distance buses depart from the Bus Port transit centre on the corner of Gheringhap and Brougham Sts.

Car All the major rental companies have offices in Geelong. Budget (☎ 5222 4588) is at 115 Mercer St, Hertz (☎ 5229 1100) is on the 323 Latrobe Terrace (at the corner of Gordon Ave), Avis (☎ 5221 1332) is at 44 Latrobe Terrace, and Thrifty (☎ 5229 1233) is at 15 York St. If you're looking for something a bit cheaper, try Delta (☎ 5229 8188) at 48 Mercer St or Halloran's Rent-A-Wreck (☎ 5221 7333) at 105 West Fyne St, Newtown.

Getting Around

Bus Geelong has an extensive city bus network operated by the Geelong Transport System (GTS; ☎ 5278 5955). The main city terminus is the Bus Port on the corner of Gheringhap and Brougham Sts. Timetables and route maps are available from V/Line stations, the tourist office and from the terminus. Tickets are bought from the bus drivers.

Taxi Taxi companies include Bay City Cabs (☎ 1800 636 636 toll-free).

Bicycle De Grandi Cycle & Sport (☎ 5222 2771), at 72 Mercer St, has bikes for hire from around $25 a day. On weekends during the holiday seasons, you can hire bikes at the Barwon Valley Fun Park, near the Barwon River, and at Eastern Beach. There are good cycling tracks throughout Geelong, along the foreshore and particularly around the Barwon River.

GEELONG REGION WINERIES

During the 19th century the area around Geelong was one of Victoria's major wine-growing areas, and by 1877 there were over 100 wineries in the region. But in the 1880s the vine-root disease phylloxera was discovered in the region and the government ordered all the vines pulled out.

Wine growing was re-established in 1966 when the Idyll Vineyard was planted in Moorabool. Two years later, Mt Anakie was planted, followed closely by Tarcoola and Rebenburg. Today there are a dozen or so wineries in the Geelong region – mostly small, individual wine makers, and the area is particularly known for its outstanding pinot noir and cabernet-sauvignon wines.

The **Idyll Vineyard & Winery** at 265 Ballan Rd in Moorabool (open daily except Monday from 10 am to 5 pm), and the tiny **Asher Vineyard** at 360 Goldsworthy Rd in Lovely Banks (open weekends from noon to 5 pm) are both about 8km north of Geelong.

The rustic **Mt Anakie Estate** (open daily, except Monday, from 10.30 am to 5 pm; 11 am to 6 pm on Sunday) and **Staughton Vale Vineyard** (open Friday to Monday from 10 am to 5 pm) are both in Staughton Vale Rd, Anakie, which is about 37km north of Geelong on the Ballan road. Staughton Vale also has its own restaurant/tearoom. **Mt Duneed Winery** on Feehans Rd in Mt Duneed, off the Surfcoast Hwy about 10km south, is open on weekends from 11 am to 5 pm. There are also several wineries on the Bellarine Peninsula. **Kilgour Estate** is open Saturday from 1 to 6 pm and Sunday from 11 am to 6 pm (open daily from Christmas to Easter). On weekends you can visit the historic **Spray Farm Estate** near Portarlington. The old homestead and stables are currently being restored and the property has recently been planted with vines – ring ☎ 5251 3176 to check opening hours.

Bellarine Peninsula

Beyond Geelong, the Bellarine Peninsula is a twin to the Mornington Peninsula, forming the northern side of the entrance to Port Phillip. Like the Mornington Peninsula, this is a popular holiday resort and boating venue.

Queenscliff is a fashionable seaside resort noted for its upmarket guesthouses, historic hotels and fine cafes and restaurants (there's also a hostel). It's also the departure point for ferries across to the Mornington Peninsula. Farther west, Ocean Grove and Barwon Heads have excellent ocean beaches and are popular summer resorts. There are also a couple of good wineries on the peninsula (see the previous section).

Accommodation prices soar on the peninsula between Christmas and the end of January. Many caravan parks have a minimum stay requirement at this time, although if you just have a small tent you might be able to stay overnight only. Limited tourist information is available at A Maze 'N Things (☎ 5250 2669) on the Bellarine Hwy – they also have a table full of great puzzles to play with.

Getting There & Away

McHarry's Bus Lines (☎ 5223 2111) operates the Bellarine Transit service with frequent buses daily from the Bus Port transit centre in Geelong and most places on the peninsula, including Barwon Heads and Ocean Grove (both $3.60 one way) and Queenscliff and Point Lonsdale (both $5.55).

Car and passenger ferries operate daily between Queenscliff, Portsea and Sorrento. See the Mornington Peninsula Getting There & Away section for details.

Getting Around

Geelong & Bellarine Mopeds (☎ 5258 4796) rents mopeds for $45 a day. You don't need a licence. It would be foolish to take one of these slow machines on a major road such as the Bellarine Hwy, but for getting around, say, the Queenscliff area, they would be good.

PORTARLINGTON, INDENTED HEAD & ST LEONARDS

These three small towns are on the north and east coasts of the peninsula. All three

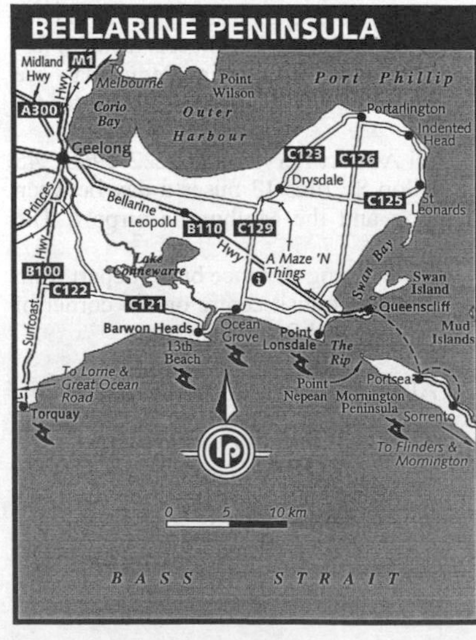

are quiet residential communities, and are popular, if low-key, resorts for fishing and summer holidays, especially with families, who flood into the local camping and caravan parks during summer. Because all three face into the bay, there's no surf.

On the north coast is **Portarlington**. During the 19th century, a string of bay steamers called regularly at the jetty to take farm produce to Melbourne. Not much evidence of the good old days remains, apart from the Grand Hotel (1886), which overlooks the foreshore park and pier, and the **steam-powered flour mill**, which was in danger of being demolished until the National Trust restored it and turned it into a historical display. Built around 1856, the massive, three-tiered building is open from 2 to 5 pm on Sunday from September to May, and on weekends and Wednesday during January ($2).

Indented Head is where Matthew Flinders landed in 1802, one of the first visits to the area by a European. In 1835 John Batman landed at this same point, on his way to 'buy' up the land that was to become Melbourne. **St Leonards** is another popular little resort just south of Indented Head.

QUEENSCLIFF

• **pop 3850**

Queenscliff was originally established as a settlement for the sea pilots, whose job it was to steer ships through the treacherous Port Phillip Heads. They weren't always successful – the coast along here is littered with the wrecks of ships that didn't make it.

The first land sales took place in 1853, and Queenscliff quickly became one of the favourite settlement areas for diggers who had struck it rich on the goldfields. Later it developed into a popular seaside resort, and during the era of 'Marvellous Melbourne' in the 1880s, Queenscliff was fashionably known as the 'Queen of the South'.

Wealthy Melburnians and the squattocracy of the Western District flocked to the town, travelling on paddle steamers such as the *Ozone* or on the Geelong-to-Queenscliff railway line, built in 1879. During these years some extravagant hotels and guesthouses were built.

Benito Bonito's Treasure

Local legend has it that the pirate Benito Bonito, who made a career out of plundering Spanish ships, was sailing the local seas in 1798 when he was spotted and chased by a British ship. Bonito is said to have come ashore near Queenscliff and buried his booty in a cave and then fled, never to return. The rumours inspired generations of treasure hunters, one lot even going so far as to form a mining syndicate – they spent two years digging but found nothing. Most of the locals have their own theories about the treasure and who knows, maybe one day it might turn up.

Mark Armstrong

But as the years passed, holiday makers moved on to other destinations and Queenscliff returned to its origins as a sleepy fishing village.

Queenscliff has been 'rediscovered' in recent times and is again a fashionable getaway town. Many of the fine Victorian-era buildings have been restored into guesthouses and upmarket hotels; these are complemented by good cafes and restaurants, a great golf course and numerous other attractions.

Things to See & Do

The best way to get an overview of the (small) town centre is on the horse-drawn double-decker bus that leaves from outside the Vue Grand Hotel ($5).

The most impressive old buildings are along Gellibrand St, where you'll find the **Ozone Hotel**, **Mietta's Queenscliff Hotel**, **Lathamstowe** and a row of old **pilots' cottages** that date back to 1853. Hesse St, the main drag, also has some great buildings, in particular the **Vue Grand Hotel** with its ornate and opulent interiors.

Fort Queenscliff was started in 1863 and finished in the 1880s. It was built to protect

Melbourne from the perceived threat of Russian invasion, and its gorge, keep and loopholed wall were designed to withstand assaults from both sea and land. But the Russians never made it, and the fort became the home of the Australian Army Command and Staff College in 1946. There are guided tours of the military museum, magazine, cells and Black Lighthouse, on weekends and public holidays at 1 and 3 pm ($4 adults, $2 children) and on weekdays at 1.30 pm ($5/2). Unfortunately, the government has decided to close the college and sell the fort. It will probably become an upmarket housing project – see it while you can.

Run by a group of rail enthusiasts, the **Bellarine Tourist Railway** (☎ 5258 2069 or 1900 931 452 for recorded information) has a large collection of old locomotives and carriages. The line was originally built when the fort was under construction, to supply men and raw materials from Geelong. Historic steam trains run every Sunday, plus Tuesday and Thursday during school holidays, and daily from late December to late January. Queenscliff to Drysdale takes 1¾ hours return – the train departs at 11.15 am and 2.30 pm, and the return fares are $12 for adults, $8 for kids. There is also a shorter trip to Laker's Siding, which takes 35 minutes and costs $6 for adults, $4 for kids.

The peninsula is something of a mecca for **diving and snorkelling** enthusiasts. Tanks can be filled at the general store in King St, and the Queenscliff Dive Centre (☎ 5258 1188), at 37 Learmonth St, and Dive Experience (☎ 5258 4058), at 8 Wharf St, both run diving trips and courses and hire out equipment.

Bikes can be hired from 'Mr Queenscliff' (☎ 5258 3403) near the pier, and one recommended excursion is to take the old steam train to Drysdale and cycle back – it's downhill all the way.

A market is held in Symonds St on the last Sunday of every month between September and May, and there are quite a few interesting galleries, craft and antique shops to browse in, mostly along Hesse and Hobson Sts.

The **Queenscliff Historical Centre**, on Hesse St, is probably the ugliest building in

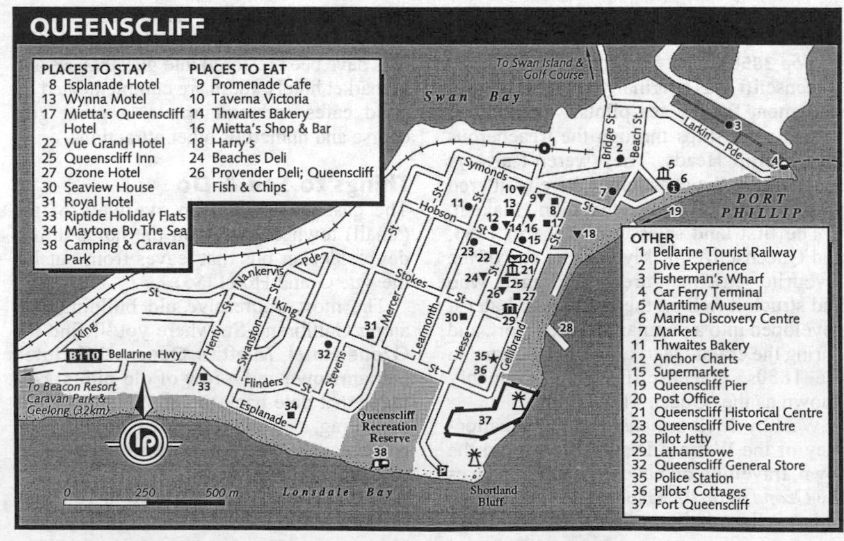

town. It displays various old relics from the town's past and opens daily from 2 to 4 pm.

The **Marine Discovery Centre** (☎ 5258 3344), on Weeroona Parade, is the educational unit of the Institute of Marine Sciences, and it holds a series of programmes and excursions that are good fun and a fascinating way to discover the hidden wonders of Port Phillip. Programmes are held regularly over summer and at other times by demand (groups of six or more). They also run a great range of trips, including 'snorkelling with the seals' (about $40), two-hour canoe trips ($12), marine biology tours, rock-pool rambles, boat cruises to the kelp forests of Pope's Eye and the bird paradise of Mud Island, nocturnal spotlighting tours of local rock platforms and tidepools, and lots more. Ring them to find out what's on.

Several other operators run similar 'snorkelling with the seals' (and dolphins) trips. We've heard good reports about Sea-All Charters (☎ 5258 3889), which charges $50/40 for adults/children, or $35/25 for non-snorkelling sightseers.

The small **Queenscliff Maritime Museum**, beside the Marine Studies Centre, has a collection of exhibitions and educational displays. It's open on weekends and every day during school holidays; admission costs $4 for adults and $1.50 for children.

For those interested in the maritime history of this and the Great Ocean Rd area, author, historian and yarn spinner, Jack Loney, has written over 100 books centred around local shipping history and legends. The books are widely available along the coast and are reasonably priced, and include titles like *Mysteries of the Bass Strait Triangle*, *Wrecks in the Rip* and *The Loch Ard Disaster*. The **Boat Bar** at the Ozone Hotel also has a collection of old photos worth seeing.

Anchor Charts, on Hobson St, is a small second-hand bookshop specialising in maritime books and maps.

Places to Stay

Camping & Caravan Parks Queenscliff has four camping and caravan parks. Most central is the simple council-run ***Queenscliff Recreation Reserve*** *(Mercer St)*, with camping and caravan sites around the Victoria Park oval ranging from $16.50 to $25.

On the Bellarine Hwy, 3.5km west of the centre, the large and modern ***Beacon Resort Caravan Park*** *(☎ 5258 1133)* has sites from $18.50 to $28 and units from $40 to $63 a night.

Hostels The friendly Queenscliff Inn guesthouse has always kept a few rooms for travellers, and at last it has been accepted as a YHA. ***Queenscliff Inn YHA*** *(☎ 5258 4600, 55 Hesse St)* has dorms for $15 and singles/doubles for $25/40. It's a nice place.

When it isn't full of divers, Queenscliff Dive Centre (☎ 5258 1188, 27 Learmonth St) offers dorm beds to backpackers for $30, including breakfast. It also has a pool, spa and the usual communal facilities.

Self-Contained Units The lights on the sign may have dimmed a little, but not much else has changed since the 1950s at ***Riptide Motel & Holiday Flats*** *(☎ 5258 1675, 31 Flinders St)*. Fibro on the outside, lino and laminex on the inside – they ain't glamorous, but starting from $80 a night for four people, these self-contained two-bedroom flats and motel rooms are good value.

Guesthouses & B&Bs In the centre of town the two storey Edwardian ***Queenscliff Inn*** *(☎ 5258 4600, 55 Hesse St)* has genial hosts and a relaxing, old-world ambience. Downstairs there's a cosy drawing room with open fires and a large dining room, and the guestrooms upstairs are decorated in period style with shared bathroom facilities. Singles are $50 and doubles range from $75 to $90, including breakfast. There is also a hostel section – see Hostels, earlier.

Maytone by the Sea *(☎ 5258 4059, corner the Esplanade and Stevens St)* is an elegantly renovated two storey guesthouse, with nine double rooms, a dining room and guest lounge with sea views. Singles/doubles start from $70/100 for B&B. ***Seaview House*** *(☎ 5258 1763, 86 Hesse St)* has its own gallery, tearoom and restaurant. Rooms with private bathrooms are $88/110. There are many other B&Bs.

Historic Hotels Most of Queenscliff's old pubs have been renovated and offer accommodation. The cheapest of these is the ***Esplanade Hotel*** *(☎ 5258 1919, corner Gellibrand and Symonds Sts)*, with rooms from $35. The ***Royal Hotel*** *(☎ 5258 1669, 34 King St)* has eight period-style rooms with balconies and shared modern bathrooms from $70/80.

The ***Ozone Hotel*** *(☎ 1800 804 753 toll-free, 42 Gellibrand St)* was built in 1881 and later converted into a hotel. It has been impressively restored and retains many fine period features. All rooms have en suites, and B&B ranges from $135/150 to $150/180 for a room with sea views.

Mietta's Queenscliff Hotel *(☎ 5258 1066, 16 Gellibrand St)* is a jewel of old-world splendour. Classified by the National Trust, the hotel has been restored rather than modernised, and the accommodation is just as it was 100 years ago: small rooms, furnished in the Victorian-style, and no telephones, TVs or radios; bathrooms are shared. Rather than spending time in your room watching TV, relax in the comfortable guest lounges. There's also a wonderful restaurant and bar (see Places to Eat). Dinner, bed and breakfast packages range from around $105 to $210 per person – prices depend on when you come and what you eat.

The ***Vue Grand Hotel*** *(☎ 5258 1544, 46 Hesse St)* looks deceptively modest from the outside, but the interior is quite grand. It has a magnificent tiled foyer with marbled columns and a very over-the-top dining room. Even if you can't afford to stay here, it's worth wandering in and having a look. Tariffs start from $125/210 for B&B.

Places to Eat

Hesse St has a collection of take-aways and, as befits a seaside town, a couple of decent fish and chip shops – try ***Queenscliff Fish & Chips*** at No 77. The ***Provender Deli*** at No 67 has good cappuccinos as well as sandwiches, cakes, salads and pastries, and across the road, ***Beaches Deli*** is also pretty good. ***Thwaites Bakery***, near the corner of Hobson St, sells good take-aways, including seafood rolls for $3.35.

Harry's, in the foreshore park in Gellibrand St opposite the pier, is known by the locals as the 'bog and grub' because it's sandwiched between two toilet blocks. But don't let that put you off – it's a quirky place with a fun beachy atmosphere and good food, especially the seafood. Mains are mostly under $20. Harry's opens for lunch and dinner during summer and closes over winter.

At 1 Symonds St, the ***Promenade Cafe*** is a good place for a casual breakfast or lunch. They have a small dining area, tables out the front and also do take-aways.

The ***Ozone Hotel*** has simple meals in the public bar and there's also a bistro serving upmarket pub food with mains around $18, and you can either eat in the Boat Bar, which is hung with a fascinating collection of photos of ships that have been wrecked along this coastline, or in the beer garden out the back.

If you want to indulge yourself and/or someone else, head for ***Mietta's*** *(☎ 5258 1066)* at the Queenscliff Hotel. The setting is a magnificently restored Victorian-era hotel, with a delightfully sophisticated ambience and consistently superb food. There's a grand, formal dining room with a set menu at $62 a head, or a pretty courtyard bistro out the back with main courses around $20.

Behind the hotel, with an entrance at the north end of Hesse St, ***Mietta's Shop & Bar*** is part bar, part gift shop and part eatery. There's a lovely sunny courtyard with a fragrant herb garden, delicious snacks like bruschetta, gourmet sandwiches or sticky toffee, and fine wines by the glass.

POINT LONSDALE

Five kilometres west of Queenscliff (it's a pleasant walk along the beach between the two towns), Point Lonsdale is a laid-back little town centred around its **lighthouse**, built in 1902 to help guide ships through the Heads and into the bay. The turbulent passage of water that leads into the bay is known as 'the Rip', and it's one of the most dangerous seaways in the world. The **Rip View lookout** is one vantage point from which you can watch freighters and other vessels negotiating the Rip – **Point Lonsdale pier** is another.

The foreshore around the headland is a marine wonderland at low tide, when an array of rock pools and caverns become natural aquariums – bring your mask or goggles.

Below the lighthouse is **Buckley's Cave**, where the 'wild white man' William Buckley, who lived with Aborigines for 32 years after escaping from the settlement at Sorrento, spent some time. Actually, this area is dotted with Buckley caves! (See the 'Buckley's Chance' boxed text in this chapter.) The town's **cemetery** has the graves of early pioneers, pilots, lighthouse keepers and shipwreck victims.

Point Lonsdale has two rocky beaches, the calmer bay beach or the surf beach, which is patrolled by a life-saving club over summer.

You can rent bikes for $6 an hour from the hardware shop on the main street.

Places to Stay

The council-run ***Royal Park Caravan Park*** *(☎ 5258 1765)*, on the foreshore, has campsites for $16.50 – it only opens between December and Easter.

Terminus B&B & Lighthouse Resort Motel *(☎ 5258 1142, 31 Point Lonsdale Rd)* is a cosy old-fashioned guesthouse with a tennis court, pool, comfortable lounges and a restaurant specialising in local seafood, which opens on Saturday nights. There are four refurbished rooms, with their own bathrooms, from $120 to $175 a double for B&B, smaller rooms for $90/98, or motel units out the back ranging from $55 to $95 a night.

There's also the ***Queenscliffe Point Lonsdale*** *(☎ 5258 2970, 4 Kirk Rd)* with units from $70 to $98 a double.

Places to Eat

On Point Lonsdale Rd, the main street, ***Pasquini's Deli*** has a tantalising array of gourmet goodies on offer. Next door, Pasquini's has a restaurant with main courses around $20. A couple of doors along, ***Cafe Angelina*** is a narrow little bistro with a mod decor and Italian-influenced food; mains are around $15.

OCEAN GROVE

Ocean Grove is a large, sprawling and unattractive town, but it's on the ocean side of the peninsula and the beach at the surf life-saving club is very popular with surfers. There is good scuba diving on the rocky ledges of the bluff, and farther out there are wrecks of ships that failed to make the tricky entrance to Port Phillip. Some of the wrecks are accessible to divers.

The **Ocean Grove Nature Reserve**, on Grubb Rd to the north of town, is a large area of natural bushland with 11km of marked walking tracks and lots of native flora, fauna and birdlife. The 143-hectare reserve is conserved and managed by a staff of volunteers. It's about the only example of surviving coastal bush on flat ground. All the other reserves are on rugged land that wasn't worth clearing for farms or towns.

Places to Stay & Eat

This is a popular family-oriented summer resort, with about half a dozen caravan parks, four motels and a few holiday flats.

On the west side of town, ***Riverview Family Caravan Park*** *(☎ 5256 1600)* has campsites between the Barwon River and the foreshore ranging from $15 to $25 – you'll need to book during summer.

The ***Ocean Grove Motor Inn*** *(☎ 5256 2555, Wallington Rd)*, 1km north of the centre, has doubles from $60 to $114. The views from ***Ocean House*** *(☎ 5255 2740, 86 Presidents Ave)* are unbeatable and doubles in this friendly place range from $120 to $140.

There's a range of food outlets in town, including Mexican and Chinese

Buckley's Chance

William Buckley (1780-1856) was transported to the recently discovered Port Phillip District on the *HMS Calcutta* in 1803. Shortly after arriving in Port Phillip Bay, the settlers set up camp near present day Sorrento. Buckley and three other convicts managed to steal a gun and escape – one was shot dead in the process. The remaining three set off around the bay, thinking they were heading to Sydney, but two of them lost their nerve and turned back. They were never seen alive again.

Shortly after, unable to find sufficient water, the *Calcutta* abandoned camp for Van Diemens Land (Tasmania) leaving Buckley to come to terms with the fact he was 'indeed a lone man'.

Buckley wandered for weeks, surviving on shellfish and berries, and was eventually found by two Wathaurong (Koori) women. Recognising the spear Buckley was carrying (he had unwittingly plucked it from the grave of a Wathaurong warrior) they believed him to be the reincarnation of their kinsman and took him back to his 'family'. Buckley spent the next 32 years with the clan who taught him their local customs and language as they moved across the Bellarine Peninsula (and as far afield as the Otway Ranges) in search of water food and trade.

In 1835, another ship sailed into the bay. Not sure how he, a convict, would be received, and no longer able to speak his native tongue, Buckley tentatively approached them. The white settlers were startled by the 6 foot 7 inch Koori emerging from the bush; they were even more surprised to discover he was an Englishman and they soon dubbed him the Wild White Man.

Gradually Buckley regained his English language and a pardon was arranged to allow him to become an interpreter. Many commented that his mediation saved unnecessary bloodshed between the British and the Kooris. As more settlers arrived, the task became bigger than the man and, with neither side paying much attention to his advice, he became disillusioned. Buckley subsequently left the colony for Tasmania, where he lived until his death.

So next time you hear the phrase 'you've got Buckley's', spare a thought for the real Buckley who beat the odds and not only survived, but thrived, as 'a wanderer among the Aborigines'.

LA TROBE COLLECTION, STATE LIBRARY OF VICTORIA

Portrait of William Buckley from the *Picturesque Atlas of Australasia* (1886)

Joyce Connolly

restaurants. The ***Bon Apetit Deli***, in the centre, does good sandwiches, snacks and cakes and opens for dinner on Saturday night.

BARWON HEADS

Barwon Heads is a smaller, quieter and prettier resort 4km west from Ocean Grove, at the mouth of the Barwon River. It was the location for the popular TV series 'Sea Change'. It has sheltered river beaches and around the headland, **Thirteenth Beach** is an excellent surf beach.

The magnificent **Barwon Heads Golf Club** (☎ 5254 2302) is one of Victoria's best courses, set among rolling coastal hills and sand dunes with inspirational ocean views. It's open to the public most days and green fees are $50 – yep, $50.

Places to Stay & Eat

The council runs the excellent ***Barwon Heads Park*** *(☎ 5254 1115)*, which is on the foreshore. Tent sites range seasonally from $15 to $23 and there are cabins and cottages for $50 to $170 a double. Over the summer months, there are also good tea tree shaded campsites between the river and the foreshore. You'll need to book during school holidays.

The ***Barwon Heads Hotel*** *(☎ 5254 2201, Ewing Blyth Rd)* overlooks the river and has motel units from $70 to $110 a double. It also has a flashy restaurant and cheaper bar meals.

Early Settlers Motel *(☎ 5254 2369, 67 Hitchcock Ave)* has good units from $64 to $89 a double.

The ***Barwon Heads Golf Club*** *(☎ 5254 2302)* has classy accommodation and a formal restaurant available for registered golf members. All inclusive overnight rates are $125 per person and residents get to play a round of golf for a more reasonable $15.

Hitchcock Ave is the main shopping area, and there are a few take-aways, although most of the eat-in places close during winter. Presumably summer will see a crop of hopefuls opening new places.

North-West from Melbourne

The Western Hwy (A8) heads west out of Melbourne to Ballarat, and there are several points of interest just off the freeway, including the towns of Trentham and Blackwood, the Lerderderg Gorge and the Wombat State Forest.

There are also some worthwhile stopovers and detours along the route of the Calder Hwy (A79), which heads north-west to Bendigo and beyond.

BACCHUS MARSH

Bacchus Marsh is just 49km from Melbourne, and just off the Western Hwy. It has some fine old National Trust-classified buildings as well as a noteworthy **Avenue of Honour**, and is a good base for walks and picnics in the vicinity. The area is noted for its apple orchards and market gardens, and there are roadside fruit and vegie stalls along the roads leading into town.

TRENTHAM & BLACKWOOD

These two charming little towns are on the edge of the **Wombat State Forest** and Wombat Ranges, a very pretty area that is highly recommended for a day or two of scenic car touring, combined with some great bushwalking and exploring.

Gold was first discovered in the area in 1854 by Harry Athorn and Harry Hider, who had wandered up the Lerderderg River looking for lost bullocks. When their discovery (the gold not the bullocks) became public knowledge, thousands of miners flooded into the densely forested area and searched the gullies and hills for gold. The miners built complex systems of water races to carry river water to their mining sites, and many of these races have now been turned into walking tracks. After the gold rush, the forests were heavily harvested for timber, but this has been controlled since the start of the 20th century.

The **Wombat Forest Drive** is a 50km route starting in Blackwood and looping through Trentham and Lyonville past lookout points, gardens and mineral springs. It's a nice drive, but you'll also see the havoc caused by logging.

Two kilometres west of Blackwood, the **Garden of St Erth** is not to be missed by garden lovers. Built around an 1860s stone cottage, the four hectare garden consists of shaded lawns and stone paths, fragrant flower beds and dappled pools, formal gardens and sustenance gardens. It's open daily from 10 am to 4 pm and entry costs $5 for adults and nothing for kids (though at the time of writing a rise was being considered – to $6 or $7). It is closed in June and July and 1-25 December. Blackwood also has its own **mineral springs reserve** in Golden Point Rd, with walking trails to the pretty **Shaw's Lake**, which is a good spot for a swim in warm weather.

Katteminga Lodge (☎ 5424 1415), a horse-riding ranch on a scenic property midway between Blackwood and Trentham, has horse trail riding for $15 an hour or $65 a day.

Places to Stay

Mineral Springs Caravan Park *(☎ 5368 6539)* in Blackwood has a lovely setting beside the Lerderderg River, with sites for $11 and a couple of on-site vans for $30 a double. The ***Blackwood Hotel*** *(☎ 5368 6501)* has three motel-style rooms at $50 a double for B&B.

The previously mentioned ***Katteminga Lodge*** *(☎ 5424 1415)* has a row of good self-contained motel-style units overlooking a beautiful valley that cost $75 a double, as well as modern dorms (self-catering groups only) and one self-contained cabin with a spa at $95 a double; breakfast is available. Facilities include tennis courts, an indoor pool and spa, and horse trail rides through the forest.

Blue Mount B&B *(☎ 5424 1296)*, in Newbury (midway between Trentham and Blackwood), has a cosy studio-style cottage in a pretty garden setting costing from $120 a night. There's also a newer one bedroom self-contained cabin on the same property that costs $130 a night.

Cosmopolitan Corner *(☎ 5424 1616, corner High St and Cosmo Rd)*, in Trentham, is a quaint old pub from the gold-rush era that has been restored and converted into a B&B, gallery and cafe (Wombat Forest Cafe; see Places to Eat). There are six comfy rooms, most with private bathrooms, costing $55/85 a single/double. ***Fir Tree Guesthouse*** *(☎ 5424 1549)*, at the other end of High St, is another converted quaint old pub with B&B from $85 a double.

Places to Eat

In Blackwood, the ***Blackwood Hotel*** is a good old pub and a lively spot for a feed, while farther along Martin St, ***Lerdies Restaurant*** is set in the former First National Bank Building (1874) and serves up country-style cooking, including popular Sunday roast lunches.

Trentham has a couple of good eateries. The vegetarian-oriented ***Wombat Forest Cafe***, near the corner of High St and Cosmo Rd, serves up light lunches, Devonshire teas and home-made pies and quiches etc from Wednesday to Sunday, and opens for dinner on Thursday and Friday nights. The previously mentioned ***Fir Tree Guesthouse*** has its own casual restaurant that is open on Saturday evening. The food is Mediterranean/Asian influenced and pretty good value. At the time of writing, Trentham even had an interesting looking Thai restaurant.

LERDERDERG GORGE & STATE PARK

The dominant feature of this 13,000 hectare state park are the spectacular gorges of the Lerderderg River. The park itself is in rugged and scenic escarpment country, and it's a great area for bushwalking, with numerous difficult and steep, long walks along the river and others that follow old water races cut by gold miners. Overnight hikers can bush camp anywhere in the park. This area is especially popular with bushwalkers during summer, with good swimming holes and sandy beaches along the river.

The main access road for the northern sector is O'Brien's Rd, signposted off the main road 3km south of Blackwood. The southern access road is north of the Western Hwy off the Bacchus Marsh-to-Gisborne road. Note that the roads through the park are rough and may be closed after rain. For more information, contact the Parks Victoria office (☎ 5367 2922) in Main St, Bacchus Marsh.

THE CALDER HIGHWAY

The Calder Hwy (large and increasing sections are freeway) takes you north-west out of Melbourne towards Bendigo. The route itself isn't terribly exciting, but there are a few pleasant surprises not far off the highway.

Melbourne to Gisborne

Take the Tullamarine Freeway and follow the Bendigo signs. Just beyond the outskirts of Melbourne you'll pass **Calder Thunderdome** raceway, where large crowds gather to watch cars go round in circles very quickly.

On the other side of the highway is the pretty and little-known **Organ Pipes National Park**. This area was stripped of vegetation in the early days of settlement and intensively farmed. Subsequent erosion exposed some fascinating geological structures – hexagonal basalt columns that look like giant organ pipes and form a natural outdoor amphitheatre. Most of the area was once covered with noxious weeds, but the weeds have been eradicated and native vegetation has been replanted. There are good picnic spots and walking trails, plus a visitor centre. You can't camp here.

Five kilometres east of the highway, the satellite town of **Sunbury** was the site for a number of large Australian Woodstock-style rock festivals in the early 1970s. On Sunbury Rd are two of Victoria's most historic wineries. **Goona Warra** and **Craiglee** were both built and first planted in the 1860s – both are open daily and are well worth a visit.

Sunbury is also where **the Ashes** originated. If you haven't heard of the Ashes you must live in a barbaric non-cricketing country, but I'll try to explain. In the 19th century, after a visiting cricket team from the Mother Country was defeated by a bunch of colonials, a Sunbury woman burned a bail (one of the wooden thingys that sit on top of the stumps – which are those three posts; there's a set at either end of the pitch, also known as the wicket – yes, as in 'sticky wicket') or perhaps a cricket ball (the legend varies), put the ashes in an urn and presented it to the England captain to mark the death of English cricket. Ever since, Australia vs England test series (a test series is typically five matches; a test match lasts for five days and often results in a draw, which is not the same thing as a tie) have been played to win or retain the Ashes. The tiny, unremarkable urn is the Holy Grail of cricket in England and Australia (which had a national cricket team before it was a nation). Although Australia regularly wins or retains the Ashes (especially in the last decade or so), the fragile urn remains at Lords in London (the home of the crusty Marylebone Cricket Club, which is also the England – not English – team). Got it? Good. For information on the extraterrestrial origins of cricket, see the *Hitchhikers Guide to the Galaxy* by Douglas Adams.

Back on the highway and 11km farther, you can turn off to the pretty township of **Gisborne**, which was once a coach stop on the goldfields route and still has some interesting historic buildings.

Ten kilometres east of Gisborne in Riddells Creek is the **Dromkeen Homestead Children's Literature Museum**, with an extensive library, a gallery of works-in-progress, and a historical room with original sketches and prints from well-loved Australian works, including *The Magic Pudding*, *Blinky Bill* and *Snugglepot and Cuddlepie*. There are barbecue and picnic facilities in the extensive gardens. Dromkeen is open from 9 am to 5 pm on weekdays, noon to 4 pm on Sundays. Entry is free.

Mt Macedon

- **pop 1250**

Just north of Gisborne you can turn off the Calder Hwy and head past the small town of Macedon to Mt Macedon, a 1013m-high extinct volcano. Following the boom years of the gold rush, this was where many of Melbourne's wealthy families built their summer

Macedon Wineries

Despite its proximity to Melbourne, the Macedon wine region is one of Victoria's best kept secrets. It may be overshadowed by the larger and more fashionable regions like the Yarra Valley and Mornington, but this is a great area for leisurely tours and explorations, with a dozen or so small and picturesque wineries scattered around an often rugged and spectacular countryside.

The area's altitude favours cool-climate varieties like chardonnay and pinot noir, and sparkling whites are a regional speciality.

At Romsey, the **Cope-Williams Winery** (☎ 5429 5428) is built around a magnificent homestead with a walled English garden. On Saturday and Sunday, they serve casual lunches in the tasting room ($10 for two courses) that overlooks the lovely cricket ground – social matches are held most weekends.

Eight kilometres north is Lancefield. On Shannon's Rd, the owners of the **Cleveland Winery** (☎ 5429 1449) live in a restored 1890s homestead, and have converted the old stables and coach-house into a restaurant (lunches on Sunday). There are also two guestrooms (soon to be expanded to six) up in the loft – tariffs are $135 to $150 a double for B&B. Four kilometres west of Lancefield, the **Glen Erin Grange Winery** (☎ 5429 1041) has an impressive modern restaurant that serves lunches and dinners Thursday to Sunday and on public holidays, and other days by appointment. East of Lancefield along the Kilmore road you'll find the **Mt William Winery** and **Portree Vineyard**, which has a cellar door at the Antique Centre in Lancefield.

The scenic **Burke & Wills Track**, the route taken by the ill-fated explorers when they left Melbourne in 1860, heads north-west from Lancefield to Heathcote. Along the track, about 16km from Lancefield, you'll find **Knight's Granite Hills**, which has a fine reputation for its wines. Nearby, you can also visit the idyllic **Cobaw Ridge**, with its mud-brick house and winery.

The **Hanging Rock Winery** (☎ 5427 0542), signposted off the Calder Hwy and overlooking the rock itself from a nearby hillside, is the region's largest winery – try their excellent *méthode champenoise* sparkling wine.

Brochures, maps and guides to the region's wineries are available from local information centres and all wineries.

homes, planted exotic gardens and came to escape the city heat. Although the town was devastated by the Ash Wednesday bushfires of 1983, many of these grand homes have been rebuilt and the gardens replanted. There are several Devonshire tearooms and a pub on the mountain. The region has an informative website (www .macedonranges.com.au).

The 'scenic route' up Mt Macedon Rd takes you up and over the mountain, past the mansions with their beautiful gardens and into some pretty countryside beyond. At the summit of Mt Macedon there is a memorial cross. Beyond the summit turn-off, the road leads to Woodend, or alternatively take the first tarred road on the right to Hanging Rock. The nearby Camel's Hump is popular with rock climbers.

The **Barringo Wildlife Reserve** (☎ 5426 1680), signposted about 10 minutes drive east of Mt Macedon, is a nature reserve with emus, kangaroos, peacocks and deer running free. It's open daily from 10 am to 5 pm ($6 adults, $3.50 children).

Places to Stay & Eat Mt Macedon makes a good base from which to explore the surrounding area as there is a wide range of accommodation on offer. The ***Mountain Inn*** *(also called Mount Macedon Hotel, ☎ 5426 1755)* is a very popular English-style pub with old-fashioned rooms with shared bathrooms at $55 a double ($70 on weekends) or with en suites from $70 ($95 on weekends). The hotel also has a good restaurant and in the gardens at the back are croquet lawns and a tennis court.

Huntly Burn *(☎ 5426 1411)* is a large, rambling garden property opposite the pub. Its old stables have been converted into a romantic self-contained getaway cottage. The tariff starts at $125 a night.

Other self-contained accommodation includes ***Milindi*** *(☎ 5426 2209)*, a pleasant bedsitter in the Barringo Valley, and ***Braeside*** *(☎ 5426 2025)*, a four-bedroom, four-star, home on 27 acres. One of the better B&Bs in the area is ***Horley*** *(☎ 5426 2448)*.

The ***Mt Macedon Trading Post*** *(☎ 5426 1471)* is open seven days a week and does breakfast, lunch and afternoon tea.

Woodend

- **pop 3000**

Back on the Calder (but soon to be bypassed), Woodend is an attractive town nestled on the northern fringe of the Black Forest. In the gold-rush days, bushrangers roamed the forest, robbing travellers en route to the goldfields.

Places to Stay & Eat ***Keating's Country Hotel*** *(☎ 5427 2510, 79 High St)* is a cosy and evocative old pub with good, inexpensive accommodation upstairs and good food at reasonable prices. It's $20 per person, $25 on weekends. Until the highway bypasses the town, you don't want a room at the front.

On the north side of town, ***Bentinck Country House*** *(☎ 5427 2944)* is a charming English-style guesthouse set in landscaped gardens with period-style guestrooms with private facilities, cosy lounges and a restaurant. Dinner and B&B costs from $270 a double and weekend packages are $420. The elegant restaurant is also open to the public, with a three course meal costing $38.

Hanging Rock

Hanging Rock, made famous by Joan Lindsay's novel and the subsequent film *Picnic at Hanging Rock* about the disappearance of a group of schoolgirls, has a peculiar haunting mystique. Like the Camel's Hump clearly visible on Mt Macedon, the rock is a former volcanic 'plug' that has eroded to its present bizarre formation. It's also a sacred site of the Wurrenjerrie Aboriginal tribe, and formerly a refuge for bushrangers, including the notorious Mad Dog Morgan.

The reserve is a popular spot for picnics, and there are walking tracks and good lookouts with superb views from higher up – watch out for koalas along the way. There's a good cafe serving light lunches and Devonshire teas. The **Hanging Rock Picnic Race Meetings**, held here every year on New Year's Day and Australia Day, have a great atmosphere and draw large crowds.

The Hanging Rock Reserve (☎ 5427 0295) is 6km north-east of Woodend; admission costs $5 per car. There are daily V/Line trains from Melbourne to Woodend ($8.60) – from there, a taxi (☎ 5427 2641) to the rock costs about $11, or it's a fairly easy bicycle ride.

Lancefield

- **pop 1150**

Lancefield is a peaceful country town with tree-lined streets and weathered old buildings that date back to the gold rush. Burke and Wills passed through here on their ill-fated expedition north – the road to Mia Mia is named in their honour and a cairn marks their passing (see the 'Burke and Wills' boxed text in the Facts for the Visitor chapter). There's a small **history museum** in the old courthouse in Main Rd, which was closed at the time of writing but is likely to re-open occasionally for special exhibitions.

Several wineries are worth visiting between Woodend and Lancefield; **Hanging Rock Winery** (☎ 5427 0542), north-west cf the rock, makes an award winning sparkling white and **Glen Erin Grange Winery** (☎ 5429 1041), south-west of Lancefield has a good restaurant (see the Macedon Wineries boxed text).

AROUND MELBOURNE

Places to Stay ***Lancefield Caravan Park*** *(☎ 5429 1434, Chauncey St)* has tent sites from $12 and cabins from $35. ***Centrevic Motor Inn*** *(☎ 5429 1777, Main Rd)* is a modern colonial-style motel with a restaurant; units cost from $75/85 for singles/doubles.

The Yarra Valley

The Yarra Valley, not far beyond the north-eastern outskirts of Melbourne, is a place of great natural beauty and well worth exploring. It's a good area for bicycle tours or bushwalks, there are dozens of wineries to visit, and the Healesville Wildlife Sanctuary is one of the best places in the country to see Australian wildlife.

Orientation & Information

The Maroondah Hwy (B360) takes you eastwards from central Melbourne out to Lilydale, the 'gateway' to the Yarra Valley, and then continues north-east through Coldstream to Healesville and Alexandra. Meanwhile, a couple of kilometres past Lilydale, the Warburton Hwy (B380) branches off and continues eastward through Woori Yallock, Yarra Junction and Warburton – this area is known as the Upper Yarra Valley. At Coldstream, the Melba Hwy (B300) branches off the Maroondah Hwy and takes you north to Yarra Glen and the Kinglake Ranges.

The Yarra Valley Visitor Information Centre (☎ 5962 2600), in an old Court House a block off the highway in Healesville, is the main information centre for the region. It's open daily from 10 am to 5 pm (to 6 pm on Saturday). Maps and brochures are also available from many general stores, shops and wineries in the area. There is also a Visitor Centre in the Upper Yarra Valley, in the impressive new Warburton WaterWheel building, on the highway at Warburton. It is open daily, 9 am to 5 pm, has maps and brochures, and provides an accommodation booking service.

The NRE publishes all sorts of information and maps about the area. These are available from their Outdoor Information Centre, 8 Nicholson St, East Melbourne.

WARRANDYTE STATE PARK

Warrandyte State Park, one of the few remaining areas of natural bush in the metropolitan area, is just 24km north-east of Melbourne. The park is made up of several sections, including Pound Bend, Jumping Creek, Whipstick Gully and Black Flat. Walking and cycling tracks are well marked, there are picnic and barbecue areas, native animals and birds, and an abundance of native wildflowers in the springtime. Although it's a suburb of Melbourne, Warrandyte has, to a degree, managed to retain the feel of a country village. Artists and craftspeople have always been attracted to the area, and there are quite a few galleries and potteries dotted throughout the hills.

There's an information section in Warrandyte's community centre on the corner of Yarra and Webb Sts (open weekdays from 10 am to 4 pm and Saturday from 10 am to 1 pm) where you can pick up walking maps and brochures. At 111 Yarra St, the **historical society museum**, which opens Wednesday, Saturday and Sunday from 1 to 4 pm, has a display of old photos and records.

One of the best ways to explore the river and park is in a canoe. Several operators, including Adventure Canoeing (☎ 9844 3323) hire canoes and equipment, and organise canoeing trips.

YARRA RANGES NATIONAL PARK

This newly declared park protects catchment areas of Melbourne's water supply. It has some rugged and beautiful bushland, including mountain ash forests and cool-climate rainforest. The endangered Leadbeater's possum lives here. Lake Mountain and Mt Donna Buang often have snow in winter.

Scenic road routes through the park include the Acheron Way (Warburton to Marysville), the Warburton to Healesville road, and the drive across Black Spur, on the Maroondah Hwy past Healesville. There are several picnic places along the way.

Because it's a catchment area, access is limited, but you can camp at the Upper Yarra Reservoir Parklands.

See the Bushwalks, Scenic Drives & Other Attractions section later in this chapter for more information on this area.

HEALESVILLE WILDLIFE SANCTUARY

Healesville Wildlife Sanctuary (☎ 5962 4022) is one of the best places to see Australian native fauna in the whole country. The park was originally used by Sir Colin McKenzie in his studies of Australian marsupials, and in 1929 he talked the government into declaring the area a reserve for native animals. The sanctuary is in a natural bushland setting, and a circular track takes you through a series of spacious enclosures, aviaries, wetlands and display houses. The sanctuary's residents include wallabies, kangaroos, dingoes, lyrebirds, Tasmanian devils, bats, koalas, eagles, snakes and lizards. The Platypus House is likely to be the only place you'll see these amazing creatures, and certainly the only place you'll see their underwater activities.

The staff give regular demonstrations such as snake shows. The best is the amazing Birds of Prey presentation, where raptors, including a huge wedge-tailed eagle, dive and swoop above your head. It's held at noon and 3 pm (weather permitting), but get there early for a good seat in the little amphitheatre. In summer the sanctuary have open-air music concerts featuring popular local acts.

There are barbecue and picnic facilities throughout the park, as well as a well-stocked Australiana and souvenir shop, bistro and take-away, and several kiosks. The sanctuary is open from 9 am to 5 pm daily and admission is $14 for adults, $10.50 for students (any country but you need ID) and $7 for children.

One reader had a less enthusiastic reaction to the sanctuary:

> OK, Healesville is good, but the *long* drive through endless urban areas to get there is not so good. If you just want to see some kangaroos, take the tram to the Melbourne Zoo.
>
> **Birgit Moller**

GALEENA BEEK LIVING CULTURAL CENTRE

Near the entrance to Healesville Wildlife Sanctuary, Galeena Beek (☎ 5962 1119, 22 Glen Eadie Ave) has an exhibition on Aboriginal history before and after the arrival of Europeans (including information on the reserves) and offers a short interpretive bushwalk. You can usually try boomerang and spear throwing and, if you're here at the same time as a school group, you might be able to sit in on story-telling and didgeridoo playing. Galeena Beek (which means 'cleanse the earth') is open on weekdays from 10 am to 5 pm and admission costs $6.50 for adults, with various discounts for different ages of children.

WINERIES

The Yarra Valley is one of Australia's most respected wine-growing regions, and there are more than 30 wineries scattered among these beautiful hills and valleys. The region is particularly noted for its pinot noir, chardonnay, cabernet sauvignon and sparkling 'méthode champenoise' wines. Being less than an hour's drive from Melbourne, the valley is one of Victoria's most accessible wine regions and a popular day trip from the city.

Wineries were flourishing in the cool valley climate way back in the 1860s, and the early wines of St Hubert's, Yeringburg and Chateau Yering achieved worldwide reputations. The valley's replanting and rebirth as a wine region began in the 1960s, and is still growing despite the high cost of land.

Wineries that are open daily include **Domaine Chandon** (the Australian operation of the famous French Möet & Chandon company), **Lillydale Vineyards**, **De Bortoli**, **Fergusson's**, **Coldstream Hills**, **Kellybrook**, **St Hubert's** and **Yarra Burn** – see our map Wineries of the Yarra Valley for more info on which wineries open when, and see Places to Eat later for details of wineries with restaurants. Many of the wineries charge a $2 or $5 tasting fee, which is refundable if you buy a bottle.

While it is an enjoyable way to see such pretty places, it's worth noting that buying

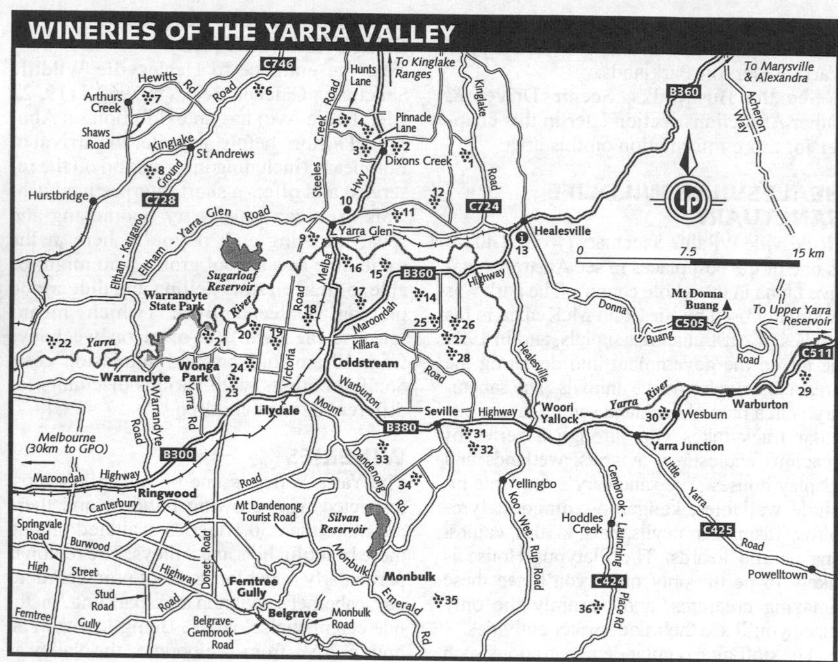

directly from the cellar is not necessarily the cheapest way to buy wine. Often the same wines are available at better prices from major discounters in Melbourne.

GULF STATION

A couple of kilometres north of Yarra Glen, Gulf Station is a National Trust-classified farm dating back to the 1850s. The farm remained in the same family until recent times, and little has changed over the years. William and Mary-Ann Bell built and developed the farm and had eight kids, six of whom lived on the property all their lives.

With the old slab-timber farmhouse, barns, stables and slaughterhouse, the original implements and the replanted sustenance gardens and orchards, Gulf Station gives an interesting insight into 19th century farm life. It's open Wednesday to Sunday and on public holidays from 10 am to 4 pm, and admission is $7 for adults ($5 concession), $4 for children.

KINGLAKE NATIONAL PARK

Known as the Forgotten Ranges, Kinglake National Park is the largest national park near Melbourne, and one of the least visited. The park covers a huge eucalypt forest on the slopes of the Great Dividing Range, and was established back in 1928 to protect and preserve the native flora and fauna. There are dozens of walking tracks, good picnic areas and scenic lookout points in the three sections of the park. An admission fee is charged in some areas. For information about the national park or to book a camping site, contact the Park Office (☎ 5786 5351) in National Park Rd, Pheasant Creek.

A scenic way to get here from the city is to drive out through Eltham (stopping to visit the **Montsalvat Gallery**), then up

WINERIES OF THE YARRA VALLEY

WINERIES OPEN EVERY DAY
- 3 Fergusson Winery & Restaurant
- 4 De Bortoli Winery & Restaurant
- 15 Domaine Chandon
- 21 Kellybrook Winery & Restaurant
- 28 Coldstream Hills
- 30 Yarra Burn Vineyard & Restaurant
- 32 Lillydale Vineyard
- 34 St Huberts Vineyard
- 2 Monbulk Winery
- 8 Lovegrove of Cottlesbridge
- 9 Yarra Ridge Vineyard
- 12 Long Gully Estate
- 16 Yering Station Vineyards
- 17 Shantell Vineyard
- 20 Yarra Edge Vineyard
- 22 Lochvie Wines
- 24 Lirralirra Estate
- 27 Warramate Vineyard
- 29 Brahams Creek Winery
- 33 Oakridge Estate
- 35 Mount Delancy

WINERIES OPEN ON WEEKENDS & PUBLIC HOLIDAYS
- 1 Chum Creek Winery
- 6 Diamond Valley Vineyards
- 7 Eltham Vineyards
- 11 Tarrahill Estate
- 14 Yeringberg
- 18 Mount Mary Vineyard
- 19 Tarrawarra Vineyard
- 23 Halcyon Daze Vineyard
- 25 Maddens Lane Winery
- 26 Yarra Yering Vineyard
- 31 Seville Estate
- 36 Gembrook Hill Vineyards

WINERIES ONLY OPEN BY APPOINTMENT
- 5 Yarra Yarra Vineyard

OTHER
- 10 Gulf Station Historic Farm & Homestead
- 13 Yarra Valley Visitor Information Centre

through Kangaroo Ground, Panton Hill and St Andrews.

In the centre of the park, **Kinglake** is a small township with a pub and a few shops and galleries (but no lake!). Eighteen kilometres east, **Toolangi** was the home of the poet and writer C J Dennis from 1915 to 1935. He wrote many of his famous works here, including the *Sentimental Bloke*. The *Singing Garden* tearooms and gardens are named after his last published book. Describing Toolangi in autumn, he wrote: 'Earth crammed with heaven and every common bush afire with God'.

Also in Toolangi is the NRE's impressive **Forest Discovery Centre** (☎ 5962 9314), with educational displays and videos on the various aspects of forest use. It's open daily from 10 am to 5 pm and entry costs $2 for adults, $1 for children. You can pick up leaflets here for the many bushwalks and scenic drives around here.

Places to Stay & Eat

Camping areas in the national park include the ***Gums***, on the Eucalyptus-Glenburn Rd 10km north-east of Kinglake. It's a pretty area with a small stream nearby, and there are eight tent sites and three caravan sites. There's another camping area north of Toolangi called the ***Murrindindi Scenic Reserve***, which is on the Murrindindi River and contains some great walks to places like the **Cascades** and the **Wilhelmina Falls**, which are quite spectacular when the snow melts in spring.

The ***Panton Hill Hotel*** *(☎ 9719 7270, Main Rd, Panton Hill)* is a very popular country pub with good, inexpensive meals. The back verandah looks out over the surrounding hills and fields, and they often have live music on weekends. ***Adams of North Riding*** *(☎ 9710 1461, Kinglake Rd, St Andrews)* is a very well-regarded country restaurant with an inexpensive bistro section.

BUSHWALKS, SCENIC DRIVES & OTHER ATTRACTIONS

Much of the valley's early history relates to the timber industry. More timber passed through Yarra Junction than any town in the world except for Seattle in the USA. Evidence of the old mills, timber tramlines and charcoal plants can still be found throughout the forests. **Powelltown**, 16km south-east of Yarra Junction, was a busy timber town during the 19th century, and timber tramlines and tunnels were built to transport the timber to the railway line.

A collection of excellent forest walks follow old tram routes. Shorter walks from Powelltown include the Reid's Tramline

Walk, the Ada Tree Walk (past a 300-year-old, 76m-high mountain ash) and Seven Acre Rock Walk. The two day, 36km **Walk into History** track takes you all the way from Powelltown to Warburton. The Parks Victoria/NRE office (☎ 5964 7088) in Woori Yallock has information.

There are some great scenic drives. The Warburton, Healesville, Marysville triangle takes you through some great countryside (for instance, along the **Reefton Spur** between Marysville and Warburton). There are several different routes and plenty of great off-the-beaten-track spots to explore. Both the Acheron Way and Woods Point Rd are excellent drives along good gravel roads.

In Yarra Junction, the interesting **Upper Yarra Historical Museum** is open on Sunday and public holidays from 1.30 to 5 pm ($3).

Warburton is a pretty little town set in a lush, green valley by the river, with rising hills on both sides. This area was a popular health retreat in the 19th century, and droves of city folk came to Warburton's guesthouses to breathe the fresh mountain air. The township still has a sleepy old charm to it. It's a short drive from Warburton up to **Mt Donna Buang**, which during winter is capped with the closest snow to Melbourne. 'Donna' was where generations of Melbourne kids got their first look at snow, rode their first toboggan and cried as their first-ever Mr Snowman melted and slid off the bonnet of the family Holden as it descended the mountain.

In summer the mountain has some pretty walks and lookouts. If you're reasonably fit, you can do a 6km walk to the summit of Mt Victoria from near the Warburton Golf course. Other good walks include the Cement Creek track, to the Ben Cairn lookout and to La La Falls.

In Wesburn, the **Sam Knott Hotel** is named after an old prospector who worked in a pub in the area around the end of the 19th century. Sam was immortalised by a Carlton & United Breweries beer poster, which depicted him standing at a bar, beer in hand, saying 'I allus has wan at eleven'. Sam died before the poster was published, but he lives on in (what's left of) the memories of all Australian beer drinkers. There's a woodcarving of him on top of a huge log in front of the pub's bottleshop.

The **Yellingbo State Fauna Reserve**, to the south of Woori Yallock, is in several sections and is the last remaining refuge of the rare helmeted honey-eater.

The **Centenary Trail**, which follows a railway line, has recently been extended to run all the way between Warburton and Lilydale. At 38km it's a good bike ride, but also offers good walking.

ORGANISED TOURS

Yarra Valley Winery Tours (☎ 5962 3870) offers bus tours of the wineries from Melbourne and Eco Adventure Tours (☎ 5962 5115) offers a wide range of tours of the area's natural attractions, including nocturnal spotlighting walks and forest and waterfalls tours.

Go Wild Ballooning (☎ 9890 0339) and Balloon Aloft (☎ 1800 028 568 toll-free) both offer dawn balloon flights over the valley, followed by champagne breakfasts at a winery.

PLACES TO STAY

B&Bs are proliferating in this area. Check with the Visitor Information Centre for more.

Healesville

Ashgrove Caravan Park *(☎ 5962 4398)* is 4km south-east of the centre of Healesville, close to the Sanctuary, and has campsites from $11 and on-site cabins and units from $45 a double.

Also near the Sanctuary and in a peaceful bushland setting, ***Sanctuary House Motel*** *(☎ 5962 5148)* has units from $45/60 to $55/70 for singles/doubles, plus a pool, spa, sauna and restaurant. ***Strathvea*** *(☎ 5962 4109, Myers Creek Rd)*, 9km north of Healesville, is a restored Art Deco-era guesthouse and gourmet getaway. Tariffs are $110 a double, or $140 for an en suite room – children aren't welcome.

Yarra Glen

The ***Grand Hotel*** *(☎ 9730 1230, Bell St)*, in the centre of town, was built in 1888 and is classified by the National Trust. It has been wonderfully restored in period detail and is one of the best country hotels in Victoria. Rooms cost from $120.

Launching Place

Hill 'n' Dale Farm Cottages *(☎ 5967 3361)*, on a forested property between Launching Place and Healesville, has three stylish, self-contained two-bedroom cottages that cost from $110 for two people.

Warburton

The cosy ***Motel Won Wondah*** *(☎ 5966 2059)*, on the fork in the Donna Buang Rd, has comfortable motel-style rooms with singles/doubles from $50/60. The ***Alpine Retreat Hotel*** *(☎ 5966 2411, 2 Main St)* is a renovated Art Deco-period hotel with upmarket accommodation at $68/98 on weekdays and $78/108 on Saturday, including breakfast.

Warburton Grange *(☎ 5966 9166)*, off the Warburton Hwy just south of the town, is an old-world guesthouse beside the river, with guest lounges and reading rooms with open fires. It hosts a lot of conferences, so ring ahead to check that there's room for individuals. The B&B tariff for doubles is $140.

There are quite a few B&Bs in the area – try ***St Lawrence B&B*** *(☎ 5966 5649, 13 Richards Rd)*, which charges from $105 a double.

PLACES TO EAT

If you're after a pub feed, the ***Alpine Retreat Hotel*** in Warburton and the ***Sam Knott Hotel*** in Wesburn both have good bistros and reasonably priced meals.

The ***Grand Hotel*** in Yarra Glen has a magnificent, formal Victorian dining room where you can have two courses for about $35 or three courses for $45, or there's a more casual bistro.

Several local wineries also have their own restaurants. ***Domain Chandon*** *(☎ 9739 1110, Green Point, Maroondah Hwy)* offers gourmet platters. On the Melba Hwy, 5km north of Yarra Glen, the rustic restaurant at ***Fergusson's Winery*** *(☎ 5965 2237)*, opens daily for lunch. It has with slab tables and a fun atmosphere. Lunches start from $7, and on Sunday they have set menus at $30 for two courses or $35 for three courses. A little farther along the same road in Dixons Creek, ***De Bortoli*** *(☎ 5965 2271)* has an upmarket Italian-style restaurant overlooking the vineyards, and serves up northern-Italian dishes for $18 to $22. It's open daily for lunch ($48 set menu on Sunday) and Saturday night for dinner.

Kellybrook Winery *(☎ 9722 1304, Wonga Park)* opens for dinner on Friday and Saturday and lunch on Saturday and Sunday. ***Yarra Burn Vineyard*** *(☎ 5967 1428, Settlement Rd, Yarra Junction)* and ***Lovey's Estate*** *(☎ 5965 2444, near Yarra Glen)* also have their own restaurants, and ***Domaine Chandon*** has a stunning glass-walled tasting room overlooking the vineyard – when you buy a glass of champagne you also get a small platter of bread, cheese, berries etc.

GETTING THERE & AWAY

The Met's suburban trains go as far as Lilydale: two bus companies operate services from Lilydale train station into the Yarra Valley.

McKenzie's Bus Lines (☎ 5962 5088) has daily services from Lilydale to Healesville (Zone 3 Met ticket) and Yarra Glen. It also operates direct services to Healesville from the Spencer St coach terminal in Melbourne (Zone 1, 2 & 3 Met ticket).

Martyrs Bus Service (☎ 5966 2035) runs regular buses from Lilydale train station to Yarra Junction and Warburton – fares are cheaper if you show your Met ticket.

The Dandenongs

On a clear day, the Dandenong Ranges can be seen from the centre of Melbourne – Mt Dandenong is the highest point at 633m. The hills are about 35km or an hour's drive east of the city, and their natural beauty has long made them a favoured destination for those wanting to escape the city.

Melbourne's early settlers were more interested in their natural resources than their natural beauty. The area was intensively logged, and by the end of the 19th century most of the natural forests of majestic mountain ash had been cleared. In an attempt to mimic the European landscapes they had left behind, the pioneering settlers planted deciduous trees – oaks, elms, poplars – and the landscape is now made up of a unique blend of exotic and regrown native trees with a lush understorey of tree ferns. These same settlers also built guesthouses, cottages and churches from local timber and stone, and established the network of quaint villages that are scattered throughout the hills.

Despite the encroaching urban sprawl and constant droves of visitors, the Dandenongs have managed to retain much of their unique charm and appeal. The attractions include magnificent public gardens and plant nurseries, tearooms and restaurants, potteries and galleries, antique shops and markets, birdlife and native animals, and bushwalks and picnic areas. With so much on offer, things can get a little hectic on the narrow winding roads, particularly on weekends during spring and autumn – midweek visits are usually much more sedate and relaxing.

Information

Dandenong Ranges & Knox Visitor Information Centre (☎ 9758 7522) is at 1211 Burwood Hwy in Upper Ferntree Gully.

The Parks Victoria office (☎ 9758 1342) is in the Lower Picnic Ground in Upper Ferntree Gully, at the start of the Mt Dandenong Tourist Rd. Rangers can supply maps of the parks and walking tracks – opening hours vary seasonally.

DANDENONG RANGES NATIONAL PARK

The Dandenong Ranges National Park is made up of the three largest areas of remaining forest. Some small sections of forest that escaped the attentions of the loggers and settlers were set aside as reserves in the 19th century, and since 1950 the Victorian government has progressively bought back sections of land for both conservation purposes and to improve fire protection.

There are three main sections, all with barbecue and picnic areas and good walking tracks. The **Ferntree Gully National Park**, named for its abundance of tree ferns, has four good walking trails of around two hours, including the educational **Living Bush Nature Walk**, which starts from the stone archway at the top of the car park.

Sherbrooke Forest has a towering cover of mountain ash trees and a lower level of silver wattles, blackwoods, sassafras and other exotic trees, as well as the ubiquitous tree ferns. The trees are home to a large number of birds, including rosellas, kookaburras, robins, currawongs and honeyeaters. The forest was also famous for its superb lyrebirds, but unfortunately a rampant population of feral cats has killed many of them, and only a few remain. The **Doongalla Forest**, on the western slopes of Mt Dandenong, is not as accessible as the other two areas, and the forest areas there are less crowded.

WILLIAM RICKETTS SANCTUARY

The William Ricketts Sanctuary (☎ 13 1963) on the Mt Dandenong Tourist Rd on Mt Dandenong is one of the best places to visit. A plaque inside the entrance proclaims that:

> In this sanctuary there is one theme only: expressing reverence for life in the New World Environment.

The sanctuary and its sculptures are the work of William Ricketts, who worked here up until his death in 1993 at the age of 94. His work was inspired by the years he spent living with Aboriginal people in central Australia and by their affinity with the land. His personal philosophies permeate and shape the sanctuary, which is set in damp fern gardens with trickling waterfalls and sculptures rising out of moss-covered rocks like spirits from the ground. It's open daily from 10 am to 5 pm (last entry 4.30 pm) and admission costs $5 for adults and $2 for children (free if you're under 10). There are also concerts here in the summer. Phone the sanctuary or check *The Age* for details.

GARDENS

The high rainfall and deep volcanic soils of the Dandenongs are perfect for agriculture, and the area has always provided Melbourne's markets with much of their produce. Botanists and gardeners have also been attracted by the growing conditions and in spring, gardens and nurseries overflow with visitors who come to see the colourful displays of tulips, daffodils, azaleas, rhododendrons and others. The gardens are at their best in spring (for flowers) and autumn (for the colours of the deciduous trees), but are worth a visit anytime.

The **National Rhododendron Gardens** on the Georgian Rd are next to the Olinda State Forest. Giant eucalypts tower over shady lawns and colourful flower beds. There are groves of cherry blossoms, oaks, maples and beeches, and over 15,000 rhododendrons and azaleas. The gardens are open from 10 am to 4.30 pm, and until 5 pm during the autumn and spring festivals and daylight savings. Admission is $6.50/4.50 for adults/kids during spring and autumn, and $5/4 at other times.

The **Alfred Nicholas Memorial Gardens**, on Sherbrooke Rd in Sherbrooke, were originally the grounds of Burnham Beeches, the country mansion of Alfred Nicholas, cofounder of Aspro and the Nicholas pharmaceutical company. At their peak in the late 1930s these were the best private gardens in the country, and they have in recent years been restored by Parks Victoria. A downhill walk leads to the very pretty ornamental lake. The gardens open from 10 am to 4.30 pm, and admission costs $4 for adults, $2 for children.

Around a couple of bends to the east, the **George Tindale Memorial Gardens** are also worth a visit. These gardens are smaller and more intimate, and are open from 10 am to 4.30 pm daily. Admission is $4/2. Off the Olinda-to-Monbulk road, the **Pirianda Gardens** have many rare plants, and there are also many commercial plant nurseries in the area.

PUFFING BILLY

One of the major attractions of the Dandenongs is *Puffing Billy* (☎ 9754 6800 for bookings and recorded information, or visit the Web site at www.pbr.org.au), a restored steam train that puffs its way through the hills and fern gullies. Billy is the last survivor of a series of experimental narrow-gauge railway lines that were built to link rural areas to the city at the end of the 19th century.

The train operates four times a day on weekdays outside school holidays, departing the Belgrave Puffing Billy station at 10.30 and 11.15 am, noon, and 2.30 pm. The 11.15 am train takes the newly extended route to Gembrook, the others run to Emerald Lakeside Park. On the noon train you have the option of travelling in a 1st class carriage and eating a lunch of soup. Travel time to Gembrook is 1¾ hours and the return train departs at 3 pm; the trip to Lakeside takes an hour and return trains depart at 12.30, 2.25, 3.50 and 4.30 pm.

On weekends trains depart Belgrave at 10.30 and 11.45 am, and 1.30 and 3.15 pm. The 10.30 am and 1.30 pm trains run to Gembrook, the others to Lakeside. Trains return from Gembrook at 1.15 and 4.20 pm, and from Lakeside at 1.30, 2, 4.35 and 5.05 pm.

There are also dinner trips on Friday and Saturday night for about $70 per person.

On days declared Total Fire Ban days for the Central Region (or for the whole of Victoria) Puffing Billy doesn't run, but there is a diesel-hauled train running a reduced service. Phone for times.

Return fares to Gembrook are $25 for adults, $14 for children and $71 for families; to Lakeside $18 for adults, $10 for children and $51 for families.

The Puffing Billy train station is a short stroll from Belgrave train station, the last stop on the Belgrave suburban line.

At Menzies Creek train station, a historic **Steam Museum** has a collection of old steam trains, carriages and machinery, and is open on weekends and public holidays from 10 am to 4.30 pm. At the pretty town of Emerald, the **Lakeside Park** is centred around Lake Treganowan and has picnic areas, a water slide and swimming pool, paddle boats for hire and the **Emerald Lake Model Railway**, the largest model railway in Australia, with over 2km of tracks and miniature hills, tunnels, towns, shops and people.

OTHER ATTRACTIONS

In Olinda, the **Edward Henty Cottage Museum** is a prefabricated cottage that was the original home of Victoria's first permanent settler. It was later moved up here, and now houses displays of antiques and furnishings from the 1850s.

A few of the townships in the Dandenongs hold regular market days, including Gembrook (last Sunday of every month), Kallista (first Saturday of every month) and Olinda (second Sunday of every month).

PLACES TO STAY

There are numerous motels, guesthouses, B&Bs and self-contained cottages, and a few options for budget travellers.

Travelling to a hostel by steam train is not a common experience, but you can in Emerald. ***Emerald Backpackers*** *(☎ 5968 4086)* is on the edge of the Lakeside Reserve in Emerald. It's a comfortable and friendly hostel with about 40 beds, good facilities and an attractive setting, and the owners can often find work for travellers in local nurseries and gardens. Dorm beds cost $13. There's also the new ***Dougie's Place*** *(☎ 5958 3297, 22 Kings Rd, Emerald)*, with only 10 beds and run by an experienced traveller. Beds in two or four-bed rooms cost from $15. In Belgrave, ***Jaynes Retreat*** *(☎ 9752 6181, 27 Terrys Ave)* is a B&B aimed at budget travellers, with good meals (from just $6.50 for dinner), big old verandahs and Sherbrook Forest nearby. Prices start a around $20 per person.

Opposite the Rhododendron Gardens in Olinda, ***Arcadia*** *(☎ 9751 1017)* is an impressive two storey cedar homestead in a delightful garden setting. The main house has full-length windows and a glass conservatory and is furnished with a quaint collection of antiques and nick-nacks. The excellent 'Treetops Suite' upstairs costs from $130 to $160 a double for B&B. There are also three well-equipped self-contained cottages in the gardens, all a bit different, with tariffs ranging from $145 to $165 a night. Highly recommended for a splurge.

There are a couple of other good places in Olinda along the Mt Dandenong Tourist Rd: ***Kenlock Manor*** *(☎ 9751 1680)* is an old English-style mansion with lovely gardens, a good restaurant and three double guestrooms upstairs from $120 to $135, and ***Como Cottages*** *(☎ 9751 2264)* has three charming self-contained cottages with period furnishings in a garden setting costing from $160 a night for two or four people.

In Sassafras, ***Monreale Country House*** *(☎ 9755 1773)* also has an excellent reputation. It's a 1920s guesthouse that has been stylishly renovated and has four doubles with en suites, a sitting room with open fires and, again, pretty gardens. Singles/doubles range from $70/100 to $80/150. They also have a cottage available from $110 to $190 per night.

PLACES TO EAT

There is an abundance of restaurants and tearooms in the Dandenongs, many of them in charming and rustic old buildings and garden settings. You don't really need to plan where to go – just cruise around the hills and, when you feel hungry, there's bound to be an eatery just around the next bend.

There are some fun and rather quirky tearooms, such as the terribly English ***Henry the Eighth*** and ***Miss Marple's***, the latter named and decorated in honour of the famous Agatha Christie character. Both are on the Mt Dandenong Tourist Rd in Sassafras. These places offer Devonshire teas, snacks and light lunches, and most are crowded on weekends in season.

On the Mt Dandenong Tourist Rd in Olinda, the ***Cuckoo*** *(☎ 9751 1003)* is a popular mock-Bavarian smorgasbord restaurant with lunches daily from $23 to $26 and dinners on Friday, Saturday and Sunday from $30 to $33, complete with a German floor show (singing, yodelling, cow bells etc). If that all sounds a bit much, the ***Snooty Fox*** nearby has the cosy feel of an English country house and a good reputation for its food.

GETTING THERE & AWAY

You really need your own transport to explore the Dandenongs properly. From the city, take either Canterbury Rd to Montrose or the Burwood Hwy to Upper Ferntree Gully – the Mt Dandenong Tourist Rd runs between these two roads and through the ranges.

The Met's suburban trains run on the Belgrave line to the foothills of the Dandenongs. From Upper Ferntree Gully train station it's a 10 minute walk to the start of the Ferntree Gully National Park. Belgrave train station is the last stop on the line and the starting point for Puffing Billy, and its a 15 minute walk from the station to Sherbrooke Forest. US Buslines (☎ 9754 8111) also run buses from both stations along Mt Dandenong Tourist Rd.

Mornington Peninsula

Mornington Peninsula, a boot-shaped peninsula between Port Phillip and Western Port, is a little over an hour's drive from the city centre. Because of its great beaches and other attractions, it has been a favourite summer resort for Melburnians since the 1870's, when paddle-steamers used to carry droves of holiday-makers down to Portsea and Sorrento from the city.

The narrow spit of land at the end of the peninsula has both calm beaches on Port Phillip (known as the 'front beaches') and rugged, beautiful ocean beaches (known as the 'back beaches'). At the far end of the spit, Portsea has a reputation as a playground for the wealthy, while nearby Sorrento has the peninsula's best range of accommodation and eateries.

The coastal strip fronting Bass Strait is protected as part of the Mornington Peninsula National Park, and along here you'll find stunning coastal walking tracks and great surf beaches. There are also good swimming and surf beaches in Western Port. Inland, the peninsula is a picturesque blend of rolling hills and green pastures, terraced vineyards and dense forests. It's a great area for leisurely tours and explorations – you can visit dozens of wineries and vineyards, pick your own fruit in orchards and berry farms, shop at craft and produce markets, wander through the bush on foot, or discover some of the many fine local restaurants.

Orientation & Information

Melbourne's urban sprawl extends down the peninsula to Mt Martha and beyond, with a string of adjoining seaside suburbs continuing all the way around Port Phillip to Sorrento and Portsea. Clusters of holiday houses extend along the Bass Strait coast from Sorrento as far as Rye, but the coastal areas between Rye, Cape Schanck and Flinders are mostly national park and largely undeveloped.

There's a string of small townships along the Western Port coast, including Flinders, Shoreham, Point Leo, Somers and Hastings. The interior of the peninsula is quite sparsely populated and mostly consists of farms, vineyards and forests, and includes the Point Nepean National Park and the Arthur's Seat State Park.

Peninsula Tourism's main Visitor Information office (☎ 5987 3078; 1800 804 009 toll-free) is on the Nepean Hwy in Dromana. It's open from 9 am to 5 pm daily. Other information centres are at the Cape Schanck Lighthouse, at Redman's Hardware in Sorrento, and, during the summer holiday season, there's an information caravan on the Nepean Hwy in Rosebud.

Activities

Swimming and surfing would have to top the list of peninsula activities, but there are plenty of other water sports to get your teeth

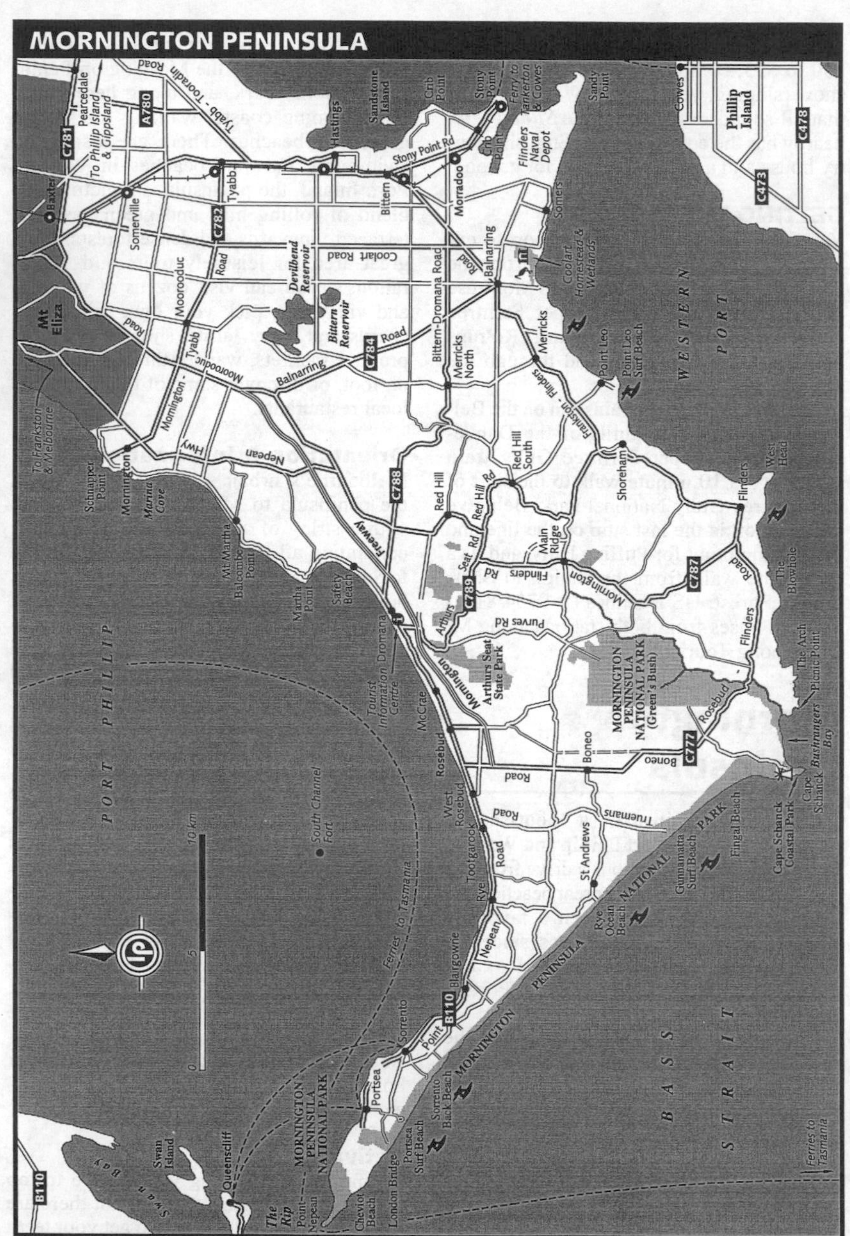
MORNINGTON PENINSULA
PORT PHILLIP
WESTERN PORT
BASS STRAIT
Mt Eliza
Mornington
Schnapper Point
Marina Cove
Mt Martha
Balcombe Point
Martha Point
Safety Beach
Dromana
Tourist Information Centre
McCrae
Rosebud
West Rosebud
Tootgarook
Rye
Blairgowrie
Sorrento
Portsea
Point Nepean
The Rip
Queenscliff
Swan Island
Swan Bay
Cheviot Beach
London Bridge
Portsea Surf Beach
Sorrento Back Beach
Rye Ocean Beach
Gunnamatta Surf Beach
Fingal Beach
Cape Schanck Coastal Park
Cape Schanck
Bushrangers Bay
Picnic Point
The Arch
The Blowhole
West Head
Flinders
Shoreham
Point Leo
Point Leo Surf Beach
Merricks
Merricks North
Balnarring
Coolart Homestead & Wetlands
Somers
Red Hill
Red Hill South
Main Ridge
Arthurs Seat State Park
MORNINGTON PENINSULA NATIONAL PARK (Green's Bush)
MORNINGTON PENINSULA NATIONAL PARK
MORNINGTON PENINSULA NATIONAL PARK
Boneo
St Andrews
Devilbend Reservoir
Bittern Reservoir
Moorooduc
Somerville
Tyabb
Baxter
Pearcedale
Hastings
Sandstone Island
Crib Point
Stony Point
Bittern
Morradoo
Flinders Naval Depot
Ferry to Tankerton & Cowes
Sandy Point
Cowes
Phillip Island
To Frankston & Melbourne
To Phillip Island & Gippsland
South Channel Fort
Ferries to Tasmania
Freeway
Nepean Hwy
Mornington - Tyabb Road
Moorooduc Road
Balnarring Road
Bittern-Dromana Road
Coolart Road
Stony Point Rd
Tyabb - Tooradin Road
Frankston - Flinders Road
Mornington - Flinders Rd
Red Hill Rd
Arthurs Seat Rd
Purves Rd
Flinders Road
Boneo Road
Truemans Road
Rosebud
Point Nepean Rd
C781
A780
C782
C784
C788
C789
C787
C777
C473
C478
B110
0
5
10 km

into, including snorkelling and scuba diving, fishing and sailing. This is a great area for bushwalkers, with some good trails through the Point Nepean National Park on the tip of the peninsula and a series of interconnected walking tracks traversing the spectacular ocean coastline from Portsea to Cape Schanck.

There are a couple of horse-riding ranches offering rides along the peninsula's beaches. You can also take a boat cruise into Port Phillip to see, and even swim with, the bay's resident dolphins (see Organised Cruises & Dolphin Trips in the Sorrento section). Portsea, Rosebud, Cape Schanck and Flinders all have excellent golf courses that are open to the public, and of course touring the wineries and tilting the elbow is perennially popular – and lots of fun.

Markets

The peninsula is an excellent place to check out craft and produce markets, as there's usually one each week somewhere in the area. The Red Hill market is the best known, and has been growing since it started in 1975. It's held at the Red Hill Recreation Reserve on the first Saturday morning of every month, except during winter. Other markets and times include: the Emu Plains (Balnarring) and Boneo markets (third Saturday of each month); the Rosebud market (second Saturday of each month); and the Tootgarook and the Sorrento Community markets (fourth Saturday of each month).

Places to Stay

There are dozens of motels, hotels and caravan parks along the peninsula, particularly along the Nepean Hwy, as well as a growing collection of guesthouses and B&Bs and a good backpackers' hostel in Sorrento. During the busy seasons (mid-December until the end of January, and Easter), tariffs go up and the entire peninsula is chock-a-block with holiday makers, so during this time you'll need to book in advance.

The peninsula is a happy camper's paradise – there are more campgrounds and caravan parks than you can poke a tent peg at. The main concentration of caravan parks is along Port Phillip from Dromana to Blairgowrie, and there are great camping reserves along the bay foreshore at Rye and Sorrento, which are filled to overflowing during summer. There are other good caravan parks on the Western Port side at places like Hastings, Somers, Point Leo and Shoreham, and many of these are in more scenic and natural settings. During the summer season, most sites are booked out well in advance – some for years ahead.

Getting There & Away

Train/Bus The Met's suburban trains from the city to Frankston take about an hour and you'll need a Zones 1, 2 and 3 ticket, which will cost $5.30 for two hours or $9.50, all day (see the Getting Around section of the Melbourne chapter for information about the Met). From Frankston train station, Portsea Passenger Buses (☎ 5986 5666) runs along the Nepean Hwy to Portsea between 7 am and 7 pm, which costs $6.90 one way.

The railway line also extends from Frankston to the Western Port side of the peninsula. You change trains at Frankston, and an old diesel chugger goes as far as Hastings, Crib Point or Stony Point – see the French Island and Phillip Island sections for details of the ferry service from there.

Car & Motorbike The Nepean Hwy runs all the way around Port Phillip from the city to Portsea, and is the most direct route to the peninsula. If you're in a hurry, there are freeway sections running parallel with and inland from the highway from Edithvale to Frankston and from Mornington to Rosebud, and via the freeways you can make the trip in just over an hour. If you're in no hurry, it's a much prettier, much slower and more sedate drive on local roads around the bay.

Ferry Peninsula Searoad Transport (☎ 5258 3244) operates a car and passenger ferry that links Sorrento with Queenscliff on the Bellarine Peninsula. It runs every day of the year and takes about half an hour to make

Round the Bay in a Day

One of the best ways to appreciate Melbourne's bayside location is to circumnavigate Port Phillip Bay, making use of the ferry services between Queenscliff and Sorrento. It's an easy day trip by car (about 200km of driving), but you could make it a two day trip, staying overnight on either of the Bellarine or Mornington peninsulas. You could also do it by public transport or bicycle.

Going anticlockwise from Melbourne, the first highlight is the view from the West Gate Bridge, with the city skyscrapers behind you, the industrial areas to the west and the bay stretching south to the horizon. It's a quick 70km down the freeway to Geelong, a city built on the wealth of Western District wool – the National Wool Museum there is worth seeing. Look carefully for the road that takes you the 30km to Queenscliff: although it's signposted, it's easy to miss. There are ferry services between Queenscliff and Sorrento (see the Mornington Peninsula Getting There & Away section). Book your ticket then look around Queenscliff, particularly the old fort and the grand old hotels.

You can see Port Phillip Heads from the ferry, but it gives them a fairly wide berth to avoid the dangerous current known as the Rip. You might see dolphins frolicking around the bow of the boat, as well as lots of sea birds around Mud Island and the unfinished island fortress called Pope's Eye. The ferry runs parallel to the coast past Portsea, and you'll have a good view of the luxury cliff-top houses that overlook the bay. As you come in, the Sorrento beachfront is particularly attractive with its tall pine trees and old-style bandstand rotunda.

There's wonderful coastal scenery on the southern tip of the Mornington Peninsula, on both the Bass Strait side and the bay side, and especially in the Mornington Peninsula National Park. Heading back towards the bright lights, you can take the Nepean Hwy, which follows the coast, or the freeway, which runs farther inland. Take the more leisurely coastal route if you want to find out about urban sprawl. From Frankston to the city is over 40km of non-stop suburbia, although there are pretty little beaches along the way.

V/Line's Round Bay Tripper ticket is a good idea if you want to take a (very) quick look at some pretty towns and scenery – it's valid for only one day. It takes you clockwise from Melbourne to Sorrento, across to Queenscliff on the ferry, to Geelong by bus and back to Melbourne by train. It costs $35 and is not available for travel on weekends.

Mark Armstrong

the crossing, departing from Queenscliff at 7, 9 and 11 am, 1, 3 and 5 pm and returning from Sorrento at 8 and 10 am, noon, 2, 4 and 6 pm. During the peak seasons (Friday and Sunday from mid-September to mid-December and then daily until Easter Tuesday), there are additional departures from Queenscliff at 7 pm and from Sorrento at 8 pm. Cars cost $32 to $36 plus $3 per adult and $2 per child; a motorcycle and rider costs $17; and pedestrians cost $7 for adults, $5 for kids. Pedestrian tickets are valid for 12 months.

Getting Around

Portsea Passenger Buses (☎ 5986 5666) runs a regular service along the Nepean Hwy between Portsea and the Frankston train station, but apart from that there's no regular public transport on the peninsula.

MORNINGTON TO SORRENTO

Mornington and **Mount Martha** are attractive residential suburbs, but apart from their excellent bay beaches they hold little interest for travellers. You could call in at **Studio City** at 1140 Nepean Hwy in Mornington, which is full of memorabilia relating to TV, cinema and radio; it opens daily from 10 am to 5 pm. Also on the Nepean Hwy in Mt Martha is the **Briars Historic Homestead**, which opens daily from 11 am to 5 pm.

If you're not in a hurry, turn off the Nepean Hwy at Mornington and take the slower but much more scenic route around the coast, which rejoins the highway at Dromana.

Arthur's Seat State Park

Arthur's Seat State Park is just inland from Dromana and signposted off the Nepean Hwy. A scenic drive, signposted near the information centre, winds up to the summit lookout at 305m, and you can also get there via the **Arthur's Seat Scenic Chairlift**, which operates between 11 am and 4.30 pm daily from September to April, and on weekends and holidays at other times. A return trip costs $7.50 for adults and $5 for kids.

The park has quite a few tourist attractions, including good picnic and barbecue facilities, a series of walking tracks, an old viewing tower, a kiosk and restaurant and a pottery and craft cottage. **Seawinds**, a public garden near the summit, enjoys great views of the bay and peninsula from several lookouts. The garden is dominated by big cypress pines and contains several sculptures by William Ricketts. It opens daily from 10 am, but often closes over winter. A small **Fauna Park** has a collection of native animals, and the **Pine Ridge Car Museum** has a collection of old cars and motoring memorabilia. Both are open at the same times as the chairlift.

On the slopes of Arthur's Seat, at 8 Charles St in McCrae, is the **McCrae Homestead**, a National Trust property. The timber-slab cottage was built from local timber and completed in 1846. It houses a collection of colonial furniture and the paintings and writings of the pioneering Georgina McCrae. It's open daily from noon to 4 pm; entry costs $5/4.

Places to Stay & Eat

There are plenty of caravan parks along this stretch of coast and, on the Rye foreshore, ***Rye Foreshore Reserve*** *(☎ 5985 2405)* has campsites from $10, bookings are necessary during summer school holidays.

Near the top of Arthur's Seat in Dromana is ***Gazebo Lodge Motel*** *(☎ 5987 2975, Purves Rd)*, a modern motel in a bush setting with B&B starting at $70.

On top of Arthur's Seat is ***Arthur's*** *(☎ 5981 4444)*, a formal restaurant with sensational views, a wine list featuring local wines and outstanding French-influenced food. There's also a casual (and less expensive) bistro downstairs with light snacks and meals, as well as a kiosk. On Purves Rd, about 4km over the summit, is the ***Pig and Whistle*** *(☎ 5989 6130)*, which is set up in the style of an English country tavern. It has a cosy bar, complete with dartboard and Bass, Tennent's and Tetley's beers on tap, snacks for around $6, and an earthy restaurant serving hearty main meals from $16 to $20 – leave room for dessert, as they have great puddings.

SORRENTO

Sorrento is the oldest town on the peninsula, and it has a delightful seaside atmosphere. During the summer silly season it's a frenetic and fashionable resort, whereas

Out in the Bay

Apart from the seals, dolphins and sea birds, you'll see some unusual and interesting sights when you take one of the cruises from Sorrento pier out into the bay. The **South Channel Fort** is a small artificial island near the entrance to the bay. It was built in the 1880s to protect Melbourne against a perceived threat of Russian invasion. Many of the 19th century fortifications and underground passages remain intact, and the island is also a protected haven for birdlife. **Pope's Eye** is the foundation ring of another (unfinished) fort that is now home to a seal colony, and the **Mud Island Wildlife Reserve** is a bird haven.

Mark Armstrong

AROUND MELBOURNE

during the colder winter months it's more akin to a sleepy little village. It has some fine 19th century buildings that were built from locally quarried limestone, including three grand old pubs, the Sorrento (1871), Continental (1875) and Koonya (1878). It also boasts fine beaches, a very good range of accommodation and some excellent cafes and restaurants. Dolphin-watching cruises in the bay are incredibly popular, and while you're here be sure to take a trip across to Queenscliff on the ferry.

The **Nepean Historical Society Museum**, in the old Mechanic's Institute building on Melbourne Rd, is open on Sunday, public holidays and during school holidays from 1.30 to 4.30 pm ($3). There's also a rather damp and cold little **Marine Oceanarium** that opens daily.

History

Sorrento was the site of the first official European settlement in Victoria. An expedition consisting of 308 convicts, 51 marines, 12 civil officers, 17 free settlers and a missionary and his wife arrived from England in October 1803, intending to forestall a feared French settlement on the bay. Less than a year later, in May 1804, the project was abandoned and moved to Van Diemen's Land. The main reason for the settlement's short life was the lack of water; unaware of the discovery of the Yarra River early in 1803, they had simply chosen the wrong place.

The settlement's numbers included an 11-year-old boy, John Pascoe Fawkner, who 30 years later would be one of the founders of Melbourne. It also included William Buckley, a convict who escaped soon after their arrival in 1803 and lived with the Aborigines for the next 32 years (see the 'Buckley's Chance' boxed text in this chapter). Not much evidence of the settlement remains, apart from four graves that are believed to hold the remains of the 30 people who died during the settlement's short life. A small stone monument marks the site at Sullivan Bay, and a display centre tells the story of the settlement – it opens from 1 to 4.30 pm daily during summer school holidays and on Sunday between April and November.

Organised Cruises & Dolphin Trips

Several operators offer a combination of sightseeing cruises of the bay, fishing trips and dolphin-watching cruises. They include Polperro Dolphin Swims (☎ 5988 8437), Dolphin Discovery Tours (☎ 018 392 507) and Moonraker (☎ 018 591 033). All cruises depart from Sorrento pier.

Dolphin cruises run for four hours and cost $35 for sightseeing or $50 if you want to swim with the dolphins, with all gear supplied. There are also various sightseeing cruises and fishing trips.

Places to Stay

Hostels ***Bell's Environmental YHA Hostel*** *(☎ 5984 4323, 3 Miranda St, Sorrento)* is a great place to stay. The hostel was purpose-built and the facilities are of a high standard. Horse trail rides and snorkelling trips can be organised and the nightly charge is $12 for YHA members ($14 in peak season). To get here from Melbourne take a train to Frankston, then bus No 788 to stop 18.

Pubs & Motels ***Hotel Sorrento*** *(☎ 5984 2206)* has motel-style rooms with doubles from $90 to $160. The town's other cheap pubs have made way for new developments.

Down near the back beach, the ***Oceanic Motel*** *(☎ 5984 4166, 234 Ocean Beach Rd)* has neat budget units from $45/90 to $55/100.

Guesthouses, B&Bs & Apartments ***Carmel B&B*** *(☎ 5984 3512, 142 Ocean Beach Rd)* is a historic limestone cottage in the centre of Sorrento. It's been tastefully restored in period style, and has a cosy guest lounge, four guestrooms with private bathrooms ranging from $120 to $150 a double, and two self-contained units out the back from $120.

Near the back beach, ***Whitehall Guesthouse*** *(☎ 5984 4166, 231 Ocean Beach Rd)* is a rambling old two storey guesthouse with old-fashioned rooms with shared bathrooms, large guest lounges and its own restaurant. Singles/doubles range from just $35/60 to $100/110.

Next to Hotel Sorrento, ***Sorrento on the Park*** *(☎ 5984 4777)* is an impressive complex of modern timber apartments that range from $120 to $220 a night.

Places to Eat

Ocean Beach Rd is the main shopping centre, and has two good bakeries and a health-food shop, the usual take-aways and a couple of good deli/cafes for lovers of gourmet food (and good coffee). ***Stringer's***, opposite the Continental Hotel, is a great spot for breakfast or lunch, with good cooked breakfasts, sandwiches and cakes. ***Just Fine Food***, next to the Continental, is an outstanding (if somewhat pricey) gourmet deli with sensational cakes and pastries, handmade chocolates, pâtés, smallgoods and lots more.

Sorrento's three pubs all serve counter meals – the ***Koonya*** bistro is the cheapest. ***Big Joe's Bistro*** *(77 Ocean Beach Rd)* is a casual pizza and pasta parlour, with a take-away section at the front and dining area out back.

Buckley's Chance *(174 Ocean Beach Rd)* is a busy pancake joint. The menu is mostly crêpes, and pancakes from $6.50 to $12, and desserts from $6.50 to $8, and they have a few other meals from $9 to $12. They also have an inexpensive lunch menu. The ***Smokehouse*** *(☎ 5984 1246, 182 Ocean Beach Rd)* is a stylish and very popular place – you'll need to book during the peak season. They serve great gourmet pizzas from a wood-fired oven ($10 to $15), pastas, risottos and grills ($12.50 to $16.50) and main meals from $14 to $22.

Entertainment

Like most seasonal resorts, the peninsula comes alive in summer and buzzes for three months before going into hibernation for the rest of the year. The peninsula's pub scene is always lively, with two of the most popular spots being the ***Continental Hotel*** (with a nightclub that stays open till late) in Sorrento and the ***Portsea Hotel*** in Portsea.

PORTSEA

Portsea, at the eastern tip of the peninsula, is where many of Melbourne's most wealthy families have built their seaside mansions, and the small town has an unmistakable but subtle air of privilege. And not so subtle. That little blue bathing box on the beach? It was snapped up for $185,000 in 1999.

Portsea has some great beaches. At the back beach there's the impressive natural rock formation known as **London Bridge**, plus a cliff where hang-gliders leap into the void. This ocean beach has good surf and can be dangerous for swimming, so head for the life-saving club and swim between the flags where the bronzed Aussies can keep an eye on you. The front beaches are safer for swimming, and if things get too hot on the sand you can always wander up to the pub and enjoy a drink in the pretty (and usually pretty crowded) beer garden that overlooks the pier.

Diving & Snorkelling

Portsea is a popular diving centre, and there are a couple of companies on Nepean Hwy, near the pub, that operate trips. Dive Victoria (☎ 5984 3155) offers one-day beginner's dives (from $120, including gear and two dives) and snorkelling trips ($30 plus $15 for gear hire).

Mornington Peninsula National Park

After being off-limits to the general public for over 100 years because it was a quarantine station and army base, Point Nepean National Park on the tip of the peninsula was opened to the public in 1988. It has since expanded (and been renamed) to include the ocean beaches up to Cape Schanck and another large chunk called Green Bush.

There's an excellent Visitors Centre (☎ 5984 4276) near the entrance. Admission costs $8.50 for adults, $4.50 for children and $19 for families if you want to take the two to four-hour bus tour, less if you want to walk. You need to book if you're taking the bus tour and even if you aren't, booking is a good idea because visitor numbers are restricted.

At the entrance to the park are two historic gun barrels that fired the first Allied shots in both WWI and WWII.

There are several good walks, some quite long, and you can find yourself alone on wild surf beaches. Swimming is dangerous. The visitors centre has details of walks. On the fourth weekend of every month, the park holds 'bike & hike' days where, for a reduced entry fee of $5.50, cyclists and walkers can explore the park at their leisure. If you're cycling, you'll need a helmet and a lock – bikes aren't allowed on the walking tracks, so you'll have to leave them beside the roadway to explore the best parts of the park.

Places to Stay

Accommodation in Portsea is somewhat limited, and generally more expensive than elsewhere on the peninsula. The cheapest option is the ***Portsea Hotel*** *(☎ 5984 2213)*, which has comfortable and clean rooms with shared facilities from $60 plus a few en suite rooms from $110. Nearby, ***Portsea Village*** *(☎ 5984 8484)* is an executive-style multi-level complex with one, two and three-bedroom apartments ranging from $175 to $400 per night.

The ultimate in luxury accommodation is the ***Peppers Delgany Portsea*** *(☎ 5984 4000)*, an international standard resort hotel in a magnificent old limestone castle on five hectares of private gardens. Rooms range from $275 to $395 a night, and dinner B&B packages start from $368 a double. See also Places to Eat.

Places to Eat

Portsea has a couple of cafes and takeaways, as well as the ever-popular ***Portsea Hotel***, which serves upmarket pub food and has a great beer garden that overlooks the pier and the bay. Mains range from $12 to $20.

At the other end of the price scale is the dining room at the exclusive ***Peppers Delgany Portsea***. The food will be wonderful, the service impeccable. This place is very expensive for dinner (about $70 a head plus drinks), but they have good Sunday lunches at $40 for two courses or $48 for three courses.

> **The First Shot**
>
> In August 1914 a German ship was on its way out from Melbourne to the Heads when news of the declaration of war came through on the telegraph. A shot across its bows at Portsea resulted in its capture. The first shot in WWII turned out to be at an unidentified Tasmanian freighter!
>
> **Mark Armstrong**

OCEAN BEACHES – PORTSEA TO FLINDERS

The south-western coastline of the peninsula faces Bass Strait. Along here are the beautiful and rugged ocean beaches of Blairgowrie, Rye, St Andrews, Gunnamatta and Cape Schanck. There are a series of points and bays and a backdrop of cliffs, sand dunes, spectacular scenery and tidal rock pools – this is the fragile natural habitat of coastal birdlife, surfers and rock-fishing people.

Surf life-saving clubs operate at Gunnamatta and Portsea during summer. There have been quite a few drownings along this stretch of coast, so only swim in patrolled areas.

At Cape Schanck is the **Cape Schanck Lighthouse Station** (☎ 5988 6154), an operational lighthouse built in 1859 with a kiosk, museum and information centre. It's open daily from 10 am to around 4 pm and admission to the site is $2. Guided tours are held half-hourly in summer, less often at other times, and cost $6 for adults, $4 for children. Cape Schanck is now part of the Mornington Peninsula National Park (see the earlier section) but admission to this section of the park is free during the week and $3.50 per car on weekends. There are some great walks here.

Main Creek, which runs up the centre of the peninsula from Cape Schanck, is the dividing line between the infertile and sandy areas to the west, and the rich and fertile soils on the eastern side of the creek.

Off the road from Cape Schanck to Flinders is a gravel turn-off to the **Blowhole**, and the rock platforms along here are accessible at low tide.

Places to Stay

Ace-Hi Ranch *(☎ 5988 6262)* in Cape Schanck is a family-style horse riding ranch with self-contained four to seven-berth cabins costing $50 a double, plus $15 per extra adult. A short horse ride costs $15, a two hour ride is $25 and a 2¾ hour bush and beach ride is $35.

WESTERN PORT – FLINDERS TO HASTINGS

Western Port Bay starts at the town of **Flinders**, which is a pretty village with a busy fishing fleet, good rocky point breaks for surfers, excellent oceanside golf course and views across to Phillip Island from the point at West Head. A naval gunnery range based here fires at offshore targets, so don't panic if you hear the occasional loud explosion (unless you're in a boat about 3km offshore). On one side of the point is a protected harbour with a jetty, and the oceanside beaches are more rugged and windswept. If the wind is south-easterly, you'll often see hang-gliders launching off the cliff-tops here.

Towns on this coast are not as developed and crowded as those on Port Phillip, and the natural environment on this part of the peninsula is more fertile and 'European', with pine trees and rolling green hills – in stark contrast with the sand dunes and coastal scrub of the western side of the peninsula. There are good beaches all the way along here at Shoreham, Point Leo (which also has good surf beaches), Merricks, Balnarring, Somers and Hastings.

Head inland from Shoreham for some great scenic drives and good exploring around Red Hill and Main Ridge. The hills and bushlands make an appealing change from the coastal scenery, and there are some great craft galleries, produce stores and wineries to stumble across (see Wineries below).

Coolart Homestead, on Lord Somers Rd in Somers, is a historic mansion with some interesting old photos, landscaped gardens, nature displays and a great wetlands sanctuary with a wide variety of birdlife – it has seven distinct habitats and 150 bird species. It opens daily from 11 am to 5 pm.

In Baxter is **Mulberry Hill**, the former home of Joan and Sir Daryl Lindsay, which opens on Sunday for tours at 1.30, 2.15 and 3 pm. (Joan wrote *Picnic at Hanging Rock*, Sir Daryl was a noted Australian painter.)

Places to Stay

Flinders The ***Flinders Hotel*** *(☎ 5989 0201)* has a few motel-style units behind the pub from $65/75 for singles/doubles, or there's ***Flinders Cove Motel*** *(☎ 5989 0666)* across the road, which has a three day minimum stay, with rooms from $99.

Shoreham ***Black Rabbit*** *(☎ 5989 8500, Hillcrest Rd)* is a modern limestone villa on a bushland property with fine views of Western Port. The two double rooms in the main house start at $150 and self-contained units at $130. It also has a synthetic-grass tennis court.

Main Ridge ***Pines Ridge Retreat*** *(☎ 5989 6170, Main Creek Rd in Main Ridge)* is a B&B with singles/doubles from $75/95.

Places to Eat

Flinders The bistro at the ***Flinders Hotel*** has a reputation for serving food a cut above the standard pub fare, and also specialises in local wines at reasonable prices. On Cook St, the ***Flinders Bakery*** bakes wonderful natural breads in old-fashioned wood-fired ovens.

Red Hill Red Hill also has a few good restaurants, which are harder to find because they're tucked away inland among the hills and trees. ***Poffs'*** *(☎ 5989 2566)*, on Red Hill Rd not far from the recreation reserve, is an atmospheric and very popular local eatery. The chef is Russian and the menu has Baltic influences but is broadly international, with mains mostly in the $20 to $24 range. It's open Thursday to Sunday for lunch and Friday to Sunday for dinner.

In the small shopping centre in Red Hill Rd, ***Red Hill Bakery*** is a local favourite – everything is freshly baked, and the aromas are enough to whet any appetite.

It's quite an experience to dine at ***Villa Primavera Vineyard*** *(☎ 5989 2129)*. They serve hearty Italian provincial-style lunches on Sunday and dinners on Friday and Saturday, where everyone sits at the same long table. Expect to pay around $40 a head, wine is extra. They have a range of wines available.

WINERIES

In the last decade the Mornington Peninsula has blossomed into one of Victoria's prime wine-producing regions. Wedged between the two bays, the peninsula's fertile soils, temperate climate and rolling hills are now producing consistently good wines, although they tend to be relatively expensive due to the high cost of real estate this close to Melbourne. The region is particularly noted for its pinot noir, but also produces good shiraz, chardonnay and other wines.

There are dozens of wineries, mostly in the elevated central area around Red Hill and Main Ridge. Most of these are small-level producers, and many are individually run. More than 20 of the wineries are open to the public on weekends, and those open daily include **Dromana Estate**, **Hann's Creek Estate**, **Hickinbotham of Dromana**, **Main Ridge Estate**, **Red Hill Estate**, **Stonier's Winery at Merricks**, the **Briars Vineyard** and **T'Gallant at Darling Park**.

A map and brochure is available from information centres and from the wineries themselves, or you can contact the Mornington Peninsula Vigneron's Association on ☎ 5987 3822.

FRENCH ISLAND

Off the coast in Western Port, French Island was once a prison farm and is virtually undeveloped. Only around 70 people live on the island, two-thirds of which is now an 11,000 hectare national park, and the main attractions are bushwalks, bike rides, mutton-bird rookeries and the thriving koala population. Actually, the koalas are thriving too much for their own good, and 200 a year are deported to the mainland to keep the numbers at a sustainable level.

There are whole day, half-day and shorter walks and bike rides starting at Tankerton Foreshore Reserve.

For information call ☎ 5980 1241; there's a ranger station by the ferry pier.

There's accommodation at the remote old prison farm (☎ 5678 0155) 2km from the ferry. Pick-ups can be arranged for $10 per person or included as part of a package. Cells cost $15/25, and family dorms are $55 – if you prefer your windows without bars, try the guesthouse for $65 per person. Alternatively you can camp in the national park. There are toilets and drinking water (the only water available in the park) at the Fairhaven campsite on the western shore. Note that you aren't allowed to light fires at any time, so bring a fuel stove. Tankerton General Store is the only place to buy supplies, and the stock is limited.

Inter Island Ferries (☎ 9585 5730) runs between Stony Point on Mornington Peninsula and Phillip Island via French Island, charging $8 one way. There's at least one trip each day all year. A train runs between Melbourne and Stony Point; see the Mornington Peninsula Getting There & Away section for details.

Phillip Island

At the entrance to Western Port, and 125km south-east of Melbourne by road, Phillip Island is a very popular holiday resort for Melburnians. Its winter population of around 5000 swells to 40,000 in summer. The island's main claim to fame is its selection of excellent beaches, from the world-renowned surf at 67 and the other south coast beaches, to sheltered bay beaches on the north side. Inland, the island has mostly been cleared for farming and isn't especially attractive.

Phillip Island's penguin parade is one of Australia's most popular tourist attractions.

The island was used by Aborigines as a pantry until they were hunted off by 19th century sealers.

Orientation & Information

The island is about 100 sq km in area. It is connected to the mainland by a bridge across the Narrows from San Remo to Newhaven. San Remo has quite a few shops, motels and a couple of pubs, and it's home to most of the island's fishing fleet – the co-op near the bridge sells fresh fish and crayfish.

Cowes, on the north coast, is the main town on the island and has pleasant sheltered beaches, as well as banks, pubs, motels, caravan parks, restaurants, snack bars and other amenities, most of which are along Thompson Ave (the road in from Melbourne) or the Esplanade.

The south of the island has surf beaches like Woolamai, Berry's Beach and Summerland (home of the famous penguin parade). Rhyll is a small fishing village on the east of the island and has the island's main boat ramp, while Ventnor is another small settlement on the west coast.

The island's information centre (☎ 5956 7447) is on the main road near Newhaven, just after you cross the bridge. It is open daily from 9 am to 5 pm.

PENGUIN PARADE

Every evening at Summerland Beach the Little Penguins that nest there perform their 'parade', emerging from the sea and waddling resolutely up the beach to their nests – seemingly oblivious of the sightseers. The penguins are there year-round, but they arrive in larger numbers in the summer when they are rearing their young. The parade takes place like clockwork a few minutes after sunset each day and it is a major tourist attraction. There are crowds of up to 4000 people, especially on weekends and holidays, so bookings should be made at the information centre near Newhaven, or at Phillip Island Nature Park (☎ 5956 8300 for recorded information) – the name of the penguin reserve. There's a visitor centre, open from 10 am every day.

The admission charges for the Penguin Parade are $9.50 for adults, $5 for children or $24.50 for families.

SEAL ROCKS & THE NOBBIES

Off Point Grant, the extreme south-west tip of the island, a group of rocks called the Nobbies rises from the sea. Beyond these are Seal Rocks, which are inhabited by Australia's largest colony of fur seals. The rocks are most crowded during the breeding season from October to December, when up to 6000 seals arrive.

The new **Sea Life Centre**, (☎ 1300 367 325) has some interesting displays, including live close-up video of the seals, but the really exciting project is a planned 2km submarine tunnel out to the rocks themselves. That's some way off yet. At the moment admission is a hefty $15 for adults, $7.50 for children.

See Organised Tours, Flights & Cruises for cruises to Seal Rocks.

BEACHES

The ocean beaches are on the south side and there's a life-saving club at Woolamai – this beach is notorious for its strong rips and currents, so swim only between the flags. If you're not a good swimmer, head for the bay beaches around Cowes, or the quieter ocean beaches such as Smith's.

There are quite a few surf shops that rent equipment, and plenty of excellent breaks from Cat Bay to Woolamai. Island Surfboards (☎ 5952 3443) at Smith's Beach has surfing lessons for $25.

Dive Phillip Island (☎ 5674 2382) rents diving equipment and runs NASDS courses.

KOALAS & OTHER WILDLIFE

Phillip Island was once promoted as a good place to see koalas 'in the wild'. However, as development increased, their habitat was degraded to the point where they were living in defoliated trees in badly managed roadside reserves. Introduced diseases and road accidents were also taking their toll.

Nowadays the best place to see koalas is at the **Koala Conservation Centre** at Fiveways on the Phillip Island Tourist Rd. There's a visitor area and elevated boardwalks (so you can see what goes on in the treetops) running through a bush setting. Admission is $5 for adults and $2 for kids; the centre opens from 10 am to 6 pm.

Phillip Island Wildlife Park, on Thompson Ave about 1km south of Cowes, has a good range of animals and is open daily. Admission costs $9 for adults, $4.50 for children, $25 for families. Off the island, on the highway about 10km from San Remo, **Wildlife Wonderland** also has native animals, plus giant Gippsland earthworms. Admission costs $10.90/5.90 for adults/children, and it's open from 10 am.

Birds

There are mutton-bird colonies, particularly in the sand dunes around Cape Woolamai. These birds, which are actually called shearwaters, are amazingly predictable: they arrive back on the island on exactly the same day each year – 24 September – from their migration flight from Japan and Alaska. They stay on the island until April. Your best chance of seeing them is at the penguin parade, as they fly in low over the sea each evening at dusk in the spring and summer months, or at the Forest Caves Reserve at Woolamai Beach.

You'll also find a wide variety of water birds, including pelicans (which are fed at Newhaven daily at 11.30 am), ibis and swans in the swampland at the Nits at Rhyll.

OTHER ATTRACTIONS

The old **Motor Racing Circuit** was revamped to stage the Australian Motorcycle Grand Prix in 1989. After moving to Sydney it has returned to Phillip Island and seems set to stay here. There's a visitor centre open from 10 am daily.

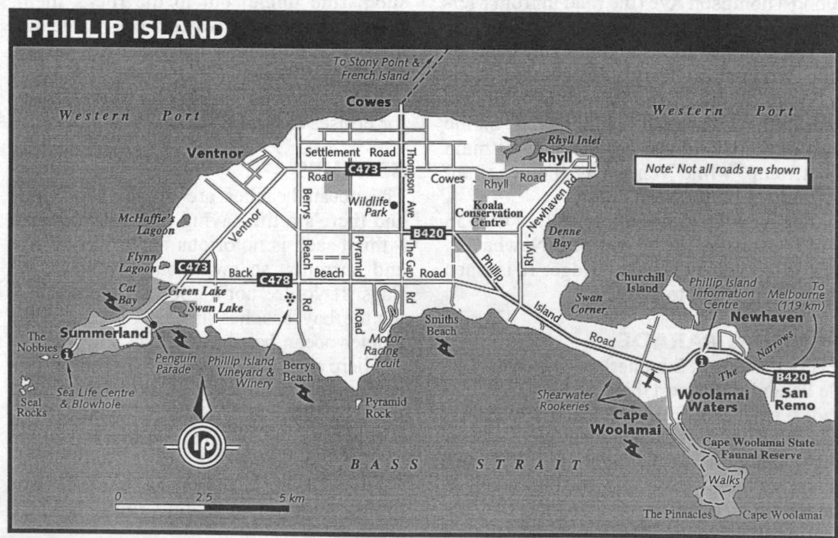

There are some walking tracks and a few cycling tracks. Rugged **Cape Woolamai** with its walking track is particularly impressive. Access to the signposted walking trail is from the Woolamai surf beach near the life-saving club. The information centre and Amaroo Park Backpackers have information on other walks.

Small **Churchill Island** has a historic homestead and beautiful gardens. The island is connected to Phillip Island by a narrow bridge and the turn-off is signposted about 1km out of Newhaven. Very occasionally a combination of high tides and wind closes the bridge. The island is open from 10 am to 4 pm daily, and admission costs $5 for adults and $2 for kids.

There's a **museum** in the Heritage Centre on Thompson Ave in Cowes. It's open on Saturday morning and Sunday afternoon all year, plus some weekday afternoons during school holidays. Admission is $1/20c for adults/kids.

ORGANISED TOURS, FLIGHTS & CRUISES

Island Scenic Tours (☎ 5952 1042) runs trips most nights from Cowes out to the penguin parade ($18, which includes entry). Other tours include a three hour scenic tour ($18). Amaroo Park Backpackers also operates an evening service out to the penguin parade. Phillip Island airport (☎ 5956 7316) operates scenic flights ranging from a 15 minute zip around Cape Woolamai $32 per person) to a 45 minute loop around Western Port ($80 per person).

Bay Connections Cruises (☎ 5678 5642) runs a variety of cruises, including trips to Seal Rocks ($35), and to French Island ($40; includes a bus tour of the island) from Cowes' jetty, and evening 'shearwater cruises' ($27) from San Remo. You can book at the rotunda on Cowes foreshore or at King Neptune Crafts (☎ 5678 5642) at 139 Marine Pde in San Remo. Cruises are much more frequent in summer and school holidays, but there are some in the off season.

Surefoot Explorations (☎ 5952 1533) introduce you to various aspects of the island's history, ecology and wildlife: from rock pools to stargazing.

PLACES TO STAY

Phillip Island is a very popular holiday destination, so there are all sorts of hostels, guesthouses, B&B's, motels, holiday flats and campsites in Cowes, Newhaven, Rhyll, Ventnor and San Remo.

Vacancies can be scarce at Christmas, Easter and during school holidays. Tariffs are also higher during these times. The island's information centre has an accommodation booking service.

Unless otherwise stated, the places mentioned below are all in Cowes.

Camping, Caravan Parks & Hostels

Note that you aren't allowed to camp or even sleep in your car in any public area on the island.

There are about a dozen caravan parks and about half of them are in Cowes. Generally, sites range seasonally from $15 to $27, and on-site vans and cabins cost anywhere from $35 to $85 per night.

The best backpackers' accommodation is at the very friendly ***Amaroo Park YHA*** *(☎ 5952 2548, corner Church and Osborne Sts)*, close to the centre of Cowes. It's a good and popular hostel attached to a caravan park and charges $14 in dorms ($17 for non-members) doubles at $17 per person ($20 for non-members) and tent sites at $7 per person ($10 for non-members). The facilities are good and a number of excursions can be arranged. V/Line bus drivers will usually drop you off at the door and the hostel also runs Duck Truck packages, with three nights accommodation, two meals, entry to the Penguin Parade, an island tour, bike hire and transport to and from Melbourne – all for $75.

The caravan park has sites from $14 to $16, on-site tents for $16 and vans and cabins from $35 to $77 a double.

Other caravan parks in the vicinity include ***Anchor Belle Holiday Park*** *(☎ 5952 2258, 272 Church St)* and ***Kaloha Caravan***

Park (☎ *5952 2179, corner Chapel and Steele Sts)*, which is about 200m from the beach and close to the centre.

Pubs & Motels

There are more than 20 pubs and motels on the island, so you have plenty to choose from.

The ***Isle of Wight Hotel*** (☎ *5952 2301)* is in a prominent position opposite the beach in Cowes on the Esplanade, and has motel rooms out the back from $37/47 a single/double. Prices rise in summer.

Farther along the Esplanade is ***The Continental*** (☎ *5952 2316)*, a modern executive-style complex with two restaurants, standard rooms from $109 a double and deluxe suites from $169 a double. Also on the Esplanade is ***The Anchor at Cowes*** (☎ *5952 1351)*, with a good restaurant, motel units and suites ($62 to $72) and self-contained townhouses (from $92).

There are several motels along Thompson Ave, the main road into Cowes. They include the ***Hollydene Motel*** (☎ *5952 2311)* at No 114, with a good restaurant and rooms from $48, and ***Banfield's*** (☎ *5952 2486)* at No 192, a large family-style motel with a bistro, cinema, swimming pool and singles/doubles from $68/75.

Holiday Units

Flats are an option worth considering if you have a few people together, want to cater for yourself and intend to stay for a while. ***Bayside Holiday Units*** (☎ *5952 2058, Beach St)* has units sleeping from four people and costing from $60 to $100 a night, with a laundry, pool and spa. ***Parkview Luxury Flats*** (☎ *5952 1496, 2 Park St)* are in a quiet part of Cowes, and these two-bedroom units cost up to $170 a night, depending on the time of year and the number of people.

Guesthouses, Cottages & B&Bs

Rothsaye on Lovers Walk (☎ *5952 2057, 2 Roy Crt)* is on the beach and offers very well-equipped cottages from $120 to $160. ***Rhylston Park*** (☎ *5952 2730, 190 Thompson Ave)*, near the centre of Cowes, is a restored 1886 homestead with period fittings and furnishings, set in two hectares of gardens. They have five guestrooms, one with an en suite and the others with shared facilities; singles/doubles cost from $85/95.

Narabeen Cottage (☎ *5952 2062, 16 Steele St)* is a 'gourmet getaway' in a comfortable old timber cottage with five guestrooms and a small restaurant. B&B costs from $110 a double, or $195 with dinner included.

Cliff Top Country House (☎ *5952 1033, 1 Marlin St)* overlooking Smiths Beach is a great place to unwind while enjoying stunning views from private verandahs or the comfort of a hammock. Doubles start at $140 in this kid-free retreat.

Closest to the Penguin Parade, and signposted from the main road, is ***Penguin Hill Country House B&B*** (☎ *5956 8777)*. Doubles are tastefully furnished with period pieces and cost from $120.

PLACES TO EAT

Cowes

Cowes has the standard collection of greasy-spoon take-aways, pizza joints and Chinese restaurants, as well as quite a few good restaurants. Most eateries are along the Esplanade or Thompson Ave, which intersect.

Isola de Capri on the main corner has a good reputation. It's a bustling Italian bistro overlooking Western Port, with pizzas and pastas from $12 to $15 and chicken, steak and seafood dishes from around $14. At 81 Thompson Ave, ***Wing Ho*** serves up Chinese tucker at reasonable prices. Along the Esplanade you'll find the more upmarket places. The ***Jetty*** (☎ *5952 2060)*, on the main corner, has an attractive dining area on four levels, an upstairs cocktail bar and a cheaper cafe, ***TVR***, next door. The food is good – they specialise in seafood but also have steaks, pastas, game and vegetarian dishes – with most mains in the $17 to $20 range. Farther along, the ***Isle of Wight Hotel*** has fairly straightforward pub meals in either the bar or the upstairs bistro area. Specials can cost as little as $5. A little farther along, ***The Clock Cafe*** is a very pleasant place for a coffee or a light meal.

RICHARD NEBESKY

Studying the form, Caulfield Racecourse

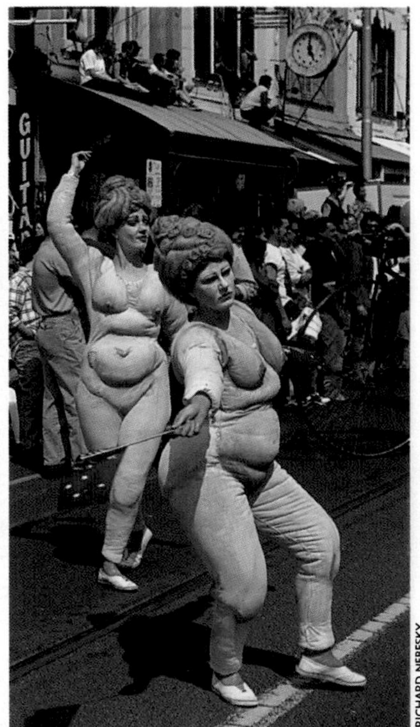
RICHARD NEBESKY

Fringe Festival parade, Brunswick Street, Fitzroy

RICHARD NEBESKY

St Kilda beach sunset

RICHARD I'ANSON

A beautiful river red gum frames Flinders Peak, You Yangs Forest Park

RICHARD I'ANSON

Boatshed in autumn, Alfred Nicholas Memorial Gardens, Dandenong

Charmandene Cottage *(☎ 5952 1386)*, set in a quaint timber cottage at 27-31 Osbourne Ave (the westward continuation of the Esplanade), specialises in old-fashioned roast dinners – beef, pork and lamb with vegies, salads and great puddings and desserts – all for $20 a head. They're open every weekend and daily during holiday seasons – it's a good idea to book.

Around Cowes

There are a couple of other good eateries outside Cowes. At the ***Phillip Island Vineyard & Winery*** on Berrys Beach Rd, you can sample their wines and at the same time tuck into gourmet platters of cheese, terrine, smoked salmon, pâté etc all of which are relatively inexpensive.

Dutchie's Stone Grill *(☎ 5956 6000, corner Phillip Island and Woolamai Rds, Woolamai)* is an interesting place. You cook your own steak, chicken or seafood grills at your table over red-hot stones, and they have a three course menu at $27 a head.

ENTERTAINMENT

During the high season the island is fairly lively, with live bands playing at several of the pubs, but at other times things can be pretty quiet. The ***Isle of Wight Hotel*** in Cowes has live bands, including good jam sessions in its intimate 'cocktail bar'.

Banfields Theatre Bar & Bistro *(☎ 5952 2088, 192 Thompson Ave, Cowes)* has a reasonably priced bistro with a bar and live music most Saturday nights. They also have a 200-seat cinema that screens latest releases on most nights and during the day in the holiday seasons.

GETTING THERE & AWAY

Car & Motorbike

From Melbourne, take the South-Eastern Arterial (M1; soon to become a toll-road) and take the Phillip Island exit onto the South Gippsland Hwy (M420) around Cranbourne. The alternative to the M1 is a slow trip out St Kilda and Dandenong Rds on the Princes Hwy.

Bus

V/Line's daily bus service between Melbourne and Cowes costs $13.50 and takes 2¼ hours. See the earlier Camping, Caravan Parks & Hostels section for the Duck Truck.

Ferry

Inter Island Ferries (☎ 9585 5730) runs between Stony Point on Mornington Peninsula and Phillip Island via French Island, charging $7.50. There's at least one trip each day all year. A train runs between Melbourne and Stony Point (see the Mornington Peninsula Getting There & Away section for details).

Bay Connections (☎ 5678 642) also runs a ferry between Stony Point and Cowes ($15), via French Island but not daily and not at all in winter.

GETTING AROUND

There is no public transport around the island. You can hire bikes from Phillip Island Bike Hire (☎ 5952 2381), 11 Findlay St in Cowes, and from Amaroo Park Backpackers.

Great Ocean Road & South-West Coast

The Great Ocean Road (B100), which runs between Anglesea and Warrnambool, is one of the world's most spectacular coastal routes. It takes you on a journey of dramatic contrasts around the south-west coast of Victoria. It has lush rainforests, sheer and ragged cliffs, idyllic sandy beaches, mountains and forests of towering eucalypts, intriguing rock formations, great state and national parks and charming seaside settlements.

Until the road was built, the small coastal settlements were only accessible by boat or rough inland roads. Coach tracks were built along some sections, but these were never linked and were impassable in bad weather.

The idea for the Great Ocean Rd originated with the head of the Country Roads Board, who foresaw a tourist road 'of world repute, rivalling California'. The project was dedicated to those who gave their lives in WWI. Construction started in August 1918, employing over 3000 ex-servicemen. During the Great Depression, unemployed men or 'susso workers', as they were called, were hired on sustenance pay to work on the road. It was finally completed in 1932.

The most famous section of the Great Ocean Rd is the Port Campbell National Park, which features an amazing collection of natural rock sculptures, including the Twelve Apostles, London Bridge and the Loch Ard Gorge, all carved out of the soft limestone headland by fierce ocean waves.

Perhaps the most spectacular section of the road is between Lorne and Apollo Bay, featuring the beautiful contrast of the ocean on one side and the forests and mountains of the Otway Ranges on the other. This is an area of great natural beauty and well worth exploring, with scenic drives, walking trails, waterfalls and tiny hillside townships. Within the Otways, the Angahook-Lorne State Park features some of the best and most

HIGHLIGHTS

- Playing the kangaroo-covered golf course (preferably without collecting a roo) at Anglesea
- The beaches, bushwalks, bike rides and horse rides of Aireys Inlet
- Lorne's beaches, cafes and restaurants, cottages and cabins, and great bushwalks in the nearby Angahook-Lorne State Park
- The Apollo Bay Music Festival
- Otway Ranges, for hiking and leisurely scenic drives
- The Great Ocean Road
- Port Campbell National Park's bizarre rock formations
- Port Fairy's historic guesthouses and B&Bs and the Port Fairy Folk Festival in March
- The Great South-West Walk, which winds from Portland to Nelson

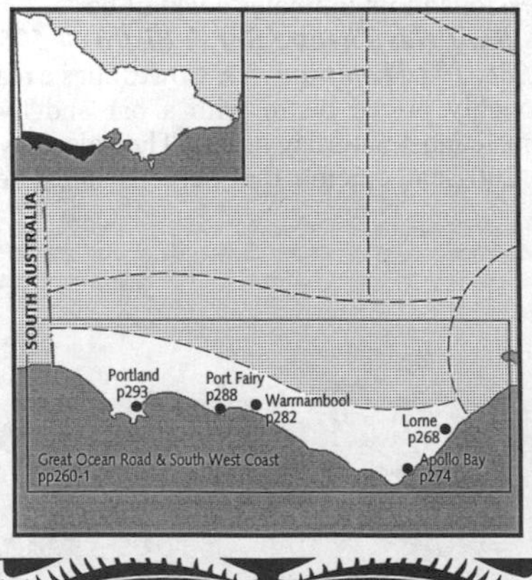

GREAT OCEAN ROAD

popular bushwalks in the state. The Otway National Park, at the southernmost tip of this coast, is another natural wonderland.

Lorne is the most popular of the coastal townships along the road, combining great beaches, bushwalks and good food with a wide range of accommodation. Apollo Bay is another great spot.

Beyond Warrnambool there's Port Fairy, a historic fishing village; Portland, the site of Victoria's first permanent European settlement; the Lower Glenelg National Park; and the Discovery Bay Coastal Park.

Information

The accredited visitor information centres are in Lorne, Apollo Bay, Warrnambool, Port Fairy and Portland – all are open daily from 9 am to 5 pm. In addition, there are smaller tourist offices in Torquay and Port Campbell.

There are several Parks Victoria offices throughout this region – contact details are listed under individual towns throughout this chapter, or you can call the Parks Victoria hotline on ☎ 13 19 63.

Activities

There are some great swimming and surfing beaches along the stretch of coast between Torquay and Apollo Bay. The beaches between Capê Otway and Warrnambool are much more rugged and less accessible, but there are good surfing and swimming beaches farther west around Warrnambool, Port Fairy and Portland.

This is a spectacular area for bushwalkers, with plenty of short and long walking trails through the lovely Otway Ranges in the hinterland between Aireys Inlet and Cape Otway. For longer hikes, the Shipwreck Trail follows the treacherous coastline from Princetown to Port Fairy, and the 250km Great South-West Walk takes you through the coastal wilderness between Portland and Nelson.

You'll find horse-riding ranches right along the coast, canoeing trips from Lorne and through the Lower Glenelg National Park near Nelson, mountain-bike tours (see Organised Tours following) and lots more.

A word of warning for cyclists, however – the Great Ocean Rd may be very scenic, but it's also narrow and dangerous, and is not a recommended cycling route. Head for the hills instead, where the roads are quieter and the countryside very beautiful.

There are plenty of fishing opportunities for keen anglers – pick up a *Fishing Guide* brochure from the Torquay tourist information centre.

Organised Tours

The larger bus-tour companies run tours along the Great Ocean Rd from Melbourne. Some smaller companies such as Autopia Tours (☎ 9326 5536) and Let's Go Bush Tours (☎ 9662 3969) run fun-oriented small-group tours for backpackers to this area. See the Organised Tours section in the Melbourne chapter for details.

Another good way to see this part of the country is on the Wayward Bus (☎ 1800 882 823 toll-free), which does a three day ramble from Melbourne to Adelaide following the coast all the way. See the Bus section in the Getting There & Away chapter for more details.

Otway Discovery Tours (☎ 9654 5432) runs day tours from Melbourne that visit many of the attractions for $50. Melbourne Sightseeing (☎ 9663 3388) also offers day trips ($83 for adults, $50 for YHA members).

A range of mountain-bike tours through the Otway Ranges and the Angahook-Lorne State Park are available from Great Ocean Road Adventure Tours (☎ 5289 6841). They cost from $30 a day depending on numbers. It can also arrange bushwalks and short bus tours, and offers special deals and accommodation for backpackers.

For information on other specialised tours, see the Organised Tours sections under individual towns in this chapter.

Accommodation

Accommodation along this coastal stretch is always heavily booked during the holiday seasons, particularly during the Christmas school holidays and Easter. Prices are higher during these times, and many places have a minimum stay of two nights or one week – book ahead.

There's a good range of campgrounds and caravan parks right along the coast. There are also some good budget accommodation options, with excellent backpackers' hostels in Lorne, Apollo Bay and Torquay, and other hostels in Anglesea, Fairhaven (near Aireys Inlet), Port Campbell, Warrnambool, Port Fairy and nearby Yambuk, and at Cape Otway.

You'll find plenty of motels along the coast, and the number of guesthouses, B&Bs and farmhouses offering accommodation is always increasing – it's impossible to list them all here, so check with the tourist offices for more options.

Often prices are higher in the peak season. Unless otherwise specified where two prices are quoted in this chapter they refer to off peak/peak season.

Getting There & Away

V/Line buses operate from Geelong train station along the Great Ocean Rd as far as Apollo Bay ($18) via Torquay ($4.50) and Lorne ($11.20) three times daily Monday to Friday, and twice daily on weekends. On Friday, a V/Line bus continues around the coast from Apollo Bay to Port Campbell and Warrnambool. All V/Line prices listed in this chapter are one-way fares.

McHarry's Bus Lines (☎ 5223 2111) has frequent bus services from Geelong to Torquay ($4.35 one way).

TORQUAY

• **pop 6000**

Torquay is a popular holiday town and the capital of Australia's booming surfing industry. There are loads of surf shops in town, with the big names like Rip Curl and Quicksilver based at the Surfcity Plaza complex

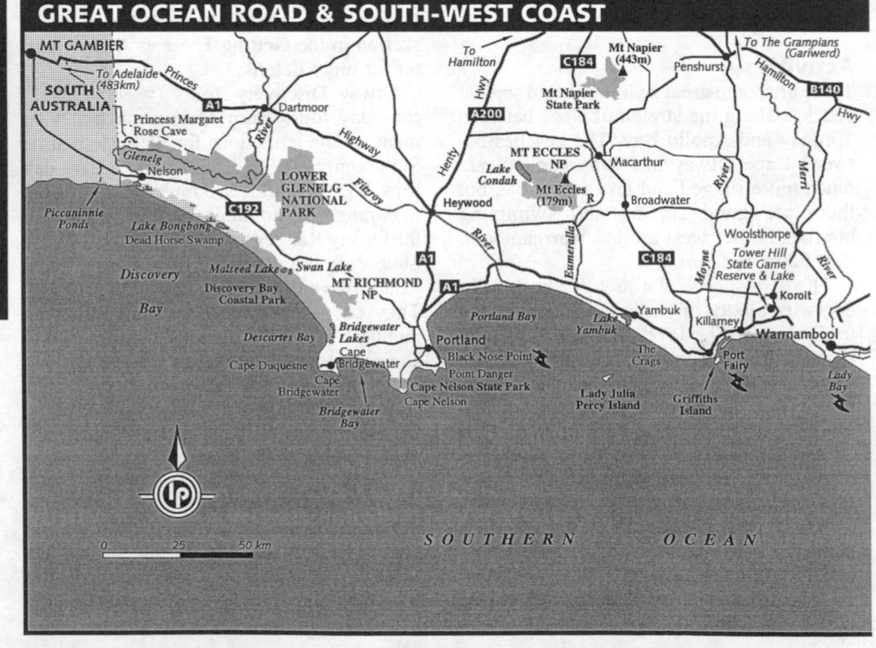

on the Surfcoast Highway. This complex is currently being extended to represent every major surfing label, so if you're in the market for surfboards, wetsuits, surf wear or equipment, this is the place to head for.

Information

The tourist information centre (☎ 5261 4219) is in the same building as Surfworld Australia Surfing Museum at the rear of the Surfcity Plaza complex. It has an impressive array of brochures on the region and also sells interesting surfing books. Its opening hours are weekdays from 9 am to 5 pm and weekends from 10 am to 4 pm.

Things to See & Do

At the rear of the Surfcity Plaza complex on the highway, the excellent **Surfworld Australia Surfing Museum** (☎ 5261 4606) features the Australian Surfing Hall of Fame, a wave-making tank, board-shaping demos, surf videos and lots more. Its opening hours are the same as for the information centre and entry costs $6 for adults ($4 for children, $16 for families).

Most of the action in Torquay revolves around the local beaches, which cater for everyone from paddlers to world-champion surfers. **Fisherman's Beach** is popular with families as it is protected from ocean swells. The **Front Beach** is ringed by Norfolk Island pines and sloping lawns, and the **Back Beach** is patrolled by members of the surf life-saving club during summer. About 3km south-west of Torquay, **Jan Juc's** sandy beaches are more exposed to the ocean swells – good news for serious surfers but a potentially dangerous spot for children or inexperienced swimmers.

Surfing gear can be hired at a number of shops on the highway opposite the Surfcity

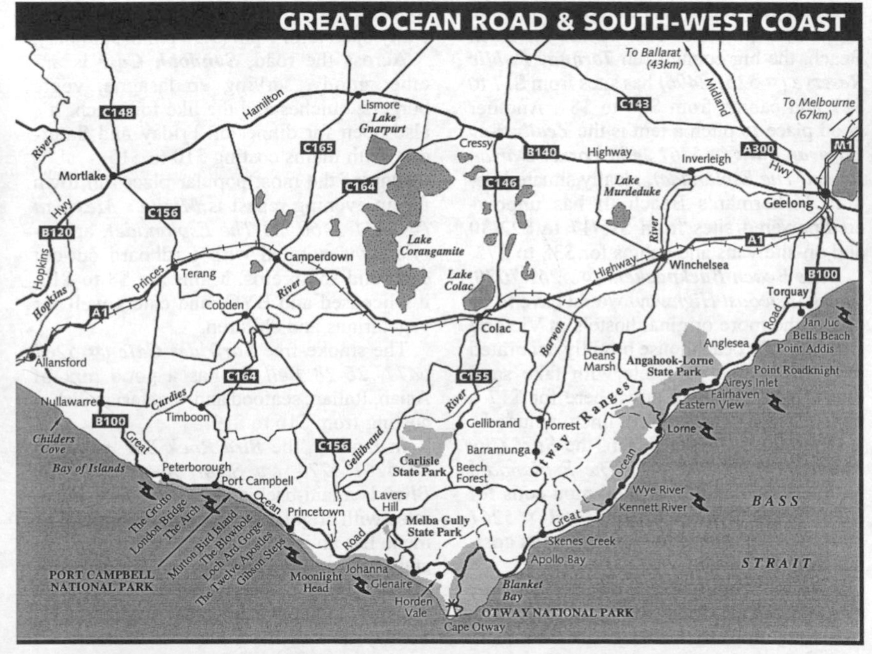

Plaza, or try the second-hand surf shops close by in Baines Court if you want to buy your own. To be taught by a professional, book surfing lessons with either Go Ride a Wave (☎ 5263 2111) or Westcoast Surf School (☎ 5261 2241). Two-hour group lessons for adults cost $30 and $25 respectively, with boards and wetsuits provided.

A great place to entertain the kids is **Tiger Moth World Adventure Park** (☎ 5261 5100), 5km north-east of Torquay on Blackgate Rd. It has daily air shows, canoes, a flying fox and loads of games, along with a cafe and aviation museum. It's open daily from 10 am to 5 pm and costs $7 for adults, $6 for children or $25 for families. It also has three vintage Tiger Moths – joy flights cost from $80, and longer tours in modern planes to places like the Twelve Apostles cost $70 per person for six people.

Places to Stay

Over summer and Easter, Torquay is flooded with campers and it can be hard to find a site in the caravan parks. Just behind the Back Beach, the big council-run ***Torquay Public Reserve*** *(☎ 5261 2496)* has sites from $17 to $27 and cabins from $60 to $87. Another good place to pitch a tent is the ***Zeally Bay Caravan Park*** *(☎ 5261 2400, corner Darian Rd and The Esplanade)*, ideally situated behind Fisherman's Beach. It has unpowered/powered sites from $15/17 to $22/30 and on-site vans and cabins for $38 to $75.

Bells Beach Backpackers *(☎ 5261 7070, 51-53 Surfcoast Highway)* would have to be one of the more original hostels in Victoria – it's a 1960s beachhouse brightly decorated in a surf theme complete with fake sand dunes. You can bunk down here for $17 a night ($20 in peak season), linen included.

Opposite the Front Beach, the ***Surf City Motel*** *(☎ 5261 3492, 35 The Esplanade)* has pleasant doubles with all mod cons for $79 to $134. ***Torquay Hotel/Motel*** *(☎ 5261 6046, 36 Bell St)* has basic motel units costing from $70 to $80.

For a more intimate getaway, try ***Torquay Beach B&B*** *(☎ 5261 4127, 6 Pride St)*, a two storey modern home close to the beach. Doubles cost from $100 to $130, which includes a magnificent breakfast. Another good option is ***Potter's Inn B&B*** *(☎ 5261 4131, 40 Bristol Rd)* where singles/doubles cost from $60/85, including breakfast served on a lovely garden deck. Pottery lessons can be arranged here with the host, professional potter Laurie Close.

Places to Eat

Gilbert St, which runs at a right angle to the Esplanade, is the main shopping area and has a supermarket, an organic fruit and vegie shop, a bakery and several delis and take-aways. At the beach end of Gilbert St, ***Yummy Yoghurt*** provides healthy fare such as flat bread sandwiches, felafels, cakes and great banana smoothies. Famous surfers have scribbled testimonials on the walls.

At the other end of Gilbert St, ***The Lapin Agile Cafe*** is a relaxed and inviting spot for a bite or cuppa, with great 1950s furniture and a good selection of magazines. It serves soups, bagels, muffins and pastas and is generally open until 7 pm (9.30 pm in summer).

Across the road, ***Sandbah Cafe*** is another goody, serving up lasagne, vegie burgers, quiches and the like for lunch. It's also open for dinner on Friday and Saturday, with mains costing $10 to $15.

One of the most popular places in town for an evening repast is ***Micha's Mexican*** *(☎ 5261 2460, 23 The Esplanade)*, appropriately decorated with cardboard cut-out cacti and sombreros. Mains are $8 to $13, it's licensed and BYO, and caters well for vegetarians and children.

The smoke-free ***Surfrider Cafe*** *(☎ 5261 6477, 26-28 Bell St)* has a good mix of Asian, Italian, seafood and vegetarian dishes costing from $16 to $19.

In Jan Juc, the ***Bird Rock Bar & Bistro*** *(☎ 5261 4774, cnr Stuart Ave and Ocean Blvd)* is a laid-back and inviting spot, decorated with bright murals and surf photos. The menu has an interesting mix of Italian, Thai and Mexican food and servings are generous and tasty, with mains costing from $9 to $15. It's open in the evening from Wednesday to Sunday, as well as for lunch on Sunday.

Getting There & Away

McHarry's Bus Lines (☎ 5223 2111) has frequent services from Geelong to Torquay ($4.35). In Torquay the buses arrive and depart from the corner of Pearl and Baston Sts, behind the Gilbert St shopping centre.

TORQUAY TO ANGLESEA

The Great Ocean Rd between Torquay and Anglesea heads slightly inland, with a turn-off about 7km from Torquay to the **Bells Beach Recreation Reserve.** The powerful point break at Bells has worked its way into surfing folklore and is the site of a world-championship surfing contest every Easter (see the boxed text 'Bells Surfing Classic'). Nine kilometres south-west of Torquay there's a turn-off to **Point Addis** – it's 3km down to the car parks, from where there are walking trails to the beaches, popular with surfers, hang-gliders and swimmers. Also here is the signposted **Koori Cultural Walk**, a 1km circuit trail to the beach through the **Ironbark Basin**, a nature reserve with abundant birdlife.

The **Surf Coast Walk** follows the coastline from Jan Juc to Moggs Creek, south of Aireys Inlet. The full distance takes about 11 hours, but the walk can be done in stages. The *Surf Coast Touring Map*, available from tourist offices in Geelong and along the coast, has this walk marked on it.

ANGLESEA

• **pop 2000**

Anglesea is a popular family-oriented seaside resort with good beaches and campgrounds. The town is built around the Anglesea River, which cuts through the hills from the north to the coast. There are numerous artists' galleries and studios in the town and surrounding areas, many of which are signposted off the main road.

Brochures are available from a tourist information board in the main shopping centre.

Things to See & Do

Anglesea is well known for the scenic **Anglesea Golf Club** (☎ 5263 1582), home to a large population of kangaroos that graze blithely on the fairways and around the greens as golfers fire golf balls around them. The course is in Noble St and is open to the public, with an 18 hole round costing $25 and club hire another $15.

There are some good beaches here, such as the sheltered **Point Roadknight**, which is popular with families. There are also great places to surf, and equipment can be hired from the Anglesea Surf Centre (☎ 5263 1530) on the corner of the Great Ocean Rd and McMillan St.

Good bushwalking areas and trails around the town include the Surf Coast Walk (see the Torquay to Anglesea section earlier). **Coogoorah Park** is a small bushland nature reserve beside the river, with a playground, picnic facilities and walking paths. These wetland areas are home to abundant birdlife.

Sea-Mist Stud (☎ 5288 7255), 17km north-west of town at Wensleydale, offers rides several times a day through state forest, costing $14 for one hour or $26 for two hours. The **Anglesea Hang Gliding School**

Bells Surfing Classic

Officially known as the 'Rip Curl Pro & Sun Smart Women's Classic', this world-championship tour event is one of the world's longest-running professional surfing contests, having been held annually since 1964.

Every year at Easter, Bells Beach attracts the world's top professional surfers and thousands of spectators over the five days of the contest. Heats and semis are run from Thursday to Easter Sunday, with the finals being held on the Monday. Autumn produces the biggest swells of the year, and waves have reached up to 6m during the contest.

General admission tickets cost $10 per day, or you can buy a cheaper four day pass. Contact Surfing Victoria (☎ 5261 2907) for more details.

Andrew Tudor

(☎ 015 841 107) offers introductory tandem flights as well as full certificate courses.

If your fishing skills need fine-tuning, **Anglesea Outdoors & Angling** (☎ 5263 3021) offers tuition, or if you're after some entertainment for the kids, try **Eco Logic Education & Environment Services** (☎ 5263 1133), which conducts activities such as 'marine rockpool rambles' and 'possum prowl nightwalks'.

Places to Stay

There are three caravan parks in Anglesea. Within earshot of the sea, the ***Anglesea Family Caravan Park*** *(☎ 5263 1583, Cameron Rd)* has powered sites from $17 to $24 and self-contained cabins and cottages from $47 (from $511 per week during summer and Easter). The well established ***Narambi Caravan Park*** *(☎ 5263 1362, 11 Camp Rd)* has sites from $15 and standard cabins from $40.

Anglesea Backpackers *(☎ 5263 2664, 40 Noble St)* is a spotless place run by a local surfie. Dorm beds cost from $15 to $17 and doubles with en suites cost from $20 per person. Noble St runs off the main road at the bridge and the hostel is a couple of blocks back this intersection.

The 1920s-style ***Debonair Guesthouse & Motel*** *(☎ 5263 1440, fax 5263 3239)* on the main road overlooking the Anglesea River offers guesthouse rooms (some with shared bathrooms) for $75 to $95 a double, including breakfast. There are also motel-style units available for $65 to $75. The guesthouse is due to be renovated, so these prices probably won't last.

There are a couple of modern motels on the main road: the friendliest of the two, ***Anglesea Motel*** *(☎ 5263 2600, 109 Great Ocean Rd)*, offers doubles costing from $99 to $149.

Perched on a hill with excellent panoramic bush views, ***Thornton Heath B&B*** *(☎ 5263 2542, 33 Pickworth Dve)* is sunny, homey and good value with tariffs from $50 per person per night.

Heading towards Lorne on the main road, the attractive ***Roadknight Cottages*** *(☎ 5263 1820, 26 Great Ocean Rd)* has self-contained cottages sleeping up to six people. Prices are based on a two night minimum stay – from $230 for four people plus $10 per extra person per night. Make sure you ask for a room with a view.

Sea-Mist Stud *(☎ 5288 7255)* has a bunkhouse and a unit, with B&B for $35 per person (see Things to See & Do earlier).

Places to Eat

In the main group of shops you'll find a bakery, a pizza/pasta restaurant, and ***Off Shore Cafe***, a good spot for breakfast and lunch with a selection of focaccia and ciabatta. Opposite, the excellent ***Olive Tree Cafe*** *(☎ 5263 1010)* is airy and inviting with a selection of fine fare for lunch and dinner. Evening meals such as salmon steaks and curries cost from $12 to $17.

The big, modern ***Anglesea Hotel*** *(☎ 5263 1210, 1 Murch Cres)* has a bistro where mains cost from $11 to $17. ***Shelles By The River*** *(☎ 5263 2500, 113 Great Ocean Rd)* is a fully licensed restaurant in a cosy cottage with open fires. Main meals are around $17 (though the menu is not extensive). ***Digger's***, behind the Shell service station on Diggers Pde, is a low-key little bistro with pastas, pizzas and other dishes for $7.50 to $12.50.

AIREYS INLET

• pop 760

Just south of Anglesea, the Great Ocean Rd finally meets the coast and starts its spectacular coastal run. Aireys Inlet, midway between Anglesea and Lorne, was originally established as a terminus for the Cobb & Co coach service from Geelong. In 1891, the lighthouse and keeper's cottages on Split Point were built, and the town gradually grew into a coastal holiday village. Many of the older beach-houses were destroyed by the Ash Wednesday bushfires of 1983, but much of the town has since been rebuilt.

Aireys has a good vibe, having largely managed to sidestep overdevelopment, and is popular with those who find Lorne just a little too trendy.

Things to See & Do

The **Split Point Lighthouse**, nicknamed the White Lady, sends out a beacon that can be seen from 30km offshore. There are walking tracks and a lookout point beside the lighthouse, and the former stables have been converted into a tearoom (which, incidentally, serves a fine cuppa).

There are some great **beaches** in Aireys, backed by tall volcanic cliffs with tidal pools along the foreshore, and volcanic rock stacks such as Eagle Rock and Table Rock rising from the ocean. Eagle Rock Pde runs around the foreshore, and there are car parks and walking tracks down to the beaches.

The **bark hut**, signposted off the main road, is a replica of an 1852 settler's hut which was destroyed by the 1983 fires. The hut was rebuilt by the descendants of its original owners, Thomas and Martha Pierce.

The Surf Coast Walk continues along the coast here, and there are also excellent bushwalks through the nearby Angahook-Lorne State Park. Signposted trails start from **Distillery Creek picnic ground**, 2.5km north, and the **Moggs Creek picnic ground**, 3km west of Aireys Inlet.

Blazing Saddles (☎ 5289 7322), about 2km inland, has good **horse rides** costing from $20 for 1¼ hours to $35 for a 2¼ hour beach ride.

Honey Anderson, of Bush to Beach Guided Walks (☎ 5289 6538), offers **wild-flower and cliff-top walks** ranging from one hour to a full day.

Places to Stay

The ***Aireys Inlet Caravan Park** (☎ 5289 6230, 19-25 Great Ocean Rd)* has camping sites from $15 to $20, standard cabins with en suite bathrooms from $45 to $65, and self-contained timber cottages for $80 to $95 a night.

***Bush to Beach B&B** (☎ 5289 6538, 43 Anderson St)*, a two storey, cedar cottage tucked away in a bushy setting, has two en suite guestrooms and doubles from $90. It's signposted but can be a bit tricky to find among all the dirt roads.

Set on a windswept cliff beside the White Lady, the stylish and homey ***Lighthouse Keeper's Cottages** (☎ 5289 6306, Federal St)*, which date from 1891, are two impressively converted self-contained cottages, comfortably fitted out with antique furniture and mod cons. Prices range from $140 to $165 a double.

Two kilometres inland in an idyllic farm setting beside the state forest, ***The Glen Farm Cottages** (☎ 5289 6306, Hartleys Rd)* is a collection of six self-contained mud-brick cottages that sleep from four to seven people and cost from $110 to $140 a night.

***Aireys Inlet Getaway** (☎ 5289 7021, mobile 0417 897 021, 2-4 Barton Court)*, back in town, consists of five massive villas, with all mod cons, that sleep up to eight people. They're good value with prices ranging from $220 to $300 per weekend for four people, with each extra person costing another $20 per night. Facilities include a swimming pool, spa and tennis court.

***The Lightkeeper's Inn** (☎ 5289 6666, 64 Great Ocean Rd)* is a motel with modern units costing from $70 to $100 a double.

In Fairhaven, 1.5km towards Lorne from Aireys, ***Surf Coast Backpackers** (☎ 5289 6886, mobile 0419 351 149, 5 Cowen Ave)* is an excellent hostel. A bunk bed in an airy, light-filled room with en suite facilities costs $17 a night.

Places to Eat

Next door to the quaint Aireys Inlet General Store on the main road, ***Crumps Cafe*** serves a range of sandwiches, bagels and cakes at good prices. The staff are friendly and there are plenty of magazines to keep you amused.

Ernie's Cantina** (☎ 5289 6327, 34 Great Ocean Rd)* is an attractive restaurant with a small bar and tasty Tex-Mex cooking; most mains are around $13. You'll get a friendly greeting from Ernie ('Butch' to his friends). Across the road, the cosy ***Aireys Inlet Hotel *(☎ 5289 6270)* has good bistro meals from $10 to $16.

AIREYS INLET TO LORNE

South of Aireys Inlet, the Great Ocean Rd is wedged between the ocean and steep cliffs, and runs past a series of sandy beaches and through a string of small townships – **Fairhaven, Moggs Creek** and **Eastern View**. A surf life-saving club patrols the beach at Fairhaven during summer, and Moggs Creek is popular with hang gliders who launch themselves from the cliff-tops and land on the beach below. In the stretch between Aireys Inlet and Fairhaven, you'll see some striking houses that seem to balance on the cliff face.

At Eastern View, 11km before Lorne, a timber arch spanning the road marks the official start of the construction of the Great Ocean Rd; there's a commemorative plaque for those who fought in WWI.

ANGAHOOK-LORNE STATE PARK

This park covers 22,000 hectares of coast and hinterland between Anglesea and Kennett River. Within the park are some stretches of magnificent coastline, blue-gum forests, cool-temperate rainforests, cascades, and numerous well signposted walking tracks, many of which follow the old timber tramlines that were used to cart cut timber out of the forests.

The park has an abundance of wildlife, including swamp wallabies, brushtail and ringtail possums, echidnas, bats, kangaroos and bandicoots. More than 150 species of birds have been recorded in the area, including the rare crested penguin and peregrine falcon.

Much of this area was devastated by the Ash Wednesday fires, but surveys have shown that plant species, birdlife and mammals have all since made a remarkable recovery. There's good fishing in many of the creeks in the park – fishing licences are available through the Lorne Foreshore Committee on ☎ 5289 1382.

The main access roads into the park are the unsealed Bambra Rd, which runs from Aireys Inlet to Bambra; the sealed Deans Marsh-Lorne road, which heads north out of Lorne; and the sealed Erskine Falls Rd, which runs from Lorne to Erskine Falls. This last road continues on to the Mt Sabine-Benwerrin road, which runs along the spine of the Otway Ranges.

There are seven designated camping areas in the state park. These are bush sites with no facilities. You can't book these sites – they're available on a first-come first-served basis. Parks Victoria produces excellent brochures and walking maps to the park, which are available from local Parks Victoria offices and visitor information centres. For more information, contact the Lorne Parks Victoria office (☎ 5289 1732) at 86 Polwarth Rd, Lorne.

Most of the walks near Lorne start from either the **Blanket Leaf** or **Sheoak Creek picnic areas**, or the **Erskine Falls car park**. You can drive to these areas for walking, or simply picnicking. Following are some of the most popular walks:

Cora Lynn Cascades Walk Starts from the Blanket Leaf picnic area. A moderate 6km one-way walk through blue-gum forests to the Cora Lynn Cascades car park.

Kalimna Falls Walk Starting from the Sheoak Creek picnic area, this is an easy 8km circuit walk along an old timber tramway via both the upper and lower Kalimna Falls.

Sheoak Falls Walk Also starting from the Sheoak Creek picnic area, this 8.6km return walk takes you to the 15m waterfalls and brings you back via the Castle Rock lookout.

Erskine Falls Walk Starting from the car park, this 7.5km trail follows the Erskine River past Straw Falls and Splitter's Falls to Erskine Falls, and continues all the way back to Lorne (about three hours).

Teddy Lookout Walk A moderate, three hour walk from the township up to Teddy Lookout, which has great views of the coastline and the winding Great Ocean Rd.

Shipwreck Walk An easy, one hour coastal stroll from Lorne that takes you past a series of plaques commemorating some of the shipwrecks along this coast.

There are many other fine walks around Lorne and its environs, and you can link up several trails and use the campsites if you want to do longer overnight treks. Contact the visitor information centre or the rangers at the Parks Victoria office for more information.

LORNE

• **pop 1100**

Lorne is the most popular and fashionable town along this stretch of coast; during the peak seasons there may be traffic jams leading into town and accommodation could be booked out. At other times life here is fairly quiet and peaceful. Despite the hordes, Lorne has managed to retain most of its charm.

Built around the Erskine River and the shores of Loutit Bay, Lorne and the surrounding areas have been renowned for their natural beauty since the earliest days of European settlement. Rudyard Kipling visited Lorne in 1891 and, inspired by its beauty, wrote the poem *Flowers*, which includes the lines: 'Gathered where the Erskine leaps, Down the road to Lorne...'

Information

At 144 Mountjoy Pde,The Lorne Visitor Information Centre (☎ 5289 1152) is open daily (except Christmas Day) from 9 am to 5 pm. It has excellent information on the town and surrounding areas, including good maps and guides to the bushwalks through the Angahook-Lorne State Park.

Parks Victoria (☎ 5289 1732) has an office at 86 Polwarth Rd.

Beaches

Lorne's lovely white-sand beaches, backed by rows of big old pine trees, are great for swimming, surfing, sunbathing and other beach activities. A surf life-saving club patrols the main beach, and you can hire boogie boards and wetsuits from the Lorne Surf Shop (☎ 5289 1673) at 130 Mountjoy Pde.

Bushwalks

There are more than 50km of wonderful walking tracks through the forests and hills of the Angahook-Lorne State Park behind Lorne (see the Angahook-Lorne State Park section earlier for more details).

Other Attractions

If you don't have the time or the inclination for bushwalking, at least take a scenic drive through the hills behind the town. Drive up to **Teddy Lookout**, follow the Deans Marsh-Lorne road into the Otways or take the popular **Erskine Falls Rd** inland. At Erskine Falls, a viewing platform overlooks the large waterfall and, if you're feeling energetic, a series of steps leads down to the base of the falls. The Erskine Falls Tearooms are nearby in case you need sustenance before or after the walk.

The **Lorne Historical Society**, on the corner of Otway St and the Great Ocean Rd, has a display of old photos depicting the construction of the Great Ocean Rd and the development of Lorne. It is open on weekends from 1 to 4 pm.

Qdos Arts (☎ 5289 1989), Allenvale Rd, is an excellent contemporary gallery in a bush setting with interesting outdoor sculptures. Exhibitions change regularly and lunch is available daily (except in winter) in the licensed cafe next door.

The **Lorne Golf Course** (☎ 5289 1267), high in the hills above Lorne, has one of Australia's most picturesque (and demanding) nine hole layouts. A round costs $12, and club hire is another $7.

Organised Tours

Paddle with the Platypus (☎ 5236 2119) offers excellent half-day canoeing trips ($65 including transport) to the mysterious and lovely Lake Elizabeth in the Otways, where you have a good chance of seeing platypuses. Dawn is the best time to go. There's a minimum of two people and a maximum of six for all tours.

Special Events

New Year's Eve is usually a fairly wild time in Lorne. During the first week of January, the popular Pier to Pub Swim sees several thousand swimmers splash their way across Loutit Bay to the Lorne Hotel.

The Great Otway Classic Foot Race is a gruelling test of any runner's endurance – this prestigious event is held on the Queen's Birthday weekend in June.

Places to Stay

Lorne has a tremendous range of excellent accommodation, for bush and beach lovers alike. It's impossible to list it all here so check with the visitor information centre for other options or contact an agency such as the Great Ocean Rd Accommodation Centre (☎ 5289 1800, 136 Mountjoy Pde).

Camping & Caravan Parks The Lorne Foreshore Committee *(☎ 5289 1382)* manages five good caravan parks. The main booking office is at the ***Erskine River Caravan Park***, which is pleasantly sited beside the river and is open year-round. The ***Kia Ora Caravan Park***, also open all year, is nearby on the southern side of the river. ***Ocean Road Park***, ***Queens Park*** and ***Top Bank*** caravan parks are only open at busier times of the year. If you're planning to camp over Christmas or Easter, you'll need to book well in advance.

Costs vary seasonally, with campsites costing from $12 to $20, powered sites from $15 to $25 and on-site cabins from $45 to $60 for two people. Over Christmas (19 December to 23 January) and Easter, cabins

can only be booked weekly; prices range from $500 to $850 per week at these times.

Hostels The laid-back ***Erskine River Backpackers*** *(☎ 5289 1496, 6 Mountjoy Pde)* is a top spot to hang out with other travellers. It's light and airy, and has rooms opening onto a wide veranda which surrounds the building. Dorm beds cost $17 and doubles are available for $50 (shared bathroom).

Great Ocean Road Cottages & Backpackers *(☎ 5289 1070, Erskine Ave)* is a complex of modern timber cottages in a bushy hillside setting, with a separate backpackers section. Bunk beds cost $16 for YHA members, $18 for nonmembers. If you ask nicely, the V/Line bus can stop 200m from the front gate. (See also Self-Contained Cottages & Holiday Apartments in this section).

Pubs & Motels Both of Lorne's pubs have rooms, although it's worth noting that both are live band venues, so nights can be noisy. The ***Lorne Hotel*** *(☎ 5289 1409, corner Mountjoy Pde and Bay St)* has motel-style doubles costing from $80 to $110, self-contained units from $120 to $160 and a noticeable poker machines presence. The ***Grand Pacific Hotel/Motel*** *(☎ 5289 1609, 268 Mountjoy Pde)* isn't as grand as it once was, although there are plans for renovation. The guestrooms in the main building are a bit shabby but they're spacious and have balconies with great bay views. Doubles cost from $70 to $110, as do the motel-style units out the back.

There are half a dozen motels in Lorne. The ***Ocean Lodge Motel*** *(☎ 5289 1330, 6 Armytage St)* is the oldest, cosiest and one of the cheapest. It has an inviting 1950s holiday feel and singles/doubles (most with great views) cost from $60/70 to $95/105. Right in the thick of things, the ***Sandridge Motel*** *(☎ 5289 2180, 128 Mountjoy Pde)* is also good value with pleasant standard rooms costing from $60 to $100.

Guesthouse, B&B & Resort Hotel ***Erskine House*** *(☎ 5289 1209, fax 5289 1185)* between Mountjoy Pde and the beachfront is a splendid, rambling 19th-century guesthouse with distinctive Art Deco alterations and several hectares of sweeping gardens. The bedrooms are nothing special but the facilities are excellent and include a bar and dining room, magnificent guest lounges with open fires, grass tennis courts, croquet lawns, an 18-hole putting green and table tennis. Tariffs range from $95 to $140 a double (from $120 to $165 with en suites), including breakfast.

Perched on the corner of William and Otway Sts, ***Stanmoor*** *(☎ 5289 1530, fax 5289 2247)* is a delightful B&B getaway with wide open verandas, elegantly furnished rooms and a warm atmosphere. Doubles cost from $110 to $150 a night.

The huge ***Cumberland Lorne Resort*** *(☎ 5289 2400, fax 5289 2256, 150-178 Mountjoy Pde)*, a modern conference centre and resort hotel, dominates the streetscape along Loutit Bay. It's luxurious but lacks character. The spacious apartments range in price from $175 (one bedroom, garden views) to $285 (two bedrooms, ocean views).

Self-Contained Cottages & Holiday Apartments There are some excellent self-contained cottages in and around Lorne. The pick of the bunch would have to be ***Allenvale Cottages*** *(☎/fax 5289 1450)*, 2km north-west of Lorne along Allenvale Rd, which is ideal for couples and families alike. There are five spacious and superbly fitted-out timber cottages in an idyllic setting amid shady old trees, a bubbling brook and luscious lawns. Prices for two range from $95 to $125 per night, with good deals available for longer stays.

Back in town, ***Great Ocean Road Cottages & Backpackers*** *(☎ 5289 1070, Erskine Ave)* has attractive cottages in a bush setting, with verandas, air-con and heating, TVs, en suites and other mod cons. They sleep up to six people and cost from $95 to $175 a night.

On the Erskine Falls Rd, 6.8km north of town, is the delightful ***Lemonade Creek Cottages*** *(☎ 5289 2600)*. As sweet as their name, these one and two-bedroom timber cottages in a tranquil setting cost from $115 to $150 a night – a minimum booking of one week applies in the peak season.

For style and simplicity, you can't go past ***Phoenix Apartments*** *(☎ 5289 2000, 60 Mountjoy Pde)*. They're the ultimate in slick, with polished wood floors, individual balconies and ocean views. Studio apartments, which sleep two, cost $110 a night midweek and $260 for a two night stay on weekends.

Places to Eat

Lorne is the gastronomic capital of the Great Ocean Rd and has some fine (if somewhat pricey) cafes and restaurants along Mountjoy Pde. Most are open day and night during summer, but in winter many places have shorter trading hours, and some close altogether.

Kafe Kaos *(☎ 5289 2639, 50a Mountjoy Pde)* is a good place for a healthy, filling lunch. It's an earthy cafe/deli with massive tofu and vegie burgers, tasty antipasto platters, focaccias, smoothies and the like. Try the nearby ***Loutit Bay Bakery*** for homemade pies, pastries and bread and good strong coffee. Next to the bakery, the ***Lorne Ovenhouse*** has a wood-fired oven and specialises in pizza, pasta and focaccia.

The Arab *(☎ 5289 1435, 94 Mountjoy Pde)* is something of a local landmark, having opened here in 1956. It's a bustling, cosmopolitan eatery that opens all day every day. There are tables on the footpath for the warmer weather, and it has good coffee and breakfasts, pasta dishes from $10 to $15 and other main evening meals for around $18.

For a good vibe, head to ***Reif's*** *(☎ 5289 2366, 84 Mountjoy Pde)*, an inviting bar and cafe fronted by outdoor terraces. This place has light meals like gourmet burgers and sandwiches, pasta dishes from $12 to $15 and a dinner menu that includes plenty of seafood; mains cost from $14 to $20.

Kosta's Tavern *(☎ 5289 1883, 48 Mountjoy Pde)* has a rowdy atmosphere and a Greek-influenced menu that makes good use of local seafood. Main courses cost between $18 and $22, desserts are $8.50 and there's a light lunch menu on Sunday. Kosta's is probably Lorne's most popular restaurant – you'll need to book during the holidays.

Mark's *(☎ 5289 2787, 124 Mountjoy Pde)* is elegant and upmarket and has a good reputation for innovative food – mains such as quail, kangaroo fillets or prawn risotto cost between $11 and $20 for lunch and dinner, and there is a good selection of wines by the glass. Mind, this is not the best place for vegetarians.

Marine *(☎ 5289 1808, 6a Mountjoy Pde)*, another fine restaurant, is open daily for breakfast, lunch and dinner. It's spacious yet snug and evening mains are around $20.

The ***Lorne Pier Seafood Restaurant*** *(☎ 5289 1119, Pier Head)* is a low-key seaside cafe with a great outlook over the ocean, complemented by the sound of waves lapping at the shore. Brunch and snacks are available from 11.30 am, and the dinner menu features mostly seafood with mains costing from $19 to $25. Right next door, the ***Lorne Fisheries Co-op*** offers a wide range of fresh seafood, and complimentary poetry pasted inside the front windows.

Entertainment

The ***Lorne Theatre*** *(☎ 5289 1272, corner Mountjoy Pde and Grove Rd)* screens movies daily during the peak season and less often at other times (closed July and August).

The ***Lorne Hotel*** has bands in the bottom bar on most weekends, and nightly over summer, and the grungy ***Grand Pacific Hotel*** is also a popular band venue.

Getting There & Away

V/Line's daily bus services along the Great Ocean Rd stop at the Commonwealth Bank in Mountjoy Pde. Services to/from Lorne include Melbourne (train/bus, $21.90), Geelong ($11.20) and Apollo Bay ($4.90).

Getting Around

For a taxi, call the Lorne Taxi Service (☎ 5289 2300). During the main holiday periods, bicycles are available for hire from Erskine House (see Places to Stay earlier).

OTWAY RANGES

These beautiful coastal mountain ranges, which stretch from Aireys Inlet to Cape

Otway, provide a spectacular backdrop to the Great Ocean Rd. If you have time it's worth heading inland to explore the area. The ranges are fertile, natural wonderlands, with rich volcanic soil, high rainfall and dozens of small streams, cascades and waterfalls.

This area contains lovely scenic drives, and small and picturesque settlements like Forrest, Gellibrand, Barramunga, Weeaproinah (which has the highest rainfall in the state) and Beech Forest. Especially worth searching out are the interesting **Feral Gallery** (☎ 5236 6472), in a restored chapel in the sawmilling town of Forrest, the **Red Rock Winery** (☎ 5233 8466) on the Gellibrand Rd 12km south of Colac, and **Gellibrand Pottery** (☎ 5235 8246) signposted off the Gellibrand-Beech Forest road. It's a good idea to phone these places for opening hours before heading out.

This is also a great area for bushwalking, with walking trails following the many timber tramlines that were once used to cart cut timber to the sawmills. One of the most popular trails is along the old railway line that used to connect Beech Forest and Colac. Most of the coastal section of the Otways is part of the **Angahook-Lorne State Park** (see the Angahook-Lorne State Park section earlier).

Most of the waterfalls are signposted off the main roads, and you'll find car parks, picnic areas and walking tracks leading down to the various falls. The major falls include the **Sabine Falls** (off the Skenes Creek-Forrest road, north of Haines Junction), **Stevenson's Falls** (west of Barramunga), **Triplet Falls** (between Lavers Hill and Beech Forest), **Beauchamp Falls** and **Hopetoun Falls** (both south of Beech Forest).

The **Aire Valley Picnic & Camping Reserve** off the Aire Valley Rd is very pretty, and a great place to pitch a tent.

Contact Parks Victoria (☎ 5289 1732) in Lorne for more information on the landscapes, plants, animals and attractions of this region.

Places to Stay

As well as camping areas in the Angahook-Lorne State Park, there are numerous cottages, B&Bs, pubs and guesthouses scattered throughout the Otways. On the main street in Forrest, the former Colac bowling club has been converted into the ***Forrest Country Guesthouse*** *(☎ 5236 6446)*, comprising five quirky, individually themed guestrooms. Singles/doubles cost $55/95, including breakfast served whenever you are ready. This place is really relaxed – there's not even a set check-out time.

About 6km south of Forrest and close to Stevenson's Falls, ***Barramunga Cabins*** *(☎ 5236 3302)* is a set of three rustic timber cabins in a peaceful bushland setting. Each sleeps up to 12 people and costs from $150 a double for a weekend.

The architect-designed ***King Parrot Holiday Cabins*** *(☎ 5236 3372, mobile (015 519 567)*, 8km west of the town of Deans Marsh, are a bit tricky to get to along the potholed Pennyroyal Valley Rd, but it's well worth the effort. The cabins, built from local hardwood and recycled timbers, overlook the picture-book Pennyroyal Valley, complete with abundant wildlife. They've been stylishly finished and cost $55 per person per night. There is just one down side – beware the resident blue heeler.

LORNE TO SKENES CREEK

This is one of the most spectacular sections of the Great Ocean Rd, a narrow twisting roadway carved into sheer cliffs that drop away into the ocean. This stretch takes you past the small towns of **Wye River** and **Kennett River** and the walking track to **Cumberland Falls**.

There are a few opportunities for scenic detours into the Otway Ranges from here: the rough Old Wye Rd from Wye River and the unsealed Grey River Rd from Kennett River. Both Roads take you to the Mt Sabine-Benwerrin road, which runs along the spine of the range.

Places to Stay & Eat

Seven kilometres south of Lorne is the ***Cumberland River Holiday Park*** *(☎ 5289 1790)*, a scenic camping reserve beside a rocky gorge with good walking trails and

PAUL SINCLAIR

Cumberland Falls, one of many beautiful waterfalls in the Otways.

fishing. Campsites cost from $10 to $17, and on-site cabins start at $38 (in winter).

The small town of **Wye River**, 17km south-west of Lorne, has the ***Wye Valley Caravan Park*** *(☎ 5289 0241)* and the ***Rookery Nook Hotel*** *(☎ 5289 0240)*, a sweet little pub overlooking a pretty bay. On a sunny day its front balcony is a top spot for a meal and a beer, and there are simple motel units for $50 to $100 a double.

Ten kilometres west of Wye River on the Great Ocean Rd, ***Whitecrest Holiday Resort*** *(☎ 5237 0228)* has modern apartments with open fireplaces, and balconies providing excellent views of the pounding sea. Nightly tariffs range from $95 to $145 per double midweek. On weekends, there's a minimum booking of two nights which costs between $480 and $560 a double, including two three-course dinners, and breakfasts. Dinner is served in the in-house restaurant which is also open to the public from Thursday to Monday. Mains cost around $20.

About 2km towards Apollo Bay is the turn-off to ***Wongarra Heights B&B*** *(☎ 5237 0257)*, 'a view with a room' as its brochure proclaims. It's an old-fashioned farmhouse with simple accommodation, perched high on a bluff with incredible ocean views. There are five guestrooms with singles/doubles for $45/85.

SKENES CREEK

Six kilometres east Apollo Bay is the small town of Skenes Creek, squeezed between the ocean and steeply rising hills. From the centre of the town, the sealed Skenes Creek Rd winds steeply up into the heart of the Otways. There are some very good eating and accommodation options high in the hills above the town.

Places to Stay & Eat

Beside the foreshore is the basic ***Skenes Creek Camping Reserve*** *(☎ 0418-367 499)*, with grassy campsites costing from $6 per person.

Chris's Restaurant and Villas at Beacon Point *(☎ 5237 6411, Skenes Creek Rd)* is set high on a cliff-top, with spectacular views of the coastline. This restaurant is one of the best and most popular in the state – and not without reason. The decor is quite casual with simple timber furniture, but the food, wine list, service and views elevate the place to great heights. The food combines Mediterranean flavours with local produce, and main meals cost around $20. The accommodation comprises six, quite flash, self-contained two-bedroom villa units, costing from $180 a night midweek. There's a two night minimum stay on weekends, when the tariff is $220 per night.

On the same hill you'll find ***Beacon Point Lodges*** *(☎ 5237 6218)*. These brick-and-timber self-contained holiday cabins are in rows on four levels, all with great views. The tariff starts at $95 a double, and on weekends and holidays at $135 with a two night minimum stay.

APOLLO BAY

• **pop 1000**

The pretty port of Apollo Bay is a fishing town and another popular summer beach resort. It's a little more relaxed than Lorne and a lot less trendy; in addition to all the fishing folk, quite a few artists and musicians live in and around the town.

Majestic rolling hills, reminiscent of northern Scotland, provide a picture-perfect backdrop to the town while broad white-sand beaches dominate the foreground. A breakwater protects the jetties from which the fishing boats operate – the main catch is shark and crayfish (lobster).

Information

The Great Ocean Rd Visitor Information Centre (☎ 5237 6529), on the left as you arrive from Lorne, is open daily from 9 am to 5 pm. In the same building there's an impressive 'eco-centre' with displays on Aboriginal history, rainforests, shipwrecks and the building of the Great Ocean Rd.

Things to See & Do

The **Old Cable Station Museum**, on the Great Ocean Rd 2km north of the town centre, has local artefacts and a large photographic display. It's open on weekends and during school and public holidays from 2 to 5 pm ($2). There's also a **shell museum** at 12 Noel St, open daily from 9.30 am to 8 pm.

It's a 1km (signposted) drive from town up to **Marriner's Lookout** – from the car park a 500m walking trail climbs the hilltops, with great views of the town and back along the coast. There's a good picnic area at the aptly named **Paradise Valley**, 8km west of town (signposted off the Beech Forest-Apollo Bay road).

The pretty Apollo Bay Golf Course (☎ 5237 6474) costs $10 for nine holes, $15 for 18 holes and $5 for club hire. A small **open-air market** operates on the foreshore between the visitor information centre and the surf life-saving club on Saturday morning. This is also the site of the town's 'creative village' – an interesting display of sculpted cypress poles.

Wild Dog Trails (☎ 5237 6441), based at a ramshackle farm 2km inland on Wild Dog Rd (it's signposted off the Great Ocean Rd 2.5km north-east of Apollo Bay), offers one to three-hour **horse rides** along the beaches ($25 for two hours or $70 all day). You can hire a plane for a **flying tour** over the Port Campbell National Park for $210 (seats three) from 12 Apostles Great Ocean Road Air Tours (☎ 5237 7370).

Apollo Bay Boat Charters (☎ 5237 6214) offers 50-minute **scenic cruises** ($15) and half-day **fishing trips** ($55). Apollo Bay is also very popular for **hang-gliding**, and the Wingsports Flight Academy (☎ 0419-378 616) is based here.

Special Events

The Apollo Bay Music Festival, held over a weekend in mid-March, features blues, jazz, rock and folk music, as well as buskers and markets. Venues include local restaurants, the pubs and marquees along the foreshore. Weekend passes cost $55 – phone ☎ 5237 6761 for more information.

Places to Stay

Surprisingly, there's not much in the way of inspiring accommodation – motels seem to be all the go (there are 10 in town).

Camping & Caravan Parks There are five caravan parks, including ***Pisces Caravan Resort*** *(☎ 5237 6749)* on the Great Ocean Rd 1.5km north of town. Powered sites cost from $17 to $30 for two, and on-site standard cabins from $40 to $70.

There's also the attractive ***Waratah Caravan Park*** *(☎ 5237 6562)* in Noel St, beside the golf course, with sites for $16 to $28 and on-site vans/cabins starting at $35/48.

Hostels Of the two hostels here, ***Surfside Backpackers*** *(☎ 5237 7263)*, on the corner of the Great Ocean Rd and Gambier St, is the closest to the ocean. It's small and homey with bunk beds for $13/16 (YHA members/nonmembers), and doubles for $45. Guests have free use of surfboards, a windsurfer and skin diving equipment.

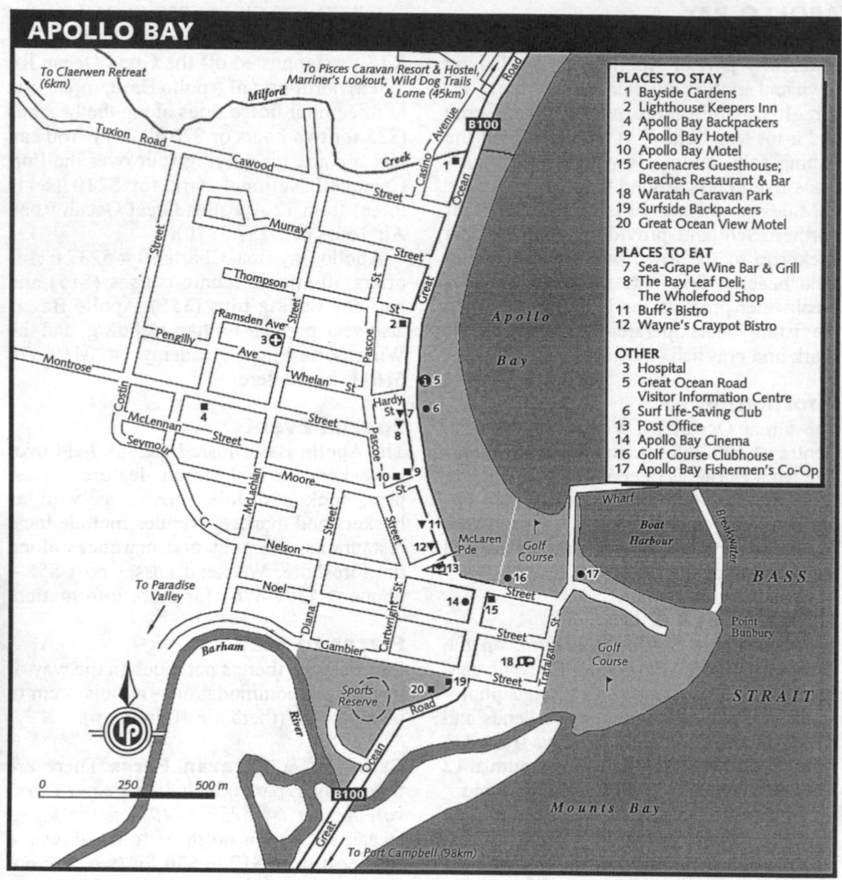

Another good option is the larger *Apollo Bay Backpackers* (☎ *0419 340 362, 47 Montrose Ave)*. Traveller's reports about it are good and it costs from $12 to $15 (linen included).

Motels & Holiday Units The modern *Lighthouse Keepers Inn* (☎ *5237 6278, 175 Great Ocean Rd)*, north of the town centre, is good value with five comfortable units with ocean views costing from $70 to $110 a double. Also good value, the *Great Ocean View Motel* (☎ *5237 6527, 1 Great Ocean Rd)* at the other end of town has doubles for $55 to $88. And it does actually have great ocean views.

The *Apollo Bay Hotel* (☎ *5237 6250, 95 Great Ocean Rd)* in the centre of town has a few basic motel-style units out the back costing from $60 to $80 a double. Behind the pub in Moore St, the *Apollo Bay Motel* (☎ *5237 6492)* has rooms from $79 to $99.

Bayside Gardens (☎ *5237 6248, 219 Great Ocean Rd)* has comfortable (though a little bland) self-contained units surrounded by gardens. There are budget units from $65, and ocean view units for $80 to $180 a double.

Guesthouse & Retreat On the corner of the Great Ocean Rd and Nelson St, ***Greenacres*** *(☎ 5237 6309)* is a 1950s-era guesthouse with tennis court, guest lounge with pool table, an outdoor heated spa, and bar and restaurant (see Places to Eat following). It has six rooms (most with balconies) with excellent bay views, a number of other guesthouse rooms and basic motel units out the back. Nightly prices for a double cost from $55 (motel unit, midweek, low season) to $180 (bay-view guesthouse room, peak season), including a continental breakfast.

Stunningly situated, 6km north of Apollo Bay on the corrugated-dirt Tuxion Rd, ***Claerwen Retreat*** *(☎ 5237 7064)* has unrivalled views of the coast and surrounding areas. Guests can stay in the modern, new age-style home from $95/120 a single/double, including breakfast, or in one of the well appointed self-contained cottages with spectacular views from $180 per night (sleeps up to six adults). If it suits your budget, this is definitely the pick of the crop.

Places to Eat

An excellent place for breakfast and lunch, ***The Bay Leaf Gourmet Deli*** *(131 Great Ocean Rd)* in the centre of town has an innovative menu, real coffee and a buzzy, friendly atmosphere. Vegetarians should definitely try the sweet potato bagel. ***The Wholefood Shop***, another good vegetarian option nearby, is an earthy health food place with reasonably priced soups, rolls, felafels and bulk foods.

An offshoot of the renowned cliff-top Chris's Restaurant in Skenes Creek, ***Sea-Grape Wine Bar & Grill*** *(☎ 5237 6610, 141 Great Ocean Rd)* is a top spot for a meal or beverage any time of the day. The menu is Mediterranean influenced, with evening mains costing around $20.

Visit the ***Apollo Bay Fishermen's Co-operative*** at the entrance to the harbour, if you're in for a fresh cray (crayfish) and other seafood. Or try the popular ***Wayne's Craypot Bistro*** *(☎ 5237 6240, 29 Great Ocean Rd)* at the 'top pub' if you'd rather not cook it yourself. The ***Apollo Bay Hotel*** (or the 'bottom pub') has bistro meals for $12 to $17 and cheaper bar meals.

Cosy ***Buff's Bistro*** *(☎ 5237 6403, 51 Great Ocean Rd)* is an inviting BYO and licensed restaurant, with friendly service and dishes such as Thai and Indian curries and gado-gado. Mains cost from $13 to $18 and there are delicious cakes and desserts.

The spacious Art Deco-influenced ***Beaches Restaurant & Bar*** at Greenacres guesthouse specialises in local seafood with main courses in the $17 to $22 range. The small bar next to the restaurant is an ideal spot to linger over coffee and port.

Entertainment

During holiday periods, a ***cinema*** operates from the local hall near the corner of the Great Ocean Rd and Nelson St. Both pubs in town have live bands during summer and on weekends.

Getting There & Away

There are daily V/Line buses along the Great Ocean Rd as far as Apollo Bay, where they stop at the Visitor Information Centre. A one-way ticket costs $18 from Geelong or $26.90 from Melbourne. On Friday, a V/Line bus continues to Port Campbell and Warrnambool ($20.80).

CAPE OTWAY & OTWAY NATIONAL PARK

From Apollo Bay the road temporarily leaves the coast to climb over Cape Otway. The coast is particularly beautiful and rugged on this stretch, but it is dangerous and there have been many shipwrecks.

The main road winds its way through the centre of the Otway National Park with its relatively untouched rainforests, fern gullies and tall forests of mountain ash. The cool-temperate rainforest is made possible by the sheltered conditions and high rainfall of the area. Closer to the coast are areas of low coastal scrub and grasslands. Over 250 species of birds have been recorded in the park, half of which breed here and half are migratory. There are also more than 45 types of native mammals, including 10 species of bat, 20 of reptile and 50 of fish.

A couple of unsealed roads lead off the highway and run through the park to the coast – they are generally in good condition and present no problems for most cars.

The first turn-off, about 6km south-west of Apollo Bay, leads to the **Elliot River picnic area** and **Shelly Beach**. There are toilets and wood barbecues in the reserve. A short walking track leads down to the beach, and the 4km Elliot River Walk starts from the car park and loops past the coastline and river.

Seventeen kilometres past Apollo Bay is **Maits Rest Rainforest Boardwalk**, a 20 minute walk along elevated boardwalks through a spectacular rainforest gully, with ferns sheltered by a thick protective canopy of myrtle beeches.

About 2km farther on is the Otway Lighthouse Rd, which leads 12km down to Cape Otway. In the middle of the 19th century, it was decided a lighthouse was needed on this remote and windswept headland to warn ships of the treacherous waters. Charged with this mission, Charles J La Trobe wrote in his map notes:

> I do not know of a single spot on the whole line of coast from the Hopkins (Warrnambool) to Cape Otway where a landing could be effected with any chance of certainty.

La Trobe reached the cape on his third attempt, and a plaque commemorates his efforts. The **Cape Otway Lighthouse**, built in 1848 using more than 40 stonemasons, is 20m high and stands on the edge of a cliff 78m above sea level.

The lighthouse is open daily from 9 am to 5 pm for self-guided tours. Entrance fees are $6 for adults, $4 concession, $3 for children and $15 for a family.

GREAT OCEAN ROAD

Places to Stay

Signposted off Otway Lighthouse Rd about 3km before the lighthouse, ***Bimbi Park*** *(☎ 5237 9246)* is a campground and horse-riding ranch in a remote bushland setting of sand dunes and forest, with some good bushwalking tracks leading to remote beaches. Trail rides along beaches, rivers and through forest cost $18 an hour or $32 for a half-day trip ($14/20 for people under 15). This place is also a hostel, with backpackers' beds in on-site vans from $12 or in canvas army tents from $10. There are also campsites from $11 and on-site vans from $25.

At the ***Cape Otway Lightstation*** *(☎ 5237 9240)*, self-contained accommodation is available in two huge heritage sandstone residences, which feature wood fires and spectacular views of the lighthouse and ocean. The larger house can sleep up to 16 people. Prices vary but a three day package (Friday, Saturday and Sunday nights) for four people costs $445 (non-holiday period). Two studio apartments with a similar package cost $245 for two.

The Blanket Bay Rd leads off the Otway Lighthouse Rd across to **Blanket Bay**, where there are picnic and barbecue facilities, walking tracks and a few bush campsites which you'll need to book during summer – phone Parks Victoria (☎ 5237 6889) in Apollo Bay.

HORDEN VALE & GLENAIRE

After Cape Otway, the Great Ocean Rd straightens out somewhat and runs in a series of sweeping curves around the large and fertile Horden Vale flats, which are mostly occupied by dairy farms. The road returns to the coast briefly at Glenaire (which is just a hill – there's no town as such) after a long and steep climb past a scenic car park and lookout point.

Places to Stay

To really get away from it all, head to ***Cape Otway Cottages*** *(☎ 5237 9256)*, 7km along Horden Vale Rd (off the Great Ocean Rd), which leads down to the mouth of the Aire

River. There's a good two-bedroom stone cottage available from $110 a night, and three studio units, custom-built for cosy couple escapes, costing from $130 a double. There's a minimum stay of two nights, and fully catered gourmet dinners are available on request.

On the side of the hill at Glenaire are the ***Glenaire Log Cabins*** *(☎ 5237 9237)*, four secluded cabins with views back across the valley. These pine-lined, two-bedroom cabins are simple and comfortable with open fireplaces and good facilities; they cost from $270 a double for a weekend, plus $10 per extra person.

JOHANNA

From Glenaire, the road returns inland and starts the climb up to Lavers Hill. Six kilometres north of Glenaire you can take the scenic Red Johanna Road. This winds down through magnificent rolling hills dotted with grazing cows to the small coastal district of Johanna, known for its rugged windswept beaches and great surf (they can be dangerous for swimming).

There's a very basic ***campground*** near the beach car park. Camping fees apply – phone Parks Victoria on ☎ 5237 6889 to organise payment, or wait for the ranger to come and collect your fees. Located in a tranquil bush setting 3km inland, ***Glow Worm Cottages*** *(☎ 5237 4238, 70 Stafford Rd)* are fully self-contained and cost from $245 to $325 a double for three nights on weekends (minimum stays apply). Be sure to visit the glow-worms at night.

Truly stunning are the architect-designed ***Boomerang Cabins*** *(☎ 5237 4213)* on the Great Ocean Rd close to the Red Johanna Rd turn-off. These three cabins (shaped, funnily enough, like boomerangs) feature vaulted ceilings, polished floorboards, lead-lighting, spas, and sweeping views of the Johanna Valley and ocean – very swish. This place is relatively new so the gardens aren't well established, but it's still fantastic value with doubles costing from $110 to $150 per night ($25 per extra person). The largest cabin sleeps seven people.

LAVERS HILL

Lavers Hill is at the Otway Junction, where the Great Ocean Rd meets the roads to Colac and Cobden. This small and often mist-shrouded hilltop town was once a thriving timber township, but things are pretty quiet nowadays. There are two large Devonshire tea-house near each other on top of the hill, the **Blackwood Gully Tearooms** and the **Gardenside Manor Tearooms**.

The ***Lavers Hill Roadhouse*** *(☎ 5237 3251)* at the Shell petrol station on the road to Port Campbell has basic bunkroom accommodation for $30 a double, campsites for $10 and on-site vans from $25. The ***Otway Junction Motor Inn*** *(☎ 5237 3295)* is a modern motel with good views and doubles costing from $68 to $95.

MELBA GULLY STATE PARK

Seven kilometres south-west of Lavers Hill is the small and very beautiful Melba Gully State Park, named after the Australian opera singer Dame Nellie Melba. There's a scenic picnic area with fireplaces and toilets below the car park. A marked **nature walk** leads through the park, with its canopy of blackwoods and myrtle beeches and fern-filled rainforest. You'll also find a giant 300-year-old messmate eucalypt (unimaginatively nicknamed 'Big Tree'), which is 27m in circumference.

After dark, **glow-worms** (the larvae of the fungus gnat) can be seen in the park, but they are highly sensitive to light and noise. During the holiday season, guided night-time tours are held – ask at the Great Ocean Rd Visitor Information Centre (☎ 5237 6529) in Apollo Bay for details.

MOONLIGHT HEAD

From Lavers Hill, the road heads south again towards the coast. About 16km from Lavers Hill is the turn-off to the romantically named Moonlight Head, so dubbed by Matthew Flinders as he sailed past on his way around Australia in 1802. Near the turn-off is the historic **Old Wattle Hotel**, formerly a stopover on the coastal coach routes and now privately owned.

A bumpy 5km dirt and gravel road leads down towards Moonlight Head itself. Near the coast, the road forks: to the left is the **Moonlight Head cemetery** and a walking track along the cliff-tops, while to the right is a car park from where a track leads down onto **Wreck Beach** – you can see the anchors of two of the many ships that met their fate along this coast. The *Marie Gabrielle* sank off here in 1869, and in 1891 the *Fiji* was driven aground in a storm and 12 sailors were drowned.

The **Shipwreck Trail** starts at Moonlight Head and follows this treacherous coastline all the way to Port Fairy. Commemorative plaques have been mounted at points overlooking the sites of 25 shipwrecks.

Based near here, **Seareach Horse Treks** (☎ 5237 5214) offers rides along the coastal cliffs and beaches, costing $25 for two hours or $50 a day.

Three kilometres after the Moonlight Head turn-off the road crosses the Gellibrand River. From here a scenic but rougher alternative route, the Old Ocean Rd, follows the river and rejoins the Great Ocean Rd at Princetown.

PRINCETOWN

There's not a lot of town in Princetown, apart from a post office, general store (the closest store to the Twelve Apostles), an eatery called ***Talk of the Town*** and the ***Apostles Camping Park*** *(☎ 5598 8119).* You can pitch your tent here for $8 (with pretty good views over the Gellibrand River), or bed down in one of their teensy, musty units for $12 ($15 if you need linen).

PORT CAMPBELL NATIONAL PARK

This narrow coastal park stretches through low heathlands from Princetown to Peterborough. This is the most famous and most photographed stretch of the Great Ocean Rd. Sheer limestone cliffs tower 70m above the often fierce seas, with waves and tides relentlessly pounding the soft rock in an ongoing process of erosion and undercutting. Over thousands of years, natural sculptures have been carved out of this soft tertiary limestone, creating a fascinating series of rock stacks, gorges, arches and blowholes.

The **Gibson Steps**, carved by hand into the cliffs in the 19th century (and more recently replaced by concrete steps), lead down to the treacherous Gibson Beach. This beach, and others along this stretch of coast, are not recommended for swimming – you can walk along the beach, but be careful not to be stranded by high tides or stormy seas. Opposite Gibson Steps is the 1869 **Glenample Homestead** (open for visitors) where the survivors of the famed *Loch Ard* shipwreck recovered (see later in this section).

The **Twelve Apostles** is the best known rock formation in Victoria. These tall rocky stacks have been abandoned to the ocean by the eroding headland. These outcrops also are being constantly pounded by waves; one day, they too will submit to the inevitable and drop into the sea. Today only seven apostles can be seen from the viewing platforms: the fate of the missing apostles is unknown. Either there were originally 12 and five have been consumed by the sea, or the formation was named with a touch of poetic licence.

At present, timber boardwalks run around the cliff-tops and provide viewing platforms and seats. A visitor amenity facility and massive car park are planned for the rear of the site outside the national park. Pedestrian access to the Twelve Apostles will then be via a walking trail running beneath the Great Ocean Rd. This development is due for completion in September 2000.

Loch Ard Gorge has a sad tale to tell. In 1878 the iron-hulled clipper Loch Ard was driven onto the rocks around Mutton Bird Island at 4 am on the final night of its long voyage from England. Of the 55 people on board there were only two survivors. Eva Carmichael, a nonswimmer, clung to a piece of wreckage and was eventually washed into the gorge, where she was rescued by apprentice officer, Tom Pearce. Tom heroically climbed the cliff the next day and raised the alarm at a local farmhouse, but no other survivors were found. Eva and Tom were both 18, and the romantic aspects of the rescue led the press of the time to speculate on the possibility of a romance between the two, but Eva soon returned to Ireland and they never saw each other again.

Four of the victims of the *Loch Ard* are buried in the small cemetery here, and a sign at the gorge relates the story.

Short walking trails around the gorge lead to the cemetery and other interesting formations nearby, including the **Blowhole**, **Elephant Rock** and **Mutton Bird Island**, which is home to a large colony of short-tailed shearwaters (called mutton birds by the early settlers).

Places to Stay

Macka's Farm *(☎ 5598 8261)*, a working dairy farm on the Princetown-Simpson road about 5km inland from the Twelve Apostles, has comfortable self-contained lodges costing between $85 and $100 a double, plus $15 per extra person. Guests can join in various farm activities, and even go trout fishing. On a nearby dairy farm, Macka's daughter runs ***Cath's Place*** *(☎ 5598 8106)*, a farmhouse B&B with one double room with private bathroom costing $95.

Three kilometres inland from the Twelve Apostles on Booringa Rd is the friendly ***Apostles View Motel*** *(☎ 5598 8277)*, with good motel units on a pleasant little farm costing $70 to $90 a double. There's a playground and animal nursery for the kids and home-cooked meals are available.

PORT CAMPBELL

This small windswept village has one pub and a cluster of motels and take-away places catering for the passing parade of tourists who come to see the local sights. The town is set on a natural gorge that looks artificial because of its almost perfectly rectangular shape. At the end of the inlet is a pleasant sand beach, a great place for fish and chips and one of the few decent swimming spots along this stretch of coast.

Information

The Parks Victoria Information Centre (☎ 5598 6382) in Morris St has good information on Port Campbell National Park and is open weekdays from 10 am to 4 pm and at varying hours on weekends. At the front of the centre is the anchor from the *Loch Ard*, which was salvaged by divers in 1978.

Things to See & Do

The **Loch Ard Shipwreck Museum**, opposite the general store at 26 Lord St, has an interesting collection of shipwreck relics and a video on the sinking of the *Loch Ard* (open daily from 9 am to 5.30 pm; $4 adults, $1 kids). There's a cafe/restaurant at the front of the museum, open daily until late.

The museum is also the booking office for Port Campbell Boat Charters (☎ 5598 6463), which runs fishing trips (from $50 for four hours), 1½ hour scenic cruises to the Twelve Apostles and Bay of Islands ($30), and scuba diving trips ($35 for one dive, $60 for two). There's a dive shop in Lord St (behind the general store) where you can hire gear.

The **Discovery Walk** provides an introduction to the area's natural and historical features. You can pick up a map from the Parks Victoria office, cross the caravan park and creek and explore the western headland area (about an hour).

Next to the Port Campbell Hotel, the **Old Hall Gallery** has an interesting collection of old photos, records and memorabilia from the local district plus a few shipwreck relics. It's open daily, except Monday and Friday, from noon to 4 pm.

Places to Stay & Eat

The ***Port Campbell Caravan Park*** *(☎ 5598 6492)*, on Tregea St, overlooks the gorge and has campsites from $12 to $15 and on-site cabins from $55 to $80. Opposite is the ***Port Campbell YHA Hostel*** *(☎/fax 5598 6305, 18 Tregea St)*, which has several bunkrooms and a huge kitchen and dining area. Dorm beds are $13 a night for YHA-members, $16 for nonmembers.

Port O'Call *(☎ 5598 6206)*, opposite the pub, is more homey than the average motel. The A-frame rooms have nice high ceilings and are great value at $55 to $70 a double.

More slick is the ***Southern Ocean Motor Inn*** *(☎ 5598 6231)* at the eastern entrance to the town, offering doubles from $92 to $117. It's also home to ***Napiers Restaurant***, which overlooks the port and specialises in local seafood.

The ***Port Campbell Hotel*** *(☎ 5598 6320)*, the only pub in town, has inexpensive bar lunches and the ***Cray Pot Bistro*** out the back, with mains for between $12 and $15. ***Emma's Cottage Tea Rooms*** *(☎ 5598 6458)*, in a cosy timber cottage next to the general store, has good meals, light snacks and Devonshire teas.

PORT CAMPBELL TO PETERBOROUGH

West of Port Campbell, the next feature is **The Arch**, a rocky archway offshore from Point Hesse. Nearby is **London Bridge**, which was once a double-arched, rock platform linked to the mainland. Visitors could walk out across a narrow section over one of the arches and onto the small island. But in 1990, one of the arches collapsed into the sea, stranding two surprised tourists on the island – they were eventually rescued by helicopter. On clear moonlit evenings, this is a good spot to view penguins as they retire for the night.

Other formations along here include **The Grotto** and the aptly named **Crown of Thorns Rock**.

PETERBOROUGH

A small and somewhat old-fashioned coastal township just off the Great Ocean Rd, Peterborough is built around the mouth of the Curdies River, which opens into a broad inlet before it enters the sea. It is a great fishing and swimming spot. There are some good beaches around Peterborough and this place is popular with families for low-key summer holidays.

Beside the river, the ***Great Ocean Road Tourist Park*** *(☎/fax 5598 5477)* has campsites from $12 to $15 and cabins from $44 to $60. Attached to the nearby pub, the ***Shomberg Inn Motel*** *(☎ 5598 5285)* has double units from $50 to $75.

PETERBOROUGH TO WARRNAMBOOL

Eight kilometres west of Peterborough is the **Bay of Islands**. A two hour walk from the car park here takes you along the coastline to magnificent lookout points over the bay.

The 'Great' part of the Great Ocean Rd effectively ends at the Bay of Islands. From here, the road heads inland through some fairly unspectacular flatlands and farming communities all the way to Warrnambool, although there are a couple of worthwhile detours and stops along the way.

Signposted about 16km north-east of Peterborough is the wonderful **Timboon Farmhouse Cheese** (☎ 5598 3387) on Ford and Fells Road. Its tasting room, 'The Mousetrap', is open daily from 9.30 am to 4 pm. Generous (free) tastings take you through a range of award-winning biodynamic cheeses such as bries, fetas, camemberts and triple-creams. Cheese platters, sandwiches, Devonshire teas and wine are all sold here and can be enjoyed in the pleasant garden when the weather's fine.

In the pretty town of **Timboon**, the friendly and quirky ***Koo-Aah Coffee Shop and Restaurant*** *(☎ 5598 3533, 15 Main St)* is open for lunch and dinner. It has a terrific selection of tucker with house specials such as Pakistani lamb curry or raspberry salmon fettuccine, and it's very cosy in winter.

WARRNAMBOOL

• **pop 26,000**

Like most of the towns along this coast, Warrnambool was originally settled as a humble whaling and sealing station. It was first named 'Warnimble', an Aboriginal word meaning 'plenty of water', and is sited on Lady Bay between the Hopkins and Merri rivers. This was chosen as a settlement site because of the supposedly safe and sheltered harbour of Lady Bay. More than 30 shipwrecks lying off the coast suggest there was no such thing as a safe harbour along the Shipwreck Coast.

Nowadays Warrnambool is a major industrial and commercial centre, and the town's major employer, Fletcher Jones &

Southern Right Whales

Warrnambool's Logans Beach is a major breeding ground and nursery for southern right whales. Each year around May, these majestic whales migrate to the ocean waters around Port Fairy and Warrnambool, staying until September or October. There's a car park and several lookout platforms on the sandy cliff-tops above Logans Beach – a pair of binoculars will come in handy.

The southern right whale was hunted from whaling stations in Victoria and Tasmania from the earliest days of European settlement. It was considered the 'right' whale for hunters for several reasons – it was an easy target due to its slow swimming speed and preference for shallow water, and as an added benefit, it floated after being killed.

By 1940 it was estimated that there were fewer than 1000 southern right whales left. Although the species has been protected since 1935, today these whales still number only around 1200 to 1500. You can be fined up to $100,000 for interfering with whales. Boats have to keep at least 100m away, and you can't swim or dive within 30m.

For the latest information on sightings, contact the Warrnambool Visitor Information Centre on ☎ 5564 7837 or drop in there and pick up a copy of the free annual publication, *Whales at Warrnambool*.

Mark Armstrong

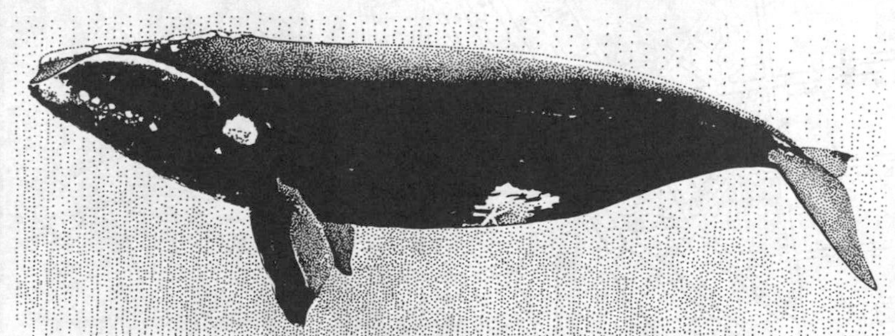

The southern right whale, once hunted to the brink of extinction, can now be seen each winter at breeding and nursery grounds off Logans Beach.

Staff, is one of Australia's best known clothing manufacturers. Despite its growth, Warrnambool maintains a relaxed seaside feel. The city centre has some historic buildings, and many of the main streets are lined with Norfolk Island pines and pohutukawas (New Zealand Christmas trees). The town is a popular family summer resort, with some good sheltered swimming beaches as well as open surf beaches. There are also great fishing spots around here, with a choice between the two rivers or more-adventurous ocean fishing.

Warrnambool also has a large student population attending the Warrnambool campus of Deakin University – as a result, there's an active nightlife and quite a few good pubs, bars, cafes and restaurants.

Information

The excellent Warrnambool Visitor Information Centre (☎ 5564 7837), signposted

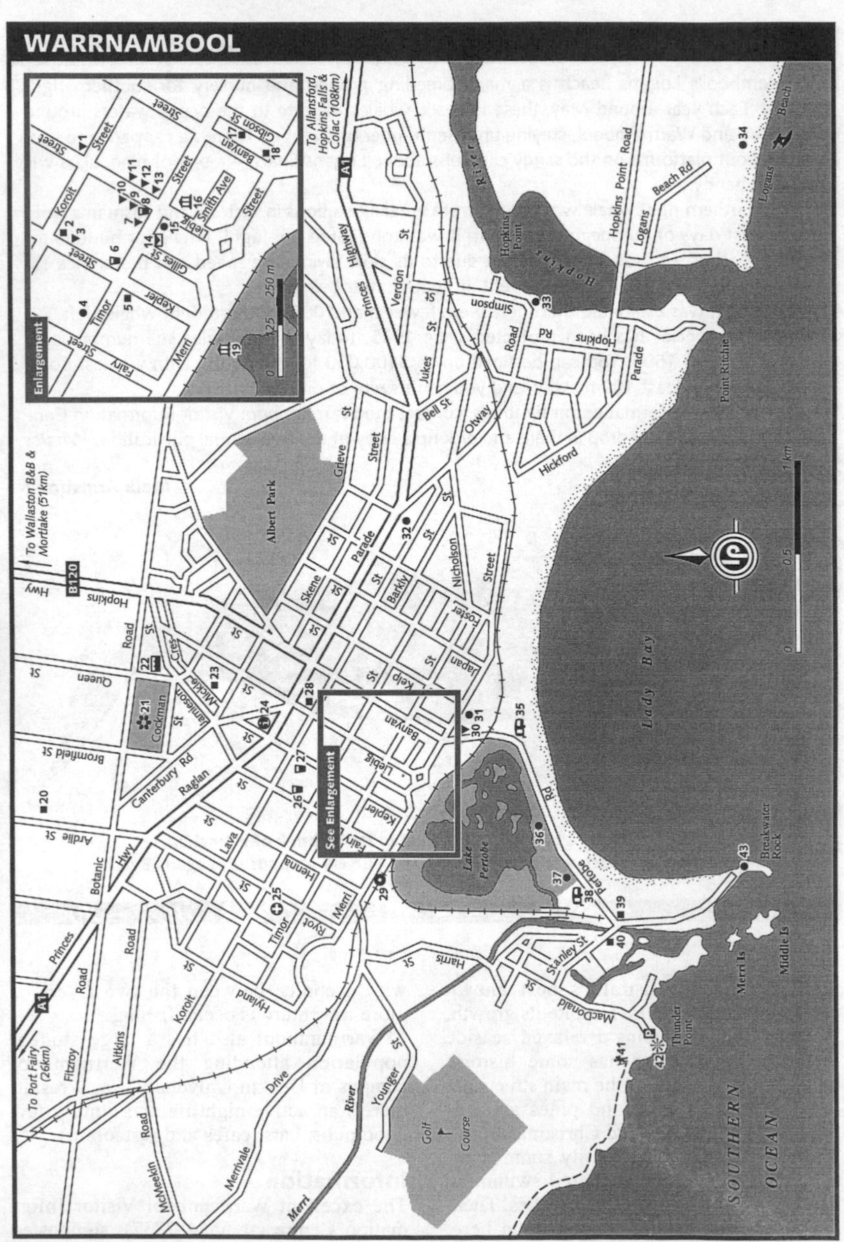
WARRNAMBOOL
Enlargement
See Enlargement
To Port Fairy (26km)
To Wallaston B&B & Mortlake (51km)
To Allansford, Hopkins Falls & Colac (108km)
Albert Park
Cockman
Lake Pertobe
Golf Course
Merri River
Hopkins River
Hopkins Point
Point Ritchie
Breakwater Rock
Thunder Point
Merri Is
Middle Is
Lady Bay
Logans Beach
SOUTHERN OCEAN

WARRNAMBOOL

PLACES TO STAY
2 Hotel Warrnambool
5 Western Hotel Motel
17 Pertobe B&B
18 Olde Maritime Motor Inn
20 Merton Manor
23 O'Brien's B&B
28 Backpackers Barn
35 Surfside Holiday Park
38 Ocean Beach Holiday Village
39 Lady Bay Hotel
40 Warrnambool Beach Backpackers

PLACES TO EAT
1 China City Chinese Restaurant
3 Sea Change Cafe; Capitol Cinema
7 Balenàs
9 Fishtales Cafe; Bojangles
10 Malaysia
11 Freshwater Cafe
12 Beach Babylon
13 Images; Seanchai
30 Mahogony Ship Bar & Restaurant

OTHER
4 Laundrette
6 Gallery Nightclub
8 Whaler's Inn Hotel
14 Post Office
15 Warrnambool Performing Arts Centre
16 Warrnambool Art Gallery
19 History House
21 Warrnambool Botanic Gardens
22 Olympic Swimming Pool
24 Visitor Information Centre
25 Hospital
26 Caledonian Hotel (The Cally)
27 Criterion Hotel
29 Train Station
31 Flagstaff Hill Maritime Village
32 Fletcher Jones Factory & Gardens
33 Proudfoot's Boathouse
34 Logans Beach Whale-Watching Platform
36 Lake Pertobe Adventure Playground
37 City of Warrnambool Lawn Tennis Club
41 Start of Mahogony Walking Trail
42 Thunder Point Car Park & Lookout
43 Lady Bay Breakwater

off the Princes Highway (A1) at 600 Raglan Pde, is open daily from 9 am to 5 pm. The centre produces the handy *Warrnambool Visitors Guide* which has detailed information on sights, accommodation, eating and transport, as well as regular 'what's on' listings.

Parks Victoria (☎ 5561 9900) has an office at 78 Henna St, and the RACV (☎ 5562 1555) is at 165 Koroit St.

Flagstaff Hill Maritime Village

Warrnambool's major tourist attraction is the impressive Flagstaff Hill Maritime Village (☎ 5564 7841). At the entrance, an elaborate tapestry depicts the major themes of the village, linking Aboriginal history, sealing and whaling (see the boxed text, 'Southern Right Whales' in this chapter) with exploration and settlement. The whaling display features a whaling boat that was built in the workshops here.

A small theatre continually screens old maritime films and documentaries such as the brilliantly narrated 1929 classic *Around Cape Horn*.

The village itself is modelled on an early Australian coastal port. The lighthouse, keeper's cottage and chartroom were moved here from Middle Island (near the mouth of the Merri River) in 1872, and you can see the original cannon and fortifications built in 1887 to withstand the perceived threat of Russian invasion. Other buildings include the Ship Chandler's office, a shipwreck museum and the Public Hall, in which the superb Loch Ard Peacock is displayed. This colourful porcelain peacock, which was made in England by Minton Potteries and was on its way to Melbourne for the Great International Exhibition, was one of the few items recovered after the tragic sinking of the *Loch Ard* in 1878. Miraculously, it was washed ashore in its packing crate.

On the small lake are two restored historic ships, the old Tasmanian steamer *Rowitta* and the sailing cargo ship *Reginald M*. There's also a working blacksmith's shed and shipwright's workshop, several gift and souvenir shops and a tearoom, bar and restaurant (see Places to Eat later).

Flagstaff Hill is open daily from 9 am to 5 pm; admission costs $9.50 for adults, $8 for students/pensioners, $4.50 for children and $26 for a family.

Warrnambool Art Gallery

This gallery, at 165 Timor St, has a large permanent collection that includes early Australian colonial paintings, a collection from the Melbourne modernism period (1930-50) which includes Arthur Boyd's *Portrait of Max Nicholson*, 19th century European paintings and more than 600 contemporary prints. It's open daily from noon to 5 pm; admission is $3 for adults (free for students and people under 16).

Warrnambool Botanic Gardens

On the corner of Queen and Cockman Sts, these pretty gardens with their velveteen-like lawns are just the spot to take a pleasant stroll beneath exotic trees. There's a fernery, a band rotunda and a small lake where kids can feed the ducks. Like many of Victoria's provincial gardens, their development was fostered in the middle of the 19th century by Baron Ferdinand von Mueller, then director of the Royal Botanic Gardens in Melbourne. They were designed in 1877 by his successor, William Guilfoyle.

Mahogany Walking Trail

The Mahogany Walking Trail, which starts at the Thunder Point coastal reserve on the western edge of town, is a 22km coastal walk along beaches and sand dunes between Warrnambool and Port Fairy that takes you past the possible site of the fabled Mahogany Ship (see the boxed text).

Even if you don't stumble across the old ship, an interesting aspect of this walk is imagining what the surrounding landscape was like before European settlement – this whole area was once an extensive coastal forest, but was cleared for agriculture by the early settlers.

Other Attractions

The historic **Proudfoot's Boathouse**, classified by the National Trust, is on the banks of the Hopkins River at the end of Simpson St. The boathouse has been restored and converted into a sports club with a bar, tearooms and an impressive restaurant, Proudfoots on the River.

The Mahogany Ship

The *Deliens World Map*, published in 1567, included a mysterious landmass called 'Java La Grande' in the vicinity of the then-unknown Australian continent. Historians and researchers have speculated that a secret voyage by the Portuguese mariner and explorer, Cristovao de Mendoca, in 1522 may have been the basis for this map, which charts the southern coastline of this landmass but stops abruptly near present day Warrnambool.

Mendoca's expedition included three ships. Researchers and speculators have suggested that one of the ships may have sunk near Warrnambool, causing Mendoca to abandon the expedition.

In 1836, two shipwrecked sailors reported having seen the remains of a large mahogany ship in the sand dunes near Armstrong Bay, between Warrnambool and Port Fairy. There were numerous other reported sightings of the ship between 1836 and 1870, After which it is thought the ship may have been covered by shifting sand dunes.

The fabled Mahogany Ship may be the product of imagination, then again it may not. If such a ship were discovered, it would rewrite Australian and world history. In the early 1990s, the Victoria government posted a $250,000 reward for the discovery of the ship – the offer has since expired without the reward being claimed, but perhaps one day someone will discover the remains of the Portuguese caravel and prove that Mendoca's expedition did reach Australia in the 16th century.

Mark Armstrong

Warrnambool has some very pleasant beaches, with the main swimming beach being the sheltered **Lady Bay**. You can drive out to the breakwater here where there is a partially sheltered harbour for fishing boats. **Logans Beach** is the best surf beach, but there are other good breaks at Levy's Beach and Second Bay (near the golf course). **Hopkins Falls**, known locally as 'mini Niagara', is 13km north-east of Warrnambool.

The **Lake Pertobe Adventure Playground** is a good place to take the kids. On weekends and during the holidays, you can hire canoes, paddleboats and mini-power boats, walk across suspension bridges to islands on the lake, play minigolf or brave the flying foxes.

The Visitor Information Centre has maps and brochures of some of the **walking trails** in and around Warrnambool – for example, you can wander along to the **Thunder Point Coastal Reserve**, or take the 3km **Heritage Trail** which starts at the information centre and takes you past some of Warrnambool's historic sites.

History House on the corner Gillies and Merri Sts is the local historical society museum and houses exhibits of old photos and documents from the area. It's open on the first Sunday of each month (every Sunday in January) from 2 to 4 pm.

Local clothing manufacturer, **Fletcher Jones**, has a factory at the corner of Flaxman St and Raglan Pde. The company is very proud of the rather quirky but very popular **gardens** at the front of its offices on the Princes Hwy.

Special Events

Warrnambool has three main annual festivals. Each February there's the Wunta Festival. 'Wunta' is a local Aboriginal word for fish, and the festival celebrates the fishing industry with a wine and seafood fair, a whale boat race, concerts and other events.

The May Racing Carnival is a three day horse-racing festival held early in May. It features Australia's longest horse race, the gruelling Grand Annual Steeplechase. This hellish 5.5km jumps race is held on the first Thursday in May. The carnival draws large crowds and you'll need to book accommodation in advance.

The Melbourne-Warrnambool cycling race, known as the 'Holy Grail', finishes here each October, as it has done every year since 1895.

Places to Stay

Camping & Caravan Parks The ***Surfside Holiday Park*** *(☎ 5561 2611)* on Pertobe Rd is less than 1km south of the centre and right on the beach. Powered sites cost from $15 to $23, and on-site cabins (one room) from $45 to $75.

Another good caravan park on Pertobe Rd is the ***Ocean Beach Holiday Village*** *(☎ 5561 4222)* with sites from $18 to $23 and cabin-vans from $38 to $64.

Hostels & Pubs There are four hostels in town. Closest to the sea, the friendly ***Warrnambool Beach Backpackers*** *(☎/fax 5562 4874, 17 Stanley St)* has a huge living area, bar, Internet access and offers free pick-up from the train and bus station. Dorm beds cost $15, doubles $35. In the town centre, ***Backpackers Barn*** *(☎ 5562 2073, corner Liebig and Lava Sts)* at the Victoria Hotel has beds for $14 ($13 for YHA members).

Rooms for budgeters are also available at the recently renovated ***Western Hotel Motel*** *(☎ 5562 2011, 45 Kepler St)*, with standard singles/doubles for $18/30. ***Hotel Warrnambool*** *(☎ 5562 2377, corner Koroit and Kepler Sts)*, has comfortable, old-fashioned (though noisy) rooms for $30/60, including breakfast (shared bathrooms).

Motels On Merri St, opposite Flagstaff Hill Maritime Village, the ***Olde Maritime Motor Inn*** *(☎ 5561 1415)* is one of the best of the 23 motels here. Standard units are $75, and suites cost from $85 to $130.

On Pertobe Rd near Breakwater Rock, the ***Lady Bay Hotel*** *(☎ 5562 1544)* has budget motel singles/doubles from $35/45 (plus $5 in summer).

B&Bs You may never want to leave ***O'Brien's B&B*** *(☎ 5562 6241, 8 Mickle*

Cres), a charming Edwardian home with elegant period features and private guest living and dining rooms. Tariffs are $75/85 a single/double. The central ***Pertobe B&B*** *(☎ 5561 7078, 10 Banyan St)* is a lovely sandstone cottage, and excellent value with rooms for $40/60. The whole house is available for $150 a night (sleeps seven).

More upmarket is ***Merton Manor*** *(☎ 5562 0720, 62 Ardlie St)*, an impressive 1880s Italianate villa. The guest suites lack character, but the main house is incredibly grand, overflowing with antiques and offering a full-size billiards table and grand piano. Rooms cost $95/130, including breakfast.

Places to Eat

Liebig St is Warrnambool's major shopping strip, and many of the eateries are along here. The excellent ***Fishtales Cafe*** at No 63, is a groovy and friendly eatery/take-away open all day, every day. Its delicious fare includes burgers ($5 to $7), gourmet fish and chips, vegetarian specials ($7 to $10), seafood and Asian dishes ($10 to $15) and superb breakfasts (try the 'Monster Plate', if you're game).

Next door, ***Bojangles*** is a popular Italian bistro with pastas and pizzas for $10 to $14, and steak, veal and chicken dishes for $15 to $20. ***Malaysia***, nearby at No 69, serves up fairly good Malaysian and Chinese tucker plus a few Aussie specials, with mains in the $12 to $16 range. The walls and windows are covered with photos of famous, semi-famous and not-at-all-famous people who have eaten here.

Across the road, ***Freshwater Cafe*** *(☎ 5561 3188, 78 Liebig St)* has an elegant, atmospheric dining room and a modern menu with mains for $15 to $21. A few doors south, ***Beach Babylon*** *(☎ 5562 3714, 72 Liebig St)* is a bustling and inviting pizza/steak/pasta joint. Steaks cost from $17 to $19, pasta dishes are around $13 and there's a cheaper children's menu. Another good option for families is ***Images*** *(☎ 5562 4208, 60 Liebig St)*, a massive bistro with a children's play area. Mains cost from $10 to $17.

Around the corner, ***Balenàs*** *(☎ 5562 0900, 158 Timor St)* is an understated and elegant dining venue, with mains in the $13 to $20 range and a good cocktails list.

If you're looking for pub grub, ***Hotel Warrnambool*** *(☎ 5562 2377, corner Koroit and Kepler Sts)* has tasty bistro mains for $10 to $19. ***Sea-Change Cafe*** *(52A Kepler St)*, near the cinema, is a good place to head for breakfast, yummy focaccias and good strong coffee served with a smile.

On Koroit St, near the Liebig St corner, the ***China City Chinese Restaurant*** has all-you-can-eat deals for $6 at lunchtime and $11.50 at dinner.

The ***Mahogany Ship*** *(☎ 5561 1833)*, right next to the Flagstaff Hill Maritime Village on Merri St, has a cosy tavern bar and restaurant, both with great views across Lady Bay. The restaurant has mains for $11 to $18.

Entertainment

Warrnambool's nightlife is centred around the pub scene. The ***Criterion Hotel*** *(151 Kepler St)* is a grungy rock pub with live music every Saturday night. The ***Caledonian Hotel*** (The Cally), in Fairy St, has a big entertainment lounge with pool tables, video games and the like. The ***Whalers' Inn Hotel*** *(corner Liebig and Timor Sts)* is one of the most popular spots, with live bands on Wednesday, Friday and Saturday.

A great spot for some genuine Irish hospitality and Guinness on tap is ***Seanchai*** *(62 Liebig St)*, where there's live music every weekend. Disco fans could head to the ***Gallery Nightclub*** *(cnr Timor and Kepler Sts)* – it's a good idea to watch your back here!

Capitol Cinema *(☎ 5562 2709)* in Kepler St screens films daily. ***Warrnambool Performing Arts Centre*** *(☎ 5564 7885, corner Liebig and Timor Sts)* is the major venue for live theatre, ballet and music. Phone to find out what's on.

Getting There & Away

Warrnambool's V/Line station is on Merri St at the south end of Fairy St. There are daily services between Melbourne and Warrnambool (three trains each weekday, two on Saturday and one on Sunday). The trip

GREAT OCEAN ROAD

takes about three hours and economy/1st class fares are $34.20/47.80.

Connecting V/Line buses continue west to Port Fairy ($4.30), Portland ($12.20) and Mt Gambier ($26.90). There are also weekday bus services to Ballarat ($18) and Hamilton ($6.10).

On Friday only, a bus heads along the Great Ocean Rd to Apollo Bay ($20.80) and Geelong ($38.90).

WARRNAMBOOL TO PORT FAIRY

Tower Hill State Game Reserve

Midway between Warrnambool and Port Fairy, this 614 hectare reserve is based around the remains of an extinct volcanic crater. Tower Hill became a state game reserve in 1961, and thousands of native trees and shrubs have been planted in an attempt to regenerate the natural bush and attract native wildlife and birds. There's abundant birdlife on and around the lake, and the reserve's mostly friendly residents include koalas, grey kangaroos, emus, sugar gliders and peregrine falcons.

A one-way ring road circles the central crater lake, and along the way there are lookout points, car parks and picnic areas. Don't feed the animals or you'll be liable for a hefty fine, and drive very slowly as it's more than likely an emu will step out to greet you. The **Natural History Centre** has an educational display explaining the history of the reserve, and there are several walking tracks if you want to explore on foot. The reserve is open daily from 9.30 am to 4.30 pm and there is no admission fee.

Koroit

• **pop 1000**

Seven kilometres north of Tower Hill and the highway, Koroit is a charming little township settled by Irish immigrants in the 1840s and 50s. Set amid rolling green pastures speckled with black and white cows, the sign at the town entrance proclaims this 'A green and pleasant land...'

Koroit's main street is lined with old verandah-fronted buildings, and among the shops there are some interesting galleries, craft and antique shops, and pottery works.

Places to Stay & Eat In the centre of town, the ***Koroit Hotel*** *(☎ 5565 8201)* is a great old country pub that's very popular for St Patrick's Day celebrations. The exterior is an unusual blend of Art Nouveau and Victorian architecture, and the cosy heritage-style bedrooms upstairs cost $25 per person for B&B. The pub's dining room serves country-style dinners for around $10 on Friday, Saturday and Sunday nights.

The Croft *(☎ 5565 8721, 145 High St)* is a cute little timber cottage that has been brightly renovated. It's self-contained, has two bedrooms and costs from $90 a night.

Killarney

Back on the highway 8km east of Port Fairy, Killarney is another area originally settled by Irish immigrants. The modern ***Killarney Hotel/Motel*** *(☎ 5568 7290)* replaced a historic pub that burnt to the ground in 1993. A big block of bluestone at the front of the pub has been christened the 'Blarney Stone'. The pub has cheap bar meals for $6 to $9 or bistro meals for $8 to $12, and there are three motel units costing from $50 to $70 a double.

From the highway it's about 2km down to the crescent-shaped **Killarney Beach**, which is a noted fishing spot, especially for King George whiting. There's a basic ***camp-ground*** here beside the football oval – bookings can be made through the Killarney General Store (☎ 5568 7381).

PORT FAIRY

• **pop 2600**

This historic seaside township was one of the earliest settled areas in Victoria, dating back to 1835. The first arrivals were whalers and sealers, and Port Fairy is still the home port for one of Victoria's largest fishing fleets. You can walk along Fisherman's Wharf and watch the fishing boats unload their catch of crayfish and abalone.

The town has a relaxed and salty feel, with its old bluestone and sandstone buildings, whitewashed cottages, colourful fishing boats alongside the wharf, and streets lined with Norfolk Island pines. For a time it was known as Belfast and, although the name was changed back to Port Fairy in 1887, there's still a northern Irish flavour about the place (and the Belfast Bakery on the main street).

Some 50 of the fine old buildings are classified by the National Trust. One of them, the Caledonian Hotel, claims to be Victoria's oldest continuously licensed premises. There are several unfinished rooms at the hotel – apparently, during the 1850s, the workers downed tools and joined the rush to the goldfields, and the work was never completed.

Orientation & Information

The Moyne River runs parallel to Port Fairy Bay. The narrow strip of land between the bay and river provides a natural port for the fishing fleet. Two bridges cross the river to the narrow headland.

The town centre is along Bank St to the west of the river. The Port Fairy Visitor In-

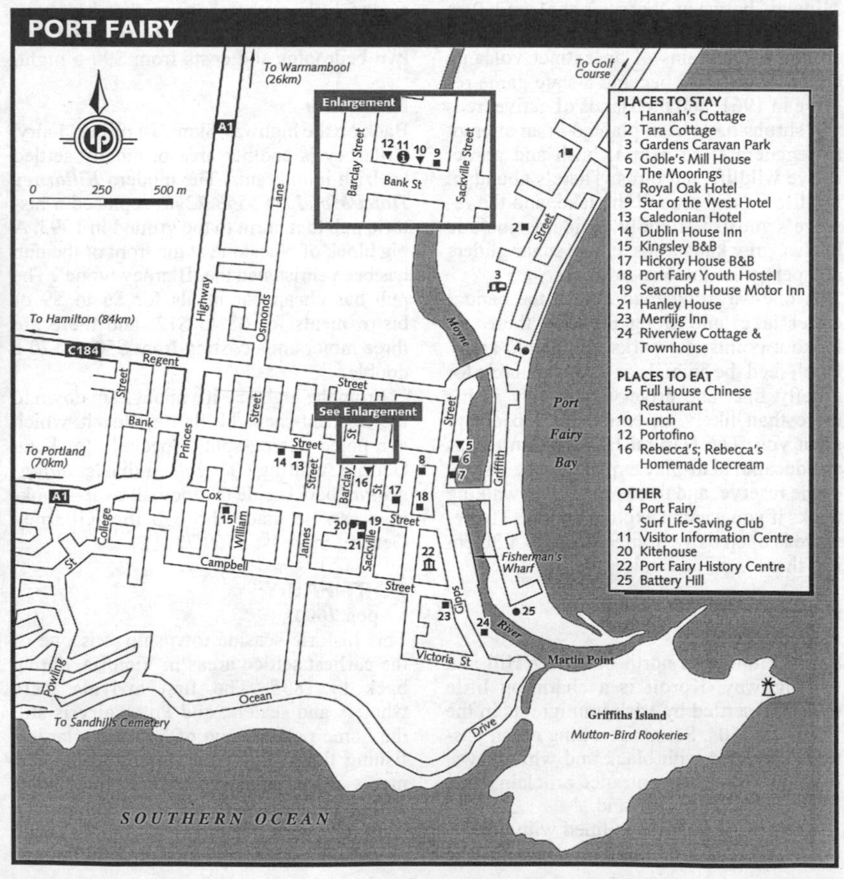

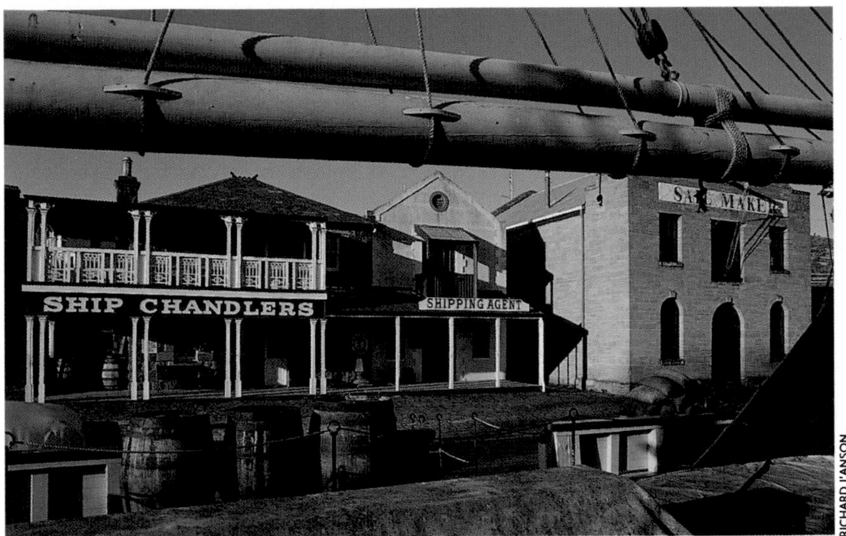

RICHARD I'ANSON

Flagstaff Hill Maritime Village, Warrnambool

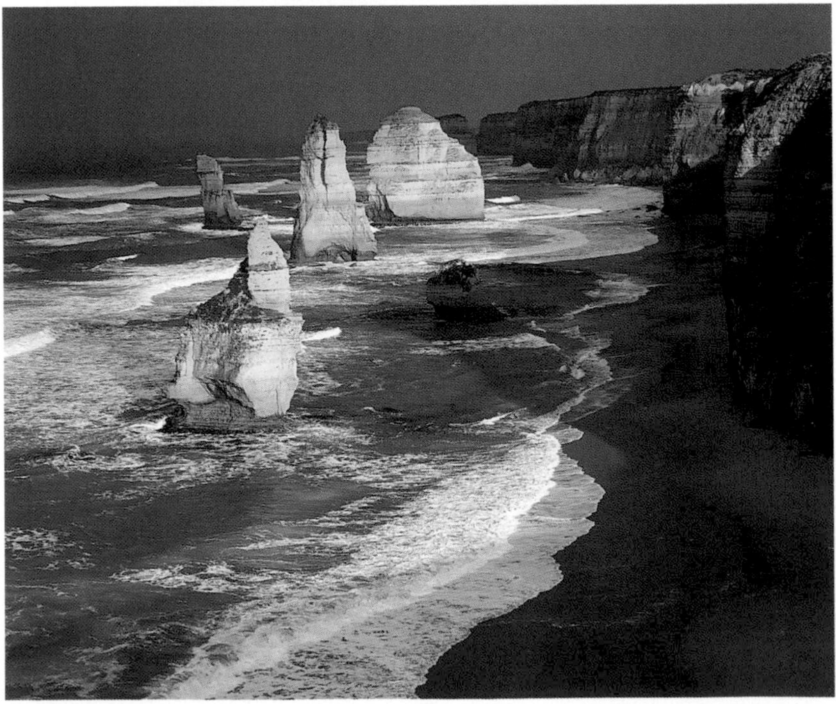

RICHARD I'ANSON

Morning at the Twelve Apostles, Port Campbell National Park

HUGH FINLAY

The endless Warrnambool coastline

GLENN BEANLAND

Cape Nelson Lighthouse, near Portland

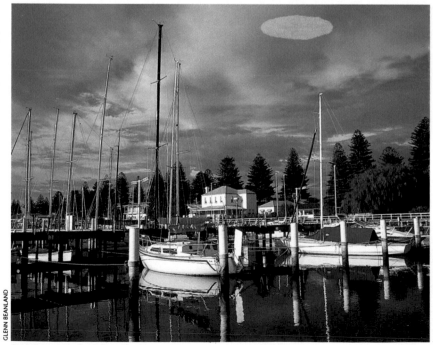

GLENN BEANLAND

Port Fairy waterfront from the Moyne River

formation Centre (☎ 5568 2682), on Bank St between Sackville and Barclay Sts, is open daily from 9 am to 5 pm. A new centre is planned for the old railway site on Bank St near the river. Opening hours will remain the same.

Things to See & Do

A brochure is available from the Visitor Information Centre for the **Shipwreck Walk**, comprising three short walks which highlight the sites of some of the many wrecks along this coastline.

For those interested in Port Fairy's rich architectural heritage, there's a signposted **History Walk** around the town – a walk map (20c) is available from the Visitor Information Centre, as is the booklet *Historic Buildings of Port Fairy* ($1).

The **Port Fairy History Centre**, housed in the old bluestone courthouse in Gipps St (complete with mannequins acting out a courtroom scene), has shipping relics, old photos and costumes and a prisoner cell. It's open from 2 to 5 pm on Wednesday, weekends, and daily during school holidays ($3 for adults, 50c for children).

On **Battery Hill**, there's a lookout point and old cannons and fortifications that were here in the 1860s.

In the 1830s, local whaling operations were based on **Griffiths Island**, which is joined to the mainland by a narrow strip of land. A bluestone lighthouse was built here in 1859, and still shines its beacon to warn local shipping. Today the island is home to a colony of mutton birds (short-tailed shearwaters). These birds, a protected species in Victoria, have a remarkably regular life cycle, returning to their nesting grounds on the island within a few days of 22 September each year. Each bird returns to the same nest burrow it occupied the previous year, and generally mates with the same partner throughout its breeding life. The birds lay their eggs in November (which hatch in January), and leave with their young for the Kamchatka Peninsula in Siberia every April. When they're in town, you can see the memorable sight of tens of thousands of birds returning to their nests at dusk to feed their young. Take a torch and stick to the tracks, as you will collapse the birds' nests if you stray and walk across the dunes.

The very scenic **Port Fairy Golf Course** (☎ 5568 1654) overlooks the coast about 6km north of town. It's open to the public most days, and a round costs $12.

Organised Cruises

Mary S Tours (☎ 5568 1480, mobile 014 807 054) and Mulloka Cruises (☎ 5568 1790) both offer half-hour scenic cruises for $10 (children free) as well as fishing trips. Cruises depart from Fisherman's Wharf.

Special Events

The Port Fairy Folk Festival, one of Australia's foremost music festivals, is held here on the Labour Day long weekend in early March. The town is flooded with festival-goers so it's impossible to get a bed unless you have booked well in advance; otherwise camping is the only possibility.

'Rhapsody in June', held over the Queen's Birthday weekend, is a showcase for local artists, craftspeople, musicians and dancers. There's also the popular Spring Music Festival (classical and jazz music) in mid-October.

The Moyneana Festival is held between Christmas and the Australia Day weekend in late January – the New Year's Eve procession is always a highlight.

Places to Stay

Port Fairy has an excellent range of accommodation, including an outstanding collection of B&Bs, guesthouses and self-contained cottages. It's impossible to list them all here so check with the Visitor Information Centre for other options, and bear in mind that accommodation is usually heavily booked during holidays.

Camping & Caravan Parks A few of Port Fairy's six caravan parks only open over summer. The closest place to town is the spacious and well set-up ***Gardens Caravan Park*** *(☎ 5568 1060, 111 Griffiths St)*, with campsites for $12 to $15 and two-bedroom timber cabins for $50 to $70.

On the Princes Hwy 2km north of the centre, ***Learnean Anchorage Caravan Park*** *(☎ 5568 1145)* has powered sites for $17 to $22 and on-site vans and cabins for $30 to $72.

Hostel & Pubs ***Port Fairy Youth Hostel*** *(☎ 5568 2468, 8 Cox St)* is in the former home of merchant William Rutledge, built in 1844. It's a friendly, relaxed and well set-up hostel, offering a choice of bunk beds in the main house or a bed in the modern units out the back. The nightly cost is $13 for YHA members and $16 for nonmembers.

The ***Star of the West Hotel*** *(☎ 5568 1715, corner Bank and Sackville Sts)* has basic pub rooms for $20 per person ($12 if you're travelling on the Wayward Bus – see Organised Tours at the beginning of this chapter), including breakfast. Further down Bank St, the ***Royal Oak Hotel*** *(☎ 5568 1018)* has B&B for $30 per person (shared bathroom).

Motels The recently renovated ***Dublin House Inn*** *(☎ 5568 2022, 57-59 Bank St)* has a self-contained unit in the Old Bakery for $120 and other cosy doubles from $75 a night.

Seacombe House Motor Inn *(☎ 5568 1082, corner Cox and Sackville Sts)* has motel units from $95 a double, quaint hotel-style rooms in the original 1847 inn for $30 per person, including breakfast, and National Trust-classified cottages that sleep up to four people and have their own kitchen, lounge, spa and open fire, costing from $150 to $200 a double (plus $20 per extra person).

The ***Caledonian Hotel*** *(☎ 5568 1044, 41 Bank St)* has motel units costing from $60 to $75 a double.

Guesthouses & B&Bs Undoubtedly one of the top B&Bs in this part of the world, ***Goble's Mill House*** *(☎ 5568 1118, fax 5568 1178, 75 Gipps St)* is a divine bluestone building, formerly a flour mill and later a butter factory, that stands imposingly on the banks of the Moyne River. It's stylish, solid and snug with doubles costing from $100 to $150 (for a loft room with river views).

For a home-away-from-home experience, stay at ***Hanley House*** *(☎ 5568 2709, 14 Sackville St)*, a peaceful place dating from the mid-1850s with cosy rooms and a welcoming Morton Bay fig out the front. Renowned singer/songwriter Archie Roach liked this place so much he recorded his latest CD here. Singles/doubles start at $65/85.

Also good are the elegant ***Hickory House B&B*** *(☎ 5568 2530, 4 Princes St)* with rooms from $85/100, and the well restored Federation-era ***Kingsley B&B*** *(☎ 5568 1269, 71 Cox St)*, which has rooms for $55/85.

The ***Merrijig Inn*** *(☎ 5568 2324, corner Campbell and Gipps Sts)* is a favourite with those escaping the city. Dating from 1842, this restored inn has its own bar and restaurant (see Places to Eat later), several inviting spots to curl up in front of an open fire, cosy attic rooms for $90 and downstairs suites for $110.

Self-Contained Cottages & Apartments There are numerous restored cottages that can be rented overnight or longer. ***Tara Cottage*** *(☎ 9818 2532, 131 Griffith St)* is a cute-as-a-button bluestone and sandstone cottage set in pretty gardens. It sleeps two and costs from $175 for a weekend or $375 for a week. Nearby, ***Hannah's Cottage*** *(☎ 5568 1583, 177 Griffith St)* is a simple, three bedroom timber place that sleeps up to seven people. Nightly costs range from $80 to $100 a double, plus $15 per extra person.

If you're after something more modern, ***The Moorings*** *(☎ 5562 6824, 69 Gipps St)* is a pair of stylish, two storey architect-designed townhouses on the riverfront. They're equipped with all the mod cons, sleep up to six people and cost $120 a double, plus $10 per extra person (minimum two night stay). Also down by the river, ***Riverview Cottage & Townhouse*** *(☎ 5568 2324, 17 Gipps St)* has a cottage costing $110 a night for four people, and a townhouse for $120 a double.

Places to Eat

A top spot for a daytime bite is ***Rebecca's*** *(☎ 5568 2533, 72 Sackville St)*, a cheery cafe with a pleasant vibe, diverse lunch menu (with a good vegetarian selection), and sticky date pudding to die for. Lunch costs around $8 and it's open daily from 8 am to 6 pm. And for ice cream freaks, ***Rebecca's Homemade Icecream*** is right next door – yum!

Lovely ***Lunch*** *(☎ 5568 2642, 20 Bank St)*, set in the old Port Fairy Town Hall (1865), is (as the owner says) the only place in Australia where you can have breakfast at Lunch for dinner. The cuisine is modern Australian and the vegetarian selection is impressive. Mains cost between $9 and $18.50. Lunch is open Wednesday to Sunday from 8.30 am to 5 pm and is also open for dinner on Friday, Saturday and Sunday.

Portofino *(☎ 5568 1047, 28 Bank St)* is a small and intimate Italian bistro. The walls are hung with photos of some of the more famous sights of Italy, and the menu has traditional Italian cuisine with pasta dishes for $14 to $16 and other mains for around $18.

The rustic corner bar of the 1844 ***Caledonian Hotel*** *(41 Bank St)* is the domain of the local fishermen. The Cally serves up the best bar meals in town, with hearty dishes like mixed grills, roast beef, fish and chips, or mashed potatoes and meat for around $7. The pub's dining room, known as The Stump, has mains in the $12 to $15 range. Also along Bank St, the ***Royal Oak Hotel*** and the ***Star of the West Hotel*** both do pretty good pub meals.

The modern ***Full House Restaurant*** *(☎ 5568 1889, 79-83 Gipps St)*, overlooking the river, serves Chinese dishes costing from $10 to $15.

Several of the accommodation places listed in the earlier Places to Stay section have restaurants. The cosy restaurant at ***Dublin House Inn*** specialises in fresh local produce with particularly good seafood and it's open every day. The well regarded restaurant at the ***Merrijig Inn*** is open for dinner nightly except Monday, with mains costing $19.50, and at Seacombe House the ***Stag Restaurant*** is also very good, with main meals around $20.

Getting There & Around

There are daily buses between Port Fairy and Warrnambool ($4.30), connecting with trains to/from Melbourne ($36.50/50.10 in economy/1st class). V/Line has daily buses heading west to Portland ($8.60) and Mt Gambier ($20.80). Buses arrive and depart from Southwestern Roadways in Bank St.

Kitehouse (☎ 5568 2782) at 27 Cox St hires out a good range of racers and mountain bikes from $20 a day.

PORT FAIRY TO PORTLAND

Signposted off the Princes Hwy, **The Crags** are 12km west of Port Fairy. Along this jagged foreshore are the calcified remains of a small coastal forest, while 8km offshore you can see the flat-topped volcanic **Lady Julia Percy Island**, known by local Aboriginal tribes as 'Deen Maar'. This island is important in Aboriginal mythology as the resting place of the spirits of the dead from the Gunditjmara tribe.

Seventeen kilometres north-west of Port Fairy is the tiny town of **Yambuk**. ***Eumeralla Backpackers*** *(☎ 5568 4204)* is an excellent new hostel in the old Yambuk school, run by a local Aboriginal trust. Facilities are good and the living room displays artwork documenting local Koori history. The cost is $10 for a bunk bed and canoes can be hired for $5 a day to paddle down the Eumeralla River to Lake Yambuk.

The bluestone ***Yambuk Inn Hotel*** *(☎ 55 68 4310)* has B&B in attic rooms for $25 per person.

PORTLAND

• **pop 9500**

Portland is Victoria's oldest town. Nowadays it's a strange blend of the historic and the industrial – a mix typified by the scenic drive around the foreshore, where you get a foreground view of old bluestone buildings in landscaped grounds, with the modern Portland Aluminium Smelter and tanker wharfs dominating the background.

From early in the 19th century, Portland was a main base for seasonal whaling and sealing operations. The first permanent settler was Edward Henty, who brought his family here from Van Diemen's Land (Tasmania) in 1834, thus establishing the first permanent European settlement in Victoria. Portland has many 19th-century buildings, many of which are classified by the National Trust.

The Portland Aluminium Smelter occupies a narrow headland. This place produces something like 300,000 tonnes of aluminium each year, making it one of Australia's biggest export earners. Although it gives the city a decidedly industrial feel, the smelter is very modern and relatively clean; thousands of trees have been planted around the plant to create an 'industrial park'.

The Portland Port is the only deep-water port between Melbourne and Adelaide, handling everything from huge tankers and carriers to small fishing boats. You can walk along some of the wharf areas to inspect the various ships and watch the fishing boats unload their catch.

Information

The Portland Visitor Information Centre (☎ 5523 2671), at the Maritime Discovery Centre (see the following entry), has a good range of information on Portland and its surrounds. The staff are helpful and it's open daily from 9 am to 5 pm.

For information about the many national and state parks in the area, call into the Parks Victoria office (☎ 5523 1180) at 8-12 Julia St.

Geothermal Energy

The visitor information centre, the swimming pools at the Portland Leisure & Aquatic Centre in Bentinck St, the hospital, library and a number of other buildings in Portland are heated geothermally from the city's water supply. The water comes from an underground source and reaches the surface at around 56°C, and the heat is captured through heat exchanges. Before this innovation, the swimming pools were heated by oil-fired burners. The new system is environmentally friendly and saves the swimming centre up to $300,000 in fuel bills a year.

Mark Armstrong

Maritime Discovery Centre

This impressive new centre, on Lee Breakwater Rd overlooking Portland Bay, explores the links between people and the sea with displays on marine exploration, whaling, wildlife of the sea and the Portland Lifeboat, Australia's oldest intact vessel. The building itself is worth a squizz; its modern metal forms and structures evoke maritime themes. The complex also houses the Portland Visitor Information Centre and ***The Galley*** cafe, which has fine views of the working port. It's open daily from 9 am to 5 pm and admission is $7 for adults, $3 for children and $20 for families.

Portland Botanic Gardens

These gardens in Cliff St were established in 1857, when the first curator William Allitt borrowed 80 Chinese prisoners from the Portland prison to help him prepare the site. The tiny **gardener's bluestone cottage** is furnished in period style and contains various items of historical interest; it's open on Sunday from 2 to 4 pm (September to May). The gardens have many rare species, including Victoria's largest New Zealand cabbage tree. There's a large rose garden, and the colourful dahlias reach their spectacular peak in March.

Burswood Homestead & Gardens

Burswood Homestead, at 15 Cape Nelson Rd, was built for Edward Henty in 1850. The 5.5 hectare gardens were laid out between 1853 and 1856, and they remain an outstanding example of a 19th-century town garden. A tree-lined driveway leads to the homestead, and the gardens include many of the original trees and shrubs, as well as

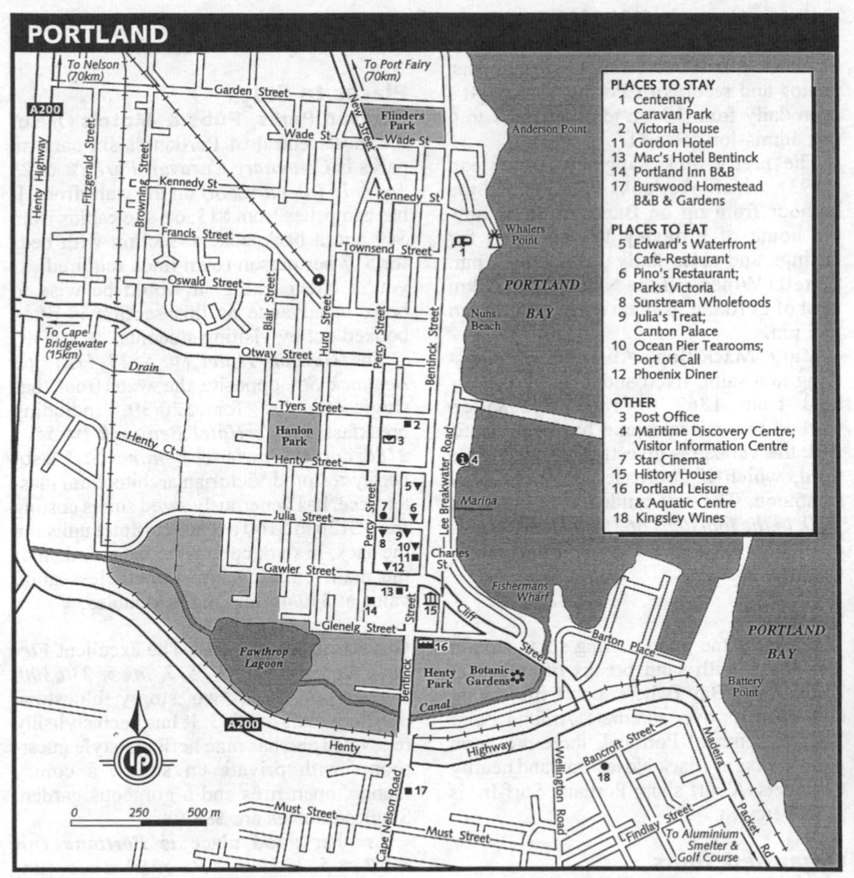

rose gardens and a conifer garden. The homestead is now a B&B (see Places to Stay later). The gardens are open daily from 10 am to 5 pm (closed during winter). Admission costs $3 for adults (free for children).

Other Attractions

The Portland **tourist drive** winds around the waterfront and port past many historic buildings and finishes at the botanic gardens. There's also a **historic walking trail** that starts from the Visitor Information Centre and, again, passes many of the town's historic buildings.

Fawthrop Lagoon, a large area of open tidal water south of the city centre, is at the end of a broad canal lined with wharfs. The lagoon is a great spot for birdwatchers, with species including swans, ducks, pelicans, herons and white ibis. There's a bird hide and barbecue area, and a walking track leads around the lagoon to the botanic gardens.

History House (☎ 5522 2266) is a history museum in the former town hall in Charles St, chock-full of interesting old documents, photos and records of Portland's past. It's open daily from 10 am to noon and 1 to 4 pm; admission costs $1.

The pretty pink Kingsley Homestead (1893), which overlooks Portland and the harbour from up on Bancroft St, is now the home of **Kingsley Wines**, open for tastings and sales daily from 1 to 4 pm. **Barretts Wines**, off the Nelson road 20km west of Portland, is open daily from 11 am to 5 pm.

Mary MacKillop, Australia's nearest thing to a saint, lived and worked in Portland from 1862 to 1866. MacKillop worked two miracles and has been beatified; the Vatican is investigating a possible third, which if confirmed may result in sainthood. The self-guided tour brochure *Walk in the footsteps of Mary MacKillop* is available from the Visitor Information Centre.

Surfing

There are some good surfing spots around this coast, with sand breaks often out at Bridgewater Bay (where a surf life-saving club operates over summer). Around Point Danger, south of Portland, there are good point breaks at Black Nose Point and nearby Crumpets. A surf shop, Portland Surf-In, is at 98 Percy St.

Organised Tours

There are free two-hour tours of the aluminium smelter every Monday, Wednesday and Friday at 10 am (and several times daily during holiday periods). Bookings are essential – phone ☎ 5523 2671.

Special Events

Every second weekend in February, Portland hosts the Go Kart Street Grand Prix, heart-pumping racing action for rookies and pros alike. More than 50 races are held over the two days with about 350 karters participating. Admission is free for spectators.

Portland also hosts the Dahlia Festival in March, always a colourful affair.

Places to Stay

Caravan Parks, Pubs & Motels One of the most central of Portland's six caravan parks is ***Centenary Caravan Park*** *(☎ 5523 1487, 184 Bentinck St)* on the waterfront. It has campsites from $13, on-site cabins from $40 and a backpackers' section with beds for $17 per person (own linen required). If you're backpacking, it would be wise to book in advance as this section is often booked out by visiting students.

The ***Gordon Hotel*** *(☎ 5523 1121, 63 Bentinck St)*, opposite the waterfront, has singles/doubles for $20/30, including breakfast. ***Mac's Hotel Bentinck*** *(☎ 5523 2188, corner Gawler & Bentinck Sts)*, a superbly restored Victorian architectural masterpiece, has generously sized suites costing from $120 to $160 a double. Motel units out the back, in stark contrast to the grandeur of the main building, are nonetheless good value at $40/46 for singles/doubles.

Guesthouses & B&Bs The excellent ***Victoria House*** *(☎ 5521 7577, fax 5523 6300, 5 Tyers St)* is a two storey bluestone dwelling built in 1853. It has been stylishly renovated and has nine heritage-style guestrooms with private en suites, a comfy lounge, open fires and a gorgeous garden. Singles/doubles are $88/98.

Another good place is ***Portland Inn B&B*** *(☎ 5523 2985, 4 Percy St)*, a cosy timber home dating from 1840 with a charming courtyard garden. There are three guestrooms from $85/95.

The resplendent ***Burswood Homestead*** *(☎ 5523 4686, 15 Cape Nelson Rd)*, built for Edward Henty in 1850 and set amid beautiful gardens, is one of the most impressive guesthouses in Victoria. It's a formal, indulgent, antique-laden mansion (get the picture?), with standard rooms from $85/110 (shared bathroom) and more-spacious master rooms with en suites from $95/145. Family rooms are available from $155. All prices include a buffet breakfast, and Devonshire tea on arrival.

Places to Eat

Julia's Treat *(5 Julia St)* – nice pun – may look like just another take-away joint, but most nights Katrina (the local ambassador for Greek hospitality) turns the place into a fun and casual restaurant. The menu is small but you can usually get Greek salads, lamb and dips, a steak or a casserole, or even fish and chips. It's BYO and meals cost up to $10 – and the coffee is great.

A couple of doors up from here, ***Canton Palace*** has a cheap Chinese smorgasbord at $6.90 for lunch or $13.80 for dinner. Across the road, ***Pino's*** is a casual Italian pizza house with pastas, schnitzels, calamari and steaks for $9 to $13. For a huge, cheap feed, head to ***Phoenix Diner*** in Gore Place. The $5 entree-size bowls of pasta and roasts are massive.

The inviting ***Port of Call*** *(85 Bentinck St)*, a cafe on the waterfront, is good value for breakfast or lunch. Close by, ***Ocean Pier Tearooms*** is also good for lunch, with hearty home-style soups, bagels, 'hot toasties', pastries and Sunday roasts ($6). ***Sunstream Wholefoods*** *(49 Julia St)* has good healthy tucker, including mountain bread rolls, lentil burgers, fresh juices and smoothies.

Portland's best, most upmarket eatery, ***Edward's Waterfront Cafe-Restaurant*** *(☎ 5523 1032, 101 Bentinck St)*, is open for breakfast, lunch and dinner. It has an extensive wine list, mains such as pasta and seafood dishes, roast quail, lamb curry and steaks for $15 to $18, plus a cake selection that will make you wish you hadn't ordered a main.

Getting There & Away

There are daily V/Line buses between Portland and Port Fairy ($8.60), Warrnambool ($12.20) and Mt Gambier ($11.20). Buses operate from Henty St, near the corner of Percy St.

AROUND PORTLAND

Cape Nelson

Along a sealed road 11km south of Portland is the **Cape Nelson State Park.** This small coastal park has a Sea Cliff Nature Walk and other walking tracks with some excellent coastal views, as well as a picnic area with fireplaces and tables. The park's vegetation is mostly coastal shrub, and includes the soap mallee, a common South Australian species that doesn't grow anywhere else in Victoria.

The 1884 **Cape Nelson Lighthouse** is classified by the National Trust and is open for tours – check with Parks Victoria or the Portland Visitor Information Centre for opening times.

Cape Bridgewater

The road to Cape Bridgewater, 21km west of Portland, is a very pleasant scenic drive. The route is lined with saltbush and passes through sand dunes and paddocks. Eventually you come to idyllic Bridgewater Bay, a lovely arc of white-sand beach backed by a handful of holiday houses.

The road climbs around the Cape to the top of a high hill, with great views back along the coast. Blowholes Rd continues out to a car park at Cape Duquesne, from where walking tracks lead to a platform overlooking the rocky **blowholes**, which spout water into the air during high seas. Another track leads to the remains of a **petrified forest** on the cliff-top.

The Great South-West Walk (see that section later in this chapter) continues around the coastline, and from the western end of Bridgewater Bay you can follow the trail up to the top of the cape and continue around to a **seal colony**. It's a steep and sometimes difficult walk of around three hours return. If you'd prefer to see these sweet creatures from the water, Seals by Sea (☎ 5526 7247) runs tours on weekends, or by appointment during the week.

Places to Stay & Eat

Sea View Lodge B&B *(☎ 5526 7276)* on Bridgewater Rd is a modern, two storey beachhouse/guesthouse with spectacular views of the bay. It's a bright, comfortable and friendly place with a nice wide veranda from which to contemplate the sea. The owners run the Marine Ecology Centre next door (entry $2) with interesting tactile displays for children. Doubles cost from $75 to $90 and there are backpacker B&B deals for

$25. The owners may be able to pick you up from Portland if you ring in advance.

Spindrift has million-dollar views from high on the hilltop, as well as tasty home-made meals and Devonshire teas. It's closed on Monday and Tuesday.

PORTLAND TO SOUTH AUSTRALIA

From Portland, you can either head north to Heywood and rejoin the Princes Hwy, or head north-west along the slower but much more interesting coastal route known as the Portland-Nelson road. This road runs inland from the coast, but along the way there are turn-offs leading down to the beaches and into some great national parks.

GREAT SOUTH-WEST WALK

This walk covers 250km of coastal wilderness between Portland and the South Australian border. Starting from the Portland Visitor Information Centre, the walk follows the coast all the way to the small township of Nelson, then heads inland along the course of the Glenelg River to the South Australian border before looping back to Portland.

To walk the full distance you'd need at least 10 days, although the walk is designed to allow people to walk shorter sections – taking anywhere from a few hours to a couple of days.

The first section of the walk, from Portland to Nelson, heads south from Portland to Nelson Bay and Bridgewater Bay. At Bridgewater Lakes you could detour via the Mt Richmond National Park, rejoining the coast at the Swan Lake camp. The coastal trail traverses Discovery Bay, with its remote and beautiful beaches, sand-dunes and inland lakes, all the way to Nelson. See the Discovery Bay Coastal Park section later in this chapter for details.

From Nelson the walk follows the Glenelg River inland for about 45km through the Lower Glenelg National Park, and then crosses into the Cobboboonee State Forest before traversing alternating sections of open forest and farmland on the way back to Portland.

The walk is clearly marked with distinctive red triangular 'emu logo' signs, and there are 16 bush camping sites at varying intervals along the way, all of which have fireplaces, toilets and fresh water supplies. A gas or fuel stove is a good idea as firewood can be scarce, and you should carry water with you along the way.

For more information on the walk, see Lonely Planet's *Bushwalking in Australia* or contact the Portland Visitor Information Centre (☎ 5523 2671). If you're interested in sections of the walk, a good booklet entitled *Short Walks on and around the Great South-West Walk* is available from the Portland Parks Victoria office for $3.

MT RICHMOND NATIONAL PARK

This is the first point of interest along the Portland-Nelson road. The park is on the site of an extinct volcano, although Mt Richmond last erupted about two million years ago and, since then, most of the evidence of volcanic activity has been buried under coastal sand blown inland from Discovery Bay. The vegetation is mainly hardy native species such as brown stringy-bark and manna gums, and the park is noted for its wonderful wildflowers and unusual plants. Over 450 species have been recorded here, including 50 different species of orchid.

The park's residents include kangaroos and wallabies, koalas and echidnas, snakes and potokangaroos. Whatakangaroos, you ask? The southern potoroo is a rarely seen, mainly nocturnal member of the kangaroo family. There's also abundant birdlife.

There are some good picnic areas with tables and wood barbecues, and a lookout tower with views to Discovery Bay and Lady Julia Percy Island. There are four main walking tracks through the park: **Benwerrin Nature Walk, Noel's Walk** and the **West Walk** all take an hour, and the **Ocean View Walk** takes around 45 minutes. A brochure guide to the local flora and fauna is available from a box at the start of the nature walk.

DISCOVERY BAY COASTAL PARK

The entire coast from Cape Bridgewater to Nelson is a protected coastal park. Discovery Bay Coastal Park is a narrow coastal strip of long sand beaches backed by high sand dunes. Behind the dunes are swampy flatlands and a number of small and pretty lakes and lagoons which are good for swimming and fishing. The ocean beaches along here are notorious for their rips and currents, and swimming in the sea should be approached with extreme caution – or better still, not done at all. Swim in the lakes instead.

This is a great area for bushwalking, fishing and birdwatching. The 200km Great South-West Walk traverses the park, and there are shorter walking trails around Swan Lake and Lake Mombeong.

There are camping areas with basic amenities at both Swan Lake and Lake Mombeong – the Parks Victoria office at Nelson issues permits for these sites. Several unsealed access roads lead into the park from the Portland-Nelson road. For more information about this park, contact the Parks Victoria office in Portland (☎ 5523 1180) or in Nelson (☎ 08-8738 4051).

LOWER GLENELG NATIONAL PARK

On the inland side of the Portland-Nelson road is the 27,000 hectare Lower Glenelg National Park, featuring deep gorges and brilliant wildflowers. The Glenelg River, which originates in the Grampians and travels more than 400km to the coast at Nelson, is at its most impressive during its last 35km – to reach the ocean, the river waters have carved spectacular gorges through soft, limestone cliffs. This park is very popular with canoeists and those who like to dangle a line; you can hire canoes, boats and fishing gear in Nelson.

The park is rich in native wildlife and plants. Over 700 different plant species have been recorded here, including a variety of orchid and even tree ferns. The wildlife includes kangaroos, wallabies, echidnas, brushtail possums and potoroos. There is also a small colony of wombats near the Princess Margaret Rose Cave, the only remaining colony in this part of the state. Birds are also abundant, and include emus, herons, ducks, kingfishers and quail.

There's an extensive network of walking tracks that in places follow fire access tracks throughout the park – many of these are alongside or lead to the river. There's also a number of picnic areas with wood fires, tables and toilets. You can camp here if you book with the ranger, but the facilities are limited.

The best way to see the park is from a canoe and there are 11 canoeists' camping sites between Nelson and Dartmoor. Most of the sites are only accessible from the water, and they provide basic facilities such as fresh water, toilets and fireplaces. The ranger's office issues camping permits for these sites, and canoes can be hired in Nelson. The river is navigable for more than 70km from Nelson and is also used by motor boats.

Parks Victoria has an information centre (☎ 08-8738 4051) in the park several kilometres north of Nelson, and this is the place to make camping reservations (not necessary outside of peak seasons). The office is open on weekdays, except Tuesday, from 9 am to 4.30 pm.

NELSON

Nelson is a small and sleepy riverside village with a few houses, a cute general store, a pub and a few motels and caravan parks. It's a popular holiday and fishing spot because of its great setting on the coast and at the mouth of the mighty Glenelg River, but because it's a bit out of the way it hasn't yet been spoiled by commercialisation and development.

Canoe & Boat Hire

Two operators, Nelson Boat Hire (☎ 08-8738 4048) and South West Canoe Service (☎ 08-8738 4141), hire out canoes and kayaks for paddling expeditions through the Lower Glenelg National Park. The daily cost is around $25, including barrels, life jacket and paddles, and both operators will drop you at your starting point so you can paddle downriver and finish back in Nelson.

There is an additional fee for drop-offs, depending on how far you're going.

Nelson Boat Hire also hires out open fishing boats and half-cabin cruisers.

River Cruises

The *Nelson Endeavour* and *Pompei's Pride* (☎ 08-8738 4191) both offer scenic cruises from Nelson up the Glenelg River to the Princess Margaret Rose Cave. *Nelson Endeavour* departs Wednesday and Saturday at 1 pm; *Pompei's Pride* departs Tuesday, Thursday and Sunday at 1 pm. Adults cost $15 and children $7.

Both boats operate less frequently in winter and more frequently in holiday periods.

Places to Stay

The ***River-Vu Caravan Park*** *(☎ 08-8738 4123)* is friendly and has good sites with private bathrooms for $15, as well as cabins from $38 a double.

The ***Nelson Hotel*** *(☎ 08-8738 4011)* in Kellett St has basic singles/doubles costing from $20/30, including breakfast, and the ***Motel Black Wattle*** *(☎ 08-8738 4008)* on Mount Gambier Rd has good doubles from $65.

On Black Swan Rd on the west side of the river, the ***Anchorage B&B*** *(☎ 08-8738 4220)* is a small, simple and friendly place with one room costing $35/50 a single/double, including breakfast. The owner used to run a restaurant in Bali, and can do home-cooked Indonesian dinners.

PRINCESS MARGARET ROSE CAVE

It's a pretty 12km drive along the border from Nelson to Princess Margaret Rose Cave. The unsealed road winds past pine forests, and through the trees you can catch occasional glimpses of the gorges of the Glenelg River.

The caves are now managed by a lessee on behalf of Parks Victoria and half-hour tours are run daily approximately every hour from 10 am to 4.30 pm and cost $5.50. There are interesting tactile displays at the entrance explaining the geological and historical nature of the caves.

Bunny's Burrow

A local grazier, Keith McEarchern, discovered some caves near Nelson in 1936 and named them after Princess Margaret in 1940 (when she was nine years old).

McEarchern found a hole in the ground on his property, and having decided to explore, he lowered himself down 17.5m on an old rope to see what he could see. He was helped by his rabbit-trapper companion, Bunny Hutchesson and his two sons, and the four of them, encouraged by the beauty of the caves and their potential, built a public entrance and carved a set of steps into the limestone. The caves were opened to the public in 1941, and Bunny acted as cave guide for years. He had no geological training but plenty of natural enthusiasm for the loveliness of the caves.

In the parklands around the caves are landscaped picnic areas with barbecues and nature walks which boast fine views of the river gorge. There are also good camping facilities, and cabin accommodation is available – to book, phone the manager on ☎ 08-8738 4171.

PICCANINNIE PONDS

The South Australian border is 4km west of Nelson. Just across the border is the turn-off to Piccaninnie Ponds, which leads down to a pretty stretch of white-sand beach, backed by a few bush camping areas and the ponds, which are famous among divers for their natural beauty.

A signboard describes the ponds and some of the local wildlife, and you can walk to a small platform at the edge of the ponds. The water is surrounded by reeds and is incredibly clear and cold, so cold that it's often too dangerous to swim without a wetsuit. If you want to dive or snorkel here, you'll need a permit from the Department for Environment, Heritage & Aboriginal Affairs (☎ 08-8735 1177), 11 Helen St, Mt Gambier.

The Western District

This south-western region of Victoria inland from the coast, contains some of the best sheep and cattle grazing pasture in the country. It's also said to be the third largest volcanic plain in the world. Hamilton, the major town of the Western District, is known locally as the 'Wool Capital of the World', and there are a few interesting things to see in and around the town.

However, the region's volcanic features are probably of most interest to travellers. South of Hamilton are the volcanic parks of Mt Napier and Mt Eccles, while the area around Colac is known as 'Lakes and Craters Country' – most of the dozens of lakes in the district are old volcanic craters.

History

The Western District is littered with signs of its volcanic past: craters and lakes, eroded lava flows, lava tubes and caves and mile after mile of stone walls made of volcanic rocks.

About 20 million years ago, much of this area was flooded by shallow seas. By about six million years ago, the sedimentary base-rock had been covered by a bed of marine limestone, which gradually eroded. Then there was a period of violent volcanic activity some 19,000 or 20,000 years ago, when the earth's crust split and volcanoes such as Mt Eccles and Mt Napier erupted. This period lasted until about 6000 years ago.

Before European settlers came, much of this area was the territory of the Dhauwurd wurrung Koori tribe. The Dhauwurd wurrung clans who lived along the coast first saw European settlers around 1810, when whalers and sealers based themselves around Portland. The Hentys were Victoria's first permanent European settlers, arriving at Portland from Van Diemen's Land (Tasmania) in 1834 and gradually extending their 'land holdings' inland. Within a few years the Hentys and other settlers had begun to move inland, grazing their sheep on rich

HIGHLIGHTS

- Stay overnight in a 19th century homestead built by the squattocracy of the Western District, such as the Elliminook B&B in Birregurra or Inverary, south-west of Hamilton.
- Enjoy a Sunday lunch at Sunnybrae in Birregurra.
- Check out the excellent and varied collection of the Hamilton Art Gallery.
- Explore the lava tubes and walking trails of Mt Napier State Park.
- Bushwalk, swim and camp at Mt Eccles National Park.
- Visit historic Matthew Cooke Blacksmith Shop in Coleraine.
- The Glenelg Fine Confectionery chocolate factory in Coleraine is perfect for those 'life is like a box of chocolates' times.
- See the fascinating architecture and perhaps stay at Warrock Homestead north of Casterton.

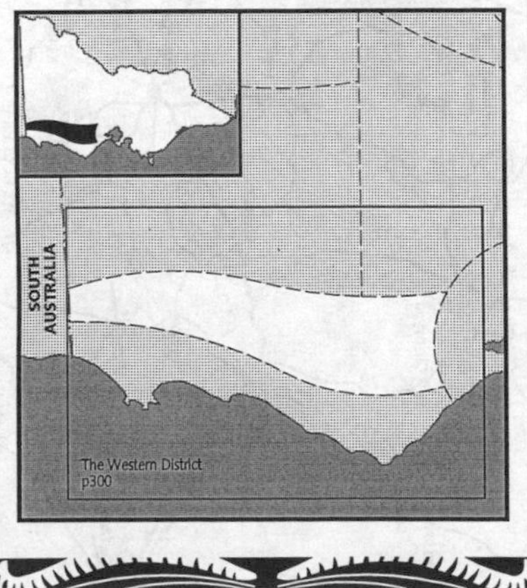

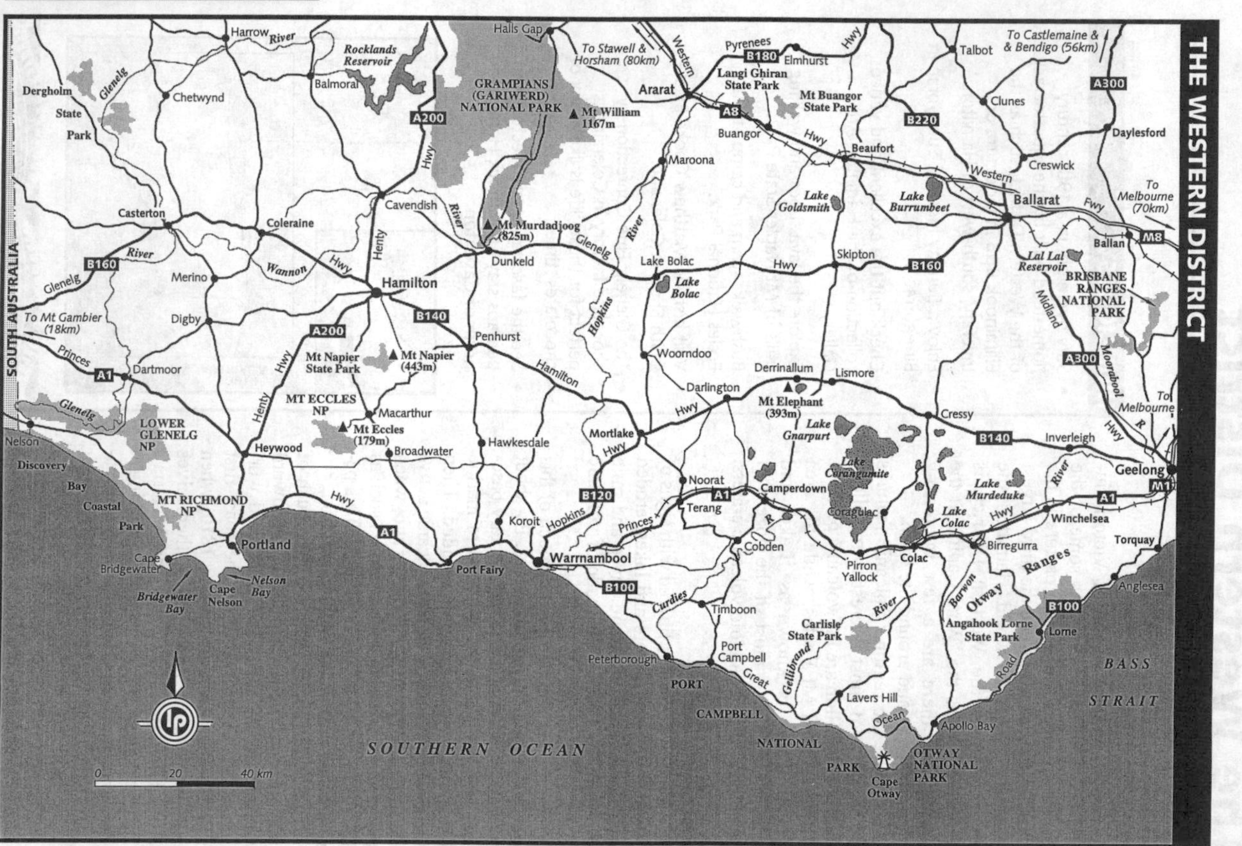
THE WESTERN DISTRICT
BASS STRAIT
SOUTHERN OCEAN
SOUTH AUSTRALIA
To Castlemaine & & Bendigo (56km)
To Melbourne (70km)
To Melbourne
To Stawell & Horsham (80km)
To Mt Gambier (18km)
Geelong
Ballarat
Ararat
Hamilton
Warrnambool
Portland
Colac
Daylesford
Creswick
Clunes
Talbot
Ballan
Torquay
Anglesea
Lorne
Apollo Bay
Cape Otway
Lavers Hill
Winchelsea
Birregurra
Inverleigh
Cressy
Lismore
Skipton
Beaufort
Elmhurst
Pyrenees
Buangor
Maroona
Lake Bolac
Woorndoo
Darlington
Derrinallum
Mortlake
Terang
Noorat
Camperdown
Coragulac
Cobden
Timboon
Port Campbell
Peterborough
Koroit
Port Fairy
Hawkesdale
Penhurst
Dunkeld
Halls Gap
Cavendish
Balmoral
Harrow
Coleraine
Chetwynd
Casterton
Merino
Digby
Dartmoor
Heywood
Macarthur
Broadwater
Nelson
Cape Bridgewater
Cape Nelson
Pirron Yallock
GRAMPIANS (GARIWERD) NATIONAL PARK
BRISBANE RANGES NATIONAL PARK
OTWAY NATIONAL PARK
PORT CAMPBELL NATIONAL PARK
LOWER GLENELG NP
MT RICHMOND NP
MT ECCLES NP
Mt Napier State Park
Angahook Lorne State Park
Carlisle State Park
Langi Ghiran State Park
Mt Buangor State Park
Dergholm State Park
Discovery Bay Coastal Park
Otway Ranges
Lake Burrumbeet
Lake Goldsmith
Lake Corangamite
Lake Gnarpurt
Lake Colac
Lake Murdeduke
Lake Bolac
Lal Lal Reservoir
Rocklands Reservoir
Mt William 1167m
Mt Murdadjoog (825m)
Mt Elephant (393m)
Mt Napier (443m)
Mt Eccles (179m)
Bridgewater Bay
Nelson Bay
Western Fwy
Western Hwy
Midland Hwy
Henty Hwy
Hamilton Hwy
Princes Hwy
Glenelg Hwy
Great Ocean Road
Moorabool River
Barwon River
Hopkins River
Wannon River
Gellibrand River
Curdies River
Glenelg River
Harrow River
A1
A8
A200
A300
B100
B120
B140
B160
B180
B220
M1
M8
0
20
40 km

pastures, many of which were traditional meeting places and sacred sites of the local clans. This eventually led to bloody conflict.

During the 1840s, the Dhauwurd wurrung people fought against the invaders, attacking settlers around Port Fairy, Mt Napier and Lake Condah. The settlers replied in force, and in one incident up to 30 Aborigines were massacred. More subtle methods such as gifts of poisoned flour were also used, and by 1846 Koori resistance had been broken. In 1841 the Koori population in western Victoria was estimated to be 7900; 22 years later, it was only 500.

After the 1840s, much of this area was owned and controlled by a select few families, such as the Hentys and the Whytes. These families were able to lock up the land and amass enormous wealth through their pastoral interests, especially during the heady days of the gold rush when there was a high and constant demand for food. They continually expanded their holdings, influenced and paid politicians to maintain their control and built extravagant homesteads on their properties. Many had exclusive townhouses in Geelong or Melbourne and holiday houses in Queenscliff, made frequent visits to Europe and sent their children to exclusive schools such as Geelong Grammar, Scotch College and Melbourne Grammar. They were the Australian aristocrats, nicknamed the 'squattocracy'. The dominance of these few families was eventually broken, and today the average property is an owner-operated holding of around 200 to 400 hectares.

Orientation & Information

This chapter is split into three sections that correspond with the three major highways that run through the district: the Glenelg Highway (B160; from Ballarat to Hamilton), the Hamilton Highway (B140; from Geelong to Hamilton) and the Princes Highway (A1; from Geelong to Warrnambool, and on to Adelaide).

There are good tourist offices in the towns of Colac, Camperdown, Hamilton and Casterton.

Getting There & Away

Train/Bus There are two to three trains daily from Geelong to Colac ($8.60 economy, $12 first class), continuing through Camperdown and Terang to Warrnambool ($24.50/34.40). On Sunday this route is serviced by buses operating along the Princes Hwy.

V/Line buses also operate daily services along the Glenelg Hwy from Melbourne to Hamilton via Ballarat, continuing on to Mt Gambier ($38.90).

Ballarat to Hamilton

The Glenelg Hwy is the northern border of the Western District. It starts in Ballarat and passes through Hamilton before meeting the Princes Hwy in South Australia, 7km east of Mt Gambier.

SKIPTON

• pop 450

The small rural town of Skipton, 50km west of Ballarat and beside Mt Emu Creek, has a few interesting buildings such as the **Skipton Hotel** (1859) and an old Gothic Presbyterian church complete with gargoyles. There's also an eel farm called Eels Australis where you can usually buy freshly smoked eels. It's in Cleveland St – coming from Ballarat, turn right at the bridge.

Near Skipton is **Mooramong Homestead** (☎ 5340 6553), a National Trust-classified building that was built in the 1870s and features the strange blend of a Californian-style exterior with an Art Deco interior. The interior was remodelled in 1937 when it was the home of the silent-film star, Claire Adams. The homestead, surrounding gardens and a nature reserve are open to the public on most days, but ring in advance to let the manager know you are coming. Admission costs $6 for adults and $4 for children. The turn-off to Mooramong is signposted off the Glenelg Hwy 4.5km west of Skipton – from the turn-off, it's another 8km along a dirt road.

The **Mt Widderin Caves** (☎ 5340 2010) are 6km south of Skipton, just off the Lismore Rd. These are part of a group of seven volcanic caves in the Western District between Bacchus Marsh and Hamilton – Mt Widderin's main cave has the largest chamber of the group. The caves are actually lava tubes, formed as streams of flowing lava cooled and the outer crust solidified, leaving a hollow centre. The caves are privately operated and open to the public on most days, but ring in advance to let the managers know you are coming. Take a torch (flashlight) and old clothes, as some clambering and climbing is necessary at the entrance. Once you're inside, a 200m walk leads to an underground lake. You can explore the cave unaccompanied for $1.

Places to Stay

Mooramong Homestead *(☎ 5340 6553)* is part of a large sheep and crop property, and the self-contained ***Mooramong Cottage***, a simple three-bedroom farmhouse, has its own gardens and chicken pen. The tariff is $75 a night for four people plus $20 for each extra adult.

You can also stay in the ***Mooramong Shearer's Quarters***, with bunkhouse accommodation at $15 per person. There are communal bathroom and kitchen facilities, with room for up to 20 people in twin rooms. Guests at both places have use of a tennis court and swimming pool and need to supply their own linen. If you're carless, the owners can pick you up from Skipton.

LAKE BOLAC

• **pop 250**

Another 50km west of Ballarat, this small highway town is on the northern edge of Lake Bolac, which is popular for fishing, boating, duck shooting and swimming. Every Easter, a sailing regatta is held on the lake.

Places to Stay

The ***Lake Bolac Caravan Park*** (☎ 5350 2329), 2km south of town, has campsites beside the lake from $11 and on-site vans from $30.

On the highway on the west side of town, the ***Lake Bolac Motel*** *(☎ 5350 2218)* has singles/doubles from $45/55. Three kilometres east is ***Lakeview B&B*** *(☎ 5350 2240)*, an Edwardian farmhouse on a sheep farm near the lake with three guestrooms costing from $70/90.

DUNKELD

• **pop 450**

The best and most scenic route into the Grampians is via the town of Dunkeld. Be sure to drop in to or stay a while at the superbly refurbished **Royal Mail Hotel** – see the Grampians National Park section in the Wimmera chapter for details.

Geelong to Hamilton

The Hamilton Hwy is the major route through the Western District, although there's not too much to see along the way. This is one of the earliest settled areas in Victoria, and there are a number of interesting old buildings in some of the small towns such as **Inverleigh** and **Cressy**.

At Derrinallum, 10km west of Lismore, the old ***Mt Elephant Hotel*** *(☎ 5597 6641)* on Main St has basic motel units from $30/50 a single/double, including breakky. Just off the highway south-west of Derrinallum is Mt Elephant which, at 240m, is one of the highest volcanic craters in the state. The volcano was last active 4000 years ago (that's not to say it's extinct – vulcanologists say a volcano is not officially dead until it's been inactive for about 10,000 years).

MORTLAKE

• **pop 1000**

Mortlake is a sleepy and historic township in the shadows of **Mt Shadwell**, an extinct volcano which is now one of the world's richest sources of olivine – an olive-coloured quartz gemstone. The town is surrounded by fertile volcanic plains, and has a number of interesting, historic bluestone buildings.

A historic walking trail has been mapped out, and brochures are available from the Mortlake Information and Tele-Education Centre (☎ 5599 2899) in Dunlop St (open 9 am to 5 pm, Monday to Friday). The trail takes you past numerous interesting historic buildings such as the old courthouse (1864) on Shaw St and a wind-powered flour mill (1856) on Mill St.

South-east of the main street, there's a pleasant park with lots of shady trees, barbecues, tennis courts, a pool, a playground and the pretty **Tea Tree Lake**.

Special Events

Over the first weekend in February, Mortlake hosts the unique annual Buskers' Festival. For inquiries, call ☎ 5599 2899 and make sure you book accommodation in advance.

Places to Stay & Eat

You can pitch a tent or pull up your van at the southern end of the aforementioned park. Unpowered/powered ***sites*** cost $8/10 – contact the caretaker on ☎ 5599 2468 for inquiries.

The ***Mt Shadwell Hotel Motel*** *(☎ 5599 2019, 128 Dunlop St)* offers motel units in converted bluestone stables for $55/65 a single/double. The restaurant in the hotel serves up pretty good counter meals from $10 to $12. A massive old bluestone wall divides the dining room from the lounge – they don't make walls that thick any more.

And Mortlake is the home of Clarke's Pies – delish! Pop into the milk bar on Dunlop St for yours.

Geelong to Warrnambool

The Geelong-Warrnambool section of the Princes Hwy passes through the heartland of the Western District, with its countryside scarred by ancient volcanic activity. The locals call this 'Lakes and Craters Country' – you'll soon see why.

Thank Tom for the Rabbits

Barwon Park is a 42-room two-storey bluestone mansion built in 1869 for the grazier Thomas Austin, who holds the dubious honour of being responsible for introducing rabbits into Australia.

A keen sporting hunter, Austin imported six pairs of rabbits (along with pheasants, foxes and quail) from England and set them free on the banks of the Barwon River. Thriving in the warm climate and having no natural predators, they multiplied a thousand times faster than Austin could shoot them, and within a few years, Australia was infested with an imported species in plague proportions.

Classified by the National Trust, Barwon Park homestead is open to the public on Wednesday and Sunday from 11 am to 4 pm. Admission costs $4 for adults and $2 for kids. Barwon Park is 3km north of Winchelsea on the Inverleigh road.

Mark Armstrong

WINCHELSEA

• pop 1000

This town was established as an early coach stop on the way from Geelong to the Western District. An old bluestone bridge crosses the Barwon River, and there are numerous historic buildings in the area, including the National Trust-classified Barwon Park Homestead (see the boxed text 'Thank Tom for the Rabbits'). The **Barwon Hotel** (1846) houses a museum with displays of local artefacts, riding equipment and farming implements.

BIRREGURRA

• pop 400

Midway between Winchelsea and Colac and 6km south of the Princes Hwy, Birregurra is a tiny one-pub township which time seems to have passed by. The main street has a row of old, faded shops fronted by sloping timber verandahs, and there are a couple of interesting handicraft shops and galleries to check out. On Sladen St, **Christ Church** is an impressive Gothic church that was erected here in 1870.

Places to Stay & Eat

On Warncoort Rd on the western side of town, ***Elliminook B&B*** *(☎ 5236 2080)* is a beautifully restored and very civilised National Trust-classified homestead, set in magnificent gardens. Four guestrooms are available ranging from $95 to $140.

Tarndwarncoort *(☎ 5233 6241)* is a historic sheep property off the Warncoort Cemetery Rd north-west of Birregurra – it can be hard to find, so ring for directions. This was where Australia's first breed of sheep, the Polwarth, was developed. Wool, sheep skins, coats and other products are available. There's also a small two-bedroom fibro-cement farm cottage which sleeps up to four people. The cottage is fairly rough and ready, but is in a scenic setting and has good views and a pretty garden; the nightly cost is from $85 for four people.

Just east of Birregurra on the corner of the Cape Otway and Lorne Rds, ***Sunnybrae*** *(☎ 5236 2276)* is a gourmet's delight, and one of the best restaurants in country Victoria. Surrounded by lovely gardens, it's set in a 19th-century farm cottage with a simple, elegant dining room and a great outlook over the Barwon Valley. It opens for dinner on Saturday and lunch on Sunday (during January, lunch daily and dinner on Friday and Saturday); meals are a combination of à la carte and set menu and range from $35 to $46. Sunnybrae also runs very good cooking classes from March to December.

Back in town, the ***Royal Mail Hotel*** serves up hearty country-style cooking in the small dining room out the back, with mains ranging from $12 to $17.

COLAC

• **pop 9750**

Before European settlers came, the Coladgin Koori tribe lived beside Lake Colac, which is the largest natural freshwater lake in Victoria. Hugh Murray was the first European to settle in the area (in 1837), and the town of Colac quickly grew into the main centre of the region, a growth fuelled by the combined wealth from the pastures of the Western District and the forest timbers of the Otway Ranges.

Colac calls itself the 'Gateway to the Otways', and while it's a good place to collect information on the district and has a couple of points of interest, the town is more of a stopover en route to elsewhere.

Orientation & Information

The Princes Hwy, called Murray St as it passes through Colac, is the main shopping street. The Colac Visitor Information Centre (☎ 5231 3730), on the corner of Murray and Queen Sts, is open daily from 9 am to 5 pm and has information about Colac, the Otway Ranges and the Great Ocean Road.

Things to See & Do

Lake Colac is well patronised by lovers of all water sports and has good fishing – it is especially renowned for redfin and perch. The **botanic gardens** are on the edge of Lake Colac at the northern end of Queen St. The lawns are shaded by old trees, and there's a barbecue, picnic facilities, tearooms and a playground adjacent to the gardens. The **Colac Historical Centre** is in Gellibrand St, beside the library and opposite the train station. This place features items of local historical significance and is open Thursday, Friday and Sunday from 2 to 4 pm.

If you're heading south from Colac, both the Colac-Lavers Hill road (via Gellibrand) and the Colac-Forrest road pass through the scenic beauty of the Otway Ranges.

Special Events

The Go Colac! Go Country! Festival, incorporating the famous Ferret Cup, is an annual event held over four days around the first weekend in November. Contact the visitor information centre for more information.

The Wallers of the Western District

Low stone walls line the sides of the road between Colac and Camperdown. When this area was first settled, these basalt plains were covered in volcanic rocks. Men called 'wallers' were paid £120 per mile to build these dry rock walls. The first walls were built in the 1860s by teams of Yorkshiremen, and the wallers had a favourite saying that 'there's a place for every stone' – which was probably another way of saying don't pick it up until you've got somewhere to put it. No mortar was used in the construction of the walls – an angled frame was built into which the rocks were tightly fitted. Most of these walls are still standing rock-solid after more than a century, a tribute to the skills of the wallers.

Mark Armstrong

Places to Stay

***Learey's Caravan Park** (☎ 5231 5337)*, on the Princes Hwy, and the ***Lake Colac Caravan Park** (☎ 5231 5971)* both have campsites for $10 and on-site vans for around $30.

***Prince of Wales Guesthouse** (☎ 5231 3385, 2-6 Murray St)*, built beside the Barongarook Creek in 1875, offers three cosy guestrooms with beautiful Federation-era beds (the kind you really have to climb into), for $30/60 a single/double. Tariffs include breakfast, served until noon.

The ***Union Club Hotel** (☎ 5231 5644, 110 Murray St)* has pub-style rooms from $25/50, or the ***Commercial Hotel** (☎ 5231 5777, 10 Murray St)* has basic motel units behind the pub from $30/40.

The ***Otway Gate Motel** (☎ 5231 3244, 52 Murray St)* is a good budget motel with singles/doubles from $47/57. There's also the ***Colac Mid-City Motel** (☎ 5231 3311, 289 Murray St)* with a swimming pool, a good restaurant and singles/doubles from $60/69.

Places to Eat

Murray St has a range of take-aways, coffee lounges and two bakeries. A top spot for lunch is ***The Wanda Restaurant Café** (23 Murray St)* which serves up delicious lunches around the $5 mark and caters well for vegos.

For some pub grub, try the ***Austral Hotel** (185 Murray St)* which has bar meals for $5 and bistro meals from $11 to $14, or the ***Commercial Hotel***, which has good meals for similar prices. The ***Sing-Bo Chinese Restaurant** (253 Murray St)* serves up tasty Cantonese dishes in the $8 to $16.50 range.

COLAC TO CAMPERDOWN

The road from Colac to Camperdown skirts a series of volcanic lakes and craters, and there are some worthwhile stopovers and detours along the route. Five kilometres west of Colac is the turn-off to the **Red Rock Lookout**, near the town of Coraguluc. This is a set of twin volcanic peaks with great views of the surrounding flatlands and lakes – you can drive right up to the top.

At Pirron Yallock, 17km west of Colac, is the **Floating Islands Reserve**, in which six large peat islands float in a lagoon and move about according to the wind. Though an interesting phenomenon, the islands sound more exciting than they are – it has to be very windy (or you have to be very patient) for any noticeable movement to occur. A walking trail leads from the car park to the reserve.

Nearby on the highway, the ***Koala Motel & Roadhouse** (☎ 5235 1277)* has basic motel units at $25/35 a single/double. The roadhouse is open from 6 am to midnight, and has a small fauna park where kids can talk to the animals.

North of Pirron Yallock is **Lake Corangamite**, the largest lake in Victoria, which, because it has no outlet or overflow, has a salt concentration three times that of sea water and is a good spot for bird watching.

South of the town of Weerite, **Lake Purrumbete** has good fishing, especially for trout and quinnat salmon. The lake is also home to large numbers of water birds, and has a campground (see Camperdown's Places to Stay section).

CAMPERDOWN

• **pop 3150**

Camperdown is a lovely town. The main street is divided by a central plantation of English elm trees, and dominated by a red-brick Gothic **clocktower**. The tower, constructed in 1896, is 30m high – on the first Sunday of every month you can climb to the top and enjoy the fine views.

Information

The Camperdown Tourist Information Centre (☎ 5593 3390) is in the courthouse on Manifold St, and opens weekdays from 9.30 am to 5 pm, Saturday to 4 pm, and Sunday, 11 am to 4 pm.

Things to See & Do

A signposted **heritage trail** winds past many of the town's historic brick and bluestone buildings – pick up a *Heritage Walks* leaflet from the tourist information centre. The **Camperdown Historical Society Museum** at 241 Manifold St is open on Tuesday, Friday and Sunday from 2 to 4 pm. Admission costs $2 for adults and 20c for kids. The **Buggy Museum** (☎ 5293 1119) is in Ower St – head towards the train station and it's on your right. This ramshackle museum has a collection of old buggies and traps in various stages of restoration. It's open most days and admission is by donation.

There are two volcanic crater lakes, side by side, a few kilometres west of Camperdown. **Lake Gnotuk** is the lower and saltier of the two. Farther south, **Lake Bullen Merri** has good fishing and swimming. Near the lakes are the **Camperdown Botanic Gardens** on Park Rd, which are a fine spot for a picnic, with barbecue facilities, an arboretum and a lookout over the lakes. Within these Victorian gardens are some rare examples of Himalayan oak trees. There's also a campground between the lakes.

For a fine view of Camperdown and its surrounding lakes and farmland, drive up to the **Mt Leura lookout** – turn off the Princes Hwy at Adeney St.

Places to Stay

There are two caravan parks within cooee of Camperdown. The ***Camperdown Caravan Park*** *(☎ 5593 1253)* is 5km west of Camperdown between lakes Gnotuk and Bullen Merri and adjacent to the Botanic Gardens. It has sites from $10, on-site vans from $29 and cabins from $48. The ***Lake Purrumbete Camping Park*** *(☎ 5594 5377)* is on the shores of the lake, 13km east of town, and has sites from $10 and cabins from $35 a double.

There are three old pubs in Camperdown's main street, all with fairly basic hotel rooms upstairs. The Edwardian ***Commercial Hotel*** *(☎ 5593 1187, 115 Manifold St)* offers B&B for $25/40 a single/double (shared bathroom).

There are also three motels in town. The inviting ***Amble Inn Motel*** *(☎ 5593 1646)*, on the Melbourne side of the highway, has good budget rooms from $35/50 a single/double (if you're lucky, you might score a room with a water bed). Also good, the ***Manifold Motor Inn*** *(☎ 5593 2666, 295 Manifold St)* has rooms from $66/76 for singles/doubles.

The Mill *(☎ 5593 2200, 3-5 Curdie St)*, Camperdown's original historic mill transformed into three individually stunning luxury apartments, is a magical place to stay with kitchens, spas, balconies, living areas and oodles of charm. Prices range from $180 per night (four guests) to $260 (six guests).

Places to Eat

There are a few take-aways and cafes in Manifold St. ***Lizzie's on Manifold*** is good value for breakfast and lunch, with a lovely garden courtyard and gourmet pies a speciality. The low-key ***Clocktower Cafe*** is good for snacks and lunches while the ***Hampden Hotel*** has cheap bar meals and good bistro food.

The most happening place for a meal is ***Madden's Bistro*** *(☎ 5593 1187)* at the Commercial Hotel. It's pretty upmarket for a bistro, with evening mains ranging from $12 to $17 and lunches around the $7 mark – forget it if you're vegetarian though.

COBDEN

• **pop 1400**

Originally known as 'Lovely Banks', Cobden is near the Curdies River and is a commercial centre for the surrounding dairying district. Dominating the townscape is the huge Bonlac factory which processes the output of over 134,000 cows in the region.

If you're after somewhere to stay here, the ***Cobden Motel*** *(☎ 5595 1140)*, next to the Shell service station on the Camperdown road, has singles/doubles from $38/48. Or for something really swish, head to the divine ***Heytesbury House B&B***, an Edwardian home surrounded by a secluded garden complete with croquet lawn and fish pond. Doubles are available from $130 to $140 (ask for the front room with the cosy little attic) and there's also a lovely cottage out the back available for $300 (four people).

TERANG

• **pop 1850**

A double row of English oaks, plane trees and cottonwood poplars line the main street through Terang. Planted in the 1890s, these historic trees have been classified by the National Trust.

The saddlery and souvenir shop at 105-107 High St has a small information section.

Things to See & Do

Terang has some interesting examples of late 19th and early 20th century architecture along High St – a *Heritage Trail* brochure describing these is available from the information centre. The post office and clocktower were built by public subscription in 1903. The courthouse next door was built by the same builder at about the same time. The Thompson Memorial Church was built in 1894 and modelled on Scots Church in Collins St, Melbourne.

Six kilometres north of Terang is the pretty and tiny hamlet of **Noorat**, which in 1902 was the birthplace of Alan Marshall, one of Australia's greatest writers. His most famous novel is the autobiographical *I Can Jump Puddles*. Try to get hold of a copy of his *Collected Stories*, a collection of simple and distinctively Australian tales some of which are set in this area. One story, *Tell Us About the Turkey, Jo,* opens at Lake Corangamite.

Noorat is at the foot of Mt Noorat, a green hill, which is actually a large, dry volcanic crater 310m high and was once a trading place for local Koori tribes. The **Alan Marshall walking trail** climbs to a cairn on the summit which overlooks the crater – it takes just under an hour return.

Twenty kilometres south of Terang, the **Ralph Illidge Sanctuary** (☎ 5566 2267) is of particular interest because it is home to native birds and animals including rare species such as the white goshawk and the potoroo (a small member of the kangaroo family and the first animal Captain Cook saw when he stepped off the *Endeavour* onto the shores of Botany Bay). Ralph Illidge bought the land here in 1958, and rather than clear it he preserved the property as a nature reserve. It's one of the few examples of what the landscape around here might have been like before European settlers set about stripping it of its natural vegetation. There's a series of walking tracks through the 96-hectare sanctuary, an extensive array of birdlife, plus barbecues and picnic facilities. The sanctuary is signposted off the Cobden-Warrnambool road, and is open on weekends and public holidays. Admission is by donation.

Places to Stay

The Old Manse *(☎ 5592 1635, 1 McWilliam St)* is a gorgeous old homestead with wide halls and verandahs and splendid gardens. B&B costs $100/120 a single/double and dinner can also be arranged for another $35 per person.

In town on the Princes Hwy, the ***Dalvue Motel*** *(☎ 5592 1566)* has singles/doubles from $48/55, and the mint-green ***Terang Hotel*** (☎ *5592 1291, 40 High St)* on the main drag has clean old-style pub rooms at $20/30.

Hamilton to the South Australian Border

The Glenelg and Hamilton highways meet at the south-eastern entrance to Hamilton. From here, the Glenelg Hwy continues across the South Australian border, and the Henty Hwy (A200) runs south to Portland and north to Horsham and beyond.

HAMILTON

• pop 9250

Known as the 'Wool Capital of the World', Hamilton is the major town of the Western District and the commercial and retail centre for one of the richest and the most intensively grazed wool-growing areas in the world. The area was settled in 1837 soon after Major Thomas Mitchell passed through on his journey of discovery.

Orientation & Information

Ballarat Rd (the Glenelg Hwy; B160) is the main road into Hamilton from the east, taking you past Lake Hamilton and across the Grange Burn waterway into the town centre. The highway takes a couple of twists through town – along Cox St, Lonsdale St and then Pope St – and immediately west of the centre you can take a left along Portland Rd (the Henty Hwy; A200) to Portland or continue straight along Coleraine Rd (the Glenelg Hwy; B160) towards Mt Gambier.

The Hamilton Visitor Information Centre (☎ 5572 3746) is in the centre of town in Lonsdale St, and opens daily from 9 am to 5 pm. The main shopping precinct is along Gray St, which runs parallel with Lonsdale St one block south.

Things to See & Do

The **Hamilton Art Gallery** in Brown St is an excellent provincial gallery with a varied collection, including Australia's largest holding of paintings by the English watercolourist, Paul Sandby. There is also a series of satirical engravings by William Hogarth, 19th century and contemporary Australian paintings, Oriental and European ceramics, glass, silverware, furniture, tapestries and some interesting Tibetan and Indian pieces. The gallery was established in 1958 after a bequest by local graziers, Herbert and May Shaw. The gallery is open Monday to Friday from 10 am to 5 pm, Saturday from 10 am to noon and 2 to 5 pm, and Sunday from 2 to 5 pm. Admission is by donation.

On Coleraine Rd 2km west of the centre, **The Big Woolbales** consists of five linked buildings that look like oversized wool bales, containing an assortment of wool-related displays such as shearing and farming equipment, videos and wool samples. There's a souvenir shop and kiosk, and shearing demonstrations are sometimes held in one of the 'bales'. It's open daily from 9.30 am to 4 pm (5 pm over the warmer months) and entrance is free.

The pretty **botanic gardens** on the corner of Thompson and French Sts are well worth a visit. Some of the trees such as Californian redwoods and weeping elms date back to 1870, and there's a central pond, walk-through aviary, Victorian band rotunda, playground and barbecues.

Lake Hamilton is large, artificial, unspectacular and popular for water sports and fishing. A cycling/jogging track circles the lake. There's a barbecue and picnic area, and a playground at the end of Rippons Rd.

For garden lovers some of the properties in and around Hamilton open their private gardens to the public – ask at the information centre for details.

Sir Reginald Ansett began his empire in Hamilton in 1931, when he started a passenger service to Ballarat. He gradually expanded and by 1937, backed by local money, he was able to launch Ansett Airlines, which today is one of Australia's major airlines. The **Sir Reginald Ansett Transport Museum** on Ballarat Rd was set up using the remains of one of the company's original aircraft hangars. The museum houses various displays relating to the Ansett empire, including a replica Fokker Universal, old uniforms and photos. It's open daily from 10 am to 4 pm and costs $2 for adults and $1 for kids.

The **Hamilton History Centre**, in the old Mechanics Institute Hall next to the post office at 43 Gray St, has items of local history, photos and records, and is open daily (except Saturday) from 2 to 5 pm. Next door there's a small **Aboriginal Keeping Place Museum**, although it's seldom open to the public – check with the tourist office.

Hamilton is the last refuge of the eastern barred bandicoot, a rare and endangered Australian marsupial. The bandicoot looks a bit like a bush rat, with a long pointy nose, a short white tail and several pale bars across its hindquarters. The bandicoot colony on the banks of the Grange Burn Creek is the last on mainland Australia, and the **Hamilton Institute of Rural Learning**, 333 North Boundary Rd, is trying to establish new colonies. There's a nature trail in the institute's parklands where you can wander around and see different examples of native flora and fauna.

Special Events

Hamilton's major event is the Hamilton Sheep-vention, a trade show featuring sheep and wool products and related farming inventions. It's held on the first Monday and Tuesday of August and attracts crowds of up to 20,000.

Places to Stay

Camping & Caravan Park & Hostel The *Lake Hamilton Caravan Park* (*☎ 5572 3855, 8 Ballarat Rd*) is well located near the lake and has excellent facilities. Campsites cost from $10, on-site vans from $28 and on-site cabins from $38 to $50. Next door, *Peppercorn Lodge* (*☎ 5571 9046*) is a good place for budgeteers with rooms in prefab buildings accommodating up to three people each. Beds cost $12/20 a single/double.

Pubs & Motels The *Commercial Hotel* (*☎ 5572 1078*), on the corner of Lonsdale and Thompson Sts, is an old pub with a heritage colour scheme and very basic rooms upstairs with shared bathrooms at $20/33. The *Grand Central Hotel* (*☎ 5572 2899, 141 Gray St*) is a more contemporary pub with quite good rooms at $25/35. This pub has live bands on Saturday nights.

Hamilton has 10 motels. One of the cheapest, *Lenwin on the Lake Motor Inn* (*☎ 5571 2733, 2 Riley St*), has singles/doubles from $45/58. Riley St. It's off the Glenelg Hwy – coming from Melbourne, turn right after the Ansett Transport Museum.

The *Botanical Motor Inn* (*☎ 5572 1855, corner Thompson and French Sts*) has doubles from $85, while the *Grange Burn Motor Inn* (*☎ 5572 5755*) at 142 Ballarat Rd (the Glenelg Hwy; B160) has doubles from $99 to $104.

B&Bs There are also some excellent B&Bs in Hamilton. The central *Hewlett House* (*☎ 5572 2494, 36 Gray St*), a classical two-storey Victorian mansion, is a friendly and comfortable place with singles/doubles with their own bathroom costing from $80/110.

Mourilyan B&B (*☎ 5572 4989*), 200m west of the centre at 22 Pope St (the Glenelg Hwy; B160), is a cosy 1920s family home with friendly hosts, a dream upstairs bathroom and singles/doubles for $65/80 with a continental breakfast, or $70/90 with a cooked breakfast.

Another good place, 24km south-west of Hamilton near Branxholme, is *Inverary* (*☎ 5578 6212*). It's an impressive two-storey bluestone homestead surrounded by pretty gardens on a large merino sheep farm. The house was built in 1867, has three guestrooms and good facilities. Doubles range from $95 to $115, which includes a fully cooked breakfast and a tour of the property.

Places to Eat

The majority of Hamilton's eateries are along Thompson and Gray Sts. You'll find the usual range of cafes and take-aways, plus quite a few good restaurants and pubs.

Gilly's, at 106 Gray St, is a good cafe/restaurant that opens for breakfast, lunch and dinner – it has a pasta and salad bar with all-you-can-eat deals ($7.50 for lunch or $10.50 for dinner). Down at 175 Gray St, the bustling ***Gallery Corner*** is a good spot for lunch (especially if you like baked spuds) and a cuppa. It's open seven days.

De Niro's, at 127 Thompson St, is a simple and modern restaurant offering pizza, pasta and $6 Mexican dishes. For a pub meal, try the nearby ***Commercial Hotel,*** which has good bistro meals ranging from $10 (fried whiting) to $15 (a huge Fisherman's platter, big enough for two). Cheaper bar meals are also available.

The Verandah *(☎ 5572 1844, 213 Gray St),* at the George Hotel, is a recently renovated and very inviting spot to eat. Meals can be ordered from the bar downstairs or off the innovative restaurant menu which includes dishes such as Camembert wrapped in bacon, and yabby and scallop kebabs. There's a small indoor eating area but dining alfresco on the wonderful wide verandah is the way to go.

Hamilton's best restaurant is ***The Strand*** *(☎ 5571 9144, 56 Thompson St)*. The food is excellent, wine list extensive and the atmosphere superb – the Mediterranean-yellow building dates from the 1870s and has a casual cafe at the front, more formal separate dining rooms and an inviting courtyard. Evening mains are around the $19 mark.

Getting There & Away

V/Line's bus service from Melbourne to Hamilton ($38.90), continuing on to Mt Gambier ($18), operates twice daily on weekdays and once a day on weekends. There are also weekday services south to Warrnambool and north to Horsham.

Buses leave from beside the train station, which is at the end of Brown St (three blocks south of Lonsdale St).

MT NAPIER STATE PARK

Mt Napier erupted around 7000 years ago. A professor of vulcanology said of Mt Napier in 1945, 'I have visited all the main volcanic areas of this globe...What impresses me so much is that there is such a diversity of volcanic features in this one lava field'.

The three main aspects he was referring to are the volcanic cone, the surrounding lava flow and the lava tubes or caves. Mt Napier itself is 447m high, and its crater 25m deep. You can walk up to a lookout point on the summit. The **Stony Rises** is an eroded area of lava flow. The most interesting aspect of the park is the **Byaduk Caves**, a series of lava tubes which were formed as the outer crust of the lava flow cooled and solidified, leaving the molten lava to flow through the hollow centre. The caves can be entered and explored by climbing down holes at ground level. You'll need a decent torch; look for the interesting ferns and mosses growing in the caves. The largest cave is Church Cave, which is about 50m long and 7m high.

The **Mt Napier State Park** is 15km south of Hamilton. There are no camping facilities here, and the park is jointly managed with Mt Eccles by Parks Victoria. Ask for maps at the Visitor Information Centre in Hamilton.

MT ECCLES NATIONAL PARK

The Mt Eccles National Park is about 9km west of the small town of Macarthur, which in turn is 36km south of Hamilton.

Mt Eccles erupted around 19,000 years ago, and the lava flow covered the countryside in all directions, with one massive tongue of lava flowing 30km to the coast and continuing another 19km out to sea – Lady Julia Percy Island is a formation of this flow (see the Great Ocean Road & South-West Coast chapter).

The main features here are Mt Eccles itself, the very scenic Lake Surprise (which is rimmed by three volcanic craters and makes a great swimming spot), several lava caves, a series of vents and craters, a huge koala population and a number of marked walk-

Lake Condah Aboriginal Mission

Lake Condah, on the western side of the Mt Eccles National Park, is the former site of the Lake Condah Aboriginal Mission. This area is also of unique and important historical significance. There is evidence that before European settlement, the local Aborigines lived here on a semi-permanent basis, rather than living the fully nomadic lifestyle traditionally associated with hunter-gatherers. They were able to live here because of an abundant and constant supply of food, particularly fish from the lake, and they set up relatively sophisticated systems to harvest fish and eels.

Lake Condah was formed when Mt Eccles erupted around 19,000 years ago. The molten lava from the volcano flowed along the paths of many local streams, blocking the water and resulting in the formation of this shallow lake at the edge of the lava plains.

This south-western part of Victoria was the tribal territory of the Dhauwurd wurrung Aboriginal people, also known as the Gundidjmara. The tribe was made up of around 56 different clans. One of these clans, the Kerupmar (water people), lived around Lake Condah. The Kerupmar built U-shaped stone houses and complex stone water channels and traps to catch fish and eels. The traps were designed to divert water from the lake and through a series of gaps in the stones, behind which were placed plaited baskets to catch the fish.

When the European settlers invaded the area in the 1830s and 1840s, the local tribes were driven from their traditional lands, and the majority of them were killed off in the subsequent years.

In 1858 a government select committee recommended that Aboriginal reserves be set up to protect the interests of the remaining Aboriginal people. In 1869, the Church of England established a mission at Lake Condah and members of various Dhauwurd wurrung clans formed a community there. At first they lived in *mia-mias* (bark lean-tos) and later a series of houses and a mission church were built. The community maintained traditional hunting and food-gathering practices, while at the same time the Christian missionaries were trying to 'Europeanise' and convert it to Christianity.

While the missions weren't the ideal environment, they at least enabled the tribe to occupy its own land and sacred sites, as well as maintain self-sufficiency and retain its traditional culture and knowledge. However, in 1886 the Victorian government passed the notorious Aborigines Protection Law Amendment Act, which prohibited part-Aborigines under 35 from living on missions. The gradual effect of this was that the community was splintered and some families were forcefully split up. By 1890, the population at the mission had fallen from 117 to 20, and the decline continued until the mission was closed in 1918.

In 1984, the federal government passed land-rights legislation that led to 53 hectares of the former mission reserve being given back to the Kerupmar community. It now manages the site and it is no longer open to tourists.

Mark Armstrong

ing tracks. The **crater nature walk** follows the rim of the craters and takes about an hour, and there's a shorter walk around the lake. Another walk follows the lava canals and takes you to **Tunnel Cave** (four hours return). The whole area makes for interesting exploring.

The park has good camping, picnic and barbecue facilities. Parks Victoria has a ranger's station in the park (☎ 5576 1338) and an office in Macarthur (☎ 5576 1014) at 21 Huntly St; ring for camping bookings and inquiries.

COLERAINE

• **pop 1100**

On the Glenelg Hwy 34km west of Hamilton, Coleraine is a fairly sleepy little place with some interesting old buildings and an excellent native garden, plus a few other points of interest.

Signposted off the highway, the **Coleraine Tourist & Exhibition Centre** (☎ 5575 2733) is housed in the town's beautifully restored old train station. As well as being the local information centre, it has a selection of local arts and crafts for sale, and opens most days from 9 am to 5 pm.

In the centre of town at 91 Whyte St, the **Matthew Cooke Blacksmith Shop** (1884) is a fascinating old timber building that still operates as a blacksmith's shop, using all the original equipment. It's open on Saturday from 10 am to noon, or by appointment.

Coleraine is also the place where **Helena Rubenstein** started her famous cosmetics empire. She came out here to work in her uncle's grocery shop, and during the three years she lived here she started importing cosmetics. That grocery shop is now an antique and gift shop on the main street – coming from Hamilton, it's the last shop on the left (before you cross the bridge).

Chocolate-lovers take note: in a green and cream building on the main street is **Glenelg Fine Confectionery**, a small chocolate factory selling gift boxes and packaged chocolates.

The **Peter Francis Points Arboretum**, 2km south of Coleraine on the Portland road, is an excellent picnic and/or walking spot, especially for anyone interested in Australia's native trees and shrubs. In 1968 members of the local community started planting this 37-hectare disused quarry, and today the site has the largest number of eucalypt species in the southern hemisphere as well as many other species. Entry is free, and there are barbecues and picnic areas,

Warrock Homestead

On a bushland property north of Casterton, Warrock Homestead (☎ 5582 4222) is one of the most significant remnants of Victoria's early architectural heritage.

The land was bought by George Robertson, a Scottish cabinet-maker, in 1843. Over the next 17 years he built some 40 timber buildings in a unique combination of Gothic revival style and his own imagination and skill. Most of these buildings remain, including the main house, a cottage, stables, a blacksmith's shop and woolsheds. Descendants of Robertson's nephew lived on the property until 1991, maintaining it in its original condition; most of the original tools, machinery and craft equipment are still there.

The homestead is classified by the National Trust, and is being gradually restored by the owners. There is currently one self-contained four-bedroom cottage available if you want to stay overnight, and the owners are planning to offer several other cottages for rent as well as bunk-style accommodation in the old shearers' quarters. Also on the drawing board are plans for a restaurant and an old-style movie house. Ring the owners, Gavin and Caroll Larkins, to find out the latest before heading out.

The property is open daily from 10 am to 5 pm and admission costs $5 for adults, $3 for concessions and $1 for kids. It's a lovely 25km drive north of Casterton through lush, rolling hills – there's a signpost beside the National Bank in Casterton.

Mark Armstrong

walking trails, lookouts and a playground for the kids.

CASTERTON

• pop 2000

Casterton, the ancient Roman word for 'walled city', takes its name from the fact that it's surrounded by hills, in the manner of a castle ringed by battlements – well, that's what the early settlers thought, anyway. This area was settled by the Henty brothers back in 1846. The town is on the Glenelg River, and has quite a few historic buildings along Henty St (the Glenelg Hwy; B160).

The Visitor Information Centre (☎ 5581 2070), just off the highway in Shiels Terrace, is open daily from 9 am to 5 pm. There's a small picnic area beside the centre. The **Casterton Historical Society Museum** is in the old train station just off the main street, but it's seldom open.

Bailey's Rocks, about 30km north-west of Casterton (on the Casterton-Naracoorte road, near Dergholme), is a popular and scenic picnic area and walking reserve featuring a collection of unusual giant green granite boulders.

Places to Stay

The ***Albion Hotel*** *(☎ 5581 1092)* on Henty St is a red-brick pub with white trim that was built in 1906. It has very basic pub rooms at $27/45 for B&B, or newer motel rooms at $48/55. The large bistro at the back of the hotel serves inexpensive counter meals. Another pub in town, the ***Casterton Hotel*** *(☎ 5581 1122, 101 Henty St)*, has rooms for $20 per head ($25 with a cooked breakfast), should not be confused with the ***Casterton Motel*** *(☎ 5581 1317, 29-31 Mt Gambier Rd)*, which has singles/doubles for $38/48.

The Wimmera

The Wimmera is one of Victoria's major wheat and wool districts. Much of the land has been cleared for farming and there are seemingly endless expanses of wheat fields and sheep properties. The bleakness of these cleared lands contrasts starkly with the majesty of the two national parks in the area, which remind us of what the natural environment of this region would have been like before European settlers arrived.

The area takes its name from the Wimmera River, which Major Thomas Mitchell discovered during his expedition of 1836. In his journal, Granville Stapylton, Mitchell's second-in-command, wrote of the river and its tributaries, 'Wimare (is the) native name of these streams'.

The major attraction of the Wimmera is the spectacular Grampians National Park, a collection of four rugged granite and sandstone mountain ranges that are renowned for their flora and fauna, colourful wildflowers, fine bushwalks, superb mountain lookouts and excellent rock-climbing areas. Another natural feature in this district is the Mt Arapiles State Park, known as the 'Ayers Rock of the Wimmera' and Australia's most famous rock-climbing venue.

The Little Desert National Park, bordered by South Australia and the Western and Wimmera highways, is a wonderful wilderness area. Though not actually a desert, the soil in this park is predominantly sandy which, unlike the surrounding clay-soil areas, is what saved it from being cleared for agriculture. The park is remote and not easily accessed, which leads to what is probably one of its best features – no crowds! There are extensive walking and 4WD tracks, and a fascinating array of hardy native species that have adapted to the extremes of this harsh environment.

HIGHLIGHTS

- The mystical grandeur, wonderful bushwalks, wildflowers, panoramic lookouts, wildlife and Aboriginal rock art of the Grampians
- Brambuk Living Cultural Centre, an Aboriginal heritage centre near Halls Gap
- The wineries around Great Western; don't miss the underground cellars at Seppelt's or the rustic charm of Best's
- The Stawell Gift foot race held at Easter in Stawell
- The Mack Jost collection at the Horsham Art Gallery
- Rock climbing at Mt Arapiles State Park
- Exploring Little Desert National Park

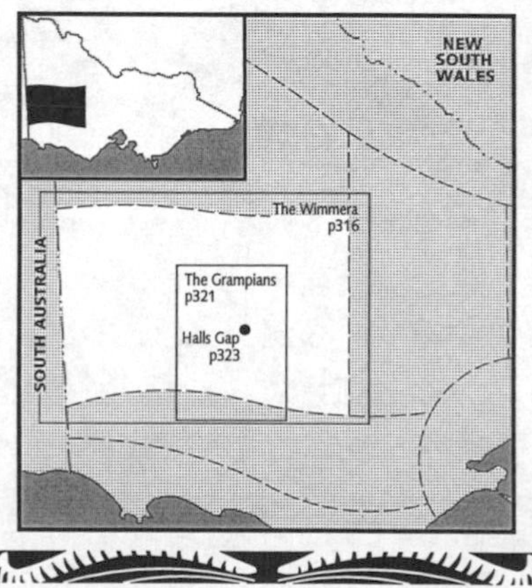

Orientation & Information

The main road through the Wimmera is the Western Highway (A8), which also happens to be the main route between Melbourne and Adelaide. Horsham is the Wimmera's largest town and the hub of the region – it's where all the major highways intersect. The only other towns of any size are the former gold-mining towns of Ararat and Stawell, both on the Western Hwy to the east of the Grampians.

There are tourist information centres in Ararat, Stawell and Horsham, and Parks Victoria has an excellent visitor centre in Halls Gap which has information on the Grampians.

Activities

Most of the activities in the Wimmera are tied to the area's national and state parks. The Grampians has always been a favourite area for bushwalking, camping, rock climbing, wildlife watching and generally communing with nature: the Little Desert National Park is popular for similar reasons, and a lot less crowded during peak seasons. Mt Arapiles is Australia's premier rock-climbing venue.

There are numerous wineries to visit and if you're into fishing inland waters you'll also find some pretty good places to dangle a line – surprisingly, Horsham hosts one of the country's richest fishing competitions.

Getting There & Away

The daily *Overland* train between Melbourne and Adelaide runs through the Wimmera, stopping at Ararat, Stawell, Horsham and Dimboola. V/Line has train/bus services that run between Melbourne and the major towns in the Wimmera.

From Horsham, you can take a bus north to Mildura, west to Naracoorte or south to Hamilton.

LANGI GHIRAN STATE PARK

The dominant physical features of this small park, off the Western Hwy 14km east of Ararat, are the two granite mountains, **Langi Ghiran** and **Gorrin**. At 950m, Mt Langi Ghiran is the higher of the two and from its summit there are great views across to the Grampians. The area is carpeted with huge granite boulders and native vegetation including red gums, yellow box, banksias and wattles, and in spring, colourful wildflowers. There are some good walks, ranging from a short walk to the Langi Ghiran reservoir to a full day trek to the summit of Mt Langi Ghiran.

Langi Ghiran is the Aboriginal name for the yellow-tailed black cockatoo, which is found here along with many other species of birds including corellas, robins, honeyeaters and finches. Spring is the best time for birdwatching.

This area was a significant site for local Aboriginal clans, and there are several rock art sites, shelters and scar trees in the park.

For more information regarding the park, contact the Parks Victoria office in Beaufort (☎ 5349 2404).

Mt Langi Ghiran Vineyard is in a great setting at the foot of the mountain and is renowned for its peppery shiraz wines. It's

The yellow-tailed black cockatoo, a spectacular inhabitant of Langi Ghiran State Park

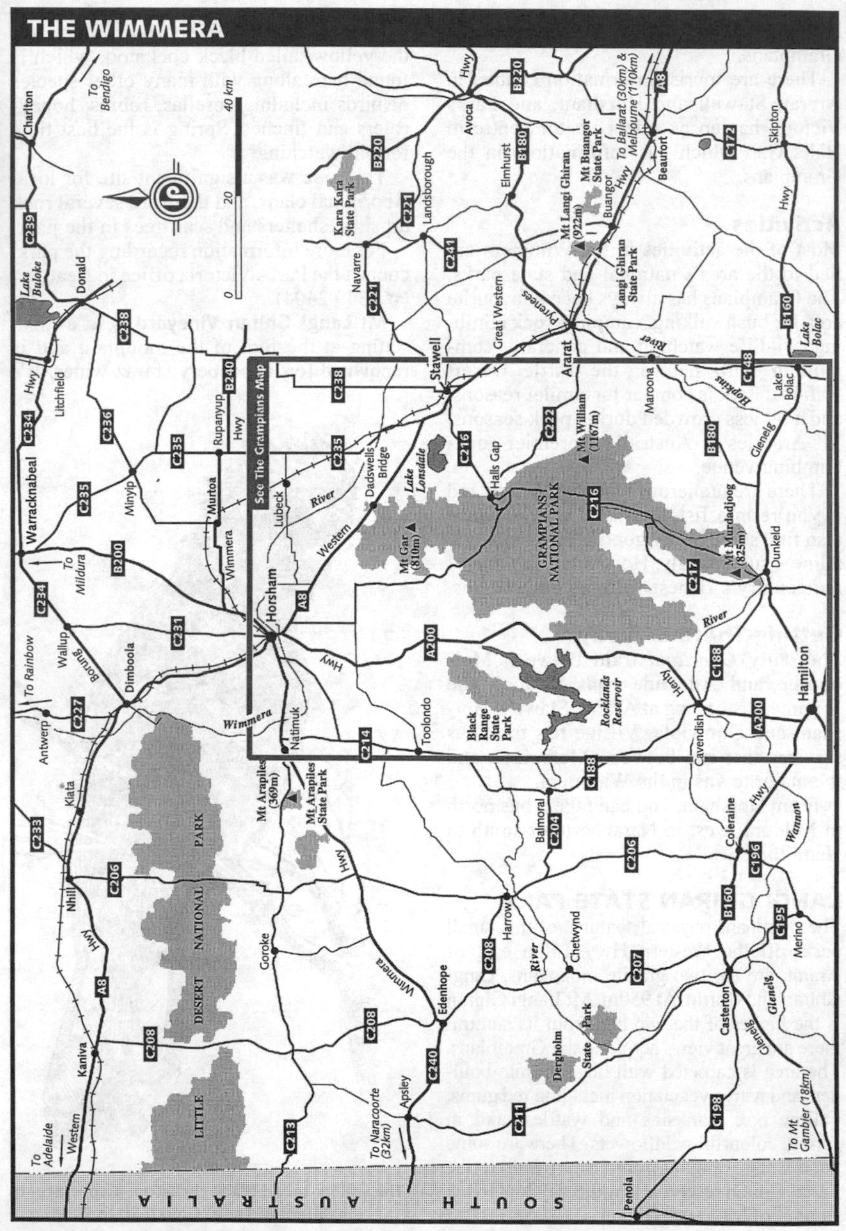
THE WIMMERA
0
20
40 km
To Bendigo
Charlton
C239
Lake Buloke
Donald
C238
Hwy
C234
Litchfield
B240
Rupanyup
Hwy
C236
C235
Minyip
Murtoa
Warracknabeal
C235
Wimmera
B200
To Mildura
C234
Wallup
Borung
C231
Dimboola
To Rainbow
C227
Antwerp
Kiata
C233
Nhill
C206
Hwy
A8
Kaniva
C208
Western
To Adelaide
LITTLE
DESERT
NATIONAL
PARK
Mt Arapiles (369m)
Mt Arapiles State Park
Natimuk
Wimmera
Horsham
A8
Hwy
See The Grampians Map
Lubeck
River
Western
Dadswells Bridge
Lake Lonsdale
C238
C235
Stawell
Mt Gar (810m)
C216
Halls Gap
Great Western
C222
Mt William (1167m)
GRAMPIANS NATIONAL PARK
C216
Ararat
Pyrenees
Hwy
Mt Langi Ghiran (922m)
Langi Ghiran State Park
Buangor
Mt Buangor State Park
Elmhurst
B180
Beaufort
To Ballarat (30km) & Melbourne (110km)
A8
B220
Avoca
Hwy
Landsborough
C221
Navarre
C221
C241
Kara Kara State Park
B220
River
Maroona
Hopkins
C148
Lake Bolac
B180
Glenelg
Lake Bolac
B160
Hwy
Skipton
C172
Mt Murradjoog (825m)
Dunkeld
C217
River
Henty
C188
Hamilton
A200
Cavendish
A200
Hwy
Toolondo
C214
Black Range State Park
Rocklands Reservoir
C188
Balmoral
C204
C206
Harrow
Coleraine
Hwy
Wannon
C196
B160
C195
Merino
Glenelg
C207
Chetwynd
River
C208
Goroke
Wimmera
Edenhope
C208
C240
Apsley
To Naracoorte (32km)
C213
C211
Dergholm State Park
Casterton
Glenelg
C198
To Mt Gambier (18km)
Penola
SOUTH AUSTRALIA

signposted off the Buangor-to-Warrak road, and is open weekdays from 9 am to 5 pm and weekends from noon to 5 pm.

On this same road is **Wilde's Caravan Museum**; the oldest exhibit dates back to 1910 and looks like a Coolgardie safe on wheels.

ARARAT

• pop 7000

Chinese miners who were travelling overland from Adelaide to the Ballarat goldfields found gold in Ararat in 1857. They stayed and mined here until the early 1860s when the gold ran out, but the town continued to grow as a commercial centre for the surrounding agricultural district.

The Ararat Tourist Information Centre (☎ 1800 657 158 toll-free) is on Town Hall Square on Barkly St and is open daily from 9 am to 5 pm.

Things to See & Do

There are quite a few historic buildings in town, and several have been classified by the National Trust. Some of the better examples are **Pyrenees House** beside the hospital in Girdlestone St, and **Ararat Town Hall** in Vincent St, which was built in 1898.

Next to the town hall is **Ararat Art Gallery**, which is mainly devoted to the works of contemporary artists working with fibres and textiles. The gallery is open weekdays from 11 am to 4 pm, and on Sunday and public holidays from noon to 4 pm; entry is $2 for adults.

The **Langi Morgala Museum**, in Queen St just off Barkly St, is the local historical museum – of particular interest is the Mooney collection of Aboriginal artefacts. The museum opens on weekends from 1 to 4 pm. Admission costs $2 for adults and 50c for kids.

The **Alexandra Gardens**, in Vincent St, are set around a central lake and have picnic facilities, an orchid glasshouse, a playground and garden fernery with waterfalls. Behind the gardens is an imposing old bluestone jail which until recently was a prison for the criminally insane. Ararat's historic **J Ward** is open for tours on weekdays at 11 am and on Sunday from 11 am to 3 pm; tours cost $6 for adults, $3 for children.

The **YMCA Recreation Centre**, 78 High St, is an impressive complex that combines an old church, a brick basketball stadium and a modern 25m indoor pool. The other facilities include a spa, sauna, gym and squash courts. The complex is open to the public and a swim, sauna and spa cost $5.

On the site of the old **Canton Lead Mine**, which is signposted off the Western Hwy west of the centre, work has begun on the construction of a pagoda-style Chinese museum to record the history of the Chinese in this area.

Four kilometres east of town is **Green Hill Lake**, which is a good local fishing spot, especially for brown trout. It's also popular for boating and swimming.

Montara Vineyards is a small and friendly family winery 3km south of Ararat, set high on a hill. There's a slab-timber table in front of the tasting room, which makes a good spot for a picnic lunch, and the winery is open for tastings daily.

Places to Stay

Acacia Caravan Park *(☎ 5352 2994)*, 1km north of the centre on the Western Hwy, has campsites from $11.50 to $14 and on-site vans and cabins from $25 to $55.

There are five pubs on Barkly St with accommodation: cheapest is the ***Shire Hall Hotel*** *(☎ 5352 1280)* at $18/25 a single/double, including a light breakfast. The ***Grampians Hotel*** *(☎ 5352 2393)* has rooms at $20/30 a single/double and also does weekend packages.

There are about half a dozen motels in town. ***Chalambar Motel*** *(☎ 5352 2430)*, on the Western Hwy 2km north of the centre, has comfy rooms from $34/40. ***Colonial Lodge Motel*** *(☎ 5352 4644, 6 Ingor St)* is the closest motel to the centre of town and has modern units from $69/79, and a BYO restaurant.

Places to Eat

Pyrenees Country Kitchen *(330 Barkly St)* is a casual BYO restaurant that serves up hearty, country-style cooking with mains around $12. It is open for dinner from Thursday to Saturday and for lunch on Sunday.

The hotels on Barkly St have counter meals.

Getting There & Away

Ararat train station is near the centre of town at the north end of Queen St. There are three or four services to/from Melbourne daily – train to Ballarat and connecting bus to Ararat. The trip takes just over three hours and a one-way, full fare is $26.90.

GREAT WESTERN

Great Western is a tiny and charming town midway between Ararat and Stawell. There are three wineries in the area, and the town is surrounded by vineyards. 'Great Western' is synonymous with Australian 'champagne' (which must now be called 'sparkling wine' after protests from French champagne makers) – see the boxed text on Grampians' wineries. The famous Champagne Race meeting is held at the racecourse here on Australia Day.

Places to Stay & Eat

The *Great Western Hotel* (☎ *5356 2270)* serves good bistro meals and has motel units next to the Tudor-style pub, from $32/38 for a single/double.

An excellent, self-contained, two bedroom cottage, ***The Hermitage at Great Western*** (☎ *5356 2361)* is set in lovely gardens. Tariffs are $95/110 per couple on weekdays/weekends.

At ***Allanvale*** (☎ *5356 2201)*, a sheep property 3km east of Great Western, you can stay in restored shearers' quarters for $15 per person.

STAWELL

• **pop 6250**

Stawell is bypassed by the Western Hwy, although a string of motels and petrol stations have sprung up along the highway about 5km south of the town centre. Born of the gold rush of the 1850s the town is now best known as the home of the Stawell Gift, a world famous running race.

Gold was found near here in May of 1853. The alluvial gold in the area soon ran out, but the discovery of rich quartz reefs in the Big Hill area lead to the development of large-scale mining operations which lasted until the 1920s and extracted something like 58 tonnes of gold. The 1870s were the boom years for Stawell, and many of the most impressive old buildings, including the town hall and most of the pubs, date back to these times.

Nowadays, Stawell is a busy commercial centre for the surrounding agricultural areas and is still a substantial producer of gold. The main shopping area is in and around the Gold Reef Mall in the centre of Main St. Stawell is a popular base for visitors to the nearby Grampians, and a bus service links the train station with Halls Gap.

Information

The excellent Stawell & Grampians Tourist Information Centre (☎ 1800 246 880 toll-free) is on the Western Hwy, before the turn-off to Halls Gap. It's open weekdays from 9 am to 5 pm, weekends from 10 am to 4 pm, and has a good range of information about Stawell, the local wineries and the Grampians, as well as an accommodation booking service.

Things to See & Do

Central Park, the local football and cricket ground, has been the venue for the Stawell Gift since 1898. The impressive set of iron entrance gates were erected in 1903 in memory of local men who served in the Boer War, and a Victorian timber grandstand, which was built in 1899, has recently been restored.

The unassuming **Stawell Gift Hall of Fame** is in Main St, opposite the Railway Hotel. The museum is open weekday mornings and by appointment (check for times, ☎ 5358 1326), and has a collection of videos, photos and memorabilia documenting the history of the Stawell Gift race meeting. There are also a few souvenirs for sale. Admission costs $2.50.

On London Rd, just out of town, is **Casper's World in Miniature**, a large tourist park with pavilions housing displays devoted to different countries, cultures and eras. It's all fairly kitsch – some of the displays are simple while others are quite quirky and sort of interesting, with things like a pyramid, a miniature Eiffel Tower and a replica gold mine. The park is well spread out so it takes a while to walk around. There's an extensive souvenir gallery and the park attracts tourists by the bus load. Casper's is open daily from 9 am and costs $7.50 for adults, $3.50 for kids.

Sisters Rocks, just off the highway south of Stawell, is a collection of huge granite rocks that have been extensively painted with colourful graffiti – it's a matter of opinion as to whether this is art or vandalism. This ugly sight is very clearly signposted from the highway about 6km from town.

Bunjils Shelter, 11km south of Stawell and signposted off the road to Pomonal, is one of the most significant Aboriginal rock art sites in the state. Bunjil is the creator spirit of the Kooris of this region. For those with a taste for the monstrosity of Sisters Rocks this simple, subtle painting will fail to excite. The painting is enhanced by the contours of the rock and makes sense only within its context. Two dimensional sketches of the painting suggest a 'primitive' quality that doesn't exist in the original.

Special Events

The Stawell Gift has been run here on Easter Monday since 1878. The Easter race meeting features a variety of sprint and distance-running events, but the prestigious 120m dash is the main event. The Gift is the richest and most famous foot race in the country, attracting up to 20,000 visitors each year, so if you're planning to visit during the Gift, you'll need to book your accommodation ahead – preferably, a year in advance.

Places to Stay

Camping & Caravan Parks ***Stawell Park Caravan Park*** *(☎ 5358 2709)*, on the Western Hwy, has campsites from $10 and cabins from $35 to $45.

Pubs & Motels In the town, the only pub with accommodation is the ***Town Hall Hotel*** *(☎ 5358 1059)* in Main St, which has basic rooms from $25/35, a single/double, including a light breakfast.

There's a string of motels along the Western Hwy. ***Coorrabin Motor Inn*** *(☎ 5358 3933)* is one of the cheapest with good units ranging from $30/50 to $40/60. ***Magdala Motor Lodge*** *(☎ 5358 3877)* is more upmarket with an indoor pool, an à la carte restaurant and a range of rooms from $70/92 to $80/102.

In town, the ***Diamond House Motor Inn*** *(☎ 5358 3366, 24 Seaby St)* is a local landmark. The motel is fronted by an 1868 building with a fa ade decorated with brown and white quartz stones in a diamond pattern. Rooms cost from $45/55 to $60/80 and the restaurant is excellent – see Places to Eat.

B&Bs & Cottages ***Wayfarer House B&B*** *(☎ 5358 2921, 30 Patrick St)* is a historic Victorian home with three B&B guestrooms, each with an ensuite (two with spas); rooms cost $100 to $130 a double. ***The Ambers*** *(☎ 5358 2383, 40 Main St)*, set in a beautiful shady garden, provides B&B for $110 a double in a self-contained area of the house.

Stawell Holiday Cottages *(☎ 5358 2868)*, signposted off the Western Hwy, are in Errington Rd on a small bush property about 2km from Stawell. There are six simple and comfortable, self-contained cottages, each sleeping up to six people. The facilities include a playground and barbecues. The tariff ranges from $60 to $70 a double, plus $10 for each extra person.

Places to Eat

Cafe Rasuli *(139 Gold Reef Mall)* serves coffee, cakes and a variety of sandwiches throughout the day and that familiar mix of Asian, Italian and traditional Australian food termed 'modern Australian cuisine' for dinner with mains from $11 to $16. The ***restaurant*** in the Diamond House Motor Inn (24 Seaby St) is excellent; main meals cost around $17 and the cellar is full of local wine. The ***Railway Hotel*** (*13 Main St)* has good bistro meals and on weekdays there are lunch specials.

Getting There & Away

Stawell is on the Melbourne to Adelaide train line; the train station is about 1km south of the centre in Napier St. In addition to the daily Adelaide train there are three to four services daily to/from Melbourne – train to Ballarat and connecting bus to Stawell. The trip takes over 3½ hours; a one-way, full fare is $31.60.

A bus service connects Stawell with the Grampians – see Getting There & Away in the following Grampians National Park section for details.

GRAMPIANS NATIONAL PARK

Major Thomas Mitchell named the spectacular mountain ranges the Grampians after the mountains in Scotland. In 1836, he eloquently described them as:

> ...a noble range of mountains, rising in the south to a stupendous height, and presenting as bold and picturesque an outline as a painter ever imagined.

Major Thomas Mitchell,
an early European admirer of the Grampians

The Grampians are one of Victoria's most outstanding natural features. The area was declared a national park as recently as 1984.

The array of attractions for visitors here includes an incredibly rich diversity of wildlife and plant species, spectacular wildflower displays, unique and unusual rock formations, Aboriginal rock art, fine bushwalking, an extensive network of creeks, streams, cascades and waterfalls and some excellent rock climbing.

The entire national park is a natural wonderland of flora and fauna. Over 900 species of native trees, shrubs and wildflowers have been recorded here, with everything ranging from fern gullies to red-gum forests. There are almost 200 species of birds, 35 different mammals, 28 reptiles, 11 species of amphibians and six types of freshwater fish living here, so you never know what you might see in your wanderings.

The mountains are at their best in spring, when the incredible range of wildflowers (including 20 species that don't occur anywhere else in the world) are at their peak, although there's always something flowering. The Grampians are worth visiting at any time of year, although it can often be extremely hot in summer and very wet in winter.

In 1991 the Grampians' name was officially changed to include the Aboriginal name, Gariwerd, but it was changed back again when the Kennett government came into office.

Orientation

The Grampians lie immediately west of Ararat and stretch some 90km from Dunkeld in the south, almost to Horsham in the north.

The Grampians are made up of four different mountain ranges: the Mt Difficult Range in the north, the Mt William Range in the east, the Serra Range in the south-east and the Victoria Range in the south-west. Halls Gap, the only town in the Grampians, lies in a valley between the northern tip of the Mt William Range and the southern tip of the Mt Difficult Range.

The 40km drive along the unsealed Mt Zero road from Halls Gap to Mt Zero, Mt

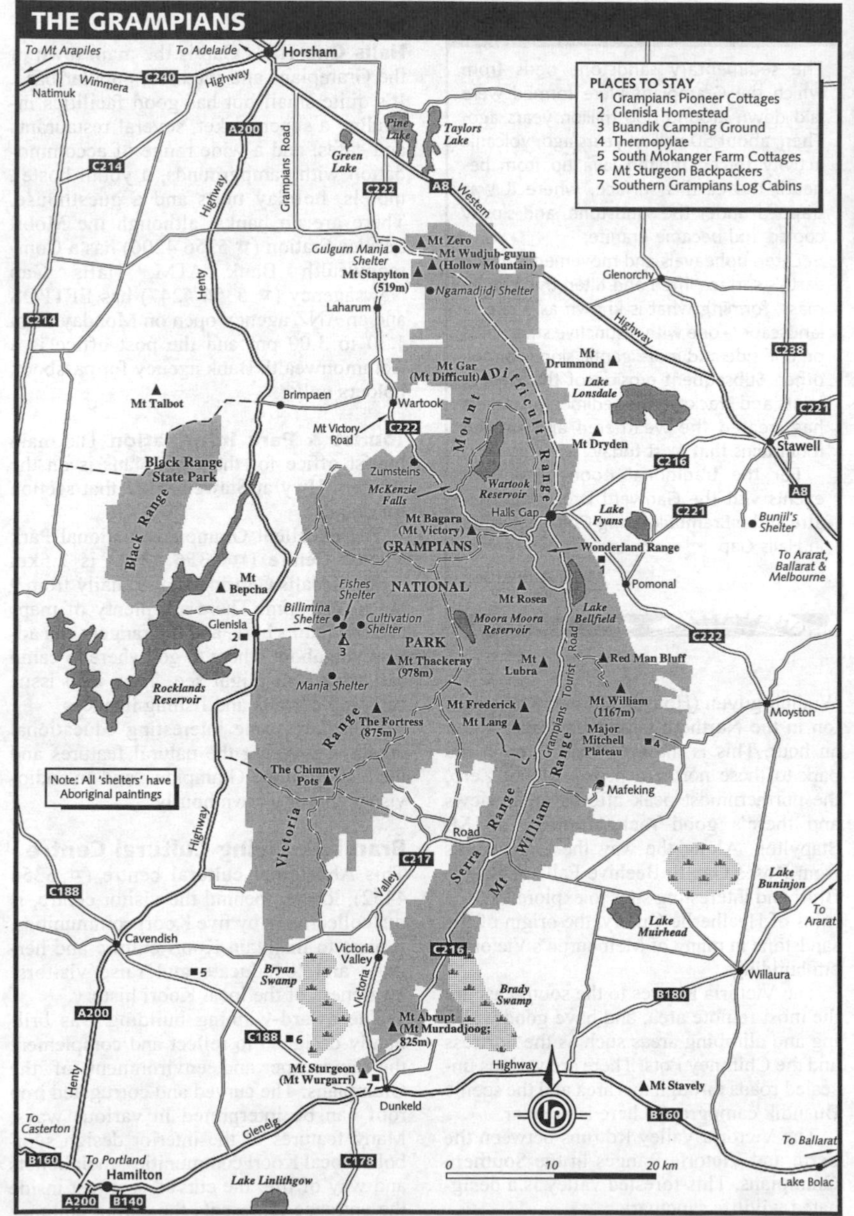
THE GRAMPIANS
PLACES TO STAY
1 Grampians Pioneer Cottages
2 Glenisla Homestead
3 Buandik Camping Ground
4 Thermopylae
5 South Mokanger Farm Cottages
6 Mt Sturgeon Backpackers
7 Southern Grampians Log Cabins
Note: All 'shelters' have Aboriginal paintings
To Mt Arapiles
To Adelaide
Horsham
Natimuk
Wimmera
Highway
C240
A200
C214
Grampians Road
Pine Lake
Taylors Lake
Green Lake
C222
A8
Western
Highway
Henty
Gulgurn Manja Shelter
Mt Zero
Mt Wudjub-guyun (Hollow Mountain)
Mt Stapylton (519m)
Ngamadjidj Shelter
Laharum
Glenorchy
C238
Mt Gar (Mt Difficult)
Mount Difficult Range
Mt Drummond
Lake Lonsdale
Mt Talbot
Brimpaen
Wartook
Mt Victory Road
C221
Mt Dryden
Stawell
C216
Black Range State Park
Black Range
Zumsteins
McKenzie Falls
Wartook Reservoir
Halls Gap
Lake Fyans
Bunjil's Shelter
Mt Bagara (Mt Victory)
GRAMPIANS
NATIONAL
PARK
Wonderland Range
To Ararat, Ballarat & Melbourne
Mt Bepcha
Fishes Shelter
Mt Rosea
Pomonal
Billimina Shelter
Cultivation Shelter
Glenisla
Moora Moora Reservoir
Lake Bellfield
Rocklands Reservoir
Mt Thackeray (978m)
Mt Lubra
Red Man Bluff
Grampians Tourist Road
Manja Shelter
Mt William (1167m)
Mt Frederick
Moyston
The Fortress (875m)
Mt Lang
Major Mitchell Plateau
Victoria Range
The Chimney Pots
Serra Range
Mt William Range
Mafeking
Road
C217
Valley
C188
Lake Buninjon
To Ararat
Lake Muirhead
Cavendish
Victoria Valley
C216
Bryan Swamp
Brady Swamp
Willaura
B180
Mt Abrupt (Mt Murdadjoog; 825m)
Mt Sturgeon (Mt Wurgarri)
Highway
Mt Stavely
Dunkeld
B160
To Casterton
Glenelg
To Ballarat
To Portland
Hamilton
A200
B140
C178
0
10
20 km
Lake Linlithgow
Lake Bolac

Creation of a Mountain Range

The sedimentary sandstone beds from which the Grampians were formed were laid down around 500 million years ago. Then, about 50 million years ago, volcanic activity forced molten lava up from beneath the earth's surface, where it was trapped under the sandstone, and slowly cooled and became granite.

Later, upheavals and movements of the earth's surface lifted and tilted this granite mass, forming what is known as a cuesta landscape – one with distinctive steep cliffs on one side and more gentle slopes on the other. Subsequent erosion of the weaker joints and cracks in the sedimentary layers has created the weathered and rugged mountains that exist today.

For the traditional Koori version of events visit the Gariwerd Dreaming Theatre in the Brambuk Living Cultural Centre in Halls Gap.

Mark Armstrong

Wudjub-guyun (Hollow Mt) and Mt Stapylton in the Northern Grampians takes about an hour. This is the only road through the park to these northern peaks. Mount Zero, the northernmost peak affords great views and there's good rock climbing on Mt Stapylton. Along the way there are walks from Roses Gap to Beehive Falls or Briggs Bluff and interesting sites to explore like the ruins of Heatherlie Quarry, the origin of the sandstone in many of Melbourne's Victorian era buildings.

The Victoria Ranges to the south-east are the most remote area, and have good walking and climbing areas such as the Fortress and the Chimney Pots. There are various unsealed roads through this area and the scenic Buandik campground here is popular.

The Victoria Valley Rd runs between the Serra and Victoria Ranges in the Southern Grampians. This forested valley is a designated wildlife sanctuary.

Information

Halls Gap Halls Gap is the main town of the Grampians and the most popular base. It's quite small but has good facilities including a supermarket, several restaurants and cafes, and a wide range of accommodation with campgrounds, a youth hostel, motels, holiday units and a guesthouse. There are no banks, although the Mobil Service Station (☎ 5356 4206) has a Commonwealth Bank ATM, Halls Gap Newsagency (☎ 5356 4247) has EFTPOS and an ANZ agency open on Monday from 1.30 to 3.00 pm and the post office is a Commonwealth Bank agency for passbook holders only.

Tourist & Park Information The main tourist office for the Grampians is on the Western Hwy at Stawell – see that section for details.

The excellent Grampians National Park Visitor Centre (☎ 5356 4381) is 2.5km south of Halls Gap and is open daily from 9 am to 4.45 pm. There are plenty of maps and brochures here, and the rangers can advise you about where to go, where to camp and what you might see. They also issue camping permits and fishing licences.

There are some interesting educational displays covering the natural features and the history of the Grampians, and an audiovisual film is shown hourly.

Brambuk Living Cultural Centre

This Aboriginal cultural centre (☎ 5356 4452), located behind the visitor centre, is run collectively by five Koori communities. It aims to maintain Koori culture and heritage and to educate and raise visitors' awareness of the local Koori history.

The award-winning building was brilliantly designed to reflect and complement the landscape and environment of the Grampians. The curved and corrugated iron roof can be interpreted in various ways. Many features of the interior design symbolise local Koori communities, their beliefs and way of life: the curved seat just inside the entrance represents the caring embrace of Bunjil, the creator spirit, the ramp upstairs is the eel dreaming, the theatre ceiling depicts the Southern Right Whale (totem of the Gundjitmara people). The area around the centre has been landscaped and planted with native plants used by Aboriginal people for food and medicine.

The displays in the centre tell the history of the Koori people, from the customs and lifestyles before European settlement to persecution by European settlers and the history of local Aboriginal missions. There are examples of Koori art, clothes, weapons and tools on display, a souvenir shop and a bush-tucker cafe.

During the peak holiday periods there are demonstrations of Koori music and dance on the ceremonial ground. Organised tours of the rock art sites are run from here. They also run education and holiday programmes.

The centre is open daily from 10 am to 5 pm and admission is free. Entrance to the Gariwerd Dreaming Theatre – a multi-media narration of traditional stories of the region – costs $4 for adults, $2.50 for children.

Aboriginal Rock Art

There is an extensive collection of rock art within the Grampians National Park, but not all of it is publicised or accessible. In the Northern Grampians near Mt Stapylton the main sites are Gulgurn Manja Shelter and Ngamadjidj Shelter. In the Western Grampians near the Buandik campground the main sites are Billimina Shelter and Manja Shelter.

These rock paintings were made with either ochre or white clay, and are mostly drawings or stencils such as hand prints, animal tracks or stick figures. The paintings are in rock overhangs and are protected by wire fences. The Brambuk Living Cultural Centre takes tours to these sites.

Wonderland Range

The Wonderland Range is close to Halls Gap and has some of the most spectacular and accessible scenery in the Grampians. There are good scenic drives, picnic grounds and excellent walks ranging from an easy half-hour stroll to Venus Baths to a four hour walk to the Boroka Lookout.

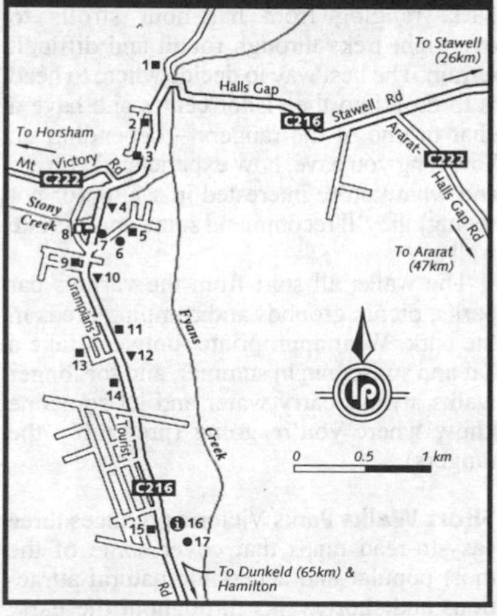

HALLS GAP

PLACES TO STAY

1 Marwood Villas
2 Halls Gap YHA Hostel
3 Grand Canyon Motel
5 Halls Gap Kookaburra Lodge
8 Halls Gap Caravan Park
9 Mountain Grand Guesthouse
11 Halls Gap Motel
13 Grampians Wonderland Cabins
14 Kingsway Holiday Flats
15 Brambuk Backpackers

PLACES TO EAT

4 Flying Emu Cafe
10 The Kookaburra Restaurant
12 Suzy's Halls Gap Tavern

OTHER

6 Halls Gap Fun Park & Bike Hire
7 Halls Gap General Store, Newsagency & Post Office
16 Grampians National Park Visitor Centre
17 Brambuk Living Cultural Centre; Bush Tucker Cafe

Walking tracks start from Halls Gap and also from the Wonderland picnic ground.

Halls Gap Wildlife Park & Zoo

This small wildlife park, on the Pomonal Rd behind Halls Gap, houses an interesting variety of animals in a natural bush setting. There are native species such as kangaroos, wombats, emus and possums as well as deer, monkeys and ostriches. The park is open Wednesday to Monday from 10 am to 5 pm and admission costs $7 for adults, $5 for kids.

Zumstein

Zumstein is a reserve in the Western Grampians where large numbers of kangaroos congregate. They are generally tame but shouldn't be fed or touched. The reserve is named after Walter Zumstein, a beekeeper and naturalist who settled in the area in 1910 and developed it into a wildlife reserve. There are picnic facilities here and a walking track follows the river to the base of the spectacular McKenzie Falls.

Lake Bellfield

This lake is just south of Halls Gap. Years ago an old homestead and guesthouse stood on the present lake site, but the valley was flooded to create a water-storage area. The lake has also been stocked with rainbow and brown trout.

Dunkeld

This small township on the Glenelg Hwy (B160) has a picturesque location at the foot of the Southern Grampians, in the shadows of Mt Abrupt (Mt Murdadjoog) and Mt Sturgeon (Mt Wurgarri). The Grampians Tourist Rd, which runs from Dunkeld to Halls Gap, is the most scenic route into the Grampians, although most people approach from the north.

The town was established in the 1860s, but many of the buildings were destroyed by bushfires in 1944. There's a historical **society museum** in an old bluestone building in Templeton St with a local history collection including Aboriginal artefacts and old photographs. It's open on Sunday and public holidays from 1 to 5 pm and admission costs $2.

Dunkeld has one hotel, a couple of takeaways, a craft shop and tearooms, and a couple of places to stay. (See Dunkeld under Other Accommodation, later in this chapter.)

Activities

Adventure Activities Base Camp & Beyond (☎ 5356 4300) runs two to five-day rock climbing and abseiling courses most weekends and during holiday periods, costing from $60 per day.

Action Adventures (☎ 5356 4654) run a two hour introductory abseiling course ($25 for adults), one-day rock climbing and abseiling courses ($65 for adults), as well as canoeing and bicycle tours.

Grampians Adventure Services (☎ 5356 4556) offer a full range of outdoor activities: rock climbing, abseiling, canoeing, bike tours, bushwalking and caving. They also combine two or three of these activities into a day at a cost of $40 to $60 for adults.

Bushwalking There are more than 150km of well-marked walking tracks through the park, ranging from half-hour strolls to overnight treks through rough and difficult terrain. The best way to decide where to head is to drop into the visitor centre and have a chat to one of the rangers – depending on how long you have, how experienced you are and what you're interested in seeing (or not seeing) they'll recommend some appropriate walks.

The walks all start from the various car parks, picnic grounds and camping areas in the park. Wear appropriate footwear, take a hat and sunscreen in summer, and for longer walks always carry water and let someone know where you're going (preferably the rangers).

Short Walks Parks Victoria produces three easy-to-read maps that cover some of the most popular and accessible natural attractions and short walks throughout the Park;

you can buy these at the visitor centre where copies are on the counter for browsing.

Fishing Permits are required to fish in the local streams and creeks. A permit costs $10 for 28 days and is available from the visitor centre and the local petrol stations.

Horse Riding In Brimpaen, about 50 minutes drive north-west of Halls Gap, The Grampians Coach House (☎ 5383 9255) offers good horse rides ranging from $25 for an hour to $80 for half a day (including morning tea).

Joy Flights & Balloon Rides Grampians Balloon Flights (☎ 5358 5222) in Stawell offer morning flights for $175 with champagne and breakfast included and Stawell Aviation Services (☎ 5357 3234) offers joy flights by plane from $40.

Organised Tours

In the Halls Gap Newsagency, which is on Main St, the Grampians Central Booking Office (☎ 5356 4654), takes bookings for rock climbing, abseiling, cycling, ballooning, horse riding and bushwalking tours. You can book Grampians Bushwalking Company tours here. Their walks and tours range from a two hour King Koala Hunt costing $5 for adults, to a four hour sunrise or sunset tour costing $48 with breakfast or dinner.

Grampians National Park Tours (☎ 5356 6221) run full-day, 4WD tours of the national park which depart from Halls Gap at 10 am daily and include short walks, lunch and afternoon tea for $75 per person.

Bicycle Outback (☎ 9484 0284) run three-day bike tours through the national park over the long weekends for $235 per person. Transport to and from Melbourne and all meals are provided. It's BYO bicycle and tent, although hire is available.

For other tours from Melbourne see the Getting Around chapter.

Brambuk Living Cultural Centre (☎ 5356 4452) runs tours to Aboriginal rock art sites, departing from the centre most days at 9 am. Tours cost $12 for adults and you need to book 24 hours in advance.

Special Events

Halls Gap is the centre point for some good local festivities, including the Grampians Jazz Festival in February, the Grampians Gourmet weekend in May, the Halls Gap Spring Art Exhibition in September, the Halls Gap Wildflower Exhibition in October and the Halls Gap Film Festival in November.

Places to Stay

During the busier seasons it can be hard to find accommodation in Halls Gap. The helpful Grampians Accommodation Booking Service (☎ 1800 246 880 toll-free), at the Stawell & Grampians Tourist Information Centre, can make bookings and give advice on vacancies and rates.

While Halls Gap is the most central and popular base, accommodation is also available in Dunkeld, Glenisla, Cavendish and Wartook.

Camping in the Park Parks Victoria maintains more than 10 campsites in the national park, all with toilets, picnic tables and fireplaces, and most with at least limited water. There's no booking system – it's first in, best site. Permits cost $8.60, which covers one car and up to six people, and you can self-register or pay at the visitor centre.

Bush camping is permitted anywhere outside the designated campsites except in the Wonderland Range area, around Lake Wartook and in parts of the Serra and Victoria Ranges.

When camping in the park pay close attention to the fire restrictions – apart from the damage you could do to yourself and the bush, you stand a good chance of being arrested if you disobey them. Remember that you can be jailed for lighting *any* fire, including fuel stoves, on days of total fire ban, and the locals will be more than willing to dob you in.

For a more organised camping trip, High Spirit Outdoor Adventures (☎ 019 403 620) have a campsite beside the Moora Moora

Reservoir in the Victoria Valley where accommodation, meals, transport to bushwalks, use of canoes, a bush sauna and more costs $30 a day.

Caravan Parks – Halls Gap, Wartook & Dunkeld There are around a dozen caravan parks in and around the Grampians.

In the centre of Halls Gap, ***Halls Gap Caravan Park*** *(☎ 5356 4251)* has campsites from $12, on-site vans from $36 and cabins from $45 to $95. ***Halls Gap Lakeside Caravan Park*** *(☎ 5356 4281)*, 5km south on the scenic shores of Lake Bellfield, has sites from $13 and on-site cabins and holiday flats ranging from $38 to $94.

At Wartook on the western side of the Northern Grampians, ***Happy Wanderer Log Cabins & Caravan Park*** *(☎ 5383 6210)* has a scenic setting overlooking the mountains; facilities include a playground, pool, tennis courts and a nine-hole bush golf course. Ensuite sites cost from $15, on-site vans from $37 and self-contained log cabins from $47.

In Dunkeld on the Glenelg Hwy, ***Southgate Grampians Caravan Park*** *(☎ 5577 2210)* has sites from $10.

Other Accommodation There is a range of other types of accommodation available in the area.

Halls Gap Brambuk Backpackers *(☎ 5356 4250)*, opposite the visitor centre on the Grampians Tourist Rd, has dorm beds from $15 to $20 per night depending on the season, and a large kitchen, dining room and lounge. The smaller ***Halls Gap YHA Hostel*** *(☎ 5356 6221)* is 1km from the centre on the corner of Grampians Tourist Rd and Buckler St. Dorm beds here cost $13 ($16 for nonmembers), and there are family rooms at $16 per person. A new, larger YHA hostel will be built soon.

Mountain Grand Guesthouse *(☎ 5356 4232)*, on Grampians Tourist Rd (aka Main Road), is a gracious, old-fashioned timber guesthouse. It's well run and friendly, and has comfortable lounges, two licensed eateries (see Places to Eat), and good guestrooms with ensuites costing from $98 a double including a cooked brekkie. The popular weekend getaway package is great value at $180 a double; bookings are essential.

There are about half a dozen motels in Halls Gap. A couple of the cheaper ones are ***Halls Gap Motel*** *(☎ 5356 4209)*, doubles from $59 to $85 and ***Grand Canyon Motel*** *(☎ 5356 4280)*, doubles from $55 to $93: both are on the Grampians Tourist Rd. Close to the centre, ***Halls Gap Kookaburra Lodge*** *(☎ 5356 4395, 14 Heath St)* has good double units from $70 to $90, and an excellent restaurant (see Places to Eat).

There are also quite a few self-contained units and cottages to choose from. ***Kingsway Holiday Flats*** *(☎ 5356 4202, Grampians Tourist Rd)* is one of the cheapest and has good budget flats from $45 to $55 a double. ***Grampians Wonderland Cabins*** *(☎ 5356 4264, Ellis St)* have self-contained, two bedroom units from $85 to $135 a double.

One of the most luxurious self-contained accommodation options in the area is ***Marwood Villas*** *(☎ 5356 4231)* where, if a king size bed, a colonnaded spa, a log fire, stereo, TV and CD aren't enough, you can order extras like chocolates and red roses. Doubles cost from $195 to $260 a night.

Midway between Halls Gap and Pomonal, ***Grampians Pioneer Cottages*** *(☎ 5356 4402)* consists of three rustic/modern cottages. They're each a bit different and quite isolated, with open fires and the usual mod cons. Tariffs range from $80 to $95 a double, plus $20 per extra adult.

For a farm stay that includes farm activities, ***Thermopylae*** *(☎ 5354 6245)*, near Moyston, has self-contained or fully catered accommodation from $150 for a weekend.

Dunkeld The recently, stylishly renovated ***Royal Mail Hotel*** *(☎ 5577 2241)*, in the centre of town, has rooms from $70/90 a single/double. ***Southern Grampians Log Cabins*** *(☎ 5577 2457)*, on Victoria Valley Rd, has eight self-contained log cabins in a bush setting. They're well equipped with TVs, open fires and barbecues, and range from $80 to $145 a double, plus $10 per extra adult.

Five minutes from Dunkeld on the Cavendish Rd, ***Mt Sturgeon Backpackers*** *(☎ 5577 2241)* has beds for $20 per night in a fully equipped house on a working sheep property. It's BYO bedding and towel.

Glenisla & Cavendish Two large properties on the western side of the Grampians have good accommodation on offer.

Glenisla Homestead (☎ 5380 1532), an elegant 1873 homestead on a 700 hectare sheep property, offers very good B&B accommodation in its three guestrooms with private ensuites. Tariffs are from $100/196 a single/double, which includes farm activities and guided tours. Home-cooked meals are available.

If you're feeling energetic at ***South Mokanger Farm Cottages*** *(☎ 5574 2398)* you can join in the farm work. There are two self-contained cottages on this 1800 hectare sheep and cattle property. They cost $95 to $110 a night for up to four, plus $15 per extra adult and cooked breakfasts are available.

Places to Eat

In the small shopping centre in the centre of Halls Gap you'll find a general store with a cafe and a take-away section and a well-stocked supermarket. Nearby in the shopping complex next to Stony Creek you'll find a bakery – 1998 winner of Jeff Kennett's state-wide vanilla slice competition, a butcher, a casual pizza, pasta and pancake restaurant and the ***Flying Emu Cafe***, which serves a good range of gourmet foods including sandwiches, pastries, muffins, smoothies and coffee.

The ***Kookaburra Restaurant*** *(☎ 5356 4222)*, on Grampians Tourist Rd, has earned an excellent reputation over the years. The menu makes great use of fresh local produce such as Western District lamb, freshwater fish and home-reared venison. Main meals range from $15 to $22; try to leave room for the wonderful desserts. The Kookaburra opens nightly for dinner; you'll need to book ahead, especially on weekends and holidays.

At the Mountain Grand Guesthouse, the upstairs ***The 'Balconies' Restaurant*** serves fine country cuisine, and has live jazz on weekends and holidays; they also have a casual licensed cafe downstairs. ***Suzy's Halls Gap Tavern*** is a spacious and modern colonial-style tavern and bar offering three-course set meals for $10 and kids' meals from $5; you can also order à la carte, with pastas and entrées from $9 and main courses around $16.

At the ***Bush Tucker Cafe*** at the Brambuk Living Cultural Centre you can get a range of bush snacks; a 'roo burger or kebab costs $6.

Getting There & Away

V/Line has a daily train/bus service from Melbourne to Halls Gap. Trains leave Melbourne every morning to Ballarat. A connecting bus takes you to Stawell and another bus takes you from Stawell to Halls Gap. The trip takes about four hours and a one-way, full fare is $38.90.

There are buses from Halls Gap back to Stawell every afternoon. The Halls Gap-to-Stawell bus section costs $7.30 for a full fare.

The road from Stawell to Halls Gap is flat so it's an easy cycle of about 25km. You can take your bike on the *Overland* train (Melbourne to Adelaide) to Stawell, although the train arrives at Stawell at 1.43 am. It's a longer and hillier ride from Ararat to Halls Gap (via Moyston) but still fairly easy.

Getting Around

Car & Motorbike The major roads through the Grampians are the Grampians Tourist Rd from Dunkeld to Halls Gap, the Mt Victory Rd from Halls Gap to Wartook and the Silverband Rd, which completes the loop around the Wonderland area. These roads are all sealed.

The unsealed roads in the park are in good condition, although some are closed during winter and after heavy rain.

Bike Hire Halls Gap Fun Park and Bike Hire (☎ 5356 4348), behind the main shopping centre, has mountain bikes for hire from

Wineries of the Grampians

Great Western is the centre point of the wine-growing district now known as the Grampians region, and there are three excellent wineries to be visited within a barrel's roll of the township.

The most famous of these is **Seppelt's Great Western**, one of Australia's oldest and largest producers of sparkling wines. The highlight of a visit here is a tour of the huge old underground cellars, which were dug by hand in the 1860s. The winery is open daily from 10 am to 5 pm. Tours are held from Monday to Saturday at 10.30 am, 1.30 pm and 3 pm; $5 for adults and $2 for kids.

On the Ararat side of Great Western is **Garden Gully Wines**. This is relatively new winery in the region but the vineyard was planted about 40 years ago by Seppelt's. The tasting room is a modern brick building on the site of the famous 1870s Salinger Winery. The winery is a co-op run by local wine workers and is open daily from 10.30 am to 5 pm.

Best's Winery, just north of Great Western, has been producing wine since 1868 and is imbued with a sense of history. The tasting room is an old slab-timber hut full of character and the walls are lined with old photos. Visitors are free to wander on a do-it-yourself tour of the winery, which is beyond the rustic tasting room. Best's is open weekdays from 9 am to 5 pm, Saturday from 9 am to 4 pm and Sunday, during holiday periods, from noon to 4 pm.

The **Gap** winery, formerly known as Boroka, is located 5km east of Halls Gap on the Pomonal Rd. It is owned by Mount Langhi Ghiran Vineyards and wines available for tastings and sales include estate grown Mt Langhi Ghiran and Four Sisters Wines. It's open from Wednesday to Sunday, 10 am to 5 pm.

Other wineries in the district include **Mt Langi Ghiran** (see Langi Ghiran State Park section), **Kimbarra Wines**, 422 Barkly St, Ararat, open Monday to Friday from 9 am to 5 pm, and **Montara Winery** (see the Ararat section).

$15 a day; they also have a drop-off service if you want to ride to/from a particular area.

HORSHAM

pop 12,600

The area around Horsham was first settled in 1841, when James Darlot put down roots here. In 1849 a post office and general store were built, and from these humble beginnings the town has grown to become the main commercial centre of the Wimmera. It's a bustling and progressive country town with modern retail facilities that service the surrounding wheat and sheep farms.

There's not a great deal to see in the town itself, but it's a good base for exploring the nearby Little Desert National and Mt Arapiles State parks.

Orientation & Information

Firebrace St, which runs off the Western Hwy, is the main shopping strip. There are several large supermarkets and a K-Mart complex in town, as well as plenty of other shops and eateries.

The Horsham Tourist Information Centre (☎ 5382 1832), 20 O'Callaghan's Parade, has good information on Horsham and the surrounding areas. It's open daily from 9 am to 5 pm.

Things to See & Do

The **Horsham Art Gallery**, 80 Wilson St, is well worth a visit. It's main feature is the Mack Jost Bequest, a private collection of significant Australian artists that includes works by Rupert Bunny, Sir Sidney Nolan,

John Olsen and Charles Blackman, but it also houses an impressive Australian photography collection. The gallery opens Tuesday to Friday from 10 am to 5 pm, and on Sunday from 1 to 4.30 pm. Entry costs $1 but may go up after renovations are finished.

The wide, brown **Wimmera River** meanders through the town, and its banks are lined with river red gums. The **Botanic Gardens**, on the banks of the river at the end of Firebrace St, were established in the 1870s and designed by the then curator of Melbourne's Royal Botanic Gardens, William Guilfoyle. Behind the entrance gates is a large bunya pine, and these pleasant gardens have shady trees and lawns, rose gardens and picnic facilities.

The **Wool Factory**, in Golf Course Rd, is a community project that provides employment and skill development for handicapped people. It produces ultra-fine wool from merino sheep, and there's a walk-through sheep shed, a cafe and souvenir shop where you can buy wool products. Tours are held daily at 10.15 am, 11 am, 1.30 pm and 2.30 pm; the cost is $4 for adults, $2 for kids.

The **Horsham Golf Course** (☎ 5382 1652), on Golf Course Rd, was recently rated number one in country Victoria and is open to visitors. Clubs are available for hire from the clubhouse.

Green Lake, 10km south-east of Horsham, has a small beach and is the most popular local spot for swimming, boating and fishing.

At Laharum, 32km south and on the fringe of the Grampians, ***Big Spring Mount*** *(☎ 5383 8235)* native flower growers can take you on a tour of their flower shed and the nearby olive plantation. Tours are by appointment only and cost varies according to the number of people on the tour.

Special Events

Horsham's Apex Fishing Competition is held on Labour Day long weekend in March on the Wimmera River. Organisers of the first contest, held in 1972, got the surprise of their lives when around 3,500 keen anglers turned up. Since then, the competition has grown into one of the richest and most popular in the country.

Other events include the Agricultural Show in September, the Horsham Spring Garden Festival in October and the Kannamaroo Festival in November, which includes a raft race.

Places to Stay

Camping & Caravan Parks The ***Horsham City Caravan Park*** *(☎ 5382 3476)*, at the end of Firebrace St between the botanic gardens and the river, has good facilities with campsites from $10 and on-site vans and cabins from $40.

Pubs & Motels There are a few pubs in town with rooms. The ***Bull and Mouth Hotel*** *(☎ 5382 1057, Wilson St)* has pretty basic rooms for $15/25 a single/double. A better choice would be the historic ***Royal Hotel*** *(☎ 5382 1255, 132 Firebrace St)*, which has rooms for $20/35 a single/double and includes a continental breakfast.

There are more than 15 motels in Horsham. One of the cheapest is the ***Glynlea Motel*** *(☎ 5382 0145, 26 Stawell Rd)*, which has good rooms from $48 to $52 a double. There's also the ***Majestic Motel*** *(☎ 5382 0144, 56 Stawell Rd)* with singles/doubles from $39/48. Another good option is the ***Olde Horsham Motor Inn*** *(☎ 5381 0033)* on the Western Hwy on the southern outskirts of town. Standard doubles are $62 and executive units are $70.

See the tourist centre for information on the B&Bs in the area.

Places to Eat

Cafe Bagdad, Wilson St near the corner of Firebrace St, is open Monday to Saturday and has good meals from $5 to $10. The decor is reminiscent of an early 80s Melbourne cafe and the coffee is excellent. It's a popular spot for climbers heading to Mt Arapiles.

The ***Fig Tree Cafe*** in Firebrace St is another good spot for coffee and cake.

The bistro and counter meals at the pubs are popular, particularly ***The Commercial*** in Wilson St. Most of the motels also have restaurants.

Getting There & Away

Train Horsham is on the Melbourne to Adelaide train line; the train station is in Railway Ave, about 1km north of the centre. However the only passenger train it carries is the Overland from Melbourne every night except Wednesday and Saturday. There are four train/bus services daily (three on Sunday) to/from Melbourne; train between Melbourne and Ballarat and bus between Ballarat and Horsham. The trip takes about 4½ hours and the one-way, full fare is $41.30.

Bus Several private companies operate the following bus services from Horsham: south along the Henty Hwy (A200) to Hamilton (daily Monday to Friday; ☎ 015 851 642); west along the Wimmera Hwy (C240) to Naracoorte (daily Monday to Friday; ☎ 014 472 025); north along the Henty Hwy (B200) to Mildura (Tuesday, Thursday and Friday; ☎ 5381 1871); north to Rainbow via Dimboola (Thursday only; ☎ 5352 1501). All these buses leave Horsham from the old Police Station, 24 Roberts Avenue.

There's no direct service from Horsham to the Grampians – take the V/Line bus to Stawell and another bus from there.

MINYIP

• **pop 475**

This tiny and historic township, 55km north-east of Horsham, is better known as Coopers Crossing, the former home base of the *Flying Doctors* TV series. The town was established in the 1870s and Main St is lined with 19th century buildings including two grand old pubs trimmed with iron lace work.

The ***Club Hotel*** *(☎ 5385 7281)* and the ***Commercial Hotel*** *(☎ 5385 7271)* both have pub rooms for $15 a single including light breakfast; both serve counter meals.

MT ARAPILES STATE PARK

Mt Arapiles is widely regarded as Australia's best venue for rock climbing. It has more than 2000 different routes, ranging from basic to advanced climbs, with colourful names such as Violent Crumble, Punks in the Gym and Cruel Britannia. Rock climbers come here from all around the world, and on most days you can see climbers scaling the mountain from all directions. The park is also popular for walks and picnics, and has over 500 species of native plants as well as kangaroos, possums, goannas and some rare bird species including the peregrine falcon. Dogs shouldn't be taken into the park.

The mountain is 37km west of Horsham and 12km west of the sleepy town of Natimuk. So great is its attraction that Natimuk is now home to quite a few climbers who have moved into the area, bringing with them tastes and attitudes not usually associated with small rural towns in Australia.

Approaching Mt Arapiles from the Wimmera Hwy, you'll soon see why it's known as the 'Ayers Rock of the Wimmera' as it looms up on the horizon. You can drive to the summit of the mountain along the sealed Lookout Rd – a short track leads from the car park to the lookout.

Centenary Park is a picnic area and campground at the foot of the mountain. This area was named in 1936, 100 years after Major Mitchell climbed and named the mountain. The pine trees that were planted at the same time provide good shade and protection. There are picnic tables, fireplaces, bore water and toilets here.

There are also two short and steep walking tracks from Centenary Park to the top of Arapiles, and another rough road leads around the boundary of the park.

Climbing Instruction

Several operators, including the Climbing Company (☎ 5387 1329) and Arapiles Climbing Guides (☎ 5387 1284), offer climbing and abseiling instruction. Group instruction costs around $30 for a half-day, or private tuition is around $180 a day for individuals or $250 a day for small groups.

Places to Stay & Eat

There's a popular campsite (known locally as 'the Pines') in Centenary Park at the base of the mountain – facilities are limited to toilets and a washbasin. The ***Natimuk Lake Caravan Park*** *(☎ 5387 1462)* is beside Lake Natimuk about 4km north of Natimuk and has full facilities. Campsites cost from $8 a night and there are on-site vans from $30.

In Natimuk, The ***National Hotel*** *(☎ 5387 1300, 65 Main St)* has comfortable pub rooms for $17.50 per person, breakfast is extra. The pub serves counter meals from Wednesday to Saturday nights for around $10. They also have self-contained cabins with a double bed and four bunks for $50 a double, plus $10 for each extra adult.

Quamby Lodge *(☎ 5387 1569, 71 Main St)* provides comfortable accommodation in a relaxed and friendly household. Beds are $15 per night with breakfast. Even if you're not sleeping there you can have a shower in their newly renovated bathrooms for $3 and do your laundry for $3.50.

Seven kilometres east of Natimuk and midway between Horsham and Mt Arapiles, the friendly ***Tim's Place YHA*** *(☎ 5384 0236)* has dorm beds at $15 per person, which includes breakfast. There are also three double rooms at $35. The hostel has heaps of information about local activities and can arrange climbing and abseiling instruction. You can hire mountain bikes for $5 a day, go fishing, yabbying, horse riding, swim in the dam or enjoy an emu steak on the barbie. The hostel also runs a Koori cultural issues evening three times a week for $15.

Natimuk Gallery and Cafe is open weekends from November to May and has excellent coffee and cakes. The vegetarian meals are delicious and cost around $10.

If you're into milkshakes, the local milkbars are famous for them.

Getting There & Away

The weekday bus service between Horsham and Naracoorte will drop people at Mt Arapiles ($4.50). See the earlier Horsham Getting There and Away entry for details.

If you're planning to stay at Tim's Place (see the previous Places to Stay entry) ring to find out about transport/accommodation packages.

EDENHOPE

• **pop 775**

Edenhope is a fairly uninspiring town with one pub, one motel and a caravan park next to Lake Wallace. The lake has good fishing, and there's a walking/jogging track around its perimeter. If you're looking for a stopover between Melbourne and Adelaide, the ***Edenhope Motor Inn*** *(☎ 5585 1369)* on the Wimmera Hwy has rooms from $45/52 a single/double.

One point of interest here is the **Johnny Mullagh Memorial Cairn**, a simple stone obelisk standing in the grounds of the local school, which commemorates the first Aboriginal cricket team to tour England. The team trained here before departing in 1868. The cairn lists the team members – Dick-a-Dick, Charles Lawrence (captain), Johnny Mullagh, Twopenny, Redcap, Mosquito, King Cole, Peter, Cuzens, Tiger, Jim Crow, Bullocky, Dumas and Sundown – and their tour record: they won 14, lost 14 and drew 19 matches.

KANIVA

• **pop 775**

Kaniva is a quiet country town with echoes of a more prosperous past. A broad central plantation divides the main street, which is lined with weathered old buildings and historic verandah-fronted pubs.

The Apricot House coffee lounge, 41 Commercial St, has a small tourist information section (☎ 5392 2418); it's open weekdays from 9 am to 5 pm and weekends from 10 am to 2 pm. There's a **Historical Museum** at 111 Commercial Rd but it's only open by appointment.

The historic and disproportionately large **Serviceton train station** (1887), about 24km west of Kaniva and 3km off the Western Hwy, is classified by the National Trust – what's left of it, that is.

Places to Stay & Eat

The ***Commercial Hotel*** *(☎ 5392 2230, corner of Commercial and Madden Sts)* has basic pub rooms for $20/30 a single/double with light breakfast, and the ***Kaniva Colonial***

Motor Inn *(☎ 5392 2730, 134 Commercial St)* has rooms from $49/59 a single/double.

There isn't a great choice of eateries in Kaniva – a couple of take-aways and road-houses on the main street, a restaurant in the Kaniva Colonial Motor Inn, which is open every night, or bistro meals in the Commercial Hotel.

NHILL

• pop 1900

Although Nhill is an Aboriginal word meaning 'mist over the water', there's not much water around these parts. Lake Nhill is usually a dry lake bed. The town is a wheat industry centre, as evidenced by the huge grain silos and flour mills.

Nhill's main claim to fame is that it was once the home of the Australian lyric poet John Shaw Neilson. Neilson's simple slab cottage from his birthplace, Penola in South Australia, has been restored and erected beside the Western Hwy on the western edge of town.

The Nhill-to-Harrow road (C206) heads south through the centre of the Little Desert National Park. The **Stringybark Nature Walk** starts just off this road about 20km south of Nhill. For details, see the Little Desert National Park entry later in this chapter.

Places to Stay

In the centre of Nhill the old verandah-fronted ***Union Hotel*** *(☎ 5391 1722, 41 Victoria St)* has rooms upstairs for $20/40 a single/double, including a light breakfast. ***Motel Halfway*** *(☎ 5391 1888)*, on the Western Hwy, has budget rooms from $38/42, while ***Zero Inn*** *(☎ 5391 1622)*, also on the highway, has more modern rooms from $58/65 and a bigger pool and restaurant.

Little Desert Lodge is 16km south of the town – see the section on the Little Desert National Park later in this chapter for details.

DIMBOOLA

• pop 1550

The pretty town of Dimboola, just off the Western Hwy, is a historic country town with some fine old buildings and is worth a detour. It's also the 'Gateway to the Little Desert', according to a sign over the timber archway on the road to the Little Desert National Park (the park starts 4km south of the town).

Made famous in 1969 by Jack Hibberd's play *Dimboola*, about a country wedding, and the subsequent film, the town is set on the Wimmera River, which is lined with river red gums and has some good shady picnic spots along its banks.

Pink Lake is a colourful salt lake beside the Western Hwy about 9km north-west of Dimboola.

Ebenezer Aboriginal Mission Station was established in Antwerp, 18km north of Dimboola, by Moravian missionaries in 1859. The historic buildings, once in ruins, have been classified by the National Trust and are being restored. You can wander around and visit the small cemetery. The mission is signposted off the Dimboola-to-Jeparit road.

Walkabout Tours (☎ 5381 1691) run Koori tours in this area that include a visit to the mission. Tours costs $15 per person.

Special Events

Held here on the Wimmera River every November since 1884, the Dimboola Rowing Regatta is the biggest regatta in country Victoria.

Places to Stay

The ***Riverside Caravan Park*** *(☎ 5389 1416)* is in a scenic setting beside the Wimmera River with grounds that are shaded by an assortment of eucalypt and pine trees. Campsites cost from $9 and on-site vans from $30.

The ***Victoria Hotel*** *(☎ 5389 1630, Wimmera St)* is a well-preserved 1920s pub with renovated single/double rooms for $30/45. The hotel is family owned and run, and is a cut above the normal standard of country pubs. ***Motel Dimboola*** *(☎ 5389 1177)*, on the Western Hwy on the edge of town, has rooms from $42/50.

On an attractive bush property, ***Little Desert Log Cabins & Cottage*** *(☎ 5389 1122)* has two simple, comfy and well-equipped two-bedroom timber cottages that cost from $65 to $75 a double, plus $10 per extra adult. It is 4km south of town and on the edge of the Little Desert.

Getting There & Away

Dimboola is on the Melbourne to Adelaide train line, and there are two daily services to/from Melbourne – train to Ballarat and bus to Dimboola; a one-way, full fare is $42.90.

LITTLE DESERT NATIONAL PARK

The name of this park is quite misleading, and if you come here expecting large expanses of windswept sand dunes you'll be in for a surprise. The soil in the park is mainly sandy, but there's a rich diversity of native plant species which thrive in this harsh environment. It is famous for its brilliant springtime displays of wildflowers.

The park covers a huge area of 132,000 hectares, between the Wimmera River in the east and the South Australian border in the west. The vegetation varies substantially due to the different soil types, climate and rainfall in each of its three constituent blocks (central eastern and western), which are separated by roads running south from Nhill and Kaniva. The rainfall ranges from about 400 to 600mm per year, but most of the rain falls in winter. Summers are dry and very hot.

When the Wimmera was settled and cleared for agriculture, the Little Desert was ignored as it was considered to be an infertile wilderness. But in the late 1960s, the state government announced a controversial plan to clear and subdivide the entire area for agriculture. Conservationists and environmentalists protested, and the Little Desert developed into a major conservation issue. The government insisted that the park would be cleared, until it lost a safe seat in a by-election over the issue – shortly after, the Little Desert was declared a national park and it was expanded to its present size in 1986.

Two sealed roads between the Western and Wimmera highways pass through the park: the Edenhope-to-Kaniva road and the Harrow-to-Nhill road. There's also a good gravel road from Dimboola into the park. The tracks in the park itself are mostly sandy and only suitable for 4WD vehicles or walking, and some of these tracks are closed to 4WDs in the wet season (from July to the end of September).

The park is rich in wildlife and plants. There are over 670 indigenous plant species here, and in spring and early summer the landscape is transformed into a colourful wonderland of wildflowers. Over 220 species of birds have been recorded here, and you may also see possums, kangaroos and reptiles such as the bearded dragon and stumpy-tailed lizard. The best-known resident here is the mallee fowl, an industrious bird which can be seen in an aviary at the Little Desert Lodge. See the boxed text in the Mallee chapter for more on this unusual bird.

Bushwalks

If you want a brief introduction to the park there are several short walks in the eastern block. South of Dimboola there's the **Pomponderoo Hill Nature Walk**, south of Nhill is the **Stringybark Walk**, and south of Kiata is the **Sanctuary Nature Walk**. A variety of longer walks leave from the campground south of Kiata including a 12km trek south to the Salt Lake. These walks are all well signposted. On longer walks, water should always be carried and the rangers notified before you set out. The rangers will also give you advice on where to go and what to look out for at different times of the year.

Organised Tours

Oasis Desert Adventures (☎ 5389 1957), 6km south of Dimboola, run a large variety of tours in and around the Little Desert.

Little Desert Lodge (see Places to Stay, following) also runs tours of the park.

Places to Stay

***Little Desert Lodge** (☎ 5391 5232)*, run by Whimpey Reichelt (one of Victoria's 'living treasures'), is on the edge of the national park about 16km south of Nhill. The lodge caters mainly for schools and groups, but takes individuals when there are vacancies.

The B&B tariff is $45/60 for singles/doubles in an ensuite room or $25 in the bunkrooms; tariffs include a continental breakfast, or for another $5 you can have a cooked breakfast. There's a dining room and licensed bar, and three-course dinners cost $18. There's also a campground with sites for $9 ($12.50 with power), an environmental study centre and a mallee-fowl aviary ($5 entry). The lodge also runs 4WD tours of the park for $25 for half a day and $38 for a full day (including lunch), as well as evening spotlight walks to see and feed sugar-gliders.

Parks Victoria has ***campgrounds*** at Horseshoe Bend and Ackle Bend, both on the Wimmera River south of Dimboola, and another one about 10km south of Kiata. All sites have drinking water, toilets, picnic tables and fireplaces and cost $7.90 per night.

You can bush camp if you're doing overnight walks in the central and western blocks, but if you're planning to do so, speak to the rangers first at the Parks Victoria office, Wail Nursery Rd, south of Dimboola (☎ 5389 1204).

Getting There & Away

There is no public transport from Dimboola into the park. The only way in, if you don't have a car, is to take an organised tour.

The Mallee

The Mallee, in Victoria's north-west corner, is the least populated part of the state. Wedged between the South Australian and New South Wales borders, this dry area includes the one genuinely empty part of the state – the semi-arid wilderness known as 'Sunset Country'. You don't have to visit central Australia to get a taste of the Outback.

The Mallee takes its name from the mallee scrub that once covered the entire area. A mallee is a hardy eucalypt with chunky roots and multiple slender trunks. Mallee roots are twisted, gnarled, dense chunks of wood, famous for their slow-burning qualities and much sought after by wood-turners.

Coming from the city, or from a region where trees are tall and the odd hill breaks the skyline, the Mallee can appear desolate. Huge horizons, hot skies and an apparent infinity of undulating sandy soil covered in dense, twisted mallee scrub combine to heighten a sense of agoraphobia. However, it's just this sense of isolation and expanse that many find exhilarating.

Away from the cleared farming areas the mallee gums are canny desert survivors – root systems over 1000 years old are not uncommon – and for the Aborigines the region certainly wasn't desolate. The land yielded plentiful food, including waterbirds and fish in the huge but unreliable lakes, kangaroos and other marsupials, emus, and the many edible plants that thrive in this environment. 'Mallee scrub' is actually a diverse and rich biosystem.

The first European intruders set about clearing the land for farming by a process known as mullenising, which involved crushing the scrub with heavy red-gum rollers pulled by teams of bullocks, then burning and ploughing the land. The only problem was that, after rain, the tough old mallee roots regenerated and flourished, and more than a few of the earlier pioneers eventually gave up and moved elsewhere.

When the railway line from Melbourne to Mildura was finally completed in 1902, the government decided that the Mallee was ripe for settlement, and much of the region was divided into small blocks. Apart from the ongoing problems with clearing the mallee, the farmers had to deal with rabbit and mouse plagues, sand drifts and long droughts, but today the Mallee is a productive sheep-grazing and grain-growing district. Wheat and oats are still the staples ('sheep-wheat' is a common description of a farm here) but more exotic crops, such as lentils, are appearing.

HIGHLIGHTS

- The Victoria Hotel in Ouyen – a classic old country pub
- Wyperfeld National Park – its rugged beauty, its isolation, the diversity of its native plants and animals
- Murray-Sunset National Park
- Ancient landscapes and big skies

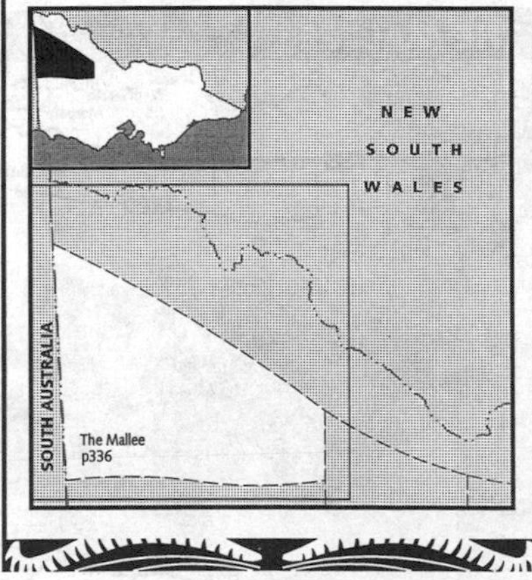

Orientation & Information

The region is bordered by the Murray River in the north and east, by the South Australian border in the west, and by the

Western (A8) and Borung (C243) highways in the south. The main road through here is the Sunraysia Highway (B220), which runs from Ballarat to Mildura (it becomes the Calder (A79) at Ouyen) through the heart of the Mallee.

The largest towns are Warracknabeal, Ouyen and Charlton. The only real attractions (other than huge horizons and friendly little towns) are the remote and semi-arid wilderness areas such as the Wyperfeld National Park, the Big Desert Wilderness and the Murray-Sunset National Park. Collectively these parks cover over 750,000 hectares and are particularly notable for their abundance of native plants, spring wildflowers and birds.

Organised Tours

Sunset 4WD Tours (☎ 5023 1047), based in Ouyen, runs several different 4WD tours of the Murray-Sunset, Wyperfeld, Big Desert and Hattah-Kulkyne national parks. Tours range from day trips to longer expeditions.

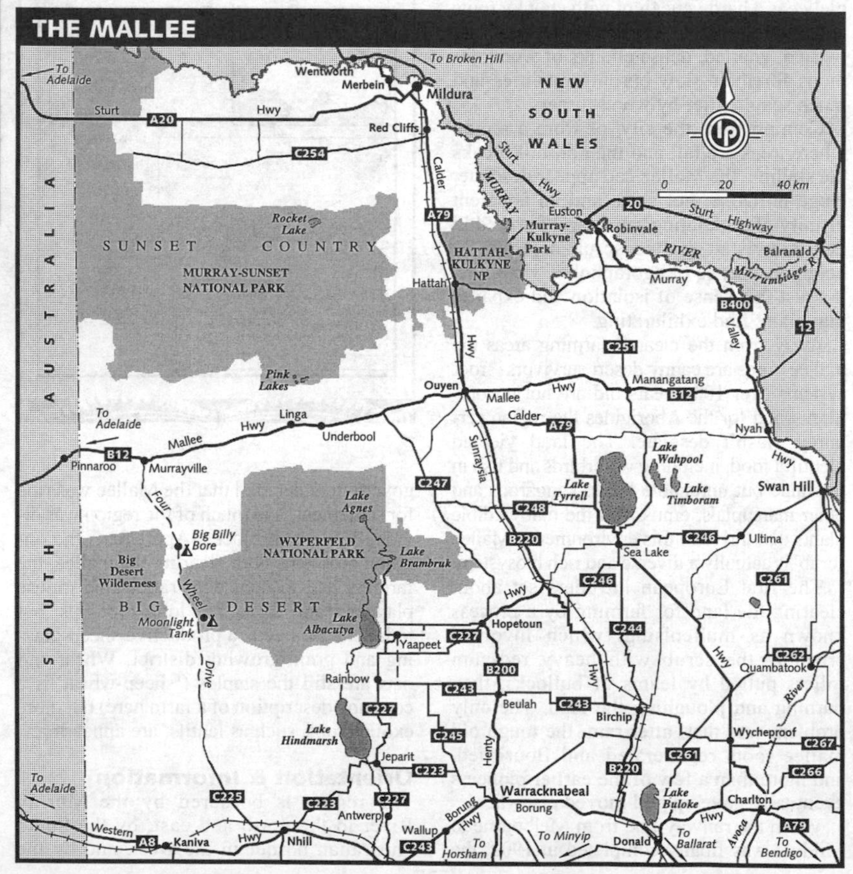

If you have your own 4WD, you can tag along for a special rate. Tours depart from either Ouyen or Mildura.

Mallee Outback Experiences (☎ 5021 1621) runs tours to Hattah-Kulkyne National Park – see the Mildura section in the Murray River chapter for details.

Getting There & Away

V/Line operates an overnight bus service from Melbourne nightly except Saturday through the heart of the Mallee to Mildura ($53.60) via Donald ($36.50) and Ouyen ($49.20). Alternatively, take a train to Bendigo and catch a bus from there.

The Henty Highway Coach (☎ 5382 4260 or 5023 5658) runs due north/south between Horsham and Mildura three times a week, stopping at many towns along the way. The one-way fare between Warracknabeal and Mildura is $38.

CHARLTON

• **pop 1100**

The small town of Charlton grew from a crossing point on the Avoca River. An inn was built here in 1863, and four years later a bridge was built across the river. The town has been frequently flooded when the river spills its banks.

Charlton is a pretty town with some interesting historic buildings and churches. Trees line the river and main streets and huge grain silos dominate the skyline. There are a couple of banks (Commonwealth and National) and one ATM.

The **Golden Grain Museum** ($2) is in the old Mechanics Institute building (1882) next to the shire offices. It has an interesting collection of local memorabilia, photos and historical items, but it's only open by arrangement. Call into the shire offices and they'll get someone to show you through, or phone one of the numbers displayed at the museum entrance.

Places to Stay & Eat

The small ***Gordon Caravan Park*** *(☎ 5491 1968)*, on the highway just north of town, has powered sites for $9 for two people.

The ***Foundry Palms Motel*** *(☎ 5491 1911, 86 High St)* has good rooms from $45/55 for singles/doubles. On the Calder Hwy (A79), the ***Charlton Motel*** *(☎ 5491 1600)* has older rooms at similar prices, and a licensed bistro.

For food try the ***Bush Poet Cafe*** in the centre of town, or the trendier ***Vale of Avoca Cafe***, in a delicensed pub just across the bridge.

DONALD

• **pop 1400**

This small highway town on the banks of the Richardson River and in the centre of the wheatbelt has a couple of points of interest. Signposted off the main road, the **Bullock's Head**, a tree in the middle of the river with a growth on one side that looks exactly like a bullock's head in profile – horns and all! Probably the best reason to have a look is the walk by the river to get there. On the Charlton road, there's an **agricultural museum** at the front of the local showgrounds. It's a tin shed with an open wire front, and you can look in at the collection of old farming machinery and harvesting equipment.

Off the Western Hwy, there's a small picnic area on **Scilleys Island** – a footbridge crosses the river to the reserve. Opposite this reserve there's a collection of historic buildings on the site of the original **police camp**, which was established in 1865. The collection includes the Banyenong Police Camp (1874), a slab-timber shepherd's hut (1850s), a colonial brick oven (1880s) and an old police lock-up.

Donald's slogan is 'Duck Country', maybe due to the Disney fowl of the same name but also in recognition of the duck shooting that takes place (in season) on nearby Lake Buloke.

Places to Stay

Donald Caravan Park *(☎ 5497 1764)* is north of town and charges $12/8 for a powered/unpowered site and has on-site vans from $25 a double.

There are a couple of old pubs with accommodation but the best place to stay is

MALLEE

Donald Motor Lodge (☎ 5497 1700, 34 Woods St), which has good rooms for $65/75. Diagonally opposite, ***Motel Avalon*** *(☎ 5497 1488)* charges $40/45.

WARRACKNABEAL

• **pop 2500**

Warracknabeal is one of the largest towns of the Mallee, and a commercial centre for the surrounding wheat fields. It was established in 1867 when a store was built on the banks of Yarriambiack Creek, which is lined with ancient river red gums. Six of the town's old buildings are classified by the National Trust.

There's a tourist information centre (☎ 5398 1632) on Scott St next to the post office (a startling mock-Tudor edifice), open daily. The **Warracknabeal Agricultural Machinery Museum** is on the Henty Hwy (B200), 3km south of town, and has an interesting collection of old tractors, buggies, harvesters and wagons. It's open daily from 10 am to 5 pm. There's also the **Historical Centre** ($3), at 81 Scott St, which is open daily from 2 to 4 pm, except Saturday.

Places to Stay & Eat

Warracknabeal Caravan Park *(☎ 5398 2350)*, in Lyle St beside the Yarriambiack Creek, has camping sites from $6 and on-site vans from $28.

There are four pubs along the main street. The ***Warracknabeal Hotel*** *(☎ 5398 1849, 44 Scott St)* has basic singles/doubles from $18/28, including breakfast. There are three motels; the quietest is probably the ***Warrack*** *(☎ 5398 1633, 2 Lyle St)*, charging from $40/50.

Even quieter and much more interesting is ***Leura Log Cabin B&B*** *(☎ 5398 1154, johgra@netconnect.com.au)*, which is a mud-brick-and-wood building incorporating the first permanent residence in the district. It's on a property a few kilometres outside town (phone for directions) and is crammed with interesting and antique items. Even the kerosene lamps (there's no electricity yet) are originals. At $95 a double it isn't cheap, but it's a great experience. The owners are planning a similarly interesting restaurant nearby.

Counter lunches at the ***Warracknabeal Hotel*** can cost under $5 or there's an inexpensive Chinese restaurant up the street at the ***Commercial Hotel***. For more formal meals, ***Empress King Garden***, at 160 Scott St, is a modern Chinese restaurant (closed Tuesday). For a ***picnic*** there's a pleasant grassy area just across the creek from the top end of the main street. It's also a 'Flora & Fauna Reserve', which means that there are a few cages of well-fed birds and some bored kangaroos.

HOPETOUN

• **pop 670**

This small, historic town on the Henty Hwy was established around Hopetoun House, which was built in 1891 by Edward Lascelles, one of the pioneers of the Mallee district. This historic homestead, which is privately owned, is classified by the National Trust.

In the middle of the town's main intersection is a round white fountain, which was built as a memorial to Lascelles. The main street is lined with old, weathered verandah-fronted shops.

Beside Lake Lascelles there's a small picnic area. A **historical society museum**, in the old school in Austin St, is open Sunday from 2 to 5 pm.

JEPARIT

• **pop 400**

Jeparit, at the southern end of Lake Hindmarsh, is famous as the birthplace of former prime minister Sir Robert Menzies. One kilometre south of town, the **Wimmera-Mallee Pioneer Museum** is worth a look – it consists of an interesting collection of old buildings, antiques and farming machinery. There are good beaches and swimming spots at the lake, 6km north-west of town, and it's apparently a pretty good fishing spot too.

The ***Hindmarsh Hotel*** *(☎ 5397 2041, Roy St)* is a surprisingly grand pub with fairly comfortable pub-style rooms upstairs; B&B starts at $28/40 for singles/doubles.

MALLEE

You can camp at the extravagantly titled ***Sir Robert Menzies Caravan Park*** *(☎ 5397 2193)* from $7.50 and there's also camping on the shore of Lake Hindmarsh for $7.50.

WYPERFELD NATIONAL PARK

This large park (356,800 ha) contains a string of lake beds, which are linked by Outlet Creek. The creek and the lakes are dry, except on the rare occasions when the Wimmera River floods and fills Lake Hindmarsh, which in turn fills Lake Albacutya, and so on. In recent memory the Wimmera has only flooded three times – in 1918, 1956 and 1976. There are woodlands of river red gum and black box alongside the creek and lake beds, but rolling seas of ancient mallee are the main attraction. Emus and kangaroos are plentiful, and there's always lots of birdlife. There's a good network of walking and cycling tracks.

The visitor centre is at Wonga Campground, at the end of the main access road about 7km north of the entrance. Casuarina Campground is some way north and accessible by 4WD only – or by foot. It would be a good walk along a dry creek bed. Both campgrounds have pit toilets, fireplaces and rainwater. A site for six people and one vehicle costs $8.60 ($3.75 for additional vehicles). Contact the ranger's office (☎ 5395 7221) at Yaapeet for more information.

The main access road is signposted off the Dimboola-to-Hopetoun road which passes through Rainbow and Jeparit. The access road takes you north past Lake Albacutya into the centre of the park.

BIG DESERT WILDERNESS PARK

Unlike its southern cousin, the Little Desert National Park, this 113,500 ha park really is a desert wilderness. There are no roads, tracks or facilities, and no water. Walking and camping are permitted but you should only do so if you are experienced and can use a map and a compass. You have to be totally self sufficient, ie carry your own food and water, take out your rubbish and use a camping stove for cooking. In summer, the temperatures are usually way too high for walking. Notify the rangers in Wyperfeld National Park (☎ 5395 7221) before going.

The area is mostly sand dunes, red sandstone ridges and hardy mallee, and because of its isolation and sandy infertility it has been virtually untouched by Europeans. There's an abundance of flora and fauna: 93 species of birds have been recorded, and there are some interesting small mammals here, such as the Western pygmy-possum and Mitchell's hopping mouse. Over 50 species of lizards and snakes have also been recorded.

There are no access roads into the Big Desert. A dry-weather road from Murrayville on the Mallee Hwy (B12) to Nhill on the Western Hwy separates this park and the Wyperfeld National Park. The road is buffered from the park by a five-kilometre wide strip of state forest. This dirt road is very rough in sections and it may be impassable after rain.

There are basic but adequate camping sites in buffer zones at Big Billy Bore, the Springs, Moonlight Tank and Broken Bucket Reserve, all on the eastern side of the park, as well as other even more remote site on the southern border.

OUYEN

- **pop 1250**

Ouyen (pronounced *o*-y'n) started life in the early part of the 20th century as a train station on the Melbourne-to-Mildura line. Since then it's grown to become one of the main towns of the Mallee and is a busy transport centre for the produce of the surrounding district – mainly wheat, oats, wool and lambs. There's not too much here to interest the tourist, although if you've worked up a thirst on the long hot drive you should stop at the Victoria Hotel for refreshment (see Places to Stay & Eat) – it's a beauty.

Ouyen is also the base for Sunset 4WD Tours, which runs tours of the region's parks and wilderness areas – see the Organised Tours section at the start of the chapter.

If you're here in late October you might catch the **Vanilla Slice Contest**, with competitors from all over the state baking their version of this humble confectionary.

MALLEE

The Mallee Fowl

The rare mallee fowl is one of Australia's most fascinating birds. The mature birds are about the size of a small turkey and mainly grey in colour. Their wings and backs are patterned in black, white and brown, which helps to camouflage them in the mallee scrub, and they can fly short distances if necessary. Until the establishment of the Mallee's national parks, the mallee fowl was threatened with extinction.

The life cycle of the mallee fowl is an amazing story of survival and adaptation. The mallee fowl is the only one of the world's 19 mound-building birds that lives in an arid area – all the others are found in tropical areas. The species has developed incredibly sophisticated incubation methods to maintain its egg mounds at stable temperatures until the eggs hatch.

The male bird spends up to 11 months of the year preparing the mound for the eggs. First he digs a hole, or opens up an old mound, fills it with leaves, bark and twigs and covers the lot with sand to create the main egg chamber. He then waits until the mound has been saturated by rain and the organic material has started to decompose. At the end of winter he builds up the mound by covering it with sand, and by this stage the mounds can be up to a metre high and five metres in diameter. He tests the core temperature of the mound every day by sticking his beak into it and when the temperature is stable at 33°C he lets the female know that she can start laying her eggs.

The female lays between 15 and 20 eggs each year, which hatch at various stages over spring and summer. All this time, the male checks the mound temperature daily, and if it varies from 33°C he adjusts it by covering the mound or removing sand.

After hatching the chicksare are immediately self-sufficient. They dig their way up to the surface and, although they can run within a few hours of hatching and fly on their first day out, the mortality rate is very high. The parents don't recognise or help their own young, and while an average pair of mallee fowl will produce around 90 chicks in their lifetimes, only a few will survive to reproduce.

The male mallee fowl preparing his enormous mound; the liberated female needs only to lay her eggs, the male cares for them until they hatch, then they are on their own.

Places to Stay & Eat

Ouyen Caravan Park *(☎ 5092 1246)*, on the Calder Hwy, has campsites from $10 and on-site vans and cabins from $28 to $45. The ***Ouyen Motel*** *(☎ 5092 1397)*, also on the Calder Hwy, has rooms from $44/50 a single/double. There are a couple of other motels charging about the same.

The Calder Hwy is separated from the town centre by the railway line. Cross over and turn into Rowe St, where you'll find the ***Victoria Hotel*** *(☎ 5092 1550)* at No 22.

This is one of Victoria's best remaining examples of a classic country pub – a two-storey, red-brick, verandah-fronted delight, with emerald green wall tiles up to window level. Once you get inside, it feels as though time has stood still, or at least moved a little more slowly here than elsewhere. If you decide to stay the night, there are simple pub rooms upstairs with shared bathrooms from $25/40.

Oke St, which runs parallel to Rowe St one block back from the railway line, is the main shopping centre. There's a supermarket and the ***Fairy Dell Cafe***, which is part milk bar, part cafe and part take-away, plus the similar ***Mallee Bakery***. In Pickering St, the ***Community Club*** serves dinner every night and lunches from Thursday to Sunday. It also hosts other entertainment and occasionally screens films.

MANANGATANG

Manangatang is what's known as a 'one horse town', although twice a year this small, sleepy township comes to life when the farmers (and more than a few outsiders) come to town for the famous Manangatang Races. The town is on the Mallee Hwy 55km east of Ouyen and surrounded by harsh country of rich red earth and scrub. The racecourse is truly a bush track – a few of the fairways from the adjacent golf course even pass through it!

Race meetings are held in mid-March and mid-October. The ***Manangatang Hotel*** *(☎ 5035 1210)* has motel-style rooms for $28/32 a single/double.

MURRAY-SUNSET NATIONAL PARK

This is one of Victoria's newest national park areas, proclaimed in 1991. It covers an area of 633,000 hectares, making it the state's second largest national park (after the Alpine National Park).

Its creation was the subject of a good deal of controversy as much of this area was productive agricultural and grazing land. The park was established in an attempt to prevent the eradication of much of the area's unique native fauna, which has suffered greatly as more than 65% of the mallee scrub has been cleared.

The park includes the older **Pink Lakes State Park**. These lakes get their pink colour from millions of microscopic organisms on the surface which concentrate an orange pigment in their bodies. The lakes have a high level of salinity, and leave thick salt crusts when they dry out. Salt was extensively harvested from the lakes when this area was first settled.

The park is arid and mainly inaccessible. An unsealed road leads from **Linga** on the Mallee Hwy up to the Pink Lakes at the southern edge of the park, where there's a basic campground, but beyond here you need a 4WD. Don't go exploring in a two-wheel drive – remember that in this area, one hour's driving equals one day's walking, and you won't see any water or passing traffic.

For more information contact the rangers in Underbool (☎ 5094 6267), on the Mallee Hwy or Werrimull (☎ 5028 1218), on the north side of the park.

The Murray River

The Murray River is Australia's most important inland waterway, flowing from the mountains of the Great Dividing Range in north-eastern Victoria to Encounter Bay in South Australia – a distance of more than 2700km. This makes it the third-longest navigable river in the world – only the Nile and the Amazon are longer.

It's also an unusual river, in that very long stretches receive little or no water from the country through which it passes. This, combined with the huge dam near the source and the heavy demands of irrigation along most of its length mean that the river's ecology changed dramatically in the 20th century, and 'old man Murray' is in serious danger.

The river's source is in New South Wales (NSW), close to Mt Kosciuszko, but soon after it forms the border between NSW and Victoria. The river itself is deemed to be in NSW. Most of the places of interest are on the Victorian side, although there's almost always a 'twin' town on the NSW side, a legacy of the days before Federation when the states levied tariffs on goods carried across their borders: all major river crossings were likely to have customs houses on each bank.

The Murray is a river with a history. It was travelled along by some of Australia's earliest European explorers, including Mitchell, Sturt and Eyre, and later became a great trade artery and a means of opening up the interior.

Long before roads and railways crossed the land, the Murray was an antipodean Mississippi, with paddle steamers carrying supplies and carting wool to and from remote sheep stations and homesteads. The township of Echuca became Australia's leading inland port, as trading boats travelled for hundreds of kilometres along the Murray's winding waterways to other thriving river towns like Swan Hill and Mildura, as well as up and down the Murrumbidgee, Goulburn and Darling rivers. Wool from the isolated

HIGHLIGHTS

- Paddle-steamer cruises along the Murray River – you can go from Mildura, Swan Hill or Echuca
- Mildura, a lively oasis with lots of sunshine
- The great golf courses along the length of the Murray
- The Hattah-Kulkyne National Park south of Mildura
- The Historic Port of Echuca
- Echuca itself has a wonderful riverside atmosphere, interesting attractions, good eateries and accommodation
- Touring the wineries around Rutherglen – great fun on a bike
- The Herb & Horse – a guesthouse and horse-riding farm overlooking the Hume Weir about 60km east of Albury-Wodonga
- The spectacular and unspoilt mountain country of the Upper Murray (around Corryong)

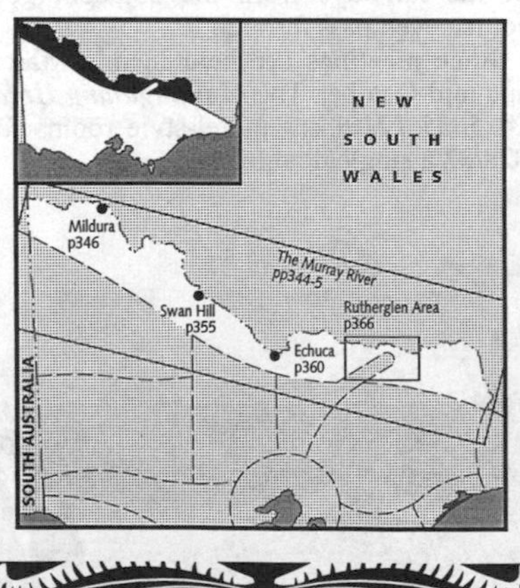

Bourke (NSW) district could reach London in just six weeks. That's somewhat faster than a sea mail parcel today.

Many of the river towns carry evocative reminders of their river-boat days, including historical museums, old buildings and well preserved paddle steamers.

The Murray is also of great economic importance as it supplies the vital water for the irrigation schemes of northern Victoria that have made huge areas agriculturally viable.

In the 1880s Alfred Deakin, Australia's commissioner for public works and water supply (and later prime minister), recognised the agricultural potential of developing irrigation projects in the state's north. He encouraged the Canadian irrigation experts, the Chaffey brothers, to move to Mildura, where they established an irrigation settlement and designed and installed pumps and irrigation systems to feed the land with the Murray's water, attracting thousands of new settlers.

The Murray and its irrigation projects support dairy farms, vineyards, market gardens, orchards and huge citrus groves which provide fresh fruit and supply the thriving dried fruit industry, which exports its produce around the world. After years of irrigation, however, soil salinity has become a major problem, one which poses a long-term threat to the economic viability of much of this area.

The river is also famous for its magnificent forests of red gum, its plentiful bird and animal life, and as a great place for adventurous canoe trips, relaxing river-boat cruises or leisurely riverbank camping.

Orientation & Information

The Murray Valley Highway (B400) is the main route along the river's southern side. You'll find good tourist information centres in all the major towns and tourist centres along the way – Mildura, Swan Hill, Echuca, Yarrawonga, Rutherglen and Albury-Wodonga.

Activities

The Murray is one of the state's great watersports playgrounds and is used for a huge range of activities, including fishing, swimming, canoeing, water-skiing, houseboat holidays and boat cruises. The Murray region is also a golfer's paradise, with plenty of excellent riverside courses on both sides of the river.

Getting There & Away

Train The Melbourne-Swan Hill line connects Melbourne and the Murray; trains run daily via Bendigo. There is also a daily train/bus service between Melbourne and Echuca – you change from train to bus at Bendigo.

Bus Greyhound Pioneer Australia and McCafferty's both go through Mildura daily on the Sydney to Adelaide run.

V/Line operates the Murraylink bus service, which connects all the towns along the Murray River between Mildura and Albury. It operates from Mildura on Tuesday, Wednesday, Friday and Sunday; and from Albury on Monday, Wednesday, Thursday and Saturday. You need a reservation on the Mildura-Kerang sector. V/Line's daily Speedlink service between Adelaide and Albury (connecting with the XPT train to Sydney) runs between Echuca and Albury, taking a fairly roundabout route. You need a reservation.

Car & Motorbike The main route along the Murray is the Murray Valley Hwy, which starts near Mildura and follows the river south-east to Corryong.

While the Murray Valley Hwy links all the major riverside towns, it runs right beside the big river for only a few sections of its length. For most of the journey it is separated from the river by flood plains, subsidiary waterways and forests of river red gum. Sometimes you're separated from the forests by bleak paddocks and this can be unattractive. If you want a taste of less tamed river country, get some good maps and follow the web of minor backroads on the northern bank. This will add hours to your travel time though. The alternative is to use the Murray Valley Hwy while taking

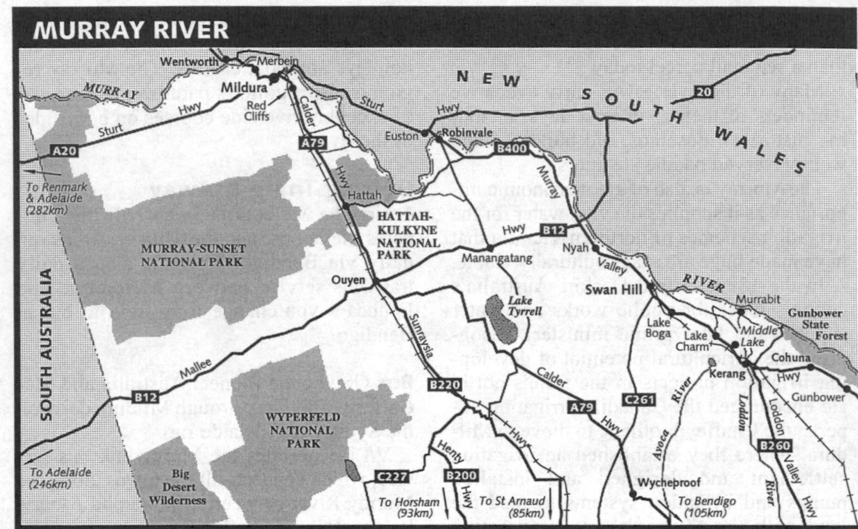

advantage of the fairly frequent tracks (often marked 'River Access') which lead you to the banks.

On a round trip between Melbourne and Mildura, consider taking the Calder Highway (A79; via Bendigo) or the Sunraysia Highway (B220; via Ballarat) on your way to the river and then following the Murray Valley Hwy south-east on the way back. Reaching the oasis of Mildura after hours of long, straight roads through very harsh Mallee country is the best way of appreciating what rivers mean to inland Australia.

MILDURA

• **pop 24,000**

After driving for hours through a dry and desolate landscape of windswept deserts and pale brown wheat fields, you reach this thriving regional centre – a true oasis town, watered by the mighty Murray River.

The name 'Mildura' (pronounced 'milld-*yoo*-ra') means 'red soil'.

The main road into the town centre, Deakin Ave, is impressively lined with palms and gum trees, and at night the street is one continuous strip of flashing neon lights outside motels and take-away food shops. It's easy to forget you're in the midst of Victoria's arid region when you see the lush green golf courses, endless orange groves, orchards and vineyards for which Mildura is renowned.

As well as being one of the richest agricultural areas in Australia, Mildura is a popular tourist town – it promotes itself as a place of endless blue skies and sunshine, and is perfectly placed on both the Melbourne-Adelaide and Sydney-Adelaide routes.

Mildura owes its existence to the Chaffey brothers and their irrigation systems. The early years were tough and full of frustrations, but when the Melbourne to Mildura railway line finally opened in 1902, the town's future was assured.

Orientation

Once you penetrate the thick rind of tacky development that extends kilometres from the city centre, central Mildura is reasonably compact. Deakin Ave, a wide boulevard, is the main street and runs east to the Murray

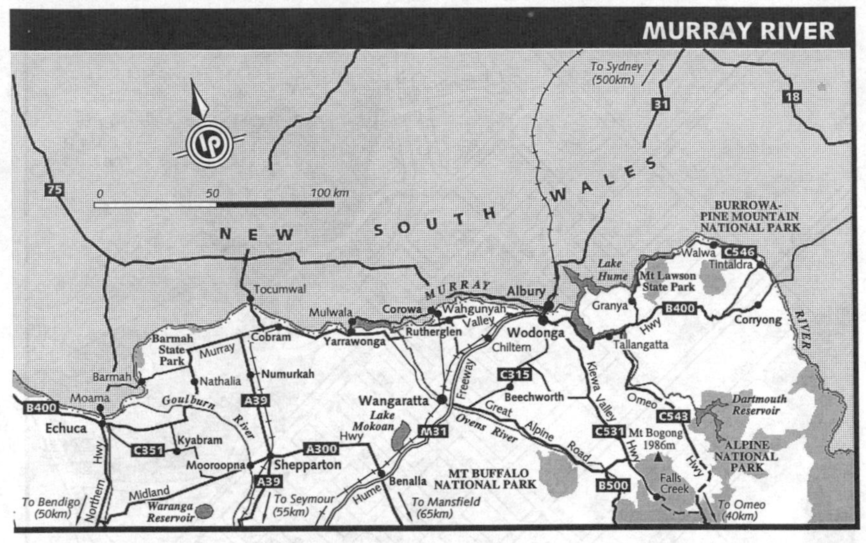

River. Langtree Ave, running parallel to Deakin (and a block north) between Eleventh and Seventh Sts, is the main shopping street.

Mildura's urban sprawl extends south as far as Red Cliffs, a quiet little town with a big tractor – see the boxed text on Big Lizzie.

Information

The tourist information centre in Mildura (☎ 5021 4424 or 1800 039 043 toll-free for bookings), on the corner of Deakin Ave and Twelfth St, is open from 9.30 am to 5.30 pm daily except Sunday when it closes at 5 pm. This place has a good range of information, including various displays, and can also book tours and accommodation.

The Coles supermarket on the corner of Lime and Eighth Sts is open 24 hours daily. The post office is on the corner of Eighth St and Orange Ave.

Useful Organisations The RACV office (☎ 5021 3272) is on the corner of 9th St and Lime Ave. There is a Natural Resources & Environment (NRE) office (☎ 5022 3000) at 253 Eleventh St.

The Australian Trust for Conservation Volunteers (☎ 5021 0970) has several projects in the area.

Fruit-Picking Work If you're interested in fruit-picking work, contact Madec (☎ 5021 3359), a private employment agency on Deakin Ave just west of 10th St. The harvest season runs from about January to March (call Madec's Harvest Office, ☎ 5022 1797, from November) but casual work on farms and orchards is available year-round.

After a few days, you'll get used to the back-breaking 10-hours-a-day labour. The official hourly rate for casual labour is $11.34. Some farmers provide a place to pitch a tent but often you'll need to stay in town, so your own transport might be necessary. At least one of the backpacker hostels shuttles people to work.

Mildura Arts Centre & Rio Vista

This excellent complex is well worth a visit, combining an art gallery, a theatre and a historical museum at Rio Vista, the former home of WB Chaffey. The modern art gallery has a

large collection that includes a European section with various works by Sir William Orpen (a leading British society portrait artist), Sir Frank Brangwyn and the most prized painting, *Woman Combing Her Hair at the Bath*, by the French impressionist painter Edgar Degas. Australian paintings include works by Fred McCubbin and Arthur Streeton, and there is an interesting Australian sculpture collection.

Next door is the historic Rio Vista. This grand homestead has been beautifully preserved, and the interior is set up as a series of historical displays depicting life in the 19th century, with period furnishings, costumes, photos, and an interesting collection of letters and memorabilia. The gallery and museum are open weekdays from 9 am to 5 pm, weekends from 1 to 5 pm. Entry costs $2.50.

Other Attractions

The tourist information centre has a handy brochure called *The Chaffey Trail*, which guides you around some of Mildura's more

MILDURA

PLACES TO STAY
2 Yerre Yerre
3 Mildura Park Motel
4 Mildura Country Club Motel
5 Riverboat Bungalow
7 Buronga Riverside Caravan Park
8 Riviera Motel
16 Mildura Grand Hotel; Stephano's Restaurant
17 Commodore Motor Inn
27 Rosemont Guest House
28 Mildura International Backpackers

PLACES TO EAT
10 Sandbar
11 Siam Palace
12 Copacabana
18 ADFA Shop
19 Restaurant Rendezvous; Liaisons
20 Jackie's Corner
23 Mildura Workingman's Club

OTHER
1 Old Mildura Homestead
6 Mildura Arts Centre & Rio Vista Museum
9 Coles Supermarket
13 Train Station; Bus Depot
14 Buronga Boatman
15 Mildura Wharf
21 Post Office
22 Deakin Twin Cinemas
24 Madec Employment Office
25 NRE Office
26 Tourist Information Centre

interesting sights, including the paddleboats wharf, the Mildura weir and lock, Old Mildura Homestead, the Mildara Blass Winery and the Old Psyche Bend Pump Station.

Seven kilometres north of town across the Murray in NSW, is an interesting attraction with one hour tours on tractor trains around the property daily at 10.30 am and 2.30 pm. This is a fascinating introduction to how citrus fruits are produced. There's also a nursery, packing shed, lookout tower and winery to visit. Tours cost $6 for adults, $3 for kids.

The **Golden River Zoo**, signposted off Eleventh St, 4km north-west of Mildura on the banks of the Murray, is a privately owned zoo in a parkland setting. It houses various native and exotic species including kangaroos, wombats, camels and a puma. Many of the animals can be fed and touched, and there's also an aviary. The zoo has barbecue areas, and is open daily from 10 am to 5 pm; it costs around $10 for adults and $5 for kids (prices vary with different promotions).

The **Old Mildura Homestead**, a cottage that was the first home of William B Chaffey, is in a heritage park on the banks of the Murray in Pioneer Way. There are a few other historic buildings in this pleasant park, which has picnic and barbecue facilities, and is open daily from 9 am to dusk.

Activities

Paddle-Steamer Cruises The famous PS *Melbourne* (☎ 5023 2200) is one of the original paddle steamers and is the only one still driven by steam power – you can watch the boiler operator stoke the original boiler with wood. Two-hour cruises depart daily at 10.50 am and 1.50 pm, and cost $16 for adults and $6 for kids. The fastest of the river boats, the PV *Rothbury* (☎ 5023 2200) operates various day cruise trips to the Golden River Zoo and to Trentham Estate Winery; both cruises cost $35 for adults, $15 for kids, including lunch.

Showboat Avoca (☎ 5021 1166) has two-hour upstream cruises daily ($16 adults, $7 children) and night cruises with dining, live entertainment and dancing on Thursday and Saturday nights.

Cruises depart from the Mildura Wharf at the end of Deakin Ave. Cruises operate more often during school holiday periods.

There are also overnight cruises – see the following Organised Tours section.

Golf The Mildura Golf Club (☎ 5023 1147) is an excellent members' course and is open to the public at $15 plus $10 for club hire. The Riverside Golf Course is also good, and is a bit cheaper.

Boat Hire The Buronga Boatman Boat Hire, on the NSW side of the Murray River opposite Mildura Wharf, hires kayaks, canoes, power boats etc daily.

Hot-Air Ballooning Cameron's Balloons (☎ 5021 2876) offers hot-air balloon trips daily, weather permitting. Flights last about 40 minutes and cost from $130 per person, including champagne afterwards to celebrate your safe landing.

Swimming In summer you may want to use the pool behind the tourist information centre. You'll be pleased to hear that it's heated during winter when the weather's chilly, and that a new indoor pool and a wave pool are being built on the same site.

The Chaffey Brothers

The Canadian brothers, George and William Chaffey, were famous 19th century irrigation engineers who were to set up an irrigation colony at Mildura.

A promotional scheme was launched in 1887 to attract settlers, and by 1890 there were more than 3000 people living in the area, clearing scrub, digging irrigation channels and building fences. Two massive pumping-station engines were shipped from England, one of which now stands in front of Rio Vista (the home William built).

The early years of the settlement weren't easy. Along with the economic collapse of the 1890s, there were the nightmares of trying to clear the mallee scrub, rabbit plagues and droughts. George became disillusioned during the hard early years, and in 1896 returned to the US.

In 1889, William started building Rio Vista, a grand riverside homestead for his wife and family that was to be his expression of confidence in the new settlement. But his wife, Hattie, died in childbirth before the building was finished, and their newborn son also died five months later. William later married his deceased wife's niece, also named Hattie, and lived in Mildura until he died in 1926 at the age of 70.

Mark Armstrong

Rio Vista, the grand homestead built by George Chaffey for his family, is now a museum of 19th century life.

Swimming in the mighty, muddy Murray might not seem so appealing, but it's something you should try. Just be careful of snags, and never jump into water when you can't see the bottom, or what's below the surface.

Other Activities There's a huge range of holiday-oriented entertainment. You know, that tacky stuff like minigolf, tenpin bowling and gokarting that's somehow irresistible when you're on vacation. Check the tourist information centre for details.

Organised Tours

Several Aboriginal operators run tours of the area, concentrating on culture, history (which covers 45,000 years if you go to Lake Mungo) and wildlife. The best known is Harry Nanya (☎ 5027 2076), which has a wide range of tours, including a day trip to Mungo National Park for $43. Also good is Ponde Tours (book at the tourist information centre).

Mallee Outback Experiences (☎ 5021 1621) is run by a former ranger and wildlife officer, and offers a good range of tours, for a minimum of two people, in and around Mildura. It includes day trips to Mungo National Park (see the Around Mildura section for details of the park) and to the Hattah National Park ($45 for adults and $20 for children on each tour).

On Monday, Wednesday and Friday, the Broken Hill Express Coach has day trips from Mildura to Broken Hill via Wentworth ($69 or $45 one way). Book at the tourist information centre.

Paddleboat Coonawarra (☎ 1800 034 424 toll-free) has three and five day cruises from around $400.

Special Events

Mildura's main festivals include an Easter Arts & Crafts Festival, the International Balloon Fiesta in the first week of July, Country Music Week during the September school holidays and the Jazz & Wine Festival in October/November. The Mildura Show (mid-October) is one of the largest in rural Victoria.

Places to Stay

Camping & Caravan Parks There are nearly 30 caravan and campgrounds around Mildura. Prices are relatively high, especially in school holidays.

Not the flashest but one of the best located is the ***Apex Caravan Park*** *(☎ 5023 2309)*, on Cureton Ave, about 4km west of the town centre. It's across the road from the river and has sites from $11, on-site vans from $26 to $36 and cabins from $40 to $65 (all prices for two people). ***Buronga Riverside Caravan Park*** *(☎ 5023 3040)*, just across the river from the centre of town but a kilometre or two by road, has a river frontage. Tent sites cost from $11 and cabins from $35 a double. ***Golden River Holiday Park*** *(☎ 1800 621 262 toll-free)* is also on the river, 5km north-west of the town centre, and has excellent facilities. It has sites from $15, and self-contained cabins from $35 to $60 a double.

There's a cluster of places along Fifteenth St (the Calder Hwy) about 3km south-west of the centre of town. These include ***Cross Roads Holiday Park*** *(☎ 1800 675 103 toll-free)* and ***Mildura & Deakin Caravan Park*** *(☎ 1800 060 705 toll-free)*. Both charge from $16 for sites; Cross Roads has cabins from $38 to $74 a double and Mildura & Deakin charges $44 to $55.

Guesthouses & Hostels Friendly ***Rosemont Guest House*** *(☎ 5023 1535, 154 Madden Ave)* is a cosy old timber guesthouse with simple units out the back. Doubles with bathroom cost from $45 and singles with shared bathroom cost $22. This place is also a ***YHA Hostel*** and members are charged $15. All rooms have air-con, there's a good pool, and rates include a generous breakfast.

Mildura International Backpackers hostel *(☎ 5021 0133, 5 Cedar Ave)*. Cedar Ave runs between 12th and 11th Sts, a block back from the tourist information centre. All rooms have two beds (not bunks), at $14 per person. Ros and Fi are good hosts who will help you find work, and their Saturday night BBQ (about $5) is worth waiting around for. The hostel has a van so you might be able to arrange a lift to work if you don't have a car.

Riverboat Bungalow *(☎ 5021 5315, 27 Chaffey Ave)*, the newcomer, is in a nice old house and fairly close to most things. It's well equipped and dorm beds cost around $15.

There's another hostel in Red Cliffs, ***Red Cliffs Backpackers*** *(☎ 5024 2905, 63 Indi Ave)*. It's over 15km from central Mildura, but might come in handy if you're here for work. Beds cost $13.

Motels & Hotels There are dozens of motels but at various times, mainly school holidays, vacancies are scarce at the more central places and prices rise.

Most motels are strung out along major roads and suffer from the usual problem of traffic noise. A good choice for a quiet night is the ***Mildura Park Motel*** *(☎ 5023 0479, 250 Eighth St)*. It's in a residential area a kilometre or so west of Deakin Ave and charges from $45/49 a single/double to $79/84. There's also a pool. Opposite the train station the ***Riviera Motel*** *(☎ 5023 3696, 157 Seventh St)*, is one of the cheapest places with rooms from $38/42.

The ***Commodore Motor Inn*** *(☎ 5023 0241)*, well located on the corner of Deakin Ave and Seventh St, has units ranging from $69 to $110 a double. The ***Mildura Country Club Motel*** *(☎ 5023 3966)*, at the north-western end of Twelfth St, is the place for golf enthusiasts. The motel-style accommodation units are right on this excellent golf course and doubles range from $75 to $95.

The palm-fronted Mildura ***Grand Hotel*** *(☎ 5023 0511)*, on the corner of Deakin Ave and Seventh St, is a Spanish mission-style building. Architecturally it combines a few different periods, reflecting Mildura's development. This place would probably be more comfortable than a motel in summer, as it was built to withstand the heat (and it has air-con anyway). Rooms range from $58/81 to $102/127, with cooked breakfast. There are also suites.

Holiday Units There are also plenty of self-contained holiday flats. One of the better places for value is ***Yerre Yerre Holiday Flats*** *(☎ 5022 1526, 293 Cureton Ave)*, opposite the river, about 1km north of the town centre. There are four two-bedroom flats, each with a kitchen, laundry, TV and air-con. Each sleeps six people, and nightly rates are $46 to $68 for two people. Weekly rates are a little lower.

Houseboats Staying on a houseboat is a great way to see the river at close quarters. And you can move if you don't like the view. Houseboats range from two to 12 berth and from modest to luxurious, and are priced accordingly.

There are over 20 different companies and most have a minimum hire of three days with prices starting from around $100 a night or $600 a week, dramatically more in summer and school holidays. Contact the tourist information centre or the RACV for more details.

Places to Eat

The main restaurant precinct is along Langtree Ave, between the mall and the river.

Sandbar, at the corner of Langtree Ave and Eighth St, is a lively and fun bar with a good garden courtyard and live entertainment from Wednesday to Saturday nights. It serves an interesting range of snacks and meals in the $9 to $15 range. Across the street, ***Restaurant Rendezvous*** *(34 Langtree Ave)* is a modern, classy place with entrees around $12 and mains around $20. Next door and run by the same people, ***Liaisons*** is a bar and bistro with a pleasant courtyard – and lower prices.

Siam Palace at No 35 has tasty Thai and Chinese meals and competitive prices, especially at lunch. Further down, ***Copacabana*** at No 19 isn't quite sure what it is. A seafood brasserie? A noodle bar? A pizza place? Whatever, it's large and relaxed and the food is good.

The ***Grand Hotel***, at the river end of Deakin Ave, has several bars and dining rooms, including a casual wine bar and Italian cafe. Down in the old cellars is the atmospheric, award-winning ***Stefano's Restaurant*** *(☎ 5023 0511)*, a candle-lit restaurant serving five course banquets of northern Italian cuisine based on fresh local produce. Bookings essential.

Jackie's Corner, on the corner of Deakin Ave and Eighth St, serves cheap and reasonably good Chinese food. It's mainly a take-away, although there's a tiny eat-in section. The ***Mildura Workingman's Club***, on Deakin Ave, once boasted the longest bar in the world, but some fool cut it down so they could fit in more poker machines. Oh well, there's a tavern bistro where you can sit and watch all the action on the lawn-bowling greens; lunch specials start at $3.

The ***ADFA Shop*** *(33 Deakin Ave)* is the retail outlet of the Australian Dried Fruit Association. Mildura was founded before modern refrigeration and transportation meant that fresh fruit could be sent around the world – or even around Australia. Dried fruit was the main produce. Today the ADFA Shop sells dried fruit plus health food products, as well as snacks and light meals.

The ***gambling clubs*** on the NSW side of the Murray River have good bistro meals at bargain prices to entice gamblers across the border, and they even provide free transport from Mildura.

Entertainment

Mildura has a small but lively nightlife scene, with several nightclubs in the centre. The ***Sandbar***, on the corner of Langtree and Eighth Aves, has live music on Wednesday to Saturday nights. At ***Deakin Twin Cinemas*** *(☎ 5023 4452, 93 Deakin Ave)* most shows cost $6.

Getting There & Away

Air Mildura airport is about 10km west of the town centre, off the Sturt Highway (A20). Kendall Airlines (book through Ansett ☎ 13 1300) operates daily services between Melbourne and Mildura ($183 one way), as does Southern Australia Airlines (book through Qantas ☎ 13 1313). Smaller local operators fly to other destinations including Adelaide and Broken Hill.

Bus Between Melbourne and Mildura, V/Line has a direct overnight bus every night except Saturday, as well as several daily train/bus services via Bendigo or Swan Hill. The trip takes around eight hours and costs $52. V/Line also has a four-times-weekly bus service connecting all the towns along the Murray River – fares from Mildura include Swan Hill ($29.30), Echuca ($34.20) and Albury ($55).

Greyhound and McCafferty's both have daily services between Mildura and Adelaide ($35) or Sydney ($74); Greyhound and Sunraysia Bus Lines have twice weekly services to Broken Hill ($37).

Long-distance buses operate from a depot at the train station on Seventh Ave.

Train There are no passenger trains between Melbourne and Mildura, although there is a train from Melbourne to Bendigo which connects with a bus service to Mildura.

Getting Around

There are regular bus services around town and as far out as Red Cliffs and Merbein, mostly during the week but there are a few on weekends. The tourist information centre has timetables. Free coaches to the NSW gambling clubs leave from various pick-up points, including in front of Ron's Tours & Charters at 41 Deakin Ave.

Mildura Taxis (☎ 5023 0033) operate 24 hours a day.

AROUND MILDURA

You don't have to travel far from this riverside oasis to get a taste of the outback. The Sturt Hwy runs arrow-straight to Adelaide – the South Australian border is 130km west of Mildura.

A popular trip is to cross the Murray into NSW to visit one of the oldest towns on the river, **Wentworth**, which is 32km west of Mildura. Here you can visit the Old Wentworth Gaol and the Pioneer Museum, and see the impressive confluence of the Murray and Darling rivers. There's also a big, red sand dune just north of town.

Another popular excursion is to **Lake Mungo National Park**, 110km to the north. The park covers an ancient, dry lake bed, and a long crescent-shaped dune running along the eastern shore has been dubbed the 'Walls of China'. It's a fascinating formation of layers of sand, salt and clay which have built up and eroded into weird shapes over tens of thousands of years. More importantly, the dune yields evidence of 45,000 years of continuous occupation by Aborigines whose intricate culture was destroyed by the arrival of European settlers a very few decades ago. Spend a night camping in the bush behind the Walls and feel the ancient spirits.

Note that the road to Mungo becomes impassable after heavy rain.

At Dareton, 19km north-west of Mildura, the **Tulklana Kumbi Gallery** has an excellent collection of locally made Aboriginal arts and crafts on sale.

Wineries

There are several wineries in and around Mildura that you can visit. Twenty kilometres south of Mildura, **Lindeman's Karadoc Winery** (☎ 5051 3285) is an interesting place to visit – this huge complex is part of the largest winery in the state. There's a cafe (open noon to 3 pm) and picnic and barbecue facilities. The winery is signposted off the Calder Hwy south of Red Cliffs. It's open daily from 10 am to 4.30 pm.

Mildara Blass specialises in fortified wines. It's on the Murray River at Merbein, 9km west of Mildura, has good barbecue and picnic facilities beside the river and opens weekdays from 9 am to 5 pm and weekends from 10 am to 4 pm. During the week there are guided tours at 11 am and 2.30 pm.

Also on the river, over the border in NSW and 12km from Mildura, the small and charming **Trentham Estate Winery** opens daily from 9 am to 5 pm. It has picnic and barbecue facilities, plus a restaurant that opens for lunch daily except Monday. You can also get here on a paddle-steamer cruise from Mildura – see Activities in the Mildura section earlier for details.

HATTAH-KULKYNE NATIONAL PARK

Hattah-Kulkyne is a beautiful and diverse park. The eastern section of the park around the Murray River is called the Murray Kulkyne State Park, but the two areas are managed as one unit. The vegetation ranges from dry, sandy mallee scrub country to the

The Strange & Touching Story of Big Lizzie

Red Cliffs is primarily notable as the final resting place of 'Big Lizzie', a huge steam-engine tractor.

The tractor, a massive monument to one man's inventiveness and stubborn persistence, was the brainchild of Mr Frank Bottrill, who designed it to cart wool from the outback sheep stations around Broken Hill in central New South Wales (NSW). It was built in a backyard factory in Richmond, Melbourne, in 1915.

With a travelling speed of 1.61 km/h and a turning circle of 60 metres, Lizzie wasn't built for city living, and once finished, Frank and his family set out on the journey north. Two years later they reached the Murray River, where Frank stumbled on the one small flaw in his plan – he couldn't get Lizzie across the border into NSW, as the river was in flood. So instead of Broken Hill, Lizzie was put to work in the Mallee, where she worked happily for many years clearing scrub and trees.

Lizzie was saved from rusty oblivion and brought to Red Cliffs in 1971, and now stands proudly in a small park on the Calder Highway, opposite the train station, where a taped commentary tells her story.

Mark Armstrong

PAUL SINCLAIR

Peak hour at Dimboola

PAUL SINCLAIR

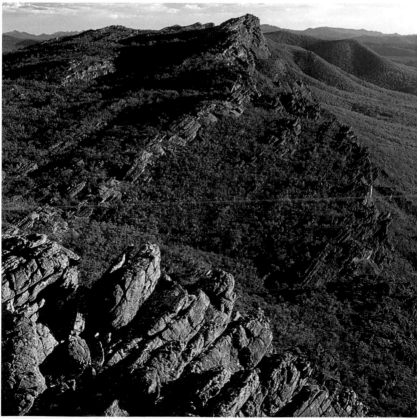

Mt Difficult Range, Grampians National Park

CHRIS MELLOR

The paddle-steamer *Alexander Arbuthnot* (in the background) at Echuca's historic wharf

RICHARD I'ANSON

Salt-encrusted ground at Pink Lakes, Murray-Sunset National Park

fertile riverside areas closer to the Murray, which are lined with red gum, black box, wattles and bottlebrush.

When the area was recommended as a park in 1976, it was said to be the most rabbit infested part of the state. The rabbits were largely eradicated, but then it was decided that the huge population of kangaroos was responsible for the degradation of the land. In 1990 the park hit the headlines when the state government decided to cull (shoot) some of the 20,000-odd kangaroos that inhabit the park – it has been estimated that the park can only carry around 5000 kangaroos without harming the fragile environment. Of course, any operation involving the killing of native animals is bound to be controversial, and this one was no exception. The irony of this management dilemma is that while the huge kangaroo population is causing the degradation of the park environment, and inevitably many of the kangaroos will die during the drought seasons anyway, their numbers can't be culled because the issue is too politically sensitive.

The **Hattah Lakes** system, which fills when the Murray floods and supports many species of water birds. The many hollow trees are perfect for nesting, and more than 200 species of birds have been recorded here. Apart from the kangaroos, there are many native animals, mostly desert types that are active in the cool of the night or wetland species such as the burrowing frog, which digs itself into the ground during the dry season and waits until there is enough water to start breeding. There are also a few reptiles, one of which, the mountain devil, is the inspiration for the great Aussie saying 'flat out like a lizard drinking' because of the way it draws surface water into its mouth by lying flat on the ground. The vegetation varies considerably from season to season, and over 1000 plant species have been recorded, 200 of which are listed as rare or endangered.

The main access road is from the small town of **Hattah**, 70km south of Mildura on the Calder Hwy. About 5km into the park is a good information centre. There is a network of tracks through the park, but many are impassable after rain – check at the information centre before venturing onward. There are two nature drives through the park, the Hattah and the Kulkyne, and there's a good network of old camel tracks which are great for cycling, although you'll need thorn-proof tubes. Tell the rangers where you're going and carry plenty of water, a compass and a map.

There are camping facilities at Lake Hattah and Lake Mournpoul, but note that there is limited water and the lake water, when there is any, is muddy and undrinkable. Camping is also possible anywhere along the Murray River frontage, which is actually the Murray-Kulkyne State Park. There's a charge of $8.60 for up to three people.

For more information contact Parks Victoria (☎ 13 1963) or the Hattah ranger's office (☎ 5029 3253).

ROBINVALE

• pop 1750

Robinvale, 13km north of the Murray Valley Hwy, is a small, quiet and somewhat nondescript town which is almost ringed by a loop of the river.

There's an information centre (☎ 5026 1388) at the top of the main street.

The local Aboriginal Co-Op (☎ 5026 4070) runs eco-cultural tours but only for groups. A garden of indigenous plants has been planted by the Koori community on Riverside Dve.

Robinvale is at the centre of a busy grape and citrus growing area, and there are two wineries here. **McWilliams Wines** is in the industrial sector, and opens on weekdays from 9 am to noon and 1 to 4.30 pm. The **Robinvale Winery** is open daily from 9 am to 6 pm (from 1 to 5 pm on Sunday) for tastings and sales.

Places to Stay & Eat

Riverside Caravan Park *(☎ 5026 4646)* on Riverside Dve, has campsites from $14, on-site vans and cabins from $35 to $50 a double, and a boat ramp for river access. ***Homestyle Motel*** *(☎ 5026 3513)*, on Ronald

St, is exactly what the name suggests, a motel set up in a cosy country house. Singles/doubles cost from $38/46. The ***Robinvale Hotel*** *(☎ 5026 0272)*, on the corner of Perrin and George Sts, is a good pub with accommodation and meals. There's also a ***Chinese restaurant*** on Bromley Rd and a few ***cafes*** and ***take-aways***, but perhaps the best bet for food is to duck across the river to the gambling club at Euston, 5km north of Robinvale in NSW.

SWAN HILL

• pop 9400

Swan Hill, the low hill on which the current town sits, was named by Major Mitchell in 1836 after he was kept awake by swans in the nearby lagoon. The area was settled by sheep graziers soon after and the original homesteads of the two major properties in the area, Murray Downs and Tyntynder, are open to visitors.

Swan Hill is a major regional centre surrounded by fertile irrigated farms that produce grapes and other fruits. It has the easy pace of a country town, and while it's mainly an agricultural and commercial settlement, it has quite a few points of interest for travellers.

Information

The visitor information centre (☎ 5032 3033 or 1800 625 373 toll-free) in Swan Hill, at 306 Campbell St, is open daily.

Swan Hill Pioneer Settlement

Swan Hill's major attraction is a re-creation of a riverside port town of the paddle-steamer era, and the entrance to the township is through the old PS *Gem*, one of the largest river boats to serve on the Murray.

The settlement is well worth a visit and has displays including an old locomotive, a blacksmith's workshop, a bakery, a stereoscope, a general store (with very tasty boiled lollies), a great collection of old cars, trucks, carriages and buggies, and an old-time photographic studio. The paddle steamer PS *Pyap* makes short cruises along the Murray, which cost $8.50 for adults, $4.50 for children. Other attractions include vintage car rides, free horse-drawn wagon rides and Devonshire teas, and all the settlement workers are dressed in period costume.

There's also an example of the first prefabricated house in Australia. These prefabs were shipped to Australia en-masse to accommodate the sudden and dramatic increase in the population during the gold-rush years.

The settlement is open daily from 8.30 am to 5 pm, and admission costs $13 for adults and $6.50 for kids.

Every night at dusk a 45 minute **sound & light show** is held, a dramatic journey through the settlement in a motorised transporter. The show costs $8.50 for adults and $4.50 for children.

Murray Downs Homestead

A couple of kilometres east of Swan Hill in NSW, this historic 1886 homestead and working property is open to the public Tuesday to Sunday from 9 am to 4.30 pm. The place has been home to a series of wealthy pioneers, one of whom was Alfred Felton, an avid art collector who bequeathed his collection to the National Gallery of Victoria.

The homestead was built in a keep formation (like a fort) for defence against bushrangers. At that time it was a totally self-sufficient community, home to the settlers, their farm hands and an assortment of trappers and drovers.

The homestead is now surrounded by formal English gardens and has a small animal park with deer, wallabies and other animals, and a nursery. Inside there are some interesting historical displays of original letters and photos, furnishings and artworks, and there's a craft and souvenir shop. Admission costs $7.50 for adults and $3.30 for children, and includes an interesting one hour tour.

Other Attractions

Swan Hill Regional Art Gallery, opposite the Pioneer Settlement, concentrates on the works of contemporary artists and has an interesting collection. Admission costs $2.

MV *Kookaburra* (☎ 5032 0003) has **lunch cruises** on the river. The information centre sells tickets.

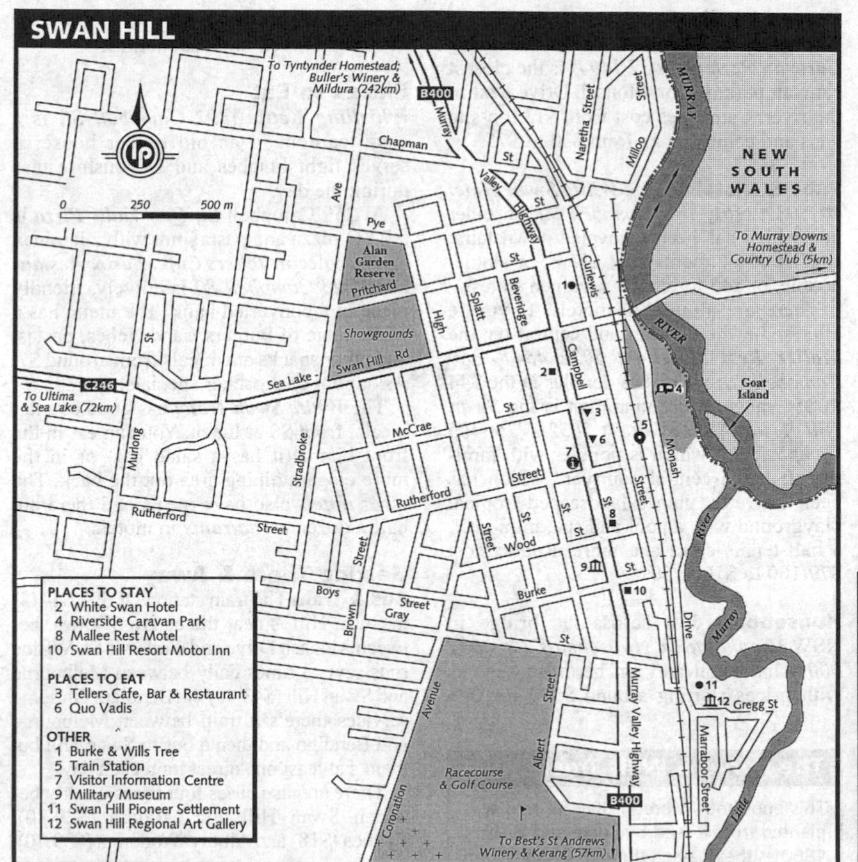

Tyntynder Homestead, 16km north of the town, has a small museum of pioneering and Aboriginal relics, and many reminders of the hardships of colonial life, such as the wine cellar! Admission is $7.50, which includes a tour, and the homestead is open daily.

Buller's Caliope Winery is 14km north of town on the Murray Valley Hwy, and opens from Monday to Saturday from 9 am to 5 pm (and Sunday during holiday periods).

Best's St Andrews Vineyard, the sister winery to Best's in Great Western, is 2km south-east of the town of Lake Boga, which is 17km south of Swan Hill. It specialises in fortified dessert wines and brandies, and opens weekdays from 9 am to 5 pm, Saturday from 10 am to 4 pm and Sunday from noon to 4 pm. There are free tours on weekdays at 11 am and 3 pm.

Murray Downs Country Club is on the NSW side of the Murray River, 5km from Swan Hill. It has a fine golf course, poker machines and cheap bistro meals.

Places to Stay

Camping & Caravan Parks ***Riverside Caravan Park*** *(☎ 5032 1494)* is the closest caravan park. It's on Monash Drive next to the river. Campsites cost from $13, on-site vans and cabins range from $30 to $75.

Pubs & Motels At the ***White Swan Hotel*** *(☎ 5032 2761, 182 Campbell St)*, an older pub which has been renovated downstairs; small budget rooms cost $25/35 a single/double, or $45 for doubles with en suites.

There are almost 20 motels. If you're after somewhere cheap and central try the ***Mallee Rest Motel*** *(☎ 5032 4541, 369 Campbell St)*, which has doubles in the $44 to $54 range. More upmarket is the ***Swan Hill Resort Motor Inn*** *(☎ 5032 2726, 405 Campbell St)*, which is popular with families. It has a central courtyard which has been converted into a landscaped tropical playground with a pool and spa, mini-golf, a half-tennis court and more. Rooms cost $79/100 to $100/150.

Houseboats Just across the bridge in NSW, ***Kookaburra Houseboats*** *(☎ 5032 0003)* has eight and ten berth houseboats with prices starting around $500 for two weekend nights from May to October or $800 for a week in those months.

The Burke & Wills Tree

This enormous Moreton Bay fig tree was planted from a seed by Burke and Wills in 1860 as they passed through Swan Hill on their ill-fated journey to the Gulf of Carpentaria. It was planted in the home of a Dr Gummow, who hosted the explorers and their party and was probably looking forward to their return visit to show them the progress of their tree, but they never made it. The tree, the largest of its kind in the country – we're talking a very big tree – is in Curlewis St opposite the bowling green (or from Campbell St drive through the bottleshop of the Commercial Hotel).

Mark Armstrong

Places to Eat

Whistling Kettle *(392 Campbell St)* is a cosy tearoom in an old timber house; it serves light lunches and Devonshire teas during the day.

At 259 Campbell St, ***Quo Vadis Pizza*** is a BYO pizza and pasta joint with a laminex and lace decor. ***Tellers Cafe, Bar & Restaurant*** *(223 Campbell St)* is a lively, friendly place in a converted bank. The menu has a wide range of burgers, sandwiches, pastas, and other snacks and meals from around $7. Ask about backpacker specials.

The ***White Swan Hotel*** has good counter meals, from $6 at lunch. You can eat in the front bistro (it has a salad bar) or in the more elegant dining area out the back. The other ***hotels*** also have meals and there are half a dozen ***restaurants*** in motels.

Getting There & Away

Bus & Train The train station (☎ 5032 4444) in Swan Hill is near the centre of town, between Monash Drive and Curlewis St. V/Line runs several times daily between Melbourne and Swan Hill ($43.40) via Bendigo. On some services there's a train between Melbourne and Bendigo and then a bus to Swan Hill but there's at least one direct train each day.

There are also buses four times weekly between Swan Hill and Mildura ($29.30), Echuca ($18) and Albury-Wodonga ($39.70).

SWAN HILL TO KERANG

This section of the highway takes you through the fertile red-soil flatlands south of the Murray, and past a string of lakes including Lake Boga, Kangaroo Lake, Salt Lake (from which salt is commercially harvested) and Lake Charm. This area is best known for the huge flocks of ibis that breed on the 50 or so lakes here. Middle Lake, 9km north of Kerang, is the best place to see the rookeries; there's a small bird hide on the lake.

Lake Boga was a base for **flying boats** during WWII and a small museum tells the story. Admission is $5 ($2 children).

KERANG

• **pop 3900**

Kerang is on the Murray Valley Hwy and the Loddon River about 25km south of the Murray. It's mainly a commercial centre with not much to offer from a tourism point of view. You can climb to a lookout tower in the **Lester Smith Water Tower**, which also houses the local tourist information office (☎ 5452 1860). The **Kerang Historical Museum**, next to the caravan park, is open on weekends from 1.30 to 4.30 pm.

Places to Stay & Eat

Kerang Tourist & Holiday Park *(☎ 5452 1161)*, on Riverwood Dve, has tent sites from $11, and on-site vans and cabins from $30 to $42 a double. ***Motel Loddon River*** *(☎ 5452 2511)* on the highway has rooms from $45/54 a single/double. The ***Commercial Hotel*** *(☎ 5452 1031 corner Victoria and Wellington Sts)*, has basic pub rooms at $25/35 with breakfast.

For sandwiches or take-away food, try the ***bakery*** on the corner of Scoresby and Fitzroy Sts. ***Kwong Ling*** *(14 Victoria St)* has a typically huge Chinese menu, with most mains around $10.

COHUNA

• **pop 2000**

Cohuna (pronounced 'ko-*hoo*-na'), a quiet and peaceful town, is famous for its family-oriented Easter tennis tournaments, when the town takes on a carnival atmosphere and fills to the brim with servers and volleyers. Cohuna is also the gateway to the Gunbower State Forest, which is linked to the town by a bridge across the Gunbower Creek.

Places to Stay

Cohuna Caravan Park *(☎ 5456 2562)* is on Island Rd, just across the bridge from the centre of town and surrounded by river forests, has tent sites from $10.50 and on-site vans and cabins from $36 to $55 a double.

The ***Cohuna Hotel/Motel*** *(☎ 5456 2604, 39-41 King George St)* is a solid two storey pub on the corner. It has motel-style rooms out the back with en suites from $35/45 to $40/55. The pub has a good bistro which is very popular, especially on weekends.

The ***West End Motel*** *(☎ 5456 2547)* on the Murray Valley Hwy has good doubles from $45 to $60.

GUNBOWER STATE FOREST

The superb Gunbower State Forest is actually on Gunbower Island, which covers an area of 26,400 hectares and is almost 50km long, stretching from Koondrook in the north to near Torrumbarry in the south. The island is enclosed by the Murray River on one side and the Gunbower Creek on the other.

Gunbower was declared a state forest back in 1874, and features forests of magnificent river red gums and large areas of swamps and marshes. The forests have been extensively milled since the 1870s, supplying timber for hundreds of piers and bridges in Melbourne and along the Murray, for house stumps, railway sleepers, fence posts and paddle-steamer fuel in the river-trade days. Red gum is an incredibly beautiful and dense timber, a rich 'tawny port' red in colour, but because of its wide availability in Victoria it has always been taken for granted as a common building material.

Gunbower has abundant animal and birdlife. The more visible forest residents include kangaroos, possums, emus, goannas, turtles and snakes, and more than 160 bird species have been recorded here, including many water birds.

Cohuna is the main access point to the forest, although there are numerous marked tracks in from the highway. There's a network of dirt tracks throughout the forest which, though maintained, are all on old river mud and turn impossibly slippery after rain – 4WD only in the wet. There are also plenty of walking tracks.

Apart from the caravan park (see the previous Cohuna section), there are more than 100 numbered riverside campsites with fireplaces and picnic tables between Torrumbarry and Koondrook.

You may see a male emu looking after his chicks at Gunbower State Forest.

Organised Cruises

Gannawarra Wetlands Cruises (☎ 5453 3000), based at a mooring 16km north of Cohuna, is a family-run tour company which has built the *Wetlander* cruise boat to take visitors into the wetland areas of the forests. The tours operate daily from mid-August to mid-May – during winter, the creek level is too low to navigate due to irrigation channelling. Two hour nature cruises operate daily except Thursday and cost $17 ($9 children). There are also 3½ hour dinner cruises with live entertainment on most Saturday nights for $40.

ECHUCA

• pop 10,000

Echuca is located at the spot where the Goulburn and Campaspe rivers join the Murray. Appropriately, 'echuca' (pronounced 'e-*choo*-ka') is an Aboriginal word meaning 'the meeting of the waters'.

Today, Echuca is one of the state's most popular tourism centres, with the recreational benefits of the Murray River including water-skiing, swimming, paddle-steamer cruises and houseboat holidays. There are also some excellent tourist attractions, most notably the tourist facilities around the old Port of Echuca.

History

The town was founded in 1853 by the enterprising ex-convict Harry Hopwood. Hopwood was born in Lancashire in 1813, and in 1834 he was transported to Australia for receiving stolen goods. He served 12 years as a convict in Van Diemen's Land, and when released came to the mainland. In 1853 he settled on the banks of the Murray, and converted some rough sheds into an inn and a store. He then established the area's only punt and ferry crossings over the Murray and Campaspe rivers, and with his transport monopoly and the gold rush in full swing, he profited handsomely. Hopwood built the Bridge Hotel in 1858, and lived his remaining years in Echuca as a wealthy man. By the time he died in 1869, he had watched his town grow from nothing into the busiest inland port in Australia.

At the peak of the riverboat era there were more than 100 paddle steamers operating along the Murray, Darling and Murrumbidgee rivers, carting wool, timber and other goods between Echuca and the outback sheep stations. The Melbourne to Echuca railway line was opened in 1864, and the boom years of the riverboat trade extended from this time until the mid-1880s, when the more efficient railways reached the more remote areas.

At the peak of the era the famous river red-gum wharf was just over a kilometre long and lined with shops and hotels all the way along the waterfront, but much of the wharf was gradually dismantled as the riverboat trade fell away towards the end of the 19th century. Most of the timber was eventually carted to Melbourne during WWII and burned as firewood.

Information

The tourist information centre (☎ 5480 7555) is off Heygarth St, not far east of Hare St, and is open daily from 9 am to 5 pm. There's an accommodation booking service (☎1800 804 446 toll-free) at the information centre.

There's a combined RACV and NRMA (the NSW equivalent) office (☎ 5482 1711) at 555 High St. For camping gear and other odds and ends, go to Echuca Camping or, next door, to Echuca Disposals, on High St. The Coles supermarket on High St (corner of Darling St) never closes. There's a coin laundry on Darling St near the corner of Hare St.

Historic Port of Echuca

The best feature of the old port area is that everything is original, so you're exploring living history rather than re-created history. The attractions are spread out along the waterfront, and instead of separate admission tickets you buy a 'passport' which admits you to the three main sections, the Star Hotel, the wharf and the Bridge Hotel.

The ticket box is at the entrance to the **wharf** via the old train station building. There's an interesting collection of vintage trains, carriages and a railway crane to inspect. In the wharf's cargo shed, there's a push-button audiovisual presentation and a series of dioramas which depict life on the river boats. You can then walk down along the various levels of the massive wharf and onto the restored historic paddle steamers *Pevensey* (which featured in the TV series *All the Rivers Run*) and *Adelaide* which are moored alongside. The massive wharf was built with three tiers because of the changing river levels, and there are gauges marking the highest points the river has reached during flood years.

Across the road at the **Star Hotel** (1867) you can escape through the underground tunnel that was built to help drinkers avoid the police during the years when the pub was a 'sly grog shop'. At the **Bridge Hotel**, your ticket admits you to a historic upstairs gallery. This pub is now a restaurant and bistro.

The Port of Echuca is open daily from 9 am to 5 pm, and tickets cost $7/5 for adults/children; admission plus a paddleboat cruise costs $16/9.

Other Port Area Attractions

There are various other attractions along the waterfront and around the old port area. The **Red Gum Works** is a historic sawmill that recreates the timber-milling days and has workshops where you can watch woodturners and blacksmiths at work using traditional equipment. You can also purchase redgum products made from beautiful recycled and aged redgum. Admission is free, and the works are open daily from 9 am to 5 pm.

Sharp's Magic Movie House & Penny Arcade on Murray Esplanade has a great collection of authentic and fully restored penny-arcade machines, including a fortune teller and strength test. These accept old predecimal pennies, which are included in the admission fee. In the same building there's a movie house that projects old movies on authentic equipment. The programme includes mainly Australian short films, comedies and archival footage, as well as Buster Keaton and Laurel & Hardy classics. It is open daily from 9 am to 5 pm. Admission costs $10/6 for adults/children, and as the ticket is valid all day you can come and go as you like. The **Murray River Aquarium** shows denizens of the river deep such as a Murray cod. Admission is $5/2.50.

The World in Wax, at 630 High St is modelled on Madame Tussaud's renowned London establishment and features a cast of some 60 famous and gruesome characters ranging from the British royal family to Paul Hogan. It's open daily from 9 am to 5 pm, and entry costs $6/3.

You can take a tour in a horse-drawn coach or carriage for $4/2 with Cobb & Co (buy tickets at the PS *Canberra* office) and Flynn (PS *Pride of the Murray* office).

There are free wine tastings at the Port at **Murray Esplanade Cellars** in the old Customs House on the corner of Leslie St. There's also the **William Angliss Wine Tasting Centre** on the corner of Radcliffe St and Murray Esplanade.

Other Attractions

Echuca's **Historical Society Museum** is at 1 Dickson St in the old police station and

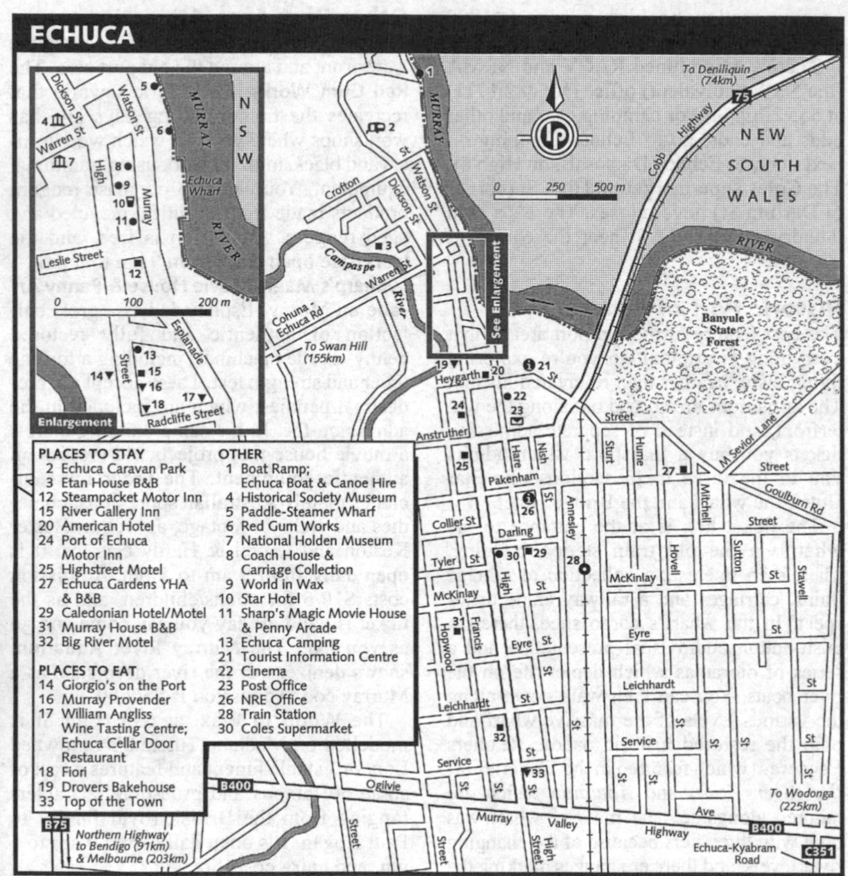

lock-up buildings, which are classified by the National Trust. It has a collection of local history items, some charts and photos from the riverboat era, and early records. It's open Monday, Wednesday, weekends and holidays from 1 to 4 pm ($2/1).

At 7 Warren St, the **National Holden Museum** houses a collection of more than 40 restored Holdens and associated memorabilia – one for the car buffs. It opens daily from 9 am to 5 pm, and entry costs $5/2.50.

Activities

A **paddle-steamer cruise** along the Murray is almost obligatory, and at least four steamers offer cruises throughout the day. Head down to the river next to the old port and check out the sailing times. PS *Emmylou* (☎ 5480 2237) is a fully restored paddle-steamer driven by an original engine, offering one and 1½ hour cruises ($12 and $15 for adults, $5 and $6 for children). *Emmylou* also offers two-day and two-night cruises departing Wednesday evening (from $365 per person), and an overnight cruise, usually on Saturday night (from $135 per person). She sleeps 18, so it wouldn't be too hard to get a group together to book the whole boat, and thus receive a discount.

One hour cruises are offered by PS *Alexandra Arbuthnot* ($12/5), PS *Canberra* ($10/5), PS *Pevensey* ($12/5) and PS *Pride of the Murray* ($9/5).

PS *Adelaide* is the oldest wooden hulled paddle-steamer still operating anywhere in the world, and occasionally takes passengers on a cruise. There's also MV *Mary Ann* (☎ 5480 2200), not a paddle-steamer but a cruising restaurant offering lunch and dinner cruises.

Based at the Victoria Park boat ramp about 700m north of the old port, Echuca Boat & Canoe Hire (☎ 5480 6208) has **motor boats, kayaks and canoes** for hire. It also offers canoe cruises to places like Albury, the Barmah State Forest and Picnic Point – it drives you upstream, you paddle back. A four hour paddle costs $50 for two people, three day trips are $140 per two person canoe. A 10 day marathon from Yarrawonga to Echuca costs $285 per two-person canoe.

Several operators offer **water-skiing** trips and classes – ask at the tourist office for details.

For **horse-riding** in the area, contact Billabong Trail Rides (☎ 5480 1222), Firedust Horse Riding (☎ 5482 5314) or Tarragon Lodge (☎ 5884 3387). Expect to pay around $15 for an hour.

Special Events

On the Queen's Birthday weekend in June, the Steam, Horse & Vintage Rally features a collection of classic and historic vehicles powered by all imaginable methods. A food and wine festival is held in early November. Various other events are held throughout the year, generally on long weekends.

Places to Stay

Camping & Caravan Parks ***Echuca Caravan Park*** *(☎ 5482 2157)*, near the end of Dickson St, is well placed beside the river, and is close to the centre of town. The facilities are good and there are large grassy areas shaded by river red gums. For two people, tent sites cost from $13, on-site vans from $35 and on-site cabins from $48. The other caravan park close to the town centre is ***Moama Riverside Caravan Park*** *(☎ 5482 3241)* across the bridge in Moama (NSW), which has sites and cabins for similar prices.

Hostels & B&Bs ***Echuca Gardens YHA & B&B*** *(☎ 5480 6522, 103 Mitchell St)* is a 10 minute walk from the town centre. There are two sections – a small hostel in an old and comfy house with dorm beds at $16 ($19 nonmembers; everyone pays a small surcharge on long weekends and some major holidays), and the pleasant ***Echuca Gardens B&B***, with doubles with en suites at $100, including breakfast ($120 between Friday and Sunday). The hostel is on the edge of the Banyule State Forest and near the river, and is well run by the multi-talented Kym Kelly, who's a good source of information on things to see and do. There are free bikes.

If you like the idea of staying in an elegant B&B, ***Etan House B&B*** *(☎ 5480 7477, 11 Connelly St)* is highly recommended. It's a beautifully restored homestead in a quiet street, with friendly owners and good facilities including comfortable lounges, a guest kitchen, a grass tennis court and pool. Doubles with en suite start at $120.

Another good place, ***Murray House B&B*** *(☎ 5482 4944, 55 Francis St)*, is a charming B&B with four guestrooms (each with bathroom). Singles/doubles are from $95/165. A self-contained two bedroom cottage is also available at around $100 a night.

River Gallery Inn *(☎ 5480 6902, upstairs 578 High St)* has eight elaborately decorated theme rooms from $130 on weekdays and from $140 on weekends, when you'll probably have to stay two nights.

Pubs There are plenty of options if you want to stay in one of Echuca's old pubs. The ***American Hotel*** *(☎ 5482 5044)*, on the corner of Hare and Heygarth Sts, is a good pub that draws a lively young crowd. Basic pub rooms upstairs cost from $25/40 a single/double, including a continental breakfast. The ***Palace Hotel*** *(☎ 5482 1461)*, on the opposite corner, is slightly more upmarket, with clean rooms also from $20 per person.

Motels There are around 20 motels, including a couple of good budget motels close to the town centre: the ***Big River Motel*** *(☎ 5482 2522, 371 High St)* has good clean singles/doubles from $40/50 to $48/58, while a bit closer to the centre of town ***Highstreet Motel*** *(☎ 5482 1013, 439 High St)* has budget units at similar prices.

The ***Caledonian Hotel/Motel*** *(☎ 5482 2100, 110 Hare St)* is an old pub that has been extensively and tastefully renovated, and has new motel units at the back, with spas and all mod cons; doubles range from $70 to $85.

Right by the old port is the ***Steampacket Motor Inn*** *(☎ 5482 3411)*, on the corner of Murray Esplanade and Leslie St, housed in a National Trust-classified building. Units cost from $64/87.

At the upper end of the motel market, the ***Port of Echuca Motor Inn*** *(☎ 5482 5666, 465 High St)* is a luxury motel and conference centre with all the mod cons imaginable and units from $120 to $140 a double.

Houseboats Hiring a houseboat is a great way to experience river life. The boats generally sleep from four to 12 people, and are fully equipped with cooking and bathroom facilities, sundecks and chairs, TVs etc. Some boats provide linen.

There are three hire periods – weekend (three nights), midweek (four nights) and full week (seven nights). The rates vary according to the season and the size of the boat. For example, a boat with two double bedrooms costs around $800 per week between May and late December (except during school holidays), rising as high as $1600 per week from late December to the end of January. The tourist information centre has full details and a booking service.

See the earlier Activities section for overnight cruises on PS *Emmylou*.

Places to Eat

High and Hare Sts both have quite a collection of bakeries, cafes, restaurants, pubs and take-aways. ***Murray Provender*** *(568 High St)* is a good gourmet deli. ***Drovers Bakehouse*** *(513 High St)* is open during the day for light meals. There's a pleasant deck at the rear overlooking the Campaspie River. In the historic Star Hotel building on Murray Esplanade, ***Pygall's on the Port*** sells cakes, snacks and light meals during the day.

For a pub feed, try the ***American Hotel***, which has good bar meals from $7 and a pleasant bistro. The ***Caledonian Hotel*** is a renovated pub with an upmarket dining area.

Oscar W's at the Wharf is right on the wharf and overlooks the river. It claims to be the only restaurant overlooking the Murray in the country (and the world, for that matter), which is a bit of an indictment of restaurateurs, really. Prices, especially at lunch, aren't as high as you might expect, with snacks from $7.50 and main courses from $10 at lunch.

The atmospheric ***Echuca Cellar Door Restaurant*** *(☎ 5480 6720, 2 Radcliffe St)* at the William Angliss Winery has lunches for around $13.50 and a three course dinner for $19.50. Bookings are preferred.

Fiori, on the corner of Radcliffe and High Sts, is a smart Italian place with good food at reasonable prices, with entrees around $10 and mains around $20. Another good Italian place, and a bit more formal, is ***Giorgio's on the Port*** *(527 High St)*, which is not really on the port. It's open nightly from 6 pm.

Across the river in Moama, the big ***Rich River Golf Club*** complex and the opulent ***Moama Bowling Club*** have a range of eateries, some are very good value.

Top of the Town *(corner High and Service Sts)* claims to be the best fish and chippery in the state. That might or might not be the case, but it does have a good range of the piscine, including river fish such as redfin and yellowbelly. It isn't often that you get the chance to sample these.

Entertainment

There are quite a few good pubs in town, some of which have live music – try the ***American Hotel*** or the ***Shamrock Hotel***.

There are four gambling clubs across the river in Moama – ***Rich River Golf Club***, the ***Bowling Club***, the ***Sports Club*** and the ***RSL***. Some show free movies and they all have courtesy coaches that will pick you up from wherever you're staying – check with your host.

Getting There & Away

V/Line has a daily service between Melbourne and Echuca ($26.90), changing from train to bus at Bendigo (just $6.10 from Echuca, thanks to a pricing anomaly). Four times a week V/Line buses connect Echuca with Albury-Wodonga ($34.20), Swan Hill ($18) and Mildura ($34.20). There's also a daily bus to Albury-Wodonga which takes you to destinations in southern NSW.

BARMAH STATE PARK

This state park is a significant wetland area created by the flood plains of the Murray River. The low-lying alluvial plains are forested with old river red gums, and the swampy understorey is usually flooded in winter, creating a complex wetland ecology which is important as a breeding area for many bird species. It's the largest remaining redgum forest in Australia (and thus the world).

The **Dharnya Centre** (☎ 5869 3302) is both the visitor information centre and a good little museum ($2) with displays on Aboriginal heritage and the park. It's open daily from 10.30 am to 4 pm. The centre is run by members of the Yorta Yorta people.

Although evidence in the area dates Aboriginal occupation at 'only' a thousand years or so, this is probably because the river's floods and changes of course have destroyed older evidence. It isn't very far away, on drier land, that evidence of more than 40,000 years of continuous occupation has been found. The Yorta Yorta people's Native Title claim for the area was rejected by the Federal Court in 1998. The claim was opposed by the Victorian and NSW governments, along with a mining company or two and other commercial interests.

The park starts 9km north of the small town of **Barmah**, which is 36km north-west of Echuca via Moama. The main access road from Barmah is a reasonably good dirt road which leads to the Dharnya Centre and camping areas. Beyond here, there's a forest nature drive and a network of walking tracks, but they may be flooded, so check on road conditions at the centre. The centre also has track notes for the walks.

The park is popular for birdwatching, fishing and walking, although in the wet seasons many of the tracks are flooded and a canoe is the best way to get around.

Gondwana Canoe Hire (☎ 5869 3347), midway between the town of Barmah and the Dharnya Centre, hires canoes for $45 a day (less for longer rentals) and can advise on canoe trails of varying length. Staff can pick you up from as far afield as Echuca (for a fee). The cruise boat *Kingfisher* (☎ 5869 3399) runs good two hour cruises through the state forest on Monday, Wednesday, Thursday and Sunday (more often during holiday periods) for $16, children $10.

Places to Stay

You can camp for free anywhere in the park or at the Barmah Lakes camping area. The ***Dharnya Centre (☎ 5869 3302)*** has good dorm accommodation at $15 per person, but it's designed for groups and the minimum charge is $150. Still, with a group of five that isn't too bad. BYO bedding and food.

There are also two ***caravan parks*** and a ***hotel/motel*** in the town of Barmah.

COBRAM

• **pop 3900**

With Cobram situated close to the banks of the Murray, the township, local economy and tourism all revolve around the big river. The surrounding area produces peaches, citrus fruit, tomatoes, wheat, wool and much more.

The main tourist attraction is the river itself, and Cobram has some excellent sandy 'beaches', the best of which is **Thompson's Beach** just north of the town.

Cobram is known as the 'Home of Peaches and Cream' because of the festival of that name held here in odd-numbered years for 10 days around the Australia Day weekend (late January).

The tourist information centre (☎ 5872 2132), in the centre of town on the corner of Main and Station Sts, is open daily from 10 am to 4 pm.

There are a few wineries around here. One of them, **Heritage Farm Wines** on the Murray Valley Hwy, is quite novel in that the vineyard and orchards are worked with old horse-drawn farm equipment. It's open daily from 10 am to 5 pm.

Places to Stay

The closest caravan park to the centre of town is the ***Apex*** *(☎ 5872 2223)*, on the corner of Punt and Campbell Rds, which charges from $13 for a tent site, $33 for vans and $40 for cabins. On the outskirts of town, 2km east of the centre ***RACV Club Cobram*** *(☎ 5872 2467)*, is a large, family-style holiday complex with tennis courts, a pool and playground. Sites cost from $20 a double. On-site cabins cost $38 to $70 a double (BYO bedding) and self-contained apartments cost $80 to $110 a double; extra adults cost about $10.

The ***Royal Victoria Hotel*** *(☎ 5872 1009)*, on the corner of Mookarii (the Barooga road) and Warkil Sts, has simple pub rooms with shared bathroom from $20/35.

The ***Regency Court Motel*** *(☎ 5872 2488, 1 Main St)* is the most central motel, and has rooms from $63/78 – there's little discount for singles. Next door, the ***Charles Sturt Motor Inn*** *(☎ 5872 2777)* is a modern motel with a pool and spa and good rooms from $80 to $118 a double.

Places to Eat

Maidment's Tea Rooms *(24 Punt Rd)* is a good coffee shop and deli that serves lunches, breakfasts and snacks, and makes good take-away sandwiches. ***Chefoo*** *(87 Punt Rd)* is a licensed restaurant with good Chinese food at reasonable prices, with mains from $6.50. Across the road ***Cafe da Marrello*** has snacks from $3.50 and more substantial Italian dishes.

More upmarket is ***Old Currency*** *(☎ 5872 2990)*, on the corner of Main and Station Sts, a very pleasant BYO restaurant in a section of the former State Bank of Victoria building. It's open for dinner most evenings, but bookings are essential.

YARRAWONGA

- **pop 3400**

On the western edge of the large Lake Mulwala, Yarrawonga is known for its fine and sunny weather, a host of aquatic activities including windsurfing, swimming, power boating and water-skiing, and as a retirement centre.

Lake Mulwala was formed in 1939 by the completion of the Yarrawonga Weir which was in turn part of the massive Lake Hume project (near Albury) to harness the waters of the Murray for irrigation purposes. There are some good foreshore parks alongside the lake in Yarrawonga which have picnic and barbecue areas.

Yarrawonga's twin town, Mulwala, is across the other side of the lake in NSW. The poker machines, cheap meals and other facilities attract a steady stream of visitors from the Victorian side.

Information

The tourist information centre (☎ 5744 1989) is on Irvine Pde on the shores of Lake Mulwala, just beside the bridge. You can book accommodation and tours here. It is open daily from 9 am to 5 pm.

Byramine Homestead

This is the former home of Elizabeth Hume, sister-in-law of the explorer Hamilton Hume. She was the first permanent European settler in this area and built this substantial homestead in 1842, designed to provide protection against bushrangers. The house is 15km west of town off the Murray Valley Hwy. It's open from Thursday to Monday, and admission is $4.

MURRAY RIVER

Other Attractions

The **Clock Museum** is signposted on Lynch St. This cosy museum, inside a simple Tudor-style house, has hundreds of clocks of all shapes and sizes simultaneously ticking and tocking – it's an ominous sound, the time of your life ticking away. Admission costs $4.50.

Across in Mulwala you can visit a **Pioneer Museum** ($3) and the **Linley Park Animal Farm** ($6).

Organised Cruises, Boat Hire & Water Sports

Two paddle steamers, the *Lady Murray* and the *Paradise Queen*, operate cruises along the lake and the Murray River. Both have 1½ hour barbecue cruises at noon ($15) and a scenic cruise at 2 pm ($10). There are dinner cruises during summer.

Phil and Val Smith's Ski Rides (☎ 0419 211 122) rents a huge array of water craft, from canoes ($12 per hour, $40 a day) to fishing boats ($40 a half day) to catamarans ($70 a half day). It also offers water skiing ($40 per half hour), para-sailing ($50 per flight) and other boat-towed thrills. You'll find them on the foreshore at Mulwala.

Places to Stay

There are something like 10 caravan parks, 20 motels and a plethora of time-share resorts in Yarrawonga. If you're confused or can't find a place to stay, the information centre has a booking service.

Yarrawonga Caravan Park *(☎ 5744 3420)*, on the banks of the Murray River at the end of Piper St, is very central and has sites from $9 to $12 and cabins from $30 to $50 a double.

Several pubs have accommodation, including the ***Victoria Hotel*** *(☎ 5744 3009, 35 Belmore St)*, with basic pub rooms from $20 per person, and motel-style rooms from $30 to $40.

The ***Central Yarrawonga Motel*** *(☎ 5744 3817, 111 Belmore St)* is the most central motel and one of the cheapest, with doubles from $55 to $75. ***Scalzo Lake-View Motel*** *(☎ 5744 1555)*, on Hunt St, opposite the information centre and the lake, is also quite reasonable with rooms from $50 to $75. There are many others to choose from.

Places to Eat

In Belmore St you'll find a bakery, quite a few cafes and take-aways, and an inexpensive Chinese restaurant for meals on the run. For cheap club meals head across the river to one of the gambling clubs in Mulwala.

Shag's Nest Restaurant & Wine Bar *(40 Belmore St)* is a good country restaurant in a historic building. It has several dining areas including a courtyard, and a small menu which changes daily. Next door, ***Left Bank*** (it's in a disused bank) is a good place for breakfast or lunch, with sandwiches, roasts, burgers and cakes. Most nights it becomes an affordable BYO bistro with main courses around $15.

Lussino's *(132 Belmore St)*, opposite the Tuckerbag supermarket car park, is a popular pasta bar and Italian restaurant with pasta from $10 and other main meals around $16.

Getting There & Away

There are daily V/Line buses to/from Benalla which connect with trains to/from Melbourne (total fare $31.60). The Murraylink bus service which runs along the Murray Valley Hwy from Mildura to Albury-Wodonga also stops in Yarrawonga.

RUTHERGLEN

- **pop 1900**

Rutherglen is at the centre of one of Victoria's major wine-growing districts, a food-and-wine buff's paradise. It's a quaint little town, and as well as being a popular base for touring the wineries it has a few interesting sights and a rustic atmosphere.

Rutherglen was born during the gold-rush days, and Main St is a historic precinct lined with weathered timber buildings, antique and bric-a-brac shops, tearooms, verandah-fronted pubs and the like.

The **Rutherglen Historical Society Museum** is in the old common-school building (1872) in Murray St behind the Victoria

Hotel. It's open on Sunday from 10 am to 1 pm, and admission is free.

Information

The Rutherglen Visitor Information Centre (☎ 02-6032 9166), inside the historic Jolimont Wines complex on the corner of Main and Drummond Sts, opens daily from 9 am to 5 pm.

Note that this Victorian town is in the NSW telephone area, so you need to add 02 to the beginning of the phone numbers if calling from a state other than NSW.

Special Events

The Winery Walkabout Weekend is a local wine and produce festival of long standing. It's held on the Queen's Birthday weekend in June. There's a wide range of events, as well as eating and drinking, of course.

Other festivals include the Tastes of Rutherglen, held on the Labour Day weekend in March, and the Winemakers' Legends Weekend in mid-November. The Tour de Muscat, a bike ride around the wineries, is held in early November.

Accommodation in the area is likely to be tight during these festivals.

Places to Stay

Rutherglen Sites start at $15 and on-site vans at $30 in the ***Rutherglen Caravan Park*** *(☎ 02-6032 8577, 72 Murray St)*.

The National Trust-classified ***Victoria Hotel*** *(☎ 02-6032 8610, 90 Main St)* has old-fashioned budget rooms at around $30/40 for singles/doubles and en suite rooms from $58 a double; $78 with breakfast. Rates might be lower midweek. Nearby, another historic pub (but not quite as charming), is the ***Star Hotel*** *(☎ 02-6032 9625)* with basic rooms upstairs from $15 per person ($20 with breakfast) and motel units out the back for $39 a double during the week and $49 on weekends. Most of the pub rooms have access to an impressive balcony and the publican has plans to renovate them soon.

There are a few motels in the area. The two nearest the centre of town are ***Motel Woongarra*** *(☎ 02-6032 9588)*, on the corner of Main and Drummond Sts, which has doubles from $48 to $62, and ***Wine Village Motor***

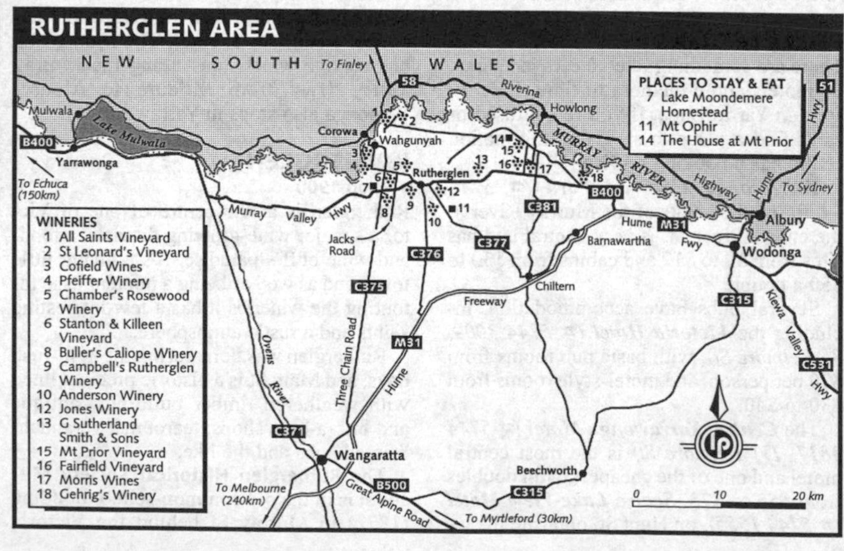

Wineries of the Rutherglen Region

Rutherglen is one of Victoria's major wine-growing districts, an area world famous for its fortified wines and one which also produces a wide range of high-quality table wines. There are more than a dozen within striking distance of the town of Rutherglen, which makes for a perfect day or two of winery touring. One of the best ways to get around is to cycle from winery to winery – the countryside is scenic and fairly flat, and bikes can be hired in Rutherglen.

Listed below are some of the area's wineries. Pick up the *Touring Guide* brochure from the Rutherglen information centre for a complete list.

Jones Winery is off the Chiltern road a couple of km south-east of Rutherglen. It's the smallest operation in the area and the winery is made up of a fairly ramshackle collection of sheds and old buildings – try the vintage port.

Eleven kilometres east of Rutherglen, off the Murray Valley Hwy, is **Fairfield Vineyard**. This historic winery, owned by the great-grand-daughter of its founder, has guided tours through the wonderful restored mansion daily during school and public holidays at 11 am and 1 and 3 pm. Nearby is the famous **Morris Wines**, renowned for its range of fortified wines, in particular its muscat – the glass-sided cellar door looks into the old barrel room. A few km north of here is the **Mt Prior Vineyard**, with its outstanding accommodation and restaurant – see the Places to Stay & Eat sections in Rutherglen.

Twenty-one kilometres east of Rutherglen on the Murray Valley Hwy is **Gehrig's Winery**, Victoria's oldest and set around the historic Barnawartha Homestead (1870). There are picnic facilities and restaurant.

One kilometre north-west of Rutherglen on the Corowa road is **Chamber's Rosewood Winery**, which is full of character and history, and well known for its ports, muscats and tokays. To the west of Rutherglen, the first winery you come to is **Campbell's**, a modern winery complex with a sloping roof, as featured on its label. Across the road is the **Stanton & Killeen Vineyard**. Further along, on the corner of Three Chain Rd, is **Buller's Calliope Winery**, which has some great aged fortified and shiraz wines, a picnic area and an interesting aviary.

South of Wahgunyah is **Pfeiffer Wines**, which has a rustic old brick and tin winery complex and a tasting room full of character (and wine).

One kilometre north-east of Wahgunyah, **All Saints** is one of the area's most impressive wineries, with a tree-lined driveway leading to a huge red-brick winery with a strange medieval castle-like facade. The tasting room is crowded with barrels, and old photos and documents on the walls tell the history of the place. It has its own restaurant (open daily for lunch and on weekends for dinner), picnic facilities and the Winemakers Hall of Fame.

Four kilometres north-east of Wahgunyah is **St Leonard's Vineyard**, which has a delightful picnic area overlooking the river and an excellent bistro.

There are a couple of exceptions, but most of the wineries in the region open daily from 9 am to 5 pm (on Sunday from 10 am). The wine-makers of Rutherglen produce an excellent free map and brochure. It has a few paragraphs on each of the wineries and details their wine ranges, specialities and opening times, and is available from the information centre or from the wineries.

Inn *(☎ 02-6032 9900)*, across the road, which is a bit more modern and has a swimming pool and doubles from $60 to $85.

Carlyle House *(☎ 02-6032 8444, 147 High St)* and ***Cannobie*** *(☎ 02-6032 9524)*, on Grahams Lane, are two high-quality B&Bs, charging from around $100 a room.

Around Rutherglen There are some excellent upmarket accommodation houses in this area.

Mt Ophir *(☎ 02-6032 8920)* is a historic vineyard property 6km south-east of Rutherglen that is now an emu and elk farm. The old homestead has been restored and has four guestrooms. B&B tariffs are from $130 to $150 a double, and dinner B&B ranges from $180 to $240 a double. There's also a self-contained four bedroom homestead on the property, with doubles costing from $120 a night with a three night minimum. There's also a spa suite in an old winery building ($200 a double) and the impressive tower suite at $500.

Lake Moondemere Homestead *(☎ 02-6032 8650)* is 6km west of Rutherglen off the Murray Valley Hwy on a 600 hectare sheep property. The homestead has three homey guestrooms with their own bathroom and lounge. The B&B tariffs start at $90/110 for singles/doubles ($120 for a double with en suite).

Fourteen kilometres north-east of Rutherglen at the Mt Prior winery, ***The House at Mt Prior*** *(☎ 02-6026 5256)*, in Howlong Rd, is a luxurious gourmet retreat in a restored historic mansion. B&B costs between $105 and $150 per person, but bring some spare cash to spend in the excellent restaurant.

Places to Eat

There are several good eateries along Main St. For light lunches and teas try ***Shanty*** or ***Rutherglen Tearooms***. Both of the historic pubs in Main St, the ***Victoria Hotel*** and the ***Star Hotel***, serve good bistro meals, and the Victoria has a very pleasant beer garden out the back.

The ***Shamrock*** *(152 Main St)* is in a lovely old verandah-fronted two storey red-brick building. Hearty dishes are reasonably priced. ***Rendezvous Courtyard*** *(68 Main St)* is open for dinner nightly and has a Mediterranean-influenced menu.

Several wineries have cafes and restaurants, including ***All Saints*** (lunch and snacks daily), ***St Leonards*** (weekend lunches), ***Cofield*** (pre-order a picnic pack, daily), ***Gehrig's*** (lunch Thursday to Sunday), ***Lake Moodemere*** (pre-order a barbecue pack, daily) and ***Pfeiffer*** (pre-order a picnic hamper, daily).

The ***House at Mt Prior*** *(☎ 02-6026 5256)*, at the Mt Prior winery 14km north-east of Rutherglen, is probably the most highly rated restaurant in this area. The setting is superb and the food outstanding. It's pricey but worth it. There's also the less expensive ***Terrace*** restaurant here, which opens for lunch on weekends.

Getting There & Around

The only transport to/from Rutherglen is the V/Line bus which runs to Wangaratta ($4.30) and connects with the Melbourne train on Wednesday, Friday and Saturday.

You can hire bikes for leisurely cycle tours from Walkabout Cellars, at the information centre.

WAHGUNYAH

This small, historic riverside township is 9km north-west of Rutherglen. The town was established in 1856, and at the height of the riverboat era was a thriving port town and trade depot. Things are somewhat quieter now, and the town's economy revolves around the local wine industry. Across the bridge in NSW is the large provincial centre of Corowa, which has a wide selection of gambling clubs and accommodation, including riverside caravan and campgrounds.

CHILTERN

• **pop 1100**

Just off the Hume Fwy, tiny Chiltern is one of Victoria's most historic and charming colonial townships. Originally called Black Dog Creek, the town was established in 1851 and prospered when gold was discovered here in 1859. Mining continued until the early 1900s, and not much has changed since then.

Conness St, the main street, is lined with old buildings and shops fronted with sloping verandahs. The entire streetscape has been preserved intact, and the buildings all look so quaint and authentic that the town has often been used as a film set for period pieces.

On the outside, most of the shops look as if they haven't been touched since they were built over 100 years ago – and some look that way on the inside.

Things to See

The historic **Lake View Homestead** was built in 1870 and is classified by the National Trust. It's a small red-brick house surrounded by sloping verandahs and simple gardens. The house is significant as the one-time home of a famous early Australian author, Henry Handel (Florence Ethel) Richardson, who lived here with her family in 1876 and 1877. She wrote of life here in the book *Ultima Thule*, the third part of her trilogy *The Fortunes of Richard Mahony*. Richardson's other works include *The Getting of Wisdom*, an autobiographical account of her schooldays at Presbyterian Ladies College in Melbourne. Lake View is in Victoria St overlooking Lake Anderson and is open to the public on weekends, public holidays and during school holidays from 10 am to noon and 1 to 4 pm, and at other times by appointment.

The **Atheneum Library & Museum**, now the local historical society museum, is housed in the former town hall (1866) and has a collection of local memorabilia, art, photos and equipment from the gold-rush days. It opens at various times, usually from 1 to 4 pm on Sunday and public holidays, and admission costs $2.

The **Star Hotel/Theatre**, in the centre of town, was once the centrepiece of Chiltern's social and cultural life, with the theatre used for plays and dances. A grapevine growing in the hotel's courtyard is entered in the *Guinness Book of Records* as the largest in the southern hemisphere. The Star is now a historical museum and is open Tuesday and Sunday from 10.30 am to 5 pm.

Pick up a copy of the booklet *A Walk into Chiltern's Past*, available at several businesses on Conness St, for a walking tour.

Places to Stay

Lake Anderson Caravan Park *(☎ 5726 1298)*, on Alliance St, has campsites from $8 and on-site vans from $40.

Chiltern Colonial Motor Inn *(☎ 5726 1788, 1 Main St)* is a modern motel with its own restaurant and good units from $60 to $70 a double. ***The Mulberry Tree*** *(☎ 5726 1277, 28 Conness St)* is a good B&B in an old bank. Singles/doubles cost $75/100.

In Springhurst, just off the highway south of Chiltern, ***Springhurst Tour-Tel Accommodation Centre*** *(☎ 5726 5343)*, on Anzac Rd, offers very inexpensive B&B accommodation – just $23 per person. It's designed for groups but there's usually room for individuals. A three course dinner costs $14. Trains running between Melbourne and Albury (but not the XPT) stop at Springhurst.

Places to Eat

There are several cafes, take-aways and tearooms along Conness St, and the weathered old ***Telegraph Hotel*** serves counter meals. The ***Council Club Tearooms*** *(43 Conness St)* serves reasonable Devonshire teas, sandwiches, cakes and the like, and is also the local pizzeria. A rather bizarre feature of its dining room is a circular staircase that does not lead anywhere.

CHILTERN STATE PARK

An area of 4500 hectares around Chiltern has been declared a regional park to conserve the environment and relics of early mining activities. There are two main sections of the park, on either side of the Hume Fwy.

There's a network of gravel tracks through the park. The main road, the Chiltern Historic Drive, starts from Chiltern and takes you through the park past the old open-cut **Magenta Mine**, the remains of the **Indigo Cemetery** and **Donkey Hill**. You can also hike through the park, but if you leave the main tracks watch out for old mine shafts. There are picnic areas at various sites, and you can camp here – but contact the local Parks Victoria/NRE office first (☎ 5726 1234).

This is the last remnant of box-ironbark forest in this part of the state. The forest also puts on a colourful display of wildflowers each spring, and is a haven for birdlife with over 150 species having been recorded here.

Brochures on the park and the historic drive are available from Parks Victoria and the Athenaeum Library in Chiltern.

WODONGA

• pop 25,800

The twin towns of Albury and Wodonga are separated by the broad banks of the Murray River, and several kilometres of farmland. Together, these two towns form the main economic, industrial and bureaucratic centre for the northern Victorian and southern NSW region.

The Albury-Wodonga Development Corporation was a population-decentralisation project formed by the Whitlam Labor Government in 1974, which was intended to oversee the expansion of these two towns into Australia's major inland growth centre. The corporation projected a population of around 300,000 by the year 2000. At last count the two towns collectively were about 230,000 residents short of the target.

Wodonga is mainly a commercial centre and there's not too much joy in the town itself from a tourism point of view.

The **RAA Ordnance Corps Museum** is at Bandiana, 4km south-east of Wodonga. This army museum displays a variety of war weaponry and documents, and is open Tuesday to Friday from 10 am to 3 pm and weekends until 4 pm.

Information

There's a good range of information on both Victoria and NSW at the Gateway Tourist Information Centre (☎ 1800 800 743 toll-free), on Lincoln Causeway between Wodonga and the Murray River. It's open daily from 9 am to 5 pm.

Places to Stay

There are plenty of caravan parks in this area but none near the town centre. The closest is ***Wodonga Caravan & Cabin Park*** *(☎ 02-6024 2598, 186 Melbourne Rd)*, about 2km west. Sites cost $13 a double, on-site vans are $30 and cabins cost from $35.

There are two hostels across the river in Albury. ***Albury Wodonga Backpackers' Hostel*** *(☎ 02-6041 1822)* is on Hume St. Beds cost from $13 a night, there's a free pick-up service, and you can hire bikes and canoes. There's also ***Albury Motor Village YHA*** *(☎ 02-6040 2999, 372 Wagga Rd)*, on the Hume Fwy, nearly 5km north of central Albury. It's in a converted motel, so the rooms and facilities are quite good. A bed in a shared room costs $14 for members.

There are quite a few motels, with the main clusters along Melbourne Rd which leads into the town, and along High St which is the main street. On Melbourne Rd, a few kilometres from the town centre, the ***Stagecoach Motel*** *(☎ 02-6024 3044)* is a friendly place, with rooms and suites of a good standard ranging from $72 to $125 a double. In High St, there's the ***Provincial Motel*** *(☎ 02-6024 1200)*, at No 10, with rooms from $50 to $60, and the ***Terminus Hotel*** *(☎ 02-6041 3544)* has clean and basic pub rooms from $30/40 for singles/doubles.

Places to Eat

There's the usual range of cafes and takeaways along High St, but probably the best bet for meals is to head across the river to Albury, where you'll find a wide range of restaurants and cheap bistro meals at the gambling clubs.

Getting There & Away

Wodonga's train station is in the centre of town near the intersection of the Hume Fwy and Murray Valley Hwy. There are daily services to/from Melbourne, and the one way fares are $38.90/54.40 in economy/1st class.

MURRAY RIVER

WODONGA TO CORRYONG – THE UPPER MURRAY

The Murray Valley Hwy continues east of Wodonga through **Tallangatta**, a small township with an interesting history. In the 1950s, following the construction of the Hume Weir, the original site of Tallangatta was flooded by the rising waters of the Mitta Mitta River, a tributary of Lake Hume. Most of the actual township had already been relocated to what is known as New Tallangatta. Seven kilometres east of the town, there's a lookout point from which you can see the streetscape of Old Tallangatta, especially if the waters are low. A map shows the old layout of the town.

Fifteen kilometres west of Tallangatta, there's a turn off to the town of **Granya**. Both the turn-off road and the main road have been called the Murray Valley Hwy at different times by different organisations. Regardless of the names, the road to the north rejoins the Murray River and follows it all the way around to Towong and Corryong, via Tintaldra which is worth a detour if you have a day or two to spare. Tintaldra has a friendly hotel, campground and good trout fishing. The main road also leads to Corryong, but by a slightly quicker and more direct route.

About 6km north of Granya is the ***Herb & Horse*** *(☎ 02-6072 9553)* – run by a friendly family, it's a great place to stay for a while and has been recommended by quite a few travellers. It's an 1890s homestead on a lakeside farm and riding ranch, with home-cooked meals, excellent horse riding and canoe trips. You can stay in the homestead, in the restored barn or stables, or in a quaint and rustic little cottage overlooking the river. Shared rooms are from $25, doubles from $75 and cottages with B&B from $70 per person. The staff can usually arrange free transport from Albury-Wodonga if you ring in advance.

An area of 13,000 hectares around **Mt Lawson** has recently been declared a state park to protect the abundance of native flora and fauna, particularly the rich birdlife. Mt Lawson is north-east of the town of Granya, and the park stretches some 20km south from the half-moon-shaped loop in the Murray River and is about 10km wide. There are few facilities, but you can camp or hike here.

BURROWA-PINE MOUNTAIN NATIONAL PARK

This rugged and remote area was always considered too rocky and steep for farming, so luckily for us it was never cleared. Some areas have been mined for silver and gold or have been logged, and a few of the access tracks remain from these activities, but on the whole the area is intact. Burrowa Pine is a significant vegetation reserve and is very popular for a range of outdoor activities, including bushwalking, nature observation and rock climbing.

The park, in the north-eastern corner of Victoria, covers an area of 18,400 hectares and is in two separate mountainous sections. The northernmost section is centred around the red granite **Pine Mountain** (1062m), which is covered in black cypress-pine and has great views of the Snowy Mountains and the Murray River from its summit. This section of the park is botanically significant for its large number of rare plant species such as the phantom wattle, branching grevillea and pine mountain grevillea.

The southern or Burrowa section is dominated by **Mt Burrowa** (1300m), made up volcanic rock. The vegetation in this section is mainly eucalypts, with peppermint and blue gums in the lower areas, and alpine ash and snow gums higher up.

Wildlife is abundant here, with kangaroos, wallabies, wombats and more than 180 species of birds, including the lyrebird.

The main access road into the park is the road between Walwa and Cudgewa North, which, if you just want a quick look, is a great scenic drive. The other tracks through the park are 4WD-only roads. The facilities in the park are limited, with a picnic and camping area at Bluff Creek and two other small camping areas at Blue Gum and Hinces Creek. Some good walking tracks start from these areas, and two leaflets, the *Walking Track Guide* and *Bluff Falls Nature Walk*, are available at the park or from Parks

Victoria. If you want to hike overnight here, you can camp independently but you have to notify the ranger first. Contact the Parks Victoria/NRE office (☎ 02-6076 1655) in Corryong for more information.

CORRYONG

• pop 1200

Corryong, the Victorian gateway to the Snowy Mountains and the Kosciusko National Park, is a pretty township. It's ringed by mountains and the main street is lined with liquid-amber trees. The surrounding area is a natural playground, perfect for a range of activities including fishing, canoeing, cycling, and bushwalking.

This is also a great area for scenic drives. No matter which way you head from Corryong, you'll be surrounded by spectacular countryside. A good guide to four of the area's most scenic routes is available from Corryong's newsagencies, and from the historical museum.

There is no official tourist office but both of the newsagencies (on opposite sides of Hansen St) have information sections with a selection of brochures.

Jack Riley's Grave

This simple memorial of stone and timber is engraved with the words: 'In memory of the Man from Snowy River, Jack Riley, buried here 16th July 1914'. The town's pretty hillside cemetery is at the top of Pioneer Ave and signposted off the main road.

Man from Snowy River Folk Museum

This museum at 55 Hansen St isn't actually dedicated to the legend, but is more of a local history museum. Still, it houses a fascinating collection of items, and you can spend hours wandering around looking at the weird and wonderful bits and pieces. There's a large collection of old skis dating back to 1870, an amazing flying jacket that was handmade from scraps by a prisoner of war during WWII, old photos, farming machinery and tools, an old jail cell, a slab timber hut set up as a dairy, and a collection of beautifully intricate handmade 19th-century costumes. The museum is open from 10 am to noon and 2 to 4 pm (closed between June and August). Admission costs $4.

MURRAY RIVER

The Man from Snowy River

Corryong's main claim to fame is as the last resting place of Jack Riley, the hero of *The Man from Snowy River*. Banjo Paterson's famous poem was first published in the *Bulletin* magazine in 1890, and more recently the successful Australian film consolidated the 'Man's' fame worldwide. Paterson is said to have based his hero on Riley, a tailor turned mountain man who worked this district. While some people dispute the claim, Riley is nevertheless well remembered in the area, as the last lines of the poem foreshadowed:

And down by Kosciusko, where the pine-clad ridges raise
Their torn and rugged battlements on high,
Where the air is clear as crystal, and the white stars fairly blaze
At midnight in the cold and frosty sky,
And where around the Overflow the reed-beds sweep and sway
To the breezes, and the rolling plains are wide,
The Man from Snowy River is a household word today,
And the stockmen tell the story of his ride.

Mark Armstrong

Activities

Across the border in Khancoban (27km west of Corryong), you'll find quite a few companies that are set up to help you make the most of this spectacular and unspoilt mountain country.

The area around Corryong and Khancoban is great for canoeing, and Alpine Hideaway Canoe Hire (☎ 02-6076 9498) hires canoes for $35 a day. Khancoban Trail Rides (☎ 02-60769455), based at Tom Groggin Station on the Alpine Way about 50km south of Khancoban, has good horse-trail rides for $55 a half day or $90 a full day, as well as overnight safaris from $180 a day all-inclusive.

Special Events

Each year in March, Corryong holds the Corryong High Country Festival, which includes a bush market, a commemorative ride along the route of 'Riley's Last Ride', a drover's dance and a stockmen's muster.

Places to Stay & Eat

Corryong ***Mt Mittamatite Caravan Park*** *(☎ 02-6076 1152)*, 1km west of town, has tent sites from $10 and on-site vans and cabins from $20 to $40.

Corryong Country Inn *(☎ 02-6076 1333, 7 Towong Rd)* is a very nice motel with doubles from $68 to $96. The ***Corryong Hotel*** *(☎ 02-6076 1004, 54 Towong Rd)* has motel-style units for $30/40 a single/double. ***Alpine Gateway Lodge*** *(☎ 02-6076 1269, 96 Hansen St)* is a sort of motel in an old family home, with old-fashioned and simple accommodation from $39/60, with breakfast.

Jardine Cottage *(☎ 02-6076 1318)*, in Jardine St, just off the main road, is a cafe/teahouse in a very attractive Victorian-style timber cottage. Accommodation prices start at $75 a double. It's also a good place for Devonshire teas and light lunches and is also open for dinner nightly, with home-style main meals.

Khancoban Across the border in Khancoban, ***Khancoban Alpine Inn*** *(☎ 02-6076 9471)* has a backpacking and fishing lodge with bunkrooms at $17 for one person, $24 for two, and a wide range of other rooms starting at $62/75 a single/double, up to $100 a double for a room with a spa.

Goldfields

The Goldfields region of central Victoria is one of the state's most interesting areas to visit, with reminders of the rich heritage of the gold-rush days wherever you go. It's a great area to explore, with its blend of quaint little townships, impressive regional centres and some pretty countryside. It's also a place of dramatically contrasting landscapes, ranging from the green forests of the Wombat Ranges to the red earth, bush scrub and granite country up around Inglewood. Unless you're in a hurry, take to the backroads and just go exploring. This is also a great area for bike touring, or if you have a few days you could even hire a horse-drawn gypsy-style caravan (see the Bridgewater-on-Loddon section).

Ballarat and Bendigo are Victoria's largest inland centres, and both have a rich architectural heritage and numerous attractions that are linked to the gold rush era. Sovereign Hill, the re-created gold-mining township in Ballarat, is one of Australia's most popular tourist attractions and should definitely be on your itinerary. Ballarat also has an excellent gold museum and a fine art gallery, while Lydiard St is one of the most impressive Victorian-era streetscapes in Australia.

Bendigo also boasts an abundance of classic Victorian architecture, and it's one of the few places in Victoria with reminders of the thousands of Chinese diggers who worked the goldfields during the 1800s. The Golden Dragon Museum and Chinese joss house are well worth a visit, and the Bendigo Easter Fair features two famous Chinese processional dragons, Loong and Sun Loong. Other popular attractions include underground tours of the Central Deborah Gold Mine, lovely gardens, an excellent art gallery and a handful of wineries.

Speaking of wineries, central Victoria is a major wine-producing area and has more than 40 wineries to visit. The major regions are the Pyrenees Ranges near Avoca, the Heathcote region and around Bendigo.

HIGHLIGHTS

- The re-created 1860s gold-mining township of Ballarat's Sovereign Hill
- The historic Craig's Royal Hotel in Ballarat and Shamrock Hotel in Bendigo are wonderful places to stay
- The historic township of Maldon
- Spas, massages, bushwalks, galleries, gardens, eateries and guesthouses in Daylesford & Hepburn Springs
- Superb cafes and restaurants such as L'Espresso in Ballarat, Frangos & Frangos in Daylesford, the Bull & Mouth in Talbot, and Ruby's at Calder House in Maldon
- A spring visit to the magnificent gardens at Buda in Castlemaine
- Maryborough's amazing (and extremely large) train station
- Winery tours of the Pyrenees Ranges – for a great splurge, stay and eat at Warrenmang Vineyard Resort
- Horse-drawn gypsy-caravan holidays through the Golden Triangle
- Bendigo Art Gallery, exhibiting a fine collection of Australian art

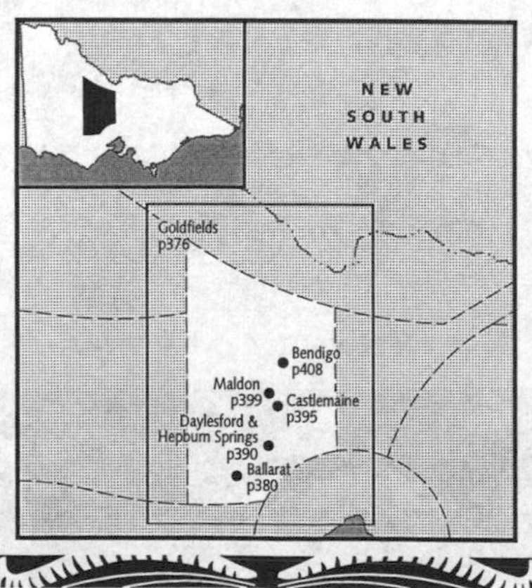

Castlemaine is another impressive old gold town, and is surrounded by a cluster of charming and historic hamlets. Maldon is steeped in history and is a popular tourist town, or if you want to hit the backroads and explore there are plenty of forgotten little towns to discover – places like Moliagul, Tarnagulla, Rushworth and Talbot.

Last but by no means least are the twin towns of Daylesford and Hepburn Springs. Set in the scenic central highlands region, these towns were popular health and rejuvenation centres throughout the 19th century, famous for the regenerative qualities of their mineral spa waters. In recent decades they've gone through something of a renaissance, and are again a popular escape for overworked city folk. As well as the new Hepburn Spa Complex and the wonderful Convent Gallery, the town boasts masseurs and naturopaths, gardens and craft shops, restored old guesthouses and cottages, plenty of great eateries and lots more.

Orientation & Information

Ballarat and Bendigo are the two major 'hubs' in central Victoria, with most of the main highways intersecting at one or the other. If you have time, detour off the highways and explore – this is a great area to get lost in, with plenty of interesting sights and unusual discoveries along the backroads and byways.

This chapter is (dis)organised in roughly the following sequence: from Ballarat north via Daylesford and Hepburn Springs to Castlemaine, then out west to Maryborough, north to Wedderburn, south-east to Inglewood and Bendigo, east to Rushworth, and south to Heathcote. As I said, it's a great area to get lost in.

Not to worry, you'll find plenty of helpful tourist information centres along the way. The main ones are in Ballarat, Bendigo, Daylesford-Hepburn Springs, Castlemaine, Maldon, Kyneton and Maryborough.

Activities

Yep, there's still gold in them thar hills. The old diggers dug up most of the stuff, but even today this is a popular area for prospectors, and every now and then you hear stories of significant nuggets being unearthed. Metal detectors and other prospecting gear can be bought or hired in many of the towns, or if you don't want to get your hands dirty there are quite a few working gold mines and tourist mines that open up for public tours.

Highlights for keen bushwalkers include the numerous trails and rambles around Daylesford and Hepburn Springs (including the recently opened Great Dividing Trail between Daylesford and Castlemaine), the rugged granite countryside of the Kooyoora State Park, the Pyrenees Ranges near Avoca, and the hills and forests around Maldon and Bendigo.

There are some fine golf courses in this area, as well as lots of good freshwater fishing spots and numerous horse-riding ranches. For the warmer weather, most of the towns have good public swimming pools.

Accommodation

The accommodation options in this region are excellent and can be booked through the toll-free Goldfields Accommodation Hotline (☎ 1800 240 077).

Getting There & Away

Train & Bus There are two main train lines through the Goldfields: the Melbourne-Swan Hill line (via Kyneton, Castlemaine and Bendigo) and the Melbourne-Ballarat-Adelaide line.

V/Line buses service most of the regional centres, with the majority of services radiating out of Ballarat and Bendigo.

Car & Motorbike If you have your own transport, the well-signposted **Goldfields Tourist Route** makes an interesting excursion for a couple of days. It takes in all the major gold-rush centres, and in a clockwise direction from Ballarat goes through Linton, Beaufort, Ararat, Stawell, Avoca, Maryborough, Dunolly, Tarnagulla, Bendigo, Maldon, Castlemaine, Daylesford and Creswick.

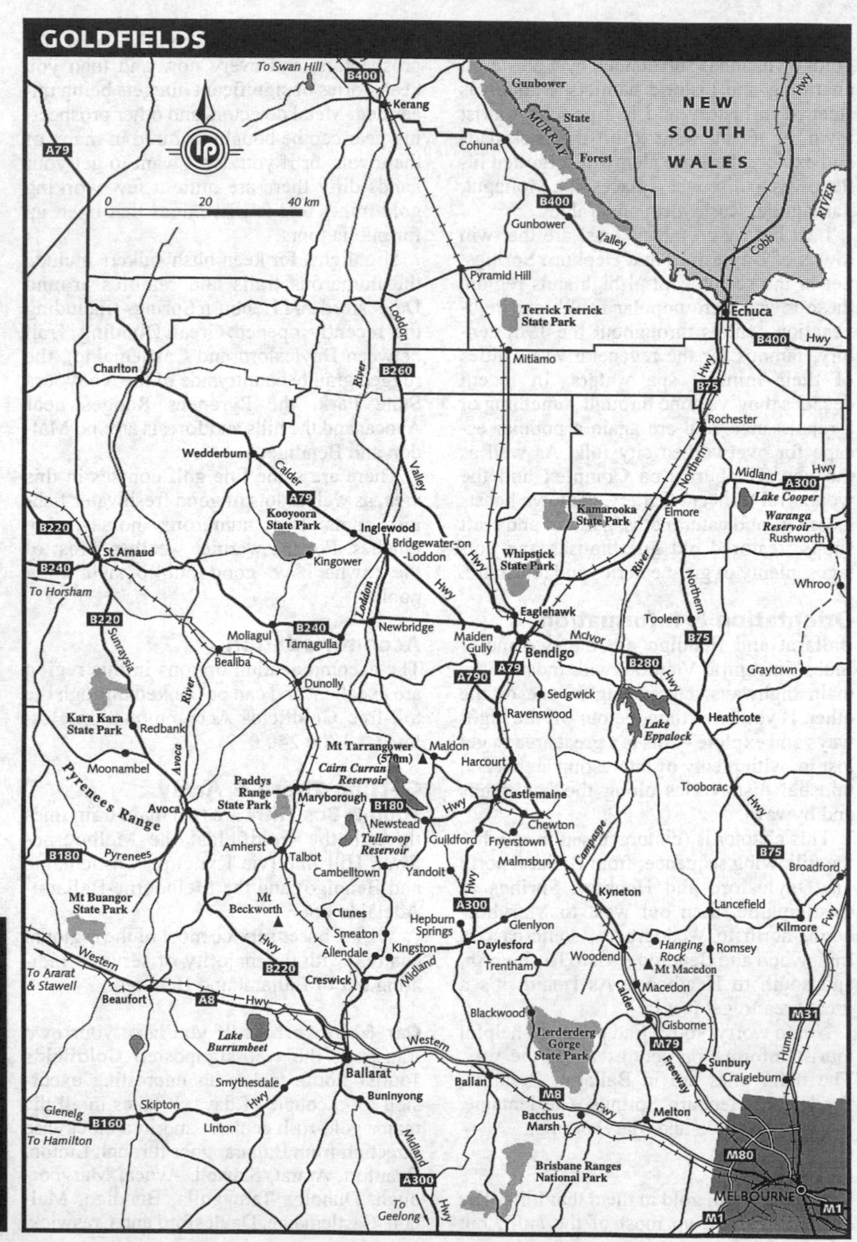
GOLDFIELDS
To Swan Hill
B400
Kerang
A79
0
20
40 km
Gunbower
MURRAY
State
Forest
Cohuna
NEW
SOUTH
WALES
RIVER
Hwy
B400
Gunbower
Valley
Cobb
Pyramid Hill
Terrick Terrick
State Park
Echuca
B400
Hwy
Mitiamo
Loddon
River
B260
Charlton
Hwy
B75
Rochester
Wedderburn
Calder
Valley
Northern
Midland
Hwy
A300
Lake Cooper
Waranga
Reservoir
Rushworth
A79
Kooyoora
State Park
Kamarooka
State Park
Elmore
B220
St Arnaud
Inglewood
Bridgewater-on
-Loddon
Kingower
Whipstick
State Park
Hwy
River
Northern
B240
To Horsham
Loddon
Hwy
Whroo
B220
Eaglehawk
Tooleen
Sunraysia
Moliagul
B240
Tarnagulla
Newbridge
Maiden
Gully
McIvor
B75
Bendigo
Bealiba
A79
B280
Graytown
River
Dunolly
A790
Hwy
Sedgwick
Kara Kara
State Park
Redbank
Avoca
Ravenswood
Lake
Eppalock
Heathcote
Moonambel
Mt Tarrangower
(570m)
Maldon
Cairn Curran
Reservoir
Harcourt
Pyrenees Range
Paddys
Range
State Park
Maryborough
Tooborac
Avoca
B180
Castlemaine
Hwy
Hwy
Newstead
Chewton
Tullaroop
Reservoir
Guildford
Fryerstown
B180
Pyrenees
Amherst
Talbot
Campaspe
B75
Malmsbury
Campbelltown
Yandoit
Broadford
Hwy
Mt Buangor
State Park
Mt
Beckworth
Kyneton
A300
Lancefield
Clunes
Hepburn
Springs
Glenlyon
Fwy
Kilmore
Hwy
Smeaton
Western
Allendale
Kingston
Daylesford
Hanging
Rock
Romsey
Woodend
To Ararat
& Stawell
B220
Midland
Trentham
Mt Macedon
Creswick
Calder
Macedon
Beaufort
A8
Hwy
Blackwood
M31
Gisborne
Lake
Burrumbeet
Western
Lerderderg
Gorge
State Park
M79
Hume
Freeway
Ballarat
Sunbury
Smythesdale
Ballan
Craigieburn
Hwy
Buninyong
M8
Skipton
Fwy
Glenelg
B160
Linton
Bacchus
Marsh
Melton
To Hamilton
Midland
M80
Brisbane Ranges
National Park
A300
MELBOURNE
To
Geelong
Hwy
M1
M1

A route map is available from most of the tourist information centres along the way.

BALLARAT

• pop 65,000

The area around presenxt-day Ballarat was known to the local Kooris as 'Ballaarat', meaning resting place. European settlers first arrived in the district in 1837 and established pastoral runs here.

When gold was discovered at nearby Buninyong in August of 1851, the rush was on and thousands of diggers flooded into the area. Ballarat's alluvial goldfields were but the tip of the golden iceberg, and when deep shaft mines were sunk they struck incredibly rich quartz reefs. The mines were worked until the end of WWI, and about 28% of the gold unearthed in Victoria came from Ballarat.

As the riches were claimed, the original shanty town of canvas tents and bark and timber huts was gradually replaced with more permanent dwellings, and Ballarat eventually grew into a major provincial town. Today there is a wealth of gracious Victorian architecture here, a reminder of the prosperity of the days of gold.

Ballarat's main drag, Sturt St, is a wide boulevard lined with some impressive old buildings and divided by central plantations. The popular theory for its width is that it had to be three chains wide (60m) to allow for the turning circle of the bullock wagons that brought supplies to the town before the rail link was built. Lydiard St is a historic precinct that contains some of the finest examples of Victorian architecture.

Ballarat's major attraction is Sovereign Hill, but there are plenty of other points of interest in and around the town. The range of accommodation is good, and you'll also find some excellent restaurants and cafes here.

Information

The well-stocked Ballarat Visitor Information Centre (☎ 5332 2694) is in a small building on the corner of Sturt and Albert Sts. It's open daily from 9 am to 5 pm.

The Royal Automobile Club of Victoria (RACV) office (☎ 5332 1946) at 20 Doveton St North has an information section and an accommodation-booking service.

Parks Victoria (☎ 5333 6782) has an office on the corner of Doveton and Mair Sts.

Sovereign Hill

You should allow at least half a day for a visit to this fascinating re-creation of a gold-mining township of the 1860s. It's probably the best attraction of its type in Australia and has won numerous awards.

The main street features a hotel, a post office, a blacksmith's shop, a printing shop, a bakery and a Chinese joss house. It's a living history museum with people performing their chores dressed in costumes of the time. There's even a re-creation of an early bowling alley – the Empire Bowling Saloon – where you can have a game.

The site was mined back in the gold era so much of the equipment is original, as is the mine shaft, and there's a variety of above-ground and underground diggings. You can pan for gold in the stream, and with luck may find a speck or two among the gravel.

There are at least four places around the 'town' offering food of various types, from pies and pasties at the Hope Bakery to a full three-course lunch at the United States Hotel.

Sovereign Hill is open daily from 10 am to 5 pm and admission is $18.50 for adults, $13.50 for students, $9 for children and $48 for families – expensive but well worth it. The ticket also gets you into the nearby Gold Museum which is also worth seeing.

Sovereign Hill also opens at night for the impressive sound & light show 'Blood on the Southern Cross', a simulation of the Eureka Stockade battle (see the 'Eureka Rebellion' boxed text). The show runs twice nightly from Monday to Saturday – commencement times vary depending on the time the sun sets and therefore the time of year; the first show starts between 6.45 pm (in winter) and 9.15 pm (summer) and the second show between 8 and 10.30 pm. Show-only tickets are $22.50 for adults,

Victoria's Gold Rush

In May 1851, EH Hargreaves discovered gold near Bathurst in New South Wales (NSW). It was not the first gold discovery in Australia, but the sensational accounts of the potential wealth of the find caused an unprecedented rush as thousands of people dropped everything to try their luck.

News of the discovery reached Melbourne at the same time as the accounts of its influence on the people of NSW. Sydney had been virtually denuded of workers and the same fate soon threatened Melbourne. Victoria was still in the process of being established as a separate colony, so the loss of its workforce to the goldfields would have been disastrous.

A public meeting was called by the young city's business people and a reward was offered to anyone who could find gold within 300km of Melbourne. In less than a week gold was discovered in the Yarra but the find was soon eclipsed by a more significant discovery at Clunes. Prospectors began heading to central Victoria and, over the next few months, the rush north across the Murray was reversed as fresh gold finds and new rushes became an almost weekly occurrence in Victoria.

Gold was found in the Pyrenees, the Loddon and Avoca rivers, at Warrandyte and Buninyong. Then in September 1851 the greatest gold discovery ever known was made at Ballarat, followed by others at Bendigo, Mt Alexander, Beechworth, Walhalla, Omeo and in the Great Dividing Range.

By the end of 1851 about 250,000 ounces of gold had already been claimed. Many workers downed tools to join the rush and some employers had no choice but to follow. Hopeful miners came from England, Ireland, Europe, China and the failing goldfields of California. During 1852 about 1800 people a week arrived in Melbourne.

The government introduced a licence fee of 30 shillings a month for all prospectors, whether they found gold or not. This entitled the miners to a claim, limited to eight square feet, in which they could dig for gold. The licence also provided the means to govern, and to enforce the laws that were improvised for the goldfields.

The administration of each field was headed by a chief commissioner whose deputies, the state troopers, were empowered to organise licence hunts and to fine or imprison any miner who failed to produce the permit.

$11.50 for children; dinner-and-show tickets are $41/25.50. Bookings are essential – phone ☎ 5333 5777.

Gold Museum

Over the road from Sovereign Hill and built on the mullock heap from an old mine, this excellent museum has imaginative displays and samples from all the old mining areas in the Ballarat region, as well as gold nuggets, coins and a display on the Eureka Rebellion (see the boxed text). It's open daily from 9.30 am to 5.20 pm and is well worth a visit. Admission is included in the Sovereign Hill ticket, or separate admission costs $5 for adults and $2.50 for kids.

Ballarat Fine Art Gallery

This gallery is the oldest and one of the best provincial galleries in the country, and is highly recommended. The collection of predominantly Australian art is housed on two levels and includes early colonial paintings, works from noted Australian artists (including Tom Roberts, Sir Sidney Nolan, Russell Drysdale and Fred Williams), and contemporary works. A separate section of the gallery is devoted to the work of the famous and

Victoria's Gold Rush

In his book *Australia Illustrated*, published in 1873, Edwin Carton Booth wrote of the goldfields in the early 1850s:

...it may be fairly questioned whether in any community if there ever existed more of intense suffering, unbridled wickedness and positive want, than in Victoria at [that] time...To look at the thousands of people who in those years crowded Melbourne, and that most miserable adjunct of Melbourne, Canvas Town, induced the belief that sheer and absolute unfitness for a useful life in the colonies...had been deemed the only requisite to make a fortunate digger.

While the gold rush certainly had its tragic side and its share of rogues, including the notorious bushrangers who regularly attacked the gold shipments being escorted to Melbourne, it also had its heroes who eventually forced a change in the political fabric of the colony. (See the Eureka Rebellion boxed text, under Ballarat.) Above all, the gold rush ushered in a fantastic era of growth and material prosperity for Victoria and opened up vast areas of country previously unexplored by Europeans.

During the first 12 years of the rush, Australia's population increased from 400,000 to well over a million, and in Victoria alone it rose from 77,000 to 540,000. To cope with the moving population and the tonnes of gold and supplies, the development of roads and railways accelerated.

The mining companies, which followed the independent diggers, invested heavily in the region over the next couple of decades. The huge shanty towns of tents, bark huts, raucous bars and police camps were eventually replaced by the timber and stone buildings that were the foundation of many of Victoria's modern provincial cities, most notably Ballarat, Bendigo and Castlemaine.

It was in the 1880s that the gold towns reached the height of their splendour, but although gold production was gradually to lose its importance, the towns of the region by then had stable populations. In many areas agriculture and other activities steadily supplanted gold as economic mainstays.

Mark Armstrong

multi-talented Lindsay family who lived in nearby Creswick. You can also see the remnants of the original Eureka flag here. The gallery is in the centre of Ballarat's historic precinct at 40 Lydiard St North. It's open daily from 10.30 am to 5 pm; entry costs $4 for adults, $2 for students and $1 for kids.

Lake Wendouree

Formerly the Black Swamp, this large artificial lake near the centre of Ballarat is something of a focal point for the town and was used as the rowing course in the 1956 Olympics. Wendouree Parade, which circles the lake, houses much of Ballarat's best residential architecture. There are old timber boat sheds along the lake's shore, and you'll often see rowing boats stroking their way from one end to the other. The jogging and walking track around the lake is also popular, and a favourite training venue for local hero and Olympic marathon runner Steve Moneghetti.

Botanic Gardens

Ballarat's excellent 40 hectare botanic gardens are beside Lake Wendouree. First planted in 1858, these beautiful and serene

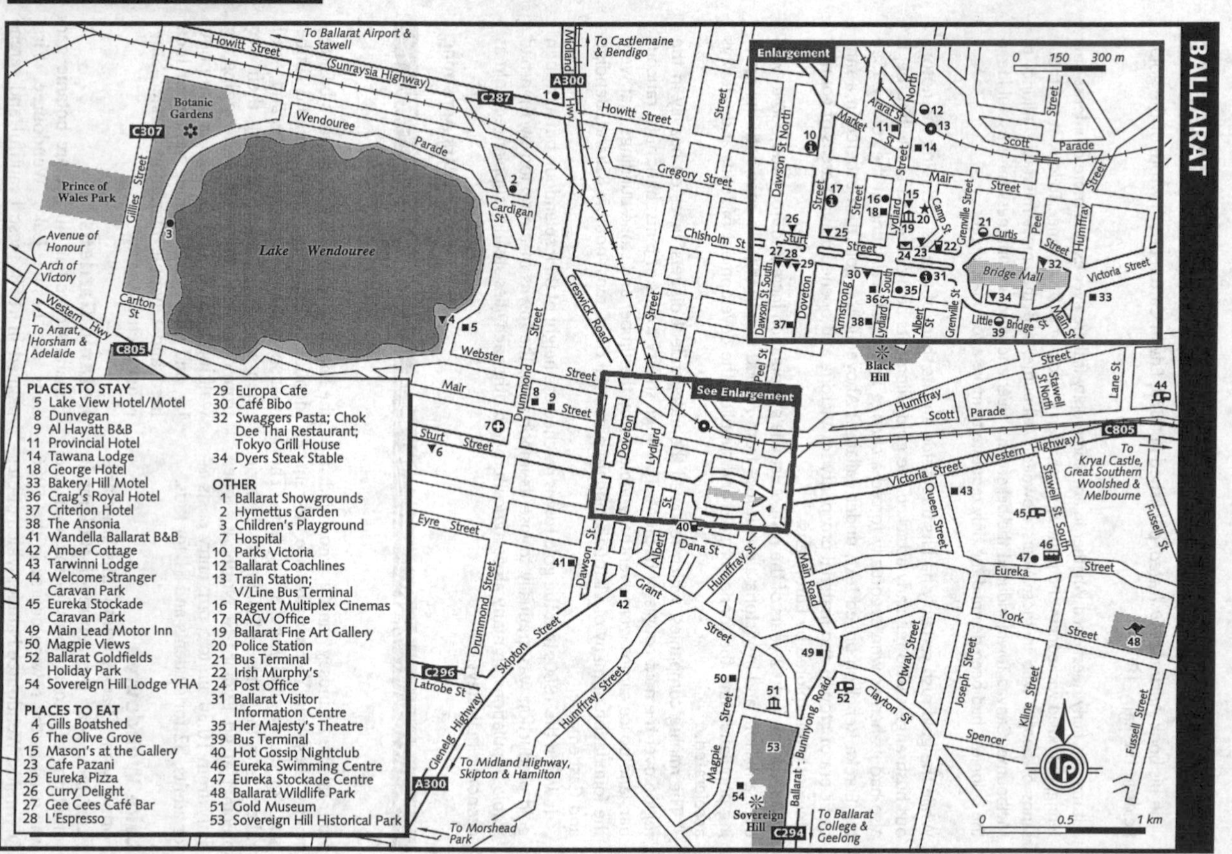
BALLARAT
Enlargement
0 150 300 m
See Enlargement
PLACES TO STAY
5 Lake View Hotel/Motel
8 Dunvegan
9 Al Hayatt B&B
11 Provincial Hotel
14 Tawana Lodge
18 George Hotel
33 Bakery Hill Motel
36 Craig's Royal Hotel
37 Criterion Hotel
38 The Ansonia
41 Wandella Ballarat B&B
42 Amber Cottage
43 Tarwinni Lodge
44 Welcome Stranger Caravan Park
45 Eureka Stockade Caravan Park
49 Main Lead Motor Inn
50 Magpie Views
52 Ballarat Goldfields Holiday Park
54 Sovereign Hill Lodge YHA
PLACES TO EAT
4 Gills Boatshed
6 The Olive Grove
15 Mason's at the Gallery
23 Cafe Pazani
25 Eureka Pizza
26 Curry Delight
27 Gee Cees Café Bar
28 L'Espresso
29 Europa Cafe
30 Café Bibo
32 Swaggers Pasta; Chok Dee Thai Restaurant; Tokyo Grill House
34 Dyers Steak Stable
OTHER
1 Ballarat Showgrounds
2 Hymettus Garden
3 Children's Playground
7 Hospital
10 Parks Victoria
12 Ballarat Coachlines
13 Train Station; V/Line Bus Terminal
16 Regent Multiplex Cinemas
17 RACV Office
19 Ballarat Fine Art Gallery
20 Police Station
21 Bus Terminal
22 Irish Murphy's
24 Post Office
31 Ballarat Visitor Information Centre
35 Her Majesty's Theatre
39 Bus Terminal
40 Hot Gossip Nightclub
46 Eureka Swimming Centre
47 Eureka Stockade Centre
48 Ballarat Wildlife Park
51 Gold Museum
53 Sovereign Hill Historical Park
To Ballarat Airport & Stawell
To Castlemaine & Bendigo
To Ararat, Horsham & Adelaide
To Kryal Castle, Great Southern Woolshed & Melbourne
To Midland Highway, Skipton & Hamilton
To Morshead Park
To Ballarat College & Geelong
Lake Wendouree
Botanic Gardens
Prince of Wales Park
Avenue of Honour
Arch of Victory
Black Hill
Sovereign Hill
Bridge Mall
Howitt Street
(Sunraysia Highway)
Wendouree Parade
Gillies Street
Carlton St
Western Hwy
Midland Hwy
Cardigan St
Gregory Street
Chisholm St
Creswick Road
Webster Street
Mair Street
Drummond Street
Sturt Street
Eyre Street
Dawson St
Doveton
Lydiard
Albert
Dana St
Grant Street
Humffray St
Main Road
Skipton Street
Latrobe St
Glenelg Highway
Humffray Street
Magpie Street
Ballarat - Buninyong Road
Clayton St
Otway Street
Joseph Street
Kline Street
Spencer
York Street
Eureka Street
Queen Street
Victoria Street
(Western Highway)
Scott Parade
Stawell St North
Stawell St South
Lane St
Fussell St
Fussell Street
Peel St
Dawson St North
Dawson St South
Armstrong
Lydiard St South
Grenville St
Grenville Street
Little Bridge St
Main St
Curtis
Camp St
Ararat St
North
Market
Peel Street
Humffray
Victoria Street
A300
C287
C307
C805
C296
C294
0 0.5 1 km
GOLDFIELDS

gardens are immaculately maintained and a delight to stroll through, with their extensive rose gardens, wide lawns, old trees and colourful begonia glasshouse. The cottage of the poet, Adam Lindsay Gordon, is also here – apparently he (and his poor horse) tragically jumped to their death in the Blue Lake in Mount Gambier. You can also come face to face with the likes of Bob Hawke, Paul Keating and John Howard in the Prime Ministers' Avenue, a collection of bronze portraits.

A tourist tramway operates around the gardens on weekends and public and school holidays, departing from the tram museum south of the gardens. Close by, on the other side of Wendouree Pde, is a fantastic wooden children's playground.

Eureka Stockade Centre

This new centre stands on the site of the Eureka Rebellion (see boxed text) and takes you through multi-media galleries simulating the battle. If you're a bit exhausted after all the fighting, you can move into the 'contemplation space' to be soothed by the sound of running water. The centre is in Eureka St (just look out for the huge Eureka sail), and is open from 9 am to 5 pm daily (except Monday). Admission is $8/4 for adults/kids.

Kryal Castle

Surprisingly, this modern bluestone 'medieval English castle' is a very popular attraction, no doubt helped along by the daily hangings and whippings (volunteers not called for). Kids love it, but adults may find it tacky. The castle is 8km from Ballarat, towards Melbourne, and is open daily from 9.30 am to 5 pm. On weekends and during school holidays, entry costs $12.50 for adults, $9.50 for concessions, $7 for kids and $37 for families; at other times, these prices are $11/8.50/6/32.

Ballarat Wildlife Park

This private zoo, on the corner of York and Fussel Sts in East Ballarat, has a collection of native animals and reptiles, plus a few exotic species. Residents include koalas, kangaroos, wallabies, Tasmanian devils, wombats, crocodiles, emus, snakes and eagles. A guided tour is held daily at 11 am; on weekends there are regular programmes, including a koala show at 2 pm, a wombat show at 2.30 pm and crocodile-feeding at 3 pm. The park is open daily from 9 am to 5.30 pm and costs $10.50 for adults, $8.50 concession and $5 for kids.

Other Attractions

Lydiard St is one of Australia's finest and most intact streetscapes of Victorian architecture. A walk along here will take you past some of Ballarat's most impressive buildings, including Her Majesty's Theatre, the art gallery and Craig's Royal Hotel. The *Historic Lydiard Precinct* brochure is available from the Visitor Information Centre.

The **Ballarat Aviation Museum** at Ballarat airport on the Sunraysia Highway (B220) houses a collection of vintage and military aircraft and associated bits and pieces. The museum is open on weekends and public holidays from 1 to 5 pm.

When Hymettus won the Caulfield Cup in 1898, the horse's owner used the winnings to build a house which he named **Hymettus**. The original home, at 8 Cardigan St, is surrounded by beautiful period gardens – formally arranged flower gardens at the front and cottage gardens with herbs and vegetables at the rear. The gardens are open daily from 10 am to 6.30 pm, and admission costs $4 for adults and $1 for kids.

The Great Southern Woolshed, on the Western Highway (A8) on the eastern outskirts of town, has shearing demos, trained dogs and woolly displays. Entry costs $9 for adults, $4 for children.

At the Ballarat Showgrounds on Creswick Rd, there's a fine **Trash & Trivia market** every Sunday morning.

Activities

If you want to try finding some gold for yourself, visit the Gold Shop at 8A Lydiard St North, in the old Mining Exchange building. They sell miner's rights and hire out metal detectors.

The Eureka Rebellion

As the easily won gold began to run out, Victorian diggers came to recognise the inequality that existed between themselves and the privileged few who held the land and governing power.

The limited size of claims, the inconvenience and brutality of police licence hunts and the fact that while the miners were in effect paying taxes they were allowed no political representation, all fired the unrest that led to the Eureka Rebellion at Ballarat.

In September 1854, Governor Hotham ordered that the hated licence hunts be carried out twice a week. A month later a miner was murdered near a Ballarat Hotel after an argument with the owner, James Bentley. When Bentley was found not guilty, by a magistrate who just happened to be his business associate, miners rioted and burned his hotel down. Though Bentley was retried and found guilty, the rioting miners were also jailed, which further fuelled distrust of the authorities.

Creating the Ballarat Reform League, the diggers called for the abolition of the licence fees, the introduction of the miners' right to vote and increased opportunities to purchase land.

On 29 November about 800 miners tossed their licences into a bonfire during a mass meeting and then set about building a stockade at Eureka where, led by an Irishman called Peter Lalor, they prepared to fight for their rights.

On 3 December, having already organised brutal licence hunts, the government ordered the troopers to attack the stockade. There were only 150 diggers within the makeshift barricades at the time and the fight lasted only 20 minutes, leaving 25 miners and four troopers dead. (See the painting *Eureka, 3 December 1854* opposite page 384.)

Though the rebellion was short-lived the miners were ultimately successful in their protest. They had won the sympathy of most Victorians, and with the full support of the goldfields' population behind them, the government deemed it wise to acquit the leaders of the charge of high treason.

The licence fee was abolished and replaced by a Miners' Right, which cost one pound a year. This gave them the right to search for gold; the right to fence in, cultivate and build a dwelling on a moderate-sized piece of land; and the right to vote for members of the Legislative Assembly. The rebel miner, Peter Lalor, actually became a member of parliament some years later.

For the warmer weather, Ballarat has four large outdoor pools – the closest to the centre being the Eureka Swimming Centre in Eureka St.

Organised Tours

Timeless Tours (☎ 5342 0652) offers half-day guided tours around Ballarat's heritage sites ($20), as well as day trips to destinations further afield, including the Brisbane Ranges and Lerderderg Gorge.

Special Events

Ballarat's 100-year-old Begonia Festival attracts thousands of visitors. Highlights include some sensational floral displays, a street parade, fireworks, art and music. The festival takes place in early March.

The Eureka Jazz Festival is held during April. In September/October there's Australia's oldest eisteddfod, the Royal South St Eisteddfod – during this time accommodation can be hard to find as the competition draws people from all around the country.

Places to Stay

Camping & Caravan Parks There are several caravan parks in and around Ballarat. The ***Ballarat Goldfields Holiday***

Park *(☎ 5332 7888, 108 Clayton St)* is the closest to Sovereign Hill, and has tent sites from $14, on-site vans from $37 and standard cabins from $45. The ***Eureka Stockade Caravan Park*** *(☎ 5331 2281)* is also convenient in Stawell St, with tent sites at $11 and on-site vans from $25.

There are has excellent facilities at the ***Welcome Stranger Caravan Park*** *(☎ 5332 7722)*, 3km east of the city centre on the corner of Water St and Scott Pde. Tent sites are $14.50 and on-site vans and cabins range from $37 to $55.

Hostel & Pubs Adjacent to Sovereign Hill, ***Sovereign Hill Lodge YHA*** *(☎ 5333 3409)* has eight to ten-bunk dormitories costing $16 for members ($19 for non-members) or singles/doubles from $27/46 (with en suites from $86/95). The facilities here are excellent (and it's often fully booked).

The ***Provincial Hotel*** *(☎ 5332 1845, 121 Lydiard St)*, opposite Ballarat train station, has basic pub rooms for $20/40 a single/double. The ***Criterion Hotel*** *(☎ 5331 1451, 18 Doveton St South)*, also has old-fashioned pub rooms for $26/42.

The sprawling ***Wandella Ballarat Bed & Breakfast*** *(☎ 5333 7046, 202 Dawson St South)* is popular with students and travellers, with budget rooms from $28.50/44.50 a single/double, including breakfast.

Historic Hotels Some of Ballarat's grand old pubs have been restored and offer gracious accommodation. The best of these is ***Craig's Royal Hotel*** *(☎ 5331 1377, 10 Lydiard St South)*, so named after it hosted visits by the Prince of Wales and the Duke of Edinburgh. This pub will delight aficionados of Victorian architecture – wander into the bistro and the old ballroom/function room upstairs. There are various standards of accommodation, from old-fashioned budget rooms at $40, en suite rooms from $70 to $90 and more swish suites from $120 to $160.

The George Hotel *(☎ 5333 4866, 27 Lydiard St North)* is another pub with a rich history – the rooms here are more modern and singles/doubles (including breakfast) start at $35/50, or $50/65 with en suites.

Boutique Hotel For an upmarket retreat, ***The Ansonia*** *(☎ 5332 4678, 32 Lydiard St South)* exudes calm and peace with its minimalist design, polished cement floors and light-filled atrium. There's also a cafe where you can breakfast all day. Prices range from $110 (studio apartment, sleeps two) to $180 (family suite, sleeps four).

Motels If you're after a motel, Ballarat has about 25 to choose from. One of the cheapest central options is the ***Lake View Hotel/Motel*** *(☎ 5331 4592, 22 Wendouree Parade)*, overlooking Lake Wendouree. It has units for $50/60 a single/double. ***Tawana Lodge*** *(☎ 5331 3461)*, right beside the train station, is a ramshackle old private hotel/motel with quaint and well-worn rooms ranging from $25/40 with shared bathrooms to $49/58 for xmotel-style rooms.

One of the best and most central motels is the ***Bakery Hill Motel*** *(☎ 5333 1363, 1 Humffray St)* which has singles/doubles from $76/88. There are also quite a few motels near Sovereign Hill, including the ***Main Lead Motor Inn*** *(☎ 5331 7533, 312 Main Rd)* with rooms from $80.

B&Bs & Cottages Quite a few of Ballarat's old homes have been converted into B&Bs and self-contained cottages. ***Dunvegan B&B*** *(☎ 5332 2505, 806 Mair St)* is a centrally located 1857 homestead with drawing and billiards rooms and four comfortable guestrooms with en suites. Singles/doubles start at $75/100.

Close by ***Al Hayatt B&B*** *(☎ 5332 1396, 800 Mair St)* is a lovely Edwardian home built in 1916 for an English colonel. 'Al Hayatt' means 'the key to good health and happiness' in Egyptian so you're bound to have a pleasant stay, especially if you score the upstairs front room with adjoining sun room. The cost is $70/90 for a single/double.

Tarwinni Lodge *(☎ 5331 9979, 3 Queen St South)* is a lovely Victorian timber home with three guestrooms costing $90 to $100 a double. It's good for couples and families – children of all ages will love the room with the tree inside.

If you're after something self-contained, try ***Magpie Views*** *(☎ 5341 3362, 14 Magpie St)*, a very sweet cottage perched on a hill overlooking the city and also convenient to Sovereign Hill. It sleeps four and costs $125 a double plus $30 per extra person.

Places to Eat

Ballarat has plenty of excellent cafes and delis, many of them on Sturt St with pleasant footpath table settings in the warmer months. ***L'Espresso*** *(☎ 5333 1789, 417 Sturt St)* has the cafe business down pat – it's stylish, friendly and atmospheric, the food and service is terrific and, most importantly, its coffee is superb. It also has an extensive CD library with CDs for sale or to enjoy while you sip your latte.

A couple of doors down, the warm and inviting ***Europa Cafe*** serves all-day breakfasts, lunches such as Turkish pide or Spanish omelettes, and Mediterranean-style evening mains ranging from $15 to $18. Also good for a meal at any time is the friendly ***Gee Cees Cafe Bar*** *(427 Sturt St)* nearby.

Further east is the truly hip ***Cafe Bibo*** *(205 Sturt Street)*. Its walls are lined with pages from 1960s *Women's Weekly* magazines and boxed shelves holding hundreds of decorated coffee cups belonging to the cafe's regulars. The food is delicious and good value. Across the road, ***Cafe Pazani*** *(102 Sturt St)* is a European-style bar/restaurant complete with designer decor and in-vogue food. Evening meals range between $15 and $20, or you can just pop in for coffee and cake.

The Olive Grove *(1303 Sturt Street)*, up towards the lake, is a fantastic deli, chock-full of gourmet delights, including a good selection of pies, focaccias, bagels, cakes and cheeses – the perfect place to stock up for a picnic.

If you're going to the art gallery, pop in for lunch or cake at ***Mason's at the Gallery***, a daytime cafe which brews a fine cuppa and has lunch in the $8 to $10 range.

There's a cluster of eateries in Bridge Mall. ***Swaggers Pasta*** has evening pasta dishes for $8.80 ($6.80 at lunch), while the fully licensed ***Chok Dee Thai Restaurant*** *(☎ 5331 7361, 113 Bridge Mall)* has tasty Thai mains between $12 and $16. Next door is the ***Tokyo Grill House*** *(☎ 5333 3945)*, a Japanese restaurant with teppanyaki and sushi dishes in the $15 to $19 range, or banquet menus between $22 and $37 per person.

The best place in town for a steak is ***Dyers Steak Stable*** *(☎ 5331 2850, 28 Little Bridge Street)*, a long-established local favourite where you'll pay between $17 and $40 for a great steak – they also have duckling and seafood dishes.

For some pub grub, there are plenty of pubs with cheap bar meals and good bistros to choose from. The bistro at the ***Lake View Hotel/Motel***, by the lake on Wendouree Parade, is always popular, and the ***Criterion Hotel*** *(18 Doveton St)* is also quite good with mains in the $9 to $12 range.

Eureka Pizza *(316 Sturt St)* is a casual and lively BYO (bring your own alcohol) Italian bistro with pasta, pizzas and other dishes such as veal parmigiana and calamari from $8 to $12. Nearby, ***Curry Delight*** *(418 Sturt St)* serves up fine Indian fare in the $9 to $13 range, catering well for vegos and carnivores alike.

Gills Boatshed, on Lake Wendouree's eastern shore, serves up great coffee, cakes, meals and alcohol along with excellent lake views.

Entertainment

With its large student population, Ballarat has a lively nightlife. There are a few good nightclubs – the most happening place is ***Hot Gossip*** *(102 Dana St)*, which plays funky dance music and has occasional live bands. Also popular is ***21 Arms*** *(21 Armstrong St)*, in a converted pub.

The local pub scene is also pretty strong. ***The George Hotel*** *(☎ 5333 4866, 27 Lydiard St North)* is one of the better venues for live bands, as is the charming ***Irish Murphy's*** *(36 Sturt St)*, the 'drinking consultants', where there's also plenty of Guinness on tap.

THE SOVEREIGN HILL MUSEUMS ASSOCIATION: EUREKA STOCKADE CENTRE

George Browning, *Eureka, 3 December 1854* (oil on canvas, 1989)

GLENN BEANLAND

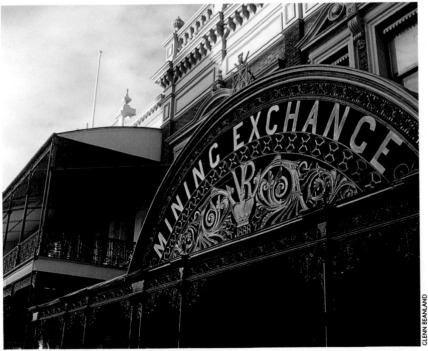

The Mining Exchange building in Lydiard Street, Ballarat

GLENN BEANLAND

Main Street, Maldon

GLENN BEANLAND

One of many delightful B&Bs in Castlemaine

RICHARD NEBESKY

Inside the Chinese Joss House, Bendigo

Ballarat's main venue for the performing arts is the wonderful ***Her Majesty's Theatre*** *(☎ 5333 5800, 17 Lydiard St South)*, while the main cinema complex is the ***Regent Multiplex Cinemas*** *(☎ 5331 1399, 49 Lydiard St North)*. Ring them both to find out what's on while you're in town.

Getting There & Away

Ballarat train station is near the centre of town in Lydiard St North. Trains run frequently between Melbourne and Ballarat (via Bacchus Marsh), with 10 trains each weekday, six on Saturday and five on Sunday. The trip takes about 1¾ hours and fares are $13.80/19.40 in economy/1st class. Buses continue on through Ararat ($11.20) and Stawell ($15.20).

V/Line has daily bus services from Ballarat to Geelong ($9.80) and Mildura ($46.90) via St Arnaud ($16.50), and weekday services to Warrnambool ($18), Hamilton ($24.50), Maryborough ($7.50) and Bendigo ($18) via Daylesford ($8.60) and Castlemaine ($13.80).

Both Greyhound-Pioneer-Australia and McCafferty's buses stop at the coach bay at the Ballarat train station on their way between Melbourne and Adelaide.

Getting Around

The local bus service, Ballarat Transit, is operated by Davis Bus Lines (☎ 5331 7777). There are two main terminals on either side of Bridge Mall; one in Curtis St and one in Little Bridge St. Timetables are available from the Visitor Information Centre or the train station. Bus No 2 goes to the train station, and Bus No 15 goes to the botanic gardens and Lake Wendouree. Two buses go to Sovereign Hill, the No 9 and No 10.

For a cab, call Ballarat Taxis on ☎ 131 008.

AROUND BALLARAT

Buninyong

Buninyong, 11km south of Ballarat, was the site of one of the earliest discoveries of gold in this area back in 1851. A signposted **historic walk** takes you past points of interest, and the surrounding areas are popular with bushwalkers. There's also a great lookout point on Mt Buninyong.

Places to Stay ***The Eyrie*** *(☎ 5341 2259, 505 Warrenheip St)*, a spacious unit above a plant nursery in the former Eagle Hotel is self-contained, has two-bedrooms and the tariff for singles/doubles is $65/80 ($75/90 on weekends). ***Woodside B&B*** *(☎ 5341 3451, 120 Fisken Rd)*, a couple of kilometres north of Buninyong, is a country-style B&B with two guestrooms in a farmhouse on a four-hectare garden property. B&B costs $50/80 (including port and chockies). It's a bit tricky to find, so call for directions.

Great value for families, the ***Coach House*** *(☎/fax 5341 3615, corner Somerville and Allan Sts)* is a bright and spacious fully self-contained dwelling with lovely rural views. It's very 'kid friendly' with cots, portable beds, high chairs, videos, toys, games and a playground all available. The cost is $90 a double plus $10 per child, or $400 a week.

Smythesdale

At Smythesdale, 19km south-west of Ballarat, is the **Yellowglen Winery**, one of Australia's better known producers of sparkling '*méthode champenoise*' wines. It's a modern, fairly characterless complex with a small barbecue area for visitors beside the winery, and opens daily from 10 am to 5 pm (weekends from 11 am) for tastings and sales.

Places to Eat ***Louisa's*** *(☎ 5342 4705)* is off the Glenelg Highway (B160) a couple of kilometres back from Smythesdale towards Ballarat. It's a middle-European style licensed restaurant in a modern colonial homestead, with mains ranging from $18 to $20. Roast duckling is the speciality of the house – at last count they were up to duck number 5300.

CRESWICK

• **pop 2300**

Creswick, another old gold-mining town and the home of forestry, is 18km north of Ballarat. At the height of the rush, the town had a population of 60,000 diggers. In 1882,

Creswick was the site of Australia's worst mining disaster when the Australia No 2 mine flooded and 22 miners were drowned. Creswick is also noteworthy for having produced a few famous Australians, including John Curtin (who became prime minister in 1941), Lady Peacock (Australia's first female member of Parliament) and the artist and writer Norman Lindsay.

Nowadays Creswick is a quiet highway town and agricultural centre with some interesting old buildings. There's a **historical museum** in the old town hall at 68 Albert St which opens on Sunday from 1.30 to 4.30 pm and costs $2. **St George's Lake**, 2km east of Creswick, has a good picnic and barbecue spot and walking tracks through the bush.

One kilometre north along the Castlemaine Rd is **Springmount Pottery** and the quirky **World of Dinosaurs** bushland theme park.

Places to Stay

The ***Victorian School of Forestry*** *(☎ 5321 4100)* in Water St is a forestry management study centre and backs on to 20 hectares of forest. The school has an eclectic but good range of budget accommodation (bunkrooms, dorms, motel units and tiny cabins) which range in price from $16 to $35 per person (single beds only).

Hillview Farm *(☎ 5345 2690)*, 3km north of Creswick on Spittle Rd, is a host farm with a simple self-contained cottage that overlooks a lovely valley. The cottage sleeps up to four and is good value for $60 (four people).

CRESWICK TO CAMPBELLTOWN

The area to the north of Creswick is an interesting and attractive region for scenic drives, with a cluster of historic hamlets and tumbledown towns which have a few hidden treasures.

In Kingston you'll find the delightful ***Kirkside Cottages*** *(☎ 5345 6252)*. There's an enchanting bluestone chapel, home to the lovely owners, as you enter the grounds. Set back from the church are three fully self-contained dwellings, their design based on an old miner's cottage but fitted out with all the mod cons. The tariff per double for B&B ranges from $120 (weekdays) to $150 (weekends – two night minimum stay), with each extra person costing $20 to $30.

The impressively restored **Anderson's Mill** in Smeaton, is a gigantic bluestone flour mill beside Birch Creek. Built in 1862, it has been fully restored and is open to the public on Sunday afternoons, from noon to 4 pm. Great spot for a picnic.

At the ***Tuki Trout Fishing Complex*** *(☎ 5345 6233)*, off the Newstead road 8km north of Smeaton, you can go fishing for fresh trout and then have your catch filleted, barbecued and served with bread, salad and herb potatoes. There's a rustic restaurant in a converted shearing shed, and a lunch-and-fishing package deal costs $20 for adults and $10 for kids. If you just want to fish, admission is $5/2.50 for adults/children, rod hire is another $3 each and the trout you catch costs $9.50 per kilogram, cleaned and packaged. If you'd like to stay a while, there are also two lovely self-contained cottages overlooking the trout ponds available from $110 to $135 per night mid-week or from $320 to $395 on weekends, including two nights accommodation, breakfasts and a three-course dinner.

CLUNES

- **pop 850**

Clunes, a charming little town 32km north of Ballarat, was the site of Victoria's first significant gold discovery in June of 1851. Although other finds soon diverted interest from Clunes, there are still many fine buildings as reminders of the golden riches that were unearthed in the surrounding areas. There is also a small museum, the **William Barkell Arts & Historic Centre**, in a double-storey bluestone building at 36 Fraser St.

The small hills around Clunes are extinct volcanoes. Nearby **Mt Beckworth** is noted for its orchids and birdlife, and you can visit the old gold diggings of **Jerusalem** and **Ullina**.

Places to Stay

The ***Clunes Caravan Park*** *(☎ 5345 3278)* in Purcell St has sites starting at $8 and on-site vans and cabins from $30 to $40 a double.

Keebles of Clunes (☎ *5345 3220*) at 114 Bailey St is an elegant period-style guesthouse and gourmet getaway in a restored country pub. There are six guestrooms with en suites, a cosy lounge with an open fire, a sunny dining area and over a hectare of gardens. The B&B tariff ranges from $140 to $190 a double and the restaurant is à la carte and open to the public on Saturday night, with a set menu for guests only on other nights.

TALBOT

Talbot, well off the beaten track and 18km north-west of Clunes, is another old gold mining centre that has been all but abandoned to time. A wander through these quiet and empty streets reveals a wealth of history and some great old buildings, but at times the place resembles a ghost town.

Speaking of ghost towns, all that remains of **Amherst**, another gold-rush centre 5km north-west, are the ruins of a few buildings and a very big cemetery.

Places to Stay & Eat

The *Bull & Mouth* (☎ *5463 2325*), in Ballaarat St, is a fantastic old bluestone pub that has been converted into a well-regarded licensed restaurant and bar. It serves up hearty country food with mains for $20, and is open for dinner Thursday to Sunday and for lunch on Sunday.

The pub also has five cottages set in delightful gardens beside it and ranging in price from $75 to $95 a double.

DAYLESFORD & HEPBURN SPRINGS

• **pop 3300**

Set among the scenic hills, lakes and forests of the central highlands, the delightful twin towns of Daylesford and Hepburn Springs are enjoying a booming revival as the 'spa centre of Victoria'.

The well preserved and restored buildings show the prosperity that visited these towns during the gold rush, as well as the lasting influence of the many Swiss-Italian miners who expertly worked the tunnel mines in the surrounding hills.

The health giving properties of the area's mineral springs were known before gold was discovered here, and by the 1870s Daylesford was a popular health resort, attracting droves of fashionable Melburnians. It was claimed that the waters could cure any complaint, and the spas and relaxed scenic environment could rejuvenate even the most stressed-out 19th-century city-dweller.

The current trend towards healthy lifestyles has prompted a revival of interest in Daylesford/Hepburn Springs. The restored spa complex is again a popular relaxation and rejuvenation centre, and the towns also boast masseurs, craft and antique shops, gardens, galleries, excellent cafes and restaurants, and dozens of charming guesthouses, cottages and B&Bs.

As well as attracting regular visitors from Melbourne, this area is also an increasingly popular place for escapees from the city rat race, and the population is made up of an interesting blend of alternative-lifestylers and old-timers. There's also a thriving gay and lesbian scene.

Orientation & Information

Daylesford is the larger of the two towns, set around the pretty Lake Daylesford. Its two main streets are Raglan St (the Midland Highway; A300) and Vincent St, which is the main shopping and eating precinct.

Hepburn Springs is a delightful residential settlement just north of Daylesford, centred largely around the spa resort (see the following entry). The twin towns are connected by 'urban sprawl'.

The Daylesford Visitor Information Centre (☎ 5348 1339) is next to the post office on Vincent St; it's open daily from 9 am to 5 pm. The lovely staff here are very knowledgable about the area.

Warning

It's not advisable to drink water from the taps in this area or you could catch a bug. The problem's being rectified at the time of writing, and tap water should be drinkable by the end of 1999 – check with the Visitor Information Centre to be sure. Of course, you can always fill up bottles with water from the mineral springs at the Hepburn spa resort.

Spa Resort

The modern Hepburn Spa Resort (☎ 5348 2034) in the Mineral Springs Reserve is an impressive relaxation and rejuvenation centre with a wide range of services, including heated spas, plunge pools, floatation tanks, beauty treatments, massages and saunas. A splash around in the indoor pool and spa costs $9, aero spas with essential oils cost $21/30 for singles/doubles, massages start at $36 for half an hour and floatation tanks are $50 an hour (weekend rates). This place gets pretty packed on weekends, so prices are lower during the week.

The complex is open weekdays from 10 am to 8 pm and weekends from 9 am to 8 pm.

Things to See & Do

There are some wonderful long and short **walking trails** around both Daylesford and Hepburn Springs, to and from places like Sailors Falls, Tipperary Springs and the Central Springs Reserve – the Visitor Information Centre has maps and walking guides.

Daylesford's most popular attraction is the **Convent Gallery**, a massive 19th-century convent brilliantly converted into a craft and art gallery and set in lovely gardens, with a great cafe (see Places to Eat, later in this section). The gallery is in Daly St on Wombat Hill, opens daily from 10 am to 6 pm and admission costs $3.

The lovely **Wombat Hill Botanic Gardens**, on top of the hill in Central Springs Rd, are well worth a visit. There's a great picnic area and you can climb to the top of a lookout tower which has fine views of the surrounding countryside.

Lake Daylesford is a popular fishing and picnic area close to the centre of town; boats and kayaks are available for hire. Even prettier is **Jubilee Lake**, about 3km south-east of town, another good picnic spot where you can hire canoes. There's also a kiosk and campground by the lake.

There's an excellent **Historical Society Museum** beside the fire station at 100 Vincent St, which is open weekends and during school holidays from 1.30 to 4.30 pm. Entry is $2.50 for adults, 50c for kids.

The **Central Highlands Tourist Railway** (☎ 5348 3503) operates rides on old railway trolleys and restored trains along the line that used to connect Daylesford with Carlsruhe on the main Melbourne-to-Bendigo line. Trips leave from the Daylesford train station five times every Sunday between 10 am and 2.45 pm and cost $5 for adults, $3 for kids and $16 for families. Also on Sunday at the train station, the **Daylesford Sunday Market** is held between 8 am and 2 pm.

The extinct volcanic crater of **Mt Franklin** is 10km north of Daylesford and quite 'otherworldly', with lush vegetation and exotic trees. There are walking trails and a beautiful picnic area here, and a lookout at the summit.

Activities

Daylesford and Hepburn Springs are all about health, relaxation and the inner-self. As well as the spa complex, you'll find plenty of local operators offering traditional massage, reiki, shiatsu, spiritual healing, tarot readings and all sorts of other services. There's a brochure available at the Visitor Information Centre listing many of the town's healers.

The Hepburn Springs Golf Club (☎ 5348 2185) out on Golf Links Rd is a very pleasant 18-hole public course.

There are also numerous walking trails, including the new Great Dividing Trail between here and Castlemaine; Parks Victoria has information.

Horse lovers could head to the Boomerang Holiday Ranch (☎ 5348 2525) on Tipperary Springs Rd, 1km west of Daylesford, which runs leisurely one-hour trail rides in the state forest for $15. This place also has accommodation – see Places to Stay following.

Places to Stay

Between them, Daylesford and Hepburn Springs have a tremendous range of excellent

GOLDFIELDS

accommodation – at last count there were more than 3500 tourist beds available. It's impossible to list every place so check with the helpful Visitor Information Centre for other options or contact the Daylesford Accommodation Booking Service (☎ 5348 1448), although this service hasn't exactly received glowing reports from travellers. If you're after a self-contained cottage, try booking through the well-regarded Daylesford Cottage Directory (☎ 5348 1255) which manages more than 50 cottages in the area.

Unfortunately, there isn't too much in the way of budget accommodation here, apart from the caravan parks and an alternative guesthouse in Hepburn Springs.

Due to the area's booming popularity, it can be difficult to find somewhere to stay on weekends and during holiday periods, so make sure you book ahead. Also, bear in mind that most places stipulate a minimum two-night stay on weekends.

Daylesford The ***Jubilee Lake Caravan Park*** *(☎ 5348 2186)*, beside Lake Jubilee, 3km south-east of Daylesford, has tent sites starting at $9 and on-site cabins from $35 to $70. There's also the ***Victoria Caravan Park*** *(☎ 5348 3821)*, 1.5km south on the Ballan road.

The ***Boomerang Holiday Ranch*** *(☎ 5348 2525)*, 1km west on Tipperary Springs Rd, is a ranch-style horse-riding farm. Its bunkroom accommodation (BYO linen) is popular with families and school groups. The nightly tariff is $75 for adults and $35 to $45 for kids, which includes horse-riding and three meals a day.

Daylesford has some excellent small B&Bs. Romantic ***Pendower House*** *(☎ 5348 1535, 10 Bridport St)*, a beautifully restored Victorian-era home, is one of the best. Doubles range in price from $120 to $160. ***Ambleside B&B*** *(☎ 5348 2691, 15 Leggatt St)* is a restored Victorian cottage overlooking Lake Daylesford. It has three bedrooms with en suites – be sure to ask for one with a view – and B&B ranges from $135 to $185 a double.

Double Nut Guesthouse *(☎ 5348 3981, 5 Howe St)* is excellent value. It comprises four very spacious and tasteful suites, each with its own kitchenette (microwave, but no stove). Tariffs are $80 to $100 a double, including a light breakfast.

For a splurge, try ***Lake House*** *(☎ 5348 3329)* in King St, a cluster of stylish and modern units near the lakeside. There's a guest lounge, tennis court and spa/sauna room, and it's just a short walk from the popular restaurant of the same name. The tariff ranges from $90 to $145 per person per night, including breakfast.

If you're after a motel, try the ***Central Springs Inn*** *(☎ 5348 3134, corner Howe and Camp Sts)* where you have a choice of old-fashioned rooms in the 1875 Provender Store building or modern units at the back; doubles range from $85 (standard) to $150 (spa and fireplace room).

Pete's Palace *(☎ 5348 6531)*, a fantastic bush hideaway about 5km out of town along the Ballan Rd is ideal for budgeteers. The self-contained 'shack' is no Hilton but it's cute and cosy and has excellent views of the Hepburn Regional Park. It sleeps five people and costs $13 per person, or you can rent the whole cottage for $50 a night. It's a good idea to ring for directions or, if you are carless, the lovely owners can pick you up in town.

Hepburn Springs The rambling ***Continental House*** *(☎ 5348 2005, 9 Lone Pine Ave)* is an old timber guesthouse with a laid-back alternative vibe, a vegan cafe serving excellent buffets on Saturday nights ($10), a superb open-verandah sitting room and a music room. A bed for the night costs between $12 and $20 (BYO linen).

The charming 1930s ***Springs Hotel*** *(☎ 5348 2202, 124 Main Rd)* has good rooms upstairs with superb shared bathrooms from a bygone era for $55/65 a single/double.

Mooltan Guesthouse *(☎ 5348 3555, 129 Main Rd)* is an inviting, friendly place with a terrific topiary hedge and broad verandahs overlooking the Mineral Springs Reserve. Midweek B&B singles/doubles cost from $50/75 (shared bathroom), or weekend packages start at $170/240, including two

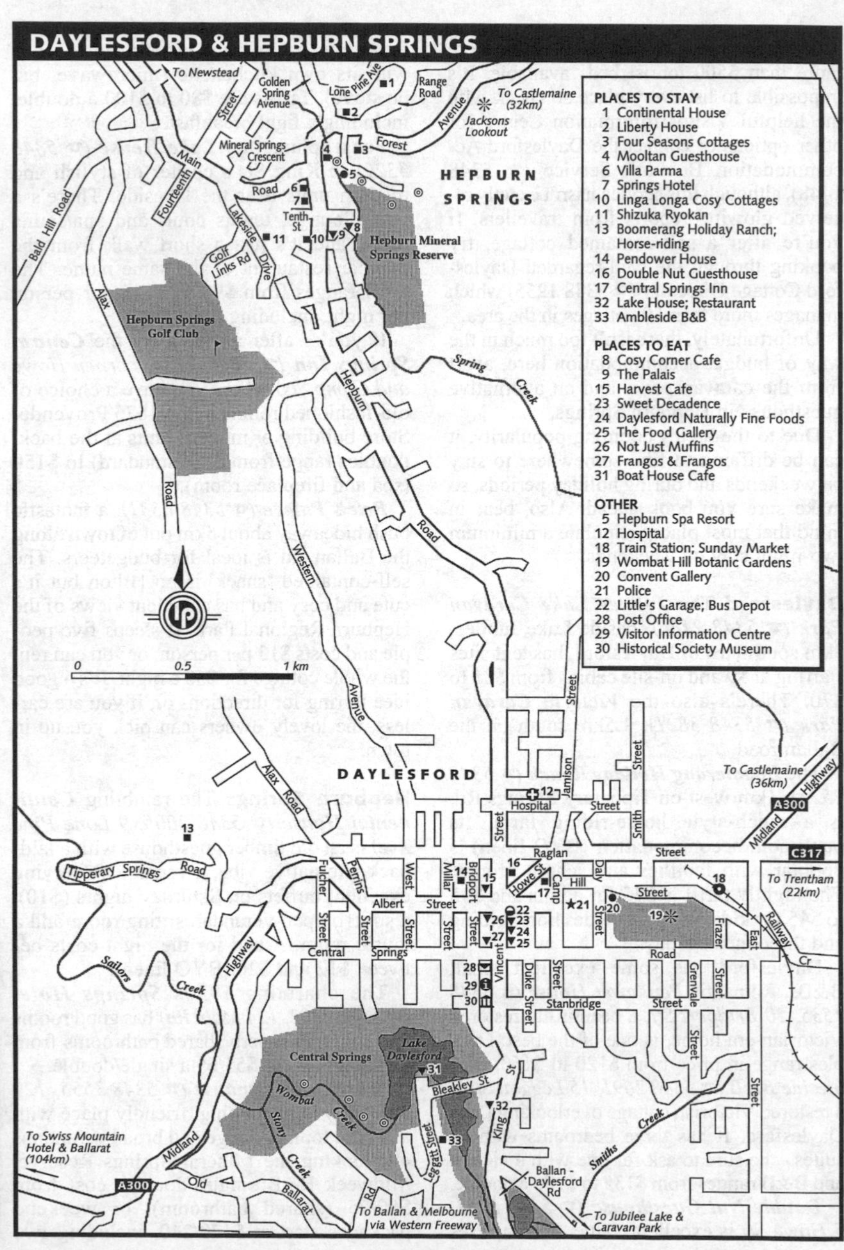
DAYLESFORD & HEPBURN SPRINGS
PLACES TO STAY
1 Continental House
2 Liberty House
3 Four Seasons Cottages
4 Mooltan Guesthouse
6 Villa Parma
7 Springs Hotel
10 Linga Longa Cosy Cottages
11 Shizuka Ryokan
13 Boomerang Holiday Ranch; Horse-riding
14 Pendower House
16 Double Nut Guesthouse
17 Central Springs Inn
32 Lake House; Restaurant
33 Ambleside B&B
PLACES TO EAT
8 Cosy Corner Cafe
9 The Palais
15 Harvest Cafe
23 Sweet Decadence
24 Daylesford Naturally Fine Foods
25 The Food Gallery
26 Not Just Muffins
27 Frangos & Frangos
31 Boat House Cafe
OTHER
5 Hepburn Spa Resort
12 Hospital
18 Train Station; Sunday Market
19 Wombat Hill Botanic Gardens
20 Convent Gallery
21 Police
22 Little's Garage; Bus Depot
28 Post Office
29 Visitor Information Centre
30 Historical Society Museum
To Newstead
Golden Spring Avenue
Lone Pine Ave
Range Road
To Castlemaine (32km)
Jacksons Lookout
Forest Avenue
Mineral Springs Crescent
Main Street
Fourteenth Street
Bald Hill Road
Road
Lakeside Drive
Tenth St
Golf Links Rd
HEPBURN SPRINGS
Hepburn Mineral Springs Reserve
Hepburn Springs Golf Club
Ajax Road
Spring Creek
Hepburn Road
Western Avenue
0
0.5
1 km
DAYLESFORD
Ajax Road
Jamison Street
Smith Street
Street
To Castlemaine (36km)
Midland Highway
A300
Hospital
Street
Raglan Street
C317
Tipperary Springs Road
Fulcher Street
Perrins Street
West Street
Millar Street
Bridport Street
Howe St
Camp Hill
Daly Street
To Trentham (22km)
Albert Street
Street
Vincent Street
Frazer Street
East Street
Railway Cr
Highway
Central Springs
Road
Sailors Creek
Duke Street
Stanbridge Street
Grenvale Street
Street
Central Springs
Lake Daylesford
Bleakley St
King St
Wombat Creek
Stony Creek
Smiths Creek
To Swiss Mountain Hotel & Ballarat (104km)
Midland
A300
Old Ballarat Rd
Leggatt Street
Ballan - Daylesford Rd
To Ballan & Melbourne via Western Freeway
To Jubilee Lake & Caravan Park
GOLDFIELDS

breakfasts and a three-course dinner. ***Liberty House*** *(☎ 5348 2809, 20 Mineral Springs Cres)* is an English-style guesthouse with bright rooms. B&B ranges from $40 to $50 for singles and $75 to $100 for doubles.

If you're driving along Main Rd and suddenly think you're in Tuscany, you've probably just driven past ***Villa Parma*** *(☎ 5348 3512)*. Set in cottage gardens, this evocative pensione is crammed with antiques and charisma. There are three guestrooms all sharing one bathroom; B&B costs from $120 to $160 a double.

Another unique place is ***Shizuka Ryokan*** *(☎ 5348 2030, Lakeside Drv)*, which is inspired by ryokan inns, traditional places of renewal and rejuvenation in Japan. This serene, minimalist getaway has guestrooms complete with private Japanese gardens, tatami matting, rice paper shoji screens and plenty of green tea. Weekend packages cost $540 a double, including two breakfasts (Japanese or Australian) and dinner in the central dining area. Remember to leave your shoes at the door.

If you're after a self-contained cottage, try the ***Four Seasons Cottages*** *(☎ 5348 1221, 3 Forest Ave)*, two and three-bedroom Victorian cottages ideally situated close to the spa resort. There's a two-night minimum, and they range from $170 to $250 for two nights, depending on the cottage. Also good are the ***Linga Longa Cosy Cottages*** *(☎ 5348 3317, 112 Main Rd)*, which sleep between two and 10 people and start at $220 a double for a weekend stay.

Places to Eat

Daylesford Daylesford's Vincent St has plenty of good eateries. ***Daylesford Naturally Fine Foods***, a wholefoods shop at No 59, is good value for lunch with filling fare such as sandwiches and rolls, chilli-bean pies and vegetable pasties. At No 57 is the appropriately named ***Sweet Decadence***, a tiny cafe with good food and, of course, great cakes and chocolates. At No 77 ***The Food Gallery*** is an excellent gourmet deli with a tantalising array of delicacies on offer.

Around the corner on Albert St, ***Not Just Muffins*** is a bakery that is famous (or should be!) for its sensational home-made muffins and shortcakes. The ***Harvest Cafe*** *(☎ 5348 3994)*, across the road at 29 Albert St, is a terrific place that serves up innovative vegetarian and 'aquatic' cuisine using biodynamic and organic produce. Evening mains are in the $10 to $14 range. The cafe is closed on Tuesday and Wednesday.

The popular ***Convent Gallery*** in Daly St has a sunny Mediterranean-style cafe which serves light lunches as well as morning and afternoon teas to the visiting hordes. The views are great and you can tuck into soup, focaccia, pasta, cakes and pastries, ranging in price from $5 to $13.

Daylesford's most upmarket restaurant is the ***Lake House*** *(☎ 5348 3329)*, where you can dine in stylish surrounds with a fine view over Lake Daylesford. This licensed restaurant is among the best in the state. Main meals are around $25 (lunch and dinner) and on Saturday night there's a fixed price three-course menu at $58 a head.

Set in an old boatshed extending out over the lake, the ***Boat House Cafe*** *(☎ 5348 1387)* is another very popular local cafe/restaurant. The setting is particularly appealing, and it's a great place for a meal, especially when it's warm enough to eat outdoors. Mains range from $12 to $15 at lunch, and from $14 to $19 at dinner – you'll need to book on weekends.

Back in the main street is the fabulous ***Frangos & Frangos*** *(☎ 5348 2363)*, well up there with the top restaurants/cafes in the state. This newish coffee palace, wine bar and restaurant, with its terrific food, service and atmosphere, is bound to become an institution. Mains are in the $14 to $25 range and it's open all day, every day.

The ***Swiss Mountain Hotel***, 12km west of town on the Midland Hwy, is a charming and historic little pub with a cosy restaurant out the back. Stop in for a thirst-quencher if you're motoring past.

Hepburn Springs The (very) ***Cosy Corner Cafe*** *(☎ 5348 3825)* in Tenth St is an inviting BYO and licensed cafe/restaurant. It caters well for vegetarians and carnivores alike, with dishes such as stir-fried tofu with Asian greens, warm tempeh salad, fillet steaks, and pasta dishes with vegetarian, fish and red-meat sauces. It's open for breakfast, lunch and dinner on weekends and from Thursday to Monday for dinner only. Evening mains range between $15 and $19.

The Palais *(☎ 5348 1254, 111 Main Rd)* is a dazzlingly refurbished and atmospheric 1920s theatre with a restaurant, cafe and cocktail bar. It's open for lunch, dinner and everything in between from Thursday to Monday, with evening mains around the $20 mark. After dinner, you can relax in lush lounge chairs, play pool or even have a boogie – there's live (mostly) jazz and blues music every Friday, Saturday and Sunday night. Not to be missed.

Getting There & Away

There are daily buses connecting Daylesford with the train station at Woodend ($4.30), from where you can continue to/from Melbourne by train. The Melbourne-Daylesford trip takes about two hours; the economy/1st-class fares are $12.20/15.60.

V/Line also has weekday buses to Ballarat ($8.60), Castlemaine ($4.30) and Bendigo ($8.60). The buses run from Little's garage at 45 Vincent St.

Getting Around

A shuttle bus runs back and forth between Daylesford and Hepburn Springs four times a day (weekdays only).

Daylesford Bicycle Hire (☎ 5348 1518) at 121 Vincent St has mountain bikes for hire, and can deliver them to wherever you're staying.

DAYLESFORD TO MALMSBURY

Glenlyon, a sleepy hollow 12km north-east of Daylesford along the scenic Daylesford-to-Malmsbury road, is a tiny settlement with its own mineral spring. The ***Glenlyon General Store*** *(☎ 5348 7519)* has two simple, self-contained, motel-style cabins which cost from $50 to $70 a double.

Signposted 1km north-east of Glenlyon is the magnificent ***Holcombe Homestead Country Retreat*** *(☎ 5348 7514)*, a grand country homestead built in 1891 on a large sheep property. It's been meticulously restored and elegantly furnished with period antiques and is fully self-contained. The facilities available here include a pool, tennis court and trout-stocked dam, and the tariff is $350 for a weekend for two ($45 a night per extra person). The lovely owners have also built ***Holcombe Lodge Country Retreat*** nearby, another good self-contained option. It's a modern, luxurious house with impressive stonework. A weekend for two costs $400.

Nearby, on Porcupine Ridge Road (off the Daylesford-to-Malmsbury road), is the exceptional new ***Tarascon Village*** *(☎ 5348 7773)*, a cluster of superbly decorated self-contained cottages in a peaceful country setting, reminiscent of an Amish village. Each cottage is fitted with modern facilities and has its own character and personal touches. Tariffs range from $130 to $160 a double, including breakfast. There's also a licensed cafe on the property.

Cliston Farm *(☎ 5423 9155)* is a host farm signposted about 7km south-west of Malmsbury, offering a simple cottage with all the modern facilities and great valley views. Prices start at $130 a night for four people.

YANDOIT

Yandoit, in picturesque surrounds about 22km north of Daylesford off the Newstead Rd, was settled by Swiss Italians during the gold-rush era. A few historic buildings remain in the town, and the surrounding area is scattered with the ruins and remains of what was once a bustling settlement.

A little further north on the Yandoit Creek Rd, the ***Jajarawong Country Cottages*** *(☎ 5476 4362)* is an attractive 29 hectare bush property, with five self-contained cottages built from mud brick, stone, timber and iron. There's no electricity (gas lights) and no TV; just the sound of the birds in the trees – a great escape. The tariff ranges from $80 to $90 a double, plus $20 per extra adult and there's a two night minimum stay.

CASTLEMAINE

• pop 6700

Settlement of this district dates back to the 1830s when most of the land was taken up for farming. The discovery of gold at Specimen Gully in 1851, however, radically altered the pastoral landscape as 30,000 diggers worked a number of goldfields known, collectively, as the Mt Alexander Diggings.

The town that grew up around the government camp at the junction of Barker's and Forest creeks was named Castlemaine in 1853, and soon became the thriving marketplace for all the goldfields of central Victoria.

Castlemaine's importance was not to last, however, as the district did not have the rich quartz reefs that were found in Bendigo and Ballarat. The centre of the town has been virtually unaltered since the 1860s when the population began to decline as the surface gold was exhausted.

These days Castlemaine is a charming and relaxed country town, home to a diverse group of artists, with the legacy of its rapid rise to prosperity evident in its splendid architecture and gardens.

Its diverse claims to fame include being the original home of the Castlemaine XXXX beer-brewing company (now based in Queensland), producing 'Castlemaine Rock', a popular sweet dating back to the gold-rush days, and being the 'Street Rod Centre of Australia', building hotrods since 1962.

Information

The Visitor Information Centre (☎ 5470 6200), located in the magnificent Castlemaine Market building on Mostyn St (see later entry under Other Attractions), is open daily from 9 am to 5 pm. The friendly staff will help you sift through the reams of literature on the region, which includes useful information on historic town walks and vehicle tours.

Buda Historic Home & Garden

Dating from 1861, Buda, on the corner of Hunter and Urquhart Sts, combines interesting architectural styles of the original Indian villa influence and the later Edwardian-style extensions. Home to a Hungarian silversmith and his family for 120 years, the house has permanent displays of the family's extensive art and craft collections, furnishings and personal belongings. The impressive gardens feature a massive clipped cypress hedge. It's open from 9 am to 5 pm, and admission is (a rather steep) $7 for adults and $3 for children.

Castlemaine Art Gallery & Historical Museum

This impressive gallery in a superb Art Deco building in Lyttleton Street, has a collection of colonial and contemporary Australian art, including work by well-known Australian artists such as Frederick McCubbin and Russell Drysdale. The museum in the basement provides a unique insight into the history of the region. Opening hours are from 10 am to 5 pm, Monday to Friday, and noon to 5 pm on weekends. Admission is $3 for adults and $7 for families.

Castlemaine Botanical Gardens

These majestic gardens, among the oldest in Victoria, strike a perfect balance between sculpture and wilderness. This is an excellent spot for 'getting back to nature', assisted by the many awe-inspiring National Trust-registered trees. Electric barbecues are available, along with a rather misplaced children's plastic playground. The main entrance is on Walker St.

The Old Castlemaine Gaol

This imposing sandstone building provides excellent views of the town from a hilltop on Bowden St. There's a lingering eerie atmosphere to the place despite the tourist overkill. Guided tours of the gaol are available on weekends and public holidays at 11 am, 1 and 3 pm and cost $4/2 for adults/children. And if you'd like to do some time, see the Places to Stay section.

Other Attractions

The **Castlemaine Market**, the town's original market building on Mostyn St, is fronted with a classical Roman basilica facade with a statue of Ceres, the Roman goddess of harvesting, perched on top. This magnificent space is home to the Visitor Information Centre, a diggings interpretive display, a kiosk and shire offices and is also used for functions.

An institution in itself, **The Restorers Barn** in Mostyn St is chock full of interesting bric-a-brac for sale. It's open from 9 am to 5.30 pm daily, and is an ideal place to while away an hour or five.

There are more attractions in the surrounding area, see the Around Castlemaine section in this chapter.

Special Events

Every odd-numbered year the town hosts two festivals. The State Festival in April is one of Victoria's leading arts events, featuring theatre, music, art and dance programmes. During the Garden Festival, held in November, over 50 green-fingered locals open their properties to the public. Booking accommodation in advance is essential if you plan to visit during either of these festivals.

Places to Stay

Accommodation choices around this area are numerous – we can't list every place so check with the tourist centre for other options. The Mount Alexander Shire Council provides a free accommodation booking service (☎ 5470 5866).

Camping & Caravan Parks The ***Botanic Gardens Caravan Park*** *(☎ 5472 1125, Walker St)*, ideally situated next to the gardens and public swimming pool, has camping sites available from $10 and on-site vans from $31.

Hotels The ***Commercial Hotel*** *(☎ 5472 1173, corner Forest and Hargreaves Sts)* has basic rooms for $30/45 a single/double. Away from the town centre, the ***Northern Hotel*** *(☎ 5472 1102, 359 Barker St)* offers singles/doubles for $20/30.

Motels The impressive facade of ***Campbell St Motor Lodge*** *(☎ 5472 3477, 33 Campbell St)*, in an inviting National Trust-classified building dating from 1886, belies a relatively bland interior. However, it is a pleasant place to stay, with doubles ranging from $65 to $85 and family units for $115.

Castlemaine Colonial Motel *(☎ 5472 4000, 252 Barker St)* has more traditional motel accommodation, with singles/doubles from $66/76.

Guesthouses & B&Bs The quality, quantity and diversity of B&B-style accommodation in town is impressive. The ***Midland Private Hotel*** *(☎ 5472 1085, 2-4 Templeton St)*, which has been sheltering travellers since 1879, features a magnificent Art Deco entrance foyer and dining room, and a Victorian club-style lounge with two open fireplaces and a belvedere ceiling. Singles/doubles are great value for $60/90 (shared bathrooms), including breakfast, which may come with homemade ricotta cheese courtesy of the friendly Sicilian owner.

The recently opened pseudo-French provincial ***Yellow House*** *(☎ 5472 3368, 95 Lyttleton St)* is another delightful place. Perched high on a hill, its one twin and two double rooms have excellent views of the town. B&B costs $90/120 on weekdays/weekends. It also houses a contemporary art gallery and studio of the lovely resident artist.

Looming over the town, ***The Old Castlemaine Gaol*** *(☎ 5470 5311, Bowden St, corner Charles St)* has B&B accommodation in converted cells for $45 per person, or $65 with dinner as well. ***Broadoaks*** *(☎ 5470 5827, 31 Gingell St)* was the last home of the famous Australian explorer Robert O'Hara Burke, who was superintendent of police in Castlemaine before setting out in 1860 on his ill-fated journey from Melbourne to the Gulf of Carpentaria. Doubles are available for $85, including breakfast.

The tastefully renovated garden cottage on the property of ***Barrington*** *(☎ 5470 5163, 162 Hargreaves St)*, a splendid Victorian-style residence, offers seclusion for

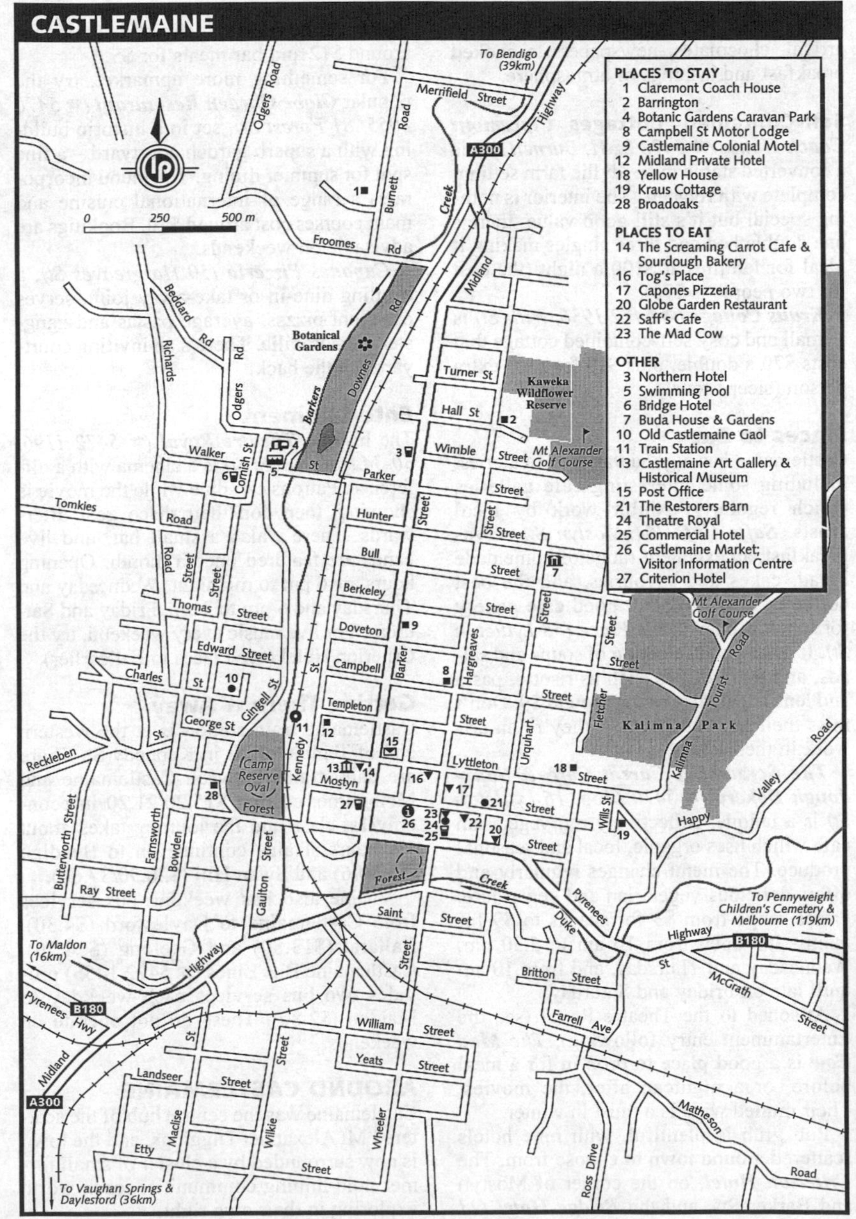
CASTLEMAINE
PLACES TO STAY
1 Claremont Coach House
2 Barrington
4 Botanic Gardens Caravan Park
8 Campbell St Motor Lodge
9 Castlemaine Colonial Motel
12 Midland Private Hotel
18 Yellow House
19 Kraus Cottage
28 Broadoaks
PLACES TO EAT
14 The Screaming Carrot Cafe & Sourdough Bakery
16 Tog's Place
17 Capones Pizzeria
20 Globe Garden Restaurant
22 Saff's Cafe
23 The Mad Cow
OTHER
3 Northern Hotel
5 Swimming Pool
6 Bridge Hotel
7 Buda House & Gardens
10 Old Castlemaine Gaol
11 Train Station
13 Castlemaine Art Gallery & Historical Museum
15 Post Office
21 The Restorers Barn
24 Theatre Royal
25 Commercial Hotel
26 Castlemaine Market; Visitor Information Centre
27 Criterion Hotel
To Bendigo (39km)
To Pennyweight Children's Cemetery & Melbourne (119km)
To Maldon (16km)
To Vaughan Springs & Daylesford (36km)
0 250 500 m
A300
B180
Botanical Gardens
Kaweka Wildflower Reserve
Mt Alexander Golf Course
Kalimna Park
Camp Reserve Oval
Forest
Merrifield Street
Froomes Rd
Barkers Creek
Downes Rd
Midland Highway
Pyrenees Hwy
Tourist Road
Happy Valley Road
Duke St
McGrath Street
Matheson Road
Ross Drive
Farrell Ave
Britton Street

GOLDFIELDS

$85 to $100. This includes a bite to eat on arrival, chocolates, newspapers, a cooked breakfast and lashings of atmosphere.

Self-Contained Cottages ***Claremont Coach House*** *(☎ 5472 2281, Burnett Rd)* is a converted stable in an idyllic farm setting, complete with roosters. The interior is nothing special but it's still good value: there's one double bed and three singles making it ideal for families at $100 a night (the cost for two people is $70).

Kraus Cottage *(☎ 5472 1936, Wills St)* is a small and cosy self-contained cottage that costs $70 a double, plus $10 for each extra person (sleeps four).

Places to Eat

Castlemaine has a good variety of eateries, including some interesting cafe galleries which regularly exhibit work by local artists. ***Saffs Cafe*** *(64 Mostyn St)* serves breakfast, an excellent range of homemade bread, cakes and savouries, and the best coffee in town. Another good cafe gallery for lunch is cosy ***Tog's Place*** *(58 Lyttleton St)*. It has a good selection of soups and salads, and main dishes such as risotto, pasta and lentil dhal, all costing around $9. Don't miss their hot chocolates – they're an artwork in themselves.

The Screaming Carrot Cafe & Sourdough Bakery *(☎ 5470 6555, 16 Lyttleton St)* is a unique, collectively run vegetarian cafe which uses organic, local and seasonal produce. The menu changes regularly and offers delicious vegetarian and vegan fare. Prices range from $3 for snacks to $9 for mains. It's open from 10 am to 5.30 pm, Wednesday and Thursday, and from 10 am until late on Friday and Saturday.

Attached to the Theatre Royal (see the Entertainment entry following), ***The Mad Cow*** is a good place to drop in for a meal before, or a nightcap after, the movies. Their mulled wine is a must in winter.

Pub grub is plentiful, with nine hotels scattered around town to choose from. The ***Criterion Hotel***, on the corner of Mostyn and Barker Sts, and the ***Bridge Hotel*** *(21 Walker St)* both offer bistro-style mains for around $12 and bar meals for $5.

For something more upmarket, try the popular ***Globe Garden Restaurant*** *(☎ 5470 5055, 81 Forest St)*, set in a historic building with a superb garden courtyard – a fine spot for summer dining. The menu incorporates a range of international cuisine and main courses cost around $20. Bookings are advisable on weekends.

Capones Pizzeria *(50 Hargreaves St)*, a bustling dine-in or take-away joint, serves excellent pizzas, average pastas and gangster memorabilia. There's an inviting courtyard out the back.

Entertainment

The historic ***Theatre Royal*** *(☎ 5472 1196, 30-34 Hargreaves St)* is a cinema with a difference. Patrons can dine while the movie is showing, then don their disco gear afterwards. There's also a small bar, and live bands are featured once a month. Opening hours are 6 pm to midnight, Wednesday and Thursday and 6 pm to 3 am, Friday and Saturday. For live music every weekend, try the Criterion Hotel (see Places to Eat earlier).

Getting There & Away

Castlemaine train station is at the western end of Templeton St in Kennedy St. There are daily trains between Castlemaine and Melbourne, costing $15.20/21.20 in economy/1st class and the journey takes about 1¾ hours. Trains continue on to Bendigo ($4.30/6) and Swan Hill ($26.90/37.60).

V/Line also has weekday bus services from Castlemaine to Daylesford ($4.30), Ballarat ($13.80) and Geelong ($24.50). Castlemaine Bus Lines (☎ 5472 1455) provides two bus services each weekday to Maldon ($2.80). These do not operate on weekends.

AROUND CASTLEMAINE

Castlemaine was the central hub of the scattered Mt Alexander Diggings, and the town is now surrounded by a cluster of small former gold-mining communities, each worth exploring in their own right.

Off the road heading south-east to Chewton is the sombre **Pennyweight Children's Cemetery**, a small cluster of tiny graves of children who died during the gold-rush years. **Chewton** is a charming and historic township, with some interesting antique and bric-a-brac shops along the main street and a very sweet town hall. Nearby, you can visit the **Forest Creek Historic Gold Mine**, which has tours on weekends from 1 to 4 pm for $7.50. One kilometre north of the town is **Garfield's Water Wheel**, the remains of Victoria's largest water wheel, which provided power for an ore-crusher at the Garfield Mine. Also near Chewton is the **Dingo Farm**, which gives you an opportunity to learn a little more about this much maligned creature. It opens daily from 9 am to 6 pm; entry costs $5 ($2 for kids).

It's a pretty drive south from Chewton to **Fryerstown**, another historic settlement. Here you'll find the **Heron's Reef Gold Diggings**, a former mine site that has been preserved and has examples of the different methods used for extracting gold as well as old miners' huts and other relics. Tours of the diggings are conducted on Saturday at 2 pm and Sunday at 10 am and 2 pm, and cost $10 for adults and $5 for kids.

Vaughan Springs, about 10km south along the Midland Hwy is also worth a visit, and has its own mineral springs and swimming hole and some great walking tracks. The turn-off is at Yapeen.

Turner's Horsefarm (☎ 5476 4288), off the Midland Hwy 16km from Castlemaine on the road to Daylesford, takes trail rides through the nearby state forest for $30 for two hours (see also the following Places to Stay entry).

Places to Stay

Tranquil Valley *(☎ 5472 2118 Hoopers Rd Chewton)* is a delightful cottage attached to a historic farmhouse. The farm is in an idyllic little valley, and this self-contained cottage costs from $75 to $85 a double. It's a bit tricky to find, so best to phone for directions.

Sage Cottage B&B *(☎ 5473 4322)* in Fryerstown, is a charmingly restored two-bedroom miner's cottage with a good view of the surrounding bushland. B&B costs from $85 to $95 a double.

At Guildford, on the Midland Hwy 16km south of Castlemaine, is the resplendent ***Tara*** *(☎ 5473 4205)*, a lovely old homestead, set in magnificent gardens, with two tastefully decked-out cottages available. They cost $110 a double, with breakfast provisions included. The gardens are also open to the public from 10 am to 5 pm from March to May, and September to November ($4).

A little further south on the Midland Hwy, ***Turner's Horse Farm*** *(☎ 5476 4288)* has a simple and rustic two-room cabin out in a paddock, with an open fire, gas lights, and outdoor shower and toilet. It has bunks and couches that sleep up to eight, and costs $100 a night.

HARCOURT

• pop 400

Harcourt, the 'Apple Centre of Victoria', is a small town on the Calder Highway (A79) 29km south of Bendigo. It's at the foot of Mt Alexander and has some wineries worth checking out.

On the Melbourne side of town is the **Harcourt Valley Vineyards** in a large building made from local granite (open daily from 11 am to 6 pm), while nearby is the **Blackjack Vineyards** (open weekends and public holidays). Three kilometres north of Harcourt is the **Mt Alexander Winery and Cidery** which, in addition to wine, sells apple ciders, mead and a pear brandy (open daily from 10 am to 5.30 pm).

And of course, you can't go past the delicious, crispy Harcourt apples, with varieties such as Royal Gala, Mutsu, Red Fuji, Pink Lady and Lady Williams. They're available from roadside fruit and vegetable stalls on the highway.

MALDON

• pop 1250

The current population of Maldon is a scant reminder of the 20,000 who used to work the local goldfields. Nevertheless, the whole town is a well-preserved relic of the era with many fine buildings constructed from local stone.

In 1966 the National Trust named Maldon Australia's first 'notable town', an honour given only to towns where the historic architecture was intact and valuable. In fact Maldon was considered so important in the history of Victoria that special planning regulations, the first of their kind in the state, were implemented to preserve the town for posterity. Consequently, the whole town oozes charm and is now a very popular tourist spot.

Information

Maldon Visitor Information Centre (☎ 5475 2569), at the shire offices in High St, is open daily from 9 am to 5 pm.

Things to See & Do

The Visitor Information Centre has a handy *Information Guide* and a *Historic Town Walk* brochure, which guides you past some of the most historic buildings around town and along the verandahed main street. Interesting places include **Dabb's General Store** (now the supermarket); the **Maldon**, **Kangaroo** and **Grand** hotels; the 24m-high **Beehive Chimney**; and the **North British Mine & Kilns**.

Carmen's Tunnel Goldmine is 2km south of town, off Parkin's Reef Rd. The 570m-long tunnel was excavated in the 1880s. It took two years to dig, yet produced only $300 worth of gold. Candle-lit tours through the mine take place on weekends, public holidays and during school holidays between 1.30 and 4 pm and cost $3.50 for adults and $1.50 for kids.

Maldon's train station was built in 1884, but the train service to Castlemaine stopped in 1936. For rail enthusiasts, the local Railway Preservation Society runs **steam-train trips** along the original track into the Muckleford Forest and back. The trips leave on Sunday, public holidays and Wednesday during school holidays at 11.30 am, 1 and 2.30 pm and on other Wednesdays at 11.30 am and 1 pm. The return fare is $10 for adults, $6 for kids and $29 for a family ticket.

The **historical museum** is in the town's former marketplace in High St. It has a large collection of interesting relics from Maldon's past, and is open weekdays from 1.30 to 4.30 pm and on weekends and public holidays from 1.30 to 5 pm.

Nearby, **Mt Tarrangower** has a great lookout tower and good picnic areas and walking tracks. There are other good walks at **Anzac Hill** and in the **Nuggetty Ranges**, 4km north of the town, where you'll also find the historic cemetery.

Porcupine Township, on the Bendigo road 2.5km out of Maldon, is a quaint re-created gold-mining village with original slab buildings. It's open daily from 10 am to 5 pm and costs $7 for adults, $5 for kids and $20 for families.

Cairn Curran Reservoir, 12km south, is large and scenic with good boating, swimming and picnic facilities.

Special Events

Maldon's main event is the excellent Maldon Folk Festival. It's held in early November and features a wide variety of world music. The town also hosts the Maldon Easter Fair.

Places to Stay

There are loads of good places to stay in Maldon. Listed here is a small selection; check with the Visitor Information Centre for other places.

Camping & Caravan Park The ***Maldon Caravan Park*** *(☎ 5475 2344, Hospital St)* has tent sites from $10 and on-site vans and cabins from $29 to $48.

Hostel It's mostly used for youth camps but the architecturally intriguing ***Derby Hill Accommodation Centre*** *(☎ 5475 2033, Phoenix St)* has motel-style rooms (available weekends and school holidays) for $30 per adult per night (children $10).

Motel Even motels in this town have loads of appeal. ***Maldon's Eaglehawk*** *(☎ 5475 2750)* has comfortable units in pleasant grounds, with doubles from $84.

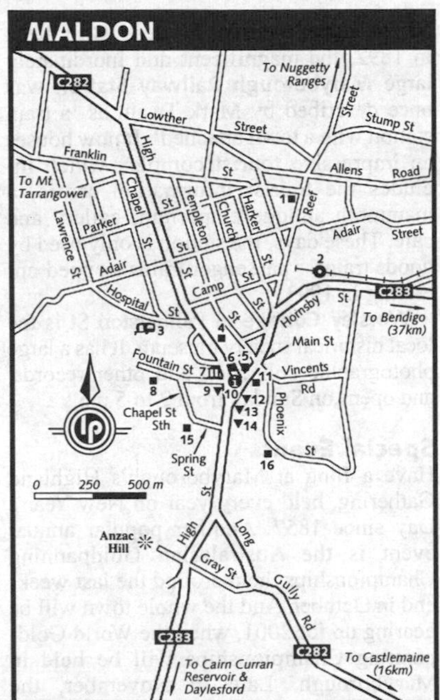

MALDON

PLACES TO STAY
1 Maldon's Eaglehawk
3 Maldon Caravan Park
4 Tressider's Cottage
5 McArthur's B&B & Restaurant
6 Calder House; Ruby's at Calder House
8 The Terraces
11 The Barn & Loft; Cornflowers at the Barn
15 Spring Cottage
16 Derby Hill Accommodation Centre

PLACES TO EAT
9 Kangaroo Hotel
12 Cafe Maldon
13 Berryman's Cafe & Tearooms
14 Cumquat Tree Tearooms

OTHER
2 Maldon Train Station
7 Historical Museum
10 Maldon Visitor Information Centre

Guesthouses & B&Bs The rest of Maldon's accommodation is mainly up-market B&Bs in restored old buildings. There are some very charming and quirky places such as ***The Barn & Loft*** *(☎ 5475 2015, 64 Main St)*, a rustic two-storey barn which has been converted into two guest units. Doubles range from $85 to $95 a night, including breakfast. Next door, owned by the same people, is ***Cornflowers at the Barn*** *(☎ 5475 2015)*, a pretty two-storey, self-contained cottage, ideal for romantic escapes. Doubles range from $130 to $150, including a cooked breakfast.

Other B&Bs include the formal and grand, yet very inviting ***Calder House*** *(☎ 5475 2912, 44 High St)*, with superb features and guestrooms costing from $70/95 to $95/120 a single/double; and ***McArthur's B&B*** *(☎ 5475 2519, 43 Main St)*, behind the restaurant of the same name, with two doubles from $75, including breakfast.

Self-Contained Cottages There are also plenty of self-contained cottages to rent, many of which are managed by Heritage Cottages of Maldon *(☎ 5475 1094)*. One of the best places on their list is the delightful ***Spring Cottage*** *(13 Spring St)*, an idyllic little miner's cottage nestled in pretty gardens, available from $85 to $100 a double (minimum two-night stay on weekends).

Tressider's Cottage *(☎ 9325 4447, High St)* is a larger cottage full of period furniture that sleeps up to eight people. It costs $95 a double (minimum two nights, four people). ***The Terraces*** *(☎ 9818 8512, Fountain St)* sleeps up to four and costs $175 a weekend for a double, with $15 per night for each extra person.

Places to Eat

There are several cafes and tearooms along the main street which serve good afternoon teas and lunches – try ***Berryman's Cafe & Tearooms***, ***Cafe Maldon*** or the quaint ***Cumquat Tree Tearooms***. For a pub meal, head to the ***Kangaroo Hotel*** in High St, which has a cosy bar and excellent bistro, with mains ranging from $9 to $16.

McArthur's (☎ 5475 2519, 43 Main St) is a lovely old-fashioned restaurant with open fires and a garden courtyard. The extensive menu ranges from toasted sandwiches to whole trout; evening mains cost from $13 to $16. The set-menu roasts are good value ($8 for lunch).

Ruby's at Calder House (☎ 5475 2912) is one of the state's best restaurants. Set in an elegant Victorian dining room, its 'creative country cuisine' (as the chef calls it), incorporates fine local produce. Vegetarians are catered for and the delicious mains range from $15 to $20. Make sure you book.

Getting There & Away

Castlemaine Bus Lines (☎ 5472 1455) runs two buses each weekday (none on weekends) between Maldon and Castlemaine ($2.80) which connect with the trains to and from Melbourne. The total journey takes about two hours.

MARYBOROUGH

• pop 7400

The district around Charlotte Plains was already an established sheep run, owned by the Simpson brothers, when gold was discovered at White Hills and Four Mile Flat in 1854. A police camp established at the diggings was named Maryborough, and at the height of the gold rush the population swelled to over 40,000. Gold mining ceased to be economical in 1918 but Maryborough had by then developed a strong manufacturing base and is today one of the district's major industrial and production centres.

Information

Central Goldfields Visitor Information Centre (☎ 5460 4511) is housed in the Maryborough train station complex (see the following Things to See entry), and opens daily from 9 am to 5 pm.

Things to See

Maryborough boasts plenty of impressive Victorian-era buildings, but the local train station leaves them all for dead. Built back in 1892, the magnificent and inordinately large **Maryborough Railway Station** was once described by Mark Twain as 'a train station with a town attached'. It now houses an impressive tourist complex which includes the tourist information centre, a mammoth antique emporium, gallery and cafe. These days, the station is only used by goods trains – passenger trains stopped operating in 1993.

Worsley Cottage in Palmerston St is the local historical society museum. It has a large photographic collection and other records, and opens on Sunday from 2 to 5 pm.

Special Events

Have a fling at Maryborough's Highland Gathering, held every year on New Year's Day since 1857. Another popular annual event is the Australasian Goldpanning Championships, held around the last weekend in October. And the whole town will be gearing up for 2001, when the World Goldpanning Championships will be held in Maryborough. Late in November, the RACV Energy Breakthrough Festival focuses on alternative energy sources and lifestyles, with events such as the low energy grand prix.

Places to Stay

The *Maryborough Caravan Park (☎ 5460 4848, 7 Holyrood St)*, pleasantly situated by a lake, has camping sites for $10 and on-site cabins from $40 to $60.

The historic *Bull & Mouth Hotel (☎ 5461 1002, 119 High St)* has decent pub rooms for $30 a double, or $40 with en suites.

Maryborough has several motels, *Wattle Grove Motel (☎ 5461 1877)*, on the Ballarat road, is the cheapest, with rooms starting at $42/48 a single/double. A bit more up-market is the *Junction Motel (☎ 5461 1744, 2 High St)* with rooms from $55/65.

Bella's Country House B&B (☎ 5460 5574, 39 Burns St) is an impressive red-brick Victorian homestead with a magnificently restored interior, complete with comfy lounges and open fires. The beds are particularly inviting with lashings of white linen. Tariffs range from $90 to $150 a double (less $20 for singles).

Four kilometres south of town on Majorca Rd, ***Davoren*** *(☎ 5461 2934)* is a very sweet mud-brick and stone cottage in a bushy setting – a top hideaway and good value at $70 a double.

Places to Eat

The ***Bull & Mouth Hotel*** on High St is a good place for a pub feed. In the train station complex, ***The Station Cafe*** is an excellent daytime cafe with tasty focaccias, cakes and coffee.

Goldfields *(☎ 5461 3033)*, 2km south on the Ballarat road, is a licensed restaurant in a mud-brick building. It serves up a three-course set menu spit roast for $17 per person, and opens on Saturday night (with live music) and Sunday for lunch.

The ***Moonlight Inn*** *(☎ 5461 4598)*, 5km west of town off the Avoca road, is an excellent BYO French restaurant set in a French-style farmhouse. Entrees are $10 and main meals are around $18. It's signposted but hard to find, so telephone first to get directions. You'll need to book anyway.

Getting There & Away

The trip to/from Melbourne involves a train/bus changeover at either Ballarat or Castlemaine; the one-way fares are $21.90 (economy) and $27.50 (1st class) and the journey takes about three hours.

AVOCA & PYRENEES RANGES

Avoca, with a population of 950, is a small agricultural town and the centre of one of Victoria's most rapidly expanding wine-growing regions. The town, at the junction of the Sunraysia and Pyrenees highways, is the gateway to the nearby Pyrenees Ranges, so named by Major Thomas Mitchell in 1836 because they reminded him of the Spanish Pyrenees. Despite the major's delusions, these mountains are distinctively Australian, and as they are covered by eucalypt forests they take on a blueish tinge in certain light. Mt Avoca, the highest peak, reaches 760m. There are plenty of good walking tracks and waterfalls throughout the ranges, including the 18km Pyrenees Trail, which starts from the Waterfall Picnic Area 7km west of Avoca.

North-west of Avoca are the two tiny hamlets of **Moonambel** and **Redbank**, both relics from the gold-mining era.

Information

There's an information centre (☎ 5465 3767) on the main street next to the post office, open most days (depending on volunteer availability), from 10 am to 4 pm. Pop in and pick up an excellent *The Pyrenees & Grampians Wine Trail* brochure.

Special Events

The annual Pyrenees Vignerons' Gourmet Wine & Food Anzac Day Race Meeting (phew!) on 25 April features local wines and foods, as well as the horses, of course. This is also the home of petanque festivals, with two held every year – over the third weekend in March and the last weekend in November.

Places to Stay

Camping & Caravan Parks The ***Avoca Caravan Park*** *(☎ 5465 3073)*, beside the golf course in Liebig St, has powered sites for $12 and on-site vans from $25.

Hotel & Motel The ***Avoca Hotel*** *(☎ 5465 3018, 115 High St)* has pub rooms for $25/45 a single/double, including a continental breakfast. ***Avoca Pyrenees Motel*** *(☎ 5465 3693, 102 High St)*, possibly Victoria's most welcoming, has themed rooms from $40/$45 a single/double.

B&Bs The ***Old Avoca Vicarage*** *(☎ 5465 3630, 102 Rutherford St)* is a century-old, red-brick house converted into a period-style gourmet getaway. There are two guestrooms and singles/doubles cost from $65/85 for B&B. Dinner can also be arranged for $25 per person.

Also in Rutherford St at No 124, The ***Avoca Heritage School B&B*** *(☎ 5465 3691)* is a renovated old school building with a

Wineries of the Pyrenees Ranges

There are at least eight wineries in and around the Pyrenees Ranges which are open for tastings and sales, and they can all be easily visited in one day. Cycling from winery to winery is a popular way of getting around, but you'll need to be in training – the area is steep and hilly.

The closest winery to Avoca is the **Mt Avoca Vineyard**, at the foot of the mountains in Moates Lane 6km west of the town (open weekdays from 9 am to 5 pm; weekends from 10 am).

The lovely **Blue Pyrenees Estate**, formerly Chateau Remy, is an impressive complex in Vinoca Rd 7km west of Avoca. Set in peaceful gardens with barbecue and picnic areas and a *petanque piste*, it sells the Blue Pyrenees Estate, Leydens Vale, Fiddlers Creek and Columba labels. It's open weekdays from 10 am to 4.30 pm and weekends to 5 pm. Gourmet lunches are available in its restaurant on weekends and public holidays.

From here, head north-west to Moonambel, where you'll find another five wineries in and around the town. **Summerfield Vineyard** has a tasting room on the edge of Moonambel (open daily from 9 am to 6 pm; from 10 am Sunday).

The other wineries are all west of Moonambel and signposted off the Stawell to Avoca road. **Warrenmang** in Mountain Creek Rd is an outstanding winery, restaurant and accommodation complex – see the Places to Stay & Eat sections under Avoca & Pyrenees Ranges in this chapter – and the nearby **Mountain Creek Vineyard** opens on weekends from 10 am to 6 pm.

Taltarni (an Aboriginal word meaning, appropriately, 'red earth') is the largest and oldest of the Moonambel wineries. It's in Taltarni Rd and opens daily from 10 am to 5 pm. Just beyond Taltarni, **Dalwhinnie** is a tiny vineyard in an idyllic valley setting. The tasting room has spectacular views, and this place is particularly noted for its fine chardonnay and shiraz wines (open daily from 10 am to 5 pm).

Redbank, makers of the world-famous Sally's Paddock cabernet wine, is just south of the town of Redbank on the Sunraysia Highway (open daily from 9 am to 5 pm; from 10 am Sunday).

guest wing with three guestrooms costing from $85 to $95 a double.

Winery In the heart of the Pyrenees winery district, about 20km north-west of Avoca, the ***Warrenmang Vineyard*** (☎ *5467 2233)* is a winery with a wonderful restaurant and an accommodation complex of 12 impressive timber cottages. The cottages overlook the vineyards, and each is divided into two heritage-style units with two double bedrooms. Tariffs include dinner, B&B, winery tours and use of the tennis courts, pool and spa and start from $120 per person midweek or from $140 per person on weekends.

Places to Eat

The charming ***Avoca Bakehouse & Cafe***, in an old bank building at 114 High St, offers a good selection of freshly baked goodies. For a pub meal, try the ***Avoca Hotel*** at 115 High St.

The ***Commercial Hotel*** in Moonambel also has good meals, including excellent fixed-price roasts on Saturday night and Sunday lunch ($15 for three courses).

The award-winning restaurant at the ***Warrenmang Vineyard*** (see the preceding Places to Stay entry) is one of the best in Victoria. The dining room is sophisticated but relaxed, with a large open fire in winter and an outlook over a valley filled with vineyards. The food is always superb and imaginative, making use of local produce, including rabbit, yabbies and trout. Lunch is a la carte with main courses in the $14 to $18 range, while dinners can be chosen from a three-course fixed-price menu for $55 per person.

Getting There & Away

V/Line has bus services to Avoca from Melbourne every night (except Saturday) on the overnight bus to Mildura, arriving in Avoca in the wee hours. There's also a train/bus service via Ballarat on Friday. The one-way fare is $21.90. The bus trip takes about four hours; by train and bus it's three hours.

MOLIAGUL, TARNAGULLA & DUNOLLY

The rich alluvial goldfields in this area, around 20km north of Maryborough and known as the Golden Triangle, produced more gold nuggets than any other area in the country, including the world's largest gold nugget, the 65kg Welcome Stranger. The stranger was found in Moliagul in 1869 by John Deason and Richard Oates, who hid it for two days before concealing it in a wagon and taking it to Dunolly, where it was cut into pieces because it was too big to fit on the scales!

Moliagul

Now a tiny, tumbledown village with a scattered collection of old buildings, Moliagul has a memorial near the site of the discovery of the Welcome Stranger nugget. Another memorial in the town commemorates the Reverend John Flynn, founder of the Royal Flying Doctor Service, who was born here in 1880.

Tarnagulla

Tarnagulla also has some interesting architectural relics from the gold-rush days, including an inordinate number of churches and the **Victoria Hotel & Theatre**, a former dance hall and vaudeville theatre. Beside the **Methodist church** there is a memorial recording the discovery of the Poverty Reef, which yielded over 13 tonnes of gold during its life span. The mine was discovered by a Captain Hyatt, who named it after a bay in New Zealand where he was rescued from a shipwreck by a beautiful Maori maiden, with whom he promptly fell in love and married. They are buried together at the cemetery nearby. The town's **historic reserve** features still more churches, and a charming timber pavilion at the local cricket ground.

The ghost town of **Wanyarra**, just south of Tarnagulla, is well worth a visit and has numerous historic sites.

Dunolly

This is the largest of these three towns and also has a few points of interest. The **Goldfields Historical Museum** on Broadway has an interesting collection of mining relics, tools, equipment, weapons and photos, as well as replicas of some of the nuggets found in the area. In front of the museum is the anvil on which the Welcome Stranger was cut up. The museum is open on Sunday and public holidays from 1.30 to 5 pm and is worth a visit.

A shop called **Finders Prospecting Supplies** (☎ 5468 1333), in the main street at 90 Broadway, hires out prospecting equipment and metal detectors, just in case you think the old-timers left anything behind.

Places to Stay

Dunolly *Dunolly Caravan Park (☎ 5468 1262, corner Thompson and Desmond Sts)* has tent sites for $9 and on-site vans from $25. *Golden Triangle Motel (☎ 5468 1166)* on Maryborough Rd has singles/doubles from $45/55.

Tarnagulla The *Golden Triangle Caravan Park (☎ 5438 7329, Poverty St)* has tent sites for $8 and on-site vans and cabins from $25.

ST ARNAUD

• **pop 2650**

This solid country town is bordered by both the mountains and the goldfields. Beyond the town, the barren and flat Mallee district stretches north all the way to Mildura.

St Arnaud's main street, Napier St, is now a heritage precinct and has been classified by the National Trust. The street is lined with old pubs and verandah-fronted shops that date back to the gold-rush days, some looking as though they haven't been touched since the gold ran out and others having been recently restored. There are also plenty of other interesting old buildings scattered around the town, and an extensive lawn tennis complex.

Information

The Visitor Information Centre (☎ 5495 1268) is next to the old post office at 4 Napier St, open from 9 am to 5 pm daily.

Places to Stay & Eat

St Arnaud Caravan Park (☎ 5495 1447) has sites from $10 and on-site cabins from $35.

The ***Old Post Office Tearooms & B&B*** *(☎ 5495 2313, 2 Napier St)* is a solid old building (1866) which has been converted into a tearoom, gallery and B&B. Upstairs, there is cosy accommodation for up to four people, with a private bathroom, a guest lounge and a very pleasant breakfast balcony. The tariff is from $90 to $110 a double, including a fully cooked breakfast.

The tearooms, gallery and info centre downstairs is open daily (except Tuesday) from 11 am to 5 pm. This place has the best food in the area, with freshly baked, home-made goodies like pies, pastries, soups and salads – don't leave town without trying Josephine's famous apple and butterscotch pie. The restaurant opens at night for house guests and by arrangement – which means you need to book.

The historic ***Botanical Hotel*** *(☎ 5495 1336, corner Napier and Inkerman Sts)* with its magnificent cast iron lacework, has pub rooms for $20/30, and is also a great place for some grub with mains around the $12 mark. The ***St Arnaud Hotel*** *(☎ 5495 1004, 20 Napier St)* also has simple pub rooms upstairs at $25/30 for B&B.

The ***Motel St Arnaud*** *(☎ 5495 1755)*, on the Ballarat road, has budget singles/doubles from $43/48.

WEDDERBURN

• **pop 700**

The area around Wedderburn was one of the richest during the early days of the gold rush. There's still some evidence of the heady days of gold, mainly in the form of rusting old mining equipment scattered around the area and some historic buildings along the main streets, but the town itself is fairly quiet nowadays.

General Store Museum

This museum, at 51 High St, is set up as a late-19th-century general store, with some interesting, cluttered and dusty displays, including old jars and bottles containing all sorts of snake-oil remedies. The cellar has a collection of old photos, bottles and pots and there are old buggies and carts out in the back yard. This rather ramshackle museum is open daily from 9 am to 5.30 pm, except Monday; admission costs $2 for adults and $1 for kids.

Christmas Reef Mine

If you're interested in authentic gold mining, head out to the Christmas Reef Mine, 5km east of Wedderburn in the bush. It's a working mine that is open to visitors from noon to 3 pm daily. The best part about visiting here is that the mine is actually being worked (with a combination of some fairly antiquated equipment and fierce enthusiasm). You can walk through the mine, which has been blasted and dug by hand, see the ore crusher in operation, and get an insight into the less-than-glamorous reality of searching the earth for hidden gold. Tours cost $6 for adults and $2 for kids.

Places to Stay

The ***Wedderburn Pioneer Caravan Park*** *(☎ 5494 3301)* is set in the town's old botanic gardens in Hospital St, a pretty setting shaded by gums and pines. This place has camping sites from $10, on-site vans from $24 and self-contained cabins from $40.

The ***Wedderburn Motel*** *(☎ 5494 3002, 43 High St)* has singles/doubles from $32/42.

BRIDGEWATER-ON-LODDON

• pop 1600

As the name suggests, Bridgewater is on the Loddon River, which in summer is a great spot to go for a cooling swim if you're suffering from on-road heat. You might also want to visit the local winery, **Water Wheel Vineyards**, which is in Lyndhurst St and opens weekdays from 9 am to 5 pm (from 10 am on Saturday and noon on Sunday) for tastings and sales.

The town is also the base for a rather unique and wonderful way of exploring the backroads and bush areas of the Golden Triangle. The ***Colonial Way*** *(☎ 5437 3054)* hires out horse-drawn, gypsy-style caravans pulled by friendly Clydesdale horses. The caravans, which sleep up to five people, are fully equipped and self-contained, and the owners give you a map and visit you at the start of each day to check on your progress. The caravans cost between $620 and $820 for a week.

INGLEWOOD & AROUND

Seven kilometres further along the Calder Hwy, Inglewood is another town with its roots firmly planted in the goldfields. The town is now a peaceful rural centre, nicknamed 'home of the blue eucy', with distillation of eucalyptus oil being one of its main industries. Eucalyptus has been distilled here for more than 100 years, and there's an old distillery in the town and many eucalyptus farms in the area. Inglewood was also the birthplace of aviation and transport pioneer Sir Reginald Ansett.

When gold was discovered in the area in 1859, a rough shanty town built of calico, bark and tin sprang up to house the itinerant population. A fire in 1862 destroyed most of the town, and Inglewood claims to be 'the only town in Australia to have 10 pubs burnt down in 30 minutes'.

Eleven kilometres west of Inglewood is **Kingower**, a tiny settlement where you'll find the **Passing Clouds** and **Blanche Barkly** wineries, both well worth a visit. They're open most days for tastings and sales, but it's best to call first to let them know you're coming. Kingower is another former goldfield, and the area was known as the 'potato diggings' because finding gold nuggets here was as easy as plucking spuds from a potato patch. Back in 1857, the 49kg Blanche Barkly nugget was found near here, and hopeful prospectors still comb the area. As recently as 1980, the 27kg Hand of Faith nugget was found in the old schoolyard.

Kingower is also on the edge of the **Kooyoora State Park**, a 3500 hectare area that has recently been declared a park because of its scenic beauty and recreational values. It's a distinctive area of striking contrasts – red earth and granite, gum trees and wattles – and has some great areas for bushwalking, rock climbing, orienteering and exploring. The highest point is Mt Kooyoora, at 480m. There are good walking tracks, scenic drives and camping areas. In the western section of the park are the **Melville Caves**, named after the gentleman bushranger, Captain Melville, who used to hide out here. You'll understand why when you stand on the lookout point – from up here, he would have had plenty of warning of anyone coming looking for him. Apart from the climb from the lower car park to the lookouts and the caves, there are more walking tracks and some good picnic reserves at the caves.

Places to Stay

Inglewood Motel & Caravan Park *(☎ 5438 3232)*, on the Calder Hwy, has powered sites from $10, on-site caravans and cabins from $25, and budget motel singles/doubles from $38/50, including breakfast.

There are also good bush camping areas in the Kooyoora State Park.

BENDIGO

• pop 60,000

The solid, imposing and, at times, extravagant Victorian-era architecture of Bendigo is a testimony to the fact that this was one of Australia's richest gold-mining towns.

When gold was discovered at Ravenswood in 1851, thousands upon thousands of diggers converged on the fantastically rich Bendigo Diggings, which covered more than 360 sq km, to claim the easily obtainable surface gold. As this began to run out and diggers were no longer tripping over nuggets, they turned their pans and cradles to Bendigo Creek and other waterways around Sandhurst (as Bendigo was then known) in their quest for alluvial gold.

The arrival of thousands of Chinese miners in 1854 caused a great deal of racial tension at the time, and had a lasting effect on the town. Bendigo still has a rich Chinese heritage, and is one of the few places in Victoria where reminders of the thousands of Chinese diggers who came to Australia during the gold rush can be seen.

By the 1860s the easily won ore was running out and the scene changed again as reef mining began in earnest. Independent miners were soon outclassed by the large and powerful mining companies, with their heavy digging and crushing machinery. They poured money into the town as they extracted enormous wealth from their network of deep mine shafts. Some 35 quartz reefs were found, and the ground underneath Bendigo is still honeycombed with mine shafts – local legend has it that you can walk underground from one side of town to the other. The boom years of reef mining were from the 1860s to the 1880s, and this is the period when many of the town's most impressive buildings were built. The last of the mines was worked until the mid-1950s.

Today Bendigo is a busy and prosperous provincial city, with an interesting collection of mines, museums, historic buildings and other relics from the gold-mining era. It also has one of the best regional art galleries in Australia, as well as some great wineries in the surrounding district.

Information

Bendigo Visitor Information Centre (☎ 5444 4445) and excellent interpretive centre, in the historic former post office on Pall Mall, opens daily from 9 am to 5 pm.

The RACV (☎ 5443 9622) has an office at 112 Mitchell St, while the Parks Victoria office (☎ 5444 6620) is at 57 View St.

Central Deborah Gold Mine

This 500m deep mine, worked on 17 levels, became operational in the 1940s, and was connected with the two other Deborah shafts which date back to the early days of the goldfields. About 1000kg of gold was removed before it closed in 1954. The mine is now being reworked and has been developed as one of Bendigo's major tourist attractions. It's well worth a visit as there are lots of interesting exhibits and many photographs taken from the mid-1800s onwards. You can take a self-guided surface tour ($6 entry), but if you have time take the interesting 70-minute underground tour. After donning hard hats and lights, you're taken 61m down the shaft to inspect the ongoing operations, complete with drilling demonstrations. Underground tours cost $15.50 for adults and $8 for kids. The mine is in Violet St – you can't miss it – and is open from 9 am to 5 pm daily.

A combined ticket for the mine tour plus a ride on the 'talking tram' (see the later Talking Tram entry) costs $21 for adults and $11 for kids.

Chinese Joss House

The Chinese Joss House, on Finn St in North Bendigo, is the only one remaining of four that existed during the gold rush, and one of the few practising joss houses in Victoria. It is built of timber and handmade bricks and painted red, the traditional colour for strength. The entrance is guarded by a pair of *kylin* – mythical guardian beasts. Exhibits include embroidered banners, figures representing the 12 years of the Chinese solar cycle, commemorative tablets to the deceased, paintings and Chinese lanterns. The house is open from 10 am to 5 pm daily (closes 4 pm in winter) and admission is $3 for adults and $1 for kids.

There's a Chinese section in the White Hills Cemetery on Killian St and also a prayer oven where paper money, and other goodies for the spirits of the dead, were burnt.

Bendigo Talking Tram

A vintage tram makes a regular tourist run from the Central Deborah Mine, through the centre of the city and out to the tramways museum (which is free if you have a tram ticket) and the Chinese Joss House, with a commentary along the way. It departs Monday to Friday at 9.30 and 11.30 am and 1.30 and 3 pm from the Central Deborah Mine, or five minutes later from the Alexandra Fountain in Charing Cross. On weekends, the tram departs every hour between 9.30 am and 3.30 pm (except 12.30 pm). The fare is $8 for adults and $4.50 for kids.

Sacred Heart Cathedral

Construction of the massive Sacred Heart Cathedral, the largest Gothic-style building in Victoria outside Melbourne, began in the 19th century and was completed in 1977. Inside, there's a magnificently carved bishop's chair, some beautiful stain-glass windows and wooden angels jutting out of the ceiling arches. The pews are made from Australian blackwood and the marble is Italian. On the corner of Short and High Streets, it's worth a visit.

Bendigo Art Gallery

The Bendigo Art Gallery is the largest and definitely one of the best provincial galleries in the state. It has an outstanding collection of colonial and contemporary Australian art, including work by Louis Buvelot, Fred Williams, Clifton Pugh, Rupert Bunny and Lloyd Rees. It also has a surprising and valuable collection of 19th-century European art. There are guided tours of the permanent collection daily at 2 pm. The gallery is at 42 View St and is open daily from 10 am to 5 pm; entry costs $2 for adults, $1 for children.

Shamrock Hotel

This magnificent hotel, built in 1897 on the corner of Pall Mall and Williamson St, is a fine four-storey example of elaborate Italianate late-Victorian architecture. Its size and opulence give some indication of just how prosperous the town was in the goldmining era when, so the story goes, the floors were regularly washed down to collect the gold dust brought in on the miners' boots. There are tours of the hotel on Saturday and Sunday at 2.30 pm; the $7.50 fee includes Devonshire tea. And of course, you can drop in for an ale, or stay a while (see Places to Stay later in this chapter).

Golden Dragon Museum & Gardens

The excellent Golden Dragon Museum in Bridge St houses the two Chinese processional dragons, Old Loong and the world's longest dragon, Sun Loong, which are the centrepieces of the annual Easter Fair parade. The museum has also brought together an interesting collection of Chinese heritage items and costumes. It opens daily from 9.30 am to 5 pm and admission costs $6 for adults, $3 for children and $18 for a family. There are also classical Chinese gardens on the site, admission to which costs $2 for adults and 50c for children (admission is free if you've paid the museum entry fee).

Gardens

Just north of Pall Mall, **Rosalind Park** features open lawns, big old trees, picnic tables and the fabulous 'Cascades' fountain. You can climb to the top of a lookout tower for sensational 360 degree views, or go for a stroll through the shady green fernery. The **Conservatory Gardens**, at the front of Rosalind Park and beside the law courts, have a wonderful rose garden, sculptures and a flower conservatory. The **White Hills Botanic Gardens**, on the Midland Hwy 6km north of town, feature many exotic and rare plant species, a small fauna park and aviary, as well as barbecue facilities.

Other Attractions

Bendigo's rich gold-rush heritage is evident in the city's impressive Victorian architecture, especially in and around the city centre. The most striking examples are along Pall Mall, where the grand old **Shamrock Hotel**, along with the **law courts** and former **post office**, form a trio of late-Victorian splendour. If you have time, go for a wander inside all three – the interiors are just as elaborate as the exteriors. The old **town hall** at the end of Bull St is also impressive.

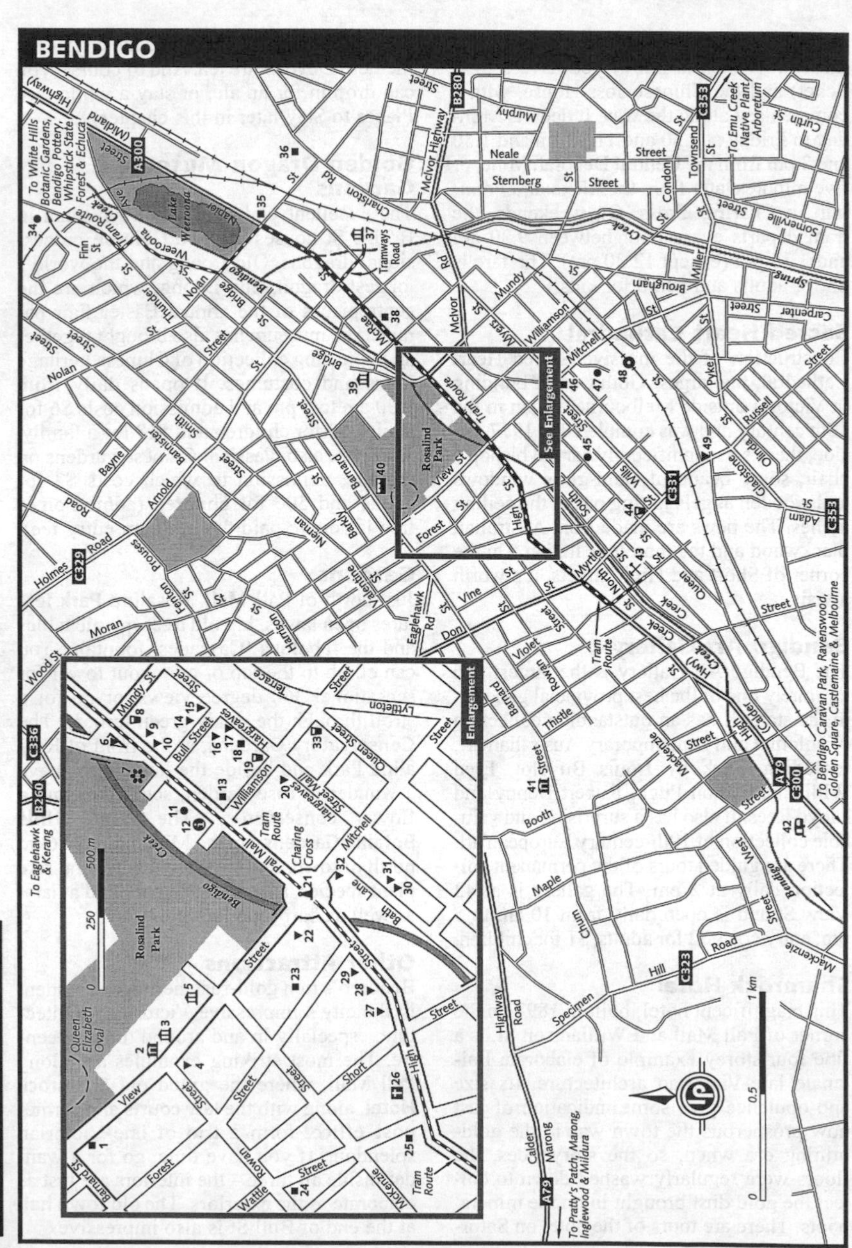
BENDIGO
To White Hills Botanic Gardens, Bendigo Pottery, Whipstick State Forest & Echuca
To Emu Creek Native Plant Arboretum
To Bendigo Caravan Park, Ravenswood, Golden Square, Castlemaine & Melbourne
To Pratty's Patch, Marong, Inglewood & Mildura
To Eaglehawk & Kerang
Lake Weeroona
Rosalind Park
See Enlargement
Enlargement
Queen Elizabeth Oval
Charing Cross
Tram Route
Pall Mall
Bendigo Creek
Midland Highway
McIvor Highway
Calder Highway
Neale Street
Sternberg Street
Mitchell St
Williamson St
High St
View St
Forest St
Hargreaves St
Bull Street
Mundy St
Lyttleton Terrace
Queen Street
Myrtle St
Don St
Vine St
Booth St
Maple St
Specimen Hill Road
Holmes Road
Arnold St
Nolan St
Barnard St
Eaglehawk Rd
A300
B280
C353
C331
C329
C336
B260
A79
C300
C323
0 250 500 m
0 0.5 1 km

BENDIGO

PLACES TO STAY

1 Bendigo Central Motor Lodge
13 Shamrock Hotel
18 Old Crown Hotel
23 City Centre Motel
24 Marlborough House
25 Cathedral Terrace B&B
35 Julie-Anna Inn Motel
36 Fleece Inn Hotel
38 Jubilee Villa
42 Central City Caravan Park
46 Hopetoun Hotel

PLACES TO EAT

4 Rifle Brigade Pub Brewery
6 Bazzani
9 Clogs
10 Café Kryptonite
14 The Match Bar & Bakehouse
15 Darby O'Gills
16 Cafe La Vache
17 The House of Khong
20 Gillies' Pies
22 Whirrakee Restaurant & Wine Bar
27 Rasoyee
28 Mexican Kitchen
29 Jo Joe's
30 Bath Lane Cafe
31 Green Olive Deli
32 Cafe au lait
49 Queens Arms Hotel

OTHER

2 Dudley House
3 Bendigo Regional Arts Centre (Capital Theatre)
5 Bendigo Art Gallery
7 Conservatory Gardens
8 Sundance Saloon
11 Law Courts
12 Visitor Information Centre; Old Post Office
19 Eclipse
21 Alexandra Fountain
26 Sacred Heart Cathedral
33 Studio 54
34 Chinese Joss House
37 Tramways Museum
39 Golden Dragon Museum & Gardens
40 Aquatic Centre
41 Fortuna Villa
43 Central Deborah Gold Mine
44 The Vine
45 Bendigo Cinemas
47 Discovery Science & Technology Centre
48 Train Station

View St, which runs uphill from the Alexandra Fountain in Charing Cross, is a historic streetscape with some fine buildings, including the **Capital Theatre**, which houses the Bendigo Regional Arts Centre, and next door, **Dudley House**, which is classified by the National Trust and is the home of the Bendigo Historical Society.

Fortuna Villa, Chum St, is a stately mansion with a large decorative lake and beautifully kept gardens. It was built and owned by George Lansell, Bendigo's richest and most famous gold baron who was known as the 'Quartz King'. The villa is only open to the public on Sunday for a two-hour guided tour at 1 pm. The tour costs $8 which includes Devonshire tea served in the ballroom.

Much of the town's best **residential architecture** was built along the ridge of a hill just north of the city centre, and it's worth going for a walk or a ride along streets like Barkly, Forest, Vine and Rowan.

The **Discovery Science & Technology Centre**, with a wide range of interesting and educational exhibits, is in Railway Place opposite the train station and opens daily from 10 am to 5 pm. Admission costs $7.50 for adults, $4.50 for children and $24 for a family.

See also the Around Bendigo section in this chapter for other points of interest in the area.

Activities

Bendigo has several good golf courses, the best being the Bendigo Golf Club (☎ 5448 4206) in Epsom, about 9km north, which has a population of resident kangaroos. An 18-hole round costs $13 and club hire is $10.

For the warmer weather, Bendigo has four excellent outdoor swimming pools – the Aquatic Centre in Barnard St is the closest to the centre of town. There are also ice skating and roller skating/blading rinks and an indoor go-kart track – ask at the information centre for details.

Organised Tours

Bendigo Double-Decker Bus Tours (☎ 5441 6969) has a restored double-decker bus doing a shuttle service around Bendigo's major sights and attractions. Tickets cost $8 for adults, $4 for kids, and you can get on and off anywhere along the route.

Bendigo District Wineries

There are some very good wineries in the Bendigo district – three within 10km of the town and another dozen or so that can easily be visited from here. A map and guide to the wineries is available free from the Visitor Information Centre or from the wineries themselves.

Balgownie Vineyard was the first modern-era winery (1969) established in the area. Its success led to the development of this region as a wine district, particularly noted for shiraz wines. Balgownie is in Maiden Gully, 7km west of Bendigo, signposted off the Calder Highway, and open Monday to Saturday from 10 am to 5 pm for tastings and sales.

Chateau Leamon is also well regarded for its wines, particularly its riesling and shiraz wines. It's on the Calder Hwy about 10 km south of Bendigo, at the base of Big Hill, and opens daily from 10 am to 5 pm.

Chateau Dore is the area's most historic vineyard, established and built in 1856. The great-grandson of the original wine maker has re-established the vineyard, and the old stone-and-timber cellars and tasting rooms are steeped in history and well worth a visit. It's in Mandurang, 8km south-west of Bendigo, and opens Monday to Friday, 9 am to 5.30 pm, Saturday to 2 pm and Sunday, 10.30 am to 5 pm.

Special Events

Bendigo's major festival is the annual Easter Fair, which attracts thousands of visitors with its carnival atmosphere and colourful and noisy procession of Chinese dragons. The Bendigo Agricultural Show is held in October each year, and the Bendigo Cup race meeting in November is part of the Spring Racing Carnival.

Perhaps Bendigo's most curious attraction is the annual November 'Swap Meet', which draws enthusiasts from all over the country in search of that elusive vintage car spare part. While this may sound quite unremarkable as a community event, it actually draws in tens of thousands of people, and accommodation is at a premium at this time. The Bendigo 5000 Madison, a cycling event at the local velodrome, also attracts large crowds each March.

Places to Stay

Camping, Caravan Parks & Hostel There are about ten caravan parks in and around Bendigo. One of them, the ***Central City Caravan Park*** *(☎ 5443 6937, 362 High St)* has a basic hostel section in prefab cabins with four bunks each, and separate cooking and bathroom facilities. Beds cost $12. There are also tent sites for $12 and on-site vans and cabins from $32 to $55. This place is about 2km south of the town centre – you can get there on a Kangaroo Flat bus from Hargreaves St.

The ***Bendigo Caravan Park*** *(☎ 5447 1773)*, 7km south on the Calder Hwy, has tent sites from $12 and on-site vans and cottages from $32 to $59.

Pubs The ***Hopetoun Hotel*** *(☎ 5443 4871)*, close to the train station on the corner of Wills and Mitchell Sts, has singles/twins for $25/40, although it's pretty grim and shabby. A much better option is the central ***Old Crown Hotel*** *(☎ 5441 6888, 238 Hargreaves St)* with old-fashioned but comfortable pub rooms with shared bathrooms at $30/48, including a continental breakfast.

The ***Fleece Inn Hotel*** *(☎ 5443 3086, 139 Charlston Rd)*, opposite the cattle saleyards, has B&B at $20/40. Bear in mind that things can get kind of smelly around here at auction times.

Motels Bendigo has a seemingly endless string of motels (actually, there are about 25 in town). Two of the cheaper and more central ones are the ***City Centre Motel*** *(☎ 5443 2077, 26 Forest St)* and the ***Bendigo Central Motor Lodge*** *(☎ 5443 9388, 181 View St)*, which both have doubles from $55.

For somewhere more up-market, try the ***Julie-Anna Inn Motel*** *(☎ 5442 5855, 268*

Napier St) which has rooms from $100 (standard double) to $170 (suite).

Hotels, Guesthouses & B&Bs There are a few different levels of accommodation at Bendigo's historic and splendid ***Shamrock Hotel*** *(☎ 5443 0333)* in Pall Mall – in more ways than one. There are old-fashioned rooms with shared bathroom for $65 a double, motel-style rooms with en suite for $95 a double, or spacious two-room suites such as the one the famous soprano singer, Dame Nellie Melba, stayed in, ranging from $125 to $150 a night.

Marlborough House *(☎ 5441 4142, corner Wattle and Rowan Sts)* is an elegant and up-market Victorian-era guesthouse. The cosy guest lounge has an open fire and there's also a lovely glass-enclosed winter garden. The B&B tariff starts at $110 a double.

Close to the centre, ***Jubilee Villa*** *(☎ 5442 2920, 170 McCrae St)* is an 1887 homestead with a separate accommodation section in the restored former servants' quarters. It's well set up, with two bedrooms, a breakfast room and bathroom with spa; B&B costs $110 to $135 a double.

Cathedral Terrace B&B *(☎ 5441 3242, 81 Wattle St)* is a lovely Victorian-era home with splendid views of the Sacred Heart Cathedral opposite. Its two guestrooms fitted with period features are available from $110 to $130 a double.

Ravenswood *(☎ 5435 3284)*, just off the Calder Hwy seventeen kilometres south of Bendigo, is a magnificent Georgian mansion classified by the National Trust. Accommodation is available in the refurbished servants quarters for $120 a double, including breakfast. Dinner, B&B packages are also available.

Places to Eat

Bendigo has an excellent range of cafes, pubs and restaurants. The cafes worth a visit for breakfast and lunch include ***Cafe La Vache*** *(47 Bull St)*, crammed with goodies, including superb olive bread, ***Cafe au lait*** *(20 Mitchell St)*, for light meals, yummy cakes and strong coffee, and the ***Bath Lane Cafe*** and award-winning ***Green Olive Deli***, both in Bath Lane.

There are several other excellent cafe/restaurants that also open for dinner. ***Cafe Kryptonite*** *(☎ 5443 9777, Pall Mall)* has interesting, contemporary art exhibited on its red walls and serves up excellent fare such as risotto, pasta, lamb souvlaki, salads and a special fish and chips done 'the Kryptonite way'. Prices range from $9 to $16. ***Bazzani*** *(☎ 5441 3777)* in Howard Place, close to the Conservatory Gardens, is a stylish venue with a pleasant outdoor eating area. The menu is diverse and innovative, with both an Italian and Asian influence, and evening mains range from $11 to $22.

Clogs *(☎ 5443 0077, 106 Pall Mall)* is a stylish pizza restaurant/bar with an inviting alfresco area out the back. Light meals such as focaccias and salads are available ($6 to $10) and there's an extensive pasta and pizza menu with prices ranging from $10 to $18. Another good place for pizza and pasta is ***Jo Joe's*** *(☎ 5441 4471, 4 High St)*, a bustling fully licensed restaurant with a take-away section and tables out on the footpath.

In the Hargreaves St Mall, ***Gillies'*** pies are regarded by connoisseurs as among the best in Australia. A Bendigo institution, you queue at the little window, order one of their five or so varieties, then sit in the mall to eat it.

Some of Bendigo's best food is found in its pubs, of which there are plenty. ***Darby O'Gills***, on the corner of Bull and Hargreaves Sts, has a good selection of food ranging from focaccias ($8) to steak and seafood dishes (around $14). They also have Guinness (and many beers) on tap and live music every Thursday, Friday and Saturday night.

The popular ***Rifle Brigade Pub Brewery*** *(137 View St)*, has inexpensive bar meals such as burgers, sausages and schnitzels from $6 to $8. There's a good bistro section and a shady courtyard. They also brew their own beers, including Ironbark Dark, Old-fashioned Bitter and Rifle Lager. Also popular is the corner bistro at the ***Shamrock Hotel***.

The ***Queen's Arms Hotel*** *(25 Russell St)*, is down to earth with bar meals for around $5, and a good bistro.

Bendigo also has a few BYO ethnic restaurants that are good value. Try the self-explanatory ***Mexican Kitchen*** *(28 High St)*, or for Indian food, head to ***Rasoyee*** *(40 High St)*. Both of these places have filling mains for around $11, and also do take-aways. For good Chinese food, try ***The House of Khong*** *(200 Hargreaves St)*, which has an $8.50 smorgasbord lunch every weekday.

For a huge and tasty steak in historic surrounds, head out to the ***Golden Gully Steakhouse*** *(☎ 5447 0070)*, *(78 Woodward Rd)* in Golden Square (a suburb about 2.5km south-west of the centre). Steaks and other mains range from $17 to $23.

The sophisticated ***Whirrakee Restaurant & Wine Bar*** *(☎ 5441 5557, 17 View St)* has a small wine bar with cosy sofas, and a restaurant serving excellent 'modern Australian' cuisine (yes, including kangaroo) with mains in the $14 to $19 range.

One of the best places to eat is the rustic and charming ***Pratty's Patch*** *(☎ 5449 6341, 35 Monsants Rd)* off the Calder Hwy in Maiden Gully, 7km west of Bendigo. The restaurant is in a historic stone cottage and serves hearty home-cooked country cuisine with mains ranging from $18 to $23. It's open daily for dinner and on Friday, Saturday and Sunday for lunch.

Entertainment

Bendigo has a fairly lively nightclub scene. ***Eclipse***, on the corner of Williamson and Hargreaves Sts, has a contemporary hits dance floor on one level and a yesteryear hits disco upstairs, where you can hear all those good old 60s and 70s numbers over and over.

On the corner of Williamson and Queen Sts is ***Studio 54***, a huge warehouse-style multi-level high-tech nightclub complete with smoke machines and pool tables, and sometimes live bands.

There are also some pretty good live music venues in town. One of the best is ***The Vine*** *(135 King St)*, which has regular jam sessions and features local and Melbourne bands playing a wide variety of music styles. The ***Sundance Saloon***, on the corner of Pall Mall and Mundy St, is a historic pub converted into an old-Western-style pool hall – it also has live bands on weekends.

Bendigo Regional Arts Centre *(☎ 5441 5344)*, in the beautifully restored Capital Theatre at 50 View St, is the main venue for the performing arts. The ***Bendigo Cinemas*** *(☎ 5442 1666)* are at 107 Queen St.

Getting There & Away

Train Bendigo's train station is in Railway Place off Mitchell St, quite close to the centre of town. V/Line has regular services each day to and from Melbourne, with six trains each weekday and four a day on weekends. The trip takes about two hours and the one-way economy/1st-class fares are $20.80/29.20. Trains continue on to Swan Hill ($23.30/32.60).

Heading south from Bendigo to Melbourne, stops along the way include Castlemaine ($4.30/6), Kyneton ($7.50/10.60) and Woodend ($9.80/13.80).

Bus V/Line buses from Bendigo include daily services to Castlemaine ($4); weekday services to Ballarat ($18) and Geelong ($29.30); and Monday to Saturday services to Echuca ($6.10). There are also daily buses to Mildura ($46.90) via Swan Hill ($23.30).

Getting Around

Bendigo and the surrounding area are quite well serviced by public buses. There are two companies operating in the region: Walkers Buslines (☎ 5443 9333) and Christian's Buslines (☎ 5447 2222). Route maps and timetables are available from the Visitor Information Centre; tickets cost $1.30 and are valid for two hours.

For a taxi call Bendigo Associated Taxis (☎ 5443 0777).

AROUND BENDIGO

Bendigo Pottery

Bendigo Pottery, the oldest pottery works in Australia, is on the Midland Hwy at Epsom, 6km north of Bendigo. The pottery was founded here in 1857 and is classified by the National Trust. As well as roofing tiles and the like, which keep the works financial, the historic kilns are still used to produce fine pottery. There's a cafe, a sales gallery set among historic kilns, and you can watch potters at work in the studio. The pottery opens daily from 9 am to 5 pm; entry is free.

Whipstick State Park

The 2300 hectare Whipstick State Park, about 19km north of Bendigo, is a state park established to conserve the distinctive whipstick mallee vegetation and protect the abundant birdlife found there. There are picnic areas sited near old eucalyptus distilleries, walking tracks, and those with a Miners' Right can fossick for gold in designated areas. Hartland's Eucalyptus Oil Factory, close to the Whipstick Forest, was established in 1890 and the production process can be inspected; it's only open on Sunday from 10.30 am to 4 pm ($4). There are bicycle rides you can do through Whipstick Park and also a couple of designated camping sites – contact Parks Victoria (☎ 5444 6620) in Bendigo for more details.

Lake Eppalock

This large lake, about 30km east of Bendigo, provides the town's water supply and is popular for all sorts of water sports, including water-skiing, boating and fishing. There are camping facilities, swimming spots, boat-launching ramps and a kiosk. The lake can be reached via the Bendigo to Redesdale road or the McIvor Highway (B280).

Other Attractions

About 20km south of Bendigo near Sedgwick, the popular **Sedgwick's Camel Farm** (☎ 5439 6367) is in an attractive bush setting. It offers a wide range of camel rides and treks, including 10-minute rides ($7 for adults, $5 for kids), half-hour rides ($10/7), sunset treks with barbecue dinners ($30/18, during daylight savings times only), and overnight treks into the bush ($145/95 all inclusive). The farm opens on weekends and school and public holidays between September and May (10 am to 5 pm) and weekdays by appointment only. Entry costs $2 for adults and 50c for kids.

The **Emu Creek Native Plant Arboretum** is a forest of Australian native plants around a central lake, and is open on weekends and holidays ($2). It's 12km south of Bendigo off the Bendigo-to-Redesdale road.

The large undercover **Epsom Sunday market** at Epsom, 9km north of Bendigo, attracts large crowds and is reported to be very good.

ROCHESTER

• **pop 2550**

Rochester, on the Northern Highway (B75), 65km north-east of Bendigo, was first settled in the 1840s and has been a rich agricultural area since irrigation was introduced in the 1880s. These days nearly 800 sq km of land in the Rochester region is serviced by irrigation canals from the Campaspe Weir and Waranga Reservoir.

The town is on the banks of the Campaspe River (named by Major Mitchell after a beautiful courtesan of Alexander the Great's). Today it's a solid and typical country town, with some impressive old buildings, including the wonderful **Random House** in Bridge Rd. This grand and historic homestead, built beside the river in 1852, has been restored and converted into a museum, tearoom, restaurant and guesthouse (see Places to Stay & Eat). It's open for tours and teas (by arrangement, ie ring first) from Wednesday to Friday and on Sunday between 10 am and 4.30 pm, and admission costs $3.

Places to Stay & Eat

The ***Rochester Caravan Park*** *(☎ 5484 1622)* is in Church St beside the river and has sites from $10 and on-site vans and cabins from $35 to $45. The ***Rochester Motel*** *(☎ 5484 1077, 24 Echuca Rd)* has singles/doubles from $39/50 and family rooms available from $74.

Random House *(☎ 5484 1792, 22 Bridge Rd)* is a gracious guesthouse and gourmet retreat. The four period-style rooms each have en suites and lounges with open fires, and there are lovely gardens to stroll in. The tariff is from $130 a double with a cooked breakfast. Dinners are also available by arrangement, costing $25 a head for three courses.

RUSHWORTH

• **pop 975**

This historic town, about 65km south-east of Rochester, was originally settled as a stopover for travellers between the Beechworth and Bendigo gold diggings. In 1853, after local Kooris took a party of travelling diggers to see some 'pretty stones' in a gully, Rushworth soon had a gold rush of its own. Once the rich alluvial gold was exhausted, dozens of deep mine shafts were sunk to follow the gold-bearing quartz reefs underground, and by the 1880s there were more than 50 reefs being mined.

After the golden years, Rushworth developed into a thriving timber town. At one stage, the surrounding forests (known as 'golden ironbark country') supported seven sawmills.

The town has a rich architectural heritage, and in 1983 the National Trust classified High St as a historic precinct. The street is divided by a central plantation and has some interesting old buildings, including an old Victorian band rotunda. There's a **Historical Museum** in the old Mechanics Institute in High St, which is open Saturday from 10 am to noon and Sunday from 2 to 5 pm (entrance by gold coin donation).

Whroo Historic Reserve

Seven kilometres south of Rushworth, this reserve is in the centre of the Rushworth State Forest. Whroo (pronounced 'roo') is an old gold-mining ghost town, and the reserve was established to preserve the relics of the gold-rush era: old mine shafts, cyanide vats (used for dissolving and separating the gold from quartz) and puddling machines. Although at its peak the town had over 130 buildings, the ironbarks and native scrub have largely reclaimed the site.

Whroo's old cemetery (also classified by the National Trust) is an evocative place with headstone inscriptions that bear testimony to the hard life experienced by those who came in search of gold.

There are walking tracks and signposted nature trails through the reserve, one of which leads to a small waterhole used by the Kooris who inhabited this region. There's also a signposted camping site close to the newly established visitor information centre (☎ 5856 1561) and cafe. The friendly staff will be glad to answer any questions you have about the reserve.

Other Attractions

From Whroo, it's a rough and bumpy but interesting drive south to **Graytown**, another gold-mining ghost town. It's basically just two signs a few hundred metres apart saying 'Graytown' – with nothing in between them.

The **Waranga Basin**, 6km north of Rushworth, is a huge irrigation reservoir and a popular spot for water-skiing, fishing, swimming and boating.

Places to Stay

The leafy and friendly ***Miners Pick Caravan Park*** *(☎ 5856 1550)*, in Neill St, has sites for $10 and on-site vans for $25 a double. There is another caravan park 5km north on the edge of Lake Waranga, and you can also camp in the nearby Whroo Historic Reserve (see the earlier entry).

The National Trust classified ***Criterion Hotel*** *(☎ 5856 1433)*, standing sentinel over the town's historical main street, has basic old-fashioned pub rooms at $20 for B&B – it's also a good spot for a counter meal. The ***Rushworth Motel*** *(☎ 5856 1090, 4 School St)* has rooms from $40/45 a single/double.

HEATHCOTE

• **pop 1550**

Heathcote is a pleasant little highway town south of Rushworth, with a gold-mining past and a wine-making present. The (incredibly long) main street has some inter-

Heathcote Wineries

The rich and ancient soils around Heathcote support a cluster of excellent wineries which are well known for their distinctive, peppery shiraz. A tour around these wineries makes for an enjoyable day, both for the quality of the wines and the diversity of the countryside.

The **Heathcote Winery** is in a historic building at 183 High St near the centre of town. This place breaks the local mould by producing excellent chardonnays – it opens daily from 10 am to 6 pm. On the northern edge of town is the ramshackle but charming **Zuber Estate**, which has a tasting room in a tin shed and produces some honest and earthy reds that were built to last – they're great value, too. Zuber opens daily from 10 am to 6 pm.

The highly regarded **Jasper Hill** winery is 6km north-west of Heathcote, signposted off the Northern Highway. Jasper Hill specialises in shiraz wines, with the grapes coming from paddocks named after the owners' daughters. Its rieslings are also excellent. It opens weekends from 10 am to 6 pm between August and October (when new wines are released) and other times by appointment. The smaller **Huntleigh Vineyard** (☎ 5433 2795), another 2 km further on, opens for cellar-door sales on weekends from 10 am to 5.30 pm and usually weekdays also.

McIvor Creek Winery is 3 km south of Heathcote, signposted off the Northern Hwy, and sells some interesting preserves and souvenirs as well as wine. It's open daily from 10 am to 5 pm.

Another winery worth visiting is **Osicka Wines** near the remote gold-mining ghost town of Graytown, 27km north-east of Heathcote. It's open Monday to Saturday from 10 am to 5 pm (from noon on Sunday).

esting old buildings and shops and there are a few points of interest in addition to the wineries.

Heathcote's Visitor Information Centre (☎ 5433 3121) is on the corner of High and Barrack Sts and open daily from 9 am to 5 pm.

The **Pink Cliffs Reserve** is an area that was eroded by the frantic sluicing activities of the early gold miners, and now the stained granite resembles a colourful moonscape of pinks and ochres.

It's a good sized town to wander around – ask at the Visitor Information Centre for a map that will lead you up past a **historic powder magazine** to the **Devil's Cave** and up to the **Viewing Rock Lookout**.

Another great lookout spot is at the top of the **Mt Ida Flora Reserve**, a wildflower reserve 5km north of the town on the road to Echuca.

Places to Stay

The ***Queens Meadow Caravan Park*** *(☎ 5433 2304)* has sites for $10 and on-site vans from $35. The ***Commercial Hotel*** *(☎ 5433 2944)* in High St has budget motel-style rooms at $45/60 a single/double, or the ***Heathcote Motor Inn*** *(☎ 5433 2655, 257 High St)* has generous sized doubles from $57.

Argyle Lodge B&B *(☎ 5433 3413)*, 5km south of Heathcote on Newlans Lane, is a mud-brick and sandstone home surrounded by lovely gardens and budding vineyards. There are three rooms in a separate guest wing, with doubles here ranging from $95 to $110.

Places to Eat

Stop in at ***A Gaggle of Geese*** *(97 High St)*, a good coffee shop and sandwich bar with hearty home-made food. It stays open until

8 pm or later (depending on the traffic) on Friday and Sunday night, but it's mainly a daytime place.

TOOBORAC

At Tooborac, 13km south-east of Heathcote on the McIvor Hwy, the old Tooborac Hotel is now the ***Stag's Head Hotel & Restaurant*** *(☎ 5433 5201)*. It's an inviting English-style tavern with a restaurant downstairs that serves lunches and dinners from Wednesday to Sunday. The food is hearty country-style fare, with pastas from $8 and mains around $17. They also offer a self-contained cottage next door, available from $100 a double.

KYNETON

• pop 3750

During the gold rush, Kyneton developed as the gateway to the goldfields. It was the main coach stop, and also became the centre of the local agricultural industry that supplied the diggings with fresh produce. This is another town with a rich architectural heritage from the Victorian era, and many of the more impressive structures were built from local bluestone. **Piper St** is a historic precinct lined with tearooms, antique shops, museums and restaurants.

Information

Just off High St on the south-eastern outskirts of town, Kyneton Visitor Information Centre (☎ 5422 6110) is open daily from 9 am to 5 pm.

Things to See

The **Kyneton Historical Museum** at 67 Piper St is an old bank building (1855) that now houses a display of local history items, farming machinery, furniture and ornaments – the upper floor is furnished in period style. It's open from Friday to Sunday and public holidays from 11 am to 4 pm and costs $3 for adults, $1 for kids.

Kyneton's **botanic gardens**, beside the Coliban River in Clowes St, were established in the 1860s by Baron Ferdinand von Mueller, and are a wonderful place to stroll and appreciate the wonders of nature. There's a good picnic and barbecue area beside the river.

Four kilometres north of the town, signposted off the Calder Hwy, are Kyneton's **mineral springs**, another good picnic spot. The **Lauriston Reservoir**, 9km west, is popular for fishing and water sports.

Flynn & Williams (☎ 5422 2228) is a tiny vineyard and winery in Flynn's Lane, on the northern outskirts of Kyneton, that opens by appointment.

Places to Stay

Kyneton ***Kyneton Caravan Park*** *(☎ 5422 1612)* has tent sites from $9 and on-site vans from $30. It is in a lovely setting beside the river and the botanic gardens.

Kyneton Motel *(☎ 5422 1098, 101 Piper St)* is the cheaper of the town's two motels, with rooms from $40/46 a single/double.

For something more up-market, try the ***Kyneton Country House*** *(☎ 5422 3556, 66 Jennings St)*. It's a magnificently restored National Trust-classified homestead in a lovely garden setting with four guestrooms, which include use of a sunroom, library and dining room. Mid-week B&B is available for $125 a double, and weekend packages start at $350 a double (shared bathroom); this includes two nights accommodation, breakfasts and a scrumptious four-course dinner.

Another excellent B&B is ***Moorville*** *(☎ 5422 6466, 1 Powlett St)*, an elegant Edwardian-era home close to the Campaspe River and botanic gardens. The tariff is $135 a double.

Around Kyneton About 5km east of Kyneton, in Chasers Lane, the romantic ***Pond Cottage*** *(☎ 5422 1447)* is a delightful self-contained, double-storey cottage set in pretty gardens. It overlooks a beautiful trout-filled lake and the excellent facilities include a tennis court and pool, and the B&B tariff ranges between $165 and $195 a double.

Fifteen kilometres from Kyneton, on Sidonia Rd, ***Bringalbit*** *(☎ 5423 7223)* is a superb 1870s stone homestead set in acres of magnificent gardens that are a veritable bird sanctuary. B&B ranges from $60/100 to $75/125 a single/double. The gardens are also open to day visitors at certain times of the year ($3).

Places to Eat

A top spot for lunch or a cuppa is the ***Kyneton Steam Mill*** *(18 Piper St)*, a historic flour mill and bakery. The store also sells special flour, bread tins and recipes, and houses a fascinating collection of old millstones and other flour making equipment. The ***Steam Mill Bakery*** *(10 High St)* is an offshoot of the mill – it's elegant for a bakery and sells delicious doughnuts.

For pizza perfection, head to the ***Mud Brick Pizza Cafe***, a friendly and inviting place in Piper St that's popular on weekends. Excellent pub meals can be had at the ***Club Hotel*** *(41 Mollison St)*, which also has Guinness on tap.

Opposite the Kyneton museum, ***Babette's*** *(☎ 5422 2581)* is a fully licensed French restaurant, open for lunch from Friday to Sunday and daily (except Tuesday) for dinner, with evening mains costing from $16 to $21.

Getting There & Away

Kyneton's lovely old train station is in Mollison St. There are several daily trains for the one-hour journey to Melbourne and the one-way fare is $11.20 economy, $15.60 1st class.

MALMSBURY

- **pop 500**

Malmsbury, a tiny settlement on the Calder Hwy, is 10km north-west of Kyneton. Apart from its distinctive and solid bluestone buildings, points of interest here include a magnificent **bluestone viaduct**, built in 1859 across the Coliban River by a crew of 4000 men, and the **botanic gardens**, first planted in 1863, with lovely shady old trees and a small ornamental lake. There's a good picnic area beside the **Malmsbury Reservoir**.

Places to Stay & Eat

Hopewell Cottage *(☎ 5423 2470)* on Ross St, is a sweet three-bedroom miner's cottage, with an open fire and B&B costing $80/110 a single/double plus $40 for each extra person.

The ***Malmsbury Bakery***, on the highway, is a good spot to stop for a bite, especially for one of their pies or wicked custard tarts.

The Mill *(☎ 5423 2267)*, on the Calder Hwy, is a magnificent old bluestone flour mill that has been restored and converted into a gallery and restaurant. The restaurant opens on Friday and Saturday night for dinner and on Saturday and Sunday for lunch. At dinner, main meals cost from $16.50 to $22.50; lunches are lighter and less expensive. The food is imaginative and the setting is great. Morning and afternoon tea and light lunches can also be enjoyed in the gallery downstairs from Friday to Monday, 10 am to 5 pm. The owners have also recently completed building several classy B&B units, available from $135 a double.

The High Country

Victoria's High Country is actually the southern end of the Great Dividing Range. This massive mountain range runs all the way along the eastern side of Australia from Queensland, through New South Wales (NSW) and into the north-eastern corner of Victoria, where it continues almost to Ballarat, fades away and then reappears in a spectacular finale as the Grampians mountain range in the state's west.

The High Country isn't particularly high in world terms – the highest point, Mt Bogong, reaches 1988m – but it contains some of the state's most spectacular and diverse countryside. It's a fragile and beautiful environment, and several large sections of the High Country have been declared national and state parks. Victoria's largest national park, the Alpine National Park, encompasses the greatest proportion of the High Country. Other parks include the Mt Buffalo National Park, Baw Baw National Park and Lake Eildon National Park.

The High Country's greatest asset is its unspoilt, natural beauty, and there's a huge variety of ways you can enjoy this area (see the Activities section, later). Highlights include the resorts and snowfields for both downhill and cross-country skiing; the historic former gold-mining towns in the north-east, especially Beechworth and Yackandandah; and the all-seasons towns in the foothills of the mountain ranges – particularly Mansfield, Bright and Mt Beauty.

It's worth remembering that this is an alpine environment, and weather conditions can change dramatically and without warning at any time of year. Bushwalkers should be self-sufficient, with a tent, a fuel stove, warm clothes and a sleeping bag, and plenty of water. In the height of summer, you can walk all day in the heat without finding water, and then face temperatures below freezing at night.

HIGHLIGHTS

- The Australian Alps Walking Track and the Alpine National Park
- Marysville's scenic beauty, charming guesthouses and B&Bs
- Lake Mountain's cross-country skiing trails
- A houseboat holiday on Lake Eildon
- The drive from Jamieson to Walhalla via Woods Point
- Horse-trekking safaris through the High Country
- Dinner Plain, a designer alpine village inspired by early cattlemen's huts
- Skiing at the 'big three' – Falls Creek, Mt Hotham and Mt Buller
- Bright's Spring and Autumn festivals
- Mt Buffalo National Park and the historic Mt Buffalo Chalet
- Milawa's gourmet trio – the bakery, cheese factory and Brown Brothers Winery

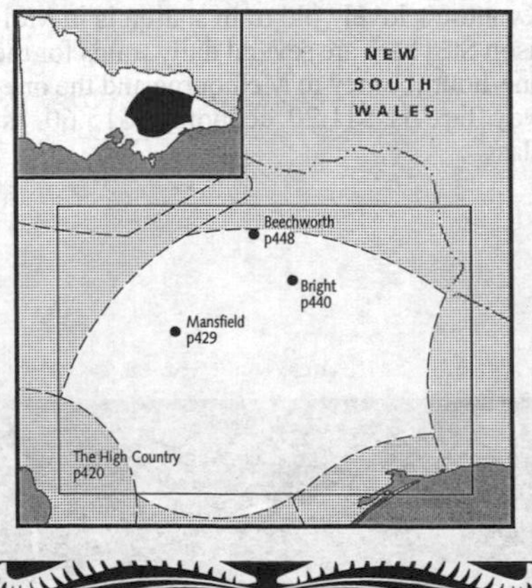

Orientation & Information

The High Country's major tourist information centres are at Mansfield, Beechworth, Mt Beauty and Bright – these places can furnish you with plenty of information on all the attractions of the region.

All the major ski resorts have their own Alpine Resort Management Boards which also have on-mountain information offices, and most of these are open year-round. There are no banks in any of the ski resorts.

For a report on snow conditions in any of the ski resorts, ring The Official Victorian Snow Report (☎ 1902 240 523, www.snowreport.vic.gov.au).

Activities

This area provides the setting for a huge range of outdoor and adventure activities, including snow skiing, bushwalking, canoeing and white-water rafting, fishing, rock climbing, hang-gliding, para-gliding, and, especially since *The Man from Snowy River* films were shot on location in the area, horse-trekking.

The High Country also contains a number of towns below the snowline that are good bases for the ski fields in winter and for a range of other activities year-round. For more detailed information on such activities, see the Activities chapter at the start of this book.

Getting There & Away

There are direct bus services into the High Country from Melbourne, as well as connecting services from the train stations at Benalla and Wangaratta. There are also local services from the various 'base towns' such as Mansfield, Mt Beauty and Harrietville. Most of these services vary seasonally – see the individual town listings for more details.

Many of the roads through this area can become impassible during winter, and some roads will be closed. It's a good idea to check road conditions with the Official Victorian Snow Report recorded information service (☎ 1902 240 523) before heading out. During winter all roads into the ski resorts can only be travelled if wheel chains are carried, and the regulation is enforced with fines.

MT DONNA BUANG

- **elev 1250m**

Mt Donna Buang is the closest snowfield to Melbourne – 95km north via Warburton – but is mainly for sightseeing and tobogganing. Parks Victoria manages the mountain from their Woori Yallock office (☎ 13 1963) on Syme St. Accommodation and toboggan hire are available in **Warburton**, 18km south (see the Yarra Valley section in the Around Melbourne chapter for details), and toboggans can usually also be hired on the mountain. There is a food van at the car park if there is snow during winter.

The entrance fee only during the snow season is $5 per car at the time of writing, but is likely to rise.

There's no public transport from Warburton to Mt Donna Buang but it's a short drive.

BAW BAW NATIONAL PARK

This national park is a southern offshoot of the Great Dividing Range, and encompasses the Baw Baw plateau and the valleys of the Thomson and Aberfeldy rivers. The highest points are Mt St Phillack (1566m) and Mt Baw Baw (1564m). The vegetation ranges from open eucalypt forests to wet gullies and tall forests on the plateau.

There are various long and short walking tracks through here, including the Australian Alps Walking Track which starts its 655km journey at Walhalla. The only camping area is at Aberfeldy River, in the north-eastern section. The main access roads are the Baw Baw road from Noojee and the Moe-to-Rawson road via Erica. If you're heading up this way, a detour to Walhalla is highly recommended – see the Gippsland chapter for details.

The higher sections of the park are covered with snow in winter, and the Mt Baw Baw ski resort and the Mt St Gwinear cross-country skiing area are both within the park.

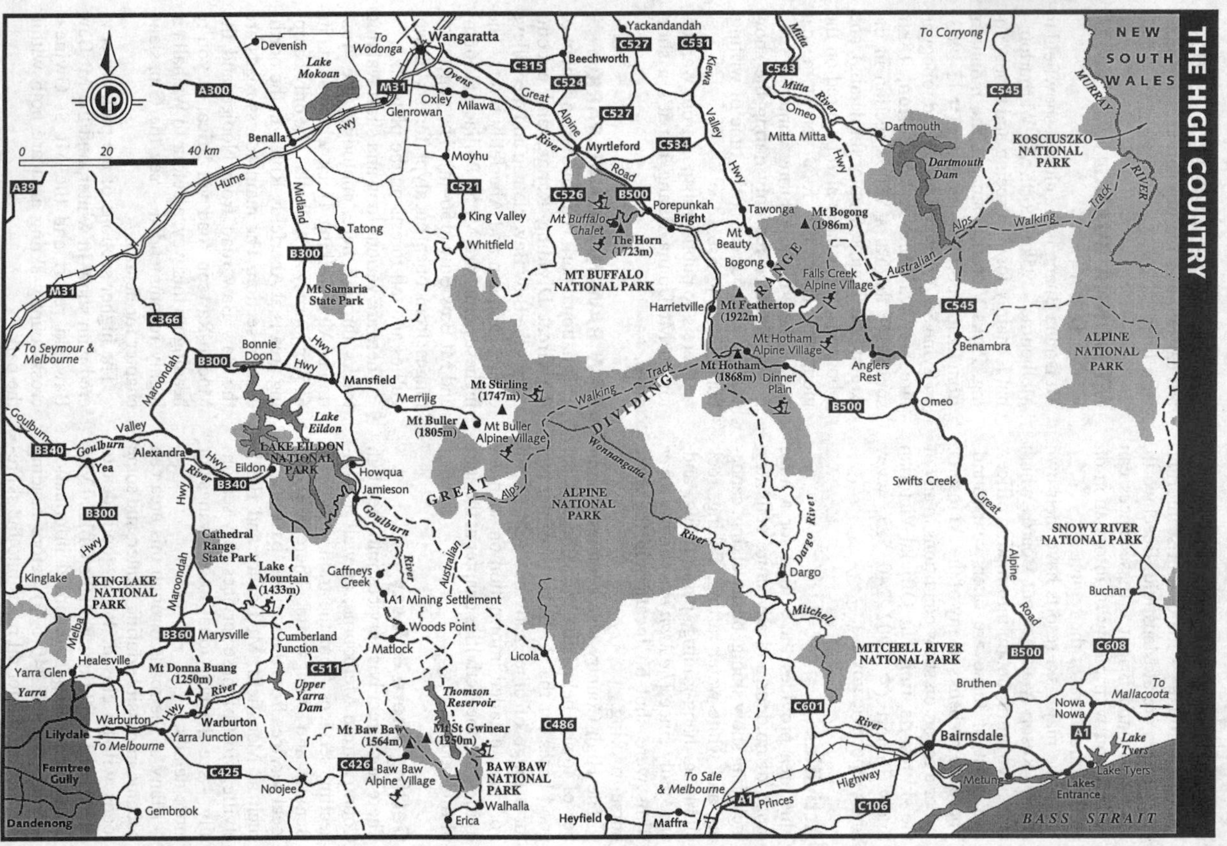
THE HIGH COUNTRY
NEW SOUTH WALES
MURRAY
RIVER
KOSCIUSZKO NATIONAL PARK
ALPINE NATIONAL PARK
SNOWY RIVER NATIONAL PARK
MITCHELL RIVER NATIONAL PARK
MT BUFFALO NATIONAL PARK
BAW BAW NATIONAL PARK
LAKE EILDON NATIONAL PARK
KINGLAKE NATIONAL PARK
Mt Samaria State Park
Cathedral Range State Park
GREAT DIVIDING RANGE
Australian Alps Walking Track
BASS STRAIT
To Corryong
To Mallacoota
Dartmouth
Dartmouth Dam
Benambra
Omeo
Anglers Rest
Mitta Mitta
Mt Bogong (1986m)
Falls Creek Alpine Village
Mt Hotham Alpine Village
Mt Hotham (1868m)
Dinner Plain
Mt Feathertop (1922m)
Tawonga
Mt Beauty
Bogong
Harrietville
Bright
Porepunkah
Kiewa Valley Hwy
Yackandandah
Beechworth
Myrtleford
Great Alpine Road
The Horn (1723m)
Mt Buffalo Chalet
Wangaratta
Oxley
Milawa
Moyhu
King Valley
Whitfield
Glenrowan
Tatong
Mt Stirling (1747m)
Mt Buller (1805m)
Mt Buller Alpine Village
Merrijig
Mansfield
Howqua
Jamieson
Goulburn River
Gaffneys Creek
A1 Mining Settlement
Woods Point
Matlock
Licola
Wonnangatta River
Dargo
Dargo River
Mitchell River
Swifts Creek
Buchan
Bruthen
Nowa Nowa
Lake Tyers
Lakes Entrance
Metung
Bairnsdale
Princes Highway
To Sale & Melbourne
Maffra
Heyfield
Walhalla
Erica
Thomson Reservoir
Mt St Gwinear (1250m)
Mt Baw Baw (1564m)
Baw Baw Alpine Village
Noojee
Upper Yarra Dam
Cumberland Junction
Lake Mountain (1433m)
Marysville
Eildon
Lake Eildon
Bonnie Doon
Alexandra
Maroondah Hwy
Midland Hwy
Benalla
Lake Mokoan
Devenish
Hume Fwy
To Wodonga
To Seymour & Melbourne
Yea
Goulburn Valley Hwy
Melba Hwy
Healesville
Kinglake
Yarra Glen
Yarra River
Warburton
Mt Donna Buang (1250m)
Yarra Junction
To Melbourne
Lilydale
Ferntree Gully
Dandenong
Gembrook
0 20 40 km
A1 A39 A300 B300 B340 B360 B500 C106 C315 C366 C425 C426 C486 C511 C521 C524 C526 C527 C531 C534 C543 C545 C601 C608 M31

MT BAW BAW

• **elev 1564m**

Mt Baw Baw village (1480m) is a small ski resort in the centre of the Baw Baw National Park and on the edge of the Baw Baw plateau. While it doesn't receive the attention of Falls Creek and Mts Buller and Hotham, it's a good option for novices and families, and tends to be more relaxed, less hectic and less hyped than the three main resorts. It's popular on weekends, but is seldom overcrowded.

There are eight lifts, a good range of beginner to intermediate runs, and a few harder runs. The skiable downhill area is 25 hectares and the runs are 25% beginners, 64% intermediate and 11% advanced, with a vertical drop of 140m. It's also an excellent base for cross-country skiing, with plenty of trails, including one that connects to the Mt St Gwinear trails on the southern edge of the plateau.

All year there's a small alpine village with a tourist centre (toilets and lockers), while during the snow season there are several ski-hire places, two licensed restaurants (Kelly's Cafe and Village Hotel) and a couple of take-away food places. The day car park is close to the village and lifts.

If you're just after somewhere to ski, and you're not too concerned about the social or après-ski side of things, Mt Baw Baw is a good option and has some reasonably priced places to stay.

Information

There is an administration and information office of the Mt Baw Baw Alpine Resort Management Board (☎ 5165 1136, email mtbawbaw@bawbawar.com.au) in the centre of the village.

Costs

Gate entry fees are $17 per car for the day car park only during the snow season. The lifts only operate if there is snow and tickets for a full day cost $44 per adult, $22 per child; combined lift-and-lesson packages cost $58 per adult, $37 per child. The cross-country daily trail fee is $3.

Places to Stay

There are three main places to stay here, although more of the private lodges are now taking bookings – the Mt Baw Baw Alpine Resort Management Board office can advise you about accommodation options. Outside of the winter season you also need to book ahead as none of the lodges are staffed year-round.

Everest Lodge *(☎ 5823 2466)* is in the village and has bunk rooms in club-type accommodation with a good standard of facilities. In summer a bed is $15 per person and during the ski season it's $25 a night mid-week and $70 for the weekend per person.

The ***Cascade Ski Apartments*** *(☎ 9764 9939 or 1800 229 229 toll-free)* has good self-contained flats with kitchenettes. The units sleep from two to five people and cost around $445 for a weekend, and $560 for five nights during mid-week. In summer, there is a minimum two night stay and a bed costs $25 per person.

Getting There & Away

By car, Mt Baw Baw is 176km and an easy three hour drive from the centre of Melbourne. You can either take the Princes Highway (A1), or go via Yarra Junction and Powelltown, to Noojee, from where you take Baw Baw Rd. The last section of the drive from Noojee is slow but very scenic, and takes about an hour as the road is unsurfaced in sections (it's to be fully surfaced by early 2000), and steep and winding.

There is no public transport between Melbourne and Mt Baw Baw.

MT ST GWINEAR

• **elev 1250m**

Mt St Gwinear is a cross-country skiing area in the Baw Baw National Park, managed by Parks Victoria (☎ 5165 3204). It's 171km from Melbourne, the main access route being the Princes Hwy to Moe, then north via Erica.

The main trail is 9km long across the Baw Baw plateau, connecting to the alpine village at Mt Baw Baw. Various other shorter marked trails (1km to 3km) are set up during the season. Facilities are limited – there's a car park, day shelter and toilets year-round, while during the snow season there's also a ranger's office, toboggan hire and take-away food huts. Accommodation, ski equipment and chain hire are also available at Erica. Nordic ski patrols operate only on weekends.

The day entry fee is $8 per car during the snow season – no fees apply if you're snow camping overnight.

MARYSVILLE

• **pop 625**

This delightful little town was established as a private mountain retreat back in 1863, and later developed into a European-style resort town. By the 1920s there were over a dozen guesthouses here, and the town became known as Melbourne's honeymoon capital. Today, Marysville is a popular getaway town, with its beautiful mountain setting, old-fashioned timber guesthouses, flower gardens, streams and waterfalls, fern gullies and bushwalks through the forests. The area is particularly pretty in autumn, when the deciduous trees start dropping their leaves in a blaze of colour. In winter, Marysville is the main base for the cross-country ski fields of Lake Mountain, 21km to the east.

The quite unique statues at **Bruno's Art & Sculptures Garden** at 51 Falls Rd, depict various cultures in a fabulous native garden setting. The gallery is open weekends and public holidays from 10 am to 5 pm, while the garden is open daily. Admission to both for adults is $4 and children under 12 years old are free. Another new attraction is **The Marysville Museum** at 49 Darwin St, just behind the General Store. It has a superb collection of vintage cars, motorcycles, a fire engine and a Romany caravan. It's open daily from 10 am to 5 pm. Admission costs $8 adults, free for children under 12, $5 under-18s.

There are many bush tracks to walk, especially to Nicholl's Lookout, Keppel's Lookout and Mt Gordon. The Department of Natural Resources & Environment (NRE) publishes *Marysville Forest Walks* and various other brochures and guides to the area's natural attractions – these are available from the tourist information centre or Parks Victoria/NRE's offices.

Steavenson's Falls, which are the state's highest, and among the most spectacular, waterfalls, are beautifully floodlit until midnight each night, and visitors can hand-feed the possums here. **Cumberland Scenic Reserve**, with numerous walks and the Cora Lynn and Cumberland Falls, is 16km east of Marysville.

The **Lady Talbot Drive**, which starts in Marysville and takes you in a 48km scenic loop past some of the area's prettiest spots and most spectacular features, is one of Parks Victoria's Great Forest Drives of Victoria – a map and brochure to the drive is available from its offices.

Information

The Mystic Mountains Tourism tourist information centre (☎ 5963 4567, www.mm.tourism.com.au) is on Murchison St and is open daily from 9 am to 5 pm.

Parks Victoria (☎ 5963 3310) and NRE have an office in 38 Lyell St.

Activities

You can take two hour to full day trail or overnight horse rides at the Black Spur Trail Riding Centre (☎ 5963 7191) in Narbethong, about 12km from Marysville.

Special Events

The Wirreanda Festival is held annually over the Melbourne Cup weekend in early November. It's a celebration of spring, and features garden open days, a parade, an art show and other events. To celebrate autumn, there is the Marys-festa-Ville, during early April, with a Sunday market and musical performances.

Places to Stay

Marysville has a good range of guesthouses, cottages and B&Bs, most are reasonably up-market and many offer package deals that include dinner, bed and breakfast. Great if you're looking to splurge, but there aren't too many options for budget travellers.

Camping, Caravan Parks & Bunkhouses One inexpensive option is the popular and scenic ***Marysville Caravan Park*** *(☎ 5963 3443)*, on Buxton St, beside the river. You can get a tent site from $12 to $14 or an on-site van from $38 to $44. They also have two 12-bed bunkrooms with cooking facilities; a bed costs $10 to $14 per person, depending on the season.

Motels The cheapest of the motels is the rambling ***Crossways Motel*** *(☎ 5963 3290)*, on Woods Point Rd, which has budget log cabin-style motel units from $50/55 for singles/doubles. The ***Tower Motel*** *(☎ 5963 3225, 33 Murchison St)* has rooms from $72/84.

Guesthouses, Cottages & B&Bs Guesthouses include the enormous ***Marylands Country House*** *(☎ 5963 3204, 22 Falls Rd)*, which has B&B from $190 a double, or $260, including dinner; and the ***Mountain Lodge*** *(☎ 5963 3270, 32 Kings Rd)*, which has rooms from $80 per person, including all meals.

The ***Dalrymple Guest Cottages*** *(☎ 5963 3416, 18 Falls Rd)* has four attractive, spacious and romantic timber cottages with open fires from $110 for doubles.

If you're looking for somewhere self-contained, try the ***Blackwood Cottages*** *(☎ 5963 3333, 38 Falls Rd)* – it has two bedroom, self-contained units that sleep up to five people and cost $75 to $170 a night.

Mathilde's of Marysville *(☎ 5963 3697, 19 Red Hill Rd)* is a stylish two storey timber cottage in a bushland setting with three smallish guestrooms. B&B is from $140 a double, and three course dinner is $50.

Places to Eat

There are several take-away food places and the ***Bakery*** is a popular place for lunch. ***Marysville Hotel Motel*** *(42 Murchison St)* has excellent pub-style food, and the menu at ***Steavensons Restaurant***, also on Murchison St, is small but the food is good.

The ***Fruit Salad Farm*** *(☎ 5963 3232)* on Aubrey-Couzens Drive, has superb food. The rather twee restaurant is in a garden setting and bookings are recommended for Saturday nights.

Getting There & Away

McKenzie's Bus Lines (☎ 9853 6264) runs a daily bus service from the Spencer St bus terminal in Melbourne to Marysville costing $11.20 one way. The journey takes around 2 hours and these buses continue on to Alexandra and Eildon.

LAKE MOUNTAIN

• **elev 1430m**

Lake Mountain is 120km and less than two hours drive from Melbourne, via Marysville. The cross-country skiing facilities are world class, with an extensive system of about 40km of trails that are groomed daily. The trails are divided evenly between beginners, intermediate and advanced, and there are seven toboggan runs. Ski patrols operate daily during the season.

Gerraty's is the main parking area at the summit. The Lake Mountain Alpine Resort Management Board (LMARMB) has an information centre (☎ 5963 3288) which is open daily during the snow season from 7 am to 6 pm and the rest of the year weekdays from 8 am to 4.30 pm. They also provide an EFTPOS facility for withdrawing cash. Nearby, there's a year-round visitor's shelter with toilets and a public telephone, while during the snow season there's also a ski and toboggan-hire hut, a ski school and a kiosk.

There's no accommodation on the mountain. The closest is at Marysville, 21km to the west. Summer and snow camping are allowed – there's no fee, but you must notify the LMARMB office of your intentions before heading out.

The day entry fee is $18 per car during the snow season. The daily trail fee is $8 for adults and $4 for kids.

Getting There & Away

V/Line has a daily bus service from Melbourne to Marysville operated by McKenzie's Bus Lines (see the Getting There & Away section for Marysville). On weekends when there is skiable snow, the LMARMB runs the complimentary Fallon's Bus Service (☎ 5772 1768) from Marysville to Lake Mountain, departing Marysville at 9 am and returning at 4.30 pm. The journey takes about 45 minutes. Otherwise, the Australian Adventure Experience (☎ 5772 1440 or 0417 028 004) runs 4WD chartered services from Marysville to Lake Mountain. They also have ski package tours, including accommodation, transport, ski hire and instruction from $108 per day.

CATHEDRAL RANGE STATE PARK

The Cathedral Range State Park is roughly 10km north-west of Marysville, and offers excellent bushwalks and camping. It's a small park of approximately 3500 hectares, dominated by the 7km-long razorback ridge of the ranges, which reach a height of over 800m.

The vegetation in the park varies dramatically – from tall open forests to damp sheltered gullies, and subsequently there is a wide variety of animal and birdlife here. This area has long been a favourite spot for all types of outdoor activities, including bushwalking, rock climbing, fishing, camping and hang-gliding.

There are several access roads to the park off the Maroondah Hwy (B320) and Marysville Rd, although you should check on road conditions during the wet seasons.

Places to Stay

There are four campsites in the park, at Ned's Gully, Blackwood Flat, Cook's Mill, and the Farmyard. For more information on the park, contact the Parks Victoria/NRE offices in Marysville or Alexandra.

The YHA-associated ***Australian Bush Settlement*** *(☎ 5774 7378, email bushlife@mynet.net.au)*, west of the park, on the Maroondah Hwy between Buxton and Taggerty, is an adventure camp and youth hostel on a farm property. It costs $15 a night ($20 for nonmembers). This place is about 15km north of Marysville.

ALEXANDRA

• pop 1850

Alexandra is another former gold-mining town that developed into the centre of a thriving timber industry. There is an extensive narrow-gauge steam railway system that was built through the area's forests to link the network of bush sawmills to the town.

While it's the largest town in this area and still sports an interesting collection of historic buildings, Alexandra is now more of an administrative and commercial centre than a tourist destination. One point of interest is the **Timber & Tramways Museum** (☎ 5772 2392), in the old train station in Station St, which opens every second Sunday from 10 am to 4 pm; entry costs $7 for adults, $2.50 for children.

The information centre (☎ 5772 1100) is on Grant St, opposite Rotary Park. It's open daily from 9 am to 5 pm.

The NRE has an office (☎ 5772 0200) at 46 Aitken St.

Places to Stay & Eat

There are numerous motels and B&Bs in and around Alexandra. The ***Shamrock Hotel*** *(☎ 5772 1015, 80 Grant St)* is an emerald-green 1920s pub that has been fully restored. It has good pub rooms upstairs from $20/40 for singles/doubles (including a continental breakfast), an excellent bistro and cheap bar meals.

The ***Redgate Motel*** *(☎ 5772 1777)* on Rose St, off the main road, is a neat older-style motel with rooms from $56/60.

Eleven kilometres north-west of Alexandra, ***Mittagong Homestead*** *(☎ 5772 1586)* is a farm where you can either stay in the luxury guest wing of the homestead, or in one of the units in the converted old woolshed; B&B is from $120 to $150 a night.

Pendaven *(☎ 5772 2452, email pendaven@mynet.net.au, 159 Halls Flat Rd)*, is about 1km south of Alexandra, and is a place with style and grand panoramic views of valleys and mountains. The modern, stylish rooms are $190 a double or $160 a night for a weekend two night package, including breakfast.

EILDON

• **pop 700**

The town of Eildon was originally built in the 1950s to house people working on the Eildon Dam project. Since then it has developed into a popular recreation and holiday base for both Lake Eildon and the surrounding Lake Eildon National Park. It's a small town, with one pub and a small shopping centre, and most of the accommodation is in motels or caravan parks. The main boat harbour is 2km north of the town.

From the town centre, you can drive across the top of the dam's massive retaining wall. On the other side is a lookout point, boat launching ramps and the state park. A road leads around the lake to the Jerusalem Inlet.

Lake Eildon, created as a massive reservoir for irrigation and hydro-electric schemes, has a shoreline of over 500km and is one of the state's favourite water-sports playgrounds – water-skiing, fishing, sailing, sail-boarding, jet-skiing and houseboat holidays are all popular.

Information

There's a tourist information centre (☎ 5774 2909) on Main St, opposite the small shopping centre. It's open from 10 am to 2 pm daily.

Things to See & Do

The **Snobs Creek Visitor Centre** is a trout farm and hatchery run by the NRE. Visitors can watch two short films on the fish hatchery, feed the fish and visit the series of aquarium tanks with 22 different kinds of fish, eel and frog. The centre is on the Goulburn Valley Hwy (B340) 6km south-west of Eildon and opens daily during the school holidays from 10 am to 4 pm, and the rest of the year from Saturday to Wednesday from 11 am. It costs $5 for adults and $2.50 for concessions and kids.

Lake Eildon Holiday Boats (☎ 5774 2107), with moorings in the Eildon boat harbour, hires boats for skiing, fishing or cruising on the lakes. Horse rides, from short trots to overnight rides, are offered by Great Divide Adventure Rides (☎ 5774 2122) on Skyline Rd, Eildon.

Places to Stay & Eat

There's a wealth of caravan parks in and around Eildon, as well as campsites in the Lake Eildon National Park – you'll need to make a booking for these sites during the holiday seasons by phoning the ***Lake Eildon Camping & Cabins*** *(☎ 5772 1293)*.

The ***Eildon Caravan Park*** *(☎ 5774 2105)*, on Eildon Rd, is a good campground beside the pond, with plenty of trees and barbecues. Campsites cost $15 to $17, and on-site vans and en suite cabins $42 to $62.

The ***Golden Trout Hotel/Motel*** *(☎ 5774 2508)*, on Eildon Rd, is a timber motel with older units from $45/50 for singles/doubles and modern units from $65/70. The pub has a good bistro with meals from $11 to $15, or bar meals in the Sportsman's Bar from $5 to $8. The ***Eildon Lakes Motel*** *(☎ 5774 2800)* on Girdwood Parade, has rooms ranging from $50/65.

Lake Eildon Holiday Boats *(☎ 5774 2107)*, with moorings in the Eildon boat harbour, hires houseboats that sleep between six and 10 people and cost from $750 to $4950 a week – houseboats can also be hired for a weekend (three nights) or midweek (four nights).

The modern ***Coco's Restaurant & Bar*** *(☎ 5774 2866)*, overlooking the boat harbour, has an interesting international-style menu with dinner mains from $15 to $20, and a cheaper, more casual lunch menu. It's open for dinner from Thursday to Sunday and for lunch on weekends.

Eucalypt Ridge *(☎ 5774 2033, 546 Skyline Rd)*, about 11km north-west above Eildon town, is one of the most luxurious B&Bs with a spectacular vista of Lake Eildon and the Victorian Alps. The prices are as high as the ridge at $500 per person, but it has marble bathrooms, deluxe furnishings, French champagne and dinner is included.

Getting There & Away

McKenzie's Bus Lines (☎ 9853 6264) in Melbourne runs a daily service to Eildon ($18, one way) via Marysville ($10.70) and Alexandra ($15.20).

LAKE EILDON NATIONAL PARK

The Lake Eildon National Park surrounds the southern and central sections of the huge and sprawling Lake Eildon, covering an area of over 27,000 hectares. The park is very scenic and provides excellent opportunities for bushwalking and camping.

From the middle of the 19th century, the areas around Lake Eildon were logged and mined for gold, so most of the vegetation is regrowth eucalypt forest.

There are several lakeside camping areas at Coller Bay in the Fraser section, which are equally popular with campers and kangaroos – you'll need to book during summer by phoning the ***Lake Eildon Camping & Cabins*** office *(☎ 5772 1293)*. A kiosk sells basic supplies at the gate to the bay and the entry fee is $6 per car. There are various walking tracks throughout the park, including the **Candlebark Nature Walk**.

In the Jerusalem section, the main camping areas are at Jerusalem Creek and along the Eildon to Jamieson road, which forms the southern boundary of the park. This road is steep, winding, and unsealed in sections, but particularly scenic. Various 4WD tracks lead off the road into, and across the park to the lake. Camping areas are in high demand over summer, and can be booked through the ***Lake Eildon Camping & Cabins*** office *(☎ 5772 1293)*.

BONNIE DOON

This small lakeside town, spread around the northern arm of Lake Eildon, is a good base for activities like water-skiing, yachting, fishing, canoeing and horse riding. The Mansfield/Melbourne bus stops at Bonnie Doon town centre on Maroondah Hwy but there is no public transport to the places to stay, following.

The ***Lakeside Leisure Resort*** *(☎ 5778 7252)*, on Hutchinsons Rd, about 2km east of town, is a modern caravan and tourist park on the lake's edge. It has a YHA-associated hostel with four eight-bed bunkrooms costing $14 for YHA members ($17 nonmembers). Campsites cost from $9, and self-contained cabins from $75. The facilities are good, including sailboards and boats for hire.

The ***Lakeland Resort Hotel*** *(☎ 5778 7335)*, on Maroondah Hwy, is a large, modern, colonial-style hotel with motel units from $60/70. The ***Mountain Bar*** is a good spot for a drink, and their ***bistro*** has mains in the $9 to $17 range.

Starglen Lodge *(☎ 5778 7312)*, 10km north, is a 200 hectare bush property in the foothills of the Strathbogie Ranges. It has 20 small en suite units, and lodge facilities include a pool, spa, tennis courts and a guest lounge. The tariff for dinner, B&B costs $180 a double. It also offers guests or casual visitors horse-trail rides, costing $15 an hour or $95 a day.

Peppin Point Houseboats *(☎ 5778 7338)*, based 9km south of Bonnie Doon, hires houseboats that sleep up to 10 people and cost from $1250 to $2350 a week – houseboats can also be hired for weekends (three nights) or mid-week (four nights).

JAMIESON

The road from Jamieson to Eildon is quite spectacular, climbing and twisting through the edge of the Eildon State Park.

Jamieson is a sprawling country village in a scenic setting on the tip of the south-eastern arm of Lake Eildon. The area attracts a blend of people – water-skiers, power boaters, 4WD enthusiasts, bushwalkers, duck-shooters and hunters. It tends to get crowded in the holiday seasons (and especially so at the opening of duck-hunting season), but at other times it's a fairly quiet and remote backwater.

Jamieson was a thriving frontier town during the gold-rush days of the 1860s, and once had nine pubs and two breweries. Some of the few remaining historic buildings have been converted to cater for visitors to the area. There is a post office but no bank.

The **Historic Jamieson Courthouse** on Nash St has a local goldmining exhibit and is also the tourist information centre. It's open from 10 am to 6 pm, weekends and public holidays, between November and Easter. Admission is $2 for adults; $1 for children.

Places to Stay & Eat

The ***Jamieson Caravan Park*** *(☎ 5777 0567)*, on Nash St, has campsites from $14 and on-site vans and cabins from $30 to $45. The ***Courthouse Hotel/Motel*** *(☎ 5777 0690)* has motel-style rooms for $25/40 for singles/doubles and also serves counter meals. The ***Lakeside Hotel*** *(☎ 5777 0515)*, on the Eildon road 3km from Jamieson, has old motel-style rooms from $30/45.

Duck Inn Jamieson *(☎ 5777 0554, email duckin@bigpond.com)*, on Bank St, is a guesthouse and restaurant set in the charming old Colonial Bank building (1866). They have three double rooms with a guest lounge and open fire, and B&B starts at $80 for doubles. The restaurant serves Devonshire tea, lunch on weekends and dinner on Saturdays. Lunches range from $9, dinner is a three course, fixed price menu at $30 a head.

JAMIESON TO WALHALLA

There are some spectacular drives from Jamieson. An unsealed road heads east, and then south to **Licola**, 91km from Jamieson. This road is rough, steep and winding, and is often closed during winter.

The pick of the scenic routes, and one of the best drives in the whole state, is the 135km route south from Jamieson to Walhalla. This road is unsealed and rough in sections, winding alongside the Goulburn River, through forests and hills, and past a series of derelict gold-mining settlements, many of which were destroyed by the tragic bushfires of 1939. As well as some fascinating relics of the gold-mining era, you'll find some good camping and picnic spots along the route.

Conventional vehicles are okay for the main road, but if you want to head off the beaten track, you'll need a 4WD. This is some of the best 4WD territory in Victoria, and there's an abundance of backroads and tracks through this spectacular and unspoilt mountain countryside.

Eleven kilometres south of Jamieson, the old and helpful ***Kevington Hotel*** *(☎ 5777 0543)* has basic pub rooms at $25 per person, including continental breakfast. South of Kevington, at the Tunnel Bend Reserve, there's a ***campground*** with picnic facilities, and some good swimming spots in the Goulburn River.

Continuing south, you pass through the small mining settlements of **Gaffneys Creek** and the **A1 Mining Settlement**.

Woods Point, 55km south of Jamieson, is a tiny and historic gold-mining town set in a valley on the upper reaches of the Goulburn River. There's a pub, a tiny museum, a general store and a petrol station here. The friendly ***Commercial Hotel*** *(☎ 5777 8224)* is a great pub with accommodation at $35/70 for singles/doubles, or $80 a double with en suite – tariffs include a cooked breakfast, and the pub's bistro serves lunch and dinner.

Matlock, eight kilometres south-east of Woods Point, is another former gold-mining settlement with spectacular views and a handful of houses. From there, you can head 55km west to **Cumberland Junction** (and from there either south to Warburton or north to Marysville), or continue east and then south, down to Walhalla.

MANSFIELD

• **pop 2550**

During the ski season Mansfield is the gateway to Mt Buller. It's also one of the High Country's best base-towns, with a good range of accommodation, some excellent restaurants and easy access to places like Mt Stirling and nearby Lake Eildon.

The area around Mansfield was first settled as a pastoral run in 1839. The town was established during the gold-mining era, and later became a centre for the local timber and farming industries. Today it's a progressive country town and a popular all-seasons destination – apart from skiing in winter, other activities in the area include horse riding, bushwalking, canoeing, water-skiing and even camel trekking.

The graves of three police officers killed by Ned Kelly at Tolmie in 1878 are in the **Mansfield cemetery** (at the end of Highett St), and there's a monument to them in the centre of the roundabout on the corner of High and Highett Sts.

Information

The Mansfield visitor information centre (☎ 5775 1464, email infocent@mansfield.net.au), in the old train station on High St, opens daily from 9 am to 5 pm – they also run an accommodation booking service (☎ 1800 060 686 toll-free). While you're here, pick up a copy of the glossy tourism brochure called *Mansfield Lakes, Rivers & High Country*, which has details activities, tours and accommodation.

The NRE has an office (☎ 5733 0120) at 33 Highett St.

Activities

There are quite a few companies in this region that take people on horse-trail rides through the High Country, such as Stoney's Bluff and Beyond (☎ 5775 2212), Watson's Mountain Country Rides (☎ 5777 3552) and Merrijig Lodge (☎ 5777 5590).

Mountain Adventure Safaris (☎ 5777 3759, email mas@mansfield.net.au) offers a wide range of tours in the area, including mountain-bike rides, white-water rafting, trekking, abseiling and more. High Country Camel Treks (☎ 5775 1591), 7km south, offers one hour rides ($18), as well as one, two and five-day alpine treks.

You can enjoy the region from a hot-air balloon with Global Ballooning (☎ 9428 5703), or by helicopter with High Country by Helicopter (☎ 018 376 619).

Special Events

Mansfield's Mountain Country Festival, held annually over the week leading up to the Melbourne Cup, is a family festival featuring a mountain-horse race, art exhibitions, bush markets, fireworks, concerts and a grand parade. There is a Balloon Festival on the weekend closest to Anzac Day in late April, and for fine food and wine there is the Harvest Festival in early March.

Places to Stay

Camping & Caravan Parks The *James Holiday Park Caravan Park* (☎ 5775 2705), on Ultimo St, is quite close to the town centre and has tent sites from $14 and on-site vans from $35.

Hostels The *Mansfield Backpackers' Inn* (☎ 5775 1800, 112 High St) is now part of the *Travellers Lodge*. It's well set up with good, modern facilities, including a laundry, drying room, lounge and kitchen. It's in a stylishly restored heritage building with doubles, four and six bunk rooms from $15 per person per night ($20 in winter). The motel-type rooms cost from $60 a double. They can also arrange discounts for guests on some restaurant meals and local tours and activities.

Pubs & Motels The two pubs on diagonally opposite sides of the main roundabout, the *Mansfield Hotel* (☎ 5775 2101) and the *Delatite Hotel* (☎ 5775 2004), have pub rooms from $20 and $25 per person for B&B, respectively.

The modern *Mansfield Valley Motel* (☎ 5775 1300), on the Maroondah Hwy, has good rooms at $100/110 a night. The *Mansfield Motel* (☎ 5775 2377, 3 Highett St) is a bit older but has comfortable double rooms from $61 to $73. Both have swimming pools.

Guesthouses, Resorts & B&Bs The *Alzburg Resort* (☎ 5775 2367, 39 Malcolm St) is a large holiday complex built around a century-old convent. It's now a rambling motel-cum-guesthouse, with good facilities, including a restaurant, bar and disco, swimming pool, spa and sauna, tennis courts and ski hire. The rooms sleep up to six people, some have kitchenettes and prices start at $55 in summer and $75 in winter per double.

Highton Manor *(☎ 5775 2700)*, on Highton Lane, is a historic two-storey homestead built in 1896 for Francis Highett, a tennis champ and tenor who sang with Dame Nellie Melba. They have six beds in the loft for roughly $35 per person, and not-too-flash motel-style, dark, guestrooms in the old stables from $75 to $95 a double, or luxurious B&B rooms in the homestead from $150. Breakfast and Saturday (only) evening meals are served in the homestead's dining room.

The ***Alpine Country Cottage*** *(☎ 5775 1694)*, on The Parade, has a simple and tiny one-bedroom timber cottage, and a larger two-bedroom cottage, in the backyard of a house. B&B starts at $125 a double. Extras that other B&Bs don't include are a bowl of fruit, newspapers, orange juice and condiments.

Places to Eat

There are plenty of eateries in Mansfield. ***Bon Apetit*** *(39 High St)* is an excellent deli

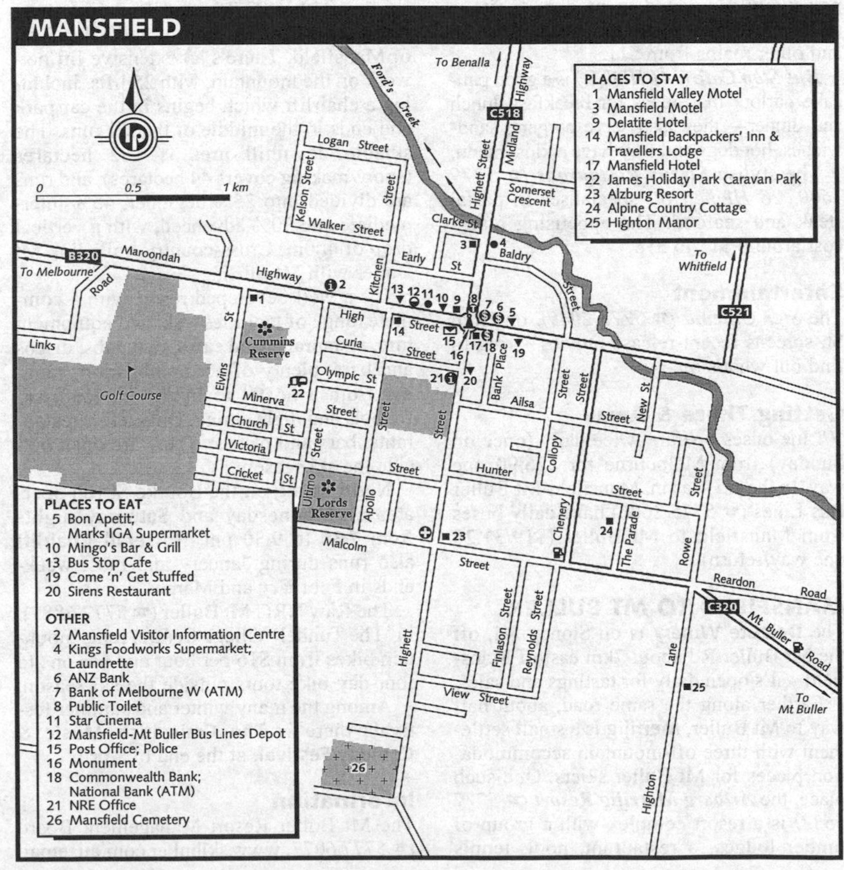

and cafe with tasty goodies such as pasta, cheese, olive, cake and smallgoods, and they also make gourmet sandwiches. For a pub meal, try the bistros at either the ***Mansfield Hotel*** or the ***Delatite Hotel*** – both have mains from $9 to $16.

Come 'n' Get Stuffed on High St has a very inventive international menu for breakfast, lunch or dinner from $4 to $17. Try the Moroccan Lamb and one of their desserts, or just have a drink at the bar.

Mingo's Bar & Grill *(☎ 5775 1766, 101 High St)* is a good place for lunch or dinner. The split-level dining room has been impressively renovated in modern heritage style. The dinner menu has pastas from $8 and other mains from $11.

Bus Stop Cafe *(141 High St)* is a good pancake parlour that opens for breakfast, lunch and dinner – they also serve burgers, sandwiches, hot dogs and they have a kids' menu.

The stylish ***Sirens Restaurant*** *(☎ 5779 1600, 28 Highett St)* specialises in pasta, steak and seafood. The appetising mains cost around $13 to $18.

Entertainment

The ***Star Cinema*** *(☎ 5775 2049)*, on High St, screens recent-release movies – ring to find out what's on.

Getting There & Away

V/Line buses operate twice daily (once on Sunday) from Melbourne for $26.90 one way. In the ski season, Mansfield-Mt Buller Bus Lines (☎ 5775 2606) have daily buses from Mansfield to Mt Buller ($19/31.20 one way/return).

MANSFIELD TO MT BULLER

The **Delatite Winery** is on Stoney Rd, off the Mt Buller Rd about 7km east of Mansfield – it's open daily for tastings and sales.

Farther along the same road, about half way to Mt Buller, **Merrijig** is a small settlement with three off-mountain accommodation places for Mt Buller skiers. One such place, the ***Arlberg Merrijig Resort*** *(☎ 5777 5633)* is a resort complex with a group of timber lodges, a restaurant, pool, tennis courts and motel-style rooms from $55 to $80 a double.

Between Merrijig and the base of Mt Buller there are several B&B's and other places to stay scattered along the roadside. Another 3km farther from Merrijig is ***Willawong B&B*** *(☎5777 5750)*, overlooking the valley of the Delatite River. The modern and cosy rooms cost from $90 a double, including breakfast.

MT BULLER

• elev 1600m

Mt Buller is Victoria's largest and busiest ski resort. It's 237km and less than three hours drive from Melbourne and 47km west of Mansfield. There's an extensive lift network on the mountain, with 25 lifts, including a chairlift which begins in the car park and ends in the middle of the ski runs. The skiable downhill area is 162 hectares (snow-making covers 44 hectares), and runs are divided into 25% beginner, 45% intermediate and 30% advanced, with a vertical drop of 400m. Cross-country trails link Mt Buller with Mt Stirling.

It's a well developed resort with a complete range of facilities – ski and equipment hire, restaurants and cafes, two pubs, discos and bars, plenty of accommodation (ranging from a hostel to luxury chalets), ski schools and night skiing. Only a few restaurants, bars and places to stay are open outside the ski season.

Night skiing on the Bourke St run operates on Wednesday and Saturday nights from 7.30 to 9.30 pm. **Horsehill Chairlift** also runs during January and most weekends in February and March.

The Raw NRG Mt Buller (☎ 5777 6887), in 'The Tunnel' Village Centre, rents mountain bikes from $16 per hour and has one to four-day bike tours outside the ski season.

Among the many winter and summer festivals there is **The Craic Irish Music & Comedy Festival**, at the end of April.

Information

The Mt Buller Resort Management Board (☎ 5777 6077, www.skibuller.com.au, email mbresort@mansfield.net.au,) shares premises in the village with the post office on Summit Rd. It's open weekdays from 8.30 am to 5 pm and weekends in summer 10 am to 4 pm. In winter the information office is 100m farther along Summit Rd, opposite the Village Centre Building and is open daily from 8.30 am to 5 pm, although these hours can vary.

Costs

Gate entry fees are $18 per car, for the day car park only, during the snow season. Lift tickets for a full day cost $62 for an adult, $32 for a child. (Half day tickets are only available in the afternoon.) Combined lift-and-lesson packages cost $95 for an adult, $55 for a child.

Places to Stay

There are over 7000 beds on the mountain. There are all sorts of different rates – for high and low seasons; mid-week and weekends; summer and the number of people sharing a room.

Mt Buller Central Reservations (☎ 1800 039 049 toll-free) can book accommodation in commercial lodges from around $75 per person. Club lodges generally have bunk accommodation and kitchen facilities; prices start from around $45 per person. Most commercial lodges don't have kitchen facilities for the guests, but the tariffs usually include breakfast and sometimes dinner.

The ***Mt Buller Youth Hostel*** *(☎ 5777 6181)* is, of course, the cheapest commercial place on the mountain. It's only open during the ski season, and the nightly rate is $45 for members, $49 for nonmembers. You'll need to book well in advance – ring (☎ *9670 3802*). The ***Preston Alpine Lodge*** *(☎ 5777 6336)* at the end of Stirling Rd has beds in summer from $15 per person and in winter from $50.

The ***Kooroora Hotel*** *(☎ 5777 6050)* is another winter-only place with very basic, budget, three or four-bed rooms with en suites around $70 per person on the weekends or $60 mid-week – tariffs include breakfast. ***Avalanche Lodge*** *(☎ 9663 0811)*, which has doubles from around $55 in summer and $75 per person in winter, including breakfast.

The luxurious ***Mt Buller Chalet Hotel*** *(☎ 5777 6566)*, on Summit Rd, has rooms from $150 a double in summer and up to $440 in winter. The hotel also has a swimming pool (open to the public), restaurant, cafe and a sports centre.

Places to Eat

If you're staying somewhere with kitchen facilities, there's a licensed supermarket in the Moloney's building in the village centre, but in summer it's not well stocked. In winter there are various kiosks and takeaway places scattered around the mountain, selling the usual range of microwaved pies and hot dogs.

Koflers is a ski-in bistro at the base of the Summit Run, where you can enjoy the views while you eat. Another winter only place is the ***Kooroora Hotel*** in the village, which has a large and varied breakfast, lunch and dinner blackboard menu.

Of the numerous restaurants, one of the best is ***Pension Grimus*** *(☎ 5777 6396)* on Breathtaker Rd, next to the Bourke St ski school. It's open nightly during the season (around $50 per person for three courses) and on weekends for lunch (around $25 per person).

The restaurants, bars and cafes at the ***Mt Buller Chalet Hotel*** and the ***Arlberg Hotel*** are open all year.

Entertainment

The dreary ***Arlberg Hotel*** and ***Kooroora Hotel*** both have discos and regular live bands. For a quiet drink, the ***Abomb*** on Summit Rd has plenty of atmosphere, or try the cocktail bars at the ***Alpine Retreat*** or ***Breathtaker*** lodges. All of these places are only open during the snow season.

Getting There & Around

V/Line has buses twice-daily from Melbourne to Mansfield, $26.90 each way; Mansfield-Mt Buller Buslines (☎ 5775 2606) runs winter-only connecting bus services to

Mt Buller, for $19/31.20 one-way/return. Mt Buller Snowcaper Day Tours (☎ 1800 033 023 toll-free) have winter-only day trips on weekends $110 and midweek $100, which include return transport from Melbourne, lift tickets and a lesson; gear hire is another $20.

Car parking during the ski season at Mt Buller is below the village. There is a 4WD taxi service that moves people around the village and to and from the car parks; fares are $4 within the village and $8.50 between the car parks and the village.

If you're coming just for the day you can take the quad chairlift from the Horsehill day car park into the skiing area and save time by bypassing the village – ski hire and lift tickets are available at the base of the chairlift. However, there is a free day-tripper shuttle bus service between the day car park and the village. Outside the ski season the above mentioned services don't operate and it's possible to park in the village.

MT STIRLING

• **elev 1757m**

Mt Stirling is an excellent cross-country ski area, a few kilometres north-west of Mt Buller alpine village and 40km from Mansfield, with no public transport access. There is an extensive range of over 60km of mostly groomed cross-country ski trails here. The trails link Mt Stirling with the alpine village at nearby Mt Buller, but are only useable for a short time during the season when the snow line is low. Ski patrols operate daily on the main trails.

The Mt Buller Rd from Mansfield is the main access route – the turn-off to Mt Stirling is 16km south of Mt Buller, just before the entry gates at Mirimbah at the base of Mt Buller.

There's no accommodation on the mountain and the facilities are limited. At the Telephone Box Junction car park area, there's a year-round visitors' shelter, and during winter there's the Mt Stirling Alpine Resorts Management Board information office (☎ 5777 5624), a cross-country ski school, ski and toboggan hire, a bistro and kiosk.

The day entrance fee is $17 per car during winter only. The daily trail fee is $8 for adults, $4 for kids and $22 for families.

ALPINE NATIONAL PARK

The Alpine National Park was declared in December 1989. The park covers an area of 646,000 hectares, a substantial proportion of the High Country of the Great Dividing Range, and joins the high country areas of NSW and the Australian Capital Territory (ACT). It is divided into four separately managed units: the Bogong, Wonnangatta-Moroka, Cobberas-Tingaringy and Dartmouth areas.

Most of the ski resorts in the state are in or near the park's boundaries, but apart from these the area is largely undeveloped. Large areas which are now part of the park were used for many years for cattle grazing, but this is now being restricted.

There are plenty of access roads to and through the park, although in winter a number of the roads are closed. The opportunities for recreation and ecotourism in the area are outstanding. During winter, downhill and cross-country skiing are the main activities, but once the snow melts the area attracts bushwalkers, campers, photographers and artists, hang-gliders, horse trekkers, balloonists, cyclists, anglers, canoeists and scenic-drivers. There are a number of camping areas and picnic grounds, and bush camping is allowed in most parts of the park. The area's many walking tracks include the Australian Alps Walking Track, which extends 655km through the park from Walhalla to the outskirts of Canberra.

The park is a spectacular and fragile environment, and the vegetation throughout is quite diverse. Eucalypt forests are typical, ranging from stringybark and peppermints in the lower reaches, to blue gum and mountain ash, and alpine ash and snow gums in the higher areas. In spring and summer, the areas above the snowline are carpeted with beautiful wildflowers. More than 1100 plant species have been recorded in the park, including 12 that aren't found anywhere else in the world.

RICHARD I'ANSON

Sunset view to the Buffalo Plateau from the Mt Hotham Road

RICHARD NEBESKY

Paper daisies near Mt Hotham

RICHARD I'ANSON

Snow gum trunks ablaze with vibrant colour, Baw Baw National Park

RICHARD NEBESKY

Letter boxes at Piries, Lake Eildon

RICHARD NEBESKY

Chinese burning towers, Beechworth Cemetery

RICHARD NEBESKY

Powder magazine courtyard, Beechworth

RICHARD I'ANSON

Autumn in the parkland beside the Ovens River, Bright

Parks Victoria manages the park and has a number of offices in the region. The rangers are always a good source of information and advice, and have a good range of brochures, maps and guides to the park areas.

Nature Tours

During the no-snow seasons, Jill Dawson of Alpine Nature Rambles (☎ 5758 3492) in Falls Creek takes visitors on alpine nature walks looking at the High Country ecology, everything from insects and butterflies to plant species. The walking tours cost from $20 per person for a three hour trip; day trips are also available.

HARRIETVILLE

Harrietville, 24km south of Bright, is a pretty little town nestled in a valley at the foot of Mt Feathertop, at the point where the Ovens River forks into its east and west branches. It's also the gateway to the ski resort of Mt Hotham, although the road is sometimes closed because of snow, so check on conditions before heading up the mountain. During the ski season a shuttle-bus service connects the town with Mt Hotham.

Like most of the other towns along the Ovens Valley, Harrietville started out as a gold-mining town in the 1850s. Mining activities continued into the 1950s, and the surrounding areas bear the scars and signs of the incessant digging and dredging.

The town is also the starting and finishing point for various alpine walking tracks (including the Mt Feathertop bushwalk, one of the most popular walks in Victoria, the Razorback Ridge and the Dargo High Plains walks), and is popular on long weekends outside the ski season.

Places to Stay & Eat

The ***Harrietville Caravan & Camping Park*** *(☎ 5759 2523)* has a good spot beside the Ovens River and has sites from $5 and on-site vans from $30.

The ***Snowline Hotel*** *(☎ 5759 2524)* has motel-style units starting from $35/50 for singles/doubles and standard pub meals.

The ***Alpine Lodge Inn*** *(☎ 5759 2525)* is a motel-style lodge with units from $30/60. A continental breakfast is available for another $5.50, and the facilities include a pleasant bar and lounge, a spa and pool, and drying rooms. The ***Cas Bak Holiday Flats*** *(☎ 5759 2531)* are a collection of self-contained one and two bedroom timber cabins. They don't win any awards for interior decorating, but the setting is pretty, with a swimming pool. Cabins start at $60 a double.

The ***Lavender Hue B&B*** *(☎ 5759 2588)* is on a lavender farm, which also includes a pleasant cafe. The spacious double overlooks the Ovens River and is $110, including continental breakfast. On arrival you get Devonshire Tea and scones.

MT HOTHAM

- **elev 1750m**

Mt Hotham is 373km from Melbourne. The skiing is good – there are 13 lifts, and the skiable downhill area is 245 hectares (with about 4 beginners, 34 intermediate and 37 advanced runs), with a vertical drop of 428m. The lift system at Hotham isn't as well integrated as the other major resorts and some walking is necessary, although the 'zoo cart' (see Getting There & Around in this section) along the main road offers some relief. There is night skiing at the Big D and the Village Chairlift runs during January.

Mt Hotham is a smaller and more intimate resort than Falls Creek and Mt Buller. It's also a skiers' mountain, with more emphasis on skiing and less on après-ski activities. Off-piste skiing in steep and narrow valleys is good. Cross-country skiing is also good and ski touring on the Bogong High Plains, which you can cross to Falls Creek, is excellent. This is also the starting point for trips across the Razorback to beautiful Mt Feathertop. Below the village, on the eastern side, there is a series of trails which run as far as Dinner Plain. All these and other trails can also be hiked during summer when Mt Hotham becomes and excellent base for hikes in the High Country.

Information

The Mt Hotham Alpine Resort Management (☎ 5759 3550, www.hotham-fallscreek.com.au) has an office in the village administration centre which opens from 8 am to 5 pm daily during the snow season and weekdays the rest of the year.

Costs

The daily entry fee is $17 per car only during the ski season. Lift tickets for a full day cost $64 for adults, $33 for children. Combined lift-and-lesson packages cost $87 for adults, $59 for children.

Places to Stay

There are some 90 private and commercial lodges as well as hotels and apartments on the mountain. The Mt Hotham Accommodation Service (☎ 1800 032 061 toll-free, email hotham@netc.net.au), based in the Lawlers Apartments, can book accommodation – mainly club lodges from around $45 per person – or give advice on costs and availability of rooms. The Mt Hotham – Falls Creek Reservation Centre (☎ 1800 354 555 toll-free) in the Hotham Central building can book accommodation on the mountain. Skicom (☎ 1800 657 547 toll-free),

Mountain Pygmy Possum

For 70 years the Mountain Pygmy possum (*Burramys parvus*) was thought to be extinct, as the only evidence of its existence was fossilised remains. However, a live specimen was found at Mt Higginbotham in 1966, and today there are an estimated 3000 possums roaming the High Country. They live above an elevation of 1400m, in a restricted rocky environment of subalpine and alpine regions of Victoria and New South Wales. Their limited diet is essential to their survival and is restricted to the Mountain Plum pine, Snow Beard heath and Rambling bramble. Thus, it's not surprising that the Mountain Pygmy possum is an endangered species.

The possum's life cycle is governed by the alpine seasons, as it hibernates from April to September. The breeding season is in October and November and the female carries her offspring for a month before giving birth. The young mature quickly, becoming independent by January.

Like most animals the possum is sensitive about its environment, and increasing human activity in the alpine regions is endangering its chances of survival. Their known concentrated populations are at Mt Higginbotham, Mt Buller, Mt Bogong, Mt Loch and the Bogong High Plains, which are becoming increasingly popular for winter and summer activities. At the Mt Hotham ski resort, the ski lift company wanted to install a new ski lift at the Blue Ribbon area – a known possum habitat. In the end, the go ahead was given for the construction of the lift but only after so-called 'love tunnels' were created, so the possums could continue to hibernate and breed in the area.

Richard Nebeský

based in the Last Run Bar, is another accommodation booking service which deals mainly with apartments.

Some of the cheapest apartments are in the ***Jack Frost Lodge** (☎ 5759 3586)*. They have two sizes of self-contained apartments: the studio-style apartments sleep up to two people and cost up to $1218 per week, the two-bedroom apartments sleep up to six people and cost up to $2800 per week.

***Zirky's** (☎ 5759 3518)* has six double rooms that cost $110 per person, including a continental breakfast.

The ***Arlberg** (☎ 9809 2699)* is a large multilevel block of apartments with a bar, restaurant, disco, and licensed supermarket. They have two to eight-person self-contained apartments: the two-bed apartments cost $216 to $480 in the high season; an eight-bed apartment costs $495 to $1100 for two nights in the high season. During summer a double is $70 per night with a minimum two night stay.

Most places are closed in summer but the above mentioned accommodation services can help you. The ***Snowbird Inn** (☎ 5759 3503)* has beds in dorm-style rooms for $15 per person and rooms with en suite for $30/50 a single/double, but in winter this place is not a bargain.

Places to Eat

If you're staying somewhere with kitchen facilities, there's a small General Store supermarket next to Big D. There are several restaurants as well as a few kiosks and takeaways where you can get sandwiches, pies, hot dogs – like the other resorts, this food is generally uninspiring, microwaved and overpriced. However, ***Bedrock***, in the village administration centre, is an exception and is open all year, as is the eatery in the General Store serving pizzas and pastas.

The following places are only open in winter. ***Zirky's*** in the centre of the village is a good option for a bite. This place opens from 10 am to 1 am and serves bistro-style lunches such as lasagne, stroganoff and hot dogs. At dinner, main meals are European style, and there's also a piano bar here.

Two other more expensive but very good restaurants are ***Frawley's** (☎ 5759 3586)* at Jack Frost, where the international menu changes daily, and ***Herbies Bar & Grill** (☎ 5759 3626)* below the White Crystal with bistro-style lunches and a varied international menu for dinner.

Entertainment

The ***T-Bar*** at Hotham Central has live entertainment, and apart from the ***General Store*** bar, is the only places open year-round. There's ***Katz*** disco on the third floor of the Arlberg. The bar at ***Jack Frost*** is usually pretty lively, as is ***Herbies Bar & Grill*** in the White Crystal complex in the centre of the village.

Getting There & Around

By car, Mt Hotham can be reached by taking either via the Hume Fwy (M31) and Harrietville or via the Princes Hwy and Omeo. The trip takes about 4½ hours but 5½ hours via Omeo. Ring Mt Hotham Alpine Resort Management (☎ 5759 3550) to check on road conditions before deciding which route to take.

In winter, Trekset Snow Services (☎ 9370 9055) have daily buses from Melbourne to Mt Hotham (twice on Friday), costing $75/105 one way/return. They also have daily services between Hotham and Myrtleford, Bright ($30/40) and Harrietville ($25/35).

If you want to ski Falls Creek for the day, jump on the 'Helicopter Lift Link' for $49 return if you have a valid lift ticket; they are transferable between the resorts – the six minute flights are only possible on clear days. The flight costs more if you don't have a lift ticket.

The village is on a ridge near the top of the mountain, and is spread along the road. Luckily, there are free shuttle mini-buses that run frequently all the way along the ridge from 7 am to 3 am next morning; the free 'zoo cart' takes skiers from their lodges to the lifts between 8 am and 6 pm. Another shuttle service operates to Dinner Plain.

DINNER PLAIN

Dinner Plain is an architect-designed alpine village in the heart of the High Country, 11km east of the Mt Hotham ski resort. The whole town was built from scratch in the mid 1980s – all of the houses, lodges, shops (and the great pub) were built from local timber and stone and inspired by the early cattlemen's huts, with a few quirky additions.

In winter the town is used as a base for skiers. A shuttle bus runs to Mt Hotham and there are also some excellent cross-country skiing trails around the village itself, some of which lead to Mt Hotham. There is one lift for skiers. In summer it's an excellent base for enjoying the High Country, and there's plenty of accommodation available year-round.

Activities

Apart for some of the best hiking in the country you can also enjoy horse riding with Dinner Plain Trail Rides (☎ 5159 6445), who offer anything from one hour to seven day overnight rides on the High Plains and its valleys all year.

The Walk About Gourmet Adventures (☎ 5159 6556, email WalkaboutAus@compuserve.com) has luxury tours in the High Country which specialise in fine food. A five day tour is $865 per person, including all meals and accommodation.

Contact Dinner Plain Central Reservations (☎ 5159 6451 or 1800 670 019 toll-free) about mountain bike and tennis court hire.

Places to Stay

There's no cheap accommodation in the village, but ***Dinner Plain Central Reservations*** *(☎ 5159 6451 or 1800 670 019 toll-free, email dinnerplain@b150.aone.net.au)* can tell you what's available and for how much. Choices range from cabins, lodges and B&Bs to a resort hotel. As an indication of price, in the summer you can expect to pay a minimum of $160 a night for an apartment which sleeps up to six. In winter that same apartment starts at $640 for a weekend. The centre can also provide some tourist information.

Currawong Lodge *(☎ 9827 3996)* is a bargain in summer with a bed from $25 per person, but in winter the price creeps up to $140 during peak season.

High Plains Lodge *(☎ 5159 6455)* is the only hotel-type establishment, where doubles are $100 in summer and $225 in winter. They also have a restaurant.

Places to Eat

Dinner Plains Hotel is well worth a visit – with its split-level interior of huge timber poles and slabs plus roaring open fires, it looks somewhat like an overgrown mountain hut. The bistro serves lunches and dinners, with mains around $15.

There are three or four other eateries in town, including ***Brandy Creek Bar & Restaurant*** *(☎ 5159 6488)* on Big Muster Drive.

FALLS CREEK

• **elev 1780m**

Falls Creek, on the edge of the Bogong High Plains and overlooking the Kiewa Valley, is one of Victoria's best ski resorts. It's 375km and a 4½ hour drive from Melbourne. Falls Creek is the only alpine village in Australia where you can ski directly from your lodge to the lifts and from the slopes back to your lodge.

The skiing is spread over two main areas, the Village Bowl and Sun Valley. There are 19 lifts and the skiable downhill area is 451 hectares, with runs divided into 17% beginners, 60% intermediate and 23% advanced. The vertical drop is 267m. On Wednesday and Saturday from 7 to 9 pm there is night skiing in the Village Bowl. The Halley's Comet Chairlift also runs in January.

You'll also find some of the best cross-country skiing in Australia here. A trail leads around Rocky Valley Pondage to some old cattlemen's huts, and the more adventurous can tour to the white summits of Nelse, Cope and Spion Kopje. Australia's major cross-country skiing event, the Kangaroo

Hoppet, is held on the last Saturday in August every year. The event is part of the Worldloppet series of long-distance citizen races, and comprises a 42km course, a 21km Birkebeiner race and a 7km juniors' race.

Falls Creek is probably the most upmarket and 'fashion conscious' of the Victorian ski resorts, and combines good skiing with plenty of nightlife. The village is large and well developed, with a full range of facilities – ski and equipment hire, ski schools, restaurants and cafes, pubs, discos and bars, and a good range of accommodation – although not much in the budget range. Car parking for day visitors is conveniently at the base of the village, right next to the ski lifts.

Falls Creek is also more of an all seasons resort than the others, with a good range of accommodation open year-round. Check out the Special Summer Events Program listings from the tourist office for activity weekends during summer.

Information

The Falls Creek Tourist Information Centre (☎ 5758 3490 or 1800 453 525 toll-free), at the bottom of International Poma ski lift, is open daily from 9 am to 6 pm during the season, but closes at 5 pm in summer. They also have a Web site (www.skifallscreek.com.au).

Costs

The daily entry fee is $17 per car during the ski season only. Lift tickets for a full day cost $64 for adults, $33 for children. Combined lift-and-lesson packages cost $87 for adults, $59 for children.

Summer Activities

Some of the best hiking trails start at Falls Creek but there are many other activities, such as horse rides with Daily Trail Rides (☎ 5758 3655), or mountain biking; bikes can be hired from Viking Lodge.

Places to Stay

There is very little cheap accommodation in Falls Creek in winter. ***Falls Creek Central Reservations*** *(☎ 1800 033 079 toll-free)* can help you find accommodation on the mountain any time of the year.

The cheapest accommodation is found in the club lodges such as the ***Alpha Lodge*** *(☎ 5758 3488)*, which in summer has bunk beds from $17 per person and about $40 in winter.

The ***Viking Lodge*** *(☎ 5758 3247, email viking@fallscreek.albury.net.au)* has two to six-bed rooms and communal kitchen facilities. A bed in two to six bed-rooms with en suite costs around $28 in summer to around $84 per person in the winter high season.

The ***Silver Ski Lodge*** *(☎ 5758 3375 or 9886 8587)* has double rooms with en suites from $70 per person in low season to around $105 per person in high season – the tariff includes breakfast and dinner.

At the top end of the market, ***Astra Lodge*** *(☎ 5758 3496)* has luxurious private double rooms and great facilities, and costs around $85 per person in summer and around $180 per person in high season.

Places to Eat

There's a licensed supermarket (open all year) in Snowland Centre at the bottom of Halleys Comet Chairlift, and the usual range of kiosks and snack bars selling pies, hot dogs and sandwiches (winter only).

Cafe Max, in the village bowl, is a popular and lively licensed bar/bistro with an outdoor balcony that serves breakfast, lunch and dinner, offering such dishes as gourmet burgers, soups and pastas at reasonable prices. The ***Charcoal Grill Steakhouse*** at Silver Ski Lodge is the place for fine steaks and wines. Both are open only during the ski season. If it's pizza you're after try ***The Man***, all year.

Winterhaven *(☎ 5758 3243)* is one of the best restaurants on the mountain. It's in a small and simple timber-lined room upstairs in the Winterhaven apartments and is open nightly for dinner – even most weekend evenings during summer.

Entertainment

The two main nightspots in winter at Falls Creek are ***The Man***, a bar and nightclub that has live music on most nights (cover charge from $5 to $10), and the ***Frying Pan Inn***, which has a disco and often live entertainment. Also popular is the Harvey Hour on Tuesday and Thursday from 3.30 pm at the ***Falls Creek Motel***.

For a quieter drink, try the ***Cock 'n' Bull*** English-style pub, the bar at ***Cedarwood Lodge*** or the ***piano bar*** at the Man. During summer, one of the few bars that is open regularly is at The Man.

Getting There & Around

During the winter, Pyle's Coaches (☎ 5754 4024) operates buses between Falls Creek and Melbourne every day for $60/100 one way/return, it also has daily services to and from Albury ($30/52) and Mt Beauty ($17/29).

If you want to ski Mt Hotham for the day, jump on the 'Helicopter Lift Link' for $49 return if you have a valid lift ticket; the tickets are transferable between the two resorts – the six minute flights are only possible on clear days. The flight costs more if you don't have a lift ticket.

On the mountain, a tracked, over-snow transport service operates between the car parks and the lodges from 8 am until midnight, and until 2 am on Friday night ($19 return per person).

MT BEAUTY

• **pop 1650**

Nestled at the foot of Mt Bogong, Victoria's highest mountain, Mt Beauty and its twin town of Tawonga South are the gateway to the Falls Creek ski resort and the Bogong High Plains. The town was built in the 1940s as a base for workers on the Kiewa Hydro-Electric Scheme. Nowadays it's a handy base for skiers in winter and for a range of activities in other seasons.

Subsequently, there's a good choice of accommodation in the area year-round. Rates are generally higher during the ski season, but this is still a good base for day trips to Falls Creek, and there are plenty of facilities such as ski hire and regular transport to the mountain in winter.

Information

The tourist information centre (☎ 5754 4531) on Kiewa Valley Hwy (C531) is open daily from 9 am to 5 pm. Next to the information centre (ask them to open the museum) is a small Kiewa Valley Heritage Museum with a collection of old photos, documents and memorabilia from the area – admission is by donation.

Parks Victoria (☎ 5754 4693) is on the Kiewa Valley Hwy in Tawonga South.

The Commonwealth Bank (with an ATM) and ANZ Bank have branches in the Mt Beauty shopping centre.

Activities

Bogong Horseback Adventures (☎ 5754 4849) runs excellent overnight horse-riding trips and treks from their farm 4km along Mountain Creek Rd (turn off the Kiewa Valley Hwy at the Bogong Hotel in Tawonga) to the Bogong High Plains. Other activities include bike tours (book with Mountain Logistix; ☎ 5754 1676); Powered Hang Gliding (☎ 0417 496 264); fishing with Angling Expeditions (☎ 5754 1466); hiking, canoeing, ski touring and cross-country skiing with Ecotrek and Bogong Jack Adventures (☎ 5727 3382). For more information about these and others like hang gliding, buggy riding, rafting and hiking contact the tourist information centre.

Places to Stay

The tourist information centre has a good accommodation booking line (☎ 1800 808 277 toll-free).

The ***Tawonga Caravan Park*** *(☎ 5754 4428)* on Mountain Creek Rd (turn off the Kiewa Valley Hwy at the Bogong Hotel in Tawonga) is in a beautiful setting beside the Kiewa River. It has campsites from $12, on-site vans from $35 and cabins from $40.

Baenschs *(☎ 5754 4041, 16 St Bernaud Dve)* in Tawonga South is a modern brick homestead/lodge, with accommodation for up to 20 in two and four-bed rooms. There are communal cooking and laundry facilities, a lounge and drying room and it costs $30 per person in doubles.

Carver's Log Cabins *(☎ 5754 4863)* on Buckland St, Tawonga South, is a group of five self-contained, three bedroom cabins. They're fairly bare and basic but are good value, sleeping up to six people and priced from $75 to $110 a night for the whole cabin ($110 on mid-winter weekends).

The ***Bogong Hotel*** *(☎ 5754 4482)*, on the Kiewa Valley Hwy in Tawonga, has restored pub rooms with shared bathrooms at $30 per person, including a continental breakfast.

The cheapest of the motels is the ***Meriki Motel*** *(☎ 5754 4145)* on Tawonga Crescent, with rooms from $55 to $80 a double, including breakfast. The ***Valley View Lodge/Motel*** *(☎ 5754 1033)*, in Allamar Court in Tawonga South, has motel-style units with doubles from $90, including breakfast.

Modern luxury accommodation in the High Country is at its best in Tawonga South at ***Dreamers*** *(☎ 5754 1222)*, where every cottage has different design aspects, including magnificent views of Mt Bogong. The self-contained cottages start at $150 a night for two, including breakfast.

Places to Eat

There are a couple of cafes and take-aways and a good bakery in the Mt Beauty shopping centre in Hollonds St.

In Tawonga, the ***Roi's Diner*** *(☎ 5754 4495)* is an Italian-style restaurant with good pasta and meat dishes for $17.

Sasha's *(☎ 5754 4737)* on the Kiewa Valley Hwy is a well regarded, licensed restaurant with a homely dining room and good views over the Kiewa Valley. The food is European-influenced with main meals such as pasta, roasted duckling or chateaubriand.

Getting There & Away

Pyle's Coaches (☎ 5754 4024) in Tawonga South operates buses to Albury once a day all year and to Falls Creek only in winter. They also have 4WD tours to Mt Feathertop outside the snow season for $65 a day. V-Line operates a train/bus service via Wangaratta on weekdays only.

BRIGHT

• **pop 1900**

Bright is a pretty and popular holiday town in the heart of the Ovens Valley in the foothills of the Alps. The streets, and the banks of the Ovens River, are lined with deciduous European trees which shed their leaves in a colourful exhibition every autumn, and the town is perfectly placed to provide access to the wonders of the **Alpine National Park**, the ski resorts, and a wide range of outdoor activities. In fact, Bright has become one of Victoria's centres for outdoor adventure activities. Another attraction is that it has a wide range of places to stay and eat that will suit most budgets.

The town grew as a centre for the Ovens Valley goldfields after gold was found in nearby Buckland Valley in 1853. In 1857 the notorious Buckland Valley riots took place near here, when diligent Chinese gold miners were forced off their claims and given less than a fair go.

It's about an hour's scenic drive from Bright to the snowfields of Mt Hotham and Falls Creek, which makes the town a fairly good base during the ski season. The ever popular **Mt Buffalo National Park** is about half an hour's drive from here.

Information

Bright's tourist information centre (☎ 5755 2275) is at 119 Gavan St and is open daily from 9 am to 5 pm.

Parks Victoria has an office (☎ 5755 1577) at 46 Bakers Gully Rd, which has brochures on the Wandiligong Valley, walking trails and national parks in the area.

Things to See & Do

The **Bright & District Historical Society Museum** is in the old train station building, and is open on Tuesday, Thursday and Sunday from 2 to 4 pm during school holidays and festivals, and only on Sunday the rest of the year. Around the corner on Mill Rd is the **Lotsafun Amusement Park** with dodgem cars, skating, bike hire etc. **Centenary Park**, beside the Ovens River, has some good picnic areas and swimming spots.

Activities

There are plenty of walking trails around here, including strolls along the Ovens River and Morses Creek and climbs to various lookout points around the town. The tourist office has a *Short Walks around Bright* brochure, which details eight great walks from 1.5 to 5km long.

The Bright Sports Centre (☎ 5755 1339) hires mountain bikes, and Getaway Trailbike Tours (☎ 5752 2336) can take you on bike tours. Freeburgh Horse Trails (☎ 5755 1370) offers horse rides, from short trots to overnight treks.

If you want to get airborne, Alpine Paragliding (☎ 5755 1753) and the Eagle School of Hang-Gliding (☎ 5750 1174) both offer introductory flights and full certificate courses. For the less adventurous there is the powered hang glider flights with Bright Microlight Centre (☎ 5750 1555).

Rapid Descents (☎ 02-6076 9111, email rafting@rapiddescents.com.au) offers rafting tours, while River Mountain Guides

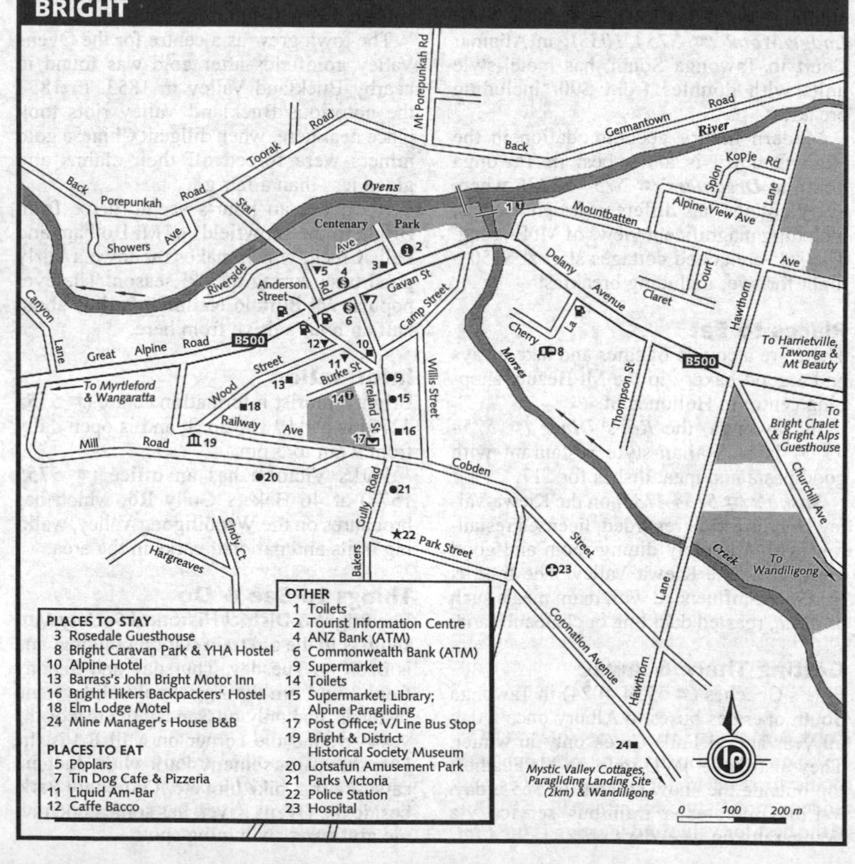

(☎ 1800 818 466 toll-free) has hiking, skiing, canoeing and canyoning trips.

Special Events

Bright's two main festivals celebrate the town's seasonal colour changes. The Autumn Festival, held over the last week of April and the first week of May, celebrates the colourful falling of the leaves with music, a street fair, parade and fun run. During the Spring Festival, held at the end of October, many of the gardens in the area are open to the public.

Places to Stay

Bright has a wide range of accommodation, especially holiday flats, but during holiday seasons rooms are often scarce. The tourist information office (☎ 1800 500 117 toll-free) has a helpful accommodation booking service.

Camping, Caravan Parks & Hostels At the ***Bright Caravan Park*** *(☎ 5755 1141, email yhalodge@bright.albury.net.au)*, on Cherry Lane, there is an excellent YHA-associated hostel which was recently purpose-built. The main communal areas are in an attractive building of stone and timber, with a modern kitchen, large dining area and lounge room with wood heater. There are 10 four-bunk rooms and a bed costs $16 for YHA members, $19 nonmembers. Campsites are also available in the park from $17, and on-site cabins range from $48 to $82. If you have your own transport, there are another half dozen caravan and camping parks out of town and alongside the Ovens River between Bright and Harrietville.

The modern and well-equipped ***Bright Hikers Backpackers' Hostel*** *(☎ 5750 1244, email gwhite@netc.net.au, 4 Ireland St)* has dorm beds at $15 and twins/doubles at $32 – the owners can help with arrangements for numerous activities.

Pubs & Motels The ***Alpine Hotel*** *(☎ 5755 1366)* on Anderson St is a restored pub with rooms for $30/45 for singles/doubles and modern motel-style rooms at $35/50. One of the best for value and location is the ***Elm Lodge Motel*** *(☎ 5755 1144, 2 Wood St)* with rooms from $38/47 and discounts for backpackers and hostellers.

If you're after somewhere more upmarket, ***Barrass's John Bright Motor Inn*** *(☎ 5755 1400, 10 Wood St)* is a modern motel with excellent facilities; rooms and suites range from $90 to $100 a double.

Guesthouses & B&Bs The ***Bright Alps Guesthouse*** *(☎ 5755 1197, 83-85 Delany Ave)* has 19 rooms of a good standard with shared bathrooms and a guest lounge and dining room. The B&B tariff is from $60 a double, which includes a cooked breakfast. They also have a self-contained apartment sleeping from two to five people from $80 a double. The ***Rosedale Guesthouse*** *(☎ 5755 1059, 117 Gavan St)* is a large 1890s timber cottage with 16 guestrooms ranging from a single to a six bed family room. It's an old fashioned, rambling and relaxed guesthouse, and the tariff of around $40/65 includes a cooked breakfast. Home-cooked dinners are also available, and dinner plus B&B costs around $60 per person.

Mine Manager's House B&B *(☎ 5755 1702, 30 Coronation Ave)* has rather twee en suite bedrooms, including a lounge with a fireplace for $105 a double.

Self-Contained Cottages The ***Mystic Valley Cottages*** *(☎ 5750 1502)*, in Mystic Lane, is a set of five modern, brick-and-stone, one and two-bedroom holiday units on a three hectare property, from $90/100.

Places to Eat

Bright has plenty of restaurants, take-away places and two supermarkets. The ***Liquid Am-Bar*** *(8 Anderson St)* is a modern, fun and trendy cafe/bar with an interesting range of food, good music and a 10% discount for backpackers. Pasta, cajun chicken, jaffles, burgers and steak are around $10 to $15 and there's a cheaper kids' menu. Another trendy place that is well regarded is ***Caffe Bacco*** *(2D Anderson St)*, which serves Asian-type noodles and pasta for under $20.

Poplars (*☎ 5755 1655*), on Star Rd, is a good upmarket restaurant, with a stylish but relaxed dining room and main meals specialising in local produce such as beef, veal and rainbow trout, from $16 to $20.

Tin Dog Cafe & Pizzeria, on the corner of Gavan and Barnard Sts, is a more casual place with pizzas, pastas from $7 and a Mexican menu with mains from $7.50 to $12.50.

Getting There & Away

V/Line from Melbourne to Bright costs $38.90, with daily trains to Wangaratta and a connecting bus service continuing on to Beechworth and Bright.

AROUND BRIGHT

The idyllic former gold-mining area of **Wandiligong Valley** and town, 6km south of Bright, has been allowed to revegetate and recover from the violence of years of mining activities, and the valley's landscape and old cottages are classified by the National Trust. A walking track alongside Morses Creek passes many of the historic sites – a brochure is available from Parks Victoria.

Whichever direction you go from Bright, you're taking a great scenic drive. A brochure outlining some of the drives is available from the information centre.

Boynton's of Bright, about 8km northwest of Bright on the Great Alpine Rd is an excellent winery and well worth a visit. The tasting room sits on a rise overlooking the vineyards and the road, and is open daily for tastings and sales.

MT BUFFALO NATIONAL PARK

This is the oldest national park in the Victorian Alps. It was declared back in 1898, and since then has always been one of the state's best loved and most popular parks. It covers an area of 31,000 hectares. The park is 333km and about a four hour drive from Melbourne. The main access road leads off the Great Alpine Road at Porepunkah.

Apart from Mt Buffalo itself, the park is noted for its spectacular scenery of huge granite outcrops, pleasant streams and waterfalls, an abundance of birdlife and some fine walks. The mountain was named in 1824 by the explorers Hume and Hovell on their trek from Sydney to Port Phillip – from a distance, they thought its bulky shape resembled a buffalo.

The mountain is surrounded by huge granite tors – great blocks of granite broken off from the massif by the expansion and contraction of ice in winter and other weathering effects. There is abundant plant and animal life around the park, and over 90km of walking tracks. Self-guided nature walks are at the **Gorge Nature Walk**, **View Point Nature Walk** and the **Dickson's Falls Nature Walk**. A road leads to just below the summit of the 1723m Horn, the highest point on the massif.

In summer, Mt Buffalo is a hang-glider's paradise (definitely not for beginners) and

The Bogong Moth

Bogong moth (*Agrotis infusa*) is a brown moth that grows to a length of about 5cm. It's a migratory creature which breeds and lives during autumn, winter and spring in the lowlands of New South Wales. However, during summer, when the food in the lowlands is exhausted and it gets too hot, the moth migrates to the High Plains.

At Mt Buffalo and other parts of the alpine region, it hides in the cracks and crevices of rocks. Once the sun sets, the moths leave their hiding spots and fly around, becoming easy prey for ravens, kestrels and pied currawongs. The Aborigines also used to follow the moth to the High Country as it was considered a delicacy. It was commonly roasted and the wings and legs were separated from the body. Usually, the body was made into a paste with a nutty flavour. At the end of summer the moths return to the lowlands to lay eggs and the cycle begins again.

Richard Nebeský

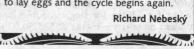

the near-vertical walls of the Gorge provide some of the most challenging rock climbs in Australia. **Lake Catani** is good for swimming and canoeing, while in winter Mt Buffalo turns into a ski resort with downhill and cross-country skiing. There's an excellent camping area at Lake Catani with toilets, showers and fireplaces, and there is accommodation at the historic Mt Buffalo chalet – refer to the following section for details.

MT BUFFALO

• **elev 1500m**

Mt Buffalo is Victoria's smallest ski resort and is managed by Parks Victoria. However, a private operator manages the Mt Buffalo Chalet and Lodge, the ski lifts, the handful of downhill runs, along with some more challenging cross-country skiing areas that are popular with beginners and families.

There are two skiing areas: Cresta Valley and Dingo Dell. Cresta is the main area, with five lifts – the skiable downhill area is 27 hectares, and runs are 45% beginner, 40% intermediate and 15% advanced, with a vertical drop of 157m. The chairlift also operates on weekends in January. There's a day visitors' centre which has a cafe, kiosk, ski hire, and the Mt Buffalo Lodge attached. Parks Victoria also has a historical audiovisual program in the theatre next to the cafe. Cresta Valley is the starting point for many of the cross-country trails. Dingo Dell has a day visitor shelter with a kiosk.

Information

Parks Victoria has an office (☎ 5755 1466) at the resort with plenty of brochures and maps. Their *Mt Buffalo National Park Visitor's Guide* is available from the entrance station and the office for $3 – elsewhere, it costs about $5.

Costs

The entry fee to Mt Buffalo National Park is $8 per car ($11 in winter but only if ski lifts are operating) and payable at the Mt Buffalo entrance station. Lift tickets for a full day cost $35 per adult, $21 for children. Combined lift-and-lesson packages cost $37 for adults, $27 for children.

Activities

Adventure Guides Australia (☎ 5728 1804) have abseiling, rock climbing, caving, ski touring/snow camping and other activities. Horse rides suitable for children can be arranged at the Chalet or by phoning (☎ 1800 037 038 toll-free).

Places to Stay & Eat

The ***Mt Buffalo Chalet*** *(☎ 5755 1500, email buffalo@netc.net.au)* is a huge, rambling mountain guesthouse which was built in 1909. It retains a wonderfully old-fashioned feel, with simple bedrooms, large lounges and games rooms with open fires, and a choice of four different types of room. The basic rooms with shared bathrooms cost around $115 per person; spacious rooms with en suites cost around $145 per person – tariffs include all meals. The chalet is open all year round.

The cafe is open daily to the public, while the chalet's dining room, in the former ballroom, is open to the public when it's not booked out by house guests. The fixed price, three course, buffet-style lunches cost $30 a head, and dinners are $35 a head.

The ***Mt Buffalo Lodge*** *(☎ 5755 1988)* is a large inn with both motel-style units and four-bunk rooms with shared bathrooms. The basic motel units cost from $75 per person for B&B plus dinner; the backpacker bunkrooms cost up to $24 ($27 to $32 in winter). The inn has its own restaurant and ski hire.

During summer there are campsites available at the ***Lake Catani camp ground*** for $14. Remote camping is also allowed at Rocky Creek but strict conditions apply – get a permit from the Parks Victoria ranger at the Mt Buffalo entrance station.

Entertainment

Opera in the Alps is held at the end of January in the grounds of Mt Buffalo Chalet. The program includes highlights from popular operas; tickets start at $46 per person.

The First Ski Trails

Kooris were regular summer visitors to the Victorian Alps for thousands of years. Surprisingly, they left only a handful of remains in such places as Mt Buller's Baldy, where a sharpening stone and three axe heads were found. The first white men to see the Victorian Alps were the explorers Hume and Hovell in 1824.

The first skiers in Australia were apparently fur-hunters in Tasmania; and in Victoria were Norwegian miners in the Alps, in the 1860s. During those early days skis were used as a form of transportation to deliver supplies and mail. There are few records left, but skiing is first mentioned as a recreational activity at the Mt St Bernard Hospice (between Harrietville and Mt Hotham) in 1863.

In Victoria skiing as a sport was not as popular as in New South Wales, where the first ski club in the world is claimed to have been established at Kiandra in 1861. It was not until the 1880s when members of the Bright Alpine Club started regularly skiing in the vicinity of the Mt St Bernard Hospice that skiing began to catch on in the state. Nevertheless, Mt Buffalo became the most popular ski area from 1890 until the 1920s. The popularity of Mt Buffalo was largely due to the 1890 winter ascent that resulted in the construction of a lodge, and the formation of the Mt Buffalo National Park in 1898. This was followed by the construction of the first section of the Mt Buffalo Chalet in 1910 to accommodate the ever increasing number of visitors to the mountain. However, it wasn't until the establishment of the Ski Club of Victoria in 1924 that skiing really took off. Exploration of the Victorian Alps commenced that same year, with Mt Buller, Mt Donna Buang and the Bogong High Plains.

In those days skiers didn't have it easy and went through much agony and discomfort in the name of the sport. Equipment and clothing were not water resistant, and worse, there were no ski lifts, so every descent on skis meant a much longer walk back up the slope.

It was the development of the ski tow that made skiing popular and easy for the masses. It was again at Mt Buffalo where the first rope tow was installed in August 1937. However, the main resorts didn't see a major development of lodges and ski lifts until the late 1940s.

Richard Nebeský

Getting There & Around

There is no public transport to the plateau. The closest you can get is to Bright – from there, a taxi to Mt Buffalo costs about $40. If you're staying at the chalet or the lodge, transport from Wangaratta train station can be arranged.

MYRTLEFORD

• **pop 2700**

Myrtleford, the self-proclaimed 'gateway to the Alps', is at the foot of Mt Buffalo. It's an agricultural town in the heart of the Ovens Valley, a district dominated by hops and tobacco growers. The town is mainly of interest as an overnight stop en route to the High Country or the snowfields, and has few accommodation options.

Beside the Great Alpine Road on the north side of the town is the **Phoenix Tree**, the trunk and roots of a massive red gum that has been loosely sculpted – a signboard explains the symbolism of the work. The **Old School Museum** in Elgin St is the local history museum, and is open Sunday from 2 to 4 pm, September to May.

Places to Stay & Eat

One of the best places to stay around Myrtleford is ***Happy Valley Hotel*** *(☎ 5751 1628)* in Ovens, 5km south-east of Myrtleford. This old country pub (1870) looks rather ordinary from the outside, but it has seven rooms decorated in period style, with old brass beds and canopies, hand basins and shared bathrooms. They're excellent value at $35/55 for singles/doubles, including a light breakfast.

Back in Myrtleford, the ***Myrtleford Caravan Park** (☎ 5752 1598)* on Lewis Ave is close to the town centre and has sites from $12 and on-site vans from $25. The ***Myrtleford Hotel/Motel** (☎ 5752 1078)* on the corner of Standish and Smith Sts has basic pub rooms from $20/30 or with en suites from $30/45, and the ***Railway Hotel/Standish Street Motel** (☎ 5752 1583)* on Standish St is restored and has good pub rooms from $35 and modern motel rooms from $38/58. This pub also has a good bistro with mains from $12 to $16 and bar meals from $5 to $12.

The recently refurbished ***Golden Leaf Motor Inn** (☎ 5752 1566)* on the Great Alpine Road has rooms from $62/67. ***Basil's*** is a licensed restaurant in the motel and has steak and seafood mains from $14 to $19.

THE SNOW ROAD

The Snow Road, which runs from the Hume Fwy near Glenrowan and Wangaratta east to Myrtleford, linking it with the Great Alpine Rd, is one of the main access routes for travellers to the Victorian snowfields and High Country. It also has a few points of interest along its route, especially around the twin towns of **Milawa** and **Oxley**.

Milawa is a small town with one pub, the **Earthly Gems Museum**, a few scattered buildings, and the surrounding area which has developed into a regional gourmet centre, with some good wineries, restaurants, a cheese factory and a few other local producers that are worth visiting on your way through.

The most famous of these is the **Brown Brothers Winery** at Milawa. Their first vintage was in 1889 – the winery has remained in the same family ever since and has become one of Australia's largest and most successful. It's a huge winery with a wide range of wines and a great reputation. As well as the large tasting rooms, there's a good restaurant (see Places to Eat, following) and pleasant picnic areas, with barbecues for the use of visitors. Brown Brothers opens daily from 9 am to 5 pm.

At Oxley, there are three wineries at the other end of the scale – **John Gehrig Wines** (some of the best wine in the region), **Ciavarella Wines** and **Read's Winery**, all family-run, smaller operations. All three are open daily for tastings and sales.

The **Milawa Cheese Co** is 2km north of Milawa and has opened a restaurant. They sell an excellent assortment of cheeses, including a particularly fine and pungent washed-rind cheese. A visit there and a trip to the **Milawa bakery** makes a great combination – now all you need is some wine!

Places to Stay

The ***Milawa Caravan Park** (☎ 5727 3203)*, just behind the pub, is a bit ramshackle but has sites from $6 and on-site vans from $22. The ***Milawa Lodge Motel** (☎ 5727 3326)* is a colonial-style motel with modern units from $65/70 for singles/doubles.

In Milawa, on the main road, ***Ercildoon Homestead** (☎ 5727 3222)* is a huge, rambling old homestead with country-style B&B rooms from $55/90.

Places to Eat

The ***Milawa Bakery*** comes highly recommended, and is a good spot to stop for supplies of fresh bread and pastries, but only from Thursday to Sunday. It also serves light lunches and teas. The ***Milawa Hotel*** has good counter meals in the $9 to $14 range.

At Brown Brothers, the ***Epicurean Centre*** opens daily for lunch and snacks from 11 am to 3 pm. It's a spacious and rustic dining room, and serves an excellent range of gourmet meals, each matched with an appropriate glass of wine.

In Oxley, a couple of kilometres west, is the ***King River Cafe*** which has become known for its excellent cuisine. It's open for lunches and dinners, Wednesday to Sunday.

BEECHWORTH

• pop 2950

Beechworth, a picturesque and historic town in the northern foothills of the Victorian Alps, is rated by the National Trust as one of Victoria's two 'notable' towns. From 1852, the town developed into the main centre for the rich Ovens Valley goldfields, and today many well preserved and restored buildings remain from the gold era, 32 of which are classified by the National Trust.

Many of the public buildings were built with distinctive honey-coloured local granite, including a huge old jail where both Ned Kelly and his mother were imprisoned, and the courthouse where Ned was tried. The broad tree-lined streets are full of other historic buildings, including charming miners' cottages, grand hotels trimmed with cast-iron lace, the tower-topped post office and the grand facade of the Goldfields Hospital.

Beechworth's attractions have always been a drawcard for visitors – in 1927, the town won the Melbourne *Sun News Pictorial's* 'ideal tourist town' competition. It's still a popular destination. Apart from the attractions of the town itself – gracious gold-era architecture, public parks and private gardens, galleries and craft shops, historic museums and sites, and a wide range of accommodation and eating options – the scenic countryside surrounding the town is also excellent for walking, cycling and exploring.

ROSS BARNETT

The magnificent facade of Ovens Goldfields Hospital

The town is 35km east of Wangaratta, and if you're travelling between Wangaratta and Wodonga the detour through Beechworth makes a worthwhile alternative to the frenetic pace of the boring Hume Fwy.

Information

The Beechworth tourist information centre (☎ 5728 3233, www.beechworth-index.com.au) is inside the old Shire Hall on Ford St, and opens daily from 9 am to 5 pm. A local historian presents several sessions on Ned Kelly and his association with Beechworth in the mornings, Monday to Saturday, during school holidays.

NRE has an office (☎ 5728 1501), at La Trobe University's Beechworth Campus on Albert Rd, which opens in summer from 9 am to 4.30 pm, Monday to Friday and the rest of the year until 1 pm Tuesday to Thursday, to 4.30 pm on Friday and closed Monday – this place has good information about the walking tracks around the town, the Beechworth Forest Dve, the Gorge Scenic Dve and the Woolshed Falls Historic Walk. Pamphlets about these are also available from the tourist information centre.

Things to See & Do

The very well presented and interesting **Burke Museum**, in Loch St, has three display areas and an eclectic collection of relics from the gold-rush era. The displays include old photos, machinery, birds, rocks and gems, tools, weapons and a 'street of shops', an arcade with 16 shopfronts presented as they were over 100 years ago. The museum was named after the hapless explorer, Robert O'Hara Burke, who was Beechworth's superintendent of police during the early days of the gold rush, before he set off on his historic trek north with William Wills. It's open daily during school holidays from 9 am to 4.30 pm and the rest of the year to 3.30 pm. It's well worth the entry fees of $5 for adults, $3 for concessions and kids, and $14 for a family.

The **Gorge Scenic Drive** is a 5km tour around the outskirts of Beechworth, through old gold-mining territory and past a few historic sites, including the 1859 **Powder Magazine**. The small stone building is surrounded by solid granite walls, and is open daily from 10 am to noon and 1 to 4 pm, but only in the afternoons from February to August. Admission costs $1.30 for adults and 70c for kids, and a taped commentary describes the history of the building.

The **MB Historic Cellars**, on the corner of Last and William Sts, is also worth a visit. In the cellar of this old beer and stout brewery, an interesting collection of old bottles, machinery and tools has been set up, and upstairs you can buy some of their bar syrups and cordials. Admission is free and it's open daily from 10 am to 4 pm.

The **Golden Horseshoes Monument** on the corner of Sydney Rd and Gorge Scenic Dve, is near the spot where, in 1855, a horse was shod with golden shoes and ridden into town on polling day of the first Victorian parliament by Donald Cameron, who was elected to a seat in the parliament.

The **Beechworth Cemetery** is fronted with solid granite gateposts and surrounded by trees. Within the grounds are the graves of many pioneers, and in the Chinese section, a set of ceremonial burning towers and rows of marked and unmarked Chinese graves – all that remains of the town's large Chinese population during the gold-rush days.

The **Historic Courthouse** on Ford St was the site of Ned Kelly's first court appearance and the place where he was committed to trial for the murders of constables Scanlon and Lonigan in August 1880. The courtrooms are open daily from 10 am to 4 pm and cost $2 for adults and $1 for kids. Across the road and in the basement behind the **Shire Hall**, you can see the cell where Ned was held. Also on Ford St is the **Left Bank Artists Co-operative** where local artists exhibit and sell their commendable art.

The **Carriage Museum**, run by the National Trust, is in a former goods shed in Railway Ave and has an interesting collection of old horse-drawn carriages, including a funeral hearse, a Cobb & Co coach and a horse-drawn bus! It's open daily from 10 am to noon and 1 to 4 pm, but on weekends and in February it's only open in the afternoon; entry costs $1.50.

The **Beechworth Stagecoach** offers horse-drawn carriage rides around town ($5). The interesting two hour Historic Town Tours operated by Beechworth Bus Lines can be booked through the visitor information centre ($12.50). If you prefer to see Beechworth from a Harley Davidson contact Harley Heritage Tour Rides (☎ 018 085 579). Horse rides are offered by Woorage Trail Rides (☎ 5728 7282).

Special Events

Beechworth's three main festivals are the Golden Horseshoe Festival, held over Easter, the Harvest Festival held in May and the Celtic Festival held in early November.

Places to Stay

Camping & Caravan Parks The *Lake Sambell Caravan Park (☎ 5728 1421)*, on McConville Ave and near the lake, has campsites from $11, on-site vans from $28 and cabins from $40.

Pubs The restored old pub *Tanswell's Commercial Hotel (☎ 5728 1480, 30 Ford St)* has good rooms with shared bathrooms from $25/40 for singles/doubles ($35/55 on weekends). The tariff includes a continental breakfast.

Motels If you're looking for a motel room, try the *Armour Motor Inn (☎ 5728 1466, email armour@dragnet.com.au, 1 Camp St)*, which is central and has cosy rooms from $70/75, including a pool, spa and sauna, or the *Carriage Motor Inn (☎ 5728 1830, email carriage@albury.net.au, 44 Camp St)*, which has comfortable rooms from $70/80.

Guesthouses & B&Bs Beechworth has a great selection of B&Bs and country cottages, all of which include a cooked breakfast in the tariff. One of the best

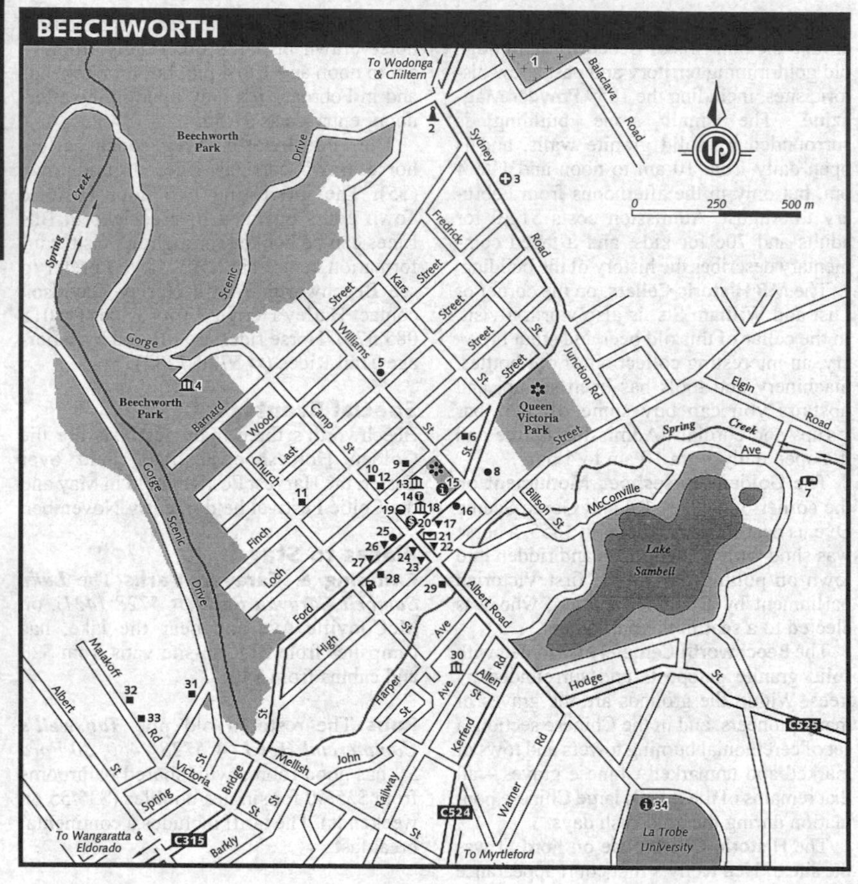

places is the ***Rose Cottage*** *(☎ 5728 1069, email ros-cot@hotkey.net.au, 42 Camp St)*, an 1876 timber cottage with a pretty front garden and four charming en suite guestrooms. The rooms are all romantically decorated in heritage style and nicely cluttered, plus there's a cosy guest lounge. B&B is from $65/90.

Kinross Guesthouse *(☎ 5728 2351, 34 Loch St)* is a restored, double fronted homestead, blending heritage style with a few modern touches, and has five guestrooms with private bathrooms. The B&B tariff starts at $120/148. ***Burnbrae B&B*** *(☎ 5728 1091)*, on Gorge Rd, is a more casual and rambling Victorian cottage. It's on the edge of town overlooking the gorge and has relaxed country-style guestrooms, a cosy lounge and pretty gardens – doubles that share bathrooms are from $98 and with en suite are $110. ***Foxgloves B&B*** *(☎ 5728 1322, email mead@magnet.com.au, 21 Loch St)*, opposite the Burke Museum, is another restored cottage with rooms from

BEECHWORTH

PLACES TO STAY
6 Kinross Guesthouse
7 Lake Sambell Caravan Park
9 Foxgloves B&B
10 Carriage Motor Inn
11 Finches of Beechworth
12 Rose Cottage
28 Tanswell's Commercial Hotel
29 Armour Motor Inn
31 Burnbrae B&B
32 Alba Country Rose
33 Country Charm Swiss Cottages

PLACES TO EAT
17 The Bank
22 Beechworth Provender
23 Chinese Village
24 Beechworth Bakery
26 The Parlour & Pantry; Commonwealth Bank (ATM)
27 Beechworth Pizza; Goldfields Greengrocer

OTHER
1 Beechworth Cemetery
2 Golden Horseshoes Monument
3 Ovens District Hospital
4 Powder Magazine
5 MB Historic Cellars
8 Beechworth Prison
13 Burke Museum
14 Public Toilets
15 Shire Hall & Tourist Information Centre
16 Historic Courthouse
18 Left Bank Artists Co-operative
19 Beechworth Animal World
20 Bank of Melbourne W (ATM)
21 Post Office
25 Foodtown Supermarket
30 Carriage Museum
34 NRE Office

$80/110. ***Alba Country Rose*** *(☎ 5728 1107, 30 Malakoff Rd)* is a modern home surrounded by 1.2 hectares of rose gardens. The two suites range from $65/80, including cooked breakfast.

The new and modern ***Country Charm Swiss Cottages*** *(☎ 5728 2435, 22 Malakoff Rd)* is the best value in town, with excellent views of the gorge and Beechworth. Each wooden cottage is equipped with open fire place and spa, and starts at $120 a double, including breakfast.

At the top end of the guesthouse market is ***Finches of Beechworth*** *(☎ 5728 2655, email finches@netc.net.au, 3 Finch St)*. It's a beautifully restored, formal Victorian guesthouse, richly and elegantly decorated. The guestrooms have private en suites and there's a guest lounge, sitting room and dining room, and overpriced B&B costs from $170 a double, or $260 with dinner.

Self-Contained Cabins Five kilometres north of Beechworth at Woolshed Falls, the ***Woolshed Cabins*** *(☎ 5728 1035)* is a group of four timber holiday cabins on a farm near the falls. They are self-contained and sleep up to five people. The rates are from $67 a double plus $8 for extra adults.

Places to Eat

The ***Parlour & Pantry*** *(69 Ford St)* is an excellent (if somewhat pricey) deli, coffee shop and restaurant. The décor is country-heritage style; the food is delicious and all home-made, and they serve the best coffee in town. Gourmet snacks and take-aways are $6 to $10, lunch mains from $9 to $16, and dinner mains from $15 to $19.

The ***Beechworth Bakery*** in Camp St has an irresistible selection of hot bread, cakes and home-made pies. The tables on the footpath are an excellent place for a coffee and fresh croissant breakfast on a sunny morning. The ***Beechworth Provender*** *(18 Camp St)* is a gourmet's paradise: a small deli crammed with cheeses, smallgoods, wines, preserves and local produce – not cheap, but a great spot for supplies for a gourmet bush picnic.

Tanswell's Commercial Hotel *(30 Ford St)* has a popular bistro with main meals from $10 to $15. A better pub bistro is at the ***Hibernian Hotel*** on the corner of Camp and Loch Sts.

The ***Chinese Village*** *(11-15 Camp St)*, has reasonably good Chinese food at affordable prices, including take-away lunches for around $5. Very good, although more expensive pizzas are found at ***Beechworth Pizza*** *(57 Ford St)*.

Beechworth's most upmarket restaurant is ***The Bank*** *(☎ 5728 2223, 86 Ford St)*, a sophisticated and formal licensed restaurant in a stylishly restored former bank.

Getting There & Around

V/Line has daily services between Melbourne and Beechworth ($34.20), changing from train to bus at Wangaratta. Wangaratta Coachlines (☎ 5722 1843) runs local buses to Albury-Wodonga, Bright, Rutherglen etc. Tickets for V-Line, Country Link and Greyhound buses can be booked at Beechworth Animal World (☎ 5728 1374, 36 Camp St), near the bus stop. Mountain bikes can also be hired from this unfriendly place.

AROUND BEECHWORTH

Five kilometres out of town on Chiltern Rd, **Woolshed Falls** is a popular picnic area and the site of a major alluvial goldfield which yielded over 85,000kg of gold in 14 years. There are numerous **walking tracks** in the area, including one that leads from the Gorge Falls to the Woolshed Falls and takes about half a day. Other sites around Beechworth worth a visit include the picturesque **Fletcher's Dam** and old mining sites such as the **Wallaby Mine**.

Another 7km farther north is the **Mt Pilot Yeddonba Aboriginal Art Site** with faint rock face drawings of a Tasmanian Tiger, a lizard and a snake.

The town of **El Dorado**, west of Beechworth, was named after the legendary city of gold. It's a fairly unremarkable country town now but it was once the site of a gold rush. A few historic buildings remain, including an interesting **Historical Society Museum** in the old red-brick school building. It's open from 2 to 5 pm on Sunday and from 10 am to 5 pm on public holidays. Also of interest is an **old dredge**, a massive piece of rusting machinery partly encased in a slapped-together tin building long-since abandoned.

YACKANDANDAH

• **pop 600**

Yackandandah is another well preserved former gold-mining town. The main street is a walk back through time – an avenue of trees lined with charming and rustic old buildings which now house a collection of craft and gift shops, bric-a-brac and antique shops, galleries and tearooms. Like Beechworth, the town is set amidst beautiful hills and valleys, and is so historic that the entire town has been classified by the National Trust.

Needless to say, all of this charm attracts plenty of visitors. Apart from browsing through the shops, you can enjoy a Devonshire tea, call into one of the two pubs for a cool ale, or wander down to the river and try your hand at trout fishing. Most visitors to the town are day-trippers, although there's a caravan park, motel, several B&Bs and both pubs have basic accommodation. The Yackandandah tourist information centre (☎ 02-6027 1988) is in the Athenaeum on High St and has irregular opening hours.

The town has many fine buildings, including the 1850 **Bank of Victoria**, at 21 High St, which is now a historic museum and opens on Sunday, public holidays and daily during school holidays from noon to 4 pm (adults $2, children 50c). The **Soldiers' Memorial Gardens** in High St, opposite the post office, are small but very picturesque with their tall palm trees, trimmed lawns and timber pavilion.

The very gripping **Kars Reef Goldmine Tour** takes you to a 150m-long gold-mining tunnel (1888) where you see many artefacts and get a step-by-step description of gold mining. The tours are at 10.30 am, noon, 1.30 and 3.30 pm on weekends, public and school holidays. They depart from 2 Kars St (☎ 02-6027 1757) and cost $7 for adults and $4 for children.

Places to Stay

The ***Yackandandah Caravan Park*** *(☎ 02-6027 1380)* is beside the Yackandandah Creek and a good spot for trout fishing. They have sites from $10 and on-site vans from $30.

The tiny and historic ***Star Hotel*** *(☎ 02-6027 1493, 30 High St)* has a few basic but clean pub rooms which it rents out occasionally for $25/40 for singles/doubles. The new *Yackandandah Motor Inn* (☎ *02-6027 1155, 18 High St)* has spotless rooms for $45/65, including breakfast. There are several B&Bs, including ***Serendipity B&B*** (☎ *02-6027 1881, 9 Windham St)* has a cottage for $80 a double or a room in the house at $50/90, including breakfast.

Places to Eat

Wildon Thyme Tearoom is in the back section of a collectables shop, and serves Devonshire teas, snacks and lunches. ***Yackandandah Bakery*** is fine for snacks and drinks. The ***Star Hotel*** has good pub food and ***Yackandandah Hotel*** has decent bar and pub meals for lunch and dinner. These are all on High St, the main street, and easy to find.

Getting There & Away

Wangaratta Coachlines (☎ 5722 1843) runs bus services between Beechworth, Yackandandah and Wodonga, on weekdays, but only on Tuesday and Thursday during school holidays. The one way fare from Yackandandah is $1.65 to Beechworth and $3.20 to Wodonga.

OMEO HIGHWAY

The only major route through the heart of the High Country is the Omeo Hwy (C543) which stretches from the Murray Valley Hwy (A16) near Tallangatta to Omeo, and the Great Alpine Rd which continues to Bairnsdale – a distance of almost 300km. On its journey from the coast to the Murray River, it passes through some of Victoria's most scenic and diverse countryside. The highway is unsealed in several sections (between Anglers Rest and Mitta Mitta) and often snow-bound during winter, but at any time it is a memorable drive.

The first section of the road, from Tallangatta to Mitta Mitta, follows the flatlands of the Mitta Mitta River. **Mitta Mitta** is a tiny town in an idyllic valley (accommodation available). It's a former gold-mining settlement, and a track leads from the highway to the former Pioneer Mine site, an open-cut mine that was one of the largest hydraulic sluicing operations in Victoria and yielded some 15,000 ounces (425,250g) of gold over 16 years.

From Mitta Mitta, the highway leaves the river and climbs into the mountains, reaching its highest point near Mt Willis (1750m). Seventy kilometres south of Mitta Mitta, a turn-off leads to the Bogong High Plains and the Falls Creek alpine village – this road is closed during the ski season. At **Anglers Rest**, beside the Cobungra River, is the ***Blue Duck Inn Hotel*** (☎ *5159 7220)*, which is especially popular with anglers, canoeists and bushwalkers. There's no town or shops here, just a long colonial-style timber building with seven self-contained units, a bar that also serves meals and a good barbecue area by the river. The tariff starts at $45 for a double room to $65 for an six-bunk unit. You need to bring sheets but pillows and doonas are provided.

About 30km south of Anglers Rest is Omeo, the only sizeable town along the highway and the turn-off point for Dinner Plain and Mt Hotham.

OMEO

• **pop 300**

This small town is the southern access route to the snowfields of Mt Hotham during winter, although the road is sometimes snowbound – check conditions before heading this way. In summer it's a popular base for explorations of, and activities in, the Alpine National Park – bushwalking, rafting trips, horse trekking, mountain biking and more.

Omeo's origins date back to the gold-rush days of 1851, when gold was found in the area. This was one of the toughest and most remote goldfields in the state. When the gold ran out early in the 20th century, some of the miners stayed on and established market gardens, sheep and cattle runs.

Omeo still has a handful of interesting old buildings, despite two earthquakes and one disastrous bushfire since 1885. They include the old **log gaol** (1858), the old **courthouse** (1892), the **state school** (1860) and several churches. The **historical society museum**, on the bend of Day Ave, is open during weekends or by appointment at other times. The **Petersen's Gallery** on Day Ave is also worth a look.

There's an unofficial information centre in the **German Cuckoo Clock Shop** on Day Ave. The Bank of Melbourne is also on Day Ave. Information and bookings for accommodation, horse riding, fishing, rafting, bike riding and hire, gold panning and ski hire is available from Omeo & High Country Booking Service (☎ 5159 1600 or bookings ☎ 1800 888 633 toll-free). The High Plains overnight droving, mustering and trail ride trips offered by High Plains Droving (☎ 5145 6055, treasure@tpgi.com.au) are highly recommended. They start $240 per person for two days.

Places to Stay

The ***Holston Tourist Park*** *(☎ 5159 1351)* has campsites from $11 and on-site vans from $28. The cheapest accommodation is at the ***Omeo Alpine Camp*** *(☎ 5159 1228)* on Day Ave next to the Catholic Church in the former convent. A bed in the five bunk rooms is $15 per person.

Colonial Bank House *(☎ 5159 1388)*, on Day Ave, has accommodation units at the rear of the main building. These four small, one-bedroom units are self-contained, with kitchenettes and a shared laundry, from $45/60 a single/double.

Livingstone Holiday Units *(☎ 5159 1308)*, on the northern outskirts of town, is a set of four self-contained timber holiday units from $85 a double. ***The Manse*** *(☎ 5159 1441)*, on the corner of Day Ave and the Omeo Hwy, is a fully restored guesthouse with four rooms, each with en suite. The B&B tariff is from $65/75.

The ***Omeo Motel*** *(☎ 5159 1297)* has smaller units at $40/50 and larger units from $60 a double. The best place to stay is the ***Golden Age Private Hotel*** *(☎ 5159 1344)* on Day Ave. It has been revamped into a luxury hotel. The smart rooms start at $85 a double.

Places to Eat

The ***Hilltop Hotel*** on Day Ave has the usual counter meals. Down the hill, the ***Omeo High Country Tavern*** *(☎ 5159 1273)* on Day Ave has good but overpriced main meals in the $11 to $20 range, and service is a bit slow. The upmarket restaurant in the ***Golden Age Private Hotel*** has been recommended.

Getting There & Away

Omeo Bus Lines (☎ 5159 4231) run daily buses between Omeo and Bairnsdale taking about two hours. During the ski season there is a bus on most days to Dinner Plain and Mt Hotham.

Hume Freeway & Goulburn Valley

Back in the early days of European settlement, the main route connecting Melbourne with Sydney was known as the Port Phillip Track. It was literally a track, and a slow and arduous trip for early travellers, not made any easier by the many river crossings. The route gradually developed and bridges were built across the rivers, with towns springing up around many of these river crossings.

Today the Hume Freeway (M31) is Victoria's busiest freeway. For most of its length the Hume is a multilane freeway bypassing the towns along its route. As a transport route, it's fast and efficient, but from the traveller's viewpoint it's not a particularly thrilling or scenic drive.

There are a few points of interest: the Ned Kelly-inspired tourist attractions of Glenrowan, the pleasant country towns of Benalla and Wangaratta and a handful of wineries to visit.

West of the Hume is the Goulburn Valley, Victoria's fruit bowl. It's a small but rich agricultural district producing some 25% of the state's total rural output in dollar terms. While fruit orchards make up the bulk of the area's produce, other important agricultural activities include grain growing, sheep, beef and dairy farming and market gardening. The valley's other main crop is wine and there are several wineries worth a visit, most notably Chateau Tahbilk and Mitchelton, both just south of Nagambie.

The Goulburn River winds its way through the heart of the district before meeting the Murray River just east of Echuca. The Goulburn provides the irrigation source which, from about 1912, enriched and transformed this entire area from a pastoral dust bowl into a paradise of fruit orchards and market gardens.

HIGHLIGHTS

- Chateau Tahbilk and Mitchelton wineries near Nagambie
- Wangaratta's Jazz Festival
- Airworld aviation museum at Wangaratta
- Historic Chiltern
- The lazy Goulburn River

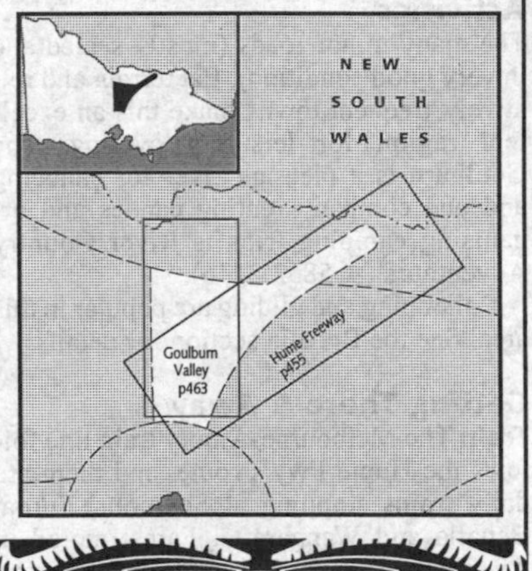

Of course, before the sheep and cattle arrived it hadn't been a dust bowl but a complex system of rivers, creeks and billabongs which must have provided an idyllic home to the peoples who lived here for many thousands of years before being shunted into near-oblivion by the pastoralists. If you get off the main roads you can still find some nice (if tiny) pockets of riverine ecology. The old waterways still have their occasional fling, and despite the best efforts of modern engineering, floods regularly damage crops and towns.

Orientation
Shepparton is the Goulburn Valley's major town, and the tourist information centre has good information on all of the valley's other attractions. Wangaratta and Benalla, included in the Hume Fwy section of this chapter, are the region's other main centres.

The Hume Fwy runs along the eastern edge of the Goulburn Valley, separating the valley from the foothills of the High Country.

The Goulburn Valley overlaps or borders several other regions, so you'll probably find yourself flipping back and forth between the Murray River (for the Rutherglen area) and High Country (for places east of the freeway) chapters while exploring it.

Activities
The many minor roads (mostly sealed and in very good condition), flat terrain and relatively frequent towns make this an excellent region for leisurely cycling. The Goulburn is a pleasant river for canoeing and one company renting canoes and organising camping trips is River Country Adventours (☎ 5852 2736).

Ballooning and gliding are popular in this area. See the Benalla section for details.

Getting There & Away
Train The Melbourne-Albury train line follows the Hume Fwy's route, and there are daily trains stopping at Seymour, Euroa, Benalla and Wangaratta. Fares quoted in this chapter are for V/Line trains. You can also take the XPT (Melbourne-Sydney via Albury), which is run by the New South Wales railway company Countrylink. The XPT is faster but the fares are slightly higher and you'll need a reservation.

Bus Quite a few V/Line services pass through this region.

From Melbourne there's a weekly (Friday) bus between Melbourne and Albury stopping in Wodonga, Wangaratta and Euroa; a weekday bus to Echuca stopping in Shepparton and Kyabram; a weekday bus to Cobram stopping in Seymour, Murchison, Shepparton and Numurkah; a Sunday bus to Shepparton stopping in Seymour and Murchison; and a daily bus to Barmah stopping in Kyabram.

There are also buses between Bendigo and Albury, stopping in Shepparton and Wangaratta. The daily Speedlink service between Adelaide and Sydney via Albury stops in Shepparton, Benalla and Wangaratta.

Buses connect with several train services to smaller towns in the region. Some towns east of the freeway (see the High Country chapter) are serviced by V/Line buses from Shepparton, Benalla and Wangaratta.

Hume Freeway

KILMORE
• **pop 2700**

Kilmore developed as an early coach stop on the Melbourne to Sydney route, and reached its prime during the gold-rush years. Along the main street are some impressive old bluestone and brick buildings from this era, including the town's three pubs and the twin post office and courthouse buildings (1863). A tourist information centre opens in the old courthouse on Sunday.

Whitburgh Cottage is a simple and solid bluestone cottage with a twin-peaked slate roof. It was built in 1857 and has been preserved as a historic museum, opening on Sunday from 2 to 4 pm. The cottage is in Piper St and signposted off the main road.

Places to Stay
Kilmore Country Motel *(☎ 5782 1346, 95 Sydney St)*, north of the town centre, has singles/doubles from $35/50. ***Bindley House*** *(☎ 5781 1142, 20 Powlett St)* has well-equipped cottages sleeping up to four people, for $80/110.

SEYMOUR
• **pop 6300**

Seymour, 100km north of Melbourne, is an industrial and agricultural centre on the banks of the Goulburn River. The Hume Fwy bypasses the town, but the Goulburn Valley Highway (B340) passes through it.

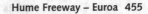

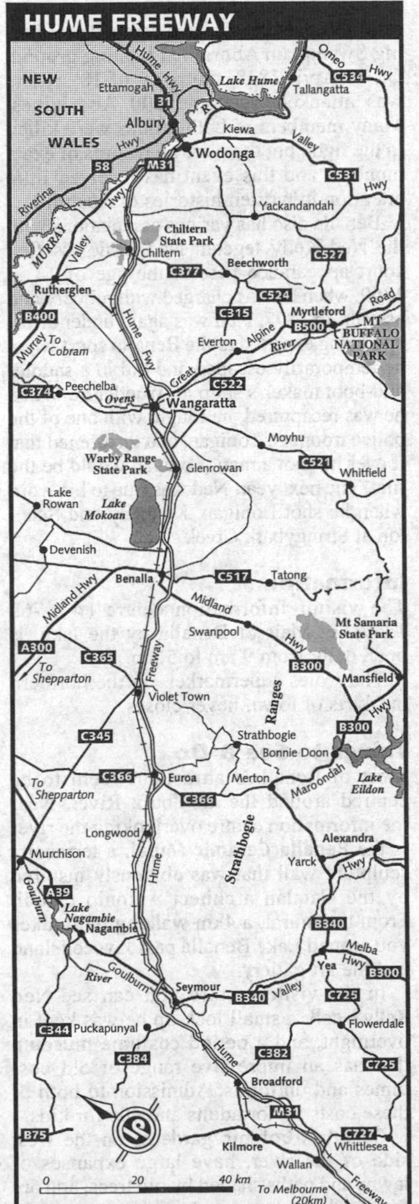

There's not much that will attract tourists off the freeway into Seymour, although in the surrounding area there are a few wineries, an alpaca farm and an army tank museum.

Things to See & Do

The **RAAC Tank Museum** is at the Puckapunyal Army Base, 18km west of Seymour. The museum houses a large collection of vintage armoured vehicles and tanks, including Australia's earliest, the Vicker MKII, as well as antitank weapons, smaller guns and various historic army displays. It's open daily from 10 am to 4 pm and entry costs $6 for adults and $3 for kids.

In an octagonal-shaped building on the old Hume Highway, **Somerset Crossing Vineyard**, on Seymour's western edge, is open daily for tastings and sales. There's an information desk in the tasting room.

Places to Stay

In Progress St on a bend of the Goulburn River, the ***Goulburn River Caravan Park*** (*☎ 5792 1530*) has camping sites for $10 and on-site vans and cabins from $25 to $42.

There are five motels along the old Hume Hwy (Emily St). The cheapest is the ***Seymour Motel*** (*☎ 5792 1500*), which has singles/doubles from $36/44. The ***Wattle Motel*** (*☎ 5792 2411, 9 Emily St*) has better rooms from $56/66.

Places to Eat

Somerset Restaurant (*☎ 5799 1097*) is a good restaurant on the old Hume Hwy on the western side of town. It's part of the Somerset Crossings Vineyard complex, and is in a modern octagonal-shaped building beside the Goulburn River. The hours vary seasonally – ring to find out when they're open.

EUROA

• **pop 2700**

The Hume Fwy bypasses Euroa, but the old highway still passes through the outskirts of town. This section of the road is lined with petrol stations and roadhouses with the usual greasy take-away food.

Euroa (pronounced 'yoo-*ro*-a') is pretty quiet nowadays, and seems to have been bypassed by more than just the freeway. It's notable for its large number of solid red-brick buildings – all symbols of past prosperity. Most of these are late Victorian and Edwardian, and the more impressive examples are found along Binney and Railway Sts.

In December 1878, the Kelly gang raided the nearby Faithful Creek Station (a sheep farm) and later robbed the Bank of Euroa (the building was demolished in 1975).

Places to Stay & Eat

The ***Seven Creeks Hotel*** *(☎ 5795 3034)*, on Clifton St, is an old two-storey hotel with simple pub rooms at $20/30 a single/twin, or $40 for a double with a bathroom.

Castle Creek Motel *(☎ 5795 2506, 53 Clifton St)* has rooms from $44/50 a single/double, and at 28 Clifton St, the ***Jolly Swagman Motel*** *(☎ 5795 3388)* has more modern units from $59/66.

At Longwood, 13km south-west of Euroa, ***Taffy's*** *(☎ 5798 5325)* has rustic, self-contained cottages in the foothills of the Strathbogie Ranges which start at $120 a double including breakfast.

If you want to avoid the roadhouses, head down Binney St, the town's main drag, which has a few take-aways, cafes and two bakeries. Back on the old Hume Hwy, ***Haygun's*** is a small restaurant with lunch-time pastas and other dishes from $7 and a dinner menu with mains around $17.

BENALLA

• **pop 8600**

Benalla is a relaxed country town on the banks of the Broken River and off the Hume Fwy. The river is dammed in the town centre to make an attractive lake; just the place for a dip to break a hot drive on the Hume.

Back in 1836, Major Thomas Mitchell crossed the Broken River near Benalla on his journey of exploration around Victoria. 'Benalla' is probably a variation on a local Aboriginal word meaning 'crossing place'.

Two years later, the first European settlers arrived in the area with several thousand sheep and cattle, and camped at Winding Swamp, an Aboriginal hunting ground. On 10 April 1838, the party of 18 settlers was attacked by some 300 Aborigines. Many members of both groups were killed in the fight, but there are no records of exact numbers and this event has received little attention in written histories of Australia.

Benalla also has various associations with the Ned Kelly legend: Ned made his first court appearance here at the age of 14 in 1869, when he was charged with robbery and assault. In 1877, Ned was again under arrest and being escorted to the Benalla court when he temporarily escaped and hid in a saddle-and-boot maker's shop in Arundel St. When he was recaptured, he fought with one of the police troopers, Lonigan, and threatened that if ever he shot a man, Lonigan would be the first. The next year, Ned was true to his word when he shot Lonigan, Kennedy and Scanlon at Stringybark Creek.

Information

The visitor information centre (☎ 5762 1749), in Mair St Benalla by the lake, is open daily from 9 am to 5 pm.

The Coles supermarket, on the northern outskirts of town, never closes.

Things to See & Do

Most of Benalla's attractions seem to be centred around the Goulburn River. Near the information centre overlooking the river is the **Benalla Ceramic Mural**, a terracotta sculpture wall that was obviously inspired by the Catalan architect Antonio Gaudi. From the mural, a 4km **walking path** takes you around Lake Benalla past Jaycee Island and the art gallery.

In the visitor centre you can see **Ned Kelly's cell**, a small lock-up he was kept in overnight, and a **period costume museum** that has an impressive range of old costumes and uniforms. Admission to both of these costs $3 for adults and 50c for kids.

Benalla's **botanic gardens**, on the west side of the river, have large expanses of lawns and paths shaded by old trees, and are fronted by a long stretch of rose gardens which, when blooming from late October to April, are very colourful.

In the gardens, facing the main road, is the **Weary Dunlop Memorial**. Sir Edward Dunlop, born in Benalla, was an army doctor who tended fellow POWs in the appalling Japanese camps on the Thai-Burma railroad during WWII. He was regarded as something of a saint by the men he helped to survive. It says something about Australia that two of its best-known war heroes – Dunlop in WWII and Simpson (of 'Simpson's donkey' fame) in WWI – were noncombatants.

Also in the botanic gardens is **Benalla Art Gallery**, a very impressive, modern gallery with a spacious and light design and a good collection of Australian art which includes paintings from the Heidelberg School and more recent works by artists such as Leonard French, Fred Williams and John Brack. It's open daily from 10 am to 5 pm and costs $3.

Benalla is known as a **gliding centre**. The Gliding Club of Victoria (☎ 5762 1058) has a base at the airport here, which is 2km from the town. Joy flights and training courses are available, or you can go and just watch the gliders. Balloon Aloft (☎ 1800 028 568 toll-free), takes passengers on dawn **balloon rides** in this region, which cost around $200 including a champagne breakfast.

North-west of Benalla, the **Winton Motor Raceway** (☎ 5766 4235) is one of Victoria's main motor-racing circuits, and has events programmed almost every weekend. Ring to find out what's on.

Special Events

Benalla's major festival is the Rose Festival, held over 10 days in early November and featuring the botanic rose gardens, parades and fireworks.

Places to Stay

Motor Village Caravan Park *(☎ 5762 3434)*, about 2.5km north of the centre on the Winton road, has sites starting at $8 and on-site vans and cabins from $29 to $42 a double.

There are nine motels to choose from. ***Benalta Family Inn Motel*** *(☎ 5762 5600, 27 Bridge St West)* is one of the cheapest, with singles/doubles for $39/49. (In the last edition of this book, 'Benalta' was printed as 'Benalla'. That typo was the reverse of a 19th century government typo which almost saw Benalla named Benalta.) ***Top of the Town Motel*** *(☎ 5762 4866, 136 Bridge St)* has a good standard of rooms from $48/58, rising to $83 for doubles.

Yaridni B&B *(☎ 5764 1273)* is a host farm near Goorambat 17km north of Benalla where you can experience life on a 600-hectare sheep property. The B&B tariffs start from $75/100.

Places to Eat

The ***Commercial Hotel***, near the bridge on Bridge St, has a pizzeria and counter meals.

Edible Deli, at 52 Nunn St, is an eat-in or take-away gourmet deli with tasty home-made goodies such as filled focaccia bread, pasta, beef-and-burgundy pies, sandwiches and felafel rolls, mostly around the $6 mark. Across the road is ***Cafe 1***, serving modern dishes at around $19 and the more formal ***Raffertys***.

Georgina's *(☎ 5762 1334, 100 Bridge St)* has a very good local reputation and has been in business 40 years. It's friendly and the food is good. Main course pasta or risotto costs $9. Other main meals such as braised rabbit, baked eggplant or fish of the day range from $10 to $19.50. There are some good special deals.

Getting There & Away

Benalla train station is in Mackellar St. Daily trains between Melbourne and Benalla cost $24.50/34.40 in economy/1st class.

V/Line buses also connect Benalla with Shepparton ($7.50; Monday, Wednesday and Friday) and Yarrawonga ($8.60; daily).

GLENROWAN

Ned Kelly's legendary bushranging exploits came to their bloody end here in Glenrowan in 1880. The story of Ned and his gang has since become something of an industry in this small town. You can't possibly drive through Glenrowan, which is 24km north of Benalla and bypassed by the Hume Fwy, without being confronted by the commercialisation of the Kelly legend.

Kellyland

This computerised, animated theatre is the highlight of Glenrowan's tourist attractions, although it's certainly not cheap. The theatre

The Kelly Gang

CHRIS MELLOR

Glenrowan's statue of Ned Kelly, wearing the home-made armour in which he fought his last battle

Ned Kelly is probably Australia's greatest folk hero. His life and death have been embraced as a part of the national culture, and Ned himself has become a symbol of the Australian rebel character.

But before he became a cult hero, Ned was a common horse thief. Born in 1855, Ned was first arrested when he was 14 and spent the next 10 years in and out of jails. In 1878, a warrant was issued for his arrest for stealing horses, so he and his brother Dan went into hiding. Their mother and two friends were arrested and sentenced to imprisonment for aiding and abetting. The Kelly family had always considered themselves victims of persecution by the authorities and the jailing of Mrs Kelly was the last straw.

Ned and Dan were joined in their hide-out in the Wombat Ranges, near Mansfield, by Steve Hart and Joe Byrne. Four policemen – Kennedy, Lonigan, Scanlon and McIntyre – came looking for them, and in a shoot-out at Stringybark Creek, Ned killed Kennedy, Lonigan and Scanlon. McIntyre escaped to Mansfield and raised the alarm.

The government put out a £500 reward for any of the gang members, dead or alive. In December 1878 they held up the National Bank at Euroa, and got away with £2000. Then in February 1879, they took over the police station at Jerilderie, locked the two policemen in the cells, and robbed the Bank of New South Wales wearing police uniforms. By this time the reward was £2000 a head.

On 27 June 1880, the gang held 60 people captive in a hotel at Glenrowan. A train-load of police and trackers was sent from Melbourne. A plan to destroy the train was foiled when a schoolteacher warned the police. Surrounded, the gang shot it out from the hotel for hours wearing heavy armour made from plough-shares. Ned was shot in the legs and captured, and Dan Kelly, Joe Byrne and Steve Hart, along with several of their hostages, were killed.

Ned Kelly was brought to Melbourne, tried and hanged on 11 November 1880. On her last visit, his mother told him to die like a Kelly. He met his end bravely, and depending on who you read, his last words were either, 'Ah well, I suppose it has come to this' or 'Such is life'.

His death mask, armour and the gallows on which he died are on display in the Old Melbourne Gaol.

Mark Armstrong

is a unique and innovative type of entertainment. The audience moves through four different rooms – depicting a railway waiting room, a shoot out scene, a burning building and, for the finale, the Old Melbourne Gaol – and the story is told by a cast of surprisingly lifelike computerised characters.

Be sure to read the promotional rhetoric on the two painted boards out the front, which compels visitors to go inside with words like '...most visitors to Glenrowan wouldn't know if the country shithouse fell on them!', and audaciously asks what you're doing in Glenrowan in the first place if not to see this display. Anyhow, if you can't afford the show, at least read the boards for some free entertainment. For a startling change from overly polite switchboards, phone Kellyland (☎ 5766 2367).

The show runs for 40 minutes and starts every half an hour between 10 am and 4 pm, with extended hours during school holidays. Tickets cost $15 for adults and $8 for kids (though the show could be a bit too scary for young children). Family tickets are $42. The theatre also has a souvenir shop and an information section.

Places to Stay & Eat

Glenrowan Caravan Park *(☎ 5766 2288)* is in a very pleasant and relaxed bushland setting 2km north of the town, and has sites from $11 and on-site vans and cabins from $26 a double.

On Main St, ***Glenrowan Kelly Country Motel*** *(☎ 5766 2202)* has rooms from $40/45 a single/double.

The ***Glenrowan Hotel***, also on Main St, is refreshingly free of Kelly paraphernalia and serves bar and bistro meals – there's a pleasant, covered courtyard at the back of the pub.

Wineries

There are four wineries near Glenrowan, all signposted from town and all well worth a visit. **Auldstone Cellars** (with lunches on weekends) and **Booth's Taminick Cellars** are both about 15km north of Glenrowan in Booth's Rd, Taminick.

Bailey's Bundarra Vineyards is about 10km north of Glenrowan on the corner of Taminick Gap Rd and Upper Taminick Rd. **HJT Vineyards** is 10km south-west of Glenrowan near Lake Mokoan.

Bailey's and Booth's are open daily for tastings and sales, HJT's is open on Friday and Saturday and Auldstone is open from Thursday to Sunday and every day during school holidays.

Warby Range State Park

North of Glenrowan, this low range of steep granite slopes has been preserved as a state park because of its scenic value (and, as usual, because it wasn't worth farming). Features of the park include fast-flowing creeks and waterfalls after rain, wildflowers in spring, some great picnic spots and an abundance of birdlife.

The park is in several sections and from Glenrowan it extends about 20km to the north. It's bordered on the western side by the Glenrowan-to-Boweya road and on the east by the Warby Range and Yarrawonga Rds – there are good sealed roads through the larger northern section of the park, which run between these two roads. There are also some good walking tracks, lookout points, picnic areas and a campground in the park – a map and brochure outlining these are available from information centres.

WANGARATTA

• pop 15,500

Wangaratta (pronounced 'wan-ga-*rat*-a' and commonly called 'Wang') is at the junction of the Ovens and King rivers. Its name comes from two local Aboriginal words meaning 'resting place of the cormorants'.

The first buildings were established here in the 1840s, based around a punt service to take passengers across the rivers. The punt operated until the first bridge was built in 1855. The town grew slowly as a minor rural centre until the middle of this century. The Wangaratta Woollen Mills and Bruck Mills were established here after WWII, leading the way for Wangaratta to become an industrial centre and a major textile town. Today the town is a modern rural centre. Accommodation options are mainly motels and caravan parks, but there are some good restaurants.

Wangaratta is the turn-off point for the Great Alpine Rd, which leads to Mt Buffalo, Myrtleford, Bright and the northern ski resorts of the Victorian Alps.

Orientation & Information

As with most towns along the Hume in Victoria, Wangaratta's main street, Murphy St, once doubled as the old Hume Hwy. The visitor information centre (☎ 5721 5711) is just south of the town centre on the corner of the old highway and Handley St. It's open daily from 10 am to 4 pm.

The Royal Automobile Club of Victoria (RACV, ☎ 5722 1292) has an agency at 10 Templeton St. The Coles supermarket on Greta Rd, just off the old highway, is open 24 hours a day. The Natural Resources & Environment (NRE) office (☎ 5721 5022) is in Tara Court on Ford St.

Things to See & Do

Wangaratta's main tourist attraction is **Airworld**, an aviation museum at the Wangaratta airport, signposted 4km east of the freeway. In a huge aircraft hangar, the museum has a collection of 40 vintage flying aircraft and aviation memorabilia. There's also a cafe and souvenir shop. The museum is open daily from 9 am to 5 pm and costs $6 for adults, $4 children and $12.50 for a family ticket.

The visitor information centre features **Mrs Stell's House in Miniature**, a house built to a one-sixth scale. Mrs Stell was 70 years old when she started the house, which took her 10 years to build using only a saw, a Stanley knife and a file. Kitsch? You bet, but curiously fascinating. The admission price of $2.50 goes to charities. If you're travelling further up the Hume, be sure to see the similarly kitsch Marble Marvel in the Gundagai (NSW) information centre. Which is odder?

At the Wangaratta Cemetery is the grave of **Dan 'Mad Dog' Morgan**, one of Australia's most notorious and brutal bushrangers. The grave contains most of Morgan's remains – his head and scrotum were cut off after he was fatally shot at nearby Peechelba Station in April 1865. The head was taken to Melbourne for a study of the criminal mind; the scrotum was supposedly fashioned into a tobacco pouch. The cemetery is off the old highway south of the town centre.

One of Wangaratta's most impressive buildings is the **Holy Trinity Anglican Cathedral** on the corner of Ovens and Docker Sts. The church was begun in 1909 and wasn't finished until 1965. The **Apex Park** beside the Ovens River bridge has picnic and barbecue facilities and a playground.

North-west of the town, the **Warby Range State Park** is a scenic spot for picnics and hiking (see that section earlier).

Special Events

The Wangaratta Jazz Festival, first held in 1990, has quickly grown into one of Australia's premier music festivals, and features a great programme of traditional, modern and contemporary jazz. It's held on the weekend before the Melbourne Cup horse race, which is held on the first Tuesday in November.

The ANA Carnival, an athletics meeting featuring the Wangaratta Gift, is held around Australia Day, in late January. The Easter Air Show, held on Easter Sunday, features a range of vintage and modern aircraft from the museum and from around the country.

Places to Stay

Of the three caravan parks, ***Painters Island Caravan Park*** *(☎ 5721 3380)*, in Pinkerton Crescent, on the banks of the Ovens River, is the most central. It has camping sites from $12 and on-site vans and cabins from $25 to $45 a double.

The ***Pinsent Hotel*** *(☎ 5721 2183, 20 Reid St)* is a renovated pub with reasonable motel-style rooms upstairs at $45/65 a single/double including continental breakfast. More traditional pubs include the ***Royal Victoria Hotel*** *(☎ 5721 5455, 25 Faithful St)* with pub rooms for $20/30 and the ***Bill-***

abong Hotel (☎ 5721 2353, 12 Chisholm St), from $24/40.

There are about a dozen motels in town. Approaching from Melbourne, the first one you come to on the old Hume Hwy is ***Crana Motel*** *(☎ 5721 4469)* with good budget rooms from $37/42 a single/double. On the northern side of town on the highway, ***Millers Cottage*** *(☎ 5721 5755)* is another good budget motel with rooms at $36/43.

The ***Hermitage Motor Inn*** *(☎ 5721 7444)*, on the corner of Cusack and Mackay Sts, just off the highway near the KFC outlet, has good standard rooms with doubles from $80 to $100. ***Gateway Wangaratta*** *(☎ 5721 8399, 29 Ryley St – the old Hume Hwy)* is a modern motel and convention centre with standard rooms from $80/89, and more expensive suites with spas.

Places to Eat

There are plenty of cafes, bakeries and takeaways, mainly along Murphy St (Wangaratta Rd) and Reid St, which crosses Murphy St in the centre of town.

Scribbler's Coffee Lounge *(66 Reid St)* is a daytime cafe with good food at reasonable prices. The walls and tables are covered with the work, letters and poems of local writers. This is a good place for breakfast. Down Reid St, on the corner of Bickerton St and across from the gardens, ***Vespas*** is another modern cafe. ***Zippis*** *(6 Roy St)* has a Tex-Mex menu plus other dishes. There are nightly specials, including all-you-can-eat deals on Friday and Saturday.

In the Bull's Head hotel on Murphy St, ***Martini's*** is a big and bustling restaurant with wood-fired pizzas and a range of other dishes, mainly Italian. The food is surprisingly good and reasonably priced. ***Satchmo's Wine Bar & Restaurant***, on Victoria Pde (parallel to and a block north of Murphy St) is popular. Another reasonable place is ***Peter's Cellar*** *(54 Ryley St)*.

For a good pub meal, head out to the ***Vine Hotel*** *(☎ 5721 2605)*, a charming old pub with underground cellars and innovative Asian and Mediterranean-influenced food. The Vine is about 4km north of town, on the road to Eldorado, and opens Monday to Saturday for dinner and Sunday for lunch.

Getting There & Away

Wangaratta train station is just west of the town centre in Norton St. Daily trains between Melbourne and Wangaratta cost $29.30/41 economy/1st class. They continue on to Albury ($11/18 economy/1st class).

V/Line buses run daily to Bright ($9.80) via Beechworth ($4.90) and Myrtleford ($6.10), and there's a daily (except Saturday) service to Rutherglen ($4.30) and Corowa ($4.90).

A bicycle and walking trail is being developed on disused railway lines which will eventually connect Wangaratta with Wahgunyah (near Rutherglen) to the north, Beechworth to the east, Whitfield to the south and Bright to the south-east. The Beechworth and Bright sections will be finished first. The great thing about paths on rail systems is that the grades are never steep.

GOULBURN VALLEY

Goulburn Valley

NUMURKAH

• pop 3100

Numurkah is just off the Goulburn Valley Hwy. A sign at the town's entrance proclaims it as the 'town of lakeside and roses', a reference to the Numurkah Rose Gardens, beside the Broken Creek Lake. The town has a rose festival each year at Easter.

The **historical society museum**, in a former bank building on the corner of Melville and Knox Sts, opens on Sunday from 2 to 4 pm and Wednesday from 1 to 3.30 pm.

El Toro Motel *(☎ 5862 1966)*, a Spanish-looking place on the corner of Melville and Brennion Sts, has singles/doubles from $40/50, and a restaurant open for dinner from Monday to Saturday.

NATHALIA

• pop 1500

Nathalia is an attractive small country town on the Broken River. Its main street is divided by a wide tree-lined plantation, and there are some interesting old buildings (including three pubs) along both the main street and the river. The town has a few points that may be of interest as you pass through. The Barmah State Forest (see the Murray River chapter) is about half an hour's drive north-west of here.

The **memorial gardens** here are small but quite significant – the 64 rose bushes at the entrance are dedicated to the 64 locals who gave their lives in WWI and WWII. At the rear of the gardens is a unique war memorial to the soldiers – a large rock bound in chains and surrounded by name plaques.

There's a local **historical society museum** here in the old Mechanics Institute building, but it only opens on the second Sunday of each month from 2 to 5 pm.

Places to Stay & Eat

Nathalia Carotel Caravan Park *(☎ 5866 2615)*, on the Murray Valley Hwy, has sites from $15 and cabins from $45 a double. ***Riverbank Caravan Park*** *(☎ 5866 2821)*, on Park St about a kilometre east of the town centre, is cheaper and also has on-site vans from $20 a double.

KYABRAM

• **pop 5700**

Kyabram is a bustling commercial centre, with modern retail facilities for the surrounding farming communities. 'Kyabram' (pronounced 'ky-*ab*-r'm') is a local Koori word meaning 'dense forest'.

The main point of interest for tourists is the excellent **Kyabram Fauna & Waterfowl Park**, devoted to native species. It's very well set up, with modern enclosures and natural habitat settings. You can see most of the animals at close quarters, including kangaroos, koalas, Tasmanian devils, wombats and dingoes. There's a large number of bird species in aviaries and a variety of water birds in the wetlands section, plus a historic cottage and farming machinery display. The park, just south of town, is well signposted from the town centre. It's open daily from 9.30 am to 6.30 pm (to 5.30 pm in winter) and costs $7 for adults and $3.50 for kids.

The indigenous people of this area called the Murray River the **Tongala**, which is the name taken by a small town off the Murray Valley Highway (B400) between Echuca and Kyabram. The **Golden Cow** centre here has displays on the dairy industry (including its own small farm) as well as what are claimed to be the best milkshakes in Australia. Admission is $5 for adults, $2.50 for children.

Places to Stay & Eat

If you decide to stay in town, ***Kyabram Caravan Park*** *(☎ 5852 2153, 14 Anderson St)* has camping sites from $10.50 and on-site vans and cabins from $28 to $35 a double. The ***Commercial Hotel*** *(☎ 5852 1005, 217 Allan St)* has motel units behind the pub for $40/50 for singles/doubles, cheap bar meals and a reasonable bistro.

Country Roads Motor Inn *(☎ 5852 3577, 363 Allan St)* is the best of the town's motels, with doubles costing from $54 to $72.

For a good meal, the best bet is the big ***Kyabram Hotel***, corner of Allan and Union Sts.

SHEPPARTON

• **pop 31,900**

Shepparton is the regional centre of the Goulburn Valley, a modern town at the junction of the Midland and Goulburn Valley highways. It's also at the junction of the Goulburn and Broken rivers.

Shepparton started out in 1850 as a river crossing on the Goulburn River, when McGuire's punt and inn were built beside the river (near the present site of the town's historical museum). There was no great rush to join McGuire – by 1870 there were still only half a dozen buildings in the town – but in 1912 irrigation technology came to the Goulburn Valley, leading to a sudden influx of settlers and a steady growth in the local agricultural industries. Today, the city's major industrial employers are the Shepparton Preserving Company (SPC), Ardmona Fruit Products and Campbell's Soups.

Information

Shepparton's visitor information centre (☎ 5831 4400 or 1800 808 839 toll-free) is in Wyndham St at the southern end of the Victoria Park Lake and opens daily from 9 am to 5 pm.

The RACV has an office (☎ 5821 9522) at 330 Wyndham St.

Fruit Picking From January to April it's fruit-picking season in the Goulburn Valley – a good time to be looking for casual work.

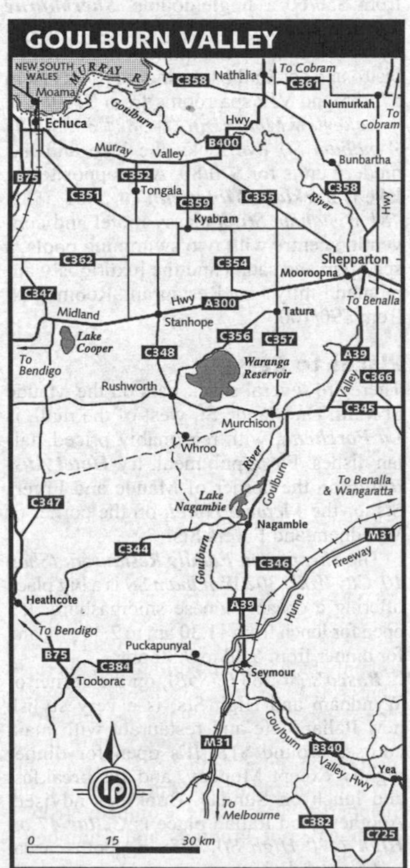

It's best to start looking in December as demand for jobs is high when the apricots, then peaches and pears ripen. The Harvest Office (☎ 1300 720 126), at 361 Wyndham St, arranges employment. Some orchards offer basic accommodation or tent sites, but for others you'll probably need to stay in town and use your own transport.

Shepparton City Historical Museum

This is one of the best historical museums in country Victoria, and the most interesting attraction in Shepparton – it ought to be open every day! You could easily spend several hours wandering around looking at the thousands of items, which are maintained by volunteers. The museum is divided into separate galleries, with sections devoted to transport, local agriculture, colonial clothing, shopping and communications. A highlight is the huge 100-year-old four-faced post office clock, which is in full working order and chimes on the hour.

The museum is on the corner of High and Welsford Sts, close to the original site of McGuire's punt. Although it's only open on even-dated Sundays, the museum will also open at other times by request – ask at the visitor information centre and one of the volunteer curators will happily show you around. Admission costs $2 for adults and 50c for children.

Shepparton Art Gallery

The art gallery is between the town hall and the municipal offices in Welsford St. It has a good permanent collection of Australian art including a large collection of ceramics and paintings by Margaret Preston, John Perceval, Arthur Boyd, Frederick McCubbin, Arthur Streeton and Rupert Bunny. *Goulburn River near Shepparton* (1862) by Eugene von Guèrard is an early landscape which depicts McGuire's punt across the river.

A separate gallery is devoted to temporary and touring exhibitions. The gallery is open Tuesday to Friday from 10 am to 5 pm and on weekends from 2 to 5 pm; admission costs $1.

Other Attractions

Good views of the Goulburn Valley and Shepparton can be seen from the **telecommunications tower** (near the post office in the mall) which is open Monday to Saturday from 9 am to 5 pm.

On Parkside Dve, the **Aboriginal Keeping Place** has displays on the area's original owners and a cultural officer to answer questions. It's open daily from 9 am to 7 pm.

Just south of the town centre on Wyndham St is the **Victoria Park Lake**. The lake is a popular venue for various water sports and is surrounded by lawns and trees and some very pleasant picnic and barbecue areas. Beside the lake, on Tom Collins Drive, is the **Raymond West swimming complex**, with several pools and a large water-slide. The complex is open from November to March. There's also a **bike hire** place by the lake.

You can tour the **SPC cannery** (the largest in the southern hemisphere) during the canning season from January to early April. Tours operate on weekdays between 8.30 and 11 am and between noon and 3.30 pm – book at the tourist information centre.

There are several wineries around Shepparton, and more are opening all the time. The closest is **Broken River Wines**, 8km east of town, which is open from Thursday to Sunday for tastings and sales.

Places to Stay

Camping & Caravan Parks There are half a dozen caravan parks in or near Shepparton. The most central is ***Victoria Lake Caravan Park*** *(☎ 5821 5431)*, which is right beside the lake and the tourist information centre in Wyndham St, about a kilometre south of the town centre. It has camping sites from $9 and on-site vans and cabins from $30 to $48 a double.

Hostel At ***Backpackers International*** *(☎ 5831 8880, 129 Benalla Rd)* you can get help in finding work, and transport to get you there. Weekly rates are around $105, but you should phone before arriving to check the current situation.

Pubs ***Hotel Australia*** *(☎ 5821 4011)*, on the corner of Maude and Fryers Sts, has old-style pub rooms which are plain but clean and cost $25/40 a single/double. The ***Victoria Hotel*** *(☎ 5821 9955)*, on the corner of Wyndham and Fryers Sts, also has old pub rooms with shared bathrooms from $29/39 and motel-style units at $45/55.

Motels There are almost 20 motels here to choose from, all fairly pricey. ***Tudor House Motor Inn*** *(☎ 5821 8411, 64 Wyndham St)* is central and fairly economical with rooms from $50/60 a single/double. ***Sherbourne Terrace Motel*** *(☎ 5821 4977, 109 Wyndham St)* is a large and modern motel with a bistro and cocktail bar, standard rooms from $75/85 and VIP spa rooms from $110/120.

Lakeview Motor Inn *(☎ 5821 3355, 505 Wyndham St)* overlooks the lake and has modern units for $70/80. Also opposite the lake is ***Parklake Motor Inn*** *(☎ 5821 5822, 481 Wyndham St)*, a classy motel and convention centre with two swimming pools, a spa, gym and sauna and the luxuriously appointed Emily Jane Restaurant. Rooms cost from $90/100.

Places to Eat

There are several snack bars on the Maude St Mall. On Maude St, west of the mall, is ***La Porchetta***, with reasonably priced Italian dishes. For a pub meal, try ***Hotel Australia***, on the corner of Maude and Fryers Sts, or the ***Victoria Hotel***, on the corner of Wyndham and Fryers Sts.

The ***Shepparton Family Restaurant*** *(Shop 10, City Walk, 302 Wyndham St)* is a big place offering a cheap Chinese smorgasbord. It's open for lunch from 11.30 am to 2.30 pm, and for dinner from 5.30 to 9.30 pm.

Bosco's *(☎ 5831 5858)*, on the corner of Wyndham and High Sts, is a very stylish new Italian cafe and restaurant with main courses around $18. It's open for dinner nightly except Monday, and for breakfast and lunch on Sunday. Bookings advised. Another good Italian place is ***Cellar 47 on High*** *(170 High St)*, offering both casual and formal dining.

REG URQUHART

Welcome to Gippsland Art Gallery, Sale

RICHARD I'ANSON

Wetlands, The Lakes National Park

CHRIS MELLOR

Patersons Curse, a glorious purple carpet, displacing the pasture near Lake Hume

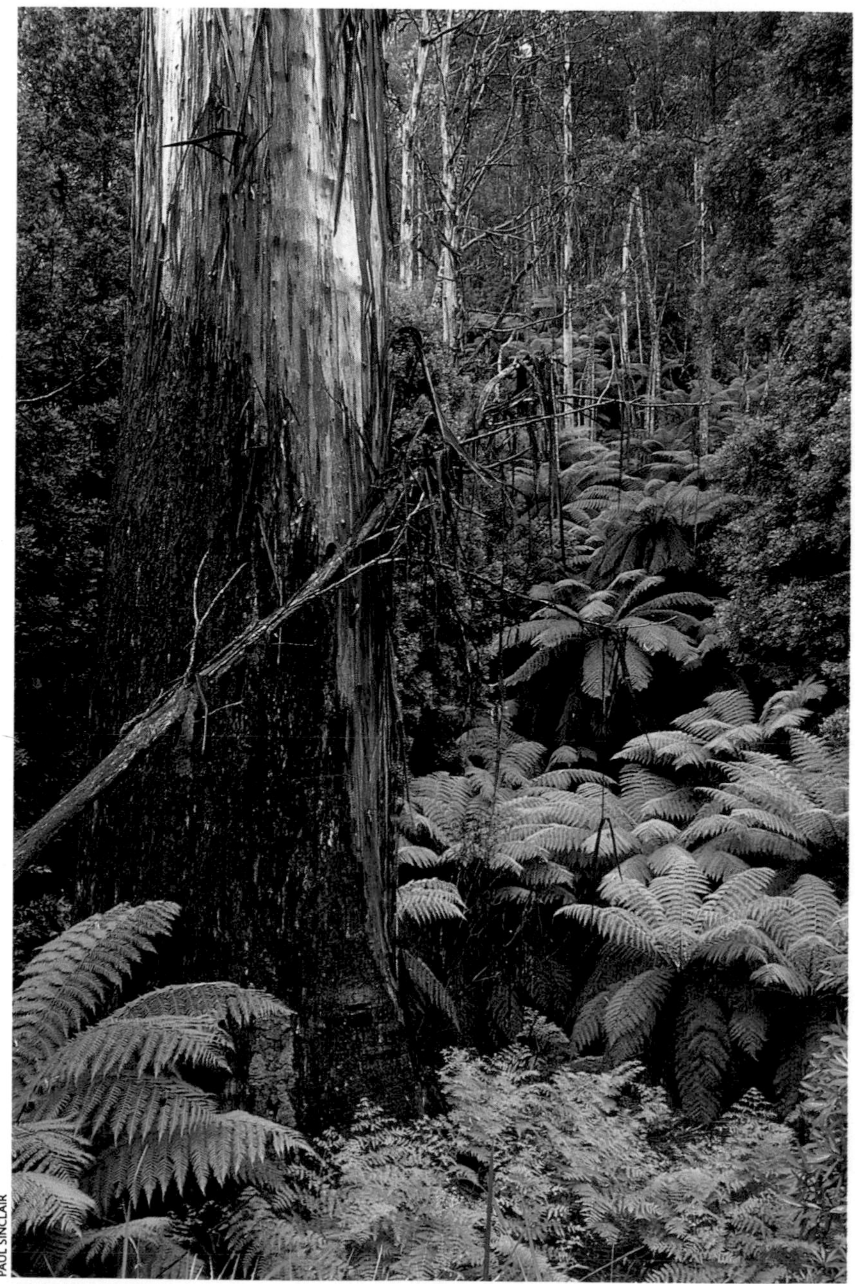

PAUL SINCLAIR

Majestic mountain ash forest at Result Creek, Errinundra National Park

Getting There & Away

Shepparton train station is south of the town centre in Purcell St. There are daily trains and buses to Melbourne $23.30/$32.60 in economy/1st class); connecting buses continue on to Cobram ($75).

V/Line buses also connect with Albury ($24.50) and Benalla ($7.50) daily, and with Mildura ($39.70) and Bendigo ($9.80) three times a week.

TATURA

• pop 2800

Tatura is a small farming community 20km west of Shepparton. During WWII a number of prisoner-of-war and internment camps were set up in the area between Tatura, Rushworth and Murchison, and there's a small museum here which records that period.

Irrigation & Wartime Camps Museum

Tatura's historical society museum has a separate section devoted to the history of this area's prisoner-of-war and internment camps, with a fascinating collection of photos, records, books and memorabilia.

At the outbreak of WWII, all 'enemy aliens' living in Australia were rounded up and confined to internment camps. During the war, more than 25,000 prisoners of war (1658 Germans, 18,432 Italians and 5637 Japanese) were also held in various camps throughout Australia. There were seven different camps in this area, ranging from temporary tent camps to the historic homestead at Dhurringile, which housed German officers from the Afrikan Korps, the Luftwaffe and sailors and officers from the ship *Cormoran*.

The original section of the museum is devoted to local history with special displays on the history of irrigation. The museum, on the corner of Hogan and Ross Sts, is open on weekend afternoons.

German Military Cemetery

This cemetery was established by the German government in 1958, when the remains of all German prisoners of war and internees who died in Australia during WWI and WWII were exhumed from other cemeteries in Australia and reburied here. The cemetery is signposted off the Midland Highway (A300) and is 2km west of Tatura.

Places to Stay

Country Gardens Caravan Park *(☎ 5824 2652)*, on Rushworth Rd, has tent sites from $8 and on-site vans and cabins from $24 to $40 a double. ***Whim-Inn Motel*** *(☎ 5824 1155)*, on the corner of Hogan St and Dhurringile Rd, has good rooms at $50/60 plus a licensed restaurant.

MURCHISON

• pop 630

Murchison is a small township on the Goulburn River just off the Goulburn Valley Hwy. There's not much to see here, although there are a number of historic buildings as well as a very pleasant picnic park on the banks of the Goulburn River.

South of the town on Old Weir Rd, **Longleat Winery** is worth a visit and is open daily from 9 am to 5 pm (Sunday from 10 am) for tastings and sales. The winery also sells gifts and souvenirs and has a pleasant picnic area under a vine-covered pergola.

Beside the local cemetery is the **Italian Ossario**. This pretty little chapel-style building, with rows of cypress pines, houses remains of Italian prisoners of war and detainees.

Across the river from town is the old **Bridge Hotel** (1868). It is now a private dwelling, so you can't poke around, but it's an atmospheric sight.

Whroo Forest Wagons (☎ 5826 2420) offer a chance to travel slowly in a caravan drawn by a Clydesdale draught horse. The vans sleep up to five and cost $95 a day. You need to bring food and sleeping bags.

Places to Stay

Murchison Caravan Park *(☎ 5826 2546)* is on River Rd 2km north of town and has sites from $8 and on-site vans from $25 a double. ***Murchison Motel*** *(☎ 5826 2488)*, on High St, has singles/doubles from $35/40.

Places to Eat

The best place for tucker around here is the ***Murchison Gallery Tearooms*** *(12 Robinson St)*. This tiny gallery/tearoom is in a historic two-storey building and serves good soups, sandwiches, cakes and pastries at reasonable prices. It's open during the day between 10 am and 5 pm from Thursday to Monday.

NAGAMBIE

• **pop 1300**

Nagambie (pronounced 'na-*gam*-bi') is on the shores of **Lake Nagambie**, which was created by the construction of the Goulburn Weir back in 1887.

This area's main attractions are **wineries** and **water sports**. Lake Nagambie and Goulburn Weir are popular for water-skiing, canoeing, sailing, fishing and swimming. Two of the best-known wineries in Victoria, Chateau Tahbilk and Mitchelton, are just south of the town (see the boxed text).

A great way to visit both these wineries is to take a **cruise** with Goulburn River Cruises (☎ 5794 2877). Cruises run from October to the end of April on weekends, holidays and Wednesdays, with one cruise on Friday. Most run between Chateau Tahbilk and Mitchelton, and include a light lunch or a picnic. The rest of the year there are cruises on Sunday. There are two and four-hour options, plus a 90 minute scenic cruise from Chateau Tahbilk.

Nagambie itself has a number of historic buildings, including the **Nagambie Folk Museum** which is in the former courthouse and shire hall at 344 High St. The museum has a collection of local history items and memorabilia, and is open on Sunday afternoon.

Information

The Nagambie Lake visitor information centre (☎ 5794 2647), at 145 High St, has a good range of information on the entire region and the local wineries. It's open daily from 9 am to 5 pm.

Places to Stay

Nagambie Caravan Park *(☎ 5794 2681, 143 High St)* has camping sites for $10, on-site vans from $18 and holiday units from $47 a double.

Motels range from the ***Nagambie Goulburn Highway Motel*** *(☎ 5794 2681, 143 High St)*, which charges from $34/38 a single/double, to the ***Nagambie Motor Inn*** *(☎ 5794 2833, 185 High St)*, which has good units from $65 to $85 a double.

Wineries around Nagambie

The **Chateau Tahbilk Winery**, 8km south-west of Nagambie off the Goulburn Valley Highway, is an absolute must if you're in this area. One of Australia's most historic wineries, this place is full of character. You can explore the musty underground cellars, dusty and fascinating tasting sheds, stables and other areas at your leisure. Chateau Tahbilk is open Monday to Saturday from 9 am to 5 pm and Sunday from 11 am to 5 pm.

The nearby **Mitchelton Winery** is a startling contrast. A modern and stylish operation, this is one of Victoria's largest and most successful wineries. There are tours of the cellars, river-boat trips, a wine library/museum, several dining areas and panoramic views to be had from the top of the observation tower. Mitchelton opens Monday to Saturday from 9 am to 5 pm and Sunday from 10 am to 5 pm.

On the northern edge of Nagambie is the smaller **David Traeger Wines**. David is one of the region's most respected wine makers, and has a good range of table wines that includes an interesting verdelho. His winery is open daily from 10 am to 5 pm.

Other local wineries include the tiny **Twelve Acres**, at Bailieston 16km north-west of Nagambie (open weekends from 10 am to 6 pm), **Longleat** (see the Murchison section) and **Plunkett Wines** at Avenel, 19km south-east of Nagambie.

Gippsland

Gippsland forms the south-eastern corner of Australia and is often overlooked by travellers as they take a more direct route between Sydney and Melbourne. By doing so many are missing out on some of the most diverse and attractive scenery on the continent. Bordered by the mountains of the Great Dividing Range to the north, the waters of Bass Strait to the south and Western Port to the west, Gippsland also includes the Lakes District and Wilderness Coast areas which are covered in separate chapters of this book.

The western part of Gippsland covered in this chapter is divided into two distinct halves; the Latrobe Valley, through which the Princes Highway (A1) passes; and South Gippsland, the coastal section of which includes the wonderful Wilsons Promontory National Park. The contrast between these two areas is stark. The Latrobe Valley is Victoria's industrial heartland. It contains one of the world's largest deposits of brown coal, and its mines and power stations supply most of Victoria's electricity, while the offshore wells in Bass Strait provide most of Australia's petroleum and natural gas.

The major towns along the Princes Hwy are predominantly residential and industrial centres for the valley's and the strait's work forces. While the thought of all these coal mines, paper mills, power plants, smoke stacks and factories probably conjures up visions of the David Lynch film *Eraserhead*, the regions surrounding this industrial landscape are surprisingly beautiful. The Princes Hwy provides access to a number of very scenic areas, including the historic former gold-mining township of Walhalla and the delights of the Gourmet Deli region.

South Gippsland is an area of great natural beauty, with rolling hills, forested mountains and a rugged and spectacular coastline. An extremely fertile area, it is also the focus of Victoria's dairy industry. The main road through here is the South Gippsland Hwy (B440), but the backroads through the hills, and the coastal route, are more scenic and worth exploring if you

HIGHLIGHTS

- Take a day or overnight hike through magnificent Wilsons Prom, or simply laze on the beach at Tidal River
- Discover Victoria's very own 'ghost town' in the tiny old gold-mining township of Walhalla set in an idyllic, small, steep sided valley
- Follow the Gourmet Deli Trail to taste some of Gippsland's most delicious home grown produce
- Cool down with a rainforest walk through Tarra Bulga National Park – the last of the magnificent forests that once covered all of South Gippsland
- Horse ride, drive or take a horse-drawn carriage through the rolling blue hills of the Strzelecki Ranges
- Hunt for dinosaurs at Bunurong Marine Park

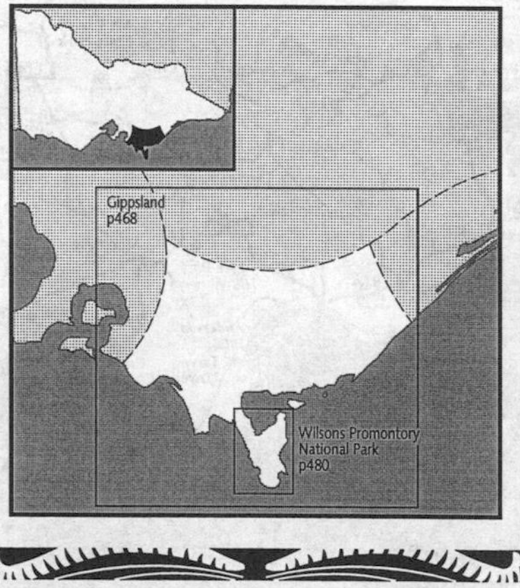

have enough time. South Gippsland has one of Victoria's most loved and most popular national parks, Wilsons Promontory, commonly known as Wilsons Prom and even more simply as the Prom.

Orientation & Information

Gippsland's major townships are strung along the Latrobe Valley, although these residential centres have good facilities for the valley's 75,000 inhabitants, and plentiful motels and campgrounds, they are of little interest to travellers except as a base for the region's attractions.

There are good tourist information and Parks Victoria centres throughout the region that can help with inquiries and accommodation booking.

Activities

Wilsons Prom is one of Victoria's most popular destinations for bushwalkers, with dozens of great walks to choose from. Beach activities abound in South Gippsland, and

there are good surf beaches along the coast between Kilcunda and Cape Paterson and at the Prom.

You can also go horse-riding in the Strzelecki Ranges or from Erica, take a tour of one of the coal mines and power stations in the Latrobe Valley, fossick for leftover gold in Walhalla or go bird-watching in the Sale Wetlands.

For a holiday with a difference, try a leisurely horse-drawn gypsy-wagon tour through the Strzelecki Ranges. Two operators, Promway Horse Drawn Gypsy Wagons (☎ 5184 1258), based at Yarram, and Tarwin Valley Horse Drawn Wagons (☎ 5681 2244), based near Foster, have fully equipped gypsy-style caravans, drawn by gentle Clydesdale horses, which sleep five or six people and cost around $90 to $120 a day.

Getting There & Away

Train V/Line has daily trains between Melbourne and Sale, stopping at all the major towns of the Latrobe Valley.

Bus There are also daily V/Line buses from Melbourne along the South Gippsland Hwy to Leongatha, Fish Creek, Foster and Yarram. There are no direct bus services from Melbourne to Wilsons Prom, although the Foster-based 'Prom Postie' runs a daily bus service down to the Prom.

Car & Motorbike The two major routes through Gippsland are the Princes Hwy through the Latrobe Valley, and the South Gippsland Hwy, which heads south-east to Phillip Island then passes through Leongatha and Foster before rejoining the Princes Hwy at Sale.

Scenic Drives There are also some great scenic drives. If you're heading to the Prom and have time, take the coastal route via Cape Paterson and Inverloch. The Grand Ridge Rd, which runs along the ridge of the Strzelecki Ranges, is a spectacular but rough alternative route to the South Gippsland Hwy. Farther north, 'Gourmet Deli Trail' through Neerim South and Noojee, and the mountain drive from Moe to Erica and Walhalla are two excellent drives.

Latrobe Valley

From Melbourne, the Princes Hwy follows the powerlines back to their source in the industrial heartland of the Latrobe Valley, before heading on to Sale.

The region between Moe and Traralgon is the site of one of the world's largest deposits of brown coal. The power stations built on the coal fields at Yallourn, Morwell and Loy Yang provide 85% of Victoria's power requirements. The immense Loy Yang power station is the largest in the southern hemisphere.

WARRAGUL

• **pop 9000**

A regional centre for the district's dairy farms, which provide most of Melbourne's milk, Warragul is the first major town east of Dandenong. The excellent **West Gippsland Arts Centre** (☎ 5624 2456) – part of Warragul's Civic Centre – showcases all local and visiting art, both performance and visual. Of interest is a large wall panel carved from timber which depicts the history of the region. Warragul's **historical society museum** (☎ 5625 3763), in the old shire hall on the corner of Queen and Smith Sts, is open on Sunday from 2 to 4 pm (every second Sunday in winter).

Warragul has a Mardi Gras celebration in December and a Springfest in October.

The **Darnum Musical Village**, signposted off the Princes Hwy 8km east of Warragul, has a collection of old and modern pianos, organs and other musical instruments in three historic buildings. There's a workshop, cafe and picnic areas, and the village is open daily from 10 am to 4 pm. Admission including a tour costs $8/3 for adults/children.

Places to Stay & Eat

There are a few motels and hotels offering accommodation and ***Warragul Caravan***

GIPPSLAND

Park *(☎ 5623 2707, Burke St)*, surrounded by parklands, has camping sites from $12 and on-site vans from $28. ***Southside B&B*** *(☎ 5623 6885, 20 Korumburra Rd)* is central and has doubles with a full cooked breakfast for $90.

South of town, ***Clearview Farm*** *(☎ 5626 4263, Van Ess Rd)*, in Ferndale near Mt Worth State Forest, has single/double B&B on a mixed organic farm for $65/90. It also has tearooms open on weekends with delicious chutneys and jams for sale.

Warragul has a good choice of restaurants that includes the ***Flamin' Bull*** *(☎ 5623 2377, 9 Mason St)*, a rustic pioneer-style restaurant specialising in steaks and bush tucker. Mains range from $12 to $20, and it's open nightly for dinner. The ***Courthouse Cafe*** *(☎ 5622 2442)*, housed in the restored courthouse building, has pizzas and pasta from $14 to $20 and is open daily for lunch and dinner. The multi-award-winning ***Bukhura Restaurant*** *(☎ 5622 0015, 12 Napier St)* is a licensed and BYO Indian restaurant with good value lunch packs.

GIPPSLAND

Getting There & Away

Warragul's train station is in the town centre, off Queen St. Daily trains run between Melbourne and Warragul, and the one-way fare is $10.90/15.30 in economy/1st class.

GOURMET DELI REGION

The West Gippsland area to the north of **Drouin** (a pretty town off the Princes Hwy with hotels, a motel and camping) and Warragul is being promoted as Victoria's 'Gourmet Deli Region'. It's a truly picturesque area of rolling hills, lush cattle farms and small villages, and there's a good range of fruit and berry orchards, deer farms, cheese factories, trout farms and country gardens to visit. The Gourmet Deli Trail is signposted off the Princes Hwy west of Drouin. Pick up a copy of the *Gourmet Deli* brochure available from tourist information centres and most attractions en route.

The friendly ***Robin Hood Hotel*** *(☎ 5625 4884, Drouin West)*, also signposted from the highway, makes a good base for exploring the region and has motel rooms from $45 to $49. It also has a great restaurant with mains from $14 to $18. Alternatively, ***Glen Comrie Park*** *(☎ 5626 8212)*, off the main Neerim road, is a 45 acre area of bushland with walking tracks that has tent sites from $9.

From Drouin head north-east to **Jindivick** and the ***Jindivick Smokehouse*** *(☎ 5628 5217)*, with a tearoom, and tastings and sales of smoked hams, bacons, chicken, trout etc.

To the east is **Neerim South**, a small, modern village with the rustic ***Old Bakehouse***, which serves up Italian cuisine, pizzas, pastas and chicken dishes; check out the wood fired oven bakery behind it. Just north of the town is the **Tarago River Cheese Co**, home of great local cheeses including Gippsland Blue and Blue Orchid (a kind of gorgonzola). The factory is open daily for tastings ($8.50/9.50 cheese plate for one/two people) and sales.

From Neerim South continue past the **Tarago Reservoir**, a haven for water birds, north to **Noojee**, a tiny, ramshackle township surrounded by green hills and spectacular countryside. Just south of the township is the **Noojee Trestle Bridge**, a massive timber bridge, built in 1919, spanning a deep fern gully. The bridge is classified by the National Trust and the surrounding area is managed by the Department of Conservation & Natural Resources. In the town itself is a pretty picnic ground, general store, trout farm, a couple of tearooms and the ***Outpost Restaurant and Retreat*** *(☎ 5628 9669, Loch Valley Rd)*, which has a char grill restaurant and bar. It also has log cabins sleeping from one to eight people from $80 to $160 per night.

North-east of Noojee are the scenic **Toorongo Falls**. Follow the signs to Mt Baw Baw then take the signposted left turn to the falls, which are a short walk from a bush ***camping*** area. There's another, rougher track to the nearby **Amphitheatre Falls**, which are also well worth a visit.

From the falls head to Willow Grove and **Blue Rock Lake**, a popular boating and fishing venue with some good picnic areas. From there head south to **Trafalgar**, which has antique and craft shops, and ***Nelson's*** *(☎ 5633 1730, 215 Contingent St)*, a cosy licensed restaurant.

To the west, **Yarragon**, a small highway town midway between Warragul and Moe, has a ***motel*** *(☎ 5634 2655)*, hotel and more antique, craft and souvenir shops to cater to the passing parade. The ***Commercial Hotel*** has a good bistro and ***Gippsland Food & Wine*** is a large deli, tearoom and bakery, specialising in local produce.

MOE

• pop 15,500

Moe is a large commercial centre on the northern side of the Princes Hwy. A railway line runs through the town centre, dividing the place in two.

The main attraction of this coal-mining centre is **Gippsland Heritage Park**, beside the Princes Hwy and the first turn-off to Moe, where a 19th century community has been re-created on three hectares of parklands. The 30 or so buildings are authentic, having been collected from all over Gippsland and reassembled here – at least one is classified by the National Trust. The place has a realistic feel to it, and there's a number of working displays of old crafts, as well as rides in horse-drawn vehicles. The excellent collection of restored carriages, buggies and wagons is a highlight. Old Gippsland is open daily from 9 am to 5 pm; entry costs $4/2/12 for adults/children/families.

A short distance from Moe is the **Yallourn Power Station** – the township of Yallourn was moved lock, stock and barrel to provide access to the brown coal deposits underneath. The hill behind the town site has a lookout with some information for visitors and views of the vast open-cut mine.

Places to Stay

The ***Moe Gardens Caravan Park*** *(☎ 5127 3072)* has tent sites from $9 and on-site units from $35. There are few motels along the highway, but just to the east of town, in Newborough, is ***Brigadoon*** *(☎ 5127 2656, 106 Haunted Hills Rd)*, which has individually designed cottages in a pleasant natural setting. Doubles, including breakfast, start at $110.

Getting There & Away

Moe's train station is in Lydiard St. There are daily trains between Melbourne and Moe, and the one-way fare is $14.80/20.70 in economy/1st class.

WALHALLA

Tiny Walhalla, 46km north of Moe, is one of Victoria's most historic and charming towns. It has much greater appeal and authenticity than most of the state's more heavily promoted and commercialised 'historic townships', and is well worth a visit. Though the population has declined, there's plenty to see, and the drive up to the town is quite beautiful. The town itself is in a small, idyllic valley, with a cluster of historic buildings and old miners' cottages scattered around and set into the hillsides. Stringer's Creek runs through the centre of the town, winding through a steep and narrow cutting, and crumbling stone walls line the streets.

Things to See & Do

Most of Walhalla's attractions only open on weekends and during school or public holidays; at other times it's fairly quiet up here. The best way to see the town is on foot – take the circuit walk that leads from the car park by the information shelter as you enter town. It passes the main sights before climbing up the hill to follow the old timber tramway back to the car park. There are longer walks to Thomson Bridge, Poverty Point or on to the Baw Baw Plateau. South of Walhalla, there is a car park and marked trail to the summit of Mt Erica, the start of the Australian Alps Walking Track. Warning: there are many mine shafts in the area so keep to the marked tracks.

Guided tours of the **Long Tunnel Extended Gold Mine** are held Friday to Wednesday at 1.30 pm (and 2.30 and 3.30 pm on weekends and school holidays). The mine has a museum and blacksmith's shop, and tours cost $4/2 for adults/kids. You can also take a 40 minute ride on the **Walhalla**

Goldfields Railway (☎ 0055 11788); it operates from Thomson Bridge and trains depart at 11.30 am, and 1 and 2.30 pm on Saturday; and 11 am, and 12.30, 2 and 3.30 pm on Sunday and holidays. Return fares cost $7/5/20 for adults/children/families.

Back in town, a set of steps lead up a steep hillside to the **Walhalla Cricket Ground**. A famous sign at the base of the steps says, 'Warwick Armstrong, Australian cricketer, played here in 1907. He wagered he could hit a sixer into Stars Hotel yard. He failed however and only scored eleven runs.'

The **Walhalla Cemetery** gives a sombre insight into the history of the area and those who came and stayed. There's a group of restored shops on the main street, one of which contains the **Walhalla Corner Stores & Gold Era Museum**, with a good photographic collection; it's open most days and entry costs $2.

Most Sundays, Mountain Saddle Safaris (☎ 5165 3365) operates excellent horse trail rides from Erica up to Walhalla through the steep hills ($80 including lunch at the Walhalla pub). It also operates a range of catered horse-riding safaris through the High Country.

Places to Stay & Eat

There are good bush ***camping*** areas along Stringer's Creek. Another option is the simple and self-contained ***Mill House*** *(☎ 5165 6227)*, which sleeps up to six people and starts at $75 a night.

The slightly more salubrious ***Windsor House*** *(☎ 5165 6237, Right Hand Branch Rd)* is a restored National Trust building

There's Gold in Them Thar' Hills

Tiny Walhalla, the quaint former gold-mining township, is bracing itself for a second, modern-day gold rush.

Gold was first discovered in Walhalla's creek towards the end of 1862 by determined prospector Edward Stringer. Within weeks he was joined by another 200 or so hopefuls and Cohen's Reef, an outcrop almost 2 miles long, was discovered. By 1865 the Long Tunnel Mine, the single most profitable mine in Victoria, was open and in the 49 years that followed over 13.5 tonnes of gold was extracted from it.

Between 1885 and 1890 over 4000 people were living in and around the town, in dwellings that clung precariously to the steep sided valley. Ironically the train from Moe, incorporating a truly amazing section of tunnels and trestle bridges, was running late and the railway line only came into service in 1910 just as the town's fortunes began to decline; it closed in 1944, but parts of it still operate today as a tourist attraction (see Things to See & Do).

After mining in the area stopped, Walhalla's population fell and the town became little more than a 'ghost town' with a weekend tourist trade. However, in December 1998 the Perseverance Corporation announced plans to mine Cohen's Reef (through the Long Tunnel Extended Mine) for gold. Perseverance believe the reef still has plenty of potential and hope to open a processing plant here by 2001. Around the same time, a new (second) hotel was undergoing construction on the former site of the Star Hotel and on 21 December 1998, Walhalla, which lies less than 40km as the crow flies from the enormous Loy Yang Power Station, received electricity from the national grid (through underground power lines) for the first time.

With all this development it seems quite likely that Walhalla could easily double its 1998 population of 19, although it's unlikely that it will ever return to its former boom town glory. Let's hope that this is the case and Walhalla retains its refreshing old world charm.

Mark Armstrong

GIPPSLAND

with five guestrooms and suites. Open on weekends only, double B&B starts at $100, or $170 with dinner.

More accommodation options lie nearby. To the east ***Rawsons Village*** *(☎ 5165 3200, 1 Pinnacle Drive)* in Rawson has motel/lodge accommodation from $50/36. Farther south, ***Crawford's Erica Hotel/Motel*** *(☎ 5165 3252, Main Rd)* in Erica has motel-style units at $50 and good bistro meals, and serves skiers' breakfasts during the snow season. The pub also has the **Logger's Museum**, an interesting collection of cross-cut saws, axes and other memorabilia.

There are a few places in Walhalla serving light lunches and teas, and the rebuilt ***Walhalla Lodge Hotel*** – the old (and legendary) pub burned down a few years ago – serves good food.

MORWELL

- **pop 14,000**

Morwell was founded in the 1880s, and before the turn of that century it became the supply centre for diggers and traders heading for the goldfields at Walhalla.

These days Morwell is an industrial town servicing the massive open-cut mine, the Hazelwood Power Station, the APM pulp mills and the local briquette works. The **Latrobe Regional Gallery** (☎ 5134 1364, 138 Commercial Rd) has changing exhibitions of contemporary art, andan opens Tuesday to Friday from 1 to 4 pm, Saturday from 11 am to 3 pm and Sunday from 10 am to 4 pm.

The **Powerworks Visitor Centre** (☎ 5135 3415), signposted off Commercial Rd, houses models and displays of the Latrobe Valley's coal-mining and power-generating activities. It also has guided tours of the Morwell open-cut mine and the Hazelwood Power Station. These leave the centre daily at 9.30 and 11 am, and 1, 2 and 3 pm. Tours cost $8/3.50/18 for adults/children/families.

The **Hazelwood Pondage**, a huge artificial lake about 10km south of Morwell, was created to provide the nearly 200 million litres of water needed every hour by the Hazelwood Power Station's steam condensers. The waters here are warm year round, and are popular for sailing and water-skiing.

Places to Stay

There are a couple of motels along the highway, but ***Southside Motel*** *(☎ 1800 358266 toll-free, 7 Maryvale Crescent)*, on a quieter side street, has single/double units for $49/57.

Places to Eat

The town's best eatery is ***Cafe Gaztronomy*** *(☎ 5134 2913, 15 Church St)*, a small two-roomed cafe/restaurant with a plush burgundy interior, slate floors and open fires. By day it has a light lunch menu with take-away tarts, pastries, gourmet cakes and sandwiches etc from $2, and eat-in lunches from $8.50 to $11. By night, it's an intimate BYO restaurant, with mains from $17 to $18.

Getting There & Away

Morwell's train station is in the centre of town. Daily trains run between Melbourne and Morwell and the one-way fare is $17.50/24.50 in economy/1st class.

MORWELL NATIONAL PARK

The small Morwell National Park (283 hectares) is about 15km south of Morwell. The area is steep and hilly, with vegetation ranging from eucalypts to fern gullies and an abundance of koalas and birdlife, including lyrebirds. The area was declared a national park partly because of the presence of the now-rare butterfly orchid, which grows on tree trunks.

There are a couple of walking tracks and a picnic area at the north of the park. From Morwell head to Churchill, from where the park is signposted.

TRARALGON

- **pop 19,000**

The original township was a rest stop and supply base for miners and drovers heading farther into the gold and farming country of Gippsland. Today Traralgon is the centre of the state's paper and pulp industry and a major electricity centre.

In front of the train station in the centre of town, the **Gippsland Shop** houses an impressive collection of arts and crafts including sculptures, pottery, prints and toys, all made by local artists, and a tourist information centre (☎ 1800 621409 toll-free) open daily from 9 am to 5 pm.

Places to Stay & Eat

There are a number of caravan parks and motels along the Princes Hwy: the ***Park Lake Caravan Park*** *(☎ 5174 6749, Park Lane)* has tent sites from $12 and cabins from $45; the ***Sundowner Motel*** *(☎ 5174 7277)* has rooms from $68.

Creek Cottage *(☎ 5174 4367, 14 George St)* is a lovely B&B with self-contained units from $85. At ***Quigley's of Traralgon*** *(☎ 5174 4088, 11 Hyde Park Rd)* there are smaller en suite single/double rooms with breakfast from $65/75.

There are heaps of take-aways and coffee lounges in Traralgon. For a pub meal, try ***Ryans Hotel*** in Franklin St. This Victorian-era pub has been well renovated and has several bars and dining areas and a large and popular bistro.

Getting There & Away

Traralgon's train station is between Princes St and Queens Pde. Trains run daily between Traralgon and Melbourne; the one-way fare is $19/26.60 in economy/1st class.

SALE

• **pop 13,500**

At the junction of the Princes and South Gippsland Hwys, Sale is a supply and residential centre for the Bass Strait oil fields. The town was settled on the banks of the Thomson River in the 1850s. It is connected by the river to the Gippsland Lakes, and during the paddle-steamer era it became a busy port town for the river-boat trade. There's nothing left of the old port now; the former site has a playground and a few boats moored to the river bank.

Sale has a few remnants from its early years, but most of its growth is quite recent and it's a modern and progressive town. It is also the centre of the significant Gippsland Wetlands, a sprawling collection of lakes, waterways and billabongs which are home to more than 135 species of water birds.

Information

The Sale Information Centre (☎ 5144 1108) on the Princes Hwy is open daily from 9 am to 5 pm.

The Wetlands Centre of Victoria, on York St near Lake Gutheridge, has information on the local wetlands and runs ecology tours of the district. It's staffed by volunteers; if there's no-one there grab one of the leaflets in the box by the door.

Things to See

To see all that Sale and its environs have to offer, pick up a copy of the Heritage Walk and Drive leaflets which will guide you past some of the area's older sights. One example is the **Cobb & Co Stables & Market Place** at 199 Raymond St. This unique building, with a high arched roof, has been transformed from stables into a market and amusement centre.

Signposted at Lake Gutheridge, the **Sale Wetlands Walk** is a 4km walking trail around the lake via **Sale Common**, a game refuge with bird hides, an observatory and other walking tracks. The common is home to many species of waterbirds including swans, pelicans, swamp hens and cormorants.

The **Gippsland Art Gallery**, in the Civic Centre at 70 Foster St, is open daily from 10 am to 5 pm; entry costs $2. There's also a **historical museum** in Foster St which opens on Sunday from 1.30 to 4.30 pm ($2).

Places to Stay

Beside the tourist office, the ***Sale Motor Village Caravan Park*** *(☎ 5144 1366)* has tent sites from $12, on-site vans from $30 and cabins from $55.

Across the road, ***The Creek B&B*** *(☎ 5144 4426, 5 Foster St)* is a lovely old red-brick homestead with three comfy double rooms, a private sitting room, a shared period-style bathroom and a very pleasant back garden.

Singles/doubles cost $85/105 including a cooked breakfast.

Another very good B&B is the ***Bon Accord Homestead*** *(☎ 5144 5555, 153 Dawson St)*, a restored colonial homestead set in spacious grounds open to the public, with excellent heritage-style guestrooms at $90/120 for singles/doubles including a cooked breakfast.

There are plenty of motels, and the ***Criterion Hotel*** has basic rooms from $25.

Places to Eat

If you're after a pub feed, ***Gippy's Hotel*** on the corner of York and Cunninghame Sts has good meals in the bar and Gaslight Room bistro.

Cafe Rossi *(☎ 5144 5855, 90 Raymond St)* is an attractive and lively bar/restaurant with tasty dishes in the $13 to $24 range. In the mall, ***Cafe Catchadeli*** has groovy artwork and good coffee and snacks. It's fully licensed and open for dinner.

Getting There & Away

Sale's train station is on the western side of town in Petit Drive. Trains run daily between Melbourne and Sale and the one-way fare is $26.10/36.50 in economy/1st class. Connecting buses continue along the Princes Hwy into New South Wales via Bairnsdale, Lakes Entrance and Orbost.

MAFFRA

• pop 4000

Maffra is a small, progressive and pleasant town on the Macalister River. It is a centre for the surrounding dairy district, and has quite a few historic buildings and tree-lined streets. The **Sugar Beet Museum**, in River St, has a historical collection and displays on the area's agriculture, and opens on Sunday from 2 to 4 pm.

Places to Stay & Eat

The ***Maffra Caravan Park*** *(☎ 5147 1323, 187 Johnson St)* has tent sites for $8 and on-site cabins from $28. The ***Metro Hotel*** *(☎ 5147 1809, Johnson St)*, has singles/doubles from $50/60.

If you're looking for something special, head out of town to ***Powerscourt Country House*** *(☎ 5147 1897)*. It's on the Maffra-Stratford road, about 4km east of Maffra. This magnificent white-brick homestead on 48 hectares of grazing pastures overlooking the adjacent **Wa-De-Lock Winery** (☎ 5147 3244) has the perfect combination – great accommodation, great food and great service. The guest bedrooms are all decorated individually in heritage-style, with four-poster or brass-and-iron beds and Victoriana en suite bathrooms, and there's a cosy guest lounge and sitting room with leather armchairs to pull up to the open fire. Of course, being worthy of so many superlatives, it ain't cheap: the courtyard rooms start at $140 a double, while a larger front room starts at $180.

The restaurant here is also highly regarded and set in the small but impressive ballroom (built by the original owner for his daughter's 21st birthday party!). A mid-week 'Indulgence package' offers dinner and B&B for $135 per person.

Powerscourt is also the venue for the Gippsland Harvest Festival held annually in March.

Getting There & Away

Maffra is connected to Sale by daily V/Line coaches; the one-way fare to/from Melbourne is $26.10/33.70 in economy/1st class.

South Gippsland

From Melbourne, the South Gippsland Hwy passes through the Strzelecki Ranges and is the quickest route to Wilsons Promontory. An alternative coastal route, via Wonthaggi and Inverloch, is slower, but more scenic and interesting.

KORUMBURRA

• pop 2750

The first sizeable town along the South Gippsland Hwy, Korumburra, on the edge of the Strzelecki Ranges, grew as a coal-mining centre following the discovery of black-coal deposits here in 1872. Mining declined after 1900, and nowadays the town is a commercial centre for the surrounding dairy farms. The South Gippsland tourist information centre (☎ 1800 630704 toll-free) is on the highway at its intersection with Silkstone Rd.

The **Coal Creek Historical Park** (☎ 5655 1811), off the highway east of town, is a very popular re-creation of a 19th century coal-mining town. It is on the site of the original Coal Creek Mine, which operated here until 1958, and comprises the mine shaft, poppet head, sawmill, old train station, miners' cottages and various old shops. It's open daily from 10 am to 4.30 pm, and admission costs $11/5.50 for adults/children.

Korumburra is the headquarters for the **South Gippsland Railway** (☎ 5658 1111), which runs between Nyora and Leongatha on Sundays and holidays. The return fare between Korumburra and Leongatha costs $12/7 for adults/children.

Whitelaw Cottage *(☎ 5655 1410, Sullivans Rd)* in Whitelaw is a restored miner's cottage B&B. It has nice gardens with views, and doubles with breakfast start at $90.

V/Line coaches stop in Commercial St, Korumburra; the one-way fare to/from Melbourne is $13.40.

LEONGATHA

• pop 4200

Another centre for the local dairy industry, Leongatha is perched among the rolling green hills of Gippsland 14km south-east of Korumburra. There's a **historical society museum** in the old Mechanics Institute in McCartin St, and a few interesting craft and food shops in the town.

To the south in Koonwarra, the ***Lyre Bird Hill Winery & Guest House*** *(☎ 5664 3204, Inverloch Rd)* has wine tasting and double B&B accommodation from $100. It also has a cottage from $80 per night, and dinner with the wine maker can be arranged.

V/Line coaches stop at Leongatha train station; the one-way fare to/from Melbourne is $14.80.

GRAND RIDGE ROAD

Between the Latrobe Valley and the South Gippsland coastal areas are the beautiful 'blue' rounded hills of the Strzelecki Ranges. These areas fiercely resisted early agricultural development, and were less-than-affectionately nicknamed the 'Heartbreak Hills' by the pioneer farmers.

The winding Grand Ridge Rd traverses the top of these ranges, running from midway between Warragul and Korumburra to midway between Traralgon and Yarram, providing a fabulous excursion through fertile farmland that was once covered with forests of mountain ash trees. You can easily get onto the panoramic road from either Trafalgar or Moe by turning south via the lovely little townships of Narracan or Thorpdale. Alternatively use the road to get to or from Tarra Bulga National Park (see the following entry).

The road is mostly gravel, and rough and bumpy in sections as it twists through the hills, but the countryside and views are quite spectacular. Take a good road map with you.

The only place of any size along the route is the pretty township of **Mirboo North**, which has the ***Grand Ridge Brewery & Restaurant*** *(☎ 5668 1647)* in the historic old Butter Factory building. This is Gippsland's only beer brewery, and the complex features a cosy bar and a large bistro with good meals in the $10 to $15 range. There's a caravan park opposite the shire hall, and ***Strathmore Cottage*** *(☎ 5668 1571, Mardan Rd)*, south of town, is self-contained with singles/doubles from $40/60.

There are also some good picnic areas and walking tracks in and around the town, including the 13km Rail Trail walking track which winds its way to **Boolara**. The renovated ***Old Boolara Pub*** *(☎ 5169 6633)* is a solid bluestone hostelry dating from 1884 and is a great spot for a beer or a bite. It even has B&B accommodation from $70/90.

Tarra Bulga National Park

Tarra Bulga, at the eastern end of Grand Ridge Rd and about 30km south of Traralgon, is one of the last remnants of the magnificent forests that once covered the whole of southern Gippsland. This small park (1230 hectares) is in two sections, 3km apart, and is an absolute delight to visit.

A canopy of magnificent, towering mountain ash trees encloses areas of cool temperate rainforest. Below the mountain ash are sassafras, myrtle beech and mulberry trees, and the ground is covered with a mass of tree ferns, Christmas-bush and mosses. Birds, including lyrebirds, parrots, robins and honeyeaters, revel in the lush environment.

There are two picnic areas in the park. The Tarra Valley picnic ground is on the western side, off Tarra Valley Rd. A 2.2km walking track leaves from here to the **Cyathea Falls**. The Bulga picnic area is in the northern section, just off Grand Ridge Rd. The park visitor centre (☎ 5196 6166) and the 2km **Fern Gully Nature Walk**, crossing the Bulga suspension bridge, are here. Camping isn't allowed in the park.

The ***Tarra-Bulga Guest House*** *(☎ 5196 6141)* is on Grand Ridge Rd near the park entrance. It's an old-fashioned guesthouse, built in the 1930s, with 11 rooms with shared bathrooms, a games room and lounge with open fire. The tariffs start at $45/75 for single/double B&B, while packages including dinner start at $55 per person. In the cold winter of 1954, the famous Russian defectors Vladimir and Evdokia Petrov spent a weekend at the guesthouse (then called 'Fern Gully') as a break from the rigours of the Petrov Royal Commission. It must have been a particularly cold winter: Mrs Petrov wrote in the visitors' book, 'A pleasant rest from the Royal Commission. Weather not unlike Siberia.'

A male lyrebird displaying his magnificent plumage

WONTHAGGI

• **pop 5900**

Wonthaggi is a former coal-mining town that has developed into a busy commercial centre, the largest in this area. In 1937, Wonthaggi was the scene of one of Victoria's worst mining disasters. During a miners' strike, a naked flame set off an underground methane gas fire, killing 18 maintenance workers.

The **State Coal Mine** (☎ 5672 3053), to the south of town, is a scattered cluster of buildings, including an interesting mining museum with great old photos from the mining days, and hard-hat tours down the mine conducted by old timers. There are seven historic mine sites to visit, and tours operate daily between 10 am and 3.30 pm; a small fee is charged.

Wonthaggi's old train station houses the local **historical society museum**, which opens on Saturday from 1 to 5 pm.

The ***Wonthaggi Hotel*** (formerly the Whalebones Hotel), on the corner of Murray St and McBride Ave, has tasty pub grub, a pair of massive whale jawbones outside the entrance and a big old stuffed crocodile on the wall in the public bar. Former barman James Dunbar used to tell amazed visitors that he caught the crocodile in the local creek – actually, he shot it up in the Northern Territory!

The helpful tourist information centre on Watt St can tell you about bush camping sites out of town, and the ***Miner's Rest Caravan Park*** *(☎ 5672 2667, 125 White Rd)* has tent sites/on-site vans from $10/28. There is also a selection of motels in town.

V/Line coaches stop at the corner of McBride Ave and Watt St; the one-way fare to/from Melbourne is $14.80.

INVERLOCH

• **pop 2450**

Inverloch is at the head of Venus Bay, at the point where Anderson's Inlet meets the sea. The foreshore and streets are lined with pine and gum trees, and together with **Cape Paterson** it's a popular family holiday destination with good ocean beaches, protected and safe swimming spots and a modern shopping centre.

There's an information centre (☎ 5674 2706) on the Esplanade, open daily from 10 am to 4 pm. The Bunurong Environment Centre (☎ 5674 3738, Ramsey Blvd) has a shop and conservation information on the local area. It also organises environmental and educational **tours** for all ages, and is open from 10 am to 4 pm from Thursday to Sunday and during school holidays.

Inverloch hosts an annual **jazz festival** each March.

Places to Stay

There's plenty of camping available in Inverloch, including at ***Inverloch Foreshore Reserve*** *(☎ 5674 1236, cnr the Esplanade and Ramsay Blvd)*, which has unpowered sites starting at $14. More camping is available opposite the beach at ***Cape Paterson Caravan Park*** *(☎ 5674 4507)* in Cape Paterson.

The ***Inverloch Motel*** *(☎ 5674 3100)*, on the Inverloch-Wonthaggi Rd, has well-equipped singles/doubles from $45/56. For B&B try ***Hilltop House*** *(☎ 5674 3514, Lower Tarwin Rd)*, which has views across Inverloch and doubles for $95. Holiday houses and cottages in Inverloch and Cape Paterson can be booked through the helpful tourist information centre.

Places to Eat

There are a few places to eat, including coffee shops, pizza joints, take-aways and pub bistros in the main shopping centre. ***Beaches and Cream*** *(☎ 5674 3366)* in the A'Beckett St mall has good snacks and lunches for around $6.

Digging for Dinosaurs

The Bunurong Marine Park, which covers 17km of coast between Wonthaggi and Inverloch, is a great area with an array of rock pools, tidal platforms, cliffs and sandy coves backed by thick vegetation. The foreshore is perfect for swimming, surfing and especially snorkelling. It is also the old stomping ground of dinosaurs.

Over 115 million years ago the rock platforms of the marine park formed a channel across a floodplain between present-day Australia and Antarctica; as the two continents began to separate the rocks moved north. Fossils were first found here in 1991, and the park is now a significant excavation site for many species of dinosaur remains, including small two-legged herbivores, small carnivorous theropods, turtles and aquatic reptiles. However, it was the discovery of the jaw bone of *Ausktribosphenos nyctos* that caused the most excitement. This tiny placental mammal lived in a polar habitat and the fossil is more than twice as old as the oldest marsupial or monotrene fossil previously found in Australia.

The Monash Science Centre Dinosaur Dreaming dig team have spent several summers diligently excavating the area – not an easy task when you consider that the main site lies beneath the high tide line. Not surprisingly they welcome volunteers. If you do fancy yourself as a bit of a palaeontologist, or are interested in hearing more about the team's discoveries, contact the Bunurong Environment Centre (see the Inverloch entry).

Joyce Connolly

GIPPSLAND

The ***Rippleside Restaurant & Brasserie*** (☎ *5674 3999)*, on the corner of the Esplanade and Cuttris St, is a classy upmarket place overlooking Anderson's Inlet. It serves modern Australian dishes, with an emphasis on fresh local produce; mains range from $12 to $18.

Overlooking the Tarwin River, 19km south-east of Inverloch, the pub at **Tarwin Lower** is a great place for a drink and a $5 lunch.

Wombats are a common sight at Wilsons Promontory National Park.

Getting There & Away

V/Line coaches stop on Beach Rd; the one-way fare to/from Melbourne is $17.50.

WILSONS PROMONTORY

Established in 1898, the 'Prom', one of the most popular national parks in Australia, covers the peninsula that forms the southernmost part of the mainland. The Prom offers superb variety including more than 80km of walking tracks and a wonderful selection of beaches – whether you want surfing, safe swimming or a secluded spot all to yourself, you can find it at the Prom. Then there's the wildlife, which abounds despite the park's popularity. There are kangaroos, a wide variety of birdlife including emus and, at night, plenty of wombats. The wildlife around Tidal River is very tame.

There's a small booth at the entrance to the park where day visitors pay the $8 per car entry fee. If you're camping here or staying overnight, the entry fee is incorporated in the cost of your accommodation.

The one access road into the park leads to Tidal River on the western coast, which has a park office and education centre, a petrol station and general store, a cinema, 500 campsites and a range of cabins and lodges, all run by Parks Victoria.

Information

The park office (☎ 1800 350552 toll-free) at Tidal River is open daily from 8 am to 6 pm. The displays are excellent, with information and many colour photos of the history of the park. It also takes reservations for accommodation and issues permits for camping away from Tidal River and is the place to pay your park entry fee if the main gate is not staffed.

Walks

It's probably walkers who get the best value from the Prom, though you don't have to go very far from the car parks to really get away from it all. The park office has detailed maps and free leaflets on a huge range of walks ranging from 15-minute strolls from Tidal River to overnight and longer hikes.

The walking tracks take you through swamps, forests, marshes, valleys of tree ferns and long beaches lined with sand dunes. For serious exploration, it's worth buying a copy of *Discovering the Prom on Foot*, available from the park office for $6.95.

The following are some of the Prom's most popular walks:

Mt Oberon Nature Walk
Starts from the Mt Oberon car park. A moderate 6.5km walk that takes about two hours it's an ideal introduction to the Prom, and the views from the summit are excellent in all directions.

Sealers Cove Track
Starts from the Mt Oberon car park. A great five hour, 19km return walk across the Prom from west to east via Windy Saddle.

Great Prom Walk
This is the most popular long-distance hike, a moderate 45km circuit across to Sealers Cove, down to Refuge Bay, Waterloo Bay, the

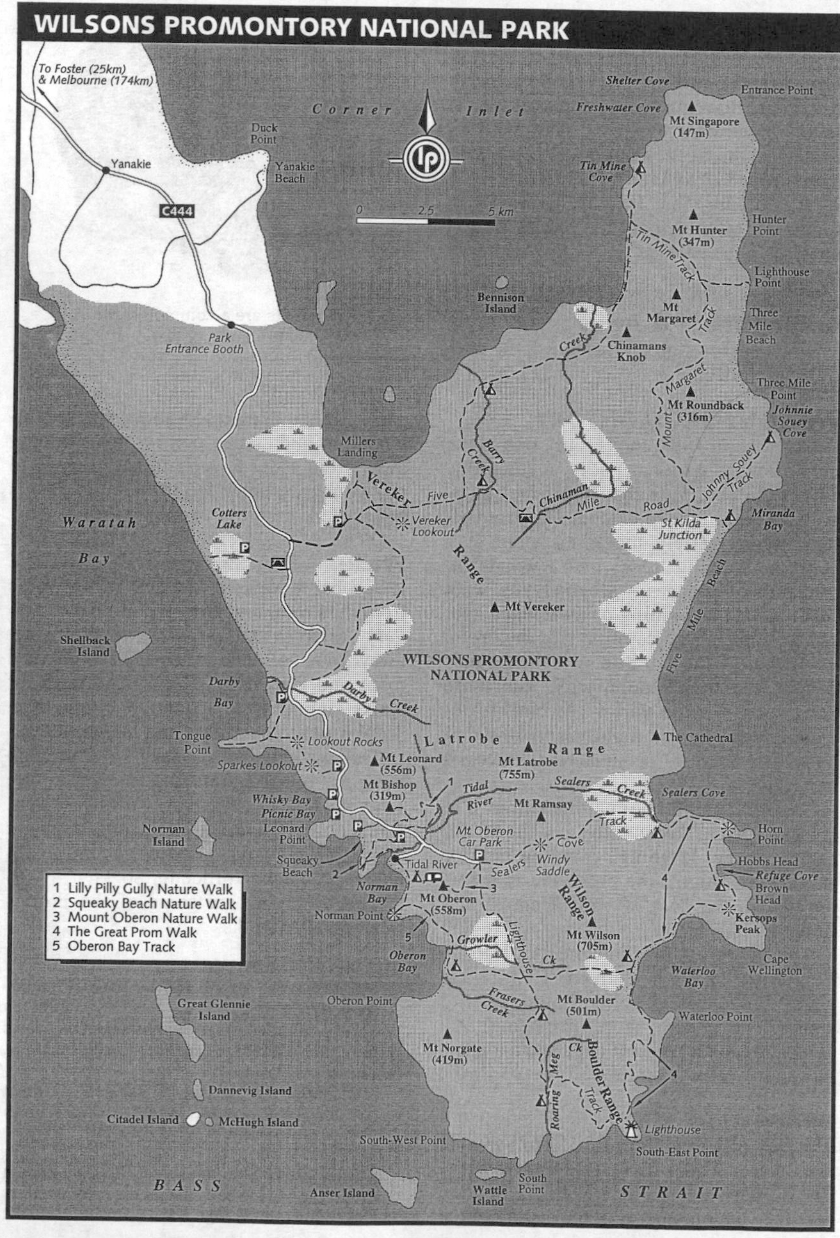
WILSONS PROMONTORY NATIONAL PARK
To Foster (25km)
& Melbourne (174km)
Corner Inlet
Shelter Cove
Entrance Point
Freshwater Cove
Mt Singapore (147m)
Duck Point
Yanakie
Yanakie Beach
C444
Tin Mine Cove
0 2.5 5 km
Mt Hunter (347m)
Hunter Point
Tin Mine Track
Lighthouse Point
Bennison Island
Mt Margaret
Three Mile Beach
Park Entrance Booth
Chinamans Knob
Creek
Mount Margaret Track
Three Mile Point
Mt Roundback (316m)
Johnnie Souey Cove
Millers Landing
Barry Creek
Vereker
Five Mile Road
Chinaman
Johnny Souey Track
Miranda Bay
Waratah Bay
Cotters Lake
Vereker Lookout
St Kilda Junction
Range
Mt Vereker
Five Mile Beach
Shellback Island
WILSONS PROMONTORY NATIONAL PARK
Darby Bay
Darby Creek
Tongue Point
Lookout Rocks
Latrobe Range
The Cathedral
Sparkes Lookout
Mt Leonard (556m)
Mt Latrobe (755m)
Mt Bishop (319m)
Tidal River
Sealers Creek
Sealers Cove
Whisky Bay
Picnic Bay
Mt Ramsay
Norman Island
Leonard Point
Mt Oberon Car Park
Track
Horn Point
Squeaky Beach
Sealers Cove
Windy Saddle
Hobbs Head
Tidal River
Refuge Cove
Brown Head
Norman Bay
Mt Oberon (558m)
Wilson Range
Norman Point
Kersops Peak
Growler
Lighthouse
Mt Wilson (705m)
Oberon Bay
Ck
Cape Wellington
Waterloo Bay
1 Lilly Pilly Gully Nature Walk
2 Squeaky Beach Nature Walk
3 Mount Oberon Nature Walk
4 The Great Prom Walk
5 Oberon Bay Track
Great Glennie Island
Oberon Point
Frasers Creek
Mt Boulder (501m)
Waterloo Point
Mt Norgate (419m)
Roaring Meg Ck
Boulder Range
Track
Dannevig Island
Citadel Island
McHugh Island
Lighthouse
South-West Point
South-East Point
BASS STRAIT
Anser Island
Wattle Island
South Point

GIPPSLAND

lighthouse and back. Allow two to three days and co-ordinate your walks with tide times as creek crossings can be hazardous. By prior arrangement with the park office it's possible to visit or stay at the lighthouse.

Lilly Pilly Gully Nature Walk
An easy 5km, two to three hour walk through heathland and eucalypt forests, with lots of wildlife – pick up the guided walk leaflet detailing the flora and fauna at the park office.

Squeaky Beach Nature Walk
Another easy stroll of 5km through coastal tea trees and banksias to a sensational white-sand beach. Go barefoot on the beach to find out where the name comes from.

The northern area of the park is much less visited, simply because all the facilities are at Tidal River. Most walks in this 'Wilderness Zone' area are overnight or longer, and mainly for experienced bushwalkers. Wood fires are allowed in the northern section, in designated fireplaces, except of course on total fire ban days. Fires are totally banned in the southern section (except in designated fireplaces in Tidal River between May and October), so carry cooking equipment with you.

Places to Stay

Camping Tidal River has 500 camping sites, and at peak times (school holidays, Easter and long weekends) booking is essential. In fact, a ballot is held in July allocating sites for Christmas, so you can forget about a casual visit then. However, the park office usually reserves a few casual campsites for overseas visitors during the holiday season, with a two night maximum stay.

During peak periods sites cost $15 for up to three people and one car, plus $3.20 per extra person and $4.60 per extra car. These rates are cheaper during the off season.

There are another 11 bush camping areas around the Prom, all with pit toilets and most with water, but nothing else in the way of facilities. Overnight hikers need camping permits ($4.20 per person), which should be booked ahead through the park office.

Huts & Units There are a number of self-contained timber huts that can accommodate two to six people. Costs range from $49 per night for a single/double in the off season to $660 in the peak season.

There are also group lodges available, accommodating up to 30 people from $486 per night.

All cabins and motor huts are usually heavily booked, so plan ahead. From September until the end of April, the flats and lodges can only be booked for a minimum of one week; at other times, they can be booked for either a weekend (three nights) or from Monday to Thursday (four nights).

Getting There & Away

Unfortunately, there isn't any direct public transport between Melbourne and the Prom. V/Line has daily buses from Melbourne to Fish Creek ($19.50) and Foster ($21.90), but both places are about 60km north of Tidal River. The owner of ***Foster Backpackers Hostel*** runs a bus service to and from the Prom (see the following Foster section).

From Phillip Island, ***Amaroo Park Backpackers*** *(☎ 5952 2548)* runs regular day trips to the Prom for $45; it's possible to stay a few nights at the Prom before returning to Phillip Island another day.

AROUND WILSONS PROMONTORY

Foster

• pop 1000

This former gold-mining settlement on the South Gippsland Hwy is now a bustling small rural community with good facilities.

A pretty creek runs through the town, and there's a good picnic area in Pearl Park. The local **historical museum**, in Main St opposite the park, opens on Sunday and daily during school holidays from 11 am to 4 pm. Next to it is the Stockyard Gallery, a small art and craft shop and information centre.

The ***Foster Caravan Park*** *(☎ 5682 2440)* on Nelson St has sites from $13 and on-site vans and cabins from $40. There are also a few motels along the highway.

Foster Backpackers Hostel *(☎ 5682 2614, 17 Pioneer St)* has lovely budget accommodation in a small mud-brick cottage with doubles for $40, and beds in dorms for $17, as well as a barbecue, laundry and sitting room. The owner also runs the postal/bus service to the Prom ($10 each way) at 9 am most mornings, returning from Tidal River at 11.15 am, and has camping gear for hire.

Hillcrest Farmhouse B&B *(☎ 5682 2769, Ameys Track)* is a couple of kilometres out of Foster and is signposted from Port Welshpool Rd. Doubles in this friendly place start at $90 per night.

The ***Black Cherry Coffee Lounge*** in the centre of Foster is a popular and reasonably priced cafe serving snacks and light lunches, eat-in or take-away; it becomes a restaurant on Saturday night. The ***hotel*** also has a reasonable bistro and children's playroom.

Fish Creek

A tiny one-pub township, Fish Creek is the self-proclaimed 'Gateway to Wilsons Prom and Waratah Bay'.

The entrance to the quirky **Fish Creek Rock & Gem Museum** leads under an old railway bridge near the eastern entrance to town. You can park in a ramshackle farmyard, cluttered with a collection of buildings, old cars, chickens, ducks, dogs and a peacock. The hundreds of rocks and gems, displayed on shelves and in old television cabinets in a bus, railway carriage and shed, are the lifetime collection of Roy and Margaret Comrie. Roy has a story for almost every fossil and gem here. The museum is open whenever he's around so just drop in; there's no entry fee, but donations to maintain the collection are accepted.

The ***Fish Creek Hotel*** *(☎ 5683 2404, Old Waratah Rd)* has backpacker accommodation upstairs at $20 per person, and motel rooms out the back from $40 to $70. It also has a good bistro. The ***Flying Cow Cafe*** *(☎ 5683 2338, 9 Falls Rd)* serves breakfast and lunch, including veggie fare, and has nice views from its verandah.

Waratah Bay

West of the Prom is the half-moon shaped Waratah Bay, with a couple of quiet and remote holiday townships and some wonderful long stretches of white-sand beach.

The ***Waratah Bay Caravan Park*** *(☎ 5684 1339)* has two good foreshore camping areas with sites from $12 to $14 and on-site vans from $40. There are no shops here, although the park office sells supplies. A couple of kilometres back from the bay, the impressive ***Waratah Park Country House*** *(☎ 5683 2575)*, beside a state park, has six double rooms with great views across to the Prom. Tariffs are $150 a double; dinner and B&B weekend packages are available for $255 per person.

Yanakie

The nearest place to the Prom, Yanakie is a tiny settlement with some nice places to stay in the surrounding area.

Yanakie Caravan Park *(☎ 5687 1295)* is in secluded bush by the waterfront at Corner Inlet. It has sites from $14 per night and on-site cabins from $45 per night.

Vereker House *(☎ 5687 1431)*, signposted off the main Prom road, has good views, and on a clear night you can use its telescope for some star gazing. Single/double B&B starts at $70/100.

Walkerville

Overlooking Waratah Bay, Walkerville is a pretty spot with a handful of holiday houses scattered across the hills. There are some great beach walks in this area, including a 14km hike down to the lighthouse at Cape Liptrap.

Right on the foreshore, the ***Walkerville Camping Reserve*** *(☎ 5663 2224)* has tent sites from $9 to $11 and on-site vans from $45 to $50.

Toora

West of Foster and close to spectacular **Agnes Falls** – the tallest falls in Victoria – Toora has some nice accommodation options making it another good base for visits to the Prom.

Woorarra Bushland Retreat *(☎ 5681 6209)* is signposted from the highway and set in natural bushland with an abundance of native flowers and birds. Tent sites here start at $10, and day visitors can also enjoy the facilities for $2.

Ambleside Country Manor (☎ 5686 2365) dates from 1896 and makes a peaceful base. Double B&B with a hearty breakfast costs from $115 to $130. A three-course dinner, using home-grown produce, can be arranged for an extra $35 per head.

PORT ALBERT

Port Albert is a quaint old fishing village with a large collection of historic buildings, combined with a few 1950s-era beach-houses. It's far enough off the main track to be fairly unspoilt, although it's a popular spot in the holiday seasons, especially with fishing fanatics.

The original buildings date back to the 1850s, and are mostly Georgian and early-Victorian in style, with simple façades and verandahs. There are over 40, many in original condition and each with a brass plaque attached, so you can wander the streets and identify what was what.

The town extends out to the end of a narrow spit of land, surrounded by sheltered waters and lined with old Norfolk Island pines. There's a good historic pub on one side and a couple of boat jetties on the other. The boathouse on the pier sells fresh fish, fishing supplies and delicious fish & chips. Boats and fishing gear can be hired or chartered from the main wharf.

There's a **historical & maritime museum** on Tarraville Rd, which opens daily from 10.30 am to 4.30 pm; entry costs $4/1.

The Old Port Trail

Just before you enter town is a roundabout with a turn off to the right which leads to the site of the first settlement in this area. From there a 2km walking track, the Old Port Trail, follows the shoreline and passes the remnants of the old port town. A sign at the start tells the history of the pioneers who explored this area and the story of how the sheltered harbour was discovered.

This area forms part of the **Nooramunga Marine & Coastal Park**, a protected offshore wilderness of islands and coastal wetlands. The vegetation is mostly low-lying coastal scrub, mangrove and salt marsh.

Places to Stay & Eat

There are two caravan parks here. The ***Seabank Caravan Park*** *(☎ 5183 2315)* is about 3km north of the town, on Old Port Rd and McMillan Bay. It has tent sites from $12 and on-site vans from $35.

Gowrie House *(☎ 5183 2401, 65 Tarraville Rd)* is a B&B in a lovely historic house, with singles/doubles starting at $78/88.

The renovated ***Port Albert Hotel/Motel*** *(☎ 5183 2212, Wharf St)*, the oldest licensed pub in Victoria, has backpacker beds for $15 and comfortable motel units out the back from $45, including breakfast. The bistro has good tucker with meals from $5.

The ***Customs House Cafe***, in yet another restored building, is open Wednesday to Sunday till 8 pm and is fully licensed, with mains ranging from $10 to $14.

YARRAM

Yarram is a remote commercial centre on the South Gippsland Hwy. It has a few historic buildings, including the renovated **courthouse**, which contains the tourist information centre and the **Regent Theatre**. Nearby in Tarraville you can see a **wooden church**, the oldest in Gippsland; it was constructed without the use of a single nail.

As you enter the town from Foster look for signs for ***Rosewood*** *(☎ 5182 5605, Hiho's Lane)*, a gorgeous, friendly B&B set in nice gardens with doubles from $95. It also has a cosy two bedroom cottage available from $85 ($100 with breakfast).

Yarram is served by V/Line coaches; the one-way fare to/from Melbourne is $26.90.

The Lakes District

Gippsland's Lakes District is the largest inland waterway system in Australia. There are three main lakes: Lake King, Lake Victoria and Lake Wellington. They are all joined and fed by a number of rivers which originate in the High Country, including the Mitchell, Nicholson, Tambo and Avon. The 'lakes' are actually shallow coastal lagoons which were once part of a large bay. Over thousands of years, sand has built up in deposits along the coastline, and the lakes are now separated from the ocean by a narrow strip of coastal sand dunes known as Ninety Mile Beach.

The main towns are Bairnsdale, a commercial centre for the surrounding district, and Lakes Entrance, a rather bizarre blend of tourist town and fishing village. Metung is one of the smaller and more pleasant of the area's bases.

Most of Ninety Mile Beach, from Seaspray to Lakes Entrance, is part of the 17,200 hectare Gippsland Lakes Coastal Park. Within this area is the Lakes National Park, including the birdwatcher's paradise of Rotamah Island. The Mitchell River National Park is another feature of the area.

HIGHLIGHTS

- Set sail on a yacht or cruiser and spend a few days (or longer) exploring the spectacular and sheltered 400 sq km lakes complex
- Surf-fish or walk along the white-sand beaches of Ninety Mile Beach and explore the sand dunes, swamplands and lagoons of its hinterland
- Cruise to a winery or secluded picnic spot on the lakes, relax on Ninety Mile Beach or dine alfresco with fish and chips at Lakes Entrance
- Explore the excellent Mitchell River National Park on walking tracks through temperate rainforest – look out for the half-stone creature, Nargun!
- Raft down the deep river gorges on the Tambo and Mitchell rivers
- Spoil yourself with a stay at Bairnsdale's Riversleigh Country Hotel – one of country Victoria's top B&Bs

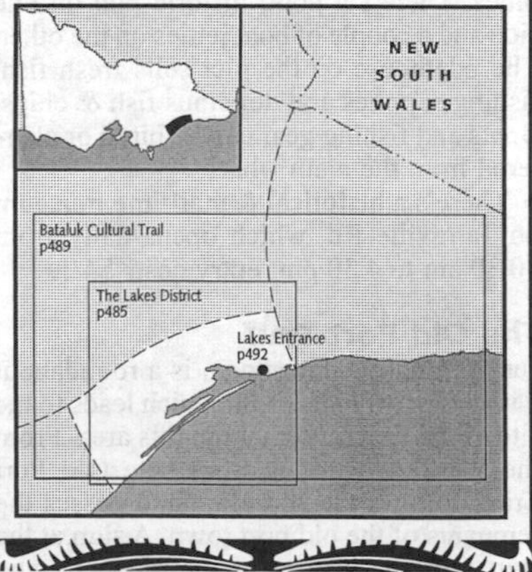

Orientation & Information

Lakes and Wilderness Tourism has good tourist information offices in Bairnsdale and Lakes Entrance (☎ 1800 637060 toll-free), both of which can help with accommodation and tour bookings for the whole region.

Activities

The Lakes District is popular for fishing, boat cruising, water-skiing, surfing and other water-oriented activities. Obviously, with more than 400 sq km of waterways to explore, the best way to appreciate the area is from a boat. Yachts and cruisers can be hired from Metung for boating holidays, and if you don't have much time you could hire a fishing boat for a few hours, or join one of the cruises that operate from Metung and Lakes Entrance (see individual entries for details).

If you prefer something a bit more adventurous, Ramrod Raft Tours (☎ 5157 5548), based 6km north of Bruthen, offers

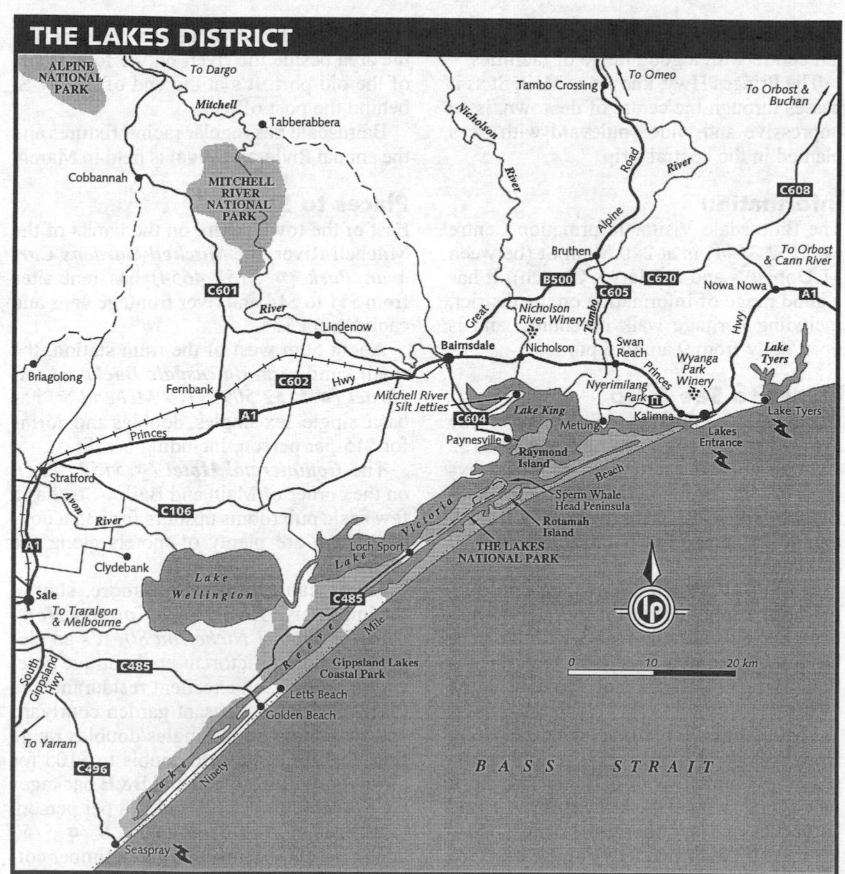

gentle and very enjoyable raft trips down the Tambo River Gorge. Trips depart at 9.30 am and cost $40/20 for adults/children, including lunch.

Getting There & Away

Bus V/Line has daily bus services along the Princes Highway (A1) from Sale into New South Wales (NSW), via Bairnsdale and Lakes Entrance. From Bairnsdale, there are also private bus services north to Omeo and south to Paynesville. See the Getting There & Away section under Sale in the Gippsland chapter for information about V/Line services from Melbourne.

The Wayward Bus Co stops at Lakes Entrance, while the Oz Experience also drops off/picks up in the area.

BAIRNSDALE

• pop 11,000

Bairnsdale, on the banks of the Mitchell River, is the major town of this district and a commercial centre for the surrounding agricultural areas. It's a large and busy retail centre with a good range of facilities.

The Princes Hwy, known as Main St as it passes through the centre of the town, is an impressive and wide boulevard with trees planted in the central strip.

Information

The Bairnsdale Visitor Information Centre (☎ 5152 3444) is at 240 Main St (between McDonald's and St Mary's Church). It has a good range of information on the district, including heritage walk brochures, and is open daily from 9 am to 5 pm.

Things to See & Do

At 37-53 Dalmahoy St there's the **Krowathunkoolong Keeping Place** (☎ 5152 1891), a cultural centre with good displays focusing on the heritage of the local Aboriginal people. It opens weekdays from 9 am to 5 pm; entry costs $3.30/2.50 adults/children.

St Mary's Catholic Church, an imposing red-brick church beside the tourist information centre, is notable for its intricate ceiling murals painted over four years by the Italian migrant artist Frank Floreani in the 1930s.

For parents travelling with children, **Howitt Park** is a very good public playground, complete with a flying fox, huge foot-swing, wire walk-bridge, BMX track, barbecues and an Aboriginal canoe tree – it's just off the Princes Hwy on the east side of town. The park also serves as the starting point for the **East Gippsland Rail Trail** leading to **Bruthen**, 30km away, which hosts a Blues Festival each February.

The **historical museum** in MacArthur St, near the city oval, has an interesting and large collection of local history items and records, and is open Wednesday, Thursday and Sunday from 1 to 5 pm. Entry costs $3/1 for adults/kids. It's signposted from Main St.

Beyond the historical museum, the **MacLeod Morass Boardwalk** is a swampy and flat wetland reserve with walking tracks, bird hides and a large range of birdlife.

The **Port of Bairnsdale** is a pleasant picnic area beside the river, on the former site of the old port. It's at the end of Bailey St behind the post office.

Bairnsdale has regular racing fixtures and the annual **Riviera Festival** is held in March.

Places to Stay

East of the town centre on the banks of the Mitchell River, the ***Mitchell Gardens Caravan Park*** *(☎ 5152 4654)* has tent sites from $11 to $14 and river frontage vans and cabins from $35.

About 50m west of the train station, the small family-run ***Bairnsdale Backpackers' Hostel*** *(☎ 5152 5097, 119 McLeod St)* has basic single-sex singles, doubles and dorms for $15 per person, including breakfast.

The ***Commercial Hotel*** *(☎ 5152 3031)*, on the corner of Main and Bailey Sts, has a few basic pub rooms upstairs for $35 a double. There are plenty of motels along the highway.

If you can afford a little more, stay at the impressive ***Riversleigh Country Hotel*** *(☎ 5152 6966, 1 Nicholson St)*. It's an elegantly restored Victorian-era boutique hotel with 22 rooms, an excellent restaurant (see Places to Eat), a pleasant garden courtyard and swimming pool. Singles/doubles range from $95 for a standard double to $105 for a two room suite; dinner and B&B packages are available from $120 to $178 per person.

In Bruthen, the ***Bruthen B&B*** *(☎ 5157 5616)* is a cute yellow and green timber cottage fronted by a garden of tall roses. There are two guestrooms, each with private bathrooms, and doubles/triples cost $85/110, including a continental breakfast.

Places to Eat

Most of Bairnsdale's eateries are along Main St. ***Oz Mex*** *(☎ 5152 4549)*, on the corner of Main and Service Sts, is a popular and fun Mexican cantina with a good range of eat-in and take-away food. The renovated ***Commercial Hotel***, on the corner of Main and Bailey Sts, has an excellent bistro with good steaks and other mains in the $12 to $16 range.

The narrow ***Strix Wine Bar Cafe*** *(☎ 5152 6909, 131 Main St)*, opposite the band rotunda, is a good spot for lunch or dinner and is open till late. ***Larrikins Cafe Deli*** *(☎ 5153 1421, 2 Wood St)*, around the corner from the Riversleigh, is open weekdays and has a good selection of snacks, salads and cakes.

The dining room at the ***Riversleigh Country Hotel*** *(☎ 5152 6966, 1 Nicholson St)* is one of country Victoria's better restaurants. It also has a more casual bistro and the menu specialises in local produce such as grain-fed beef, guinea fowl and lamb fillets, with mains ranging from $14 to $19.

Getting There & Away

Bairnsdale's V/Line station is on McLeod St, one block south of the town centre. There are daily trains between Melbourne and Sale, and connecting buses from Sale to Bairnsdale. The one-way fare from Melbourne to Bairnsdale is $33.20/43.60 in economy/1st class.

From Bairnsdale, V/Line buses operate daily farther along the Princes Hwy to Sale ($7.30), Lakes Entrance ($7.30) and Orbost ($17.50).

Omeo Buslines (☎ 5159 4231) operates a bus service every weekday (1.30 pm) from Bairnsdale to Omeo (2 hours, $23.60 one way).

AROUND BAIRNSDALE

Mitchell River National Park

Signposted about 42km north-west of Bairnsdale is the Mitchell River National Park, which covers an area of over 12,000 hectares. The park's best-known feature is the **Den of Nargun**, a small cave which, according to Aboriginal legend, was haunted by a strange, half-stone creature known as the Nargun. According to the legend, the creature would drag passers-by into its cave and, if attacked, was able to deflect spears back onto the thrower. A one hour loop walk leads to a lookout, rainforest gully and the den – it contains fragile stalactites so please don't go in.

Access tracks lead into the park off Dargo Rd. There are three ***camping*** areas within the park and some excellent walking tracks including the two day 18km . One of the most interesting aspects of this park is the dramatic contrast between the warm-temperate rainforest areas in the sheltered river gullies and the more sparse vegetation in the open and higher areas of the park. The spectacular deep gorges and valleys carved through rock by the Mitchell River are another feature, popular with white-water canoeists.

Paynesville

Paynesville is about 18km south of Bairnsdale, right on the edge of Lake Victoria. The 8km long **Mitchell River Silt Jetties**, to the north of Paynesville, are the second longest in the world. Paynesville has a few places to stay and a couple of boat-hire companies, but it also has a retirement village feel to it. However, the town does get into the swing of things when it hosts a **jazz festival** each February.

A **car and passenger ferry** runs a constant shuttle service across McMillan Strait to Raymond Island, about 200m away. The ferry runs from dawn to dusk and the return fare is $3 per car. **Raymond Island** is fairly isolated, with a few houses on the Paynesville side and large areas of bush, with some good walking tracks, an abundance of birdlife and a large population of koalas. ***Montague's B&B*** *(☎ 5156 7880, Third Parade)* in a waterfront location has good facilities including a games room and singles/doubles from $85/110.

Paynesville Bus Services (☎ 018 516 403) runs buses Monday to Saturday between Bairnsdale and Paynesville. The one-way adult/concession fare is $6/3.

Nicholson

About 4km north-east of Nicholson and signposted from the highway, the **Nicholson River Winery** (☎ 5156 8241) has daily tastings ($2 refundable with purchase) and sales. It's a friendly place where you can savour your wine in a garden overlooking the river.

Bataluk Cultural Trail

The Aborigines of Gippsland, collectively known as the Gunai (Kurnai), are estimated to have inhabited east Gippsland for over 18,000 years. Descended from their Dreamtime ancestors, Borun the Pelican and his relative Tuk the Musk Duck, the Gunai tribes lived together in relative harmony.

As the Princes Hwy cuts through Gippsland, it forms the backbone of the Bataluk (Lizard) Cultural Trail which itself follows a network of Gunai trails and trading routes. Designed and promoted by the Gunai community in Gippsland to allow a greater appreciation and understanding of their traditional lifestyle, the trail introduces and explains an abundant heritage, including arts and craft, traditional foods, dreamtime stories and tool making.

A brochure detailing the trail is available from tourist offices en route, and all the sights are well signposted from main roads. Some of the sights also have information boards explaining their significance and place in the community today.

Ramahyuck Aboriginal Corporation, Sale
Named after an Aboriginal mission established on the Avon River in 1863, this centre displays and sells locally produced arts and crafts. The corporation (☎ 5143 1644) at 117 Foster St is open Monday to Friday from 9 am to 5 pm.

Wetlands Information Centre of Victoria, Sale
Take a walk through a Gunai supermarket. This centre (☎ 5142 333) has information sheets introducing the wide variety of plants and birds used by the Gunai for food and raw materials. (Also see Things to See & Do under Sale.)

The Knob Reserve, Stratford
Sandstone rocks here were used by the Gunai as grinding stones for sharpening axe heads. It's also likely that the river here was a popular fishing spot for eels, bream, flathead and prawns.

Den of Nargun, Mitchell River National Park
It's believed that the legend surrounding this cave (see the Mitchell River National Park entry) resulted from the whistling sound of the wind in the cave and served the dual purpose of keeping Gunai children close to campsites and scaring people away from this sacred place for women's initiation ceremonies.

Howitt Park, Bairnsdale
In this park is a 'canoe tree' bearing a clearly visible 4m scar which is thought to be over 170 years old. The scar was caused by the bark being peeled away by the Gunai to build a canoe.

Gippsland and East Gippsland Aboriginal Cooperative, Bairnsdale
Incorporating the Krowathunkoolong Keeping Place (see Things to See & Do under Bairnsdale), this centre caters to the needs of the Gunai community throughout East Gippsland. It also has some fascinating and informative displays of crafts and tools used by the Gunai, as well as their Dreamtime and post-colonial history.

Bataluk Cultural Trail

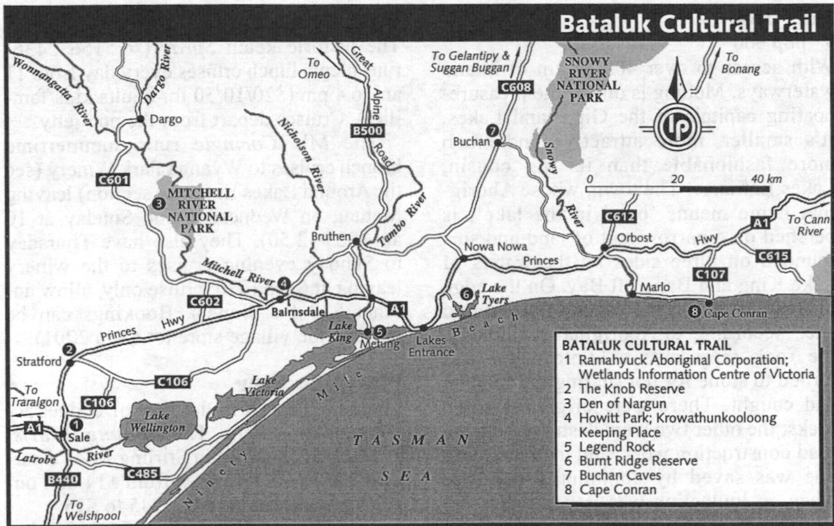

Legend Rock, Metung
Opposite the Metung Yacht Club in Bancroft Bay, this rock is of special significance to the Gunai, and is now preserved under the Heritage Act of Victoria (see Things to See & Do under Metung).

Burnt Bridge Reserve
Although the Aboriginal settlement at Lake Tyers, which became the focus of the first successful Aboriginal land rights case in 1971, is off limits to the public, Burnt Bridge Reserve (on the road between Lakes Entrance and Nowa Nowa) has a display centre detailing the history behind the community and its progress today.

Buchan Caves, Buchan
Gunai people are thought to have inhabited the caves at Buchan over 18,000 years ago, and there are many legends concerning the caves that are still recounted today (see Buchan in the Wilderness Coast chapter).

Cape Conran
The remains of a shell midden are visible just below the Salmon Rock viewing platform at Cape Conran. This was probably a Gunai venue for feasts, celebrations and ceremonies. It's also possible that weddings, which could only be held after a man had run away with a woman, could have been held here. (Also see Cape Conran Marine Park in the Wilderness Coast chapter.)

Joyce Connolly

METUNG

• pop 500

With access to over 400 sq km of inland waterways, Metung is one of the pleasure-boating capitals of the Gippsland Lakes. It's smaller, more attractive and much more fashionable than its big cousin, Lakes Entrance. The town, whose Aboriginal name means 'bend in the lake', is perched on a narrow spit of land and surrounded on three sides by the waters of Lake King and Bancroft Bay. On the edge of Bancroft Bay is the **Legend Rock** sacred site. According to Aboriginal mythology, the rock represents a hunter who was turned to stone for not sharing the food he had caught. There were originally three rocks; the other two were destroyed during road construction work, and the remaining one was saved by community pressure when an injunction was issued under the Heritage Act of Victoria.

Metung is an excellent base for all sorts of water-based activities – water-skiing, sailing, cruising and fishing – and has some very good upmarket accommodation and restaurants. In January, the town hosts a sailing **regatta**; and in March a **jazz festival** and the **Metung Classic**, featuring classical music and a boat show, take place.

Boat Hire & Boating Holidays

Award-winning Riviera Nautic (☎ 1800 815 127 toll-free) hires out a wide range of boats for cruising, fishing and sailing on the lakes. A small half-cabin motor boat takes up to six people and typically costs $80 a day, or you can have a larger traditional fishing boat for $110.

For overnight cruises, there's a minimum hire period of three days. Prices vary enormously, depending on the type of boat, season and the number of people. As a guide, a four-berth yacht costs from $835 to $1050 per week while a 10-berth cruiser costs from $2330 a week.

A competing company, Bull's Cruisers (☎ 5156 2208), has a similar range of boats for hire.

Boat Cruises

The historic ketch *Spray* (☎ 5156 2436) runs picnic lunch cruises every day from 11 am to 4 pm ($20/10/50 for adults/kids/families). Cruises depart from the pub jetty.

The MV *Coringle* runs summertime brunch cruises to Wyanga Park Winery (see the Around Lakes Entrance section) leaving Metung on Wednesday and Sunday at 10 am ($25/12.50). They also have Thursday to Sunday evening cruises to the winery leaving at 6 pm ($20; cruise only, allow another $30 for dinner). Bookings can be made at the village store (☎ 5156 2201).

Places to Stay

There isn't much in the way of budget accommodation here. The ***Metung Tourist Park*** *(☎ 5156 2306)* in Stirling Rd is a caravan park with tent sites from $14 and on-site vans and cabins from $45 to $55.

The ***Metung Hotel*** *(☎ 5156 2206)* has good rooms with shared bathrooms from $30/40; add another $10 per person for a cooked breakfast.

There are a couple of older-style holiday units that are good value. ***Maeburn Cottages*** *(☎ 5156 2736, 33 Mairburn Rd)* has four comfortable timber cottages which range from $60 to $75 a night with a two-night minimum stay.

On Shaving Point, the tasteful Mediterranean-styled ***Bancrofts by the Bay B&B*** *(☎ 5156 2216)* has modern en suite units overlooking the water that range from $110 to $140 a double. ***Clovelly of Metung*** *(☎ 5156 2428, 5 Essington Close)* has individually designed double rooms from $120. Farther out, ***Metung House*** *(☎ 5156 2352, 3 Rosherville Rd)* has cosy rooms from $95, with breakfast.

In recent years Metung has been transformed by a series of upmarket developments along the waterfront – if you're staying at one of these places, ask for a room overlooking the water. ***The Slipway*** *(☎ 5156 2469, 50 Metung Rd)* is a collection of impressively designed waterfront villas that sleep up to eight people and range from $130 to $210 a night. Nearby, the enormous

Moorings at Metung *(☎ 5156 2750)* has double motel units from $89 and one, two and three bedroom units from $115 a night. There are one, two and three bedroom cottages in a landscaped garden ranging from $95 to $300 a night behind the imposing gates of the award-winning ***McMillan's Holiday Village*** *(☎ 5156 2283)*.

Places to Eat

The ***Metung Hotel*** is a great pub perched on the edge of the lakes, with an outdoor deck overlooking Bancroft Bay. Their bistro meals range from $9 to $16 – turn up for lunch and you can join in the pelican feeding frenzy. At 57 Metung Rd, the ***Little Mariners Cafe*** has very tasty gourmet burgers, as well as good breakfasts, felafels and sandwiches. It's also open for dinner.

Morcomb's of Metung *(☎ 5156 2646, 70 Metung Rd)*, once owned by Aussie country music legend Slim Dusty, is a timber fishing cottage which has been delightfully transformed into a simple, stylish restaurant with a fantastic outlook over the lakes. It's licensed, and the small menu is based on local produce, with seafood for around $17.50.

Marrillee at Metung is another classy restaurant with outside dining, open for dinner from Monday to Friday with mains from $16 to $20.

Getting There & Away

Morning V/Line services can drop you off in Swan Reach from where you can walk or hitch the 5km to Metung.

LAKES ENTRANCE

- **pop 5250**

Lakes Entrance is probably the caravan park capital of Victoria. As well as being a popular, if somewhat old-fashioned, tourist town, it's also the largest fishing port in Victoria.

The Princes Hwy, known as the Esplanade as it passes through the centre of Lakes Entrance, reveals the two contrasting faces of the town. On one side are the gentle waters of Cunninghame Arm, backed by sand dunes and sprinkled with a fleet of colourful fishing boats, on the inland side of the road is a startling array of motels, caravan parks, minigolf courses, pubs and shops, which at night is a wall of flashing neon.

Information

The Lakes Entrance Tourist Information Centre (☎ 5155 1966) is on the corner of the Princes Hwy and Marine Parade, on the western edge of town. It's open daily from 9 am to 5 pm.

Things to See & Do

A footbridge crosses the Cunninghame Arm inlet from the centre of town to the ocean

Pelicans are common in the Lakes District.

and the **Ninety Mile Beach**. From there, you can walk along a 2.3km walking track to the 'entrance' to the lakes; the current entrance is man made, the original was near the footbridge. From December until Easter, paddleboats, canoes and sailboats can be hired by the footbridge.

The **Kinkuna Country Fun & Fauna Park**, on the Princes Hwy on the eastern outskirts, is a modern family-style amusement park which opens daily from 10 am. The adult/child admission fee of $4/4.50 includes use of the playground, games room and barbecue, but you pay extra for the high-speed toboggan rides ($2), minigolf ($2) and water slide (50c). There's a kitsch **shell museum** at 125 the Esplanade, with sea shells, an aquarium and a model railway. It has some interesting exhibits but the $4/2 adult/child entry fee is a bit steep.

Signposted off the Princes Hwy on the western side of town, **Jemmy's Point Lookout** has great views of the ocean, the lakes and the entrance – the lights of the town look spectacular from here at night.

Each January the **Lakes Summer Festival** takes place with lots of family-based activities, markets and street stalls.

Cruises & Fishing Charters

The *Corque* (☎ 5155 1508) does a two hour morning tea cruise ($18/5 adult/child), and popular all-inclusive trips to Wyanga Park Winery which include a four hour luncheon cruise ($30; daily) and dinner cruise ($45; Thursday to Sunday and holidays only) – they're popular so book ahead.

Peels Tourist & Ferry Services (☎ 5155 1246) runs three different cruise boats from the post office jetty – *Thunderbird*, *Bluebird* and *Stormbird* – and a variety of cruises, in-

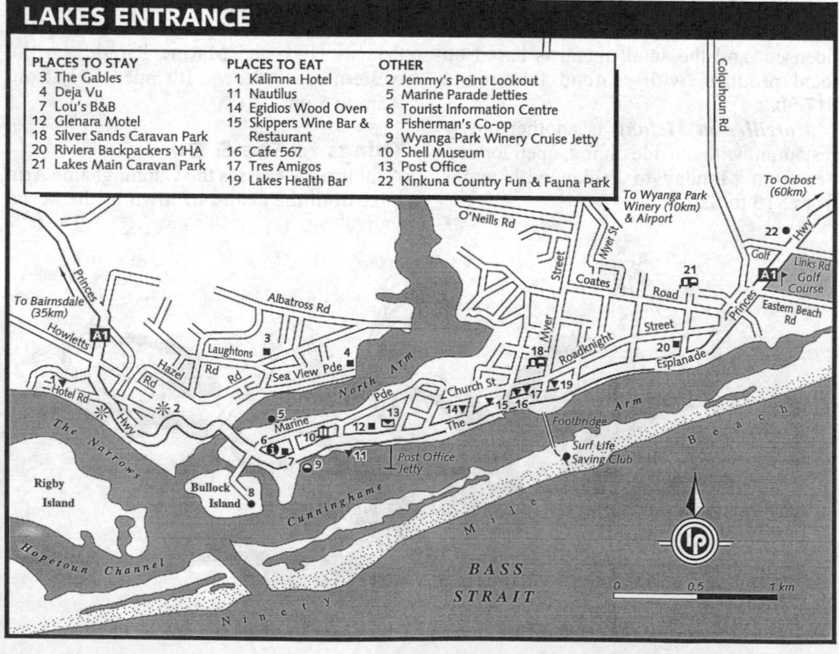

cluding four-hour lunch cruises to Metung ($25 including lunch), and two to 2½ hour lakes cruises ($15 to $24).

At Lake Tyers, the MB *Rubeena* (☎ 5155 1283) runs two-hour explorer cruises every Tuesday, Thursday and Saturday (daily during holiday seasons) costing $15/9 for adults/kids. Cruises leave from Fisherman's Landing at Lake Tyers Beach. On Mondays, the *Rubeena* joins up with the East Gippsland Carriage Co wagonette for an all-inclusive 'Lake and Bush' tour which costs $65/40 for adults/kids.

Mulloway Fishing Charters (☎ 014 943 154) has half-day fishing cruises for $25 and charters – contact them or the tourist information for details.

Boat Hire

If you want to explore the lakes independently, there are a couple of places where you can hire boats. Based at jetties in Marine Parade, just down from the tourist information centre, Victor Hireboats (☎ 5155 1888) and Portside Boat Hire (☎ 5155 3822) both have small motor boats from around $20 an hour, $60 for 4 hours and $80 for a full day.

Places to Stay

There's a huge range of holiday accommodation here – mostly caravan parks, motels and holiday units – but unfortunately few take advantage of lake views or have beach frontage.

Hostels, Camping & Caravan Parks

Riviera Backpackers YHA *(☎ 5155 2444, 5 Clarkes Rd)* is just off the Esplanade. It has about 60 beds, a swimming pool and a common room. Accommodation is in four-bunk dorms, twins or doubles, all for $13 per person.

At last count there were more than 20 caravan parks in and around Lakes Entrance. ***Silver Sands Caravan Park*** *(☎ 5155 2343, 33 Myer St)* has special $13 rates for backpackers; as with most of the other caravan parks, they also have tent sites from $14. ***Lakes Main Caravan Park*** *(☎ 5155 2365, 7 Willis St)* also has more basic beds at $10 and tent sites/on-site vans starting from $12/25.

Motels, B&Bs & Holiday Units There are dozens of motels and holiday units to choose from in Lakes Entrance, the cheaper of which advertise their rates on signs outside. The ***Glenara Motel*** *(☎ 5155 1555, 221 the Esplanade)* is one of the cheapest and most central, and has oldish but comfortable rooms starting at $40 a double.

Lou's B&B *(☎ 5155 2732, 37 the Esplanade)* is a modern (non-smoking) B&B with two units, one motel-style and one self-contained. Room tariffs start at $75 per double and dogs are welcome.

Away from the centre, overlooking town, are two tasteful B&Bs. There are unrivalled views across the lake system from ***Deja Vu*** *(☎ 5155 4330, 17 Clare St)*, and rooms start at $90 for a double. ***The Gables*** *(☎ 5155 2699, 1-9 Creighton St)* is an impressive home with a swimming pool and peaceful gardens; single/double B&B is $90/125.

Places to Eat

There are plenty of pizza/pasta joints, cafes, fish & chip shops and other take-aways along the Esplanade and most motels have restaurants open to the public. Health freaks will be cheered considerably by the ***Lakes Health Bar*** on the corner of the Esplanade and Myer St, which does tasty sandwiches, jaffles, fruit smooths, salads and, best of all, coffee and cake for $2.80. If you'd prefer a delicious handmade chocolate with your coffee, try ***Cafe 567*** *(☎ 5155 3199, 567 the Esplanade)*.

Tres Amigos *(☎ 5155 2215)* is a lively BYO Mexican cantina with main meals around $13 to $16, a cheaper take-away menu and discounts for YHA members. For pizza, try ***Egidios Wood Oven*** *(☎ 5155 1411, 357 the Esplanade)*, which is fully licensed.

The ***Fisherman's Co-op***, on Bullock Island at the western end of the Esplanade, sells all types of fish fresh off the boats, if you feel like cooking yourself a seafood feast. It's open daily from 9 am to 5 pm. For views, you can't beat the ***Kalimna Hotel***, off the highway on the Melbourne side of Lakes Entrance overlooking the lakes. It has mains from $12 to $16.

Lakes Entrance has a few upmarket places. ***Skippers Wine Bar & Restaurant*** *(☎ 5155 3551, 481 the Esplanade)* is an attractive pale-green cottage owned by a former fisherman and his wife. It specialises in fresh local seafood, but also serves game dishes, and is open for dinner daily and lunch on the weekends. ***Nautilus*** *(☎ 5155 1400)* is a licensed restaurant in a floating glass-sided barge moored in the inlet, where you can tuck into seafood.

Getting There & Away

There are daily V/Line buses between Lakes Entrance and Bairnsdale, connecting with trains to/from Melbourne ($40.10/50.50 in economy/1st class). V/Line and Greyhound Pioneer Australia also have daily buses continuing along the Princes Hwy into NSW.

AROUND LAKES ENTRANCE

Just east of Lakes Entrance, **Lake Tyers** is a small and peaceful settlement of holiday houses, caravan parks and the ***Waterwheel Tavern*** (☎ 5156 5855), complete with bistro and waterwheel – they run a courtesy bus from Lakes Entrance. The lake itself is surrounded by bush and separated from the sea (and some great sandy beaches) by a narrow strip of sand dunes. It's well worth a visit. ***Lake Tyers Camp & Caravan Park*** *(☎ 5156 5530)* overlooking the lake has tent sites from $15 and on-site vans from $23 to $55. This area is popular with surfers, with good breaks at Red Bluff and Sandy Point.

The original homestead at **Nyerimilang Park** (☎ 5156 3253) was built in 1892 as a gentleman's holiday retreat, then extended and renovated in 1928. It is a graceful blend of colonial and Edwardian style, and the walls are hung with some interesting old photos of other historic buildings from the area. The property is managed by Parks Victoria, and has beautifully maintained grounds, rose gardens, sloping lawns and a pleasant picnic area, as well as short walks ranging from five minutes to half an hour. The park is on Metung-Kalimna West Rd, which runs off the Princes Hwy about 5km west of Lakes Entrance, and is open daily from 9 am to 4 pm. There is no admission fee.

Wyanga Park Winery (☎ 5155 1508) is 10km north of Lakes Entrance, on the edge of the North Arm and near the Colquhoun Forest. ***Henry's Winery Cafe*** offers tasty lunches and dinners but can get busy so book ahead. You can get to the winery by boat (see Cruises & Fishing Charters in the Lakes Entrance section earlier in this chapter) – it's open daily for tastings and sales and is signposted from Myer St in Lakes Entrance.

The **East Gippsland Carriage Co** (☎ 5155 7383) is based near Nowa Nowa, about 23km north-east of Lakes Entrance. They run various 'Aussie experience' tours in horse-drawn carriages, including a morning or afternoon tea trip ($25/12 adults/children), a four hour lunch trip ($50/25) and a candle-light dinner trip with bush poetry ($60/25). You can book direct or through the tourist information centre in Lakes Entrance.

NINETY MILE BEACH

This is a long, narrow strip of coastal sand dunes backed by swamplands and lagoons, stretching from Seaspray to Lakes Entrance. The whole area is included in the Gippsland Lakes Coastal Park. The vegetation is quite harsh and affected by the high salinity of the lakes – typically low-lying coastal shrubs, banksias and tea tree, with native wildflowers appearing in spring. There are large numbers of kangaroos in this area, so you should drive slowly and cautiously, especially at night.

The road is generally separated from the ocean by wide sand dunes. Beaches are long, white-sand strips, and are great for surf-fishing and walking but can be dangerous for swimming as the shoreline drops suddenly from the beach into the sea, and strong rips are common.

The main access roads are from Sale to Seaspray or Letts Beach. The townships along here are small and remote with few facilities. There are shops and basic accommodation at **Seaspray** and **Loch Sport**, including ***Pelican Point*** *(☎ 5146 0011, 2328 Pelican St)* in Loch Sport which has lake views and double B&B from $90. Bush ***camping*** is allowed to the west of Loch Sport.

THE LAKES NATIONAL PARK

In the centre of the Ninety Mile Beach, the Lakes National Park is a 2400 hectare coastal bushland park made up of the Sperm Whale Head Peninsula and Rotamah Island. The park is in Lake Victoria, and can be reached by road from Sale via Loch Sport or by boat from Paynesville.

The park is sandy and swampy, with vegetation ranging from canopies of banksias and tea trees to low-lying heathlands and salt marsh scrub. In spring the park is colourfully carpeted with native wildflowers and orchids. Native animals here include large numbers of kangaroos, as well as wallabies, possums, wombats and koalas. One of the main attractions is the abundant birdlife, with over 190 species including water birds such as cormorants, pelicans, terns and sea-eagles (see the following Rotamah Island section).

There is a Parks Victoria rangers' office (☎ 5146 0278) at the park entrance near Loch Sport. It opens for an hour in the morning and in the afternoon. A loop road provides good car access, and there are well-marked walking trails and several picnic areas through the park – bring drinking water. Point Wilson, at the eastern tip of the park, is the best picnic area and a popular gathering spot for kangaroos. (Please don't feed them, though.) The only camping area is at ***Emu Bight***, which has basic facilities. Sites, which cost around $9.50 for up to six people, can be booked and paid for through the park office – call ahead.

Rotamah Island

Protected as part of the Lakes National Park, this small island is only accessible by boat. The Royal Australian Ornithologists Union has established the **Rotamah Island Bird Observatory** (☎ 5156 6398) here, with accommodation in an old homestead. The sense of isolation and the scenery are wonderful. There are various bird hides and observation points, and the wardens supervise study courses.

The lodge sleeps up to 20 people in dorms and double rooms, and the overnight tariff of $65 per person includes all meals and boat transport from the mainland.

The Wilderness Coast

This section of East Gippsland, known as the Wilderness Coast, contains some of the most remote and spectacular national parks in the state. Unlike the rest of Victoria, much of this region was never cleared for agriculture. So, instead of the vast and barren sheep pastures that characterise the Western District on the opposite side of the state, this area is a wonderland of dense forests ranging from the coastal wilderness areas of Croajingolong to the lush rainforests of the Errinundra Plateau.

The Princes Highway (A1) carves its way through the centre of the region. Happily, the coastal areas such as Cape Conran and the wonderful inlets and coastline of Croajingolong are all uncrowded, unspoiled and undeveloped. Mallacoota is the major holiday town, but even it has remained relatively untouched by commercial development, although it's usually pretty crowded in the Christmas and Easter holiday seasons.

There are four major national parks here, all of which are wonderful in their own special way – Croajingolong for its wilderness areas, inlets, creeks, forests and abundance of birdlife and animals; Snowy River for its bush and mountain scenery and river gorges; Errinundra for its sensational cool-temperate rainforests; and Coopracambra for its remoteness and sense of isolation.

HIGHLIGHTS

- Experience the wilderness of Croajingolong National Park – unspoiled beaches and beautiful, isolated estuaries – from the relative comfort of a lighthouse keeper's cottage
- Shoot the rapids on the mighty Snowy River as it carves its way through superb mountain scenery
- Follow the route of botanist Baldwin Spencer through Gippsland's diverse landscape – from dramatic coastline to cool plateaus
- Enjoy the perfect getaway at Cape Conran Cabins set in beautiful bush close to the beach
- Cruise the Mallacoota Inlet, surrounded by national park, with its spectacular scenery and abundant wildlife

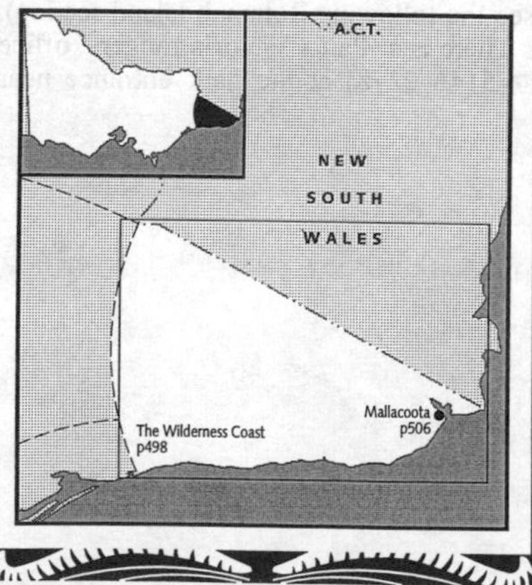

Orientation & Information

Orbost, which is the only sizeable town and the 'gateway' to the Wilderness Coast, has a useful tourist office that incorporates a Parks Victoria office and rainforest centre, with excellent displays and information on the area's natural attractions. There are other good park offices at Cann River and Mallacoota.

Mallacoota is the major holiday township in the area, with a wide range of accommodation alternatives. If you'd rather get away from it all, there are some excellent remote cabins and cottages in this area, and plenty of great camping areas in the national parks.

Parks Victoria publishes several good maps/brochures to the area, including *East Gippsland: A Guide for Visitors*, which highlights the main access roads, scenic drives, places of interest, picnic spots and camping areas and gives some good background information. The Australian Conservation Foundation also publishes *Car Touring & Bushwalking in East Gippsland*, although that book's information is somewhat outdated.

Activities

Popular activities in this area are whitewater rafting on the Snowy River, canoeing trips in the Croajingolong National Park, and sea-kayaking and mountain-biking trips from Mallacoota. Buchan is a centre for caving, climbing and abseiling. Bushwalkers have a wealth of great walks to choose from in this area's spectacular national parks.

These parts are renowned for their great fishing spots – choices range from the Snowy River estuary near Marlo, with its abundance of bream, bass and tailor, to trout fishing areas in the remote streams and creeks in the mountains.

Getting There & Away

Bus V/Line operates a daily bus service along the Princes Hwy from Bairnsdale into New South Wales (NSW). From Melbourne, take the train to Sale and connect with the bus from there.

Car & Motorbike The Princes Hwy runs through the heart of the region, and there are good sealed roads leading off the highway to Mallacoota, Marlo, Cape Conran and Bemm River. The only other major route is the Monaro Hwy (B23), which runs north from Cann River to Monaro in NSW.

Most of the other roads are unsealed and of varying standards, and some of the roads (especially those through national parks) will be closed during the wetter winter months or after floods such as those in June 1998. Check road conditions with park offices before heading off the main highways and keep an eye out for logging trucks. To explore this region fully would require a 4WD.

BUCHAN

Buchan, a tiny and beautiful town in the foothills of the Snowy Mountains, is chiefly known for its famous and spectacular limestone caves. There are a number of caves and caverns in this area, and the two major ones are managed by Parks Victoria.

Buchan Caves Reserve

The scenic Caves Reserve is just north of Buchan. The main features are the Royal and Fairy caves, but the reserve itself is also a pretty spot with shaded picnic areas, walking tracks, tame kangaroos and a small concrete swimming pool fed by an icy underground spring.

Parks Victoria has an office in the reserve, where tickets for guided tours of the caves are sold. Between April and September tours run at 11 am, and 1 and 3 pm; at other times tours of the **Royal Cave** start at 10 am, and 1 and 3.30 pm while those of the **Fairy Cave** start at 11.15 am and 2.15 pm. Each tour costs $10/5/20 for adults/children/families and a visit to either cave is worthwhile. The more adventurous can explore the Moon Hill cave system to the right of the road as you enter the park – bring a torch (flashlight).

The rangers also offer guided tours to the more remote and undeveloped caves in the area; ☎ 5155 9264 or ask at the park office for details.

Activities

Buchan is also the gateway to the spectacular Snowy River National Park. Snowy River Expeditions (☎ 5155 9353) is based at Karoondah Park and runs a wide variety of adventure tours, including one, two and four-day rafting trips on the Snowy costing $75/150/380 respectively (minimum booking of six people); half or full-day abseiling or caving trips costing $25/55; and two-day 4WD, hiking and camping trips costing $140. Most trips require a minimum of six people, and costs include transport, meals, guides, camping gear etc.

Detours Eco Adventures (☎ 5155 9464) offers adventures for the adventurous

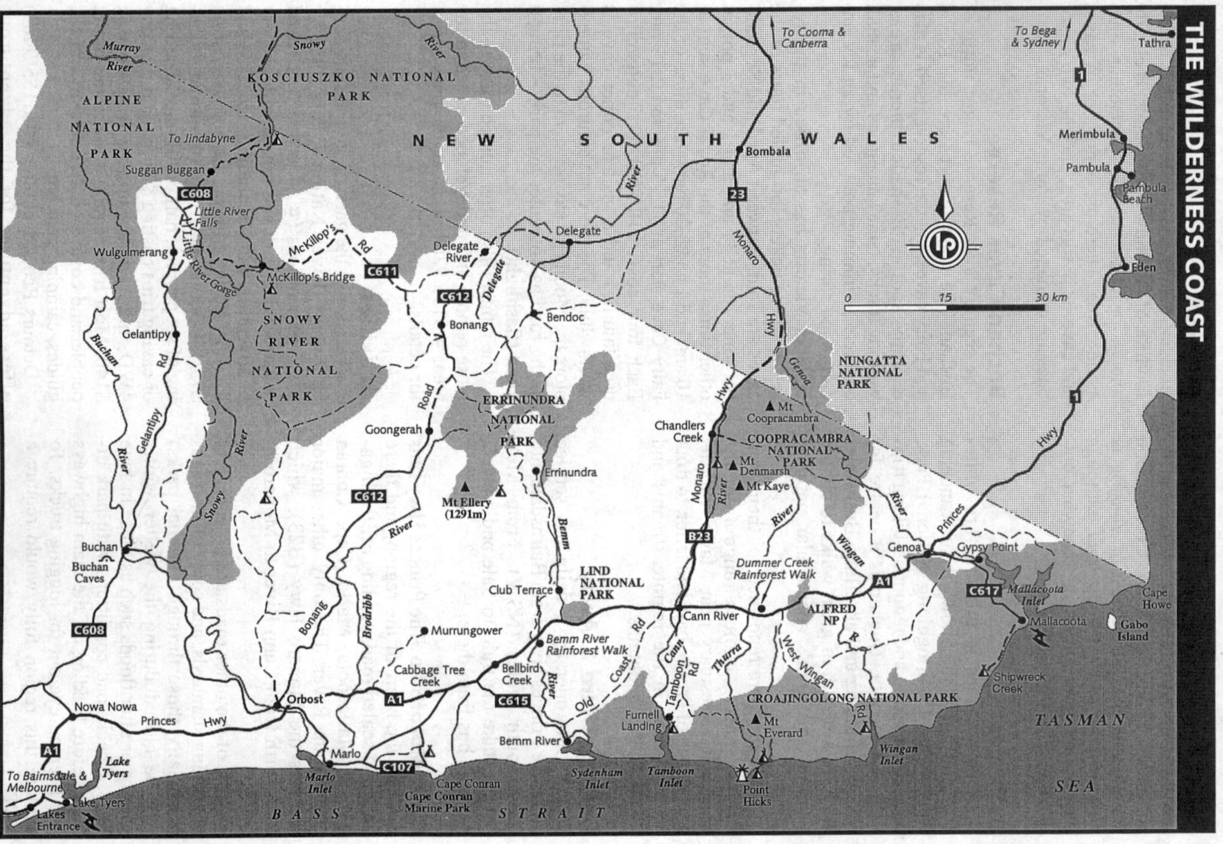
THE WILDERNESS COAST
NEW SOUTH WALES
Murray River
Snowy River
KOSCIUSZKO NATIONAL PARK
ALPINE NATIONAL PARK
To Jindabyne
Suggan Buggan
C608
Little River Falls
Little River Gorge
Wulgulmerang
McKillop's Rd
C611
McKillop's Bridge
SNOWY RIVER NATIONAL PARK
Gelantipy
Rd
Buchan River
Gelantipy
Snowy River
Buchan
Buchan Caves
C608
Nowa Nowa
Princes Hwy
A1
To Bairnsdale & Melbourne
Lake Tyers
Lake Tyers
Lakes Entrance
Delegate River
Delegate
C612
Delegate
Bonang
Bendoc
Road
Goongerah
ERRINUNDRA NATIONAL PARK
Errinundra
Mt Ellery (1291m)
C612
River
Bemm
Bonang
Brodribb
Murrungower
Club Terrace
LIND NATIONAL PARK
Bemm River Rainforest Walk
Cabbage Tree Creek
Bellbird Creek
River
Orbost
A1
C615
Old Coast Rd
Marlo
C107
Marlo Inlet
Cape Conran
Cape Conran Marine Park
Bemm River
BASS STRAIT
Sydenham Inlet
To Cooma & Canberra
Bombala
River
23
Monaro Hwy
NUNGATTA NATIONAL PARK
Genoa
Mt Coopracambra
Chandlers Creek
COOPRACAMBRA NATIONAL PARK
Mt Denmarsh
Mt Kaye
Monaro
River
B23
River
Dummer Creek Rainforest Walk
Cann River
Cann
Tamboon Rd
Thurra
Furnell Landing
Tamboon Inlet
Point Hicks
Mt Everard
CROAJINGOLONG NATIONAL PARK
West Wingan
Wingan
ALFRED NP
R
Rd
Wingan Inlet
River
Genoa
A1
Princes
Gypsy Point
C617
Mallacoota Inlet
Mallacoota
Shipwreck Creek
Cape Howe
Gabo Island
TASMAN
SEA
To Bega & Sydney
Tathra
1
Merimbula
Pambula
Pambula Beach
Eden
Hwy
1
0
15
30 km

including half-day wild caving and abseiling starting at $45. It also has a half-day mystery trip for $25. The company is based in a tipi village just outside town (see Places to Stay).

Places to Stay

Campgrounds & Caravan Parks There's a delightful campground in the Buchan Caves Reserve: the ***Buchan Caves Caravan Park*** *(☎ 5155 9264)* is very pretty, is shaded by pine trees and has good facilities. Tent sites cost from $10, and self-contained units cost from $45 to $55 a double – BYO linen.

Nagaul Tipi Village *(☎ 5155 9464)* is run by the people who operate the Detours Eco Adventures. It has occasional workshops and year-round accommodation in tipis just outside Buchan for $20 per person.

Hostel Just out of town on Saleyard Rd, the excellent ***Buchan Lodge Backpackers*** *(☎ 5155 9421)* is a modern and spacious timber-lined homestead with good facilities. It's a friendly place that's a step above most other hostels, and the owners can help organise a wide range of activities. A bed in the six to eight-bunk dorms costs $15 a night and it's advisable to book ahead for peak periods.

Motel & Self-Contained Units The ***Buchan Motel*** *(☎ 5155 9201)*, on top of a hill behind the general store, has singles/doubles with great views starting at $45/55.

The ***Buchan Valley Log Cabins*** *(☎ 5155 9494)* are about 200m north of Buchan. There are four self-contained treated-pine cabins on this sloping property; they start at $60 a double plus $15 per extra adult.

Places to Eat

The ***Caves Hotel*** in Buchan is an attractive pub with a good bistro, inexpensive meals and a covered courtyard. The ***Buchan Valley Roadhouse*** has good burgers and other take-aways, while ***The Willows***, opposite the pub, is a cottage-style restaurant with great meals for $5 and $10.

SNOWY RIVER NATIONAL PARK

This area is one of Victoria's most isolated and spectacular national parks, dominated by deep gorges carved through limestone and sandstone by the mighty Snowy River. The entire park is a smorgasbord of unspoiled and superb bush and mountain scenery. It covers over 95,000 hectares and includes a huge diversity of vegetation, ranging from alpine woodlands and eucalypt forests to rainforests and even areas of mallee-type scrub.

The two main access roads to the park are the Gelantipy Rd from Buchan and the Bonang Rd from Orbost. These roads are joined by MacKillops Rd (also known as Deddick River Rd), which runs across the northern border of the park from Bonang to just south of Wulgulmerang. Various access roads and scenic routes run into and alongside the park from these three main roads. The Deddick Trail, which runs through the middle of the park, is only suitable for 4WDs.

Along MacKillops Rd you'll come across **MacKillops Bridge**, which crosses the Snowy River. This is a spectacular and beautiful area. Near the bridge are the park's main campsites, toilets and fireplaces, as well as some good sandy river beaches and swimming spots. There are several good short walks around here, and the 15km Silver Mine walking track starts at the eastern end of the bridge. The views from the lookouts over **Little River Falls** and **Little River Gorge**, the deepest in Victoria, signposted about 20km to the west of MacKillops Bridge, are spectacular.

There are various other bush camping areas and picnic grounds in the park, where you can camp for free. Bushwalking and canoeing are the most popular activities in this area, but you need to be well prepared for both as conditions can be harsh and subject to sudden change. The classic canoe or raft trip down the Snowy River from MacKillops Bridge to a pull-out point near Buchan takes at least four days and offers superb scenery: rugged gorges, raging rapids, tranquil sections and excellent camping spots on broad sand bars. See the Activities chapter for details of commercial white-water rafting operators.

Good scenic drives in and around the park include MacKillops Rd, Rising Sun Rd from Bonang, Tullock Ard Rd from just south of Gelantipy, and Yalmy Rd, which is the main access road to the southern and central areas and places like Waratah Falls, Hick's Campsite and Raymond Falls. These roads are fairly rough and usually closed during winter.

For information about camping, road conditions and other details contact the park offices at Deddick (☎ 02-6458 0290), Orbost, Bairnsdale or Buchan.

Places to Stay

Forty kilometres north of Buchan at Gelantipy, ***Karoonda Park*** *(☎ 5155 0220)* is a cattle and sheep property and horse-riding ranch with YHA accommodation. Singles/doubles/dorms cost $14 per person and the owners may have work available for those who wish to stay a bit longer. Fully catered packages are available from $24 to $30 per person and lifts from Buchan can be arranged.

The ***Delegate River Tavern*** *(☎ 02-6458 8009)* is a fairly new hotel in a cleared valley near the NSW border. The pub is popular with trout fishers, bushwalkers and people driving 4WDs, and has good bistro meals and accommodation in the adjacent ***Tranquil Valley Resort***. The resort has 12 log cabins equipped with toasters, kettles and bar fridges – stoves are available if you want to do your own cooking. Cabins with one-bedroom have shared bathrooms and cost $45 a double, and the two-bedroom cabins have en suites and cost $65 a double plus $10 for extra people. Tariffs include a continental breakfast. There are also campsites here for $4 per person.

ORBOST

• **pop 2150**

Orbost, just off the Princes Hwy and on the banks of the Snowy River, is mainly a service centre for the surrounding farms and logging areas. It's also the gateway to the Wilderness Coast and the rainforests of East Gippsland, and is a good place to stop for information about this area's attractions.

The Princes Hwy passes just south of the town; the Bonang Rd heads north from Orbost towards the Snowy River and Errinundra national parks; and Marlo Rd follows the Snowy River south to Marlo, where the river meets the ocean, and continues along the coast to Cape Conran.

Information

Parks Victoria runs the excellent Rainforest & Information Centre (☎ 1800 637060 toll-free), which highlights this area's natural attractions, especially the many rainforests. There are visual and audio-visual displays and landscaped gardens that introduce you to the forest and plant species in the area including plants used by the Gunai. The centre, in Lochiel St, is open daily from 9 am to 5 pm, and on weekends during school holidays from 10 am to 4 pm.

Things to See

The Slab Hut (☎ 5154 2511), on the corner of Nicholson and Clarke Sts, is a historic hut surrounded by pretty cottage gardens. Built in 1872, it was moved here from its original site at the junction of the Buchan and Snowy rivers. It's open daily from 10 am to 4 pm.

Places to Stay

The central ***Orbost Camp Park*** *(☎ 5154 1097)* on the corner of Nicholson and Lochiel Sts has sites from $12 and on-site vans from $30.

The ***Commonwealth Hotel*** *(☎ 5154 1077, 159 Nicholson St)* has double B&B from $35, and, on the Princes Hwy, the ***Orbost Motel Lodge*** *(☎ 51541122)* has good double units for $40.

There are also a few modern homestead-style B&Bs close to Orbost: just off the highway, ***River View*** *(☎ 5154 2411, 15 Irvines Rd)* has doubles starting at $80.

Places to Eat

Try the ***Snowy River Cafe*** or ***Marilena's***, both on Nicholson St, for burgers, sandwiches and the like – they both have eat-in coffee lounge areas. The ***Orbost Golf Club*** on the northern side of town has the best bistro meals in town. The ***Club Hotel*** has Australian and Chinese bar meals from $5.50 and more expensive bistro meals.

Getting There & Away

Daily V/Line trains connect Melbourne and Sale: from Sale, daily buses continue east along the Princes Hwy into NSW, via Orbost. Bairnsdale to Orbost costs $17.50, Orbost to Genoa also costs $17.50. Buses stop outside the Orbost post office on the corner of Nicholson and Ruskin Sts.

BALDWIN SPENCER TRAIL

This 262km driving tour is a great way to see some of East Gippsland's most interesting and diverse natural features, from the ocean to rainforest. The route follows the trail of Walter Baldwin Spencer, a noted scientist and explorer who led an expedition through here in 1889. At the time, Orbost and Bendoc were the only settlements in the area. The circular route starts in Orbost, heads south to Marlo on the coast and then north through the cool-temperate rainforest areas of the Errinundra Plateau and on to Bendoc, then back along the Bonang Rd to Orbost.

There are various camping areas, picnic grounds and short walking tracks along the route. A brochure with a map of the route is available from information centres and park offices. Many of the roads along the trail are unsealed, narrow, winding and steep. They are often impassable in winter, so check on road conditions before heading out.

MURRUNGOWER FOREST DRIVE

This is another of the 'Great Forest Drives of Victoria' (as outlined in the Parks Victoria booklet *See How They Grow*). The 113km route starts at Orbost and takes you past dry and wet eucalypt forests, rainforests, timber harvesting areas, sawmills and various lookout points, short walks and picnic areas. It takes about three hours (without stops).

From Orbost, the drive follows the Princes Hwy east for about 16km before heading north-east along Murrungower Rd. The third section of the route, south along the unsealed Bendoc Ridge Rd back to the Princes Hwy, may be impassable in wet weather, so check road conditions first. A brochure with maps and guide notes for the drive is available from parks offices.

ERRINUNDRA NATIONAL PARK

The Errinundra Plateau is a misty and verdant wonderland that contains Victoria's largest areas of cool-temperate rainforest. The national park covers an area of 25,100 hectares, but should be much larger. Unfortunately the areas around the park are still being extensively logged, a short-sighted practice in direct conflict with the promotion of this region as a wilderness area.

The park is on a high granite plateau with a high rainfall, deep, fertile soils and a network of creeks and rivers. The 'mixed forest' vegetation is dominated by southern sassafras and black oliveberry, with tall eucalypt forests providing a canopy for the lower rainforests. This is a rich habitat for the abundant native birds and animals, which include many rare and endangered species.

The main access roads to the park are the Bonang Rd from Orbost and the Errinundra Rd from Club Terrace. The Bonang Rd passes on the western side of the park, while the Errinundra Rd passes through the centre. Both roads are unsealed, steep, slow and winding. The road conditions are variable and the roads are often closed or impassable during the wetter winter months or after floods – check with the park offices first.

You can explore the park by a combination of scenic drives and short walks. The only ***camping*** area is at Frosty Hollow on the western side of the park, and there are a few basic picnic and camping areas on the park's edges – at Ada River, The Gap and Goongerah. There's a petrol station and general store at Bonang, a public phone at Goongerah, a pub at Bendoc (closed Sunday) and another pub and cabins at Delegate River (see Snowy River National Park earlier).

Where Have all the Trees Gone?

While Far East Gippsland was always considered too remote for agriculture, it has provided a rich harvest for the logging industry since the end of the 19th century. Today the ongoing logging of these forest areas is a controversial issue, with an underlying conflict between the region's history of economic dependence on the timber industry (which employs a large proportion of the local workforce) and the current promotion of the area as a wilderness zone. This conflict is perhaps best illustrated by the case of the Errinundra Plateau, regarded as a conservation area of international significance, while logging trucks are still carting out ancient timbers from the area surrounding the national park. Due to fierce lobbying and pressure from environmentalist groups such as Goongerah Environment Centre (GECO), the national park areas have been expanded in recent years, but the government has typically tried to please everyone, with mixed success.

The situation has been further aggravated by reports that by 2020 all forest outside national parks and conservation sanctuaries is slated to become plantation style managed regrowth forest. This means that over 400,000 hectares of crown land (40% of Victoria's existing native forest) will be logged, burnt and replanted, further endangering the survival of rare species such as the spotted quoll and long-footed potoroo. With most of the logs going to woodchipping at prices reputedly as low as 8c or 9c per tonne, environmentalists are stepping up their campaigns. GECO (tel 5154 0156) is a locally-based organisation that welcomes supporters to join their peaceful protests around the Errinundra Plateau. Call either GECO or the Friends of the Earth forest network (tel 9419 8700) for the latest information before heading up there.

Be warned that while the locals are friendly, many consider the environmentalists' actions to be a direct threat to their livelihood. Unfortunately this often leads to direct conflict between the two groups, and posters such as 'greenies cost jobs' are a common sight hanging in the bars of local hotels.

Joyce Connolly

For more information contact the park office (☎ 02-6458 1456) at Bendoc weekdays from 8 am to 4.30 pm, or the park offices at Cann River or Orbost.

MARLO

Marlo, a sleepy little settlement at the mouth of the Snowy River 15km south of Orbost, has a small cluster of holiday houses, shops, a good pub with views over the inlet and a couple of places to stay. There's also a **historic cinema** – ask in the supermarket if you want to look inside. The road from Orbost to Marlo follows the Snowy on the final leg of its journey from the mountains to the ocean. The river flows into a large lagoon before entering the sea, and the area has excellent fishing and abundant birdlife around the inland waterways.

Marlo Bush Races are held here on New Years Day.

Places to Stay

Upmarket backpacker accommodation is available at the ***Snowy River Entrance Retreat*** *(☎ 5154 8504, 14 Stirling St)* for $15 per person, including an Orbost pickup and drop off.

There are two caravan parks at Marlo, both near the beach. The ***Marlo Caravan Park*** *(☎ 5154 8226)* has on-site vans from $25, self-contained cabins from $35 and motel units from $55. The ***Municipal Park*** *(☎ 5154 8268)* has sites from $10 to $14.

The nicest place in town is ***Tabbara Lodge** (☎ 5154 8231, 1 Marlo Rd)*, on the right as you enter town from Orbost. It's a small brick lodge in a garden setting, with four self-contained units that sleep up to five people and cost from $45 a double, plus $5 for each extra person.

CAPE CONRAN MARINE PARK

The 19km coastal route from Marlo to Cape Conran is especially pretty; it's bordered by banksia trees, grass plains, sand dunes and the ocean. There are some great remote white-sand beaches along this coast, and this is an excellent and undeveloped getaway place – you'll need to book accommodation during the holiday seasons, although it seldom gets crowded.

The cape is an excellent venue for snorkelling and scuba diving, boating and fishing, and in the warmer weather, swimming and surfing. There are several good picnic areas and a short nature walk from the East Cape beach to the end of the cape. A rough track leads from the cape to the mouth of the Yeerung River, which is 4km east and another good spot for swimming, canoeing and fishing. Note that there are no shops at Cape Conran.

Places to Stay

Parks Victoria (☎ 5154 8438) manages the accommodation at Cape Conran. The ***Banksia Bluff Camping Area*** is right on the foreshore and surrounded by banksia woodlands. There are toilets, cold showers and a few fireplaces, but you'll need to take drinking water. Sites cost from $11 to $15 depending on the season.

Nearby, the ***Cape Conran Cabins & Lodge*** are a set of self-contained timber cabins in a bush setting, well spaced and a short walk from the beach. The cabins are well designed, with an airy, beachy feel, and were built from 10 different local timbers. Great design, great location, great value – which is why they're usually booked out in the holiday seasons. Cabins sleeping up to eight people range seasonally from $65 to $92 for up to four people, plus $12 to $14 per extra adult. There is also a large lodge that sleeps up to 17 people from $126 per night for 12 people.

ORBOST TO GENOA

There are various rainforest walks, state forests and national parks along this section of the Princes Hwy. Roads leading to the area's four major national parks also lead off this part of the route.

Bemm River

Thirty-five kilometres east of Orbost is the turn-off to the small, old-fashioned holiday township of Bemm River, on the shores of Sydenham Inlet and close to the Croajingolong National Park. Facilities include a pub, a general store, a couple of caravan parks and a few holiday flats.

Bellbird Creek

Back on the Princes Hwy a couple of kilometres past the turn-off to Bemm River, the ***Bellbird Hotel** (☎ 5158 1239)* does bistro meals, and has comfortable single/double rooms from $20/35. It also has Sunday country music sessions.

Bemm River Rainforest Walk

Signposted off the Princes Hwy 46km east of Orbost, this walking trail follows a creek bed through a patch of warm-temperate rainforest, and takes less than half an hour to stroll through.

Lind National Park

Signposted just east of the turn-off from the Princes Hwy to Club Terrace, this small park (1365 hectares) was declared in 1926 as a scenic stopover spot for travellers along the highway. A number of creeks run through the park, and the vegetation ranges from warm-temperate rainforests and wet-gully plants alongside the creeks to open eucalypt forests in the drier areas. There are several walking tracks, a picnic area in the centre of the park and a nature drive that follows the Euchre Creek through the park from Club Terrace back to the Princes Hwy.

Cann River

• **pop 250**

Cann River is a small sawmilling centre at the junction of the Princes and Monaro Hwys. It has a pub, motels (including the ***Cann River Motel*** on the highway, with doubles from $38, including breakfast), caravan parks and a couple of service stations and cafes. There is a Parks Victoria office (☎ 5158 6351) in the centre of town that specialises in Croajingolong National Park and posts daily bulletins about road conditions, which you'll need to check on, especially in winter. Opening hours are from 9 am to 3 pm daily.

From Cann River, the Monaro Hwy heads north to the Coopracambra National Park, and the unsealed Tamboon Rd heads south to Tamboon Inlet and the Croajingolong National Park.

Drummer Creek Rainforest Walk

This reserve is 11km east of Cann River, on the northern side of the Princes Hwy. The walk starts at the picnic area and takes you through warm-temperate rainforest – allow about half an hour.

Alfred National Park

About 20km east of Cann River, the Princes Hwy passes through the centre of this small park (3050 hectares), which was burnt out in the 1983 bushfires and is still regenerating. There are no access trails or facilities here.

GENOA

Genoa is a small highway town at the junction of Mallacoota Rd. There's a general store here where V/Line buses stop and the ***Genoa Hotel/Motel*** *(☎ 5158 8222)* has motel units, but if you have time you'll be much better off heading down to Gipsy Point or Mallacoota.

GIPSY POINT

Gipsy Point is a tiny and idyllic settlement at the head of the Mallacoota Inlet. Although it's only 10km off the Princes Hwy, there's a deliciously remote feel about the place. Once you're sitting on the jetty looking out over the inlet, with a beer in one hand and a fishing line in the other, you'll feel like you're a million miles from anywhere (unless you're here during the Christmas or Easter school holidays).

Places to Stay

The ***Gipsy Point Lodge*** *(☎ 1800 063556 toll-free)* is in a peaceful setting surrounded by bush. There are two types of accommodation here: a guesthouse, and three self-contained cottages. The guesthouse is a long and low green weatherboard building with eight double en suite rooms, a games room and a guest lounge. The self-contained cottages sleep three to five people and start at $50, depending on the season and the size of the cottage. Other facilities include a tennis court and motor boats for hire. The lodge also runs a programme of packaged holidays for birdwatchers and naturalists – ring for dates and details. Nonresidents are welcome for dinner, which entails a three course set meal for $30 per person – book ahead.

The ***Gipsy Point Resort Hotel & Apartments*** *(☎ 1800 688200 toll-free)* has modern self-contained lake-view apartments starting at $95 and garden apartments from $75.

MALLACOOTA

• **pop 980**

Mallacoota is completely surrounded by the Croajingolong National Park. It's a one-road-in, one-road-out town, a sleepy and old-fashioned place populated by alternative lifestylers, retirees, abalone fishers and surfers. Everything is fairly low-key and relaxed, and life revolves around the ocean, the inlet, the bush and the one pub.

It's also a seasonal resort, and during the Christmas and Easter holiday periods it is transformed into a crowded family holiday spot. At these times, most of the accommodation is booked out, the caravan parks fill up, and tariffs are much higher. The character of the place also changes when it's full of tourists, so if possible come during the quieter times, when it's a totally different place.

Mallacoota's attractions are unique: there's access to remote ocean beaches, an extensive estuarine waterway system, the fabulous Croajingolong National Park, an abundance of birdlife, great fishing, bushwalks, surfing, swimming and plenty more.

There's a wide range of accommodation here, and a small shopping centre in Maurice Ave, where there's a pub, shops, a laundrette, a video shop, a couple of take-aways and banking facilities.

Mallacoota's major festival is **Carnival in Coota**, held during the Easter holiday period. Other festivals include a **blues weekend** in July and a celebration of forests, flowers and folk in November.

Information

Parks Victoria (☎ 5158 0219) has an information centre on the corner of Buckland and Allan Drives, opposite the main wharf. This place has good displays and information on Croajingolong, as well as brochures about the walking tracks around Mallacoota. Staff can also advise you on some excellent two and three-day walks into the more remote sections of Croajingolong between Mallacoota and the NSW border. Opening hours are weekdays from 9.30 am to midday and 1.00 to 3.30 pm.

There isn't an official tourist information centre in town, although the Mallacoota Information & Booking Service (☎ 5158 0788) at 57 Maurice Ave (actually the local real estate agent's office) has a few tourist brochures and maps. It also offers an accommodation and tour booking service, although it's better to make bookings directly if possible.

Walking Trails

A great way to see this area is on foot. There's a good range of short walks around Mallacoota, the coast and the inlet, ranging from a half-hour stroll to a four hour bushwalk. The Mallacoota Walking Track, a 7km, five-stage trail around the town, was built and developed by local school students. It starts in the centre of town, takes you down to Bastion Point, around the golf course and along the coast, and back into town through forests and heathlands.

Parks Victoria can give you maps and advice on where to go walking. For longer walks, see the Croajingolong section.

Cruises & Boat Hire

One of the best ways to experience this area's unique setting is by boat. The estuarine waters of the Mallacoota Inlet are completely surrounded by national park and have more than 300km of shoreline. There are picnic areas, walking tracks, a goanna colony, and the remnants of an old gold mine around the inlet – the brochure *Discovering Mallacoota Inlet* is a good guide to these and other features. There are plenty of options for getting around on the water and some accommodation may provide water toys for their guests' use.

Wallagaraugh River Wilderness Cruises (☎ 5158 0555) operates excellent cruises through the lakes system on board the MV *Discovery*. Its five hour 'wilderness cruise' departs from the main wharf at 10 am and costs $40/30 for adults/children, including a barbecue lunch and snacks. It also has two and 2½-hour cruises that cost $15/8 and $20/10 respectively. Cruises operate most days, depending on demand – book by phone or at its office by the main wharf.

Another local cruise boat is the MV *Loch Ard* (☎ 5158 0144), a restored old timber ferry that runs different cruises on different days: the two hour twilight cruise costs $15/8/38 for adults/kids/families. It also has a five hour Gipsy Point cruise costing $25/10/60, and a 3½ hour combined cruise and gold-mine walk costing $18/8/44. The *Loch Ard* also departs from the main wharf, and tickets can be booked by phone or at the wharf.

If you'd rather do your own thing, there are a couple of operators that hire boats. Rankin's Cruiser Hire (☎ 5158 0555), based near the main wharf, hires powered fishing boats for $20 for the first hour and $10 for every hour thereafter. Buckland's Boat Hire

(☎ 5158 0660), about 4km north of the centre of Mallacoota around Lakeside Drive, has inboard or outboard fishing boats for around $70 a day, and also hires canoes by the hour.

Places to Stay

There is plenty of holiday-style accommodation here, with caravan parks, motels and an abundance of holiday units. Prices vary significantly with the seasons, and if you're coming during Christmas or Easter you'll need to book ahead.

Camping & Caravan Parks There are several good camping and caravan grounds here, but the council-run ***Mallacoota Camping Park*** *(☎ 5158 0300)* has the best location, with good facilities and hundreds of well-grassed campsites, many of them are right on the foreshore. Sites range seasonally from $11 to $14 a night. The central ***Beachcomber Caravan Park*** *(☎ 5158 0233)* has on-site vans which start at $25 and cabins from $35; it sometimes offers discounts to backpackers.

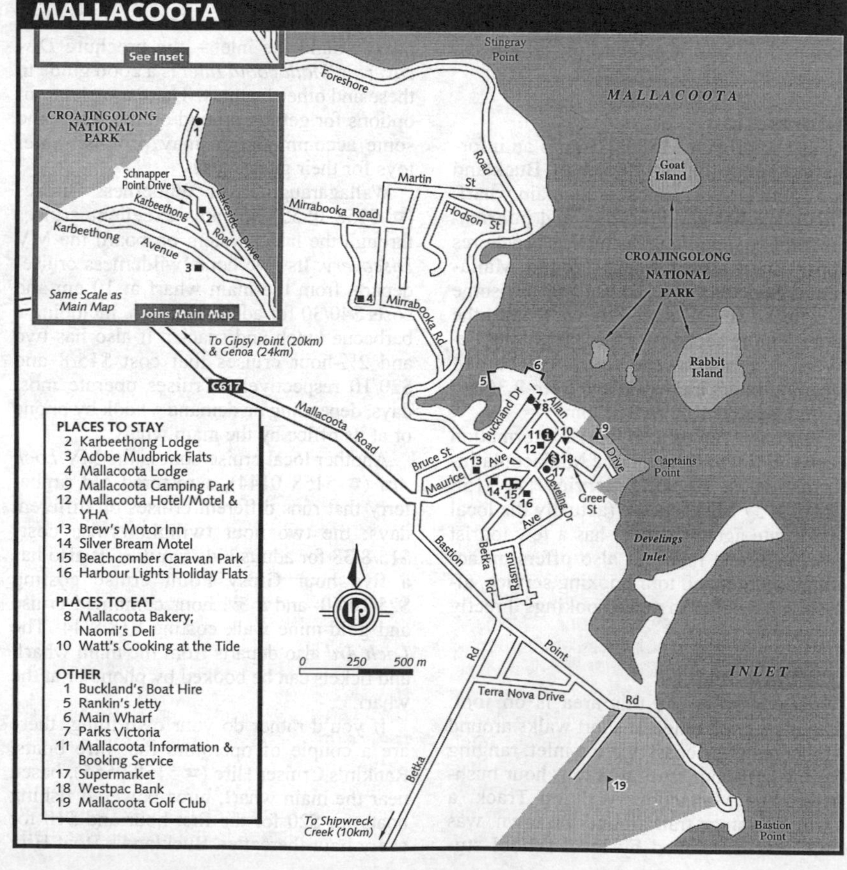

Hostel *Mallacoota Lodge YHA (☎ 5158 0455)*, conveniently attached to the pub on Maurice Ave, has singles, doubles and dorm beds starting at $15 per night.

Motels The ***Silver Bream Motel*** *(☎ 5158 0305, 32 Maurice Ave)* has doubles starting at $60. At 15 Maurice Ave, ***Brew's Motor Inn*** *(☎ 5158 0544)* has units with kitchenettes from $50 (the top units have good views across to the inlet). The ***Mallacoota Hotel/Motel*** *(☎ 5158 0455)* in Maurice Ave has modern units with doubles from $45.

Self-Contained Units The best of Mallacoota's self-contained options is the marvellous ***Adobe Mudbrick Flats*** *(☎ 5158 0329)*, on a hillside at 17 Karbeethong Ave. Built and run by the friendly Peter Kurz, it has six two-bedroom flats and two one-bedroom flats in this 'mud-brick village'. Each flat is fully self-contained and imaginatively and creatively designed, and all have good views of the inlet, Gabo Island and the lighthouse. This place is like a private wildlife park, with all sorts of birds and animals wandering around, including possums, parrots, wombats and geese (guests are welcome to bring their own pets). In winter and spring the flats cost $45 per day for up to four people plus $10 per extra person; between December and May and during school holidays the base rate goes up to $75 per day. Great value.

There are many other holiday units and flats, including the ***Harbour Lights Holiday Flats*** *(☎ 5158 0246, 88 Betka Rd)* with simple budget units starting at $34 a night.

Guesthouse ***Karbeethong Lodge*** *(☎ 5158 0411)*, on Schnapper Point Drive, a favourite with cartoonist Michael Leunig, is a classic old-fashioned timber guesthouse. Fronted by a broad, shady verandah, the guesthouse looks out over sweeping lawns and rose gardens to the Mallacoota Inlet. It's a cosy, rambling place with simple rooms, a large kitchen, a comfortable lounge and dining room, open fires and laundry facilities. Doubles with shared bathrooms range from $50 to $70, family rooms (sleeping up to five) range from $75 to $105, and rooms with en suites cost another $20.

Houseboats One well set-up houseboat for is available for hire from ***Mallacoota Houseboats*** *(☎ 5158 0775)* It has three double beds and a small single bunk. Weekly rates are $1300 between December and March and $900 during the rest of the year; there's a three night minimum hire.

Places to Eat

If you're self-catering there are two supermarkets, a butcher and a fresh seafood shop along Maurice Ave, as well as a couple of take-aways. At the Mallacoota Hotel, ***Barnacles Seafood Bistro*** offers a good range of bistro meals with main courses ranging from $10 to $16.

Watt's Cooking at the Tide *(☎ 5158 0100)*, on the corner of Maurice Ave and Allan Drive, is a modern and stylish timber bar/restaurant with full-length windows overlooking the inlet. It specialises in local seafood and opens daily for dinner, and for lunch on weekends. ***Naomi's Deli*** *(☎ 5158 0064, 14 Allan Drive)* opens daily for breakfast and lunch and has outside dining and a good selection of focaccias, cakes, meals etc.

Getting There & Away

Mallacoota is 23km off the Princes Hwy, and while buses stop at Genoa, there is no scheduled transport from Genoa down to Mallacoota. Hitching is reasonably easy, as there's only one road in; otherwise, some of the accommodation places and tour operators will pick you up from Genoa if you ring in advance.

CROAJINGOLONG NATIONAL PARK

Designated a 'World Biosphere Reserve' by UNESCO, Croajingolong is one of Australia's finest national parks. This coastal wilderness park covers 87,500 hectares and stretches for about 100km along the easternmost tip of Victoria from Bemm River to the

NSW border. Magnificent unspoiled beaches, inlets, estuaries and forests make this the ideal park for camping, walking, swimming, surfing or just lazing around. The five inlets, Sydenham, Tamboon, Meuller, Wingan and Mallacoota, are very popular for canoeing and fishing. Mallacoota Inlet is the largest and most accessible, and is covered in the previous section on Mallacoota.

Two sections of the park have been declared wilderness areas (which means no vehicles, and access to walkers only): the Cape Howe Wilderness area, between the Mallacoota Inlet and NSW border, and the Sandpatch Wilderness area, between Shipwreck Creek and Wingan Inlet.

The diverse habitat in the park supports a wide range of plants, birds and animals. In particular this place is a paradise for birdwatchers, with over 300 recorded species, including glossy black cockatoos and the rare ground parrot, and the inland waterways are home to a myriad of water birds such as the delicate azure kingfisher and magnificent sea eagle. There are many small mammals here, including possums, bandicoots and gliders, and the reptile population includes a colony of huge goannas at Goanna Bay, on the Top Lake of the Mallacoota Inlet. The vegetation ranges from typical coastal landscapes to thick eucalypt forests, with some areas of warm-temperate rainforest. The heathland areas put on impressive displays of orchids and wildflowers in the spring.

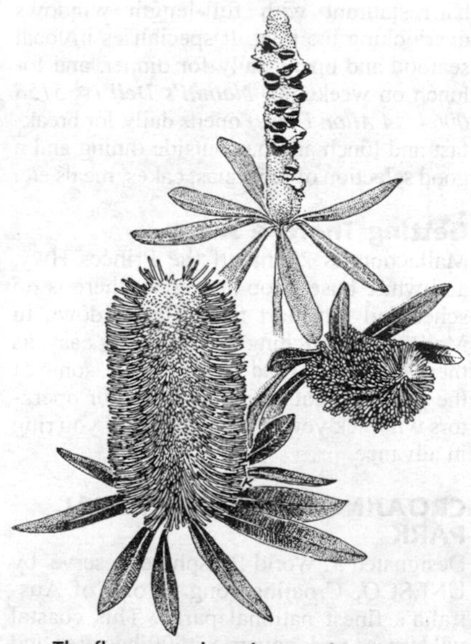

The flowers and seed cone of a coastal banksia, which is common in untouched coastal areas of eastern Victoria.

Access roads of varying quality lead into the park from the Princes Hwy. Apart from Mallacoota Rd, all of these are unsealed and can be very rough in winter, so check with the park offices on road conditions before venturing on, especially during or after rain. From the west, the first road in is Old Coast Rd, which starts 1km west of Cann River and forms the western border of the park. It takes you to the tiny village of Bemm River and to the Sydenham Inlet. From Cann River, Tamboon Rd, a good gravel road, takes you to the boat ramp at Furnell Landing. Cape Everard Rd branches off the Tamboon Rd, and leads to Point Hicks, the mouth of Thurra River and Mueller Inlet. West Wingan Rd starts about 18km east of Cann River, and is a long bumpy ride down to Wingan Inlet. From Mallacoota, Betka Rd takes you west to Shipwreck Creek.

The main camping areas are at Wingan Inlet, Shipwreck Creek, Thurra River and Mueller Inlet. The Tamboon Inlet camping area can only be reached by boat from Furnell Landing. The serene and secluded Wingan Inlet has the best facilities, with pit toilets, fireplaces, picnic tables and fresh water. Other bush camping areas (permits required) lie along the Wilderness Coast Walk but you may need to bring drinking water. All sites in the park are limited, so you'll need to book during the main holiday seasons, especially at Wingan Inlet; camping fees range from $6.90 to $11.50 depending on the site and the season.

Point Hicks was the first part of Australia to be spotted by Captain Cook in 1888. The remote yet comfortable ***Assistant Light-***

keeper's Residence (☎ *5158 4268*) can sleep up to eight and is available from $160 per night. This truly is wilderness area.

Call into the park offices in Cann River (☎ 5158 6351) or Mallacoota (☎ 5158 0219) for information and advice, to check road conditions and to get maps of the park and walking tracks.

COOPRACAMBRA NATIONAL PARK

Coopracambra is one of the most remote and least developed of the state's national parks. It was declared in 1979 and now covers an area of more than 35,000 hectares. It's bordered in the north by the NSW border and on the west by the Monaro Hwy. The landscape is rugged and spectacular, with the dramatic deep gorges of the Genoa River and a series of smaller creeks running through it. The vegetation is mainly open eucalypt forest, with a few areas of sheltered rainforest, and there are various difficult climbs to high peaks such as Mt Denmarsh, Mt Kaye and Mt Coopracambra.

One 4WD track passes through the centre of the park from the Monaro Hwy to Genoa. Apart from this route, there are no other access tracks, campgrounds or walking trails through Coopracambra, which makes it a great spot for experienced bushwalkers who want to go far from the madding crowds. On the Monaro Hwy side, the Beehive Creek Falls (signposted) is an idyllic and scenic spot, with small cascades falling into rock pools shaded by the surrounding bush – some great swimming holes for the warm weather.

It's a fascinating drive from Cann River to Bombala in NSW. The Victorian sector of the highway is very pretty, winding through national parks and thick forests, but as soon as you cross the border the landscape changes dramatically into dry, denuded sheep pastures, a landscape stripped of its natural vegetation. It's a stark and sad contrast.

Places to Stay

Coopracambra Cottage (☎ *5158 8277*) is a wonderfully remote getaway set on a scenic cattle farm about 5km south of the national park. It's a modern and attractive octagonal cottage built out of local timbers, fully self-contained with three bedrooms, log-fire heating and everything supplied. Tariffs are great value at $50 a night for up to four people, or $60 for up to six. The cottage is 16km north-west of Genoa, and well signposted.

Glossary

Listed here are some Australian words that you're likely to come across in this book, or in your travels in Australia. For further listings of Aussie slang, see the boxed text 'Transporting the Language' in the Facts about Victoria chapter.

barbie – barbecue (BBQ)
barrack – cheer on team at sporting event; to support (as in 'who do you barrack for?')
bathers – swimming costume
bikies – motorcyclists
billabong – waterhole in dried-up riverbed, more correctly a cut-off ox-bow bend
billy – tin container used to boil tea in the bush
bitumen – asphalt; surfaced road
booze bus – police van used for random breath testing for alcohol
brumby – wild horse
Buckley's (ie Buckley's chance) – no chance at all (as in 'Across the Tanami? They've got *Buckley's* in that shitbox'). The origin of this term is unclear. It may derive from the escaped convict William Buckley, who lived with the Aborigines, though his chances of survival were considered negligible; or from the Sydney escapologist Buckley, who had himself chained up in a coffin and thrown into Sydney Harbour, with dire results.
bug – germ, not insect
bull bar – outsize front bumper on car or truck as a barrier against animals on the road
bush – country, anywhere away from the city; scrub
bushranger – Australia's equivalent of the outlaws of the American Wild West (some goodies, some baddies). Ned Kelly is Australia's most famous.
BYO – Bring Your Own (booze to a restaurant, meat to a barbecue etc)

camp oven – large cast-iron pot with lid, used for cooking in an open fire
cask – wine box (a great Australian invention)
cooee – long, loud call used in the bush to attract attention; shouting distance (as in 'to be within cooee of...')
coolgardie safe – cupboard covered with wet hessian to keep food cool
counter meal (also countery) – pub meal, usually ordered and served over the counter of the public bar
cray(fish) – lobster

deli – delicatessen
didgeridoo – cylindrical wooden musical instrument played by Aboriginal men
dingo – indigenous wild dog
distillate – diesel fuel
donk – car or boat engine
droving – moving livestock a considerable distance

esky – trademark name for a portable icebox used for keeping beer etc cold

flake – shark meat, often used in fish & chips
fossick – hunt for gems or semiprecious stones

grazier – large-scale sheep or cattle farmer

Hughie – the god of rain and surf (as in 'Send her down, Hughie!'; 'Send 'em up, Hughie!'); god when things go wrong (as in 'It's up to Hughie now.')

joey – young kangaroo or wallaby

Koori (also spelt Koorie) – Aborigine (generally used south of the Murray River)

lollies – sweets; candy

main – a meal's main course
mallee – low, shrubby, multi-stemmed eucalypt; the north-west region of Victoria

March fly – horsefly; gadfly
milk bar – general store
mozzies – mosquitoes
mulga – arid-zone acacia; the bush; away from civilisation (as in 'he's gone up the mulga')
muster – round up livestock, usually on a *station*

NRE – (Department of) Natural Resources and Environment

outback – remote part of the bush
Oz – Australia

paddock – a fenced area of land, usually intended for livestock (paddocks can be huge in Australia)
pastoralist – large-scale *grazier*
pot – 285ml beer glass
potato cake – fried potato snack from a fish and chip shop; 'scallop' in some other states

RACV – Royal Automobile Club of Victoria
rego – registration (as in 'car rego')
roo bar – outsize front bumper, (see *bull bar)*

Salvo – member of the Salvation Army
sanger – sandwich
shout – buy round of drinks (as in 'it's your shout')
smoothie – thick milkshake with added fruit, ice cream, yoghurt etc
snag – sausage
squatter – pioneer farmer who occupied land as a tenant of the government
squattocracy – Australian 'old money' folk, who made it by being first on the scene and grabbing the land
station – large sheep or cattle farm
stickybeak – nosy person
stoush – fist fight; brawl (also verbal)
stubby – 375ml bottle of beer
surfaced road – tarred road
swag – canvas-covered bed roll used in the outback; a large amount

thongs – flip-flops
tinny – 375ml can of beer
togs – swimming costume; *bathers*

ute – utility, pick-up truck

Wathaurong – Koories of Geelong and the Bellarine Peninsula area
woomera – notched throwing stick used by Aborigines to aid the throwing of spears

yabby (also spelt 'yabbie') – small freshwater *crayfish*
yabbying – catching *yabbies*

LONELY PLANET

Guides by Region

Lonely Planet is known worldwide for publishing practical, reliable and no-nonsense travel information in our guides and on our Web site. The Lonely Planet list covers just about every accessible part of the world. Currently there are nine series: travel guides, shoestring guides, walking guides, city guides, phrasebooks, audio packs, travel atlases, diving and snorkeling guides and travel literature.

AFRICA Africa – the South • Africa on a shoestring • Arabic (Egyptian) phrasebook • Arabic (Moroccan) phrasebook • Cairo • Cape Town • Central Africa • East Africa • Egypt • Egypt travel atlas • Ethiopian (Amharic) phrasebook • The Gambia & Senegal • Kenya • Kenya travel atlas • Malawi, Mozambique & Zambia • Morocco • North Africa • South Africa, Lesotho & Swaziland • South Africa, Lesotho & Swaziland travel atlas • Swahili phrasebook • Tanzania, Zanzibar & Pemba • Trekking in East Africa • Tunisia • West Africa • Zimbabwe, Botswana & Namibia • Zimbabwe, Botswana & Namibia travel atlas
Travel Literature: The Rainbird: A Central African Journey • Songs to an African Sunset: A Zimbabwean Story • Mali Blues: Traveling to an African Beat

AUSTRALIA & THE PACIFIC Australia • Australian phrasebook • Bushwalking in Australia • Bushwalking in Papua New Guinea • Fiji • Fijian phrasebook • Islands of Australia's Great Barrier Reef • Melbourne • Micronesia • New Caledonia • New South Wales & the ACT • New Zealand • Northern Territory • Outback Australia • Papua New Guinea • Papua New Guinea (Pidgin) phrasebook • Queensland • Rarotonga & the Cook Islands • Samoa • Solomon Islands • South Australia • Sydney • Tahiti & French Polynesia • Tasmania • Tonga • Tramping in New Zealand • Vanuatu • Victoria • Western Australia
Travel Literature: Islands in the Clouds • Sean & David's Long Drive

CENTRAL AMERICA & THE CARIBBEAN Bahamas and Turks & Caicos • Barcelona • Bermuda • Central America on a shoestring • Costa Rica • Cuba • Dominican Republic & Haiti • Eastern Caribbean • Guatemala, Belize & Yucatán: La Ruta Maya • Jamaica • Mexico • Mexico City • Panama
Travel Literature: Green Dreams: Travels in Central America

EUROPE Amsterdam • Andalucía • Austria • Baltic States phrasebook • Barcelona • Berlin • Britain • British phrasebook • Canary Islands • Central Europe • Central Europe phrasebook • Corsica • Croatia • Czech & Slovak Republics • Denmark • Dublin • Eastern Europe • Eastern Europe phrasebook • Edinburgh • Estonia, Latvia & Lithuania • Europe • Finland • France • French phrasebook • Germany • German phrasebook • Greece • Greek phrasebook • Hungary • Iceland, Greenland & the Faroe Islands • Ireland • Italian phrasebook • Italy • Lisbon • London • Mediterranean Europe • Mediterranean Europe phrasebook • Norway • Paris • Poland • Portugal • Portugal travel atlas • Prague • Provence & the Côte d'Azur • Romania & Moldova • Rome • Russia, Ukraine & Belarus • Russian phrasebook • Scandinavian & Baltic Europe • Scandinavian Europe phrasebook • Scotland • Slovenia • Spain • Spanish phrasebook • St Petersburg • Switzerland • Trekking in Spain • Ukrainian phrasebook • Vienna • Walking in Britain • Walking in Italy • Walking in Ireland • Walking in Switzerland • Western Europe • Western Europe phrasebook
Travel Literature: The Olive Grove: Travels in Greece

INDIAN SUBCONTINENT Bangladesh • Bengali phrasebook • Bhutan • Delhi • Goa • Hindi/Urdu phrasebook • India • India & Bangladesh travel atlas • Indian Himalaya • Karakoram Highway • Nepal • Nepali phrasebook • Pakistan • Rajasthan • South India • Sri Lanka • Sri Lanka phrasebook • Trekking in the Indian Himalaya • Trekking in the Karakoram & Hindukush • Trekking in the Nepal Himalaya
Travel Literature: In Rajasthan • Shopping for Buddhas

LONELY PLANET

Mail Order

Lonely Planet products are distributed worldwide.They are also available by mail order from Lonely Planet, so if you have difficulty finding a title please write to us. North and South American residents should write to 150 Linden St, Oakland, CA 94607, USA; European and African residents should write to 10a Spring Place, London NW5 3BH, UK; and residents of other countries to PO Box 617, Hawthorn, Victoria 3122, Australia.

ISLANDS OF THE INDIAN OCEAN Madagascar & Comoros • Maldives • Mauritius, Réunion & Seychelles

MIDDLE EAST & CENTRAL ASIA Arab Gulf States • Central Asia • Central Asia phrasebook • Iran • Israel & the Palestinian Territories • Israel & the Palestinian Territories travel atlas • Istanbul • Jerusalem • Jordan & Syria • Jordan, Syria & Lebanon travel atlas • Lebanon • Middle East on a shoestring • Turkey • Turkish phrasebook • Turkey travel atlas • Yemen
Travel Literature: The Gates of Damascus • Kingdom of the Film Stars: Journey into Jordan

NORTH AMERICA Alaska • Backpacking in Alaska • Baja California • California & Nevada • Canada • Chicago • Florida • Hawaii • Honolulu • Los Angeles • Louisiana • Miami • New England USA • New Orleans • New York City • New York, New Jersey & Pennsylvania • Pacific Northwest USA • Rocky Mountain States • San Francisco • Seattle • Southwest USA • USA • USA phrasebook • Vancouver • Washington, DC & the Capital Region
Travel Literature: Drive Thru America

NORTH-EAST ASIA Beijing • Cantonese phrasebook • China • Hong Kong • Hong Kong, Macau & Guangzhou • Japan • Japanese phrasebook • Japanese audio pack • Korea • Korean phrasebook • Kyoto • Mandarin phrasebook • Mongolia • Mongolian phrasebook • North-East Asia on a shoestring • Seoul • South-West China • Taiwan • Tibet • Tibetan phrasebook • Tokyo
Travel Literature: Lost Japan

SOUTH AMERICA Argentina, Uruguay & Paraguay • Bolivia • Brazil • Brazilian phrasebook • Buenos Aires • Chile & Easter Island • Chile & Easter Island travel atlas • Colombia • Ecuador & the Galapagos Islands • Latin American Spanish phrasebook • Peru • Quechua phrasebook • Rio de Janeiro • South America on a shoestring • Trekking in the Patagonian Andes • Venezuela
Travel Literature: Full Circle: A South American Journey

SOUTH-EAST ASIA Bali & Lombok • Bangkok • Burmese phrasebook • Cambodia • Hill Tribes phrasebook • Ho Chi Minh City • Indonesia • Indonesia's Eastern Islands • Indonesian phrasebook • Indonesian audio pack • Jakarta • Java • Laos • Lao phrasebook • Laos travel atlas • Malay phrasebook • Malaysia, Singapore & Brunei • Myanmar (Burma) • Philippines • Pilipino (Tagalog) phrasebook • Singapore • South-East Asia on a shoestring • South-East Asia phrasebook • Thailand • Thailand's Islands & Beaches • Thailand travel atlas • Thai phrasebook • Thai audio pack • Vietnam • Vietnamese phrasebook • Vietnam travel atlas

ALSO AVAILABLE: Antarctica • Brief Encounters: Stories of Love, Sex & Travel • Chasing Rickshaws • Not the Only Planet: Travel Stories from Science Fiction • Travel with Children • Traveller's Tales

Lonely Planet Journeys

JOURNEYS is a unique collection of travel writing – published by the company that understands travel better than anyone else. It is a series for anyone who has ever experienced – or dreamed of – the magical moment when they encountered a strange culture or saw a place for the first time. They are tales to read while you're planning a trip, while you're on the road or while you're in an armchair in front of a fire.

These outstanding titles explore our planet through the eyes of a diverse group of international writers. JOURNEYS books catch the spirit of a place, illuminate a culture, recount a crazy adventure or introduce a fascinating way of life. They always entertain, and always enrich the experience of travel.

ISLANDS IN THE CLOUDS
Travels in the Highlands of New Guinea
Isabella Tree

This is the fascinating account of a journey to the remote and beautiful Highlands of Papua New Guinea and Irian Jaya: one of the most extraordinary and dangerous regions on the planet. Tree travels with a PNG Highlander who introduces her to his intriguing and complex world, changing rapidly as it collides with twentieth-century technology. *Islands in the Clouds* is a thoughtful, moving book.

SEAN & DAVID'S LONG DRIVE
Sean Condon

Sean and David are young townies who have rarely strayed beyond city limits. One day, for no good reason, they set out to discover their homeland, and what follows is a wildly entertaining adventure that covers half of Australia.

'a hilariously detailed log of two burned out friends' – *Rolling Stone*

DRIVE THRU AMERICA
Sean Condon

If you've ever wanted to drive across the USA but couldn't find the time (or afford the gas), *Drive Thru America* is perfect for you. In his search for American myths and realities – along with comfort, cable TV and good, reasonably priced coffee – Sean Condon paints a hilarious road-portrait of the USA.

'entertaining and laugh-out-loud funny' – *Alex Wilber, Travel editor, Amazon.com*

BRIEF ENCOUNTERS
Stories of Love, Sex & Travel
edited by Michelle de Kretser

Love affairs on the road, passionate holiday flings, disastrous pick-ups, erotic encounters . . . In this seductive collection of stories, 22 authors from around the world write about travel romances. Combining fiction and reportage, *Brief Encounters* is must-have reading – for everyone who has dreamt of escape with that perfect stranger.

Includes stories by Pico Iyer, Mary Morris, Emily Perkins, Mona Simpson, Lisa St Aubin de Terán, Paul Theroux and Sara Wheeler.

LONELY PLANET

Phrasebooks

Lonely Planet phrasebooks are packed with essential words and phrases to help travellers communicate with the locals. With colour tabs for quick reference, an extensive vocabulary and use of script, these handy pocket-sized language guides cover day-to-day travel situations.

- handy pocket-sized books
- easy to understand Pronunciation chapter
- clear & comprehensive Grammar chapter
- romanisation alongside script to allow ease of pronunciation
- script throughout so users can point to phrases for every situation
- full of cultural information and tips for the traveller

'...vital for a real DIY spirit and attitude in language learning'
– Backpacker

'the phrasebooks have good cultural backgrounders and offer solid advice for challenging situations in remote locations'
– San Francisco Examiner

Arabic (Egyptian) • Arabic (Moroccan) • Australian *(Australian English, Aboriginal and Torres Strait languages)* • Baltic States *(Estonian, Latvian, Lithuanian)* • Bengali • Brazilian • British • Burmese • Cantonese • Central Asia • Central Europe *(Czech, French, German, Hungarian, Italian, Slovak)* • Eastern Europe *(Bulgarian, Czech, Hungarian, Polish, Romanian, Slovak)* • Ethiopian (Amharic) • Fijian • French • German • Greek • Hill Tribes • Hindi/Urdu • Indonesian • Italian • Japanese • Korean • Lao • Latin American Spanish • Malay • Mandarin • Mediterranean Europe *(Albanian, Croatian, Greek, Italian, Macedonian, Maltese, Serbian, Slovene)* • Mongolian • Nepali • Papua New Guinea • Pilipino (Tagalog) • Quechua • Russian • Scandinavian Europe *(Danish, Finnish, Icelandic, Norwegian, Swedish)* • South-East Asia *(Burmese, Indonesian, Khmer, Lao, Malay, Tagalog Pilipino, Thai, Vietnamese)* • Spanish (Castilian) *(also includes Catalan, Galician and Basque)* • Sri Lanka • Swahili • Thai • Tibetan • Turkish • Ukrainian • USA *(US English, Vernacular, Native American languages, Hawaiian)* • Vietnamese • Western Europe *(Basque, Catalan, Dutch, French, German, Greek, Irish)*

FREE Lonely Planet Newsletters

We love hearing from you and think you'd like to hear from us.

Planet Talk

Our FREE quarterly printed newsletter is full of tips from travellers and anecdotes from Lonely Planet guidebook authors. Every issue is packed with up-to-date travel news and advice, and includes:

- a postcard from Lonely Planet co-founder Tony Wheeler
- a swag of mail from travellers
- a look at life on the road through the eyes of a Lonely Planet author
- topical health advice
- prizes for the best travel yarn
- news about forthcoming Lonely Planet events
- a complete list of Lonely Planet books and other titles

To join our mailing list, residents of the UK, Europe and Africa can email us at go@lonelyplanet.co.uk; residents of North and South America can email us at info@lonelyplanet.com; the rest of the world can email us at talk2us@lonelyplanet.com.au, or contact any Lonely Planet office.

Comet

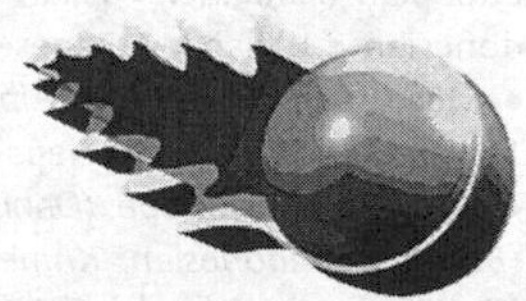

Our FREE monthly email newsletter brings you all the latest travel news, features, interviews, competitions, destination ideas, travellers' tips & tales, Q&As, raging debates and related links. Find out what's new on the Lonely Planet Web site and which books are about to hit the shelves.

Subscribe from your desktop: www.lonelyplanet.com/comet

Index

Abbreviations

NP – National Park SP – State Park

Text

C

Bold indicates maps.

Bold indicates maps.

Bold indicates maps.

Boxed Text

MAP LEGEND

BOUNDARIES

International
State

HYDROGRAPHY

Coastline
River, Creek
River Flow
Lake
Intermittent Lake
Salt Lake
Spring, Rapids
Swamp
Waterfalls

ROUTES & TRANSPORT

Freeway
Highway
Major Road
Minor Road
Unsealed Road
City Highway
City Road
City Street, Lane
Pedestrian Mall
Train Route & Station
Light Rail Route & Stop
Underground & Station
Tramway
Walking Track
Bicycle Track
Ferry Route

AREA FEATURES

Beach
Building
Cemetery
Market
Park, Gardens
Urban Area

CAPITAL ... National Capital
CAPITAL ... State Capital
CITY ... City
Town ... Town
Town ... Small Town

Place to Stay
Camping Ground
Caravan Park

Place to Eat
Pub, Entertainment
Picnic Area

MAP SYMBOLS

Airport
Bank
Cave
Church
Golf Course
Hospital
Lighthouse
Lookout
Mine
Monument
Mountain
Museum, Art Gallery
National, State Park
One Way Street
Petrol Station

Police Station
Post Office
Shopping Centre
Skiing, Cross Country
Skiing, Downhill
Stately Building
Surf Beach
Swimming Pool
Telephone
Toilet
Tourist Information
Trailhead
Transport
Winery
Zoo

Note: not all symbols displayed above appear in this book

LONELY PLANET OFFICES

Australia
PO Box 617, Hawthorn 3122, Victoria
tel: (03) 9819 1877 fax: (03) 9819 6459
e-mail: talk2us@lonelyplanet.com.au

USA
150 Linden St, Oakland, CA 94607
tel: (510) 893 8555 TOLL FREE: 800 275-8555
fax: (510) 893 8572
e-mail: info@lonelyplanet.com

UK
10a Spring Place, London, NW5 3BH
tel: (0171) 428 4800 fax: (0170) 428 4828
e-mail: go@lonelyplanet.co.uk

France
1 rue du Dahomey, 75011 Paris
tel: 01 55 25 33 00 fax: 01 55 25 33 01
e-mail: bip@lonelyplanet.fr

World Wide Web: www.lonelyplanet.com *or* AOL keyword: lp
Lonely Planet Images: lpi@lonelyplanet.com.au